FLYING FILM STARS

THE DIRECTORY OF AIRCRAFT IN BRITISH WORLD WAR TWO FILMS

First published 2014.
Red Kite
PO Box 223,
Walton-on-Thames,
Surrey, KT12 3YQ
England
Tel. 0845 095 0346

Design Amy Shore.

Printed by
Dimograf, Sp. Z o. o. Poland
Purchase this and other Red Kite books directly from Red Kite's websites;
www.redkitebooks.co.uk
www.wingleader.co.uk

First Edition
ISBN 978-1-906592-15-8

FLYING FILM STARS

THE DIRECTORY OF AIRCRAFT IN BRITISH WORLD WAR TWO FILMS

MARK ASHLEY

CONTENTS

INTRODUCTION

CHAPTER ONE, 1939 - 1945

1939 - The Lion has Wings	12 - 20
1940 - Night Train to Munich	21 - 22
1940 - Convoy	22 - 22
1941 - Freedom Radio	22 - 23
1941 - Dangerous Moonlight	23 - 24
1941 - Pimpernel Smith	25 - 25
1941 - Target for Tonight	25 - 26
1941 - Ferry Pilot	26 - 31
1941 - A Yank in the R.A.F. *1	31 - 37
1941 - International Squadron *1	31 - 41
1941 - Cottage to Let	41 - 41
1941 - 49th Parallel	41 - 42
1941 - Ships with Wings	42 - 46
1942 - The Big Blockad	46 - 50
1942 - One of our Aircraft is Missing	50 - 51
1942 - The Day will Dawn	51 - 52
1942 - The Foreman Went to France	52 - 52
1942 - The Next of Kin	52 - 54
1942 - They Flew Alone	54 - 56
1942 - Flying Fortress *1	56 - 58
1942 - Eagle Squadron *1	58 - 61
1942 - The Goose Steps Out	61 - 61
1942 - Unpublished Story	61 - 61
1942 - The First of the Few	62 - 63
1942 - In Which We Serve	63 - 64
1942 - Desperate Journey *1	65 - 66
1942 - Secret Mission	66 - 67
1942 - Went The Day Well?	67 - 67
1942 - Commandos Strike At Dawn *1	67 - 68
1943 - Nine Men	68 - 68
1943 - The Silver Fleet	68 - 68
1943 - Fires Were Started	68 - 68
1943 - Tomorrow We Live	68 - 68
1943 - Tonight We Raid Calais *1	68 - 69
1943 - The Bells Go Down	69 - 69
1943 - We Dive At Dawn	69 - 69
1943 - The Life and Death of Colonel Blimp	69 - 69
1943 - Undercover	70 - 70
1943 - The Flemish Farm	70 - 71
1943 - The Volunteer	71 - 77

1943 - Millions Like Us	77 - 78
1943 - The Adventures of Tartu	78 - 79
1944 - Big Pack	79 - 82
1944 - Western Approaches	82 - 82
1944 - Candlelight in Algiers	82 - 82
1944 - The Way Ahead	83 - 83
1944 - For Those In Peril	83 - 85
1944 - Two Thousand Women	85 - 85
1945 - The Way to the Stars	85 - 89
1945 - Journey Together	89 - 92

CHAPTER TWO, 1946 - 1950

1946 - Now It Can Be Told (School for Danger)	94 - 100
1946 - Night Boat to Dublin	100 - 100
1946 - The Captive Heart	100 - 101
1946 - Theirs Is The Glory	101 - 102
1946 - A Matter of Life and Death	102 - 103
1946 - School for Secrets	103 - 105
1947 - Frieda	106 - 106
1948 - against THE WIND	106 - 107
1949 - The Small Back Room	107 - 107
1949 - Landfall	107 - 109
1950 - They Were Not Divided	109 - 109
1950 - Odette	109 - 111
1950 - The Wooden Horse	111 - 111

CHAPTER THREE, 1951 - 1960

1951 - The Desert Fox *1	113 - 114
1952 - Angels One Five	114 - 116
1952 - Gift Horse	116 - 118
1953 - Appointment in London	118 - 120
1953 - The Cruel Sea	120 - 120
1953 - The Desert Rats *1	120 - 121
1953 - Single-Handed	121 - 121
1953 - Malta Story	121 - 126
1953 - The Red Beret	126 - 130
1953 - Albert R.N.	130 - 130
1954 - They Who Dare	131 - 131
1954 - The Purple Plain	132 - 132
1954 - The Sea Shall Not Have Them	132 - 135
1955 - The Colditz Story	135 - 135
1955 - Above Us The Waves	135 - 135
1955 - The Dam Busters	135 - 141
1955 - Cockleshell Heroes	141 - 141
1956 - A Town Like Alice	141 - 142
1956 - The Man Who Never Was	142 - 143
1956 - The Black Tent	143 - 143
1956 - Reach For The Sky	143 - 147
1956 - The Battle of the River Plate	147 - 148
1957 - Ill Met by Moonlight	148 - 149
1957 - The Steel Bayonet	149 - 149
1957 - The Bridge on the River Kwai	149 - 149
1957 - The One That Got Away	149 - 150
1958 - Carve Her Name With Pride	150 - 151
1958 - Bitter Victory *2	151 - 151
1958 - Dunkirk	151 - 152

1958 - The Silent Enemy | 152 - 153
1958 - The Camp on Blood Island | 154 - 154
1958 - Ice Cold In Alex | 154 - 155
1958 - The Wind Cannot Read | 155 - 155
1958 - Battle of the V1 | 155 - 158
1958 - The Key | 158 - 158
1958 - I Was Monty's Double | 158 - 161
1958 - Sea of Sand | 161 - 161
1958 - The Two-Headed Spy | 161 - 162
1959 - Operation Amsterdam | 162 - 163
1959 - Danger Within | 163 - 163
1959 - The Angry Hills | 163 - 163
1959 - Yesterday's Enemy | 163 - 163
1960 - Sink the Bismarck! | 163 - 167
1960 - Foxhole in Cairo | 167 - 169

CHAPTER FOUR, 1961 - 1970

1961 - The Long, and the Short, and the Tall | 171 - 171
1961 - The Guns of Navarone | 171 - 174
1961 - Very Important Person | 174 - 174
1961 - Tarnished Heroes | 174 - 174
1962 - The Password is Courage | 174 - 175
1962 - The Silent Invasion | 175 - 175
1962 - The Valiant *2 | 175 - 175
1962 - The Longest Day *1 | 175 - 182
1962 - The War Lover | 182 - 185
1963 - Mystery Submarine | 186 - 186
1963 - The Great Escape *1 | 186 - 188
1963 - Torpedo Bay *2 | 188 - 188
1963 - The Victors | 188 - 189
1964 - 633 Squadron | 189 - 197
1964 - The Secret of Blood Island | 197 - 197
1965 - Operation Crossbow | 197 - 203
1965 - The Hill | 203 - 203
1965 - Von Ryan's Express *1 | 203 - 205
1965 - King Rat | 205 - 205
1965 - The Heroes of Telemark | 205 - 207
1966 - It Happened Here | 207 - 207
1966 - Triple Cross | 207 - 208
1967 - The Night of the Generals | 208 - 209
1967 - Tobruk *1 | 209 - 210
1968 - The Long Day's Dying | 210 - 210
1968 - Attack on the Iron Coast | 211 - 211
1968 - Where Eagles Dare | 211 - 214
1969 - Hannibal Brooks | 215 - 215
1969 - Play Dirty | 215 - 215
1969 - Mosquito Squadron | 215 - 221
1969 - Submarine X-1 | 222 - 222
1969 - Battle of Britain | 222 - 236
1969 - Eagles Over London *2 | 236 - 238
1970 - Hell Boats | 238 - 240
1970 - The Last Escape *1 | 240 - 240
1970 - Too Late The Hero *1 | 240 - 241
1970 - The McKenzie Break | 241 - 241

CHAPTER FIVE, 1971 - 1980

1971 - Murphy's War	242 - 244
1971 - Raid on Rommel *1	244 - 244
1971 - Dad's Army	244 - 245
1973 - Hitler: The Last Ten Days	245 - 245
1975 - Overlord	245 - 247
1976 - Operation: Daybreak	247 - 248
1977 - Cross of Iron	248 - 248
1977 - The Eagle Has Landed	248 - 253
1977 - A Bridge Too Far	253 - 259
1978 - Force 10 From Navarone	259 - 260
1979 - Escape to Athena	260 - 260
1979 - The Passage	260 - 260
1979 - Hanover Street	261 - 264
1979 - Yanks	264 - 264
1980 - The Sea Wolves	264 - 264

CHAPTER SIX, 1981 - 1990

1981 - Escape to Victory *2	265 - 265
1981 - Eye of the Needle	265 - 269
1983 - Merry Christmas, Mr Lawrence	269 - 269
1983 - Another Time, Another Place	269 - 269
1987 - Hope and Glory	269 - 270
1989 - Return from the River Kwai	270 - 271
1990 - Memphis Belle	271 - 278

CHAPTER SEVEN, 1991 - 2000

1996 - The English Patient	279 - 279
1998 - The Brylcreem Boys	279 - 280
1998 - The Land Girls	280 - 281

CHAPTER EIGHT, 2001 - Current

2001 - to END all WARS *1	282 - 282
2001 - Charlotte Gray	283 - 283
2001 - Captain Corelli's Mandolin	283 - 284
2001 - Dark Blue World (Tmavomodry Svet) *2	284 - 289
2001 - Enigma	289 - 289
2002 - Two Men Went to War	289 - 290
2005 - The Last Drop	290 - 292
2007 - Atonement	292 - 292
2008 - Female Agents (Les Femmes de l'Ombre) *2	292 - 293
2009 - Brothers War	293 - 294
2009 - Glorious 39	294 - 294
2011 - Age of Heroes	294 - 294

*1   *Hollywood 'British' war film*
*2   *International 'British' war film*

FINAL CUT	295 - 296
DIRECTORY	297 - 366
REFERENCE	366 - 368

INTRODUCTION

This book describes every single aircraft appearing in every single feature film made or produced about Great Britain and its people during the most terrible conflict in the history of humanity, World War Two.

Every single aircraft?

Yes, every single traceable and identifiable aircraft of the World War Two era appearing in British war films made from October 1939 up to Year 2013. A period covering 74 years and 181 films in total.

This, surely, is a momentous task!

So it may seem, but one that is achievable thanks to modern technology which up till now has been the exclusive preserve of the film editor alone. Today, we can all be our own film editors in our front room, study, or bedroom. Combining the use of flat screen high-definition TV, DVD recorder, laptop computer and the Internet, minute analysis of any subject on film is possible through use of freeze-framing or stop-motion of any form of imagery. What would have taken years of expensive research in any number of film libraries is now achievable on a living room couch, a study room desk, or even on (or in) bed.

What we are going to do, through the means described above, is research and analyse each film in order to identify every single aircraft that features in it, explain its role in the plot, and pinpoint its whereabouts today or discover its fate, if known.

What, every single one of the 181 British World War Two war films listed in this book?

Fear not, the task is not so enormous as it may appear. To begin with, 44 out of the total of 181 war films have no aircraft in them at all. They receive only a brief mention in this book just to place them in context with every film that is reviewed. A further 28 have such little aviation content, or, as will become apparent in the final Chapter, use virtual reality aircraft created by computer graphic imagery (CGI), that no more than a few paragraphs are needed to complete a review of them. That leaves 109 British World War Two war films with a very significant or an extremely wide-ranging level of aircraft action in them.

During our research for this book, a number of unexpected discoveries and revelations will appear. The fact that so many British war films dealing with World War Two use aviation to such a large extent is one of them.

There are, of course, many books that detail the making of specific films in which aircraft of the World War Two era appear.

Various aviation magazines have covered particular films and detailed the actual aircraft in them. Innumerable Websites and Internet Forums attest to the extraordinary amount of interest there is among aviation enthusiasts and film fans in the actual aircraft which perform a whole series of roles in many films, covering myriads of plots, scenes, set-pieces and dramas. However, no publication has yet attempted to detail all of them. Until now.

It is for the aviation enthusiast, the film fan, the war historian, and the historic aircraft owner and collector, that this book has been written and which, hopefully, will form a valuable and beneficial part of their library. It is intended to be a reference work, but one that, like the films it describes, will entertain as well as inform.

Before proceeding with this research work, it is important we understand what we are looking at and discussing here. Not least of all, what is a British war film? The definition is not as straightforward as might be thought.

To be as precise as it is possible to be, it can be stated that a British war film is a film production that enacts a story set during World War Two, which is financed by a British film studio, produced by a British film producer working for a British film production company, using British film technicians and directed by a British film director, and is then released to the cinema by a British film distributor. During the actual War years themselves and into the decade and a half that followed, this was almost always the case. However, from the Sixties onwards the distinction became more blurred.

Despite the huge wave of success the British film industry enjoyed in the Sixties, many films made in Britain during that decade were financed by American film studios and distributed globally by American film distribution companies. Technically, the nationality and ownership of a film released to cinema is defined by the studio that funds it and by who owns the distribution rights. Thus, the epic science fiction movie "2001: A Space Odyssey" (1968), made entirely in Britain with British film crews and a British Special Effects team, is by definition an American film because it was financed and produced by the American MGM Film Studios. In reality, it is better described as a British-American co-production, but it is often thought of as a British film.

For the purposes of this book's research into British World War Two war films that feature aircraft prominently, the definition of a 'British war film' will not be based on who or what company or studio in whichever country funds it. Instead, the definition will be based on the fact that the film was made in Britain by British film crews, or was made overseas using British film technicians and British Special Effects (often known simply in the industry as Special FX, or just SFX), with post-production work taking place later in a studio in Britain.

The subject of some of these films need not be British: two feature films involving exclusively United States Eighth Air Force B-17 Flying Fortress crews, "The War Lover" (1962) and "Memphis Belle" (1990), are as American as it is possible to make them, but they are British-made war films. "Cross of Iron" (1977) is set in the Soviet Caucasus on the Eastern Front and does not have a single British character in it, but it is a British-made war film produced by Sir Lew Grade's EMI Films company.

Today, in the second decade of the 21st Century, the definition as to which country produced which film has become so globalised as to be virtually meaningless: many large-scale film productions are financed from a variety of international sources, especially through product-placement arrangements with companies providing funding in return for their products receiving prominent viewing in the final production, as happens with the James Bond films. But nobody thinks of James Bond as being anything other than a British film institution. Consequently, the most recent films reviewed in this book, while being 'British' by our definition, are more realistically multi-national productions.

There is one more definition that is being applied specifically for this book, that of the Hollywood 'British' war film. There are 17 such films included in this book. These are films that are not made by British-owned film studios, but are films produced by American production companies based in Hollywood whose subjects specifically concern Britain and Britons at war. The pioneer of these is "A Yank in the R.A.F." (1941), made in Hollywood by producer Darryl F Zanuck and starring Tyrone Power and Betty Grable. Zanuck made the film as a salute to the Royal Air Force, in which a complete RAF Fighter Command squadron appears; he also used the film to espouse his views that the United States should join the War on Britain's side against Nazi Germany, a belief then opposed by 'isolationist' Americans before Pearl Harbor. Another example is the 20th Century Fox production, "The Desert Rats" (1953), set during the siege of Tobruk, in which all the characters are either British or Australian - Americans don't feature in it at all, but it is an American-made war film with an entirely British and Commonwealth theme. It, thus, earns the distinction of being a Hollywood 'British' war film. And who thinks of "The Great Escape" (1963) as being anything other than a British war film!

Furthermore, Metro-Goldwyn-Mayer set up its Borehamwood-based MGM-British Film Studios in 1937 expressly to exploit its highly successful trend of Hollywood 'British' films, such as "David Copperfield" (1934), "Mutiny on the Bounty" (1935) and "A Tale of Two Cities" (1935), all high grossing films with very strong British themes and content that were produced at MGM's Culver City (California) studios, but would now, from 1937 onwards, be made in Britain using British talent in acting, directing, screenwriting and film production.

"Louis B. Mayer and other MGM executives had been planning to set up a British production base for several years", writes H Mark Glancy in his book, When Hollywood Loved Britain: The Hollywood 'British' Film 1939 - 1945, published in 1999. Glancy goes on to say, "From the outset of the Second World War, Hollywood's 'British' films were given wartime themes and relevance... Films such as The Sea Hawk (1940), That Hamilton Woman (1941), Foreign Correspondent (1940), A Yank in the RAF (1941) and the long-delayed Eagle Squadron (1942) are an integral part of Hollywood's (then) reputation as an industry of Anglophiles".

Thus it is that the reviews of Hollywood-backed films portraying Britons at war in World War Two deserve their place as 'British' war films in a book of this kind, as do other foreign-made and multi-national productions that take the same Britons-at-war theme. In that sense, they will be described as International 'British' war films.

There are a couple of other 'rules' to iron out before we commence this research. The films included are solely those released directly to cinema (or theater in the United States), therefore films made for TV do not count. Nor do television series; hence the Battle of Britain TV series of the Eighties, "A Piece of Cake", does not feature. More recently, films released directly onto video are likewise excluded.

Of the 181 British war films covered in this book, 50 alone were produced between 1939 and 1945, the six years of World War Two itself. All of these are covered in the first Chapter. The second Chapter details the war films made between 1946 - 1950, just 13 of them. This allows us to then cover each succeeding decade in successive Chapters. As can be seen, the Fifties and the Sixties were prolific years for British war films, their decades providing virtually half the content of this book. From the Seventies onwards the number of war films begins to diminish as time progressively separates the British conscious mind from World War Two, to the extent that when we reach the Nineties only three British-made films were released in the UK whose themes concerned that mighty conflict. The final Chapter engrosses the whole of the 21st Century to date, a period of 13 years.

This research is detailed and extensive, by necessity. It is not just a lifeless list of each film and every aircraft appearing in it. It is important for the reader to know the roles each aircraft perform, so some description of a film's plot and how the aircraft play their part in it has to be provided. Aircraft appear as principal actors, as extras, as props and as set-dressing, etc, making it essential that the context of their roles is understood.

Finally, a complete Directory of every aircraft examined in this research, giving their identity, their owner or operator at the time they appear in any film, their role, and their existing status today or their fate, where known, is provided for quick reference at the rear of this work.

Well, there's enough to be getting on with, so let's crack on.

CHAPTER 1

1939-1945

As this most crucial of periods in the history of Great Britain will show, the British film industry faced, along with the rest of the nation, the greatest crisis it has ever known. It had a straight choice: live or die. One of the unexpected discoveries made in this research is that we can see how the British film industry not only survived, but grew with such astonishing zest and purpose through the most dangerous years the British people have ever known. British cinema became literally part of the British war effort against Nazi Germany and its Axis partners.

It was a time of extraordinary inventiveness. What is it they say about necessity being the mother of? During World War Two, British cinema became a propaganda weapon aimed directly at the Third Reich, while at the same time seeking to embolden the British nation during its darkest years when it and its Commonwealth allies resisted the Nazi might alone. Never in the field of human conflict were so many lies told to so many by so few, all in the interests of serving the nation, of course.

During the War years, the British film industry pioneered the format known as the drama-documentary, a method of story-telling in which actual events are re-created often using non-professional actors, but the real people themselves who were originally involved. "Ferry Pilot" (1941) and "Big Pack" (1944) are excellent examples of these 'drama-docs', as they are styled today, having become the staple diet of re-enactment film channels such as the Discovery Channel series, The History Channel and Zone Reality. How aware are they that they owe their origin to the inventiveness of the British film industry during World War Two?

To feed the appetite of the British cinematic war industry, unique and dedicated film companies came alive whose sole purpose was to place on celluloid the courage and the heroism of the British war machine in action. Thus arose the Crown Film Unit, which in its turn gave birth to separate film units for each of Britain's major armed services. For our purposes, it is the RAF Film Production Unit which mostly supplies much fascinating material for us to admire in this first Chapter covering the War years; the film units attached to the Royal Navy and the British Army also feature to a lesser extent. It is without any exaggeration to state that without the RAF Film Production Unit, the cinema industry as a whole worldwide would be much the poorer, for so much exciting and astonishing footage of British and German aircraft in action would never have been seen.

Thanks to the Crown Film and RAF Film Production Units, the British cinema gained access to something which no other film industry anywhere in the world has been able to exploit: captured enemy aircraft. One of the revelations that emerges from this research is the number of captured Deutsches Luftwaffe fighters and bombers that were flown by British pilots in major film productions. Two examples are "The First of the Few" (1942) and "In Which We Serve" (1942). Not even Hollywood could claim access to captured enemy aircraft of the World War Two era.

As far as the author is aware, this book is the sole source for the aviation historian and enthusiast for the fullest details of the actual captured Luftwaffe aircraft that were flown in British war films, and of their respective fates. Suffice it to say, just one survives. The historian and the enthusiast of today may criticise the destruction of these historically valuable machines (two were lost in airborne accidents), but that is to forget that, in the immediate aftermath of World War Two, anything bearing the hated symbols of the Nazi Swastika and the splintered black-and-white Balkenkreuze (Beam Cross) was trashed with unabated relish.

Likewise of considerable value to the historian is the huge amount of archive film material which these film productions used, some of it extremely rare and in certain cases being sole source examples in the public domain. Discovering rare individual aircraft which have not been identified before in archive imagery used in feature films, such as Adolf Hitler's personal Focke Wulf FW.200V3 D-2600, has been one of the real personal bonuses for the author and hopefully will be of real value for present and future researchers.

What becomes apparent in this Chapter is how British war films changed and developed as World War Two progressed year upon year. At the outset we have blatant propaganda films, in which reality and honesty are only of value if they can be seen to be working in Britain's interest. German characters are unrelentingly sly, sinister and sadistic. Indeed, certain British actors, like the larger-than-life (in every physical sense) Francis L Sullivan, honed a lucrative career playing Nazi villains during the War.

As the War progressed, however, an increasing feel for realism replaced such obviously exaggerated works bordering on the ridiculously fanciful, as with "Ships With Wings" (1941), resulting in much more honest productions like "One of our Aircraft is Missing" (1942). The War was not progressing well, and no one could pretend that the country wasn't seriously threatened by the U-Boat menace, so the mendacious message of the propagandistic "The Big Blockade" (1942) - a project begun in 1940 but not released to cinema until two years later - would, for the most part, be rejected by an increasingly war-wise public.

By the time the War ended in 1945, it was possible to present honest, sensitive and realistic film productions, as with "The Way to the Stars" (1945), depicting the effect of the conflict on both military and civilian personalities, male and female.

Chapter One begins with the first British war film in history about World War Two. It is also the shortest, yet contains an extraordinary amount of aviation, much of it rare and unique, so the review of it is one of the most lengthy in the book. Not only that, it is by far the strangest and most unusual war film ever made.

THE LION HAS WINGS

(Released: November 1939)

"In war, truth is the first casualty". So declared ancient Greek dramatist and poet, Aeschylus, some 2,500 years before the start of World War Two.

Within one month following Great Britain's declaration of war against Nazi Germany on 3rd September 1939, "The Lion Has Wings", the first British war film to be made, proved Aeschylus right in just about every respect. Produced to demonstrate to the British government that cinema could contribute valuably to Britain's war effort by using propaganda to strengthen the nation's morale, "The Lion Has Wings" makes bold with the truth from virtually its delusional beginning to its self-deceiving end.

This, however, is not reason to dismiss what is now a most important piece of film and aviation history. "The Lion Has Wings" is a drama-doc, mixing archive and newsreel footage with material filmed exclusively for the production. Genuine British military personnel appear alongside familiar British film actors, particularly Ralph Richardson and Merle Oberon: they portray a most unlikely and unconvincing married couple, both as devoted to their nation as much as they are to each other, he as a serving Royal Air Force Fighter Command Operations Controller, she as a Red Cross nurse.

The sole purpose of "The Lion Has Wings" is to propagandise Britain and the nation's people as a freedom-loving, peaceful nation that, up to 3rd September 1939, had successfully defied tyranny in Europe for 800 years. Nazi Germany, on the other hand, was characterised by Adolf Hitler's treacherous nature and by the remorseless, soul-devouring authority of National Socialism which had imprisoned the minds of all people under its control. This was not difficult for the film to achieve, taking into account the events of 1939 in Europe, beginning with Germany's and Hungary's annexation of Czechoslovakia in March, followed by Germany's invasion of Poland on 1st September.

But the film's message that Britain's armed forces were fully equipped, and that the nation's industries were properly prepared to supply and support them, was pure camouflage on the part of producer Alexanda Korda and of the three directors he employed to film "The Lion Has Wings" in a remarkable 12 days.

When the film was edited and completed inside one month, then released to the cinemas in the UK during early November 1939, the question would surely have to be asked as to whom its message was mostly aimed at. Surely not just the British public alone, as the film's commentary within the first few minutes would have brought jeers of disbelief from any cinema audience in London's East End, or from many of those watching in the impoverished inner cities of the Midlands and the North of England.

"A new Britain, in which everyone of us might have a home of which he was proud", exclaims the commentator. "A gigantic task we undertook ("we", presumably, being the British Government), to re-house the urban population in well-built, well-lighted, well-ventilated flats to replace the tumbledown slums of the past", he continues, as the camera pans over the then new Kensal House complex in Notting Hill.

Many a cinema-goer in late 1939 would know only too well that the only real alternative to the inner city slums were small, single-level, temporary prefabricated buildings constructed from plasterboard and corrugated iron: "prefabs", as anyone from the generations before the Seventies will remember them, and so temporary that they were still being used as principal dwelling homes more than 20 years after the War's end.

If Korda and his production team of directors and editors thought they could foist just this one falsehood alone onto a contemporary British cinema audience, then it really does beg the question as to whom they were really trying to convince. The film is riddled with other social, economical and industrial distortions, but it is not the purpose of this book to examine them all here.

Undoubtedly, "The Lion Has Wings" was aimed at the German government of 1939, and especially at the new German Air Force, der neu Deutsches Luftwaffe. Whether the film had any significant effect at all on the German political and military mindset is very questionable, as any blatant piece of propaganda is certain to be rejected for what it obviously is. For instance, the film's claim that the Kiel Kanal Raid by RAF Bomber Command on 4th September 1939 was a complete success would have exposed such a lie to the German authorities immediately – the Raid had hardly any effect at all on the Deutschen Kriegsmarine Panzer Schiffen (German Navy armoured ships) it was targeted against.

Any neutral observer might also have been left considerably unimpressed by the film's message, such as the CBS Radio news reporter, William L Shirer. He criticises the film in his celebrated book, "Berlin Diary", in which he describes his eye-witness accounts of the rise of Nazi Germany in the Thirties and the effect of the War upon that nation until the Nazis expelled Shirer in 1941. Shirer writes of "The Lion Has Wings" as being a very bad film, which he considers so "supercilious and silly" as to be not worth taken seriously. He was shown the film in the Reich's Propaganda Ministry, so it could be said he had to accommodate his hosts in his review of it; but Shirer had a reputation for accuracy and honesty in his reporting, so it has since been taken as fact that he was expressing his genuine opinion.

Therefore, if all the above is taken into account, to whom was the film's message really meant to be delivered? The primary target audience for whose benefit Korda produced the film can only have been the British government of 1939 itself. The image of Britain compared to Nazi Germany, and particularly the lifestyle that the British government is proclaimed in the script for having created for its nation's people, was the kind of flattery that Korda must surely have wanted to bestow upon Prime Minister Neville Chamberlain and his War Cabinet.

Korda had good reason to, because "The Lion Has Wings" was made not just to propagandise Great Britain as she stood beside her ally France to face down Hitler's war machine, but to save the British film industry from being closed down by Chamberlain's government. Korda feared that what happened between 1914 – 1918, when the then British government shut down the new, fledgling film industry as an inessential luxury during The Great War, would be repeated again in 1939, from which it might never recover.

In this regard Korda succeeded, as "The Lion Has Wings" was warmly welcomed by the government. In so doing, it is probably not an overstatement to say that Korda saved the British film industry in total for posterity: as all the films which follow in this book will illustrate, cinema played its part in portraying and reflecting – sometimes accurately, sometimes a good deal less so – the role of military aviation in contributing to both Britain's victories and her defeats.

Looked at in this light, "The Lion Has Wings" is an absolute gem of aviation history, even though it tells lies at the outset of war and aims to deceive the Luftwaffe in particular about the Royal Air Force's capabilities. The film illustrates the level of deception that Korda and his team, on behalf of the British government, felt incumbent to practice on both the enemy and on their own population, in pursuit of creating the image of a mighty power and a just people standing ready and prepared to face and defeat a monstrous foe. Michael Powell, one of Korda's three directors, himself denounced the film several years after its release, admitting that it was "full of half-truths". But that does not denigrate its place in cinematic history as being the single production which ensured the British film industry's future at a most dangerous and uncertain time, and, as a vehicle of the kind of propaganda promoted more than 70 years ago, it is worth its weight in gold as an important historical study.

The principal medium that carries the message of "The Lion Has Wings" is British aviation, and in particular, the Royal Air Force. But before the first aircraft in the film appears in view, the audience is treated to an elegant preamble of the virtues of the British way of life compared to the dark tyranny of Nazi Germany. This takes up the opening third of the film, and is the section that was received in British cinemas with most of the derision directed at the production at the time: the claims about healthy working conditions for all and free health care throughout the land insulted the British audiences' collective intelligence, they knowing full well that the exact opposite was true in a heavily industrialised Britain of the Thirties when hardship and poverty was rife for a good one-third of the nation.

It is during this preamble showing Britain as a peace-loving country preparing for war – illustrated with shots of the Royal Navy battleships HMS Warspite and HMS Nelson ploughing through heavy seas, before speeded-up footage of Mk.VI 'Vickers' Light Tanks (obsolete before the War began) attempts to portray the British Army as an armoured fast manoeuvre force that would be a match for any opponent (within six months the Wehrmacht's 'Blitzkrieg' tactic would destroy that deception) – when "the youngest service of them all" first appears in the film. The Royal Air Force is given an interestingly curious introduction by the narrator that appears to reflect as to how the then 21-year-old service was regarded at the time:

"In the war of 1914 – 1918, the Royal Air Force grew from the small, experimental force to become undisputed masters of the sky. Each following year, the Hendon Pageant of the Royal Air Force demonstrated breath-taking skill and parade ground precision in this new element of war".

At this point in the film, a significant section is devoted to the annual Royal Air Force Display held up until 1937 at RAF Hendon on the northern outskirts of London. Footage of some of these Displays, popularly known as the Hendon Air Pageants, are easily obtainable today on the Internet, particularly that of the newsreel coverage shown in cinemas during the Thirties by British Pathe. However, the image quality of much of this footage is limited. Thanks to digital remastering techniques, the DVD release of "The Lion Has Wings" has vastly improved this imagery, so that the footage of the 1937 Hendon RAF Display shown in the film is of the best quality available.

A shot of the Royal Air Force Ensign, with a billboard of The Star newspaper superimposed over it proclaiming "Britain Creates Mighty Air Force", belies the fact that successive British governments in the Twenties and Thirties had been progressively reducing the RAF in size, until it became obvious that war could not be avoided and that aircraft production had to be increased rapidly. True, a re-armament White Paper released by the government in March 1937 called for a home air defence force of 1,750 aircraft by the end of that year, and there were already Air Ministry specifications on the table for new fighter and bomber designs. What makes "The Lion Has Wings" of special interest is that several of these new experimental designs appear in the film, albeit briefly.

Archive footage from British Pathe provides a panoramic scene-setting shot of the packed spectator areas at Hendon, showing four unique new aircraft lined up on static display in front of the crowd barriers. All were experimental designs. Three of them were destined to remain as such and to disappear as virtual unknowns in a relatively short space of time; the fourth would find itself subjugated to a low-priority role, after initially receiving a large Air Ministry order as a light bomber that would be subsequently cancelled when the government, not for by any means the only time, changed its mind.

Clearly seen in the British Pathe footage to be heading the static line is a squat, sturdy, radial-engined bi-plane that has the appearance of a beefed-up cross-breed between a Fairey Albacore and a Gloster Gladiator. It is nothing of the sort, but is an extremely rare and early design of a pilot-less target drone: the Airspeed Queen Wasp, serialled K8887. The concept of using unmanned drones as aerial targets is much older in invention than many today may realise. The Airspeed Queen Wasp was built to meet the Air Staff requirement for a military pilot-less target drone to replace the de Havilland Queen Bee, an unmanned, radio-controlled version of the ubiquitous Tiger Moth trainer already in RAF service. Described at the time as a "wireless-controlled target machine", Flight magazine was moved to comment on the Airspeed Queen Wasp as looking "much too comfortable and private-ownerish to shoot down into the sea!". The Queen Wasp would never supercede its Queen Bee drone predecessor, being too underpowered; the Queen Bee was destined to drone on for the Army's Royal Artillery anti-aircraft gunners to practice aiming at.

Next to the Queen Wasp in the static line is a sleek, low-slung and quite fearsome-looking experimental prototype of a combat aircraft, built for a specification which the Air Staff cancelled without explanation later the same year. This is the second prototype of the Fairey P.4/34, serialled K7555, built by the Fairey Aviation Company to meet Air Staff specification P.4/34 for a light bomber with dive bombing capabilities. The Air Ministry, against all common sense at the time, cancelled this specification, largely it is thought due to a prejudice in RAF Bomber Command against dive bombing as a technique, possibly led by exponents of the fast twin-engined bomber of which the Bristol Blenheim was their champion. The Fairey P.4/34 did survive in another guise, however, as the basis for the Fleet Air Arm's first monoplane fleet fighter, the Fairey Fulmar. The second Fairey P.4/34 itself was retained by its manufacturer for flight testing wing and tail-plane designs for its future fighter projects, the Fulmar and the Firefly.

Third in the static line seen at Hendon in 1937 is another light bomber that appeared destined at the time to succeed where the Fairey P.4/34 had failed, the Hawker Henley prototype K5115 (officially the Hawker P.4/34). The Air Ministry had already ordered a large quantity of Henleys when the 1937 Hendon RAF Display was held, but, as described, the Air Staff were subsequently to change their minds about P.4/34 and to cancel the single-engined, light bomber requirement altogether; the Henley found itself demoted in RAF service to the rank of target-tug for anti-aircraft co-operation units.

Last shown in the static line is a fighter for which, at the time, there were high hopes: the Gloster F.5/34, described by Flight as the newest British single-seat, multi-gun fighter. Powered by a Gloster Mercury radial engine, the F.5/34 was built to the Air Staff specification of that same number for a new monoplane fighter in competition with the Hurricane and the Spitfire, being the latest of the three designs to fly and which lost out to its rivals from Hawker's and Vickers Supermarine, partly because F.5/34 selected the Rolls Royce Merlin engine as the powerplant of choice for the winning design. The Hurricane and Spitfire were both designed to incorporate the Merlin from the outset; the Gloster design was not, hence it ruled itself out. Nonetheless, in appearance the Gloster F.5/34, serialled K5604, had a purposeful and powerful airframe, but it was underpowered compared with its two rivals. Much of its design is owed to the last bi-plane fighter built for the RAF, the Gloster Gladiator, with the same nose, engine cowling, and cockpit layout, while the single low wing is taken from the Gladiator as well. It has been alleged that Glosters permitted the then neutral Imperial Japan in the late Thirties to examine the Gloster F.5/34 design, resulting in certain elements of it supposedly appearing in the future Mitsubishi A6M 'Zero'.

Finally, seen in the film engine running behind the four experimentals is an example of one of the most elegant and sleek airliner designs to appear pre-World War Two, the beautiful de Havilland DH.91 Albatross, carrying the Class B serial of E.2. The DH.91 was designed as a 22-passenger trans-Atlantic airliner for Imperial Airways, powered by four Gipsy Twelve engines designed in-house which gave this beauty a maximum speed of 225mph. Seven were built, but they never got the chance to fly across 'The Pond' due to the onset of war; they completed their days flying wartime civil airline routes from Britain to Portugal and Iceland. Technological know-how from the DH.91 Albatross's design led to the development of the de Havilland Mosquito.

"The Lion Has Wings", therefore, is important as the sole source of public film imagery for these original and unique British aircraft designs, created experimentally while the threat of war was growing.

The 1937 Hendon RAF Display was of special interest at the time because it was held soon after the Coronation of King George VI, with the new Monarch and Queen Elizabeth (destined to become the Queen Mother, when her elder daughter ascended the Throne as Queen Elizabeth II in 1953) were in attendance on Saturday 28th June. They and an estimated 300,000-plus audience witnessed an RAF Display that was designed to show the newly expanded Royal Air Force to the world, and in particular to send a message that the RAF was a major air power to be reckoned with. Mass formations of over 250 aircraft from 25 RAF squadrons powered overhead, but, as the footage reveals, by far the greatest quantity of aircraft involved were of bi-plane designs – the RAF still had a great deal of modernising to do. And it was two years earlier that Adolf Hitler had told British government ministers visiting Germany during March 1935 that the Luftwaffe had achieved parity with the Royal Air Force.

Moreover, the formations passing over Hendon contain no large bomber aircraft, a serious deficiency in the RAF's armoury in the latter half of the Thirties. Designs such as the short-lived Handley Page Harrow (a converted transport type) and Hampden, plus the new Vickers Wellington, were at the prototype phase, but such bombers that were on show at Hendon in 1937 were antiquated Handley Page Heyfords. It is hard to imagine the Luftwaffe, with their new Dornier Do.17 and Heinkel He.111 bomber designs, considering the RAF with its mass of bi-plane fighters and out-dated bombers as a force to be reckoned with.

The most significant monoplane type in the formation fly-pasts is the Avro Anson general purpose reconnaissance aircraft: 30 Avro 652A Anson Mk.Is, all, according to Flight, from No.224 (GB) Squadron, form the centrepiece column of the formations by flying in six successive 'Vics' of five Ansons each. They are flanked on both sides by two lengthy columns of bi-plane aircraft, also in successive 'Vics' of five: the inside columns are comprised of Hawker Hind light day bombers, while the outside columns are filled by Gloster Gauntlet fighters, adding up to five squadrons each of Hinds and Gauntlets.

The entire formation fly-past of three-quarters of a mile in length formed progressively up from the north-west, the four exterior flanks of light bomber and fighter columns coming together with the Ansons' column over Dunstable at a height of 2,000 feet, with each 'Vic' stepped marginally down behind the five-ship in front until the final 'Vics' were passing overhead at 1,350 feet. It took the massive formation of 250 aircraft nearly five minutes to over-fly RAF Hendon at a level speed of 130mph.

The fly-past is filmed by British Pathe both from the ground and air-air. The extent and breadth of the formation columns is nothing less than astonishing, especially when seen filmed from the camera aircraft (this probably is footage of one of the several full-scale rehearsals in the week before the RAF Display, filmed from one of the 'whipper-in' machines accompanying the formations). However, despite its apparently awesome array of RAF fire power and aerial discipline, nothing can hide the fact that the 1937 RAF formation fly-past is made up of aircraft that were becoming obsolete at that very time and were completely unrepresentative of the kind of Royal Air Force that would face the Luftwaffe just short of three years to come.

The Royal Air Force's love affair with formation aerobatics is given full expression in the footage of the RAF Display shown in "The Lion Has Wings". Five Gloster Gauntlets of No.66 (F) Squadron illustrate the tradition long since kept alive into the 21st Century of using coloured smoke – the black-and-white film can't convey the colourful manoeuvres, but apparently 66 (F) favoured using green, orange and white smoke using the same principal as The Red Arrows of today, that of squirting dyed fluid through their Bristol Mercury radial engines' exhausts. The film's editors, though, make much liberal use of engine noise taken from the fly-pasts and other large-scale set-pieces staged in the Display, which they have matched with the Gauntlets' aerobatics but have thereby created a completely false and over dramatic impression of how the five-ship team actually sounded to the ear.

The imagery of nine Hawker Fury I fighters of No.25 (F) Squadron in virtually perfect line-abreast formation, with the

bars adjoining the roundels atop each of their wings making an almost mathematically straight line as it was possible to achieve in flight, creates as special a sight today as it was when it was flown at Hendon on 28th June 1937. When seen filmed air-air at very close quarters, the steadiness of all nine Furies, with their accurate station keeping in line with each other, is nothing less than truly admirable. Furies K2053, K2055 and K2051 are identified in the imagery filmed from what looks like the front seat of a Hawker Hart Trainer flying extremely close to the formation.

You can understand a nation's pride in such airmanship, even if it was being flown in an eye-catchingly beautiful fighter which was only being kept on in service due to production delays affecting its famous successor from the same manufacturer, the Hawker Hurricane. Had the Hurricane been produced according to schedule – design changes from the Merlin I to the Merlin II engine were the cause of the delay – the RAF's first monoplane fighter would have dominated the 1937 RAF Display and would have given justification to the claim made by the character played by Ralph Richardson to his screen wife, Merle Oberon, that, "Some of these new buses are quite good": the "new buses" weren't there, at least not in RAF service as the film implies, so the scriptwriter was being wantonly economical with the truth again.

Interestingly, the Hawker Hurricane prototype was present at the 1937 RAF Display but did not fly, probably so as not to reveal anything to certain interested parties of its qualities as the RAF's new-to-be monoplane fighter (the Spitfire prototype did not appear at all). The watching interested parties were German Wehrmacht visitors in civilian guise, as portrayed in the film. The General de Flieger, Erhard Milch himself, had attended the 1936 RAF Display and is parodied in "The Lion Has Wings" as Schulemberg, Chief of the German Air Staff, watching the RAF Display and discussing with his German Reich Ministry colleague that the British are "becoming air-minded, but not war-minded".

Best of all is the footage showing the four-ship diamond of No.1 (F) Squadron's Hawker Fury I aerobatic team, flying beautifully precise loops, wing-overs and rolls, and again filmed both air-air and from the ground. One shot is filmed from a camera fixed to the top wing of the team leader's Fury, facing backwards, which dramatically captures the team in a join-up loop flown at very fast pace. Although it is not shown in the film, this was the first time an RAF aerobatic team had flown a display which involved formation changes during certain manoeuvres, described at the time as advanced formation flying. The four Hawker Fury Is are K5673 (Leader), K2881 (No.2), K2043 (No.3) and K2879 (Slot).

This time the editing team of "The Lion Has Wings" have done their job properly, capturing the reverberating rasp of the Furies' Kestrel engines properly in tune with the manoeuvres flown.

There is a very accurately built, full-scale replica of Hawker Fury I K5673 on display today in the Brooklands Museum, Surrey, painted in the same markings as the original K5673 when it was the lead ship of No.1 (F) Squadron's aerobatic team. The real K5673 was lost in a fatal landing accident at RAF South Cerney, Gloucestershire, on 7th December 1938 when it was being operated by No.3 Flying Training School.

Judging how the massed crowds swivel to follow the path of flight of some of the displays, it appears that more than one aircraft was performing directly over their heads. Unthinkable today. And the way the spectators are so densely packed together, it would not do to have been claustrophobic at Hendon, or to need to answer the call of nature in a hurry. Deodorant was a luxury afforded by few in the Thirties, so the combined scent of humanity from literally the great unwashed (the average bath time for the majority was once in seven days, in those times) mixing with pipe tobacco and other unmentionable aromas, is definitely not desirable to imagine.

The film creates a celebratory picture of the 1937 RAF Display, but these were hard times for the majority of the British public and they were soon to get much harder.

At this point the film switches scenes to depict Britain's aircraft factories in full production, most particularly that of the aforementioned Hawker Hurricanes and of Vickers Wellington bombers. "British pilots and crews shall have only the finest aircraft that our factories can produce", the commentator asserts. "The British Royal Air Force shall never be let down by its aircraft". Oh dear, if only history could confirm the accuracy of that statement, especially relating to RAF Bomber Command in the earliest phase of the war. And it is to RAF Bomber Command that "The Lion Has Wings" now turns its attention in the central section of the film.

The opening shots are of Vickers Wellington Mk.I bombers dispersed close to trees and bushes, and even right beside cottages just outside the air base fence, as their crews "await orders to avenge the outrage of the Athenia", claims the commentator. This places the scene as representing a Bomber Command airfield on the day following Britain's declaration of hostilities with Germany: the British steamship, the SS Athenia, was torpedoed off the West Coast of Ireland on the evening of 3rd September 1939, with the loss of 118 passengers (including 38 Americans) sailing to America, just eight hours after Britain's and France's final ultimatum to Hitler to withdraw his troops from Poland had passed without response.

The claim that the Kiel Kanal Raid by Bomber Command on 4th September was carried out with orders to avenge the sinking of the Athenia is pure dramatic licence on the part of Korda's scriptwriters. No such raid could be planned and put into effect within less than 24 hours notice, as is being implied in the film. Shipping moving through the Kiel Kanal entrances of Brunsbuttel and Kiel-Holtenau, plus moored in the German port of Wilhelmshaven, were marked as primary strategic targets well before war broke out, and plans were in place to strike at them at the earliest opportunity after hostilities had commenced. But news of Bomber Command's attack on Brunsbuttel would easily have been accepted in the British public mind as representing a blow against Nazi Germany in revenge for the Athenia, so Korda would have had little difficulty in securing the cinema audience's belief that this was the real motive for conducting the Kiel Kanal Raid.

Korda sent a 2nd Film Unit headed by director Michael Powell to RAF Mildenhall in Suffolk, then a Bomber Command base housing the Wellington Mk.Is of No.149 Squadron. This was one of two Wellington Bomber Command squadrons which committed aircraft to attack Kriegsmarine warships steaming past

Brunsbuttel at the mouth of the western entrance of the Kiel Kanal on the evening of 4th September. Various reviews of "The Lion Has Wings" claim that Powell's 2nd Unit filmed the Wellingtons taking off on the raid and landing back afterwards: this was not the case, as the 2nd Unit did not film at Mildenhall until some two weeks after the event. However, film taken by a GPO Film Unit camera crew of the take-offs and landings on 4th September have been edited into the scene, along with footage gained by the 2nd Unit.

The dispersal of the Wellingtons seemingly haphazardly on lengthy, uncut grass close to woodland and to neighbouring cottages is of note, as these images illustrate Bomber Command's policy right at the start of the War to park and conceal its bomber assets in such a manner that they were best protected from low-level attack by marauding fighter-bombers. No.149 Squadron's Wellingtons are easily identified by their distinctive 'OJ-' code letters in white, which appear to off-set the bombers' low visibility camouflage and roundels. The logic of the time was that squadron code letters should be clearly visible, even if this did clash with the purpose of an aircraft's camouflage in concealing it as much as possible from the enemy's view, for the benefit of Royal Artillery anti-aircraft gunners in being able to recognise the aircraft as friendly.

Among the Wellingtons shown parked, starting engines and taxying for take off at RAF Mildenhall, the following are recognisable in varying degrees of picture quality: Wellington Mk.Is L4229/OJ-K and L4259/OJ-L in full; Wellingtons OJ-J, OJ-O and OJ-Q are identifiable by their codes only, while OJ-G shows the latter two digits '---14' of its serial number under its wing (probably L4214); another Wellington reveals part of its serial as '---67' under the starboard wing, making it possibly Wellington Mk.Ia N2867, a newly-delivered example from the Weybridge production line (its individual code letter following 'OJ-' is obscured). The Wellington carrying code letters OJ-T clearly has had its serial painted over; as this Wellington makes more appearances than any other in the film, it is possible Ministry of Information (MoI) or Air Ministry censors required its identity to be concealed when the 2nd Unit was filming.

What is of note among the first shots of the Wellingtons at dispersal is that one of them parked by the fence literally right beside a cottage carries the entirely different code letters of VF-G (its serial is not visible). 'VF-' are the code letters for No.99 Squadron, which was based at nearby RAF Newmarket at the time. The terrain of the airfield on which it and other Wellingtons stand is noticeably different from that of RAF Mildenhall, which suggests that the 2nd Unit also filmed at RAF Newmarket, although these shots have clearly been taken 'over the fence', ie, outside the airfield.

Of the Wellingtons that appear on film, one in particular deserves individual mention: this is L4259/OJ-L, which failed to return after the Raid. This means that "The Lion Has Wings" briefly shows footage of one of the first, if not the first, British military aircraft to be shot down in World War Two. This footage also confirms that it was taken by the GPO film crew either on 4th September before No.149's departure for the Raid, or on a date closely preceding it: L4259 obviously could not have been filmed two weeks later by the 2nd Unit.

There is a noticeable difference in picture quality and in presentation between the imagery taken by the two film crews, both ground-air and air-air. Some of the imagery of aircrew in front of their aircraft, and of the Wellingtons themselves engine running, is clear, smooth and steady, but other imagery is not, being of scratchy picture quality, jerky in motion (suggesting a hand-held camera) and speeded up: the latter was almost certainly filmed by the GPO crew, or even by a film crew from RAF Mildenhall itself.

The Wellingtons seen taking off on the actual raid are filmed in long shot, with RAF Mildenhall's distinctive hangars as a back drop (the same two hangars exist today, exactly as they appear in the film). This imagery is not creative, nor dramatic, which suggests that it was not taken for any purpose other than as a matter of record of the event. Also, the bombers were heavy, ie, bombed up; the GPO Film Unit crew was obviously not going to risk filming from a position close to the runway, in the event of one of the aircraft piling in with its full bomb load on board.

Other imagery of the Wellingtons taking off, however, is of much more clear quality, and with creativity of image and dramatic effect in mind. They are taken from a position very close to the lift off point of the Wellingtons from the grass runway. These images were surely taken by the 2nd Unit, on a date following the Raid and with the bombers almost certainly empty, filmed for "The Lion Has Wings". Other shots show three Wellingtons filmed from the ground making three-ship fly-overs in 'Vic', or making passes in either tactical spread formation or in line astern. The fly-overs appear to have been staged – probably over RAF Mildenhall itself – and cut into the film to portray the Wellingtons on their attack runs over the Kiel Kanal.

There is also a difference in quality and in style of the air-air shots of the Wellingtons in flight. Some have clearly been taken from within a Wellington itself, but again are less creative: this suggests it is GPO footage provided by the MoI we are looking at here, filmed on an earlier occasion than 4th September for stock footage. Noticeably, one image shows four Wellingtons, with three in 'Vic' and the fourth more distant, filmed with the starboard airscrew of the camera-ship clearly in view in the foreground. It is obviously that of a Vickers Wellington; it would be possible to obtain such a picture through the fuselage side windows built into the Geodesic airframe that is such an original feature of this bomber's design. The imagery is noticeably stable, with no camera shake, which suggests that the Wellington was a very steady aircraft to fly producing little in the way of vibration.

Other air-air imagery in the film is most clearly not stable, with the camera visibly shaking due to the vibrations from the aircraft in which it is mounted. However, the film imagery is much more clear, which suggests this was taken by the 2nd Unit and involved three Wellingtons that were assigned to fly various profiles with the camera-ship. But if the GPO's camera was not shaking when it was filming air-air, why then is the 2nd Unit's film shuddering like it was being taken in a train repeatedly running over points?

The answer almost certainly was that the 2nd Unit were filming from a different aircraft, and one that inflicted its own version of St Vitus's Dance on all those on board.

The possible culprit is seen in one shot lurking in the background from beneath the wing of a Wellington as it runs engines before take off. It is a clear example of the type of inadequate aircraft which RAF Bomber Command had foisted upon it at the start of the War, and which equally clearly gives the lie to the film's claim that only the finest aircraft from Britain's factories would be used by RAF pilots and crews. The aircraft in dubious question is a Bristol Bombay troop transport and medium bomber that was late and obsolete from the day the first production example flew in March 1939.

A twin-engined, heavy, all-metal ponderous beast of an aeroplane, the Bristol Bombay employed out-moded features like a high wing and fixed undercarriage, guaranteeing that it would go nowhere fast. It would almost certainly induce the shakes in a film camera.

Ruled out of bombing operations over Europe even from the beginning of the War, only 50 Bristol Bombays plus the prototype were built and equipped four RAF squadrons, three of them operating in the Middle East and North Africa campaigns. The sole British-based Bombay squadron, No.271, a transport unit that flew supplies to the British Expeditionary Force in France, didn't form up until May 1940, seven months after "The Lion Has Wings" was released. The example used may have come from the batch that was allocated to No.216 Squadron in Egypt in October 1939, and loaned to Powell's 2nd Unit before delivery, as it was not a priority asset for the RAF's European war theater, or it could have been the actual prototype, K3583, on Air Ministry charge.

One small mystery occurs during the air-air sequences. A Wellington clearly identified as L4346 appears in close-up to display the tail gunner's position, but also visible are the squadron code letters of 'UX-'. These are the codes of No.214 Squadron; no other Wellington in the film is seen with these codes, so why a No.214 aircraft suddenly appears can only remain unknown.

The interior sequences of the crew of the lead Wellington during their flight over the North Sea and of their attack on the German warships are probably the most convincing and the best element of "The Lion Has Wings". The sequences were filmed inside a Wellington - albeit, a very stripped-out one in terms of on-board equipment - and depict the stages of the attack as carried out by the aircrew in 1939 quite realistically. However, the crew are portrayed by actors, with the pilot in what appears to be a white flying suit; with his soft leather flying helmet and long leather gloves, plus what seems to be a lot of facial cream make-up, he has the appearance of an alien spaceman! An error in detail is the fact that the crew are not wearing life jackets, which they most certainly would have done on an over-water mission.

The film's portrayal of the attack on the German cruisers is where it departs from reality in this section. The attack is shown to be a complete success, and it is likely that initial reports in the British press conveyed the same message. Quite probably cinema audiences cheered aloud at this sequence.

The reality is that the Kiel Kanal Raid on 4th September achieved very little. The two pocket battleships, as the script describes them, were in fact the Panzer Schiffe (later, redesignated Schwer Kreuzer: heavy cruiser) Admiral Scheer and the light cruiser Emden. Neither was damaged. Two Wellingtons were lost, one being the aforementioned L4259, the first RAF losses of World War Two.

For attacks on the Wellingtons by Luftwaffe fighters, Korda and his editorial team have had to rely on stock MoI footage of Spitfires and Fairey Battles, as they had no archive footage of German fighters available to them at this earliest stage of the War.

"They drew first blood in a war that was not of their making", proclaims the commentator, over shots of the Wellingtons landing back at base – again a mix of the GPO Film Unit's and Powell's 2nd Unit footage. At this point, the commentator admits that what is being shown is a reconstruction, thus confirming that Powell's 2nd Unit had filmed the Wellingtons on a separate occasion. But what unquestionably is true is the statement by the commentator that, "the men you now see stepping out of these bombers are the officers and the men of the RAF who actually carried out that heroic raid". Propaganda always was, and always will be, a mix of fact and falsehood.

"The Lions Has Wings" now moves to the final third of the film's message, carried by RAF Fighter Command.

Powell's 2nd Unit was given access to No.74 Squadron at RAF Hornchurch, Essex, and their Vickers Supermarine Spitfire Mk.Ia fighters, then the most advanced fighter type in Royal Air Force service. No.74 have traditionally been known as 'The Tigers', due to the tiger's head in their squadron emblem. They were most famously known well after the War for being the first RAF fighter squadron to mount a full aerobatic team on the English Electric Lightning, the first British supersonic jet fighter to enter squadron service. In the film, Powell includes a shot of the squadron's crew tent beside their Spitfires, labelled the "The Tigers Den" and with a "Wanted!" poster of Hitler taped to it.

No.74 Squadron provided six of its Spitfires for Powell's 2nd Unit, acting as 'A' and 'B' Flights of Nos.299 and 301 Squadrons. Neither of these two squadrons existed at the time. The real No.299 Squadron did not form until 1943, as a troop-carrying glider-tug outfit on Vickers Venturas, whilst No.301 was destined to become the second of two Polish bomber squadrons in the RAF formed in 1940, first with Fairey Battles, then later on the Vickers Wellington.

This final third of the film is intended to portray RAF Fighter Command, along with the barrage balloon units, the anti-aircraft gun divisions and the Observer Corps, combining to defeat German air raids. It has to be remembered that the Battle of Britain was 10 months into the future when the film was made and that the earliest Luftwaffe raids on Britain mostly involved mine-laying operations at harbour entrances during the first few months of the 'Phoney War'. Therefore, what is shown in "The Lion Has Wings" is a fictional portrayal of RAF air defence, as the large-scale interceptions as shown in the film had yet to take place.

It is a most deeply flawed representation of Fighter Command in action, but it was sending out a message to the German High Command that Britain could defend itself day and night. In so doing, it was sending a coded message to Germany that Britain had a secret weapon and that the Luftwaffe would suffer in British airspace, no matter when it attacked. It is noteworthy that the film appears to be informing the British public at the outset of the War, that the expectation was that the Luftwaffe would bomb only at night. This was probably based on the experience of the previous Great War, when Imperial German Air Force Zeppelin airships and Gotha bombers did conduct their raids on Britain during night-time for greater protection against fighters. But "The Lion Has Wings" is telling the audience, and with it the Luftwaffe, that the RAF's Spitfire squadrons were capable of intercepting and shooting down enemy aircraft in the dark. This was completely untrue at the time, as aerial night fighting had yet to be developed successfully by either side.

However, "The Lion Has Wings" was being truthful in hinting at Germany that Britain had a secret weapon which enabled British fighter pilots to see the enemy coming and to be prepared for them. Radar, or more correctly radio direction finding (RDF), was very much a secret weapon in the RAF's armoury in 1939; it is unlikely that Korda and Powell were privy to its capabilities, but nonetheless they clearly had been given sufficient information to allow them to threaten Nazi Germany in their film with the message that aerial attacks on Britain could be successfully intercepted and repulsed.

In this sense, "The Lion Has Wings" is now being used as a weapon itself against Germany, aimed at sowing doubt in the minds of the enemy. The possibility of using film aggressively against a would-be invader undoubtedly did much to persuade the War Office of the viability of what could be called cinematic warfare, and thus ensured its support for the film industry during the dark years to come.

Nonetheless, some of the film's claims about Britain's air defences are simply rubbish, such as the supposed threat posed by barrage balloons in deterring attacks due to the risk of aircraft flying into their cables. True, that was the purpose of the barrage balloon defence, but the Luftwaffe was never once deterred by the balloons' infestation over London, simply because it never flew low enough to strike their cables.

And the commentator's claim that the balloons would force the German bombers to fly higher, and thus lose accuracy in bombing, exposes the lack of knowledge in the film about bombing techniques. Korda and Co appear not to be aware of the contradiction of their making exaggerated claims for the RAF's bombing methods aided by scientific instruments, such as the bomb sight, while assuming that the Luftwaffe would not have the same or equivalent aids. Moreover, the film can today be shown to confirm the complete lack of knowledge within the RAF's Air Staff about the Luftwaffe's Knickebein navigational beam system, which enabled German bombers to attack selected targets much more accurately than their British counterparts when 'The Blitz' attacks began in late 1940.

Much of this final part of the film focuses on RAF Fighter Command's Operations Centre and its system of plotters. Although broadly accurate, it seems that Korda was only given sufficient information by the Air Ministry for him to create at Denham Studios his idea of what an Operations Centre may appear to be. For instance, in reality there was the one main plotting table, not a second "action table" as the film depicts.

Ralph Richardson's character is an Operations Commander at a mythical RAF Fighter Station. He brings a sharp edge to the otherwise fixed stereotypical role he is asked to play. Again, the film portrays Korda's interpretation of what an RAF fighter station's Operations Room appeared to be; "Angels One Five" (1952), made six years after the end of World War Two, shows a much more accurate and realistic Fighter Station Operations Room in action.

What follows in this part of the film contains many errors in the depiction of aircraft flown, partly because at this time so little archive or stock footage of Luftwaffe aircraft was available to Korda's editorial team, requiring them to be "creative" with what they could use. It also exposes their lack of knowledge of aircraft types to an embarrassing degree.

For instance, among the first shots of No.74 Squadron's Spitfires at rest on the grass at RAF Hornchurch, two lines of Fairey Battle light bombers suddenly appear; the quality of their imagery is clearly inferior to the 2nd Unit's footage of the Spitfires, so the Battles obviously haven't been filmed by Powell's crew and must be stock material from the MoI or the Air Ministry. This error must have been made in the editing suite, the editors inserting the Battles' line up by mistaking them for Spitfires! "Fast machines: fighters, interceptors, pursuit 'planes" claims the commentator, everything the lumbering, obsolete Fairey Battle was not.

We shouldn't be too surprised at the film's depiction of robotic-like Luftwaffe bomber aircrews receiving their orders from their rigid, authoritarian Commander, all very World War One-like in appearance, adorned head to foot in leather as if they are about to board Fokker or Albatros aircraft. In effect, this is the image that Korda and Powell have tried to create because they next show a long line-up of German bombers turning massed propellers before take off to attack Britain: the bombers are obsolete 1936-vintage Heinkel He.51C bi-planes.

The Heinkel He.51 fighter and light attack aircraft only really knew success with the German Legion Kondor that fought alongside General Franco's Nationalist Forces in the Spanish Civil War. By the time World War Two broke out, it had been relegated to being a trainer, having been surpassed by much more modern monoplane fighter and attack designs. It was a big brute of a bi-plane and the imagery in "The Lion Has Wings" of this massed array of He.51Cs, all whirling propellers and bulged exhaust housings, is extremely rare. Obviously Korda used it because similar imagery of much more representative and threatening Dornier and Heinkel bombers was not available at the time. The Luftwaffe never risked the Heinkel He.51 in the skies above Britain.

To depict Luftwaffe bomber formations approaching Britain, Korda's editorial team have had to resort to using archive footage of 27 Junkers Ju.52/3M tri-motor transports, flying in what appears to be a ceremonial display, with three waves of nine Ju.52s each, possibly either over Berlin or Nuremberg. Any newsreel footage of Luftwaffe bombers in action over Poland had yet to become available in September 1939. The Ju.52 footage is immediately followed by more archive footage from the same aerial parade, this time of 18 Dornier Do.23G medium bombers. The Do.23 had a short service life with the Luftwaffe during the early to mid-Thirties, being a slow, lumbering twin-engined design with a poor safety record. The imagery of the Do.23Gs (and of the Ju.52s) in "The Lion Has Wings" dates this ceremonial parade as probably being no later than that of 1936, as the Do.23 had been withdrawn from Luftwaffe service and replaced by the much faster, more modern Heinkel He.111 when Fall Weisse (Case, or File, White), the Wehrmacht's code name for the invasion of Poland, was put into effect on 1st September 1939. Again, this confirms that Korda had no up-to-date film material of the Deutsches Luftwaffe to use in his production.

"Tonight's the night", exclaims the Air Officer Commanding (AOC) Fighter Command, who, for some unknown reason at the director's behest, wears his RAF cap at a slanted angle, making him look slightly drunk. The raids on the plotting table shown approaching the east coast of England are comically small – of five, eight and 12 aircraft respectively – compared with what was to become the overwhelming reality in 1940, revealing again the limited knowledge of the film's production team, and possibly that of the Air Ministry, at the time.

Group Control gives the order to "Braxted Fighter Station" to alert 'A' Flight, 299 Squadron. Richardson orders 'A' Flight to "Take off": no mention of the command, "Scramble" – clearly the term had yet to become RAF fighter pilot lore. 'A' Flight pilots dash in white flying suits from their crew tent, in complete darkness – Korda, Powell and the Air Ministry are definitely taking liberties with reality here.

The imagery we then see is that taken by Powell's 2nd Unit at RAF Hornchurch, showing pilots running not too hurriedly to their Spitfires, strapping on parachutes, entering their cockpits and starting engines. What is noticeable is that the Spitfires are filmed in almost complete shadow, masking any squadron code letters and serials. The scene is meant to be taking place at night, so this partly explains the effect, but the intention may also have been to obscure the Spitfires' markings for security reasons. If this was the case, one wonders what security was being achieved because No.74 Squadron's emblem is clearly shown at the beginning of this section of the film. Also, only a limited attempt was made to conceal the Wellingtons of No.149 Squadron, an interesting contrast. Perhaps Korda and Powell had to deal with the different security requirements of two different Commands in the RAF, Bomber and Fighter, whose approach to war fighting was significantly different (which indeed it was: there were times, especially in the early part of the War, when the two Commands rarely spoke to each other).

Powell's direction of the Spitfires' take off sequence is sharp and neatly edited to convey the urgency of 299 Squadron's call to action. What is particularly of note is the sight in the background, represented by black dots in the sky, of the barrage balloon defences over London – no doubting the reality of the situation being depicted here, but compare the few balloons seen in this footage with the massed clusters of the big bags shown in later films of the War.

In fact, Powell's sequence with the Spitfires is arguably the best cut and edited in the film overall. The six Spitfire Mk.Ia fighters of No.74 Squadron allocated to Powell's 2nd Unit are then mostly seen making passes in two separate 'Vics' of three, to portray the pursuit and interception of the German raiders.

Here again Korda has had to resort to what was available to him, to show in-coming Luftwaffe raiders approaching Harwich. Air-air imagery of five Fairey Battles try to convince us they are German bombers; their picture quality in flight appears cleaner than stock footage, so they may have been filmed 'upstairs' by the 2nd Unit. However, there are no air-airs of the Spitfires.

When 'Cornflower Raid', the operational name for 'A' Flight, sight the five 'Bandits', one of the Spitfire pilots lets out an inexplicably loud and unintelligible bellow into his mike, seeming to represent a war cry that prompts a response from Richardson listening in the Ops Room: "Here we go".

The enemy then changes into a single Focke Wulf FW.200 airliner, whose imagery has been reversed by the editors so that the Swastika emblem on the tail is displayed spiralling in the reverse direction to that which the Nazi Party adopted for their infamous use of this ancient symbol. The FW.200 is filmed with its undercarriage retracting on take-off. For the film's editors, it was a case of anything would have to do. They use this same image of the FW.200 several times in this sequence, the final time showing the airliner flying in the correct direction, as its Swastika's position confirms.

The quality of the footage is dark and poor, which prevents any successful attempt at identification of the aircraft. However, Focke Wulf FW.200 airliners operated by Lufthansa had a distinct dark blue cheat line running the length of the fuselage, which ended near the tail section where the civilian registration letters were displayed. There is clear enough imagery of this FW.200 to detect a cheat line, but no registration letters are discernable close to the rear fuselage's junction with the tail section as they should be. Adolf Hitler had been allocated a personal FW.200, the third prototype serialled D-2600 and named Immelmann III, after the World War One German air ace, Max Immelmann. It is possible that this is footage of Hitler's personal aircraft, the only known public source of it on film; the smaller serial number 'D-2600' would be more difficult to discern, making the FW.200 appear anonymous as it does in the film. Most pictures of Hitler's personal FW.200V3 show the aircraft in its military garb and serial during the War; before the War, the same aircraft appeared in a colour scheme very similar to the FW.200s flown by Lufthansa. Newsreel footage of it would be available to Korda's team, possibly filmed taking off with Der Fuhrer on board on a pre-War occasion; using it to depict the enemy taking off to attack Britain would have been logical for Korda to use.

More archive footage is then used, British this time, of five Bristol Blenheim Mk.I bombers in formation with three Spitfires peeling off from them – the footage is of poor quality. No.74 Squadron's Spitfires tail chase each other, to give the impression of dog-fighting, while actors playing their pilots either yell out loud during the fight or nonchantly chew gum – yes, RAF pilots could fly and chew gum at the same time (note: Spitfire pilots in white flying suits, German bomber pilots in black). Several shots of a single Lufthansa Junkers Ju.52/3M are also used here. Model miniatures of very basic quality are used to depict crashing German bombers.

'B' Flight of 299 Squadron is then ordered to take off and intercept the second raid coming in. A formation of eight unidentified b-iplanes (due to their height and distance on film) is used to depict this. Powell uses this sequence to film anti-aircraft and searchlight batteries in action, again accurately and effectively.

'A' Flight returns to base to refuel and re-arm: "In the ghostly shrouded blackness of the aerodrome, everything goes with clockwork smoothness, as if they were working in broad daylight", announces the imaginative commentator. One wonders what the Spitfire pilots themselves thought of this blatant distortion of their real operational methods. Perhaps, if it spoofed the enemy, then fine.

The film now foists the ridiculous fantasy onto the audience that the balloon barrage could deter German bombers and cause them to abandon their raid. More footage from the ceremonial parade showing the Junkers Ju.52s is used to depict this raid, as well as similar footage of trios of Heinkel He.51 bi-planes from probably the same event, not to mention that back-to-front FW.200 as well. The scene has the Luftwaffe pilots desperately pulling back on their control columns, to avoid flying into the cluster of balloons!

The commentator claims that the bombers have been forced to climb too high for accurate bombing, so they turn and make for home, pursued by Spitfires of 301 Squadron out over the North Sea. Here, the film editors have at last been able to make brief use of a piece of darkened archive footage of three Heinkel He.111 bombers in 'Vic' formation, the only accurate footage presumably available to them. But the three He.111s then turn into three RAF Vickers Wellesley single-engined day bombers, so ruining the impression (the Wellesley was another piece of kit RAF Bomber Command could well have done without at the start of the War).

The final air battle is depicted by a close up of Richardson's face, displaying his tension as he listens to cannon fire and shouting from the Spitfire pilots coming through the Ops Room's speakers. But the raid is successfully repulsed. The film ends, after Merle Oberon's impassioned and patriotic speech about standing up for freedom and fairness, with a final sight of the massed fly-past at RAF Hendon.

Several years after its release, Michael Powell expressed his regret at making this film, largely because the course of the War for Britain had exposed too many of its deceptions and distortions. Reportedly, Ralph Richardson later disliked being associated with it. But one man was satisfied with the result: Alexanda Korda. For, with this film, he achieved what he had really set out to do – to save the British film industry from being dismantled by the government, from which it might never have sufficiently arisen again. Korda was right. The impact of "The Lion Has Wings" was everything that the British government wanted at the time, and from then on gave its full support to cinema as a vital morale-booster to a war-damaged population.

It might not be too much an exaggeration to state that, had the government closed the British film industry down in 1939, it is unlikely it would ever have produced in the years following World War Two such classics as the Ealing Comedies, the Hammer Horror films, and produced stars like Alec Guinness, Peter Sellers, Sean Connery and Michael Caine. Just think, no James Bond, no Harry Potter. So, if you watch "The Lion Has Wings", treat it with the respect it deserves – despite all the lies it has to tell.

NIGHT TRAIN TO MUNICH

(Released: August 1940)

Released when the Battle of Britain was raging at its height, "Night Train to Munich" is an espionage thriller based on the Nazi Occupation of the city of Prague and on the battle of wits between British Military Intelligence and the German Gestapo in trying to secure the services of a brilliant Czech scientific metallurgist who has designed a new, more effective form of armour. Both sides want to make use of his design. The plot's time period covers from 15th March 1939, the day Wehrmacht forces enter Prague to "protect" the city, up to 3rd September 1939, the day Britain declares war on Nazi Germany.

Technically, "Night Train to Munich" is much more of a spy film in the Bulldog Drummond mould than a war film, but Britain had been at war with Germany for just a few days short of one whole year when it was released. The Royal Air Force and the Luftwaffe were fighting daily air battles in the skies overhead, while the whole population was preparing to face the expected imminent German invasion of Britain. To say it does not qualify as a war film is to nit-pick at the most obdurate level.

Aviation plays only a limited role in "Night Train to Munich", but what is shown is significant. Nearly all of it is archive material and is used right at the beginning of the film, when the Czech scientist is trying to escape from Prague with his daughter, played by the fascinatingly beautiful Margaret Lockwood. German war 'planes power over Prague, depicted by an archive shot of 12 Messerschmitt Bf.110 Zerstorers flying in successive 'Vics' of three aircraft apiece. Clearly this is footage of an aerial formation parade, but what makes its imagery of particular note is that it has been filmed from a location in a public street, not in a ceremonial parade ground itself, because the Bf.110s can be seen to disappear behind the roof of a house that the cameraman is standing next to. One wonders if this is unofficial film footage, taken by a cameraman not endorsed by the Nazi authorities and filmed from a vantage point he had found along the route of the fly-past. Perhaps it was subsequently passed to one of the newsreel agencies in Britain, or may even have been clandestinely filmed footage smuggled out of the country in which it had been shot (Czechoslovakia?).

As if to endorse the possibility that this is unofficial footage, another shot follows soon after it, this time of 25 unidentifiable aircraft flying at height in a large formation of conjoined 'Vics' over a metropolitan area. They are flying at a considerable distance away from the camera position, which is located at ground level next to what appears to be an apartment block with a domed church tower beyond it. There is a terrace at the end of the block, on which a tall, thin figure can clearly be seen standing watching the formation as it powers away in the distance amid clear skies and cumulous clouds. In the bottom right hand corner of the screen an engraved metal sign can be seen, with the letters 'O I B' clearly visible above a curved rim. There are smaller engraved letters below contained within the upper and lower bars of the rim: they do not seem to match any recognisable lettering.

But when this image is viewed with the aid of a mirror placed in front of and held towards the screen, the combined set of letters appear to read 'BIO MODERNA' (the footage has been cut into the film in reverse). The sign they form might translate as 'Modern Life'. In what city and what European country this footage was taken is anyone's guess (it might have been Prague), and what message it is meant to convey with the mystical-sounding words below the mysterious figure beyond watching the massed formation of aeroplanes passing away, can only be guessed at. There is no doubt that this shot was staged, with the cameraman ready and waiting for the formation to pass over, while the lone figure was placed fully in view above the curious lettering to watch the aerial parade. For what reason, we may never know.

The only aircraft in the film that is not shown in archive footage is a bi-plane parked in a hangar in the background of a scene that is presumably intended to be taking place at Prague-Ruzyne Airport. The scientist is standing by the door of the aircraft which is about to fly himself and his daughter to England (the fuselage is a studio prop of no specific aircraft type). Unbeknown to him, his daughter has been arrested by the Gestapo. An open-top car driving Gestapo officers and led by two motorcycle outriders speeds through a gate in the airfield's fence and heads towards him. The scientist has to get on board fast as his aircraft moves to take off.

As the motorcycles and car race onto the airfield, they pass a hangar with its doors open. What looks like a Hawker Hart Trainer can be clearly seen inside the hangar. Which airfield location this is that is being used for Prague-Ruzyne Airport isn't identifiable, but a windsock in the background clearly carries the letters 'X L G' printed on it. Presumably these letters form either the Ministry of Transport code for the airfield, or a logo for a company which provided the windsock.

The scientist manages to escape from Prague on board the aircraft bound for England. To illustrate his escape, either newsreel or archive footage of Lockheed 14W Super Electra G-AFGN of British Airways appears, presumably filmed taking off from Heston Airport outside London from where British Airways operated prior to World War Two. The Civil Aviation Authority (CAA) database shows that Super Electra G-AFGN came onto the British civil aviation register on 20th June 1938. It is a notable aircraft, having inaugurated British Airways' non-stop London-Stockholm-London service on 18th September 1938. But its most public claim to fame is that it was in this Super Electra that Prime Minister Neville Chamberlain flew back to Heston from Munich on 29th September 1938, to proclaim his fateful "Peace in our time" message after his final meeting with Herr Hitler. Therefore, using imagery of this actual aircraft in "Night Train to Munich" is particularly apt from an historical perspective, while at the time of the film's release on 31st August 1940 this actual Lockheed Super Electra would probably have been very recognisable to British cinema audiences. Super Electra G-AFGN is recorded as being permanently withdrawn from use on 11th August 1939, having crash landed at Luxeuil, France, just seven days after the Bill the government had presented to form the British Overseas Airways Corporation (BOAC) received its Royal Assent.

From this point onwards in the film's plot, aviation does not feature again in "Night Train to Munich". But despite this, the film is an enjoyable romp that delights in poking the Gestapo in the eye, which would have been well received by British audiences in 1940. Directed by Carol Reed - he of "The Third Man" (1949) fame to come - "Night Train to Munich" is pacey, while being a spin-off from the Alfred Hitchcock classic thriller, "The Lady Vanishes" (1938), which also starred Margaret Lockwood. British war film fans might be interested to know that the climax, in which the Bulldog Drummond-style hero played by Rex Harrison escapes from the Gestapo by jumping from one cable car to another, inspired the cable car fight scene in "Where Eagles Dare" (1968).

CONVOY

(Released: September 1940)

"Convoy" was Ealing Studios' first feature-length war film. It is naturally propagandistic in style, but nowhere near to the level of "The Lion Has Wings" (1939). Michael Balcon was the producer, as he was for all of Ealing Studios' war films made between 1939 – 1948. Later Sir Michael Balcon, he was head of production for Ealing Studios from 1938 – 1959, during which time this prolific British film company produced such classics as "Kind Hearts and Coronets" (1949), "The Blue Lamp" (1950) and "The Lavender Hill Mob" (1951), all of which may never have seen the light of day if it was not for Alexander Korda's success in saving the British film industry with "The Lion Has Wings".

The Royal Navy and the Merchant Navy take centre stage in "Convoy". Its theme is the protection of North Sea convoys from German U-Boats and surface raiders, like the pocket battleship Deutschland. The term 'pocket battleship' was coined by the Admiralty at the outbreak of war as a definition for the heavier class of cruiser that the Kriegsmarine had in service, whose 11-inch guns were significantly longer in range than the eight-inch guns of the Royal Navy's lighter but faster cruisers. In Kriegsmarine service, warships of the Deutschland's class were termed Panzer Schiffe (armoured ship). At the time of the film's production, the Deutschland had been renamed Lutzow on Hitler's orders, due to his fear that the morale of the German people might be harmed if the warship bearing the name of their Fatherland should be sunk by the enemy. It, along with other Panzer Schiffen of the Deutschland's class, had been redesignated by the Kriegsmarine in 1940 as Schwer Kreuzer (heavy cruiser) class warships. The original Deutschland was one of three such heavy cruisers, the others being the Graf Spee (scuttled in December 1939 off Montevideo, when cornered by three British cruisers) and the Admiral Scheer, which "The Lion Has Wings" claimed was successfully bombed by the RAF on 4th September 1939.

The plot of "Convoy" has the Royal Navy cruiser HMS Apollo nobly sacrificing itself to take on the much more powerful Deutschland, to protect the convoy it is escorting. What makes "Convoy" of real interest to military historians is that much of it was filmed during an actual wartime convoy protection task, and that the destroyers and cruiser which feature in it were actually on operations escorting merchant vessels.

The aviation elements of "Convoy" are not many and all involve stock footage taken pre-War. In one sequence, to show Fleet Air Arm aircraft launching off the deck of the fictional aircraft carrier HMS Aquila (depicted by footage of the converted battlecruiser HMS Glorious, an appropriate image to use as this pre-War aircraft carrier conversion met her end in the North Sea when, on 8th June 1940, she was sunk by the German battlecruisers Scharnhorst and Gneisenau), two Fairey Swordfish Mk.I torpedo bombers are seen being hand-cranked into starting engines. A third Swordfish, distinctly in pre-War markings and not carrying a torpedo, is seen starting its take off roll from what was probably HMS Glorious's flight deck; while a final shot filmed from a Swordfish's air gunner's position looks back at the departing flight deck, with a host of Swordfish ranged together on it with folded wings.

The most significant aviation element is the shot of HMS Apollo launching her reconnaissance aircraft, to locate the Deutschland. This is depicted by very brief imagery of a Hawker Osprey fighter reconnaissance floatplane being launched by catapult from the deck of a Royal Navy cruiser. The use of this imagery is not accurate for the period of the film's plot because, by the time of the outbreak of World War Two, all Hawker Ospreys had been withdrawn from front-line Fleet Air Arm service.

The Osprey was the navalised version of the RAF's Hawker Hart day bomber, converted for maritime fighter and reconnaissance tasks, and was produced either with landing gear and arrestor hooks for operations off carriers, or with floats for catapult launching off cruisers. By 1935, the Second Cruiser Squadron of the Home Fleet had a number of cruisers carrying Hawker Ospreys, but these were withdrawn in 1939. Which actual Osprey appears in "Convoy" is not easily identifiable due to the indifferent quality of the brief footage in which it is shown, but its '034' code number is clearly visible.

The Osprey is later shown attacking the Deutschland, represented by a very crude and obvious studio miniature, even allowing for the SFX limitations of the day. When seen searching for the heavy cruiser, the film editor has resorted to brief footage of a Saro London flying boat to represent HMS Apollo's spotter aircraft.

No more aviation elements appear in "Convoy", an early British war film which has earned plaudits for balancing realism with the inevitable propaganda message of British courage and self-sacrifice on the high seas in the face of a powerful and implacable enemy.

FREEDOM RADIO

(Released: February 1941)

This unusual British propaganda film was aimed at a wartime German and Austrian population, in an attempt to convince them they had been lied to by the Nazi Party. Not that they would have had much chance of seeing the film, but its screenplay was written by an Austrian who wanted the free world to know that there were Germans and Austrians who had actively opposed the Nazis up to the date of the invasion of Poland. The title is based on the forbidden radio station set up by an Austrian gentleman who is described in the film as being Hitler's former doctor, to counter the broadcasts by the Reich's Propaganda Ministry. Aircraft do not appear in "Freedom Radio".

DANGEROUS MOONLIGHT

(Released: June 1941)

This dark and enigmatic war film owes much to its dark and enigmatic star, Anton Walbrook, an Austrian-born actor who left his native country in 1936 when the Nazis were growing in strength and came to England, where he remained throughout the War years and became a British national. "Dangerous Moonlight" made Walbrook's name like no other, his intense, saturnine good looks suiting well this chiaroscuro-esque film classic, one which impacted emotionally on wartime British audiences more so than almost any other production during the War years. Walbrook's appeal to female film fans had not a little to do with its popular reception.

Adding to the film's allure is the performance by the truly lovely British actress, Sally Gray, playing very convincingly an American journalist, Carol Peters, who falls in love with Walbrook's Polish fighter pilot, Stefan Radetzky, during a German air raid on Warsaw. But the film is most remembered for its signature music, "The Warsaw Concerto", a classical piano composition still played today in concert performances to audiences who, for the most part, are probably unaware that it was composed especially for "Dangerous Moonlight". Radetzky happens also to be Poland's leading classical pianist, according to the story's plotline.

The title refers to the danger of going out on a moonlit night because, as the common belief of the time held, German bombers favoured attacking cities when the moon was bright. The title becomes especially poignant when one realises that The Blitz had only just ended the month prior to the release of this film. "Dangerous Moonlight" was produced literally at the height of The Blitz.

Radetzky and Peters fall in love the night before Poland surrenders to the advancing Wehrmacht forces. The next day Radetzky and his fellow surviving Polish Air Force comrades must fly their final mission before the surrender at midday. But four of them are to fly the last four Polish fighters to Romania. They draw lots to choose the fortunate four. Radetzky wants to stay to fight, but his colleagues fix the draw without his knowledge to ensure that he is one of the chosen, because they want him to draw the world's attention to Poland's suffering wherever he performs his piano concerts.

The last Polish Air Force wave of bombers departing on their final mission, from which the aircrews know they will not return, is portrayed by MoI footage of three Bristol Blenheim Is in 'Vic' formation. The fighter that Radetzky is to fly to Romania is a Spitfire Mk.Ia with a large Polish military quadrant pasted over its port fuselage roundel. Obviously there was no footage available

at the time of real Polish Air Force aircraft that could be used. The Spitfire is seen being wheeled out of a hangar, in readiness for Radetzky's flight to Romania. An extraordinary goof immediately follows, with footage of a Luftwaffe Dornier Do.17 being used to portray Radetzky taking off! How the film's editor came to make such an obvious howler defies explanation.

Radetzky flies over the bombed-out city of Warsaw, saying, as he looks pityingly down on the destroyed city, "I'll be back one day. One day I'll be back". Whether it literally is the ruins of Warsaw that are shown – filmed from a slow-flying aircraft with a high wing configuration, judging from the shadow it casts, perhaps a Fieseler Storch – cannot be known to anyone outside of Poland itself. If it is, then this can only be footage released by the Reich Propaganda Ministry, to show the world what destruction the Luftwaffe could wreak.

The bulk of the film concerns the struggle between Radetzky and Carol Peters in their relationship after they marry and move to New York, where he is torn between playing concerts to promote support for Poland in the United States or whether he should go to England to join the Royal Air Force. This reveals the main purpose of the film, it being a propaganda vehicle to send the message to isolationist America that it needs to join the fight against Nazi Germany. At the time of the film's British release, America was still determinedly neutral. Ironically, "Dangerous Moonlight" did not achieve theatrical release in the United States until April 1942, by which time Japan and Germany had made certain that America would be fully engaged.

Aviation plays no part in this central section of the film. But eventually Radetzky leaves Carol for England and joins a Polish fighter squadron in the RAF. For this part of the story footage from the MoI and imagery of an RAF fighter squadron in action is mixed with film of a Spitfire loaned to the production company, RKO Radio British Productions, to portray the RAF fighter that Radetzky flies (it also carried the Polish quadrant earlier in the film, to impersonate the Polish Air Force fighter in which Radetzky escapes to Romania). The Air Ministry made available Spitfire Mk.Ia R6774 for this purpose, which flies without any squadron codes and has the smaller lower wing tip roundels that were in use at the start of the War, but which were abandoned soon afterwards. As "Dangerous Moonlight" was filmed in 1941, this suggests that Spitfire Ia R6774 could not have been a squadron aircraft, as no operational Spitfires were carrying these small wing tip roundels by the time the film was made. According to a report issued in July 1940, Spitfire Ia R6774 was used by the Aircraft & Armament Experimental Establishment (A&AEE) to air test the de Havilland variable speed airscrew against Spitfire Ia N3171 fitted with the Rotol constant speed airscrew. The latter was found to be marginally superior in performance, resulting in all new-build Mk.II Spitfires being automatically fitted in production with the Rotol airscrew, while in-service Mk.I and Mk.II 'Spits' were retrofitted with the same propeller.

The Spitfire Aircraft Production Website shows that Spitfire Ia R6774 was on charge with the Royal Aircraft Establishment (RAE) at Farnborough from October 1940 onwards, where it remained until it was reduced to instructional airframe status with

No.3 School of Technical Training in March 1943. It would thus have been with the RAE when it was loaned to RKO Radio British Productions for its appearance in "Dangerous Moonlight".

In a 'Scramble' sequence, images of 'ZD-' coded Spitfire Mk.IIa fighters of No.222 (Natal) Squadron appear, probably taken at RAF Hornchurch where No.222 was based during and after the Battle of Britain. Of the six Spitfires in shot, ZD-D and ZD-G are identifiable. Another 'Scramble' shows a line of Spitfire Mk.Is of No.19 Squadron at RAF Duxford, distinguishable by their two-bladed propellers which indicates that the footage was taken either pre-War or at the start of the War, almost certainly by the GPO Film Unit; by 1940, No.19 had changed to the three-bladed Spitfire Mk.Ia. More No.222 Squadron Spitfires are seen taxying for take-off, ZD-J among them, before the film cuts to imagery of an entire squadron of Spitfires taking off en masse – 12 aircraft – in four 'Vics' of three from an all-grass airfield. Four more Spitfires are seen dispersed around the edges of the airfield, as the massed formation roars impressively off the grass.

Reich Propaganda Ministry footage of nine Messerschmitt Bf.110s leading 18 Messerschmitt Bf.109s in a ceremonial fly-past is used to portray an incoming Luftwaffe raid – this footage is also used in "Reach For The Sky" (1956), although in "Dangerous Moonlight" it has been reversed. Equally reversed is air–air footage of a Heinkel He.111H, clearly identified with the aid of a mirror as 9K+FP of Kampfgeschwader 51 (KG.51). More reversed Reich Propaganda Ministry footage follows, this time of massed formations of Luftwaffe bombers comprising five He.111s leading no less than 30 Dornier Do.17s. Flying to intercept them are the 12 Spitfires of No.222 Squadron in very untactical four 'Vics' astern – RAF Fighter Command learnt the hard way that the 'Vic' formation only offered Bf.109s a large, easy target and provided no tactical advantage at all. What is very clear is that the editor has made sure the Spitfires are shown flying in the correct order, with ZD-A, ZD-B, ZD-R and ZD-V all clearly visible, as well as the previously identified ZD-G and ZD-J, whereas he has reversed all the imagery of the Luftwaffe aircraft. Was this his way of showing the difference between the good guys and the bad guys?

If so, his enthusiasm to portray the Luftwaffe in as bad a light as possible seems to have gone to the extreme when he has inserted a shot of the incoming raid shown flying upside down! This might appear to be the goof of goofs, but not necessarily, not when one realises that the director and editor were working amid the terror of The Blitz on London. What more obvious way for them to convey their utter contempt for the enemy that is bombing their cities than to portray him as twisted and back-to-front, achieved by reversing his image in the shape of the Luftwaffe on screen. Other commentators have criticised the makers of "Dangerous Moonlight" for making what appear to be such clumsily distinct errors, but they overlook the grim realities facing both the production team and the cinema audiences in 1941. Thus, these reversed and inverted images are no accident: they are the film's deliberate insult to Nazi Germany and a means by which the director and the editor are fighting back.

In the climactic dog-fight, the editor has had to resort to using similar material of RAF bombers to represent Luftwaffe types as the Alexander Korda team had to do, due to the lack of footage of German aircraft in combat at the time. Thus a Bristol Blenheim I makes several appearances in the dog-fight as a Luftwaffe bomber, although a gun-camera Special Effects shot of a Heinkel He.111 streaming smoke is used for Radetzky's first shoot-down. The quality of this SFX is exceptionally good for the 1941 period, making the shoot-down look very realistic

It has been suggested that shots in "Dangerous Moonlight" of fighters milling around the sky were taken during an actual dog-fight, but careful freeze-frame analysis of the aircraft involved confirms that they are all Spitfires. They also total 12, so they almost certainly are the No.222 Squadron Spitfires flying pre-planned profiles of peel-offs and tail chases for the camera.

Radetzky – flying without his face mask, so he neither needs oxygen nor his radio while he stays good looking for the audience – shoots down a second He.111 in a real gun-camera shot that has been frequently used since in other films and documentaries. This is the first gun-camera footage of an aircraft being shot down to be used in any feature film in the world. No doubt the MoI and the Air Ministry were keen for it to be seen by the British cinema audience.

Judging from the imagery used in this dog-fight, a single Spitfire Mk.IIa performed various solo manoeuvres for the camera, shots of which were then mixed with the mass of No.222 Squadron Spitfires flying tail-chases. This Spitfire is not R6774 (it has the larger underwing roundels than those worn by R6774, applied from 1940 onwards), which was filmed only at the airfield that is portraying the RAF air station from which Radetzky's Polish RAF fighter squadron flies. Neither is this Spitfire a No.222 Squadron machine because it does not have any squadron code letters. Due to the angles at which it is filmed, its serial is unreadable; therefore this Spitfire remains a mystery.

The fight ends with Radetzky deliberately ramming a German bomber. He survives but suffers total memory loss. He recovers when he begins playing "The Warsaw Concerto" and discovers that Carol has returned to him. The film ends as it began, with Radetzky telling Carol that it is not safe to go out at night when the moon is bright, thus showing her that his memory has fully recovered and that they can be reunited.

"Dangerous Moonlight" is a slow film by today's standards, and it suffered, like other British war films, at the hands of the American distributor by having a significant chunk cut from it when it was released States-side. It was also released in the United States under the title "Suicide Squadron", presumably due to Radetzky ramming the German bomber at the end. But its beautiful musical score and the charm of its love story have ensured it has remained a classic of its time, while for aviation enthusiasts and historians the imagery of No.222 Squadron's Spitfires is what makes "Dangerous Moonlight" a classic worthy of being in any collection. It also makes cinematic history by being the first major film production to feature the Battle of Britain.

PIMPERNEL SMITH

(Released: July 1941)

Film producer/director/actor Leslie Howard re-worked his 1935 performance as "The Scarlet Pimpernel" in this, his own aggressively-produced propaganda attack on the Nazis, portraying an archaeological professor who uses his supposed research into the Aryan race in Germany as a cover to help members of the opposition to escape. Allegedly, Reich Propaganda Minister Josef Goebbels was so enraged by Howard's direct attack on the Nazi regime in this film that he ordered the famous British and Hollywood actor's assassination. Aviation does not feature at all in "Pimpernel Smith".

TARGET FOR TONIGHT

(Released: July 1941)

In today's film and television terminology, "Target for Tonight" would be classified as a drama-documentary. It is filmed on an actual wartime air base, with real RAF personnel portraying themselves as they prepare for and take part in an actual air raid on Germany. When it was released, "Target for Tonight" was classified as a straight documentary and went on to win an honorary Hollywood Academy Award in 1942 as best film in the category for short documentaries. In so doing, "Target for Tonight" became the first British war film to win an 'Oscar'.

This film was made by the Crown Film Unit, formed in 1940 by the Ministry of Information to make films – both documentaries and dramas – about life in Britain during the war years for public release at home and abroad. Many familiar British actors of the period took part in these productions made between 1940 – 1945. Despite being only 47 minutes long and not having any professional actors in it, "Target for Tonight" was released to British cinemas as a leading feature, with a supporting full-length film as the 'B' feature.

"Target for Tonight" begins by showing an explanation to the audience that certain facts and details have been changed in order not to provide helpful information to the enemy. It then displays the following proclamation:

"This is the story of a Raid on Germany – how it is planned and how it is executed. Each part is played by the actual man or woman who does the job – from Commander-in-Chief to Aircrafthand".

Indeed, the then C-in-C of RAF Bomber Command, Air Marshall Sir Richard Pierse, does appear in the film, as do the aircrew of No.149 (East India) Squadron, the same squadron that appeared in "The Lion Has Wings" (1939). The same air base, RAF Mildenhall in Suffolk, is also used, although its identity is disguised by being named "Millerton Aerodrome", one of the pieces of misinformation applied in the film to deceive the Reich Propaganda Ministry, which would certainly have obtained a copy (as was intended).

Filming was completed in a similar short period of time as that for the first British wartime propaganda film, director

Harry Watt and his crew spending four weeks at RAF Mildenhall in March and April 1941, as well as at Bomber Command headquarters at High Wycombe, before completing the production by having the crew of one bomber act their real roles inside a struck-off airframe. "Target for Tonight" was then released to the public within three months of filming being wrapped at RAF Mildenhall. It was very well received by British filmgoers who, only two months since the end of The Blitz, now welcomed the chance of seeing RAF Bomber Command "giving it back" on their behalf to the Germans. It was also praised for its realism, without any of the false and exaggerated claims of military success which came to mar "The Lion Has Wings". It also went on to have a strong influence on the making of the classic British war film, "One of our Aircraft is Missing" (1942).

The target of the film's title is a strategic one, a new fuel dump that the Germans have created concealed in woods beside a canal outside the small town of Freihausen in Bavaria. The target was real and reflected the policy of Bomber Command during the earlier war years to hit strategically important industrial and supply facilities, rather than attack major cities with the aim of destroying the morale of German citizens, as became Bomber Command's principal strategic policy later in World War Two with the use of carpet bombing.

The film opens with an Avro Anson I reconnaissance aircraft over-flying an open field and dropping a parachute-retarded canister (the parachute only partially opens, resulting in the canister landing forcefully but intact). It is collected by an RAF Corporal who carries the canister into an underground bunker concealed in a forest. Inside the canister is film, which is developed and shown to reveal the fuel dump at Freihausen. The imagery is examined by RAF Intelligence Officers: although not revealed in the film, this would have to be at Medmenham in Buckinghamshire, close to RAF Bomber Command HQ at High Wycombe. The decision is taken by the C-in-C that the target must be bombed immediately. The No.33 Group squadrons at Millerton Aerodrome are selected for the operation.

In order to conceal the true target from the Germans, the majority of Millerton Aerodrome's bomber force is briefed to attack Channel ports on the Occupied French coast, a regular bombing 'Ops' mission of the time. The intention is to divert the Luftwaffe in particular from the separate 'A' Flight of five bombers detailed to hit the fuel dump at Freihausen. To increase accuracy, the bomb runs must be made at low-level. Two lead bombers will drop incendiaries, to mark the target, 15 minutes ahead of the remaining three, each of which will be carrying an HE (high explosive) bomb load, among which will be one delayed action bomb in each load intended to explode some time after the others, to cause more death and destruction to troops on the ground trying to put out the oil fires. Because Freihausen is a new target and will be trying to conceal itself in the hope that it has not been identified by British Intelligence, it is expected its flak crew will be unlikely to fire on the bombers until the first incendiaries hit. From then on, though, 'A' Flight can expect plenty of attention from the defending flak crews.

During the briefing and then into the operation itself, the focus is entirely upon the No.149 Squadron aircrews and their Vickers Wellington Mk.Ic bombers. In particular, one aircrew and their Wellington, 'F for Freddie', becomes central to this drama-documentary. Five out of the six aircrew of 'F for Freddie' are genuine No.149 Squadron airmen, but the sixth is not: he is Squadron Leader Charles 'Pick' Pickard, drafted in from No.311 (Czech) Squadron to portray the one fictional character in the film, the pilot of 'F for Freddie', Squadron Leader Dickson. 'Pick' Pickard was already gaining a reputation as an outstanding pilot and leader in RAF Bomber Command - he already held the Distinguished Flying Cross (DFC) and Distinguished Service Order (DSO), and would go on to lead the famous Amiens Prison Jailbreak Operation by Mosquito bombers in 1944, among other daring exploits – so it seems that the decision was taken, probably by RAF Bomber Command HQ in return for providing facilities for the Crown Film Unit, to have its own 'star' in a leading role in "Target for Tonight".

'F for Freddie' is actually Vickers Wellington Mk.Ic P2517/OJ-F, as is clearly seen in one shot as the crew prepare to board their aircraft. P2517 was built as a Wellington Mk.Ia but was modified, as were many others of the same Marque, into a Mk.Ic with the addition of a sixth crew member who acted as waist gunner. It was No.149 Squadron that learnt to its and Bomber Command's cost in late 1939 of the vulnerability of the Vickers Wellington to beam attacks by Luftwaffe fighters.

'F for Freddie' is to be the last of the three HE-carrying Wellingtons in 'A' Flight to bomb Freihausen. The other two are 'A for Apple' and 'B for Bertie'. The leading two incendiary-carrying Wellingtons are 'C for Charlie' and 'R for Robert'. All are seen in the film during take off for the mission, as directed by the flare path controller, identified by their respective codes of OJ-A, OJ-B, OJ-C and OJ-R. Their serials, however, do not appear in shot.

Actually, Wellington Mk.Ic P2517/OJ-F was not fully equipped operationally, but was used instead by No.149 Squadron as an aircrew familiarisation and flying standards aircraft. Each bomber squadron had one such aircraft in its quota assigned to this task. Therefore, although 'F for Freddie' is the subject aircraft in the film, the actual Wellington on which director Harry Watt and his cameraman flew on the Operation they filmed was a different machine. P2517 transferred in September 1941 to No.3 Group Training Flight at RAF Newmarket.

Not everything is genuine in "Target for Tonight"; however, the anti-aircraft tracer fire streaming up at the Wellington from which Watt was flying and filming most definitely is. Along with Hollywood director William Wyler's famous documentary about B-17F Flying Fortress Memphis Belle, this is one of only a few feature films to show real flak aimed at the bomber the camera is filming from. For the film production itself, however, the actual target being bombed is a studio-made miniature, and of reasonable quality for its time. There is no film of the real Freihausen target being bombed. German flak gunners are seen only in silhouette; this is deliberate, because they are British Royal Artillery anti-aircraft gunners wearing German helmets, not real German flak

gunners in Wehrmacht film footage, as has been supposed in some sources. The giveaway is the Bofors anti-aircraft gun they are manning, a type of AA gun not used by the Wehrmacht but widely employed by Royal Artillery anti-aircraft units.

One other part of the film which is not genuinely taking place at RAF Mildenhall is when a meteorologist takes readings of weather conditions with the assistance of a WAAF NCO before the Operations briefing. Behind him is a Gloster Gladiator with its engine cowling under wraps. No code or serial is visible. This Gladiator would be a strange resident at an RAF Bomber Command air station, so the assumption must be that this scene was filmed separately at a location different from RAF Mildenhall.

Finally, credit must be given to director Harry Watt and his team for not falling into temptation to portray the crew of 'F for Freddie' as outstandingly heroic and completely successful on their operation. Their bomber takes a hit, with the wireless operator injured in the leg. Dickson manages to nurse the bomber home, with a failing port engine. The return flight, the controlled concern of the Operations Staff back at base at knowing one of their aircraft is overdue, the tension that mounts as Millerton Aerodrome becomes fogbound at dawn, and the final landing in difficult conditions – all are handled with a real sense of growing danger and drama, relieved only when 'F for Freddie' finally lands on. The post-Operation debrief reveals that three out of four HE bombs missed their target, but that the fourth caused a large amount of red flame and black smoke, indicative of a direct hit on a fuel cell. With no reference to hits by the other bombers in 'A' Flight, the assumption must be that this was the only successful strike, accurately representative of success rates achieved by RAF Bomber Command before it switched to using radio navigation aids to increase targeting accuracy.

The manner in which Watt increases the tension by building the engine noise progressively the closer 'F for Freddie' gets to Millerton, while the fog thickens more and more, remains as dramatically effective today on DVD as when the film was first seen by cinema audiences in 1941. "Target for Tonight" remains as fascinating and engrossing a depiction of RAF bomber aircrews in action for the viewer in the 21st Century, as it did for the bomb weary British public over 70 years ago whose spirits it was created to lift. There is no doubt of the film's success.

FERRY PILOT

(Released: 1941)

Filmed by the Crown Film Unit the same time as "Target for Tonight" was in production, "Ferry Pilot" adopts the same drama-documentary style in using actual service and civilian personnel to 'act' the roles they actually carried out operationally. In this case, it is the Air Transport Auxiliary, or ATA, that is the theme. Director Pat Jackson added genuine drama to what could be perceived as an interesting but otherwise mundane subject by managing to get the Luftwaffe to play the bad guys in the film, albeit without their voluntary co-operation.

"With the full co-operation of pilots of the Air Transport Auxiliary, the Royal Air Force and the British Aircraft Industry", proclaims the film's credits during the opening scene, when hangar doors are pulled back and Armstrong Whitworth Whitley V Z6669 is wheeled out into the sunshine. Its code letters of A-B are visible either side of the fuselage roundel, but the leading code is blocked off by the wing flap; however, there is a strong chance it was letter 'Z', making the full code ZA-B. This would make Whitley V Z6669 a No.10 Squadron aircraft. This Whitley was lost on 28th December 1942 after returning from an anti-submarine patrol when it was serving with No.10 Operational Training Unit at RAF St Eval, Cornwall. A thick sea fog, for which Cornwall can be notorious, had enveloped St Eval, causing the pilot, Sergeant F Charlton, to divert to RAF Chivenor further up the coast in North Devon. But, being very low on fuel, Sgt Charlton ordered his crew to bale out before he flew the Whitley to an unpopulated area, where he would likewise bale out. Tragically the engines failed before he could achieve this and he was killed in the subsequent crash.

The narrator tells the audience that "the smoke trails over southern England have now moved to northern France. But to keep the Royal Air Force on the offensive, hundreds of aircraft must be flown each day between the factories, the maintenance depots and the aerodromes". As he speaks these words, two Vickers Wellington Ia bombers parked at RAF Mildenhall are seen in shot: they wear the low visibility markings of the first period of the War and No.149 Squadron's 'OJ-' code letters, suggesting this is an out-take from "The Lion Has Wings" (1939). A follow-up shot shows a Westland Lysander parked in the foreground (too dark to identify), with a Vickers Wellington beyond it carrying cowls wrapped around its engines, while an Airspeed Oxford waits patiently in the background.

"The RAF can't take on the job, they're too busy on active service". A stock shot, probably from the MoI, of six Vickers Supermarine Spitfire Mk.Is of No.19 Squadron appears next, all in a neat line turning propellors at RAF Duxford.

"It's done for them by the ATA, the Air Transport Auxiliary". To illustrate this, a group shot with two Spitfires (one of them a Mk.II), three Wellingtons, plus an Oxford landing beyond them, is used.

"A civilian air force of men and women operating aircraft from their own Pools or Stations scattered all over Britain". The Spitfire Mk.II taxyies out of the line, representing yet another delivery en route to an RAF fighter station.

The scene switches to No.15 Air Ferry Pool, where some 50 pilots of all nationalities muster every day to fly whatever type of aircraft that needs delivering to whichever unit is expecting to receive them. The narrator mentions that some of these pilots have experience of flying up to 80 different types of aircraft in their logbooks. They come from all manner of pre-War civilian professions, with advertising executive, teacher, dramatic critic and "stunt pilot" listed among some. "In peacetime, they flew their Puss Moths for a hobby (Ah, so they were well-off compared with the majority of the population); today it's Spitfires to four-engined bombers".

Among the names of pilots being assigned their flying tasks is "Mollison": this is Jim Mollison, already a famous name to the British public due to his record-breaking flights before the War, as well as to his highly public marriage to the even more famous Amy Johnson, also an ATA pilot. Their exploits and controversial relationship was due to be portrayed in the 1942 film, "They Flew Alone", also explored in this book (by the time "Ferry Pilot" was being produced in 1941, Amy Johnson was dead, having died on ATA duty at the beginning of the year). Jim Mollison is seen in several shots, playing chess with an American ATA pilot, while waiting to be assigned a ferry task.

Integral to the successful ATA operation was its own fleet of transport and communications aircraft - "taxi aeroplanes" - which flew ferry pilots to whatever location in the country they had to go to, to collect an aircraft and ferry it to the destination that required it, then had to be collected themselves and flown back to the Air Ferry Pool where they either picked up another 'kite' or prepared themselves for the next day's task/s. This fleet was made up primarily of sturdy, reliable Avro Anson Is, of which a goodly number are seen in this film. Identifiable are Anson Is N5100 and L7909/5, seen parked up, waiting to carry out this "aerial bus service"; three others accompany them, but are not identifiable.

Anson I L7909 was sold after the War to British Air Transport Limited (BATL) operating from Redhill Aerodrome in Surrey, being placed on the British civil register as G-AKVW. In July 1950, BATL sold Anson G-AKVW to Gulf Aviation, who operated the aircraft until selling it to Aden Airways in January 1953. G-AKVW was subsequently "reduced to produce". An Anson carrying the G-AKVW serial is preserved today in a museum at Sharjah, United Arab Emirates, but this is not the real former L7909.

Two characters who feature prominently in the film are ferry pilots "Thompson" and "Talbot": the former is British and is destined to encounter his first Whitley, but the second is American from Alabama and is referred to throughout as 'Alabam' by his ATA colleagues. Due to his strange, languid drawl, it is hard to decide if 'Alabam' is real, or a put-up job to make the film appealing to an American audience. One aviation Website Forum has a contributor claiming that 'Alabam' was his cousin, but whether in the UK or USA isn't clear.

Thompson, 'Alabam', Mollison and two other ATA pilots are ferried in Anson I N9972 to collect their respective delivery aircraft of the day. More ATA pilots board Anson I N5100, which jumps straight into take off from its parking position. Anson I N5289 follows. Another Anson I, which cannot be identified because unlike all its compatriots in the film it has large mid-wing roundels under each wing where the serial would normally be, takes off directly over the camera position, missing by not much more than 10 feet - brown pants job for the camera operator! It does show you can get some fun in flying the prosaic old Anson. A shot looking the opposite way has the Anson suddenly flying in very low over the camera, then sweeping away just over the top of a group of five Miles Magisters parked in the sun.

When Anson I N5089 lands at another airfield, it taxyies past North American BC-1 Harvard Is P5856, N7128/51 and N7126/49. The BC-1 Harvard I was the initial version of the famous T-6 Texan/Harvard series of world-beating pilot trainers, with its distinctive rounded tail rudder as opposed to the pyramid-shaped tail of the instantly recognisable T-6. The Harvard Is were the RAF's first monoplane trainers and, as public footage of them is not altogether common, their brief appearance in this film is welcome.

As Anson N5089 taxyies in, the narrator mentions that the Air Ferry Pool located at the airfield where it has landed is staffed entirely by women pilots. A shot shows a group of these pilots walking out, with an ATA de Havilland DH.87B Leopard Moth wearing RAF roundels and camouflage parked behind them; this same shot is used in "They Flew Alone" (1942), when the scene of Amy Johnson joining the ATA appears. Although the narrator describes the female ferry pilots as flying Spitfires, Hurricanes and Lysanders, he qualifies this by saying they mostly flew training aeroplanes and then, to ameliorate any suggestion that this might be an easier and softer job than flying fighters, describes the trainers as being just as demanding to fly. He also underlines that the female ATA pilots faced just the same perils as their male counterparts, including the risk of running into a wandering 'Jerry'. As this narration is given, a number of female ATA pilots are seen getting into a de Havilland DH.89A Dominie, whose serial is not visible.

The film switches to Anson I N9972 "landing at a Spitfire factory in the Midlands", clearly meant to be Castle Bromwich but with its name not used, so as not to be helpful to the enemy (the Anson is actually filmed landing back at the same No.15 Air Ferry Pool airfield it has taken off from, as the same parked Miles Magisters attest). In the film's story, Thompson and 'Alabam' are to pick up two Spitfires.

Cue some of the most remarkable film you can ever expect to see of a master Spitfire performer in action. We are talking about Vickers Armstrong chief test pilot, Alex Henshaw. "Ferry Pilot" is host to some extraordinary footage of Henshaw aerobating a Vickers Supermarine Spitfire Mk.Ia. We are not talking Ray Hanna or any other famous airshow Spitfire pilot of today. We are talking about the performance of a genius, who is shown in "Ferry Pilot" displaying a Spitfire in a manner that could never be allowed under the strict rules governing airshow flying in the 21st Century. Nowhere, and I mean nowhere, will you see a Spitfire perform a zoom climb from low-level up to inverted at the top, then be held inverted right the way through the dive out and continue to be held inverted through the following fly-past. The Spitfire's amazing inverted performance has never been demonstrated to such astonishing effect as seen in "Ferry Pilot", which alone makes acquiring this valuable piece of British aviation history on film such a must. And how about a vertical diving roll? Henshaw frequently flew this kind of Spitfire demonstration at Castle Bromwich for various visiting dignitaries, including Prime Minister Winston Churchill.

The film shows Henshaw being watched by two enthralled female ATA pilots preparing to ferry aircraft, while 'Alabam' comments, "He really knows his stuff!". As he and Thompson walk to their aircraft, they pass yet another ATA Anson I, this time N9719 - how many did the ATA have?

The women ferry pilots are seen taxying away in two Miles Masters, T8902 being one of them. The word to describe the Miles

Master is, useful. As an advanced pilot trainer, it was faster than its rival, the North American T-6 Harvard II, and with more than 3,000 built during the War it is curious why the RAF continued to operate the American design as well. It could double as a short-range fighter - even a small number were developed as such - although the project was not continued with. Master T8902 seen in "Ferry Pilot" is an M.19 Master Mk.II variant powered by a Bristol Mercury XX radial engine. Publicly available film footage of the Miles Master is rare, so "Ferry Pilot" scores high again for the aviation historian in providing some excellent studies of this feisty RAF monoplane.

Thompson and 'Alabam' walk to the Spitfires they are going to ferry. "We're not into this Schneider Trophy, you know", Thompson warns the American. "OK, I'll keep a tight harness on it", quips 'Alabam'. The curiosity about this scene is that a mix of eight different Spitfires is used to enact the start up, take off and delivery flight of the two Spitfires the ATA pilots are meant to be flying.

Thompson walks to a Spitfire Mk.II, of which 'P799-' of its serial is in shot. He is then seen in the cockpit of three different Spitfires! We can confirm this because firstly he is filmed in one Spitfire which has lettering stencilled on its fuselage below its cockpit; frustratingly, the film frame cuts off the lettering, which is stencilled in a scripted style. Then, in the next shot, Thompson is sitting in a Spitfire without stencilling on the fuselage at all. Following that, Thompson is seen in another cockpit shot with more lettering below the cockpit sill, but this is stencilled in an entirely different style. Again, these letters are cut off by the bottom of the film frame. Because of the way these shots have been filmed, reading whatever is stencilled onto the sides of these Spitfires is not possible.

The first Spitfire to be definitely identified is Vickers Supermarine Spitfire Mk.Ia R7157 - some excellent footage of the start-up procedure for a Spitfire is filmed in the cockpit for this sequence, perfect for Spitfire fans to study. This Spitfire first flew on 27th February 1941 and was taken on charge by the RAF on 1st March. R7157 was issued to No.124 Squadron on 7th May, then was relegated to an operational training role when it joined No.52 OTU on 3rd November. It had a short service life, which ended on 26th September 1942 when it dived into ground near Quedgeley in Gloucestershire, being consequently written off.

R7157 appears to have no stencilling on its forward fuselage. But as Thompson gives the signal to the two 'Erks' helping with the start-up procedure to move the chocks, a two-worded name can be clearly seen below the cockpit of the Spitfire he is now sitting in. Due to the faintness of the lettering and the diffused quality of the imagery, deciphering the two words isn't possible, even with careful freeze-frame analysis. So, one Spitfire without stencilling can be identified, but the two with stencilled lettering on them can't be. Frustrating.

The Spitfire with 'Alabam' in it cannot be identified either because no serial appears in shot. When the two Spitfires line up together for take off, Thompson's Spitfire is seen without any stencilling below its cockpit, so presumably he is in R7157. When the Spitfire 'Alabam' is flying moves forward on its take off run, it can clearly be seen to be carrying no serial at all. What is noticeable is that, judging by the slightly more pointed propeller boss of his Spitfire, compared with the more rounded one of Thompson's Spitfire, 'Alabam' is sitting in a Spitfire Mk.II, whereas Thompson appears to be in a Spitfire Mk.Ia. As he moves off, a Hawker Hurricane appears in shot in the background.

However, as the two Spitfires roll in formation they have suddenly acquired squadron code letters! Careful analysis shows them to be Spitfire Mk.IIs, each carrying the 'UO-' code of No.266 (Rhodesia) Squadron, with the Spitfire nearest the camera appearing to be UO-O. Director Jackson appears to have used various Spitfires at Castle Bromwich to film Thompson and 'Alabam' in-cockpit and lining up for take off, but clearly he was not given Spitfires for any actual take off shots - to acquire those, he had to source stock footage from the Crown Film Unit and, unavoidably, had to use imagery of squadron Spitfires, as opposed to the Spitfires he filmed for "Ferry Pilot" which had no squadron codes.

A take off shot shows the full production works of Castle Bromwich, much targeted by the Luftwaffe during the first years of the War but never successfully damaged. There follows a beautiful sequence of air-airs of two Spitfires in flight together over the English countryside, played out to a delightful musical score composed by Brian Easdale and conducted by prolific wartime conductor, Muir Mathieson (his name appears as music conductor or arranger on the credits for a whole host of British war films).

"These ships sure do handle nice", muses 'Alabam', as his Spitfire sways gracefully alongside the camera aircraft. He is now flying Spitfire N3111, but when close-ups of him in the cockpit are shown, the tops of the same stylised scripted letters of the Spitfire Thompson was filmed in appear!

Spitfire N3111 is historically a very interesting machine. It began life as a Spitfire Mk.Ia when it first flew on 24th October 1939. It served with No.54 Squadron, but was off front-line duties with Air Services Training when the Battle of Britain took place. In August 1940, N3111 was converted by Heston Aircraft, Ltd, at Benson into the photo reconnaissance PR.III prototype. It underwent F.24 camera trials with the RAE at Farnborough, to prove the Spitfire PR.III as a capable airframe for the photo reconnaissance (PR) role.

During these trials Spitfire PR.III N3111 undertook a vitally important PR mission on 22nd February 1941, when Flying Officer W K Manifould photographed at low-level the previously undiscovered Freya radar system at Cap de la Hague, Auderville, France. Thus we are seeing a very significant Spitfire here in "Ferry Pilot".

After successful completion of these trials in April 1941, Spitfire PR.III N3111 was converted again by Heston Aircraft, Ltd, this time into the sole PR.V variant with an oblique camera fitting located just behind and below the cockpit on the port side. N3111 was issued to the PRU at Benson on 21st June 1941. It later went on to serve with No.543 Squadron in 1942 until it spun into the ground on 27th February 1943 at Worlington in Devon.

It is possible that Spitfire N3111 is seen in "Ferry Pilot" as the PR.V prototype, filmed by the Crown Film Unit in formation with another PRU Spitfire during the summer of 1941. If so, this would make these air-air studies unique and rare footage indeed.

Suddenly a Hawker Hart Trainer appears, filmed air-air and too dark to identify. "Well, ol' fellah", exclaims 'Alabama' in his Southern drawl, "you'll have one of these before long. Good luck, fellah".

A study of a balloon barrage appears next, filmed by the passing camera-'plane, the sun streaming out of the clouds beyond them. The passage of English countryside, a country in the grip of War, yet the studies of clouds, sun and the carpet of fields below, all accompanied by Easdale's delightful score, would have moved the wartime cinema audience to feel a special pride in their country and to value fighting for it. Just the feeling Jackson would have wanted to have created in them.

The Spitfires arrive at Walbrooke, where Thompson has to collect the Whitley he is due to fly. Before doing so, he taxyies the Spitfire he has flown to a parking position close to the fence bordering the airfield. This shot reveals that yet another Spitfire is being used, with its serial partly obscured, just showing 'P80--', but enough to confirm it is a Spitfire Mk.II. After handing the Spitfire over, Thompson sets off across the field towards his destiny with the Whitley.

Jackson films the Armstrong Whitworth Whitley in question from imposing angles, creating the effect that this is a rather formidable machine to fly. Thompson cuts a lonely figure as he walks across the grass towards the leviathan waiting for him. Mathieson's conducting helps build the tension. What is this thing going to do, as Thompson the minnow confronts the Whitley the whale? He looks the beast over, as if uncertain how to approach it. Interesting to note the background leafless trees and dull, grey sky: gone is the sunshine and summer of the Spitfires sequences, the Whitley scenes were obviously filmed before Spring had sprung in 1941.

The Whitley in question is Whitley V Z6635, with no code. Jackson obviously enjoyed filming it because he lets the camera focus at will on its angular airframe and greenhouse-like frontal area. Thompson consults the company test pilot, who asks rather disconcertingly, "Well, what have you flown?" when Thompson confesses he hasn't handled a Whitley before. The test pilot reminds him that, on approach to land, to remember that he has "a lot of aeroplane behind you". You can say that again!

'Alabam' climbs into the main cabin while Thompson straps himself into the cockpit. As they prepare for take off, No.15 Air Ferry Pool are alerted to a German air raid building in the direction that Thompson is about to fly. A call is put through to Walbrook to cancel the flight but, too late, the Whitley is airborne. The Whitley is filmed from the ground flying in the distance amid big stratocumulous, while farm workers gathering hay watch it pass. Strange how the trees have suddenly sprung into leaf!

"Old Thompson heading straight for a bunch of Jerries, have to leave him with the fighter boys", comments the Air Ferry Pool Commander matter-of-factly, as if it's all a bit of a pickle that no one can do anything about. Perhaps that was the way to look at it in those days: as there was strict radio silence imposed on ferry pilots whilst in transit, all one can do is shrug, as there is no way of warning Thompson.

This part of the film is where Jackson has built in a sequence of drama, to show to the cinema audience the very real risk ATA pilots faced when flying defenceless aircraft to their destinations through skies where the enemy could be lurking behind the next clump of cloud.

Sure enough, the enemy raid is building. The film cuts to Reich Propaganda Ministry archive footage of a formation of two Heinkel He.111H bombers flying in echelon starboard, posed just off the wing of the lead Heinkel He.111H they are being filmed from. Quite possibly this formation is part of the five-ship of He.111s seen leading the formation of 30 Dornier Do.17s that we saw in "Dangerous Moonlight", as the Heinkels are flying tight together in what looks like ceremonial pose, not a tactical grouping. The He.111H nearest to the camera has a brightly painted letter 'B' behind its fuselage Balkenkreuze and a much darker painted letter 'L' beyond it, but the bomber's wing obscures the Geschwader code letters ahead of the Kreuze. Another air-air shot of a Heinkel He.111H immediately follows, filmed from inside a He.111H in formation with it off its port wing. This He.111H can be clearly identified, its 9K+FR code indicating that it was on the strength of Kampfgeschwader 51 (KG.51) Edelweiss when this film was taken. The digitally re-mastered footage used in "Ferry Pilot" provides an excellent view of it. Another He.111H is next seen swinging behind the aircraft it is being filmed from; as it is filmed head-on, it cannot be identified. Immediately after it, archive footage of two Messerschmitt Bf.110C Zerstorers appears, the nearest Bf.110, in making a fast pass over the camera, displaying the letter 'K' under its starboard wing. This is immediately followed by cropped footage of eight Bf.110s, part of two Bf.110 Kettes (Chains) flying in a ceremonial formation.

The use of this Reich Propaganda Ministry imagery in "Ferry Pilot" confirms that the British film industry was now gaining access to more and more contemporary footage of Luftwaffe aircraft.

Meanwhile, Thompson flies blissfully on through the clouds, totally unaware of what he is heading into.

Cut again to more Reich Propaganda Ministry archive footage, this time of another Heinkel He.111 filmed air-air and carrying markings noticeably different from the He.111Hs seen earlier: it carries the letters 'OIG' on the fuselage behind the Balkenkreuze symbol (again, the wing is obscuring the code ahead of the cross) and is painted differently as well, with camouflaged top surfaces and grey under surfaces. It also appears to be a different version of He.111 from the He.111H series most commonly seen in Reich Propaganda Ministry footage. Research suggests that this is a Heinkel He.111B-2 and that almost certainly the numbers '72' would be adorning the fuselage ahead of the Kreuze symbol, making the complete code of this aircraft 72+OIG. This would make it an early model He.111B-2 of Kampfgeschwader 157 Boelcke, which was formed at Hannover-Langenhagen on 1st April 1937. KG.157 only kept this nomenclature until 1st May 1939, when it was re-numbered as KG.27. Therefore, this footage of He.111B-2 72+OIG in "Ferry Pilot" must have been filmed pre-War.

The next image that follows clearly identifies another Heinkel He.111, this being V4+AU, making it an He.111H

variant of KG.1 Hindenburg. This is a genuine Battle of Britain veteran aircraft, as KG.1 were involved in attacks on Great Britain from Adlertag (Eagle Day, 13th August 1940) onwards. KG.1 were assigned RAF Biggin Hill as their target for Adlertag. There are two surviving photoes of He.111H V4+AU in action, including a similar study as shown in "Ferry Pilot", on the Deutches Bundesarchiv Website, taken through the cockpit window of an accompanying He.111 and dated September 1939 over Poland.

As 'Alabam' settles down in the back of the Whitley to read a Western novel, "The Lone Eagle", archive footage shows four Bf.110 Zerstorers in echelon starboard formation closing in. The observer/gunner in the lead Zerstorer spots a single aircraft flying below them above clouds and alerts his pilot. A close-up of a Bf.110C breaking to starboard heralds the attack on Thompson's Whitley; the Zerstorer teasingly reveals a small part of its code letters on the fuselage but they are unreadable, although the letter 'L' is discernable under the starboard wing.

The air battle sequence which director Jackson now weaves into this drama-documentary is very significant, as this footage established a development in British war films that the British film industry was in a unique position to exploit. It also demonstrates the ability of the Crown Film Unit - and subsequently that of its successor, the forthcoming RAF Film Production Unit - to have access to any part of the Royal Air Force they wanted to film, and to use the RAF's assets to maximum effect for the purposes of exploiting propaganda, contributing to newsreel reports, and providing realistic, as well as actual, enactments of air combats for cinematic productions.

In short, the Crown Film Unit was able to use captured Luftwaffe warplanes being evaluated by the RAF and film them in staged set-pieces against Royal Air Force fighters, something that no other country's film industry among the Allies, including the United States, was in a position to do. "Ferry Pilot" was the first such British war film to stage a rehearsed set-piece, using a captured German fighter dog-fighting with a British fighter.

Whether the dog-fight was filmed specifically for "Ferry Pilot", or whether it was a set-piece staged separately by the Crown Film Unit, in order for it to be used in whatever format the British government's Ministry of Information, the Air Ministry, and the Royal Air Force itself felt fit, is not known, but from the time of its use in "Ferry Pilot" out-takes of this dog-fight sequence have appeared time and again in a variety of film productions and television documentaries on air warfare. "Ferry Pilot", however, is the only film in which this set-piece is shown in its entirety.

The dog-fight is staged between a Messerschmitt Bf.110 Zerstorer (Destroyer) and a Vickers Supermarine Spitfire. The Zerstorer was on charge with the RAF's Air Fighting Development Unit at the time of filming, being captured Messerschmitt Bf.110C-4 AX772. This Bf.110C-4 was formerly 5F+CM (Werke Nummer 2177) of Luftwaffe reconnaissance outfit 4(F)/14, when it was forced down on 21st July 1940 and had to make an emergency landing at Goodwood Aerodrome in Sussex. It was taken to RAE Farnborough, where it was brought back into flying condition using parts from another shot down Bf.110. It was painted in RAF markings and given the serial AX772, taking to the air again from Farnborough on 15th February 1941.

The pursuing Spitfire was a trials aircraft from the RAE, it being Vickers Supermarine Spitfire Mk.IIa P8441. This Spitfire had an interesting career with the RAE after it was first delivered to the RAF on 4th June 1941. Between 15th July 1941 and 8th November 1942, Spitfire Mk.IIa P8441 was used to air test a de Havilland-designed spring tab attachment to ailerons and was involved in Oboe and GEE-H precise bombing and radio navigation systems trials for RAF Bomber Command, presumably simulating an opposing enemy fighter. But this Spitfire's most interesting duty was to perform comparison trials with captured Messerschmitt Bf.110C-4 AX772. It was probably during this trials period that the dog-fight set-piece was filmed, amid the summer of 1941.

Spitfire Mk.IIa P8441 returned to RAF service on 8th November 1942, spending various periods with No.39 Maintenance Unit, No.277 Squadron and No.610 Training Unit before it was struck off charge on 30th December 1944.

It is believed that the camera aircraft was a Bristol Blenheim Mk.IV, with much of the filming done from its dorsal gun turret (guns removed, of course); what supports this belief is that a Blenheim IV was used as camera-ship for another dog-fight set-piece, involving a Spitfire and another captured Luftwaffe aircraft, at about the same time the Bf.110C-4/Spitfire IIa dog-fight was being filmed (see, "The First of the Few", 1942).

Spitfire P8441 is seen in "Ferry Pilot" making runs at Bf.110C-4 AX772 from a variety of angles, the latter being filmed mostly from head-on running at the camera with the Spitfire charging in behind it. The British pilot flying this captured Bf.110 obviously had full confidence in his charge because he is seen throwing the Zerstorer around the sky like a wild thing. On one weaving pass, Bf.110C-4 AX772's RAF camouflage and roundels can be clearly seen. One particular shot has been used as an out-take in a host of film productions and documentaries: the Bf.110C-4 heads directly for the camera, growing in size on the screen as it swoops over the camera-ship's dorsal turret, while Spitfire P8441 closes in behind it. It is a classic dog-fight image, and was used extensively in newsreel footage during the War, giving the British public immense satisfaction in seeing a German fighter being bounced by an RAF Spitfire. Many thought it was genuine dog-fight footage. Most notably, this shot has appeared in classic TV documentaries about World War Two, such as the BBC TV's "The Valiant Years" in the Sixties and ITV's highly acclaimed "The World At War" series in the Seventies. Among the films we shall come across using this out-take shot is "Reach For The Sky" (1956), while believe it or not, the same out-take appears in the 1980 spoof airline disaster movie, "Airplane!".

What was definitely filmed for "Ferry Pilot" are the in-cockpit shots of the Bf.110's pilot and gunner, providing a unique view of what the inside of a Zerstorer looked like - unobtainable anywhere else, and a further example of the value of this historic British war film. The pilot and gunner were presumably played by Bf.110C-4

AX772's actual aircrew from the RAF's Air Fighting Development Unit, made up to look suitably Teutonically superior until, "Achtung! Spitfire!", throws them into a most satisfying panic.

The dog-fight sequence in "Ferry Pilot" also utilises more archive footage, both from the Reich Propaganda Ministry and from the Crown Film Unit's own stocks released by the MoI. Some of it is of Heinkel He.111Hs already seen before in this film. A brief air-air of a Whitley appears, but whether it is of the same Whitley Z6635 in the film is questionable because no other air-air of it is used. Well used stock footage of three Spitfires in a dive is shown, plus that of two Spitfires filmed making repeated runs at what may have been one of the captured Heinkel He.111s in the possession of No.1426 (Enemy Aircraft) Flight, based at RAF Duxford. This same footage is also very familiar, and has likewise been used in a number of other films and documentaries. A different shot of a single Spitfire Mk.I in an earlier pre-Battle of Britain scheme (without codes) breaking to port leads into a shot of Spitfire P8441 unleashing its Browning machine guns. A gun-camera shot of the shoot-down of what looks like a Heinkel He.111 is spoilt by the aircraft taking hits being almost out of picture at the bottom of the screen. The audience would have been delighted by the close-up of a Luftwaffe Balkenkreuze symbol being peppered by machine gun bullets. The shoot-down of the threatening Bf.110 is completed through the use of archive footage of an aircraft diving vertically into the English countryside and exploding in a huge blast; this archive shot is also repeated in a number of other British war films and is believed to be that of the death throes of a Junkers Ju.88.

Throughout all this mix of staged and actual aerial mayhem, Thompson stooges on whistling to himself at the controls of the Whitley, blissfully ignorant of the carnage that is supposed to be going on around him, while 'Alabam' remains totally engrossed in the adventures of "The Lone Eagle". The only time either of them return to consciousness is when it's time to land the Whitley. For this sequence, footage of a different Whitley V, bearing the codes of ZA-O, is seen landing, making it another No.10 Squadron aircraft - No.10 were the first Whitley-equipped squadron in RAF Bomber Command at the outbreak of World War Two.

"I shan't forget my first Whitley flight", says Thompson with relief, as he shuts the engines down.

The film ends with sunset shots of Ansons landing. "And now at dusk", the narrator informs us, "the taxi aeroplanes return to their home aerodrome, reporting another day's quota of deliveries, adding to the striking force of the RAF".

"That wasn't your first Whitley, really, was it?", asks 'Alabam' of Thompson, with a sudden note of anxiety in his voice. Time for a beer.

In total, 88 aircraft can be counted in this historically fascinating, 60-minute long drama-documentary film.

A YANK IN THE R.A.F.

(Released: September 1941, USA) Hollywood 'British' war film.

This, the first and most Hollywood of all the Hollywood 'British' war films included in this Chapter, cannot be ignored because its producer, Darryl F Zanuck, was self-declaredly pro-British and had this movie made partly to inspire young American males to do precisely what the title says, become a Yank in the RAF. Never mind that this was in direct defiance of the Neutrality Act, Zanuck openly espoused his belief in 1940 that the USA should enter the War on the side of Britain and its Commonwealth Allies, claiming, as President Franklyn D Roosevelt privately believed, that the United States would have to do so sooner or later anyway. Thus, "A Yank in the R.A.F." is a blatantly obvious propaganda vehicle, targeted at what Zanuck considered to be patriotic Americans who were opposed to the considerable number of isolationists in the USA (those who believed America should isolate itself from becoming involved in another European war).

Zanuck believed - again, as did 'FDR' - that if Britain fell, Hitler would eventually expand the Nazi empire around the world to the point that it would directly threaten America. At the time, Bolshevik Russia and Nazi Germany had signed a non-aggression pact; the nightmare scenario of these two powers combining (very few suspected Hitler of planning to invade Russia, before Operation Barbarossa exploded as it did on 22 June 1941) would mean that North America would be confronted by an overwhelming force dominating most of Europe which would eventually be turned on Canada and the United States.

Thus, "A Yank in the R.A.F." has to be viewed from the perspective of Zanuck's motivations and aspirations in pre-Battle of Britain 1940, and not simply be seen as a vehicle for an all-American flyboy-anti-hero-made-hero going gung-ho to prove he can out-fly and out-seduce British fighter and bomber pilots. Made at 20th Century Fox Film Studios, it stars both the Tom Cruise of the 1940 generation, Tyrone Power, as the flyboy in question, Tim Baker, and 'The Pin Up Girl' herself, Betty Grable, a kind of Forties prototype for Britney Spears, whose famous legs had yet to be insured for $1 million with Lloyds of London but which get plenty of showing when she combines being a nightclub showgirl with being a volunteer RAF nurse. Grable plays Baker's former girlfriend, Carol Brown, who he chances upon in wartime London, not knowing she has volunteered her services to the RAF. He then tries to rekindle their romance - having previously walked out on her ("I know, honey, I'm a worm") - in a manner that might have been acceptable in Hollywood in the Forties, but which could constitute sexual harassment by today's standards.

The aerial battle of the finale takes place over Dunkirk, because the evacuation of the British Expeditionary Force from France was the defining event of 1940 when the shooting script was finalised and production began. As Zanuck saw it, Dunkirk rammed home the need for a film of this kind.

By the time of the film's premier at Grauman's Chinese Theater in downtown Los Angeles on 26th September 1941 - with both Power and Grable in attendance before a crowd of 10,000 movie fans - the attack by Japan on Pearl Harbor was little more than two months away. American flyers were still volunteering to join the RAF, while US Navy officers were sailing as observers aboard Royal Navy warships on convoy protection duty in the Atlantic. The feeling in America was that war was coming, one way or the other, sooner or later. "A Yank in the R.A.F." was thus popularly received in the USA, especially with the pulling-power of its two lead stars.

Interestingly, an alternative title of "The Eagle Squadron" was considered while the film was in production, under which it might have been released, but "A Yank in the R.A.F." better conveyed its message, as Zanuck saw it. "A Yank in the R.A.F." actually exploits a popular trend that Hollywood had created for American movie audiences in the late Thirties, the 'Yank Film'. This had its genesis in MGM's "A Yank at Oxford" (1938), with the studio-contracted star, Robert Taylor, playing an over-confidant American 'yahoo' of an under-graduate who continually challenges the strict traditions and manners of the Oxford University establishment. Powers's flyboy Baker is exactly in the same mould, who keeps coming up against British, and RAF in particular, attitudes and disciplines.

Two more Hollywood war films about the RAF, "International Squadron" (1941) and "Eagle Squadron" (1942), are also 'Yank Films' in that they both have a leading American character who is a brilliant pilot joining the RAF but who repeatedly comes into conflict with British military discipline; in fact, the plots of all three of these 'Yank Films' are so extraordinarily similar that Zanuck was convinced - probably with good reason - that his original plot had been ripped off by the other two productions. "Eagle Squadron" is reviewed later in this Chapter; "International Squadron" - which also tried to name itself "Eagle Squadron" before Zanuck threatened to get legal - is reviewed next.

The plot of "A Yank in the R.A.F." is simplistic in its style, while the film production is largely naive in its depiction of what Zanuck and his team thought squadron life was like in the RAF (all filmed in Hollywood), especially in their treatment of RAF bomber pilots suddenly switching to becoming Spitfire pilots overnight (mind you, not as risible as that of Boeing Stearman flyboys jumping straight into Spitfires, to "teach those Brits how it's done", as in the facts-defying "Pearl Harbor", 2001).

The film opens patriotically with the Royal Air Force March Past being played as the title credits appear over the RAF badge and motto, 'Per Ardua, Ad Astra'. The following dedication then appears: "The producers wish to express their appreciation to the officers and personnel of the Royal Air Force whose cooperation, under difficult conditions, made possible the filming of the aerial scenes in this production". A poster advertising the film in the USA held this declaration: "The aerial battles in 'A Yank in the R.A.F.' are authentic and were filmed over Germany, France and England with the full cooperation of the British Air Ministry!".

This is blatant Hollywood promotional invention-ism of the shameless kind in order to sell a movie - the aerial battles are far from authentic, and certainly no filming took place over Germany and France, the Luftwaffe would have had something to say about that. It has been claimed that the Ministry of Information made available a considerable amount of aerial combat footage, but if it did, none of it was used. The air battle in the film's finale is achieved entirely by the use of studio miniatures and props. There wasn't even any filming over England, the Spitfires shown on screen were flown in Scotland.

British cinematographer Ronald Neame, later to become a prolific film director and producer both in the UK and the USA, was contracted by 2nd Unit director, Major Herbert Mason, MC, of the Crown Film Unit, to head the camera team in Britain that would film aerial scenes with RAF fighters. His camera operator was Austrian-born Otto Kanturek, assisted by aerial photographer Jack Parry (uncredited). Tragedy struck when a Hawker Hurricane that was being filmed air-air by these two over Norfolk from an Avro Anson, after they had finished filming with Neame for "A Yank in the R.A.F.", collided with their camera aircraft, killing them both. Zanuck's 20th Century Fox studio's publicity department dressed up their deaths by putting out a news release claiming they had been shot down by German aircraft while engaged in filming, thus making their deaths appear more heroic.

The opening shot of "A Yank in the R.A.F." could hardly be more un-British, it being of six North American AT-6 Harvard II trainers rasping across what could not be a more American skyline, and Californian in particular. It then cuts to what purports to be the international border crossing between Canada and the United States, but which is a film set on North American Aviation (NAA)'s Inglewood plant in California, where the Harvards were built. Parked up on a road bisecting the 'border' are two North American AT-6 Harvard IIs. What are they doing there? Ropes from a tow truck marked 'Maple Leaf Garage', so that we know the truck is from the Canadian side, are attached to the lead Harvard on the US side. As this happens, a narrator explains that under the terms of the Neutrality Act, the United States of America was forbidden to fly American-built military aircraft into the airspace of a belligerent nation, as Canada was. The Act didn't say anything about towing them across the border: "Democratic ingenuity and a stout rope did the rest", the narrator proudly proclaims.

Harvard II RCAF 3781 is the first to be pulled across. Four more Harvard IIs are seen behind it, awaiting their turn, when the ground crews, garage mechanics and border guards suddenly have their attention diverted skywards by the sound of an aircraft approaching. This is another Harvard II, only it isn't waiting to join the queue but instead just powers over the border crossing accompanied by the distinct growl of its Pratt & Whitney Wasp radial engine. An air-air shot gives a good view of what looks in black-and-white film like an all-white Harvard, but which, of course, was painted all-over bright yellow: the serial number RCAF 3817 is clearly visible. This is our introduction to Tyrone Power's Tim Baker, flagrantly breaching the Neutrality Act by flying direct from American airspace into Canadian airspace - a scene that probably reflected Zanuck's contempt for the Act.

The scene switches to a close-up of a signboard for the Royal Canadian Air Force Training Station of Trenton, Ontario. RCAF Station Trenton was indeed a major training base under the British Commonwealth Air Training Plan in World War Two. The plot has Baker flying the Harvard II he is delivering into RCAF Trenton, over-flying a line of eight Harvard IIs at dispersal as he does so. This scene was also filmed at NAA's Inglewood plant and airfield, with eight RCAF Harvard IIs fresh from the factory on the line ready for delivery; Harvard II RCAF 3027 is clearly visible among them - the earlier serial number suggests this scene was filmed on a date sometime before that of the border crossing scene. Baker lands on, but now he is aboard Harvard II RCAF 3016, definitely confirming an earlier film date than that of the previous scene. The huge expanse of flat plain beyond the Harvard is very different terrain from that of the real RCAF Trenton.

Baker tries to defend his breaching of the Neutrality Act by pretending he was flying to Trenton, New Jersey (in a RCAF Harvard?), but had landed at Trenton, Ontario, by mistake (that's some mistake of the navigational and geographical kind!). As he dismounts his aircraft, Harvard II RCAF 3763 can be seen heading the line of parked trainers in the background - another, and later, date change for Power to be filmed at Inglewood doubling as RCAF Trenton.

After getting a carpeting by the Station's Wing Commander and being told he won't be allowed to ferry any more aircraft into Canada from the USA, Baker is offered the chance to ferry Lockheed Hudsons from Canada to England, at $1000 a trip. He doesn't need to be asked twice.

Zanuck's film production team did a lot of filming at Lockheed's Burbank facility in California, where the Hudson light bomber was built. A shot of a Lockheed Hudson in RAF camouflage and markings taking off from Burbank is significant in showing the aircraft to be flying without its dorsal gun turret installed. As this shot is meant to portray Baker leaving Canada en route to England across the Atlantic, his delivery flight over some thousands of miles of open sea was going to be rather draughty! The serial of this Hudson is not visible. An air-air shot of Baker's Hudson is that of a fairly convincing miniature.

After Baker has tried the patience of his co-pilot and radio operator aboard the Hudson, with his money-making schemes of making four flights a month across the Atlantic at $1000 a trip, the film moves into romantic third gear as Baker discovers Carol in London, which means that aviation takes a decided back seat for the next ten minutes. But then the pomp of the Royal Air Force March Past and the RAF's seal and motto herald the appearance of what is meant to be an RAF bomber base. In fact, it is Lockheed Burbank doubling as such - no filming of RAF bombers in Britain is used in "A Yank in the R.A.F.". The bombers are all Lockheed Hudsons, all in RAF camouflage and markings grouped together on Burbank's sandy and decidedly un-English-looking airfield, and in reality awaiting their delivery across the Atlantic. An RAF armed guard and some sporty British cars try to create the effect of this being somewhere in England. Five Lockheed Hudsons are filmed parked close to a boundary fence, but unfortunately the serials under the wings of the two closest to the camera aren't readable.

However, we're still in romance mode here because this scene has Carol in WAAF uniform driving past the parked Hudsons, only to have a car driven by the 'other man to be' in her life, Wing Commander John Morley (played by suave, urbane John Sutton in the charming style that Americans of the Forties liked to imagine Englishmen to be) back out and collide with hers. It cannot be ignored that Betty Grable did a lot for what Hollywood thought a WAAF uniform looked like.

As Carol parks her car by the fence, Lockheed Hudson Mk.V AM870 appears in shot beyond her; presumably all the other RAF Hudsons seen in the film are of the same Marque. Another shot has Baker in RAF uniform walking with a large group of officers past a whole rank of Lockheed Hudsons on the Burbank ramp; he appears not to have had any problem in joining up in rapid time. The Hudson passing closest to the camera has the number '2970' stencilled on its nose, unlike any of the other Hudsons: this does not approximate to any British military serial, so it has to be assumed that it is this Hudson's United States Army Air Corps (USAAC) serial number minus its fiscal year (FY) prefix. All Lend-Lease aircraft from the United States built for Britain, as are the Hudsons seen in "A Yank in the R.A.F.", were allocated USAAC serials beginning with a FY prefix prior to delivery, as they were officially taken on charge by the Air Corps; however, a Hudson with a corresponding USAAC serial of '2970' and FY prefix hasn't been traced.

As unlikely as the script has it, Baker spots Carol who just happens to be visiting the air base. He starts trying to impress her again, complaining that these Hudsons "are just bombers". "Hey, where are all those cute little Spitfires?", Carol eagerly wants to know. That's what Baker would like to know as well, he didn't join the RAF to fly bombers, of all things. The Battle of Britain must have become etched large on the American consciousness when this scene was filmed, because the Spitfire had caught the imagination of the American public by September 1940 when newspaper reports and newsreels in movie theaters of Britain's most famous fighter in action had become commonplace. This suggests that the Burbank scene with Gable and Power was probably not shot before October 1940 at the earliest.

Baker thinks that his flying time in the USA on mail work and flight testing makes him more experienced than any of his RAF counterparts and bemoans the fact that he has to undergo operational flying training. Quite likely this scene influenced the "Pearl Harbor" (2001) scriptwriters, who out do it in preposterousness by having American flyboys jump from Stearmans to Spitfires without any training at all.

Baker shows that he is still a wise guy by 'popping' a chocolate drop into the air and then catching it in his mouth, as the RAF Wing Commander is briefing squadron pilots on a shot-down Messerschmitt Bf.109. Such crass behaviour would have earned him a transfer off squadron in real life, but Power was just acting the role of Baker being a real Yank in the fashion the Forties American audience would have wanted him to do. For this

scene, the art department have created their interpretation of a Messerschmitt Bf.109 facsimile, which, even allowing for the standard of film art work of the time period, is so obviously a wooden mock-up. The studio backcloth to this scene shows more Lockheed Hudsons in ranks at Burbank.

Morley tries his own luck at charming Carol as she gets into her car by playing out an odd little scene against the backdrop of the five parked Hudsons seen earlier, AM870 among them. Carol can't get her car to start. Morley tells her he has removed her distributor. OK, he wants to introduce himself to her, but by stealing her car's distributor?

The film is making use here of an actual law in Britain during the early 1940 'Phoney War' period, requiring all car drivers to disable their vehicles after parking them. The big fear at the time was of 5th Columnists or German parachutists in disguise stealing cars and using them to get about the country to spy on British military installations. The fear was real, although disguised German parachutists also inspired plenty of jokes among the British public, the most popular of which warned people to watch out for nuns parachuting down.

Back to Carol's own leggy charms in the nightclub, and now we have to follow Morley's attempts to woo her. There's no shortage of aviation in "A Yank in the R.A.F.", but there's no shortage of Betty Grable's romantic exploits as Carol in between.

Meanwhile, Baker has completed his operational flying training and has been assigned to No.61 Squadron at Tadchester, Kent. And who should the CO of No.61 Squadron be? Why, Wing Commander Morley, no less. How coincidental is that? Some see the hand of Zanuck in this unlikely set-up, as it was he who altered the script to have a love rivalry between a Yank and a Brit for Carol's favours, and thus make the film more popular with the American movie audience. Zanuck had a talent for spotting what worked with the movie-going public in the USA, and thus increase a film's takings at the box office; whether believable or not, the rivalry between the British Wing Commander and the American flyboy Pilot Officer, played by heart throb 'Ty' Power, for the best pair of legs in Hollywood, owned by 'Pin Up Girl' Betty Grable, was box office dynamite in 1941.

Baker makes no secret of being cheesed off with being on a bomber squadron. He doesn't believe he will see much action stooging around over the Ruhr for five - six hours at a time. Morley promises to try and see he gets as much action as he can wish for. Much to Baker's disgust, his first operation is a propaganda leaflet drop over Berlin: "I'm not in a war, I'm back carrying the mail!", he complains.

We're still only one third of the way through the film at this stage. The limitations imposed on Zanuck's 20th Century Fox team means that Lockheed Burbank doubles as No.61 Squadron's Tadchester base, and the Hudsons are portraying the squadron's bombers. The Lockheed Hudson never served with RAF Bomber Command and never operated over Germany. The real No.61 Squadron was equipped with Handley Page Hampdens at the time "A Yank in the R.A.F." was in production, based at RAF Hemswell in Lincolnshire.

Shots of three Hudsons taking off at sunset from Burbank are used; noticeably, they are all fitted with dorsal gun turrets. They are too dark to be identified. If it is the same three aircraft, they are filmed air-air in 'Vic' formation silhouetted over the sea, presumably the Pacific doubling as the North Sea. Later, the scene changes to three miniatures. When it comes to the leaflet raid over Berlin, the SFX becomes far less effective. A comical element has Baker hurling whole packs of leaflets out, rather than breaking them open and let them flutter out en masse. He manages to score a direct hit on a searchlight, knocking it out! One can imagine the mirth in the packed movie theaters that this scene probably provoked.

We have to be diverted by more romancing of Carol, but Baker proves he's still a worm when he prefers going on a bender in London with an American ferry pilot buddy rather than taking her out. This means that Morley now has a chance, as Carol is convinced - for good reasons - that Baker hasn't changed.

After a prolonged exchange between first Carol and Morley, then between she and Baker, the film gets back to the business of war when Hitler invades Holland and Belgium on 10th May 1940. No.61 Squadron has been assigned the marshalling yards at Dortmund for a concentrated bombing raid: the reason for choosing such a target is not explained in the plot, it can only be assumed that it was a key railway hub for transporting vital military equipment to the new Occupied Territories. Was it believed by Zanuck and his team that the Nazi High Command had timed its invasion of The Lowlands on the German railway timetable, as was the case with Imperial Germany's attack on the Maginot Line in World War One?

Back to Burbank as Tadchester, with three Hudsons turning propellers on the grass - the same three seen before? A line of five Hudsons are next seen moving off one by one, the example closest to the camera bearing the code letter 'U' next to its starboard fuselage roundel, the first Hudson to be seen with any kind of code identity. Then, in line astern, five Hudsons parting one after the other into the sunset, with darkened countryside and the single sharp steeple of a church tower below; the location cannot be confirmed, but is believed still to be in California. An air-air of five Hudsons in 'Vic' formation silhouetted against a sunlit sky and flying over a distinctly un-European coastline follows, leading into more air-airs of presumably the same five Hudsons flying through clouds. It seems that Lockheed Burbank had generously made at least five Hudsons available to fly in "A Yank in the R.A.F.", obviously with the approval of the customer, the British Air Ministry.

From now on the film resorts to miniatures and SFX to depict the attack on the Dortmund marshalling yards. Inaccurately, Baker is shown making more than one attack as bomb aimer with more than one stick of bombs, something the Hudson could not do. The attack height of 2,000 feet in the plot is not just unrealistic, but suicidal against the flak defences.

Morley and Baker happen to be flying in the same Hudson. They have lost one engine and are losing power. Baker belly-lands the Hudson on what is meant to be the flat Dutch coastline, but in reality is a Californian Pacific beach - the crash landing is achieved by a SFX miniature Hudson on a studio model beach set of a quality that would have been reasonably realistic for the time. The film now follows Baker's and Morley's escape in a boat from

invading German troops in Holland.

Baker wakes up in England in a maternity ward converted into bed space for wounded troops, having been unconscious for more than 40 hours. He wastes no time in pursuing Carol again and forces an engagement ring onto her finger in a manner that would constitute physical assault today, but was considered to be appropriate passion in 1941. He then has to report for duty, as there is "a general flap on". The "general flap" is Dunkirk, and every available pilot is needed to protect the evacuation of 325,000 troops from constant bombardment by the Luftwaffe. Here the film's plot goes into fantasy mode, by having Baker convert instantly from being a Hudson bomber pilot into a Spitfire fighter jockey.

We do now, though, get to see Spitfires and plenty of them, an entire squadron, in fact. They were filmed by Ronald Neame and his fellow 2nd Unit cameramen at Prestwick in Scotland early in 1941 and consist of the entire 12 Vickers Supermarine Spitfire Mk.Ia fighters of No.602 (City of Glasgow) Squadron, a Royal Auxiliary Air Force fighter unit carrying the 'LO-' squadron code letters. No.602 Squadron was resting and regrouping at Prestwick, having been in the forefront of the Battle of Britain flying from Westhampnett in Sussex, when its services were required for "A Yank in the R.A.F.".

It was an appropriate choice, as No.602 Squadron ("Glasgow's Own") had already acquired a distinguished reputation within the Royal Air Force, not just for its exploits in the Battle of Britain, but for claiming a role in shooting down the first German aircraft in British skies during World War Two. It had also been the first Royal Auxiliary Air Force squadron to be formed, in 1925, and the first Auxiliary squadron to be equipped with the Spitfire; plus, it had two famous pre-War pilots in its ranks, The Marquis of Douglas & Clydesdale (the future Duke of Hamilton) and Flight Lieutenant David MacIntyre, who both achieved fame for being the first pilots ever to fly over Mount Everest.

In the Battle of Britain itself, No.602 Squadron was the longest serving unit in No.11 Group's front-line in South-East England, it suffered the lowest loss rate of pilots, and claimed the second highest total of enemy 'kills' of any No.11 Group squadron. No wonder the Air Ministry selected it for the prestigious role of appearing in a major Hollywood film starring two of America's most popular actors.

When we first see them in "A Yank in the R.A.F.", No.602 are called upon to act as more than one squadron returning to refuel and re-arm after fighting over Dunkirk. A good close-up of one Spitfire Mk.Ia shows that, by early 1941, No.602 Squadron had adopted the white spinners and white rear fuselage bands that characterised Spitfires post-1940. This particular Spitfire Ia still had the smaller underwing roundel close to the elliptical wing tip, as borne by the earliest Spitfires to enter the War. Unfortunately, the fuselage band close to the tail and the first letter 'L' of the squadron code are masking part of this Spitfire's serial, but the final two numbers '2' and '7' can clearly be seen. In between the fuselage band and the letter 'L', the number '6' can also be discerned, making it the first of the four numbers of this Spitfire's serial, but the second number and the prefix serial letter are both completely masked from sight.

From a process of elimination, however, this is either Spitfire Mk.Ia R6627 or R6927, as no other Spitfire serials of the Mk.Ia production range can offer the numbers '6' followed by a blanked number and then the numbers '2' and '7'. Likewise unfortunately, the individual code letter is blocked out of sight by the wing, while the film editor has seen fit to cut this Spitfire Ia's imagery into the film in reverse, meaning identification has had to be achieved by means of a mirror.

A shot of two armourers underneath a Spitfire show them preparing to re-arm it, while Spitfire Ia coded LO-R can be seen taxying out in the background - the fuselage band on this Spitfire totally obscures its serial. This scene gives us a very good close-up study of the method of installing the Browning machine gun cartridge cases into a Spitfire's underwing ammunition boxes.

Three Spitfire Mk.Is are seen landing in 'Vic' formation, portraying the arrival of Baker and two others as part of the replacement pilots' pool. Immediately obvious is the combined rasping of Pratt & Whitney engines, meaning that 20th Century Fox did not have any recording of Rolls Royce Merlin engines noise to match to this imagery. What is also of interest is that this particular piece of imagery appears to have been filmed at a different location at a different time of year, and are not of No.602 Squadron Spitfires as they are not carrying any code letters. Trees in the background are in full leaf, contrasting with the shots filmed at Prestwick where the trees are clearly seen to be leafless, denoting a wintertime period for filming.

To show Baker being marshalled into dispersal in his Spitfire, a taxying shot of a Spitfire Mk.Ia showing serial R662-, but with the final number covered by the fuselage band and coded LO-E, is used; Spitfire Ia LO-D can be seen parked up in the background. But then Baker's Spitfire swings right round guided by an 'Erk' holding each wingtip and, lo and behold, we see between the fuselage band and the code letter 'L', the numbers '6' followed by the masked second number and then the final two of '2' and '7'. It is the same imagery of the reversed Spitfire seen just before, now edited in the correct way round! It also means we can now nail this Spitfire Mk.Ia down to be R6627/LO-E.

Spitfire Ia R6627 first flew on 24th May 1940 and was delivered the next day to No.12 Maintenance Unit. Within six days it was transferred to No.19 Squadron, then, on 8th September 1940 it was passed on to No.234 Squadron but suffered a flying accident the same day. It was repaired by Heston Aircraft Ltd at Benson, Oxfordshire, and delivered to No.602 Squadron at Prestwick on 24th January 1941, so it was a relatively new squadron aircraft when it was filmed for "A Yank in the R.A.F.". R6627 went on to serve with No.124 Squadron but spent much of its wartime career with No.52 Operational Training Unit. On 22nd March 1944, it joined No.1 Tactical Exercise Unit, but was declared written off on 18th August the same year.

Another battle scarred Spitfire Ia is refuelled to the tune of more Pratt & Whitney radials growling in the background - don't laugh.

The call to 'Scramble' is given which leads into one of the most classic pieces of film footage that has ever been used both in films and documentaries portraying Spitfire pilots running to their aircraft. Eleven of No.602 Squadron's pilots are seen dashing from the large four-storey building that housed their crewroom at Prestwick, with one Spitfire Ia parked close to it with its engine running. The pilots dash past the camera position and out onto the dispersal, where ten more Spitfire Is are all waiting with propellers turning and Aircrafthands - 'Erks' - ready to assist each pilot into their cockpit. It still is a marvellously historic piece of footage that captures superbly RAF fighter pilots springing into action; no wonder it has been used again and again in other productions and documentaries. It is a credit to Ronald Neame's film work.

Baker straps into the cockpit of his Spitfire, only it is not a real Spitfire that Tyrone Power is being filmed climbing into but that of a 20th Century Fox studio prop which bears very little resemblance to an actual Spitfire cockpit. The No.602 Squadron Spitfires seen beyond him are footage of the 'Scramble' blown up onto a large studio backcloth. Spitfire Ia LO-R can be seen closest in shot. The engine noise recording used here again sounds very much like that of Pratt & Whitney Wasp radials turning over. Then two shots appear, both showing five Spitfire Is taking off in a 'Scramble', rasping away like Harvards!

Next, stock footage of three Spitfire Is taking off in 'Vic' formation appears, with Spitfire Ia SH-D leading SH-E and SH-J, marking them out as No.64 Squadron Spitfires. This squadron actually fought above the skies of Dunkirk, so use of this footage is fitting. However, they didn't sound like Harvards when they took off!

Finally, a fine panoramic study of wartime Prestwick Airfield is shown, with all 11 Spitfires of No.602 Squadron climbing out over their stationary 12th Spitfire Ia left forlornly alone on the ground - perhaps either it, or its pilot, was sick. As they sweep away over the church and village houses of Monkton bordering Prestwick Airfield, a solitary Bristol Blenheim I can be seen being worked on by 'Erks'. It appears to be painted in night fighter black and probably formed part of the air defence of Glasgow.

Air-air shots of No.602 Squadron Spitfires follow next. First, two Spitfire Is are shown, the leader of which appears to be LO-C. Then a close-up of Spitfire Mk.Ia LO-Q follows, showing the last two numbers of its serial, '2' and '9'; the fuselage band and code letter 'L' mask its serial's prefix letter and first two numbers. Research indicates that the only possible candidate is Spitfire Mk.Ia X4829, which first flew on 29th November 1940 and was delivered to No.12 MU on 5th December. It arrived with No.602 Squadron on 26th February 1941, which gives us a good indication as to when the 2nd Unit filmed the squadron at Prestwick. This Spitfire did not stay long with No.602, transferring to No.52 OTU on 18th July 1941, then, very shortly after that, moving on to No.61 OTU on 8th August that same year. It suffered a flying accident on 10th April 1942, was deemed beyond repair on site but was salvageable for use as a ground instructional airframe.

X4829 re-appeared at No.82 MU on 2nd October 1942. It appears that this Spitfire was packed aboard the Danish merchant vessel, Peter Maersk, on 8th November 1942 and was part of that unescorted ship's cargo that was lost at sea on 7th December 1942, as a result of being torpedoed by U-Boat U-185. The Peter Maersk was listed as carrying 4,601 tons of British government stores, including Spitfire Ia X4829, plus 643 tons of commercial stores, and was en route from Liverpool to Saldanha Bay, Aden, then to Alexandria in Egypt, when she was sunk with all hands and her entire cargo.

An air-air of nine Spitfires flying in three separate 'Vics', with a tenth 'whipper-in' Spitfire alongside them, appears next - they cannot be identified as No.602 Squadron Spitfires, as they are too distant. This is more than likely to be stock footage provided by the MoI. Careful study of aerial shots of Spitfires in "A Yank in the R.A.F." appears to show that a maximum of three No.602 Squadron Spitfires were filmed air-air.

The big set-piece of the film is the bombing of British troops on the beaches of Dunkirk. This was filmed on a Californian beach, with American Hollywood extras acting as British 'Tommies' withstanding constant air attacks by the Luftwaffe. All of the German Stukas and Messerschmitt Bf.109s are very obvious studio miniatures, flying like giant insects over the heads of the 'Tommies', while the full-scale facsimile of the Bf.109 used much earlier in the film is also brought into play. Likewise, a very crude looking studio Spitfire facsimile has Tyrone Power in its un-Spitfire-like cockpit for close-ups of Baker going into action.

Two of No.602 Squadron's Spitfire Is, X4829/LO-Q and another marked LO-B, are filmed peeling off into attack. What is revealed here is that these are the same two Spitfire Is which perform the peel-off manoeuvre that has also been used as stock footage in other films and many documentaries; it is obvious that this footage, along with all else that was filmed by Neame of No.602 Squadron's Spitfires, was passed to the Air Ministry for use in propaganda films and newsreels in return for providing facilities to 20th Century Fox. The two Spitfires are identified by X4829/LO-Q having the later wartime larger roundels under the wings, while LO-B has the smaller underwing roundels applied close to the wing tips of the style of pre-War Spitfires. Mystery solved.

Both of these two No.602 Squadron Spitfires were filmed air-air making a number of peel-offs close to the camera aircraft - most likely the Anson in which two of Neame's colleagues died soon afterwards - specifically for "A Yank in the R.A.F.". They are the last real Spitfires we see in the film.

The entire dogfight over Dunkirk is created by the use of SFX miniatures cut with the Spitfire and Bf.109 facsimiles, the latter two large-scale props being made to roll longitudinally in the studio, with the actors playing the pilots strapped into them. The air battle Special Effects were probably considered exciting enough in 1941, but they appear wild and amateurish by today's obviously more advanced and sophisticated standards. This was probably the first aerial dog-fight scene created for a Hollywood film about World War Two. It gives the lie to the studio's claim that actual air combat footage is used in "A Yank in the R.A.F.".

One shot may puzzle anyone viewing this film, as it shows Tyrone Power as Baker in his Spitfire's cockpit with blood trickling from his mouth. This is due to the original ending having Baker being killed in action. However, the Air Ministry itself appealed to Zanuck to change the ending as they were concerned that the sight of Baker being killed

might deter potential American volunteer pilots from joining up. Film preview audiences in America prior to the planned release date also protested at Tyrone Power losing his life at the end - in those days, he was expected to get the girl in a happy ending.

This meant that Zanuck had to order a re-shoot of a different ending, delaying the film's premier until a date later than was planned. The new ending has Baker being reported to have been shot down over Dunkirk, but turning up on the last ship with rescued troops to dock at Dover. Carol walks off arm in arm with both Baker and Morley. American film fans and the British Air Ministry were equally satisfied.

"A Yank in the R.A.F." is Hollywood through and through, but its storyline was intended to stir up support in America for the British cause against the Nazis. Its portrayal of the RAF at war against the Luftwaffe won admiration on both sides of the Atlantic. American it may be, but "A Yank in the R.A.F." is undoubtedly deserving of being a Hollywood 'British' war film. The late Darryl F Zanuck would surely have proudly agreed.

INTERNATIONAL SQUADRON

(Released: August 1941, USA) Hollywood 'British' war film.

Note straightaway that this Hollywood 'British' war film was released to American movie theaters one month before "A Yank in the R.A.F.", but to maintain sequential order Zanuck's film was made first and only had its release date delayed due to the Air Ministry's request that he re-shoot the ending to allow Tyrone Power's character to live. Had there been no delay, "A Yank in the R.A.F." would have pre-dated the release of "International Squadron" by some months.

Also, "International Squadron", produced by the Warner Bros Studio, has an almost like-for-like plot compared with Zanuck's production: an all-American 'Yank' pilot named Jimmy Grant, who is famous in 1940 America as a fearless test pilot - played by Ronald Reagan who, in real life, had a serious fear of flying which prevented him from completing his wartime USAAF service career - and who, like Tyrone Power's Tim Baker, flies a bomber from the States to Britain, joins the RAF and tries to beat the Brits at flying, fighting and winning the girl.

And the similarity didn't end there - Warner Bros' production was also, like Zanuck's film, originally named "Eagle Squadron".

Small wonder Zanuck smelled a Hollywood rat when he learnt what Warner Bros were planning. He wrote to the head of Warner Bros, Hal B Wallis, protesting about their "Eagle Squadron" and demanding that they hold back their film for at least 60 days after the release of "A Yank in the R.A.F.", a demand which Wallis not only ignored but he actually sanctioned the release of the Warner Bros' production ahead of Zanuck's (although, as explained, Zanuck had to delay the release of his film anyway). However, Wallis made some concession to Zanuck by ordering the re-naming of Warner's production as "International Squadron" and in having the plot changed so that Reagan's 'Yank' joins an RAF fighter squadron made up of pilots of different nationalities flying and fighting in England.

As we shall discover, a third film production named "Eagle Squadron" was also in the works at the same time, which was yet another 'Yank film' and which did finally get a release (reviewed later in this Chapter) - this "Eagle Squadron" did have British Air Ministry involvement, whereas "International Squadron" did not. Therefore, no RAF aircraft were used in the Warner Bros production, only stock images of them appear. Directors Lothar Mendes and Lewis Seiler had to rely on exclusively US-based aircraft, mostly air racers, to act the roles of RAF fighters. Their appearance makes them look extremely incongruous, but for an American movie audience not yet at war they probably looked convincing enough. Most of them don't actually fly in the film - very obvious-looking studio miniatures perform that role - although already renowned (in the States) stunt pilot, Paul Mantz, who would become world famous for his daring aviation performances in film and TV productions, was contracted to operate some of them.

The film opens with the following dedication: "To the men of the Royal Air Force and to those exiled flyers who still fight for their homelands in England's skies this story is respectfully dedicated". Such a statement confirms H Mark Glancy's affirmation in his book, "When Hollywood Loved Britain" (referenced in the Introduction section), that Hollywood film studios were unashamedly pro-British in what was still neutral America, while in "International Squadron" Hal B Wallis's Warner Bros clearly sympathised with pilots from the nations conquered by Nazi Germany who were fighting with the RAF. Neutral comes nowhere near it in this film.

The first aircraft we see in "International Squadron" appears right after this opening dedication. Grant is demonstrating, in impossible fashion through the use of a studio miniature, to a senior RAF officer (who is married to Grant's ex-girlfriend from Texas - yes, it's that kind of plot) the new American fighter the RAF apparently want to buy. Acting the role of the new fighter is the sole example of the Brown B-3 air racer NX266Y, designed and built by Lawrence W Brown of Montebello, California, where he established his Brown Aircraft Company to build racing aeroplanes. He built three: the B-1 in 1933, which is the sole survivor and is preserved today in the Wings Over Miami Museum; the B-2, which became the most well known of Brown's racers, named Miss Los Angeles and which crashed in 1939; and the B-3, a closed cockpit two-seater version of the B-2 built more for touring than racing, powered by a Menasco C6S-4 Super Buccaneer inline piston engine developing 290hp with a maximum speed of 205mph. This B-3 was destroyed in a hangar fire in 1943 at what is today Van Nuys Airport, California - the Los Angeles Metropolitan Airport in 1940.

The B-3 is the aircraft that makes the most appearances in "International Squadron", first as the new fighter (unnamed, and to replace the Spitfire!), then later as a Spitfire! It is seen taxiing

in, by Paul Mantz, showing a very streamline shape which is not dissimilar to the then contemporary Caudron C.460 racer. The senior RAF officer tells Grant and the fighter's owner, "Of course, we shall have to wait for official confirmation, but as far as I am concerned the order's in the bag for you". He being married to Grant's ex-girlfriend, and having taught Grant to fly, suggests a serious conflict of interest on his part! Incidentally, this B-3 had another walk-on part in the famous Humphrey Bogart movie, "Casablanca" (1942), in the background at what is meant to be Casablanca International Airport (actually, Los Angeles Metropolitan) as Bogart and Claude Rains walk away in the finale.

While watching Grant's demonstration, the cockpit and bracing wires of a bi-plane can be seen behind the RAF officer. This is Travel Air D-4000 NC406N, which is seen later in the film performing aerobatics. The Travel Air Model 4000 series of tough, durable bi-planes were extremely popular in the USA of the Twenties and Thirties, being capable of performing a whole variety of roles. Its chief rival was the world famous Boeing Stearman series.

Just as Tyrone Power's Baker did, Ronald Reagan's Grant flies a new American bomber across the Atlantic to Great Britain (Grant got paid $2,000USD for doing so, whereas Baker only got a measly $1,000 bucks). The bomber is depicted by a poor studio miniature of a Lockheed Electra painted in RAF roundels and camouflage. When Grant arrives over Britain at night, the whole country is covered in fog. In a ridiculously unbelievable scene, Grant manages to find the airfield he is flying to and lands the bomber without being able to see a thing ahead of him, wise-cracking all the time over the radio. He is treated by the RAF officers not only as a hero, but as if he is the sole Yank to fly one much-needed bomber to Britain. Part of this scene was filmed, like "A Yank in the R.A.F.", at Lockheed's Burbank facility, with a Lend-Lease Lockheed Hudson doubling as the bomber in the background.

As with Zanuck's 20th Century Fox 'Yank' British war film, everything just so happens in "International Squadron". It just so happens that the airfield where Grant has flown the bomber to is where his senior RAF officer friend is based. It just so happens that Grant meets his ex-girlfriend from Texas there. It just so happens that the same senior RAF officer commands the fighter squadron at the airfield made up of different nationalities, including Czech, Polish and Belgian pilots as well as American, and that they need another Yank. Grant is reluctant to join up but in one affecting and much more realistic scene where he witnesses a bombing raid on London, he changes his mind after being moved by the courage shown by Londoners under fire. It's quite likely this scene was very moving to American movie theater audiences and had strong propaganda value in winning their support for Britain's cause in the face of Nazi aggression.

A brief, darkened shot of a Vickers Wellington is used in this scene to portray a German bomber dropping bombs on London, followed soon after by a similar shot of a Heinkel He.111. An air-air of a Heinkel He.111B, similar to that seen in "Ferry Pilot", is also used, although it clearly bears wartime Luftwaffe markings and is filmed releasing small bombs. The He.111B was used more as a trainer than as a front-line bomber, so more than likely this imagery was filmed for training as well as for propaganda footage. The Balkenkreuze stands out clearly on this Heinkel's fuselage, but its Geschwader codes are indistinguishable.

However, unlike Baker in Zanuck's film, who joins the RAF with simplistic ease and switches from being a bomber pilot to a Spitfire pilot overnight, Grant does have to go through elementary flying and physical training, even enduring the humiliation of having to make a solo flight before gaining his RAF pilot's wings. This enables directors Mendes and Seiler to make use of stock film footage of the correct type of RAF aircraft to appear in "International Squadron". To depict Grant making his solo flight, they have acquired footage of de Havilland DH.82A Tiger Moth II N6921, carrying the code number '4'on its engine cowling, making a bounce on landing before settling down for a nice 'three-pointer'. How they acquired this footage is anybody's guess, but it definitely appears to have been filmed on an air station somewhere in England, judging by the leafy backdrop. The Tiger Moth is also painted in the correct RAF Flying Training Command colour scheme of camouflaged upper surfaces and yellow undersides, with the fuselage roundel separating the two paint schemes ringed by a white circle and the white diamond atop the upper rear fuselage. Also briefly shown is an Airspeed Oxford in the same colour scheme, confirming it too is an RAF Flying Training Command aircraft, making a fast fly-past, followed by a quick shot through an open office window of an Avro Anson I taxying by.

While he makes his solo flight Grant loses patience with RAF discipline and begins a hairy series of aerobatics, causing aircrew and ground staff to think he is crashing. The aerobatics are flown in Travel Air D-4000 NC406N and are filmed from the air, looking down on the Travel Air as it spins, loops and rolls above a distinctly Californian-looking airport below it. This shows the original terminal building of Los Angeles Metropolitan Airport. Hollywood filmed a large number of aviation action scenes for movies at the Metropolitan Airport in the Twenties and Thirties. A variety of aerobatic bi-planes used for stunts in movies were based there. Travel Air D-4000 NC406N was a very busy performer in Hollywood movies, with "Sky Bride" (1932), "Mystery Squadron" (1933), "Tail Spin Tommy" (1934), "Living on Velvet" (1935) and "Sky Parade" (1936) among its many credits. It is believed that the aerobatic sequence seen in "International Squadron" was lifted from the aviation action-thriller, "Murder In The Clouds" (1934). Travel Air D-4000 NC406N is extant today, in private ownership in the USA.

After completing his flying training, Grant is assigned to "Squadron 242". Whether the choice of this squadron number in the film's plot is coincidental, or whether Wing Commander Douglas Bader and his No.242 (Canadian) Squadron had acquired some public status in the USA in 1940 - 1941, is not known.

Now we have "Spitfires", or what passes for them, in action. To the fore is the Brown B-3 racer, now painted in RAF camouflage, roundels and codes. Parked alongside it are two Ryan ST-A Special air racers, also painted up in RAF markings. The ST-A Special was the most advanced of the original Ryan ST series of racers, powered by a 150hp Menasco Pirate C-4S inline engine. Which actual ST-A Specials are acting as Spitfires in the film isn't known.

A fourth racer parked at the end of the line is a Travel Air R-2002 'Mystery Ship', designed by Wichita-based Travel Air Aircraft Company in complete secrecy for the National Air Races in 1929. Five were built, with the fifth being sold to the Italian government. The example seen in the film is stated by the French Aeromovies Website to be NR613K and owned by Paul Mantz. It also appeared in "Tail Spin Tommy". According to the Aerovintage.com Website, this 'Mystery Ship' exists today, preserved with the Skyfire Corporation at Wilmington, Delaware.

Acting as the RAF air station where the "Spitfires" are lined up is Alhambra Airport in California.

To depict the "Spitfires" taking off, stock footage of the real thing is briefly used. This is imagery reproduced in poor quality by the film editor of three No.19 Squadron Spitfire Mk.Is taking off in 'Vic' formation from RAF Duxford, which will be seen in other films. As previously stated, none of the air racers actually fly in the film.

Unlike 20th Century Fox's Zanuck, Warner Bros' directors Mendes and Seiler did acquire stock footage of actual Deutsches Luftwaffe aircraft to use in "International Squadron", which begs the question as to why Zanuck did not do so for his production. Seen making a paired take off are two Heinkel He.111H bombers which are unidentifiable because they are filmed in silhouette against the sun, although a white letter 'G' can be seen next to the Balkenkreuze on the nearest example. A brief shot of an He.111 pilot and navigator follows, which cuts to a fine study of three Junkers Ju.87R Stukas making a fly-by in 'Vic' formation, or Kette as it would be known in the Luftwaffe. Although the imagery of them is clear, identifying them isn't possible as their Stukageschwader code letters on their fuselages are too dark to stand out. They appear to have a white letter identifier behind their Balkenkreuzen: the lead Stuka has what looks like a white 'K' but this is difficult to confirm as it as not shown clearly enough and the editor, typical of the time, seems to have cut this imagery into the film in reverse.

A fine air-air study of a Heinkel He.111P appears next; however, the editor has cast the image too dark to read its Kampfgeschwader codes, only the white letter 'A' behind the Balkenkreuze being visible. After two more shots of He.111 aircrew inside their aircraft another air-air of a Heinkel He.111P appears, filmed close-up from its front starboard quarter - if it was not reproduced so dark, it would be an excellent study. Almost certainly Mendes and Seiler obtained this material from footage released by the the Reich Propaganda Ministry; interestingly, none of this stock footage appears in any other war film covered by this book.

In this part of the plot, Grant disobeys orders to fly at the rear of a formation of four Spitfires to protect them from attack from behind; instead he breaks formation to attack a single German bomber. Because of this, one of the other three Spitfires is shot down in a surprise attack and the pilot killed. Grant's battle with the German bomber is depicted by very amateurish studio miniatures of the Brown B-3 and what is meant to be a Heinkel He.111. For some extraordinary reason, Grant is shown carrying a floor mop with him in the cockpit which he sets light to (!) and then holds out of the cockpit to make the German pilot believe he has been hit! This unbelievably ridiculous scene illustrates only too clearly the often completely fanciful ideas Hollywood had about aviation and, in the early Forties, about air warfare in particular.

Stock footage of what is believed to be a Junkers Ju.88 diving vertically into the ground and exploding massively, which is used in other films reviewed in this book, depicts the He.111 being shot down.

Grant is carpeted for selfishly breaking formation and is held responsible for the death of his fellow Squadron 242 pilot. The theme of the plot is that of a single-minded fly-boy who has to learn the hard way to be a dependable squadron pilot. "There are no aces in this war, only squadrons", the Wing Commander tells him. Despite that, and in another unbelievable scene, Grant is shown to have skived off a patrol he was detailed to fly just so that he can date the WAAF girlfriend of another pilot, and persuades his American buddy on the squadron to fly the patrol for him. The result is that Grant's buddy is shot down and killed. The dog-fight in this scene has the appearance of the three Spitfire Mk.Ia fighters of No.74 Squadron that were flown for "The Lion Has Wings" (1939), which means that Warner Bros acquired these out-takes from that film. As Alexander Korda had, by 1941, moved to Hollywood as a producer, it is almost certain he provided them.

Grant arrives back at base from his clandestine date just in time to witness his buddy's aircraft crashing and burning. The scene used to depict this appears to have been lifted from another, unidentified film made in the Thirties with a miniature version of the Travel Air 'Mystery Ship' crashing and bursting into flames.

The chief difference between "A Yank in the R.A.F." and "International Squadron" is that the 'Yank' in the latter film is shown to be a fallible character, as opposed to the courageous show-off played by Tyrone Power in the former. Reagan's 'Yank' has caused the deaths of two comrades due to his irresponsibility, as well as bringing about further division between himself and a third pilot by messing around with that pilot's WAAF girlfriend. The plot has Grant redeeming himself by taking on a suicide mission assigned to Squadron 242. The type of mission exposes yet again Hollywood's, then, lack of knowledge of military tactics: the mission is to send a single fast 'plane at night armed only with four bombs to destroy a large concentration of enemy fuel and ammunition on the French coast. The 'plane will have to glide down onto the target to avoid detection, drop the bombs, then make a fast dash for home. A large bomber force has been ruled out because the enemy would be waiting for them in strength.

No fighter of the Spitfire type could carry four bombs. The use of a single fast 'plane is illogical because its bomb-load would be inadequate to destroy the target. Gliding down before attacking is nothing short of Hollywood fantasy. A large bomber force would be exactly what would be sent against such a target, with a large fighter escort, but the likelihood of the Germans locating such a store close to the French coast is not believable anyway. But the motto of Hollywood is, Don't let reality get in the way of a good story.

So, the finale of "International Squadron" has Grant fly the suicide mission and die a gallant and courageous death in the process of destroying the target, thus wiping his reputation clean and exonerating himself from causing the deaths of his two comrades. The International Squadron drink a toast to his memory in the Officer's Mess.

The final attack is achieved through the use of a studio miniature of the Brown B-3 painted as a Spitfire and an obvious-looking model ammunition dump. But the really interesting part of this finale is the use of Reich Propaganda Ministry-released footage of Messerschmitt Bf.109 fighters starting engines and taking off. This actual footage features Messerschmitt Bf.109E 'Emil' fighters of one of the Deutsches Luftwaffe's most prestigious units, Jagdgeschwader 51 (JG.51).

JG.51 became one of the highest scoring fighter wings of the Luftwaffe in World War Two, fighting in all major campaigns and claiming more than 800 victories. It was heavily engaged in the Battle of Britain and suffered more losses than any other Jagdgeschwader. By May 1941, JG.51 was credited with destroying nearly 350 enemy aircraft, making it one of the Luftwaffe's top-scoring fighter units with no less than 10 'Aces' among its pilots. It is not surprising, then, that it was selected by the Reich Propaganda Ministry for its pilots and aircraft to be filmed for publicity purposes at home and overseas. This film may have been taken at an airfield in Occupied France, probably before the Battle of Britain began in earnest.

What is shown is one pilot being assisted into the cockpit of his Messerschmitt Bf.109E, with the number '2' clearly seen ahead of the port side Balkenkreuze. No Staffel badge is visible. A stripped off ground crewman vigorously hand-cranks the 'Emil' into life, confirming that this film was taken well into summer. Then a second Messerschmitt Bf.109E appears starting its engine, with two ground crewmen on its port wing - it is definitely a different 'Emil' because there is a Staffel badge on the port side below the cockpit between the two Luftwaffe 'Erks'. Then comes a close-up of one ground crewman moving out of shot after securing the cockpit canopy; as he moves away, the Staffel badge comes clearly into view, as does the aircraft's number '12' beside it - the badge is a shield with a sad-looking owl holding a furled umbrella under its left wing. This is the badge of VI/JG.51. The next shot is of three Messerschmitt Bf.109Es taking off in 'Vic' formation, all of them VI/JG.51 'Emils': the number of the lead Bf.109E is obscured by its wing, but '12' is nearest to the camera while '5' makes up the starboard wingman furthest away.

The VI/JG.51 Staffel badge can be seen on an 'Emil' from this unit today. This is Messerschmitt Bf.109E-3 Werke Nr 1342 'Yellow 8' of Paul Allen's Flying Heritage Collection at Everett, Washington, one of two genuine 'Emils' flying in the world. This was the Bf.109E-3 flown by Eduard Hemmerling that crashed on a French beach on 29th July 1940 after a fierce dog-fight over the South Coast of England. Hemmerling died in the crash and his Bf.109E-3 was gradually submerged by sand until it was recently discovered and salvaged. Today it flies together with Paul Allen's Focke Wulf FW.190A-5. As the restoration of Bf.109E-3

'Yellow 8' confirms that it was this version of the 'Emil' flown by Hemmerling in July 1940, it is almost certain that the 'Emils' seen in the Reich Propaganda Ministry footage in "International Squadron" are Bf.109E-3s 'Yellow 5' and 'Yellow 12' of VI/JG.51, plus a third example unidentified.

Immediately following this imagery of the Bf.109E-3s, footage of three Junkers Ju.87D-5 Stuka dive bombers appears next taking off as a three-ship framed in the foreground by the nose, fuselage and tail of a Junkers Ju.52/3M turning its motors. What is noteworthy about this Ju.52 is that it has a dorsal machine gun turret atop the fuselage, confirming that some examples of this rugged transport carried an aft-facing machine gun to provide some element of self defence.

Mendes and Seiler now demonstrate their lack of knowledge about Luftwaffe aircraft as they use imagery of Stukas to portray Luftwaffe fighters attacking Grant's Spitfire. An air-air of a Kette of three Junkers Ju.87B-1 Stukas in very close formation, filmed from the rear cockpit of the starboard wingman, leads into this final sequence of the film. Other archive footage of three Ju.87 Stukas making very low, fast passes in trail, which will appear in several British war films, follows; then an air-air of a Spitfire Mk.IIa filmed from the dorsal turret of a Heinkel He.111 making a run at the German bomber's tail - the origin of this footage will be revealed in the reviews of other films in this Chapter, but suffice it to say its source would be the British Ministry of Information, not the Reich Propaganda Ministry, probably released to newsreels. An unidentified aircraft dives vertically into the ground screened by rows of chimney stacks on rooftops.

Round and round goes Grant's miniature Brown B-3. "Two down, one to go", he says, grimacing through the pain of his wounds. He shoots down the third German fighter with straightforward ease. The enemy aircraft is seen striking the sea, only it is imagery of a Westland Lysander flying above the surface in a steep bank, with its port wing high, before it strikes the sea and cartwheels in. This footage must be of a coastal patrol Lysander that obviously got unlucky and must have been filmed somewhere off the English South Coast. It is the final piece of aviation seen in "International Squadron", Warner Bros' take on the 'Yank' theme in Hollywood 'British' war films that proved so popular in America before the United States was drawn into World War Two.

COTTAGE TO LET

(Released: September 1941)

The innocuous-sounding title of this film disguises a wartime thriller which reflected the still strong fear in Britain of large-scale infiltration of the country by Nazi agents and domestic 5th Columnists. Set in Scotland, the plot has a cottage in the grounds of a large private estate being advertised for let which is actually a front for a research laboratory where an eccentric boffin is developing a new bombsight for RAF Bomber Command. The same boffin had successfully designed a new, self-sealing fuel tank in British aircraft which the Germans appear to have mysteriously

acquired and installed in Luftwaffe bombers. The Security Service and RAF Intelligence believe that there is a leak from the Scottish research laboratory to German Intelligence and suspect the boffin's assistant, who studied in Germany before the War.

Adding to the mystery is the arrival of an RAF Spitfire pilot who has apparently parachuted into a loch from his aircraft which has been shot down by a Dornier tail gunner (if British Intelligence had been on the ball, they would have realised the Dornier Do.17/Do.217 series had no tail gunner, while a check on the squadron he said he came from would have revealed he did not exist). The film quickly lets us know that the Spitfire pilot, played by John Mills in one of his first main acting roles and out of character as a 'baddie', is an Abwehr agent who is part of a Nazi spy ring set in place to kidnap the boffin and convey him to Berlin via a Luftwaffe seaplane that will land at night on the loch.

Although there is a strong aviation theme to the plot, no actual aircraft appear in the film. It is, however, historically interesting for a number of reasons. The idea of a German agent parachuting into Scotland has strong echoes of Rudolph Hess's desperate mission in similar circumstances in May of the same year the film was in production - surely no coincidence. One character is described as "the man from MI5": the existence of the Security Service was never admitted to by the British government, the military and any part of the official establishment during and long after the War, so how this line in the script got past the wartime censor is a real curiosity. Also, another character played by the wonderfully creepy Alastair Sim, who turns out to be another MI5 agent, asks Mills about "the new Tornados which are replacing the Spitfires and Hurricanes" - surely this has to be a deception message aimed at any German Intelligence Officer watching the film.

Released as "Bombsight Stolen" in the USA two years after its cinematic release in Britain, "Cottage to Let" is still an entertaining film worth having in one's collection for historical reasons. Note George Cole as a 'Jack-the-Lad' East End evacuee kid, 38 years before he created the ultimate image of the Cockney 'Ducker-and-Diver', Arthur Daley, in the original 1979 TV series, "Minder".

49TH PARALLEL

(Released: November 1941)

Made as a wartime propaganda piece by the soon-to-be prolifically creative film-making duo of producer Emeric Pressburger and director Michael Powell, with a plot involving the survivors of a German U-Boat sunk in Canada's Hudson Bay threatening defenceless Canadian civilians, "49th Parallel" was aimed primarily at an American audience with the hoped-for intention that its message would help to increase Uncle Sam's support for the British and Canadian war effort (Pearl Harbor had yet to happen when the film was made, although it had done so five months earlier by the time of its release in the USA). The film did achieve success in the USA, with Pressburger being awarded an 'Oscar' at the 1942 Academy Awards for Best Original Story (the film was his concept, and he also wrote the screenplay as well as producing it).

The film's title is taken from the 49th Parallel North that is the circle of latitude 49 degrees north of the Earth's equatorial plane, and along which the border between Canada and the United States of America extends from the Atlantic Ocean to the Pacific Ocean.

The open and trusting values of the Canadian homesteaders, and the way their decent ways of life are at first exploited, then brutally put in danger by the more ardent Nazi members among the U-Boat crew, as they try to find a way to escape from Canada, was intended to convey the message that Nazism threatened exactly those same values held by the people of the United States. Therefore, the film's additional message to the US authorities was that any German Kriegsmarine personnel, especially from U-Boats, seeking asylum in the United States should be interned and not be allowed to return to Germany.

Aviation appears early in the film in the shape of Royal Canadian Air Force (RCAF) bombers searching for and destroying the U-Boat. A full-scale facsimile of a submarine was actually blown up for the production: the author admits that initially he believed it was a real decommissioned Royal Canadian Navy submarine that was used, so realistic is the facsimile. Interestingly, the number given to the U-Boat in "49th Parallel" is U-37: the real U-37 was one of the most successful U-Boats in the Kriegsmarine, sinking more Allied shipping than most others in the U-Boat 'Wolf Packs'. The Royal Navy's Admiralty would have been aware of U-37's success through Enigma code traffic intercepts mentioning the U-Boat's number whenever a sinking took place. It is possible that Powell and Pressburger were made aware of U-37's reputation, and that using its number for the U-Boat in the film was another propaganda scoring point they were trying to make.

The RCAF staged a formation of six bombers over-flying coastal patrol boats, filmed air-air by cameraman 'Skeets' Kelly, to portray the all-out search for the dangerous U-Boat. 'Skeets' Kelly was a British combat cameraman with the RAF Film Production Unit based at Pinewood Studios in 1941, and had worked on major film productions before the start of the War. He became an accomplished aerial cameraman long after the War, with such aviation-related films as "Those Magnificent Men in their Flying Machines" (1965), "The Blue Max" (1966) and "Battle of Britain" (1969) among his credits, but tragically was to lose his life while filming air-air sequences for the World War One drama, "Zeppelin", in 1971.

The RCAF formation is made up of four Lockheed Hudson Mk.III maritime patrol aircraft and two Douglas Digby Mk.I medium bombers. Also briefly shown is a distant shot of a Westland Lysander, too small to identify and almost certainly a Mk.II variant, as the Mk.III had not yet entered production in Canada when the film was made.

The aerial maritime search sequence is factual in its representation, as the RCAF's Eastern Air Command was heavily engaged in anti-U-Boat operations during World War Two and successfully sank several submarines off the Canadian Atlantic coast.

Two RCAF aircraft were actually made available for "49th Parallel" for individual sequences. Clearly seen is Lockheed Hudson Mk.III RCAF 778/OY-P of No.11 (Bomber Reconnaissance)

Squadron, first taking off, then later making a run past the camera as the bombing attack on the U-Boat begins. This Hudson was an ill-fated aircraft, as it was lost in a crash at its base of RCAF Dartmouth, Nova Scotia, while it was being filmed there.

This may explain why a major continuity goof in the film occurs at this point, when the Hudson turns itself into a Douglas Digby (or the Douglas B-18A Bolo, in US service) that is filmed actually carrying out the attack on the submarine. Presumably, as the RCAF's most potent anti-submarine warfare asset in 1941, another Hudson and crew could not be spared, so a Douglas Digby had to complete the submarine attack sequence in its place.

The Douglas Digby must stand out as one of the strangest and most ungainly-looking aircraft designs ever built, but its ancestry as the aerodynamic forerunner of the Douglas DC-3 is all too evident when seen from beneath in plan-form: the wing-shape is pure DC-3, although it is actually based on the earlier model DC-2. Footage of this chunky hybrid of a bomber and transport is extremely rare, which alone makes "49th Parallel" of special interest as a collector's item (leaving aside the remaining drawn-out plot-line of honest Canadian values prevailing in the face of Nazi tyranny). Seeing the Douglas Digby filmed in action is like discovering a long-forgotten, extinct species, virtually unknown to a 21st Century aviation film audience.

In its coastal bomber role, the Douglas Digby Mk.I was operated by No.10 (Bomber Reconnaisance) Squadron of Eastern Air Command. The Digby used in the film is serialled RCAF 744/PB-D, which actually conducted 10 (BR) Squadron's first operational mission in wartime on 17th June 1940. This same aircraft was lost when it crashed at sea on 29th December 1941, less than two months after the British release of "49th Parallel".

The film's plot has the U-Boat survivors taking settlers prisoner and reverting to their base Nazi nature by murdering a number of them. This includes the two-man crew of a relief supply floatplane, which the crew hijack in the hope of flying to the neutral United States. The floatplane used in the film is Fairchild 71C CF-BJE of Canadian Airways Limited, a high-winged, radial-engined seven passenger monoplane built under licence in Canada. The design was not new, having first flown by the Fairchild Aircraft Company in the USA in 1926. As it appears in the film, the floatplane has a distinctly vintage appearance compared with the Lockheed Hudsons and even the Douglas Digby. The Fairchild 71C was used for both passenger and freight purposes in Canada; the floatplane version was developed exclusively in Canada and was marketed as the Fairchild Super 71.

While trying to reach Lake Winnipeg the Fairchild runs short of fuel and crash lands on water. Powell's production team cause a goof to happen here, when the mock-up of the rear fuselage and tail of the floatplane they have built and placed sticking vertically up out of the water shows the Canadian civil registration letters of 'CF-A', when they should have been 'CF-B' (the remainder are submerged). Quite why they managed to make this goof isn't clear.

Fairchild 71C CF-BJE was, in fact, a composite rebuild from two other Fairchild 71s after suffering an earlier mishap. It was subsequently sold to Canadian Pacific Airlines, but ultimately ended its days after making a forced landing in trees near Franquelin,

Province of Quebec, on 4th January 1943, caused, somewhat coincidentally with its fate in the film, by running out of fuel.

Following the crash of the Fairchild 71 in "49th Parallel", aviation makes only one further brief appearance towards the end of the film when Lockheed Lodestar CF-TCH is seen filmed air-air. A Trans-Canada Air Lines machine, Lodestar CF-TCH is in natural metal scheme with no markings or titling on its fuselage other than its registration.

SHIPS WITH WINGS

(Released: November 1941)

When it is said, "They don't make 'em like that anymore", such words could not be more aptly applied than to this blatantly propagandistic and flagrantly ridiculous film. And after this production – an Ealing Studios one as well, all the more surprisingly – films like "Ships With Wings" didn't get made anymore. Such embarrassing nonsense was simply no longer defensible as public entertainment, with the nation being faced with the obvious realities that the progress of the War was having on Great Britain in late 1941.

The question has been asked as to how the Royal Navy allowed itself to be associated with this film, so far-fetched is its plot concerning naval aviation, even allowing for the nation's need for morale boosting entertainment. In reality, there was probably little the 'Senior Service' could do about it, because the flying elements involving actual Fleet Air Arm aircraft were all taken from a documentary, "Find, Fix, and Strike", that the Royal Navy had given full support to. The documentary was about the training and operational roles of Fleet Air Arm pilots, much of it filmed aboard HMS Ark Royal, then the most modern aircraft carrier in the world. The director and producer simply added a fictional plot about a cashiered pilot having to redeem himself with honour and glory in the face of overwhelming odds, and in so doing help save the Fleet and win a major battle.

It has been reported that Winston Churchill, after seeing the film, wanted "Ships With Wings" withdrawn from public viewing because it seemed to send the message that the Fleet was unable to defend itself without relying on the heroic actions of just one man. However, the public took a different view and received the film well, despite the panning it took from critics.

The plot is ridiculously adolescent. A Fleet Air Arm squadron test pilot falls pathetically in love with a Vice Admiral's daughter and wants to impress her by flying a new fighter while she is accompanying her father to visit the Royal Navy's newest aircraft carrier, HMS Invincible. When told that the fighter is in a dangerous condition, he throws a petulant tantrum and says he is going to fly it anyway. Not only that, he allows the younger brother of the object of his desire, a junior Naval pilot, to fly with him. Against the rules, he performs fly-bys in the fighter (a Fairey Fulmar Mk.I) over HMS Invincible, as a result of which the wings begin to fail. He orders his beloved's brother to bail out, then does likewise without realising the other young pilot has hidden himself in the cockpit and is now

trying to fly the fighter with boyish enthusiasm! He crashes onto the deck of HMS Invincible and dies of his injuries. The test pilot is Courts Martialed and drummed out of the Navy.

He becomes an embittered pilot flying for a shoestring airline on a Greek island. There he discovers a Hun plot to trap the Royal Navy, which is sailing to defend the mythical Greek island of Panteira from Italian and German invasion. He gets shot down by Italian fighters but is picked up by the Fleet and, unbelievably, is allowed to rejoin his squadron on Invincible. They attack the enemy on Panteira, whose fighters, bombers and tanks are portrayed by the most laughable miniatures surely ever used in a film. The Italians bomb HMS Invincible, leaving a large hole at either end of her flight deck. Using more miniatures that couldn't fool a five-year-old, the film's director and scriptwriter genuinely ask the audience to believe that Fleet Air Arm pilots would try to land on the flight deck, then take off again from it – leap-frogging their aircraft over the jagged holes – to bomb a dam and thus flush the enemy out of Panteira. The hero redeems himself by landing his Fulmar fighter on top of a German bomber, piggyback-style, then steers both locked-together aircraft into the dam!

It beggars belief that, even taking into account the need for a (very) large amount of dramatic licence, the Ealing Studios team could serve up such rubbish as this to embolden the War-ravaged public. But, however incredulous it may seem, there was an appetite in Britain in the Forties for such adolescent-like heroic entertainment as this, which lasted well after the War years published in the shape of small, one shilling comic books usually penned by equally adolescently-minded authors. These comics illustrated grossly exaggerated stories of British military heroism in the face of dastardly Hun behaviour, in exactly the same style as this film. The target audience were teenage boys, to encourage them to believe that Britain would always prevail against the Nazis and who would thus be ready to sign up for the War effort once they reached the age to do so.

"Ships With Wings" can lay claim to be the only film ever made to have one of its star performers sunk during the same month of its public release. HMS Ark Royal played the role of the fictional HMS Invincible in the film. Ark Royal was torpedoed by U-Boat U-81 150 miles east of Gibraltar on 13th November 1941 and, despite desperate efforts to quell the on-board fires and to take her under tow, she listed and sank on the 14th, taking her complement of 60 aircraft with her. Ark Royal's loss created a huge hole in the Royal Navy's fleet disposition in the Mediterranean, rendering the relief of Malta and the protection of convoys to Alexandria much more difficult to achieve.

However, the saving grace of "Ships With Wings", as far as aviation enthusiasts are concerned, is the priceless imagery of World War Two Fleet Air Arm aircraft in action. It is probably accurate to say that such fine imagery is unlikely to be obtained from any other source. As all the aerial shots and those taken aboard HMS Ark Royal are from "Find, Fix, and Strike", the ideal option would seem to be to obtain the documentary alone and thus avoid this embarrassing film; however, they are only available on a combined DVD, so there's no relief.

As it is the aviation elements which save "Ships With Wings" from deserved ignominy, let's examine the aircraft they show in detail. The opening shots has the camera installed in the rear cockpit of an aircraft, possibly a Swordfish, flying past the massive grey wall of HMS Ark Royal's superstructure and up over her flight deck. The thought of such a mighty steel leviathan rusting hundreds of fathoms down seems scarcely credible, but as Mother Nature put paid to the even larger Titanic, so one torpedo was obviously enough to deliver the coup de grace to the pride of the Royal Navy's fleet.

While the credits roll, three Fairey Swordfish torpedo bombers are seen filmed air–air floating sedately in 'Vic' formation, like large maritime birds sailing aloft in the airstream. Their squadron codes are clearly visible beneath their starboard upper wings: '2A', '2F' and '2L', of 810 Squadron. With the credits still rolling, HMS Ark Royal is given star billing along with the leading actors. More film credits follow as a Blackburn Skua, not the world's most successful dive bomber, bounces clumsily down onto Ark's flight deck, is folded up, and is dropped through the deck on one of Ark's three aircraft lifts – surely this must have seemed the pinnacle of aviation and nautical technology at the time. Another Skua is brought up on the lift and pushed back to join others grouped at the stern end of the deck.

The director's name rolls, Sergei Nolbandov; as he was one of the four scriptwriters as well, he bears a heavy responsibility for this film.

The film proper opens with the launch of HMS Ark Royal in 1937, although in the plot the scene is that of HMS Invincible being launched in 1936. The crusty old Vice Admiral Wetherby - played by Leslie Banks, a prolific British character actor on the stage and screen in the Thirties and Forties, whose facial disfigurement from injuries he received in the trenches during World War One is visibly prominent here - is an exponent of the battleship and does not think the aircraft carrier is good for anything more than aerial reconnaissance. Captain Fairfax argues that she is the future, and that she is indeed invincible. How did these words register with cinema audiences in November 1941, one wonders, now that they could not avoid knowing that Ark Royal had proven herself to be anything but invincible.

The scene changes to the then new Royal Naval Air Station Yeovilton (although it is not named in the film), where three Gloster Sea Gladiators are playing like frivolous larks above the Somerset countryside. RNAS Yeovilton, with its four hardened runways and large aircraft parking ramps, would have been a very advanced airfield compared with most air stations of the day.

As the Fleet Air Arm's premier air base, it would have been natural to have chosen it to feature in this film. Shots of Sea Gladiators and Blackburn Skuas parked on the northern-most ramp show a scene that is still recognisable today, as much of this area is now occupied by the Fleet Air Arm Museum complex.

The three Sea Gladiators performing aerobatics were on strength with the Fleet Fighter School, one of the first units to be established at RNAS Yeovilton in September 1940. It had a mix of aircraft types in its inventory, including Blackburn Skuas and Rocs (seriously considered to be fighters, until wisdom prevailed), as well as four Sea Gladiators. The serials of the trio flown in the

film are not readable, although one Sea Gladiator clearly carries the code letter 'E'. The Sea Gladiator had been withdrawn from front-line service by the time of this film's release, having been badly exposed during the Norway campaign as being no match for the modern, faster monoplane fighters of the Luftwaffe.

After a tedious portion of the film that involves the principal character, Lieutenant Dick Stacey (no, not Dick Tracey) falling for Celia Wetherby, the Vice Admiral's daughter, the hero is chosen to test fly a new fighter. This fighter is portrayed by a Fairey Fulmar Mk.I, regrettably not identifiable as its serial is unreadable, while it bears no squadron codes or markings.

What is noticeable is that RNAS Yeovilton was still very much under construction when this film of the Fulmar was taken, with piled, dug up earth alongside the runways and hard standing. In one shot, the large hangars which are still used today to house Royal Navy Lynx and Sea King HC.4 helicopters, can clearly be seen among the earthworks. The scenery suggests that the Fulmar was filmed during winter, judging by the leafless trees bordering the air station, suggesting a late 1940 - early 1941 time period. What is of interest are the three civilians seen clearly on film standing at the runway end, watching the Fulmar come in over the threshold. Certainly they have nothing to do with the storyline. The best guess is that they were from the Air Ministry, watching the Fulmar's progress as it worked up in Fleet Air Arm service, or were possibly Fairey Aviation personnel. This rare imagery of a not exactly ideal fleet fighter – and one with which the word manoeuvrable was rarely associated – is certainly welcome to view. The Merlin-engined Fulmar appears fast in these shots, but nothing like as agile as the contemporary Spitfire Mk.II or Bf.109E.

The Fleet Air Arm could not be considered fortunate with its allocation of aircraft assets in the early part of World War Two. If the Fairey Fulmar fleet fighter did not exactly give the enemy sleepless nights, the same could equally be said of the Blackburn Skua dive bomber. It had occasional successes, most noticeably sinking the cruiser Konigsberg in Bergen Harbour in April 1940, but all too often it suffered losses to flak and Luftwaffe fighters. As the Skua was being withdrawn from front-line service in the first half of 1941, its appearance as part of HMS Ark Royal's air group in "Ships With Wings" gives a timescale as to when filming took place on board the aircraft carrier, probably during the previous year.

The build up to the attack on the German and Italian forces on the fictional Greek island of Panteira allows for film taken of Ark Royal's air group above and below deck to be used. "Skuas on deck!" is the bellowed command, as Blackburn Skua Mk.II coded '6K' of 800 Squadron is manhandled onto one of the aircraft lifts and is speedily brought up into the sunlight. When it reaches the deck it has become Skua II L2967/6M. Six Skua Mk.IIs are seen turning their props on Ark's stern deck. They are obviously not on operations because they are not armed up. '6M' rolls almost daintily down the deck and neatly departs the carrier over a noticeably smooth sea. It is followed by Skua Mk.IIs '6K' and '6A', while '6B' appears later. Skua Mk.II '7K' of 803 Squadron, the second Ark Royal-embarked dive bomber unit, is next to depart, dropping rather alarmingly off the bow end of the deck. This Skua was almost certainly filmed prior to June 1940, as 803 Squadron was decimated that month during an attack on the German Schlacht Kreuzer (battlecruiser) Scharnhorst; it was not reformed until the following October, on Fulmars, and was then transferred to HMS Formidable.

Next up are Fairey Swordfish Mk.I torpedo bombers, with '2Q' of 810 Squadron being loaded into the bottom lift and with '2L' emerging on deck. Shots of Swordfish Mk.Is being prepared for launching show the following coded aircraft: '2C' of 810 Squadron, '4G' and '4H' (the latter identified as K8357) from 820 Squadron, and finally '5A' and '5C' of 818 Squadron. The Swordfish coded '5A' will probably strike an accord in the minds of many aviation enthusiasts, as Fairey Swordfish Mk.II LS326 of the Royal Navy Historic Flight did for much of its career on the UK airshow circuit carry the '5A' code letters of the lead aircraft that attacked the German Schlachtschiffe (battleship) Bismarck, as applied for its appearance in the film, "Sink The Bismarck!" (1960). In that film, Swordfish LS326 was portraying the lead aircraft of both 'A' Flight from 825 Squadron, operating off the carrier HMS Victorious, and 'A' Flight from 818 Squadron off HMS Ark Royal.

For many, the Fleet Air Arm wartime coding system is confusing because the same codes appear to crop up on different aircraft from different squadrons flying from separate aircraft carriers. The explanation lies in the coding system relating to squadrons making up each aircraft carrier's air group. This means that there were two Swordfish torpedo bombers bearing the code '5A' that attacked the Bismarck in May 1941: Lieutenant Commander (Acting) E K Desmond's '5A' of 825 Squadron off Victorious on 24th May, and Lieutenant Commander T P Coode's '5A', believed to be Swordfish Mk.I P4219 of 818 Squadron from Ark Royal, which led the decisive attack against Bismarck on 26th May that crucially damaged her steering gear.

Thus it is the wing of Swordfish Mk.I P4219/5A of 818 Squadron which is shown in "Ships With Wings", while in the background is the wing of Swordfish Mk.I L9726/5C, the actual aircraft flown by Sub-Lieutenant J W C Moffatt that was destined to deliver the fatal torpedo into Bismarck's rudder, causing so much damage that the mighty commerce raider's fate was sealed. But these momentous events were still many months into the future when the scenes shown in "Ships With Wings" were filmed on Ark Royal's flight deck. They are nonetheless priceless glimpses of important British naval aviation history.

Swordfish Mk.Is '5G', '5H' and '5F' are all seen taking off from Ark Royal's flight deck, filmed from the carrier's island as well as from an aircraft directly overhead, the camera looking vertically downwards as a Swordfish travels sedately along the flight deck and floats off over the bow. Another excellent shot shows a Swordfish turning to starboard after take-off, to fly astern of a large battleship. The film then cuts to a view from the rear of a Swordfish's cockpit, as the torpedo bomber flies past the same battleship steaming ahead of Ark Royal. The warship can clearly be identified as a Queen Elizabeth Class battleship. This could help pinpoint the period in time when this particular footage was taken, as the Queen Elizabeth Class battleship HMS Barham provided escort to HMS Ark Royal when the carrier sailed from Liverpool to Gibraltar between 3rd – 6th November 1940, before both ships then joined Force H on convoy protection duties in the Mediterranean. A film crew joining Ark Royal as she steamed with HMS Barham close to Gib in the Med in November 1940 seems perfectly feasible.

It was during November 1940 that the attack by Swordfish from HMS Illustrious on capital ships of the Italian Regia Marina moored in Taranto Harbour took place, while later the same month Ark Royal launched her aircraft as part of Force H's attack on the Italian fleet off Cape Spartivento, Sardinia. Ark Royal herself was straddled by bombs from Regia Aeronautica SM.79 bombers during this battle. It is likely that these actions, plus the attack by Ark Royal's Swordfish against the Tirso Dam in Sardinia the following February, strongly influenced the part of the plot showing HMS Invincible sending her aircraft to dive bomb and torpedo similar Axis targets on the fictional island of Panteira.

The attacks on the Italian and German forces on Panteira are depicted by the use of the aforementioned embarrassingly poor miniatures, cut between imagery of Blackburn Skua Mk.II dive bombers, Fairey Swordfish Mk.I torpedo bombers and Fairey Fulmar Mk.I fleet fighters filmed for "Find, Fix, and Strike". Each type is filmed as a sub-Flight, two Skuas in the first such Flight, and three each of Swordfish and Fulmars in the second and third Flights; operating in two- or three-ship sub-Flights in co-ordinated attacks upon a target from different directions was the standard tactical method for Flights of Fleet Air Arm squadrons embarked aboard aircraft carriers in World War Two.

Among the imagery are two clear shots of live torpedo drops made by Swordfish, while a third shows a torpedo skipping like a porpoise across the surface of the sea. Then, curiously, a shot of another Swordfish Mk.I, clearly identified as L2865/V, suddenly appears. This is definitely not an Ark Royal carrier group torpedo bomber as it has the wrong code letter, while it noticeably bears an all-over camouflage scheme normally adopted by land-based Swordfish. Also, it is flying without an observer or air gunner aboard. Another similarly camouflaged and configured Swordfish Mk.I, coded 'F', but whose serial is unreadable, appears soon after. Later, a carrier-borne Swordfish Mk.I coded 'B' is shown filmed air–air, but this does not look like an Ark Royal group torpedo bomber either, as it does not show a carrier group sub-Flight number. Presumably the film editor had this imagery to hand and inserted it for effect, as they show fine close-ups of wartime Fairey Swordfish.

Air–air shots of the two Blackburn Skua Mk.I dive bombers likewise reveal that they are neither 800 nor 803 Squadron aircraft. They both wear wrap-around fuselage camouflage representative of land-based Skuas, whereas carrier-borne Skuas had their colour schemes divided between camouflage on the top fuselage and wings, with grey for the lower fuselage half and underwing areas. The Skuas seen taking off from Ark Royal are clearly bearing the carrier-borne scheme, but the two filmed air–air are definitely different.

The three Fairey Fulmar Mk.I fleet fighters, which appear to be intercepting the Regia Aeronautica bomber formations threatening the fictional HMS Invincible, are definitely not from Ark Royal's air group but are from the same unit that the solo Fulmar seen earlier in the film came, based at RNAS Yeovilton. Very English countryside can be seen briefly below them as they make line astern breaks to simulate attacks. No Fulmars are seen above or below deck on Ark Royal, or taking off from the carrier. Ark Royal embarked 808 Squadron equipped with Fulmar Mk.Is in October 1940, but the Fulmars in the film do not carry any codes, let alone those of the type that would be used by a carrier air group.

The candidate unit for these three Fulmars is, again, the Fleet Fighter School at RNAS Yeovilton, which was tasked with training Fleet Air Arm pilots in air fighting tactics. It is almost certain the two Skuas are from the same unit as well, as the Fleet Fighter School operated the Skua alongside the Sea Gladiator and the Fulmar at the time "Find, Fix, and Strike" was filmed.

"Ships With Wings", therefore, borrows heavily from the "Find, Fix, and Strike" promotional film for the Fleet Air Arm, as well as utilising footage shot between late 1939 and early November 1940 aboard HMS Ark Royal during several different cruises in that famous aircraft carrier's short but active career, which is then mixed with other footage shot at RNAS Yeovilton whilst that new air station was working up towards the end of 1940 and into the first dark months of 1941.

The actors in the feature film never appear alongside the actual aircraft shown in "Find, Fix, and Strike"; instead, all-too-obvious studio shots of the actors in the foreground posed against backcloths of Sea Gladiators and a Fulmar are used. The limited and naïvely created studio scenes of the air station control tower and of what the production team thought life aboard a then modern aircraft carrier represented, clash jarringly with the images of the real Ark Royal in action. As for the dialogue, well, the four scriptwriters (yes, four!) have much to answer for.

Even allowing for the time period in which it was made, "Ships With Wings" cannot escape from being recognised for what it is: a cheap attempt to exploit a documentary film intended to promote the Fleet Air Arm, by tagging an embarrassingly bad fictional plot onto it as wartime propaganda for the masses. The embarrassing truth is that, at the time of its release, it worked.

THE BIG BLOCKADE

(Released: March 1942)

Following in the wake of "The Lion Has Wings" (1939), the need to maintain British public morale through the means of cinematic propaganda became increasingly important as the War began to develop. It became essential to the British government, the armed services and the Intelligence Ministries to convince the people of Britain that the nation had the means - not just militarily, but equally politically and economically - to withstand and to erode Adolf Hitler's monstrously dominating war machine. Hence this mock-documentary and play-acting propaganda film, which was intended to be released in 1940 but actually reached the cinema screens two years later soon after the United States had entered the War.

To understand "The Big Blockade", it has to be realised that this film was added to and up-dated with extra scenes and newsreel material as the War progressed, so the end result is a mixed-up jumble of scenarios which criss-cross various time periods before and after the start of the War for Britain. Even when it was released it must have had a dated look to the audience, especially in relation to certain scenes depicting events leading up to 3rd September 1939 and what had taken place subsequently. Its presentation definitely conveys an impression that the intention was to release "The Big Blockade" to a 1940 audience, as its propaganda style fits with that time period when the Ministry of Information wanted a film made to convince the British public that their government could break Germany economically, as well as militarily. Trying to convey that message in early 1942 was definitely a 'stable door, bolting horse' situation, as it would then have been obvious to the British people that the former had not been achieved while the latter now only looked possible since America was no longer neutral.

There is no explanation for why this production was not completed in 1940, although something seems to have reached the screens then because certain sources give that year for the film's release. The origins of "The Big Blockade" lay in a request by the MoI for a two-reel film documentary on the work of the newly-created Ministry of Economic Warfare (MEW), to describe how Britain was successfully (so the MoI wanted the public to believe) blockading Germany's access to essential raw materials and undermining her industrial output supporting the Wehrmacht. It is perhaps this short propaganda piece that went on view alongside a newsreel and a full feature film in the cinemas of 1940.

Producer Michael Balcon placed Ealing Film Studios in the forefront of making such government information 'two-reelers', but he also developed the idea of making full feature films out of them which he believed, correctly, would appeal much more to a wider audience and would thus get the intended message over more effectively (he would also get a bigger return on his investment, as the MoI were hardly big spenders on short documentaries). Bringing in established and popular actors of the day to play cameo parts in the film added to the audience's enjoyment. "The Big Blockade" provides a veritable 'Who's Who' of British big name performers of the Thirties and Forties; playing 'Spot The Actor' was part of the fun of watching it.

"The Big Blockade" is extremely important to the aviation historian because it contains considerable footage of an unsung RAF bomber in service at the outbreak of the War which is not available in any other film: the Handley Page Hampden. In other film productions, it is firstly the Vickers Wellington bomber which takes centre stage (which we have already seen in "The Lion Has Wings" and "Target for Tonight"), then later the 'heavies', the Short Stirling, the Handley Page Halifax and, of course, the ultimate British World War Two bomber, the Avro Lancaster. But, in "The Big Blockade", the Handley Page Hampden has its one chance to be in the limelight.

The film opens with the following acknowledgment: "This film has been produced with the fullest co-operation and advice of the MINISTRY of ECONOMIC WARFARE, with the assistance of the ROYAL NAVY, the WAR OFFICE and the ROYAL AIR FORCE". The film then goes on to "gratefully acknowledge" the services not only of the "artistes" involved, but also of "the following members of His Majesty's Government, The Rt. Hon. Sir Ronald Cross, BT.MP, The Rt. Hon. Hugh Dalton MP (first and second Minister for Economic Warfare respectively) and The Hon. David Bowes-Lyon, Press Officer to the Ministry of Economic Warfare" (brother to the then Queen Elizabeth and future Queen Mother, and uncle to the then Princess Elizabeth, today Her Majesty The Queen).

As the title music ends, the film cuts to a shot of a Vickers Supermarine Spitfire Mk.I flying directly toward and over the camera. This Spitfire is entirely in silhouette, so identifying it isn't possible. It is followed by shots of a tank's tracks and a warship firing a broadside; then a figure appears, that of a suited man who speaks directly to the camera, telling us, "Fighting is one side of war. There's another side; that is, stopping the enemy from fighting".

This man is Frank Owen, the film's commentator, although if we missed reading his name at the start of the title credits we wouldn't know who he was because no further clue is given as to his identity. Interesting man, Owen; he was the former Liberal MP for Hereford but made his name as a political journalist. At the time he is seen addressing the audience in "The Big Blockade", Frank Owen was the editor of the London Evening Standard and, therefore, well known to politicians on all sides of the Houses of Parliament.

What was not known publicly at the time of the release of "The Big Blockade" in March 1942 was that Owen, along with two other journalists - political correspondent of the Daily Express, Peter Howard, and Michael Foot, future editor of the London Evening Standard (as well as future leader of the Labour Party) - had secretly authored a controversial book entitled "Guilty Men", which denounced those British politicians and public figures who had pursued a policy of appeasement towards Hitler before the War. "Guilty Men" was published in July 1940, just after Winston Churchill had taken over as Prime Minister of the wartime government of national unity. Seeing and hearing Owen in this film broadcasting the message of the Ministry of Economic Warfare makes interesting watching, especially when it is realised that his shared secret authorship of "Guilty Men" is believed by some historians to have helped destroy the reputation of Prime Minister Neville Chamberlain, after he had stepped down on 10th May 1940.

Owen's address to the camera highlights the three services taking the offensive to Nazi Germany: the RAF, the Army and the Royal Navy, in that order. As he speaks, the film fades to an air-air of a Vickers Supermarine Spitfire Mk.I peeling off from the camera aircraft and banking into a dive; the image quality is poor and Owen is superimposed behind it, masking any possibility of reading any squadron code or serial, but the small, underwing tip roundels are of an early War Spitfire. Stock footage of Matilda II infantry tanks and an HMS King George V Class battleship follow, possibly that of KGV herself.

After introducing the audience to the Ministry of Economic Warfare, Owen explains how this "Fourth Arm" will deny Nazi Germany the vital raw materials her industry needs from around the world. But that industry must be attacked militarily as well as economically. "We must smash the production power of Germany by bombing", Owen forthrightly declares. As he speaks, bombs on trailers are seen being towed along a rough track with a Handley Page Hampden parked in the background. This shot cuts to that of armourers loading a 500lb bomb under the port wing of a Handley Page Hampden, then cuts again to another shot showing armourers positioning two more 500lb bombs inside the bomb bay of a Hampden, probably the same aircraft. The Hampden could carry four bombs internally and a 500 pounder under each wing, a very limited weapons load for striking at Germany's massive industrial base.

We then get a close-up of a Hampden moving right past the camera as it commences its take off run; there are no visible codes on this Hampden and its serial is masked by the starboard tail fin. Next, we see a distant shot of a Hampden getting airborne from a very open, sparse airfield with tough grass and dirt patches, no hangars or any other buildings in sight. It passes over another Hampden parked by itself on-field. "Now this squadron is one of scores that fly to Germany in raid upon raid", intones Owen dramatically. "Squadron One Oh Two Oh, Hampden bombers". There was no Squadron 1020, of course, except in the scriptwriter's imagination.

We then see the bomber's departure time being chalked up on the Ops Board. A goof occurs here: the squadron is listed as being "1052 SQDN". Then another Hampden is seen taking off from the bare, flat all-grass airfield, which must have been a very unprotected, windswept base, from a meteorological point of view. "Hampden bombers, bound for Hanover", announces Owen. This Hampden can be identified because its code letters come clearly into view as it passes the camera: XG-A, the codes of No.16 Operational Training Unit (OTU).

But the next Hampden to come into shot gives us the clue of the location. This is Handley Page Hampden I coded D-VN making its take off run. The codes are applied on the port fuselage in the alternative order to that shown on the starboard side, which would read VN-D; this application was quite common on Hampdens, although why it was used isn't easy to understand. These are the codes of No.50 Squadron, a unit which served with RAF Bomber Command throughout World War Two.

No.50 Squadron started converting from Hawker Hinds onto the Hampden I in December 1938 at RAF Waddington, Lincolnshire. It was still at Waddington on Hampdens when war broke out in September 1939. The squadron carried out its first bombing mission, on a German seaplane base, on 19th March 1940. In July of that year, No.50 Squadron re-located to RAF Lindholme, where it remained until July 1941. It is almost certain that the bare, flat, open grass airfield that the Hampdens are filmed taking off from in "The Big Blockade" is Lindholme, on the Hatfield Moors in South Yorkshire.

More take off shots follow: a Hampden flies straight towards the camera after taking off and passes low overhead, code and serial out of view; a Hampden in silhouette takes off towards the sunset, the black shape of a Vickers Wellington parked on-field nearby.

Then a shot of a Hampden I, clearly coded with the aircraft identifier letter 'A', is seen running up its engines while an 'Erk' assists the pilot as five other men look on close by. Just visible on the opposite side of the fuselage roundel is the letter 'N'; a closer check reveals that, irritatingly, this image has been reproduced by the editor in reverse, so that confirmation by using a mirror is necessary. This shows that this Hampden I must be coded VN-A of No.50 Squadron.

"These are the machines and here are the men who drive the British blockade home", Owen forcefully tells us, as we see actors Michael Rennie (fresh from "Ships With Wings") and John Mills climbing into their Hampden, 'T for Tommy'. The value of the "The Big Blockade" to the aviation and military historian is that it provides unique access to the interior of the Handley Page Hampden, quite unlike any other British bomber design. Rennie as George the pilot sits up front alone - single pilot in a twin-engined bomber (the American Douglas Havoc had a similar arrangement). Mills as the navigator/bomb aimer enters via a hatchway in the roof some eight feet behind the cockpit position. Once inside, he is able to crawl forward to speak to the pilot, but to reach his navigator's position in the belly of the Hampden he has to swing himself down through a gap into the only reasonably spacious area aboard the bomber, where the slightly built Mills is actually able to stand. Two gunners, both facing rearwards, one mid-upper who doubles as the wireless operator, one mid-lower, make up the complement of the Hampden's aircrew.

During the start-up sequence another Hampden I is seen parked in the background, no codes carried. This is a daytime shot, even though the scene is meant to be taking place at dusk. Distant trees appear to be in leaf, so this could be a summertime shot in either 1940 or 1941, probably the former if the Hampdens were filmed for the original 'two-reel' documentary. It is likely that the Rennie-Mills scenes were filmed at Ealing Studios, using a struck off charge airframe of a Hampden, at a time a good deal later than the shots filmed at Lindholme and then tagged on to the original 1940 documentary, in the same fashion as "Ships With Wings" was tagged on to the documentary, "Find, Fix and Strike".

Hampden I XG-A of No.16 OTU is used for filming 'T for Tommy' taxying out, somewhat incongruously not having any 'T' letter code! This is, however, an excellent study of the ungainly-looking Hampden moving across the ground. Another Hampden in silhouette is used for the take off shot of 'T for Tommy' into the sunset.

As they head out towards the English coast Mills tells Rennie to "Turn Oh Nine Oh degrees, magnetic". A shot then appears of the Hampden's port wing in flight above billowing white clouds; this view could have only been achieved from the mid-upper gunner's position. The shot then cuts to the first air-air in the film of a Hampden, although it is totally silhouetted. It breaks away to port towards the clouds.

The film changes at this point and moves back in time to 1939 before war had broken out. Here it commences a series of scenarios involving various familiar actors of the time who play out the propaganda message of Britain's effectiveness in economically blockading Germany. These scenes were possibly filmed for the original 1940 MoI information cinema piece, as the scenarios they depict are relative to that period. It may have been possible to persuade a British audience still affected by the 'Phoney War' that Britain had got Germany economically encircled and confined, but it surely was asking far too much to expect a Spring 1942 audience to swallow that fantastic claim. They would have been watching when Britain was still being regularly bombed by the Luftwaffe, the Eighth Army had been driven back into Egypt, Malta was under siege, while the Battle of the Atlantic was the only means of keeping the nation supplied with vital military equipment and raw materials - what was this about a Big Blockade?

The film then focuses on the role of the Royal Navy in enforcing the blockade by boarding ships suspected of carrying contraband to Germany and seizing their cargo. "They set a steel barrier across the Western sea approaches to Europe, up to the icy waters of the tip of Norway. The blockade cuts deeply into Germany's war effort", claims Owen. "The Nazis themselves admitted it, by the desperate efforts they made to break it".

Now comes the most incredible spin of the entire script of "The Big Blockade", that Hitler ordered the invasions of Norway, Denmark, Holland, Belgium and France to possess the resources of those countries because the British blockade had been so successful in starving the German nation of its own goods and materials. Such an extraordinary lie is then bolstered by a fake recording of Lord 'Haw Haw' claiming that Germany had taken control of Denmark on 9th April 1940 "to protect them (the Danes) from the effects of British aggression….to the evident satisfaction of the people".

"On the same day, Germany had gone to the rescue of little Norway, trembling before the menace of Britisher fame". The sneering voice of Lord 'Haw Haw' accompanies stock footage of a parade formation of nine Heinkel He.111s in three 'Kettes' of three. A trio of Junkers Ju.87 Stukas are seen in long-shot making shallow dives, obviously not actual combat footage. A Junkers Ju.52/3M sits on verdant ground while flame and smoke belch from what was probably a fuel dump set on fire amid forest trees in the background. All to show Norway as a "rescued" nation. Most likely all of this imagery was obtained from material released to newsreels by the Reich Propaganda Ministry.

On 10th May 1940 Holland "was made safe from the nightmare of British aggression". To, "once again, make Belgium the cockpit of Europe, Belgium too was made safe".

"Finally, the much-vaunted French Army fell to the Reich of might. France had learnt that the German military machine was irresistible. When will a weak democracy realise that the new Order in Europe has begun to take shape?"

So, thanks to the British blockade, Hitler had created the excuses he had wanted to use to justify Nazi Germany's invasion and occupation of five European countries, having already taken possession of three more: Austria, Czechoslovakia and Poland. In other words, so successful had Britain's economic war against Germany been that Hitler had resorted to the worst in his character. By taking the steps he had done, Hitler had condemned

Germany to draining that country's entire resources to hold on to its gains, which must inevitably weaken it. This is the message "The Big Blockade" was sending to the British cinema audience.

Would a war-rationed public in Britain during the Spring of 1942 have accepted such a picture as was being presented to them by the Ministry of Economic Warfare? You never know, they may have wanted to grab on to a message that time was on Britain's side and that Germany had vastly over-stretched its ambitions, especially now that the German invasion of Soviet Russia was far from going to plan and that America had entered the War.

"Hitler seizes four-fifths of Europe, but he does not break the blockade", trumpets Owen. "He does not break the economists' plan for victory, he merely enlarges the area under siege. He gains huge stocks by looting, but the blockade still works". Such an imaginative interpretation of the situation is pure King's new clothes. Whoever came up with the description of the conquest of new territories as being merely enlarging the area under siege deserves a spin doctor's 'Oscar' Award .

The scenarios with actors continue. Will Hay and Bernard Miles act out a three-minute cameo as Captain and ship's mate of a tramp steamer, discussing the merits of the Royal Navy's role in the blockade as they come under attack by an embarrassingly poor studio miniature of a Heinkel He.111, which they shoot down with ease.

Stock footage of convoys follows, with Owen saying, "And now with the help of the United States, the big". At that point Owen is cut off in his verbal prime and the image suddenly changes to a Spitfire entirely in silhouette, filmed from the dorsal turret of a bomber as it makes its run past the tailfin. This happens so suddenly and so unexpectedly that at first the viewer must wonder what is happening. What is the point of the film editor cutting Owen off and inserting this new, and completely out of context, air-air shot of a Spitfire? There is no obvious answer, but it does show that "The Big Blockade" is a film that has had changes made to it at different time periods, some of them, like this, clumsy and unrelated to the script and plot.

Freeze-frame analysis shows that the Spitfire is passing so close and so fast that the bomber's tail only appears in shot in one frame. It bears no resemblance to an RAF bomber of the period, ruling out the Blenheim, Hampden, Whitley and Wellington. What it does appear to be is the tail of a Heinkel He.111. If so, is this footage filmed from a Luftwaffe bomber as a Spitfire attacks? Undoubtedly, yes, but how would Ealing Film Studios have acquired it in 1940 - 1941? Such material could only be gained if the Reich Propaganda Ministry released it in newsreel footage. That's possible, but what would the Third Reich and the Luftwaffe gain from releasing film of one of their bombers being attacked by a British fighter? Hardly an image that Dr Goebbels would want to convey.

There is an explanation for the source of this footage, which is better explained later in this Chapter when we come to the review of "The First of the Few" (1942).

As the Spitfire dashes past, Owen states, "hero of the Royal Air Force, fresh from the Battle of Britain. They smashed the Luftwaffe out of the skies". Clearly Owen has had the first part

of his narrative about the Spitfire cut by the editor. But this does confirm that elements of the film were put together at a later period than the earlier scenes completed in 1940.

The shot of the Spitfire melds into an air-air of the Hampden playing 'T - Tommy' dropping four bombs from its bomb-bay, probably the only imagery publicly available of a Hampden doing this. Noticeably, the bombs are released individually, not collectively in a 'stick', and a total of only four of them. Further confirmation of the Hampden's limitations.

Cut to a cameo by Michael Redgrave playing the role of an unfailingly cheerful Russian sent by the Soviet Union to study the economic conditions of the Reich, who smiles his way through repeated British bombing attacks on the trains he is travelling in. Redgrave refers to the non-aggression pact existing between the Nazis and the Soviets, which Hitler broke when he launched Operation Barbarossa against Stalin's Russia in June 1941. Obviously this cameo was filmed well before that happened, as Redgrave is describing the non-aggression pact as being in existence while a German passenger complains to him about Russia's failure to deliver more than one-tenth of the oil Soviet foreign minister Molotov had promised to German foreign minister Ribbentrop. This scene must have seemed somewhat incongruous and out of place to a British cinema audience watching it in Spring 1942, with the Soviets and the Germans fighting it out amid the snows of the recent Russian Winter.

The anomaly of the confused time periods in the film are further raised in another scene that follows when actor Leslie Banks, playing the role of a director of the MEW, asks the question when discussing the U-Boat menace, "And what happens if America leaves us to stew in our own juice?". This is answered by US war correspondent, Quentin Reynolds, who was stationed in London throughout the Battle of Britain and The Blitz: "Oh, believe me, gentlemen, America is with you heart and soul". No need for these lines in March 1942, three months since Japan had brought the United States into the War.

Later in the film, Owen actually refers to the Nazi invasion of the Soviet Union and to the United States having come into the War, meaning that Balcon and his team threw in Owen's contradictory commentary, mixed among what was already on film, in little more than three months, between 7th December 1941 and the release to the cinema on 20th March 1942. "The Big Blockade" was confusing and out of date as a propaganda vehicle as soon as it went public.

Finally, the film reaches the point where RAF Bomber Command is described as being part of a combined operation with the MEW, "to hit him (the enemy) where it hurts, and to speed up, with well placed bombs, the confusion of the enemy's economy to the point where he can neither attack others nor even defend himself". Well placed bombs? The public were not on the MEW's or the MoI's list of people who needed to know, but Bomber Command's accuracy in 1940 and 1941 was more often than not wide of the target, literally. And the Hampden's hitting power was hardly widespread, as this film demonstrates only too obviously. Again, it begs the question as to why Balcon and the MEW either chose, or were given no choice but, to use a Hampden squadron to convince the British public that the RAF had the capability in the early years of the War to smash the Ruhr industries and to destroy Germany's transport system. The answer has to be that the Hampdens were filmed in the summer of 1940 for the 'two-reeler', and then cut into the 'drama-doc' that Balcon went on to create haphazardly over the next 18 months.

"British bombers hammer at the heart of German industry, destroying the mechanism of war itself". insists Owen. "Not the over-worked squadrons of 1940 (another clue as to when the Hampdens were filmed), but a brand new bomber force with further range, height and speed, and a far higher bomb load". But nothing is seen of this brand new bomber force, only the tops of a sea of white clouds. When Owen was uttering these words, only the first of the RAF's three four-engined bombers, the Short Stirling, was entering service with Bomber Command, which, while carrying a maximum 14,000lb bomb load, definitely far greater than anything the RAF or the Luftwaffe could mount with any other aircraft of the time, could not reach the industrial heartland of Germany and be capable of returning. To achieve that, the Stirling's bomb load had to be halved - no greater than that of a Vickers Wellington.

In fact, it is the over-worked bombers of 1940 that now feature in the remainder of "The Big Blockade". The shot of the clouds scenery melds into a new air-air of a Hampden acting the role of 'T - Tommy' flying amidst clouds, possibly the best aerial imagery of a Handley Page Hampden obtainable from any public source. "T for Tommy, bound for Hanover, objective: power house" announces Owen. The image cuts to John Mills at his navigator's position, playing cards and chewing gum: the ideal nonchalant British hero the audience would have loved in wartime.

From now on the action is depicted entirely with the use of studio miniatures of 'T - Tommy' attacking and destroying the power house in Hanover. The miniature sets and models are of a standard that would have been the best achievable by Ealing Film Studios at the time. The He.111 miniature seen bombing Will Hay and Bernard Miles acts as a Luftwaffe night fighter, converted into what is meant to be a Messerschmitt Bf.110 by having its single, erect tailfin replaced with a twin set of fins!

'T - Tommy' is hit while making its bomb run and has to make the return flight to Britain on fire. The wireless operator/air gunner beats out the flames using only his gloved hands, suffering badly as a result. A viewer today would probably not realise it, but this is a re-enactment of a very real situation aboard a No.83 Squadron Hampden on the night of 15th September 1940, when wireless operator/air gunner Sergeant John Hannah fought the flames of his burning aircraft, saving it at the expense of serious burns to himself. For this action, Sergeant Hannah was awarded the Victoria Cross.

The remaining shots of what is meant to be 'T - Tommy' landing back at base are of three different Hampdens obviously filmed at RAF Lindholme at the same time as when the take off shots seen earlier were achieved. What is noticeable is that the second Hampden seen landing close to the camera has a motif on its port side forward fuselage below the cockpit. When Michael Rennie is seen opening his cockpit after the engines have stopped

turning, the camera pans down to the motif which shows itself to be St George slaying the Dragon. Message well and truly driven home.

One is left to wonder why Michael Balcon, the MEW and the MoI went ahead in March 1942 with the release of such a haphazardly thrown together hotch potch of cameos and commentaries that "The Big Blockade" is as a film, the message of which had already been overtaken by events when it eventually hit the screens. Promoting the MEW was obviously one reason, but it was at the expense of credibility in certain aspects as the audience was hardly likely to buy in to the claim that Nazi expansionism was in response to Britain's supposed success in restricting Germany's acquisition of raw materials for its war effort. Balcon almost certainly wanted a return on Ealing Film Studios' investment in what was meant originally to be a short propaganda information film, scheduled for release in 1940, but went well beyond that remit when Balcon tried turning it into an extended drama-documentary.

However, "The Big Blockade" has its place in British cinema history as a valuable example of wartime propaganda. For the war and aviation historians, its unique footage of the very rarely seen Handley Page Hampden medium bomber must make it a welcome addition to their collections.

ONE OF OUR AIRCRAFT IS MISSING

(Released: April 1942)

The title of this Academy Award nominated film has become a classic in its own right, much copied or parodied by various films or TV productions over the decades since its original wartime production. The BBC TV comedy series, "Dad's Army", referenced it in one episode; a Seventies British comic film borrowed the title as a parody about a stolen dinosaur skeleton from an archaeological museum, in "One of our Dinosaurs is Missing"(1975); while Sean Connery in his second outing as James Bond 007 made play with the expression, "I'd say one of their aircraft is missing", after bringing down the 'SPECTRE Helicopter' in "From Russia With Love" (1963) (an expression itself copied soon after by an American Hollywood Tarzan, who likewise causes a helicopter to crash).

The expression, "One of our aircraft has failed to return", became an all-too familiar one to British radio listeners as they heard the cultured tones of BBC announcer, Alvar Lidell, reporting about yet another RAF Bomber Command raid over Occupied Europe. Producers/directors Michael Powell and Emeric Pressburger chose the expression to fit the plot of the story, not just because of its familiarity with a British film audience. They changed the expression slightly to give the film's title more focus.

As was normal for the time, the film had to carry a message to boost the audience's morale. In this case, it was a dedication to the courage of Dutch Resistance fighters, both male and female – which set it apart at the time, women not being seen as anything more than romantic or maternal objects in most film productions of the Forties – whose courage in aiding downed RAF aircrews to escape from Nazi Occupied Holland became an inspiration to many. By now, though, realism was also becoming a vital component of British wartime films, meaning that overly fanciful plotlines, such as that devised for "Ships With Wings", could not be justified any more. This is noteworthy in "One of our Aircraft is Missing", because one of the leading players in the film is the actor, Hugh Burden, who played the idiotically unbelievable Fleet Air Arm pilot and son of a Vice Admiral in "Ships With Wings" (1941), whereas in this production he is called upon to act in a much more mature and convincing role as the pilot of 'B for Bertie'.

'B for Bertie' is a Vickers Wellington bomber, whose crew are targeted against the Mercedes Benz works at Stuttgart. They fail to return from their mission. All six aircrew safely parachute out of the stricken 'B for Bertie' and land in Holland, but unbeknown to them 'B for Bertie' continues to fly until it loses height over the North Sea and crashes into power lines soon after pilotlessly crossing over the English coast.

The film's plot is then focused exclusively on the aircrew's efforts to evade capture by German troops searching for them, aided and supported by courageous Dutch civilians and Resistance fighters.

Aviation, therefore, appears principally during the first part of the story, covering the take-off for the raid, the raid over Stuttgart itself, and the shoot-down of 'B for Bertie'. The film has received accolades for the very realistic way in which it portrays RAF Bomber Command Wellingtons on Operations. The Air Ministry made available the same complete Vickers Wellington shell that was used only a short while earlier in "Target for Tonight" (1941), fully outfitted with power and electrical systems, which was laid out covering the entire floor of Denham Studios. The scenes filmed inside this genuine Vickers Wellington interior are far more realistic and atmospheric than the corresponding scenes inside a stripped-out Wellington filmed for "The Lion Has Wings".

Because it is acting a particular role, the actual Vickers Wellington flown in the film which portrays 'B for Bertie' has only the code letter 'B' applied to its fuselage – its real squadron codes have been masked. However, film is shown of Vickers Wellington bombers lining up and taking off on real Ops: the shots obtained are of Vickers Wellington Mk.Ic bombers of No.115 Squadron, filmed by Michael Powell's 2nd Unit at RAF Marham, Norfolk, in the Spring months of 1941. Powell had, of course, plenty of experience of filming Wellingtons on Ops, after his time at RAF Mildenhall in September 1939 filming No.149 Squadron Wellingtons for "The Lion Has Wings". Filming the aerial sequences was Ronald Neame, following his memorable work for "A Yank in the R.A.F." (1941).

Identifying the Wellingtons in "One of our Aircraft is Missing" isn't possible due to their heavily blackened squadron code letters, plus the fact they were filmed taking off on a mission at dusk, which means they are seen in very subdued light. At least six Wellingtons can be counted, while a seventh was filmed separately as 'B for Bertie' both taxying and airborne. However, the studio miniature Wellington of 'B for Bertie' can be seen carrying the No.115 Squadron codes of KO-B as it smashes into the electricity power pylon, so there is a strong indication here that the actual Wellington playing 'B for Bertie' would have carried the same codes.

A crew of six for a Wellington bomber, as depicted in the film, is correct; however, there is one noticeable alteration that the production team have made to the complement carried by the Wellington Mk.Ic, the most numerous variant of the Wellington in RAF service. In the film, the aircrew are pilot, second pilot, wireless operator, observer, front gunner and rear gunner. In fact, the observer doubled as the forward gunner, while the film's scriptwriters have omitted the all-important role of the navigator, who was also the bomb aimer. There was no dedicated second pilot, while the sixth member of the crew was a waist gunner, an important addition to the Mk.Ic version as earlier Mk.I and Mk.Ia Wellingtons, without waist guns, had been exposed as vulnerable to beam-on attacks by Messerschmitt Bf.109s and Bf.110s.

The decision by Emeric Pressburger not to use any music score in the film, but to rely instead on the constant tone of the Bristol Pegasus XVIII engines, greatly adds to the realistic effect of a Wellington bomber raid. He was influenced by the same effect created in the famous drama-documentary, "Target for Tonight", which likewise had no music score, while emphasising the roar of the engines for dramatic purposes. The Special FX of the actual attack on Stuttgart in "One of our Aircraft is Missing" is superior to that which had been seen in most war films up till now. So, too, is the SFX miniature used of Wellington 'B for Bertie' slamming into the electricity power pylon as it reaches the climax of its fatal last flight. One glitch in the plot is that, after taking the flak hit over Stuttgart which knocks out the starboard engine, the air–air shot of 'B for Bertie' weaving as it struggles to stay airborne shows both engines still running on full! Probably an asymmetric flight on a single engine was too great a risk to take, but the pilot of the actual Wellington flown for this sequence does perform some impressive evasive manoeuvres to simulate 'B for Bertie' in trouble.

After the crew bail out of the stricken bomber over Holland, no more aviation appears until right at the end of the film as a postscript to five out of the six men who flew 'B for Bertie' returning to Operations again after their successful escape from Occupied Territory. Their new bomber is totally different, the RAF's first four-engined heavy bomber, a Short Stirling Mk.I. Clearly seen in shot is a line of seven Stirling Mk.Is of No.7 Squadron, the first RAF Bomber Command squadron to be equipped with this heavier but still somewhat limited aircraft. Because of its performance limitations, the Stirling could not carry a larger bomb load than the Wellington all the way to the Ruhr and back.

At the time of the film's production, the Stirling was still being introduced to RAF Bomber Command. No.7 Squadron was paving the way – the hard way – to develop heavy bomber operations. The imagery used in "One of our Aircraft is Missing" uses MoI-released footage of No.7 Squadron Stirlings filmed at their base of RAF Oakington in Cambridge, with MG-K, MG-E and MG-B clearly visible. Stirlings MG-Z and MG-W appear in another shot. A nice study of Stirling Mk.1 MG-P taking off merges into the film's final message, which is shown as the last shot before fade-out: "The Netherlands will rise again!".

All of the MoI imagery is edited to fit with film of the main actors of the crew of 'B for Bertie' in front of a Short Stirling Mk.I, presumably a No.7 Squadron aircraft at RAF Oakington, although from the angle at which it is filmed its codes cannot be read. This single Stirling is parked in a different location on base from those seen in the MoI footage, while the image quality itself is noticeably cleaner, confirming that this scene with the actors was filmed on an occasion separate from that taken of the line-up of Stirlings.

"One of our Aircraft is Missing" has always been acknowledged as presenting as honest a view of RAF Bomber Command aircraft and aircrews in action as it was possible to achieve at the time the film was made, while simultaneously sending a message of hope to the people of Holland living under the domination of Nazi Germany.

THE DAY WILL DAWN

(Released: June 1942)

This film is dedicated to the Norwegian Resistance and its title is taken from a speech made by British Prime Minister, Winston Churchill, to the US Senate on 26th December 1941, three weeks after the Japanese attack on Pearl Harbor ensured the United States of America entered the War. Churchill refers to a "dozen famous ancient states, now prostrate under the Nazi yoke" whose masses of people "await the hour of liberation". The title is based on Churchill's words, "That hour will strike, and its solemn peal will proclaim that the night is past and that the dawn has come".

The film opens with the same Reich Propaganda Ministry footage of massed formations of Luftwaffe aircraft over-flying Nuremberg or Berlin which appears in "Dangerous Moonlight" (1941), firstly with the shot of nine Messerschmitt Bf.110s leading 18 Messerschmitt Bf.109s, then followed up with the aerial parade of 30 Dornier Do.17 bombers. Immediately coming after this footage is the same air-air shot of two Heinkel He.111Hs in echelon formation, filmed from a third and leading Heinkel He.111H, which was used in "Ferry Pilot" (1941).

The use of this Reich Propaganda Ministry imagery is intended to portray the growing threat to Europe due to Germany's invasion of Poland. Later in the film the invasion of France is depicted by a Luftwaffe dive bomber commencing its attack on French forces. However, it seems that the editor of "The Day Will Dawn" did not have access to footage of Junkers Ju.87 Stukas, so instead he has used an air-air shot of a Henschel Hs.126 peeling off from the camera aircraft, rolling over onto its back and falling into a vertical dive.

The Henschel Hs.126 evolved from an interim high wing dive bomber, the Hs.122, operated by the Luftwaffe until the Junkers Ju.87 came into service. The Hs.126 was a high parasol-winged design with strong, fixed undercarriage and powered by a BMW 132Dc radial engine. It was operated during the early period of World War Two by Luftwaffe army co-operation units, primarily as a reconnaissance and artillery spotter aircraft, but by 1943 it had been superseded by more modern types and was used mostly as a glider-tug for trainee pilots. Footage of the Hs.126 is rare, so its use in this film is welcome. However, the markings of this aircraft are not visible, so identification is not achievable.

The plot of "The Day Will Dawn" has a British journalist with Norwegian connections, played by "Boys Own"-style actor hero, Hugh Williams (he was part of the crew of 'B for Bertie' in the preceding film, "One of our Aircraft is Missing", playing a famous cricket player who had been drafted into the RAF), being recruited by Naval Intelligence as an agent and parachuted into Norway. The aircraft in which he is flown to Norway is Vickers Wellington Mk.Ic P2517/OJ-F of No.149 Squadron, which means that out-takes of 'F for Freddie' from "Target for Tonight" (1941) are being used here. However, when the agent parachutes into Norway, a shot of a parachutist exiting from the under fuselage hatch of an Armstrong Whitworth Whitley is used instead. The latter aircraft is the correct type for this sequence, as British agents were being parachuted into Occupied Territory from Whitleys operated by the clandestine No.1419 Flight from RAF Stradishall, Suffolk, at the time "The Day Will Dawn" was released. The Whitley was obsolete as a bomber at the outbreak of World War Two, but continued in service for much of the War, particularly as a Paratroop training aircraft and as a tug for large Infantry gliders. The clash between this use of footage of the Whitley and the out-takes of Wellington 'F for Freddie' from "Target for Tonight" is unfortunate, but perhaps was unavoidable at the time.

The agent's mission is to locate a hidden U-Boat base in a Norwegian fjord, then direct RAF bombers to destroy it. He is helped by Norwegian Resistance fighters who shelter him. Somewhat implausibly the agent uses torches from right inside the U-Boat base to guide the bombers and manages to survive the consequent bombing! More out-takes of 'F for Freddie' from "Target for Tonight" are used for the bombing sequence, plus air-air Crown Film Unit footage of four Bristol Blenheim IVs flying in 'Box Four' formation. Aside from this, there is only a limited amount of aviation in "The Day Will Dawn".

THE FOREMAN WENT TO FRANCE

(Released: June 1942)

Based on the true exploits of a factory foreman, Melbourne Jones, who travelled to France in May 1940 to prevent important factory machinery producing new aircraft cannon shells from falling into the hands of the invading Wehrmacht, this film exclusively uses SFX miniatures to portray Luftwaffe Messerschmitt Bf.109s and a Junkers Ju.87 Stuka.

THE NEXT OF KIN

(Released: June 1942)

This is a very important film. It must have made a strong impact upon its audience when it was first shown because it is at that audience that its message was aimed: "Keep Mum".

"The Next of Kin" refers to the dreaded message (still heard today) that the next of kin have been informed of the loss of their son, or brother, or father, in action. But the importance of the message is that they, the audience, were responsible because they were careless about what they were saying in public. The enemy was listening and overheard. Sooner or later they were able to devise what military operation that the British senior staff were planning and were waiting in strength when it was carried out.

While Britain was fighting alone, the biggest fear among military planners was of German agents living and spying among ordinary citizens and servicemen. Posters bearing messages of the "Careless talk costs lives" variety were everywhere. The War Office commissioned Ealing Studios to make a military training film for the Directorate of Army Kinematography (DAK), whose remit was "to be responsible for providing and exhibiting all films required by the Army (at home and abroad) for training, educational and recreational purposes". The original intention had been to make a feature length film for British military personnel, promoting the message that they must at all times, wherever they were and whoever they were with, not say anything that could be helpful to the enemy. Ealing Studios producer, Michael Balcon, decided that it would make a successful film for public release, and funded an expanded script.

The film succeeded in promoting its message in a very effective way, as "The Next of Kin" was a popular hit with British cinema audiences who, against the expectations of Prime Minister Winston Churchill, reacted positively to the film. What may have helped with its success was the similarity of the plotline of having a British Commando raid on a French port, with the destruction of a large dry dock for U-Boats being almost compromised by a mixture of careless talk among servicemen and careless security, with the successful St Nazaire Raid (see "The Gift Horse", 1952, in Chapter Three, and "Attack on the Iron Coast", 1968, in Chapter Four) a few months earlier. What may have added to the impression made by the film's seemingly prophetic message was the fact that two months after it was released the disastrous Dieppe Raid took place, an amphibious assault on a French port that cost many Allied soldiers' lives.

Aviation plays its part in "The Next of Kin". It first appears in a scene where an Abwehr agent is parachuted into Britain. He is depicted flying into British airspace aboard a Heinkel He.111. We have seen this He.111 before. It is Reich Propaganda Ministry footage of Heinkel He.111B-2 72+OIG of Kampfgeschwader 157, as was used in "Ferry Pilot" (1941). However, when the Abwehr agent parachutes out, it is stock footage provided by the Ministry of Information of an Armstrong Whitworth Whitley that is used, filmed from below and seen only in darkened silhouette as a parachutist drops out through its hatch in the fuselage floor.

Aviation does not appear again until nearly three-quarters of the way through the film. Abwehr agents (who seem to flourish in all parts of English society) have succeeded in obtaining copies of 'mosaics', ie, aerial photographs of the French port that is the target of the Commando attack. They manage to get them to an agent in Portugal, who flies with the pictures to Berlin. He flies aboard a Junkers Ju.52/3M. The film editor has resorted to using footage of South African Airways Junkers Ju.52/3mge ZS-AFD, instead of a Lufthansa machine - maybe he did not have access to the latter. South African Airways was formed on 1st February 1934 and built up a fleet of 15 Ju.52/3Ms. This actual Ju.52/3mge ZS-AFD, named as Sir Benjamin d'Urban, was sold to Lufthansa in 1938 and was given the German civil registration and name D-ACBO von Neubrandt; the footage of it in "The Next of Kin" was obviously taken before its sale. Another source claims it was taken on charge by the South African Air Force, but if it did become D-ACBO it underwent another registration change to M-CABO Mola in Liberia and was destroyed in a crash at Cabezabellosa, Santa deGredos, Salamander, on 29th March 1940.

The finale to "The Next of Kin" is the amphibious assault on the fictional French port of Nourville, where a U-Boat Pen has been set up by the Kriegsmarine. The plan is to destroy the Pen's lock gates and as much infrastructure as possible by means of a Commando assault, before withdrawing by sea. Air cover will be provided by the RAF. Of course, the whole theme of the plot is that the Germans have learnt about the planned assault through their extensive network of spies in Britain, and thanks to plenty of injudicious talk and slack security on the part of military personnel and civilians engaged on industrial projects associated with the Operation, German troops and armoured divisions are in position to ambush the Commandos as they come ashore. The Luftwaffe is also waiting.

Judging how the Commando assault is staged, the War Office made available to Ealing Studios no lack of resources in troops, assault boats and aircraft. This segment of the film was conducted in 1941, so it reflects the kind of assault craft that Commandos then used. They are small, fast, solid hull boats, not landing craft with front ramps that could be lowered which came into service shortly after. They operated in threes and are able to beach hard on the shingle, in order to land their Commandos.

The locations used for the beach assault were around St Austell in Cornwall, where much of the large-scale battle scenes were filmed. The battles are very realistically staged and in certain shots it appears live ordnance was used. The cosy fishing port of Mevagissey portrayed Nourville, not at all French-like in appearance. It seems the citizens of Mevagissey had to put up with full-scale street fights being staged among their cottages and in their small harbour.

During the battle the RAF makes low-level attacks with bombers and fighters. As stated, there was no holding back on resources because quite a number of different aircraft types are employed in these scenes.

First to be seen heading in from over the sea towards the 'French' headland are two Bristol Blenheim Mk.IV light bombers, followed by a pair of Curtiss P-40C Tomahawk IIb ground-attack fighters. In another shot, a Blenheim Mk.IV makes a low run over the camera position, while a single P-40C Tomahawk IIb can be seen beyond it in the distance. A 'Tommy' gives the thumbs-up to his mate at the sight of them.

One of the most extraordinary shots is that of four Spitfires running in very low over Mevagissey's breakwater before passing right through - not over - the harbour and up the hill beyond just feet over the roof tops of cottages, all filmed from a high point looking down on the Spitfires as they come racing past. Leading the flight of four is a Spitfire coded LZ-A; the others following immediately behind are too blurred due to their speed for their code letters to be read. A shot of presumably the same four Spitfires flying in echelon starboard formation appears next, sweeping low over very Cornish countryside. They are followed by three P-40C Tomahawks flying in over the harbour, strafing German troops below. A fine study of a solo P-40C appears next which, although clearly showing its markings, does not reveal any squadron codes. A Bristol Beaufort sweeps low overhead, followed by a second Beaufort which makes a run at the harbour entrance. As it passes over the breakwater a charge is detonated on the seaward side, hurling up a column of water, to simulate a bomb being dropped. A larger detonation follows, which gives the impression of the breakwater being blasted: almost certainly this would have been staged in St Austell's clay mining area.

The four Spitfires return in a cluster for a second low run through Mevagissey's harbour. What the good folk of Mevagissey thought of all this is anyone's guess! This time Spitfire LZ-F is identifiable as well as LZ-A, marking them as being No.66 Squadron aircraft. No.66 was based in the West Country at the time "The Next of Kin" was filmed in Cornwall, operating on coastal patrol and bomber escort duties equipped with the Vickers Supermarine Spitfire Mk.IIa.

Attacks on the Commandos by the Luftwaffe mean that a significant portion of stock material, some of it familiar, is used. Shown first are four Junkers Ju.87 Stuka dive bombers in a loose echelon port formation. A well-used stock shot appears next of two Ju.87 Stukas in formation, with the nearest one breaking into a dive inside of the other; this stock shot will appear in a number of other British black-and-white war films, most notably "Dunkirk" (1958). The Stuka nearest the camera carries the codes TK+HG on the starboard fuselage and under its wings, while the codes under the wings of the second Ju.87 comprise GU+AC. These do not approximate to any Stukageschwader, so they may be trials aircraft.

A solo Stuka is seen in a near vertical dive, followed by another stock shot that has been well used of three Stukas diving in line astern. A Stuka pilot is seen filmed through the front of his cockpit canopy, then bombs depart from their hard points - as they are attached side by side, they can't be dropping from a Stuka. A diving Stuka is seen pulling up from its dive. Explosions rip up the ground behind the crouching 'Tommies' - as stated, some of the explosions are not Special Effects pyrotechnics but very real ordnance being detonated.

"The Next of Kin" was the first British war film to make extensive use of Reich Propaganda Ministry imagery of the Ju.87 Stuka in action.

A Junkers Ju.88 in silhouette unleashes four bombs in a dive. Another air-air shows a Stuka starting its dive; it is painted in what may have been a very dark green scheme without any visible code letters or numbers. It is followed by a continuation of the air-air of Ju.87 Stuka GU+AC, after the first Stuka TK+HG has dived

out of shot. Then a distant shot of a Stuka in a dive is followed by that of a stick of bombs descending, leading into a succession of explosions tearing up the Cornish countryside.

Now the heavy bombers close in. An air-air of a Heinkel He.111H is shown flying close off the wing-tip of another He.111H, from which it is being filmed: its imagery is too dark to allow us to identify it. Whether taken from the same piece of footage is not clear, but another air-air from an He.111H shows three more He.111Hs in a 'Kette' some distance away beyond the propeller boss. More explosive ordnance is detonated, this time hurling dummies into the air!

Despite taking heavy casualties, the Commandos achieve their objective by destroying the lock gates and much of the harbour installations of 'Nourville'. But, as the commentator says, the enemy had been warned and was waiting due to "bad security". Out-takes of the battle scene in 'Nourville' appear in "Attack on the Iron Coast" (1968), a cheaply made film based on the St Nazaire Raid whose Special Effects are considerably inferior to those of this wartime production made 26 years earlier.

The final scene has Basil Sydney and Naunton Wayne, as the then highly popular 'Old Boy' acting duo, Charters and Caldicott, who appeared in a number of British thrillers, talking openly in a railway carriage about what a friend who runs a munitions factory is producing, while an Abwehr spy sharing their carriage listens with interest. If Charters and Caldicott can't be trusted to keep their mouths shut, who can you trust?

What the entire nation, virtually every member of the military services, and certainly the government of the time (apart from the Prime Minister himself), did not know was that the Security Service, aka MI5, and the Metropolitan Police Special Branch had rounded up every known Abwehr agent at the start of the War and soon had either caught or rendered ineffective any others that had escaped their net. Through the Double Cross system, some of these Abwehr agents were 'turned' and sent MI5-planted disinformation back to Germany. This included false information about identity cards and other items that the Abwehr needed to create false identities for their agents to use in Britain when they were to gather intelligence on British defences prior to Operation Seelowe (Sealion), the planned Wehrmacht invasion of Britain. The Abwehr inserted 25 of its agents into Britain between September - November 1940 by parachute or boat, all of whom were quickly arrested because of the inaccurate identity cards they were carrying, with some being turned as double agents to work against their former masters (source: "The Defence of the Realm, The Authorized History of MI5", by Christopher Andrew, published 2009 by Penguin Books).

It was expedient to Churchill and the Security Service that none of this would be known, and that the public and the military be encouraged to remain vigilant about what they and others were saying. Hence the value of a film like "The Next of Kin", which continued to be used by British and Commonwealth forces as a training film on security long after the War had ended.

THEY FLEW ALONE

(Released: June 1942)

Not specifically a war film as such in terms of its subject matter, but "They Flew Alone" was made by producer/director Herbert Wilcox as a morale booster for the British public mid-way through the War and ends with a rousing call to women in particular to fight for freedom by serving in such branches of the military as the Air Transport Auxiliary (ATA).

"They Flew Alone" is the story of two world record-breaking British pilots who were not only rivals, but who were married to each other. Amy Johnson became famous world-wide when she became the first female pilot who single-handedly flew a de Havilland Gipsy Moth bi-plane from England to Australia in May 1930. Scotsman Jim Mollison performed the same feat in the opposite direction. He went on to fly the first East - West crossing of the Atlantic from Britain to America, while Amy - now Amy Mollinson - flew a Puss Moth from London to Cape Town, and back. They both made an East - West crossing to America in a DH.84 Dragon, in an attempt to be the first to fly to New York from Britain, but crashed in Connecticut when their aircraft ran out of fuel.

The film's theme is that both were brilliant flyers, but they could not fly happily together; their rivalry was too strong, and all their achievements were gained when flying solo - hence the title. Moreover, their marriage was in danger because the hard-drinking Mollinson could not deal with his wife's fame and her increasing public prestige over his own. Hollywood wanted to concentrate less on their relationship and more on Amy Johnson, played convincingly by Anna Neagle, and released the film in the USA under the title, "Wings and the Woman". The DVD that is on public sale in the UK from 2010 is of "Wings and the Woman", but, unlike other British films of the period, the American distributor hasn't butchered it in the cutting room.

Obviously aircraft feature strongly in the film, but all the flying sequences are achieved with SFX miniatures, which are of reasonable quality for the early Forties. Two aircraft were acquired by Herbert Wilcox's production company and used for studio shots. The first is a de Havilland DH.60G Gipsy Moth painted - not accurately - to represent Amy Johnson's famous Gipsy Moth G-AAAH and named Jason after her father's trade mark for his company in Hull. This aircraft is only seen in the studio with Anna Neagle in the cockpit as Amy prepares to leave on her famous flight to Australia - a pilot was in the front seat out of shot doing the taxying - and for cockpit shots during Amy Johnson's flying sequences. It also doubles as a London Aeroplane Club aircraft at Stag Lane Aerodrome - to which the real G-AAAH belonged in Amy Johnson's ownership - and as Jim Mollinson's Australian-registered aircraft for his Australia to Great Britain flight, as VH-UFT.

The other aircraft also used for studio shots is a de Havilland DH.80A Puss Moth, which first acts the part of Mollinson's Puss Moth G-ABXY/The Hearts Content that he used for his East - West Atlantic crossing (there is Movietone News footage in the film of the real Puss Moth G-ABXY taking off on this flight); then

as Amy Johnson's Puss Moth G-ACAB/The Desert Cloud, which she flew to Cape Town and back.

The one other aircraft that appears in the film representing the two Mollinsons' flight to New York is the real de Havilland DH.84 Dragon G-ACCV/Seafarer, which is seen in Movietone News newsreel of their departure from Pendine Sands in South Wales amid a very large crowd of admirers. The Civil Aviation Authority Website database, GINFO, shows DH.84 Dragon G-ACCV being registered to Mrs Amy Mollinson, CBE, of Grosvenor House, Park Lane, on 1st March 1933 and then under the heading, 'Destruction or Permanent Withdrawal of Use of Aircraft', "? XI . 33", presumably meaning, "On a date unknown in November 1933".

The film, of course, is devoted to most of Amy Johnson's and Jim Mollinson's record-breaking achievements before the outbreak of World War Two. The final quarter of the film deals with their time in the ATA, up till the fatal day on 5th January 1941 when Amy Johnson lost her life delivering an Airspeed Oxford to an air base. Real female ATA pilots are seen walking to collect aircraft, with a de Havilland DH.87B Leopard Moth in RAF markings in the background - this is an out-take from "Ferry Pilot" (1941), referred to in the review of that film.

Anna Neagle climbs aboard Airspeed Oxford Mk.I T1041, which is acting the role of Oxford V3457 in which the real Amy Johnson flew her last flight. Just before she departs she speaks with Mollinson, played quite effectively by Welsh film actor, Robert Newton, who reputedly did not have to act too hard in character, he having his own real-life reputation for liking a drink or four. This is a fictional final meeting between the two famous flyers, who had divorced three years earlier; it is not known if the real Amy Johnson and Jim Mollinson ever did meet up during their days in the ATA, far less having had a final meeting before Amy Johnson took off on what was to be her last flight.

Before the Oxford departs, a Vickers-Supermarine Spitfire Mk.IIa taxies out in the background, with a Vickers Wellington parked beyond it; the serial of neither aircraft is visible.

The film ends with a re-creation of the long-held belief that Amy Johnson's Oxford ran out of fuel in thick fog over the Thames Estuary, and that, although she parachuted out, she drowned in the Thames, with her body never being recovered. Officially, she had been delivering the Oxford from Blackpool to RAF Kidlington, today Oxford Airport. Quite why such an experienced pilot who flew in all kinds of weather, and who was an expert in navigating by dead reckoning, should be so far off course - and so further south than she should have been - has never been explained. Conspiracy theorists claim that she had a passenger in her Oxford, who she was delivering clandestinely to an entirely different destination, while a former British anti-aircraft gunner went public in a 1999 newspaper interview that Amy's aircraft was shot down as an enemy aircraft when she failed to send the correct identification code after being challenged by the gun battery. No one knew at the time it was Amy Johnson who had been shot down, but when the facts emerged officialdom allegedly ordered a complete news blackout and created a cover-story about her aircraft running out of fuel in thick fog, which appears to have lasted for 58 years.

The film ends with a lot of marching, especially of female ATA pilots, superimposed over images of Anna Neagle looking patriotic as Amy Johnson. The clear message of the time was to stir up the patriotism in British women to play their part in bringing about Hitler's downfall. Also shown are a number of stock images to represent RAF aircraft flown by ATA pilots, beginning with five Bristol Blenheim Mk.Is silhouetted in echelon starboard formation and followed by a close formation shot of seven Vickers Supermarine Spitfire Mk.IIs, all with No.222 (Natal) Squadron 'ZD-' codes clearly visible and with ZD-V flying nearest to the camera: this is an out-take of No.222 Squadron Spitfires in "Dangerous Moonlight" (1941).

A solo Vickers Supermarine Spitfire Mk.II is seen flying close-up, before the film cuts to female ATA pilots filmed in what are clearly Spitfire cockpits. The final shot, with Anna Neagle's image superimposed onto it, is that of a Vickers Supermarine Spitfire Mk.Ia, distinguished by its small underwing roundels near the wing tips as applied on Spitfires early into the War, breaking away from the camera. The film then cuts from Anna Neagle's face to a dedication to "all the Amy Johnsons of today who fight for freedom - from fear - from want - from persecution". Despite this exhortation in 1942 to women to fly, it would take nearly another 50 years before women were accepted as front-line pilots in the British armed forces.

FLYING FORTRESS

(Released: June 1942, UK; December 1942, USA)
Hollywood 'British' war film.

One of two Hollywood 'British' war films released in 1942 featuring the most famous American World War Two bomber of all time, the Boeing B-17 Flying Fortress. But not the B-17s of the famous 'Mighty Eighth', the United States Army Air Forces' Eighth Air Force: all the B-17s seen in "Flying Fortress" carry RAF roundels and squadron codes, not 'Stars and Bars'. It is one of the least reported facts that two of the first films that Hollywood made to feature the Boeing B-17 concentrated on the Flying Fortress in RAF Bomber Command service, a role that has received very limited publicity.

Perhaps that is because the B-17 did not last long with Bomber Command, could not be described as a success, and involved only small quantities of the actual aircraft itself. The B-17 operated in three Marques with the RAF and was named simply Fortress: the Boeing Fortress I (B-17C), the Fortress II (B-17F) and the Fortress III (B-17G) - B-17 was the bomber's US Army Air Corps designation which was not used by the RAF. What makes "Flying Fortress" of real value to the war and aviation historian is that the film focuses exclusively on the earliest Marque, the Fortress I, imagery of which in RAF Bomber Command service being extremely rare.

A total of 38 B-17C variants were built by Boeing, 20 of which were delivered to Bomber Command in the first half of 1941. They were all assigned in May that year to No.90 Squadron, formed exclusively to operate the new bomber but which seemed to suffer from being allocated a type that was not regarded within the RAF overall as a priority as No.90 was forced to move around several air stations during its short time with the Fortress I, changing between RAF Watton, RAF West Raynham and RAF Polebrook before they relinquished their 'Forts' in February 1942 and disbanded. In the ten months that No.90 Squadron operated the Fortress I, it was discovered that its bomb load was too small, it lacked range, it did not have self-sealing fuel tanks, its guns froze at high altitude, and, most crucial of all, it could not out-climb the Luftwaffe fighters of the period, the Messerschmitt Bf.109E and Bf.109F.

Between July - September 1941, Bomber Command's primary purpose was to test whether a high-flying four-engined bomber could conduct accurate daylight bombing raids over Germany at heights of 32,000 feet and above - No.90 Squadron's Fortress Is proved that this definitely was not yet the case. In that short two month period, No.90 Squadron lost eight of its 20-strong complement of the new American-built bombers and failed to hit most of its targets. This, obviously, is not a fact revealed in the plot of "Flying Fortress" featuring No.90 Squadron's Fortress Is.

The film opens with the following dedication: "Made with the cooperation of the Royal Air Force and the Atlantic Ferry Service, which pioneered the North Atlantic Air Crossing to deliver ever increasing numbers of American Aircraft in the cause of Freedom". America was still neutral when the film was initially in production but the message Hollywood, and Warner Bros in particular, wanted to convey to the American public was that their great nation was increasingly involved in the massive fight against tyranny and was helping to arm Great Britain, whose cause Hollywood openly supported. And especially to arm Hollywood's favourite British military service, the Royal Air Force, which willingly gave Hollywood whatever facilities it wanted. Americans seeing American-built bombers in British colours taking the fight to Nazi Germany was thought to be sure-fire Hollywood box office ammunition; pity that "Flying Fortress" bombed spectacularly with the audience when it was eventually released in New York.

Two factors which worked against "Flying Fortress" was the timing of its release States-side and the way it was mutilated by the American distributor. So much was cut from it that it looked a very disjointed product when it had its US premier at the Strand Theater, New York, in December 1942. Audiences cat-called it openly. Its release date - one year since it was made and six months after its release in London - is another strange anomaly which remains unexplained, particularly as events had long since overtaken it and its message was now well out of date. Presumably Warners had to try to get some return on their investment.

Another factor that has to be noted is that it is an Anglo-American film production, mostly filmed in Britain and specifically at Teddington Studios using almost exclusively British crews. Its director, Walter Forde, was a prolific British film maker before the War, although his career dissipated after 1949, while one noteworthy name is film editor Terence Fisher, who would go on to direct the Frankenstein and Dracula series of Hammer Horror films that made the fortunes of actors Peter Cushing and

Christopher Lee. The film's lead actor was British matinee idol, Richard Greene, playing the part - unconvincingly - of American play-boy/fly-boy, James Spence, Jr, who joins the RAF along with his rival flyer in the USA, 'Sky' Kelly.

It has to be said that "Flying Fortress", for the large part, is a tedious film with a drawn-out central plot of Spence trying to win over the sister of 'Sky' Kelly, played by Carla Lehmann, who blames Spence for jeopardising her brother's flying career when Spence goes hot-shot at the controls of a touring aeroplane at the start of the film, with Kelly trying to stop him. Spence lets the passenger in the front seat take over and is then, against all logic, exonerated by the resulting investigation after the 'plane crashes and the passenger is killed. Kelly gets the blame instead, hence his and Spence's rivalry.

Greene and Lehmann are so one-dimensional that one cries out for the bomber of the title to put in an appearance. It does so, but not to substantial effect until the final quarter of the film. There is, however, some aviation activity before that.

The opening sequence, of Spence breaking aviation law and getting away with it, is achieved by the use of a typically crude SFX studio miniature of an indeterminate single-engine monoplane. However, when it nose dives into the ground and collides with a tree it has changed itself into a full-scale bi-plane, whose lower wings are noticeably shorter than the upper wings. This is a rare view of a Buhl CA-6 Air Sedan, a six-seat tourer which is carrying the serial NC8446. The Buhl Aircraft Company of Marysville, Michigan, produced a family of tourers and air racers from 1925 until 1933, when it fell victim to the Great Depression. Air Sedan NC8446 is described on the Davis-Monthan Aviation Field Register Website as having been built on 29th January 1929 and had a rather chequered career before it was involved in a fatal flying accident on 17th September 1939, with four people killed, including the pilot. The report states that the aircraft burned immediately after impact and that its registration was cancelled the same day.

At some later stage, Air Sedan NC8446 appears to have been recovered as a written-off airframe, re-assembled and used in a controlled crash for an unknown Warner Bros movie production, of which an out-take is used in "Flying Fortress". The most likely method of crashing the Air Sedan would have been to set it up on guidance rails at a 45-degree angle nose down, perhaps held in place by a crane, with the rails painted so that they blend into the background - matte art work on the film's frames in the editing suite would also have disguised them. With its engine started, Air Sedan NC8446 could have been released from the crane to run down the rails, impact the ground and run forward into a tree. The result, one convincing-looking crash.

Shortly after this scene the disgraced 'Sky' Kelly is seen looking wistfully skywards at a large aircraft sailing majestically overhead. Two air-airs immediately follow of the prototype of what would become the B-17 Flying Fortress, the Boeing XB-17 under United States Army Air Corps designation or, as Boeing called it, the Boeing Model 299. These two air-air shots show the Model 299 in its original all-silver guise without any serial applied - it acquired

the serial NX13372 soon after when it was tested by the Army. The Boeing Model 299 first flew on 28th July 1935 at Seattle, having been entirely funded by Boeing for a US Army competition begun the year before for a multi-engined bomber that could carry a ton of bombs over a distance of 2,000 miles at a speed greater than 200mph. It had a short test flight career, being lost in a crash on 30th October 1935 when an Army pilot took off with a flight control inhibitor still in place. However, the Army was already impressed and ordered 13 examples, formerly designating the Model 299 as the B-17. Legend has it that when it made its first flight, a news reporter watching described it as a "Flying Fortress" because of the many guns sticking out from various positions on the airframe - Boeing had the description trademarked.

Soon after these air-airs of the Boeing Model 299 appear in the film, Spence sees a magazine article headlined, "US BOMBERS FOR BRITAIN", showing a picture of a Boeing B-17C Flying Fortress on the page and describing how they are being ferried across the Atlantic. Volunteer pilots should contact the Atlantic Ferry Organisation - Atfero - in Montreal: "The need is urgent and many adventuresome Americans are joining daily", the article declares. Spence does not hesitate to volunteer.

He flies to St Hubert Airfield outside Montreal in Quebec, where the ferrying operation to Britain is based. Atfero was actually set up by a banker in Montreal, Morris W Wilson, who hired civilian pilots to fly US-built aircraft to Britain. His organisation was replaced in July 1941 by RAF Ferry Command, which delivered more than 9,000 aircraft from Canada and the United States to Britain right up to the end of the War.

On arrival overhead St Hubert, Spence can't resist a little low-level beating-up of the airfield in his private Beech Staggerwing. The actual airfield he is filmed over-flying is Los Angeles Metropolitan Airport and almost certainly involves another out-take from another unidentified Warner Bros movie about a risk-taking pilot. The Beech D.17S Staggerwing making the beat-up appears to be registered NC180JA, but research has failed to locate this aircraft.

Richard Greene as Spence is seen walking in front of what is meant to be a Boeing B-17C Flying Fortress being overhauled at St Hubert prior to delivery to Britain. This, in fact, is the first RAF Boeing Fortress I to be seen in the film, although it is filmed from the front so that it cannot be identified as such. This scene, and others shown later in the film, was shot at RAF Polebrook in Northamptonshire sometime during September and October 1941 after No.90 Squadron had been stood-down from its unsuccessful high-altitude bombing operations. The irony is that the film's plot has the Flying Fortress as being vital to Britain's war effort against Nazi Germany as a high altitude day bomber, when in actual fact it had been withdrawn from this role as a failure by the time filming took place. Needless to say, this reality was kept well away from the public.

Spence discovers that 'Sky' Kelly is in charge of the ferry pilots at Atfero and they have time for a little slugging match - Hollywood loves a fist fight. Then, to illustrate B-17s being flown to Britain, an air-air of three US Army Air Corps Boeing B-17Cs is shown, followed by an air-ground shot of six RAF Boeing B-17Cs lined up at an unknown airfield, bearing the all-over natural metal scheme and red tail rudders they were delivered in. This shot fades into that of a cluster of four Consolidated Liberator I transports of the Atlantic Return Ferry Service, which ferried American pilots back to the USA after they had delivered their aircraft to Britain.

Spence discovers that Kelly and he are detailed to fly a B-17C across the Atlantic. Both are overjoyed at the prospect of flying together - not. A shot of a Boeing Fortress I lifting off the RAF Polebrook runway illustrates their departure from St Hubert - the head-on angle does not permit identification. Some air-airs follow of a No.90 Squadron Fortress I flying through clouds, filmed in silhouette so as not to give away the fact this is an in-service aircraft, not a B-17C on delivery. Spence and Kelly manage to ferry their B-17C to what is described as the "Ferry Command Landing Field near London", allowing for a nice study of a Fortress I on roll-out after touch down, again filmed at Polebrook.

The film now gets bogged down with Spence chasing after Kelly's sister, who just happens to be in bomb-ravaged London as an American war reporter, and with Kelly chasing after a lady of nobility who has joined the WAAF as an RAF staff car driver. We don't see a Flying Fortress again for more than half-an-hour, during which time Spence and Kelly join the RAF. They just happen to find themselves assigned to an RAF Fortress squadron, illustrated by imagery of troops marching in front of No.90 Squadron's Fortress Is played out to very American-style patriotic music. A follow-up shot of a parade in front of a Beech AT-7 Kansan and two lines of North American AT-6 Texans is very obviously that of USAAC trainers looking incongruously out of place in the film. It becomes apparent that the plot now has Spence and Kelly training in the USA, then returning to Britain by convoy, so the shots of the RAF Fortress Is appearing first are out of sequence - possibly caused by interference by the US distributor.

We get a clue as to when "Flying Fortress" was close to completion when the plot has the squadron sent on a bombing raid over Berlin on 7th December 1941. The choice of date just cannot be coincidental. Its inclusion shows that Pearl Harbor and America's entry into the War occurred while "Flying Fortress" was in production. Releasing the film in the States 12 months later shows just how out of place it had become, hence its risible reception.

The briefing has the squadron bombing at 35,000 feet; an irony, this, as we now know that No.90 Squadron's efforts at similar heights found that the target was invariably missed and that icing was a huge problem. Still, press on with the Hollywood dictum: never let reality get in the way of a good story, even though "Flying Fortress" is not a good story.

Finally, we get to grips with the RAF's Boeing Fortress I bombers. We see them being armed and bombed up, their bomb-bays noticeably limited by being only able to carry four 1,100lb bombs each. All 20 of the RAF Boeing Fortress Is were serialled in the AN518 - AN537 range and we are able to pinpoint a couple of them in the film: Richard Greene is seen entering through the forward fuselage hatch of Boeing Fortress I AN530/WP-P, while actual squadron aircrew are seen climbing aboard Fortress

I AN536/WP-M. We get good close-up views, both inside and out, of a Fortress I, giving us the best available studies of this early version of the Flying Fortress. Filming was clearly carried out inside one of No.90 Squadron's aircraft. It appears to have been Fortress I AN530/WP-P, as it acts the role of the bomber in which Spence and Kelly fly - a fine study of it starting its take off roll is one of the best images available of an RAF Fortress I in action.

Both AN536/WP-M and AN530/WP-P were definitely flown for the film, along with an unidentified third example. They appear in a number of air-airs flying in a loose 'Vic' formation, filmed from a fourth Fortress I through the port side beam gunner's window hatch. Most of the time they are filmed in silhouette well above clouds, but one shot provides a fine study of AN536/WP-M clearly lit up by the sun alongside the camera-ship.

This being a Warner Bros production means that out-takes from other films made by Warners are used in "Flying Fortress", including some from "International Squadron" (1941). This includes exactly the same Reich Propaganda Ministry film footage of VI/JG.51 Messerschmitt Bf.109E-3 fighters taking off, followed by the same three-ship of Junkers Ju.87R Stukas climbing out from behind a Junkers Ju.52/3M in the foreground, representing the Luftwaffe 'Scrambling' to intercept the Fortress I raid.

A good close-up shows a Fortress I flying with its bomb doors open, filmed from below in its starboard front quarter. Good quality archive imagery shows four Junkers Ju.87D Stukas taking off in pairs, with more Stukas parked in the background. An air-air shows four more Ju.87D Stukas forming up in echelon port formation. The same shot used in "International Squadron" of a Spitfire making a run at a Heinkel He.111, filmed from the Luftwaffe bomber's ventral gun position, is used to depict the opening attack by the Luftwaffe fighters. The archive footage of what appears to be a Junkers Ju.88 diving vertically into the countryside and exploding appears in this sequence, as it does in other British war films, probably provided by the MoI.

Most of the air battle which follows is achieved by very obvious studio miniatures, mixed with some out-takes from "International Squadron". The film's climax, in which Spence heroically climbs out onto the port wing to smother a fire in the port inner engine, is a re-enactment of the actual exploit by Royal New Zealand Air Force Sergeant Pilot, James Allen Ward of No.75 (NZ) Squadron, who climbed out onto the wing of the Vickers Wellington that he was co-piloting to stifle a fuel leak that was on fire in the starboard engine. For this exploit, Ward was awarded the Victoria Cross. After Richard Greene re-enacts Ward's actions, "Flying Fortress" just suddenly ends. It is an unsatisfactory end to a very unsatisfactory film, but it is priceless for the rare imagery it provides of the Boeing B-17C Flying Fortress in RAF service - just fast forward to the last 20 minutes and forget about the rest of the film.

EAGLE SQUADRON

(Released: June 1942, USA) Hollywood 'British' war film.

The actual "Eagle Squadron" film that was released to theater in the United States did so the year following its two predecessors, "A Yank in the R.A.F." (1941) and "International Squadron" (1941), and almost two years after its original inception. A key factor in its eventual successful production was the involvement of the British Air Ministry with its producer, Walter Wanger, and, like Zanuck's film, the appearance in it of a real Royal Air Force fighter squadron. In fact, this squadron was the first of the three so-called 'Eagle' Squadrons to be formed in RAF Fighter Command, No.71 Squadron, staffed by American volunteer pilots.

However, the film "Eagle Squadron" very nearly didn't happen, for more than one reason. Wanger developed the project in November 1940, around the same time that Zanuck was putting together "A Yank in the R.A.F." with the help of the Air Ministry. Perhaps a competing production called "Eagle Squadron" (remember, Zanuck's film was originally called "The Eagle Squadron") was not to the Air Ministry's liking and they, at first, refused to assist Wanger. At the time, there were not that many American volunteer pilots in the RAF: a total of seven flew during the Battle of Britain. It seems that Wanger had hit upon the idea of making a film about a squadron of American pilots in the Battle of Britain, flying under the banner of the 'Eagle' Squadron and using actual Americans in the RAF to portray themselves in action. The problem was, no such squadron existed in the front-line of RAF Fighter Command during the Battle, although the idea of forming an 'American' squadron had been put into effect on 19th September 1940 when No.71 Squadron was stood up at RAF Church Fenton. Initially equipped with Brewster Buffaloes, No.71 did not become operational until 5th February 1941, after converting onto Hawker Hurricanes.

If Wanger had had his way, American movie-going audiences would have been led to believe that an American squadron in the RAF flew and fought in the Battle of Britain, which was never the case. As we know, Hollywood never allowed the truth to get in the way of a good story. But clearly the Air Ministry was going to have nothing to do with such a fiction, especially as it would have been deemed offensive by the actual squadrons formed by overseas pilots, such as those crewed by the Canadians, the Czechs and the Poles, which did fight in the Battle.

Perhaps due to its successful collaboration with Hollywood through Darryl F Zanuck, and with its own desire to encourage young American pilots to volunteer to fly in the RAF, the Air Ministry became increasingly more sympathetic to Wanger's project as the year 1941 progressed. Thus Hollywood can claim, through Zanuck and Wanger, to have influenced the creation of the American 'Eagle' Squadrons, three of them in total, all made up of Yanks in the RAF: Nos.71, 123 and 133 Squadrons. There is little doubt that the original title of "The Eagle Squadron" for Zanuck's film, then transferred to Wanger's project, was taken up by the RAF, initially for No.71 Squadron alone but later attached to all three 'Eagle' Squadrons. In its opening dedication following the film title credits, "Eagle Squadron" cites the co-operation of the British Air Ministry, the British Ministry of Information, the Royal Air Force, and "The Eagle Squadron of the RAF".

Meanwhile, Wanger was having his own problems back in Hollywood in trying to get his "Eagle Squadron" off the ground. Wanger was contracted as a producer to United Artists (UA), but had earned himself a reputation for going over budget and causing UA significant financial losses with his most recent film productions. UA refused to back "Eagle Squadron". Wanger had to hawk his new project around Hollywood as an independent producer, trying to get backing for it. Eventually, Universal Pictures agreed to take it on.

By July 1941, Wanger had got Air Ministry co-operation as well. The drama-documentary, "Target for Tonight" (1941), had made a big hit in the States, as well as winning an 'Oscar'. Wanger decided to contract its director, Harry Watt, to film No.71 Squadron in England. Thus, as in "A Yank in the R.A.F.", a British film director filmed an actual wartime RAF fighter squadron for a Hollywood film production.

Wanger had been impressed by "Target for Tonight" and wanted to copy its drama-doc style, using actual No.71 Squadron pilots and personnel acting as themselves. But due to the time delays, and to the success of the 'Yank' films, Wanger decided to opt for a fictional story along the same lines as the previous two 'Yank' movies, with the then up-and-coming young male lead star, Robert Stack (later to make his fame as the FBI gangster catcher, Eliot Ness, in the popular US TV series, "The Untouchables"), as the self-interested Yank who eventually becomes committed to Britain's cause.

When Watt filmed No.71 Squadron, it had re-equipped with Spitfires. As this did not happen before August 1941, this gives a time period for when filming took place. However, Spitfires from other squadrons also appear in "Eagle Squadron". By July 1941, Wanger was said to be in possession of several thousand feet of film shot by Watt, which could not have been of No.71 Squadron Spitfires. Watt clearly had to get Spitfires from other RAF squadrons to fill in.

One significant factor in "Eagle Squadron" which separates it from the other Hollywood 'British' war films about the RAF is that it uses actual RAF units in its script, not only making direct reference to No.71 Squadron but also to No.56 Operational Training Unit, which trained fighter pilots at Sutton Bridge for RAF Fighter Command, using Hurricanes, when the film was in production. Using the identities of actual RAF units in a feature film made during World War Two was extremely unusual, as it could be construed as giving information to the enemy. One wonders if the Air Ministry's reticence towards Walter Wanger may have been caused by doubts in the minds of Whitehall mandarins as to how safe vital information about the RAF was in his possession.

The Air Transport Auxiliary also gets a look-in when Stack's Yank in the RAF makes patronisingly chauvinistic comments to a female ATA pilot, along the lines of "Hey, you're a girl" and "You'd better let me land this thing in the dark". It would have been an eye-opener to American movie audiences in 1942 that women flew aircraft in the RAF.

The studio set of an RAF Operations Room is the most realistic to be seen in any Hollywood 'British' war film to date and indicates that Wanger's production team must have had access to such an Ops Room. The five squadrons listed on the Ops Board - Nos.98, 232, 87, 71 and 89 Squadrons - were all actual operational units at the time the film was being made, although Nos.98 and 89 were not fighter squadrons and only No.232 actually fought in the Battle of Britain, stationed in Scotland.

One shot has a close-up of No.71 Squadron's badge as a shoulder patch on the uniform worn by American actor Leif Erickson. It clearly displays the spread-winged eagle with the letters 'E.S.' stitched above it. No.71's motto was, "First from the eyrie". Its squadron code letters were 'XR-'. When its Spitfires were filmed by Watt's 2nd Unit, No.71 Squadron was based at RAF North Weald. It received the Spitfire IIa in August 1941, but these were replaced by the Spitfire Vb just one month later - the latter Marque appears in the film, so it seems that Watt and his film crew were at North Weald during September and, perhaps, into October 1941.

The first establishing shot of No.71 Squadron shows five of its Vickers Supermarine Spitfire Mk.Vb fighters grouped around the perimeter track at RAF North Weald, being worked on by 'Erks', with Spitfire Vb coded XR-L the most clearly visible. But, as stated, Watt filmed Spitfires from other units as well as those of No.71 Squadron, almost certainly earlier in the year. When armourers begin loading Browning .303 machine gun ammunition into the wing boxes of an 'Eagle' Squadron Spitfire, they do so into a Spitfire Mk.Ia bearing the codes 'MV-'. This almost certainly was a Spitfire Ia from No.53 Operational Training Unit, which was based at Heston Airfield in Middlesex during the first half of 1941, training Spitfire pilots. It would have been an easy task for Watt's 2nd Unit to 'borrow' a No.53 OTU Spitfire Ia for this scene, in which other shots of Spitfire Vbs being armed and refuelled are included as well - the two Marques are distinguishable by the Browning machine gun ports in the Mk.Ia's wing leading edge and the Hispano Mk.II cannon embedded in the Mk.Vbs' wings.

Because of the delays in the production Wanger and his director, Arthur Lubin, plus his script writer, Norman Reilly Raine, had to change the plot from a Battle of Britain theme to the actual period when No.71 Squadron was operational on Spitfires in the latter half of 1941. It was engaged on bomber escort duties and fighter sweeps over Occupied France at this time, and it is on just such a sweep that we see Stack, Erickson and their 'Eagle' Squadron comrades taking off in the first piece of action in the film.

Curiously, when pilots reach their aircraft and climb aboard with the assistance of 'Erks', a shot of three Spitfire Mk.Ia variants is first used, all of them without any unit code letters on their fuselages. Perhaps they are No.53 OTU Spitfires, but there is no way to confirm this. The next shot shows two Spitfire Mk.Vb cannon-armed fighters of No.71 Squadron, with Spitfire Vb coded XR-C closest to the camera displaying the spread-winged eagle badge of the squadron on its port side engine cowling ahead of the cockpit,

while Spitfire Vb coded XR-A sits beyond it. Another Spitfire Vb coded 'P' is fired up with the use of a battery starter trolley.

But what comes as a real surprise is a shot of what is meant to be the 'Eagle' Squadron's Spitfires all stationed around the perimeter track. The camera pans across seven Spitfires parked on either side of the peri track, some turning engines. There is something familiar about this shot, as if it has been seen somewhere before. As the camera pans to the right, a Spitfire coded LO-R comes into shot, so this is not a scene depicting actual No.71 Squadron Spitfires but those of a very different unit. And we have seen this shot before: it is of the Spitfire Mk.Ia fighters of No.602 (City of Glasgow) Squadron filmed early in 1941 at Prestwick for "A Yank in the R.A.F.". How did this shot get into "Eagle Squadron"? The answer must be that it was provided by the Air Ministry and/or the Ministry of Information: they held the rights to use footage of No.602 Squadron's Spitfires for promotional and propaganda purposes in return for providing facilities for Darryl F Zanuck's film unit. A photograph of this exact scene, with the Spitfire Ia coded LO-R in the foreground, appears on the 602 (City of Glasgow) Squadron Museum Website.

One wonders if Walter Wanger knew he was using material filmed for a rival production about Yanks in the RAF. We will probably never know, but if Wanger did, he almost certainly had a good chuckle about it.

Shots of Stack, Erickson and other Hollywood actors in Spitfire cockpits are filmed in the studio or on the back lot in California, using a quite well produced wooden facsimile of a Spitfire. Images of Spitfires taxying in the background are of Watt's 2nd Unit material projected onto a backcloth. One glaring error, however, is that like Zanuck's 'Yank' movie, Wanger's production didn't use the correct engine noise for the 'Eagle' Squadron's Spitfires - indeterminate radial engine noise stands in for the distinctive Rolls Royce Merlins. Take off shots first show a group of ten Spitfires 'Scrambling' together from an all-grass airfield which may be North Weald - they are too distant to identify their squadron codes. This melds into an aerial shot of nine Spitfires filmed from an unidentified camera aircraft taking off en masse in three 'Vics' of three each. Again, they are departing an all-grass airfield and climbing out over what looks like heathland-type terrain, with a straight road cutting right through it below them.

For the air-airs of the 'Eagle' Squadron, yet another unit deputises for No.71. Whether they were filmed specifically for "Eagle Squadron", or whether we are looking at Air Ministry/MoI-provided footage filmed by the RAF Film Production Unit (the more likely), what we are now seeing are 12 Spitfire Mk.Vb fighters of No.315 (City of Deblin) Polish Fighter Squadron. As they pass the camera-ship, the 'PK-' code letters are just about discernible despite serious camera shake, with Spitfire Vb PK-V visible. But full confirmation comes soon afterwards with very impressive air-airs of the No.315 Squadron Spitfires clearly showing the Polish national red-white quadrant on their starboard engine cowlings, with Spitfire Vb PK-A closest to the camera. In another shot, Spitfire Vb PK-E is visible, and in yet another Spitfire Vb PK-R comes into view.

No.315 Polish Fighter Squadron was formed at RAF Acklington, Yorkshire, in January 1941, firstly with Hurricanes. By July 1941, it had moved to RAF Northolt outside West London and had re-equipped with the Spitfire Mk.IIa. However, as with No.71 'Eagle' Squadron, this was a temporary change-over, as in August No.315 Squadron acquired the Spitfire Mk.Vb which it operated on offensive fighter sweeps over Occupied Europe until November 1942. The air-air shots of its Spitfires in "Eagle Squadron" must, therefore, have been filmed post-August 1941, probably during its work-up on the type.

Impressive are the peel-off shots of the 12 Spitfires breaking from a long echelon port into dramatic dives to starboard, although sounding nothing like the real things. The Special FX of air battles and of strafing a German airfield in France are quite effectively achieved for the time period, using studio miniatures and F/S facsimiles of both a Spitfire and a Messerschmit Bf.109. In this regard, "Eagle Squadron" is markedly superior in comparison to the SFX used in "A Yank in the R.A.F." and in "International Squadron".

Another out-take of No.602 Squadron Spitfires from the first 'Yank' film is used in "Eagle Squadron", being the air-air of Spitfire Ia X4829/LO-Q and Spitfire Ia coded LO-B peeling away from the camera aircraft. Again, the Air Ministry or the MoI would have provided this footage.

Stack's character has to bale out over the Channel. This provides for an air-sea rescue sequence, with a Westland Lysander bearing the 'TV-' codes of No.IV Squadron setting out to search for him. No.IV Squadron was operating in the coastal patrol and air-sea rescue roles in 1941. However, when seen filmed air-air, a different Lysander appears without any codes. Two Spitfire Mk.Ia variants are also seen getting airborne to search for Stack; they also are devoid of codes and may be part of the unit operating the three uncoded Spitfires seen earlier.

Watt did film a number of No.71 Squadron Spitfires landing in pairs and threes at North Weald, to depict the 'Eagle' Squadron returning from its sweep over France. One of the Spitfires is badly shot up and has to make a crash landing. The 'crash wagon' is called for by the Ops Room. It is seen driving past a Spitfire Mk.Vb coded ZD-Y of No.222 (Natal) Squadron; no surprise, really, as No.222 were co-located at RAF North Weald with No.71 from August 1941 onwards. No.222 Squadron's Spitfires appear in more World War Two war films than those of any other RAF fighter squadron.

In a later air raid scene, stock footage is used of a Spitfire crashing inverted into the sea which appears in other British war films and in documentaries about the air war. Another out-take of No.602 Squadron pilots filmed at Prestwick running to 'Scramble' appears, eight Spitfire Mk.Ia fighters being shown. Stock footage of a low flying Vickers Wellington is used to depict a German bomber making a low-level attack. A brief shot of a single Luftwaffe Messerschmitt Bf.109 is also shown. No doubt the MoI provided this material.

In total, four Spitfire squadrons appear in "Eagle Squadron" representing the 'Eagle' Squadron of the title: No.71 (Eagle) Squadron itself, No.222 (Natal) Squadron, No.315 Polish Fighter Squadron and No.602 (City of Glasgow) Squadron, plus Spitfires from No.53 Operational Training Unit.

It has to be borne in mind that Harry Watt completed his filming in 1941 before the Japanese attack on Pearl Harbor, but when Walter Wanger and Arthur Lubin commenced filming in California with their main actors at the start of 1942 America was at war. Thus, "Eagle Squadron" commenced with American volunteer pilots in the Royal Air Force while the United States was neutral, but was completed with them as fully fledged combatants and watched by audiences at home in a nation newly at war. In this respect, "Eagle Squadron" is unique compared with other war films, either British or American.

THE GOOSE STEPS OUT

(Released: August 1942)

An Ealing Studios comedy propaganda film starring and co-directed by the then popular British comic actor, Will Hay, which, as the sleeve notes state, "Pokes fun at the Hun!". Its title mocks the Nazi military parade ground marching style of striding in a very exaggerated, leg-forward fashion, known as 'Goose Stepping'. As a comedy, it has to be judged in relation to the time of its release, with the intention of mercilessly caricaturing overly-exaggerated Nazis. Hay plays a clumsy British schoolteacher who just happens to be the exact double of a Nazi General, who he is asked by the War Office to impersonate in Germany while seeking information about a new secret weapon the General has knowledge of. Probably the funniest scene in the film is where Hay manages to persuade a class of Hitler Jugend training to be spies to give V-sign salutes to the portrait of Der Fuhrer, making them believe it is a familiar British sign of respect.

Aviation does feature in the film, particularly right at the beginning when the Nazi General is trying to escape from Britain in an airliner flying from Croydon to Lisbon. A partially-created studio prop of a Lockheed Electra is used here. Later, Hay has to parachute into Germany. An out-take from the Ealing Studios production earlier in the year, "The Big Blockade", of a Handley Page Hampden studio miniature is used to depict the aircraft he is parachuting from.

The only time a real aircraft is seen in the film occurs when Will Hay, now masquerading as a senior Nazi, is being flown to meet the Fuhrer but who, with the help of Hitler Jugend students who want to escape the Third Reich (including one played by a very young Charles Hawtrey of "Carry On" films fame), hijack the 'plane and fly it in very slapstick fashion to London. Briefly, close-up shots of a sizeable twin-engined aircraft being released from its parking chocks and taxiing forward is used as the introduction to this section of the film. One shot reveals the aircraft to be a Heinkel He.111B, filmed from in front as it taxies towards the camera. The distinctive bulbous nose of this version of the He.111, with a forward-firing machine gun, is clearly identifiable, a marked difference to the glazed nose design of the mass produced He.111H and He.111P variants.

It would be interesting to know how this footage was acquired, as it is not of the familiar parade style imagery favoured by the Reich Propaganda Ministry. Possibly it was obtained from a neutral source, perhaps from the Intelligence Ministries of countries like Sweden or Portugal which might have had easier access to such material.

The aircraft in which Hay and his student chums fly farcically to London is an all-too obvious studio miniature He.111.

UNPUBLISHED STORY

(Released: August 1942)

Richard Greene and Valerie Hobson play newspaper reporters in London during The Blitz who discover that a peace movement advocating no resistance to Nazi Germany is a cover organisation for German spies. The only aviation that appears in "Unpublished Story" is a brief use of the same archive shot of nine Messerschmitt Bf.110s and 18 Messerschmitt Bf.109s, over-flying what was probably a Nuremberg Rally, which was previously used in "Dangerous Moonlight" (1941) and "The Day Will Dawn" (1942).

THE FIRST OF THE FEW

(Released: September 1942)

"The First of the Few" is a propaganda film that blatantly romanticises the birth and the reputation of the Spitfire. It was produced and directed by actor Leslie Howard, he of "The Scarlet Pimpernel" (1934) and Ashley Wilkes fame in "Gone With The Wind" (1939). Howard was destined to lose his life one year after this film's release, shot down in a civilian former KLM Douglas DC-3 by Junkers Ju.88C-6s of V/KG.40 over the Bay of Biscay, supposedly in mistake for Winston Churchill who was flying out of Algiers at approximately the same time. Another suggestion has it that Howard was deliberately targeted for assassination by Josef Goebbels, the Reich's Propaganda Minister, in revenge for the success of not only this film but even more so for that of Howard's previous production, "Pimpernel Smith" (1940), which had mocked the Nazis mercilessly.

Howard plays designer R J Mitchell (completely unlike the real man), while Hollywood actor David Niven portrays Supermarine test pilot Geoffrey Crisp, a composite characterisation of the legendary Supermarine and Vickers test pilots, Jeffrey Quill and 'Mutt' Summers, who did much of the earliest Spitfires' test flying.

The film is today an aviation historian's and archivist's dream, containing unique imagery of a Spitfire Mk.I acting the role of the prototype, Supermarine Type 300 K5054, being aerobat'd in superb style by Quill over the Spitfire's birthplace, Eastleigh Aerodrome outside Southampton, filmed in 1941 specifically for "The First Of The Few". Most eye-catching of all is Quill's vertical upward roll in the convincing-looking 'K5054', followed

immediately by him pulling through inverted, then half rolling out into a powerful dive straight down at the camera.

In September 1941, RAF Fighter Command made available a complete Spitfire squadron for Howard's film unit, No.501 Squadron based at RAF Warmwell in Dorset with a mix of Spitfire Mk.IIa and Vb fighters. Nearby RAF Ibsley, Hampshire, was also drafted in, with Spitfire Vb-equipped No.118 Squadron loaning both pilots and aircraft temporarily wearing No.501 Squadron 'SD-' codes. They were acting as the fictional No.227 'Hunter' Squadron. Both Nos.501 and 118 were tasked on fighter escort duties for 'Ramrod' and anti-shipping raids, as well as defensive 'Scrambles', when they were filmed for "The First of the Few"; filming actually taking place between Ops.

No.501 Squadron Spitfires identified in the film at RAF Warmwell are: P8664/SD-C, P8256/SD-D, W3840/SD-G, and W3626 coded SD-K. Two more bearing codes SD-W and SD-X are No.118 Squadron Spitfires in disguise. A 'Scramble' is a re-use of the 'Scramble' scene staged by No.602 Squadron at Prestwick for "A Yank in the R.A.F.", with nine of 602's Spitfire Ia fighters turning propellers as their pilots race towards them - again, this footage would have been made available by the Air Ministry.

The 'Boss' of 118, Squadron Leader Frank J Howell, DFC and Bar, appears in a scene with David Niven (gone from Spitfire test pilot to RAF Station Commander) helping him out of a 'pranged' Spitfire Vb (118 Squadron P8789 in No.501 Squadron SD-E codes) and saying determinedly, "I need a Spitfire, not an ambulance!" Howell was a Battle of Britain veteran with several 'kills', and was among a number of 501 and 118 Squadrons' pilots who actually had speaking parts in "The First of the Few". By the time of the film's release, some had been lost in action.

The development of the Spitfire from the famous Supermarine racing seaplanes which won the Schneider Trophy outright for Great Britain is largely told in the first half of the film by the use of all-too obvious model miniatures, although the full-scale facsimile of the Supermarine S.5 with working propeller is accurately created.

Archive footage from the 1923 Schneider Trophy shows the British Supermarine Sea Lion III entrant and a Wright NW-2 entered by the US Navy, held at Cowes. Some of the Schneider Trophy footage used is now only accessible via "The First of the Few" itself, the original film taken having long been lost to posterity. This means that the footage used of the 1925 Supermarine S.4 is the sole source available of this, R J Mitchell's first monoplane seaplane racer design. Footage is also used of the Supermarine S.6A N247, the 1929 winner, but although this is meant to portray that win it actually shows the same racer bearing race number '2', which it bore as the reserve S.6A to N248 in the 1931 Schneider Trophy competition. Therefore, this footage of N247/2 is from the 1931 race which sealed the Schneider Trophy permanently for Britain. Tragically, S.6A N247/2 killed its pilot in a take off accident at Calshot, where the Schneider Trophy was held in 1931, during practice. Footage is also shown of Supermarine S.6B S1596, another unlucky racer which sank off Calshot before the 1931 Schneider Trophy race and world speed record attempt took place.

Wartime footage is used of Luftwaffe Messerschmitt Bf.109Es and Heinkel He.111s; from an historical perspective the air-air shots of a quartet of '109s in classic 'Rotte' formation is of particular interest. Some very familiar and since much used gun-camera shots of shoot-downs are also employed. One in particular is noteworthy: a Dornier Do.17 plunging vertically to earth over West London. This is Do.17Z-2 Werke Nr 2361, coded F1+FH of I/KG.76, minus its entire tail section and outer wings and falling on the London Borough of Fulham on 15th September 1940. The tail section landed on Victoria Railway Station. The long-standing myth about this crashing Do.17 is that it was about to bomb Buckingham Palace when it was rammed by Flight Sergeant Raymond Holmes in his No.609 Squadron Hurricane. In fact, it was attacked by a number of 609 and 504 Squadron Hurricanes, whose pilots may have believed that Buckingham Palace was its target due to its line of flight; however, apparently this Do.17 had developed engine trouble and had trailed behind its main bomber formation. For a Luftwaffe bomber flying alone over West London there was only going to be one outcome – two of its four-man crew survived by bailing out.

The film's finale of an aerial dog-fight is achieved with a mix of air-airs of No.501 Squadron Spitfire Vbs (obviously not 1940-era Spitfires, but still looking realistically the part, albeit with their Hispano cannon removed), genuine wartime footage, model miniatures, and something especially rare compared with other war films made on either side of the Atlantic: "The First of the Few" uses a genuine operational wartime Luftwaffe bomber.

This is an Heinkel He.111H-3 which had been captured intact and was on the growing strength of the RAF's No.1426 (Enemy Aircraft) Flight at RAF Duxford when the film was made. The Heinkel bomber in question is He.111H-3 Werke Nr 6853, coded 1H+EN of II/KG.26, an anti-shipping Kampfgeschwader operating out of Denmark, which force-landed at North Berwick Law, Scotland, on 9 February 1940 after being shot up by a No.602 Squadron Spitfire. One of the crew was killed but the other three were taken prisoner. The He.111 was only slightly damaged after the pilot made a brilliant crash landing in a field, with the bomber tipping up onto its nose. It bore the RAF serial AW177 when operated by No.1426 Flight and was used in a training film for United States Army Air Corps gunners, "Combat America", directed by Hollywood actor in US Army uniform, Captain Clark Gable.

He.111H-3 1H+EN/AW177 did not survive the War: it was reportedly destroyed whilst taking evasive action avoiding an airborne collision with another of its captured colleagues, a Ju.88, in November 1943.

Stripped of its codes but with Luftwaffe Balkenkreuzen and Swastikas applied, the He.111H-3 looks every inch the menacing part in "The First Of The Few" when filmed air-air, with Spitfire IIa P8074/SD-L of No.501 Squadron making repeated runs at it from a variety of angles. The Heinkel is filmed from P8074's cockpit, to create the effect of attacks seen from the fighter pilot's perspective, while the camera-ship filming both the Spitfire and the He.111 in action is a Bristol Blenheim IV. This Blenheim is actually captured in view in one shot from P8074, thus for the audience creating the

impression of a second Luftwaffe bomber beyond the He.111.

(The Spitfire seen in "The Big Blockade" (1942) , filmed apparently from a Heinkel He.111, was almost certainly filmed from He.111H-3 1H+EN/AW177, probably by a Crown Film Unit cameraman).

Spitfire P8074 is filmed close-up unleashing the power of its Browning machine guns. A No.118 Squadron Spitfire Vb, coded NK-B, is also included in one shot, perhaps as a credit to 118's otherwise disguised contribution to the film, portraying Niven's aircraft pursuing a Bf.109 which has had the temerity to shoot down Niven's colleague. "I'm going to get that swine if it's the last thing I do", declares Niven, before uttering among some of the worst last lines used in any film, as he stares mystically up at the clouds: "They can't take the Spitfires, Mitch, they can't take 'em".

Corporal Jones put it so much better.

IN WHICH WE SERVE

(Released: September 1942)

Made at the same time as "The First Of The Few" was being produced, "In Which We Serve" was, and still is today, regarded as a classic British war film and one of the best of its genre. It is probably not an exaggeration to state that if a compendium was made of all the British films featuring World War Two as their theme, to decide which of them was the best, most film critics and analysts would place "In Which We Serve" in the top ten.

What makes the film outstanding compared with most on the subject is its realism, especially when one takes into account the time period when it was made. The War was running two-and-a-half years hot for Britain when the film went into production under the joint direction of playwright and stage director Noel Coward and film editor David Lean. The film was Coward's inspiration, based on the wartime experiences of his friend, Lord Louis Mountbatten, who had been the captain of HMS Kelly, a Royal Navy destroyer that was sunk by Luftwaffe bombers off the coast of Crete in May 1941. By this time, the British public could not be assuaged by blatantly exaggerated propaganda of the fantastical kind as proffered by "The Lion Has Wings" (1939) and "The Big Blockade" (1942). They were facing too much hardship under German bombs and there was no disguising the severity of reverses for British forces in North Africa and Crete, not to mention the shipping losses in the Atlantic and the Mediterranean. Coward judged the country's mood correctly in making a genuinely believable piece that was well received by all who saw it, especially the Royal Navy itself who used it as a promotional film to illustrate what life was really like in the Service.

Coward acts the role of the Captain of HMS Torrin, a destroyer like the Kelly which is sunk by German low-level bombers. He and other members of the ship's crew cling to an inflatable life raft in the oil-soaked sea, having to endure being strafed periodically as each crew member recalls in flash-backs their lives, loves and experiences back home in "Blighty".

Aviation plays a limited but significant role in the film. In so doing, "In Which We Serve" shares with "The First Of The Few" the almost unique achievement of using a genuine Luftwaffe bomber which had been captured and was being operated by the Royal Air Force in 1942. This was Junkers Ju.88A-5 Werke Nr 6073, coded M2+MK, which, like the Heinkel He.111H-3 in "The First Of The Few", was on the strength of No.1426 (Enemy Aircraft) Flight at RAF Duxford when it was filmed in July 1942 by Two Cities Films at Heston Airport. It plays the part of successive German bombers which attack and sink HMS Torrin quite early on in the film's plot.

Ju.88A-5 M2+MK of II/Kuestenfliegergruppe 106 (II/KGr.106), a coastal attack unit, was spoofed by the 'Meacon' radio countermeasures system that mimicked the Luftwaffe's navigational radio beacons, sending false returns which fooled German aircrews into thinking their nav aids were telling them one thing, when in fact they were being sent completely false bearings by the British 'Meacon' operators. The Ju.88A-5's crew thought they were back in French airspace on the night of 26th November 1941 and landed at RAF Chivenor, North Devon, unintentionally delivering a completely intact Junkers Ju.88 light bomber into British hands.

After evaluation by the RAF's Air Fighting Development Unit, Ju.88A-5 M2+MK was repainted in RAF camouflage and roundels, and was assigned British military serial HM509. It spent some time at RAE Farnborough before being based at RAF Duxford. It appears in a number of photographs of No.1426 (Enemy Aircraft) Flight aircraft, which are easily obtainable on the Internet, and was used together with captured examples of Messerschmitt Bf.109, Bf.110 and Focke Wulf FW.190 fighters, plus the above-mentioned Heinkel He.111, on enemy aircraft recognition and experience visits to various RAF fighter and bomber stations around the country.

This Ju.88A-5 was written off after ground-looping at RAF Thorney Island during an aborted take off on 19th May 1944; it was broken up for spares to support other Ju.88s being operated by No.1426 (Enemy Aircraft) Flight and by the Experimental Flying Department at RAE Farnborough. It was the first of seven Ju.88s to be captured and evaluated by the RAF during World War Two, and may have been the Ju.88 involved with the fatal crash of Heinkel He.111H-3 AW177/1H+EN in November 1943.

For "In Which We Serve", Ju.88A-5 HM509 was repainted in Luftwaffe markings and with its M2+MK code re-applied; however, the painted-over RAF roundels can be seen on the underwing surfaces. Its code can be clearly observed in a number of shots, taken as the Ju.88 makes repeated low-level attack runs over HMS Torrin; it is, in fact, meant to be portraying a series of Ju.88s making attacks in successive passes, but freeze-framing confirms it is the same Ju.88A-5 on each pass, whilst the code M2+MK provides the evidence that it is a captured enemy aircraft being used and not wartime footage of a Ju.88 in action.

However, we the audience are being very successfully spoofed here by Coward's Special FX team. While Ju.88A-5 M2+MK was definitely filmed for "In Which We Serve", many of the low-level attack passes were performed by an extremely accurately made large-scale radio-controlled (R/C) model of the Luftwaffe bomber. This was created by the leading exponents of aircraft model-making of the wartime period, Woodason Aircraft Models (WAM), located at Heston who specialised in creating many of the aircraft recognition models used by RAF squadrons to identify both friend and foe in the air. WAM undoubtedly used Junkers Ju.88A-5 M2+MK as the pattern for its R/C Ju.88 used in the film.

The accuracy of detail in the R/C model stands out in the photo of WAM company boss Victor Woodason holding it after completion. Nonetheless, some important changes had to be made to it once Two Cities intended using footage of the real Ju.88A-5 alongside that of the model. The dive brakes on the model had to be removed as they were not operated on HM509/M2+MK. Because No.1426 (EA) Flight removed the RAF camouflage to expose the original Luftwaffe markings, WAM had to change the paint scheme they had chosen for the R/C model to match that exactly of M2+MK, even including the faint circular patches of the removed RAF roundels under each wing and shifting the underwing Balkenkreuzen closer to the engine nacelles.

It is the R/C model Ju.88 which is seen in the film very realistically releasing two bombs during several attack runs at low-level. However, another trick is also used: when the bombs are released they appear to be quite streamlined as they descend, but when one of them is seen in close-up its shape is very different, being shorter and much more stubby. Careful freeze-framing reveals that the editor has used footage of a 250lb inert bomb being dropped from a completely different, and real, aircraft. The editor has almost cropped this aircraft out of shot, so as to convey the intended impression that the bomb has been dropped by the Ju.88. But he has not been quick enough to defeat a modern DVD player's technology (not that he would ever have guessed that such technology would eventually become available to the home viewer): freeze-framing reveals very briefly what aircraft it is that is dropping the inert 250 pounder - a Curtiss P-40 Tomahawk, with its big RAF fuselage roundel briefly very visible. The explosions of the bombs in the sea are footage of depth charges erupting, cut into the sequence.

To add to the effect of the attacks by the Ju.88s on HMS Torrin, a studio prop of a ship's mast was set up on the film lot, designed to move as if the ship is rolling and with the R/C Ju.88 filmed running in to attack beyond it and over it. Intercut with the shots of the attacking Ju.88 are those of the destroyer's gun crews in action: the anti-aircraft guns are real and so are their crews, who were loaned by the Royal Navy for the production, while the ammunition they are firing from their ship was live. White smoke bursts are maroons, also fired each time the R/C Ju.88 ran in towards the camera, simulating flak.

To portray the Ju.88 that scores a direct hit on the Torrin before it is shot down itself, wartime long-shot footage of what appears to be a Heinkel He.115 diving vertically into the sea is used. Noticeably its elongated rear fuselage, distinctive of the He.115's design, is twisted to starboard, indicating that the stricken twin-engined torpedo bomber has broken its back as it plunges to its, and its aircrew's, death.

Later in the film, Coward's character recalls the Torrin's first action off Norway, in which it was damaged by shell fire and had to be towed back to harbour. During this time it is attacked by Ju.87 Stukas, but this is only shown as a written record by the Captain in the ship's log. When the Torrin nears harbour it receives RAF fighter protection, depicted by Ministry of Information footage of four Spitfires in 'Box' formation. The variants can't be confirmed, but for the time period they are most likely to be Mk.Vs, while the imagery does not permit their squadron codes to be identified. This is the only other appearance of aviation in "In Which We Serve".

One of the film's principal messages that Coward sought to portray was that the Torrin's crew and their stalwart families and friends are ordinary people caught up in extraordinary and dangerous situations during war, who continue to serve their country faithfully while enduring sometimes terrible strife and loss. "In Which We Serve" conveys that message with totally credible impact, which explains the film's success in the cinema and with critics. It even allows for a ship's member (Richard Attenborough, in his first screen role, uncredited) to show fear and panic, so adding to the realism – something which Hollywood film productions did not permit their actors to show in American war movies.

DESPERATE JOURNEY

(Released: September 1942, USA) Hollywood 'British' war film

Speaking of American war movies, "Desperate Journey" is the second Hollywood 'British' war movie featuring the Boeing Fortress I to be released in 1942, although it preceded "Flying Fortress" in the USA by several months and was much better received. That had much to do with its leading star, Errol Flynn, who plays the pilot of an RAF Fortress I shot down on a mission over Germany and who leads the survivors from its crew on a desperate journey through Nazi-held territory as they try to escape back to England. Flynn's star was riding particularly high in America in 1942 and "Desperate Journey" was one among three Hollywood Flynn vehicles that year which did much to embolden American morale during a very dark period for the nation.

Flynn's character is an Australian Flight Lieutenant in the RAF, one of the few roles in which he was able to play someone of his own nationality. The film borrows certain aspects of "International Squadron" (1941), in that the crew of the bomber Flynn leads are multi-national. Ronald Reagan re-appears, this time as a Canadian RAF Flying Officer, but with the same gung-ho spirit of the role he played in "International Squadron". Similar to that film, "Desperate Journey" was made entirely in California, including one scene at Los Angeles Metropolitan Airport, while Lockheed Burbank was called upon once again to provide aircraft assets to the production.

Although it has an RAF theme, the plot does not feature aviation to a large extent except at the beginning and in the dramatic final climax. Whilst driving in an open-top truck to their 'plane at the start of their mission (played out against the worst and most obvious backcloth to be seen in any film), Flynn and his crew watch wishfully as three Spitfires fly past overhead. "Say, look at those new fighters!", Flynn exclaims. "Gee, that's where I'd like to be, flying one of those babies".

"Things like that in the air, and we've got to fly an ice-wagon!", complains Reagan. Very Hollywood Royal Air Force.

The "ice-wagon" Reagan is complaining about is waiting for them, props already turning, at what looks like the corner of a rough-looking airfield. A continuity goof occurs here because soon afterwards they start engines before taking off. Their bomber is meant to be an RAF Boeing Fortress I, although an American movie audience would only know of it as a Flying Fortress. Technically, they would be correct as the actual aircraft is a Boeing B-17B Flying Fortress, one of 39 that the USAAC had taken on charge in 1939 after evaluating 13 Boeing YB-17 variants at Langley Field, Virginia. Quite possibly this particular B-17B was operated by the 7th Bomb Group using this first in-service version of the Flying Fortress at Marshall Field in California. It is filmed in low light conditions from a distance and, therefore, cannot be identified. It is recognisable as a B-17B by the oval bulged waist and ventral gun blisters seen in shot as the crew board the Flying Fortress through the fuselage side door - these blisters were replaced on subsequent versions of the B-17 by more blended waist gun windows and by a ventral 'bathtub'-style machine gun turret (itself later replaced by the rotating ball turret on the B-17E, B-17F and B-17G models).

A real goof occurs when the command is given to "start port outboard engine", and the starboard inner engine starts instead! In fact, the engine shown turning over is not that of the B-17B, but of a Lockheed Hudson - all the engine starting shots that follow are of a Hudson's engines. What this reveals is that no more shots of the B-17B are used; quite why this is the case isn't known. Only close-ups of what is meant to be the B-17B's engines and wheels are shown, followed by a shot of a main wheel on a different aircraft filmed by a camera fixed to the wheel housing during its take off run. A twin-engined aircraft seen parked nose-on in the distance has the appearance of an Armstrong Whitworth Whitley, but is too small in image to confirm.

All the following shots of the B-17B, painted to represent an RAF Fortress I, are achieved by means of a studio miniature, from take off, through the bombing raid, and then to its shoot down and crash landing within a forest. The miniature is of reasonably good standard for the time period and the crash is quite effectively achieved.

No aircraft appears again in "Desperate Journey" until nearly three-quarters of the way through the film when a tri-motor transport painted in Luftwaffe markings purports to be a Junkers Ju.52. In fact, this is an example of a Stinson Model A, a three-engined, eight-seat feeder-liner designed by the Stinson Aircraft Company for American Airlines, the prototype making its first flight on 27th April 1934. A total of 30 were produced for American Airlines, Central Airlines and Delta Airlines. Which actual example is used in the film isn't known, but it was filmed acting as a Ju.52 at Los Angeles Metropolitan Airport.

By today's standards, the escapades by Flynn, Reagan and Co as they traverse Nazi Germany, using their fists most of the time to give the Hun a good beating, is far-fetched stuff but was welcomed as much-needed patriotic adventurism in 1942. The plot has the RAF crew discovering a secret Messerschmitt factory, where the new "Messerschmitt 114" is being built. They have to get across

Germany and then through Nazi Occupied Holland, in order to escape to England with this vital information. Only three of them make it and they do so in dramatic fashion. By chance, when they go in search in the Dutch countryside of petrol for the German staff car they have stolen, they come across a hidden airfield.

Concealed beneath camouflage netting is a captured RAF bomber. Flynn and Co overhear a plan in which this bomber will fly ahead of a major German bomber force and, in using a large bomb, flatten Battersea Power Station in London. This will put out of action half of London's water pumping stations. The bomber force following up will be carrying incendiaries, to cause a fire storm in London which the fire services will be unable to cope with. Flynn realises they must steal the RAF bomber back and fly it to England, thus foiling the Nazis' dastardly plan.

Representing the captured RAF bomber (and the earlier B-17B engine-starting shots) is Lockheed Hudson III T9386, one of a large batch produced under Lend-Lease by Lockheed Burbank. Hudson III T9386 is painted up with spurious black slashes all over its earth-and-green RAF camouflage, but after Flynn and Co seize it - using the Boulton Paul machine gun turret to mow down plenty of German troops - all these black marks have disappeared. The escape sequence is very dramatically staged, with Hollywood stuntmen acting as German aircraft groundcrewmen having to genuinely get out of the way of the Hudson at the last second as it lifts off from a plain somewhere outside Los Angeles - the countryside looks anything but Dutch. Clearly the Air Ministry gave the OK to Lockheed at Burbank to permit this Hudson to be used pre-delivery in "Desperate Journey", a fast-paced Hollywood 'British' war movie that is still enjoyable to watch today.

SECRET MISSION

(Released: October 1942)

This somewhat simplistic and rather 'Boys Own'-ish style espionage war film sees British Army agents inserted into Nazi Occupied France, to capture information about enemy fortifications and an underground military control centre prior to an attack by Paratroopers. The team of four agents are led by a British Army Major played by Hugh Williams, who we saw a few months earlier as another agent behind the lines in "The Day Will Dawn" (1942) and whose urbane Public School charm and manner appealed to the ladies in British cinema audiences, but less so to their men. Among the team is a French Army officer played petulantly by a young James Mason, whose sister, acted by little-known-today but popular-in-the-Forties Canadian actress, Carla Lehmann (also seen a few months earlier in "Flying Fortress"), is divided between her belief the British betrayed the French in 1940 and her growing feelings for Williams.

What's all this to do with aviation? Nothing, for virtually the whole of the film, apart from a studio-created backcloth of a distant fly-past by Luftwaffe aircraft, there is not a hint of aviation until the finale. But what is then shown is of real value to the student of both British military and aviation history.

"Secret Mission" has some of the best publicly available, and possibly unique, archive imagery of the Armstrong Whitworth Whitley V bomber/transport in action, some of it filmed air-air which, until this film's release, was not known of unless similar such shots appeared in newsreels during the War. Certainly, air-air footage of the Whitley has not surfaced before their appearance in this film, and have not emerged in any subsequent productions.

Of even more historical significance is the probable fact that, by the use of this footage in a feature film, the British public was being given its first sighting of a new form of warfare applied in action by the British Army and the Royal Air Force: the 1st Airborne Division, forerunner of the Parachute Regiment. The Whitleys are seen dropping Paratroopers of the 1st Airborne Division, probably during a training exercise. The green light to show footage of these para-drops was probably given as a consequence of the 1st Airborne Division's initial success on enemy territory, the airborne capture and removal of a German Wurzburg radar set from the French coast, close to the village of Bruneval, on the night of 27th-28th February 1942 - the Bruneval Raid. The airborne attack by British Paratroopers on the German underground control station in "Secret Mission" is undoubtedly a salute to the Bruneval Raid, although, in October 1942, much of its details was still a military secret unknown to the British public.

To portray the airborne raid on the underground bunker, a number of shots of Whitleys are shown. First, we see a flight of five Whitleys filmed heading towards the camera's position on the ground, spread wide apart in a gaggle that would allow the Paratroopers from each aircraft to descend without colliding with those jumping from the Whitley nearest to them.

Then, a very rare air-air shot of a single Whitley V is shown, in which this ungainly-looking aircraft's elongated airframe and wing design is clearly displayed to the camera. We have seen close-up studies of the Whitley on the ground, as well as taking off and landing, in "Ferry Pilot" (1941), but as clear an air-air study as this of the big twin-engined monster has as yet to be shown to us. Paratroopers are next seen inside what is a studio-created fuselage interior, wearing their circular protective headgear used in the early days of airborne operations. From the crude studio set of the fuselage interior, it appears the film's art department were given no insight into what a Whitley looked like inside and built what was their best guess, although one would have thought they could have used footage from "Ferry Pilot" as a guide.

The next shot is of another single Whitley V filmed from the ground and making a fly-over. Its code letters of OA-S are distinctly visible on the fuselage side. A shot of the Paras inside getting the green light is followed by footage of Paratroopers dropping out of the hatch in the fuselage floor of Whitley V OA-S, which, in its turn, is followed by a second such Whitley V. A fine air-air study appears next of Paras dropping out of the belly of Whitley V OA-D. This study is taken from Crown Film Unit footage of some of the earliest Paratroop training drops filmed sometime in 1941.

Research does not throw up a Whitley-equipped RAF squadron that carried 'OA-' codes. No.51 Squadron provided the Whitleys that air-dropped the 1st Airborne Division Paratroopers in the Bruneval Raid, but they carried 'MH-' code letters. When "Secret Mission" was in production spanning the end of 1941 and into 1942 the principal unit which trained Paratroopers using the Whitley V was the Parachute Exercise Squadron based at RAF Netheravon in Wiltshire, ideally located for para-jump exercises over nearby Salisbury Plain. It was later numbered No.297 Squadron, but with 'XH-' codes. As a best guess, the 'OA-' coded Whitleys seen in "Secret Mission" are possibly Parachute Exercise Squadron aircraft filmed in late 1941 - early 1942 before they became No.297 Squadron Whitleys on 22nd February 1942: the 'OA-' code letters were not then being used by any of the other four RAF squadrons that subsequently carried these same codes over various different time periods during World War Two.

The final shots show a large number of Paras descending from three Whitleys departing in the distance and landing on very flat terrain. They are likely to be the same Whitleys seen in the previous shots. When the Paras attack the underground bunker, they are still wearing their circular flat headgear, an error of fact because the Paras traditionally put on their famous red berets as soon as they landed and went straight into action.

It is these iconic and extremely rare studies of a very original and decidedly old British aircraft design that makes "Secret Mission" a film worth having in any British aviation historian's collection.

WENT THE DAY WELL?

(Released: December 1942)

The film which is credited as helping to influence author Jack Higgins in his plot for his book, "The Eagle Has Landed", and likewise the plot of the film of the same title reviewed in Chapter Five. It is based on fictitious events involving German Paratroopers disguised as British soldiers taking over a peaceful English village prior to an equally fictitious invasion of Britain. Made in 1942, it played on still then widely held fears that a German invasion of Britain was still possible, but significantly opens and closes with a scene portraying Germany as defeated and World War Two as over. It is also credited as being one of the most important and effective British propaganda films of the wartime period.

However, important though the film is in its place in British film history, it contains no aviation elements at all. The German Paratroopers are not shown being parachuted into England. The title, incidentally, is a line taken from an epitaph written for war memorials by Greek scholar, John Maxwell Edmonds: "Went the day well? We died and never knew. But, well or ill, Freedom, we died for you".

COMMANDOS STRIKE AT DAWN

(Released: December 1942, USA) Hollywood 'British' war film

"Dedicated to the officers and men of the armed forces of Canada, Great Britain and Fighting Norway who participated in the filming of this picture", is the tribute paid right at the beginning of this Hollywood propaganda movie. The Commandos of the title are British, but the principal characters are almost all Norwegians under the yoke of Nazi tyranny. Austrian-Hungarian born Jewish actor, Paul Muni, plays the role of a peaceful Norwegian villager who becomes a Resistance fighter when he finds he can no longer tolerate the atrocities committed by the German military against his own people.

Canada deputises for Norway, in particular, British Columbia. British actor Robert Coote, who had moved to Hollywood four years before World War Two and who plays the Captain leading the Commandos, was a serving officer in the Royal Canadian Air Force when he made this film, having joined up after Canada declared its intention to fight alongside Great Britain against Nazi Germany.

"Commandos Strike At Dawn" provides a unique opportunity to see military aircraft of British design painted with German Swastika and Balkenkreuze markings, so that they can portray Deutsches Luftwaffe machines. All the aircraft were provided by the Royal Canadian Air Force, and seeing Bristol Bolingbrokes and Westland Lysanders wearing German markings is a sight to behold. The scenes in which they appear involve a secret airfield built by German troops in a Norwegian forest close to the North Sea, from where the Luftwaffe intend to attack Allied convoys sailing from Britain to Murmansk in Russia. This airfield is discovered by Muni's Resistance fighter, who decides to escape to Britain by boat with four comrades and warn the British about it. The "Commandos Strike At Dawn" scenario is a planned Commando raid on the airfield.

A careful study of the big battle scene involving the Commandos' raid reveals that the RCAF loaned two Bristol Bolingbroke Mk.IV bombers, the Canadian manufactured version of the Bristol Blenheim Mk.IV, and two Westland Lysanders, to be set up as either static props or as taxying aircraft. The nearest German approximations to these types would probably be the Junkers Ju.88 light bomber and the Henschel Hs.126 army co-operation aircraft. The film is in black-and-white, but it is likely the Bolingbrokes and the Lysanders were painted dark green overall, then had the Balkenkreuzen and the Swastikas applied. It seems unlikely that the RCAF would have taken two valuable Bolingbroke Mk.IVs off maritime patrol duties, their principal role, so probably the two examples seen in the film are Bolingbroke Mk.IVT trainer/communications variants.

The airfield where the big battle scene, using live explosives, was staged was a newly-created air base at the time; today, it is Victoria International Airport at North Saanich in British Columbia.

One other scene involving aviation in "Commandos Strike At Dawn" has Muni's character being flown from London to Scotland, to join up with the Commando force. A brief and rather distant shot of a Douglas DC-3 in bare metal scheme is used to depict this, which fades into what is meant to be a scene at an RAF bomber base. In actual fact, this has to have been filmed at Patricia Bay Airport, British Columbia (now also part of Victoria International), because lined up to the left of the screen are five Handley Page Hampden light bombers. A sixth taxyies towards the camera, while a seventh Hampden can be seen parked in the distance.

Patricia Bay was the sole location in Canada where Hampden bombers were based. Nearly 80 out of the 160 of the type that were built by the Victory Aircraft consortium were operated from Patricia Bay by No.32 Operational Training Unit, Royal Air Force, training bomber crews in the greater safety of Canadian airspace (the remaining Victory Aircraft-built Hampdens were sent to England). This shot of the seven Hampdens was probably included in the film as a "Thank you" to the authorities at Patricia Bay Airport for allowing their facility to be used.

The only other use of aviation in the film appears early on when Hitler breaks his promise to the Low Countries and the Nordic nations that he will respect their neutrality, this being depicted by archive material showing a single Heinkel He.111 flying low over a wintry-looking valley while headlines are displayed, stating "Hitler promises peace to Holland" and "Denmark Occupied". In which country this archive shot was taken - and used twice - is not known. When the headline, "Norway Invaded", appears, a close-up of another Heinkel He.111 taking off over the camera is used.

When this type of Hollywood propaganda movie was being made after America's entry into the War, the British were always portrayed as being brave, resolute and determined, the ally the Americans admired most. In fact, no American character appears in "Commandos Strike At Dawn", although most of the cast are American - the heroes are all Norwegian and British. Hence, this Hollywood movie has to be a Hollywood 'British' war film.

NINE MEN

(Released: February 1943)

Even allowing for the wartime period and limited budget allocated to this production, the wooden acting by its cast renders this a very dated film to watch. The "Nine Men" are nine British troops left behind enemy (Italian) lines in the North African desert (Tunisia?), who have to defend an old Arabic fort. The actors performing these roles were all serving in the armed forces at the time, who were released from their units to take part in the production, including a very young Gordon Jackson - he had more than 30 years to go before, as CI5 chief George Cowley, he had to handle the likes of agents Bodie and Doyle in the hit TV drama series, "The Professionals".

Director Harry Watt had, until this film, made drama-documentaries, his most notable being "Target For Tonight" (1941) reviewed in this Chapter; his lack of experience with real actors probably explains why Watt could not bring out convincing performances from the cast, he having always worked with actual serving personnel in documentary style up till now.

There is one brief element of aviation in the film, when the nine soldiers are strafed by a very ineffective Special FX miniature of a Messerschmitt Bf.109. It is clearly a studio model that is being swung round on a wire loop. But, oddly enough, this limited piece of footage of the miniature Bf.109 is used as an out-take in the Sixties war film, "Attack on the Iron Coast" (1968), reviewed in Chapter Four.

THE SILVER FLEET

(Released: March 1943)

This unusual and understated propaganda film about Dutch resistance to Nazi Occupation, named after the Spanish treasure fleet captured by Piet Hein, Holland's greatest naval hero at the time of the Spanish Armada, is devoid of any aviation.

FIRES WERE STARTED

(Released: April 1943)

Also released under the title of "I Was A Fireman", this drama-documentary is not only a tribute to the men and women of the Auxiliary Fire Service (AFS) but is also considered a classical piece of British cinema, scripted and directed by Humphrey Jennings and using actual AFS personnel, not actors. Humphrey Jennings is regarded as being possibly the most lyrical and poetic of film directors in British cinema history and "Fires Were Started" is looked upon as his best piece of work. Although the fires were staged, using bomb sites and derelict buildings, nonetheless they very realistically re-create the terror of the London Blitz. Luftwaffe bombers are heard overhead London throughout the single night that the film portrays, but are never seen. The one element of aviation that is shown is a fine shot of a Barrage Balloon being inflated aboard a Thames River Barge, with Battersea Power Station in the background.

TOMORROW WE LIVE

(Released: April 1943)

A film that probably had a strong impact on a wartime British cinema audience in early 1943, especially with the warning given right at the beginning that the events being shown were based on fact and could "have happened to us". The film's plot is about the effects of the German Occupation on a small French port, its people resentful of the crude yet relatively benign domination by the Wehrmacht, which changes when the SS are brought in and begin committing atrocities to terrorise the population into betraying each other. However, even though there are two bombing attacks by the RAF in the film, the bombers are never seen.

TONIGHT WE RAID CALAIS

(Released: April 1943, USA) Hollywood 'British' war film

The irony behind the title of this 20th Century Fox production is that there is no raid on Calais. In the plot, a British agent being inserted by landing craft into Nazi Occupied France is told he can escape after completing his mission by reaching Calais on a particular night when a British Commando raid will take place and join up with the Commandos when they withdraw by sea. However, right at the end of the film he is seen rowing out to sea on his own, with no Commando raid at all!

Very Colonial English actor, John Sutton, plays the agent: Sutton had forged a successful Hollywood career as a suave, handsome but cruel bad guy, especially in swashbucklers, such as "The Adventures of Robin Hood" (1938), opposite Errol Flynn, and "The Three Musketeers" (1948), opposing Gene Kelly. In "Tonight We Raid Calais", he plays an agent who joins up with a French farmer's family whose son, Pierre, has been killed in action and whose identity he adopts to disguise himself from the Germans. The plot has an unusual twist, in 21st Century terms, in that the sister of Pierre - played by French actress, Annabelle, who acted only under her adopted single first name - is a Nazi sympathiser and is opposed to the British because Pierre was a sailor in the French Navy who was killed in the Royal Navy's action against the French fleet at Oran, Algeria, on 3rd July 1940.

The sinking of the French fleet in the port of Mers-el-Kebir, Oran, on the orders of Prime Minister Winston Churchill, after the Admiral of the French fleet refused Churchill's request that he send his ships to join up with the Royal Navy, is an event that today's generation may know little about concerning the history of World War Two. The action took place to prevent the French Vichy government, which had agreed an armistice with Nazi Germany, from surrendering the French fleet to the German Kriegsmarine.

The film is not just a very obvious propaganda booster in support of the British fighting the Nazis, but also directs a very strong message to French citizens who, like the young Frenchwoman played by Annabelle, feel they have reason to support the Germans but who come to realise that their true purpose is to join the British in their fight to set France free. There is an underlying message that the Americans are also on the side of France, as in the plot Free French forces are about to join with British and American troops in Operation Torch, the invasion of North Africa on the coasts of Algeria and Tunisia (which had taken place six months before the release of "Tonight We Raid Calais").

The mission of Sutton's agent is to identify a factory complex the Germans have built that is manufacturing a new type of 88mm shell that can penetrate any type of armour the Allies have and thus devastate Operation Torch. The RAF is going to bomb the factory on a pre-arranged night and Sutton, as 'Pierre', must find a way to signal the correct target at night to the bombers. He achieves this by having the widows of French farmers who have

been shot by the Germans, including Odette's parents in a starkly brutal firing squad scene even by today's standards, set fire to their cornfields in a ring around the factory. The RAF see the ring of fire and successfully bomb the factory. This involves the only scene using aircraft in "Tonight We Raid Calais", an out-take of the five Lockheed Hudson Vs in "A Yank in the R.A.F." (1941); it seems Hollywood still didn't have access to stock footage of RAF bombers on Operations at the time.

From an historical perspective, "Tonight We Raid Calais" is a useful Hollywood film to study for the propaganda messages it was sending. It was very pro-British, with a very English action hero, but it also wanted to galvanise Frenchmen and Frenchwomen to fight for their freedom against Germany, using Annabelle's character Odette who turns against the Germans for murdering her parents and now supports the British, who she had previously blamed for the death of her brother. Apart from John Sutton and Annabelle, plus British actors playing Commandos in the opening scene, all the actors are Americans portraying French and German characters, and all the action is Fox Studio-based. Note the appeal to American movie theater-goers to buy US government War Bonds following the film's final credits.

THE BELLS GO DOWN

(Released: May 1943)

Released just one month after the 'drama-doc' "Fires Were Started", this is a fully fictionalised tribute to both the Auxiliary Fire Service and the London Fire Brigade during the first two days of the London Blitz in September 1940. Comic actor Tommy Trinder takes a lead role as a Cockney 'Ducker and Diver' who volunteers, with other familiar English actors of the time, to join the AFS. Trinder is Marmite, so some who watch the film might find it trying because Trinder has the same effect on audiences as does the savoury paste spread on some people's tastes. As with "Fires Were Started", the drone of Luftwaffe bombers are heard overhead London as the firemen fight the blazes and dodge the bombs exploding close by in "The Bells Go Down" (a wartime fire fighter's expression for the alarm bells being rung), but the Dorniers and Heinkels are never seen.

WE DIVE AT DAWN

(Released: May 1943)

A fictional film plot of a Royal Navy submarine's pursuit of an equally fictional German battleship, named the Brandenburg. The only appearance of aviation in the film is a brief shot of an unidentified floatplane acting the role of a German reconnaissance aircraft, seen from the submarine Captain's perspective through the periscope. The aircraft has more of the appearance of being a seaplane racer than a military type.

THE LIFE AND DEATH OF COLONEL BLIMP

(Released: June 1943)

This famous yet curious production by the increasingly imaginative Michael Powell/Emeric Pressburger teamship, which Churchill reportedly wanted to have banned because he thought it made the archetypal British Army officer look foolish (shows he failed to understand the film's message that old fashioned British values had been changed forever by World War Two), does not have any aviation in it.

UNDERCOVER

(Released: July 1943)

This rather embarrassingly bad dedication to the heroes of the Yugoslav Partizans in their fight against Nazi Occupation of their land - filmed in very obvious English locations and acted by very British Partizans and Germans - has only one shot of aircraft in it. This is an air-air of two CANT Z.1007 tri-motor bombers of the Italian Regia Aeronautica unloading their bombs at height, with a snow-covered mountain range in the background. The nearest Z.1007 can clearly be seen to be carrying the number '21' on the white fuselage band close to the tail; however, the number of the furthest Z.1007 is too faint to read.

The CANT Z.1007 did take part in the bombing campaign of the invasion of Yugoslavia by the Axis Forces during the Spring of 1941, so use of imagery of these two Regia Aeronautica bombers is appropriate in "Undercover". Presumably, the MoI obtained this imagery of these rarely-seen Italian bombers from newsreel footage released by the then Fascist government in Italy. The title of the film is not explained.

THE FLEMISH FARM

(Released: September 1943)

This is the kind of film that a 21st Century audience might find difficult to appreciate because the values it espouses and the motivation of the central character to return to his Nazi-Occupied country for the reason he chooses to do is unlikely to be considered logical today.

The essential plot has an Aeronautique Militaire Belge (AMB, or Belgian Air Force) fighter pilot, who has escaped to Britain before Belgium is overrun by the Wehrmacht Blitzkrieg on the Low Countries, being parachuted back into his now occupied country for the sole purpose of finding his squadron's standard. It was buried in secret by a fellow fighter pilot in a field close to a farm where the last Hawker Hurricanes of the Belgian Air Force are based before Belgium's surrender on 28th May 1940. This is the Flemish farm of the film's title.

The story is supposed to be based on fact but if it is, it is difficult to understand what part of the plot is factual and which is fiction. The difficulty with the film by today's standards is that it is scarcely credible that a Belgian fighter pilot, now serving with the Royal Air Force, would be allowed to parachute back into his country for the sole purpose of digging up and bringing back his squadron's flag. However, the film's message that people will go to great lengths to preserve a symbol that is inspirational and has real meaning for them would be plausible to most people in wartime. When the film was made in 1943 it served as a morale booster for British cinema audiences and as a tribute to the courage of a small nation like Belgium in the face of Nazi tyranny.

Although the Belgian fighter pilot's character is central to the film's story, in fact aviation itself only features during the first quarter of the plot and again very briefly in the finale. The opening scene-setting shot shows an obvious miniature of the Flemish farm in question, with model Hawker Hurricanes parked in front of it. A miniature set had to be used because clearly there was no Flemish-style farm building in Britain that was available for filming.

An acknowledgment is given at the beginning of the film for the support of the Belgian Government in Exile and of the Air Ministry. The latter made available four Hawker Hurricane Mk.II fighters to be flown in the production, at least two of them painted temporarily with AMB roundels and camouflage. One Hurricane is seen briefly with its RAF roundel in place on its fuselage and with its RAF squadron code letters showing faintly through the mock camouflage, but unfortunately they are unreadable due to the angle at which this Hurricane is filmed. All four of the Hurricanes had their serials painted over as well, so identification of individual aircraft is not possible.

It is believed that the Hurricanes were flown in the film by actual former AMB pilots, hence the acknowledgment to the Belgian Government. If so, they would be No.350 (Belgian) Squadron pilots, then current on Spitfires, but if they were Belgian fighter pilots some of them may have had experience of flying the Hawker Hurricane before Belgium fell and they escaped to Britain.

The Hurricanes are seen taking off amid shell bursts as the Wehrmacht forces close in on the farm, achieved with both the real Hurricanes and with the miniatures which are reasonably realistic SFX for the period. All four Hurricanes are ordered to fly to Beauvais to join with the French forces and are saluted by their Commanding Officer as they pass overhead. The Hurricanes are not seen again until the final act of the film, when the rescued standard is paraded before the Belgian pilots in England with the Hurricanes lined up as a back drop.

Aviation only features in "The Flemish Farm" again when the surviving Belgian fighter pilots make their way to Britain and join the RAF. To illustrate this, superimposed images of the pilots' faces are shown over an air-air shot of two Spitfire Mk.Vbs flying in formation, with the squadron code letters of SD-A and SD-Y clearly visible. These indicate they are No.501 Squadron aircraft and that the imagery is almost certainly an out-take from "The First of the Few" (1942). However, neither of these Spitfires appear in that film, so it is probable that an unused out-take has been inserted here.

What is annoying about this imagery of these two Spitfires is that it is obviously reversed. Why film editors of the time repeatedly, and quite obviously deliberately, committed this kind of goof is difficult to fathom today; copyright issues in using footage from a previous film production might be one explanation. It is understood that the repeated use of reversed imagery of Luftwaffe aircraft in British war films represented an intended insult to the enemy.

More Spitfire imagery appears soon after to represent the participation of Belgian Air Force fighter pilots in the Battle of Britain. First, stock MoI-released footage of nine Spitfires lined up with turning propellers and pilots running towards them is seen. This is the same MoI footage as used in "Dangerous Moonlight" of Spitfire Mk.Is of No.19 Squadron at RAF Duxford, only again it has been reversed by the editor of "The Flemish Farm". Next, a clear shot appears of Spitfire Mk.Vb coded NK-X of No.118 Squadron taking off, this time shown in correct order; again, this is an unused out-take from "The First of the Few", as is a shot of another unidentified Spitfire taking off and of a third Spitfire landing.

Returning to the Hurricanes in the film before we complete this review of aircraft seen in "The Flemish Farm", the events as depicted of the Hurricanes taking off to escape Wehrmacht shell fire definitely do not accord with historical fact. The Belgian Air Force lost nearly all of its Hawker Hurricanes it had on strength the day Hitler opened his Blitzkrieg on the Low Countries, 10th May 1940. Belgium had ordered 80 Hawker Hurricane Mk.Vs in 1938, to be built under licence by the Avions Fairey S A company (never fulfilled).

When the Wehrmacht invaded Belgium on 10th May 1940, 15 British-built Hurricane Mk.Is were in service with the Belgian Air Force. They equipped the 2nd Squadron of the 1st Group of the 2nd Air Regiment at Schaffen Air Base. Schaffen was bombed and strafed by Luftwaffe bombers and fighters on 10th May, setting fire to four Hurricanes and damaging six more. Another Hurricane was lost in a ground collision with a Gloster Gladiator during the confusion. Three Hurricanes escaped to Beauvechain Air Base. There is no record of them being used in combat, or of them escaping to France, as depicted in the film.

THE VOLUNTEER

(Public Pre-Release Showing: October 1943)

This little-known about short drama-documentary was written, produced and directed by Michael Powell and Emeric Pressburger for the Ministry of Information, expressly to encourage young men and women to volunteer to join the Fleet Air Arm. Apparently, following its general release to cinema in January 1944, it had the desired effect because the numbers of volunteers applying to join this air arm significantly increased.

The film opens with the following declaration, presented as thus: "This film was made with the cooperation of THE ROYAL NAVY and is dedicated to THE FLEET AIR ARM". It has to be said that, along with the flying elements from the documentary, "Find, Fix and Strike", used in "Ships With Wings" (1942), no

finer film record of the Fleet Air Arm in action during World War Two exists in the public domain. Short the film may be (just over 40 minutes), but it is long on naval aviation and offers the viewer unprecedented access aboard three wartime Royal Navy aircraft carriers, HMS Indomitable, HMS Formidable and HMS Argus.

Basically, the plot follows the fortunes of a young man who volunteers at the outset of World War Two to join the Royal Navy and who becomes an aircraft handler aboard an aircraft carrier. He shows courage under fire and the film ends with his investiture at Buckingham Palace when he is awarded the Distinguished Service Medal by HM The King. The young man in question is known as Alfred Davey, called simply 'Fred', and is played by jobbing actor, Pat McGrath.

However, the principal character of the plot is a certain Lieutenant Commander (Air) Ralph Richardson RNVR, as he is described in the title credits, who appears as himself - the already famous theatrical and Shakespearian actor - and who narrates much of the film's commentary. Richardson was a real-life volunteer who signed up with the Royal Navy Volunteer Reserve at the start of the War, beginning as a sub-Lieutenant with the Fleet Air Arm and rising to the rank of Lieutenant Commander. He earned himself the nickname, 'Pranger' Richardson - perhaps unfairly - after he made a forced landing in the Fairey Swordfish he was flying near Blackwater Pond, on Baddesley Common, not far from Southampton. Richardson had taken off in the Swordfish from Eastleigh Aerodrome on 22nd November 1939 and was flying to RNAS Worthy Down, near Winchester, Hampshire, when the 'Stringbag' got into engine trouble. Richardson was unhurt in the crash landing but his Telegraphist/Air Gunner received some injury.

Another, even more famous British film, stage and Shakespearian actor, Laurence Olivier no less, also volunteered to join the Fleet Air Arm after he returned from making such famous classics in Hollywood as "Wuthering Heights" (1939) and "Rebecca" (1939), reaching the rank of Lieutenant. He and Richardson served together at RNAS Worthy Down for a period; however, Olivier's service career did not last as long as Richardson's - after he had wrecked one aircraft and damaged two others just by taxying them, the Navy decided he might cause more attrition than the Luftwaffe could inflict and allowed Olivier to return to the London West End, where he could be more patriotically productive as an actor (Olivier makes a very brief cameo appearance in this film).

Richardson did not serve in the front-line aboard ship during the War but he did get to fly a number of aircraft types on second-line duties with the Fleet Air Arm. A short way into the body of the film we get to see what Richardson's naval career involved. But firstly we are shown Richardson fully made up as Othello before he takes the stage in the West End, on a day just before Great Britain declared war on Nazi Germany. This is where the link between the actor Richardson and Fred is revealed - Fred is Richardson's dresser, and a more ham-fisted one is hard to imagine. Fred has a talent for wrecking just about everything, grinning inanely all the time while doing so. Despite this, Fred is determined to join up if Britain is going to war and seeks Richardson's advice about which service to apply for.

Fred chooses the Royal Navy and is trained up as an aircraft handler. He becomes a very good one, despite his destructive talents as a theatrical dresser. This is the message that the MoI wanted the film to convey to its target audience, that no matter what skills - or lack of them - a volunteer had, the Royal Navy could turn him into a skilled tradesman performing vital crafts on behalf of the Fleet Air Arm. Fred and his fellow recruits are told by the CO of the Naval Training Establishment they have been sent to that the pilots fly the aircraft, but they - the aircraft handlers - own them and without their technical skills the War could not be won.

The film fast-forwards two years and Richardson is now a fully-fledged pilot and naval officer. He receives a letter from Fred who says he is pleased to hear that his 'guvnor' has joined the Fleet Air Arm and that he hopes one day to be able to service his aircraft. Richardson is filmed reading Fred's letter as he sits beneath the wing of an aircraft that some fitters are working on at the Royal Naval Air Station (RNAS) where Richardson is based. It is in this scene that the first aircraft to be seen in "The Volunteer" appears.

In the background and in front of an open hangar a Fairey Fulmar I fleet defence fighter taxyies into shot, noticeably with some of its engine cowling panels removed. It has no squadron markings but the letters LSR are carried on the fuselage ahead of the roundel. It passes beyond Richardson before this shot is cut.

The letters LSR give the clue as to the location of this scene. The first two letters 'LS' are the code for the RNAS which this Fulmar operates from. Almost certainly they stand for RNAS Lee-on-Solent in Hampshire, close to the south coast of England. The third letter 'R' is this aircraft's identifier within the unit it operates.

Confirmation that this scene is filmed at RNAS Lee-on-Solent is revealed by the fact that Lieutenant Commander (A) Ralph Richardson was stationed here during 1942 - along with Lieutenant Lawrence Olivier - so this scene must have been filmed at 'Lee' sometime during that year. Fulmar I coded LSR (its serial is not visible) was most likely on the strength of 739 Squadron, a multi-tasked, second-line unit operating a mixed bag of aircraft types, including the Fulmar, Swordfish, Avro Anson I, Airspeed Oxford and de Havilland DH.89A Dominie. Very likely Richardson flew with 739 Squadron, which was formed at RNAS Lee-on-Solent in 1942 and transferred to nearby RNAS Worthy Down in February 1943.

Soon afterwards Richardson is filmed flying "his" aircraft. It is a surprising and unusual type, a Vought OS2U-3 Kingfisher I observation floatplane, not usually associated with the Fleet Air Arm and footage of which in British military service is virtually unknown. The Vought Kingfisher that Richardson is meant to be flying carries no identification at all, being painted in standard Fleet Air Arm camouflage and grey undersides for aircraft operating close to or over land. No serial is visible. It is first seen filmed from a distance making a rather wobbly splash-down onto the sea, then surface taxiing across the water towards the slipway where it is being filmed from. Trolley wheels are attached beneath the large central float before this big beast of a 'plane is manhandled up

the ramp in what looks like a complicated and arduous method needed to bring the Kingfisher on land.

Richardson sits in the cockpit throughout this process before climbing out once the floatplane is secured. Whether Richardson actually flew the Vought Kingfisher in Fleet Air Arm service isn't known: it looks a challenging machine to fly. Under Lend-Lease, 100 Vought Kingfishers were delivered to the Fleet Air Arm in 1942. They were intended to be operated as catapult-launched observation floatplanes, the role they were designed for in the US Navy, aboard Armed Merchant Cruisers (AMCs) but noticeably they did not replace the long-serving Fairey Swordfish in this role. They were not popular with their aircrew and did not have a distinguished career in Fleet Air Arm service - the scene in which the example filmed for "The Volunteer" appears shows it to be an unwieldy and complicated piece of kit. All 100 Fleet Air Arm Vought Kingfishers were returned to the United States by 1944.

The scene where this Vought Kingfisher was filmed water taxiing and being manhandled up the slipway may be Sandbanks, beside Poole Harbour in Dorset, where 765 Squadron operated 13 examples of this floatplane on coastal patrol tasks. Sandbanks is not a million miles from Lee-on-Solent on the same coast.

In his narration, Richardson says his job in the Fleet Air Arm involves him making visits to aircraft carriers returned to home waters from active duty overseas: however, he does not say exactly what job it is he does aboard these carriers. He flies to the aircraft carrier training area off Scotland: the location is not revealed in the film. The aircraft he uses to fly there is a Supermarine Walrus I amphibian. Richardson is filmed at Lee-on-Solent running to catch the engine-running Walrus parked on the grass flight-line. As he does so, he passes two Grumman F-4F-4A Martlet II fighters parked next to the Walrus, also running their engines: the Martlet/Wildcat series of fleet defence fighters feature strongly in "The Volunteer", as we shall see.

Richardson climbs up into the Walrus's cockpit but enters the co-pilot/observer's position, not that of the pilot. Again, it is not explained if Richardson actually flew the Walrus during his wartime career.

The Walrus is filmed over-flying an estuary which may be close to Arbroath, as the Fleet Aircraft Carrier HMS Argus can be seen in shot moored in mid-stream. This long-serving 'flat top' was used for carrier landing and launching training by Fairey Swordfish pilot trainers based at nearby RNAS Arbroath from February 1943 onwards, after spending a good deal of time in the Med on Malta relief convoy duties and supporting the Operation Torch landings in Algeria and Tunisia. This would mean that the Walrus shots were probably filmed sometime in Spring 1943; it is seen taxiing up a slipway from the sea with self-evident spritely ease compared with the lumbering Vought Kingfisher.

Richardson takes a ship's lighter out to the aircraft carrier he is to visit. As he boards the lighter a metal film container is placed on board as well. The film inside it will prove very significant in "The Volunteer", especially in relation to aircraft action. The aircraft carrier which Richardson boards is HMS Indomitable, an Illustrious-Class

Fleet Aircraft Carrier commissioned in October 1941. Again, a Spring 1943 period is a likely time when filming aboard Indomitable took place, as the carrier was in home waters during this time working up at Scapa Flow before deployment to the Med in June. Scapa, then, is the likely location where filming took place aboard HMS Indomitable, possibly between April and May 1943.

This section of the film now covers a good deal of aircraft action. It is some of the best footage filmed anywhere aboard a British aircraft carrier in World War Two and is priceless in value for both the aviation and naval historian. Each piece of footage is described in sequential order as it appears:

a) A Grumman Martlet II, with wings folded, is brought up on deck by one of the aircraft lifts, while a Fairey Fulmar II is ranged behind it with wings fully spread. This footage shakes noticeably, presumably caused by vibrations from the ship's engines which would suggest the camera was filming from a fixed position.

b) A Vickers Supermarine Seafire Ib is brought up on the lift to the deck (the storyline has it that this is Fred's Seafire, he being a Naval Airman aircraft handler aboard this carrier).

c) Three Seafires are seen turning propellers on deck.

d) Vickers Supermarine Seafire IIc coded 8D takes off. The take off technique from the carrier's flight deck is very revealing to watch. Seafire IIc 8D is one of four Seafires grouped right at the stern end of the flight deck. As soon as the pilot opens the throttle he simultaneously pushes his stick forward, so that the tail lifts immediately the instant the Seafire starts to roll. No take off aids, such as catapult or RATOG (rocket- assisted take off gear), are used. The camera pans with the Seafire as it powers past its position, filming from the edge of the flight deck. What is noticeable is that, as the Seafire's tail passes out of shot, land can be seen beyond the flight deck. The low, flat kind of terrain visible is very suggestive of the Orkney Islands, where the natural harbour of Scapa Flow is located, the Royal Navy's main naval base during the War. The flat, calm water confirms that this location was well sheltered from the open sea and was thus ideal for aircraft deck landing and launch training.

An Online contributor to the Airfix Tribute Forum mentions Seafire IIc MB307 as carrying 8D codes of 807 Squadron. If so, this would give a time period of May 1943 for this and other shots of Seafires taking off being filmed, as it was in this month that 807 Squadron joined HMS Indomitable in preparation for the Sicily and Salerno landings. Seafire.IIc MB307 is recorded by the Spitfires.ukf.net Website as having joined 807 Squadron in May 1943 but it was only on strength for three months. It spent much of its wartime career with the RAE at Farnborough as a RATOG and catapult trials Seafire, conducting some of this work in 1944 off the carrier HMS Illustrious.

e) Vickers Supermarine Seafire IIc coded 8Y is next to roll in the same manner. Noticeably it carries its code with the number '8' ahead of the roundel and the letter 'Y' behind the roundel; Seafire IIc 8D had its number and letter placed together ahead of its roundel - inconsistent marking by the handlers.

f) A third Vickers Supermarine Seafire IIc powers forward for take off; its code is unreadable.

g) The fourth and final Vickers Supermarine Seafire IIc gets away in the same style as the previous three; again, its code is unreadable.

Note - the first three Seafires each have a single cannon fitted in the leading edge of each wing, whereas the fourth Seafire has no cannon fitted. The Seafire Mk.IIc variant was converted from the land-based Spitfire Mk.Vc and carried the same armament as the latter, comprising two 20mm Hispano Mk.II cannon and four .303in Browning machine guns. This weaponry is next seen being tested in live firing footage which follows.

h) Aerial gunnery training by the four Seafires. Cannon fire hits spurt up from the sea; a Seafire makes a low run over the sea, cannon fire erupting ahead of it; Richardson and other officers, along with the flight deck aircraft handlers, watch from the stern.

Richardson and Fred then converse, with Fred describing his experiences in action on the previous tour (the names of the places where the carrier was in action are spoken of indistinctly by McGrath as Fred, probably deliberately to avoid giving information away to the enemy).

j) The four Seafires suddenly run in low over the flight deck in Finger-Four formation, with the handlers watching in the foreground.

k) A Seafire IIc makes a fast, low pass alongside the carrier.

l) What is meant to be Fred's Seafire lands on. The landing technique is fascinating to watch: the Seafire bounces off the deck as its hook catches a wire, bringing it to a very sudden halt. The narrow undercarriage must have been under considerable strain and, not surprisingly, quite a few Seafires suffered undercarriage collapses during such a violent arrester technique. The pilot cuts back on the throttle as soon as his Seafire is hooked.

m) A Seafire IIc is manhandled by flight deck crew to the lift and is swung round a full 180 degrees before the lift descends, with the pilot remaining in the cockpit. Fred jumps onto the wing to speak to him as the lift goes down. There is no visible code on this Seafire IIc, which means it is not one of the four filmed taking off - a different Seafire IIc was obviously used for these shots.

n) Seafire Mk.IIc MB309/L appears in the next frame, acting as Fred's Seafire reaching the hangar aboard the carrier. This Seafire first flew on 8th January 1943 and was delivered three days later to No.15 MU. In March, it was allocated to 884 Squadron at Turnhouse. On 8th April 1943, MB309/L was flown into the crash barrier aboard training aircraft carrier HMS Argus but was undamaged. The very next day it repeated the same incident - it was flown by the same pilot on both occasions! Later in April, MB309 was allocated to 895 Squadron at Machrihanish but this Seafire went missing the same month whilst flying en route from Machrihanish to Donisbristle, with its pilot killed.

o) Seafire IIc MB309/L is again swung round 180 degrees when the lift reaches the floor and is then pushed back into the capacious hangar and parked. This variant of the Seafire did not have folding wings but does not appear to take up too much space in the hangar.

It is very likely that this hangar scene, and others filmed below deck among parked aircraft, were filmed aboard Argus, and not Indomitable. This would make sense because to have a film crew below deck in an aircraft carrier busy working up before its next deployment would not, to say the least, be desirable. MB309/L's record showing that it was aboard Argus in April 1943 suggests that the shots of it in the hangar were filmed on board this deck landing training carrier, where the film crew could have had more freedom in using ratings aboard ship as extras, which would not have been possible aboard a fully operational aircraft carrier. Furthermore, the hangar is almost empty, which would not have been the case on board Indomitable. MB309/L's record also appears to confirm that April 1943 was the month when this part of the filming took place.

It has to be stated that the aircraft carrier Richardson and Fred are aboard is not named in "The Volunteer". Richardson attends a film show for the ship's crew below deck. This is the film that was brought aboard along with Richardson and purports to show the carrier's last tour. It is, in fact, a mix of film taken aboard two aircraft carriers, Indomitable and her sister ship, HMS Formidable, together with footage filmed by Powell's and Pressburger's crew and MoI-provided imagery of attacks on British warships. Some of the footage aboard Formidable was filmed at sea by a camera team working for the Royal Navy Instructional Film Unit, while more footage taken aboard ship while the carrier was moored in Algiers and Gibraltar was filmed by members of the ship's own crew themselves.

While this film is shown a naval officer provides a running commentary of the scenes shown. Although his face is not seen, the voice of this officer would have been very familiar to British wartime cinema audiences. He is BBC radio commentator, Tommy Woodruffe, who, like Richardson, had joined up at the start of the war and attained the rank of Lieutenant Commander. Woodruffe's name is cemented in BBC folk lore for his live drunken commentary of the Royal Review of the Fleet off Spithead in 1937: he repeated over and over, "It'sh a wonderful shight. The Fleet'sh all lit up!", before being taken off air.

First, film taken on deck of Formidable arriving in the port of Algiers is seen, with five Seafires lined up nose to tail at the stern end. Various shots of deck sports follow, with one Seafire parked in the background. These shots taken in Algiers were obviously filmed shortly after the port fell to the Allies during the Operation Torch landings in North Africa during November 1942, with the French Vichy authorities now under Allied control.

After various shots of Algiers' famous, or infamous, Kasbah and of General de Gaulle arriving for a visit, the bulk of the film that follows is of aircraft launching from and being 'trapped' back on the flight deck. Many of these shots were filmed aboard Formidable and Argus, and are of excellent quality, providing unrivalled studies of the Fleet Air Arm operating off aircraft carriers in World War Two. The first couple of shots don't quite fit in with this style and standard, however - they are played backwards and show aircraft taking off from the carrier flight deck in reverse direction and upside down!

First to go, or rather to fly inverted backwards onto the deck, is a Fairey Swordfish coded 5Z: "We don't want the enemy to know we can do this!", quips Woodruffe. It is immediately followed by a second Swordfish, code obscured, performing the same inverted reverse-flying manoeuvre. Catcalls issue from the ratings in the

ship's audience to the matelot who is operating as projectionist, to get the film reel playing in the right order.

Next, and the right way up from now on, a Swordfish is filmed in the distance from the flight deck dropping a dummy torpedo during practice attack runs, turning away immediately the torp is released. A Fairey Albacore, the Swordfish's unloved and supposed successor, follows behind and releases its inert torpedo.

A Fairey Albacore, filmed from the carrier's island, lands on at the stern and is trapped. Two Seafires can be seen parked up on deck alongside, one coded 8F, while the other uncoded example is distinctive in being fitted with a Vokes tropical filter. The presence of an 807 Squadron Seafire indicates that this shot was filmed aboard HMS Indomitable and that the Albacore probably belonged to 831 Squadron.

A change of scene, with four Grumman F-4F-4B Wildcat IV fighters ranged on deck with their wings being unfolded. The lead Wildcat IV can be seen carrying the code 09-Z, marking it down as FN121 of 893 Squadron which embarked 10 Wildcat IVs aboard HMS Formidable in October 1942. They provided fighter protection for the Operation Torch landings the following month. The quality and style of imagery of these four Wildcat IVs noticeably differs from the other imagery shown in this part of the film, suggesting it was filmed at a different time and location, quite possibly soon after they embarked on Formidable as they carry standard Fleet Air Arm markings, whereas they swapped these for the combined FAA/US Navy markings of a single white star on a blue circle adopted by all British Torch naval fighters assigned for the North Africa landings. Also, this shot is the only one of 893 Squadron Wildcats; all other such Wildcats and Martlets seen in "The Volunteer" are from 888 Squadron.

The next shot is of Grumman F-4F-4A Martlet II, coded 07-B of 888 Squadron, being catapult launched off the bow flight deck. 888 Squadron were another Formidable-embarked squadron and it is their fighters which we see in "The Volunteer" from now on. The imagery of these Martlets is very clear and of very good quality. They are also filmed at more than one location and at different time periods, especially, as later shots show, that 888 Squadron converted from the Martlet II to the Wildcat IV, probably in early 1943. What is particularly noteworthy in these shots of 888 Squadron Martlet IIs, and of the preceding 893 Squadron Wildcat IVs, is that they carry a stylised digit 0 in their codes which have been painted as a white vertical oblong with a diagonal line running from the top right corner to the bottom left corner. This symbol was adopted by Fleet Air Arm Martlets and Wildcats during North Africa campaign operations in late 1942 and early 1943. It was applied to ensure the digit 0 was not mistaken for the letter O.

Martlet II 07-W is catapult launched next, followed by a third Martlet II whose code is unreadable. These shots are unique in clearly showing the earliest form of aircraft catapult launch system on a World War Two-era aircraft carrier in operation. They discount the description given on an Online Website about the earliest types of aircraft carrier catapult as only being operated athwartships (from the stern part of the deck, launching the aircraft away from the rear of the carrier) and being discontinued in use during the latter half of the War. The Martlets seen in this film are clearly being catapult launched from the flight deck over the bow of the carrier, during very calm sea conditions, it has to be said.

The catapult system looks extremely basic and simple compared with the highly sophisticated steam and electro-magnetic catapult launch systems used aboard US Navy aircraft carriers today. It is essentially a single groove in the flight deck stretching from almost the lip of the deck over the bow down no more than approximately 50 feet to a point behind, and to the left of, the bow aircraft lift. The Martlet sits on its main and tailwheel undercarriage astride a white line painted on either side of the groove. Ahead of these white lines, and slightly angled in on each side towards the catapult groove, are two narrow braces which are probably intended to counteract the Martlet's direction in its initial forward momentum following release, in the event of the aircraft swinging either to port or to starboard, thus keeping it straight on track as it is catapulted. The Martlet is held at full power and the pilot instantly raises the tail as soon as his aircraft starts to move. The launch run looks remarkably short and the Martlet is actually airborne just before it reaches the bow.

Freeze-frame analysis appears to show that the Martlet is attached to the catapult by a short strop or cable below its rear fuselage, which detaches at a point three-quarters of the way along the catapult groove. The instant this connecting apparatus is detached the Martlet becomes airborne. It is at least five feet into the air as it crosses the bow end of the flight deck. The little fighter flies away, gear down, with no impediment and with no discernable drop in height towards the sea. Flight deck handlers immediately rush to prepare for the next launch.

What is noticeable is that throughout the launch process the pilot sits in the open in his aircraft's cockpit, with the canopy hood pushed right back. Obviously this would be his only chance of escape if things went pear-shaped, either on deck or into the sea.

The shots of these Grumman Martlets being catapulted off deck appear to have been filmed in the aircraft carrier training area within the surrounds of Scapa Flow, as landscape corresponding to that part of Scotland comes clearly into view as each Martlet flies away. Interestingly, in his commentary Woodruffe describes them as "training Martlets". This appears to confirm that these shots of 888 Squadron's Martlets being catapult launched were filmed at a different, and probably earlier, time and location than much of the footage which follows.

The next shot is of Vokes-fitted Vickers Supermarine Seafire Ib MK345/K of 885 Squadron taking off conventionally from the flight deck of Formidable. This was probably filmed at sea in the Med during Formidable's tour of operations there in early 1943. This take off shot is interesting because, as the Seafire reaches the bow end of the flight deck, steam rising to the left of the fighter is blown by its slipstream. The steam is shown to be rising from exactly the position where the catapult is placed, which is unmanned in this shot. This is interesting because it is widely accepted that the steam-powered aircraft carrier catapult launch system was not developed until the early 1950s. What we seem to

be seeing here in "The Volunteer" is evidence that a rudimentary form of steam catapult was used to launch Fleet Air Arm fighters aboard HMS Formidable, certainly up to early 1943.

Seafire Ib MK345 began life as Spitfire Vb AR445, which was part of a batch converted into Seafires for the Fleet Air Arm by Air Services Training at Hamble, being first delivered to No.76 MU on 10th July 1942. It was shipped on 20th July and was on strength with 801 Squadron by January 1943. One month later it was coded 'K' with 885 Squadron aboard Formidable, confirming the time period when this shot of it taking off from the carrier was filmed. Seafire Ib MK345 was an accident-prone aircraft, or its pilots certainly were: it made an emergency landing on 24th May 1943 with oil obscuring its windscreen, it ran into the crash barrier aboard ship on 27th June, then, after transferring to 761 Squadron at RNAS Henstridge - a satellite to RNAS Yeovilton - it ran into a petrol bowser on 9th May 1944 which fortunately did not explode. It was last heard of taxying into a vehicle at St Merryn in Cornwall on 21st November 1945, suffering wing damage, while operating with 748 Squadron.

Back to more Martlet or Wildcat action, with a Martlet II landing on while oil stains run like rivers across the flight deck. This shot cuts immediately to Grumman F-4F-4B Wildcat IV FN123/07-J of 888 Squadron tipping right up onto its nose after being trapped, then bouncing back down again onto its undercarriage. The worst visible damage it suffers are two bent props. This shot proves what a tough little beast the Grumman Wildcat was. The pilot sits nonchantly in his open cockpit throughout the drama, while aircraft handlers rush to his assistance. The film editor has cut these two shots together to create the appearance that it is the same aircraft landing on, then tipping up, but they are definitely of two different aircraft filmed on entirely separate occasions: the first shot is grainy, the second is clear, and there are no oil stains on the flight deck.

The next two shots are of a pranged Fairey Albacore on its belly, surrounded by handlers and with its propeller and spinner removed. Then, a fine study taken from the 'Island' looking towards the stern with a Vokes-fitted Seafire Ib being waved off, while Seafire Ib MK345/K and another example further out coded 'G' are seen parked on the edge of the flight deck, sitting on their main undercarriage but with their tailwheels attached to outriggers, which means that the whole of their rear fuselages and tails are held jutting out over the sea. MK345 has had its Vokes filter panel removed while it is being worked on by handlers. The long tail hook dangling from the Seafire Ib being waved off can be clearly seen in this shot, lowered from under the fuselage at a point midway between the aft wing join and the tail.

In the next shot, of another Seafire Ib without Vokes fitted landing on, MK345/K and its G-coded colleague have been joined by a Seafire IIc parked between them, carrying 885's alternative code beginning with '06-' and the identifying letter 'B'. The Seafire which lands on does so in very hairy fashion as its hook takes the wire, swinging and bouncing wildly - no wonder so many Seafires broke their narrow-track undercarriage when being trapped on deck, such a design being very vulnerable to breakages during aircraft carrier operations. Aircraft handlers immediately rush from either side, one to release the Seafire's hook while two more run to seize hold of either wing-tip. The code of this Seafire cannot be read.

The sight of a Petty Officer running out with an inflated weather balloon in his arms, which he tosses into the air for anti-aircraft gunnery practice, draws loud laughter from the ship's crew watching the film.

The film moves on to portray Formidable's arrival at Gibraltar. Filmed from the carrier's flight deck as it passes the beacon at the harbour's entrance, three RAF Coastal Command Consolidated Catalina flying boats can be seen moored together in the distance below The Rock. There is a fine study of two King George V-Class battleships moored together in line astern - according to Woodruffe in his commentary, one of them is HMS Howe. With the ship's company standing to attention on the flight deck, five Seafires are lined up nose-to-tail at the stern end; the next shot shows Formidable moored to a jetty, with a Seafire and two Fairey Albacore torpedo bombers parked up at the bow end.

The film editor then cuts into footage of Formidable's rear-mounted Quick Firing 4.5 inch guns firing a salvo, as if in salute; however, the sea's movement past the stern shows that the ship is in motion, and not in harbour. Parked right next to these guns is Seafire IIc MB182/06-F of 885 Squadron. This Seafire was a Spitfire Vc conversion by Air Services Training at Hamble, making its first flight on 12th September 1942. It was delivered to No.15 MU three days later, then joined 885 Squadron in October when the squadron was based at Machrihanish. It remained on strength with 885 Squadron until November 1943, after which its career and fate are unknown.

885 Squadron carried '06-' codes during the Operation Torch period.

More shots of Formidable's QF 4.5 inch guns and anti-aircraft 'pom-poms' pounding away follow, then a distant shot of a high-flying aircraft with tracer fire streaming up at it appears. It has the appearance of a Heinkel He.111. A warship pouring smoke is obscured by a massive explosion close to it in the sea, then a Seafire coded 'K' (MK345/K?), and a Martlet coded 'D' (probably 07-D) parked right behind it, appear. Aircrew watch as Seafire IIc MB182/06-F takes off conventionally, but most notably its arrestor hook dangles down and scrapes along the flight deck as the fighter passes by. 'Pom-poms' pound away, with a battleship in the background from which smoke pours upwards, suggesting a direct hit - probably the same warship seen earlier. A Seafire makes a very violent-looking landing on deck: "Wants ammo", comments Woodruffe. Then a shot of what looks like three Martlets, chasing one after the other, flying above flak.

Aircraft handlers run to arm up and refuel Seafire IIc coded 06-A of 885 Squadron, its serial hidden by its tailplane. Another high-flying unidentified aircraft is fired upon by the ship's anti-aircraft guns. What looks like two bomb bursts, but which may be depth charges exploding, erupt close to the ship from which they are filmed. Another Seafire makes a wild landing: "Here's Vickers back, what's wrong?" asks Woodruffe. Two more bombs burst close to a ship almost out of shot to the left of the screen.

In what is obviously a staged sequence Fred is seen speaking with the pilot of the Seafire which has just landed with a broken airscrew. The pilot, who looks frankly ridiculous in his shorts and with his knobbly knees, orders Fred to go below and get another airscrew straightaway. A third enemy aircraft, looking like a Junkers Ju.88, is seen diving through flak.

What is seen next is a superb shot of Seafire IIc coded 06-A being catapulted off the bow. The difference between this shot and those seen earlier of the Martlets being catapulted is that the cradle which attaches the Seafire to the cat is clearly visible beneath the rear fuselage. Another difference is that this cradle enables the Seafire to be held in position prior to launch with its tailwheel lifted off the deck, so that the Seafire is poised on its two main wheels inside each brace either side of the catapult's groove in the deck. The Seafire departs the cradle just before it reaches the end of the groove and is airborne by a few feet as it passes over the bow, flying smoothly away with gear down. This cradle system is noticeably different from the strop system used by the Martlets and hints at a more sophisticated method of catapult launch. Also, the Seafire is being catapulted at sea, not in a sheltered estuary area as was the case with the Martlets; steaming ahead of the carrier as the Seafire is launched is the destroyer acting as plane-guard, in the event of the pilot needing rescuing should anything go wrong. This catapult launch shot shows just how advanced the aircraft carrier catapult system had become by 1943. For the aviation and naval historian it is a priceless record of this early method of what became one of Britain's most valuable contributions to naval sea and air power.

Fred and his mates bring a replacement airscrew up on the hangar lift. This shot cuts to that of a Junkers Ju.87 Stuka releasing its bomb in a dive, one of the best shots of a Stuka doing so and one not seen in any other film before. "Look out!", shouts Woodruffe, as the aircraft handlers with the airscrew dive for cover. "I dropped the camera", exclaims Woodruffe, as the picture goes askew amid smoke. Medics with a stretcher rush to assist casualties among the aircraft handlers - obviously staged for the camera by Powell's and Pressburger's 2nd Unit. Despite being wounded in the shoulder, Fred rushes to assist with the fitting of the replacement airscrew onto a Vokes-equipped Seafire - continuity problem here, because the Seafire which landed with a broken prop was not fitted with a Vokes filter.

The 'pom-poms' pound away behind Fred, with good reason because an enemy aircraft is coming in straight for the carrier. It is an Italian Regia Aeronautica Savoia-Marchetti SM.79II Sparveiro, filmed from the deck of a ship as the tri-motor torpedo bomber heads straight towards the camera through tracer fire. The cameraman has to be congratulated for holding his camera so steady as the SM.79II passes right over his position, with its Regia Aeronautica markings clearly visible and the long, silver tube of a torpedo attached to its port-side under fuselage – the starboard-side position is empty, showing that this Sparveiro had already launched one torp. The bravery of the pilot in command has to be admired, while this footage has to be among the best filmed anywhere of an actual air attack at sea. If this footage was taken during Operation Pedestal, the vital relief convoy that broke the siege of Malta, then this SM.79II, the torpedo bomber variant, would have come from either 109 or 132 Gruppo of the Regia Aeronautica, as both these units lost an aircraft in attacks on the convoy on 12th August 1942.

A Seafire takes off conventionally from the flight deck: "Old Vickers gets back into it, after all", enthuses Woodruffe. Yes, but he has left his Vokes filter behind - maybe he didn't need it. The Seafire flies off into the sun, before the film appropriately cuts to a shot of presumably HMS Formidable steaming through a choppy sea: "All over. There she is, still there", Woodruffe proudly proclaims amid cheers from the ship's crew as the film ends with a V-sign on to the screen by the projectionist, enthusiastically returned en masse by his shipmates.

The moral of the story is that Richardson, by watching the film aboard ship, realises that Fred has shown courage in action while wounded and goes in search of him below deck to show his appreciation. He finds Fred asleep in his hammock beside "his" Seafire and decides not to disturb him. Later, in the finale of "The Volunteer", Richardson comes across Fred outside Buckingham Palace after the courageous former bumbling theatrical actor's dresser has been awarded the DSM by HM KGVI.

As stated earlier, these below deck hangar shots were probably filmed either on HMS Argus or perhaps HMS Indomitable, but the latter is unlikely if the sister-ship to Formidable was in the throes of working up to go to sea. As Richardson walks through the hangar in search of Fred, he passes three Grumman Martlets and a Fairey Swordfish, all parked with their wings folded. Richardson pauses to give a pat to the folded wing of the Swordfish, quite probably because it was a type he knew well and in which he had earned his nickname, 'Pranger' Richardson. The Seafire in front of which Fred is sleeping is the last aircraft we see in "The Volunteer" and is probably MB309/L, as it is parked in the same position in which we last saw it. If so, this would confirm that the below-deck hangar shots were filmed aboard HMS Argus.

Again, we have a short, 40-odd minute propaganda 'drama-doc' which is chock full of some of the most fascinating imagery of British military aircraft at war, in this case all of them Fleet Air Arm types. "The Volunteer" may be a difficult film to find, but is well worth the effort by the aviation and naval historian to track down because the footage it contains of aircraft at sea is unobtainable from any other source. It is one of the most valuable of British World War Two war films to have in one's collection.

MILLIONS LIKE US

(Released: November 1943)

It might sound like a contradiction in terms to describe a British war film as heartwarming, but "Millions Like Us" comes as close as it is possible to achieve such an accolade. As its title suggests, it is about the very people who would have gone to watch this film in the cinema when Britain was completing its fourth year at war with Germany. It follows the fortunes of a family who,

like everyone else, is deeply affected and split apart by the War.

In particular, it focuses on the youngest of three sisters, Celia Crowson (played by the very heartwarmingly attractive Patricia Roc), who is called up to work in an aircraft factory in the Midlands, very much against her wishes as she dreams of joining the WAAFs or the WRNS, a far more glamorous way to serve her country, she believes, than turning out thousands of steel bracing tube sockets on the factory floor. In her dreams, she sees herself as a young WAAF officer helping a Spitfire pilot to strap into his cockpit. Beyond is a line of Spitfires, shown on a studio backcloth, with the nearest clearly bearing the code letters of 'WX-', thus confirming that these are Spitfire Mk.Vs of No.302 (City of Poznan) Polish Fighter Squadron; in total, six Spitfire Mk.Vs are seen in the line.

Earlier, during a brief episode in the Battle of Britain, an unidentified single-engined aircraft is seen diving vertically in the distance, portraying a Luftwaffe fighter being shot down. The type is too distant and the film print too old to allow for a clear identification.

The aircraft factory in which Celia has been sent to work is actually the Castle Bromwich Aircraft Factory, run by Vickers Armstrong, although its name and location are never mentioned in the film, so as not to give information away to the enemy. The nearby city of 'Stockford' is fiction for Birmingham. Castle Bromwich, of course, was the principal centre of Spitfire production and we get sight of sub-assemblies of a few of the many thousands of R J Mitchell's finest produced at this famous wartime factory. We are also shown an engine mounting being moved into place on the port wing of a four-engined bomber; as Castle Bromwich also turned out Lancasters from 1943 onwards, presumably it is a Lancaster we are seeing under assembly here.

We have to say presumably, because almost immediately after this shot the completed bomber is seen being towed out of a hangar. Except it is not a Lancaster; it is a Short Stirling. As location filming for "Millions Like Us" was mostly carried out in the Midlands, the most likely aircraft factory we are seeing in this shot is that of Cofton Hackett, south of Birmingham, an off-shoot of the famous Austin Motors Longbridge plant. Austin Aero built Stirling bombers at Cofton Hackett after Shorts moved its production away from Rochester in Kent, its factory there assembling Stirlings having been badly bombed by the Luftwaffe early in the Battle of Britain.

The Stirling Mk.I we see in shot is possibly being towed out of the Flight Shed at Austin Aero's flying ground at Cofton Hackett: the Flight Shed still existed into the Eighties, although flying from there had long since ceased post-War. The Stirling itself is not identifiable as its serial does not appear in shot. Whether it is the same aircraft or not, we next see a Stirling Mk.I taxying forward, again unidentifiable due to its serial not being shown (neither Stirling carries any code letters, so they are almost certainly new production aircraft). Finally, we see a fine shot of a Stirling Mk.I taking off from what does not look like an operational RAF air station. It heads right for the camera, which seems to be located part way down the runway - the Stirling only lifts off just as it reaches the camera position, which must have put a few years onto the cameraman, as the bomber's starboard wheel can have just missed him by no more than five feet!

The Short Stirling is to feature prominently in "Millions Like Us", as Celia falls for a young air gunner called Fred Blake, who is on Stirlings at a nearby bomber base (played by a very young and rather spotty Gordon Jackson, who was in a protected occupation as a draughtsman with Rolls Royce in Glasgow at the time). In fact, by the time of the release of "Millions Like Us" in November 1943, the Stirling was already being withdrawn from front-line service with RAF Bomber Command, it being succeeded by the Avro Lancaster and the Handley Page Halifax.

"Millions Like Us" is very much a realistic social study of life in wartime Britain and, as such, is of considerable value for historians looking to find what life was like for ordinary folk of the period. It is also a sympathetic portrayal of the diverse characters in the film played by many fine British actors of the War years. But our interest is in the aviation aspects of the story, which shows the relationship developing between Celia and Fred between his training flights and his first bomber Ops on the Stirling. The formations of Stirlings departing on Ops is depicted by fairly obvious, but not ineffective, SFX art work.

However, when Fred departs on his fatal mission soon after his marriage to Celia, it isn't Stirlings we see lined up turning props but 12 Avro Lancasters on a darkened airfield. Fred and his fellow crew members are seen boarding their aircraft, which, due to the circular windows in the fuselage, is clearly not a Lancaster. The code letter 'O' next to the fuselage roundel stands out in full view, while the first half of the serial number of 'W74--' appears on the right hand side of the screen. A process of elimination reveals that serials beginning with a 'W' prefix followed by numbers in the '7426 - 7475' range were all applied to Short Stirling Is. But when "Millions Like Us" was in production, many Stirling Is were being converted into troop transport Stirling IVs. It seems likely that Gainsborough Studios, the film production company, were given the use of one of the Short Stirling Mk.IV conversions at Cofton Hackett to film in this scene.

Fred's bomber taking off, though, is not a Stirling but an Avro Lancaster departing off a grass airfield. This presumably was a stock shot supplied by the Ministry of Information. Another MoI stock shot which immediately follows is of an Avro Manchester flying off into the distance, the Lancaster's far less successful predecessor. And with it goes the last actual shot of a real aircraft in "Millions Like Us", a moving and enjoyable film which ends with an all-round sing-song in the aircraft factory's canteen that the 1943 cinema audience would have joined in with. The feeling of unity in wartime Britain is very successfully conveyed by co-directors and co-scriptwriters, Sidney Gilliat and Frank Launder.

From the aviation historian's perspective, however, "Millions Like Us" is noteworthy for being the first feature film to show imagery of the Avro Lancaster.

THE ADVENTURES OF TARTU

(Released: November 1943)

This rather far-fetched story of a British Army Captain from the Royal Engineers being sent on a sabotage mission to Nazi Occupied Czechoslovakia was probably a hit with audiences in the War, largely due to its star performer being the highly popular Robert Donat (he of "The 39 Steps", 1935, Alfred Hitchcock film fame). His saboteur is meant to be British of Romanian extraction, hence he adopts the identity of a deceased Captain named Jan Tartu from the Romanian Iron Guard, a part of the Romanian military which sided with the Nazis. He is parachuted into Romania and is then smuggled into Czechoslovakia via Hungary.

Tartu's mission is to gain entry to an underground chemical weapons factory in Pilsen, Bohemia, and blow it up. He is chosen for this mission because he was a chemist before the War and is an explosives expert. He has to memorise the formula of a poison gas that the Nazis are developing in Pilsen, which they intend to place in the warheads of bombs and then drop them over England (perhaps he could have also got the formula for Pilsner beer while he was about it!).

Aviation features in only a limited way in "The Adventures of Tartu", but what does appear is very significant. In the early part of the film Tartu is flown from England to Romania, where he is dropped by parachute. Stock footage from the 1942 RAF Film Production Unit newsreel, "Fly Away Peter", of a Bristol Blenheim Mk.IV taking off from a coastal airfield on an RAF Ferry Command delivery flight overseas is used to depict Tartu's departure from England. The film is riddled with exaggerated and flawed events and elements within its plot, and this is one of them: Romania was far beyond the range of a Blenheim Mk.IV. Tartu is seen in the cockpit behind the pilot which, due to its size and somewhat unusual layout with glazed windows, is clearly not that of a Blenheim Mk.IV, while Tartu's exit through a hatch in the floor is also inaccurate for this aircraft. However, there is more to this scene than is apparent at this stage of the plot, as we shall discover in due course.

Aviation does not appear again in the film until right at the end of the story, but this is where enthusiasts and historians are likely to really sit up and take notice of this unusual wartime action drama. After his adventures with the Czech Resistance movement and his romantic involvement with a female member of that group, Tartu successfully penetrates the chemical weapons factory and blows it up. He and his newfound love now have to escape from Czechoslovakia. They choose the very unlikely method of stealing a Luftwaffe aeroplane and flying it to Malta, escaping from a pursuing Luftwaffe fighter in the process – a real "Boy's Own" end to the story.

With amazing ease they break into the Luftwaffe airfield and make for the nearest aircraft. What will fascinate the aviation enthusiast here is that the aircraft in question is a genuine Luftwaffe bomber from the RAF's No.1426 (Enemy Aircraft)

Flight, and one that we have seen before in a British war film. It is Junkers Ju.88A-5 HM509, as was seen bombing HMS Torrin in "In Which We Serve" (1942). Tartu holds the Luftwaffe aircrew at bay while one of the Resistance fighters, who happens to be a pilot, climbs aboard the Ju.88 and starts its engines. His Czech girlfriend also gets on board as it taxies away, with Donat as Tartu running beside it and climbing through a hatch underneath the fuselage. As the Ju.88 accelerates past the camera the letters 'MK' can be seen faintly through its RAF paint scheme beside the temporarily-applied starboard fuselage German Balkenkreuze, confirming it is Ju.88A-5 M2+MK (Werke Nr 6073), originally of II/Kuestenfliegergruppe 106 before it landed at RAF Chivenor, Devon, on 26th November 1941, a victim of the 'Meacon' navigational deception system.

Visible in the background during this sequence are three Short Stirling bomber/transports lined up on what is a noticeably muddy and sparse airfield on very flat terrain, with virtually no infrastructure in view apart from the featureless block building that Donat is running from to reach the Ju.88. When the Ju.88 takes off, it is doing so from an all-grass airfield, again without any infrastructure visible and filmed on what was a very grey winter's day. As the Ju.88 passes the camera position a Lockheed Hudson is briefly seen parked in front of a small building adjacent to the trees. This take off shot allows for study of the ungainly undercarriage retraction system employed by the Ju.88.

What is also of note is that the same glazed cockpit interior appears in this escape scene as it did for the Blenheim Mk.IV earlier in the film, confirming that the Ju.88's cockpit was used to depict the interior of both aircraft. It is a rare privilege indeed to see inside the cockpit of a real wartime Luftwaffe aircraft in a British war film, and especially that of a Junkers Ju.88. Such footage is unlikely to be found anywhere else.

As the Ju.88 takes off a Luftwaffe fighter starts engines in readiness to pursue it. This is another captured member of the RAF's No.1426 (Enemy Aircraft) Flight and, like the Ju.88, an extremely rare example to be seen in a war film made in Britain, a Messerschmitt Bf.110C-4 Zerstorer. This Bf.110C-4 was 5F+CM (Werke Nr 2177) of Luftwaffe reconnaissance outfit 4(F)/14, the same Zerstorer seen in "Ferry Pilot" (1941) with the RAF serial AX772.

In the film, a pilot is seen climbing into Bf.110C-4 AX772's cockpit; the Zerstorer is then seen turning and taxying for take-off. Luftwaffe Balkenkreuzen have been re-applied and its RAF serial painted over, but it is clearly AX772 that is being used, not just because of its very obvious RAF camouflage scheme, but due to the fact that all other Bf.110s captured and flown by the RAF and the RAE were night fighter variants, whereas this example is definitely an early model day fighter as evidenced by the twin cannon in its nose.

Just before the end of the War, Bf.110C-4 AX772 was handed over to the Central Fighter Establishment's own Enemy Aircraft Flight at RAF Tangmere in January 1945; then it was stored at No.47 Maintenance Unit at Sealand from October that year until

it was trashed, along with most other captured and redundant Axis Powers aircraft, in a huge dump at RAF Collyweston in 1947.

It is likely that the scenes with the Ju.88A-5 and the Bf.110C-4 were filmed at RAF Collyweston, as No.1426 (Enemy Aircraft) Flight had re-located there from RAF Duxford by the time "The Adventures of Tartu" went into production in 1943. RAF Collyweston was a satellite airfield to RAF Wittering in Cambridgeshire and when the bases were conjoined they formed the largest and longest all-grass airfield in Britain. That certainly fits the images of the airfield seen in this film.

BIG PACK

(Released: 1944)

Filmed between April 1942 and February 1943, this drama-documentary produced by the RAF Film Production Unit focuses on the enormous organisation that was RAF Maintenance Command. As it states in the opening blurb to the film, "Everything the Royal Air Force requires in any part of the world to carry out its vast bombing raids, its huge fighter sweeps, its endless ocean patrols - from a Lancaster bomber to an Airman's sock - has to be stored, packed and delivered by Maintenance Command. 60,000 demands a day - 6 tons of stores a minute - 2,750,000 items a month - that is the routine".

As with all such 'drama-docs', "Big Pack" uses service personnel in their actual roles within Maintenance Command to play all parts in the film. The intention is to show to the wartime British cinema audience how willingly and efficiently these men and women of all ranks could undertake the supply of aircraft, weapons, ammunition, clothing, vehicles and all other items for a major operation inside 14 days of their normal everyday tasks. The fictional Operation Storm for which they are undertaking these supply tasks is actually a cover name for Operation Torch, the Allied landings in North Africa in late 1942.

The opening shot has a map of the British Isles with markers of various Maintenance Units and Depots dotted all over it. The camera zooms in on the marker for Maintenance Command HQ in The Midlands. As it does so, the image of an air-air shot of a Lockheed Hudson is superimposed onto the marker, then the map dissolves as the Hudson breaks away from the camera aircraft. Shots within the Hudson show the pilot lowering the undercarriage and the flaps as he prepares for landing. More shots from over his shoulder and through the cabin window show the Hudson landing at a large RAF air station. When it rolls to a stop, it is noticeable that the Hudson's glazed nose has a very clear, opaque frontage, while the dorsal turret is stripped of its guns. Almost certainly this was one of the RAF Film Production Unit's own Hudsons, adapted for air-air filming. The serial is N7211, making it a Hudson I.

The Hudson has brought a senior officer within Maintenance Command to HQ, carrying instructions to get the supply task for

Operation Storm underway. As he is driven off in a staff car, an Armstrong Whitworth Whitley can be seen in the background, while in the distance a Bristol Blenheim IV takes off.

Throughout the film the various sections within Maintenance Command are shown fulfilling their roles. For the purposes of this book, we will focus on the aircraft side. An urgent requirement for Operation Storm is the provision of 70 Hurricanes - yes, 70 Hurricanes - fitted with modifications within 14 days. The mods are interesting to see, as they involve the fitment of long-range fuel tanks under the wings. Film footage or pictures of Hurricanes fitted with these tanks are very rare, so "Big Pack" should be of special interest to the aviation historian and modeller for this reason alone. 'Mac', the very Scottish Flight Lieutenant in charge of arranging the delivery of the 70 Hurricanes with the fitted mods, is seen explaining the need for all-day, all-night, round-the-clock work to the Flight Sergeant in charge of the aircraft Fitters who will have to carry it all out. They stand in front of a partly stripped-down Hawker Hurricane in a hangar with fuel tanks fitted, as they discuss the task ahead.

Hawker Aircraft Company has the responsibility of providing the Hurricanes, while Air Transport Auxiliary (ATA) pilots will fly them to No.223 Maintenance Unit (MU). The Ferry Pool HQ prepares to fly 30 Hurricanes per day from "Barchester", a cover name for Hawkers' plant at Langley, Berkshire, to No.223 MU, also a fictional MU number.

One of the most fascinating elements of "Big Pack" is the section that shows the underground ammunition depot at No.303 MU, plus the complex railway system that supports it. Bombs of all sizes are stored in tunnels carved into hills and are carted out on small trains for loading onto larger railway carriages. The Equipment Unit is shown full of aircraft sections: wings, engine cowlings, tyres everywhere. Fuel tanks and air filters have to be loaded onto a Wellington and flown to No.223 MU - "and rightaway", says the Flight Sergeant in charge.

Vickers Wellington III BJ959 is seen landing at No.223 MU, carrying the equipment load. This Wellington is not a bomber, as its lack of guns in its front and tail turrets attest; until the introduction of the C-47 Dakota in large numbers, equipment supply was flown in Wellingtons and Whitleys converted into transport aircraft. Equipment was loaded into and extracted from a large hatch in the bottom of the fuselage underneath the cockpit. Beyond the Wellington as it lands can be seen an array of parked aircraft, including an Avro Anson I, a Whitley, and a group of eight Spitfires, as well as two more Wellingtons.

Cannon-armed Hawker Hurricane IIc HV745 lands, clearly fitted with the mods needed which comprise a long-range fuel tank under each wing, twin cannon in each wing leading edge and a tropical air filter below the nose - obviously it is going somewhere hot. Behind it a Spitfire Mk.II lands, while a tank-equipped Hurricane II runs in. 'Mac', standing in front of a parked Hurricane II with chalked job checks on the fuselage below the cockpit, tells 'Flight' to, "Get these mod sets collected and checked right away".

The ATA ferry pilot who has delivered Hurricane HV745 dismounts from a Hurricane II which is clearly not HV745, because while it has the fuel tanks fitted, it is devoid of the air filter and cannon. No serial of this Hurricane is shown. The ATA pilot is a tall, slim, fair-haired young woman who says cheerfully to 'Mac', "Hello, I've brought your Hurricane". She is told she has delivered one of the 30 Hurricanes today.

Hurricane II HV863 taxyies in, fitted with the air filter and fuel tank mods but not yet with cannon. It passes another Hurricane II likewise fitted with the air filter and fuel tanks. A wider shot is meant to show the same Hurricane HV863 taxying to join a group of four Hurricanes already parked up, including Hurricane II HW267, but in fact it is a different Hurricane because although it has fuel tanks fitted, it is without an air filter. Ah, the devil is in the detail of these continuity goofs, so treacherously revealed by freeze-frame analysis. But the 1944 cinema audience did not have the luxury of such technology to expose such goofs, and probably would not have cared much anyway.

As the days progress, more and more aircraft are prepared. A Handley Page Halifax Mk.II bomber is seen undergoing preparations to its bomb bay; a Vickers Wellington is loaded up in a hangar; two Hurricanes are worked on. We get a good close-up look at a fuel tank and an air filter being attached to one Hurricane, while Hurricane IIc HV340 has Fitters swarming all over it like locusts. Four different Hurricanes are towed or pushed out of the maintenance workshops, with their new mods attached - unfortunately, their serials do not appear in shot. Hurricane IIc HV551 is seen taking off on a test flight. A Turkish Website lists this Hurricane being taken on charge by the Turkish Air Force on 31st January 1943, becoming 2740. This indicates that much of the Hurricane footage was filmed sometime in 1942.

An air-air of three Hurricanes airborne in a loose echelon port is superimposed on the map of Britain. Another Hurricane taxyies back in past two of its brethren, then parks up. A shot in one of the workshops shows both male and female Fitters working on various Hawker Hurricane sub-assemblies. A Hurricane is progressively dismantled, in preparation for shipping to wherever Operation Storm is headed (because bearskin coats are among the many items ordered, the assumption is that it is Russia). 'Mac' tells 'Flight' that he shan't be sorry to see the last of these Hurricanes.

A message comes through to 'Mac' that all Storm Hurricanes have to get airborne by 12-00 hours before fog closes in and prevents their departure from No.44 MU "packing unit". He rushes to assemble as many ferry pilots as he can.

At this point in the film a sudden change takes place. Suddenly, and with no explanation, the scene changes to a large-scale seaborne invasion, with a narrator speaking as if we know exactly what is going on (up till now, there has been no narrator). Judging by the clean footage of landing craft and of the beach assault, this is film of a rehearsal and not of an actual landing on an enemy coast. An air-air shot of six Spitfires in RAF Fighter Command camouflage and markings was obviously filmed during a period well before this rehearsed assault was staged - their squadron codes are not visible. Another air-air shows 12 Spitfires in a packed formation, the six we saw just before being part of this total. The film then cuts to another air-air, this time of four Spitfires, two of which are fitted with Vokes tropical air filters. Three out of the four are painted in desert sand-brown camouflage, but the Spitfire nearest the camera is wearing green-grey camou, a curious difference. Irritatingly, the film editor has got this imagery the wrong way round, as the reversed code letter 'B' on the nearest Spitfire attests. A study through the mirror reveals that this is Spitfire LF.Mk.IX MJ223, which was taken on charge in February 1944. Therefore, the editor of "Big Pack" has acquired use of what was for him very recent imagery of these four Spitfires, all of which are cannon-armed, low-flying, ground-attack LF.Mk.IXs, flying in loose formation near to a flat coastline.

Spitfire LF.IX MJ223 had a short service life and died in action. It served with Nos.132, 412 and 453 Squadrons between 15th June 1944 and 29th September 1944, when it was shot down by flak over Ostend.

The staged beachhead assault continues, with troops and vehicles pouring ashore from landing craft. Another air-air appears, this time of two North American P-51A Mustang II Army Co-Operation fighter-bombers in close formation, the nearest to the camera bearing the code letter 'X'. Then a ground controller informs the fighter-bombers of an enemy tank formation's map co-ordinates and directs them towards the targets. When the film cuts back to the fighter-bombers, we now see a cannon-armed Hawker Hurricane IV air-air: what is noticeable about this Hurricane is that it is painted in desert camouflage and has single detachable 40mm Vickers S cannon under each wing, not the twin installed cannon on the Hurricane IIs we saw at No.223 MU. Another air-air shows a pair of similarly configured Hawker Hurricane IIs flying over desert-like terrain. We then get a good study close-up of another such Hawker Hurricane II breaking away from the camera to begin its attack, its underwing cannon and filter under the nose clearly visible (unfortunately, the tail fin shadow obscures its serial, while there is no sign of a code letter). Next we are shown a dramatic study of a Hurricane II strafing at low-level with its cannon; this is obviously a staged shot, and not an actual combat sequence, but it is nonetheless impressive to watch. The Hurricane was a superb gun platform, and here's the proof in "Big Pack".

Next, another air-air of the same 12 Spitfires seen before, this time in parade formation of three echelons port; then a cut to a close-up of two Spitfire LF.IXs wearing the 'WR-' codes of No.40 Squadron (SAAF), the nearest to the camera being WR-D and with WR-C floating beyond. Although the latter's serial is visible, it is unreadable because of the reduced quality of the imagery. The camera is closed right up on the pilot in the nearest Spitfire, who has pulled his cockpit canopy hood back so that his moustachioed face can be clearly seen. Very annoyingly, the film editor has again cut in this footage in reverse, as can obviously be seen by the letters shown the wrong way round. How a so-called professional film editor can make such a goof is beyond guessing, unless he was under pressure to cut the film within a short space of time and simply did not check the result.

The ground controller reports 15 bandits on the way in. A formation of 11 aircraft filmed from a long distance off purports to show this raid; although not easy to confirm, the distant fighters look like Spitfires. Rough stock footage of a Ju.87 Stuka diving clashes with the cleaner imagery of most of the film. A destroyer sailing beyond depth charges it has fired, detonating with huge bursts of spray, represent the Stuka's attack upon it. Various stock shots of naval anti-aircraft guns firing follow. The well-used stock shot of two Ju.87 Stukas in formation, with the nearest one carrying the codes TK+HG breaking into a dive inside of the other bearing GU+AC, appears.

The Stuka footage cuts immediately to a dramatic air-air of a group of eight Spitfire Mk.Vc (Trop) cannon-armed fighters breaking close to the camera into a dive attack. All eight are in desert camou and have Vokes filters fitted. The Spitfire Mk.Vc nearest the camera carries the codes AN-V, but although its serial is clearly in view, very infuriatingly the code letter 'A' is painted over half of it - the serial that is visible is 'BR4--'. Beyond, other Spitfires identifiable are AN-Y, AN-W and AN-T. These codes make them Spitfires of No.417 Squadron (RCAF), which operated in the North African, Mediterranean and Balkan theaters of war. No.417 received the Spitfire Vc from February 1943 onwards, so this film footage was obviously taken after that time, indicative of the film editor using a whole mix of stock footage covering varying periods of the War to create this air battle and seaborne assault sequence. And guess what - he's gone and reversed the imagery again, with all the code letters very clearly reading backwards! How goof-laden can this film editor be?

Battle of Britain-era stock footage follows of nine Spitfires peeling off in classic dive attack mode. Solo Spitfires make runs at the camera. Crown Film Unit footage of Spitfire Mk.IIa P8441 in hot pursuit of Messerschmitt Bf.110C-4 AX772, as first seen in "Ferry Pilot" (1941), not surprisingly appears, confirming the value of the Crown Film Unit in setting up this mock dog-fight scenario for use in war films. Meanwhile, the beachhead assault continues. Sailors on the beach duck down as a P-51A Mustang II swings by very low overhead. More shots of Bf.110C-4 AX772 weaving about appear, plus the same Reich Propaganda Ministry footage of a Messerschmitt Bf.110C used in "Ferry Pilot" breaking away from the camera. Likewise, the imagery from that same film of a Spitfire making a run at the tail of a Heinkel He.111 follows, which strongly confirms that the editor simply lifted these images straight from "Ferry Pilot" and cut them into "Big Pack". The archive footage of a single Vokes filter-equipped Spitfire Vc rolling over onto its back makes an impressive study.

New to the eye is gun-camera footage of the shoot-down of a Messerschmitt Bf.110 fitted with long-range under-wing fuel tanks - the starboard tank has been hit and gushes flame and smoke, into which the pursuing fighter flies. A Stuka dives at full power into the ground and explodes - nobody felt sorry for a Stuka crew getting wiped out. Six Spitfires fly away in victory. An observer calls control and informs him, "Bandits on the run".

Aerial imagery of contemporary Luftwaffe aircraft was, by 1944, obviously plentifully available.

Then suddenly the film switches back to the Ammunition Depot, with large bombs being carefully roped down into a line of trucks before being shuttled out of the cave to a waiting train. This footage of the underground weapons stores is really priceless. The scene then changes to a dockyard, where equipment for Operation Storm is to be loaded onto merchant ships.

All this makes the insertion of the beachhead assault and air battle into the middle of the Big Pack's preparations even more strange and difficult to understand. In the author's opinion, the film editor simply made a massive goof and got what should have been the film's finale inserted into completely the wrong place. If he put it in intentionally where it is shown in the film, then only he and the director know the reason for doing so because in terms of the film's plot it makes no sense.

The dockyard comes under air attack, with some rather obvious miniatures of ships being bombed used for this scene. Three out-takes of captured Junkers Ju.88A-5 M2+MK from "In Which We Serve" (1942) are used to depict the raiders. An unidentified aircraft is seen in archive footage crashing into the sea. Apparently a truck carrying some of the bearskin coats took a hit. The driver is told not to worry, they may not be needed after all. The bearskin coats requirement was a deception, to create the impression the convoy was headed north when in fact it was going south. This was a genuine deception as part of Operation Torch, to disguise from 'Jerry' the real purpose of the invasion fleet.

The film ends with BBC radio announcer, John Snagge, informing listeners of the landings in North Africa. Archive footage has Arab tribesmen gathered together while a Spitfire Mk.Vc in the background has an engine change in the desert; another tribesman rides on his horse past a parked Hawker Hurricane II. The final shot is of a formation of seven Hawker Hurricane IIs, fitted with fuel tanks and filters, making an impressive low fly-past.

"Big Pack" is good value for money as a study of RAF Maintenance Command in action, with many fascinating shots of aircraft - especially Hawker Hurricanes - that are unique to this film. One has to overlook the misplaced invasion sequence and the stilted acting, and accept it as a valuable resource of British aviation history.

WESTERN APPROACHES

(Released: 1944)

Of even greater value to the historian is this extraordinary drama-documentary filmed in real wartime conditions aboard an Atlantic convoy and dedicated to the men of the Merchant Navy. Genuine seamen act their natural roles, some of whom had experienced being sunk more than once. Made by the Crown Film Unit between 1942 and 1943, "Western Approaches" stands out not just for its gritty realism and its real, fascinating characters, but because it was filmed by cinematographer Jack Cardiff in Technicolor, extremely rare for a British war film of the World War Two era.

Although this 'drama-doc' is centred on the ordeal of shipwrecked mariners adrift in their lifeboat in the Western Approaches - an area of the Atlantic west of the coast of Ireland through which all convoys had to pass, and therefore a prime hunting ground for German U-Boats - aviation enthusiasts and historians will still find it a richly rewarding film to watch and to have in their collection. Aviation itself plays its part, albeit in a minor role, but nonetheless a vitally important one.

In particular, early on in the film, we see a cargo ship named Leander taking on board at New York Lend-Lease materiel that include tanks, locomotives and aircraft. Most fascinating to see is the entire fuselage section, minus wings and tail but including, nose, engine and cockpit, of a Grumman F-6F Hellcat in Fleet Air Arm markings being swung aboard ship by crane. Four more Grumman Hellcats, all wrapped in what looks like polythene coverings, are shown stored together on deck - they are without their tail sections and propellers, but have their wings attached. Imagery of how these American fighters were shipped to Britain by convoy is very difficult to find, let alone to be seen in colour, so these shots make "Western Approaches" a very valuable film to own.

One interesting scene reveals a problem which occurred on actual convoys. The Focke Wulf FW.200 Condor was one of the few Luftwaffe aircraft types that had the range to probe far out into the Atlantic. They could be a menace to convoys themselves, but their primary role was to track Allied shipping and relay their positions to waiting U-Boats. As a US Navy officer points out to the assembled conference of Merchant Navy and Royal Navy Captains being briefed before the convoy sails from New York, American Flying Fortresses would be providing anti-U-Boat patrols from the sixth day out onwards. The trouble is, some Allied gunners on board ships have fired on Flying Fortresses in the past, mistaking them for the four-engined FW.200 Condors. So, the US Navy officer reminds the Captains in a long, drawn out drawl, please be sure you know the difference between a Flying Fortress and a "Farker Woolf".

For the first 600 miles air cover would be provided by Lockheed Hudsons. A sequence shows the convoy commander speaking with the pilot of a Lockheed Hudson by radio, who is filmed in the cockpit, but whether this is inside a real Hudson is difficult to tell.

The only actual aircraft seen flying in "Western Approaches" is a Consolidated PBY-5A Catalina, filmed from a ship and seen flashing a message in Morse Code from its port side observation blister. Almost certainly it was an RAF Coastal Command Catalina that is used here.

The drama of the finale, based apparently on a real-life wartime incident when a U-Boat used a lifeboat with survivors on board from a sinking as a decoy to target any ship which came to their rescue, is astonishingly realistic and believable. Virtually the whole of the production was filmed either on the high seas or off Holyhead, using Merchant Navy seamen with no acting experience and a Royal Dutch Navy Captain playing the U-Boat commander. "Western Approaches" was a huge success with the British cinema audience when it was released in 1944. As a production alone, it stands by itself and really puts the viewer right into the heart of the Battle of the Atlantic. Buy it, even though the aviation elements are limited in content.

CANDLELIGHT IN ALGIERS

(Released: March 1944)

Produced by the British Aviation Pictures company, the only thing remotely connected with aviation in this World War Two spy romp based (very) loosely on the Operation Torch landings in North Africa is archive footage of six Douglas DB-7 Havoc bombers over-flying a military parade celebrating the successful capture of Tunis. They are possibly former French Vichy Government-owned Havocs in North Africa that had been captured and commandeered by the Allies.

THE WAY AHEAD

(Released: June 1944)

A much admired war film that began life as a British Army training film for new recruits and wartime conscripts, entitled "The New Lot", directed by Carol Reed ("The Third Man", 1949) from a script by author Eric Ambler and playwright/actor/author Peter Ustinov, which was then expanded into a full-length feature film starring David Niven. Its plot involves Niven as an Army Lieutenant being given the responsibility of licking into shape a disparate and reluctant group of British civilians who have been called up against their will for wartime Army service. The film was intended to bolster public morale and to encourage more volunteers for the war effort, as well as to provide an aid to the British Army in the training of newly enlisted men. It received considerable praise at the time for Reed's, Ambler's and Ustinov's humane and sympathetic treatment of men struggling to adapt to war, after being forced to leave their safe, mundane, civilian lives behind.

"The Way Ahead" is also claimed to be the inspiration behind the much-loved BBC-TV sitcom series in the Sixties, "Dad's Army", about a similar bunch of misfits recruited into the Home Guard.

There is little in the way of aviation in "The Way Ahead", but what does appear is significant and portrays a type of aircraft not represented in many other British war films. This is one of the earliest versions of the famous North American P-51 Mustang, designated simply the North American Mustang in RAF service. The Allison V-1710-39-engined Mustang's record of service in the RAF has been much overshadowed by its world-beating Packard V-1650-7 Merlin-powered successor, the P-51D, especially due to the latter's exploits with the USAAF as a long-range escort fighter for the Eighth Air Force's B-17s and B-24s over Germany. But when it first entered RAF service – to a British pre-War specification – in January 1942, the Mustang was used as a low-level, fighter reconnaissance aircraft in the Army Co-Operation role. Initially equipped with the lower-powered Mustang I/Ia variants, the RAF's Army Co-Operation Squadrons worked the new American warplane up into a very effective close support aircraft.

A single example of the Mustang appears in "The Way Ahead", performing its fast, low-level, Army support duty in concert with tanks and troop formations on exercise. As the tanks wheel past and troop-carrying trucks follow up behind, the Mustang makes repeated low, fast runs over the columns, ready to be called into action with cannon fire should contact be made with the enemy.

The film of this military exercise used in "The Way Ahead" is that of a demonstration of British Army combined troop, artillery and armoured manoeuvres, conducted on 22nd February 1943, and released by the Ministry of Information to newsreel and film production companies for instructional, promotional and publicity purposes. The Mustang cannot be identified, but there is an excellent still photo issued at the time to the press by the MoI of the same Mustang in this demonstration running in very low over two light tanks.

There is little else concerning aviation in "The Way Ahead", except towards the end of the film when the troops, now finally welded into a close-knit and effective group of soldiers under Niven's command, are facing up to the Afrika Korps in the Tunisian desert. They come under aerial bombardment from the Luftwaffe supporting the Afrika Korps' attack. Archive footage of six Heinkel He.111s in formation is used to depict this, plus an air-air of a single He.111 filmed from the dorsal turret of a companion He.111 flying in very close formation with it over what looks distinctly like European terrain. No unit code letters or badge are visible in shot of this He.111. The version shown appears to be an He.111H-1. Imagery of Luftwaffe aircraft were now more readily obtainable from a variety of sources, not least from that released by the Reich Propaganda Ministry itself, so that more realistic use could be made of such footage in British war films.

FOR THOSE IN PERIL

(Released: June 1944)

This Ealing Studios film's title clearly refers to the hymn, "For those in peril on the sea". In this case, "those" are RAF pilots who have been shot down or have crash landed in the sea near to the British shoreline and who need immediate rescue. This is provided by the RAF Air Sea Rescue service, using a fleet of high-powered motor launches to reach downed pilots as fast as possible before the enemy or hypothermia gets them first. The film provides a fine study of these high-speed launches (HSLs) - powered by Rolls Royce Merlin engines - in action.

The script is written by Richard Hillary, an RAF fighter pilot who was shot down in the Battle of Britain and suffered severe facial burns; his exploits were made famous in his own book, "The Last Enemy", recently made into a TV film. Director is Charles Crichton, who would go on to make a number of famous films at Ealing Studios, while the producer is the prolific Michael Balcon. Basically, the plot revolves around a disgruntled Pilot Officer who has failed to make the grade as a pilot and who has been assigned to Air Sea Rescue instead. He thinks this is demeaning compared with flying, but has his eyes opened and his reputation enhanced when he has to take part in a dramatic rescue of downed flyers trapped in their inflatable dinghy amid sea mines and who are being menaced by an armed German trawler and low-level fighters.

The film opens during the Battle of Britain - 23rd August 1940, in fact - with a Lifeguard observation post on the cliffs of Dover reporting 200 enemy aircraft passing inland. To represent the enemy, the same archive footage filmed air-air of two Heinkel He.111H bombers flying in close echelon starboard to a third He.111H, that was first used in "Ferry Pilot" (1941), then subsequently in a number of other films, appears - the closest He.111H carries the code letters '--+BL'. The film then cuts to an out-take from "Ferry Pilot" of Spitfire PR.V N3111 flying in formation with the second Spitfire Ia that ATA pilots were meant to be ferrying in that film, to portray Spitfires flying to intercept the enemy.

Spitfire pilot 'Blue One' calls, "Tally Ho, Tally Ho!", then dives into the attack. A silhouetted Spitfire Mk.I is seen diving down, not very good stock imagery, before cutting to Spitfire Mk.IIa P8441 in pursuit of captured Messerschmitt Bf.110C-4 AX772, the now familiar out-take of the dog-fight first seen in "Ferry Pilot". A view of Bf.110C-4 AX772 we haven't seen before, swinging round in a tight turn, clearly shows its RAF roundels. For once, it is allowed to be the victor in the air battle, portraying a Luftwaffe Zerstorer attacking a Spitfire. As it comes into the attack, the tail of the RAF camera aircraft from which the former Crown Film Unit filmed this staged aerial dog-fight for its archive, is briefly seen in view: although not possible to confirm, it does appear to be that of a Bristol Blenheim IV, as previously supposed.

The Spitfire takes hits and the pilot calls up that he is bailing out. An early model Spitfire cockpit is used in the studio for this sequence; what is noticeable is that the panel behind the cockpit hood has been removed, not exactly making the 'Spit' safe for flight! Archive footage of an aircraft, larger than a Spitfire and streaming white smoke, is filmed from the ground while the fighter that has got it pulls away - it has the appearance of a Spitfire, despite being not much more than a speck against white cloud, while the stricken aircraft approximates to a Dornier Do.17.

The Lifeguard post alerts the Lifeboat Station that an airman has bailed out into the sea five miles off the coast. A lifeboat is sent while the pilot's comrade circles over him in his Spitfire. An archive air-air of a Spitfire Mk.IIa is used to depict this aircraft, whose serial is visible but because of camera shake is unreadable. It has no code letters. The Spitfire continues to circle the stricken pilot in the sea, but despite the lifeboat's crew's best efforts they are too late - he is dead by the time they reach him. The film's message is clear: what is needed is a much more effective Air Sea Rescue service.

The film fast-forwards to February 1944. The bulk of the plot focuses on the interaction between the principal characters, the enthusiastic leadership of Flight Lieutenant Murray (played by David Farrar) contrasting with the decidedly unenthusiastic Pilot Officer Rawlings. He certainly doesn't enjoy his first trip out to sea in rough conditions. The main stars, however, are the HSLs, powering through the waves - they alone make this film of special interest.

Aviation does not appear again until nearly 30 minutes into the film. When it does, it makes a dramatic entrance. Very clear imagery of a Douglas Boston Mk.II powering along at low-level, filmed from an accompanying Boston, shows the aggressive lines of this American-built, day-attack bomber. It carries the code letters 'OA-' forward of the fuselage roundel, identifying it as being a No.342 (Free French) Squadron Boston; these Free French Bostons carried their individual code letter separately ahead of the wing on the forward fuselage under the cockpit, which in this shot is obscured from view by the starboard engine. The serial is also too difficult to read. Forest flashes past underneath this bomber as it surges aggressively towards its target (see "The Way to the Stars", 1945, for a more detailed look at No.342 (Free French) Squadron Bostons, as they feature strongly in that film).

Another shot shows two Bostons skimming low over the sea; as they are in silhouette and, judging by their long shadows, filmed late in the day, identifying their unit isn't possible. Unlike the previous No.342 Squadron Boston with its open rear gun at the back of the cockpit cabin, these two Bostons have fared-over upper rear fuselage gun positions, making them later model Boston Mk.IIIs. Three more Boston Mk.IIs appear, again of No.342 (Free French) Squadron, flying low over the sea and almost certainly filmed on the same sortie as the previous 342 Squadron shot used in this sequence.

The intention is to create the impression that the Bostons are over-flying the HSLs en route to France on a bombing mission. "Hope they make it alright", comments Murray, "Weather looks pretty duff on the other side".

The bombing attack is depicted by archive footage released by the MoI of a low-level raid on a railway line, filmed looking back at the smoke rising from the bomb bursts and with a Douglas Marauder following in the distance. The film then cuts to a close-up of a Boston cockpit air-air, with a flight of eight Spitfires at some distance above it, flying escort. After a quick look at an in-cockpit shot of a Boston pilot, the next view is of six Douglas Bostons in parade formation flying low overhead the camera - this shot bears a strong resemblance to the same formation of six Bostons over-flying a military parade in Tunisia at the start of "Candlelight in Algeria" (1944), which, if correct, would make them ex-Vichy French Douglas DB-7 Havocs that were pressed into Allied service after their capture in North Africa.

A dog-fight ensues, using a mixture of archive and stock material along with a not-too-convincing miniature of a Messerschmitt Bf.109. Crown Film Unit footage of Messerschmitt Bf.110C-4 AX772 appears again, along with MoI-owned grainy archive material of three Spitfires flying in the classic line astern tactic adopted by RAF Fighter Command in the early stages of the Battle of Britain. An even more unconvincing miniature of a Boston being shot down is reported by a Spitfire pilot, giving the co-ordinates for the ditched bomber's location. Air Sea Rescue is alerted.

Now we reach one of the best pieces of aviation in "For Those In Peril". The call goes out to launch a seaplane to rescue the Boston's crew. "Walrus X stroke three seven four to proceed to position", orders the ASR controller. Immediately the film cuts to a close-up of a large cartoon of a white, fat and happy-looking walrus. Suddenly the walrus starts to move! Only it's not moving by itself, it is sliding on a large piece of metal to the left of the picture. Then, what is really happening emerges into view

- the cartoon walrus is painted on the nose of its namesake, a magnificent Supermarine Walrus amphibian which roars past the camera and, with surprising agility for such an ungainly pusher bi-plane, lifts nimbly off and immediately banks into a stately turn to starboard. A lovely shot, even in black-and-white, of beautiful English countryside on a fine sunny day emerges into view as the Walrus sweeps round in a majestic turn at low-level before passing in front of a very distinctive landmark. The spires of Lancing College, unmistakeably imposing in the Spring of 1944 just as they are today, slide past in the background as the Walrus glides round, giving us instantly the clue as to the location of this shot: Shoreham Airport on the West Sussex coast. The Walrus has taken off from Shoreham Airport and is seen swinging round to over-fly a scene that is not-too-dissimilar today nearly 70 years on.

Shoreham Airport was home to No.277 Air Sea Rescue Squadron for the latter part of the War and it is undoubtedly this unit that provided the Spitfires and Walrus appearing in "For Those In Peril". The Airport is still much the same today as it was in World War Two, with its classic art deco air terminal building and historic hangars of pre-War design.

The Walrus used in the film is Walrus Ia W2797. It later went on to serve with No.624 Squadron and was struck off charge in November 1945. The film has a superb shot of the Walrus flying fast and low over Shoreham-by-Sea's St Mary de Haura Church and Westminster Bank, as English a scene as is possible to imagine (no low flying rules in those days!). It is surprising to see just how fast the Walrus could fly.

Two HSLs speeding to pick up the Boston's crew in their life raft are over-flown by a Spitfire from No.277 Squadron; this squadron was changing from the Spitfire Mk.IIa to the Mk.Vb when "For Those In Peril" was being filmed at Shoreham and off Eastbourne in Spring 1944.

The Boston crew in their life raft are floating in a minefield close to the French shoreline and are covered by sea mist. The Spitfire continues to provide cover for the HSLs and is in direct radio contact with them. The Walrus spots the downed crew when the mist lifts but its pilot is unaware that the life raft has drifted into a minefield. When it lands on, it strikes a mine and is blown up, achieved through the use of convincing SFX. "What damned bad luck", comments the Boston's skipper.

A sea battle ensues between the HSLs and a German armed trawler, which is eventually seen off when two Royal Navy Rescue Motor Launches (RMLs) arrive on the scene. The Boston crew are taken on board an HSL. One of the HSLs has been hit and is taken in tow by the other. Just to make life interesting, they are shelled by a shore battery as they manoeuvre their way out of the minefield. Then they are attacked by low flying aircraft. They are meant to be Luftwaffe fighters, but the first to run in to attack is clearly a Spitfire, which the audience would have spotted straightaway. The second fighter is a North American Mustang II, flying at no more than 20 feet above the waves. Another shot has three Mustang IIs coming in head-on with no margin for error for the lead aircraft, so low is it above the sea and aiming straight for the camera. When these RAF Army Co-

Operation pilots attacked at low-level over land, they must surely have been mowing the grass at the same time as strafing the enemy.

Murray has bought it, so Rawlings has to take over and make sure he gets the HSLs and their crew back to safety. He decides that serving with the Air Sea Rescue service isn't such a boring posting after all.

"For Those In Peril" uses both professional actors and actual crewmen of RAF high speed launches, making it a mixture of both film drama and documentary, but more of the former than the latter. It is often compared with "The Sea Shall Not Have Them" (1954), which has a very similar plot and theme, suggesting that the later film was significantly influenced by this earlier wartime production.

TWO THOUSAND WOMEN

(Released: November 1944)

This very original story about British women interned by the Wehrmacht after the fall of France is both a moving and entertaining war film, with a very mixed bag of female characters and well acted by most of the leading performers; however, there are no aircraft in "Two Thousand Women", even though part of the plot involves helping three RAF airmen to escape capture by the Germans.

THE WAY TO THE STARS

(Released: June 1945)

This production was released to the cinema in the month following Nazi Germany's surrender to the Allies in the West. It was, in fact, the first British war film to be seen by a British public in peacetime following the six-year long conflict with the Wehrmacht forces. By this time war fatigue had definitely set in and the desire for Hollywood-made vaudeville spectaculars of the "Anchors Aweigh" and "Ziegfield Follies" kind were now finding greater favour with the British cinema-going public, who were wanting to look ahead to a more hopeful future, rather than look back over the dark years of war. However, that did not stop "The Way To The Stars" from becoming a very successful film in its time.

"The Way To The Stars" is a well made, well acted film, directed by Anthony Asquith from a script by playwright Terence Rattigan, and with some notable British actors starring in it, such as Michael Redgrave as an RAF Flight Lieutenant and the irrepressible John Mills, who had already by then become a welcome, household face through making so many war films. It tells the story of a succession of characters from both the Royal Air Force and the United States Army Air Force who are stationed at the fictional RAF Halfpenny Field air station during various periods in the War, and the effect they have on the lives of the people living locally, especially those who are associated with the Golden Lion Inn in the village of Shepley close by.

The title is a play on the Royal Air Force's own motto, "Per Ardua, Ad Astra": "Through Striving, To The Stars". It also references a familiar poem written by an RAF Intelligence Officer, John Pudney, during an air raid in 1941, entitled "For Johnny", which was published in a newspaper and includes the lines: "Better by far, For Johnnie-the-bright-star". Referring to an RAF pilot who has been lost in action and who has joined the stars, the film's title also relates to two pilots in the story who were given the same poem and who come to lose their own lives. Although not intended to be morbid, the title could be interpreted as reflecting the inevitable fate that so many wartime pilots experienced.

There is very little action in "The Way To The Stars", apart from a Luftwaffe air raid on RAF Halfpenny Field when John Mills's character arrives to take up a posting with a Bristol Blenheim outfit, No.720 Squadron. RAF Catterick in Yorkshire plays the part of RAF Halfpenny Field, while nearby Bedale represents the village of Shepley, first seen when five of No.720 Squadron's Blenheims roar overhead the main street while departing for a raid on Calais.

During the course of the film, told in three parts covering periods during 1940, 1942 and 1944, various characters come and go, as do the aircraft they operate which are seen departing on missions and returning, but never in action themselves. All of the aircraft in the film are genuine wartime representatives of types flown by the RAF and the USAAF.

First to be seen is an Avro Anson Mk.I, serialled R9647, flying into RAF Halfpenny Field over two Bristol Blenheim Mk.Is at dispersal. By the time the film was made most Anson Is had been disposed of, with ten squadrons remaining in 1945 out of a total of 54 RAF squadrons that had operated the type. Two of those squadrons were based overseas, so Anson I R9647 could only have come from the eight remaining in Britain: Nos.24, 116, 147, 187, 192, 437, 567 and 575 Squadrons. The majority of these squadrons used the Anson I as a 'hack' transport, as it was being replaced in the communications squadrons by its more modern successor, the Anson C.XIX. Anson I R9647 bears no squadron code letters, which suggests that it had been demoted to 'hack' status. However, R9647 clearly had once had an offensive role at some point in its career because it sports the large dorsal gun turret (bereft of its Lewis machine gun, though) that many early Anson GR.Mk.Is were equipped with.

The Anson is bringing Pilot Officer Peter Penrose, played by John Mills, a "15 hour sprog on Blenheims" from an Operational Training Unit, to his first posting. He is introduced to Flight Lieutenant David Archdale, played by Michael Redgrave, the first of the two pilots fated to fulfil the poem's and the film title's message. Within minutes of Penrose's arrival, Halfpenny Field is being bombed by the Luftwaffe. The airfield is defended by a Flight of three Hawker Hurricanes, which are seen 'Scrambling' in 'Vic' formation; in the film's plot, one of the Hurricanes fails to return.

By the time "The Way To The Stars" was being made the Hawker Hurricane had long been withdrawn from front-line RAF Fighter Command squadrons. The RAF's top-scoring fighter aircraft in the Battle of Britain was now being used only

on second-line duties (except in Burma, where it was still being operated as a ground-attack aircraft against Japanese forces), re-assigned to a host of specialised training flights and OTUs. They were effectively operated as aggressor aircraft, to use today's military terminology to describe friendly fighters which act as 'bad guys' for pilots to train against: the RAF terminology of the time was fighter affiliation. The three Hurricanes flown in "The Way To The Stars" are fighter affiliation aircraft.

They are Hawker Hurricane Mk.IIc and Mk.IV variants, and come from two different units. Leading the three-ship is a Hurricane IIc carrying the codes HQ-H (the serials are not readable as the Hurricanes are filmed from a distance). 'HQ-' are the code letters for No.56 Operational Training Unit, a former Hurricane OTU until 1943 when it was disbanded. It was reformed in December 1944 as a Hawker Typhoon and Hawker Tempest OTU at RAF Milfield, and appears to have taken on a number of Hurricane IIc's for fighter affiliation tasks to test out the ground-attack Typhoon and Tempest pilots.

The other two Hurricanes carry the codes 3K-H (closest to the camera) and 3K-C (furthest away): 3K-H is a later model Hurricane LF.IV, while 3K-C is another Hurricane Mk.IIc. Both are from No.1695 Bomber (Defence) Training Flight, based at RAF Dalton in North Yorkshire. No.1695 BDTF was a Royal Canadian Air Force outfit within RAF Bomber Command, which qualified bomber aircrews for three RCAF Handley Page Halifax squadrons stationed at nearby RAF Topcliffe; the two Hurricanes were on strength with No.1695 BDTF as fighter affiliation types and are being flown in the film by their Canadian pilots.

After the Luftwaffe attack has passed over the two surviving Hurricanes perform very low beat-ups and victory rolls, prompting the Squadron CO, played by Trevor Howard in one of his first main speaking roles, to say in disgust, "Line shoot! These fighter types, you know: top button undone, victory rolls – bad show, I think".

The Blenheim squadron Penrose has joined is engaged in mounting daily attacks on invasion barge concentrations at Calais. Penrose is sent up on an air experience flight in his Blenheim, inspiring the comment from the CO as he takes off, "Well, he managed to miss the control tower". The squadron then departs on its mission against the invasion barges, from which the CO fails to return. Archdale takes over as 'Boss' and refuses to make Penrose operational because, with only 15 hours on type, "you can't fly a Blenheim to save your life". It's a disappointing start for the over-enthusiastic Penrose.

The Blenheims are the real point of interest here. A film showing five Bristol Blenheim Mk.Is is extremely rare. These particular Blenheim Is are a curiosity because by the time this film was in production, the Blenheim in all its versions was out of service with the RAF. The Blenheim Mk.I itself was obsolescent at the outset of the War; five years later it had been withdrawn from all operations. So from where were these Blenheim Is sourced for the film?

Firstly, three out of the five Blenheims can be seen with the code letters, PJ-A, PJ-B and PJ-H. These are all No.59 Squadron codes. This squadron did fly the Bristol Blenheim during the summer of 1940, and did conduct anti-invasion barge attacks on French ports then occupied by the German forces. However, No.59 Squadron was equipped with the Blenheim Mk.IV, not the Mk.I. It relinquished its Blenheims in 1941 in favour of Lockheed Hudsons and spent much of the War on anti-submarine patrols, finishing in 1945 on the Consolidated Liberator Mk.V. Therefore, the Blenheim Is in the film may appear to be No.59 Squadron aircraft, but they are definitely not from this unit.

One close-up shot of Blenheim I PJ-A shows that the roundel and code letters have been hand-painted onto the fuselage side in rather crude and scruffy fashion. Moreover, this Blenheim's paint scheme is of note, showing what appears to be a half-completed job where the camouflage pattern on the fuselage ends below the roundel and the underside grey scheme begins. The result is a messy, fudged appearance that would get the 'Erk' who painted it a blast from 'Chiefy', while the squadron CO would likewise get a dressing down from any Air Commodore carrying out an inspection for allowing an aircraft to bear such a shabby paint-job. In the RAF, even in the Battle of Britain, aircraft could be allowed to be war-stained with oil and grease, but they had to be painted accurately – the RAF set great store by accuracy in appearance, both in peace and war.

The conclusion must be, therefore, that Blenheim I PJ-A has had a temporary paint scheme and code letters applied for the film. If it and its four co-starring extras were in operational service with the RAF, or had been taken out of storage, such a temporary paint job would not be necessary except possibly for a change of, or the addition of, the squadron codes. The only other conclusion that has to be drawn is that this Blenheim I is not an in-service RAF aircraft.

Could that be possible in 1945? The answer is, yes, and probably reveals the only source then available for Bristol Blenheim Mk.I bombers. The Finnish Air Force still operated the type, although they flew the very similarly configured Blenheim Mk.II as well as the long-nosed Mk.IV. In early 1945, Finland was no longer at war: although Finland had allied itself with Nazi Germany, its principal conflict was with Soviet Russia in what is known in Finnish history as The Continuation War. That ended in September 1944, with the signing of an armistice between Finland and Russia.

So, could Blenheim I PJ-A be a Finnish Air Force example loaned to Two Cities Films, Ltd, along with at least four other examples, to be used in "The Way To The Stars" acting as RAF Bomber Command Blenheim Mk.Is in the summer of 1940? There are two other clues about Blenheim I PJ-A that indicate this could be the case.

There was one physical exterior design difference between RAF and Finnish Air Force Blenheims concerning the Mk.I and Mk.II variants (the latter did not serve in the RAF). When the Finland State Aircraft Factory began to turn out licence-built Blenheims from 1939 onwards, they incorporated a design change to the bomb-bay to accommodate an increased bomb load. This gives the Finnish-built Blenheim Mk.IIs a slightly more convex curve to the fuselage underside, compared with the more straight and flat underside of the otherwise identical-looking British Blenheim Mk.Is. It is noticeable that the fuselage underside of Blenheim I PJ-A has the convex curve typical of the Finnish Blenheim Mk.II design.

Secondly, the RAF roundel on the fuselage side has a larger circular aura around it, suggesting it has been painted over a bigger circle showing through the temporary paint scheme. The Finnish Air Force's military symbol was a large white circle bearing an up-right blue Swastika, applied to the fuselage in exactly the position where, if it were being carried by a Finnish Blenheim, it would be seen. This suggests that the Finnish Air Force white circle, larger than the RAF roundel painted over it, is showing through the temporary camouflage paint scheme applied by the film's art department crew.

The irony is that, technically, Britain was at war with Finland while "The Way To The Stars" was being filmed. Britain had sided with its ally, Soviet Russia, when Finland lent military support to Hitler's Operation Barbarossa in 1941, and declared war on Finland, although British and Finnish forces never met in combat. After the signing of the armistice to end the Continuation War, Finland was required to demobilise its forces, including any combat aircraft, the Bristol Blenheim IIs among them; however, the Finnish Air Force got round this requirement by declaring the Blenheims as target-tugs. There was probably financial value to the Finnish government in leasing the five Blenheim IIs to Two Cities Films, Ltd (as well as enabling their aircrew to remain active on type), especially if they were now surplus under the terms of the armistice, even if they were being leased to a nation that Finland was officially at war with!

The Blenheims are shown in the film mostly as static props on the airfield, usually with no more than two in shot. When the Luftwaffe raid takes place, they are seen with some explosions going off quite close to them. Pilot Officer Penrose is seen taking off in Blenheim PJ-H. If a total of five Blenheims were loaned to the film unit, then they are all seen in loose formation thundering impressively overhead Shepley as they set course to attack Calais's invasion barges. The final shot is of three of the Blenheims returning to land after the Calais raid, with the CO gone.

We don't see the five Blenheims again in the film after this 1940-based scenario, but this is not the last time that we will come across them. As will be revealed during the reviews of several later British war films, out-takes of these Blenheims in "The Way to the Stars" proved very useful for other film productions. These out-takes contain material filmed for "The Way to the Stars", including that of the Blenheims in action, which, for whatever reason, director Asquith chose not to use in the final cut.

The film's plot now takes the audience into the lives of the many personalities with whom Penrose, Archdale and others become involved, which means that aviation, and in particular the Blenheims, bow out of the picture until the story flashes forward to 1942. At this point, a new bomber type appears which, like the Blenheim I, is a very rare beast in war films.

This is the menacing-looking Douglas DB-7 Boston, an American light day bomber operated by the RAF in several variants, as well as a night fighter version named the Havoc. In "The Way To The Stars", No.720 Squadron has converted onto the Boston, although interestingly it is heard being referred to in the film by RAF officers as the "A-20". This was the USAAF's designation for the Boston, to which it also gave the popular name 'Havoc' taken from the RAF's use. "A-20" is not a designation that would have been used by RAF aircrew, so it is a bit of a puzzle to hear it being used thus in this film, unless it was done so for American movie-goers' consumption.

Three Bostons appear in the film. The glazed nose with the bomb aimer's slanted window is clearly visible. Taking into account when the film was made, they almost certainly are the most recent of the DB-7 models operated by RAF Bomber Command, making them Douglas DB-7C Boston Mk.IIIAs (equivalent to USAAF Douglas A-20C Havocs, a version developed to meet a joint British/American specification). To portray them as No.720 Squadron aircraft, at least one of them has been given the code letters PJ-N; a second Boston is seen taking off as Archdale's aircraft coded 'O', but with no sign of any other code letters.

Unusually, the three Bostons are filmed in formation air-air, the only such footage of any aircraft in "The Way To The Stars". It is immediately obvious that they are in different markings from the three Bostons acting as No.720 Squadron bombers. They clearly bear squadron code letters of 'OA-' ahead of the fuselage roundel, but with each aircraft's individual code letter applied separately on the forward fuselage just below the cockpit. This is not the normal RAF style of displaying squadron code and individual letters. But even more distinctive are the fuselage roundels on two of the Bostons, different from the usual RAF roundel, while the entire tail fin rudders of these two Bostons have been painted top to bottom in national colours. Were this imagery to have been filmed in colour, it would immediately have shown that these two out of the three Bostons are bearing French Air Force markings. The tail rudders are painted in the French Tricolour, while the roundels stand out because French AF roundels are more pronounced than those of the RAF's. The 'OA-' codes reveal the three Boston Mk.IIIAs as OA-B, OA-P and OA-T of No.342 (Free French) Squadron.

Following D-Day, No.342 Squadron's pilots moved to their homeland in October 1944 and, with France liberated, their Bostons could therefore be repainted from RAF Bomber Command markings to Free French Air Force markings, while it continued to operate under RAF control. Quite likely this was done against Bomber Command's approval, but with the Free French pilots now back in their own country, who was going to be in a position to stop them painting their aircraft in their national colours, even though the Bostons were still Bomber Command assets. The single 'O' code letter on Archdale's Boston is probably a residue from the No.342 Squadron 'OA-' code. It is notable that one Boston is painted in a darker camouflage hue than its two colleagues.

By the time the Bostons were used in "The Way To The Stars", No.342 was converting from the Boston IIIA to the B-25 Mitchell. It is possible that these three Bostons had already been withdrawn from the squadron, freeing them up to be repainted as No.720 Squadron aircraft. The air-airs may have been filmed when the Bostons were being flown on delivery to England for the film production, possibly from an accompanying transport

aircraft that would have collected their crews for the return trip. After filming, the Bostons were probably then handed over for disposal. If they were Lend-Lease aircraft, they would have been returned to America.

The scene in which the Bostons feature prominently has Penrose, now a 43-mission veteran who is showing serious signs of strain, and the CO Archdale having what turns out to be their final conversation before taking off on a three-ship mission. Archdale is destined to fail to return from what was intended to be his final 'trip' before being re-assigned and becomes the first "Johnny in the stars" of the poem, which Penrose discovers among his late CO's possessions and passes to Archdale's wife. Penrose has to accept that he must undertake a controller's posting due to the toll of flying so many 'trips' is having on him.

Seen in the background as Penrose and Archdale walk to their Bostons to start their final 'trip' together is another Hawker Hurricane Mk.IIc, bearing the code HQ-V OF No.56 OTU.

The film's plot now moves to its final era of 1944, with RAF Halfpenny Field being taken over by the United States Eighth Air Force. A Boeing B-17G Flying Fortress Bomber Group is moving in. The film now focuses on the differences in culture and attitudes between the British characters and the USAAF bomber crews. Rattigan's script very effectively allows the characters on both sides to develop relationships of trust and understanding, permitting both the British and the Americans to overcome initial doubts and prejudices about each other, so as to develop strong bonds, and in some instances between the USAAF airmen and local female personalities, genuine affection.

A far cry from future British war films made during the Seventies, the Eighties and onwards, which all too often colluded with the increasing Hollywood propaganda that the Americans were all courageous, stronger and more effective at war fighting, while the British became increasingly weaker, more dependent on the "Yanks" and much more easily beaten in war, or, as has become the norm now, hardly of any note at all in winning World War Two. In the Forties and Fifties, relationships were much more warm and realistically equal between the "Limeys" and the "Yanks", as "The Way To The Stars" so sympathetically portrays.

There are a series of shots of B-17Gs taxiing, taking off and landing interspersed among the various personal scenes involving the principal characters. As with the RAF bomber scenes, there are no shots of the B-17s in action on their bombing missions. Director Anthony Asquith was given full co-operation by the Eighth Air Force, who assigned the 384th Bombardment Group based at RAF Grafton-Underwood, Northamptonshire, to represent the USAAF Bomb Group operating from RAF Halfpenny Field. Filming took place in late April and into May 1945. Asquith's timing was fortuitously good because the 384th BG had just come off active missions over Germany. He, therefore, had full access to a complete operational Eighth Air Force Bomb Group that had flown the largest number of bombing missions over Occupied Europe by any USAAF unit, for which it received a number of citations. This makes "The Way To The Stars" important as a war movie, it being the first feature film to portray a genuine USAAF

Bombardment Group that was operational in World War Two, not including the famous 45-minute documentary, "Memphis Belle", filmed in 1943 by William Wyler.

However, although it is the 384th BG's aircraft that feature strongly in the film, it is definitely not a 384th BG B-17G which is the first Flying Fortress that appears getting airborne. This is Boeing B-17G Flying Fortress serialled 230186 and carrying the code letter 'X' on its tail. It isn't possible to identify which Bomb Squadron or Group this B-17G belongs to because the tail code symbol and Bombardment Group Letter have been removed, or never applied. This B-17G is also devoid of any squadron code letters. It also differs in appearance with the 384th BG B-17s in being painted in olive drab; the 384th's Flying Fortresses were all-natural metal. It also is not taking off from RAF Grafton-Underwood but from RAF Catterick, so it was clearly filmed on a different occasion. It seems that this individual B-17G visited the RAF Catterick-based film unit on some purpose connected with the production, and was filmed on departure.

The second B-17 to appear in shot isn't a 384th BG Flying Fortress either. In fact, it is not a B-17G: the lack of a chin turret beneath the glazed nose clearly identifies it as an earlier model Boeing B-17F Flying Fortress, which is out of synch with all the B-17Gs in the film. Nor is it filmed at either Grafton-Underwood or Catterick, but instead at a third, entirely different airfield location. And to add to the mystery, it is filmed air-air, flying gear down very low to the runway as if it has just taken off, then it banks left, climbs and turns to pass the camera-ship above and behind. Presumably the camera was positioned in the tail gunner's turret of another Flying Fortress, filming the B-17F in formation.

This B-17F is a very important Flying Fortress. It is the first Flying Fortress in the Eighth Air Force to complete 25 combat missions successfully, and no, it is not Memphis Belle. When William Wyler made his famous documentary on B-17F Memphis Belle about its crew flying their 25th mission, he had a back-up plan in case Memphis Belle didn't make it back. It was expected that the Memphis Belle crew would be the first in the Eighth Air Force to complete 25 active missions, but flak damage to their B-17F delayed this event to a later date. In the meantime, another B-17F pipped Memphis Belle to the 25th mission mark, and Wyler had this Flying Fortress filmed as well. Had Memphis Belle failed to return from its crew's 25th mission, Wyler would have had film in the can of the actual first B-17F to score 25 completed missions and it instead would have become the subject of his documentary, not the legendary Memphis Belle. It is an out-take from Wyler's film of this B-17F, not used in the "Memphis Belle" documentary, which appears in "The Way To The Stars".

The Boeing B-17F Flying Fortress concerned is 41-24577/VK-G Hell's Angels of the 358th Bombardment Squadron, 303rd Bombardment Group, based at RAF Molesworth in Cambridgeshire, where it was filmed in May 1943. The white triangle symbol on the tail bearing the Group Letter 'C' confirms this B-17F as a 303rd BG aircraft; Memphis Belle was a 324th Bombardment Squadron, 91st Bombardment Group, B-17F

operating from RAF Bassingbourn, with the Group Letter 'A' adorning the triangle symbol on its tail fin.

It is a mystery as to how this out-take of Hell's Angels got to be in "The Way To The Stars". Perhaps it was offered to Asquith by the Eighth Air Force as a gesture of thanks for showing the 384th Bombardment Group in such a positive light in the film; it may also have been a means of getting Hell's Angels into a movie, even though virtually no one would have known anything about this B-17F and the significance of its history. Its appearance allows "The Way To The Stars" to join the ranks of other British war films that show imagery of aircraft with historically very distinct and important roles, and which cannot be seen publicly anywhere else.

Of the 384th Bombardment Group Boeing B-17G Flying Fortresses which appear in the film, the following can be identified:

B-17G 44-6923/DJ-J (with the Squadron code letters of 'JD-' incorrectly applied in the wrong order, the groundcrew applying them must have been in a hurry) of the 545th BS, 384th BG, landing but with the film screened in reverse direction for some strange reason;

B-17G 44-6909/H, bearing no Squadron code letters but the number '3' atop the fin denotes the third squadron in the Group, the 546th BS, taxying with four other B-17Gs;

B-17G 43-38757/SO-L of the 547th BS, 384th BG, leading a five-ship take-off;

B-17G 43-38016/SU-R of the 544th BS, 384th BG, acting the part of B-17 'B - Baker' flown by USAAF airman, Johnny Hollis, who has befriended David Archdale's widow and been given the poem by her. It is returning on Hollis's final 25th mission, badly shot up and with a 500lb bomb hung up in its bomb bay. This B-17G can be seen being flown low over the airfield with its port engine feathered and the bomb doors open, which confirms not only the skill of the airmanship on the part of the 384th BG pilot flying it, but that the 384th were now free to act in a film since hostilities, and their mission, had ceased. Unfortunately, the film editor has again, for some reason, cut this imagery into the film in the reverse direction. On his third attempt at landing after his crew have bailed out, and having refused to obey an order to bail out himself and thus risk 'B - Baker' crashing with a live bomb aboard on Shepley, Johnny Hollis becomes the second "Johnny in the stars" of the poem as his B-17 explodes on touch down.

The 384th BG mounted a formation of ten B-17Gs depicting a return from a raid, with three more parked on the airfield in the foreground, a scene that was all too realistic and familiar for them between May 1943 – May 1945. The Group left RAF Grafton-Underwood for Istres, France, in the same month as "The Way To The Stars" was released to become the highest grossing film shown in Britain in 1945.

"The Way To The Stars" may be slow paced and devoid of action by modern standards, and a 21st Century audience may find the relationships between the various characters cranky, if not a little strange where attitudes towards romance in the Forties are concerned; but it is another goldmine of British wartime aviation, and deserves its place among the stars of British war films that portray aircraft long lost to posterity.

JOURNEY TOGETHER

(Released: October 1945)

When filmed between May and September 1944, "Journey Together" was the 26th and largest production yet made by the RAF Film Production Unit. All the principal characters are played by well known British film actors who were serving in the wartime RAF, while the director, Captain John Boulting, one half of the successful Boulting Brothers team who became a mainstay of British cinema during the Forties, Fifties and early Sixties, was attached to the Army. Two of the leading actors, Richard Attenborough and Jack Watling, held the rank of Sergeant and Aircraftsman respectively, while a third, David Tomlinson, entered the RAF on a direct commission as a Flight Lieutenant. Names of actors and the film crew are not shown in the opening credits; instead, a simple statement proclaims that the film was "Written, produced, directed and acted by members of the Royal Air Force". It is only at the film's end that the actors' names are shown.

The film opens with the declaration, "A story dedicated to the Few who trained the Many". RAF Fighter, Bomber and Coastal Commands had all been featured in major film productions up till now, so the decision was taken to put Flying Training Command in the front seat for a change. The film's story follows three pupil Aircrewmen from their first day at an Aircrew Selection Centre through their flying training to the final part of their journey together on an operational bomber squadron. The characters are played by Richard Attenborough, who was now establishing himself as a leading actor and was to go on to have a major career in film acting and directing both at home and abroad; Jack Watling, who had a successful early career in very boyish roles but who became established as a distinguished character actor in many British TV productions; and David Tomlinson, a highly popular light character actor who acquired a reputation for playing upper class, 'silly arse' types, and who became famous in the Sixties for his roles in Walt Disney movies, especially "Mary Poppins" (1964).

The opening shot in the film shows an Avro Anson I taking off with the code number '33' painted large on its fuselage. Another shot shows this Anson performing a level turn above the camera, with the serial MG108 in large black characters under each wing. The paint scheme of the period shows this Anson to be a training aircraft, bearing standard camouflage but with what would be a large bright yellow band wrapped around its fuselage with the roundel in the centre.

This opening sequence has Richard Attenborough as a Wireless Electrical Mechanic – an 'Erk' in wartime RAF slang – bunking off from his radio servicing duties to hitch an unauthorised ride in the Anson. He is disciplined for leaving his post and taking the unapproved flight.

(Incidentally, a 21st Century reader should not make the mistake in thinking that the term 'Wireless', as used in the film, has anything to do with today's Internet technology. In World War Two, 'Wireless' was a very common term widely used to refer to both military and domestic radio sets that operated independently of electrical cables. The term remained in wide public use in reference to stand-alone household broadcast radios until the portable transistor radio was introduced in the Sixties, and became completely redundant as other broadcast devices came into use until it reappeared in the 21st Century to describe independent Internet connection systems)

During the disciplinary hearing Attenborough is described by another 'Erk', who was witness to his indiscretion, as taking the flight in aircraft number "Zero Five" – which clearly was not the Anson's number on film – and in giving him a 'V' sign (the two-fingered Victory Salute which Churchill made famous, but which Attenborough had given the wrong way round to his colleague, giving the sign an altogether well known, alternative meaning). Attenborough tells the disciplinary hearing's senior officer that when he joined the RAF he had applied to be an Aircrewman as he just wanted to fly, but became a mechanic because he had failed the written examination. After reprimanding him his senior officer recommends Attenborough's character for aircrew training because of his obvious keenness to fly.

After attending an Aircrew Selection Centre, where the three would-be pilots first meet, they are sent to No.2 Flying Grading School where their abilities are assessed. All three want to be pilots, but two of them are destined to be disappointed. Attenborough's character is a natural pilot but has great difficulty in judging his landings. Watling's role has him being a potentially good pilot, but he is lazy in his studies, especially with navigation, and only just scrapes through his final examination. Tomlinson fails to make the grade as a pilot and is selected to be an Air Bomber.

No.2 Flying Grading School was equipped with the de Havilland DH.82A Tiger Moth II and a goodly number of them appear in the film. What is interesting is that they appear to wear varying colour schemes, although all are in camouflage. Most can only be identified by their code numbers, which are either located on both sides of the forward fuselage beneath the front cockpit or on the nose cowling. In particular, Tiger Moth IIs coded '53', '14' and '101' are prominent. Attenborough flies in Tiger Moth II coded '107', which has the full Flying Training Command colour scheme of yellow engine cowling, yellow fuselage band with the roundel in the centre, and yellow patches to the ends of the upper wings carrying the wing roundels plus yellow bands around the lower wings.

Two Tiger Moth IIs are clearly identifiable. One is Tiger Moth II DF188/50, which survived the War but was scrapped on 28th March 1950. It bears the full Flying Training Command colour scheme. A goof occurs when Attenborough goes flying in Tiger Moth II coded '107', but when he tries to land he has suddenly managed to switch 'planes in mid-air and is now aboard Tiger Moth II R5035/11. This camouflaged Tiger Moth carries no yellow training markings and bears a smaller roundel on its fuselage. Clearly an earlier build aircraft, Tiger Moth R5035 was sold to a civilian buyer on 29th March 1951. Another Tiger Moth II coded '3' has the yellow engine cowling and yellow training markings on the wings, but has no fuselage band.

Watling's character goes solo on Tiger Moth II R5035/11 and taxies into the line on the same aircraft to park alongside Tiger Moth II coded '3'; but when he climbs out of the cockpit, he is doing so from Tiger Moth II coded '101'!

The scene now changes to the USA, where Attenborough and Watling are sent to complete their pilot training. The film simply gives the location as Mesa, Arizona, and does not explain the raison d'etre for RAF aircrew being trained in the USA. This is the Arnold Plan in action, the scheme developed under the Lend-Lease Agreement between the United States and Great Britain by Major-General Henry 'Hap' Arnold for the training of British pilots by American flying instructors at facilities in the USA, paid for by the British government. Under this scheme, six British Flying Training Schools (BFTS) were set up in the USA during World War Two, in which RAF pilots trained on Boeing PT-17 Stearman and North American T-6 Texan aircraft. The film does not give the official title, but the BFTS which Attenborough, Watling and other RAF student pilots have been sent to is No.4 British Flying Training School, based at Falcon Field, Mesa, Arizona.

In this sequence, famous Hollywood gangster actor Edward G Robinson makes a guest appearance as a wise and fatherly flying instructor. However, all the scenes in which he appears were filmed at Pinewood Studios in England, not at Mesa; none of the actors actually went to the USA for the Falcon Field scenes.

Set in the Arizona desert with its vast ramp space, Falcon Field is a complete contrast with the rural-style RAF airfields seen in the film. The ramps are covered with aircraft and in the opening panning shot no less than 17 North American AT-6 Texans and 19 Boeing PT-17 Stearman bi-planes can be counted. It is the latter which feature mostly in this film. All the PT-17s carry no markings other than the American 'Star-and-Bar' symbol on their all-over silver-painted fuselages and wings, plus an individual code number. No serial is visible, although usually this was carried in small characters at the lower, rear-end of the fuselage, just below and forward of the tail section.

PT-17 code numbered '13' is used primarily in the film, flown by Attenborough's character. Unfortunately for him, his problem with being unable to judge height and speed in landing finally catches him out and he crash lands when making his solo flight. This sequence is effectively created in the studio with what looks like a real Stearman but may be a full-scale facsimile (noticeably, there is no pilot in the cockpit as it crashes). Robinson and Attenborough have two studio-filmed scenes beside a complete Stearman.

Of the other PT-17s seen in the film, the following appear in various shots in the order listed: code numbers '23', '25', '14', '28', '8', '1', '4' and '2'. The AT-6 Texans only appear in a couple of shots in the background, of which just 'EP227' can be identified.

Attenborough's character has to face the reality that he will never make a pilot, but he is given the opportunity to train as a navigator. He does not take kindly to this, as he does not consider being a navigator offers the same status as a pilot. But this is where the film's message starts to play out, that the navigator is probably the most important member of a bomber's aircrew and that to believe that the supposedly more glamorous role of the pilot is of greater value is a serious misjudgement.

Attenborough is now in Canada, training – much against his will – as a navigator under the British Commonwealth Air Training Plan (BCATP), which saw thousands of British aircrew in World War Two trained by the Royal Canadian Air Force (RCAF). He has joined No.3 Air Observers School which, although not stated in the film, was located at RCAF Station Pearce in Alberta (the film mentions Toronto). It is a puzzle as to why No.3 Air Observers School is depicted in "Journey Together" because, according to Canadian historical sources, it closed in June 1943, the year before this film production began.

Avro Anson V RCAF 6331 is seen taking off and is later seen air-air when Attenborough's character is put through a challenging navigational exercise in increasingly difficult weather conditions. The Anson was licence-built in large numbers in Canada by the Federal Aircraft company and was very much a favourite of the Royal Canadian Air Force, so much so that many RCAF Ansons remained in service long after the War was over. The Anson V was more advanced than the RAF's Anson I seen at the beginning of the film, having hydraulically-operated landing gear instead of the manually-operated system on the earlier version and powered by two Pratt & Whitney Wasp Junior R-985 engines developing 450hp, as opposed to the 350hp Armstrong Siddeley Cheetah IXs equipping the Anson I. The Anson V's role in the RCAF was exclusively as a navigational trainer.

Despite his lack of enthusiasm for the role, Attenborough's character passes his navigator's exams with honours and is sent back to England to join an operational bomber squadron. He is assigned to the fictional No.522 Squadron on Lancasters. In fact, 522 Squadron is represented by a very experienced RAF unit in films, No.149 Squadron, formerly at RAF Mildenhall, Suffolk, which had contributed Vickers Wellingtons to "The Lion Has Wings" (1939) and "Target for Tonight" (1941). When it appears for a third time in a British war film, No.149 Squadron has been relocated to RAF Methwold in Norfolk and has just converted from Stirlings onto Lancasters in August 1944, at the time the RAF Film Production Unit moved in to make this section of "Journey Together". This means that No.149 Squadrons appears in the first and the last British World War Two war films to be made during the war years themselves.

Attenborough is reunited with Watling, who has also been assigned to No.522 Squadron as a Lancaster pilot. Various Avro Lancaster B.1 bombers of No.149 Squadron can be seen parked at dispersal in one scene, with NF972/OJ-H particularly visible. The Lancaster B.1 that Attenborough joins, and which Watling flies, is clearly coded OJ-L but its serial is not discernable; however, both NG355 and NG387 carried these code letters at one time or another. A Lancaster B.1 seen taking off is filmed day for night, meaning that the picture has been darkened to the extent that its serial and code letters cannot be read against its blackened fuselage.

One air-air shot sees five Lancasters in loose formation, while another incredible shot of a mass raid airborne holds no less than 77 Lancasters in frame. Much of the bombing raid action over Berlin is achieved with the use of quite effective model miniatures of Lancasters, although curiously the film's art department has created miniatures of Lancaster B.Xs, not B.1s. Much of the footage of the Lancaster miniatures in "Journey Together" carrying out the Berlin air raid and being shot down was re-used in at least two more film productions after the War was over: "Now It Can Be Told" (1946) and "Battle of the V1" (1958).

The film's climax has Watling's Lancaster being badly shot up by a German night fighter and by flak, forcing him to ditch in the North Sea. This sequence is very dramatically and realistically created in the studio at Pinewood, making it a genuinely believable scene. All the aircrew – including a very young George Cole, as seen much earlier in the War in "Cottage to Let" (1941), and still with three decades to go before he finally made his name as the decidedly dodgy Arthur Daley in the "Minder" TV series – manage to get into an inflatable life raft before their Lancaster sinks, but crucially Attenborough's navigator has been able to get a fix on their position, which the radio operator transmitted by Morse to the Air-Sea Rescue service. This is the crucial message of the film because, by doing so, Attenborough's character has saved his mates' lives and has underlined the vital role that the navigator played aboard an RAF bomber in World War Two.

The fix means that their life raft is able to be located by a spotter 'plane which, for another curious reason, turns out to be a Douglas DB-7 Boston III, not a type used by RAF Coastal Command. The Boston cannot be identified because it is filmed making very low runs over the sea towards and overhead the camera position. Its observer transmits Morse by flashlight to the survivors in the life raft that a rescue launch is two hours away and then congratulates the navigator for his almost-accurate fix. The film ends with Attenborough being praised for his efforts, thus justifying all the effort the RAF had put into training him.

"Journey Together" had a prestigious film premier at the Odeon Leicester Square in September 1945, although those on the red carpet were hardly of the celebrity generation of today. Many high-ranking officers from all three major services attended, including the Marshal of the Royal Air Force, Lord Tedder, and Viscount Trenchard, often known as the 'founding father of the RAF'. Richard Attenborough was present, still in his RAF Sergeant's uniform. With the War over, it might be thought that the film's message was no longer of any relevance, but the effects of six years of conflict was still writ large in the minds of the British public, so there was no difficulty in using a film like "Journey Together" to celebrate the nation's heroes in action. "Journey Together" was used by the RAF as a recruitment and training film for quite a number of years after its release.

CHAPTER 2

1946-1950

The immediate aftermath following the ending of World War Two in 1945 saw the war-weary British public turning to the cinema as an ever-popular means of escapism from the rigours and stresses of post-War austerity. Not surprisingly, Hollywood musicals and British romantic comedies were most in demand. Anna Neagle, now reaching her zenith as Britain's most loved of all glamorous actresses, took full advantage of the public's demand for such soft, silly, 'smoochie' movies, as with her appearances in "Spring in Park Lane" (1948) and its follow-up, "Maytime in Mayfair" (1949), before reverting to the toughest and most famous film role for which she is best remembered, as "Odette" (1950).

The initial post-War years were a good time for crime thrillers in the British cinema, perhaps because the wartime black market had sprung a bunch of spivs and crooks onto the British peacetime social scene in the late Forties and it was enjoyable to see them getting their come-uppance in films. Richard Attenborough increased his reputation for acting dexterity by playing a particularly nasty thug in "Brighton Rock" (1947), while the up-and-coming young Dirk Bogarde shook audiences with his chilling portrayal of a cop killer (unheard of, in those days) in "The Blue Lamp" (1950).

Other wartime 'Big Names' were spreading their wings dramatically. Michael Redgrave played an ambitious politician who allows his sense of decency and social conscience to become more and more compromised the higher he rises in the Cabinet, in "Fame is the Spur" (1947), a controversial subject for a film when the new Labour Government of Prime Minister Clement Attlee was striving to create the Welfare State, amidst widespread poverty in a country striving to find work for millions of demobbed servicemen. England's favourite film hero, John Mills, struck gold, however, with his performances in such highly-acclaimed productions as "Great Expectations" (1946) and as "Scott of the Antarctic" (1948).

For British war films there was still an appetite, but the hunger was for entertainment. Thus it was that in the five years following the end of World War Two and up to the beginning of the Fifties, out of the many films made in Britain during that time only 13 featured the War as its principal theme. And a mixed bunch they are too.

This time period allowed for another new development in British cinema, the re-enactment film, using the actual people involved in real events to re-enact their roles for the camera. Thus, a complete battle was re-staged in Holland where it had occurred two years earlier, using soldiers and civilians caught up in it and filmed among the still-existing ruins. This was the battle for the bridge at Arnhem, with many of the actual Paratroopers of the 1st Airborne Division re-creating their experiences for "Theirs is the Glory" (1946). Similarly, genuine British agents of the Special Operations Executive (SOE) and members of the French Resistance repeated their activities in towns and villages which had been under Nazi Occupation when they were previously present, for "Now It Can Be Told" (1946).

It is noteworthy that three out of the 13 film productions made in this period threw the wraps off the very secretive SOE, which had been disbanded following the end of hostilities and had had what was left of its assets and personnel subsumed by its wartime rival, MI6. Did Churchill, now out of work as Prime Minister, quietly urge film producers like Michael Balcon of Ealing Studios, plus others who were involved with the now defunct RAF Film Production Unit, to bring the SOE to the public eye, so that the courage and the sacrifice of its agents would be known? It's plausible, as Churchill was the inspiration behind the creation of the SOE and would undoubtedly have wanted the British people to see how important a role its agents played in the eventual liberation of Europe. All three of these SOE films - "Now It Can Be Told" (1946), "Against The Wind" (1948) and "Odette" (1950) - have very substantial and valuable aviation content in them. Two more 1946 productions, "Night Boat to Dublin" and "School for Secrets", shed light on the secretive world of British Scientific Intelligence, something else that would have been new to a British cinematic audience.

Of the other films covered in this Chapter, two are significant as being the first to establish the genre of Prisoner of War themed films, which have fascinated British cinema for decades. "They Were Not Divided" (1950) was the first British war film to feature an element in its plot that, sadly, became considered to be an absolute necessity to ensure its success in the USA, that of having an American fighting with or, totally against historical fact, leading British armed forces. Was this British cinema's contribution to the repaying of Britain's war debt to the United States? "Frieda" (1947) bravely tackles what would then have been the very unpopular subject of reconciliation with the Germans, through the story of a romance between an RAF officer and a young German woman who he brings back to England. And the continually creative duo of Powell and Pressburger came up with their extraordinary masterpiece, "A Matter of Life and Death" (1946), a film that was literally way ahead of its time in terms of creativity and production values.

But we begin with arguably one of the most fascinating of all British war films, and one which contains a large amount of very rare archival aviation film footage that, until it was released by the Imperial War Museum Collection on DVD, was inaccessible to war film fans and collectors.

NOW IT CAN BE TOLD (SCHOOL FOR DANGER)

(First Released 1946, Re-Released 1948)

"Now It Can Be Told" was originally released in 1946 through the Central Office of Information (COI, the replacement for the wartime Ministry of Information, MoI) as "School For Danger". This, however, was a shortened version; the complete film was released in 1948. Much of the filming by the RAF Film Production Unit had taken place in 1944 after the D-Day invasion of Normandy, with more conducted in 1945, but the production was not completed until 1946 due to sensitivities within the wartime MoI about whether the secretive nature of its subject should be revealed to the public. After the MoI had been disbanded post-War, its COI successor decided that release to the cinema could be allowed under certain restrictions, which resulted in the initial shorter film. When the full film was released two years later, it proved to be a revelation.

"Now It Can Be Told" is nothing more than a most compelling and extraordinary re-creation of the highly secret Special Operations Executive (SOE) organisation, using actual SOE agents and senior staff to act the roles of themselves as they organise and equip French Resistance groups to fight their German Occupiers. Two real SOE agents are central to the story: Captain Harry Ree and Jacqueline Nearne. Although they are portraying themselves in the film, they are given fictional SOE code names, 'Felix' and 'Cat' respectively – obviously a play on the popular cartoon character of the time, Felix the Cat. Ree was actually code named 'Cesar' when he was on SOE Operations in France, while Jacqueline Nearne was known simply by her first name. She also

had a sister, Eileen, working as an SOE agent known as 'Didi' who was captured and tortured by the Gestapo, an event which scarred her psychologically after the War. 'Didi' was dependent on her elder sister Jacqueline to care for her until Jacqueline died in 1982; Eileen Nearne survived until September 2010, when her name made the news headlines in the UK after her body was found in a small flat in Torquay. She had lived as a recluse and it was not until the discovery of her body that her wartime SOE papers were found, revealing who she had been. She was given a public burial with honours.

Although Ree and Nearne are shown working side by side as Resistance group organiser and Morse Code wireless operator respectively, in fact they never did so together on active duty in France. They each worked for separate Networks in France, Nearne for 15 months before she was withdrawn by Lysander pick-up aircraft in April 1944, while Ree one month later had to flee for his life, escaping to Switzerland, from where he was repatriated to England.

What makes "Now It Can Be Told" so fascinating is that much of its action takes place in recently liberated France, with real former Resistance group fighters and using actual locations where certain events took place. But for the purposes of this book it is the revealing insight the film provides to the operations that took place at the RAF's most secretive airfield, RAF Tempsford in Bedfordshire, that makes this film so well worth watching. The amount of footage the film contains of RAF Tempsford in action amounts to a priceless study of a unique organisation conducting its clandestine mission right under the noses of ordinary villagers north of London.

RAF Tempsford was, as aviation historians know, home to two of the RAF's Special Duties Squadrons, Nos.138 and 161 Squadrons, which supported SOE agents in the field. Their highly secretive roles, which involved operating almost exclusively at night, were inserting and extracting SOE agents working with Resistance groups in Occupied Europe and supplying the Resistance by air drops. Aircraft from both of these two unusual squadrons appear in the film.

The story begins with Ree's and Nearne's recruitment into SOE by Wing Commander Edward 'Teddie' Baird, who becomes their Boss and who just happens to be this film's producer and director. He, too, takes a prominent role in the film as himself, as do many of his colleagues, operating from what was SOE's headquarters at 64 Baker Street, London. The first part of the film focuses on the arduous training of agents, leading to their initial parachute drops. Although the film does not give the names of actual locations, it has to be RAF Ringway (today Manchester International Airport) where Ree and Nearne are seen using harnesses and slides inside a hangar to practice safe landings, before being introduced to the dreaded barrage balloon jump.

"The balloon jumps were the worst", comments Ree. "The awful silence as we ascended, the gathering noise of the wind as we went higher".

"The others looked green", says Nearne. "I suppose I was too".

Not surprisingly so, because they had to sit inside what was little more than a circular chamber upon a rim, with their legs hanging out the open floor and watch the ground receding as the balloon climbed. The feeling must have been claustrophobic, and the only anticipated relief – if that is what it could be called – would be from dropping through the opening they were perched around and waiting several heartbeats of silence until the static line pulled open their 'chutes.

SOE parachute training at Ringway was conducted by No.1 Parachute Training School, still in existence today based at RAF Brize Norton, Oxfordshire. Once the balloon jumps were completed, trainee agents graduated to aircraft. These appear in the film in the shape of five Armstrong Whitworth Whitleys, probably Mk.V variants, with three leading in 'Vic' and the remaining two in trail behind. A shot is then shown of one Whitley dropping parachutists. When the film opens, it gives the year as 1943 when the recruitment and training begins. By this time the Whitley was no longer in service with either No.138 or No.161 Squadron, but were still being used as Paratroop trainers. A squadron conducting this role is depicted here, probably No.297 Squadron (see "Secret Mission", 1942, in Chapter One).

Nearne comments that she found jumping from an aircraft a better experience than from the balloon: "Somehow the noise of the engines made me excited".

Ree is seen being instructed in the use of the 'Eureka', an early form of transponder with a radar mast that an agent could use to guide an aircraft to a field from 20 miles away, and in how to use the 'S-Phone', a wireless telephone that allowed an agent to talk to aircraft flying overhead from the field. Agents are given instruction by pilots from the two Special Duties Squadrons as to how to select the best available landing ground for Lysander pick-ups, using an 'L-shaped' signalling light lay-out for a field with good approach, the correct length of runway, as good a surface as possible and as far away as they can from "German interference".

Training with a real Lysander is shown, and by so doing the date when this particular part of the film was made can be pinned down. Westland Lysander Mk.III coded JR-M of No.161 Squadron is used. Although 161's code letters were usually prefixed 'MA-' this was not so for its Lysanders, which were organised into a separate Flight with 'JR-' codes. Lysander III JR-M still exists, although no longer with these codes: it is now R9125/LX-L, exhibited in the RAF Museum, Hendon. Its RAFM Individual History, prepared by Andrew Simpson and published on the RAFM Website, states that a letter confirming this Lysander's availability for use by the RAF Film Production Unit is on file and that filming with the aircraft took place between 15th – 21st November 1944. The Lysander was flown by Flight Lieutenant George Turner and the landing ground seen in the film with SOE agent trainees was at Somersham.

Interestingly, Lysander III R9125 had a very brief career with No.161 Squadron, joining on 15th October 1944, but never flew an SOE Operation in Enemy Occupied Territory – the last Lysander Operation in what remained of Occupied France was flown on the night of 5th – 6th August 1944. By that time, Allied forces had advanced sufficiently far enough to render Resistance sabotage missions unnecessary. Tempsford's

Lysanders were then used for ferry and communications work, as well as special transport services to liberated Belgium and France. When Lysander III R9125 was filmed in mid-November 1944 for "Now It Can Be Told", No.161 Squadron's special agent insertion and extraction Flight had all but been disbanded.

This Lysander was taken on charge by the RAF on 2nd August 1940 and spent its initial career with No.225 (Army Co-Operation) Squadron at Tilshead, Wiltshire, flying coastal patrols over beaches where British Military Intelligence expected German forces to land. After being modified by Westland Aircraft in September 1941 for target-towing, it then spent the bulk of its wartime career with the Central Gunnery School at RAF Chelveston and with the Central Navigation School, Cranage. By the time of the War's end, Lysander III R9125 was selected for packing and storage with the RAF Air Historical Branch (AHB), in which condition it remained for the next 12 years. The Lysander was declared obsolete as a type by the RAF in January 1946 and on 21st June 1947 R9125 was struck off charge. It was one of two Lysanders that by January 1948 was then in deep storage, indicating it was earmarked for preservation, while ten surviving examples on charge had been scrapped by the end of the same year.

Lysander III R9125 remained out of sight until during Battle of Britain Week in 1958 it was flown on 11th September at the Woolwich Tattoo, London, performing a simulated SOE pick-up mission. This Lysander then continued to spend its days in AHB storage, now at RAF Cranwell, Lincolnshire. The BBC photographed R9125 on 1st February 1963 as a pattern aircraft for BBC TV's art department to create a very obvious-looking, unpainted, full-scale facsimile of a Lysander, used in the TV series, "Moonstrike", which was based on SOE Operations and RAF Tempsford's Special Duties Squadrons.

The next time it surfaced was for a visit by HM The Queen to RAF Bicester, Oxfordshire, on 6th May 1965, before it was allocated to the burgeoning RAF Museum collection and placed in store at RAF Henlow, Bedfordshire, pending the Museum's opening. Between the end of 1967 and early 1968, this Lysander was repainted as a No.225 Squadron Army Co-Operation aircraft, bearing the squadron code LX-L (it has not been confirmed if this was R9125's code when it served with No.225 Squadron in 1940). Looking resplendent, it appeared on static display at the RAF 50th Anniversary Display held at RAF Abingdon, Berkshire, on 14th – 15th June 1968, and was again displayed during Battle of Britain Week that same year at Horse Guards Parade on 8th September. On 30th November 1971, Lysander III R9125/LX-L was placed on display in the RAF Museum, Hendon, in preparation for the Museum's opening the following year, subsequently being transferred in 1978 to the Museum's Battle of Britain Hall where it can still be seen today.

Having completed their training as agents, Ree and Nearne are selected by 'Teddy' Baird to create a Network in Occupied France, with Ree organising Resistance groups and Nearne as his wireless operator. It is at this point they receive their agents' code names of 'Felix' and 'Cat' (with no irony shown by them or by Baird). They are to be parachuted into France and have to wait at an SOE holding centre close to the airfield they will fly from. RAF Tempsford's name is not mentioned in the film, nor is that of the holding centre – a stately park in Bedfordshire called Hasell's Hall – but there is no question that these are the actual locations used in the film. It is at this point we now get our first sight of RAF Tempsford, using footage exclusive to "Now It Can Be Told".

SOE agents were driven into RAF Tempsford down a small country lane that was marked 'Closed to the public' on the edge of Tempsford village itself. What purports to be the entrance to the airfield is shown on film, but how genuine it is must be questionable as the entrance gate seen is clearly opposite residential houses, not what could be described as secretive.

The car in which 'Felix' and 'Cat' are being driven crosses the airfield on a distinctly cold, wet and murky day, RAF Tempsford having a muddy, rudimentary appearance to say the least. Two Short Stirling IV transports are seen at dispersal amid the sodden grass: the Stirling was operated on air drop missions by both Nos.138 and 161 Squadrons. The two squadrons could be distinguished from each other by No.138 Squadron bearing 'NF-' code letters on their Stirling IVs, while No.161 Squadron, although allocated 'MA-' codes, flew their Stirlings painted all-black without any code letters shown at all. The Stirlings seen in this shot are difficult to identify due to the angle from which they are filmed, but Stirling IV NF-J is visible as the furthest example from the camera, confirming that it is a No.138 Squadron aircraft; so it is safe to assume the other Stirling is from this same unit as well.

The car then approaches what must have been the most clandestine set of buildings at RAF Tempsford: "An old farmhouse that somehow managed to survive is right in the middle of the airfield", 'Felix' tells us (obviously filmed on a different day to that of the previous footage of the car passing the Stirlings, due to the dry ground and with the car driving on the grass without leaving tyre tracks). Again not named in the film but this is Gibraltar Farm, the agent reception and pre-flight preparation centre. A barn is used for the packing and storage of parachutes; this barn is all that remains of Gibraltar Farm today on what is left of RAF Tempsford. 'Felix' and 'Cat' are seen being kitted out with their maps, pistol, forged French ID papers, parachutes and, accepted with cheerful aplomb, their suicide pills – those for 'Felix' are hidden in a neatly sliding open wine cork, while the pills for 'Cat' are concealed in her lipstick.

Now it's time for them to bid farewell to 'Teddy' Baird and be driven to the aircraft from which they will para-drop into France, flown by the "best pilot on the squadron". He is introduced to them as "Wing Commander Chapman" as they arrive at his aircraft, a Handley Page Halifax A.Mk.V.Srs.1a with the No.138 Squadron 'NF-' code clearly visible on the fuselage, but with no other identifying letter or serial number visible. En route to this aircraft, 'Felix' and 'Cat' are driven in daylight on a dry day past four Halifax bombers parked at dispersal on rough, scrubby grass, but when they arrive at Wing Commander Chapman's aircraft there are clearly visible rain puddles on the tarmac where the Halifax is parked. It has also become noticeably darker, with light falling that requires Jacqueline Nearne to be lit by lamps out of shot against

the darkening sky when she is filmed against an obviously wintry background, due to the leafless trees in the distance.

Again, this gives us a clue as to when this part of "Now It Can Be Told" was filmed in 1944. Harry Ree and Jacqueline Nearne either escaped, or were extracted, from Occupied France before D-Day 6th June 1944. They did not return to France until after the Liberation. A wintry scene at RAF Tempsford, with a No.138 Squadron Halifax that 'Felix' and 'Cat' are filmed boarding, suggests a period no later than November 1944, as, by then, No.138 had relinquished all its Halifax fleet in favour of the Stirling IV.

Students of the Handley Page Halifax will find "Now It Can Be Told" extremely valuable to study, as in no other war film does the Halifax have such a prominent part to play. Two variants of the Halifax are used in the film to portray this converted four-engined bomber operating in the supply-dropping role on SOE Operations, as well as dropping small groups of operatives by parachute exiting through a hatch in the floor of the rear fuselage behind the bomb bay. Para-jumpers using static lines had to drop through the hatch with their legs stretched out straight and firmly together, and with their arms tight to their sides, in order to fall cleanly out, and then retain this position of 'falling to attention' until their parachute had fully deployed.

However, as we are learning in the course of examining British World War Two war films, not everything is as it appears in this production - what else could we expect in a film about the covert SOE. A No.138 Squadron Halifax does feature strongly, not only in the scene mentioned above with 'Felix' and 'Cat' boarding the aircraft at Tempsford, but also later and even more prominently in the film. This Halifax is a curious beast and one which needs looking at closely, especially as it poses a challenge for aircraft modellers and artists for whom the Halifax is their favourite subject.

As already mentioned, this is a Halifax A.Mk.V.Srs.1a, the final variant operated by No.138 Squadron. The complicated Marque designation reflects the many iterations the Halifax design went through during its lifetime. In essence, this variant was a slightly altered version of the Halifax Mk.II.Srs.1a that was powered by four Rolls Royce Merlin 22 inline engines, the main difference being that the Mk.II.Srs.1a was fitted with Messier landing gear whereas the Mk.V.Srs.1a was equipped with Dowty landing gear. Both had the large 'D' style tail fins, separating them from other Merlin-engined Halifax variants which were fitted with the earlier, but less stable, triangular-shaped tail fins.

What is particularly noteworthy about this No.138 Squadron Halifax is that its engines are fitted with four-bladed propellers. Imagery of the Halifax employing a four-bladed airscrew is quite rare, so the study of the Halifax A.Mk.V.Srs.1a in "Now It Can Be Told" could prove especially valuable for the modeller and the artist who may wish to re-create this layout.

The Halifax A.Mk.V.Srs.1a was primarily used in the supply-dropping role by No.138 Squadron, which meant that the bomb bay was retained when it was converted from the original bomber B.Mk.V version, but to deliver weapons and equipment containers instead of bombs. In this configuration, it retained the under-fuselage H2S radar housing behind the bomb bay, used to aid accuracy in the supply drop. The Halifax A.Mk.V.Srs.1a used in "Now It Can Be Told" has this configuration: the H2S ventral radome can be clearly seen below the 'NF-' code letters and just ahead of the roundel and the narrow fuselage hatch through which 'Felix' and 'Cat' are entering their drop aircraft. This means that this Halifax is not the Halifax from which they para-drop out of into France shortly afterwards: in order to create the fuselage floor hatch that agents dropped out of, the H2S radome had to be removed. Because the H2S is still in place on the Halifax A.Mk.V.Srs.1a used in the film means that another, and significantly different Halifax without H2S, is flown for their actual para-drop shots.

Several air-air shots of a Halifax in silhouette, reproduced day-for-night in the editing suite to create the effect of the aircraft flying in darkness, represents the journey of 'Felix' and 'Cat' to France. What is immediately apparent is that this Halifax is not a Rolls Royce Merlin-engined variant, but is being powered by four Bristol Hercules radial engines instead. It is also clearly devoid of H2S radar. Painted on its nose is a large Fleur-de-Lys symbol, which is absent from the Halifax A.Mk.V.Srs.1a seen earlier.

A clue to identifying which type of Halifax is being shown here appeared previously when the car in which 'Felix' and 'Cat' are being conveyed to their drop aircraft drives past four Halifax bombers parked on grass beside the peri-track. All four of them are radial-engined aircraft. Freeze-framing reveals the code '9W-' on one of these Halifax. This is the code of No.296 Squadron, a specialist Airborne Forces unit which had a distinguished record of parachute supply and glider towing operations in the invasions of Sicily and Normandy, as well as Operation Market Garden (Arnhem), using the Armstrong Whitworth Albemarle. In February 1945, No.296 Squadron re-equipped with the Halifax A.III; in fact, it received all 30 of these conversions and used them all in the greatest Airborne operation of all time, Operation Varsity, the Crossing of the Rhine on 24th March 1945. No.296 Squadron also undertook the parachute insertion of SOE and SAS teams, before and after D-Day.

Freeze-frame analysis of the Halifax filmed air-air with the Fleur-de-Lys symbol reveals it is a Halifax A.Mk.III coded 9W-T of No.296 Squadron. This squadron was based at RAF Earls Colne, Essex, from the end of September 1944 until it was stood down in January 1946. The Halifax A.III was a conversion for glider-towing and Special Duties teams insertion of the Halifax B.III, the most numerous of all the variants, and was powered by the Bristol Hercules XVI radial engine conferring it with significantly more power than the Merlin-engined models.

So, how is it that a No.296 Squadron Halifax is used for the air-air and para-drop shots in "Now It Can Be Told", and not a No.138 Squadron Halifax? The explanation has to be that a No.138 Squadron Halifax was not available to fly, probably because when filming took place at RAF Tempsford during the early Winter of 1944 the type had all but been withdrawn from operations there. With the tempo building throughout the Winter of 1944 - '45 towards the denouement in Berlin the following May, the availability of any aircraft type involved

in the maximum commitment would preclude their use in any film production. Thus, the contrast between the scenes meant to be of a single day's events at RAF Tempsford - dirty, wet and wintry in some shots, bright, dry and warm in others - indicates that filming took place separately over something like a six-month period. And at two different airfield locations, RAF Tempsford with Stirling IVs and a Halifax A.V.Srs.1a on base at around November 1944 and what was possibly RAF Earls Colne with four Halifax A.IIIs stood down from Airborne operations somewhere around May 1945 - very noticeably they are parked up on grass with canvas draped over their cockpits and engine cowlings as rudimentary protection from the elements, suggesting that hangarage was a luxury not on offer.

A Spring 1945 time period would fit well with other scenes filmed in liberated France, as will be described in due course. With the fall of Nazi Germany imminent, No.296 Squadron would no longer be committed to delivering troops by glider to the battlefield at this time (it was already involved in repatriation flights of PoWs before the end of the War in Europe). There would have been no restriction on making available a Halifax A.III for air-air filming, while the squadron's expertise in delivering SOE operatives and SAS sabotage teams at low-level would be ideal for the shots of 'Felix' and 'Cat' parachuting into France.

Shots of the interior of the Halifax's fuselage reveal just how narrow and cramped it was inside the converted bomber, with dispatcher and passengers having to clamber over the main central spar. 'Felix' and 'Cat' have to sit forward in order to balance the aircraft's centre of gravity. During the flight, the importance of the role of the dispatcher in caring for the agents is demonstrated, he encouraging them to rest and providing coffee and food when needed. The dispatcher shows 'Cat' that he has fixed her parachute's static line to the hook attached to the fuselage wall behind her. When the time comes for both agents to jump, they are filmed air-air leaving the aircraft through the fuselage floor hatch with the ground clearly visible below, showing that the Halifax is flying at a significantly low height. Marcus Binney, in his book about female SOE agents, "The Women Who Lived For Danger" (Hodder and Stoughton, 2002), states that agents were "dropped low at about 150 or 200 metres. This reduced the chance of their being spotted in the moonlight as they descended. It also meant that if more than one agent was dropped, there was less chance of their drifting apart or being blown off course. For this reason, it was vital to avoid the slightest hesitation in jumping".

This matches other sources, who state that the usual operating height for dropping SOE agents was 600 feet (equates to 200 metres). This explains why the ground is visible in the air-air shot when the agents are seen departing the Halifax. In another shot of 'Felix' landing and restraining his parachute, the Halifax can be clearly seen turning away in the background at low-level.

The film now focuses on the efforts by 'Felix' to co-ordinate Resistance groups, while 'Cat' sets herself up in a rented room to transmit via Morse Code to SOE's Baker Street HQ. 'Felix' decides he needs to request a supply drop from RAF Tempsford, comprising weapons, explosives, a 'Eureka' transmitter and an

'S-Phone'. He chooses a field where to receive the supply drop, then gives its map references to 'Cat' who transmits them to Baker Street. 'Teddy' Baird decides that the Network 'Felix' is organising would benefit from a full supply of weapons and HE (high explosives), in addition to the items requested.

Now RAF Tempsford's role in supplying SOE agents and Resistance groups in Occupied Europe comes into play, leading into the most fascinating section of the film. The Operations Room at RAF Tempsford is shown in full detail, with the Ops Ready Board displaying all the SOE Operations planned for the next up-coming 'Moon Period': the eight-day time period leading up to and following from the next full moon. All Special Duties Squadrons' SOE Operations are flown during each month's full moon period. The Operation for 'Felix' is code named 'Felix 1' (the first Operation for 'Felix' by the Special Duties Squadrons) and is given 'One Star' Priority, the highest priority status. 'Felix 1' is planned for the 7th night of the moon.

The film shows in detail the supply containers of the equipment to be dropped by parachute to 'Felix' being packed. Bren guns, Sten guns, plastic explosives, grenades, fuses, incendiaries, tyre busters, clam mines and limpet mines, plus tins of corn beef, tobacco, cigarettes, and chocolate (very welcome to the Resistance fighters, as chocolate was only available to their Occupiers) – all go into the mix in the supply containers, which have to be strong enough to resist being para-dropped. They are then transported in truck loads to the airfield, both day and night.

The containers are then seen being towed on low-loader by tractor to their allocated aircraft. One container load is towed to a Halifax A.Mk.V Srs.1a which has a heavily decorated nose section. It carries both the names of Haggis and Big Chief (the reasons why can only be guessed at), but most interesting of all are the mission symbols below the cockpit and beside the observer's position: they comprise eight aircraft symbols and 29 parachute symbols. One would guess that the parachute symbols represent agent drops and the aircraft symbols equipment supply drops. The Halifax A.V.Srs.1a used in this scene may well be the same Halifax seen earlier when 'Felix' and 'Cat' arrive for their flight to France. The same two Stirling IVs, plus a third example, can be seen at dispersal in the background.

However, this Halifax A.V.Srs.1a is not carrying the supply drop for 'Felix'. This again is conducted by a different Halifax A.III of No.296 Squadron which is filmed air-air in silhouette, rendering identification impossible but probably it is the same Halifax coded 9W-T; two more Halifax can be seen airborne in the distance.

'Felix' has posted guards around the receiving field, one armed with a shotgun, another with an old rifle. A small truck stands ready to convey the containers which are to be covered by faggots to conceal them. When the Halifax is heard 'Felix' details four Resistance fighters with small 4-volt torches to stand in an 'L' shape, which the observer in the Halifax manages to see. A shot which has become familiar due to its use in other films – also including the 1963 BBC TV series, "Moonstrike" – shows the Halifax passing over and releasing eight containers by parachute, one of which fails to properly open and falls heavily to

the ground. The drop is made at 600 feet. This same shot is used twice more in "Now It Can Be Told".

On the next supply drop ('Felix 2'), 'Felix' uses the 'Eureka' transponder for the first time. The in-coming Halifax picks up the emitting beacon signal ten minutes before 'Felix' and his Resistance reception party hear its engines. An interior shot shows the 'Eureka' system at work (code named 'Rebecca' aboard the aircraft): the navigator watches a green line (obviously shown white in this black-and-white film) on his screen moving horizontally across a blip that denotes the signal emitted by the 'Eureka'. He had to keep the line centred on the blip to avoid wandering off course.

An air-air shot of a stick of containers being released follows, again with the aircraft a black silhouette.

Next, 'Felix' selects a field to accept a Lysander landing. The chosen field is surrounded by woods, making it well concealed from a road, and has a flat, firm surface. Exact measurements of the field are needed, which 'Felix' paces out down one side. 'Cat' transmits these measurements to Baker Street. The Air Ministry arranges to have the field photographed from the air; 48 hours later approval is given for the Lysander pick-up of an injured agent.

An air-air of a Special Duties Westland Lysander III, with its distinctive long-range fuel tank under the fuselage, appears next – this same shot also appears in another film. Although the Lysander is in silhouette, it undoubtedly is R9125/JR-M of No.138 Squadron. It is delivering a Lieutenant and a second wireless operator, as well as collecting the injured agent. After the Lysander is seen flying through white clouds, a shot is seen from the pilot's perspective of torch lights in an 'L' shape appearing from the field. The Lysander lands on, filmed day-for-night, a shot which has likewise been used in another film.

At this point, "Now It Can Be Told" moves to a new development: sabotage. 'Felix' gives the Lysander pilot a package for 'Teddy' Baird containing "details of a factory where a new secret weapon was being stored". 'Felix' explicitly asks in his message that the RAF do not bomb the factory, but instead that his Network be given the chance of setting fire to it. In real life, Captain Harry Ree as SOE agent 'Cesar' had advised SOE that RAF bombing raids on French targets was having a counterproductive effect on the local population, turning them against Bomber Command. He advised sabotage by local Resistance groups instead. SOE agree to his Network attacking the factory where the "secret weapon", which is not specified, is stored.

The Resistance break into the factory at night and place incendiaries around packing crates containing parts of the secret weapon. Each crate has a stencilled individual number denoting which section of the weapon it contains: all are prefixed with 'V1', so it is obvious what kind of weapon the Resistance are attacking. V1 flying bombs were both stored and launched from France against London one week after D-Day 6th June 1944, until their positions were overrun by the advancing Allies.

However, the film's use of 'V1' as the weapon's prefix to each part number in their packing cases is factually incorrect. The moniker 'V1' did not come into use until after the first few flying bombs – the world's first cruise missile – were launched from the

Pas de Calais on the night 12th – 13th June and in earnest on 15th – 16th June, when in excess of 200 were fired at London. It was at this period of time that Reich Propaganda Minister, Josef Goebbels, announced to the German people that the first Vergeltungswaffen (Retaliation or Vengeance Weapons) of Germany's Vergeltung (Retaliation) programme against London had been put into effect. From this time onwards, the Fieseler Fi.103 pilotless pulse jet-powered flying warhead was designated as Vergeltungswaffe Eins (V1: Retaliation Weapon One).

The mistake made in "Now It Can Be Told" is to use the V1 designation at a time well before both D-Day had taken place and Vergeltungswaffen 1 were launched in reprisal. Until Goebbels's announcement, the V1 had been designated FZG.76. This, in fact, was an abbreviation for a cover name: Flak Ziel Gerat 76 (literally, Anti-Aircraft Objective Device No.76). This has since been interpreted as meaning Anti-Aircraft Aiming Apparatus, but British Military Scientific Intelligence Officer, Dr R V Jones, in his excellent book on British Scientific Intelligence 1939 – 1945, "Most Secret War" (Hamish Hamilton 1978, Penguin Books 2009), interpreted it to mean Anti-Aircraft Targeting Apparatus.

FZG.76 first came to the attention of British Military Intelligence via an Enigma intercept on 7th September 1943, which reported that Luftflotte III (Air Fleet 3) was making the request for immediate extra anti-aircraft defences to protect a ground organisation named Flak Ziel Gerat 76 because Abwehr (Defence) Station France was reporting the capture of an enemy agent who was given the urgent task of locating a new German rocket weapon in France. Luftflotte III believed the British intended to attack FZG.76 before it could deploy its new weapon. Jones says in his book this prompted him to write a special note to Military Intelligence on 14th September 1943, which he quotes as follows: "The Germans are installing, under the cover name of FZG 76, a large and important ground organisation in Belgium-N. France which is probably concerned with directing an attack on England by rocket-driven pilotless aircraft".

Jones's interpretation of Flak Ziel Gerat to mean Anti-Aircraft Targeting Apparatus revealed a deception to convey the impression that the Luftwaffe had developed a pilotless targeting drone for Flak forces to practice against. However, the existence of the FZG.76 organisation and the urgent need for Flak forces to protect it indicated a much more serious purpose for the pilotless aircraft.

Therefore, had the RAF FPU been accurate in their depiction of the stored secret weapon, they would have used the 'FZG.76' prefix to the packing crates' numbers, and not 'V1'. But the British public only knew of the hated 'Buzz Bomb', or 'Doodlebug', as V1; FZG.76 would mean nothing to them. So it was obvious that 'V1' would be used as the prefix on the crates, making it certain that the audience would recognise immediately what type of secret weapon the Resistance were attacking.

(See the review of "Battle of the V1" in Chapter Three for further information about FZG.76)

V1s were stored in large underground complexes in Northern France, not in unprotected factory sites as shown in the film. There was no such attack by Resistance fighters on these complexes; they would have been far too well defended for a limited group, as seen here, of three men to penetrate. The Resistance attack, therefore, is a fictitious event created for dramatic effect. Resistance groups did compile reports for British Intelligence of launch and storage sites for V1s, which were invaluable for planning air attacks against them.

According to the film's plot, the Resistance attack is unsuccessful in any case because the incendiary fires are quickly extinguished. A request is sent to bomb the factory. Stock MoI footage of flares being dropped and of a Halifax dropping bombs is mixed with that of fiery bomb damage filmed from the air. An unconvincing miniature of a Lancaster going down in flames is an out-take from "Journey Together" (1945).

'Felix' reports to London that the factory has been completely destroyed. He congratulates the RAF on the accuracy of their bombing. This is in contrast to the position taken by Harry Ree, that inaccurate bombing on French targets was turning the local population against the RAF. But here he is required to act a role praising the RAF's bombing of a French target, with no mention of French casualties or destruction to civilian property which, in reality, would have been unavoidable even with the advent of target aiming devices such as Oboe; so this is a favourable piece of propaganda that is being played out here in an RAF-made film. Hardly surprising.

The crew of the Lancaster that was shot down are being sheltered by the Resistance. The Gestapo are making a lot of arrests and the second wireless operator is detected and killed. 'Felix' decides it is imperative to get the seven-man aircrew back to England. But 'Cat' has had a narrow escape from the Gestapo and her wireless transmitter has been seized. 'Felix' gets a message to Baker Street via another Network that his operation is compromised and that he has to explain what he needs to SOE via his 'S-Phone'.

The film now shows the 'S-Phone' operation in action. Baird flies aboard a No.138 Squadron Halifax to the location in France from where 'Felix' will speak to him via the 'S-Phone' while receiving a new supply drop. Apparently reception from the 'S-Phone' was clear enough for each speaker's voice to be recognisable. As the Halifax positions for its air drop, Baird on board speaks to 'Felix' below who is hooked up to the 'S-Phone' apparatus. In reality, it is very unlikely someone as senior as Baird would have gone on such a flight because had the Halifax crashed or been shot down, with Baird killed or captured, his loss would have seriously disrupted and compromised SOE Operations. Some liberty is being taken here with the reality, but the 'S-Phone' scene is interesting in its depiction of how this unique communications equipment was used.

'Felix' and Baird agree that a Hudson aircraft should be sent to pick the Lancaster air crew up. Baird decides that it is time to relieve 'Felix' as well, so he should also go aboard the Hudson. He and the Lancaster pilot (whose crew and himself are fortunate indeed to have escaped unscathed from their burning aircraft) select a landing field large enough to take a Hudson. One problem is that it has a fence running right across the middle which the reception party will have to take down before the aircraft lands.

Back at RAF Tempsford this causes some concern, but the decision is taken to go ahead with the pick-up.

As they prepare to leave for the landing field, 'Felix' and the Lancaster pilot voice their concern about heavy rain making a landing a high risk. 'Felix' decides he has to let the Hudson land despite the risks involved because he feels it is imperative for him to get back to London to inform Baker Street of the threat to his Network, as well as getting the Lancaster crew back.

The film now depicts the use of a Lockheed Hudson of No.161 Squadron to land in Occupied Territory to perform the pick-up. The use of Lysanders in this role is well reported on and has been re-created for other films, but the use of the Lockheed Hudson for multiple person pick-ups can only be seen in "Now It Can Be Told", adding to the film's fascination. Lockheed Hudson V FK803/MA-N is the aircraft used in the film. No.161 Squadron divided its assets into two Flights: 'A' Flight for the shorter range, two person pick-up/delivery Lysanders, and 'B' Flight for the longer range, multiple person pick-up/delivery Hudsons.

When the sequence involving Hudson FK803/MA-N was used, it very clearly was filmed at a different period in time than that when Lysander R9125/JR-M was used. It was also filmed in France. The reason for the different period is that when the Hudson lands, the trees in the background are clearly in full leaf. A likely time period would have been May 1945 or perhaps a month earlier because, with France liberated and Nazi Germany on the brink of defeat, it would have been perfectly safe for actual French Resistance personnel to represent themselves in the film, while the local population were undoubtedly enthusiastic participants. No.161 Squadron had, by this time, only Stirlings and Hudsons on strength which were mostly involved with ferry and repatriation flights to and from former Occupied Countries, so there would have been far less restriction on the squadron in making one of its Hudsons available to the film production. A date after May 1945 does not seem feasible because, after that month, No.161 Squadron had ceased to exist.

The Hudson pick-up sequence re-creates an actual event when a Hudson's wheels became stuck in mud, preventing it from taking off. A fraught situation developed when it seemed the aircraft would have to be disabled and the pick-up abandoned. But almost the entire population of a local village turned out, under the noses of the German garrison nearby, to help free the Hudson. This was achieved by using oxen to pull the Hudson out of the mud, allowing it to take off safely. This actual event occurred to the pilot, Flying Officer Affleck, his passengers and his Hudson on 8th February 1944.

The film ends with the Hudson flying away into the distance with 'Felix' and the Lancaster crew on board.

"Now It Can Be Told" bears no comparison with any other film. It is a truly unique work involving actual characters from the SOE, RAF Tempsford and the French Resistance. Director/producer 'Teddy' Baird, whose project this was, worked in the film industry both before and after the War. Much credit goes to him and the RAF Film Production Unit for bringing this project to fruition, which must have seemed disjointed at the

time, with various elements filmed while SOE was at war in 1944 being joined with further sequences achieved within the next two years as Britain enjoyed its first actual 12 months of peace after six long years of hardship. Yes, the acting is stiff and wooden, but the personalities in the film are not professional actors. And, for the aviation enthusiast and historian there is no other source available that portrays in such detail the activities of RAF Tempsford and its Special Duties Squadrons. This film is a "Must Have" in any war film library, so gratitude must also be expressed to the Imperial War Museum Collection for releasing "Now It Can Be Told" from its vast archive.

NIGHT BOAT TO DUBLIN

(Released: April 1946)

The significance of this film's title will be lost on a 21st Century audience. The literal night boat to Dublin was synonymous during the War with being a conduit for various suspicious persons - criminals, black marketeers, deserters, and, possibly, spies from either side - wanting to escape from or enter into wartime Great Britain through the capital of the neutral Republic of Ireland. In this case, British Military Intelligence believe that the Nazis have gained access to a Swedish atomic scientist who has taken refuge in Dublin, and are acquiring information from him about how to develop an atom bomb. It is a race against time to track the scientist down. This is a pacey, intriguing World War Two thriller, well worth watching, but aviation - apart from a studio prop of the rear fuselage of an unrecognisable transport aircraft - does not feature in its plot.

THE CAPTIVE HEART

(Released: April 1946)

A moving and original story of British Prisoners of War interned in Germany for almost the duration of World War Two. It is, in actuality, the first of the series of PoW war films to be made, but differs from all the others in two principal effects: firstly, it deals with how the PoWs manage to cope and occupy themselves in captivity for five years, without having the usual angle about escape attempts; while secondly, it has a unique plotline that involves a Czechoslovakian Army Captain (Michael Redgrave) in the prison camp impersonating a dead British Army officer who maintains the pretence of his identity by writing letters to the dead officer's wife in England. If his true identity is discovered, the Gestapo will have him shot.

Much of the film was shot in the real Marlag Prisoner of War Camp, which had remained mostly intact in the British Zone of Occupation after the fall of the Nazi regime.

There is a single brief scene involving aviation in the film. The PoWs realise the tide has turned against Nazi Germany when they observe the contrails of United States Army Air Force bombers flying high over their Camp. "Fortresses", comments one officer. It is questionable if the PoWs would have known anything about the B-17 Flying Fortress in 1943, when this scene is meant to be taking place. All the PoWs in the film are British Army officers and men, which means that without any RAF or USAAF personnel among them, their knowledge of the types of bomber the Americans flew would have been very limited. However, this does not detract from the effect of the scene.

A careful count shows that 48 Boeing B-17 Flying Fortresses, flying in three separate waves made up of three staggered groups consisting of between four - six B-17s in each, are caught in this impressive shot filmed far below them from the ground.

THEIRS IS THE GLORY

(Released: October 1946)

The preamble to this extraordinary film really says it all:

"It was in September 1944 that the men of the First British Airborne Division   made their heroic stand at Arnhem

"One year later survivors returned to the actual battlefield amid the ruins of   Arnhem truthfully to re-enact and record for all time this most gallant action in which that had gained the admiration even of the enemy.

"This film is a tribute to every man who fought at Arnhem and an everlasting memorial to those who gave their lives"

It is a drama-documentary on a scale greater than had been achieved before, and possibly has never been equalled since. The battle-scarred ruins of Arnhem are shown in graphic detail, not least the actual bridge itself over which the action was fought between 17th - 25th September 1944. It is clearly shown in its collapsed state spanning the Lower Rhine river. The re-enactment of the stand by the 1st Airborne Division at Arnhem and neighbouring Oosterbeek is matched with actual combat footage of the action. Some 200 veterans of the real battle either portrayed themselves or other known military personnel in the re-creation directed by Brian Desmond Hurst, along with Dutch civilians who became caught up in the fighting and who re-enacted their own roles, such as Kate ter Horst, who tended to nearly 250 wounded and dying British Paratroopers in her house. The film is remarkable in using genuine captured Wehrmacht armour that were in working order after their evaluation by British military analysts, including two Panther V medium tanks.

Aviation plays a large part in "Theirs Is The Glory". Most of the aircraft shown appear in archive material, apart from some scenes where aircraft were used in the re-enactment for Desmond Hurst's cameras. Because so many transport aircraft and assault gliders are shown, there will not be an attempt made to total the actual numbers. Where aircraft can be individually identified, they will be described in sequence as they appear in the film.

Essentially the aviation elements of the film can be divided into three sections: the preparation and build-up of the airborne forces, the launch of the aerial armadas leading into the actual landings, and the perilous attempts to re-supply the besieged Paras amid fearsome anti-aircraft opposition.

The first shots show rank upon rank of RAF Airspeed Horsa infantry assault gliders lined up nose to tail on airfields, awaiting the order to commence Operation Market Garden. One Horsa is named 'The Obstinate Virgin', with a crudely drawn image of a blonde in bra and panties beside the forward loading door!

Next appears a huge line-up of USAAF Douglas C-47 Skytrain transports. The tail of the nearest C-47 shows its serial, but the poor image quality prevents it from being read. Behind it is a C-47 coded 'X5' on its nose and with the letter 'F' on its tail; behind it is a C-47 coded 'X9'.

More shots of Horsa gliders being towed by trucks into position on a runway appear next. Then, following a sermon being delivered to Paratroops by a Padre - Market Garden was launched on Sunday 17th September 1944 - troops are seen being marched up to their allotted gliders. Airspeed Horsa numbered '297' appears in shot, as do Horsas numbered '304' and '402'. Another Horsa is nicknamed 'Scroungers' Roost', while Horsa carrying the code 'D5' has been christened 'Cynthia'. Up to 700 gliders were to form part of the massive airlift, over 350 of them carrying the Air Landing Brigade of 3,000 troops in the first wave, along with their jeeps, guns, stores and rations.

Tug aircraft now appear in shot. Short Stirling Mk.IV coded 8Z-G taxyies past, identifying it as a No.295 Squadron aircraft: No.295 was an airborne forces unit, being one of the first two Allied squadrons to drop Paratroops over Normandy in the opening phase of D-Day. Stirling IV 8Z-G has been allocated the temporary airlift number '148', scrappily applied in chalk, for Market Garden. A Short Stirling IV towing a Horsa off a runway is shown next, a piece of archive footage that will appear in later films. A quite dramatic shot of a Short Stirling IV pulling a Horsa shows them both passing very close right over the camera position. Although it passes by the camera in a blur, a Short Stirling IV with the '5G-' code of No.299 Squadron flashes past with yet another Horsa in tow behind it. No.299 was formed as a Special Duties Squadron in April 1944, but took part in both Normandy and Arnhem glider landing operations as well.

Shots taken inside both gliders and tug aircraft appear next, with a Stirling IV seen from the cockpit of a Horsa being towed into the air behind it, then a look back from a tug aircraft at a Horsa coming off the runway - there are no other gliders behind it, so this was probably taken during a training or trials flight. A North American B-25 Mitchell in RAF markings pulls off a Horsa before the camera swings round to film the next Horsa being moved into position awaiting its tug aircraft. A fine shot of a Short Stirling IV wearing the codes 'ZO-' of No.196 Squadron towing yet another Horsa then appears, another piece of archive material that will be seen again in future films; the large group of people assembled by the runway to watch its departure suggests this was taken at RAF Keevil during some form of demonstration, possibly to Air Ministry and War Office staff, as No.196 was a leading Special Duties Squadron. It took a heavy toll in Market

Garden, losing 13 Stirlings and 25 aircrew to anti-aircraft fire during re-supply sorties.

The 'drama-doc's commentator says, "Dakotas of the American Ninth Troop Carrier Command, manned by American pilots and aircrews, are to carry over 2,000 men of the First Parachute Brigade". Of course, he means Skytrains, not Dakotas, but the C-47 was a Dakota to any Brit no matter whether it was an RAF or USAAF aircraft. Stock footage of C-47 Skytrains leads into the first section where aircraft are actually used in a re-enactment scene for "Theirs Is The Glory". Paratroopers are seen boarding a Douglas C-47 Skytrain carrying the code letters YAW in white on its nose, as a second Douglas C-47 Skytrain coded YCW taxiies out in front of it. Interior shots were filmed inside the cabin of one of these C-47s as well.

The next series of shots are air-air images of Stirlings towing Horsas, but one particular shot is notable for showing a Handley Page Halifax aerial towing a giant General Aircraft Hamilcar tank-carrying glider, which easily dwarfs the converted bomber ahead of it.

Four Hawker Typhoons armed with rockets break off from their echelon port formation and peel into a dive.

A dramatic study of the point of separation by a glider from its tug is shown in a shot filmed from the glider's cockpit, with the Stirling ahead of it sliding away to port, the tow cable trailing behind it. Then a shot looking down on a Horsa about to land in a field with other Horsas already down close by. A ground shot of a Horsa turning in. Another shot from a glider cockpit, this time looking at abandoned parachutes left strewn across a field and in a copse, with one tangled in a tree. Two aerial shots looking down on whole groups of Horsa gliders clustered together after landing. A dramatic study filmed through trees of a Horsa about to land port wing low, which unfortunately cuts just before impact. A shot of a Horsa landing in a cloud of dust, filmed possibly during trials as it is devoid of operational stripes.

Then Desmond Hurst cuts into shots of troops disembarking from three Airspeed Horsa gliders filmed especially for "Theirs Is The Glory". The giveaway is that the Horsas have been set up on their undercarriage in a field, completely intact; they also don't have operational stripes. A fourth Horsa has been set on fire and is burning fiercely. A jeep towing an anti-tank gun passes right under the tail of a Horsa whose serial reads HG790, making it an Airspeed Horsa I. Another Horsa numbered '111' has graffiti chalked all over its nose and forward fuselage - this appears to be archive footage, as is that of two Waco GC-4A Hadrian gliders landing.

Now it is the turn of the Paras. Their massed descent from the C-47s is filmed from a variety of angles air-air, including one spectacular shot of streams of parachutes drifting away from the Skytrains as the aircraft in which the camera is filming passes right across in front of and above the mass of aircraft. In one amazing shot the camera is being held by a Paratrooper as he leaves the C-47 and deploys his 'chute amid the flow of hundreds of parachutes all around him. This spectacular shot, and others similar to it, are replicated in the 1977 epic about Market Garden as a whole, "A Bridge Too Far" (1977, reviewed in Chapter Five), which seems to confirm that "Theirs Is The Glory" had a particular influence on that production.

Another massed drop shows the second lift coming in, half a day late due to bad weather in England. This is all filmed from the ground with troops watching. Included among this section of archive footage is a shot of a USAAF Curtiss C-46 Commando with flame streaming in the wake of its starboard engine heading for the ground - its impact occurs beyond the range of the camera. More Airspeed Horsa gliders land on.

The final section in the film featuring aviation has footage of the failed efforts by the RAF and the USAAF to re-supply the besieged 1st Airborne Division. Not only is footage of C-47s again used, but also that of three USAAF Consolidated B-24 Liberators releasing containers. It was during this phase that the majority of shoot-downs occurred. Imagery of a Curtiss C-46 Commando streaming fuel from below its starboard wing is shown, possibly the same aircraft seen earlier before the fuel caught fire - a parachute suddenly appears beside the cargo door, probably an aircrewman bailing out. A C-47 Skytrain plunges into the ground beyond Waco Hadrian gliders and erupts into flame. A B-24 Liberator is seen trailing fuel and smoke. Another C-47 Skytrain powers diagonally to earth behind a farmhouse and detonates in a massive fireball. Such a sight sums up only too well the valiant but ultimately futile effort behind the 1st Airborne Division's attempt to take Arnhem Bridge, in order to try and hasten the fall of Nazi Germany and end the War by Christmas 1944.

"Theirs Is The Glory" concentrates on the men of the 1st Airborne Division in action at Arnhem and Oosterbeek, and not on the Operational and Intelligence failures that so badly hampered their mission. The fact that Intelligence about the presence of an SS Panzer Division at Arnhem was ignored by the Market Garden Commanders was kept well away from the public's knowledge in 1946. The film also presents as simply bad fortune that the 1st Airborne were landed seven miles from their objective and had to fight their way through superior forces that they did not know were there. The serious communications problems the Paras had with radios that did not work is also not shown in the film. It is, therefore, a propaganda piece but one that does not shirk the realities and the terrible consequences the British Airborne troops faced at Arnhem. As a drama-documentary re-creation of the action, it stands out on its own and is a must for any military historian to have in their collection.

A MATTER OF LIFE AND DEATH

(Released: November 1946)

This fascinating and very original concept was regarded as being ahead of its time when it was released (it was the first film to be shown as the Royal Command Performance in cinema), and it still holds its own today. The plot concerns an RAF Squadron Leader, played by David Niven, talking on the radio from his burning Lancaster bomber to a female American ground controller, acted by Kim Hunter. He has told his crew to bale out but his own parachute has been shot up. He chooses to jump rather than die in the burning Lancaster, but mysteriously survives the fall. He meets the American controller and they both immediately fall in love.

But he has missed his time - he should have died in the fall. He has to undergo a celestial trial to win his right to continue with his life and marry his new-found love.

Because this is a story about an airman, aviation does feature but only right at the beginning. The burning Lancaster is a studio set of its cockpit and forward fuselage. When the Niven character realises he has survived the fall, he learns from a shepherd boy that an airfield is nearby. As he is told this, a de Havilland Mosquito suddenly appears overhead and shoots past him. The Mosquito cannot be identified, but freeze-framing shows it is an early model fitted with rocket rails under the wings. The nose is solid, not glazed, but appears not to have cannon fitted. Possibly it is an FB.Mk.VI variant, or a FB.Mk.XVIII version derived from it. As this scene was filmed at Saunton Sands, Devon, it may have been a Coastal Command Mosquito.

SCHOOL FOR SECRETS

(Released: December 1946)

This is an unusual film about unusual people. As the prologue following the title credits states, "The RAF has gained a reputation during the last few years, not only of being a brilliant warlike organisation, but also of inventing a new language. Among the lesser-known words which appeared in the welter of "prangs" , "scrambles" and "wizards" was the word BOFFIN meaning Scientist. The RAF linguistic experts will tell you this derivation for the new word -

"Once upon a time a Puffin, a bird with a mournful cry, got crossed with a Baffin, an obsolete Service Aircraft. Their offspring was a Boffin. This bird bursts with weird and sometimes inopportune ideas, but possesses staggering inventiveness. Its ideas, like its eggs, are conical and unbreakable. You push the unwanted ones away and they just roll back.

"This is the story of a handful of 'Boffins'".

Well, yes....

In fact, what "School for Secrets" tries to tell is the story of the scientists and inventors from completely disparate backgrounds, experiences and knowledge, who are brought together before the outbreak of war by the War Office in order to "keep ahead of the Germans in every branch of scientific warfare". The film does have a fascinating story to tell, but a 21st Century onlooker might find its eccentric approach difficult to put up with and perhaps testing of one's patience. However, considering the eccentricities of the 'Boffins' who are the subject of the film's plot, this should not be too surprising.

Add to this eccentricity the very individual personality and style of the film's director, scriptwriter and co-producer, the (literal) genius Peter Ustinov (destined to be a two-time Oscar winner and Knighted for his services to British theater, cinema and literature), and you have a very original and extraordinary concoction. We do not need to repeat Ustinov's talented and

hugely creative career, but at the time he made "School for Secrets" he had just completed his wartime service in the Army Film Unit. There, he had made documentaries and instructive films about and for the British Army, assisted by Lieutenant Colonel David Niven, the actor and Hollywood film star (see "A Matter of Life and Death" above) who Ustinov directed in his first production, "The Way Ahead" (1944), in which Ustinov himself also appeared (reviewed in Chapter One). Ustinov's first acting role had been in the well regarded "One of our Aircraft is Missing" (1942).

Ustinov had actually been Niven's batman. Niven spotted Ustinov's talents and did not hesitate to encourage them. Post-War, they became firm friends and their careers often converged in films. What was significant for Ustinov in "School for Secrets" was that Niven served in British Military Intelligence and almost certainly provided valuable information to Ustinov that enabled him to gain access to what would still have been classified material even after the War was over.

"School for Secrets" was probably the British public's first encounter with the scientific aids that helped the RAF gradually gain the upper hand over the Luftwaffe, especially in night fighting. They would be aware what radio direction finding (later, radar) was, but most probably were unfamiliar with 'AI' - Airborne Interception radar. What "School for Secrets" was allowed to do was lift the veil - albeit, only in a limited way - on some of the secret inventions that British government propaganda had decided could be made known about, to increase British prestige and the public's admiration for what their country's Scientific Intelligence community had achieved.

At its beginning the film gives credit to the Air Ministry, Admiralty, War Office, TRE Malvern College (TRE: Telecommunications Research Establishment) and RAE Farnborough for assisting the production. This presumably was technical assistance, as neither Malvern nor Farnborough as Establishments are shown in the film. In the title credits, it is stated, "Although this film deals almost exclusively with the RAF, it is intended as a tribute to all scientists, to the men and women of all ranks in the three services, and the civilians who worked side by side with them on the development of radar".

The film opens with a quite convincing studio miniature of a Handley Page HP.42 Hercules airliner flying at night through clouds. Unfortunately, it passes into the clouds, then an explosion occurs. The clouds lift to reveal the tragedy that the HP.42 has flown into a mountain, presumably the Alps, as it was en route from Zurich to London. The significance of this crash scene is that, despite the aeronautical achievements of the time - July 1939 - aircraft are still vulnerable in flight conditions where they have no visibility.

With war having broken out between Britain and Germany, the 'Boffins' - played by an assortment of British character actors, including Ralph Richardson, David Tomlinson, John Laurie and Raymond Huntley - are stationed in a Public School requisitioned by the War Office during the summer of 1940. They have managed to perfect the Radio Direction Finding (RDF) Chain Home system just in time before Britain declared war on Nazi

Germany on 3rd September 1939 and are at the rudimentary stage of installing it in aircraft for the earliest attempts at AI. The Luftwaffe attack on Ventnor RDF Station is depicted, a scene which is repeated almost word for word verbatim 23 years later in "Battle of Britain" (1969).

A 'Scramble' is portrayed, with pilots running for their aircraft from amid canvas tents. Only two Spitfires are seen beyond, mostly obscured by the tents. The Spitfire closest to the camera has a 'ZD-' code which, for the 1940 era, would make it a No.222 (Natal) Squadron aircraft. If this is the case, this then would be stock footage of a 'Scramble'; by the time of the release of "School for Secrets" six years later, No.222 Squadron had moved into the jet age with Gloster Meteors.

A stock shot of 13 Heinkel He.111s flying at height and filmed from the ground during the Battle of Britain are seen passing overhead, with flak bursts below them. Six Spitfires in a wide battle formation are shown flying to intercept: interestingly, the leading three are elliptical-winged Spitfires, while the three following behind are clipped-wing 'Spits'. This suggests that this is a mixed formation of High Flying and Low Flying Spitfires, possibly three each of the Spitfire HF.Mk.IX and LF.Mk.IX, not Battle of Britain-vintage Marques.

A formation of five Bristol Blenheims appears next, in a 'Vic'. A Spitfire - what looks like a Mk.II - is filmed air-air diving and firing its machine guns. Gun-camera footage shows a Messerschmitt Me.410 maintaining a straight course amid tracer fire streaming after it. A combined shot of a Spitfire on the tail of a Messerschmitt Bf.110 is almost certainly Crown Film Unit footage of the RAE Spitfire Mk.IIa P8441 and captured Bf.110C-5 Zerstorer AX772.

A formation break of five Luftwaffe bombers is, in fact, an out-take of the five Finnish Air Force Bristol Blenheim Mk.IIs used in "The Way to the Stars" (1945). This particular shot does not appear in that film and is a follow-on to the earlier shot in "School for Secrets" of five Blenheims in 'Vic' formation. As noted in the review in Chapter One of "The Way to the Stars", the Blenheims in that film are not seen on their bombing mission from which their CO fails to return. Here is proof that the Finnish AF Blenheim IIs were filmed for the bombing mission scene, but for whatever reason the director chose not to include it in his final cut.

The time comes for AI to be tested in action at night against an intruder aircraft. Dr McVitie, played by John Laurie, who acted a number of serious film roles during the War years before he developed his characteristically eccentric comic style in his later career, wins the toss against Ralph Richardson's Professor Heatherville to air test the AI radar on board a night fighter. Supposedly the night fighter is a Bristol Beaufighter, but imagery of it filmed in the dark means that it cannot be identified.

A quite tense scene follows in which, for the first time (as far as the film's plot is concerned), an RAF night fighter is directed onto a Junkers Ju.88 intruder using AI radar and GCI (Ground Control Interception). Because of cloud, the pilot, played by Richard Attenborough, who is in effect portraying the legendary John 'Cats Eyes' Cunningham but under a different name, cannot

get visual contact with the intruder, despite the AI cathode screen telling Dr McVitie in the back seat that they are virtually on top of it. The shoot-down of the Ju.88 is achieved with quite reasonably effective SFX. Did the GCI Controller, in reality, kiss his female assistant when Attenborough calls out that he has got the Ju.88? Very unprofessional, old chap. Attenborough is told afterwards that his success as a night fighter pilot is due to his special diet of carrots, the spoof that British Intelligence foisted onto the public at large to convince them, but more importantly 'Jerry', that carrots are very good for the eye sight at night, and thus conceal the existence of AI.

The next phase is to develop navigational aids that will improve the accuracy of RAF Bomber Command's attacks on its targets at night. Here, Ustinov has strayed into the field of unreality. He has the 'Boffin' who develops the night attack system - Oboe in fact, although this is never mentioned - fly on a night raid on Cologne, to test its accuracy because the 'Boffin' insists he is the only person capable of doing so. In reality, this would have been unthinkable. If he were to be shot down and taken prisoner, he would have been delivering the new aiming system as a free gift to the Luftwaffe, not to mention being "persuaded" to impart the extent of his scientific knowledge to the Gestapo. Ustinov appears to have dismissed this reality while pursuing sensational drama.

Stock footage of night raids on German cities is used to depict the attack on Cologne, with a superimposed black silhouette of the Short Stirling in which the 'Boffin' is flying cut into the imagery of fires and explosions. Familiar stock footage that has often been used in films and documentaries of a Handley Page Halifax over-flying a blazing city appears next. Although he is not recognisable due to his flying helmet and mask obscuring his features, the bomb aimer calculating the release of the bombs is apparently actor Kenneth More (the future Douglas Bader in "Reach For The Sky", 1956, among many other roles) in what may have been his first, and uncredited, appearance in a British war film.

The next step is to improve the system so that individual ground targets can be identified. This has the 'Boffin' played by David Tomlinson flying in daylight over urban areas in England in an aircraft which presumably is meant to be from RAE Farnborough, although this is not mentioned. Prior to the flight he is seen being briefed beside the aircraft he is going to be flying in. The serial RG876 can be clearly seen above his head on the rear fuselage behind him, plus the code letters 'AD-'. This reveals that Handley Page Halifax B.Mk.VI RG876 is being used for this scene; the 'AD-' code suggests this is a No.113 Squadron Halifax, although most likely this actual aircraft had probably yet to be delivered when it was used in the film because No.113 Squadron was a Middle East Air Force unit and did not receive the Halifax until September 1946 at the earliest. It would also mean that RG876 was a transport conversion of the Halifax B.VI, making it a Halifax A.6, which was used as a stop-gap transport aircraft post-War while its successor, the Handley Page Hastings C.1, was preparing to come into service.

However, when airborne the Halifax that is filmed air-air is clearly carrying the codes DY-C. It also noticeably has a glazed nose and a ventral fairing, which would have housed H2S radar. If so, this suggests that this is Halifax B.VI DY-C of No.102 Squadron, a heavy bomber squadron which flew three versions of the Halifax for three years until March 1945. Among No.102 Squadron's many Ops were the 'Thousand Bomber Raids' and attacks on strategic rail targets in France prior to D-Day. This Halifax was probably filmed air-air by the RAF Film Production Unit on a solo sortie well before the Halifax B.VI's withdrawal in March 1945.

In this sequence, the 'Boffin' played by David Tomlinson ignores instructions not to fly below 1,500 feet and directs the pilot - who should have overruled him - to fly at 1,000 feet so that he can test the radar system on ground targets. This involves flying over an urban area where barrage balloons are hoisted. Inevitably, the Halifax strikes the cables of one balloon and crashes, killing both the 'Boffin' and the pilot. Again, Ustinov has gone over the top here, in two respects: the pilot would never have acceded to the instruction to fly at such a low height over an area where he could clearly see barrage balloons are hoisted, while testing the radar at 1,000 feet would have been irrelevant because Bomber Command flew most of its Ops at 15,000 feet or above - the radar would need to be tested at the operational height that bombers flew over enemy territory.

The crash is achieved by the combined use of SFX art work with the tail and rear fuselage section of a Halifax, probably provided by the Air Ministry from an example that was being broken up. As if to make this crash scene more impressionable on the audience, the burning wreckage of the Halifax has been placed next to a memorial stone for those who gave their lives in the Great War of 1914 - 1918.

More stock footage of air raids over Germany are used to depict the radar targeting system operating successfully in action.

Ustinov finds a way to fit the Bruneval Raid into the plot of "School for Secrets", which probably was the first time the British public were made aware of this daring action that took place in February 1942. A much more complete description of this now famous raid by the 1st Airborne Division is given in the review of "The Red Beret" (1953) in Chapter Three. Ustinov, however, twists the facts for the benefit of his production by having the 'Boffin' played by Ralph Richardson take part in the Bruneval Raid because his knowledge of the Wurzburg radar set that was the target of this operation was essential for its success. Again, this is nonsense, for two reasons: firstly, to take a middle-aged, untrained, unfit civilian along on a very physical, high risk operation which he could all too easily hamper would not have been contemplated by the military planners, and secondly, the risk of him falling into enemy hands would not have been contemplated either. The Bruneval Raid is much more accurately re-enacted in "The Red Beret" than in "School for Secrets".

Ustinov plays around with historical facts here: he has the 'Thousand Bomber Raid' on Cologne take place before the Bruneval Raid, when in reality the assault on the Wurzburg radar took place three months before the first 'Thousand Bomber Raid' was mounted against Cologne on the night of 30th - 31st May 1942. And the Oboe system did not become established in operation by RAF Bomber Command by a good many months after that.

Although Richardson's 'Boffin' is seen departing the aircraft he and 1st Airborne Division are being carried in, they are not shown parachuting down. Consequently, no aircraft appear in this scene.

Following the Bruneval Raid set-piece, the film then jumps three years forward to a period in 1945 following the surrender of Nazi Germany but when Imperial Japan was still at war with the Allies. Richardson's character is on a barge being conveyed to a flying boat moored in an estuary, which presumably is Calshot. When asked by passengers what he did in the War, he says proudly, "I was a Boffin", and adds cheerfully that he was now on his way to "blow up Japan". Is Ustinov inferring that this character had something to do with the Manhattan Project? No confirmation is given, which contributes to the frustratingly unexplained inferences that Ustinov litters throughout the plot of "School for Secrets".

This final scene of the film does provide some shots of aircraft that have their own special but long gone place in British aviation history: flying boats. As Richardson and his fellow passengers in the studio barge are being ferried across the estuary, a backcloth shows a magnificent Short Sunderland of RAF Coastal Command at its mooring beyond them. Then, their barge draws alongside the flying boat they are taking, which is the civilian equivalent of the Sunderland: Short S45 Solent Mk.3 G-AHIU. This Solent was taken on charge by the Ministry of Supply on 23rd April 1946; taking into account the release date of "School for Secrets" in December of that same year, this means that Solent G-AHIU must have been filmed in the summer of 1946.

The fact that Solent G-AHIU was being operated by the Ministry of Supply (MoS) on civilian passenger routes one year after the end of World War Two shows that Britain was still being governed at this time under wartime emergency rules. This Solent Mk.3 continued operating under MoS contract until 24th February 1948, when it came under the Ministry of Civil Aviation's umbrella, probably operating on War Office contracts in support of British Forces overseas. It was finally taken out of service on 14th February 1956 and was recorded on the British civil aviation register as being permanently withdrawn from use on 14th May that same year.

A shot shows what is meant to be the Solent taking off from an estuary head-on towards the camera; however, with its registration and markings unseen it easily could be a Sunderland instead. For the final departure shot it has indeed turned itself into a Short Sunderland, possibly a Mk.V, wearing the all-white scheme and the two-tone blue roundel that Sunderlands operating in the Pacific Theater adopted, but having an untypical four-digit number in large figures on its rear fuselage which unfortunately, due to the image quality, is unreadable. This could make this Sunderland an aircraft operated by a squadron from a Commonwealth country.

"School for Secrets" is a rather frustrating and self-indulgent film, made by an emerging talent on the British cultural scene, but it does give us a view of how important developments in the world of scientific achievements that helped Britain to take the war to Nazi Germany, were first made known to the people they were invented to save.

FRIEDA

(Released: 1947)

This would have been a brave film to make just one year after World War Two had ended, as its subject is the then controversial one of 'enemy brides'. It probably was intended to go someway towards inspiring the British public to adopt a more concessionary attitude towards the defeated German nation. Swedish actress Mai Zetterling plays the title role, which launched her successful film career, as a young German woman who saves an RAF pilot from a Prisoner of War camp in Poland (strangely, we don't see how). In return, he marries her and brings her to live with his family in Kent. However, although leading man David Farrar plays the RAF pilot, we don't see any aircraft in the film (although we do hear a Spitfire flying overhead).

AGAINST THE WIND

(Released: February 1948)

This very well crafted, well scripted, story about SOE agents being parachuted into Occupied Belgium is a minor masterpiece – and a forgotten one, at that – of British film noir. Its tone for almost the whole of its plot is one of dark, eerie treachery and mystery, where much is not what it appears to be.

The film sets the atmosphere of doubt and confusion by opening with a Belgian priest entering what appears to be the London Science Museum, but who reveals that he is actually an agent come to meet his SOE chief in a clandestine office concealed in the museum's wall behind a life-size representation of a dinosaur. Later at night, among the museum exhibits, SOE operatives in German uniform test an agent about to go into action behind enemy lines by interrogating him as if he has been captured.

All the aviation sequences contained in this film involve the delivery and return of SOE agents into and from Occupied Belgium, under the cover of darkness. The very first shots as the film credits are run are of three agents parachuting down. Aircraft don't appear in "Against The Wind" until well into the body of the film, with the first to be seen shining under moonlight being an Avro Anson C.19, standing in as a prop for an RAF Special Duties aircraft on the airfield in England from where agents are flown. This, as we know from the review of "Now It Can Be Told", is RAF Tempsford, but no footage of the real RAF Tempsford is used in "Against The Wind".

The aircraft from which the agents will drop is a Handley Page Halifax A.Mk.9, serialled RT901 and coded 'G'. In the film, Halifax A.9 RT901/G is being used to portray a Halifax A.Mk.V.Srs.1a that was operated by No.138 (Special Duties) Squadron. Four agents are waiting to be parachuted into Belgium, in order to spring an important Resistance leader from Gestapo captivity. One of the agents, however, is a traitor.

They are seen waiting for their aircraft in the stark surroundings of a studio set of Gibraltar Farm, the SOE agent reception and pre-flight centre at RAF Tempsford.

It is not clear whether Halifax A.9 RT901/G was filmed releasing para-jumpers specifically for "Against The Wind", or whether Ealing Studios, which produced the film, acquired footage from the post-War Central Office of Information. The drops being made are clearly over English countryside during daylight; the imagery has then been darkened in the editing process, to make it appear the drops are taking place at night. Halifax A.9 RT901/G could possibly be a training aircraft, as it has a high-visibility painted top fuselage typical of that applied to four-engined types used by the RAF as trainers after the War. The footage may have been taken during a training drop for Paratroops; or, it is equally possible that this Halifax was filmed air-air for "Against The Wind", with four Paratroop Instructors exiting from the Halifax's belly impersonating the SOE agents. Research has not thrown up the unit that operated Halifax A.9 RT901/G.

Exactly the same footage of this same Halifax will be utilised in two other films with an SOE plot, the celebrated portrayal of "Odette" in 1950 by Anna Neagle and the 1958 production of "Carve Her Name With Pride", dedicated to Violet Zsabo. Footage of another Halifax performing a supply drop in "Against The Wind" is taken from the daddy of SOE war films, "Now It Can Be Told" (1946).

The bulk of the story is concerned with the SOE agents' mission to free the Resistance leader and get him to England. Credit must be given to the realism with which life in Occupied Belgium is depicted in "Against The Wind", while the atmosphere remains tense and uncertain throughout. The traitor in their midst is unmasked (played by Jack Warner, he of "Dixon of Dock Green" fame, no less!). The final part of the mission is to rendezvous with a No.161 (Special Duties) Squadron Westland Lysander III, which is filmed air-air flying at night, then landing on a rough strip to collect the liberated Resistance leader. These images are out-takes of Lysander III R9125/JR-M from "Now It Can Be Told".

However, when the agents run to the Lysander and help the Resistance leader strap in, the code letters KY-L are clearly seen on the fuselage side: these are not representative for either No.138 or No.161 Squadrons. 'KY-' code letters were adopted for a short time at around the outbreak of World War Two by No.162 Squadron, but this was a Middle East-based unit that never operated the Lysander. The same code letters were allocated to the famous No.242 (Canadian) Squadron (previously led by Squadron Leader Douglas Bader) in November 1944, but it, again, never operated Lysanders.

How it is that the Lysander used in "Against The Wind" bears code letters of a squadron which never operated this type of aircraft remains a mystery. The only supposition can be is that the KY-L code letters were painted on by the art department. To give some strength to this possibility, freeze-frame analysis shows that there is no fuselage roundel between the squadron codes of 'KY-' and the individual aircraft identifier 'L'. If it was a real Lysander provided by the Air Ministry from the ten examples it then held in store, the fuselage roundel on the aircraft would definitely be in place.

In shot, the Resistance leader can be seen climbing into the rear cabin of the Lysander, helped by one of the SOE agents. What is shown on the screen is the rear fuselage, tail fin and rudder, plus the port elevator. In the foreground is part of the long 'V'-shaped bracing strut which supported the high wing (out of shot), while the top of the port wheel faring is also visible. This is as much of the Lysander that is shown on the ground in this sequence.

The escaping Resistance leader leans out of the cockpit to shake the hand of the SOE agent, who then stands back as the pilot revs the engine before the Lysander moves away out of shot. The Lysander is heard, not seen, taking off; the camera instead focuses on the faces of the SOE agents as they watch with satisfaction, knowing their objective has been successfully achieved.

What we, the audience, are seeing is an illusion, so apt for a film of this kind. The Lysander does not move under its own power at all. It appears that it is doing so; it shakes with vibrations in the way a Lysander would, and exhaust smoke blows across the scene as would come from the engine exhaust stack (not seen in shot). But the giveaway is the ground beneath the Lysander: it is very loamy, sandy soil with scrub grass. If it was a real Lysander engine-running here, its big Bristol Mercury radial would be whipping the sand up, while when the engine increases revs to taxy away the blast from the Mercury would have sent soil and grass streaming in the Lysander's wake. Instead, the soil and grass remain flat and still, while the SOE agent merely stands back to let the port elevator pass him by as the Lysander taxyies away out of shot. If he had done this while the Lysander was really taxying under its own power, he would have faced such a blast from the slipstream that he would have been bowled over, but instead he just watches without having to either squint to protect his eyes, or to prevent the beret he is wearing from flying away!

In reality, this 'Lysander' is a partial full-scale facsimile manufactured by the art department, probably measured very accurately from a real Lysander used as a pattern (a film technique we shall see used very effectively in further productions reviewed in this book). Quite possibly, Lysander R9125/JR-M was the pattern aircraft, as it would have been available for this purpose in RAF Air Historical Branch storage. The taxying effect was achieved by having what is seen of the airframe being towed away by a machine of some kind out of shot, probably a tractor with ropes attached to it and to the facsimile Lysander's wheels. It's a very well achieved spoof, but a spoof it is.

One other factor to note about "Against The Wind": the film itself does not make any reference to the SOE, but there is no doubting that the agents portrayed in it are SOE. After all, the film is a mystery in itself: there is very little information available about it. Even the title, "Against The Wind", is enigmatic; it's origin is shown at the end, from the saying (as presented on screen): "Yet, Freedom! yet thy banner, torn, but flying, Streams like the thunder-storm against THE WIND". It doesn't help that exactly the same title is used for an Antonio Banderas film made in Mexico with a completely different storyline, as well as for an Australian TV mini-series produced in 1998, while a 1991 TV film entitled "One Against The Wind" uncannily tells the story

of escaping British and American soldiers from Occupied France aided by an English Countess. To add to the mix, Bob Seger composed a song of the same title.

The saying is a line taken from the poem, Childe Harold, written by Lord Byron, and is an elegy to Freedom. When he wrote it, Byron was escaping a life of increasing persecution in England because of his outspoken social mores. Fighting against occupation and escaping to freedom is the theme of this film, "Against The Wind".

THE SMALL BACK ROOM

(Released: February 1949)

This intriguing study of a weapons research expert fighting his private demons and a serious alcohol dependency, while trying to solve the mystery of a new type of delayed action bomb the Luftwaffe is dropping over Britain, is an absorbing film to watch but has no aircraft in it.

LANDFALL

(Released: October 1949)

This is the film version of a Nevil Shute book, "Landfall: A Channel Story". The book's title gives a better description of what the story is about than does the film's title, as "Landfall" by itself means nothing as far as the plot is concerned.

Essentially, it is the story of a young RAF Coastal Command pilot, named 'Rick' in the film and played by Michael Denison, who bombs a submarine believing it to be a German U-Boat but is later told that it was, in fact, a British sub. Mortified by his error, Rick somehow escapes a Courts Martial but chooses to leave the squadron he flies for and, at the same time, parts from the local girl, Mona, who he has fallen in love with. He redeems himself by undertaking the very dangerous task of test flying a new guided weapon launched from a Vickers Wellington bomber. Meanwhile, Mona, in a rather unlikely fashion, overhears two sailors talking in the pub where she works of a German submarine operating in the same area at the same time as Rick apparently sank the British sub. Rather implausibly, she manages to convince the Admiralty to re-open its inquiry into the sinking of the British submarine, which results in Rick being exonerated after it is found that he sank the U-Boat after all. He and Mona live happily ever after.

"Landfall" has patches of aviation in it, but the enthusiast and the historian will have to put up with the script's repeated fascination with Rick's and Mona's not very interesting relationship. The film, in large parts, is, frankly, a bore, although it was well received at the time of its release due to Michael Denison's popularity on the stage playing in very British comedies and light romances.

The first aircraft to be seen are three Avro Anson Is filmed air-air breaking formation above clouds. All three are too far from the camera aircraft to be identified. Rick is flying one of them, on coastal patrol. Filming was done inside a real Anson I, so we get a good view of what the interior cabin was like, rather cramped in fact. Coastal patrol was somewhat boring, to say the least. The dorsal turret gunner is reading a copy of "Men Only", back in the days when it was a saucy 'Penny Dreadful' and well before it became a top shelf adult magazine. The time is meant to be March 1940, a good few months before Dunkirk and the Battle of Britain, so it is 'The Phoney War' period being depicted here, hence the casual attitude towards wartime coastal patrols.

Another shot of two Anson Is parked on the airfield where Rick's squadron flies from shows Anson I NK583/MK-L in the background. 'MK-' were the code letters of No.500 Squadron, RAF Coastal Command, operating from RAF Manston, Kent, at the time "Landfall" is placed in, conducting patrols over the English Channel and the North Sea. According to its own history, No.500 Squadron made the first recorded attack of World War Two by a British aircraft on a German U-Boat, although no success was claimed. Perhaps this distinction was behind the choice to give the Anson Is in "Landfall" No.500 Squadron codes (the squadron number itself is not mentioned in the film). The Ansons were obviously not on strength with No.500 in 1949 when the film was made. In fact, the real No.500 Squadron was operational in 1949 as a Royal Auxiliary Air Force day fighter squadron on Gloster Meteor F.3s.

It is surprising that there were sufficient numbers of Avro Anson Is still available to be used in "Landfall". A total of four were found, most likely from Air Ministry stocks. It is possible that they were Avro Anson Mk.Xs, a version of the Mk.I with a strengthened cabin floor which were produced later in the War and retained all the other features of the Anson I but did not serve with Coastal Command.

A good air-air study of Anson I NK583/MK-L leads into Rick's fateful attack on what he believes must be an enemy submarine. Another shot, this time making a pass head-on to the camera, shows the Anson carrying two bombs under the fuselage - the Anson I was capable of deploying two 100lb bombs from this position, lightweight weaponry that had already rendered the Anson I obsolete at the outset of the War. The bombs in the film are released from a studio miniature.

The attack on the submarine is realistically filmed, with passes made over a real sub on the surface. A very effective mock-up of a conning tower is actually blown up in the sea, to portray the sub's destruction. Rick makes two bombing runs, dropping a pair of bombs each time, which he could not have done for real in the Anson I as its maximum bomb load under the fuselage was only two bombs. On landing back at base, he makes a wing-rocking pass to signal his success before touching down. This scene affords some good studies of Anson Is parked in the background, one bearing the code letters MK-C.

Later, of course, the Royal Navy comes to the conclusion that it was one of their submarines that Rick had sunk because a sub on delivery from refit at Harwich had gone missing at the time Rick carried out his attack. The film then slows down to concentrate on Rick's and Mona's relationship, which deteriorates due to Rick going into a blue funk over what he has done.

Despite what has happened Rick is selected to be the test pilot on a Vickers Wellington which is to launch a new form of guided weapon. Neville Shute's imagination gets the better of him here. Firstly, the British never had such a weapon in their armoury during World War Two because their research into rocket motors lagged a long way behind that of the Germans. Secondly, the Royal Navy for some reason are in charge of this project, which they never would have been in reality because they would have been incapable of launching the weapon - the Fleet Air Arm did not have an aircraft type capable of handling it, due to its size and weight.

Director Ken Annakin's art department have come up with a bomb-like thing with stubbed wings, short tail fin and squared-off elevators. Underneath the rear section is the rocket motor. The inspiration for this guided weapon was undoubtedly the German Henschel Hs.293 radio-controlled anti-shipping glide bomb launched from Heinkel He.177, Focke Wulf FW.200 and Dornier Do.217 aircraft, mostly during the invasion of Sicily and Italy in 1943 and 1944. The size, shape and lay-out of the guided bomb are similar in a number of respects to the Hs.293.

The inventor of the guided weapon is a Barnes Wallis-like character, almost identical in appearance and glasses, called Professor Legge. He tells Rick that the weapon is "a missile which guides itself to a target by a magnetic device….detonated by a proximity fuse". The fuse is giving "a certain amount of trouble at the moment". Whatever the significance is of the lettering on the lower part of the guided weapon's fin, it bears GMX in large letters.

The carrier aircraft is a Vickers Wellington which has been adapted to carry the fake guided missile, at least on taxying runs if not actually airborne. The Wellington is not identifiable due to the way it has been filmed, but it bears standard camouflaged upper surfaces and all-black undersides. It has no code letters. What is noticeable about it is that it is still fitted with both fore and aft Perspex turrets but with the guns removed. In 1949, the Wellington was still in service with the Royal Air Force, mostly as a navigational trainer or ferry aircraft; most likely the example seen in "Landfall" is a Wellington Mk.XVI from a Ferry Unit. For the period it is depicting, it is meant to be either a Wellington Mk.I or Mk.Ia.

The airfield scenes involving the Wellington have the appearance of RAF North Weald but this cannot be confirmed. What is noticeable when the Wellington taxyies out with the fake glide bomb beneath it a line of five Spitfires can be seen in the distance.

The targets for the missile are two ships. The natural magnetic signature of each ship is what will attract the missile's targeting device. Rick's first launch is a success, the missile he launches destroys a small ship. The second target is a much larger ship which has been moored east-west to reduce its magnetic signature, as compared with the larger signature it would transmit if it were moored north-south. The larger magnetic signature has the tendency to trigger the proximity fuse earlier than intended and thus put the launch aircraft at risk. Unfortunately, the second, larger ship breaks its mooring and swings round on the tide to a north-south position, just as Rick runs in and launches the missile, which detonates below the Wellington. One wing is torn off and the Wellington plunges into the sea. The effect is achieved with a studio miniature of the Wellington.

Just how we are not told, but somehow Rick survives what looks like a decidedly unsurvivable crash, another of the weaknesses of the film's plot. And it is here that the film now drags into its long, drawn-out ending with Mona trying to clear Rick's name. It is also here that we can end this review of "Landfall" because no more aircraft appear in it.

THEY WERE NOT DIVIDED

(Released: March 1950)

This fine but rather drawn out film about the Welsh Guards Armoured Division focuses on the friendship between two Lieutenants, one British, one American, through the War years up to the Ardennes Offensive in late December 1944. Directed by future James Bond film director, Terence Young, it uses tanks of the British Army of the Rhine filmed in 1949 to portray the Welsh Guards' push through France and the Low Countries in the penultimate year of World War Two.

Aviation content in the film is not large, and most of it consists of archive material, but what is seen is of historical interest. In fact, aircraft don't appear until the final quarter of the film. The first sighting is of a mass grouping of 35 Douglas B-26 Marauders filmed from the ground flying at altitude in separate formations of between five and six bombers each. Presumably this is film of a real raid because the Marauders are not in parade formation; by bombing from medium-level in one mass, with concentrations of up to six aircraft tightly packed together in sections, the USAAF Marauders could not only guarantee an absolute 'carpeting' of the target, but they could also provide concentrated defence against enemy fighters.

Next, an air-air shot of four Hawker Typhoons armed with rockets and peeling off into a dive attack is shown; film of Hawker Typhoons in action is not easy to come by, so this archive shot in "They Were Not Divided" is welcome. This same shot also appears in "Theirs Is The Glory" (1946). The rockets the Typhoon are armed with are RP3 projectiles with 60lb warheads.

For the sequence portraying Operation Market Garden, archive footage of 34 Douglas C-47s mass para-dropping is used. Added in for good measure is a shot of an Armstrong Whitworth Whitley flying alone and disgorging Paratroops, shown as seen through a pair of binoculars. The use of the Whitley footage is an error, as Whitleys were only used as glider-tugs by the time of the airborne assault on the bridges of Grave, Nijmegen and Arnhem in September 1944.

Two Douglas C-47A Skytrain transports were actually used in the film, neither of which are identifiable. One of them is in natural metal all-over scheme, and can be seen to have United States Air Force titling on its upper fuselage, despite director Young's attempt to obscure it by positioning his actors in front of this C-47A. A tail band as borne by USAF transport aircraft of the Military Air Transport Service, which came into being one year before "They Were Not Divided" was filmed, can also be seen on this same Skytrain; however, these markings are not conspicuous,

so the authentic wartime feel of this shot is not lost. It is followed by an archive shot of a USAAF Douglas C-47A Skytrain in genuine wartime camouflage flying low-level over flat countryside.

The final piece of archive footage used in "They Were Not Divided" is of a single rocket-firing Hawker Typhoon, filmed in silhouette from a distance. The film's title is a reference to the two Lieutenants facing out the War together until they are both killed during the Ardennes Offensive and are buried side by side in the snow, undivided in death as they were in life.

ODETTE

(Released: October 1950)

Starring Anna Neagle in the title role, which she considered to be her own favourite of all her film performances, this is the story of SOE agent Odette Sansom, based on the personal account of the real Odette herself. As a classic World War Two spy film about a female agent working undercover in Nazi Occupied France, one would expect aviation to feature as the means by which the SOE entered into and escaped from enemy held territory, and "Odette" does not disappoint. Actual aircraft are used alongside archive footage in this black-and-white production, some of which is very unusual.

Aviation first appears approximately one third of the way into the plot, when SOE agent Peter Churchill (played by Trevor Howard) is picked up at night from a deserted airfield by an RAF Special Duties Lysander. At least, this is what is intended to be taking place in the film, but the aircraft which appears is certainly not a Lysander. "Odette" was the third film to be made about the SOE within a four-year period immediately post-War, but unlike the previous two productions - "Now It Can Be Told" (1946) and "Against The Wind" (1948) - it does not show an actual Lysander. We learnt in the reviews of those films that the RAF had sold for scrap in 1948 ten Lysanders it still held in storage, just in time for "Odette" to miss out on using one of them (an 11th Lysander, R9125/JR-M, was in pieces in packing crates). So, as with other later productions featuring SOE agents in Nazi Occupied France, some ingenuity had to be employed when depicting a Lysander pick-up.

In the case of "Odette", two actual aircraft are used to portray the Lysander. One is seen approaching the deserted airfield at night, filmed from the ground heading towards the camera. The second aircraft is filmed taxying across the grass and coming to a halt abreast the waiting agents, Churchill and Odette, along with their French Resistance colleague.

The aircraft filmed in flight is an Auster 6A. Identifying its registration isn't possible because it appears on a darkened image flying a head-on profile. A view from the cockpit, giving the pilot's perspective as the aircraft approaches the field where three 'L-shaped torch lights are lit in the night by the agents, is also filmed from this Auster. Ahead of the lights and just in front of the Auster's nose a hardened runway of rather dilapidated condition can be seen crossing the bottom of the screen.

However, when Churchill approaches the 'Lysander' as it rolls to a stop, it has changed shape into a Fairchild F-24W Argus, a high-winged, radial-engined monoplane that could be said to bear some superficial resemblance to a Special Duties 'Lizzie', especially if filmed at night. Some 54 of this War surplus four-seater American 'hack' aircraft found their way onto the British civil register following the end of World War Two. Many of them were Lend-Lease aircraft put up for disposal; quite a few were flown during the War by female ATA pilots. The Argus shown in "Odette" is a F-24W Argus II variant, with its distinctive original Warner Scarab radial engine.

This Argus is devoid of any markings. It has not been painted with RAF roundels or camouflage, or even in Special Duties all-black. The monochrome imagery of the film gives the Argus an all-over grey appearance, although it could have been painted light blue or green. What can be discerned is the temporary paint wash obliterating completely the civil registration on the starboard side of the fuselage: the prefix 'G-' can just be made out, followed by the 'A' of the first four identifying letters, but the last three have been daubed over totally. Identifying it isn't possible, although a strong candidate is Argus II G-AIXM which was active on the British civil register when "Odette" was in production. It was often flown on air taxi and pleasure flights by former Air Transport Auxiliary 1st Officer Joan Naylor, a very experienced pilot of the time.

One wonders why this Argus was not flown in the film. It was clearly in a taxyable condition, but for whatever reason the Auster 6A substituted for it to make the actual in-flight shots.

Churchill conveys to the Chief of F (French) Section, SOE, in London, Major Maurice Buckmaster (played by the man himself, to lend authenticity to the production), a request for a large air drop of weapons and explosives for the French Resistance, le Maquis. Buckmaster confirms that 126 containers will be dropped on a particular night, this information being transmitted to Odette who informs le Maquis. They must light three bonfires at 100 metres spacing upwind, to guide the bombers in to the drop zone. This they do as the sound of the bombers' engines grows louder and louder. Then the bombers are seen overhead, from each one of which a trail of white parachutes descends.

Quite extraordinarily, producer/director Herbert Wilcox (Anna Neagle's husband) and film editor Bill Lewthwaite have used some previously unseen footage of up to eight Boeing B-17G Flying Fortresses air dropping containers by parachute whilst flying in pairs to form a large, loose formation. The B-17Gs are filmed from the ground as they unload their containers from right overhead the camera position. What is noticeable about these B-17Gs is that the containers leave each Flying Fortress from directly beneath the fuselage, which means that their ball turrets have been removed and that the containers are being released through the consequently vacant floor hatch. Also, as they make their drops, each B-17G is flying with their gear down - the reason for doing this is not apparent, unless it was for safety purposes at quite low-level.

Film of the B-17 Flying Fortress being used to air drop items by parachute is extremely rare, and in the author's experience this is the only example of such footage he has seen. The use of the B-17 to air drop supplies is also virtually unknown; in fact,

only the CIA have been known to make such drops from the Flying Fortress, in support of rebels opposing the Communist take-over of China. During World War Two, the USAAF used the B-24 Liberator as a more capable aircraft to make air drops of personnel and cargo, in the manner of the RAF Special Duties Halifax and Stirling bombers.

So, when and where this rare footage of B-17Gs conducting air drops was taken remains unknown, but presumably it was of a trials drop to test the Flying Fortress's suitability for such a role. The B-17 could only carry a limited number of small containers: study of the film footage used in "Odette" shows that each B-17G releases a maximum of 11 containers that are noticeably small, as anything larger would not be able to be passed through the ball turret hatch - compare that with the imagery of the Halifax in "Now It Can Be Told", dropping a whole stream of large weapons and equipment containers. In his book, "SOE: The Special Operations Executive 1940 - 1946" (1984), war historian and wartime SAS officer, M R D Foot, writes that a B-17 could hold a maximum of 12 containers in its bomb bay as compared with 18 in a B-24. His book has a photograph showing B-17Gs para-dropping weapons containers to French Maquis fighters on the Vercors plateau on 14th July 1944; noticeably they are doing so with their undercarriage lowered.

Aviation appears again in "Odette" when Buckmaster takes the decision to parachute Churchill - codename 'Raoul' - back into France to rejoin Odette - codename 'Lise'. To illustrate this, Wilcox and Lewthwaite have resorted to more archive footage, this time showing fine imagery of an Handley Page Halifax B.II Series I taxying out in front of a sister aircraft parked on the grass just behind it. The Halifax B.II Series I was a distinctive-looking variant of this RAF heavy bomber, being powered by Rolls Royce Merlin XX engines: the close-up shot used in "Odette" provides an excellent study of this type for the aviation historian.

The scene is obviously meant to be RAF Tempsford. A version of the Halifax B.II Series I was produced specifically for SOE missions, but the actual example shown in this archive footage is that of the bomber variant, as its Boulton Paul Type C dorsal gun turret attests (the SOE version had no dorsal turret). There is nothing to identify the actual Halifax shown: no serial is visible and it carries no codes. A third Halifax can be seen parked in the distance as the first aircraft moves past the camera.

This shot then cuts into a good study of an Handley Page Halifax B.II Series I taking off, banking noticeably port wing low as it does so. This could be the same aircraft as in the taxying shot, as its appearance is the same. The location appears to be the same airfield, as two more Halifax B.II Series Is parked on base are seen as the example taking off flies by. Recently, extra footage of this same imagery has appeared on the Web, showing that the Halifax B.II Series I taking off then gives a flying demonstration to onlookers, making very dramatic low passes. The footage was probably taken by the RAF Film Production Unit.

The Halifax B.II Series I came into service with RAF Bomber Command in March 1942. The aircraft shown in this archive footage may have belonged to a trials unit, which would place the scene shown in approximately the same time period and would perhaps explain their lack of code letters.

However, when it comes to the sequence in which Churchill parachutes from what is meant to be the No.138 (Special Duties) Squadron Halifax B.II Series I he took off in, Wilcox and Lewthwaite have unwittingly changed the Marque of this bomber. Instead of the Halifax B.II Series I, Churchill is now about to exit from an Halifax A.9 we have seen before: it is Handley Page Halifax A.9 RT901/G and the air-air footage of it in flight is exactly the same as in "Against The Wind" (1948). Actually, the footage used in "Odette" is of better and more clear quality than as it appears in the former film. The Halifax A.9 differed from the B.II Series I in being powered by Bristol Hercules 100 radial engines, having a glazed nose in place of the forward gun turret, rectangular tail fins compared with the triangular style of the other Marque, and lacking both dorsal and tail turrets (in wartime service, the A.Mk.9 was designated A.Mk.IX, the Roman numerals being changed into Arabic figures post-War). As was the case with the use of this footage in "Against The Wind", the unit which operated Halifax A.9 RT901/G is unknown. The shot of Churchill exiting the Halifax through the floor hatch is also taken from "Against The Wind".

Aviation does not appear again in "Odette" until the final quarter of the film and all of it is archive material. Wilcox uses newsreel and MoI-disseminated footage of major military advances by the Allies following D-Day, to compare the effect of these events upon the treatment of Odette by the Gestapo and the SS after her capture and incarceration in Ravensbruck Concentration Camp. Because she successfully enabled plans of the port of Marseilles to be got to London, she is blamed by the Gestapo for the sweeping invasion of the South of France and punished by being shut in complete darkness without food and with the heat from her cell's radiator turned up to suffocating levels. Among the archive footage Wilcox uses to show the invasion of the South of France, a formation of seven Martin B-26 Marauders appears ahead of film of the bombing of a port, presumably meant to be Marseilles. The Marauder formation is filmed from the ground making a ceremonial fly-past, definitely not in tactical formation.

Among more archive footage depicting the advances by the Allies in April 1945, a shot of a very low-flying Spitfire skimming over the sea beside ships and landing craft appears. Freeze-frame study shows it to be a Merlin-engined version with the standard high-back fuselage and rounded tail, placing it in the first half of World War Two. At that stage Spitfires were used to support Allied landing exercises as the more effective Mustang Is and IIs were in short supply, while cannon-armed Hurricanes and P-40 Tomahawks were needed in the North Africa campaign. So, the best guess is that Wilcox has used footage of a Vickers Supermarine Spitfire Mk.V, over-flying a Commando landing exercise, for this April 1945 sequence.

Behind the headline, "Munich Falls To The Americans", Wilcox has inserted air-air footage of a formation of three North American B-25 Mitchells filmed from the dorsal turret of a fourth example, whose tail fin gets into shot, all of which are clearly RAF examples.

However, Wilcox has made the goof of using footage of Mitchells bearing D-Day stripes, which they definitely would not have borne in 1945. This is immediately followed by an air-air of a large formation of 12 Vickers Supermarine Spitfire Mk.IXs in tactical spread, all recognisable by the Marque because they are all carrying D-Day invasion stripes - what is notable, however, is that each Spitfire is carrying a bomb under its fuselage, a rare sight indeed. Again, D-Day-marked Spitfires are wrong for the 1945 era.

This does not stop Wilcox, however. He immediately follows this air-air up with another of a D-Day-striped Douglas Boston Mk.III, coded OA-L of No.342 (Free French) Squadron, RAF, over-flying two streams of landing craft below.

Moving on through headlines of further advances by the Allies, Wilcox inserts an high-level air-air of 14 Boeing B-17G Flying Fortresses streaming their contrails in the stratosphere. This is the final shot of aviation in "Odette", a well made film about a woman who is held as a heroine of World War Two but who also created doubt in the minds of some who knew her. Incidentally, "Odette" unintentionally gave to the world a line that has been panned and mimicked mercilessly many times by comedians in spoof scenes about the Gestapo: it is the film in which Odette's Gestapo inquisitor tells her, "Ve haff vays of making you talk".

THE WOODEN HORSE

(Released: October 1950)

The first to set the trend for British Prisoner of War (PoW) escape films that proved so popular in the Fifties and the Sixties, "The Wooden Horse" is based on the true escape plan put in place by captured RAF officers in Stalag Luft III to dig a tunnel concealed by an athletics vaulting horse placed over it. No aircraft appear in this film.

CHAPTER 3

1951-1960

The first complete decade to follow the end of World War Two saw the British film industry embark upon one of its most prolific phases. Cinema was a key component in the British people's Fifties lifestyle and the box office did a roaring trade, although the feature film was already having to gear up to compete with its ever growing rival, television.

With the rise of cinema came an increasingly popular desire by the British public to relive the experience of World War Two on film, not just as victors celebrating their victory but to live through and to understand how that victory was achieved, and with what cost. Thus, more British war films were made during this decade than in any other to follow.

Real victories and real heroes, of course, were celebrated in unprecedented style. "Reach For The Sky" (1956) put Group Captain Douglas Bader high on the pedestal as the determined, unyielding British hero who triumphs over all adversity in the face of disability as well as the enemy; "The Dam Busters" (1955) made sure that the exploits of Wing Commander Guy Gibson, VC, and his fellow No.617 Squadron crew members will remain long in the memory; "Carve Her Name With Pride" (1958) made certain that it was known there were real British heroines too.

However, with the memories of World War Two so fresh in the nation's mind, and with many a scar on some cities with bomb damage still evident, as was the case with the naval port city of Plymouth, realism featured strongly in many of the productions made about the War. The first complete film about the Battle of Britain, "Angels One Five" (1952), portrayed the stark fact that many new, young fighter pilots did not survive that great conflict for long; "The Cruel Sea" (1953) was even more stark in its depiction of what a high cost was paid by sailors of the Royal Navy throughout the War; the privations and humiliations meted out by the Japanese to the thousands of British soldiers captured following the fall of Singapore and forced to work on the infamous Burma - Siam railway, was re-created on Academy Award-winning epic scale in "The Bridge on the River Kwai" (1957), although not

shown in such graphic detail as compared with its 21st Century re-make, "To End All Wars" (2001). Defeat on an epic scale was relived as well, with the highly admired "Dunkirk" (1958) setting the template for big battle films to come.

Realism also meant that in many of the productions completed by the British film industry during the Fifties, the enemy was treated with some respect and even in a few cases, admiration. Films like "Ice Cold in Alex" (1958) and "Yesterday's Enemy" (1959) showed that both the German and the Japanese soldier could act with honour to their uniform, while in "The Battle of the River Plate" (1956) Peter Finch played a particularly dignified and gracious Captain Langsdorf of the German pocket battleship, Graf Spee. In pursuit of realism and, perhaps typically British, fairness, British war films certainly differed from their American counterparts, which, in almost all cases, had John Wayne repeatedly defeating Japs who were just that, Japs, and nothing more.

A substantial number of British war films of the Fifties featured aviation in varying degrees. During the first half of the decade there were still significant numbers of Hurricanes, Spitfires, Lancasters, Mosquitos, and even Vickers Wellingtons, available for use. But, as the decade progressed, the supply dried up almost completely. This meant the beginning of ingenuity on the part of the film studios' art and Special Effects departments. Studio miniatures of certain aircraft types were relied on more frequently. Creativity became essential when portraying German aircraft types, which saw the first use of the Messerschmitt Bf.108 touring monoplane acting the role of its Messerschmitt Bf.109 fighter offspring: the Bf.108 debuts as the Bf.109 in "Operation Amsterdam" (1959).

With the majority of the productions still filmed in black-and-white, to save on costs, archive imagery could still be used plentifully. Out-takes from wartime film productions were also exploited quite widely, with the captured Junkers Ju.88 used in "In Which We Serve" (1942) and the Finnish Air Force Blenheim IIs appearing in "The Way to the Stars" (1945) being 'borrowed' for a number of productions in the Fifties.

Genuine World War Two veterans could still be found in the final years of the decade: a Hawker Hurricane plays a key role in "The One That Got Away" (1957), a real Bristol Beaufighter makes a sudden appearance in "Ice Cold in Alex" (1958), a magnificent-looking Avro York is seen thundering majestically into and out of Gibraltar in "I Was Monty's Double" (1958), while the decade ends with two Fairey Swordfish flying in "Sink the Bismarck!" (1960).

The Hollywood 'British' war film also re-emerged during the ten years to follow, along with the first International 'British' war film to be made.

THE DESERT FOX

(Released: October 1951, USA) Hollywood 'British' war film

One of two Hollywood 'British' war films covered in this Chapter, this highly regarded 20th Century Fox production is admired today but was not so at the time of its release in the USA and the UK, largely due to its sympathetic treatment of its subject, Generalfeldmarschall Erwin Rommel. The "Desert Fox", as he became famously known for his exploits with the Deutsches Afrika Korps in North Africa between 1941 and 1943, still attracted very little sympathy with both the American and British public, and especially with ex-servicemen, just six years after the War's end.

The film has a strong British influence because Rommel's North Africa campaign against the British 8th Army forms a major part of the plot, particularly during the first half. Lieutenant Colonel Desmond Young of the 8th Army, who was taken prisoner by the Afrika Korps and who met Rommel, both introduces the film and provides its closing summary when he travels to Germany to discover exactly what happened to the "Desert Fox". The North African desert scenes were filmed in California. James Mason puts in a dignified and convincing portrayal of Rommel, increasing his status as a leading film actor in Hollywood. So memorable was he that he reprised the same role two years later in another 20th Century Fox film about the North Africa campaign, "The Desert Rats" (1953), the review of which follows closely after this one.

The story follows Rommel's increasing disenchantment with Hitler and his final decision to become a member of 'The July Plot', or Operation Valkyrie, the failed assassination attempt against Hitler in July 1944.

Consequently, aviation is not a big player in this film, but the one scene where aircraft do appear is important and interesting to study. On 17th June 1944, eleven days following the Normandy invasion by the Allies, Rommel was travelling in France in his staff car while supervising the Wehrmacht forces trying to resist the Allied advance. His car was shot up by a single RAF Spitfire LF.Mk. IX, causing it to tip over onto its back. Rommel was thrown out and suffered multiple skull fractures.

Both the Americans and the British claimed the credit when Military Intelligence learnt of the strafing of Rommel. However, the American claim can only be seen as opportunistic, as the USAAF

did not operate Spitfire Mk.IXs (German sources confirmed sometime later that it was a Spitfire which strafed Rommel's staff car). There are two candidate pilots who have been credited with making the attack, one South African and the other Canadian, and both of them RAF Spitfire LF.Mk.IX pilots. The latter ironically was nicknamed the 'Flying Fox', his full rank and name being Flight Lieutenant Charley Fox. He had established a reputation for being a deadly shooter on ground-attack sorties, especially against V1 and V2 sites. Fox describes in a video interview how he believes it was he who shot up Rommel's staff car. But there is an anomaly in his description that it took place one month after D-Day; if that was the case, it would have occurred two weeks before the 'July Plot' assassination attempt on Hitler on 20th July 1944, but Rommel was in hospital recovering from his injuries at that time.

The other candidate is Squadron Leader Chris le Roux of No.602 Squadron, whose log shows that he attacked a lone German staff car on 17th June 1944 near the French village of Sainte Foy de Montgomerie (the place name could not have held greater irony for Rommel), the actual location of where the strafing took place. Le Roux would not have known it was Rommel in the staff car and possibly never knew who his victim was, as he himself was killed in an aircraft accident on 19th September 1944, just short of one month before Rommel took poison rather than undergo what would have been a fixed show trial that would have resulted in his execution and left his wife and son at the mercy of a vengeful and vindictive regime.

In "The Desert Fox", the attack on Rommel's staff car is shown being carried out by more than one Spitfire. The sequence has Rommel accompanied by a staff officer and his adjutant, plus his driver. The film's commentator states that the date is 17th June 1944 and that fatefully they were driving "near a village with the ominous name of Montgomery". Suddenly, three fighter aircraft are seen diving down on them. The driver tries to take avoiding action as first one, then a second Spitfire, strafes them at very low level. The car overturns and Rommel is thrown out onto the road.

This sequence is interesting for the way it has been achieved by the film's 2nd Unit and by the editor. It is a very effective example of the split-screen technique. To begin with, it is filmed in two separate locations in France, one on a country road, the other possibly at an airfield. It is of note that the trees in the hedgerows bordering the road are leafless, very obviously not filmed in June. In reality, the Spitfires attacking the staff car are not there. They were filmed making their attack runs at the unknown separate location, quite likely at the airfield where they were based, with only the sky as their background. Their imagery was then merged by the editor with that of the staff car on the road below them.

The two fighters which are seen strafing the staff car are definitely of the Vickers Supermarine Spitfire Mk.IX variant, which means that the film is accurate in using this type. RAF Spitfire LF.IXe squadrons were very active post-D-Day in making low-level fighter sweeps over German defences, shooting up troops, convoys, artillery positions, fuel dumps and any enemy vehicle they came across, as happens here. However, to use Spitfire Mk.IXs in the film, director Henry Hathaway had to look for a source other than the RAF because this Marque of Spitfire had been withdrawn from operational service two years before "The Desert Fox" went into production in 1950. The nearest available Spitfire Mk.IXs were in the hands of the Groupes des Chasse of the French Armee de l'Air.

At the end of World War Two France received 172 Spitfire Mk.IXs from Britain. Most were subsequently operated in IndoChina (today Vietnam) but at least one Spitfire Mk.IX-equipped Groupe de Chasse was kept at home in reserve, each of the four Groupe des Chasse in Armee de l'Air service taking it in turn to be rotated from overseas. The Spitfire Mk.IX was withdrawn by the Armee de l'Air by the end of 1950; however, Hathaway's 2nd Unit was clearly in time to make use of three of these French Spitfires.

The film being in black-and-white meant that changes to the Spitfires' camouflage schemes were not necessary. They are also all filmed head-on, flying fast and low towards the camera, so their national markings are not visible. They would have retained their Armee de l'Air roundels. D-Day invasion stripes, however, have been applied to their wings, adding to the accuracy of the scene. Their appearance takes place as follows:

Rommel's adjutant hears aircraft engines and looks up at the sky. Three fighters are seen in loose formation diving down towards the camera. Then occurs a most extraordinary goof. The film cuts to an air-air shot of what is meant to be one of the diving fighters, which is not a Spitfire but a US Navy Grumman TBM-3 Avenger! That the editor should make such a glaring mistake and be apparently not able to distinguish between not just a Spitfire and an Avenger, but also unable to tell the difference between an RAF fighter and a US Navy torpedo bomber, seems unbelievable. However, he may not have been as dumb as we may think he is. The insertion of the Avenger shot is almost certainly deliberate and the motivation for doing so was most likely to 'Americanise' this scene in an American film that has no American characters in it. The American editor may also have been thumbing his nose at the British for being given the credit for shooting up Rommel.

The first Spitfire Mk.IX comes roaring up the road at low-level in pursuit of Rommel's staff car. Its cannon are blazing and the staff officer beside Rommel in the rear seat takes a hit. This sequence is achieved by means of the car and occupants being filmed in a studio, while the Spitfire is seen behind on a backcloth. The first item to note is that this Spitfire is a clipped-wing LF.IXe variant. The muzzle flashes of its cannon have been created by art department SFX, but the Special Effects team have inaccurately made the flashes appear very close to this Spitfire's wing root next to the fuselage – they should have been flashing at mid-point along the wings' leading edges.

The next item to note is that the shot which immediately follows, showing the Spitfire over-flying the staff car and hurtling towards the camera, is of a different Spitfire Mk.IX with elliptical wing tips, making it an HF.Mk.IX. Also, by freeze-framing it is possible to confirm that the Spitfire in shot is a 'ghost', ie, it is separate imagery of a flying Spitfire merged with that of the staff car and road below it. The quality of this merged SFX, or split-

screen effect, is very well achieved and convincing. The elliptical-winged Spitfire shoots over the camera and out of shot.

A second Spitfire Mk.IX runs in to shoot up the staff car, again achieved by imagery on a backcloth and again it is a clipped-wing 'Spit' LF.IXe. The next shot is of the Spitfire catching the car up with SFX cannon fire kicking dust up from the road, but the previous shot of the elliptical-winged Spitfire HF.IX has been merged in again ahead of it – freeze-framing confirms it is the same imagery as seen before, being repeated.

This is the main involvement with aviation in "The Desert Fox". However, archive imagery is used to portray D-Day taking place, all of it American. In particular, unrepresentative footage of 17 Curtiss P-40 Warhawks (not used in D-Day) performing individual break-offs from a long echelon and impressive images of 45 Douglas C-47A Skytrains disgorging Paratroops stand out.

ANGELS ONE FIVE

(Released: March 1952)

Curiously, "Angels One Five" has provoked more discussion and questions among aviation enthusiasts, historians and researchers than any other film made about the Battle of Britain. The controversy has always been centred upon how many, and which, Hawker Hurricanes were used in the film and, specifically, whether it is either Hurricane Mk.IIc LF363 or PZ865 that appears.

The minimum number of Hurricanes most quoted is that of six, with five provided by the Portuguese Air Force and the sixth being "the last to fly with the RAF". This points conclusively, it seems, to LF363 being used, the last Hawker Hurricane to be delivered to the Royal Air Force. But other sources quote the Last of the Many, the title long borne by Hurricane Mk.IIc PZ865, the final Hawker Hurricane of 14,533 to be built by Hawkers and used by them as the company's 'hack' throughout the Fifties and Sixties.

The film itself shows a full formation of six Hawker Hurricanes. This seems to support a credible claim for a total of six Hurricanes used: five Portuguese, plus one, either RAF (LF363) or Hawkers' (PZ865).

But research has thrown up the identities of other contenders. In fact, a total of ten Hawker Hurricanes can be claimed for "Angels One Five", assembled in July 1951 at RAF Kenley, Surrey, (a genuine No.11 Group Battle of Britain fighter station, of course) for the principal scenes to be filmed of a Fighter Command air station at the height of the Battle.

Of the ten, five were loaned to the production company by the Portuguese Air Force (a sixth was based at Hawker's factory at Langley, Berkshire, as a spare but was not used). All the Portuguese Hurricanes were painted at Langley in 1940-style Fighter Command camouflage and markings before flying on to Kenley, the British pilots contracted to fly them in the film complaining that they first had to de-fumigate the cockpits because they reeked of deodorant! All were returned to the Portuguese AF after filming: the British government donated 40 Hawker Hurricanes to Portugal after the War, as a "Thank you" for allowing facilities in The Azores to be used for anti-U-Boat operations and search and rescue missions during the Battle of the Atlantic. They were only operational for a few years before the Portuguese AF began to modernise, and had been withdrawn from front-line operations by the time they were loaned for "Angels One Five".

Four Hawker Hurricanes were provided by the Royal Air Force, comprising one flyer, one taxyer, and two statics. The flyer was Mk.IIc LF363, kept on strength by the RAF for ceremonial purposes which, in 1951, involved almost solely the annual massed fly-past over London on 15th September to commemorate Battle of Britain Day, which LF363 always led along with a Spitfire. LF363 was also the personal mount of an RAF Air Vice Marshall, painted in diplomatic blue; LF363 permanently lost its blue scheme after receiving its 1940's earth and green camouflage for "Angels One Five".

The taxyable Hurricane was Mk.I P2617, then part of the RAF Air Historical Branch's substantial accumulation of both British and Axis Powers World War Two aircraft that were brought out for various ceremonial displays each year up and down the country. Today, Hurricane Mk.I P2617 has long been an exhibit in the RAF Museum at Hendon. Used as a static film prop only was Mk.I L1592, today in the custody of the London Science Museum in Kensington, while its sister, Mk.I L1591, was passed on to the film production company and used at Borehamwood Studios for a crash landing sequence and for in-cockpit shots.

The final Hawker Hurricane in "Angels One Five" is indeed Mk.IIc PZ865 of the Hawker Aircraft Company. Detractors claim this cannot be possible because at this point in time PZ865 was spending her whole life as G-AMAU on the British civil aviation register, swanning around at sumptuous Royal Aeronautical Society garden parties and King's Cup Air Races, dressed in immaculate royal gold and dark blue finery to mark her sponsorship by HRH Princess Margaret in the year of the Festival of Britain for air racing at Hatfield during the same month as filming. No way could she have swapped all that in time, to appear in grubby RAF 1940's camouflage for a film.

But, indeed, she did just that. And no less an authority than a certain Dr John D R Rawlings provides the proof, coupled with photograph, printed with his letter in an August 1951 edition of Flight magazine, showing PZ865 in "Angels One Five" wardrobe as P2619/US-B in the static park at RAF Hendon for the Daily Express-sponsored 50th Anniversary of Flight Airshow, held also in July 1951 as part of the Festival of Britain. The author, for one, is not going to argue with such an august authority as aviation historian J D R Rawlings.

PZ865 was used in "Angels One Five" to film scenes as a singleton that did not need the presence of other Hurricanes. She appears fairly early in the film air-air as P2619, without squadron codes, being flown by the main character in "Angels One Five", Pilot Officer 'Septic' Baird (played by John Gregson), a new pilot on delivery to 1320 Squadron at RAF Neethley. The air-air shots of PZ865 ('P2619') are an especially fine study, believed to be filmed over the Medway. PZ865 was then given the fictional

1320 Squadron code letters of US-B (more of this later), to act a scene when she is filmed as 'Septic' Baird's Hurricane being flown alone in pursuit of a Messerschmitt Bf.110. Hawker's test pilot Bill Bedford flew this scene, plus an exhausting series of downward spins for the cameras; he must have been as equally furious and frustrated when none of this footage was used in the film!

The shooting of PZ865 as P2619 lasted little more than a day. She retained her warpaint until after her appearance at RAF Hendon, then was washed down at Langley to reveal her 'royal' colours once more.

The appeal of "Angels One Five" is that it is about a Hurricane-equipped squadron, not that of a perennially popular Spitfire outfit. However, two Spitfires appear as background props in various scenes, while a look-out declaring to Ops during the Battle that "twelve Spitfires taking off" reveals that RAF Neethley is a joint Hurricane and Spitfire base. The imagery of two 'Vics' of Spitfires taking off comprises archive footage of six Spitfire Mk.Is, probably filmed much earlier than the Battle, as the Whitley bomber parked in the background appears to attest. The two Spitfires used as props are unidentifiable due to the way they are filmed, with no codes and serials visible; Mk.Vbs BL614 and EP120 are possible candidates, as they were being used as instructional airframes for RAF ground handling crews at the time, but there is no confirmation of this.

Other aircraft appearing in "Angels One Five" comprise two Noorduyn AT-16 Harvard IIbs, both taxying in un-warlike all-over silver and with yellow training bands around the fuselage, not at all 1940. One of them is identified as Harvard IIb FX311, but the serial of the other, while visible, is unreadable. Also in this scene is Avro Anson C.XII PH606, which actually was the airborne camera platform. The Harvards and Anson appear when RAF Neethley scrambles all remaining aircraft of the Training Flight on field before the appearance of Junkers Ju.88s overhead.

'Septic' and the Station 'Boss', Group Captain 'Tiger' Small (played by Jack Hawkins in the role which established him as a leading film actor), race for the last Hurricane, with 'Septic' winning and climbing aboard Hurricane P2617/US-B before taxying away to take off and join the fight. Obviously, this was taxyable Hurricane Mk.1 P2617 acting the role of 'Septic's Hurricane coded US-B when this sequence was filmed in July 1951. It was then intended that aerial shots of Hurricane Mk.IIc PZ865, portraying P2617/US-B and filmed on a different date, would be immediately cut into this sequence by the film editor, so that 'Septic' would be seen pursuing a Luftwaffe fighter shortly after taking off, but it appears a continuity goof got in the way here: the art department had painted 'P2619' on PZ865, not 'P2617'. This probably led to the decision by the director to edit out the aerial sequences of PZ865 as P2619/US-B; the previous shot immediately before, with 'Septic' scrambling in P2617/US-B, would clearly have exposed the goof of two different versions of the serial for what is meant to be the same Hurricane!

With this footage gone, it meant that the denouement of 'Septic' being shot down had to go as well. This was what Bill Bedford's spins in PZ865, as 'Septic' in his Hurricane crashing to earth, was intended to portray. Bedford, then a very new test pilot with Hawker's, must have felt he needn't have bothered performing all these spins, once he learnt that all of this footage had been left on the cutting room floor. As it is, the death of 'Septic' conveyed in the film by his weakening voice coming over the tannoy to his fellow officers in the Ops Room, then falling into silence, is far more moving and effective.

Before this sad ending, though, 'Septic' gets his first 'kill', and inspects the downed Bf.110 afterwards. Wreckage from a real Messerschmit Bf.110 was used. Research indicates that it was a night fighter Bf.110G-4, either Werke Nr 180850, coded 3C+BA, of Nachtjagdgeschwader 4 (NJG.4), or Werke.Nr 140655, G9+AA, of NJG.1, that had been captured intact by the Allies at the end of the War; five captured Bf.110s were ferried to Britain and given Air Ministry identity numbers. Both of these two Bf.110G-4s would have been of special interest to British military analysts because they were each found to be fitted with the latest FuG218V/R (Neptun) airborne interception (AI) radar, having been installed with it early in 1945 and were being tested against RAF Bomber Command when the Allies' overwhelming air superiority above Germany meant that night raids were no longer necessary.

The nose-mounted aerial array carried by the Bf.110G-4 in "Angels One Five" had been removed before the airframe was given to the film production company and set up to look like a Bf.110 Zerstorer crashed nose first into a field. If the array had been left in place, it would have been completely unrealistic for a scene that is meant to be taking place in the summer of 1940 - AI radar-equipped night fighter Bf.110s did not enter the fight until 1943. However, the two mounting horns for the earlier Lichtenstein aerial array can clearly be seen still attached to the upper nose section, as 'Septic's air crew mates celebrate his first 'kill'. The Neptun aerial array, smaller than that of the Lichtenstein, was attached solely by one support driven straight through the front of the nose. It appears that at some stage the nose of this Bf.110G-4 was changed with that of another, perhaps because the latest Neptun array was of greater interest and had been detached for closer examination.

The pilots carry 'Septic' back to the squadron hut on one of the Bf.110's two vertical tail fins: on it can clearly be seen the Werke Nr 180850. The same number is also applied to the remaining tail fin still attached to the downed airframe. Just discernable through the paint applied to the fuselage is the number '3', which appears to confirm that this is 3C+BA of NJG.4. This code was painted over because RAF roundels were applied to the fuselage when this Bf.110G-4 was being air tested back in Britain; the Luftwaffe Balkenkreuzen shown on the crashed Bf.110 in the film are actually covering the roundels.

Messerschmitt Bf.110G-4 Werke.Nr 180850, 3C+BA, was flown by the Kommodore of NJG.4, Major Heinz-Wolfgang Schnaufer, based at Eggebeck in Northern Germany (until December 2005, a German Naval Air Arm base, equipped with Tornado IDS tactical strike jets). Major Schnaufer was the highest scoring night fighter pilot of the War, of either side, with 121 victories: the tail fin of his Bf.110 which bore all these victory scores is on display today in the Imperial War Museum at Lambeth. According to an informed source, Major Schnaufer only flew 3C+BA five times and

did not achieve any victories in it, his last sortie being on 21st April 1945 before Eggebeck was overrun by British forces. After being ferried back to Britain, this Bf.110G-4 was exhibited at Hyde Park in London on 15th September 1945, the first Battle of Britain celebration. It did not survive long after the film was made, being buried in a mass dump along with other captured Luftwaffe aircraft. One of the five captured Bf.110G-4s which did survive is Werke. Nr 730301 of III/NJG.3, which is displayed today in the Battle of Britain Exhibition within the RAF Museum at Hendon, one of three intact surviving Messerschmitt Bf.110s in the world.

Comment has been made about the No.56 Squadron 'US-' codes borne by the Hurricanes in the film. There is also an air-air shot of two Hurricanes clearly serialled and coded N6547/AV-P and K1694/AV-X: this shot has no apparent relevance to the plot, as no other such coded aircraft appear in the film. 'AV-' codes belonged to the Spitfire IIs and Vs of No.121 (Eagle) Squadron, which did not form until 1941.

The explanation possibly lies with the film's distributor, whose sole interest would have been in getting "Angels One Five" the widest possible exposure and, with it, the greatest return on the film's investment. Box office success, in the world of movies, is spelt "A-M-E-R-I-C-A". A very British war movie had to make money in America. So, the distributor may have stepped in and told the director and producer to "Americanise" the film, even without a single American character in it. The easiest way would be to have the Hurricanes carry codes with the letters 'US', while a specially staged air-air photo shoot with two Hurricanes carrying American Eagle Squadron codes could also send its own message.

The weakest part of "Angels One Five" is the awful Special Effects art work of Luftwaffe Ju.88s bombing RAF Neethley, possibly the worst such SFX created in any war film.

The original title for the film was "Hawks In The Sun", under which it was released in the United States. No explanation has been given for the title change to "Angels One Five", but there is a clue in the person of actor Cyril Raymond. He has a major role in the film as RAF Neethley's fighter controller. Is it just coincidence that he played an identical role ten years earlier in "The First Of The Few" (1942), and that in that film he directs 227 'Hunter' Squadron to climb to "angels one five"?

GIFT HORSE

(Released: July 1952)

This is a fine, if less well known, British war film in the tradition of "In Which We Serve", telling the story of one of the fifty American Lend-Lease World War One-era destroyers taken on charge by the Royal Navy for Atlantic convoy escort and home waters patrol duties, nicknamed (sarcastically) the "Gift Horse" by its crew. It is a well made, well acted, very realistic film, gritty and uncompromising, creating a true-to-life depiction of the conditions of service on board one of these out-dated, almost unfit-for-purpose warships.

Possibly the most famous wartime action involving five of these Lend-Lease destroyers was the so-called 'Channel Dash' on 12th February 1942, when the German Kriegsmarine Schlacht Kreusers (battlecruisers) Scharnhorst and Gneisenau and the Schwere Kreuser (heavy cruiser) Prinz Eugen made a daring dash from the French port of Brest through the English Channel, to reach the safety of Wilhelmshaven and Brunsbuttel.

However, "Gift Horse" makes use of another, and this time successful, wartime operation involving one other of these 50 Lend-Lease Town Class destroyers, HMS Campbeltown, in destroying a dry dock in the French Atlantic Sea port of St Nazaire. Code named Operation Chariot, this action took place on 28th March 1942, approximately six weeks after the 'Channel Dash', and succeeded in inflicting so much damage to the dry dock that it was put out of action for the remainder of the War.

The reason behind Operation Chariot was that the Kriegsmarine Schlachtschiffe (battleship) Tirpitz, in the same Class as the Bismarck sunk less than one year earlier, was moored at Trondheim in Norway and presented the same serious threat to the Atlantic convoys as did her feared sister ship. If Tirpitz broke out into the Atlantic sea lanes, she could cause immense damage as a commerce raider and the Royal Navy would have to mount a same size-scale sea hunt as they were forced to do in May 1941 when Bismarck escaped through the Denmark Straits. However, British Naval Intelligence knew that Tirpitz could only be re-fitted after being at sea in one location: the Forme Ecluse Louis Joubert Dry Dock at St Nazaire, originally dug out for the giant (of the time) pre-War liner SS Normandie and the only dry dock large enough to take the Tirpitz. The British reasoned that if this dry dock could be put out of action, the likelihood would be that the Kriegsmarine would not risk sending Tirpitz to sea, knowing the Schlachtschiffe would have no protective harbour in which to anchor and re-fit. This is exactly what happened as a consequence of Operation Chariot: Tirpitz never put to sea in the Atlantic - although she made a brief foray into the North Sea - and was eventually capsized in Tromsofjord by Lancasters of Nos.9 and 617 Squadrons. What the British did not know at the time of Operation Chariot was that the Kriegsmarine had already been ordered by Hitler to keep Tirpitz on station in a Norwegian fjord, to guard against an imagined invasion of Norway by Britain which Der Fuhrer was obsessed with (fuelled by false information to that effect planted in the Abwehr by MI5-controlled German double agents).

In "Gift Horse", the 'St Nazaire Raid', as it became widely known, is accurately re-created. However, for the film's purpose HMS Campbeltown's name is not used. Instead, the 'Gift Horse' destroyer is HMS Ballantrae, a fictional ship, while Operation Chariot is re-named as Operation Boadicea. The actual destroyer used in the film is, in fact, one of the 50 ex-US Navy Lend-Lease destroyers, HMS Leamington, which was built in 1919 and served as the USS Twiggs until it was transferred to the Royal Navy in 1940. HMS Leamington conducted Atlantic and Baltic convoy patrols before being transferred to the Royal Canadian Navy in 1943, then, one year later, was loaned to the Russian Navy for Baltic convoys protection. In 1950, the Russians handed the

destroyer back to the Royal Navy; she was listed for disposal in 1951 but, before this happened, she was loaned to Molton Films for her role as HMS Ballantrae in "Gift Horse".

Aviation only features in one scene in "Gift Horse", when HMS Ballantrae on convoy duty comes under aerial attack by Luftwaffe bombers. Footage from various sources are used here; no actual aircraft were provided to the film production company for this scene.

The first shot shows what appear to be five Junkers Ju.88 bombers approaching the convoy in 'Vic' formation, but a closer study confirms that they are the five Finnish Air Force Bristol Blenheim Mk.IIs used in "The Way to the Stars" (1945), flying head-on towards the camera. Next they are seen breaking apart, with the Blenheim II to the right of the screen trailing smoke from its port engine. Both pieces of footage are out-takes from "The Way to the Stars" which were not actually used in that film. As stated in the introduction to this Chapter, these unused out-takes were certainly exploited by other later British war film productions, as was the case here in "Gift Horse".

Actual wartime archive footage is used in the rest of this scene, beginning with a distant shot of a Junkers Ju.87 Stuka unloading its bomb at a small merchant ship. This is a quite cleverly edited sequence, first showing the Stuka diving and pulling out of its attack, then cutting to a shot traversing down to the ship with the bomb impacting in the sea just off its port bow. Both shots are probably from the same action, with the camera positioned quite high and some distance away - possibly a good two miles - from where the Stuka is making its attack on its target. From the appearance of this footage, it looks like it is part of the film that was taken in July 1940 from the cliffs overlooking the English Channel, not far from Dover, of Ju.87 Stuka attacks on a small convoy. Footage from this film has been seen in many documentaries.

Successive bomb blasts erupt from the sea close to a ship that is being attacked. Another Ju.87 Stuka is seen unloading three bombs, a larger one from its centreline fuselage hardpoint plus two smaller bombs that were attached to either wing; then the film cuts to more bomb bursts in the sea. Dramatic footage shows bombs exploding close beside a large cargo vessel, then the anti-aircraft guns aboard HMS Ballantrae target another dive bomber. Tracer fire streams towards a small, distant aircraft which presumably is a Stuka, but is too far and too much of a speck on film to identify. A bomb explodes some distance away from a merchant ship, which appears to have been already hit and is streaming smoke; another bomb explodes closer to the vessel from where the camera is filming - both bomb impacts are noticeable for the amount of shrapnel that cuts up the water, a clear illustration how widespread the damage would be if these bombs were dropped on cities or on closely packed vehicles.

Footage is then used of two Bristol Blenheim Mk.IVs, again to give the impression of being Ju.88s, making a low pass in close formation - not a genuine attack run - over the ship from which they are being filmed. This is possibly an out-take from staged footage believed to have been filmed by the RAF Film Production Unit aboard a stationary vessel at sea, to create the effect of aerial attacks on shipping. Much more dramatic out-takes from this same footage is used to convincing effect in "Malta Story" (1953), as will be described in the review of that film in this Chapter.

A bomb explodes very close to the ship it is filmed from, to create the effect of HMS Ballantrae taking a near miss. Archive footage of an unidentified twin-engine bomber flying at altitude through flak bursts appears next; bombs send bursts of spray towering above the ship they have been targeted against; more footage of the small, unidentifiable aircraft flying high through tracer fire; then another aircraft appears which is too distant to identify, but which is flying low over the sea through flak, suggesting it is a torpedo bomber and therefore could be a Regia Aeronautica Savoia-Marchetti SM.79, although this cannot be confirmed.

The final shots of this scene have the anti-aircraft gunners on HMS Ballantrae scoring hits on an attacking aircraft, which plunges into the sea amid much cheering. The film's editor, however, has elected to use a very familiar piece of footage of a Spitfire diving inverted into the English Channel during the Battle of Britain. Clearly the editor believed that the cinema audience in 1952 would not have had time to realise it is 'one of our own' going down. No more aircraft appear in "Gift Horse" after this shot.

This is a film well worth having in one's library of war films, and is a much more realistic depiction of the 'St Nazaire Raid' - despite the limitations of the art work SFX - than was staged in "Attack on the Iron Coast" (1968) 16 years later, which also takes Operation Chariot as its theme. In the light of just how effectively the 'St Nazaire Raid' is shown in "Gift Horse", it is a puzzle to know as to why anyone bothered to make the other, less creditable film of the same operation.

APPOINTMENT IN LONDON

(Released: February 1953)

The one principal criticism that can be levelled at this otherwise well-made film about an RAF Bomber Command Lancaster squadron is its title - a less imaginative and dramatic title for a war film is hard to imagine. The distributor in the United States certainly thought so; over there, it was released under the title "Raiders in the Sky".

The meaning of the title only becomes apparent right at the very end of the film, the actual "Appointment in London" being the investiture at Buckingham Palace for two bomber pilots who are to receive Distinguished Flying Cross medals from HM The King. The film ends with a dedication to all those in Bomber Command who were unable to keep their "Appointment in London" due to being lost in action.

Leaving aside any criticism about its title, in all other respects "Appointment in London" is a fine production. This film creates more accurately than any other of its kind the atmosphere and reality of a Bomber Command base during World War Two, with believable characters and convincing acting, even if it is now redolent of its black-and-white film period. Dirk Bogarde plays Wing Commander Tim

Mason, an obsessed Commanding Officer of the fictional No.188 Squadron who is desperate to complete 90 Ops before he is ordered to fly a desk. He succeeds, of course, and has his date with destiny at the film's ending with his investiture at Buckingham Palace.

Most outstanding of all is the creative and imaginative film effects by director Philip Leacock and cinematographer Stephen Dade of the Avro Lancasters used in the production, filmed from any number of different angles to achieve the most dramatic and impressive images of these formidable bombers, which, mixed with the roar of their Merlin engines, brings their full power and energy to life.

The opening shots are of three Lancasters taking off at night in succession on a special mission. Even in black-and-white the Lancasters appear dominating and majestic. All three successfully return and are filmed landing in turn at their base which, for the film, was RAF Upwood in Cambridgeshire, an actual Bomber Command airfield with Lancasters during the War but was home to four Avro Lincoln squadrons when the film was in production there in 1952.

Various sources quote three Lancasters as being used but analysis of the film shows that four actually appear, while there is evidence that even a fifth 'Lanc' is a possibility. In addition, some of the based Lincolns of different Marques help fill the background of various shots and add to the formation of Lancasters filmed air-air as part of the climactic air raid for the finale. The three quoted Lancasters are Avro Lancaster B.VIIs NX673, NX679 and NX782. Of these three, NX673 and NX782 can definitely be confirmed through freeze-frame analysis, but by the same method NX679 cannot be identified. One explanation for these three being listed by alternative sources who have studied this film is that these same three Lancasters are said to appear in "The Dam Busters" (1955) two years later, so the assumption may have been made that they were first used in "Appointment in London". This might be a logical assumption to make, but a very careful examination of the film appears not to reveal Lancaster B.VII NX679 as a participant.

What is noticeable is that each identified Lancaster is painted with an individual identity which it retains for the whole production. Thus, each Lancaster plays one particular role and is not painted to represent different aircraft, as happens often with most British military aircraft in war films. This makes identifying each Lancaster much easier.

Lancaster B.VII NX673 acts the role of 'B - Baker' (note, the film correctly uses the Allied code wording system which the RAF adopted after the Americans assumed the leading role in the combined war effort against the Axis Powers), while Lancaster B.VII NX782 portrays 'V - Victor', the aircraft flown by Wing Commander Mason. For the film, No.188 Squadron uses the 'IH-' code letter system, which does not relate to any actual RAF squadron. Thus, NX673 is IH-B, while NX782 wears IH-V.

Both these Lancasters had previously served with famous RAF Bomber Command squadrons, NX673 with No.9 Squadron and NX782 with No.617 "Dam Busters" Squadron; however, both came on strength after the War in Europe had ended and were instead assigned to the 'Tiger Force' that was intended to be the RAF's air effort against the Japanese mainland before Japan surrendered in August 1945.

The third Lancaster which features prominently in the film carries the code letters IH-S, thus acting as 'S - Sugar'. This Lancaster is a noticeably different Marque from its B.VII sisters. It is Avro Lancaster B.I TW862, very clearly identifiable through freeze-frame analysis (which makes it a puzzle as to why the sources that identify the three B.VIIs make no mention of this actual and clearly visible Lancaster). By its serial it is a late production model that probably did not see wartime action; the B.Mk.I was the most widely produced model of the Lancaster and remained in production from the beginning to the end of the famous bomber's lifetime. It also noticeably carries a ventral radome beneath its rear fuselage, which suggests that TW862 was fitted with the H2S ground scanning radar system during part of its career.

All three Lancasters are painted all-over black with very light grey tops to their fuselages and to their propeller spinners. These obviously are not correct Bomber Command colour schemes of the 1943 period that the film's plot is covering. All three were based at RAF Upwood and were used as trainers for aircrew and groundcrew who were converting onto four-engined aircraft before being assigned to any one of the four Avro Lincoln squadrons operating from Upwood. Both B.VIIs NX673 and NX782 would have been pilot trainers, while B.I TW862, with its H2S radar, may well have been a navigational trainer. Probably repainting these Lancasters into the appropriate camouflage schemes of the period would have been too costly and taken too long for the film production company; or the Air Ministry refused permission for this to be done.

There is definitely, however, a fourth Avro Lancaster which appears in the film. It can be clearly discerned as it is the only Lancaster in the film painted in accurate-looking camouflage; it is seen fully in shot as one of the three Lancasters returning from the secret raid and has the code letters IH-C distinctly visible as it lands, but its serial cannot be read. It also, unlike the other three Lancasters, carries what looks like a Gorgon's head image painted on its nose, as well as 16 mission markings. Another shot in which it appears shows it parked beyond one of the B.VIIs, with the second B.VII and the sole B.I standing in the background - this is the only shot in the entire film in which all four Lancasters are seen together.

The supposition is that this is Avro Lancaster B.I PA474, now of the RAF Battle of Britain Memorial Flight (BBMF). However, PA474's service record for the time - 1952 - does not support this. She had been converted into a trials aircraft on loan to the Royal College of Aeronautics at Cranfield; also, she no longer had a camouflage colour scheme, while the BBMF's own history for PA474 does not include "Appointment in London" among her film credits.

There is the possibility that this camouflaged Lancaster IH-C is the unidentified Avro Lancaster B.VII NX679, meaning it either was already camouflaged or was the one Lancaster that was painted for the film. Whichever, there is still a mystery about this Lancaster because even though it is the most realistic-looking of the four in the film, it is the one that is least used. 'B - Baker', 'S - Sugar' and 'V - Victor' all appear throughout the film and have definite roles in conjunction with the actors associated with them, but 'C - Charlie' (Lancaster IH-C) does not. The hypothesis is that there may have been the intention to paint all four Lancasters in RAF Bomber Command camouflage, but that either time or cost were against the production (NX782 actually does have camouflage painted on her top wings, but nowhere else). For director Leacock and cinematographer Dade, the contrast between the camouflaged Lancaster and the black-and-light-grey other three probably meant that the camouflaged example had to be axed, otherwise its 'wardrobe' would have repeatedly conflicted with the colour schemes of its three co-stars.

Another Lancaster 'character' which appears in the film is 'R - Roger'. This Lancaster has been badly shot up in a raid which No.188 Squadron pilots believed was "jinxed". It crash lands, with all the crew on board killed. To portray this, one of the Lancasters was flown very low wheels up across RAF Upwood with its starboard outboard engine completely shut down. This imagery of such a dramatic fly-by is probably the only example available showing a Lancaster flying with the propellers of one of its engines completely stopped. Reading this Lancaster's serial is difficult because of the speed at which it passes the camera, but careful freeze-framing appears to show that it is Lancaster B.VII NX673 acting the role of the stricken 'R - Roger'.

And to add to the mystery, there is a fifth Avro Lancaster which makes a brief appearance in the film. It too represents 'R - Roger'. It is filmed air-air, with the camera 'plane looking down at it and filming it from above, as this 'Lanc' flies low over countryside. It is shown in the run-up to 'R - Roger's fly-by. The code letters OL-F are clearly visible on its fuselage, making this a Lancaster of No.83 Squadron. The excellent Avro Lancaster Heavy Bomber Register Website (www.avrolancaster.co.uk) offers several candidate Lancasters that bore these codes, but which actual one it is cannot be identified. What is noticeable is that this Lancaster was filmed on an entirely different occasion and not for "Appointment in London". The quality of the imagery is clearly inferior to that of the film production itself, so this is almost certainly stock footage of a No.83 Squadron Lancaster that is being used here.

One other aircraft has an acting role in "Appointment in London": this is de Havilland DH.82A Tiger Moth T7187, which plays the part of No.188 Squadron's 'hack'. When used in the film it was painted in the then 1950s RAF Training Command all-over yellow; in wartime, all Tiger Moths were camouflaged. Tiger Moth T7187 was built by Morris Motors, Ltd, in 1940 and was struck off charge by the RAF in 1955. It was sold onto the civilian market and became G-AOBX on the CAA Register. It actually was first owned by the RNVR Flying Group based at RNAS Ford in Sussex before being acquired in 1958 by Universal Flying Services at Fairoaks Aerodrome. In early 1966, Tiger Moth G-AOBX became part of avid sports bi-plane collector Norman Jones's collection and flew with the Tiger Club flying circus out of Redhill Aerodrome in Surrey. It then joined another airshow group in Britain, Leisure Sport, Ltd, in 1974 and was operated by them until Vintage Displays and Training Services, Ltd, took it over in 1980. From 1983 onwards G-AOBX went through several changes of private ownership until it was acquired by the David Ross Flying Group in Winchester, Hampshire, in whose care it remains to this day.

Inevitably the many Avro Lincolns based at RAF Upwood in 1952 would have to get into shot at some stage. Their family likeness to the Lancasters - in fact, the Lincolns began life as the Lancaster Mk.IV and Mk.V - obviously persuaded director Leacock that they could be used as background props. The four squadrons occupying RAF Upwood at the time were Nos.7, 49, 148 and 214 Squadrons, although some Lincolns would have been based abroad in the Far East.

The Lincolns have under-fuselage radomes, housing H2S radar, and are seen in one particular shot with their large white-painted serials on the fuselage; later, both the serials and the radomes were removed for other shots as background props. They are all painted in the same all-over black colour schemes with almost white fuselage tops as the Lancaster B.VIIs. The Lincolns are distinctive in comparison with the Lancasters in having their four-bladed propellers pointing accurately to all four 90-degree points of the compass when their engines are shut down, whereas the Lancasters' three-blade props just stand where they are left once they have stopped turning. Two particular Lincolns can be identified in shot, they both being Avro Lincoln B.IIs, RF344 and RF289, with their serials standing out large in white on their black fuselages.

The big finale of "Appointment in London" is a maximum effort by Bomber Command on what Wing Commander Mason calls "a new town built to make secret weapons". He does not mention Peenemunde by name, but it is obvious that this is what he is referring to. A little way further into the film we are shown a scene of a Luftwaffe night fighter Operations Room, with Luftwaffe controllers all speaking in German. One controller clearly uses the name Peenemunde when it is realised what the target is that the RAF bombers are aiming for. This scene has a plotting table divided into squares, each one containing a night fighter Geschwader - this is an accurate representation of how the Luftwaffe organised its night fighter units to each cover a particular part of Germany, linked by Jagdschloss plan-position-indicating radar stations.

To represent the maximum bombing raid, RAF Upwood agreed to put up a mixed formation of all four Avro Lancasters plus four Avro Lincolns, the latter comprising a single B.I and three B.IIs. They are all filmed air-air from another Lincoln, with some shots taken from this aircraft's mid-upper turret (with gun barrels appearing in the foreground) while others are taken from the rear tail turret. The Lancasters and Lincolns are seen flying in various mixed formations. One shot has the camouflaged Lancaster fitted with the mid-upper turret leading the single Lincoln B.I also equipped with a mid-upper turret, plus its ventral radome, and which is also camouflaged: this is a rare shot allowing both types to be compared, the Lincoln being noticeably longer in the fuselage than the Lancaster. This Lincoln is also seen air-air flying close formation in trail with the camera aircraft, being filmed nose-on. In another shot, all three Lancasters, NX673, NX782 and TW862, can be seen flying in 'Vic' formation; a solo shot of a Lancaster clearly shows it to be NX782/IH-V.

Archive material is used to depict Luftwaffe fighters scrambling to intercept the RAF bombers: three Focke Wulf FW.190s are seen taking off, followed by a second shot of two Messerschmitt Bf.109Ds scrambling. A solo Focke Wulf FW.190 flies very low over the camera. None of these shots are accurate; images of Lichtenstein-equipped Bf.110s or Ju.88s would have been correct. Luftwaffe flak crews in action are out-takes of the same Bofors ack ack guns, with British gun crews wearing German helmets, taken from "Target for Tonight" (1941).

Director Leacock and his editorial team have made excellent use of archive film from the Central Office of Information showing mass bombing raids on German cities. Intercut with this imagery is a re-creation of the Pathfinder Master Bomber system in action, to guide the main bomber stream over their targets. For a modern audience, it may be difficult to understand what the Master Bomber is meant to be doing, until Mason takes over the role when the two Pathfinder Mosquitos are shot down.

What adds to the effectiveness of the bomber scenes in "Appointment in London" is that not a single miniature of a Lancaster is used, only real aircraft, which sets it apart from "The Dam Busters", a film that is heavily dependent on SFX miniatures.

In all, "Appointment in London" is an extremely well directed, well acted film. It is far more believable in its portrayal of RAF bomber crews in World War Two than the stereotyped re-creation achieved two years later in "The Dam Busters". The real stars are the Lancasters, and arguably they have never been filmed better in any other production than this one. Ten years later, Philip Leacock would bring his same skill to bear on the Lancasters' famous rivals from the USAAF, the Boeing B-17 Flying Fortresses of the Eighth Air Force, in "The War Lover" (1962).

THE CRUEL SEA

(Released: March 1953)

The film version of author Nicholas Monserrat's classic account of life aboard a Royal Navy convoy escort corvette has no aviation in it apart from a long-distance shot of an aircraft purporting to be a Focke Wulf FW.200 Condor relaying the convoy's position to a U-Boat Wolf Pack, and also brief wartime archive footage of an unidentified low-level bomber flying through flak before exploding in flame.

THE DESERT RATS

(Released: May 1953, USA) Hollywood 'British' war film.

The second Hollywood 'British' war film in this Chapter. Perhaps as a means of atoning for the criticism it received for making a film about a German General that was deemed unacceptably sympathetic by American and British film audiences, the 20th Century Fox studio chose to make another war film based on the North Africa campaign in which Rommel was to feature, again portrayed by James Mason.

This time, though, Mason plays Rommel as being archetypically arrogant, as all German Generals were considered to be, and speaking in German as well.

Richard Burton is the main star, acting the role of a Scottish Captain commanding a mixed bag of Australian troops on daring raids in the desert against Rommel's Afrika Korps. Using captured Italian Army trucks they get behind enemy lines with some of the 'Aussie' troops acting as prisoners, while others wear Italian Army uniforms as their guards. Unsurprisingly, Allied fighters think the Italian trucks are part of an enemy convoy and strafe them.

Carrying out the attack is exactly the same Armee de l'Air Vickers Supermarine Spitfire Mk.IX two-ship that appear in "The Desert Fox" (1951). The film's editor has simply re-used precisely the same footage that was filmed for and used in the earlier production, which includes that intruding and inappropriate US Navy Grumman TBM-3 Avenger! This time the editor has merged the shots of the head-on attacking Spitfire Mk.IXs with that of the Italian Army trucks in the desert, in place of Rommel's staff car in the earlier film. The giveaway to reveal that they are actually edited in split-screen imagery is that the trucks are throwing shadows, while the Spitfires over-flying them at very low-level are not. Also, the same backcloth shots of the clipped-wing Spitfire LF.IXe that were used in "The Desert Fox" are used again here, this time against a studio shot taken inside a truck and looking back out of its open rear end at the cannon-firing fighter closing in.

Easily available though this imagery may have been, as it was obviously still in the possession of the studio when it was used, doing so meant that an inaccuracy occurs here: the Spitfire Mk.IXs are wearing D-Day invasion stripes, which would not have been the case in 1941 when the events in this film are intended to be taking place. Also, the Spitfire Mk.IX variant had yet to enter RAF service and did not feature in the North Africa campaign until 1943.

SINGLE-HANDED

(Released: June 1953)

This well regarded Naval action film is better known under the title it was released in the United States, "Sailor of the King". It features a number of Royal Navy cruisers acting out a C S Forester story, "Brown on Resolution", about a Naval rating single-handedly taking on a German surface raider. Well worth watching, but it does not have any aircraft in its plot.

MALTA STORY

(Released: June 1953)

Of virtually all the British war films that have been made, very few come as close to matching so effectively and realistically genuine wartime footage with imagery filmed on set by the production company's camera crew. Being made in black-and-white

makes this possible, of course, but it is the quality of the archive imagery matched with that of the film's own imagery, coupled with the quite brilliant editing of both, which makes "Malta Story" so outstanding as a production.

Added to that, one naturally has to give credit for some very fine acting performances by such as Jack Hawkins as Malta's RAF Commanding Officer, Anthony Steele as the defending Spitfire squadrons' Wing Commander, and, unusually for a war film of the period, some very strong female roles, including Muriel Pavlow's touchingly convincing portrayal of a young female Maltese air defence plotter and Flora Robson's moving performance as her mother. Strange to say, the one unconvincing performance is that given by Alec Guinness as the RAF photo reconnaissance pilot who becomes romantically involved with Pavlow's bright-eyed, yet strong-willed character. Brilliant actor though the late Sir Alec Guinness was, romantic lead was not his forte, and it shows through painfully here.

It has been speculated that the role Guinness is playing is that of Flight Lieutenant Adrian Warburton, the real-life photo reconnaissance (PR) Spitfire pilot based on Malta during 1942 whose exploits have passed into legend. The only similarity, though, is that 'Warby' and Flight Lieutenant Peter Ross, the character played by Guinness, both flew a PR Spitfire. The flamboyant, daring and sometimes downright reckless 'Warby' was the complete antithesis of the sensitive, serious, archaeology-loving Ross, and was as notorious for his open affair with an English nightclub dancer (today she would have been a pole dancer) as he was for his devil-may-care flying. Perhaps the real 'Warby' was too much of a risk to portray in the straitened and still-rationed times of post-War Britain (he was rumoured to have been involved with the black market on Malta, especially in relation to illicit supplies of food and alcohol when the island itself was on the verge of being starved into submission).

In fact, none of the characters played in the film are of actual people who took part in the defence of Malta, although the Royal Navy Admiral is obviously based on Admiral Sir Andrew Browne Cunningham, the Commander-in-Chief of the Mediterranean Fleet. Jack Hawkins' CO could be assumed to be based on Air Vice-Marshal Keith Park, who took command in July 1942 of the air defence of Malta, but in effect he was reprising his role of 'Tiger' Small in "Angels One Five" (1952) with which Hawkins was closely associated and which had placed him firmly on the cinematic map.

"Malta Story" is stacked with aviation, which means this review is going to be very detailed. So let's get stuck in.

The opening shot following the credits is that of a Lockheed Hudson flying through clouds. It is quickly revealed as a studio miniature. It is meant to be carrying Guinness, plus an RAF Intelligence Officer played by Hugh Burden (the spoilt brat Fleet Air Arm pilot in "Ships With Wings", 1941, and the skipper of Vickers Wellington 'B for Bertie' in "One of our Aircraft is Missing", 1942) and other RAF personnel. They are en route Gibraltar to Cairo, and are due to make an overnight refuelling stop on Malta. Guinness remarks that there are some interesting megalithic remains on Malta; Burden replies that there are some other more recent remains on Malta now.

Almost as soon as they have landed Luftwaffe bombs score a direct hit on the Hudson. There is no chance of Guinness and Burden getting to Cairo now. As they huddle in a crater, a miniature Fairey Albacore on a film backcloth stands in the background. Guinness's PR pilot is recruited by Hawkins's CO to replace Malta's previous PR pilot who has been medivac'd back to 'Blighty'. A scene in the Operations Room, based on the actual Lascaris War Rooms from which the defence of Malta was plotted, and where some of "Malta Story" was filmed, has a No.8 Squadron badge on a placard nailed to the wall.

There follow some of the genuine archive imagery of Luftwaffe bomb attacks on Malta and of actual bomb damage to many buildings. This imagery is very graphic and shows what the Maltese people and the British military personnel had to endure, when the island became literally "the most bombed place on earth". A Junkers Ju.87 Stuka is filmed in a vertical dive attack, the camera following its bomb as it falls. A massive blast erupts amid a Maltese town. Ack ack guns pound away. Two more Ju.87 Stukas are seen in attack.

Guinness is sent on his first PR mission, to photograph enemy shipping in an Italian harbour. He is to fly a photo reconnaissance Spitfire which, although can't be seen in a black-and-white film, has been painted in the correct all-over 'PR Blue' scheme. The limitations imposed on the film director, Brian Desmond Hurst, and his team are illustrated here. The version of the Spitfire which defended Malta was the Spitfire Mk.V. No Mk.V 'Spits' in flying condition existed when "Malta Story" was filmed in late 1952 – early 1953. Therefore, Hurst and his team had to go with what was available. To depict the PR Spitfire they made use of a Spitfire with a four-bladed propeller, clipped wings and the pointed elliptical top to the tail fin representative of a Marque much later than that of the 1942-era Mk.V.

What is noticeable about this Spitfire is that alongside the modifications described, it retains the distinctive early style of Malcolm Hood cockpit canopy, not the recognisable 'bubble' cockpit that later clipped-winged Spitfire Marques adopted. It also has the old-style 'high back' fuselage of an earlier Spitfire design. This makes the PR Spitfire in "Malta Story" compatible with a Spitfire LF.Mk.IX, as its airframe is identical with this Low-Flying (LF) variant of the highly successful Spitfire Marque Nine. But no Spitfire Mk.IXs of any variant were in service with the RAF at the time "Malta Story" was in production.

The truth, as so often, was in the middle. The PR Spitfire does indeed have a LF.Mk.IX airframe, but what it does not have is that variant's two-stage supercharged Rolls Royce Merlin 66 engine. Instead, it is fitted with a licence-built version of the same engine, a Packard Merlin 266 built in the USA by the Packard Motor Company. This makes the PR Spitfire a Vickers Supermarine Spitfire LF.XVI, a British-built Mk.IX airframe powered by an American Merlin engine and configured for the low altitude ground-attack role while also being a fighter. Externally there is virtually nothing to distinguish between the LF.IX and the LF.XVI; you have to get underneath the hood to find the difference. Both Marques were manufactured at the same time on the same production lines, the one slight alteration being a marginally raised upper engine cowling for the LF.XVI to house the Packard Merlin 266's slightly altered accessories arrangement. In all other respects, they are the same Spitfire.

However, its identity and origin are a challenge. Careful examination of various scenes in which the PR Spitfire appears reveals that its serial has been taped over. Quite why this was done is not readily apparent. It, of course, is not the only Spitfire to appear in "Malta Story". As we shall discover, all the Spitfires in the film share the same source of origin and the same assigned operator, so we will keep the mystery alive for a little longer until we examine this Spitfire LF.Mk.XVI's co-stars.

Guinness's PR pilot taxyies the Spitfire away from its parking spot, as Steele's Wing Commander gives him a good luck wave. As the Spitfire LF.XVI heads away two large aircraft appear briefly in shot in the background, parked on the opposite side of RAF Luqa, the location where the scene is being filmed – and, of course, the actual target of so much Luftwaffe bombing during the real Siege of Malta. They are both four-engined, tail wheel transport aircraft with distinctively large and high tail fins that seem out of proportion to their respective airframes. They are both Avro Tudor air freighters and provide a brief glimpse of an early post-War British civil transport design that could trace its lineage back to the Lancaster bomber.

The Tudor was built in small numbers in a series of Marques, mostly for British South American Airways and for the British Overseas Airways Corporation. The loss of two Tudors close to the Bermuda Triangle with all on board led to the Air Ministry banning any passenger-carrying flights by this aircraft and permitting it only to be used for air freight operations. The Ministry of Civil Aviation acquired two of the earliest Marque of Tudor, Avro Tudor Is G-AGRI and G-AGRJ, flying War Office military freight contracts to Gibraltar, Malta, Cyprus and the Suez Canal Zone. It seems almost certain that the two Tudors in shot at RAF Luqa are these same two aircraft. Their unintended appearance exposes the difficulties film production companies underwent in the Fifties in making British war films on airfields that, at the same time, were being used by more contemporary aircraft and which, almost inevitably, sneaked into shot.

Virtually all air-air shots in "Malta Story" of German raiders are created with the use of studio miniatures and reflect the limitations of Special Effects in the early Fifties. These miniatures are used in conjunction with archive footage of more bombing on Malta, although one brief image of a Junkers Ju.88 appears. After one raid Steele and Guinness survey the damage to RAF Luqa, with wrecked aircraft all around them. Hurst appears to have used various stored and disposed-of aircraft sections as props to create the scene of devastation, all of which appear to be that of Naval aircraft borrowed, almost certainly, from RNAS Hal Far. Predominant among the piled up debris are the wings and cockpit fuselage section of a Fleet Air Arm Fairey Firefly AS.5 and the wing, fuselage and tail of a Vickers Supermarine Seafire F.XVII carrying the code number '133' next to its fuselage roundel and with the prefix letters 'SX' of its serial under the wing, but with the actual numbers scraped off.

The Firefly AS.5 remains are shown in one shot to display the letter 'V' next to its underwing roundel, being the first prefix letter of its serial, but all of the remaining letter and numbers have been deleted. A Spitfire shell standing on its nose has the appearance of an art department-created prop, not that of a real aircraft.

More attacks take place and more archive footage is used. The same Ju.87 Stuka in its vertical dive appears again, but this time cut in by the film editor in reverse direction.

The occasion when 47 Spitfires are flown off the US Navy carrier USS Wasp and are then bombed soon after landing at Malta is a central and important part of the film's recreation of this devastating actual event. To achieve it, Hurst had all the Spitfires at his disposal fly low over Malta from a number of directions and filmed from various different angles and locations. Hurst makes the claim in his unpublished autobiography that he and his team were only able to find three Spitfires in flyable condition, but it is self evident from the film that a total of four Spitfires were used, so why Hurst has got the number wrong is a puzzle (he isn't here to explain to us now).

The high back Spitfire LF.XVI was joined by three 'razor back' Vickers Supermarine Spitfire LF.XVIs, also clipped-winged and with the same elliptical pointed tail fin. By early 1945, all Spitfire LF.XVIs were built with the cut down, 'razor back' fuselage and were fitted with 'bubble' Perspex cockpit canopies, giving all-round 360-degree vision for the pilot.

The three 'razor back' Spitfire LF.XVIs in "Malta Story" are all camouflaged and show no serials or codes. The camouflage schemes they wear are correct for Malta-based Spitfire Mk.Vs in 1943 and for Spitfire Mk.Vs and Mk.IXs operating that same year in the Sicily and Italian theaters of war, but are wrong for the 1942 Siege of Malta period that the film is covering. They are also painted with the smaller blue-red roundel of the 1943 period. Quite why Hurst's art department made this mistake is not obvious to understand, unless it was a research error.

The identities of these three Spitfire LF.XVIs and that of their source has provoked plenty of debate among enthusiasts. The reason for painting over their serials appears to be not known, unless the serial numbers would show that they were late model Spitfire LF.XVIs built before production of this Marque ceased in August 1945, thus making them even more unrepresentative of 1942-era Malta Spitfires (as if their 'razor backs', bubble canopies, clipped wings and pointed tail fins didn't make them unrepresentative enough!). The Spitfire LF.XVI was still in active service with the RAF in 1952, equipping a number of diverse second-line units, such as the Central Gunnery School, Fighter Refresher Schools and Civil Anti-Aircraft Co-Operation Units, plus Royal Auxiliary Air Force squadrons. One source suggests they were provided by No.3 Civil Anti-Aircraft Co-Operation Unit at Exeter Airport, Devon, but this conclusion may have been reached due to this unit providing aircraft for other British war film productions later in the Fifties and in the early Sixties.

Hurst himself gives a clue to these Spitfires' source in his autobiography, when he describes them as being "in cocoons for preservation", in other words, in storage. At the beginning of

"Malta Story", a tribute is paid to all those who contributed to the film, most particularly to the government and the people of Malta. Included in this tribute is the Air Ministry which, in 1952, still held responsibility for all aviation assets, military and civil, in Great Britain, as it did throughout the War years. The Air Ministry held a large number of Spitfire LF.XVIs in storage as reserves for those operating with the RAF's second-line units; probably the four which appear in "Malta Story" were taken from these stocks, brought back into flying condition, then ferried to Malta.

An independent source appears to confirm, in part, that this was the case. Aviation historian Peter R Arnold, a world authority on all things Spitfire, has trawled the movement cards of four Spitfire LF.XVIs' operational records which appear to coincide with their presence in Malta at the time "Malta Story" was being filmed. Arnold tracked down a photograph in The Times of Malta during November 1952 which showed a Spitfire LF.XVI carrying the serial TE241 at RAF Luqa. By painstakingly researching the movement cards of all other Spitfire LF.XVIs extant at this time, Arnold was able to match TE241's movements with three other examples that showed remarkably similar flight patterns. They are: RW352, TB245 and TE178. He gives TB245 as the high back LF.XVI that played the part of the PR Spitfire.

What Arnold discovered was that all four Spitfire LF.XVIs arrived at RAF Abingdon, Berkshire, between 28th – 30th October 1952 and were allocated to No.1 Overseas Ferry Unit which operated from this air station. They were then all despatched to the Middle East on 5th November, officially assigned to join Middle East Air Force Command, but were equally quickly taken off MEAF Command charge later that same month on 28th November and were back in Britain by December. Filming in Malta took place during November 1952, as well as the month both before and after, a time of year when climatically it would have been more comfortable to use external locations there.

On the face of it, this was a very short deployment of four World War Two veteran fighters from Britain to the Middle East, and in the timescale recorded they would have been turning round and flying all the way back the moment they had arrived! What a way to treat four aeroplanes that were not hot-weather equipped, let alone the pilots. And what operational purpose did it achieve?

The reason must be that the four Spitfire LF.XVIs never got further than Malta, and there was no intention of them going any further. The assignment to MEAF Command was made only to facilitate the Spitfires being based at Malta for filming; in other words, they were on operations to justify their deployment overseas on what was otherwise a non-War Office tasking (the War Office was still officially approving and ordering all British military taskings in 1952). This almost certainly explains the reason for obscuring their serials for filming; no serials meant there would be no evidence of their participation, and therefore no breach of War Office regulations governing overseas deployments by British military aircraft (appearing in a feature film in foreign airspace was definitely not covered by such regulations). It also explains why their participation in "Malta Story" does not appear in their official individual service histories, thus lifting the lid on why the identities of these four Spitfire LF.XVIs have eluded detection for so long.

The service histories of the four Spitfires are as follows:

Spitfire LF.XVIe RW352: taken on charge by the RAF on 30th July 1945, placed in storage with No.6 MU. On 5th May 1948 RW352 was allocated to No.605 Squadron, then, after suffering some minor damage, it joined No.63 Group Communication Flight on 10th May 1949. Following its brief sojourn in Malta with Middle East Air Force Command, RW352 was again placed in storage before being allocated to No.187 Squadron on 25 August 1953. This only lasted a few months before it joined No.3 Civil Anti-Aircraft Co-Operation Unit (CAACU) on 14th October 1953. Three-and-a-half years later, RW352 was sold for scrap to Enfield Rolling Mills on 5th April 1957.

Spitfire LF.XVIe TB245: taken on charge by the RAF on 4th January 1945 and placed in storage with No.39 MU, TB245 remained out of action as Air Ministry stock until it was allocated to No.102 Fighter Refresher School on 13th April 1951. After filming in Malta, TB245 returned to Air Ministry storage before being allocated to No.3 CAACU on 11th November 1953. This Spitfire was sold for scrap to Lawsons Metals on 15th May 1956.

Spitfire LF.XVI TE178: taken on charge by the RAF on 24th May 1945 and placed in storage with No.6 MU, TE178 had an earlier career than its two co-patriot Spitfires described above by joining No.2 Armament Practice Station on 16th February 1946. Following its time in Malta, TE178 next joined the HQ Home Communications Squadron on 7th September 1953. It joined TB245 in being sold for scrap to Lawsons Metals on 15th May 1956.

Spitfire LF.XVI TE241: taken on charge by the RAF on 1st May 1945, TE241 was quickly brought into service with the Central Gunnery School on 10th July 1945. It then was taken over by Vickers Armstrong on 4th June 1948 for conversion into a trials aircraft for a modified gunsight, being operated by the Aircraft & Armament Experimental Establishment at Boscombe Down from 11th June 1948 onwards until it was placed in storage before being enrolled for "Malta Story". This Spitfire was sold for scrap on 28th November 1953.

With the Spitfires identified, it is worth noting how they are used in the film. They appear in re-created blast pens and are shown a number of times flying low over very recognisable locations in Malta, especially making several passes through Grand Harbour as well as heading out towards, and running in from, Sliema.

Actual Spitfire Mk.Vb fighters operating from Malta in 1942 appear in the film in archive footage. Three such Spitfires are seen taking off from the deck of the carrier HMS Furious during Operation Pedestal in August 1942, while a total of nine Spitfire Mk.Vs are shown over-flying Furious after forming in a loose formation before heading for Malta. The former Spitfire pilot and author, Geoffrey Wellum, describes in his excellent and very readable book, "First Light", how he led one of these four formations which saw 38 Spitfire Mk.Vs launched from Furious and successfully flown to Malta.

Operation Pedestal naturally forms a key element of "Malta Story". Hurst and his production team accurately re-create how each Spitfire was received on landing and led by a motorcyclist carrying the aircraft's individual number to a blast pen that was allocated the same number. However, although this is as realistically staged in the film as it was possible to achieve using the three 'razor back' LF.XVIs, for some reason the aircraft numbers are not applied!

With a German air raid detected by radar, the Spitfires are immediately brought into action. Here some excellent archive footage is used mixed with imagery of the LF.XVIs. The archive footage is of excellent quality and has the appearance of being staged for the camera. It is likely that the RAF Film Production Unit re-created 'Scramble' shots after the Siege of Malta had been lifted by October 1942. The first shot is of a Spitfire Vb in its blast pen, with a tarpaulin covering its cockpit as protection from the sun. Next, a pilot runs past the camera to another Spitfire Vb, passing its serial as he does so, but the fast motion of the camera means the serial is seen as just a blur, so is unreadable. This footage is followed by shots of the four LF.XVIs taxiing out to take off.

More archive footage then appears, but this is of a Spitfire Mk.V taking off from a noticeably British airfield. The Spitfire flies low and fast very close to the camera position, allowing for the serial number '536' and the code letter 'J' to be read; but the prefix letters to the serial are not readable. This Spitfire is also clearly painted in the grey-green camouflage scheme of British-based fighters, not that of the sand-brown camouflage applied to Malta-based Spitfire Mk.Vs. Another Spitfire Mk.Vb is seen taking off towards the camera from the second main fighter base on Malta, RAF Ta'Qali, with a Dakota III in the background. What is noticeable about this Spitfire is that it is carrying a 250lb bomb under each wing, which means that this aircraft is operating against ground targets or shipping in the period after the lifting of the Siege of Malta – Spitfires were not operated in the ground-attack role from Malta until Kesselring's Luftflotten had given up their attacks on the island nation. A third Spitfire Mk.Vb is seen taking off from the same British airfield as the 'J'-coded Spitfire, likewise flying very low and close to the camera but this time no serial or code can be seen on it.

Mixed with shots of all-too-obvious miniatures of Luftwaffe Heinkel He.111s and Ju-87 Stukas is a dramatic air-air shot of a Spitfire Mk.Vb fitted with a Vokes filter rolling over onto its back at the start of a dive. No number is seen on it, so it is not obvious if this is an actual Malta Spitfire. An unidentified German bomber is seen diving vertically into very English-looking countryside and exploding massively, suggesting it still had its bomb load on board (this footage is also used in other films). For attacks by Ju.88s, two out-takes of captured Junkers Ju.88A-5 Werke Nr 6073/M2+MK from "In Which We Serve" (1942) appear; as such out-takes of this aircraft appear in at least three other productions, this makes this particular Ju.88 a most valuable contributor to British war films – not that the Luftwaffe intended it to be.

To portray shot down German aircraft, the film editor has used two shots of Luftwaffe aircraft being burnt on dumps, probably taken at the end of the War. One shows what appears to be a Messerschmitt Me.410, but the twisted wreckage and the close-up angle at which it is filmed do not make identification certain.

Another shot is of a Messerschmitt Bf.109E burning. The wing of a Junkers Ju.87 Stuka is seen being examined on a Maltese shoreline, while the final shot of the air battle is of a Regia Aeronautica Macchi MC.202 fighter on its belly, displaying the code number '20' on its fuselage band – whether this shot was taken on Malta is not certain, but the terrain looks typical of the island.

More archive material is used to depict air attacks on the Operation Pedestal convoy. Very dramatic pictures of bombs exploding in the sea around ships is used, as is footage of three Ju.87 Stukas in a line astern dive attack. A close-up shows an aircraft carrier with serious bomb damage; whether it is one of the four carriers in the Pedestal convoy isn't clear. Another shot is that of the carrier HMS Eagle listing to port after being torpedoed by a U-Boat – this happened just as HMS Furious was launching the 38 Spitfires she was carrying. A Junkers Ju.88 pulling up out of a dive attack through flak has smoke streaming from its starboard engine. An Italian Regia Aeronautica Savoia-Marchetti SM.79II Sparveiro is seen flying at low-level above the sea through flak, but the most outstanding piece of archive footage in this sequence is that of a second Savoia-Marchetti SM.79II Sparveiro filmed from the deck of a ship as the tri-motor torpedo bomber heads straight towards the camera through tracer fire. This is the same amazing piece of footage that was used in "The Volunteer" (1943), and may have been filmed during the actual Operation Pedestal.

To depict the Malta Spitfires attacking the Axis raiders, three archive shots of British-based Spitfires are used: first, eight Spitfires in three sections flying in echelon starboard formation are seen, followed by 11 Spitfires in four sections peeling off to attack, then a familiar piece of footage of three Spitfires diving through bombers which has been used in a number of films and documentaries on air warfare. The same footage of a Heinkel He.115 diving vertically into the sea, as was used in "In Which We Serve", appears next, followed by that of an unrecognisable aircraft totally aflame and turning to plunge into the waves.

The Pedestal sequence ends with very moving pictures of the tanker Ohio, lashed to two destroyers, being slowly and gingerly brought into Grand Harbour past Fort St Angelo with her vital cargo of aviation fuel aboard.

The final part of "Malta Story" has the tiny island going onto the offensive. Hawkins's CO tells the aircrews at a briefing, "A lot of you have been used to taking it. Now we're going to dish it out". Vickers Wellington bombers and Bristol Beaufort torpedo bombers have arrived as reinforcements from the Middle East. The targets are to be Axis convoys supplying Rommel's Afrika Korps from Italy, Greece and the Balkans.

Acting as a prop in this outdoor briefing scene on RAF Luqa is a Vickers Wellington, accurately reflecting the type of bomber the RAF used against Axis convoys in the Med from Malta. In actuality, this is a Vickers Wellington T.10, a version which was used as a utility transport and navigation trainer, and one of 270 Wellington B.Xs converted by Boulton Paul at Wolverhampton. In one shot with Jack Hawkins standing in front of it, the silver-painted covered fairing that replaced the front gun turret for navigation training can clearly be seen. This particular Wellington

will be either HF626 or NB113, attached to No.3 Overseas Ferry Unit at RAF Abingdon. They both accompanied the Spitfire LF.XVIs in their ferry flights to and from Malta, as well as being recruited for film work as props. These two Wellingtons had a busy time in films during 1952, as they also appeared in the production to follow "Malta Story", "The Red Beret" (1953).

Also recruited for "Malta Story" is a Fleet Air Arm Fairey Albacore torpedo bomber. The Albacore was intended as a replacement for the Fairey Swordfish in the same Torpedo Bomber Spotter Reconnaissance role, but was less effective than its older forbear and was withdrawn from service before the War's end. During the Siege of Malta, 828 Squadron dispatched from their parent carrier, HMS Victorious, operated from Hal Far Royal Naval Air Station from September 1941 – July 1943, so undoubtedly the Albacore in the film is representing this unit which attacked Axis shipping in the Med, mostly at night. The identity of the aircraft is not known; it is certain that it is not the only surviving Fairey Albacore today, N4389, on display at the Fleet Air Arm Museum, RNAS Yeovilton, because this aircraft was restored from the remains of two Albacores recovered in the Seventies and Eighties. Clearly the Albacore used in "Malta Story" was not preserved. It was filmed in the UK, not at Malta, and makes only a brief appearance having a torpedo installed. Actor Noel Welling makes, like quite a number of other well-known British actors in "Malta Story", an uncredited cameo appearance as the Albacore's naval pilot, which is somewhat ironic as Welling mostly portrayed German characters in British World War Two war films.

To illustrate RAF bombers and fighters dishing it out, more archive imagery is used, including some excellent studies from the RAF Film Production Unit released to Pinewood Studios by the Imperial War Museum. Three Bristol Beaufort Mk.I torpedo bombers are seen engine running, with the nearest to the camera carrying the code letter 'Z' on its nose and the aircraft in the middle having the letters 'D – T' on either side of its fuselage roundel. If these Beauforts were filmed on Malta, they would probably be of the reconstituted No.39 Squadron, formed by mixing some aircrews of Nos.39, 86 and 217 Squadrons into one unit by July 1942; however, the code letters do not appear to relate to No.39.

Two Spitfire Mk.Vb fighters operating from RAF Ta'Qali are seen next, an example coded 'C' taxiies in front of another example 'Z' taking off behind, with a USAAF Consolidated B-24 Liberator parked in the background. Both Spitfires are carrying a 250lb bomb under each wing. The use of bombs on the Spitfires and the presence of the B-24 suggests this film was taken sometime in 1943.

A superb study of a Bristol Beaufighter air-air appears before gun-camera footage is used of strafing and rocket attacks on Axis supply ships. A Bristol Beaufighter coded '2 – O' is filmed air-air firing rockets. A headline from The Times Of Malta, dated 17th October 1942, proclaims, "Malta hitting back and hitting hard".

The film's most affecting moment is the shoot-down of Guinness's PR pilot, 'Picture One', in a desperate effort to locate a vital Axis convoy, in which he is ordered by Hawkins to break radio silence and thus expose himself to searching German fighters. Although created with the use of miniatures, this scene is very realistic; it is re-used in "Reach For The Sky" (1956).

It is noticeable that the RAF air bases on Malta are listed on an Operations board in the Ops Room. The spellings reflect the phonetic pronunciation RAF personnel used for these bases, but the spellings and the pronunciations for these Maltese names are wrong. For instance, RAF Ta'Qali is spelt 'Takali', while the reserve strip at Qrendi is spelt 'Krendi' – both spellings also reflect the way these names were pronounced in English. In fact, the letter 'Q' in Maltese is pronounced as an 'H', thus meaning that Ta'Qali is actually spoken as "Ta-Hallie" and Qrendi as "Her-Rendie". RAF Luqa was always pronounced "Lookah" by the Brits, but is actually "Loo-Hah". Luqa, incidentally, is the Maltese name for Luke.

The final action is the RAF's attack on Rommel's convoy. Three Bristol Beaufort Mk.Is are filmed air-air dropping torpedoes, the nearest example clearly coded TU-Z and belonging to No.1 Torpedo Training Unit, which operated out of Turnberry Airfield in Ayrshire, Scotland. Another Bristol Beaufort Mk.I is filmed dropping its torpedo from the ship it appears to be attacking; however, careful study of this footage reveals that it is almost certainly staged and probably filmed by the RAF Film Production Unit to create the impression of what a torpedo attack from a bomber appeared like. The giveaway is that the Beaufort is flying in unhindered by flak or tracer, while the ship it is filmed from is stationary in the water. The pilot drops his torp at an angle that causes the 'tin fish' to bounce and leap out of the water like a porpoise, presumably because it was light (ie, it had no warhead).

This is followed by an even more dramatic shot of a Bristol Blenheim Mk.V unloading two bombs at very low-level across the bows of the same ship into the sea. No bursts follow, so clearly the bombs were inert. The Blenheim V was the final and least successful of the Blenheim/Bolingbroke series, it being too underpowered compared with contemporary fighter-bombers. Six RAF squadrons operated the Blenheim V in the Middle East, so presumably this example came from one of them. Nonetheless, the footage of it and the Beaufort I is very dramatic and could have been filmed to show RAF bombers in action in the Med for promotional and propaganda purposes.

"Malta Story" ends with the announcement of the 8th Army's victory over the Afrika Korps at el-Alamein. The final shot is an aerial view of Grand Harbour filmed from an aircraft flying over the huge port and out to sea, with The Three Cities in the background and an aircraft carrier moored in the Harbour. It is a fitting image of a brave island that survived everything the Luftwaffe could throw at it, and is a fine way to end what is a very fine British war film.

THE RED BERET

(Released: August 1953)

This somewhat lavish (for the period) film production sparked controversy at the time of its release by having an American Hollywood star, Alan Ladd, take the lead role in what is a profoundly British war film based on the formation and initial operations of the 1st Airborne Division, forerunner of the

Parachute Regiment. However, Ladd guaranteed box office success (the film took $8 million for a production cost of $700,000, including Ladd's fee of $200,000), especially as his most famous film, the western "Shane", was released during the same year as "The Red Beret".

Historically, this film has an important place in British cinema, as it saw for the first time the teaming of producer Albert R 'Cubby' Broccoli, director Terence Young, cinematographer Ted Moore, scriptwriter Richard Maibaum, and stunt man Bob Simmons: a decade later they would all collaborate to produce "Dr No" (1962), the first in arguably the most famous and longest-running franchise in movie history, the James Bond films.

"The Red Beret" is based largely on fact, containing almost accurate re-creations of the Bruneval Raid to capture a Wurzburg radar installation and the seizing of Bone Airfield in Algeria as part of Operation Torch. Leo Genn plays the role of Major John Snow, who is based on the actual leader of the Bruneval Raid, Major John Frost (Anthony Hopkins acts the role of Major John Frost in the epic, "A Bridge Too Far", 1977, reviewed in Chapter Five).

Ladd is 'Canada', who is actually an American who has volunteered to join the new 1st Airborne Division. He is concealing a guilty secret, which he eventually reveals to the young WAAF parachute rigger, Penny, who becomes his girlfriend. More of Canada's secret in due course.

"The Red Beret" scores with aviation enthusiasts and historians for providing the last sight of Vickers Wellington bombers in action, and in Technicolor, no less. In this regard the film is unique, for there are no other known sources of colour film imagery of Wellingtons available anywhere. As mentioned in "Malta Story", two of the Wellingtons used in that film appear in "The Red Beret" as well. In fact, they were filmed for "The Red Beret" first during September and October 1952 before flying out to Malta in November.

The film opens "Somewhere in England. The year 1940 - After Dunkirk". The "Somewhere" is meant to be RAF Ringway but is actually RAF Abingdon, home base for the Royal Air Force's No.1 Parachute Training School (PTS) which trained in 1952, as it does today, Parachute Instructors for all three of Britain's armed services. It seems an irony that the RAF trained instructors for the Army's Parachute Regiment, but Paratroop forces were in their infancy when they were first formed in 1940, with no precedent or tradition behind them. After many false starts between the Army and the RAF, the latter acquired the role of being the lead service for military parachute training through developing a technique for safe landings, based on the use of Physical Education Instructors from the RAF's Physical Education Branch: they had the best physiological knowledge of to how to impact the ground without injury. This simple idea has formed the core philosophy behind successful UK military parachute training ever since.

Both RAF Abingdon and No.1 PTS feature in two more British war films, "Carve Her Name With Pride" (1958) and "Operation Crossbow" (1965). In 1940, however, No.1 PTS was located at RAF Ringway, near Manchester (today, Manchester International Airport), so this is the "Somewhere" that RAF Abingdon is actually doubling for. "The Red Beret", though, provides a good study of RAF Abingdon itself and of No.1 PTS's operations as they were in 1952, which had not changed much after the War: the equipment was virtually the same, particularly the parachutes and the barrage balloons from which trainee Paratroopers made their first jumps. We have already seen the balloon system in action in "Now It Can Be Told" (1946); what we see of it in "The Red Beret" confirms that this basic parachute trainer was as crude and as precarious-looking in 1952 as it was in 1940. It has to be said that the parachute of Canada making his first jump takes a worryingly long time to open - good job it was obviously a dummy that was dropped from the balloon.

Having completed the regulation initial jumps from the balloon, the trainee Paratroopers now have to make their first jump from an aircraft. This means we now get a chance to see the Vickers Wellingtons in colour. It is immediately apparent that they do not bear wartime camouflage and black undersides typical of RAF Bomber Command Wellingtons. The three which are used in the film are all painted dark grey overall. One has bright yellow propeller bosses, another natural metal bosses, while those of the third appear to be painted black. All three are Vickers Wellington T.10s, with fared over turrets fore and aft. They carry 'MH-' codes in white, with MH-A and MH-D initially identifiable. The question is whether these are genuine codes, or if they have been applied especially for the film. Two squadrons in World War Two carried 'MH-' codes, but neither operated the Vickers Wellington. It is possible the all-over dark grey scheme has been applied for the film as well, particularly as Wellington MH-A does not display any serial on its rear fuselage (possibly for the same reason as the Spitfires in "Malta Story" being devoid of serials, as explained in the review of that film).

For the first take off shot seen in the film, however, an entirely different Vickers Wellington T.10 is being used. This Wellington is in all-over silver colour scheme, due to its aluminium airframe being left unpainted, and has yellow training bands around each wing, as well as red propeller bosses. This denotes that this Wellington is almost certainly a navigational trainer and carries the code letter 'P' on its silver nose turret faring. The Wellington T.10 was used as a navigational trainer from 1948 - 1953, before it was replaced by both the Vickers Valetta T.3 and the Vickers Varsity T.1.

The airfield from which this Wellington is taking off is clearly not RAF Abingdon, as the layout is very different from the Oxfordshire air station. A second silver Wellington T.10 can be seen turning on to the runway in the distance as the 'P'-coded Wellington lifts off. From its appearance, this air station bears a strong resemblance to RAF Hullavington in Wiltshire, which was home to No.1 Air Navigation School (No.1 ANS) equipped with the Wellington T.10 at the time "The Red Beret" was filmed. If so, then the 'P'-coded Wellington T.10 seen taking off would bear the full No.1 ANS code of FFK-F/P.

Another reason for No.1 ANS being the only likely unit to have provided Wellington T.10s for the film is that it was the last Air Navigation School to be operating the type when "The Red Beret" was in production during the months of August - October 1952; No.1 ANS was in the process of converting to the Varsity

T.1 when its Wellingtons were filmed. This, then, is imagery of some of the last Vickers Wellingtons in Royal Air Force service to be seen flying, making "The Red Beret" of even more special interest to the aviation historian.

A dramatic twist in the plot occurs here when the Sergeant training the new Paras, played in his first significant screen role by Welsh actor, Stanley Baker, demonstrates what making a jump is like but is killed when his parachute 'Roman Candles'. A 'Roman Candle' is a dreaded word in parachuting: it means that a parachute has deployed but has failed to fully open, trailing in a long stream above the ill-fated jumper and not arresting his fall. The twist is that the secret Canada is concealing is linked to a previous death by 'Roman Candle', which he blames himself for causing.

No actual jumps from the Vickers Wellingtons were made in "The Red Beret". Instead, the jumpers seen leaving the aircraft are actually exiting through the open bottom of the barrage balloon gondola (not seen in shot), raised to a greater height. The giveaway is that the ground seen below the Paras as they exit is not moving. A total of four Paras are seen descending as a 'Stick', the maximum number that the gondola could hold, meaning that they were experienced Paratroopers who each exited fast one after the other, to create the effect for the camera of the recruits, led by Canada, successfully descending on their first jump. At no time is any Wellington seen in shot during this sequence. Interestingly, Alan Ladd, having released himself from his parachute harness, is limping when he plays the role of Canada running to the prostrate body of the Sergeant, suggesting that he appears to have injured himself at some point during the filming of "The Red Beret".

After the trainee Paratroopers have received their Wings at a passing out parade in front of their Commanding Officer, they are prepared for their first action. Here, "The Red Beret" moves into fact, not fiction. Although the name is not used in the film, it stages an effective and, for the most part, accurate re-creation of the real Operation Biting, better known to students of military history as 'The Bruneval Raid'.

Operation Biting was a Combined Forces operation carried out on 27th February 1942 involving Airborne, Royal Navy and Royal Air Force assets to capture a Wurzburg radar set and transport it back to Britain, where it would be studied by Scientific Intelligence and technological experts. The Wurzburg was a sophisticated radar system which enabled Luftwaffe Flak units to detect RAF bombers at night and direct night fighters onto them. RAF Bomber Command's loss ratio was increasing as a result of the successful deployment of Wurzburg. One of these radar arrays had been detected on the cliff top above the Channel Coast close to the French village of Bruneval (the review of "Ferry Pilot", 1941, in Chapter One has details of the actual PR Spitfire which photographed the Bruneval Wurzburg, prior to the Raid). The plan was that Airborne forces would be dropped at night to capture the radar set, neutralise the defences, then assist an RAF radar specialist dropped with them to dismantle the array and carry it to the nearby beach below the cliffs, from where they would be picked up by Royal Navy landing craft. In short, despite many difficulties, Operation Biting was a complete success.

In "The Red Beret", the newly qualified Paratroopers are seen being briefed in a hangar by Major Snow on the forthcoming raid. They are filmed from behind in one shot all gathered together, framed through the wings and struts of a de Havilland DH.82A Tiger Moth. The Tiger Moth is only partially seen in shot and is therefore not identifiable; it can be seen to be silver overall and may have either been an Air Training Corps aircraft or perhaps was on strength with RAF Abingdon's Station Flight.

The Paratroopers are marched out to their waiting Vickers Wellingtons (in the real Operation Biting, Armstrong Whitworth Whitleys were used). Immediately, a Wellington T.10 bearing the code letters MH-L can be identified, the Wellington with the yellow propeller bosses. There is a question as to whether the three Wellingtons used in this scene, and in the earlier one depicting the Paratroopers undergoing their training, were actually in flying condition. MH-L was certainly capable of taxying because it is seen doing so head-on towards the camera.

Next, a shot taken in low light shows a Wellington in silhouette departing in the distance and being saluted by the 1st Airborne Division's CO, General Whiting (a play on the real 1st Airborne's Commanding Officer, General Browning, who would be played in controversial circumstances by Dirk Bogarde in "A Bridge Too Far", 1977). Then another shot of either the same Wellington, or a different one, also departing in low light and heading into a faint sunset, is seen framed by two female riggers waving as it heads into the distance.

However, a final shot of four Wellington T.10s in very loose formation, flying low towards the camera in what is obviously sunset light conditions, are shown by freeze-frame analysis to be silver and yellow-banded navigational trainers. Therefore, balancing these shots of flying Wellington T.10s with the earlier shot of a navigational trainer Wellington T.10 coded 'P', then adding in the ground shots of the all-over dark grey Wellington T.10s at RAF Abingdon, the conclusion must be that the latter did not fly in the film, while all those that were filmed airborne were from RAF Flying Training Command's No.1 ANS at RAF Hullavington. The extras playing General Whiting and the two riggers would have been taken to RAF Hullavington that the No.1 ANS Wellingtons flew from, and were filmed in conjunction with them taking off.

This means that seven Vickers Wellington T.10 aircraft were used in "The Red Beret": three non-flying Wellington T.10s at RAF Abingdon for the scenes involving Paratroops' training and their embarkation for the Bruneval Raid, and four flying Wellington T.10s filmed on a separate occasion at RAF Hullavington for take off and fly-over shots.

However, it is known that two of the Abingdon-based Wellington T.10s, HF626 and NB113 of No.3 Overseas Ferry Unit, were used in "Malta Story" following their appearance in "The Red Beret"; they definitely had to be in flying condition, in order to make their flights to and from the Mediterranean. Why, then, not use them as flyers in "The Red Beret"? There is probably a simple and prosaic explanation: cost. The Air Ministry obviously would have charged Warwick Films, the production company behind "The Red Beret", to fly the Wellington T.10s from No.3 Overseas Ferry Unit for certain scenes. Instead,

it was probably more affordable, let alone more expedient, to film Wellington T.10 navigational trainers during part of their normal, every day operations.

It could be claimed that the Wellingtons were filmed after their return to RAF Abingdon from Malta in late-November 1952, by which time they may have been grounded. Unlikely, for two reasons: the trees in leaf in the RAF Abingdon scenes, confirming they were not filmed during winter, and Alan Ladd's film schedule, due to he making three films in 1952; he completed "Shane" and "Desert Legion" that year as well as "The Red Beret". It is clear from the scenes he filmed at RAF Abingdon that summer was still in progress when he was there. Incidentally, the scenes at Abingdon using the trio of No.3 Overseas Ferry Unit Wellingtons were shot on what was a very grey, wet day; they clash with the late sunshine evening shot of the four No.1 ANS Wellingtons over-flying RAF Hullavington.

The shots of the Paras descending from their aircraft were filmed over a military training ground at Trawsfynydd, North Wales. The initial shot shows a stick of Paras leaving their aircraft, only the tail of which is very briefly seen. Freeze-frame analysis confirms that it is definitely not a Wellington. It is, in fact, the only aircraft of the time that Paratroopers of the Parachute Regiment in 1952 could have used for mass para-dropping: a Handley Page Hastings C.1. The Hastings was the only large four-engined transport aircraft then in service with the RAF that could deliver Paratroopers by air. Film of it dropping Paras for "The Red Beret" has been carefully edited so that only its tail is shown so quickly before passing out of shot, thus ensuring that it cannot be identified as an aircraft different from the Wellington.

Interestingly, the first shots of the Paras dropping reveal that they were not using static lines when they exited the aircraft: they are each hand-pulling their rip chords as soon as they jump. Why this was done isn't known, but it confirms that the Paras shown in this shot must have been among the most experienced jumpers in the Parachute Regiment. They are also jumping clean of any equipment, which they certainly would not have done if they were really going into battle.

The initial shots of the Paras descending from the Hastings are filmed from directly below the 'Stick'; however, further shots show a much larger mass of Paras descending, some of which have kit bags slung beneath them, while all of them have equipment packs on their backs. This confirms that these are shots of a fully kitted para drop filmed on a separate occasion. One of the perils of mass dropping is shown for real here: two Paras collide in their descent and become entangled - director Young makes use of this genuine accident by having two extras as Paras do the same thing in the studio for a close-up.

As the mass of Paratroopers descend to the ground, their jump aircraft can be seen departing in the distance: three Fairchild C-119 Flying Boxcars, flying in the standard 'Vic' formation used when dropping Paras. These would have been United States Air Force tactical transport aircraft. It is possible that the mass jump filmed here was that of a US Army Airborne battalion being dropped, but it is equally likely that they were real 'Red Devils' (the name the Paras earned from German troops in the Tunisian Campaign of 1943, due to the ferocity of their fighting and their standard practice of wearing their red berets, not helmets, in action) - the Paras regularly used USAF C-119s due to the RAF lacking sufficient numbers of transports for the task in the early Fifties. It is likely that this Battalion-sized drop was filmed in Germany, where the 16th Parachute Brigade was located as part of the British Army of the Rhine - the Brigade often jumped from Flying Boxcars during military exercises.

After the Bruneval Raid scene, Canada - whose true identity as an American named McKendrick has now been revealed - and his fellow Paras are issued with their red berets for the first time. They are also introduced to the aircraft type that became the Paratrooper's most widely used jump platform during World War Two, the Dakota. Douglas C-47A Skytrain 316048 is seen landing. There is no attempt made to disguise it as a wartime C-47 (although, by its serial number, it is a genuine World War Two veteran), it being in all-over natural metal and with United States Air Force titling on its upper fuselage (the USAF did not come into being until 1947). Almost certainly this is a stock shot from the USAF. C-47A 316048 would have been among a large number of C-47s still in USAF service in Europe during 1952.

"Good old Dakotas", comments McKendrick, as he inspects one of a number of Douglas C-47s used in the film. In reality, as an American he would not have used the British name 'Dakota' for the C-47. He is confronted by a USAF crew member who says he knows him, but McKendrick turns and leaves before he can say more. It is obvious he has something to hide.

This scene is played out in front of a C-47A which has the serial number HJ252 on its tail. This serial is either a fake - the real HJ252 was a Mosquito - or this Dakota is from another air arm that is neither British nor American. It also carries a fake USAF Star symbol without the Bars on its fuselage, as well as the code letter 'E' beside the port-side cargo door. It looks as if the Star symbol has been applied over this Dakota's actual roundel. Another noticeable feature is the rudder, which is painted white instead of being in all-over natural metal that is the scheme for whole of this Dakota.

The origin of this Dakota is something of a surprise and is revealed only very briefly when the crew member who challenges McKendick moves his head to expose the roundel on the starboard wing. The Dakota is filmed from the port side only, which means that the fake American miltary symbol and RAF serial have only been applied to that side; the starboard side retained this Dakota's true colours, including the roundel on the starboard wing, which were not intended to be in shot. However, as the crew member moves forward the wing roundel appears in view for no more than a second; freeze-frame analysis shows that it is painted with a red outer ring, white inner ring and blue centre. In other words, Dakota 'HJ252/E' is a French Air Force aircraft.

Dakotas in service with l'Armee de l'Air in 1952 bore all-over natural metal schemes and carried their fuselage roundel exactly where the fake Star symbol has been applied on 'HJ252'. The blue-white-red Tricolor on the tail was painted the full length of

the rudder, which almost certainly explains why the rudder on this Dakota has been covered entirely in white on the port side (presumably, with easily washable paint). The serial 'HJ252' has been applied exactly over where the real serial (which would have been this Dakota's original US military serial number) was carried on the tail fin; quite why a fake RAF serial has been applied to what is meant to be a USAAF C-47 isn't obvious to understand. The code letter 'E' is quite possibly genuine. This Dakota can be identified as a Douglas C-47A Dakota III.

How and why a French Air Force Dakota came to be used in "The Red Beret" remains a mystery. Two other Dakotas which appear in this scene are also in all-over natural metal schemes. The one parked ahead of 'HJ252' likewise carries a fake USAF Star symbol, which has been applied further forward on the fuselage; it also has code letters that are partially obscured by the port wing of 'HJ252', but appear to read 'NU-'. Either one of these two Dakotas has a cartoon of a gun-toting Mickey Mouse on its nose that is seen in close-up in one shot.

As McKendrick and Penny walk to his motorcycle a fifth C-47 that appears in the film can be seen parked in the distance outside a hangar. The difference with this C-47 is that its fuselage top is painted white, contrasting with its remaining all-over natural metal scheme. This is representative of post-War USAF C-47s, so it is safe to assume that this is a USAF aircraft but different to the first C-47 316048 we saw landing.

McKendrick finally reveals what's been eating him to Penny. It turns out he was a test pilot on B-24 Liberators, test firing rockets. One of them got hung up, so McKendrick has to risk landing the B-24 with the danger the rocket might explode. He ordered his co-pilot and best buddy, Robbie, to parachute out first. Robbie did so, but his parachute 'Roman Candled' and he was killed. McKendrick still blames himself for Robbie's death and has chosen to leave both the Army Air Force and the USA in disguise, and thus avoid all further responsibility as a leader.

The trouble with this scene is, it is pure George Zip. If they had never made "Airplane!" (1980), this kind of over-egged scene of self-recrimination might have got away with being taken seriously. But not after ex-fighter pilot, Ted Striker (Robert Hays), in "Airplane!" loses his nerve about flying for having caused the death of his wingman, George Zip, in a daring attack and blames himself for doing so. Just as Penny tries to help McKendrick not to blame himself for Robbie's 'Roman Candle', so Elaine Dickinson (Julie Hagerty) tries to get Striker to face up to his responsibilities and not let George Zip's death hang on his conscience. "Tell that to George Zip!", Striker replies sarcastically, and thus puts paid to any chance of a scene like this one between McKendrick and Penny of ever being taken seriously again.

Incidentally, McKendrick's claim that he was a former B-24 Liberator pilot is also full of Zip. McKendrick is shown to be one of the original volunteers for the 1st Airborne Division in 1940, just after Dunkirk. The B-24 had only just begun development flying that same year and did not come into service with the United States Army Air Force until 1941. So how could McKendrick be test flying B-24s in the USA if he was in the British 1st Airborne in 1940 sometime after Dunkirk? The screenwriter responsible for this goof has to be Richard Maibaum, who was brought in specifically to write Alan Ladd's lines for "The Red Beret", as Maibaum had done for other Alan Ladd movies.

The climax of "The Red Beret" is the attack on Bone Airfield in Algeria. Leading up to this scene is the take off by the C-47 Dakotas at the start of the long flight to North Africa. The first Dakota seen taxying out is very clearly a Royal Canadian Air Force (RCAF) aircraft, making it a Douglas C-47B Dakota IV. Again, how and why a RCAF Dakota got into "The Red Beret" will remain unknown. It too has had a false USAAF Star applied over its RCAF Clover Leaf symbol - the transfer patch is very obvious and no attempt has been made to cover up the blue cheat line that RCAF Dakotas were painted with. The appearance of this Dakota IV brings the total of C-47s used in "The Red Beret" up to six. The Dakota remained in RCAF service right up to 1989.

Penny is seen standing by the runway, waving as two Dakotas take off. The scene is definitely RAF Abingdon, with Runway Two Six being used. As RAF Abingdon was one of the Royal Air Force's principal transport air bases, the presence of Dakotas from NATO air arms was probably commonplace in 1952 and therefore using whichever of these were available as the film was made would probably have been the logical thing to do.

To depict the Dakotas en route to North Africa, archive film of wartime C-47s has been used. What is noticeable is that colour archive film is used and therefore probably originated from an American source. One shot shows seven C-47s in olive drab scheme flying over English countryside, another has 12 C-47s in loose formation.

Major Snow receives a message on board his C-47 that German troops have seized Bone Airfield. To depict the captured airfield a small control tower flying a flag with a Swastika on it is shown, with the nose and starboard engine of a Bristol Beaufighter TT.10 creeping into shot on the right hand side of the screen portraying a Luftwaffe Junkers Ju.88. The Beaufighter TT.10 is easily recognisable by the yellow undersides of the nose and engine cowling (see the review of "Ice Cold In Alex", 1958, for a more full description of the target-towing Beaufighter TT.10 variant, as an example has a particular role in that film).

When the time comes for the drop onto Bone Airfield an exterior shot of what is meant to be the rear fuselage and tail of a C-47 Dakota is used to depict Paras exiting the aircraft by static line. The effect is convincing but in reality it is the rear fuselage and tail of Handley Page Hastings C.1 TG602, which is shown in rather well used bare metal scheme with its serial number '602' repeated in large black numerals on the tail fin and the code letter 'U' just below on the fuselage. Somehow, Hastings C.1 TG602 has been placed in a raised fuselage position, with the tail wheel off the ground, allowing for the camera to be positioned just outside the door filming Paras as they exit the aircraft acting as if they are jumping by static line for real. This could only have been achieved by having Hastings C.1 TG602 supported by large jacks out of shot.

Tragically, Hastings C.1 TG602 was lost in a fatal accident at RAF Fayid in Egypt on 12th January 1953, not long after its use in "The Red Beret". Both tailplane elevators separated in mid-air after the Hastings made a steep turn after take off, followed by the tailplane itself. All nine persons on board were killed in the ensuing crash. The accident investigation found that a modification to the tail section on all Hastings C.1 aircraft had not been carried out on TG602.

Other shots show Paras leaving another Hastings C.1 in mid-air, filmed from within the Hastings itself. It has to be said that the way in which the Hastings is used in these shots is very convincing, it is very difficult to discern that it is not a Dakota that is being filmed. What is also noticeable in this scene is that the Paras making the jump are using a mix of two different coloured parachute canopies, some white and some tan brown - why this is so is not known.

A mass of equipment containers follows the Paras, all of whom land on very green grass, not desert sand and rock! German troops run in panic in front of the Beaufighter TT.10. Major Snow and his men spring into action amid a flowering of multi-coloured canopies, some blue and orange as well as tan and white - very pretty, but very untactical. Weapons containers are flung open, Brens, Stens and Lee Enfields are swiftly grabbed. The ensuing battle is filmed at several different locations, including Tawsfynydd and an airfield which is quite likely to be Llanbedr, as the white buildings in the background bear a strong resemblance to those which still exist there today. Also, RAF Llanbedr was home to No.5 Civil Anti-Aircraft Co-Operation Unit in 1952, which operated the target-towing Beaufighter TT.10 at the time. Needless to say, McKendrick comes good at the right time.

"The Red Beret" is an enjoyable British war film with a good content of historic aircraft to satisfy the aviation enthusiast, and with the added bonus of them being seen in colour. The Vickers Wellington T.10s alone make it worth being part of an historian's collection, especially as these were the last of their breed and were filmed not long before their own denouement. For this reason in itself, the film "The Red Beret" has made its own contribution to British aviation history.

ALBERT R.N.

(Released: October 1953)

The second in the series of British PoW escape films, "Albert R.N." takes its title from the ingenious trick played by captive Royal Navy officers on their German guards by creating a detachable, life-size dummy dressed in uniform. Nicknamed 'Albert R.N.', the dummy was used to replace an escapee in the head count conducted every day. There is no aviation in this film.

THEY WHO DARE

(Released: February 1954)

Set in September 1942 just prior to el Alamein, this British war film is, like "The Red Beret", unusual for its period in that it was filmed in colour. This means that wartime footage is not used. Even more unusual and of special interest for the aviation enthusiast is that genuine World War Two vintage Axis Powers bombers appear in the film, specifically Savoia-Marchetti SM.79 Sparviero (Sparrowhawk) tri-motors fully representative of the principal medium bomber of the Italian Regia Aeronautica.

The plot has Special Boat Squadron (SBS) Commandos supported by Greek Partizans landing on the island of Rhodes, with the intention of destroying what are described in the film as German bombers. According to the theme of the film, the British 8th Army in North Africa is being subjected to Luftwaffe attacks from air bases in Nazi-Occupied Greece: not wholly correct, as many Luftwaffe attacks on the 8th Army were launched from desert bases in North Africa. However, Luftwaffe bombers on the Dodecanese Islands, of which Rhodes is part, did threaten British forces in Egypt during the North African and Middle Eastern campaigns; Crete was strategically located for German bombers based there to attack British convoys in the Mediterranean Sea supplying Tobruk and Alexandria; while Regia Aeronautica bombers did likewise from bases in Italy, Sicily and from captured airfields in Albania.

The SBS are detailed to break into two Luftwaffe air bases on Rhodes and blow up as many bombers as they can. The plot is based upon an actual special forces mission in the Dodecanese that did little in reality to hamper Luftwaffe operations, but which did establish the SBS (today, the Special Boat Service) as a viable force to operate from the sea in the manner established by the SAS. The film's title is an obvious play on the SAS's famous motto, "Who Dares, Wins".

The problem for the film production company (Mayflower Pictures Corporation, for whom "They Who Dare" was their last production) was that no Luftwaffe bombers were available to use; any that had been captured during the War, and which, as we have already examined, were used in British wartime films, had since been mostly unceremoniously disposed of by the start of the new decade, while those that had been chosen for preservation were now all in non-flying condition.

The production team solved the problem by gaining access to four SM.79L Sparvieros, accurately representative of Regia SM.79s flown in the Mediterranean theater in 1942 but not, as presented in the film, over North Africa. Fascist Italian forces in North Africa had suffered badly in desert battles with the British Army under the command of General Alexander earlier in the War, and any Regia Aeronautica aircraft that might have been operating in the desert theater had long been withdrawn by the 1942 period the film is presenting. In a confusing attempt to add realism in the film, the SM.79Ls are painted with Italian Regia markings, but are called German! Both German and Italian troops are filmed protecting them on base.

Nonetheless, full colour imagery of classic wartime bombers such as these Sparvieros makes "They Who Dare" worth having in one's collection, if you can ignore the stereotypically British Commandos played by Dirk Bogarde and Denholm Elliott, who make histrionic accusations against each other along the lines of, "I hate you, I hate you, because you don't know when you're licked. I know when I'm licked!". In the six decades that have passed since "They Who Dare" was released, and now that there is no need to pretend as to what either of these two actors' natural inclinations were, any less likely persons than the artistic, sophisticated Dirk Bogarde and the sensitive Denholm Elliott playing supposedly hard drinking, hard fighting, hard living SBS Commandos, is beyond one's scope to imagine.

But where did the film makers find these SM.79s, nine years after the end of World War Two? The answer: the Lebanese Air Force, which had four SM.79L transport versions of the Sparviero in service when "They Who Dare" was made, serialled L-111 – L-114. At least two are seen taking off and airborne in a number of shots; they were probably the only two which were airworthy, especially as one scene with Dirk Bogarde scrambling over the wings of an SM.79L to plant bombs on it has him leaving long foot marks in the dust on its surfaces, suggesting that this particular aircraft had not moved for a long time. The location is believed to be Rayak Air Base in The Lebanon.

Two of the Sparvieros are carrying the serials '1928' and '1949'. These are used alongside the Regia Aeronautica markings painted on the tri-motors, which is probably accurate, as these could well have been their original Regia code numbers when these SM.79Ls were previously in service with the real Regia Aeronautica. All four SM.79Ls were donated by Italy to the fledgling Lebanese Air Force in 1949; they gave stirling service until the early Sixties. One, L-114, was captured later in the Fifties by the Isreali Defence Force/Air Force after it strayed into Israeli airspace and was forced to land at an IDF/AF air base. All three surviving SM.79Ls were returned to Italy when they were withdrawn from service: L-113 can today be seen in the Museo dell'Aeronautica Gianni Caproni in its very attractive Lebanese colour scheme, while L-112 has been painted in Regia Aeronautica colours for display in the Italian Air Force Museum.

In order to use the SM.79Ls, "They Who Dare" was filmed almost entirely in The Lebanon - then a Hezbollah-free zone - representing Rhodes, which explains the complete lack of any Greek actor taking part. The film's intended spectacular set-piece of the Sparvieros being destroyed by the SBS's planted bombs is, however, embarrassingly let down by extremely amateurish SFX of unconvincing models being blown up. "They Who Dare" exposes the limits in film technology of its time, and can't be called memorable except for the rare shots it contains of the last examples of a famous Italian World War Two bomber in action.

THE PURPLE PLAIN

(Released: September 1954)

Hollywood film star Gregory Peck was already an established leading actor in the States when he chose to make a move to Europe, to take advantage of a loophole in US federal government tax laws - Alan Ladd had done the same when he came to England to film "The Red Beret" (1953). Peck made the highly popular "Roman Holiday" (1953), a Fifties-style 'Rom-Com' with Kathleen Hepburn before he swapped the charms of Rome for the sweat and dust of Ceylon (today, Sri-Lanka) to film this adaptation of H E Bates' 1947 novel, "The Purple Plain", adapted for the screen by spy novelist, Eric Ambler.

Peck plays Squadron Leader Bill Forrester, a Canadian RAF Mosquito fighter-bomber pilot with a reputation for brilliant but high risk flying to the point of self-destruction. Forrester is moody, self-absorbed and is considered either mad or dangerous, or both, by his fellow pilots and groundcrewmen. The character of Forrester may have been based by Bates and Ambler on real-life Canadian RAF fighter pilot, George 'Screwball' Beurling, who, like Forrester, gained a reputation for being a difficult, uncommunicative personality who was shunned by other pilots and who frequently disobeyed squadron orders by going off alone while on Ops, again like Forrester. Beurling was nicknamed 'Screwball' because he constantly called everything "screwball", but he was a brilliant fighter pilot who shot down more Luftwaffe Bf.109s and Italian Macchi MC.202s than any other RAF pilot on Malta in 1942.

"The Purple Plain" is actually based in Burma, but is represented by several locations in Ceylon which were later used again in "The Bridge on the River Kwai" (1957). Whether the jungle airstrip actually existed, or was created as a film set, isn't known, but it accurately looks the part of an RAF strip in the Burmese jungle with aircraft landing and operating from it.

Peck's character Forrester is part of a South East Asia Command (SEAC) Mosquito squadron operating against the Japanese. He suffers from nightmares about bombing raids and wakes up believing that the airstrip is under attack, when in fact it is all in his imagination. His groundcrewman is convinced he has gone round the bend when Forrester tries to get his Mosquito airborne, until he is shaken out of his delusion. Later, on a five-ship Mosquito bombing raid, Forrester disobeys his CO's orders to climb above heavy flak and breaks formation to dive down and bomb the Jap ack ack guns. The Special FX of the Mosquitos and of Forrester's attack on the Japs is very sub-standard, even for the film's own time period, and is one of the weak points of "The Purple Plain".

The most interesting element of the film for our purpose are the de Havilland Mosquito fighter-bombers which appear in the film. As far as can be ascertained three Mosquitos actually appear, two of them apparently withdrawn-from-use airframes which were used either for set-dressing or in a jungle crash landing scene - the Mosquito which was set on fire was a partial airframe that was destined for the metal cutters at RAF Negombo/Katunayake, Ceylon, anyway. Apparently this was a grounded de Havilland Mosquito PR.34 which was stored in the disused aircraft compound at RAF Negombo. The other was a complete de Havilland Mosquito T.3, also stored in the same compound, carrying an all-over silver scheme typical of this trainer variant in the post-War years and coded 'Z'.; it appears as a static prop on the airstrip.

The third Mosquito was a flyer and is believed to have been a de Havilland Mosquito PR.34 of No.81 Squadron, based at RAF Seletar, Singapore, at the time of filming in early 1954. A photograph exists of a Mosquito PR.34 on the ramp outside the Aircraft Servicing Flight hangar at RAF Negombo, taken in January 1954. However, this Mosquito is very obviously in film 'wardrobe', painted in World War Two SEAC camouflage and markings, while carrying the serial 'FP136', which actually belonged to a Catalina Ib. The Mosquito has had its glazed Perspex nose replaced with a hardened nose cone bearing four cannon. It looks very similar to the Mosquito seen actually flying in the film.

According to one source, the pilot of the Mosquito for the flying sequences was Flight Sergeant 'Chick' Kirkham of No.81 Squadron. Whoever the pilot was, he was called upon to perform a single-engine landing on the jungle strip to simulate a shot-up 'Mossie' returning from a bombing mission, no mean feat in a powerful beast like a Mosquito. In portraying Forrester's aircraft, it carries the code letter 'P', but in another shot it also appears as a Mosquito coded 'F'. The serial in this shot can clearly be read as 'TF510', which appears to be entirely fictitious as it was never allocated to any aircraft type. The true identity of the Mosquito PR.34 in "The Purple Plain" seems destined to remain a mystery.

There is little action in "The Purple Plain", as the plot focuses on the psychology of Forrester's character and the reason behind his self-destructiveness, leading to a life and death struggle for survival in the Burmese jungle after he crash lands his Mosquito in Japanese-held territory. Two other aircraft appear in the film, an unidentifed North American AT-6C Harvard II which is used as a static prop on the airfield, and Avro Anson C.19 TX181, which is allowed to retain its true identity when it plays the part of the aircraft in which the rescued, and cured, Forrester returns to base. It, plus the Harvard, was also painted in SEAC colours. Presumably, both the Anson and the Harvard were operated from RAF Negombo.

"The Purple Plain" is a rather dated film and story by today's more critical standards, but it is a must-have for anyone who likes getting bitten by Mosquitos of the de Havilland kind. It is the first full-length feature film in which they appear, and there is the added bonus in that they are seen in colour.

THE SEA SHALL NOT HAVE THEM

(Released: November 1954)

Like "For Those In Peril" (1944), this film tells the story of the RAF's Air Sea Rescue HSL (high speed launch) crews and the aircrew of a ditched aircraft adrift in an inflatable life raft at sea. In fact, director Lewis Gilbert and producer Daniel M Angel have copied almost exactly the finale of the former film, with the helpless airmen drifting in sea mist into a minefield and having to be rescued by an HSL close to the enemy coast while being fired upon by a coastal gun battery. It is hard to see how Gilbert and Angel could claim that the almost identical final action sequences in both films were created coincidentally.

Gilbert and Angel are to collaborate on two more highly rated British war films included in this Chapter, "Reach For The Sky" (1956) and "Carve Her Name With Pride" (1958); Gilbert would also go on to direct three James Bond movies.

"The Sea Shall Not Have Them" - the motto of the wartime RAF Air Sea Rescue Marine Craft Units - totes a panoply of well known British film actors of the Fifties period, both starring and supporting. Michael Redgrave, already looking more recognisably filled-out physically than in his earlier lean World War Two appearances, is an RAF Air Commodore escaping enemy occupied territory with plans of a new secret weapon; Dirk Bogarde, fresh from "Appointment in London" (1953) and "They Who Dare" (1954), is a not-too-convincing Flight Sergeant; heart throb Anthony Steele is the skipper of the HSL; and Jack Watling, skipper of the shot down aircraft, endures a second spell at sea in an inflatable life raft after his first experience in one in "Journey Together" (1945). Nigel Patrick, more often seen playing well spoken officer or gentleman types, is very convincing as a rough, gruff Flight Sergeant who is 2IC on the HSL, while other all-too-familiar supporting actors of the British post-War years, like Victor Madden and Michael Ripper, also populate the cast.

As soon as the film opens, the first shot we see is of what is meant to be an RAF Coastal Command Short Sunderland flying boat standing out of the water on a wide tarmac apron. The big four-engined amphibian is filmed into sun from the rear port quarter, with its tall cabin hull and sweeping vertical tail in silhouette, which means no markings are visible. This is deliberate on the part of director Gilbert because the flying boat in shot is neither a Short Sunderland nor an RAF Coastal Command aircraft. It is a civilian Short Solent, distinguishable from the Sunderland by its curved tail fin. The Sunderland had passed out of RAF service in the UK by the time this film was in production (the last RAF Sunderland Vs were being operated only by the Far East Air Force in Singapore, until 1959), therefore Gilbert had to find a convincing substitute. In so doing, he had to ensure that the civilian markings on the Solent did not get into shot.

The Short Solent passenger flying boat, which first flew in 1946, could trace its lineage from the earlier Short Sunderland. The RAF required a much more modernised and powerful version of the Sunderland, ordered as the Sunderland Mk.IV, but the changes to the design were so substantial that the decision was taken to rename the new variant as the Short Seaford. This military flying boat embodied much of the design that became the civilian Short Solent; indeed, those Seafords in service with the RAF were converted post-War into the Solent III passenger version. Twelve Solent II series were built new for the British Overseas Airways Corporation (BOAC), which operated them between Southampton and Johannesburg between 1948 - 1950. A number of ex-BOAC Solents were acquired by Aquila Airways and flown from Southampton to Madeira and the Canary Islands until the service was withdrawn in September 1958.

Research indicates that Aquila Airways was the sole operator of the Short Solent in the UK when "The Sea Shall Not Have Them" was in production, so it is feasible that the Solent seen in the film is an Aquila Airways flying boat filmed in such a way as to conceal its non-military origin. However, there is a more likely source for the particular Solent in shot.

Online Forums quote Felixstowe in Suffolk as being the port used in the film for the HSL base. Indeed, one contributor says he was a boy living in the area when the film was being made there. Another says he was taken on board the HSL used in the film at Felixstowe Docks. What is significant is that Felixstowe was still a seaplane base in the early Fifties. Located there was the Marine Aircraft Experimental Establishment (MAEE), with its large seaplane hangars, ramp and slipway. The MAEE was controlled by the Royal Aircraft Establishment (RAE), which in its turn came under the auspices of the Ministry of Supply.

Two Short Solents were on the strength of the MAEE in 1953, the year the film was in production. One of them was actually the second production Short Seaford NJ201, which was sold to Aquila Airways that same year and converted into Short Solent III G-ANAJ City of Funchal. It flew with Aquila Airways until it was wrecked on the beach at Santa Margharita during a storm in 1956. The other flying boat was Short Solent III G-AKNS City of Liverpool, which had joined the MAEE fleet in November 1950 and been given the military serial WM759. This Solent was used by the MAEE in trials to investigate hydrodynamic problems occurring in long swell conditions. It came to a sad end when it had its wings and tail removed under a plan to join it with another Solent hull, to create a floating restaurant.

Solent III WM759 still bore a large union flag on its tail fin, which, if it is the example in shot at the beginning of "The Sea Shall Not Have Them", would explain the angle it is shown at in order to obscure this give-away symbol. Framing the Solent at the top of the screen are the engines of a second example that surely has to be Seaford NJ201.

Following the title credits, establishing shots of the RAF Marine Craft Unit base are shown to introduce us to the crews of the HSLs. Included in one of these shots is that of airmen walking past a smaller, single-engined bi-plane amphibian with two riggers standing on its lower starboard wing as they work on one of its struts. This ungainly looking flying boat has a significant role later in the film, so it would be apt to wait until it makes its full appearance to explain its identity. Beyond it in this establishing shot is the port wing and two engines of either Seaford NJ201 or Solent WM759.

In another shot showing us the newest, and clumsiest, recruit getting on board the HSL the seaplane hangars of Felixstowe Docks can be seen in the background, with the tail of one of the big Short flying boats in front of them just coming into view from the right side of the screen. It appears to have no markings at all. This being so, it may be Seaford NJ201 stripped of its military scheme in readiness for being repainted in Aquila Airways colours, which were largely natural metal overall anyway. An even clearer but distant view of this flying boat appears a few frames later, confirming that it is a completely bare metal hull. The small amphibian can also be seen parked in front of it, in the same position where it is seen in the earlier establishing shot.

HSL 2561, the high speed launch that features mostly in the film, is sent out on a standing patrol into the North Sea where it shuts down in a strong swell and waits until it is either ordered to the last known position of a downed aircraft or is told it can return to base. The scene suddenly changes to a shot of a Lockheed Hudson in trouble, trailing smoke from its bomb bay. This shot is believed to be an out-take from a pre-Pearl Harbor, Hollywood war movie, but which one is not known.

The given plot of "The Sea Shall Not Have Them" is that the crew of an RAF Hudson ditch in the North Sea and take to an inflatable life raft before their aircraft sinks. They then drift in ever worsening conditions whilst HSL 2561 tries desperately to find and rescue them before they either perish of cold or are swept onto an enemy occupied beach. Among the aircrew is the aforesaid RAF Air Commodore played by Michael Redgrave. Only he isn't quite what he appears to be. He has been sent into Nazi Occupied Holland to get hold of plans of what is later referred to in the plot as "the follow-on to the V1 and V2". Precisely which Nazi Vergelstungwaffe (Retaliation Weapon) this is we are not told. What we do learn, as Redgrave and the Hudson aircrew drift helplessly in the North Sea, is that he is carrying a brief case containing documents about this secret weapon of the Nazis which, if they are picked up by a German E-Boat before an RAF HSL can reach them, will have to be weighted down and thrown overboard.

Redgrave reveals that he spent six days on the run inside Holland before he was picked up by the Hudson. This means that the Hudson was not a bomber as the plot synopsis claims it is. We know that the RAF never used the Hudson as a bomber, but as a Coastal Command anti-submarine patrol and reconnaissance aircraft. As we have seen, Hudsons do appear as RAF bombers in Hollywood war movies made before America was forced into World War Two. However, in this film the ditched Hudson was clearly being used on an SOE-style mission to pick up a British agent inside Holland, a role, as we know from "Now It Can Be Told" (1946), that Hudsons of No.161 (Special Duties) Squadron regularly performed. Redgrave obviously felt he didn't need to disguise himself on this dangerous mission, as he is dressed in his full Air Commodore's uniform!

The actual ditching is achieved by the use of a very poor studio miniature of the Hudson. However, when the crew climb out onto the roof before getting into the inflatable life raft it looks as if the complete airframe of a real Lockheed Hudson is being used for this scene. Almost certainly it is a stripped-out Hudson airframe that has been lowered into the sea and kept afloat while extras act the role of the aircrew climbing out onto its roof and wings. Its distinct 'O-Ring' radar antenna is in place atop the fuselage just behind the cockpit, suggesting this may be a Hudson V, but its dorsal gun turret has been removed. Presumably this was a Hudson struck off charge by the RAF and kept in Air Ministry

storage, which had been given to the film production company for this ditching scene. Either that, or it is an extremely accurate and well made full-scale facsimile of a Hudson.

The author votes for the former option because freeze-frame analysis shows that this same airframe was also used for studio shots in a tank. In close-up shots, its instrumentation equipment in the cockpit can be seen. In another shot at sea, its port wing tip section can be seen to have broken off, revealing the wing join holes and torn metal skin. This detail is unlikely to have been fabricated by the art department, the damage possibly occurred when the airframe was placed into the sea. It helps to add realism to the crash scene, though. Another shot shows the Hudson almost completely submerged, apart from the tops of its twin tail fins. Whether this airframe was actually sunk at sea, or returned to the Air Ministry after filming, isn't known.

The next scene to use aircraft in the film depicts the RAF air station to which the Hudson crew were flying with the escaping Air Commodore before being shot down. To illustrate this airfield, an RAF Lancaster is seen landing. We have seen this Lancaster in this same shot before. It is an out-take from "Appointment in London" (1953) and shows Avro Lancaster B.VII NX782, carrying the codes IH-V, Lancaster 'V - Victor' as flown by Dirk Bogarde in that film (he has obviously been demoted from Wing Commander to Flight Sergeant one year further on).

A distant shot of what is meant to be a Short Sunderland is next to appear, but is so high and so indistinct on film that it could be any large four-engined aircraft.

The one aircraft to have a full acting role in "The Sea Shall Not Have Them" is the previously mentioned single-engined amphibious bi-plane. Now it is seen in full shot air-air, growling over the North Sea. It is a radial-engined amphibian of which film stock is rare, a Supermarine Sea Otter, the longer-range development and intended replacement of the Supermarine Walrus. The principal difference between the two is that the Sea Otter has a Bristol Mercury XXX 'puller' engine adjoined to the top wing, in place of the Walrus's Bristol Pegasus VI 'pusher' engine under but behind the top wing. The prototype first flew in September 1938, but the Sea Otter did not go into full production until after the Air Ministry placed an order in January 1942, which eventually totalled 592. Approximately half of these had been built and delivered to both the RAF and the Royal Navy before the War ended. They were used for coastal reconnaissance patrol, communications and air sea rescue duties by both services.

This actual aircraft can be identified as Sea Otter I JM909, on strength with the MAEE at Felixstowe. JM909 was built at Cowes on the Isle of Wight and retained by Supermarine for pilot training from Itchen. While with the MAEE it was used for Rocket Assisted Take-Off Gear (RATOG) trials off water, which must have been exciting in an aircraft of this type. Its eventual fate is not known.

In the film, Sea Otter I JM909 can be seen making a very dramatic landing in quite a swell which causes it to bounce hard back into the air after its initial touch down, then plunge back onto the sea with water spraying right over its fuselage and bottom wings while its propeller windmills frantically. A tough old bird that had to make many such heavy landings in quite rough seas, but a Godsend to downed airmen in World War Two. Even to an enemy pilot helplessly adrift, for whom imprisonment would be a preferred option to a slow, cold death on the open sea, as happens in the film when the Sea Otter picks up the German pilot who had shot down the Hudson but had been taken out himself in the process of doing so by the Hudson's air gunner.

We get some good views of the Sea Otter's cluttered interior and, in particular, a very novel sight of the radial engine at full chat, filmed through the Perspex canopy roof. Filming of the Sea Otter took place in seriously demanding and tough conditions on the open sea, making for a dramatic and unique record of this ungainly amphibian in action.

The final shot of aircraft in the film is the final shot itself as "THE END" appears above a long shot of the Marine Aircraft Experimental Establishment's hangars, with the Short Seaford/Solent and the Supermarine Sea Otter parked in front of them. For the aviation historian, this footage must be valuable to have. "The Sea Shall Not Have Them" is another classic British war film containing original images of some very original aircraft, unlikely to be found anywhere else.

THE COLDITZ STORY

(Released: January 1955)

This classic PoW escape film is, like its fellow predecessors, "The Wooden Horse" (1950) and "Albert R N" (1953), free of any aviation content.

ABOVE US THE WAVES

(Released: March 1955)

An extended drama based on the real-life X-Class midget submarine attacks on the German battleship Tirpitz moored in a Norwegian fjord. Aviation does not feature at all in this film.

THE DAM BUSTERS

(Released: May 1955)

What superlatives haven't been used to describe this classic and, indeed, most famous British war film? The author isn't going to try to add to them. Apparently acclaimed by film critics and fans as "the 43rd best British film" to be made, with its distinctive 'Dam Busters March' played over and over again by bands and orchestras (most of all, not surprisingly, by the Royal Air Force Central Band) and chanted by England football fans whenever the England football team plays the Germany football team, "The Dam Busters" is never going to lose either its appeal or its own place in film history.

It was the biggest grossing film released in Britain in 1955; it had two Royal Command Performances by popular demand because the crowds wanting to see it were too large for the Odeon Leicester Square to accommodate on what was meant to be the sole night that it was played before the Royal Family; and it was the inspiration for producer/director George Lucas in creating the spectacular finale to the first "Star Wars" (1977) film, with X-Wing Fighters replacing Lancaster bombers and the destruction of the 'Death Star' replicating the attack on the Ruhr Dams.

Having said all that, if judged objectively, "The Dam Busters" isn't that good a film, even by mid-Fifties standards. Its first 17 minutes are tediously slow, concentrating on Dr Barnes Wallis's (Michael Redgrave, again) obsessively irritating experiments in trying to perfect the method of launching bombs against the Dams, to the exasperation of War Office mandarins and while trying the patience of his loyal and patient wife and children. There is no sense of drama at all in these opening scenes, and no sense that this is wartime Britain we are meant to be seeing: Barnes Wallis fiddles about with marbles and string in the spruce garden of his flowery country home, with no sign anywhere of the privations that he and all other Britons of the Forties had to endure.

This film is about one of the most famous bombing raids in military history, but it takes almost 18 minutes before we actually see an aircraft in it. Barnes Wallis tells the Whitehall mandarin who is hectoring him for his request that a precious and much-needed Vickers Wellington bomber be released from Bomber Command Operations, so that his 'bouncing bomb' theory can be tested in reality, that he designed the actual bomber. Barnes Wallis contributed his Geodetic construction design method to the Wellington, but did not design the actual aircraft itself - that was a team effort at Vickers Aviation, Ltd's, Brooklands factory.

The film then cuts to a shot of a Vickers Wellington taking off, filmed from the end of the runway with the Wellington flying very low with wheels down right towards and directly over the camera. It is immediately recognisable as a Wellington T.10 navigational trainer variant, with its all-over silver scheme, yellow training bands on the wing, and silver painted nose faring replacing the forward gun turret. This is Vickers Wellington T.10 MF628, acting the role of the trials launch aircraft for the 'Upkeep' bomb. This is the only shot of it in the film, but Wellington T.10 MF628 had the very important task of being one of the two camera aircraft filming the air-airs of the Lancasters flown in "The Dam Busters".

Filming from Wellington T.10 MF628 took place between 19th July and 7th August 1954. Prior to this, MF628 had been kept in storage at No.19 Maintenance Unit, RAF St Athan in South Wales, but was maintained in airworthy condition. It was selected as the camera platform because, unlike all other Wellington T.10 navigational trainers, its rear turret had not been fared over and was still operable. It made an ideal platform from which to film the Lancasters air-air in forward angle positions, offering unhindered views in a wide arc behind the Wellington.

As many an aviation enthusiast and historian will know, Wellington T.10 MF628 still exists today as a proud exhibit in the RAF Museum at Hendon, although it has been converted externally back to its original 1944 condition as a Wellington B.Mk.X, with both fore and rear gun turrets restored from the remains of other Wellington survivors. After completing its filming duties, MF628 was returned to No.19 MU on 14th October 1954, where it was officially grounded. On the 24th January 1955, it was sold by the Ministry of Supply to its manufacturer, Vickers-Armstrongs Aircraft, Ltd, and flown to Wisley Airfield in Surrey. As far as it is known, this was the final flight made by a Vickers Wellington.

Vickers later presented MF628 to the Royal Aeronautical Society (RAeS) and, by now repainted in RAF Bomber Command colours but still in Wellington T.10 configuration, it was transferred to RAF Hendon on 18th November 1957 and stored, along with much of the RAeS's Nash Collection of historic aircraft. By March 1961, MF628 had been transferred to the Air Historical Branch's store at Biggin Hill, then was presented by the RAeS on permanent loan to the Ministry of Defence (Air) in mid-1964. In early 1968, MF628 returned to No.19 MU for restoration to static display standard, as, along with other historic RAF aircraft, it had been selected for display at the RAF 50th Anniversary Royal Review due to be held in June 1968 at RAF Abingdon. On 14th June 1968, MF628 was duly lined up with many other RAF aircraft dating from 1st April 1918 right up to 1968 for inspection by HM The Queen and HRH The Duke of Edinburgh.

On 26th October 1971, Wellington T.10 MF628 was transported to its present home at RAF Hendon and, on 15th November, 1972, went on public display when the RAF Museum opened its doors for the first time. It and all other RAeS Nash Collection aircraft were purchased outright by the MoD (Air) in March 1992, which in turn, in September 2004, gifted all of these airframes to the RAF Museum. Wellington B.X MF628 is today, along with Vickers Wellington B.Ia N2980 belonging to the Brooklands Museum in Surrey, one of only two complete examples of the Vickers Wellington to survive out of 11,461 Wellingtons of all versions that were built between 1936 - 1945.

In the film, Wellington T.10 MF628 is portraying the trials Wellington that conducted the initial tests of 'Upkeep' off Chesil Beach, near Portland in Dorset. It is being flown by Vickers chief test pilot, Joseph 'Mutt' Summers (played by Patrick Barr), with Barnes Wallis alongside him and actually operating the release mechanism for the bouncing bomb. In fact, because Vickers were involved with the 'Upkeep' tests, and because Barnes Wallis worked for them, there was no need for him to appeal to the Air Ministry for the release of a Wellington from RAF Bomber Command - Vickers had enough prototype Wellingtons at Brooklands that could be used. Archive film of the trials Wellington dropping 'Upkeep' off Chesil Beach is shown in "The Dam Busters", probably provided by Vickers-Armstrongs Aircraft, Ltd, or even by the real Barnes Wallis himself, as he had access to this footage which was still on the Secret List at the time the film was made.

The actual Wellington was a converted Vickers Wellington Mk.III, serialled BJ895 and modified to carry the first 'Upkeep' trials bombs, which operated out of Warmwell for the Chesil Beach trials drops.

Barnes Wallis and 'Mutt' Summers cheer the successful release of the bomb. The film is being economical with the facts here because the first drop, on 4th December 1942, saw the bomb's cylindrical outer casing disintegrate on impact, due to the structure not being strong enough; however, with 'Upkeep' still classified in 1954, it is possible that the Air Ministry kept the facts to themselves, so director Michael Anderson and scriptwriter R C Sherriff were free to make their own interpretation of what happened for dramatic purposes. They did have Paul Brickhill's book, "The Dam Busters", to refer to, and Barnes Wallis himself could have told them what really happened during the trials, assuming he was allowed to do so.

With 'Upkeep' still classified in 1954, director Anderson and his film editor, Richard Best, were required by the Air Ministry to 'doctor' the shape of 'Upkeep' departing the Wellington over Chesil Beach and bouncing across the surface of the water. They had to effectively paint a black sphere over 'Upkeep' on each frame of the archive footage they had been provided with. Quite why 'Upkeep' was still classified at the time of the release of "The Dam Busters", 12 years after the Dams Raid, has never been made known, but one possibility is that the technology involved in developing the bouncing bomb was being preserved, in case a much more modern version that could be dropped by a high speed jet bomber was developed, as research into air-launched anti-shipping missiles was still in its infancy in the UK.

The film continues to play fast and loose with the facts when Barnes Wallis tells the War Office mandarin that the 'Upkeep' trials have been completed within a month and were a complete success. The trials took far longer than one month, and the real Barnes Wallis was repeatedly frustrated by the bomb's casing continuing to disintegrate on impact, until he and his team came up with a solution. The film also does a masterly cosmetic job in having the Air Officer Commanding (AOC) RAF Bomber Command, Air Chief Marshall Sir Arthur 'Bomber' Harris, portrayed as being sceptical yet receptive to the idea of 'Upkeep'. One can't help but think that director Anderson and scriptwriter Sherriff were playing a very correct political card with this scene, as the famous fiery former AOC Bomber Command was still around in 1955 and might have aimed his own vocal version of an 'Upkeep' bomb at them if he was portrayed delivering the withering sarcasm he originally displayed when first told about Barnes Wallis's invention. 'Bomber' Harris was dead against taking any of his precious Lancasters out of Operations for 'Upkeep', and was nothing like as willing (relatively) to listen to the idea as he is portrayed as being in the film.

But at last we get to see some Lancasters, even though it has taken more than 27 minutes for the first to be seen landing on an airfield spotted with dandelions. Interesting to note, this Lancaster is landing with the starboard inner engine feathered. It is acting the part of Wing Commander Guy Gibson's Lancaster returning from a raid. It is here we are introduced to actor Richard Todd playing arguably his most famous film role of his acting career. Todd was at the zenith of his powers as the quintessential, stiff-upper-lip, tough British hero when he made "The Dam Busters", and whenever the name of Guy Gibson, VC, is mentioned, most people automatically imagine him as Richard Todd. This is why "The Dam Busters" resonates so strongly with fans of British war films, as Todd often acted roles of strong English types unyielding under pressure, exactly as Englishmen of the post-War years liked to perceive themselves as being.

Gibson and his crew dismount from their 'Lanc', among them a very youthful Robert Shaw in his first significant screen role. This scene allows us to identify the first of the four Avro Lancaster B.VIIs that were used in the film, this being Lancaster B.VII NX782. As we know, NX782 acted the role of 'V - Victor' in "Appointment in London" (1953) two years earlier, and still carried the same all-over black plus light-grey upper fuselage surface colour scheme it bore in that film. Just as in "Appointment in London", no attempt was made to repaint the Lancasters used in "The Dam Busters" into correct RAF Bomber Command markings, probably on cost grounds. For this particular scene, NX782 is carrying the squadron code letters ZN-G, the actual code letters of Wing Commander Guy Gibson's Lancaster B.I that he flew when he was Commanding Officer of No.106 Squadron before he was asked to form the new No.617 Squadron for the Dams Raid.

Lancaster B.VII NX782, along with her other B.VII sisters, had been put into storage at RAF Aston Down in Gloucestershire not long after she acted her role in "Appointment in London" in 1952. Her use as an Avro Lincoln crew trainer was no longer required, as all RAF Bomber Command Lincolns were being retired when "The Dam Busters" was in production in 1954, having been temporarily replaced by loaned Boeing B-29 Washingtons in lieu of the arrival of the first Vickers Valiant V-Bombers.

All four Lancaster B.VIIs were taken out of storage and brought back into flying condition. Much of the filming took place at RAF Hemswell in Lincolnshire, a wartime satellite Bomber Command air station not far to the north of RAF Scampton, the actual bomber base that the real No.617 Squadron operated from for the Dams Raid. Wing Commander Guy Gibson flew his fateful last raid from RAF Hemswell on 19th September 1944 when, as Squadron Commander of No.150 (Pathfinder) Squadron, he took off in a Mosquito to fly as Pathfinder Master Bomber for a bombing raid over Rheydt. Gibson's Mosquito ran out of fuel on the return trip and crashed near Steenbergen in The Netherlands, killing both himself and his navigator.

A good panoramic shot of RAF Hemswell shows the station's headquarters building and hangars, with two bombers parked beyond. This is a good likeness of RAF Hemswell during the War years, as virtually nothing had changed there since the ending of World War Two. Of the two bombers seen in the distance, one is definitely an Avro Lancaster B.VII, but the other is an Avro Lincoln B.II, recognisable by its larger airframe than the 'Lanc' and its straighter wing design (the Lancaster's wings were very slightly angled upwards outboard of the engines). When "The Dam Busters" was in production there, RAF Hemswell was a storage base for demobbed Avro Lincolns awaiting the axe. Anderson and his production team didn't waste the opportunity to use a number of them as background props, depicting Lancasters.

RAF Hemswell was home to three operational Bomber Command squadrons when filming was taking place. Nos.109, 139 and 199 Squadrons were all equipped with the then new English Electric Canberra B.2 jet bomber. Nos.109 and 139 Squadrons operated the Canberra B.2 in the pathfinder role, while No.199 Squadron was equipped with the Canberra B.2 as an electronic-countermeasures (ECM) unit which also undertook nuclear air sampling over hydrogen bomb test sites in Australia and the Pacific.

It was mostly No.199 Squadron aircrews which were recruited to fly the Lancasters, something they really enjoyed as it involved some challenging low-level flying, a complete change from the comparatively mundane high-level ECM task they normally flew. One of their Canberra B.2s actually manages to get into the film, unintentionally - more of this to come. The pilots would not have had a problem converting onto the Lancasters as they all had four-engined piston bomber experience of flying the Avro Lincoln B.II, which was still on strength with No.199 Squadron alongside the Canberra B.2 in 1954.

Filming was carried out both inside and outside RAF Hemswell's headquarters building and hangars, so "The Dam Busters" provides a last remaining record of what this Lincolnshire bomber base actually looked like. It closed for flying in 1956 and then became an RAF Bomber Command Missile base, housing Thor Intermediate Range Ballistic Missiles from 1959 - 1963. RAF Hemswell was decommissioned in 1967 and today is an industrial and retail estate, although its hangars remain in situ.

Another connection with "Appointment in London" is Australian actor Bill Kerr, who returns from his appearance in that film as a Lancaster pilot to portray Flight Lieutenant 'Micky' Martin in "The Dam Busters" - the real 'Micky' Martin became something of a national hero post-War in Australia for his participation in the Dams Raid. Also showing up is British actor Richard Leech who plays the role of Squadron Leader H M 'Dinghy' Young, so called because he held the record in Bomber Command for the highest number of ditchings in the North Sea. Sadly, the real 'Dinghy' Young was not to survive his final one on the night of the Dams Raid. We will see Leech return in another film about wartime bombers, this time USAAF B-17 Flying Fortresses, when he convincingly acts the role of an American Bomb Group Commander in "The War Lover" (1962).

After the new No.617 Squadron has formed up at RAF Scampton, their equally new Lancasters are delivered. In reality, these were Lancaster B.MK.III(Special)s, each outfitted to take a single 'Upkeep' bomb. In the film, their arrival is depicted by three Avro Lancaster B.VIIs curving in over the dandelion-carpeted RAF air station, with an Avro Anson T.21 navigational trainer parked in the foreground as a prop; the T.21 variant of the Anson did not come into RAF service until after World War Two and its all-over silver paint scheme and yellow training bands are of the Fifties era, not that of 1943. Watching is Gibson and his Flight Commanders, Squadron Leader Young and Squadron Leader Maudsley. As the three Lancasters fly by in line astern, the fourth Avro Lancaster B.VII taxies past beyond them bearing

No.617 Squadron's distinctive AJ-P code letters and a Bomber Command-style fuselage roundel - at least the art department have gone that far to achieve some measure of accuracy. We can see that this Lancaster B.VII is devoid of any mid-upper gun turret, which adds to the realism as No.617's Lancaster B.III(Special)s were operated without mid-uppers fitted. The black-and-light-grey colour scheme jars horribly, though.

At the squadron briefing, when Gibson tells the assembled aircrews for the first time that they have been formed for a secret mission which may shorten the War, the need to constantly practice low flying, day and night, is emphasized. The scene immediately cuts to three Lancaster B.VIIs over-flying the camera position in a close 'Vic' formation and heading out over a lake. More than one astute observer of "The Dam Busters" has commented Online that these Lancasters are all carrying the fake 'Upkeep' bombs below their fuselages, something they would not have been doing for real during low-level training. Director Anderson did get away with this continuity goof when the film was released to cinemas, because audiences of the Fifties would not have had time to spot it during a single showing and most would not have understood the error anyway.

When the film cuts to the next shot of the Lancasters flying very low over the lake, filmed from a position close to the waters edge with the 'Lancs' heading right for the camera, no 'Upkeep' bombs are in place. This is where "The Dam Busters", at last, comes into its own: even in black-and-white, the imagery of the Lancasters flying so low over the Upper Derwent Valley is stunning, especially one shot filmed from a hillside position looking down on a lake with a Lancaster just 60 feet above the surface heading directly for the camera and then curving majestically up and over in a surging climb. These shots fully convey the very real manoeuvrability of the Lancaster, not seen in any other war film. But then, back into another three-ship shot, heading into the sunset this time, and all three fitted with 'Upkeeps' again! Oh dear, the life of a film editor is not an easy one.

After Gibson has been introduced to Barnes Wallis for the first time and shown film of 'Upkeep' being dropped from the Wellington BJ895 trials aircraft, he is invited to see an actual test drop being made into the sea off Reculver, Kent. Whether the choice was deliberate by Anderson, or whether he was denied any further footage of 'Upkeep' test drops, isn't known, but a major goof occurs here. The test drop actually shown in the film is of Barnes Wallis's other bouncing bomb design, 'Highball', which he envisaged being used against naval targets, the most prominent being the German battleship Tirpitz moored in Trondheim Fjord in Norway. Archive imagery is shown of a Mosquito dropping 'Highball' off Reculver, which disintegrates as soon as it impacts the water. Seen in silhouette on film, the aircraft is one of two de Havilland Mosquito B.Mk.IVs which were provided by the Air Ministry for 'Highball' trials, either DK290 or DK327. More likely it is DK290/G, the 'G' suffix indicating that this Mosquito B.IV had to be guarded at all times due to the highly classified equipment it carried (Wellington B.III BJ895 also had a 'G' suffix); DK327 was held in reserve. Mosquito B.IV DK290 had a short service life, making its first flight on 23rd May 1942 and spending two periods with the A&AEE before the 'Highball'

equipment was removed in August 1943, following which the aircraft was transferred to No.27 MU at RAF Shawbury and was finally allocated to No.10 School of Technical Training at Kirkham on 3rd December 1943 as an instructional airframe.

An actual Mosquito is used in "The Dam Busters", acting the role of the 'Highball' trials aircraft flown by 'Mutt' Summers. Inaccurately, it is shown at RAF Hemswell, with the four Lancaster B.VIIs parked as props in the background (the 'Highball' trials Mosquito flew from Manston in 1943). In actual fact, however, the sight of a Mosquito at RAF Hemswell was commonplace just before "The Dam Busters" was filmed there: No.139 Squadron operated Mosquito B.35s in the target marking role for Lincolns up till December 1953, while No.199 Squadron had only just relinquished its Mosquito NF.36s in exchange for Canberra B.2s by April 1954, just before director Anderson and his production team moved in (No.199 was a joint Lincoln B.II/Mosquito NF.36 operator until the Canberra B.2s replaced the 'Mossies').

However, the Mosquito used in "The Dam Busters" was not from either of these squadrons: both No.139's and No.199's Mosquitoes were painted in the same black-and-light grey scheme as the Lincolns, a scheme clearly not borne by the Mosquito in the film. Moreover, it is neither a B.Mk.35 nor a NF.Mk.36 variant. Due to the film being in black-and-white, the colour scheme is difficult to discern, but, seen from two angles - one forward, the other broadside - this Mosquito is almost certainly painted in two-tone PR blue camouflage. The large roundel on the fuselage correlates with photo-reconnaissance Mosquitoes still in RAF service in 1954, although they were by then virtually all withdrawn from the front-line role, being replaced by the Canberra PR.3.

The most likely candidate is a de Havilland Mosquito PR.34 of No.58 Squadron, then based at RAF Wyton in Huntingdonshire, which was in the process of converting from the PR Mosquito to the Canberra PR.3 during 1954. The scene in which it appears has it waiting at RAF Hemswell for 'Mutt' Summers to fly the final and decisive test drop of 'Upkeep/Highball', the success or otherwise will decide if the War Office and Air Ministry mandarins will give their blessing to the weapon being used.

As Barnes Wallis wishes Summers good luck and gets into the waiting staff car to drive to Reculver, one of the mothballed Avro Lincoln B.II bombers used as a prop can be seen in the background through the car's window. But, more to the point, as one of the mandarins shifts position in the car, an English Electric Canberra B.2 can be clearly seen, albeit very briefly, in shot. Probably in 1955, and right up till the advent of the film's release on DVD, this goof has never been spotted until now.

Archive imagery is used of Mosquito B.IV DK290 successfully dropping 'Highball' off Reculver. The Dams Raid is on.

As is now well known, one of the film's signature scenes - that of Gibson getting the idea of using spotlights on No.617's Lancasters to accurately measure their height above water at low-level during night flying, from watching the spotlights on a dancing revue in a London West End theater - is pure theatrical invention by Anderson and Sherriff. The boffins at Farnborough came up with that technique, but this is where dramatic licence overrules fact to create an original and inventive film scene. "Genius, pure genius", claims Todd as Gibson. "We gave the idea to Farnborough, and they did the rest". In Michael Anderson's and R C Sherriff's imagination.

Now we have some superb footage of low flying Lancasters over the Derwent Valley reservoirs in the Peak District, re-enacting the actual rehearsal by No.617 Squadron testing the specially developed bomb sight by Farnborough 'boffins' against the twin towers of Derwent Dam. The imagery of three Lancasters flying low over Derwent Reservoir and between the towers of Derwent Dam is among some of the most treasured film footage of any British war film. It is an accurate representation of the real rehearsals in May 1943 and of the actual attack on the Ruhr Dams themselves. It is what makes "The Dam Busters" so special for many film fans and aviation enthusiasts.

Only one of the four Lancasters in the film made these low runs over Howden and Derwent Reservoirs, acting the role of three different Lancasters. It is filmed from a promontory just ahead of Derwent Dam itself, making several runs with its bomb doors open while flying at what certainly looks like 60 feet. In one shot it is seen to over-fly the Dam and then descend beyond it into the valley of Ladybower Reservoir below before pulling up in a left hand climbing turn. This must be Lancaster B.VII NX782, as the code letters ZN-G are clearly visible in white on its starboard fuselage when it is seen in long-shot passing low over Derwent Dam between the two towers. This, then, is a goof, but it is not an easy one to spot, and, in most of the shots, the Lancaster is heading towards the camera so low above the water that the white code letters are hardly visible behind the mass of the starboard wing, so the effect is not spoiled.

But two factors are immediately apparent about NX782 in this scene, which set it apart from each of the other three Lancaster B.VIIs in the film: first, it has camouflage over the light grey of its wings and upper fuselage surfaces, and second, it is flying with its Martin 250CE mid-upper turret still in place. No other Lancaster appears in "The Dam Busters" with its mid-upper turret attached. This suggests that Lancaster B.VII NX782 was filmed low-flying over Derwent Reservoir on a date separate from when all the other Lancaster scenes were being shot, and, as it still had its mid-upper turret still in place, probably well before the other three Lancasters underwent set-dressing as No.617 Squadron Lancaster B.III(Specials), which included having their mid-upper turrets removed. The probability is that NX782 was still wearing its paint scheme from its role as 'V - Victor' in "Appointment in London", as it had received camouflage on its upper surfaces for that film which may have been left in place when it was put into storage soon after filming was completed.

On the day of the raid, the scene is set with images of No.617 Squadron Lancasters parked at dispersal on what is meant to be RAF Scampton. These evocative shots are also much treasured by aviation enthusiasts and historians. Lancaster B.VIIs bearing the codes AJ-G (Gibson's 'Lanc') and AJ-M are discernable, but in none of these shots are the serials visible. A close-up shows the installation beneath a Lancaster B.VII of what the art department imagined an 'Upkeep' bomb appeared like, inaccurately as we now

know. Nonetheless, this fake 'Upkeep' looks impressively the part.

In what are probably the most dramatic and poignant scenes in the film, when the aircrews are bussed to their waiting 'Lancs' as Eric Coates's 'Dam Busters March' builds to a crescendo in accompaniment, the four Lancaster B.VIIs at dispersal have been joined by a single Lincoln B.II as an extra prop in the background. Bill Kerr as 'Micky' Martin walks down the length of his 'Lanc', with the serial of Lancaster B.VII NX673 clearly standing out: thus, we are able to confirm the second of the four Lancaster B.VIIs. It, too, was another player in "Appointment in London", in which NX673 appeared as Lancaster 'B - Baker'; in "The Dam Busters", it is acting the role of 'P - Popsy', the code of the real 'Micky' Martin's Lancaster.

As a youthful John Fraser, playing Flight Lieutenant John Hopgood, reaches his aircraft, we can solve the mystery of a third Lancaster: Lancaster B.VII RT686. Its serial is visible above Fraser's head as he prepares to enter through the rear fuselage hatch of what is meant to be 'M - Mother'. Interestingly, when portraying Gibson's Lancaster B.III(Special) coded AJ-G (as CO, Gibson had the privilege of using a Lancaster coded with the suffix 'G', making any such aircraft he flew identified as 'G - George'), the art department have gone for accuracy and taped the serial 'ED932' onto the rear fuselage, the correct serial of the real 'G - George' that Wing Commander Guy Gibson flew to lead the attack on the night of 16th - 17th May 1943. Which of the four Lancaster B.VIIs was given the honour of playing the role of ED932/AJ-G isn't known at this stage of the film, although a candidate is offered at the end of this review.

'G - George' appears clearly in shot when Group Captain Whitworth drives up in his staff car to wish Gibson good luck. As he steps out of his car, four Avro Lincoln B.IIs can be seen parked in the background on the far side of RAF Hemswell, of which Lincoln B.II RF446 is clearly visible with its large serial in white on its starboard fuselage.

The engine start and taxying sequences in "The Dam Busters" come close to emulating the similar scenes of Lancasters in "Appointment in London", but director Anderson and cinematographer Erwin Hillier don't quite capture the same sense of power and energy of the bombers as do their counterparts, Philip Leacock and Stephen Dade, with their imagery in that earlier film.

One thing that RAF Hemswell could not provide as a location for RAF Scampton is the scene of the take offs by the Lancasters. The shoot called for three Lancaster B.VIIs to take off in 'Vic' formation, filmed by Erwin Hillier in the rear turret aboard another Lancaster as it rolled in formation with the three-ship. This could not be achieved at RAF Hemswell, nor at RAF Scampton, as these air stations both had hardened runways which were not wide enough to take three-plus-one Lancasters in formation. Instead, the all-grass airfield of RAF Kirton-in-Lindsey was used, some 15 miles north of Lincoln and then home to a non-flying training school in 1954. These take off shots are magnificent, and are what makes "The Dam Busters" so admired by film fans and aviation enthusiasts.

Another superb shot is that of an air-air of three Lancaster B.VIIs in 'Vic' formation, carrying their fake 'Upkeep' bombs and over-flying the city of Lincoln, with Lincoln Cathedral standing out on the horizon - clearly permission was obtained from the city authorities and from the Air Ministry for this over-flight to be allowed.

The film now moves into its complete element, with the air-air shots of the Lancaster trio seen powering across the North Sea, silhouetted against the sun and the bright, glinting water, at less than 100 feet. These shots are what makes "The Dam Busters" so talked-about and sought-after by aviation film fans. No other film made anywhere carries such evocative images. Shots of the Lancasters crossing the Dutch coast were filmed over Anglesey in North Wales, The Wash close to Skegness, and Southwold in Suffolk. The immortal words, "Enemy coast ahead" - spoken countless times by real Bomber Command aircrew during World War Two - announce their arrival. Nobody minds when seeing these shots that they are, in fact, goofs: the sun is shining in the Lancaster trio's port rear quarter (in other words, the eight-o'clock direction), from the south-east, proving that the Lancasters are flying in an east - west direction. If they really were crossing the Dutch coast, the sun would be in their starboard forward quarter (two-o'clock position) and they would be flying west - east.

An air-air close-up of one of the Lancasters, filmed flying in close formation with Wellington T.10 MF628, shows that at some stage an attempt was made to apply camouflage over its light grey upper surfaces (probably it is NX782). It flies in line astern to the Wellington camera-ship, low over a canal, but not as low as the trio are flying, and filmed by Hillier from the rear turret. Another shot of this same Lancaster flying in the Wellington's Eight-o-Clock confirms that not only has camouflage been applied, but also World War Two-style roundels to its upper wings. While this helps to make this Lancaster look more realistically warlike, the near-white propeller bosses offset the effect.

The SFX of the Moehne and Eder Dams under attack and being breached are obvious miniatures reflective of the standard achievable of the Fifties period. Newsreel footage of flood damage from various natural tragedies are used to portray the deluge inflicted upon the Ruhr Valley. They include an aerial shot of a flooded airport, with the tails of two aircraft rising out of the silt. Of course, the lack of information available at the time, or that which was withheld for security/propaganda reasons in 1955, meant that the Dams Raid was portrayed in the film as causing much more damage to the Nazi war machine than was actually the case, while the loss of civilian life does not feature at all. The film's message was that a mighty blow had been struck against the Hun, and that was still cause for much celebration in Britain of the Fifties.

Although the Sorpe Dam is included as the third target in the pre-strike briefing, the unsuccessful attack upon it is completely absent from the film. "The Dam Busters" propagates the popular myth of the time that the Raid was a complete success; as we now know today, it was two-thirds of a success in terms of the targets destroyed. And it did not achieve the ultimate goal of shortening the War. It was, though, a massive morale booster for the war-torn British population and a huge public relations success for RAF Bomber Command.

The Lancaster seen landing back at RAF Scampton to the tune of 'The Dam Busters March' is actually touching down among the dandelions thronging RAF Kirton-in-Lindsay, suggesting a May - June period of filming this shot in 1954. The curved approach and easy touch down speaks volumes for the confident flying by the pilot - we won't see the Battle of Britain Memorial Flight's Lancaster PA474 being landed with such verve! At some stage, an Avro Anson T.21 had snuck in between shots, as it is seen parked up in the background; it might have been the same Anson T.21 seen earlier in the film, or a different one visiting an RAF Flying Training Command air station. It may even have been used as the Lancasters' aircrews' 'hack', to ferry them back to Hemswell if the Lancasters were to be left overnight at RAF Kirton-in-Lindsay.

The taxying-in shot of Lancaster B.VII NX673 shows that it has been dressed up by the art department to have fake flak damage to the starboard wing.

The final shot of Richard Todd as Gibson walking resolutely off into the distance was filmed at RAF Scampton, as were some other scenes, but none of the Lancaster B.VIIs flew from the real No.617 Squadron's wartime base.

Of the four Lancaster B.VIIs flown in "The Dam Busters", three have been identified by freeze-frame analysis: NX673, NX782 and RT686. The fourth cannot be identified by this method. Research shows that two other candidate Lancaster B.VIIs have been posited by four separate sources: two vote for NX671, while three out of the four are promoting NX679. Both of these Lancaster B.VIIs are claimed to be the Lancaster bearing the taped serial 'ED932' and carrying the AJ-G codes of Gibson's 'G - George'.

To examine the case for either Lancaster, let's look at each source in turn. An independent source has posted a photograph on several Websites of an Avro Lancaster B.VII in set-dressing, with a mocked-up 'Upkeep' bomb slung underneath its fuselage, making a fly-past at an airshow held at Coventry/Baginton Airport on 19th June 1954. This source gives the serial for this Lancaster B.VII as NX671.

A second Website source claims that Lancaster B.VII NX679 was another of the four used in the film, omitting RT686. This same Website also makes the identical claim that NX679 was one of the three Lancasters flown in "Appointment in London"; however, as we know, freeze-frame analysis of that film does not confirm this. Again, this Website source also failed to identify Lancaster B.I TW862 as appearing in "Appointment in London", so, in the opinion of the author of this book, the Website concerned has omitted two Lancasters for both films while making unproven claims for NX679 as a candidate Lancaster in either production.

However, Lancaster B.VII NX679 has support for acting as 'ED932/AJ-G' from two other sources, neither of which quote NX671 as being a performer. One of them is a Dutch Website, which appears to have taken its information from Jonathan Falconer's 2005 book, "Filming The Dam Busters" (The History Press). Another - British - Website quotes similar information, as well as adding some extra details of its own.

The Dutch Website states that Lancaster B.VIIs NX673/'AJ-P', NX679/'AJ-G' and RT686 were the three flyers in the film. The Website does not quote 'AJ-M' for RT686, but we have seen that this Lancaster did act as Hopgood's 'M - Mother'. The British

Website quotes the same three Lancasters as the flyers, suggesting it obtained its information from the same source as the Dutch one.

Neither refer to NX782, implying it was not a flyer, but we can confirm it definitely was.

Interestingly, both Websites mention the use of a fifth Lancaster, the British Website stating it "was used as a back-up" and for "some aerial filming"; the Dutch Website simply refers to a "vijfde (fifth) film - Lancaster".

As stated earlier, a Lancaster must have been used to film the take-off shots at RAF Kirton-in-Lindsay because the twin-engined Wellington MF628 would not have been able to sustain the same speed as the three four-engined Lancasters as they rolled across the grass airfield and powered into the air. Filming from the mid-upper or rear turret of another Lancaster was the only way to achieve these striking shots. Likewise, the shots of the trio filmed from the rear over-flying the city of Lincoln and crossing the 'Dutch coast' must have been achieved from the bomb aimer's all-Perspex position in the nose of this Lancaster, flying behind them and being able to keep pace with them - remember, Wellington T.10 MF628's nose turret was fared over. However, this fifth Lancaster probably wasn't used to film views from the pilot's and bomb aimer's perspective of flying low above Howden and Derwent Reservoirs, then crossing low over Derwent Dam and down into the valley of Ladybower Reservoir beyond; a camera in the Perspex nose of Lancaster B.VII NX782 would have caught these images - again, unachievable in Wellington T.10 MF628.

Both of these Website sources promote Lancaster B.VII NX739 as the 'fifth' Lancaster. If so, NX739 certainly does not appear in the film. The reason why is that NX739 carried a ventral radome beneath its fuselage; no ventral radome-fitted Lancaster appears in "The Dam Busters".

Lancaster B.VII NX739 was on the strength of the Aircraft & Armaments Experimental Establishment at Boscombe Down in 1954, being used as an air-air photography platform with trials aircraft, so it would have been an ideal machine to use for aerial filming in "The Dam Busters". On 13th October 1955 it was delivered by the Ministry of Supply to Blackbushe Airport to conduct air-air photography tasks, with a maintenance contract passed to Eagle Aircraft Services based there. It was flown from Blackbushe until it was delivered to RAF Wroughton on 16th January 1957, to be broken up.

If Lancaster B.VII NX739 is the 'fifth' Lancaster used for "The Dam Busters", it can only have been as a camera aircraft, not as an actor or a prop for a No.617 Squadron Lancaster. Confirmed as actors are Lancaster B.VIIs NX673, NX782 and RT686. But there is a source which finally nails down NX679 as the fourth Lancaster, acting as Gibson's 'G - George' and carrying the serial and code ED932/AJ-G. The source is the excellent Scramble Website: in its airshow reports section, an eagle-eyed spotter attending the 1956 SBAC Flying Display and Exhibition at Farnborough on 8th September notes, quote, "NX679 AJ-G Lancaster B.7 - Engineless. ED932 pasted on side. Used in Dambusters film". What would we researchers do without spotters?

It seems that Lancaster B.VII NX679 made its way to RAE Farnborough sometime after filming of "The Dam Busters" was completed, for whatever purpose is not known. At some stage its four Rolls Royce Merlins were removed, perhaps as spares to keep another Lancaster flying - PA474, maybe.

This, then, is the role of honour for "The Dam Busters" film. None of the four actor Lancaster B.VIIs have survived. Their actual fates are unknown, but almost certainly they came to an ignominious end the year after "The Dam Busters" was released, when all remaining stored Lancasters used for aircrew training in support of the equally defunct Avro Lincoln fleet were sold for scrap.

COCKLESHELL HEROES

(Released: November 1955)

Based on fact and on the book of the same title, "Cockleshell Heroes" tells the story of a group of Royal Marine Commandos who train for and execute an attack on a German-held French port using two-man kayaks to transport limpet mines, which they attach to the hulls of enemy supply ships. Directed by and starring Jose Ferrer in the role of the rather eccentric Commanding Officer, Major Stringer, who develops and initiates the plan to use kayaks, nicknamed 'Cockleshells', to penetrate the enemy coast, the film's plot makes no use of aviation except for a brief appearance by an RAF Transport Command aircraft. The trainee Commandos are required by Major Stringer to jump from the transport wearing German uniforms, then make their way back to their Royal Marines HQ avoiding capture, to test their initiative. The transport aircraft from which they jump is a Vickers Valetta C.1, a post-War 1940s' twin piston-engined design that replaced the famous Douglas C-47 Dakota in RAF Transport Command service. In the film, the Valetta is seen too briefly and at too great a height disgorging Paratroops for identification to be possible. It is, of course, an inaccurate aircraft to use for the late 1942 period that the film's plot is based on.

A TOWN LIKE ALICE

(Released: March 1956)

This highly acclaimed film adaptation of the classic novel by Nevil Shute, describing the ordeal of British expatriate women and children who are forced by Japanese soldiers to endure starvation and disease during their trek across Malaya, only has aircraft in it right at the end during the post-War period of the plot. This takes place in Australia when the women's leader, Jean Paget, played by Virginia McKenna, goes in search of the Australian Prisoner of War, Joe Harman, acted by Peter Finch, who tried to help her in Malaya and who she believed the Japanese had killed. Jean learns from the Malayan villagers who saved her life and those of the surviving women and children, that Harman was, in fact, spared by their Japanese captors and after the War had returned to his home town, Alice Springs.

Jean travels to Alice, the town of the title, where she learns she must fly on to Willstown, "a fair cow" of a town in the middle of the Outback where Harmon was last seen. To do this, she must take a trip in a typically rugged aircraft that can operate off dirt strips in the Outback. This is a de Havilland DH.90 Dragonfly five-seater, carrying the Australian civil registration of VH-UTJ. This actual DH.90 was operated by Connellan Airways of the Northern Territories when it was used in "A Town Like Alice". There is a nice picture of VH-UTJ on the airwaysmuseum.com Website, showing this DH.90 parked on very Outback-like scenery.

DH.90 Dragonfly VH-UTJ was imported into Australia in 1938 for use by North Western Airlines of Moree, New South Wales. During the War, but before Japan entered, VH-UTJ was sold to Qantas Empire Airways in October 1940, operating on internal services; it was one of four DH.90s in Australia flying these services to outlying communities. Connellan Airways of Alice Springs acquired VH-UTJ in October 1946. It suffered an accident at Amaroo, NT, on 9th January 1948 and received some fire damage, but was rebuilt. However, it was completely destroyed by fire at Tennant Creek, NT, on 9th August 1955, which must have occurred just after its appearance in "A Town Like Alice". Apparently the fire was caused by the Shell agent who was refuelling the aircraft. A sad ending for a classic de Havilland bi-plane twin prop.

Jean learns that Harman was flown all the way to London to look for her. The only thing she can do is wait for him to return to Alice Springs. The final scene has Jean waiting anxiously in the passenger terminal of Alice Springs Airport, as the 'plane carrying Harman lands. She doesn't know how he will greet her. Outside on the ramp the airliner taxyies to a standstill. Right in front of it is another Connellan Airways aircraft, this time the big brother to the DH.90, a de Havilland DH.89A Dragon Rapide. Only its nose, forward cabin, propellers and starboard undercarriage leg are in shot, so no registration is visible. Connellan Airways had two Dragon Rapides in service in 1955 when this scene was filmed, VH-AHI and VH-BKR; Connellan had operated two more, but both had been lost by the time this scene for "A Town Like Alice" was filmed at Alice Springs Airport.

Connellan Airways was founded by Australian cattle farmer, Eddie Connellan, in 1938 after making a tour of the Northern Territories in Spartan VH-UJT. There is a very interesting history of the airline on the airwaysmuseum.com Website, which provides some fascinating insight into Connellan's operations of the Royal Flying Doctor Service.

The airliner on which Harman is flying back into Alice Springs is Douglas DC-3 Dakota VH-TAN of Trans-Australian Airlines (TAA). Completed as a Douglas C-47A-30-DL at Douglas Long Beach plant on 27th May 1943 and delivered to the USAAF on the same date, it was subsequently transferred to the Royal Australian Air Force (RAAF), arriving at Amberley Air Base on 23rd June 1943 with the serial A65-12. Although operated by

No.34 Squadron, RAAF, it actually flew for Australian National Airways (ANA) during the War, being withdrawn from use and struck off charge in September 1946. DC-3 VH-TAN was registered to the Australian National Airlines Commission on 8th October 1947 and operated by TAA for nine years, flying its final revenue service for the airline on 13th August 1958. It then went into storage at Essendon Airport, Melbourne, before commencing a new career with a variety of operators throughout the Far East, including flying in New Guinea and Taiwan, before finally being scrapped in 1978.

THE MAN WHO NEVER WAS

(Released: March 1956)

This British war film claims its place in cinematic history for being the first of its genre to be filmed in Cinemascope. It tells the story - allegedly - of one of Britain's most successful Military Intelligence Operations against the Third Reich, Operation Mincemeat, the deception plan in 1943 to fool the Nazi High Command into believing the Allies would invade German Occupied southern Europe through Greece and Sardinia, and not through Sicily as happened. The corpse of a British Royal Marines Major would be found washed up on a beach in Spain, apparently drowned after the aircraft he was flying in crashed into the sea. On his person would be a briefcase containing the fictitious plans to invade Greece, which he was carrying to General Eisenhower.

In a story of this kind, aviation does not feature to any large extent. However, according to the plot, the deception plan evolved from an Airborne Forces exercise watched by the two British Naval Military Intelligence Officers charged with devising the plan. The exercise is taking place at an RAF air station that looks very much like RAF Abingdon in the film. Aircraft engine noise is heard, but no aircraft is shown on screen. A mass of equipment containers is seen dropping beneath multi-coloured parachutes. We have seen this shot before: it is an out-take from "The Red Beret" (1953), of the 1st Airborne Division's assault on Bone airfield in Algeria.

One of the containers "takes a short cut", according to the tannoy announcer, when its parachute streams in a Roman Candle. "That's what we call jumping to a conclusion, gentlemen", says the announcer.

One of the Intelligence Officers says to the other, "That parachute that failed to open - supposing we were to drop a fellow over enemy territory with papers on him saying we were going to invade Greece and with a failed parachute. The Germans would find him dead and the papers…they would say, 'They're going to invade Greece'".

"Do we tell the man who jumps and whose parachute doesn't work, that this is some sort of practical joke that he finds out about on the way down?", asks the other.

They both agree that it wouldn't work as they were unlikely to find a volunteer. But the genesis of Operation Mincemeat in planting a corpse with faked military plans on him has been created.

A sub-plot of "The Man Who Never Was" involves the American flatmate of the female assistant to the two Naval Intelligence Officers being the girlfriend of an RAF pilot. She makes the mistake of falling in love and becoming engaged to him, only to learn later that he has been shot down and killed. The significance of this sub-plot emerges when an agent of the Reich, who has been sent to London to find out if the dead Major is genuine, calls at the flat and hears the girlfriend's grief-stricken story. He thinks she is the girlfriend of the dead Major and is talking about him, not the RAF pilot, so he becomes convinced that the Major is genuine.

Before the pilot is lost, a scene shows him with his squadron. He is a Mosquito pilot and has just returned from a raid over Brussels. He is seen dismounting from his aircraft and being greeted by fellow pilots. For this scene, three de Havilland Mosquitos were brought in. All of them are painted with grey-green camouflaged upper surfaces and all-grey undersides, and have the standard solid noses with four cannon fitted. They noticeably do not have bulged under-fuselages, meaning that they are neither PR Mosquitos nor heavier bombing variants. They bear a very strong resemblance to Mosquito FB.VIs. No serials are visible. The codes 'SG-' and 'SB-F' are seen on two of them, which are fake, although No.464 (RAAF) Squadron of the 2nd Tactical Air Force carried 'SB-' codes during World War Two. None of the Mosquitos are seen flying; one is seen taxying, while another is seen winding its propellers down.

The Mosquito FB.VI was not among the variants of Mosquito still in service with the RAF in 1955, when the film was made. None bore the wartime camouflage schemes of the Mosquitos seen here. The most likely source for these three was the de Havilland Aircraft Company at Hatfield, Hertfordshire, where surplus Mosquito FB.VIs were still held for modification prior to export to nations which still operated the Mosquito as a front-line aircraft.

The scene in which the three Mosquitos appear is short, and no other aircraft appear in the film.

THE BLACK TENT

(Released: April 1956)

A lavishly filmed wartime romance between a British Army officer and a Bedouin princess in Libya which does not have any aviation content in its plot.

REACH FOR THE SKY

(Released: July 1956)

This celebrated story of amputee fighter pilot, Douglas Bader, focuses much more upon his struggle to overcome physical disability and official bureaucracy in his pursuit of his RAF flying career, despite the loss of his legs in a flying accident, than upon his exploits as a wartime fighter pilot. What is seen of

Bader's involvement in dog-fights above Dunkirk, in the Battle of Britain and over France in 1941 only occupies a portion of the film approximately two thirds of the way through the plot, but obviously they play an important part in Bader's story.

No matter how many roses of accolades "Reach For The Sky" has won from film critics and fans down the years, from aviation enthusiasts and historians it has received mostly raspberries. This is due to the completely inauthentic use of 1944-model Spitfire Mk.XVIs for 1940-era Spitfire Mk.Is and Mk.IIs. Admittedly, the film's producers had to go with what was available when filming took place (at RAF Kenley again) between August and September 1955, and that meant inevitably using Spitfire XVIs because significant numbers of this most versatile Marque were still either working or were stored during the mid-Fifties. The film's production company, Angel Productions, also painted the Spitfires XVIs in green/grey camouflage instead of painting them in 1940-period green/earth brown schemes, adding to the lack of authenticity.

Ten Spitfire Mk.XVIs were assembled at RAF Kenley. Of this total, only four were flyers. Five were static props produced from Air Ministry storage, while a sixth example was in use by the RAF as an instructional airframe and was taxyable. Three of the four flyable Spitfire XVIs came from No.3 Civil Anti-Aircraft Co-Operation Unit (CAACU) at Exeter Airport, Devon, the same unit that eight years later would provide the Mosquitos for "633 Squadron" (1964). The fourth flyer came from the RAF's No.103 Flying Refresher School (FRS). One of the Spitfire XVIs was sold to Pinewood Studios for exterior shots with actors and interior cockpit shots. It was joined by an 11th Mk.XVI that had been bought outright by MGM Film Studios after being struck off charge by the RAF.

The only shots of Spitfire XVIs filmed airborne in "Reach For The Sky" show three of the four flyers – RW352, SL574 (both of No.3 CAACU), and TE358 of No.103 FRS, as RA617/QV-S and QV-P, RV214/QV-R and AR251/QV-X respectively – performing brief 'peel offs'. Spitfire XVIe TE456 of No.3 CAACU acted as spare.

Of these 11 Spitfire XVIs, five have survived today, including one that was buried for 24 years, then was dug up and is now slowly working its way back to life again!

No less than three are with museum collections in Australia and New Zealand: TB863, a former No.3 CAACU Spitfire, was struck off charge in 1951 and was subsequently purchased by MGM Film Studios for interior and actor close up shots. It is the only surviving Spitfire XVIe from "Reach For The Sky" to be still flying today, as VH-XVI with the Temora Aviation Museum in Australia. TE288, the instructional airframe which was taxyable in the film, is now an exhibit in the Royal New Zealand Air Force Museum at Wigram, while TE456, the spare flyer, is today in the Auckland War Memorial Museum. It appears as TE425 in the film, with the strange code goof of 'PD-9'.

Of the other two survivors, flyer SL574 is on show in the United States at the Air & Space Museum, San Diego, California, while TB885, one of the Air Ministry storage Spitfire XVIs, received an extraordinary resurrection – after being used as a static prop in the film it was condemned to the fire dump at RAF

Kenley for three years, after which it was broken up and buried at Kenley, remaining in its grave until it was exhumed in 1982. Its various dismembered sections were then stored at several different locations, including the nose section with the Shoreham Aircraft Museum. In 2008, all of TB885's remains were reunited with a private collector; the Spitfire is now undergoing a slow, long-term restoration to flying condition.

One other Spitfire XVIe deserves mention: TE341, another of the Air Ministry storage examples, was sold to Pinewood Studios and was used for actor-damage risk shots, with Kenneth More as Douglas Bader climbing out of the cockpit. For some reason it was painted as 'ZD-S', with no serial, an unexplained goof, unless it was given a 'ZD-' code in error for an 'SD-' one. It is this Spitfire from which More rolls out of the cockpit, acting as Bader leaving one of his prosthetic legs behind after his collision with a Messerschmitt Bf.109 over France.

Four Hawker Hurricanes joined the Spitfires at RAF Kenley, which was called upon to portray various RAF air stations in the film, including RAF Cranwell, RAF Coltishall, RAF Duxford and RAF Tangmere, plus not least of all appearing as itself in certain scenes. The Hurricanes comprised the faithful Mk.IIc LF363, then of the RAF Biggin Hill Station Flight and the only Hurricane flyer in the film. It was joined by two of its compatriots from "Angels One Five", Mk.Is L1592 and P2617, both made taxyable. The fourth Hurricane remains a mystery to this day, and has been described by one source as a replica. It was definitely not Hawker's G-AMAU/PZ865, as it could not be spared from its tasks as a chase aircraft for the company's Hawker Hunter low speed flight test programme, pursuing earliest Marques of Hunters testing various underwing stores and changes to wing design.

Hurricane LF363 only flies briefly in "Reach For The Sky", mostly performing low-level aerobatics when Squadron Leader Bader proves to the disgruntled Canadian pilots of No.242 Squadron he has just taken charge of that he is not "a passenger with tin legs". The aerobatics are believed to have been flown by Wing Commander Peter Thompson, DFC, then Station Commander of RAF Biggin Hill, who is credited as being the inspiration behind the creation of what is today the Battle of Britain Memorial Flight. This sequence was almost certainly shot at Biggin Hill, as the image of LF363 diving straight down and disappearing, then suddenly rearing up flying directly at the camera has a distinctly familiar look of Biggin's famous 'bump' about it. Also, LF363 is clearly wearing a standard dark green/earth brown camou scheme, contrasting with the green/grey scheme it and its compatriot Hurricanes had to adopt for filming at Kenley to match the Spitfire XVIs.

In this aerobatic sequence Bader flies his Hurricane inverted towards the watching No.242 Squadron pilots. Inverted flying was, and still is, impossible in a Hurricane. The effect was achieved in the film with the use of a miniature, and likewise for one of the three low rolls that Bader flies. It is possible to distinguish between the miniature Hurricane and the real thing by the squirts of exhaust smoke produced by the latter's gravity-fed carburettor briefly cutting out as the aircraft rolls through the inverted –

the miniature Hurricane produces no such exhaust smoke. One wonders why the director, Lewis Gilbert, felt it was necessary to use an SFX model Hurricane when he had the real thing to perform aerobatics for his camera. He and his film editor, John Shirley, also use two out-takes from "The Way To The Stars" (1945), for one shot of Bader flying extremely low head-on to the camera and another of Bader's Hurricane performing a roll, while another shot of LF363 diving down is unrealistically speeded up.

The reason for using No.501 Squadron 'SD-' code letters on the Hurricanes in "Reach For The Sky" has never been explained (ironically, Hurricane LF363 bore the correct LE-D code letters of Bader's No.242 Squadron Hurricane for many airshow seasons during the Sixties and the Seventies). For 'Scrambles' and air-air formation shots, Gilbert and Shirley shamelessly borrow out-takes of Hurricanes from "Angels One Five" (1952), then reversed the images in the editing process in an attempt to disguise what they have done! A spectacular shot of five Hurricanes 'Scrambling' off grass in line abreast formation, directly towards the camera, is an out-take that was not used in "Angels" for two reasons: firstly, no matter how impressive the image, RAF Hurricanes did not 'Scramble' in this fashion in the Battle, thus making it wholly unrealistic, while secondly it clashed with other paired take-off sequences in "Angels" where the Hurricanes are using RAF Kenley's established hard runways.

Mystery footage used on two occasions has a single Hurricane diving straight down towards the camera, while two more Hurricanes tail chase behind it. The source of this footage is unknown, but most likely it is unused material filmed for either "The Way to the Stars" (which has three Hurricanes flying in it) or for "Angels One Five".

The "Reach For The Sky" editorial team's trickery did not end here, as they also stooped to lifting out-takes from "The First of the Few" (1942) to achieve Spitfire aerial shots. In this case, Spitfire XVIs suddenly morph into being Spitfire IIs and Vbs with No.501 Squadron 'SD-' codes clearly visible - perhaps Gilbert and Shirley were trying to convey the impression that the same codes seen on the Hurricanes meant that the Canadian fighter squadron had now converted onto Spitfires. But throughout "Reach For The Sky", the Spitfire XVIs all wear 'QV-' codes, no matter what squadron they are portraying – another disregard of authenticity in the film which infuriates enthusiasts and historians ('QV-' were the code letters for No.19 Squadron for a period before it switched to using 'WZ-'). The editorial team have even managed to slip in a single out-take from "The First of the Few" of captured Heinkel He.111H-3 1H+EN/AW177 being run at by Spitfire IIa P8074/SD-L.

"Reach For The Sky" does make very effective use of wartime archive footage, not relying solely on artwork miniatures to portray enemy aircraft, although there are plenty of them used as well to reasonable effect. In particular, there are some good studies of Luftwaffe aircraft, opening with dramatic footage filmed through the glazed nose of a Heinkel He.111 of two more He.111s flying ahead at low-level over the outskirts of a town, with flak bursts clearly appearing in front of the He.111 from where the cameraman, presumably the forward gunner and a cool customer indeed, is filming. The town below, with its straight angled roads and the flat countryside beyond, has the look of the Low Countries about it, so this film could have been shot on a low-level raid over Holland in May 1940. Immediately following it is more footage shot from the same position in a Heinkel He.111, flying low-level through smoke as the bomber approaches a large river carving through an industrial city, and with seven He.111s flying ahead of it. Again, the scene below of the city under attack is suggestive of the Netherlands, Rotterdam perhaps. Certainly the Luftwaffe never flew bombing raids as low over British cities as shown in this footage.

More archive footage follows to illustrate Britain under attack by the Luftwaffe, consisting of a Messerschmitt Bf.109G with underwing code letters 'G' and 'E' (the 'Gustav' variant of the Bf.109 did not appear until after the Battle of Britain); a Junkers Ju.87B clearly coded GU+AC (or it could be a stylised '6', making the code 6U+AC, which is more likely and, if so, possibly being a Stuka of ZG.1) rolling into a dive over very flat, patchwork quilt-like countryside with a small bomb attached under the fuselage, possibly filmed on a practice bombing flight somewhere over Germany; plus another example without any codes filmed at the crest of a dive, possibly for promotional/propaganda purposes. An aerial parade filmed presumably somewhere over Germany, probably before the War, of a 'Kette' of three Bf.109s leading nine Messerschmitt Bf.110s, which are in turn being followed by 18 more Bf.109s, is used to depict a raid approaching British shores (Reich Propaganda Ministry imagery which was used in several British war films during the War years themselves). A Heinkel He.111H, identified as either 1G+GT or 1G+GY (the last letter is almost invisible) of Kampfgeschwader 27 (KG.27), is filmed air-air from the No.2 aircraft, in what is a very tight formation, as the lead ship of a 'Kette' of three He.111s.

A fine shot of a Messerschmitt Bf.109E filmed from the dorsal turret of an unidentifiable bomber making a run at the tail, then turning and diving past, is used to portray Bader's Hurricane under attack from the rear. The footage is too clear to have been filmed during a real attack and the Bf.109E is clearly not firing its guns. However, a second shot of the same Bf.109E making the same approach from the rear is used slightly later in the scene of No.242 Squadron's first dog-fight in the Battle of Britain, and this time it most definitely is firing its guns, right towards the camera! Tracer fire can clearly be seen spraying from the wings of the 'Emil'. But the bomber that is meant to be the target takes no evasive action, while the tracks of the tracer shots spray past and underneath the camera-ship. What is unusual about this cannon-firing Bf.109 is that the bursts of fire show that six cannon are installed, three in each wing set close to the wing root. No version of the Bf.109 is known to have had such a set of cannon installed in this configuration, and definitely not six: all Bf.109s had nose-mounted machine guns and some had a single cannon in each wing, the latter of which show clearly in the first shot of the Bf.109E as it swings past the camera-ship, making this particular example suggestive of the Bf.109E-4 variant. Moreover, a freeze-frame study of this 'Emil' shows no cannon ports in the leading edge of either wing. The cannon fire and tracer are very cleverly

created SFX art work. The footage is probably from a staged sequence of an attacking Bf.109E-4 filmed by the Luftwaffe for propaganda or promotional purposes.

Interestingly, exactly the same cannon fire effects are seen coming from the same positions on the wings of a Spitfire, three each side close to the wing root, which also is not correct: early Spitfires had eight machine guns, four in each wing. This confirms that the cannon firing SFX was created by this film's art department on both the Bf.109E-4 and the Spitfire; the latter, incidentally, is the same No.501 Squadron Spitfire Mk.IIa P8074/SD-L filmed for "The First Of The Few" from the dorsal gun turret of captured Heinkel He.111H-3 1H+EN/AW177, making this footage another out-take from that production.

Gun-camera footage shows another Heinkel He.111 dropping its port oleo as it takes hits from what is meant to be Bader's Hurricane in the Battle of Britain. Very familiar gun-camera film of a Focke Wulf FW.190 turning and starting to dive inverted as its pilot bails out is used for another of Bader's shoot-downs, obviously inaccurate as the Battle came too early for the FW.190's entry into service. This shoot-down footage has been used in many films and documentaries about aerial warfare. It is believed to have been taken from a USAAF P-51D Mustang. It is immediately followed by footage from a fighter making a pass right at a bailed-out pilot hanging below his parachute. This was a callous tactic for which some Luftwaffe pilots were notorious, they believing it was legitimate to try to kill a pilot in the air by running past very close to him so that the slipstream would collapse his parachute canopy, or their wings would slice through the parachute rigging. It was a tactic widely reported by RAF fighter pilots as being employed by the Luftwaffe during the Siege of Malta in 1942. It is possible Allied fighter pilots did the same to German pilots: what is noticeable about the pilot below the parachute in this footage is that he is wearing a black flight suit with white boots, much more typical of a Luftwaffe pilot than an Allied flyer. Also, the gun-camera footage has to be looked at vertically in portrait, not in landscape format as one would expect; in other words, the gun-camera was installed on its side – the P-47 Thunderbolt had gun-cameras installed in this fashion, so….

More gun-camera footage shows another FW.190 taking hits on its under fuselage slipper fuel tank which detaches and explodes, the pursuing fighter from which the film is being taken having to fly right through the burst. Another Bf.109 is seen streaming glycol as it takes hits, then banking steeply to port as it starts to go down; while a third Bf.109 loses its entire left wing that nearly strikes the fighter which has caused the fatal damage. Bader attacks another Heinkel He.111, the gun-camera footage of which clearly shows tracer fire streaking into the damaged bomber before it blows up in mid-air, the pursuing fighter that is filming it having to break hard left to avoid the huge burst of flame and smoke.

The archive footage of Dornier Do.17Z-2 F1+FH falling on Fulham, minus its outer wings and entire tail section, is used in "Reach For The Sky" in the same way it is used in "The First Of The Few". An unidentifiable aircraft plunges vertically earthwards into very English-looking countryside and explodes massively, suggesting it still had its bomb load on board (this is the same footage that was used in "Malta Story", 1953, and before that in "Eagle Squadron", 1942).

Gilbert's and Shirley's pillaging of other film productions for out-takes continues with the shot of the five Bristol Blenheim IIs of the Finnish Air Force flown in "The Way to the Stars" (1945) breaking formation, one trailing smoke from the port engine. Also, they not surprisingly lift the outstanding footage taken by the Crown Film Unit, using captured Messerschmitt Bf.110C-4 AX772 being pursued by Spitfire Mk.IIa P8441, as seen originally in "Ferry Pilot" (1941).

But the most astonishing footage is of a Martin Maryland, port engine aflame, hurtling into the ground and exploding (causing the cameraman filming its spectacular crash to throw himself to the ground behind a motorcycle to escape the blast!) seconds after one of its crew escapes just before impact, his parachute opening approximately 100 feet above ground! This same footage appears in another film included in this Chapter, in which more detail about this extraordinary imagery comes to light.

Mention should be made of the Shuttleworth Collection aircraft which appear in the first part of "Reach For The Sky", covering the period of Bader's early flying career in the RAF up till his near fatal, and very fateful, crash in a No.23 Squadron Bristol Bulldog at Woodley Aerodrome, Reading, in 1931. Avro 504K G-ACNB appears prominently right at the start of the film in its dark olive and black colour scheme and with the E3404 serial it bore for many years before it was repainted and re-identified as G-ADEV/H5199 – you won't see it, or find any image of it, flying a full loop (somewhat off-angle) anywhere else other than in "Reach For The Sky"; Bristol F.2B Fighter G-AEPH as D8096 (as it is today) but in the all-over silver scheme it wore for the same length of time as E3404 wore its all-black scheme (it was used to film the air-airs of the Avro 504K, D8096's stability and spacious rear gunner's position making it an ideal camera platform); Bristol Bulldog G-ABBB, now in the RAF Museum but then of the British Science Museum, South Kensington, seen as a prop in several scenes but not flown in "Reach For The Sky"; and former Shuttleworth-owned Spartan Arrow G-ABWP for the Woodley Aerodrome scene.

Avro 504K E3404 was not yet a Shuttleworth-owned aeroplane when it was used for the scenes illustrating Douglas Bader's first experience in flying a 'plane (angry RAF instructor: "Never call it a 'plane, Bader, it's an aeroplane!"). It had been restored by Avro apprentices at Woodford and brought up to flying condition in 1955 before it appeared in "Reach For The Sky". It was also used for in-cockpit close-ups. E3404 must have suffered a small amount of damage in the process, judging by the cracked windshield in front of actor More in the rear cockpit which appears both when Bader makes his solo flight in 1928 and again in Bader's post-accident proving flight in 1933 – five years is a long time to leave an un-repaired windshield!

The appearance of a second Avro 504K, seen in the distance as Bader takes off in Avro 504K E3404 for his proving flight to the RAF in 1933, has provoked puzzlement among

aviation enthusiasts and historians concerning its identity. It has been speculated that it is a classic piece of film art work trickery, a full-scale art department painting of E3404 on a large board, set up in the background to create the impression (very effectively) of another parked Avro 504K on field (note the goof of a Spitfire XVIe creeping into shot in this scene!). However, careful freeze-framing analysis confirms that it must be a full-scale aeroplane and not a board painting because when E3404 takes off, filmed from a vehicle tracking alongside it, the positional angle of the Avro 504K in the background changes in proportion to the camera's forward momentum, which would not happen if it was a painting on a fixed board.

So, is it another real Avro 504K used as a prop in the background, or a full-scale replica? There were no replica Avro 504Ks in existence when the film was being made in 1955 (several were built later in the 20th Century), but there were two genuine candidate Avro 504Ks available at the time, owned by the Royal Aeronautical Society (RAeS) and by the British Science Museum in South Kensington respectively.

The RAeS owned sections of two redundant Avro 504Ks in the Fifties: the fuselage of G-EBJE and the wings of G-EBKN. Both had had civil careers in the Twenties and Thirties after being struck off charge by the RAF following the end of World War One. They had each suffered an "Ooh, Nasty!" while flying from Shoreham (separate incidents, several years apart), which ended their flying careers and saw their remains set aside pending any decision on their future. Eventually the RAeS acquired these remains and set about combining them to produce a 'new' complete, non-flying Avro 504K, with the serial E449. However, the RAeS did not begin its restoration until 1963, completing it in 1966. This timescale would obviously rule 'E449' out from being the 'other' Avro 504K in "Reach For The Sky". In 1968, the RAeS donated 'E449' to the Royal Air Force; since 1976 it has been exhibited in the RAF Museum at Hendon, where it can still be seen today.

The only other known candidate for being the second Avro 504K in the film was owned by the British Science Museum, which had had a specimen with the serial D7560 in its possession since 1920. Very careful study of the imagery of the two Avro 504Ks seen in shot shows a very strong comparison between the background example and that of D7560. With the film being in black-and-white, and with the subject Avro 504K being quite some distance in the background, trying to make a comparison is a challenge. But through careful freeze-framing it is possible to compare the shade of Avro 504K E3404's very dark olive/black colour scheme with that of the other aeroplane, and it can be established that the background aeroplane's scheme is definitely of a slightly lighter shade. Avro 504K D7560 wears the classic all-over olive tan dope scheme that adorned most Royal Flying Corps machines; in black-and-white, this would show up as a somewhat dark scheme on screen, just as it appears on the Avro 504K in the background. Also, D7560 wears its serial in white clearly on the rear half of its fuselage; a similarly-painted serial is visible in exactly the same position on the background Avro 504K.

Final proof that Avro 504K D7560 is the background prop is provided right at the end of the film, when the credits display the producers' gratitude to the Royal Air Force, the Shuttleworth Trust and the British Science Museum, for their assistance with the production. The puzzle is, though, that if the Science Museum's Trustees went to all the trouble of removing D7560 from its South Kensington home and transporting it by road to the film location at RAF Kenley, why then does it only make such a brief and distant appearance in "Reach For The Sky"? For the RAF Cranwell sequence, its use as an RAF College trainer prop for the scene where Bader and other new recruits are berated by a Flight Sergeant would be far more appropriate than Shuttleworth's Bristol Fighter, as was used. Perhaps getting D7560 to Kenley and re-assembling it took longer in time and was more difficult than was anticipated, while the film's budget and schedule did not allow for any delay.

Pinewood Studios built a very accurate-looking Bristol Bulldog full-scale facsimile, carrying serial K2494, for the RAF Kenley and Woodley scenes. Bulldog IIa G-ABBB was the pattern aircraft for its construction which, at this time, was carrying the incorrect serial of K2496 (previously carried by an Avro Tutor). Undoubtedly this influenced the choice of serial K2494 for the F/S facsimile Bulldog, which was dismantled to create the wreckage of Bader's Bulldog (in reality, Bader crashed in Bulldog Mk.IIa K1676). What happened to this facsimile after filming was completed isn't known, but, as it was broken up to depict Bader's crashed Bulldog it probably wasn't salvageable and, therefore, subsequently disposed of. The crash sequence at Woodley was effectively achieved through the use of a studio miniature.

"Reach For The Sky" will always remain a classic British war film, and will always be popular with fans of its genre. But, Oh those Spitfire XVIs…..!

THE BATTLE OF THE RIVER PLATE

(Released: November 1956)

"The Battle of the River Plate" stands out on its own as an accurate and faithful reconstruction of an actual sea battle in World War Two. Furthermore, this highly respected Michael Powell and Emeric Pressburger production was able to use two of the actual veteran ships of the real engagement itself, the Royal New Zealand Navy light cruiser HMNZS Achilles and the heavy cruiser HMS Cumberland, which portrayed themselves in the film.

The plot involves the search for and engagement with the Deutschen Kriegsmarine Panzerschiffe Admiral Graf Spee, off the coast of Uruguay, by the Royal Navy South Atlantic Cruiser Squadron under the command of Commodore Harwood. This Cruiser Squadron was made up of the heavy cruisers HMS Exeter and HMS Cumberland, and the light cruisers HMS Ajax and her sister ship HMNZS Achilles, the latter being part of the then fledgling Royal New Zealand Navy being built up with British Admiralty support. Cumberland was undergoing temporary refit

in the Falkland Islands when Exeter, Ajax and Achilles engaged the Graf Spee shortly after dawn on 13th December 1939.

Both Exeter and Cumberland had 8-inch main armament, significantly inferior to the 11-inch guns of the Graf Spee. They were also both smaller and had lighter armour plating than their German opponent, but they were faster and more manoeuvrable.

The British Admiralty classified the Graf Spee as a pocket battleship, or, in today's terms, a mini-battleship. The Deutschen Kriegsmarine definition for the type of ship the Graf Spee represented was Panzerschiffe (literally, armoured ship). The Royal Navy did not have a similar Class of ship of the size and striking power of these Deutschland Class Panzerschiffen, of which the Graf Spee was the third and last to be launched in 1934. Therefore, the definition pocket battleship was created by the Admiralty to define the role and offensive power of a Deutschland Class Panzerschiffe, built like the Admiral Graf Spee to apparently meet the peacetime limitations imposed on Germany under the Versailles Treaty but which breached that Treaty's terms through the installation of heavier armament than was allowed. After the Battle of the River Plate, the Kriegsmarine re-classified the Deutschland Class as Schwere Kreuzer (heavy cruiser).

Both the German and British warships in the real Battle of the River Plate carried on-board spotter floatplanes. However, the Graf Spee's Arado Ar.196 floatplane had developed a technical problem when the British cruisers were sighted and could not be launched during the engagement. HMS Exeter carried a Supermarine Walrus amphibious floatplane, but this aircraft was damaged by shell splinters from Graf Spee as it was being prepared to be catapulted, putting it out of action.

It is in the depiction of spotter floatplanes used by the Royal Navy cruisers to direct shell fire against the Graf Spee that aviation features in "The Battle of the River Plate". It also involves the one principal error in the recreation of the Battle, as the film shows HMS Exeter's spotter 'plane being catapulted and its crew reporting on the fall of shot. Because Exeter's Walrus was damaged, this obviously did not happen in reality; it was HMS Ajax's spotter 'plane that performed this crucial role. In fact, the real Battle of the River Plate was the first major naval engagement in military history in which an aircraft launched from a warship directed fire for the ships' guns.

To portray 1930's-era bi-plane floatplanes as operated by the Royal Navy aboard warships, the film production team resorted to using a genuine aeroplane of that period, plus a quite effective studio miniature. The latter is a model of a Fairey Seafox, a two seat ship-borne reconnaissance floatplane with an all-metal monocoque fuselage, which was a departure into new aero engineering technology for the time. Seafox floatplanes entered service with the Royal Navy in 1937 and operated from light cruisers in various theaters of the War until 1943. They were launched by catapult from the aft deck behind the main funnel(s) and could be recovered from the sea by crane.

The miniature used in the film is a quite realistic depiction of a Fairey Seafox being catapulted. It is only seen twice, using the same shot, representing Exeter launching its spotter during the Battle (incorrect, as we know, both in actuality and in representation of

Exeter's own spotter, the Walrus being a larger, 'pusher' floatplane than the Seafox 'puller') and that of Ajax sending its Seafox (accurate depiction) off to 'spot' the Graf Spee as she emerges from Montevideo harbour, where she had taken shelter after the Battle. The production team wisely chose not to use a miniature of the Seafox in flight, as this would have jarred with the imagery of real warships re-enacting the Battle; instead, only shots of the pilot and observer in the cockpit looking down on the Battle are used.

Another inaccuracy is the film's statement that Exeter's spotter 'plane was shot down: not the case, as we know. This is portrayed by imprisoned British merchant sailors aboard the Graf Spee during the Battle saying they can feel aviation fuel sprinkling down on them and that it must have come from Exeter's spotter after being hit. How they could feel aviation fuel while they are holed up inside the Graf Spee's hull, let alone know it came from Exeter's aircraft, is a flaw in the script which mars the otherwise very realistic depiction in this film of a naval battle.

Obviously, a genuine Fairey Seafox was not in existence for Powell and Pressburger to use, so as near as possible a substitute had to be found for the scenes of the pilot and observer boarding the floatplane before launching. The easiest option for them was to use a de Havilland DH.82A Tiger Moth, significantly smaller but contemporary with the Seafox. The Tiger Moth is only seen being started prior to launch, with the propeller, forward fuselage and cockpit, plus upper wing, being the only parts of it appearing in shot. Therefore, identifying the actual aircraft used is not possible, although this Tiger Moth displays its natural metal frontal area and has its fuselage roundel partly visible, typical of a military example in the Fifties.

The Tiger Moth was still being widely used by the Fleet Air Arm as an elementary flying trainer and all-purpose air station 'hack' in 1955 when the film was made; it would be fair to assume that this particular Tiger Moth was loaned to Arcturus Productions from any one of the Fleet Air Arm's establishments using this classic British bi-plane. It would not have been difficult to set the aeroplane up on jacks, to restrain it when the propeller is swung, either at Pinewood Studios or in a hangar for filming. No floats are shown, as the Tiger Moth was not equipped with them in Fleet Air Arm service, although civilian floatplane versions of the Tiger Moth have been flown.

"The Battle of the River Plate" was filmed in the western Mediterranean, with ships of the Royal Navy's Mediterranean Fleet made available to the production. As stated, HMS Cumberland and HMNZS Achilles played themselves in the film, although Achilles had, from 1946 onwards, been sold to the Indian Navy and was actually the INS Delhi when she re-created her role for Arcturus Productions. HMS Cumberland had been reduced to training ship status, and appears without any of her main armament installed. HMS Exeter is portrayed by the light cruiser HMS Jamaica, while HMS Ajax, the South Atlantic Cruiser Squadron's flagship, is represented by the heavy cruiser HMS Sheffield. Both Sheffield and Jamaica were genuine World War Two warships and had seen considerable action, including both performing key roles in the sinking of another dangerous Kriegsmarine warship, the Schlacht

Kreuzer (battlecruiser) Scharnhorst. The Graf Spee was portrayed by the US Navy heavy cruiser, the USS Salem.

"The Battle of the River Plate" had a huge reception on release in Britain and was Powell's and Pressburger's last independent film production together, as well as their most successful; they returned to the Rank Organisation after its completion.

ILL MET BY MOONLIGHT

(Released: January 1957)

Taking its title from a line in William Shakespeare's "A Midsummer Night's Dream", this film tells the story of a real-life SOE operation in Nazi Occupied Crete that involved the kidnapping of a German General and his transfer to British Forces headquarters in Cairo. Starring Dirk Bogarde, who, in the Fifties, seemed to be making a career out of portraying wartime British Special Forces officers operating in the Balkans, this film was the final production from the much admired Michael Powell and Emerit Pressberger partnership, which has featured strongly in this book (they made it for The Rank Organisation; their "Battle of the River Plate" was their last independent production).

"Ill Met by Moonlight" is noted for its spectacular scenery, even though it is filmed in black-and-white. The mountain scenery conveys the rough and rugged Cretan terrain, with Partizans being pursued by German troops across huge ridges and deep ravines. The whole effect is very convincing, making it easy to believe that the film is indeed taking place on Crete. In fact, it was filmed in the French Alps, which probably explains why Powell and Pressburger opted to use black-and-white film instead of their normal use of impressive colour imagery, as the Alps in summer would have had much more greenery than the stark Cretan mountain ranges. In 1956, when the film was in production, Crete had been seriously affected by a major earthquake following a volcanic eruption in the Aegean Sea, leaving the island in a state of emergency; so filming there would not have been feasible at the time.

As far as aviation is concerned in "Ill Met by Moonlight", only one aircraft appears, a Morane-Saulnier MS.505 Criquet acting the role of a German Fieseler Storch observation aeroplane searching for the SOE operatives and their Partizan allies who are frog-marching the captive General through the mountains. The Criquet is painted in Luftwaffe markings and is filmed posed dramatically against the Alpine mountain ranges. Some shots are filmed looking down on the Criquet as it passes below through deep valleys.

The origin of this Criquet is not known, but it would have been either a French or Swiss registered example. In particular, it is a version powered by a Jacobs R-755-A2 radial engine, which exposes it as being different from the German Argus engine-powered Fieseler Storch. Morane-Saulnier built the Storch when France was under German Occupation, and continued with a licence-built variant post-War for the French military forces. The Jacobs radial engine was adapted to power the recognisable Storch airframe when the last examples of the Argus engine were used up.

Named Criquet (Cricket) by Morane-Saulnier, this versatile STOL aircraft, which could literally hover when flown directly into very strong winds, remained in production in France until 1965, with more than 900 built. A significant number of both original Fieseler Storch and French MS.505 Criquet examples, plus at least one Czech K-65 Cap, are still today in private ownership or in various museums and collections throughout Europe, most of them in flying condition. The example flown in "Ill Met by Moonlight" would undoubtedly be one of these Morane-Saulnier MS.505s and may even have been provided for the film production by the French Armee de l'Air, whose pilots would have been among the most experienced in low flying amid the Alps.

THE STEEL BAYONET

(Released: May 1957)

The first of a series of British World War Two war films made in the Fifties to be set in the North African campaign, in this case just before the fall of Tunis to the Allies in 1943. "The Steel Bayonet" is very much in the spirit of the wartime "Nine Men" (1943), with a small company of British soldiers having to set up an advanced observation post close to Afrika Korps lines and defend it against overwhelming odds. It features a number of fine, recognisable British character actors and has well staged action sequences directed by the very capable Michael Carreras. However, aviation has no role to play in this film.

THE BRIDGE ON THE RIVER KWAI

(Released: October 1957)

David Lean's epic Academy Award-winning production of British and Commonwealth soldiers forced into slave labour by the Japanese on the Burma – Siam Railway has no aviation element to offer other than the brief sequence of Commandos parachuting into the Siamese jungle (today, Thailand). They are filmed making their jumps from the aircraft itself, which is meant to be an RAF Dakota. A shot of the aircraft's shadow travelling over the jungle below reveals it is a Vickers Valetta C.1, operating with the RAF's Far East Air Force. At the time "The Bridge on the River Kwai" was being filmed in Ceylon (today, Sri Lanka), RAF FEAF Valetta C.1s were regularly para-dropping Commandos into the Malayan jungle to combat the Communist insurgency against Malaya's colonial government during the Fifties.

THE ONE THAT GOT AWAY

(Released: December 1957)

This classic war movie is very well acted and directed, telling what purports to be the true story of Oberleutnant Franz von Werra, the only German pilot Prisoner of War to escape from Allied custody in World War Two and make it back to Germany. For a long time it has been believed that von Werra was the sole German PoW to escape Allied custody, but it has more recently been confirmed that a U-Boat crewman also successfully escaped imprisonment in Canada, as von Werra did, while another PoW not only escaped but settled in New York, marrying an American girl and only handed himself in to the authorities in 1952!

The film does have a carefully-worded introduction in describing von Werra as "the only German prisoner of war taken in Britain who escaped…", so there was an element of caution even then as to whether he could literally fit the description of the film's title.

Acting as this Luftwaffe pilot shot down in the Battle of Britain, Hardy Kruger is excellent and convincing in the role of von Werra. So too is the aviation in the film. In fact, it is fair to say that the other star is Hawker Hurricane Mk.IIc LF363, making its third appearance in a British war film and, by the time of the release of "The One That Got Away", a founder member of the Royal Air Force Historic Flight at RAF Biggin Hill. Today, LF363 still serves with the same Flight, renamed the Battle of Britain Flight before it was extended to include the word 'Memorial'. Hurricane IIc LF363 remains a very long-standing friend on the British airshow scene 55 years after its appearance in this production.

Von Werra had a plan to steal an aircraft and escape to Nazi Occupied Europe, a desperate plan that was very unlikely to succeed as he could not rely on getting an aircraft – even if he achieved that much – which had sufficient fuel and range to fly across Britain to Europe. The airfield he gained access to by posing as a Dutch test pilot was RAF Hucknall outside Nottingham, used by Rolls Royce during the War but described in the film as a "government Experimental Flight, very hush hush". RAF Hucknall is actually used.

The film has von Werra getting as far as strapping into the cockpit of LF363, after mechanics think that he is a ferry pilot from White Waltham "come to collect the Marque Two Hurricane, eh?". Factually, this is correct in time, as the Hurricane Mk.II variant was being introduced to service in the December 1940 period when von Werra is shown making his daring escape attempt. However, in reality he failed to make it as far to an aircraft cockpit before he was caught at Hucknall.

Whether it was intentional or not, a goof occurs when, very briefly, a 1950s' era DHC Chipmunk T.10 is seen as a back drop when von Werra gets into RAF Hucknall. The Chipmunk quickly appears on the back drop behind Hardy Kruger's head as he is being driven into RAF Hucknall. The Chipmunk's sudden appearance is so quick it is easily missed; it is possible the film director and editor thought the audience either wouldn't notice it, or might think it is an RAF aeroplane with a wartime look about it, being tailwheeled and piston-engined. Presumably the Chipmunk was on the flight line at the time when the 2nd Unit were filming the scene at RAF Hucknall that was going to be used as back drop footage, and it just got into shot. Accidents will happen.

One other piece of aviation in the film appears right at the beginning, with von Werra crash landing in his Messerschmitt Bf.109E-4. The scene is realistically created, utilising a not-too-obvious miniature for the actual impact but cutting immediately to a very accurately created full-scale facsimile of von Werra's Bf.109E-4 of Jagdgeschwader 3 (JG.3), including the French and British kill markings on the tail, taken from detailed photographs of von Werra's actual Bf.109E-4 (Werke Nr 1480). What became of this film prop isn't fully known, but another British war film made the year after "The One That Got Away" may hold the answer, as will be described elsewhere.

CARVE HER NAME WITH PRIDE

(Released: February 1958)

Starring Virginia McKenna in the role which made her name as a leading British screen star, that of SOE Agent Violette Szabo who was executed by the SS in Ravensbruck Concentration Camp and was posthumously awarded the George Cross by HM King George VI, this is a quite simple war film which is very well directed by Lewis Gilbert with an excellent British cast. Because of its subject it has a strong link with the earlier SOE films, "Now It Can Be Told" (1946), "Against The Wind" (1948) and "Odette" (1950), released 12, ten and eight years respectively before it, especially in the way it portrays RAF aircraft in the roles they employed to insert agents into Occupied France.

Foremost are the out-takes from "Against The Wind" of Handley Page Halifax A.Mk.9 RT901/G which appears in two sequences, firstly when Zsabo and her fellow SOE trainees make their first parachute jumps, then when she is parachuted into France on her fateful final mission two days after D-Day (actually, Zsabo para-dropped from a USAAF 'Carpetbaggers' B-24 Liberator with three other SOE agents). The shots of para-jumpers exiting the Halifax, both seen air-air and from within the Halifax itself looking down through its under-fuselage hatch, are exactly the same as those used in "Against The Wind".

The sequence involving McKenna and classical actor Paul Schofield, portraying Szabo's SOE field commander, Tony Fraser, undergoing parachute training was filmed at RAF Abingdon in 1957, now one of RAF Transport Command's foremost tactical transport bases. It was also, as we saw in "The Red Beret" (1953), home to No.1 Parachute Training School (PTS). Both RAF Abingdon and No.1 PTS will feature again for a third time in a British war film, "Operation Crossbow" (1965), reviewed in Chapter Four.

As we have seen before, it was the RAF's Parachute Training School based during the War at RAF Ringway, near Manchester, that trained all SOE agents who were to be parachuted into Occupied Territory. Thus, what we are seeing in the film is

accurate: Violet Szabo and her SOE colleagues would have trained in parachute jumps in the same way that Virginia McKenna and Paul Schofield are seen performing. Apparently, director Gilbert wanted a stunt double for McKenna to make the descent off the parachute tower at RAF Abingdon, but McKenna insisted on making the descent herself. She is quoted as saying she found the experience such fun that she wanted to have another go.

Szabo, Fraser and three other SOE agents have to make their final training jump by static line to qualify for their parachute badge and to be cleared for insertion into enemy territory. This jump sequence was filmed for "Carve Her Name With Pride" over No.1 PTS's satellite facility at RAF Weston-on-the-Green in Oxfordshire, ideal for parachute landings with its very flat terrain. RAF Weston-on-the-Green is clearly seen in shot below as the parachutists drop out through the belly of the jump aircraft, then deploy their 'chutes and drift away.

No.47 Squadron loaned a Blackburn Beverley C.1 to perform the role of the jump aircraft. It is, in effect, acting as the Handley Page Halifax seen in the out-take from "Against The Wind", from which Szabo, Fraser and their colleagues make their qualifying jumps. When the jumpers are seen exiting through the open hatch in the fuselage floor, the impression is meant to be conveyed that they are leaving the Halifax; but in reality, they are departing from the Beverley.

The effect is achieved very neatly. Firstly, the Beverley itself is never seen in shot. All that appears of it very briefly is the open hatch in its fuselage floor as jumpers drop through it before their 'chutes deploy and they drift away behind the Beverley over RAF Weston-on-the-Green. The Beverley had a unique design: its airframe is mostly taken up with the large cargo hold stretching from the nose to well aft of the big, high-level wing supporting the four Bristol Centaurus piston engines. The cargo hold ended in a clamshell-door sytem, which could be detached before flight and through which any manner of equipment could be air-dropped by parachute. The airframe beyond the cargo hold narrowed into a high-level tail boom which accommodated seated passengers, or could be stripped out for any purpose, including casualty evacuation. Beyond this tail boom the airframe design ended in the Beverley's distinct twin-fin tail section.

It is from an open floor hatchway in this tail boom section that the para-jumpers portraying the SOE agents are seen making their exit. They were filmed from a camera positioned on the tail-gate of the open rear cargo hold, offering an unobstructed view of the para-jumpers' exit, their 'chutes' deployment, followed by them floating away. The result is very effective: the preceding shot of the Halifax in flight, followed by the descending agents, creates the very realistic impression that Szabo and her colleagues have jumped through the floor hatchway of the Halifax.

RAF Abingdon in Oxfordshire was, at the time of the production team filming there, home to two squadrons operating the Blackburn Beverley, then the largest tactical airlift transport aircraft in service with the Royal Air Force. No.47 Squadron had received its Beverleys in 1955, while No.53 Squadron was moving in and converting on to type while the film crew were at work at Abingdon. In the scene in the hangar between McKenna and

Schofield, acting as Szabo and Fraser after they have finished their jumps off the parachute tower, a goof occurs that an eagle-eyed aviation enthusiast cannot fail to detect. Just visible through the background clutter of an RAF truck and crane equipment is the wing and tail of a Blackburn Beverley C.1 transport, a goof unlikely to have been spotted by the cinema audience and which the film crew undoubtedly did their best to obscure. The Beverley is a large aircraft and hard to hide; such are the perils of World War Two film-making after the War itself was over.

An out-take from "Now It Can Be Told" depicts Halifax V coded NF-T of No.138 (Special Duties) Squadron making a supply drop, by now a familiar piece of footage due to its use in that original film and in "Against The Wind".

The one aircraft that was hired by the production company, Keyboard Productions Limited, for the film was DHC Beaver 1 G-AMVU, which doubled as a No.161 (SpecialDuties) Squadron Westland Lysander. The Beaver is filmed at night for the sequences of Szabo boarding the 'Lysander' before embarking for France, and of her arrival and greeting by Maquis fighters. The Beaver appears crudely painted in RAF markings with the serial L2714 and the code letters of LX-T - the real L2714 was a Vickers Wellesley, but the 'LX-' codes were correct for a wartime Westland Lysander unit, No.225 Squadron which operated the 'Lizzie' in the Army Co-Operation role between 1939 - 1942 and which itself had been formed from another Lysander unit, No.614A Squadron.

G-AMVU was originally acquired in 1952 by de Havilland in the UK as its British-based demonstrator. The rugged Canadian bush 'plane had been under evaluation in 1954 by the Aircraft & Armaments Experimental Establishment at Boscombe Down for a possible MoD order. It was given the UK military serial XH455 for its evaluation by the MoD before being returned to de Havillands, with its civil registration restored. By this time de Havillands was working hard with the MoD to sell the DHC Beaver 2 concept to the British military, the single prototype of which, registered G-ANAR, was also under evaluation. The significant difference between the Beaver 1 and the Beaver 2 was that the latter was fitted with a more powerful Alvin Leonidas engine, a slightly longer fuselage and a taller, more triangular tail.

According to British CAA records, Beaver 1 G-AMVU was sold to Sierra Leone in July 1956, while Beaver 2 G-ANAR continued with firstly de Havillands, then Alvis, Ltd, until it was returned to the manufacturer in Canada in 1971. "Carve Her Name With Pride" was filmed mostly in 1957, which suggests that Beaver 1 G-AMVU had left the country by this time. Therefore, it must surely be Beaver 2 G-ANAR that appears in the film. However, the Beaver in shot clearly does not have the taller triangular tail that G-ANAR so distinctly carried, while its frontal area shows it is definitely a Pratt & Whitney Canada Wasp-engined Beaver 1, not the Alvin Leonidas-powered Beaver 2.

The only candidate Beaver for the film must then be G-AMVU which, even if sold abroad, probably had yet to depart and was still on charge with de Havillands when it was used (a photograph on the dhc-2.com Website taken in 1957 confirms that the aircraft was still in the UK). The aircraft does not fly in any of the sequences in which it appears, only taxying and taking agents on board or dropping agents off, suggesting it may have been filmed at de Havillands' Hatfield base at night for the RAF Tempsford and French landing ground scenes.

BITTER VICTORY

(Released: March 1958, USA) International 'British' war film

What is it about actor Richard Burton and the North African desert campaign of World War Two? First he makes "The Desert Rats" (1953), then he appears in the second of the "Tobruk" (1967) and "Raid on Rommel" (1971) double production. In between he made this French/American co-production and, therefore, an International 'British' war film, as a British Army Captain who has to join on a mission behind the lines in Libya with a South African Major, played by German actor Curt Jurgens, who is married to the woman Burton had an affair with before the War and abandoned. It is a complex anti-war film directed by Nicholas Ray, about who is the more honest and courageous of the two, but where aircraft are concerned it is totally empty.

DUNKIRK

(Released: March 1958)

This Ealing Studios epic of its day set the tone for realism and scale in war movies that would later be copied on both sides of the Atlantic, in particular most notably creating the template for the massive depiction of D-Day, "The Longest Day" (1962), released four years later. Filmed entirely in the south of England, despite its theme being the evacuation under fire in May 1940 of the British Expeditionary Force from the Dunkirk beaches - actually Camber Sands - "Dunkirk" was controversial for its time with its emphasis on reality, rather than perpetuating the popular myth of the British stiff upper lip in the face of adversity.

No shortage of Army assets and boats of the type used to ferry troops off the beaches were made available for the production, but for aviation the film-makers relied almost exclusively on wartime footage of Luftwaffe aircraft - all Junkers variants - cut into scenes created for the storyline. However, with the benefit of digital enhancement today, some of this footage now stands out extremely well in quality and for the most part fits effectively with the film's final product.

Early in the story John Mills (naturally, who else, and this time as a reluctant Corporal) and his mates are sitting idly in Belgium during the 'Phoney War' period, watching Movie Tone newsreels in an Army camp cinema while the Wehrmacht and Luftwaffe build up their attacks on the Low Countries.

Dramatic shots of three Junkers Ju.87 Stukas illustrate the impending attack, seen filmed from a lead aircraft taking off in echelon formation which was taken almost certainly for contemporary promotional footage in Germany. The nearest Stuka to the camera clearly carries the code letters 'LH' on its rear fuselage behind the Wehrmacht Balkenkreuze, suggesting this dive bomber may belong to the 1st Staffel of Stukagruppe 1 (I/StG.1: 1st Squadron of Dive Bomber Group No.1) and with the number '12' on its tail rudder. With their lengthened nose design and larger, more curved cockpit canopies, these Stukas appear to be Junkers Ju.87R variants, which were operated by Staffels of StG.1 in Poland and Norway at the outset of the War. The Ju.87R was a modified version of the standard Ju.87B with increased range.

What is noteworthy about these three Stukas is that they are not carrying any weapons, but clearly shown are the trumpet-shaped sirens (the 'Horns of Jericho') attached beneath the wings that produced the nerve-shredding howl of the Stuka screaming down on its target. All three Ju.87Rs are flying without wheel spats, the lack of which, plus in addition the lack of any armament, shows that these Stukas are not in combat configuration. They are filmed taking off from flat terrain and flying over what looks distinctly like Central European scenery, with a totally straight road stretching for miles without deviation across the countryside below the lead Stuka. The whole impression is of staged footage, probably filmed before hostilities commenced with the invasion of Poland on 1st September 1939, and may comprise a Stabskette (Staff Chain) of three Stukas flown by the most senior officers of the Stukagruppe (Dive Bomber Group) to which they belong. Under Luftwaffe traditions of the time, the Stabskette always led the complete Stukagruppe (up to four Staffeln of nine aircraft each) in ceremonial fly-pasts. For promotional purposes, the 1st Staffel of Stukagruppe 1 would be the ideal Luftwaffe Stuka unit to film.

Supporting this scene is further footage of three Junkers Ju.52/3M transports unloading streams of Stormtroopers by parachute, presumably also in staged footage as all three Ju.52s are flying in a neat formation 'Vic' with the Paratroopers departing the aircraft via static lines without carrying any equipment or small arms. What is particularly noteworthy is that the Paratroopers are all diving head first out of the Ju-52s! This is a clear demonstration of the different method of static line parachuting used by the Wehrmacht, as compared with the system developed by the Allies. The Wehrmacht system employed a hood over the Paratrooper's head, inside which was an umbilical-type chord attached to the parachute pack strapped to his back. A second chord led from the hood to a line attachment inside the aircraft cabin. All the Paratrooper has to do is to hurl himself head first out of the aircraft's cabin door, as the Paratroopers in this footage are seen doing. The hood is immediately yanked off his head as he departs the aircraft by the chord linked to the line attachment, which in turn causes the umbilical to instantly pull his parachute release – all achieved in a matter of seconds, from the instant of exit to the deployment of his 'chute.

Mills's troop are later strafed at low-level by a single Junkers Ju.88 that kills their CO and wrecks their trucks. Close study of the footage used reveals that two shots are out-takes of the radio-controlled model of the captured Junkers Ju.88A-5 M2+MK that appeared in "In Which We Serve" (1942). A third shot used of the

Ju.88 is presumably another out-take of the same machine, in which it is seen approaching head-on from behind a tree, but this was a shot angle that was not used in "In Which We Serve", so its progeny remains unknown. However, in two more head-on shots the Ju.88 turns into a Bristol Blenheim I, an undoubted goof but perhaps an easy mistake for the film's editor to make, as the Blenheim and the Ju.88 are distinctly similar types in role and appearance. Judging by the reduced quality of the Blenheim footage, it appears to be that of archive material which is being used here.

More stock wartime footage of Ju.87 Stukas is used for the attack on the British Army artillery position left stranded in a wooded copse, cut between vertically diving Ju.87s and timed explosions set off by the Ealing Studios Special FX team. The archive footage is extremely grainy and clashes with the clean, real film material, but there is no denying the harsh effectiveness of this scene. As the Captain commanding the artillery battery says, "They'll send in the odd shell and whistle up the Stukas. That's what we learnt in Spain and Poland, that's what we're learning now". The Blitzkreig tactic is more realistically staged in "Dunkirk" than in any other film. As one of Mills's patrol says, as they watch from a distance, "That's murder. Sheer bloody murder".

However, a not very convincing editorial cut from Mills and his men marching with other troops towards Dunkirk beach, panning up to a shot of three Stukas hurtling past overhead, is betrayed by the clash of picture quality between the modern film and the dark, grainy wartime footage.

From this point onwards, there is no more use of archive material in "Dunkirk". But most effectively re-created of all the scenes in this admirable British war film are those of the repeated attacks on the British forces spread unprotected on the Dunkirk beaches: no footage of Ju.87s and Ju.88s is used at all, while only the explosions among the dunes are seen, which works more dramatically than if the attackers were actually shown. Without question, "Dunkirk" is one of Ealing Studios' finest productions, and stands as an excellently re-created tribute to the actual Operation Dynamo that literally saved an army.

THE SILENT ENEMY

(Released: March 1958)

A well made film about the Royal Navy's frogmen - an out-of-date term today for divers - who risked their lives to defend Allied shipping moored at Gibraltar from underwater attacks by Italian divers using two-man 'Chariots': very small torpedo-shaped submarines on which divers sat as if they were riding on horseback. The central character is a real life RN Commander, Lionel 'Buster' Crabb, GM, RNVR, played by Lawrence Harvey. The real 'Buster' Crabb died in mysterious circumstances when it is believed he dived to spy on the hull design of the new Russian naval cruiser which brought Premier Nikita Kruschev to Britain in April 1956.

Aviation does not feature large in "The Silent Enemy", but what is seen is interesting, especially as much of the production was filmed at Gibraltar. Early in the film a panoramic look-down shot appears of the runway of RAF Gibraltar extending into the sea; filmed in 1957, it provides a good study of this unique military air base as it was in the Fifties. This, in fact, is the first of two such views of Gib in British war films released in 1958, as the air base also puts in an appearance in "I Was Monty's Double", the review of which follows soon after in this Chapter.

'Buster' Crabb flies into Gib from Britain to form the frogman diving team. To depict the aircraft in which he is flying, the well-used out-take of Handley Page Halifax A.Mk.9 RT901/G from "Against The Wind" (1948) briefly appears.

The only scene in which aircraft make a full appearance in "The Silent Enemy" occurs when Crabb, for whatever logical reason, decides to defuse the detonator of an Italian torpedo that was bolted to the hull of a cargo ship on the apron of RAF Gibraltar amid parked RAF bombers! No doubt the audience is meant to believe the bombers are Avro Lancasters. In fact, they are the Lancaster's descendants, Avro Shackleton MR.2 maritime reconnaissance aircraft. A detachment of Shackletons was permanently based at Gibraltar throughout the Fifties and the Sixties. When "The Silent Enemy" was in production No.224 Squadron was in residence, as evidenced by the squadron number carried on the rear fuselages of the Shackletons which appear in shot. No.224 was the permanently based squadron of Shackletons at Gibraltar, having arrived in August 1951 and was destined to remain there with its MR.2s until disbandment on 31st October 1966.

The first to be seen is Avro Shackleton MR.2 WL792/K, when the RAF Station Adjutant walks out to ask Crabb, "What the Devil do you think you are doing on my airstrip?". WL792 first flew on 1st July 1953 and was delivered to the RAF on 20th August the same year. It only had a four-year career in RAF service, being written off at Gibraltar on 14th September 1957. This Shackleton suffered a catastrophic engine failure as it approached RAF Gibraltar at low-level during its run-in for a fly-past at the Battle of Britain Display being held there. Fortunately the 'Shack' was aiming directly at the runway and the pilot succeeded in making a brilliant wheels-up landing. All of the aircrew escaped without injury. Shackleton MR.2 WL792 was struck off charge on 11th November 1957.

This unfortunate accident, however, meant that Shackelton MR.2 WL792 was able to be used in a specific role later in the film, as will be described.

Crabb has decided to defuse the Italian detonator right next to Avro Shackleton MR.2 WL741. This particular Shackleton first flew on 18th December 1952 and was delivered to the RAF on 4th February 1953. It was part of the batch of MR.2s which were converted by Hawker Siddeley Aviation at Bitteswell into Shackleton AEW.2 airborne early warning variants, serving with No.8 Squadron at RAF Lossiemouth. WL741 made its final flight on 29th May 1981 when it was flown to Manston in Kent and was assigned to the Fire School there. It was finally reduced to burnt out scrap in 1987.

A total of seven of No.224 Squadron's Shackletons can be counted in "The Silent Enemy", although WL741 and WL792 are just the two which can be identified; a third Shackleton MR.2 can be seen to be coded 'O'. Some of the others appear to be uncoded. "The Silent Enemy" provides an excellent study of these magnificent maritime patrol beasts at RAF Gibraltar, filmed in 1957, but they are of course out of place for a World War Two war film.

As mentioned, Shackleton MR.2 WL792 had another role to play in the film. Following its crash landing, the big four-engined maritime patrol aircraft was deemed damaged beyond economical repair so all surviving serviceable parts were salvaged before the airframe was disposed of. The easiest way to achieve this was to sink the broken up airframe out at sea.

Doing this enabled the film production team to add a real-life event to the plot, the crash of Consolidated Liberator II AL523 into the sea immediately after take off from RAF Gibraltar on 4th July 1943. On board this Liberator was Polish General Wladyslaw Sikorski, Commander-in-Chief of the Polish Armed Forces and Prime Minister of the Polish Government in Exile, who was killed in the crash.

There are many conspiracy theories about this crash, especially that the Soviets had Sikorski assassinated by arranging to have the Liberator's controls jammed with a partially filled mail bag in the cargo compartment, forced in between the linking rods of the tail plane's elevator. This would prevent the Liberator gaining sufficient height on take off. The finger has been pointed at the Soviet double agent, Kim Philby, who was a frequent visitor to Gibraltar at the time as the head of MI6's Iberian desk and was a trained saboteur with the SOE - the allegation is that Philby sabotaged the Liberator easily because not only was he a familiar face on Gibraltar but, more importantly, he was undetected as a Soviet mole, so his presence on the air base would not have aroused any suspicion. He is supposed to have been acting at the behest of a Soviet delegation on Gibraltar, whose transport aircraft was parked right next to General Sikorski's Liberator.

The dismantled airframe of Shackleton MR.2 WL792 is filmed on the seabed as the prop for the crashed Liberator.

In the film, 'Buster' Crabb and his team are ordered to dive on the Liberator's wreckage and retrieve the important brief case Sikorski was carrying which contains vitally important papers. Whether Crabb was so ordered in real life is not known. There is a hole in the plot here because Crabb and his divers are attacked by Italian frogmen as they search the wreckage for the brief case and an underwater knife fight ensues. How could the Italians have known about General Sikorski's brief case and make their own attempt to find it? Nonetheless, it is an exciting underwater sequence and is believed to have influenced the much larger scale fight and other underwater sequences in the James Bond spectacular, "Thunderball" (1965), to be filmed seven years later with a full-scale sunken Vulcan V-Bomber prop.

"The Silent Enemy" is naturally full of much maritime content, but the appearance of the Shackletons in it make this film an interesting study for British aviation enthusiasts and historians.

THE CAMP ON BLOOD ISLAND

(Released: April 1958)

When this controversial film was first released it attracted criticism for its graphic depiction of atrocities committed by Japanese troops against British and Commonwealth PoWs; however, it was also a big box office success in 1958 and is regarded today by historians of the cinema as being one of Hammer Films' most important productions. It has not been shown publicly either in the cinema or on TV since 1979, and nor was it released on VHS. Only in 2009 was this film put out on DVD in its original uncut version by Sony Pictures Home Entertainment Inc.

The assumption has been that this film was kept from the public eye for so long because the scenes of brutal treatment of the PoWs by Japanese prison guards, including the execution of a number of them by Samurai sword, were too extreme. In reality, the violence in the film would be considered fairly tame fare by a 21st Century audience raised on Arnold Schwarzarneggar-style 'shoot-'em ups' and "Saw"-like horror movies. The real reason why "The Camp On Blood Island" has been kept shut away for 30 years is its portrayal of Japanese prison guards as stereotypically savage and sadistic, to the extent that the film has been accused of racism by those who are labelled, or who label themselves, as politically correct. So much so, that TV and video companies have, until its release on DVD, fought shy of exhibiting it.

The plot has both male and female prisoners of the Japanese on an island just off the coast of Malaya learning by a concealed radio that Japan has surrendered. The extreme danger is that the sadistic Camp Commandant has declared that, should Japan surrender, and because he knows that due to his record of brutality he will be hanged for war crimes, the entire population of both camps will be slaughtered. The news of Japan's surrender has to be kept from the guards until an escape can be organised.

The problem is that a US Navy fighter from the Sixth Fleet has crashed on the island. The pilot, who parachutes into the jungle, knows that the war against Japan is over. The prisoners have to keep him from giving the truth away to the Japanese.

This crash scene is one of only two small elements within the film where aviation is featured. The crash is not shown, but the pilot is seen sorting himself out on the ground with the smoking wreckage beyond him. The fighter has gone into the jungle nose first and is seen with its tail stuck high in the air. Its starboard wing is still attached, but its port wing has been severed and is lying some distance away. Its US Navy star-and-bar and code letter are clearly visible on the fuselage and tail.

Freeze-frame analysis shows that the fighter bears no relation to any identifiable US Navy aircraft type. But there is something recognisable about it. A careful study reveals that the tail section is very similar in shape to a Messerschmitt Bf.109. Why would a full-scale studio mock-up of a Bf.109 be used to simulate a crashed US Navy aircraft? The answer has to be, because such a facsimile was available when there was no other alternative that could be used. Almost certainly this is the full-scale facsimile of Franz von

Werra's 'Messerschmitt Bf.109E-4' created for "The One That Got Away" (1957) released the previous year, repainted with US Navy markings and Navy dark blue overall. It is set up in such a way that it is seen only briefly from a distance among Malayan jungle foliage - actually a sandpit site in Virginia Water, Surrey - and would only have been recognisable by a very experienced eye in the cinema audience of the Fifties, although aviation enthusiasts and historians would have realised straightaway that it was not representative of a US Navy aircraft.

The Bf.109 facsimile was obviously available after its construction for and use in "The One That Got Away" (1957), and was a much more cost-effective alternative to building a full-scale mock-up for just one very brief scene. What happened to it after it was used in a dismantled state in "The Camp On Blood Island" is not known, but if it was repainted, broken up and then set on fire for the film, it was then more than likely trashed once filming was complete.

The only other sequence in which aviation appears in "The Camp On Blood Island" occurs right at the end of the film, when British Paratroopers descend on the prison camps to liberate them - although the PoWs have already done the job, albeit at considerable cost to themselves. The transport aircraft the Paratroopers are seen descending from are two Handley Page Hastings C.1s, which are obviously Fifties generation machines unrepresentative of the August 1945 period. Presumably, this imagery of them was either stock footage obtained from the Central Office of Information, or film that a Hammer Films 2nd Unit took of an exercise involving Paratroopers jumping from Hastings aircraft.

ICE COLD IN ALEX

(Released: June 1958)

This classic British war film is considered to be the epitome of its genre, with excellent and believable characters, realistic acting by some of Britain's finest of the Fifties and post-War generation, and a convincing re-creation of what was, in large, a true story. Set in the North African desert in 1942 as the British 8th Army took pounding after pounding from Rommel's Afrika Korps, the film was made in entirely correct locations representing that desperate era, namely the United Kingdom of Libya with men and material provided by the decidedly pre-Colonel Gaddafi Libyan Royal Army Service Corps (the Colonel, then Lieutenant Gaddafi, served with the Corps until he seized power after Britain continually reduced its influence over its North African dominions).

The plot, concerning a harrowing journey across the desert by a British Army ambulance from Tobruk to Alexandria (the 'Alex' of the title), with an alcoholic, self-pitying Captain played by the stalwart Brit of the Fifties, John Mills, in charge, does not inspire thoughts of aviation. But aviation does make one significant appearance in the film, portrayed by a charismatic low-level ground-attack aircraft that served with the RAF in just about every theater of World War Two in which Britain was engaged - a

Bristol Beaufighter no less, and imagery of one that was not obtained from stock wartime footage. The Beaufighter suddenly appears at low-level, seemingly to attack the ambulance, but actually drops a streamer-retarded canister bearing a message warning dispersed British personnel that the Afrika Korps was less than 100 miles of Alex.

The actual Beaufighter used in the film was a TT.10 target-towing variant, then just two years away from being withdrawn after 20 years of sterling service. A total of 35 Beaufighters were converted by Shorts into the TT.10 target-tower, with most of them based in the Middle East, Singapore and Malaya. The example appearing in "Alex" was RD788, clearly betrayed by its under-wing diagonal target-towing stripes (yellow-black, if seen in colour), but still convincingly aggressive in appearance when seen menacingly head-on to the camera. RD788 was one of two Beaufighter TT.10s then in service with the Malta Communications and Target Towing Squadron (MCTTS), based at RAF Ta'Qali, today the location for the Malta Aviation Museum. The MCTTS was a mixed-bag unit with a variety of types on charge in the Fifties, including Balliol T.1s for targets and the appropriately named Valetta C.1 as an all-purpose comms hack, providing what it said on its squadron tin for British forces in the Med and the Middle East.

THE WIND CANNOT READ

(Released: June 1958)

Although Dirk Bogarde plays an RAF Squadron Leader based in India working as an interpreter interrogating Japanese Prisoners of War, no aircraft are featured in what is a rather implausible, drawn out and, in the opinion of the author, tedious wartime romance between Bogarde and his female Japanese tutor.

BATTLE OF THE V1

(Released: August 1958)

This film opens with a dedication to "the heroes of the Polish Underground and unknown secret agents who helped to save London". It also claims that the incidents portrayed are in most essentials true to fact. Yes, in one respect certain operations involving the Polish Resistance, or the Home Army (Armia Krajowa, the AK), did occur as largely portrayed in this film, but they were mostly directed against the Vergeltungswaffe Zwei (V2, Retaliation Weapon Two) ballistic artillery rocket and not the V1 pulse jet-powered pilotless flying warhead.

This is the first of two British war films to take as its subject the Nazis' Vergeltungswaffen campaign against London during the latter half of 1944 and early 1945, and both attracted criticism for tinkering with the facts for dramatic effect. The second film, "Operation Crossbow" (1965), covered both the V1 and V2 weapons, whereas "Battle of the V1" concentrates solely upon the infamous 'Doodlebug' or 'Buzz Bomb', as the British public

against whom it was aimed called it. However, the film's plot merges actual events involving the Polish AK's own operations against the V2 with British Military Intelligence's attempts to gain information about the V1, as a means to combine the British and the Poles' war effort against both Vergeltungswaffen into one story.

The Fieseler Fi.103, to use its factory designation, was officially referred to by the Luftwaffe High Command as FZG.76, or Flak Ziel Gerat 76, until the definition for it of Vergeltungswaffe Eins (V1) was made public by Reich Propaganda Minister, Josef Goebbels, after the first V1s were launched at London on the night of 12th - 13th June 1944. Flak Ziel Gerat was translated by British Military Intelligence to mean approximately Anti-Aircraft Aiming or Targeting Apparatus which, as explained in the review of "Now It Can Be Told" (1946), was intended to conceal FZG.76's true role under the guise of it being a new pilotless target drone for Luftwaffe Flak crews to practice against.

British Military Intelligence received information about the development of a pilotless rocket 'plane from a variety of sources, most particularly when an earlier version of the drone landed intact in a turnip field on the Baltic island of Bornholm between Germany and Sweden. A Danish Resistance member successfully photographed the wreckage under the noses of German guards and smuggled the pictures to London; French and Dutch Resistance members sent information to London about the construction of long launch rails close to their coastlines, the function of which was, at the time, unknown; while, as explained in the review of "Now It Can Be Told" in Chapter Two, Enigma decoding traffic discovered the existence of FZG.76 as an organisation operating as an anti-aircraft unit that seemed to require an inordinate amount of protection from British aerial attack. Military Scientific Intelligence Officer, Dr R V Jones, gives the largest credit for revealing the pilotless rocket 'plane to a female French Resistance worker, Jeannie Rousseau, who, from her position as a translator for the Commander of FZG.76, managed to get him to boast about the new "Wunder Waffen" ("Wonder Weapons"), details of which she sent in a report to London.

The role of Polish agents at the Peenemunde Heeresversuchsanstalt (Army Research Institute) in discovering the Fi.103, as depicted in this film, has always been refuted by British Intelligence sources. However, since the collapse of the Soviet Union in 1991, links have been forged between British and Polish military historians who challenge this position. The Polish-British Historical Commission for the Investigation of Polish-British Intelligence Co-Operation has, since 2000, been calling for the release of micro-filmed documents that were allegedly smuggled by the AK to MI6 during the War. These documents will, the Commission members claim, confirm that the AK did have agents in Peenemunde among the foreign slave workforce who fed information to their leaders on both the Fi.103 and the A4 (Aggregat 4, the designation for the ballistic artillery rocket before Goebbels termed it the V2). The AK gave their Peenemunde network the code name Lombard. Reputedly, one of their prime contacts was a Polish soldier of Austrian origin in the Deutsches Heer (German Army), who held anti-Nazi beliefs and who was posted to serve as a guard at Peenemunde. From there, it is alleged, he fed the AK information about Fi.103 trials via their agents in the labour force, which the AK leadership then passed on to London. The official British position is that any documentation supplied by Polish sources that might have been in the possession of MI6 during the War has long since been destroyed.

"Battle of the V1" opens with archive footage of a Fieseler Fi.103 being fired off its launch rail before the credits roll over a not-too-convincing miniature of a Fi.103 in flight. Then, much-used but quite sensational gun-camera footage of the aerial shoot-down of a V1 is shown, with the flying bomb exploding spectacularly ahead of the fighter which flies right into the blast.

The scene then changes to Nazi Occupied Poland, where schoolteacher Stefan Novak (played by English actor, Michael Rennie, who now spoke with an American accent and whose most famous film role was as the wise and benevolent alien, Klaatu, in the cult sci fi movie, "The Day The Earth Stood Still", 1951), is summoned along with other Poles of a certain age to "volunteer" for labour at a place on the Baltic Coast. Before leaving his wife, Zofia, he is contacted by an AK member who asks Stefan to report back anything unusual he sees at this Baltic location.

Accompanied by a friend, Tadek, he is forced to work as a labourer in a camp commanded by a sadistic SS officer played "in the full fig of an oppressor" by the then up-and-coming Christopher Lee (Hammer Horror films were just around the corner for him in 1958). In his autobiography, "Lord of Misrule", Lee describes "Battle of the V1" as a "no-account picture". He confirms that the film was shot mostly in the Brighton area, with a factory site used to represent the Peenemunde rocket research complex.

After being ordered to work as cleaners in the complex, Stefan and Tadek discover by chance what looks to them like a small aeroplane, with no propeller and without a cockpit for a pilot, being worked on by technicians. They manage to report their discovery to the AK. A very realistic, full-scale facsimile of a Fieseler Fi.103 is used in this scene. It is notable that the film's set designer was Ken Adam, who went on to create award-winning film sets for most of the earliest James Bond films with Sean Connery and Roger Moore, and whose most memorable achievement was the futuristic Pentagon War Room set for director Stanley Kubrick's Cold War spoof film, "Dr Strangelove" (1964). Adam had a particular eye for detail and accuracy, and would have made certain that the Fi.103 facsimile built for "Battle of the V1" was correct in appearance down to the last nut and bolt.

The AK manage to get information about the pilotless aircraft, plus that of a large number of scientists preparing to meet at Peenemunde, to British Military Intelligence in London. An urgent meeting is convened between senior British ministerial and military staff, where it is agreed Peenemunde must be bombed as a priority over all other Bomber Command Operations. The 'Minister of Defence' who chairs the meeting, played by veteran British character actor, Geoffrey Chater, is meant in reality to be Duncan Sandys, who Churchill appointed as Chairman of a Cabinet War Committee tasked with planning the defence of London from attacks by the new rocket weapons that British Military Intelligence was aware the Nazis were developing.

When the German scientists meet at Peenemunde they are told by a senior Luftwaffe officer that the Fuhrer wanted 1,000 flying bombs launched per day at British cities, and to reach to a maximum of 5,000 per day. This is in the fantasy of the film's scriptwriters: V1 production was incapable of turning out so many flying bombs, even using slave labour. The senior officer portrayed in the film is meant to be Generalfeldmarschall Erhard Milch, in charge of production for the Deutsches Luftwaffe (V1 was a Luftwaffe asset, and FZG.76 was a Luftwaffe unit).

During this scene the scientists are shown genuine archive film of the construction and testing of the Fieseler Fi.103 (note, this designation is never used in the film, it is referred to as either the rocket aircraft or the flying bomb). The film shows a Fieseler Fi.103 on its launch ramp, with the piston and generator that propel it being attached to the ramp below its tail. A cartoon using German expressions shows how the flying bomb performs in flight before its elevator deflects when it is over its target, causing it to go into a steep dive. Slow motion footage is shown of an experimental Fi.103 being fired off its ramp.

Presumably, the actual archive film used in this scene was discovered by the Allies after they overran V1 testing and launching sites. It would have been in the possession of the Imperial War Museum, who made it available for use in "Battle of the V1".

The RAF bombing of Peenemunde is depicted by the use of genuine archive material of actual raids on German cities mixed with out-takes from the Crown Film Unit production "Target for Tonight" (1941) and from the RAF Film Production Unit's "Journey Together" (1945) and "Now It Can Be Told" (1946), all sourced from the Imperial War Museum. Among the footage used is that of Lancasters flying en masse that appeared in "Journey Together", only in "Battle of the V1" they are shown flying backwards! (How is it film editors make such mistakes?) The same shot of a Halifax releasing bombs, as seen in "Now It Can Be Told", appears twice, shown flying in either direction. Another archive shot dramatically shows a Halifax, filmed from directly overhead, flying across a mass of flame from a city burning below it. The same archive shot of incendiaries exploding, as was used in "Now It Can Be Told", likewise appears in this film. Out-takes from "Journey Together" of Lancaster miniatures also feature, plus a brief shot appears of Jack Watling piloting the Lancaster that ditches in the North Sea in that film.

Operation Hydra, conducted on the night of 16th – 17th August 1943, employed 596 Lancasters, Halifaxes and Stirlings of RAF Bomber Command against Peenemunde. Contrary to the claims in the film's script that the bombers first accurately hit the flak emplacements, then the main plant, and last of all the living quarters of the technical staff, many bombs fell harmlessly upon the surrounding woods and nearby sand dunes. The assembly hall was hit, but only enough damage was inflicted to halt production of Hitler's Wunder Waffen for a maximum of six weeks. However, the residential area was hit hard, with 178 of 4,000 personnel (including staff and families) killed, among them the head of rocket engine development, Dr Walther Thiel, a significant loss. But the majority of fatalities occurred among the foreign slave workers, who Stefan and Tadek represent in the film, penned inside the nearby concentration camp barracks. The film does not show this, but the tragedy is implied when Stefan and Tadek break out of the barracks amid the destruction being wrought by the bombing.

The real damage inflicted upon Peenemunde was the reality of the Heeresversuchsanstalt's vulnerability to Allied air attack; consequently, production of the V1 and V2 was moved to underground facilities, causing serious delays to the launch of the Vergeltungswaffen campaign against London. Thousands of slave labourers from Auschwitz concentration camp died producing the V2 in 1944 in appalling conditions within underground factories in the Harz Mountains.

The film is correct in its portrayal of rocket testing being transferred to Blizna in Poland, but is incorrect in depicting the Fi.103 flying bomb as being involved in these trials. Testing of the Fi.103 continued at Peenemunde well into 1944; it was the A4 rocket trials that took place at Blizna before it was launched against London as the V2.

With Stefan and Tadek having escaped from Peenemunde, the AK arranges for them plus Stefan's wife, Zofia, and a female AK agent, Anna, who has formed a relationship with Tadek, to go to Blizna and gain as much information on the flying bomb as they can, and especially to photograph it, if possible. The story now moves to Blizna where Stefan, Tadek and their partners get work as farmhands and where they witness the crash of a Fi.103 that explodes in a field near to them – the crash is achieved by means of quite effective SFX.

What photographs they are able to obtain are sent by the AK to London. Actor Frank Thornton, in an uncredited role as a British Military Intelligence scientist, says he needs either more complete photographs or the chance to examine a real flying bomb. He presumably is meant to be portraying Dr R V Jones, who spearheaded the Intelligence war against the Vergeltungswaffen.

The AK hatch a plan to ambush one of the trucks carrying flying bomb sections in crates, open them and photograph the contents. But in the act of doing so they are themselves attacked by German troops. Anna is captured and tortured; in fact, the water immersion technique used by SS guards in this scene was, in reality, a widely used method of torture employed by the Gestapo.

During this torture scene, when Anna is questioned by a suitably scowling SS Major conforming with the accepted image of the time of a Nazi villain at work, a curious cameo appearance occurs by an actress who was, in future, to become one of the British film industry's most recognisable faces. Throughout the scene Anna is surrounded by the SS Major, an SS Captain and the two guards, but towards the end a female German officer of striking appearance suddenly appears, as if from nowhere. Impeccably dressed and posed standing with arms folded, she watches Anna's ordeal with a permanent smile across her beautiful but otherwise cruel features. When Anna dies under the torture, she says with

an amused expression, "I'm afraid the beauty treatment is over".

The reason for the surprise appearance by this statuesque female member of the supposed 'Master Race' remains unexplained in the film. Neither the character, nor the name of the actress portraying her, are shown in the final credits. One possibility is that the director and scriptwriter inserted this mysterious personality as a representation of Hanna Reitsch, the female Luftwaffe test pilot who was an avid, unrepentant Nazi and adoring admirer of Hitler. Reitsch test flew the manned version of the Fieseler Fi.103, the Reichenberg, so she had an association with the V1 that the film may be trying to exploit here. Ardent Nazi she may have been, but there has never been any suggestion that Hanna Reitsch enjoyed attending SS torture sessions.

Even more surprising is the identity of the actress portraying this sadistic, unnamed beauty; as stated, she has been well known in British films, for decades, in fact. It is Canadian actress Lois Maxwell; in other words, Miss Moneypenny of the first 14 films of the James Bond series, starring Sean Connery, George Lazenby and Roger Moore as 007, spanning 23 years from 1962 – 1985. It is quite possible this single-line role in "Battle of the V1" was her first speaking part in a British film, after her return to the UK in 1957 from making B-Movies in Hollywood and acting in Italy.

The film now moves towards its denouement when a Fi.103 crash lands in a field close to Blizna and fails to explode. Local people retrieve it and tow it away attached to a team of horses before German troops arrive. They hide the Fi.103 in a river, then pull it out again at night. Zofia photographs it for MI6 and the AK's Intelligence Service, then a tense scene follows when Stefan and Tadek try to defuse the flying bomb's warhead.

The full-scale facsimile of the Fi.103 is used for these scenes; Ken Adam has to be congratulated on its realistic appearance. All of these scenes are representative of an actual event, but which was concerned with a V2 rocket which AK fighters retrieved after it had crashed near Blizna and was hidden by them in the River Bug.

Also representative of that same incident is the plan to fly an RAF Dakota from Brindisi in Italy to collect the hidden Fi.103 (in reality, sections of the dismantled V2). The operation was mounted by the SOE headquartered in Brindisi, although no mention of the SOE is made in the film. Air-air footage of a Douglas C-47 Dakota III, darkened to make it appear the aircraft is flying at night, is used to depict the Dakota flying en route to a disused airfield in Poland to collect the captured flying bomb. An error is made by the director and scriptwriter in showing the Dakota being flown by a single pilot; in reality, he would have had a navigator/ co-pilot. The pilot in the film is portrayed as being English, but the actual pilot who flew this highly secret and extremely dangerous mission to collect the V2 parts was a New Zealander, according to R V Jones, Flight Lieutenant Guy Culliford, alongside a Polish Air Force navigator, Flight Lieutenant Szrajer.

The Dakota that flew the real mission came from No.267 Squadron, which operated throughout the Mediterranean theater from 1942; among its varied roles was supply dropping to Partizan fighters in Yugoslavia and the Balkans. By November 1943, No.267 was based in Italy and was supporting SOE missions in Albania and Greece. No.267 Squadron was well placed to carry out the V2 collection operation in Poland.

However, the Dakota III in shot air-air is definitely not a No.267 Squadron aircraft. It is in South-East Asia Command (SEAC) markings, with the blue and white roundels clearly visible, thus making it unrepresentative of European theater RAF Dakotas. In fact, this is not even an RAF Dakota, as its squadron code letters of OM-P clearly attest. They make it a Douglas C-47B Dakota III of No.37 Squadron, Royal Australian Air Force, which operated in South-East Asia during the latter years of World War Two. Research indicates that this C-47B is almost certainly A65-73, as this serial fits with the sequence of RAAF serials and code letters allocated to C-47Bs of No.37 Squadron following their delivery as a batch from the USAAF in February 1945.

This C-47B had a long career with the RAAF, serving with No.90 Wing (Malaya) and No.91 Wing (Japan) in the immediate post-War years. It went on to serve with Nos.25, 8 and 2 Squadrons, before spending a second period in Malaya between 1964 and 1966. It became the TACAN (TACtical Air Navigation) calibration aircraft for No.10 Squadron before it was deemed damaged beyond repair on 5th November 1971 at Townsville. It was later purchased by the Channel 7 Perth TV company for use in television productions. It still exists today, loaned to the Beck Collection for static display at Mareeba, Queensland.

When the Dakota arrives overhead the airfield the AK fighters, plus many villagers, form two lines holding burning torches to create a flare path along which the Dakota can land. This sequence is filmed genuinely at night, with the location being Shoreham Airport in East Sussex. The Dakota is not seen airborne but instead emerges dramatically from the night after rolling out from landing, bearing down on the AK fighters. As it swings round it is clear that this is a civil DC-3 painted in fake RAF markings, as evidenced by the passenger windows. It carries the serial N6477, which in reality was applied to a Tiger Moth trainer. No code letters are shown.

In certain shots an airline logo beneath the cockpit window can be seen emerging through the temporary RAF paint scheme, while the word 'AIR' in capital letters has clearly been painted over. The logo shows a large circle with a winged emblem above it, while the letters 'DA' can be discerned within the circle. This is suggestive of Dan-Air's first logo. When "Battle of the V1" was in production, Dan-Air had two DC-3s in service (a third had been returned to its former operator, the Royal Air Force). Each of them was a former Douglas C-47B Dakota IV, ex-RAF aircraft. One of them, G-AMSU, was Dan-Air's first aircraft, acquired by the airline when it began operating in 1953. It was later joined by G-AMSS. If it is either one of these two Dakota IVs used in "Battle of the V1" and filmed at Shoreham Airport, they were operating from Blackbushe Airport, Surrey, at the time. G-AMSS was sold to an operator in Persia in 1968, while G-AMSU's registration was permanently withdrawn from use on 26th February 1973 when it was scrapped.

As happened to the No.267 Squadron Dakota that collected the V2 parts, the Dakota in the film gets its wheels bogged down in the rain-soaked soil. Eventually the AK fighters manage to free it by placing wooden stakes from fences under the wheels, exactly like the real drama in Poland in World War Two, as a German patrol approaches, alerted by the aircraft's engines. In the real operation, Flight Lieutenant Culliford's Dakota was rigged with explosives in the event he had to destroy the aircraft if the operation went wrong.

The film ends with more archive imagery of V1 flying bombs being destroyed over England after the Vergeltungswaffen campaign began on the night of 12th – 13th June 1944. V1s are seen in two shots to dive vertically into the countryside, while a third plunges into the sea. The message of the film is that the British government was helped to defend London from the V1 attacks, thanks to the gallant and selfless efforts of the Polish Resistance fighters in obtaining intelligence about the Vergeltungswaffe Eins despite the risk to their own lives.

THE KEY

{Released: September 1958)

This superb and very realistically created drama about sea-going tug boat men who have to rescue burning merchant ships that have been torpedoed by U-Boats has only one short sequence of aviation. This involves an attack on a tug boat skippered by Trevor Howard (marvellously rough and drunk - was he acting, or just being natural?) by a Junkers Ju.88 light bomber. This is created by the use of two short out-takes of the captured Junkers Ju.88A-5 M2+MK of 1426 (Enemy Aircraft) Flight from in "In Which We Serve" (1942).

I WAS MONTY'S DOUBLE

(Released: October 1958)

Based entirely on fact, although with a plot embellished with extra action for dramatic effect, this film is a re-telling of a British Military Intelligence operation in 1944 to deceive Nazi Germany into thinking that the forthcoming invasion of Europe would take place in the South, not, as happened, in the West. To create this belief in the minds of the German High Command, it was decided to have a 'double' of General Bernard Law Montgomery impersonate "Monty" on a tour of inspection of Allied Forces in Gibraltar and in North Africa, as if the real General was reviewing preparations for the invasion.

Lieutenant Clifton James of the Paymaster Corps was the lifelike double for Monty. In peacetime, he had had a small role as an actor. He was chosen by the Military Intelligence Officer in charge of the deception operation, British Hollywood film actor, David Niven (of

"The First Of The Few", 1942, and "The Way Ahead", 1944), who at the time held the rank of Lieutenant Colonel. Clifton James re-enacts his role in this film as "Monty's Double", but for reasons not known David Niven does not appear; instead, John Mills (yes, his third British war film to be released in 1958) plays the Intelligence Officer who discovers and grooms James.

The aviation aspect of "I Was Monty's Double" concerns the VIP aircraft in which "General Montgomery" is flown during his tour of Gibraltar and North Africa. The aircraft used is not just an accurate-looking representation of a 1944-vintage RAF VIP transport, but appears to be the actual machine which flew the fake Monty to Gib, where his arrival is observed by German agents just as British Military Intelligence intended them to do. The aircraft concerned is Avro York C.1 MW101, operated by No.24 Squadron when the real deception operation took place. No.24 Squadron was the Royal Air Force's VIP Squadron during the War years, based at RAF Hendon. However, Hendon was too small for the big Avro York, so instead No.24 operated the York C.1s in their charge from RAF Northolt, which appears in the film.

In February 1943, Prime Minister Winston Churchill had been allocated the second Avro York prototype as his personal VIP transport. According to legend, he had been less than impressed the previous month to see his Chiefs of Staff (CoS) arriving dishevelled at the Casablanca Conference (between Churchill, US President Franklin D Roosevelt and Free French Forces leader, General de Gaulle) in an RAF Consolidated Liberator bomber converted as a supposed VIP transport, while their American counterparts turned up spruce and clean in a smart, purpose-built Douglas C-54A Skymaster. Churchill later demanded that his CoS should have proper VIP aircraft available for them, so the first two production Avro York Is were diverted from delivery to British Overseas Airways Corporation, converted to C.1 standard and given the RAF serials MW100 and MW101 before joining No.24 Squadron.

Avro York C.1 MW100 became the personal aircraft of the Chief of the Air Staff, Sir Charles Portal, while MW101 was used by the real General (soon to be, Field Marshall The Viscount) Montgomery. Two years after the end of World War Two, Montgomery toured the Far East, Australia and New Zealand using this aircraft. A third York C.1, MW102, was provided for the Supreme Commander, South East Asia Command, Lord Louis Mountbatten. It has to be assumed that when it appeared in the film, MW101 was still on strength with the RAF as a VIP aircraft, although all transport York C.1 variants had been withdrawn from use by 1956. A source states that York C.1 MW101 was sold for scrap in 1955 to the British Aluminium Company, but the evidence of this film – made between 1957 and '58 – seems to suggest otherwise.

There is, however, the alternative possibility that it is not the real MW101 we are seeing in the film, but a civilian example painted to appear as Monty's personal York. BOAC were using

Yorks on air freight routes up till November 1957, but the biggest civil Avro York operator of the time was Skyways, a tour and charter airline with a fleet of 30 Yorks flying both passenger and freight services out of Heathrow and Stansted. If it is a Skyways York that is used in "I Was Monty's Double", not too much make-up would have been needed to 'dress' this civil York up to appear as MW101. Firstly, the film is in black-and-white, therefore any colour scheme changes would naturally show up less. Secondly, although the York in the film looks very much the part, in fact the real MW101 bore a different appearance when it was in No.24's and later No.511 Squadron's service: it was simply natural metal all over, with only its RAF roundels and its serial as markings. The MW101 in the film has a white upper fuselage and tail fins, and natural metal lower fuselage. The roundels and fin flashes are correct, but the serial 'MW101' is carried on the lower rear fuselage close to the tail; on the real MW101, the serial was placed high on the rear fuselage.

The fuselages of Skyways' Yorks were painted all-white upper and with all-metal lower, while a duck egg blue cheat line edged in red separated the two halves. All it would need is for the blue-red cheat line to be painted over in white; a study of the York in the film strongly suggests that this is what has been done, as a distinct white strip appears exactly where the blue-red cheat line would be. The tail fins of Skyways' Yorks were painted all-white; it would only need RAF fin flashes to be added. RAF roundels on the fuselage sides and upper wing surfaces, plus serial numbers in place, would complete a very convincing-looking personal transport aircraft for General Montgomery.

As this would mean that a civil York is being used in the film, the correct designation for this aircraft appearing in "I Was Monty's Double" would then have to be Avro York I.

A very impressive shot of the York sweeping in from the sea to land at RAF Gibraltar leads to the scene where Clifton James has to perform his first impersonation of "Monty" before a large delegation of British 'Top Brass' waiting to meet him at the air station. As the York taxies to its position a brief shot of a large military aircraft parked behind the delegation appears. The production team's intention was to create the impression of what RAF Gibraltar would appear like in 1944, where large British military aircraft were constantly to be seen. However, sharp-eyed aviation enthusiasts will immediately spot that the four-engined machine in the background is a decidedly 1950s' generation Avro Shackleton MR.2 maritime patrol aircraft. The Shackleton in the Fifties was a daily sight at Gib, as a squadron of these sub-hunters was always based there to guard NATO ships using the Straits of Gibraltar (with No.224 Squadron, as we have already seen in "The Silent Enemy", 1958).

Either it was unavoidable being able to film this scene without the based Shackleton getting into shot, or the scene was set up to include it as background scene setting. The majority of the audience would probably think it was a Lancaster. In that respect, the audience would be partly correct, due to the Shackleton's lineal descent from the

Lancaster, an ancestry which it shared with the Avro York whose own design borrowed much from the same famous World War Two bomber.

When he disembarks from the York and is greeted by the senior officers, an Admiral says of "Monty"'s aircraft, "You're lucky to get here in one of those". Clifton James responds in a perfect match for the real Montgomery's rather disdainfully nasal tone of expression, "Oh, I don't know, I think they're here to stay".

The deception plan works. "Monty" is spotted by German agents and word is sent back to Berlin that Montgomery is in Gibraltar. When he takes off in his Avro York for his inspection tour of North Africa, the principal German agent on The Rock watches the aircraft depart, knowing that the Luftwaffe are waiting to spring a trap.

Here the film departs from historical fact for the sake of dramatic effect. During his actual impersonation of General Montgomery, there was no attempt on the life of Clifton James as is portrayed in "I Was Monty's Double", although there was the genuine risk that such an attempt could be made. The film shows Luftwaffe fighters taking off to intercept the Avro York, with RAF Spitfires 'Scrambling' to protect it. This event did not happen in real life, although it does echo the rumoured attempt on the life of Winston Churchill the previous year, when the civilian DC-3 Dakota carrying the film actor and director, Leslie Howard, was shot down over the Bay of Biscay, supposedly in mistake for the British Prime Minister's personal VIP Avro York that was due to depart Algiers at approximately the same time.

Archive footage of a Messerschmitt Bf.109E-3 taking off from fairly rough soil is used to illustrate a Luftwaffe fighter launching to make the interception over the Mediterranean. In fact, the 'Emil' variant of the renowned Bf.109 was long out of front-line service with the Luftwaffe by 1944, so this footage is out of date by at least three years. The imagery shown appears to be that of a Bf.109E-3 coded 'White 5' and bearing the badge of I/JG.26. If so, this would make sense because JG.26 was one of the most prestigious and successful of all the Jagdgeschwader (Fighter Wings) in the Deutsches Luftwaffe of World War Two. Its Messerschmitt Bf.109 fighters would have been frequently filmed and shown by the Reich's Propaganda Ministry to an admiring German population, especially as JG.26 included some of the most famous and highest-scoring 'Aces' in the Luftwaffe, such as the Geschwaderkommodore himself, Oberstleutnant Adolf Galland, and the Staffelkapitan of I/JG.26, Oberleutnant Josef 'Pips' Priller (both of whom are represented in later war films, "Battle of Britain", 1969, and "The Longest Day", 1962). JG.26 operated mostly in Poland and France, and from 1st September 1939 to 31st December 1941 claimed more than 900 victories, including Galland with 94 and Priller with 58.

This Bf.109 in the film is immediately followed by archive footage of a second and different Bf.109 model, as evidenced by its larger white propeller spinner which almost certainly identifies

this Bf.109 as a 'Gustav' model, quite likely a Messerschmitt Bf.109G-2, as it does not have the upper wing fairings to accommodate the larger wheels of the G-4 variant, nor does it display the characteristic gun breech blisters on the nose of the G-6 version. Clearly visible under each wing is a fixed cannon: the Bf.109G-2 carried the 20mm MG 151/20 cannon installed in gondolas, one under each wing, to add to the firepower of its two 7.92mm MG 17 machine guns in the nose and a third MG 151/20 cannon firing through the propeller hub.

The footage shows this 'Gustav' making a very low (at about 30 feet off the ground) and fast pass in front of the camera, at a speed which causes the imagery to blur, so identification isn't possible, although there is the suggestion of another code number of '5' on the fuselage behind the cockpit. However, no Staffel badge is shown. The terrain below and beyond the Bf.109G-2 is very different to that from which the previous Bf.109E-3 is shown taking off. It is possible that the footage of this low-flying Bf.109G-2 was taken in Germany during a flight demonstration.

This footage is instantly followed by a shot of a Focke Wulf FW.190 fighter taking off from what looks, for the period, like an unusually wide tarmac'd runway. The camera is positioned right at the runway's edge, and the FW.190 is ground running at speed very close past it (the wingtip passes so close, it could not have been more than two feet away from the cameraman), making the imagery so blurred and with the aircraft passing out of shot so quickly that even with freeze-framing it isn't possible to identify either the fighter or its unit. What it does show, however, is how much of a ground run on all three wheels the FW.190 needed before it could lift its tail to gain flight speed.

The most likely model shown in this footage is a Focke Wulf FW.190A-2, with the newly introduced MG 151/20 cannon fitted to each wing (the FW.190A-1 carried wing-embedded machine guns), while there is no evidence of an under-fuselage attachment point for a bomb or a drop tank as carried by subsequent FW.190A models.

'Scrambling' to the rescue is a squadron of Spitfires, to illustrate which a mix of archive shots of different Spitfire squadrons is used. The first is a familiar piece of footage of Battle of Britain fighter pilots running from their crew room to their Spitfires outside, which is actually that of No.602 Squadron's Spitfire Mk.Ia fighters at Prestwick taken from "A Yank In The R.A.F." (1941), the review of which in Chapter One gives a more full description of this scene; this same footage has appeared in a number of films and documentaries about the Battle. Next seen is a Spitfire Mk.Ia carrying the distinctive WZ-H code letters of No.19 Squadron but wearing the different style of low-visibility roundels and camouflage adopted right at the outbreak of World War Two, which clashes with the later scheme of the Spitfires shown in the previous shot. No.19 was the first operational Spitfire squadron and operated from RAF Duxford, so presumably this is where WZ-H is filmed. Footage of a three-ship Spitfire Mk.Ia 'Vic' formation taking off, with WZ-S openly in the lead, can clearly be seen to be taken at Duxford. Nine more Spitfire Mk.Ia fighters are next seen taking off in three 'Vics' of three but from a completely different airfield, bearing the later roundels and camouflage applied in 1940; the imagery is too dark to identify their codes.

This clash of different markings and codes in these archive shots spoils the effect of this sequence, as does the obviously English locations at where the Spitfires were filmed – as far as the film's plot is concerned, they are meant to be 'Scrambling' from Malta or North Africa. Adding to the lack of realism is the use of the footage of short-range Luftwaffe fighters, as by the time in 1944 when this interception scene is meant to be taking place the Wehrmacht forces had been pushed so far back into Central Europe that there would not have been an airfield close enough to the Mediterranean for Bf.109s to use, apart from in Greece where longer-ranged Bf.110s or Ju.88s operated.

The intercepting Bf.109s are attacked and shot down by the Spitfires, although one does get through to try and put in a burst before it plunges into the Med. This sequence is achieved through the use of not very convincing miniatures of the York and a Bf.109.

"Monty" continues his North Africa theater of operations tour, during which a giveaway shot of the underside of the York's port wing confirms that it is indeed a Skyways Avro York I repainted to represent York C.1 MW101 – as "Monty" disembarks at a North African air base, the camera shot shows that the civil registration letters which would normally appear under the port wing have been painted over in white and an RAF roundel applied over them.

From this point onwards aviation ceases to have a role in the story. But "I Was Monty's Double" takes very convincing advantage of making good use of a majestic airliner to complete its own impersonation of a very personal VIP transport aircraft. Unless you look carefully, you wouldn't know the difference between the real General Montgomery and his real Avro York from both their very effective impersonators in this entertaining British war film.

SEA OF SAND

(Released: November 1958)

This story of the exploits of the Long Range Desert Group (LRDG) behind enemy lines in the North Africa desert was made at the same time as "Ice Cold In Alex" in the United Kingdom of Libya and utilised many of the same assets of the Libyan Royal Army Service Corps made available for both productions. Aviation only makes an occasional appearance in the shape of a not too convincing miniature of a Messerschmitt Bf.109, flying as "a scout aircraft" searching for the LRDG raiders.

THE TWO-HEADED SPY

(Released: November 1958)

This little-known and little-seen wartime spy drama claims to be based on fact, using a British Army Intelligence Officer with pre-War German connections as its inspiration. However, the plot has considerably added to the "facts", to the extent that the Intelligence Officer has been converted into a German General stationed, no less, than in the Nazi High Command in Berlin, with direct contact with Adolf Hitler himself! The idea is too far-fetched, but in the tradition of British spy films the story has plenty of drama and unexpected twists and turns, with a genuinely suspenseful ending. Jack Hawkins plays the lead role of the high-ranking spy of the film's title, with the elegantly lovely Italian actress, Gia Scala, as the love interest.

(It is noteworthy that British films of this period did not disguise the fact that men and women went to bed with each other, whereas in Hollywood at this time, to even suggest this happened was totally taboo).

The film opens in Berlin prior to the invasion of Poland on 1st September 1939. Archive footage of a Nazi rally shows classic images of goose-stepping troops, citizens with Swastika arm bands giving the Nazi salute en masse, and Hitler returning their devotion in kind. Overhead, parade formations of Luftwaffe bombers and fighters sweep past the Reichstag. First, a big formation of 21 Heinkel He.111 bombers, grouped in seven 'Kettes' of three aircraft each, pass over; the He.111 would have been new to many Berliners' eyes at this time. Next, a shot of nine Messerschmitt Bf.110s in three 'Kettes' appears, with the giant quadriga (chariot) and eagle symbol atop the Reichstag in the foreground below them. They are followed by three Heinkel He.111s in 'Vic', which may have been the leading 'Kette' of He.111s seen in the previous shot.

As the plot moves on, with Jack Hawkins's Nazi General spy now being in charge of supplies for the 75 Wehrmacht Divisions which invade Poland, more archive footage is used, mostly of Panzer units in action but including one shot of a Junkers Ju.88A-4 in a dive and releasing four bombs. The Ju.88A-4 became the most successful dive bomber variant of the Ju.88 series. What is significant about this shot is that the Ju.88A-4 shown is releasing its bomb load in a 45-degree angle of dive, a tactic that was developed in 1943 after dives at steeper angles were found to put the bomber at risk due to greater stresses on the airframe. Quite likely, this particular shot of the Ju.88A-4 in its 45-degree dive angle was filmed during 1943 or afterwards. The shot is very clear, suggesting it was filmed during a test drop rather than actually of this Ju.88A-4 in action.

The plot moves on to cover the Nazi invasions of Denmark, Holland, Belgium and France in 1940. For each country, archive shots of Wehrmacht armour and Luftwaffe dive bombers are used. For Denmark, footage of four Junkers Ju.87 Stukas peeling off from echelon starboard formation and rolling over into their dives appears. What is interesting about this footage is that it shows two variants of a particular model of the Stuka in action here.

The first two Stukas peeling off and diving have distinctly tapered wing-tips, not typical of most Stuka variants: the possibility is that they are both Ju.87D-5 Stukas, which introduced this type of wing design. The third Stuka peeling off in their wake is noticeably different: it has squared-off wing-tips, as did most Stuka variants, and, unusually, does not have the familiar wheel spats on its undercarriage. Possibly this is an earlier Ju.87D-2 Stuka. This footage is cut before the fourth Stuka can be seen.

Seeing different variants of Stuka in the same formation is rare. It begs the question as to whether this film shows a particular Stukageschwader equipped with two variants of the Junkers Ju.87D, perhaps converting from the D-2 to the D-5.

For the invasions of Holland and Belgium, footage of three more Junkers Ju.87 Stukas appears. By the shape of their cockpit, they appear to be early model Stukas, possibly of the Ju.87B variant. They break individually from echelon port; they don't appear to be carrying any bombs, so this is probably stage-managed footage from a Reich Propaganda Ministry promotional film.

For the invasion of France, footage of a single Junkers Ju.87D in a dive is used.

No more archive film showing aircraft appears in the film until the editor inserts various footage of Allied victories as the War progresses. Here, the editor has opted to show the Allied Tactical Air Force in action with footage exclusively of USAAF Martin B-26 Marauder medium day bombers, all covering the period of the D-Day landings and the Allies' push into France. First, three B-26 Marauders are seen air-air in 'Vic' formation, then a parade formation of six B-26 Marauders follows, looking very much like a close-up of the same shot that appears in a later film. Finally, another air-air of five B-26 Marauders releasing their bombs is used.

From this point on, no further archive material containing aircraft appears in the film. "The Two-Headed Spy" is well acted and directed, and, judging from some of the scenes, includes a certain part of West Germany that still showed bomb damage in the latter half of the Fifties. It also contains a quite brutal Gestapo torture scene, with methods that were actually employed by this criminal police force to extract information from individuals they suspected of being enemy agents or German traitors. A film worth tracking down by those who are fans of the war or spy movie genres.

OPERATION AMSTERDAM

(Released: January 1959)

A less well known, but extremely well made British war film starring a very young Peter Finch as the son of a Dutch diamond producer and filmed extensively in Amsterdam, with an enthusiastic population very willing to re-enact a desperate period in their city's history. The story is based on actual events which took place on 10th May 1940, when the British Secret Intelligence Service, or MI6, joined with Dutch industrialists and Resistance fighters to smuggle industrial diamonds out of Amsterdam before the city fell to the advancing German forces, thus preventing them

from being used by Hitler's Third Reich to increase the output of the Nazis' armaments machine.

Aviation makes three appearances in the film, beginning with archive footage of several Junkers Ju.52/3Ms taking on Wehrmacht Fallschirmjager troops to portray the Nazi invasion of Holland. As Finch, MI6 officer Tony Britton and a Dutch government representative, played by Alexander Knox, try to land by boat at an under-fire Port of Ijmuiden in North Holland, they narrowly escape a stick of bombs dropped by a Junkers Ju.88. Guess what, it's that R/C model of Ju.88A-5 M2+MK from No.1426 (Enemy Aircraft) Flight again; in other words, yet another out-take from "In Which We Serve" (1942). That film certainly proved good value in its use of the captured Ju.88A-5, out-takes of which have now appeared in no less than five other British war films.

Just before the Ju.88A-5 attacks, the three operatives look up to see a formation of five of these light bombers flying in 'Vic' formation over Ijmuiden. A close examination confirms the suspicion that they are indeed again the five Finnish Air Force Bristol Blenheim IIs that appear in "The Way To The Stars" (1945), although the shot used here did not feature in that film.

Later, as Finch and his colleagues are trying to make their way back from Amsterdam to the Port carrying the liberated diamonds, from where they are expecting to take a boat out to a waiting British warship, they are held up by escaping refugees who are blocking the road they are using. The refugee column is strafed by a single Messerschmitt Bf.109, which makes three runs at low-level. For this scene, the film's makers have resorted to using for the first time what became a familiar double in British and American war movies for Messerschmitt Bf.109s, that of using the similar-looking Messerschmitt Bf.108 Taifun, the communications variant and forerunner of the famous Me.109/Bf.109 itself, to act as the Luftwaffe fighter.

The first use of a Messerschmitt Bf.108 in a film production occurred in "The Desert Song" (1939), with Swedish actress Zara Leander portraying a female pilot flying a Bf.108B-1 registered either D-IFWA or D-IFRV. This was followed by a German film released in 1944, "The Sky is in You", about pre-War record-breaking female pilot Elly Beinhorn in which another Bf.108B-1 is used (Elly Beinhorn named the Bf.108B-1 she flew, Taifun; the name was adopted for all Bf.108s subsequently built).

In "Operation Amsterdam", the Bf.108 that impersonates the Bf.109 is Messerschmitt Bf.108D-1 PH-PBC (Werke Nr 730253) that had, since 1949, belonged to Prince Bernhard of the Netherlands, no less. It was actually built in 1944 by Nord Aviation in France before the Liberation, which means that although it is a French-built aircraft with the Argus Ar.10-C engine, technically making it a Nord 1000 Pinguoin, it would have been classified as a Messerschmitt Bf.108D-1 when operated by the Deutsches Luftwaffe, making it another genuine German World War Two-vintage military aircraft appearing in a British war film.

At some stage post-War this Bf.108D-1 came into service with the newly forged Royal Netherlands Air Force and appears to have been operated as an aircraft allocated to Prince Bernhard for his use. On 1st October 1949 it was transferred to the Prince's ownership and was based at Soestdijk. Six years later, Schreiner & Co NV became the owners of PH-PBC, basing the Bf.108D-1 at Den Haag. Interestingly, the Dutch civil register shows that an attempted sale of this aircraft was blocked on 15th October 1956. Presumably it remained with Schreiner & Co and was in their ownership when it was used in 1958 to act as the Messerschmitt Bf.109 in "Operation Amsterdam".

This Bf.108D-1 is the fifth German aircraft of the actual World War Two period to appear in a British war film. It was painted accurately in Luftwaffe markings and used battery-powered flashing lights installed in the leading edge of both wings to simulate cannon fire - an inaccurate innovation in this case, as early model Bf.109s of the 1940 era only had nose-mounted cannon and machine guns. Noticeably, it flew in the film without a propeller spinner, which equates to a photograph of the period showing it in the same configuration.

Following its appearance in the film it was sold to a new buyer in West Germany. Currently it is in private ownership at Schwabmunchen, Bavaria, registered firstly as D-EHAF, then changed to D-EBFW following a complete restoration.

DANGER WITHIN

(Released: February 1959)

A Prisoner of War film with a slight difference from its predecessors up till now, in that the British PoWs are being held by the Italians, not by the Germans, nor by the Japanese. A tense and suspenseful drama, it is the first film of its kind to have a mass escape. It also introduces an element in the plot that has been hitherto taboo in British PoW war films, in that one of their number might be a traitor. A well acted, very watchable British war film, it is nonetheless totally devoid of aviation.

THE ANGRY HILLS

(Released: July 1959, USA)

The progeny of this wartime thriller is somewhat confusing. There is no doubt that it is a British production, made at MGM British Film Studios in Borehamwood, but set entirely in Greece where all the location filming took place. However, its director is American (Robert Aldrich), its leading star is American (Robert Mitchum), and the author of its story is American (Leon Uris). It also had its first release in the United States. It suffers from the US distributor's decision to cut 14 minutes from its plot for its American release (which is the version on DVD), with the result that certain scenes do not connect properly and several principal characters suddenly appear with nothing to show where they fit into the story.

The only sight of aviation in "The Angry Hills" is that of an archive air-air shot of six Junkers Ju.87 Stuka dive bombers breaking off for the camera, without ordnance carried, probably filmed for promotional purposes.

YESTERDAY'S ENEMY

(Released: September 1959)

This is the type of war film that Hollywood, in the Fifties, would never have dreamt of making. It is an entirely studio-based, jungle warfare themed morality drama, set during the Burma Campaign of 1942, when both British and Japanese officers use ruthless methods to wage total war. Both the British Captain and the Japanese Major order their troops to commit atrocities in order to terrorise their respective prisoners into giving information. A war film that is worth having in anyone's collection, but as far as aviation is concerned, it is totally absent from the plot.

SINK THE BISMARCK!

(Released: February 1960)

This superior British war film stands as one of the best ever made that depicts naval warfare at sea during World War Two. Not only is it well acted by all the leading players and very convincingly re-created in both the studio and on board a real battleship (HMS Vanguard, just before her decommissioning as the Royal Navy's last battleship) but most outstanding of all are the very realistic SFX miniatures of the principal ships involved in this famous naval pursuit and engagement.

The success of the film is entirely dependent on the realism of not just the ships themselves, but of the environment in which they operate. The sea had to look like the actual sea in various climatic states, as did the weather conditions affecting how the ships performed. For instance, when a cruiser disappears into icy sea fog, it looks just like a real cruiser slipping into a real fog bank amid ice flows.

Most of all, in re-creating the epic sea battle between the Schlachtschiffe (battleship) Bismarck and the Schwere Kreuzer (heavy cruiser) Prinz Eugen with the battlecruiser HMS Hood and the battleship HMS Prince of Wales, then followed later in the Bismarck's final confrontation with the battleships King George V and Rodney, the film production team knew that images of shell fire and explosions had to be realistic, otherwise the whole film project would fail. To achieve this, director Lewis Gilbert and producer John Brabourne sought the services of one of the best SFX creators in the business, Howard Lydecker, who was loaned to the production by Republic Pictures Inc, plus one of the most experienced Special Effects cameramen, Skeets Kelly. Kelly was, in fact, an expert aerial cameraman who we have encountered before as far back as 1941 filming in Canada for "49th Parallel", reviewed in Chapter One, and who will feature in other major film productions involving aviation, such as "Battle of Britain" (1969), reviewed in the next Chapter.

"Sink the Bismarck!" is as faithful a re-creation of the hunt by the Royal Navy Home Fleet in June 1941 for the mighty German Kriegsmarine surface raider, the Bismarck, and of her eventual sinking as Gilbert's and Braybourne's film production team could make it. However, there are significant inaccuracies in their re-creation, largely due to a lack of knowledge of certain facts at the time when the film was made (1959) – and not least because the Admiralty was still withholding certain details of the action against the Bismarck from the public – but also due to Gilbert's and Braybourne's decision to bring a human interest element into the plot that was entirely fictitious.

 This involved a quietly evolving sympathetic relationship between the Director of Naval Operations, Captain Shepard, played by Kenneth More, and his assistant, WRNS Second Officer Anne Davis, acted by the elegant, dark-eyed beauty, Dana Wynter. Shepard is also scripted as having his only son as a naval air gunner aboard the aircraft carrier HMS Ark Royal, who goes missing at sea when his aircraft runs out of fuel, challenging Shepard's rigid self-control of his emotions that he has imposed upon himself since his wife was killed in an air raid. If he loses control of his emotions due to the possible loss of his son, this could have serious consequences for how he directs the course of the battle against the Bismarck.

The decision to have the moving interplay between More's and Wynter's characters was taken to relieve the film's plot from becoming an over-bearingly all-male re-enaction of the events leading to the Bismarck's destruction; such a scenario could have led to the loss of interest in the plot by a significant portion of the audience. It also successfully humanises what otherwise would mainly be an exercise in the planning and the execution of a military operation. However, the inclusion of these two characters meant that the real Director of Naval Operations against the Bismarck, Captain R A B Edwards, had to be excluded from the film's plot. It would not have done to have created the impression that the real Director of Operations had had other things on his mind when he was plotting the destruction of the Bismarck in May 1941.

When "Sink the Bismarck!" was made, only one photograph of Bismarck in action was known to exist. It was printed as a negative, caused by the brilliant flash of Bismarck's guns which create the impression that Bismarck was firing a broadside at HMS Hood at night. The image also led to interpreters wrongly guessing at which angle Bismarck is photographed as firing from. The picture was taken by a seaman aboard Prinz Eugen and led interpreters to believe that Bismarck is seen from her starboard rear quarter firing a broadside to starboard. This is because, until new information came to light to prove otherwise, historians believed that Bismarck was the lead ship in the engagement with the Hood and the Prince of Wales, with Prinz Eugen to the rear off Bismarck's starboard rear quarter and firing slightly closer to the British ships because

her guns had less range. This misinterpretation is reflected in the film, which also depicts the error that all four warships fired broadsides abeam to their opponent vessel; in reality, this did not happen. In other words, the film shows Hood and Prince of Wales firing to port, and Bismarck leading Prinz Eugen as they fired to starboard – the wrong way round, and with the German ships sailing in the wrong order.

Not until the most senior German naval officer to survive the sinking of the Bismarck, Leutnant-Kommandant Burkard Baron von Mullenheim-Rechberg, published his memoirs of his time aboard the battleship in the late Seventies in his book, "Battleship Bismarck: A Survivor's Tale", followed by the world famous marine geologist, Dr Robert D Ballard, publicising in 1990 his discovery of the wreck of the Bismarck, have the correct details come to light about the Battle of the Denmark Strait on 24th May 1941.

In essence, Vice-Admiral Lancelot Holland aboard his flagship HMS Hood attacked what he believed to be Bismarck from a near head-on angle, which meant only the forward main gun turrets of his battlecruiser and that of battleship Prince of Wales sailing behind could be brought to bear on the lead ship. Holland had assumed the leader of the two German warships would naturally be Bismarck; he was wrong, it was Prinz Eugen, as Mullenheim-Rechberg's book and much more information and photos subsequently released by the Bundesarchiv confirm. Bismarck was astern of Prinz Eugen due to her forward radar having failed, leaving her reliant on Prinz Eugen for forward radar coverage. Both German ships were able to bring all their main armament to bear, firing to port as they steamed west south-west out of the Denmark Strait, all of their shells aimed first at HMS Hood. The rest is history.

That one negative-like photo which existed for so long as the only known picture of Bismarck in action therefore shows the battleship to be behind and off the port rear quarter of Prinz Eugen, in the act of firing to port at HMS Hood as both ships were engaged in a turn – not ahead and in the heavy cruiser's port forward quarter, as was for so long assumed, and firing to starboard.

Vice-Admiral Holland's tactic has been described as like a boxer going into a match with one hand behind his back. It is likely that embarrassment within the Admiralty about Holland's mistake in identification and chosen tactic was a principal reason for them allowing a more favourable interpretation of the Battle of the Denmark Strait to be kept in the public knowledge, which is reflected in the film's depiction of the action. There were also many relatives of the 1,415 men who were lost aboard HMS Hood for whom the events of 24th May 1941 were still strong in the memory 18 years afterwards, and who might have made their feelings known, probably through letters to the press, had the real facts been made public.

The mistake in the portrayal of the Battle of the Denmark Strait is one among a number of errors in "Sink the Bismarck!", which have come to light since Mullenheim-Rechberg's and Ballard's books were published, but which overall do not detract from the otherwise extremely effective re-creation of the events in the Atlantic during the month of May 1941. But it is the aviation elements of the pursuit and of the eventual sinking of the Bismarck with which this review is concerned, and, as the film shows, the use of aviation was to prove crucial in bringing about the downfall of the mighty battleship. In fact, this naval action was the first to demonstrate that even the most powerful warships could be rendered vulnerable by air attack from carrier-borne aircraft, a serious game changer in the conduct of the war at sea.

The first element of aviation to feature in "Sink the Bismarck!" occurs fairly early on into the film when a photo reconnaissance (PR) Spitfire discovers and photographs Bismarck and Prinz Eugen moored in Grimstadfjord off Norway on 21st May 1941 before their break-out into the Atlantic. This actually occurred with a Spitfire PR.IV flying from Wick in Scotland, piloted by Flying Officer Michael Suckling who photographed Grimstadfjord from a height of 25,000 feet. In the scene in the film flak is fired at the PR Spitfire: in reality, this did not happen, the Germans were unaware that Bismarck had been discovered.

In the brief scene showing the PR Spitfire, two air-air shots and one ground-air shot of a Spitfire in flight are used, plus there are shots of the pilot in the cockpit; but none of these shots show a real PR Spitfire in action. In fact, the film's editor has used imagery of three different Spitfires in flight, while the cockpit is from a fourth Spitfire – all to portray one brief sortie by one aircraft!

The first Spitfire seen flying air-air is an aircraft we have seen in a British war film before: it is Spitfire Mk.IIa P8074/SD-L, the same Spitfire seen attacking captured Heinkel He.111H-3 1H+EN in "The First of the Few" (1942). This particular shot is, therefore, an out-take from that film. We then see the pilot in the cockpit. As other observers of the film have reported Online, the cockpit canopy is of a different type to that shown on the Spitfires filmed in flight. It is from a much later Marque of Spitfire, being the raised, all-perspex 'bubble' canopy that gave pilots a better all-round view, as opposed to the raised forward Malcolm Hood canopy of the earlier Marque of Spitfires shown in the film. The most likely candidate Spitfire for this 'bubble' canopy is Spitfire LF.XVIe TE341 that was sold to Pinewood Studios in 1955 for interior shots in "Reach For The Sky"(1956). "Sink the Bismarck!" was also made at Pinewood; the cockpit section would almost certainly have been retained for future usage in other productions.

Having seen the pilot looking down on Grimstadfjord, the next shot shows him turning his Spitfire in a banking turn to starboard before he is able to bring his oblique camera to bear from the compartment in the fuselage behind his cockpit. To create this establishing shot, an air-air view of his Spitfire turning away is used: it is immediately apparent that this is a different Spitfire with no squadron code letters, nor the white band wrapped around the rear fuselage forward of the tail that P8074/SD-L bears. This is archive footage of Spitfire Mk.IIa P8441, filmed by the Crown Film Unit and, of course, seen

before in pursuit of captured Messerschmitt Bf.110C-4 5F+CM of No.1426 (Enemy Aircraft) Flight: presumably no footage of Spitfire Vb P8074/SD-L performing a break to starboard was available, so alternative footage had to be found.

Finally, as flak bursts around the PR Spitfire the pilot uses his aircraft's increased level of speed over other versions of the Spitfire (due to its guns being removed and parts of its protective armoury detached, to lighten it) to accelerate away out of trouble. This is portrayed by archive footage of another unidentified Spitfire whose serial is not visible and which is not carrying any squadron codes, but it does have a white rear fuselage band. This confirms it is neither P8074 nor P8441.

It is, of course, the roles performed by the Fleet Air Arm Fairey Swordfish torpedo bombers which form two of the most crucial episodes in the pursuit and the sinking of the Bismarck. For aviation enthusiasts and military historians, it is the re-enactment of the launching of real Swordfish aircraft off a real Royal Navy aircraft carrier at sea that provides some of the most fascinating elements of the film. This took place using two Fairey Swordfish which were still in flying condition in 1959, both flown and filmed from the flight deck of the carrier HMS Centaur.

The operations the two Swordfish are re-enacting are the launches for the air strikes against Bismarck conducted first very late in the day on 24th May 1941 by nine Swordfish of 825 Squadron aboard the carrier HMS Victorious, followed on 26th May by 15 Swordfish from all three torpedo bomber-spotter-reconnaisance squadrons aboard HMS Ark Royal. The attacks on the battleships are depicted, in the main, by the use of studio miniatures of Swordfish: these are of quite high quality in their realistic portrayal of torpedo launches at low-level over sea, in keeping with the equally high quality of the ship and sea state Special Effects created for the film by Howard Lydecker and his SFX team. Two particular shots in each attack, filmed from the perspective of a Swordfish crew in their cockpit as they ply towards the Bismarck above a very realistically-created SFX high sea state – the battleship growing menacingly larger and larger on screen as the exposed bi-plane torpedo bomber closes on its target amid anti-aircraft fire spraying towards it – provides still today a most graphic and dramatic effect, and is probably the most realistic re-creation of a torpedo attack by an aircraft upon a warship to be seen in any film (apart from "Tora! Tora! Tora!", 1970).

The Fairey Swordfish attacks are shown correctly attacking in sub-Flights of three aircraft each, which, as previously explained in "Ships With Wings" (1941), was the standard method of attack adopted by the Fleet Air Arm. Miniatures are used for most of these attacks, although some shots of one of the real Fairey Swordfish flying head-on over the sea towards the camera, as well as over-flying the camera position (presumably on board HMS Centaur), are intercut with shots of the miniatures. In the HMS Victorious Swordfish attack, one Swordfish is seen blowing up in mid-air; in the HMS Ark Royal torpedo bomber attack, two Swordfish are seen diving towards the sea on fire. This is factually incorrect: no Swordfish were shot down by Bismarck, although one was written off when landing back aboard Victorious and another went down in the sea on 25th May when it became lost during the search for Bismarck – its crew ditched beside an abandoned lifeboat and spent eight days on the ocean before being picked up (this incident was adapted in the film's script as happening to Captain Shepard's son from Ark Royal, who was picked up after his Swordfish had ditched while searching for Bismarck).

It has often been pointed out that the Swordfish in the film were representing aircraft from 825 Squadron on HMS Victorious because of the '5A' and '5B' codes they bear on their fuselages. When the same two Swordfish are seen later in the film depicting Ark Royal's aircraft taking off to attack Bismarck, the presumption has been made by a number of analysts that the film production team made a mistake in not changing the codes to show a different squadron. In fact, Swordfish of 818 Squadron aboard Ark Royal also bore the same '5A' and '5B' codes, these being carrier air group codes for each particular sub-Flight from each squadron which were replicated on aircraft aboard various different aircraft carriers during World War Two. As pointed out in the review of "Ships With Wings", the real 818 Squadron Swordfish on board Ark Royal carrying the codes '5A' and '5B' that attacked Bismarck can be seen in that film. Also in view is Swordfish L9726/5C which, flown by sub-Lieutenant J W C Moffatt, delivered the fatal torpedo strike that crippled the Bismarck's rudder and thus sealed her fate.

What is not correct are the all-over dark blue-grey camouflage schemes borne by both Swordfish in the film. The correct camouflage schemes are those as seen in "Ships With Wings", with the upper half of the fuselage and upper wing surfaces being camouflaged, while the lower fuselage and undersides are painted light sea grey. The roundel on the fuselage side, bordered in yellow, is placed exactly midway between the division of these two colour schemes. The code number and letter was immediately behind the roundel, but smaller in size than that depicted on the aircraft in the film and painted in red, not large and bordered in white as shown in "Sink the Bismarck!".

The reason for not painting the two Swordfish in the correct colours and markings of the period is unknown, and appears strange as there was plenty of photographic and recorded evidence available of Swordfish in 1941 that the art department could have referred to. One possible explanation, however, is that the correct colour schemes did not stand out on film, especially black-and-white film, so the Swordfish were painted in a darker scheme which allowed for better visible contrast with their larger roundels and codes.

There are one or two goofs in the Swordfish sequences. In what is meant to be 825 Squadron Swordfish starting engines on board HMS Victorious, a close-up shot reveals that only the pilot is in the cockpit of the lead aircraft – he was going into action without his navigator and air gunner! Also, no torpedo is attached to this Swordfish, but in the next shot of it lifting off from the flight deck it has suddenly acquired one! In the sequence depicting Swordfish '5A' of 818 Squadron taking off from HMS Ark Royal, it is going into action against Bismarck without a torpedo!

The two Swordfish which appear in "Sink the Bismarck!" are well known to British aviation enthusiasts, especially the first of the two. She is Fairey Swordfish Mk.II LS326, a long-standing veteran of the UK airshow circuit. When "Sink the Bismarck!" went into production in 1959, Swordfish LS326 was in the possession of her design company, the Fairey Aviation Company at White Waltham Aerodrome in Berkshire. She was painted in the house colours of 'Fairey Blue' and was being operated on the British civil aviation register as G-AJVH. Under contract to 20th Century Fox Film Corporation, she was repainted in October 1958 in the colours as seen in the film and carried the code '5A'. She thus acts the role of the lead aircraft of 825 Squadron from HMS Victorious, flown by the Squadron Commander, Lieutenant Commander (Acting) Eugene Esmonde, as well as that of the lead aircraft of 818 Squadron aboard HMS Ark Royal, flown by that particular Squadron's Commander, Lieutenant Commander T P Coode (as stated in "Ships With Wings", the real Swordfish of 818 Squadron coded '5A' was P4219). For the film, she was flown by Fairey Aviation chief test pilot and world air speed record breaker, Peter Twiss, who flew the floatplane version of the Swordfish off armed merchant ships during the War.

After filming was completed aboard HMS Centaur, Swordfish LS326 returned to White Waltham but, in September 1960, when Fairey Aviation had become part of the Westlands Group, she was presented to the Royal Navy and stationed at RNAS Yeovilton, where she has remained ever since. Operated throughout the Sixties at many airshows by RNAS Yeovilton's Station Flight, LS326 retained her "Sink the Bismarck!" colour scheme until 1972, when she was repainted in the accurate scheme and markings of the real two '5A'-coded Swordfish.

Throughout her time with Fairey Aviation in the Fifties and during her first two decades at RNAS Yeovilton, it was commonly held that Swordfish LS326 had had an unremarkable service career with the Fleet Air Arm. The programme notes for RNAS Yeovilton's Open Day on 9th September 1967 states, "...it (LS326) never actually saw active service, being used for training and communications flying duties from the Royal Naval Air Station at Culham, near Oxford, and Worthy Down near Winchester". However, in the early Eighties LS326's complete flying record was unearthed which contradicted the earlier belief. It was revealed that she had served with 836 Squadron based at Maydown, Northern Ireland, which provided Swordfish to Merchant Aircraft Carriers (MACs) on convoy escort duties. From October 1943, LS326 served first aboard the MAC-Ship Rapana as 'L2' of 'L Flight' and then, from February 1944, with 'K Flight' operating from the Empire Ship Empire MacCallum. During this time, she flew numerous anti-submarine sorties protecting trans-Atlantic convoys, so the belief that she "never actually saw active service" was proven completely erroneous: she had been very active indeed.

As a consequence of her true career being discovered, the decision was taken within the Royal Navy Historic Flight (RNHF) to repaint LS326 in her actual wartime colours as LS326/L2 of 'L Flight', 836 Squadron, when she served aboard MAC-Ship Rapana. She has borne these colours ever since, painted high visibility white as she would have needed to be in 1943 if she had had to ditch and be easily spotted by rescue craft. Swordfish LS326 underwent a complete overhaul during the first decade of the New Millenium when corrosion was discovered in her wing spars, carried out by a combined RNHF and BAE Systems team at the place of her birth in 1943, Brough (Blackburn Aircraft at the time, making her a 'Blackfish'). Although she was returned to the air in 2008, more work proved necessary so she was grounded again until she rejoined the RNHF in full flying condition once more at the end of the 2010 airshow season. Having been in civilian hands since 1947 and been active on the British airshow scene since 1960, Fairey Swordfish LS326 must be one of the longest preserved airworthy World War Two warbirds anywhere in the world.

The second Swordfish which appears in "Sink the Bismarck!" has also long been a member of the historic aircraft preservation scene in the UK, although not as a flyer since the early Sixties and has spent a large part of her time keeping Swordfish LS326 and a second Swordfish, W5856, airborne with the RNHF, acting as a spares source. She is Fairey Swordfish Mk.III NF389 which, in Spring 1959 had been preserved by the Fleet Air Arm with 781 Squadron, based at RNAS Lee-on-Solent in Hampshire. 781 Squadron was the Fleet Air Arm's principal communications and supply unit to ship-borne squadrons and flights, and to shore-based establishments; Swordfish NF389 was kept in flying condition, but did not make many public appearances.

For the film, NF389's serial was changed to LS423, to make her more contemporary with Swordfish LS326 (there was a real Swordfish LS423 during the War, but she had yet to be built by the time of the events in the Atlantic during May 1941). NF389 acts the roles of 825 Squadron Swordfish '5B', flown from HMS Victorious by Lieutenant N G MacLean, RNVR, in the leading Flight to attack Bismarck on 24th May 1941, and of the similarly-coded 818 Squadron Swordfish flown two days later from Ark Royal on 26th May by sub-Lieutenant (Acting) E D Child.

Swordfish III NF389 is, like LS326, a 'Blackfish' built at Brough and delivered to the Royal Navy in April 1944, but was transferred to the RAF a year later. She was received back by the Royal Navy in September 1946 and was allocated to the RNAS Arbroath Station Flight in Scotland, where she remained for more than a year before she was flown south to RNAS Gosport, to become part of the Aircraft Torpedo Development Unit. She served out her Fleet Air Arm career as a torpedo development trials aircraft, moving from RNAS Gosport to RNAS Culdrose, then finally to nearby RAF St Merryn in Cornwall where the Torpedo Trials Flight was based, retiring in March 1953. Swordfish NF389 then became the responsibility of 781 Squadron.

(It is possible that the film's art department chose to have both Swordfish painted in all-over camouflage because NF389 wore such a scheme during her service life as a land-based Swordfish; painting the civilian-coloured LS326 in an identical scheme would have been perceived as expedient).

Like Swordfish LS326, she retained her "Sink the Bismarck!" markings as '5B' after filming was completed, and was flown occasionally at airshows. However, the decision was taken in the early Sixties that LS326 would be the primary display aircraft,

while NF389 would remain as a spares source at RNAS Lee-on-Solent. She spent more than 20 years there on static display until 1990, when NF389 was moved back to her Brough birthplace to act as a spares source and pattern aircraft for the restoration to flight of 'Blackfish' W5856. She then was sent to RNAS Yeovilton to support the flying roles of the other two Swordfish.

Recently there have been two attempts made to restore Swordfish NF389 to flight once more, but both times these have been put on hold for economic and practical reasons affecting the RNHF. At the time of writing, Swordfish NF389 is in the custody of BAE Systems at Brough once more, awaiting the green light for her own restoration.

The final element of aviation in "Sink the Bismarck!" involves the Consolidated Catalina I amphibious flying boat of No.209 Squadron, based at Lough Erne in Northern Ireland, which made contact with Bismarck on 26th May 1941 after all trace of the battleship had been lost for nearly 36 hours. This brief scene is depicted by archive footage of an RAF Coastal Command Catalina I, filmed air-air most likely by the RAF Film Production Unit. The aircraft is seen making a turn astern of the camera aircraft, with two depth charges attached under its starboard wing. SFX flak bursts have been added to create the effect of Bismarck's anti-aircraft guns firing at the flying boat.

"Sink the Bismarck!" is a most commendable effort at a realistic depiction of a great naval action, on both the German and the British sides. But now that the facts are fully known; and with all the technology available today in the film industry using CGI and 3D; plus the skill in creating very realistic, large-scale miniatures of ships, as have been seen in some of the James Bond films and in "Titanic" (1997); and, finally, with the possibility of having three airworthy genuine Fairey Swordfish torpedo bombers available (four, if the Canadian example can be added), what a marvellous opportunity exists to re-tell the story of the Bismarck – surely it would make a most spectacular and dramatic production.

FOXHOLE IN CAIRO

(Released: October 1960)

This made-on-the-cheap, studio-set film production is based on an actual Abwehr Intelligence Operation against the British 8th Army in Egypt, involving smuggling two German military agents into Cairo to gain intel on the 8th Army's strengths, so as to assist Rommel in his plans to take Egypt and seize the Suez Canal. The plot has a loose connection with "The English Patient" (1996), reviewed in Chapter Seven. James Robertson Justice, who in this film plays the British Intelligence chief in Cairo, reprises almost exactly the same role in "The Guns of Navarone" (1961), which he made immediately after his appearance in this production.

The film incongruously mixes black-and-white, BBC Televison-style studio scenes with very grainy archive imagery for the exterior shots. Towards the end, out-takes from the wartime Army Film Production Unit's re-creation of the Battle of el-Alamein are used to illustrate the battle itself. "Foxhole in Cairo" is also noteworthy as being one of the first films in which actor Michael Caine has a significant speaking role, while also being the fourth film in which he plays the part of a German, probably due to he being tall and very fair-haired in this early period of his long acting career.

Aviation has a small part in "Foxhole in Cairo" but what is shown is, for the aviation and war film historian, very significant. Immediately following the title credits, archive footage of several Luftwaffe aircraft and an RAF Hawker Hurricane is shown. What is significant about this footage is that none of it has appeared in any other film production before or since, making all of it, therefore, extremely rare. What is more, despite the grainy quality of this archive material, it is possible to identify several of the Luftwaffe aircraft that are shown.

First seen are two Messerschmitt Bf.109F fighters making a paired take off from a rough, dusty airfield, probably in North Africa. Unfortunately, the camera is filming into sun, so the nearest Bf.109 is almost in silhouette. However, the number '2' can be discerned on the fuselage ahead of the Balkenkreuze, which means a dash was probably on the opposite side of the German wartime national marking. Distinctly visible is the cannon protruding from the bulbous propeller boss. If taken in North Africa, the two Bf.109Fs would have been painted in desert sand brown colour schemes; the white propeller boss and white wrap-around rear fuselage band typical of Messerschmitt Bf.109s operating in this theater are clearly visible on the nearest 'Friedrich' numbered '2'.

This footage immediately cuts to a good air-air shot of Messerschmitt Bf.110E 3U+GT of 9/ZG.26 (9 Staffeln der Zerstorergeschwader 26: 9th Squadron of No.26 Destroyer Group) over-flying desolate, flat desert terrain. The aircraft identifier Staffel code letter is painted in red behind the fuselage Balkenkreuze on a white wrap-around fuselage band, which means it does not stand out as do the black ZG.26 codes; however, freeze-frame analysis brings up the suggestion of the letter 'G'. Interestingly, as the shot progresses a coastline comes into view at the top of the frame, suggesting that this is film of an aerial patrol by two ground-attack Bf.110Es close to the North African coast, possibly during the period when the Afrika Korps was gaining supremacy over the British 8th Army before the Second Battle of el-Alamein. The shot is filmed from the rear seat of the accompanying Bf.110E, of which the top part of its starboard engine nacelle can be seen in the bottom quarter of the frame.

9/ZG.26 was, in September and October 1942, operating from Kastelli on Crete, so this fits with the period assumed. The Bf.110E was a dedicated tank destroyer, whose primary weapon was a gondola-mounted 30mm Rheinmetall-Borsig RB 101 cannon attached under the fuselage in line with the cockpit. From the angle that Bf.110E 3U+GT is filmed from slightly above, its port wing is obscuring its forward under-fuselage, so it is not possible to see if the RB 101 cannon is installed; however, if these Zerstorers are on patrol looking out for enemy armour, it would be unusual for the cannon not to be fitted. The Messerschmitt Bf.110E Staffeln of ZG.26 saw action in the battles at Alam el-Halfa and el-Alamein.

Shortly afterwards another archive air-air is shown, this time of an unusual-looking Heinkel He.111 coded RD+NZ. This He.111 is filmed from the dorsal gun turret position of another He.111, part of whose starboard engine nacelle is in shot. The wide expanse of the He.111's wing, blocking any downward view, means that RD+NZ has to fly in formation slightly above the camera aircraft. The camera appears to have been fixed in position, so the pilot of the subject aircraft has to position his He.111 carefully in relation to the lens in the hope of being fully in frame; but, He.111 RD+NZ is riding slightly too high, which means that the top of its port wing and tail fin are out of shot.

What makes this He.111 distinctly unusual and of particular interest to the aviation historian is that it has a stretched nose area that is not completely glazed, as are those of most of the He.111 models, and has a stepped-up cockpit. Missing from it is the ventral gun position, while no machine gun protrudes from the nose. It might be an unarmed transport variant, while careful research suggests that the RD+NZ code is not that of a front-line Kampfgeschwader.

After detailed analysis, the author believes that this is air-air footage of a Heinkel He.111F model that is probably from a Luftwaffe training unit. What favours this decision is not just that the He.111 concerned bears a strong similarity to the early He.111B/C/D/E versions of this famous bomber, but that it has one noteworthy feature in its appearance that differs from all the others mentioned - they all have a radio antenna mast just behind and above the stepped-up cockpit, whereas the He.111F has its antenna located further back (and which would be blocked from the camera's view by the port wing, due to the angle that He.111 RD+NZ is flying in relation to the camera lens). Only the He.111A has a similar antenna configuration, but analysis shows that He.111 RD+NZ is a Junkers Jumo 211A-engined beast, whereas the He.111A was powered by very different-looking BMW VL6 liquid-cooled inline engines.

The Luftwaffe relegated the early-model He.111F bombers to become dual-control trainers when the mass-produced He.111H and He.111P variants entered service, so the vote is that what is seen here in "Foxhole In Cairo" is very rare footage of a Heinkel He.111F converted from a bomber into a trainer.

The remaining archive material then cuts to very graphic gun-camera footage of a Hawker Hurricane taking a fearful pounding from the fighter that is pursuing it right in its six-o-clock. Shells hammer into the Hurricane, which pitches up and begins to stall, causing the fighter inflicting the ferocious damage to close right in behind it. What looks like part of the cockpit canopy goes flying off, while the Hurricane's camouflage pattern and the big blue-red roundel atop its starboard wing come clearly into view. The camouflage markings stand out quite starkly in the imagery, in the way that a dark brown-and-sand brown colour scheme would do, suggesting that this could be a Hurricane used in the North African campaign that is taking the hits, or is possibly a Malta-based machine. Whichever, this shoot-down imagery of a Hawker Hurricane has not cropped up in any other war film known to the author, so again such footage is of considerable interest to the historian.

This is the last piece of aviation shown in the archive material that "Foxhole in Cairo" opens with, but one other piece of imagery appears later in the body of the film. This is imagery that has been seen before, but is no less fascinating for it being repeated. This is the same footage of a crashing twin-engined bomber that is used in "Reach For The Sky" (1956), with a crew member making a most dramatic last second escape by parachute before the bomber impacts the ground at an acute diving angle, exploding massively into flame. In the review of the previous film, the author originally identified the crashing bomber as a Junkers Ju.88, its wing-plan outline approximating very closely to that aircraft's design. However, the same imagery reproduced in "Foxhole in Cairo" is much more vivid, making the ill-fated bomber's outline stand out far more clearly. What is evident are two factors in its shape that rule out the possibility of it being a Junkers Ju.88.

Firstly, the nose stretches forward of the two engine nacelles. This does not feature in the Ju.88 design, no matter what the model; the nose length matches the same length as do the engine nacelles. Secondly, what shows in the sharper imagery in "Foxhole in Cairo", but which does not stand out in its appearance in "Reach For The Sky", is that the crashing bomber has a mid-upper gun turret - the Junkers Ju.88 did not have such a turret, again no matter what the model. It is from this gun turret that the desperate crew member is making his incredible escape.

The twin-engined bomber that is filmed plunging to earth with its port engine aflame is a Martin Maryland, a light bomber design that the RAF ordered from America under Lend-Lease. The Maryland could be considered to be in the same category as the Junkers Ju.88 and shares quite a few similarities in appearance and role with its German rival, although not nearly as effective a design, so previously mistaking it for a Ju.88 in this imagery is understandable. However, because the identical piece of imagery is reproduced much more clearly in this film, making a positive identification of the aircraft type is now a certainty.

Where this amazing piece of imagery was taken is anyone's guess, but the RAF operated the Martin Maryland as a reconnaissance bomber exclusively in the Mediterranean, the Middle East and in Cyrenaica (today, Libya). The terrain into which the bomber is crashing is mostly flat, featureless, dirt ground, with no foliage of any kind, so a North African/Middle Eastern location is a good possibility.

The air gunner who manages to get out of his turret no more than 200 feet above ground, fighting both the G-Forces and the onrushing air streaming over the steeply diving bomber, literally pulls the rip chord of his parachute as soon as he exits the stricken aircraft. His 'chute is still opening as he disappears out of shot in the top right hand corner of the screen, now no more than 100 feet above the ground. It is film of the most incredible low-level escape from a burning aeroplane that you can expect to see from any source.

CHAPTER 4

1961-1970

The Sixties was the decade of the epic in movies the world over: Roman, "The Fall of the Roman Empire" (1964); Medieval, "El Cid" (1961); Napoleonic, "War and Peace" (1965); Western, "Once Upon a Time in the West" (1968); and, of course, World War Two, "The Longest Day" (1962) and "Battle of Britain" (1969), to name just a few.

In a decade renowned for its permissiveness, its creativity in music, fashion and film, and its increasing challenges to the accepted norms and attitudes within society, it had become obvious that the War years were definitely in the past and a new generation was looking imaginatively and hopefully forward towards the future. Great Britain was putting the austerity of the post-War years behind it in a variety of new ways, with hugely successful rock bands, England winning the football World Cup in 1966, and leading the way with many highly praised and original film productions.

World War Two could now be enjoyed as a time of bold and daring adventure, never better expressed than in "The Guns of Navarone" (1961). German soldiers could be mown down or blown up wholesale, as in "Where Eagles Dare" (1968), with the comforting justification that they started it (the War), so they were asking for it. The portrayal of German officers could be more satisfyingly stereotypically arrogant, as actors like Anton Diffring and Wolfgang Preiss took full advantage of, even if privately they preferred kinder and more sensitive roles.

Black-and-white films were now becoming a minority, especially as the decade advanced. Of the 38 British war films covered in this Chapter, 13 were filmed in black-and-white, just about one third of the total. The War was fully in colour now.

For the British war film to succeed internationally, it was even more obligatory to have a major Hollywood film star in a leading role in the majority of these productions, whether appropriately so or not. Gregory Peck fitted neatly and naturally into "The Guns of Navarone" (1961) as a ruthless British Commando leader;

Kirk Douglas fitted like a square brick into a round pothole as a Norwegian atomic energy scientist in "The Heroes of Telemark" (1965). George Peppard had a knack as an American actor of playing German characters convincingly, as he does in "Operation Crossbow" (1965) - and even more so in the World War One epic, "The Blue Max" (1966) - but Clint Eastwood might as well have gone into action in the Bavarian Alps in "Where Eagles Dare" (1968) wearing his poncho from the Italian Westerns he made his name in, for all the effort he makes in trying to look and sound like an officer in the Waffen SS!

Entertainment was the key word for most British war films of the Sixties. They were directed at a new young audience that had not been born during the War itself, and so were willing to be more liberal with the realities. This meant that the studios could be more ambitious in the scale of the productions they were creating, and be marginally less sensitive when changing the facts. This allowed for an American to lead the mass break-out of PoWs in "The Great Escape" (1963), that most British of all Hollywood 'British' war films, and have him perform motorcycle stunts amid the Bavarian countryside.

The Sixties did produce the biggest challenges yet for both the British and American film industries when it came to using aircraft for World War Two war films. Making films in Technicolor and Panavision meant that archive footage could no longer be employed. Creative answers had to be found, resulting in Messerschmitt Bf.108s and North American Harvards increasingly being called upon to fill in as Luftwaffe fighters. There were still British World War Two aircraft that could be found, as the Mosquitos in "633 Squadron" (1964) and "Mosquito Squadron" (1969), a Lancaster in "Operation Crossbow" (1965) and, of course, the massing of Spitfires and Hurricanes for "Battle of Britain" (1969), attest. As the Sixties drew to a close, Hollywood was quick to 'Scramble' to join the aerial epics with huge productions like "Patton" (1970) and "Tora! Tora! Tora!" (1970). The decade ended with historic aviation on an all-time high on both sides of the Atlantic.

THE LONG, AND THE SHORT, AND THE TALL

(Released: February 1961)

This film version of the stage play, concerning disaffected British soldiers trapped in the Burmese jungle and surrounded by the Japanese, was produced entirely in the studio. Consequently, no aircraft feature in it.

THE GUNS OF NAVARONE

(Released: April 1961, Royal Premier)

If any war film made in any country has such a worldwide following as does "The Guns of Navarone", then please name it. For, without question, this is the classic war film of all time, with more repeats on television and re-runs in the cinema than any comparable production.

It has everything: genuinely believable characters at odds with each other while being faced by dangers that are virtually overwhelming, created both by humans and by Nature, as they struggle to achieve their almost impossible objective, the destruction of the mighty radar-controlled guns belching fire malevolently like monstrous dragons crouched in the mouth of their cave. Treachery, betrayal, courage, fear, cowardice, pain and love - all eight of the main characters in the plot, six male saboteurs and two female Resistance fighters, go through it all.

Let's make one thing clear: "The Guns of Navarone" is a British war film. Yes, it was backed by Hollywood's Columbia Pictures Corporation, who put up the bulk of the $6 million budget, the most expensive for a war film ever at the time (eclipsed only by 20th Century Fox's "The Longest Day", the following year). Yes, its producer and scriptwriter, Carl Foreman, was American, but Foreman had turned his back on Hollywood after becoming a victim of the investigation by the United States House of Representatives Committee on Un-American Activities into alleged Communist subversion within Hollywood, and had since devoted himself entirely to the British film industry which, in turn, had given him its total support.

Everything else about "Guns" was British, apart from its naturalised American, Russian-born theme music composer, Dimitri Tiompkin, and its Greek location, the island of Rhodes. Its premier was a Royal one, in front of HM The Queen and HRH The Duke of Edinburgh in April 1961. Its English director, J Lee Thompson, got the job (after the original director had been fired by Foreman for not being up to it) because he could handle both sensitive personal scenes, as in "Tiger Bay" (1959), and large-scale action scenes, such as those he directed in "North West Frontier" (also 1959). The special forces operation against the guns on Navarone was mounted by British Commandos (played by David Niven, Anthony Quayle and Stanley Baker), along with two Greek nationals (acted by Anthony Quinn and James Darren).

Hang on, the lead star is famous American Hollywood actor, Gregory Peck, acting the role of Captain Keith Mallory who takes over the leadership of the Commandos when Quayle's Major Franklin is crippled in a cliff fall. In fact, the nationality of Mallory's character is never revealed, but at the beginning of the film he clearly is working undercover in Nazi Occupied Crete for British Naval Intelligence. In Alastair MacLean's novel, on which the film is based, Mallory is a New Zealander. He could, therefore, be a Commonwealth officer and, in being played by American Gregory Peck, could be assumed to be Canadian. We are told he can speak Greek like a Greek, and German like a German; how, we are not told.

In effect, Mallory is British, but played by a leading American actor who wisely tries not to affect a British accent (Peck did affect a German accent in "The Boys from Brazil" (1978), portraying the escaped Nazi doctor, Josef Mengele, in South America, and suffered as a result). Actually, Peck was a great favourite with British cinema audiences because he often played heroic yet sensitive and honourable characters similar to British gentleman-types, and was often thought of as an 'honorary Englishman'. Peck did, in fact, play a British SOE agent in "The Sea Wolves" (1980), alongside, and due to the insistence of, friend and fellow actor David Niven. So, he fits naturally into the role of Mallory.

Aviation plays its part in "The Guns of Navarone", and in some unusual ways. Even before the film credits roll, a tribute appears on the screen to the Greek government, the Royal Hellenic Army, Navy and Air Force, and especially to the Greek people, "for their unstinting aid, co-operation, hospitality and friendship throughout those aspects of the production in Greece". The Greek Royal Family were still on the Hellenic throne when "Guns" was in production on Rhodes during 1960, and actually visited the film set on one occasion. The air force was the then Royal Hellenic Air Force (the King was overthrown by a military junta in 1967, allegedly backed by the CIA, and went into exile in London; the Royal Family has never returned to Greece).

The tribute also thanks the Admiralty and the War Office "for their most generous advice and assistance". For the historian, it may be of interest to note that the War Office was still in situ, 15 years after the end of World War Two. Its functions were combined with the Admiralty and the Air Ministry in 1964, to create the Ministry of Defence.

The film then leads into a prologue, narrated by the actor James Robertson Justice who plays Commodore Jensen, Mallory's boss, in the plot. The prologue explains that close to the island of Navarone is the island of Kyros (both fictional Greek islands), on which 2,000 British soldiers are marooned. In Berlin, the Axis High Command has determined on a show of strength in the Aegean Sea, to bully neutral Turkey into coming into the War on their side. The scene of the Axis demonstration was to be Kyros, only a few miles off the coast of Turkey.

An inset over the main image of Greek countryside and ruined temples shows archive footage to illustrate what the prologue is describing. This includes footage of a number of aircraft. First to be seen is the turning propeller of the starboard engine of a Vickers

Wellington. Next, a close-up of another Vickers Wellington moving off its chocks. This is followed by a Short Stirling taking off with gear still hanging. Immediately following it is footage of a pair of Armstrong Whitworth Whitleys over-flying an airfield at low-level. Then a sole Short Stirling is filmed as it performs a fly-past over a densely packed row of 13 Douglas DB-7 Boston III day bombers, the closest to the camera clearly bearing the code letter 'R'. Finally, an air-air shot of seven Bristol Beauforts in two flights brings the prologue to a close and leads into the film credits with its famous theme tune.

Immediately after the credits and theme music end, the film cuts to a night-time image of the sky with the following words imposed on it: "The first day 02.00 Hours. An Allied Airfield somewhere in the Middle East". Smoking in towards the camera is the black silhouetted shape of an Avro Lancaster bomber, with its port inner engine on fire. It is popularly held by many aviation enthusiasts and film fans that this is Avro Lancaster B.I PA474, making its first film appearance and acting the role of a stricken RAF Middle East Air Force bomber. They are correct, but only in part.

In 1960, Lancaster B.I PA474 was being operated by the College of Aeronautics (today, Cranfield University) at the former air station of RAF Cranfield in Bedfordshire. Its principal task was to operate as a flying test bed for the laminar flow wing design produced by the Handley Page aircraft manufacturing company: the wings were mounted vertically above the rear fuselage. It was loaned to Highroad Productions to portray a Lancaster in "The Guns of Navarone" returning from a failed raid on the guns' fortifications, with flames and smoke streaming from one engine. It was not asked to perform the crash landing which follows.

However, although PA474 was flown and filmed for the production, it was found that the effect director Thompson was looking to 2nd Unit assistant director Peter Yates to achieve, could not be safely or convincingly realised. An alternative way had to be found, which meant using a studio miniature Lancaster. This is what we are seeing in this opening shot of the main film. But, in effect it is Lancaster PA474 we are looking at, because the real Lancaster was used as the pattern for Highroad Productions' art department team to measure for the accurate creation of the Lancaster miniature that appears on screen.

The Special Effect was achieved by having the Lancaster miniature filmed in studio lighting, then the imagery was darkened in the editing process to create the effect of the scene happening at night. This helped to disguise the miniature Lancaster as it is 'flown' down guidance wires towards the camera (the placement of the camera in relation to the miniature confirms it cannot be a real Lancaster in shot), with flames and black smoke pouring from the port inner engine (it was the difficulty in being able to replicate an actual engine on fire that made the use of PA474 unrealistic, as the effect on screen would obviously be seen to be fake, while trying to make it look as if PA474 was really on fire would have put the aircraft at risk).

A second shot shows another angle of the miniature Lancaster heading towards the ground, leaving a long, thick trail of smoke behind it. Then the Lancaster ploughs nose first into the desert runway, rearing up with the propellers digging into the dirt. The actual crash is realistically and convincingly achieved; what spoils the effect is the suspended, motionless Lancaster hanging in the sky in the background. What induced the art department SFX team to put it there is anyone's guess. However, the author can attest that when he saw "The Guns of Navarone" for the first time as an 11-year-old sprog, he did not spot the 'hanging' Lancaster at all; his whole attention was fixed on the crashing Lancaster. Nor did he spot it when he saw several repeats of "Guns", both in the cinema and on TV, until much more recently when he acquired a video tape copy of the film. So, by the standards of 1961, the effect of the crashing Lancaster was not spoilt by the 'hanging' Lancaster.

Unfortunately, the restoration of "The Guns of Navarone" in 2002 from the original damaged film and its transfer to DVD has resulted in this and other night-time scenes being reproduced on screen as much darker than they were shown when "Guns" was first released to the cinema and later broadcast on television. As a result, even on a high quality TV screen, the Lancaster is almost unseeable against the very dark blue sky background, while the crash-landing is lost against the black surface of the airfield. The imagery is slightly more visible on a laptop screen.

In using a Lancaster in the opening scene, Thompson and Yates have avoided historical accuracy, presumably because to use the correct RAF bomber type for this sequence (the Consolidated B-24 Liberator III of No.178 Liberator Squadron, operating out of Egypt) was either not possible or it was thought it would not resonate with the cinema audience as much as would a Lancaster. The Avro Lancaster was not operated in either the Middle East or the Mediterranean theaters of war.

The first real aircraft to appear in "The Guns of Navarone" is a Consolidated PBY-5 Catalina, acting the role of an RAF Catalina I which is carrying the team of saboteurs on the next stage of their mission from Alexandria in Egypt to Castelrosso, an island port close to the Turkish border in the Dodecanese. Castelrosso was occupied by the Italians in 1941 but came under Allied control after Italy surrendered to the Allies on 8th September 1943. As Castelrosso is shown in "Guns" as having a British garrison in place, it must be that the action in the film's plot is taking place in late 1943.

The Catalina used in "Guns" is a real problem aircraft in the identification stakes. From close examination using freeze-frame analysis it appears to be a Royal Hellenic Air Force Catalina. Indeed, the author always assumed it was, as it bears what appears to be a Greek national blue-white roundel on its port rear fuselage, although the two horizontal blue stripes atop the tail fin do not look like a military fin flash. However, careful analysis of the imagery shows that the roundel is a fake RAF red-white-blue roundel.

The amphibian is painted white overall except for the engine cowlings, which appear to be light grey. Beneath the wing mounting and just aft of the main undercarriage wheel housing is a large code letter, 'Z'. There is a large, four-digit number on the Catalina's rear fuselage at the base of the tail fin. Regrettably, the number is not easy to read due to the quality of the image and the movement of the aircraft past the camera, but a best guess is that the number looks like '5583'. The Royal Hellenic Air Force of the period (1960) normally maintained the US military serials of its aircraft, as most of the reconstructed air force in Greece from 1949 onwards had been built up with American-supplied equipment under the US Military Aid Program. The serial number of the Catalina could be the 'final four' of a US military serial, if it were not for one basic fact: the Consolidated PBY Catalina never served with the Royal Hellenic Air Force, nor with the Royal Hellenic Naval Aviation.

So, where does this Catalina come from and who operated it when it was used in "Guns"? Research has not thrown up any one candidate. Indeed, the editor of The Catalina Society's newspaper himself posted a query on the Web some years ago as to its identity, and appears to have got nothing in return.

There are a couple of noteworthy features about this Catalina which offer some differences between it and most Catalinas that were operated worldwide during and after World War Two, including those that have since been preserved. Firstly, this Catalina has an antenna housing fitted atop its cockpit cabin. Not many Catalina variants carried such an antenna, and those that did were often used in surveillance or long-range maritime patrol roles. It is possible this Catalina's antenna housed a more sophisticated form of weather radar or navigational system, but for whose benefit seems destined to remain unknown. The second noteworthy feature is the layout of two cabin windows in the forward fuselage between the cockpit and the wing mounting, one small, one large: this is an unusual layout, as most Catalinas had one small cabin window in the same position and a second in the central fuselage area beneath the wing and aft of the main undercarriage wheel housing. Careful research has not thrown up any version of a Catalina with the same cabin window layout as the Catalina in "Guns"; it is suggestive of a large forward cabin with bigger windows for its occupants to look out of.

The best guess is that the Catalina in "Guns" is a civil, customised variant because of the specialised wide vision layout of the passenger cabin windows. It may be a luxury, privately owned amphibian that was loaned for the film, with RAF roundel plus fake serial number and code letter applied. Its identification and source remains unknown.

The next aircraft to appear in "Guns" is a Piper L-21B Cub observation and liaison aircraft of the Royal Hellenic Army Aviation, acting the role of a Luftwaffe Henschel Hs.126 (actually, the Royal Hellenic Air Force did operate the Hs.126 before Greece was invaded firstly by Italy, then Germany, in World War Two). "Guns" is representative of British war films that now had to rely on glaringly obvious substitute aircraft to portray German Luftwaffe types. Piper Cubs appear in a number of war films deputising for Luftwaffe spotter aircraft, in this case an Hs.126, not a Fieseler Storch, because the Hellenic Army Cub is flying too fast to replicate a Storch, while Luftwaffe Hs.126s were widely used in Greece and the Balkans.

The Piper Cub is first seen over-flying the run-down Greek caique fishing boat that the saboteurs are using to reach Navarone, then later searching for the Commandos and Resistance fighters on the island. From what can be discerned by freeze-frame analysis is that the Greek military roundels have been removed from the Piper Cub, but no Luftwaffe crosses have been applied in their place.

The Piper Cub/Henschel Hs.126 directs the attack on the Commandos and Resistance fighters by two Junkers Ju.87 Stuka dive bombers, although as shown in the film the Stukas don't actually dive onto Gregory Peck and his team - they fly through and over the ravine the British and the Greeks are taking cover in, bombing and strafing them.

Actually, three different methods are used to create the effect of the Stukas' attack: SFX art work, studio miniatures and real aircraft. What happens is that, as the six men and two women make their way through the ravine towards a cave where they can shelter from the dive bombers, the two Stukas first drop bombs on them, which thankfully all miss, then return and strafe them with cannon fire just as they finally get into the cave. No one is hurt except for one of the Greek women, who appears to have a limp and is lagging behind.

Having Stukas appear in a film when not a single Ju.87 was in flying condition in 1960, let alone was preserved anywhere (the Air Historical Branch's example was one of two rare exceptions in the world), posed a real challenge for the Highroad Productions Special Effects team. To understand how they achieved the Stukas' attack, it is necessary to study each frame in which the Ju.87s appear.

The first frame shows the two Stukas flying separately one behind the other in a straight line across the screen, each aircraft slightly banked to port, above a hillside range. Beyond, in the distance, can be seen the 'Hs.126' (Piper Cub) flying away, leaving the sky free for the Stukas to operate in. Or, it seems it must be the Piper Cub portraying the Hs.126; in fact, it is a helicopter, a Sikorsky UH-19D Chickasaw of the Royal Hellenic Air Force, which had been acting in a support and logistics role for the Royal Hellenic Army armoured units that were appearing as German light Panzer in this scene (the UH-19D was the US military designation for the Sikorsky S.55, or the Westland Whirlwind built under licence in the UK).

The two Stukas appear convincing, seen from a distance. The problem is, they are flying in too straight a line one behind the other: unrealistic for real aircraft manoeuvring aggressively at low-level. They are studio miniature Stukas being pulled along guidance wires, filmed at either Shepperton or Elstree Studios, then merged into the skyscape on the frame showing the Chickasaw flying away beyond the hills.

The second frame to show the Stukas is a continuation of the first, with the Chickasaw still in the distance, but the lead Stuka has now turned head-on towards us and is diving down in a curve to attack; the second is continuing its straight and level approach behind. The movement of the lead Stuka is unrealistic for an actual diving turn as depicted here; it is an art work SFX two-dimensional miniature superimposed onto the main picture - the second Stuka is in genuine motion, as its blurred image attests, moving along its guidance wire.

Actors Anthony Quinn, Irene Papas and Gregory Peck stop to look back at the Stukas approaching. From their perspective, we see the two Stukas heading directly towards us, flying into the ravine. The imagery has significantly changed, however: the rough terrain is different from that in the previous frames that showed the studio miniature Stukas superimposed onto them. There is also something different about the Stukas themselves: they do not have the steeply cranked wing shape of the Ju.87 design that the miniatures portrayed; instead they have a slightly downward bend of the wing brace adjoining the fuselage, while their wings themselves issue outward in a straight line. They appear to have fixed undercarriage a la Stuka, but yet they are noticeably different in shape from the Ju.87 design (at least, in freeze-frame analysis they can be seen to be different, but to a cinema audience in the Sixties there would have been no time to spot the difference).

They are, in fact, real aircraft. They are two North American T-6G Texan trainers of the Royal Hellenic Air Force deputising as Ju.87 Stukas! They are filmed approaching head-on from a distance, flying with their undercarriage down, and for the brief appearance they make they offer a superficially similar frontal likeness to the feared Luftwaffe dive bomber.

The next frame depicting a Stuka is vastly different. It shows the lead Stuka heading in fast in a weaving attack manoeuvre - far too fast to be realistic. This is art work of one of the studio miniatures superimposed onto the screen image, and even at the time of the first release of "The Guns of Navarone" in 1961 it was plainly obvious to the cinema audience that this was fake imagery. Bombs are seen falling and explosions erupt around the saboteurs and their Greek comrades.

The second Stuka now comes into the attack. It is seen from the same angle as that of the two T-6G Texans; in fact, it is one of the T-6Gs, but the film speed has been significantly increased to create the effect of a Stuka coming in fast. Too fast, actually; the film speed has been over-egged by the editor, making the effect unrealistic. The editor has also tried to make it look as if the T-6G is diving in Stuka-like fashion. To achieve this, he has moved the T-6G image in stop-motion fashion, dropping it slightly in a diagonal line on each stop and re-positioning it in each successive take of it. The result is that the T-6G appears to be dropping in a steep slant, while the aircraft itself is still flying at a flat angle of attack head-on towards the camera, so the achieved effect just looks wrong.

Stanley Baker drops the suitcase containing the team's radio. He turns to go back to collect it but sees the second Stuka coming in. A head-on shot of a T-6G Texan is again used, this time not speeded up to such an exaggerated extent. There is no mistaking the frontal shape of the T-6, whose wing design did have a very slightly cranked shape.

Another art work effect of a miniature Stuka flying in to attack appears next, again all too obvious a fake due to the over-exaggerated speed at which the aircraft is shown to be manoeuvring. A different shot shows the Stuka flying away; this, in fact, is a shot of one of the T-6G Texans that has been reversed - the ravine is the opposite way round, while the film itself is being run backwards, to create the effect of the aircraft climbing away. It is actually the same shot of the T-6G we saw before Stanley Baker takes cover, that was made to appear in stop-motion as if it is diving, but the picture itself here is turned round and the 'diving' T-6G is being played backwards, so that the 'Stuka' is 'flying' upwards, not down! If you understand that, you will realise that the entire effect has been created in the film editing suite, using a single piece of footage

of one T-6G Texan flying in a straight line towards the camera but manipulated in different ways by the editor on successive frames.

Another shot from the same reversed angle shows one Stuka diving towards the ravine while the other is flying away along the escarpment line. This is a continuation of the two studio miniatures seen at the start of the attack, with the lead Stuka diving in (down its guidance wire) while the second passes along in a straight line beyond it. The imagery has then been merged onto the picture frame of the ravine: both the merged imagery of the Stukas and that of the ravine have been reversed.

Gregory Peck turns to look behind him as his team get into the cave. He sees one of the Stukas flying towards him and hears cannon fire. A shot of one of the T-6G Texans filmed from a distance is used here, then merged art work imagery of a miniature Stuka diving in and firing cannon appears with a Texan in the distance behind it - the only shot in which a miniature Stuka and a Texan acting as a Stuka appear together in the same frame. Another art work shot of a miniature Stuka, totally unrealistically swooping into the ravine like a cartoon dive bomber while firing its cannon, finally closes this scene and with it the final act of aviation in "The Guns of Navarone".

Interestingly, a genuine Junkers Ju.87D-3 Stuka shot down by a USAAF P-38 Lightning on 9th October 1943 was salvaged from the sea half a mile off the coast of Rhodes on 5th October 2006, and is now in the Hellenic Air Force Museum at Dekeleia Air Base.

VERY IMPORTANT PERSON

(Released: April 1961)

An engaging take on the popular PoW theme of the time has James Robertson Justice as a cantankerous and overbearing military scientist who gets sucked out of a damaged RAF bomber while testing a top secret apparatus over Germany, and ends up in a PoW camp. James Robertson Justice had made an authoritative appearance in "The Guns of Navarone" during the same month as the release of "Very Important Person". His performance as the scientist, Sir Ernest Pease, echoed his role as the equally overbearing surgeon, Sir Lancelot Spratt, in the much-loved "Doctor" series of comedy films of the Fifties and Sixties.

Aviation has a short but significant part to play in "Very Important Person", when the disagreeable Sir Ernest proves the law of gravity by disappearing out through the flak shell hole in the fuselage side of the RAF bomber. To portray the bomber taking off at night, flying in German airspace and taking the flak hit, out-takes of the Vickers Wellington Ic of No.XV Squadron in the role of 'B - Bertie' in "One of our Aircraft is Missing" (1942) are used.

As an aside, the uncredited actor playing the part of the Vickers Wellington pilot in this film is Vincent Ball, the same actor who plays the part of the British Junkers Ju.52 pilot in "Where Eagles Dare" (1968).

TARNISHED HEROES

(Released: May 1961)

This lowest of low budget British war films from the Danziger Brothers' B-Movie production line in the Fifties and the Sixties has a simple storyline: a British Army Major leads a team of misfit soldiers - deserters, thieves, drunkards - on a suicide mission behind enemy lines. Sounds familiar? "Tarnished Heroes" pre-dated "The Dirty Dozen" (1967) by six years, but there is no source that suggests the famous Hollywood movie was influenced in any way by this British 75 minute-long support feature to a pretty indifferent comedy film released at the same time. One thing is for certain, the rudimentary budget did not allow for any aircraft to appear in it.

THE PASSWORD IS COURAGE

(Released: 1962)

Yet another PoW war film, and one which attracted controversy because, in making the claim that it is based on fact, it stages the same mass escape as used in "The Great Escape" (1963), which was in production at the same time. It is known for a fact that the lead character in the film, played by Dirk Bogarde, was a real PoW during the War but was not part of the "Great Escape" from Stalag Luft III. As the film uses real events, but not those involving the same real PoW, suspicion falls on "The Password is Courage" for exploiting a famous escape that was going to form the plot of a major Hollywood film due for release at almost the same time. Aviation is not involved.

THE SILENT INVASION

(Released: January 1962)

Another Danziger Brothers' B-Movie studio-based production, about the French Resistance in 1940. No aircraft are featured.

THE VALIANT

(Released: January 1962)

An Italian-British co-production, "The Valiant" portrays the attack by Italian Navy 'Human Torpedoes' on the battleship HMS Valiant and her sister ship, HMS Queen Elizabeth, as they were moored in Alexandria Harbour during December 1941 (this attack was also depicted in "The Silent Enemy", 1958). Both battleships were mined but the Valiant was damaged, not sunk, and repaid the debt to the Italians in 1943 by providing covering fire for the invasions of Sicily and Salerno.

The only part aviation plays in the film is towards the end when the Royal Navy helped to deceive the Italians into believing the Valiant had not been badly damaged because the ship remained visible above water. The Regia Aeronautica sent a photo reconnaissance aircraft which was allowed to fly unopposed over Alexandria and photograph the battleship. This is depicted in the film by the use of rather poor quality archive footage of a Luftwaffe Junkers Ju.88.

The irrepressible, or the inevitable, John Mills plays the lead role of the Captain of HMS Valiant. Ironically, Mills had played exactly the reverse role of the leader of British mini X-Craft submarines which mined the German battleship Tirpitz, in "Above Us The Waves" (1955).

THE LONGEST DAY

(Released: September 1962, France, and October 1962, USA and UK) Hollywood 'British' war film

"The Longest Day" is unquestionably a massive Hollywood epic and, until the release of "Schindler's List" (1995), was the most expensive black-and-white feature film ever made ($10 million USD). But it is also a very international film, with large parts of it filmed and directed by directors and crews of the same nationalities represented in this re-enactment of D-Day 6th June 1944: an American director filmed the American military scenes, a German director filmed the German-speaking scenes, while Englishman Ken Annakin handled both the British and French battle scenes. Because producer Darryl F Zanuck wanted to give fair and accurate representations of the roles employed by the principal nations involved on both sides in D-Day (he took a bit of flak, though, for excluding the Canadians), it would be justifiable in describing Annakin's contribution as "the British part", with the Americans and the Germans having their "parts". The French were incorporated mostly into "the British part", which was fair enough as the Free French Forces operated under British command on D-Day itself.

In fact, Annakin directed more than one third of the production and, what is significant for the purposes of this book, "the British part" contains all, bar a couple of scenes, the major elements of aviation in the film.

"Surprisingly, not a single Spitfire could be found in the British Isles", claims Richard Oulahan Jr, in his Online article on the making of "The Longest Day", entitled "The Longest Headache". That's an extraordinary claim to make, and completely out of kilter with the facts. There were five airworthy Spitfires in Britain in 1961, when "The Longest Day" was in production, of which four were operational: the ex-THUM Flight Spitfire PR.XIX PM631, operated by the RAF Battle of Britain Flight at Martlesham Heath; the Rolls Royce Derby-owned Spitfire F.XIV G-ALGT/RM689, then kept at Hucknall Aerodrome; Vickers-Armstrong Weybridge's Spitfire Mk.Vb G-AISU/AB910; and Captain John Fairey's two-seat Spitfire T.8 G-AIDN, which lived at Staverton

Airport. Air Commodore Allen Wheeler owned Spitfire Mk.Ia G-AIST/AR213 that he kept stored at Booker and which could have been made airworthy, although at the time it had been taken off the British civil register.

Two out of the five would have been contemporary Marques for the D-Day period, comprising the PR.XIX and the F.XIV, both of them Rolls Royce Griffon-engined Spitfires. However, the PR.XIX was an unarmed photo-reconnaissance Spitfire, which would have reduced its effectiveness for a role as a ground-attack aircraft in the film, although whether the audience in general would have known or cared is debatable. It certainly could have been made to look the part, especially as PR Spitfires of the period had been operational over Normandy. The F.XIV was an out-and-out fighter, but could also have made a good stand-in. The Mk.Ia and the Mk.Vb, however, would have been unrepresentative of 6th June 1944, as these Marques had long been withdrawn from front-line use by the RAF well before D-Day. The two-seater Spitfire T.8 would have been a non-starter.

Whoever was advising Zanuck about where to find Spitfires seems to have had a complete blind spot concerning these five well known Spitfires on the British aviation scene at the time; or, was there another explanation as to why Zanuck was possibly kept in the dark about them. As it is, Zanuck was offered the use of a number of exactly the correct type and Marque of Spitfire that operated over the Normandy beachhead, so perhaps the question of using British-based Spitfires that were not properly representative is immaterial. We'll look at these particular Spitfires when we come to the scene where they appear in the film.

"The Longest Day" is loaded with cameo roles by a large number of the most famous American, British, French and German actors of the early Sixties. Among them, Richard Burton plays 'Flight Officer David Campbell', according to the caption that introduces him to us (spot the probably not deliberate mistake - it should be Flying Officer, not Flight Officer), an RAF fighter pilot who becomes the last surviving member of his squadron who fought in the Battle of Britain.

"I think what always worries me about being one 'The Few', is the way we keep on getting…fewer", Campbell tells a squadron pal played by stalwart World War Two actor, Donald Houston (a real wartime serving RAF officer), about their other Battle of Britain pal, 'Johnnie', who has been shot down by flak over Calais the day before D-Day. "Now, if the big show starts tonight, he won't be in it", protests Houston's character in a creakingly cliched scene of an RAF fighter pilots' Mess. To add to the unfairness of it all, 'Johnnie' - presumably the American scriptwriters thought most British fighter pilots were called 'Johnnie' - died with Houston's boots on, not his own. At least Annakin was able to work in a neat little 'McGuffin' in what is meant to be a hackneyed scene reminiscent of all British war films about RAF fighter pilot 'types', by having a squadron member tinkling with the piano keys softly playing the film's theme tune.

The first scene in "The Longest Day" to show aircraft is that in which Luftwaffe Oberstleutnant (Lieutenant Colonel) Josef 'Pips' Priller calls his superior, General Wolfgang Hager, at the Hauptquartier (Headquarters), Luftwaffen Kommando West, in Paris, to protest at the withdrawal of all but two of his fighters from the front line. Both the film and the book versions of "The Longest Day" made the German fighter ace, 'Pips' Priller, a well known name to an international audience. Played by German actor Heinz Reincke, Priller is seen expressing the contempt he was notorious for displaying on occasions towards his senior officers, as he berates General Hager over the telephone for depleting his Geschwader when the risk of the Allies invading is high.

"Why wasn't he court-martialled?", asks Hager's adjutant, as he hands the phone to the General.

"He shot down 132 planes", answers Hager.

That is incorrect, Priller's confirmed total between May 1940 - October 1944 was 101 aerial victories, of which 68 were Spitfires, the highest number of 'kills' scored against the RAF's most famous fighter 'plane of World War Two by any Luftwaffe pilot.

"You were a rotten pilot when we flew in Russia", rants Priller at Hager. "You're flying a desk now, but you're still a rotten pilot!". Again factually incorrect, Priller never served in Russia, his wartime career following the fall of France was almost entirely conducted from captured airfields close to the Channel coast, mostly with Jagdgeschwader 26 Schlageter, of which he became GeschwaderKommodore in January 1943. Considering that the real 'Pips' Priller was one of the many military advisers from both sides on D-Day available to Zanuck and his scriptwriters, it is difficult to understand how these errors of fact got into the screenplay. By a strange twist of fate, 'Pips' Priller died of a sudden heart attack at the age of 45 in May 1961 while "The Longest Day" was in production.

"I'm squatting here on this God-forsaken airfield with only two planes, two stinking crates!", shouts Priller down the phone, watched by his long-time wingman, Heinz Wodarczyk. The "God-forsaken airfield" was Rambouillet, Normandy, in June 1944, although its name is not mentioned in the film. The "two stinking crates" were Focke Wulf FW.190A-8s of JG.26, of which Priller's personal aircraft carried the number 'Black 13'. It was in this FW.190A-8 that Priller claimed his 100th aerial victory (a USAAF B-24 Liberator) on 18th July 1944. It is almost certain the real 'Pips' Priller did not think of 'Black 13' as "a stinking crate".

Obviously, no Focke Wulf FW.190 existed in flying condition in 1961, so Zanuck had to find a suitable alternative. Thanks to British war films like "633 Squadron" (1964) and "Mosquito Squadron" (1969), we are to become familiar in the Sixties with the appearance of Messerschmitt Bf.108 Taifuns acting the roles of Messerschmitt Bf.109s. But, as we now know, by 1961 this had only been done once before in a war film, that being the use of Prince Bernhard of the Netherlands's former Messerschmitt Bf.108D-1 posing as a Messerschmitt Bf.109 in "Operation Amsterdam" (1959). Perhaps Zanuck had seen this film and decided that using Messerschmitt Bf.108s would make suitable substitutes for Bf.109s, or someone tipped him off about the idea. Whichever, France had no shortage of Bf.108 Taifun look-alikes available in the shape of the French-built Nord 1000 Pinguoin series of military liaison aircraft. In fact, La Marine Nationale were in the process of disposing of their fleet of Nord 1002 Pinguoin IIs onto the French civil market in 1961 and aircraft dealer, Alexandre Renault, had made a bid for more than a dozen of them, which he based at the airfield of Mureaux where SNCAN manufactured the Bf.108 during the Occupation and the Nord 1000 series post-War.

Almost certainly it was Alexandre Renault who was the original owner of the two retired French military Nord 1002 Pinguoin II aircraft that appear in "The Longest Day", painted in Luftwaffe camouflage and markings to give them the appearance of being Messerschmitt Bf.108s impersonating Messerschmitt Bf.109s.

It seems we get our first view of them when 'Pips' Priller walks to the window of his crewroom as he continues to argue over the phone with General Hager and looks out at two Luftwaffe fighters parked on the grass outside. We only see the fighters in this scene as back drop set-dressing, but later we see them clearly as Priller and Wodarczyk fly low, strafing British troops on the Normandy beachhead. To all appearances they are the same two aircraft, but in fact they are not: the two 'Messerschmitts' seen through the window beyond Priller are two entirely different Bf.108s than the two examples seen acting as Messerschmitt Bf.109s strafing the 'Tommies'. The paint schemes of the parked fighters do not match those of the two other 'Bf.108s/Bf.109s' seen later, there being noticeable differences between their respective camouflage patterns.

Moreover, there is a distinct feature of the two Pinguoin IIs we are looking at in the Priller - v - Hager scene which is unusual: they both have three-bladed propellers. What's unusual about that? Only that the Messerschmitt Bf.108/Nord 1000 design series all flew with twin-bladed props.

There are two possible explanations for this discrepancy. Firstly, that the art department came to the conclusion that the Nord 1002's two-bladed propeller configuration did not create a fighter-like image. So, they removed the two propeller blades and attached three for effect. Perfectly feasible.

However, it has to be recognised that the airfield scene with the two parked Messerschmitts viewed through the window behind actor Reincke is a matte image combined with the Priller studio scene in the foreground. Very often in this pre-CGI age of cinema matte backgrounds were painted on canvas, then merged as a backcloth with the foreground studio scene. So a second possible explanation is that the two Luftwaffe Messerschmitt fighters are painted images on a painted airfield, filmed as a backcloth to the scene with 'Pips' Priller.

But there is an argument against the matte backcloth airfield being a painting. It is seen in two shots behind Priller, one showing the two Messerschmitts, then another from a slightly changed angle in which two hangars can be seen through the window over Priller's shoulder. Freeze-frame study shows that this is definitely a black-and-white photograph, not a painting, of a wet and muddy airfield. Quite likely it is Mureaux, where Renault kept his collection of Nord 1002 Pinguoins.

Could they be full-scale facsimiles, or studio miniatures photographed and cut into the matte airfield image? The former seems an unnecessary waste of effort and expense if there were real aircraft available; the latter is a possibility. Three-bladed propellers could be added to the miniatures to give them a more fighter-

like appearance. But again, if miniatures were used, why not of Messerschmitt Bf.109s? Continuity with the Nord 1002/Bf.108 design has to be the reason why.

The shot of Priller shouting into the telephone with the two 'Messerschmitts' parked on the airfield outside the window behind him provides the answer to the mystery they create. It shows that the scene is a combination of matte airfield background photograph with two miniature 'Messerschmitts' modelled up against it, then merged with Priller in the foreground. The giveaway that the fighters are miniatures is that, under the studio lights, their three-bladed propellers cast shadows of themselves onto the background matte photograph of the airfield. The audience would not have noticed this at all because the shadows are so faint, but freeze-frame analysis confirms they are there. So, photograph an airfield, make two model miniature Messerschmitts and place them in position in front of a blow-up of the airfield picture, then matte the image onto the window behind Priller. There, you have your scene of Priller stranded on the airfield at Rambouillet, with the only two fighters he can call upon to attack the invasion visible outside the window as he makes his protest to his Commanding Officer.

A curious and noticeable feature of "The Longest Day" is Zanuck's decision to have the airborne part of the invasion carried out exclusively by British aircraft. In actual fact, Zanuck is in error in having the 82nd and the 101st Airborne Divisions para-drop from RAF aircraft - American Paratroopers dropped only from USAAF C-47 Skytrains. Also, Zanuck uses studio miniature Lancaster bombers as the para-dropping aircraft, a role that the Lancaster neither could nor did perform. Again, it is a mystery as to why Zanuck took this option, compounded by the miniature Lancasters looking very much like the models they are.

Zanuck had gone 'European' when he made "The Longest Day". He and the studio bosses at 20th Century Fox were not exactly on good terms in 1961 when the film was in production, largely because of the massive budgetary and time schedule over runs afflicting the studio's greatest project in cinema history, the epic "Cleopatra", being filmed in Italy and starring Elizabeth Taylor in the title role and Richard Burton as Mark Anthony. "Cleopatra" nearly broke 20th Century Fox; "The Longest Day" saved it. Zanuck had emigrated to Europe to avoid the continuing flak he was getting from the heads of 20th Century Fox and had virtually given up on being an American. He had become a close friend of Lord Louis Mountbatten, who gave a lot of assistance to "The Longest Day", and liked to swear like an Englishman, using the expression "bloody" a lot. Zanuck made sure his French girlfriend, Erina Demich, got a leading role in the film as a heroine of the French Resistance. This 'Europeanisation' of Zanuck may explain why he opted for only British aircraft in the Paratroop and glider assault scenes.

The scene involving the attack by a glider-borne unit of the British 6th Airborne Division on the Orne River Bridge is very effectively and realistically created with the use of studio miniatures and a full-scale facsimile of an Airspeed Horsa troop glider. Zanuck apparently contracted a furniture-making firm in England to build two full-scale Horsas, which was achieved with such a degree of accuracy that they could be said to be the real thing. They didn't actually fly, however.

Both Horsas appear in several different scenes throughout the film. One of them first appears when John Wayne, as Lieutenant Colonel Benjamin Vandevoort, addresses his troops of the 82nd Airborne in a hangar with a Horsa in the background. It is accurately painted in RAF markings and camouflage with D-Day stripes. For some reason, the nose has been completely detached. Again, though, this scene is inaccurate, as US troops that landed in Normandy by glider did so either in USAAF Horsas acquired under Reverse Lend-Lease or in Waco GC-4A Hadrian assault gliders,

In the Orne River Bridge assault scene, one of the Horsas is dragged by unseen ropes through barbed wire fencing and shrubs to create the effect of the assault glider landing. The same shot was used three times in succession and speeded up by the film editor. The battle scene itself was actually filmed at the Caen Canal Bridge that was stormed and seized at the same time as the Orne River Bridge, today known as Pegasus Bridge in honour of the Pegasus Horse badge worn by the British Airborne forces and now the site of a museum dedicated to the first part of France to be Liberated in World War Two.

Both Horsa facsimiles can be seen in the background to the scene involving US Paratroopers meeting up outside the strategically important town of Ste Mare Eglise.

The 'Omaha' Beach scenes were filmed on Corsica, using ships of the United States Navy's Sixth Fleet that were supporting an amphibious exercise on the French island colony, to portray part of the massive Allied armada crossing the English Channel. Seen twice over-flying some of the Sixth Fleet's warships, and darkened in the editing to create the impression of the armada sailing at night, is a four-ship of Douglas AD-4 Skyraiders flying in 'Finger-Four' formation. Their appearance is an attempt to create the effect of American warplanes flying toward Normandy to attack targets ahead of the beach landings. The Skyraider might look the part, but it came into United States Navy service one year after World War Two ended. The four seen in "The Longest Day" could be from the US Navy aircraft carrier attached to the Sixth Fleet (which had to be kept out of shot because aircraft carriers were not used in the D-Day invasion), or from the French Air Force which also operated the AD-4 Skyraider. All four carry drop tanks under the wings. Operationally, it would have been easier for Zanuck to liaise with the Admiral commanding the Sixth Fleet, to arrange for over-flights by four Skyraider aircraft, than it would have been with the French Air Force, so it is more likely they are US Navy AD-4s we are seeing in the film, and not French.

The two most prominent scenes in "The Longest Day" involving actual aircraft both consist of strafing attacks by a pair of fighters, the first by what are meant to be Messerschmitt Bf.109s (as mentioned, in reality, Focke Wulf FW.190A-8s) and the second by Spitfire Mk.IXs.

The 'Messerschmitt Bf.109s' are French-built Nord 1002 Pinguoin II F-BFYX and Nord 1002M Pinguoin II F-BGVU. As stated earlier, they are believed to be part of the batch of former Armee de l'Air and Marine Nationale Nord 1002s purchased by aircraft dealer Alexandre Renault at Mureaux. They are used to portray the strafing attack by Oberstleutnant 'Pips' Priller and his wingman, Heinz Wodarczyk, on what in reality was 'Sword' Beach on 6th June 1944, but which is depicted as being 'Gold - Juno' Beaches in the film.

Heinz Reincke as Priller is seen filmed in what looks like a larger cockpit than that of the Nord 1002, and certainly much larger than the narrow, squared-off cockpit of a Messerschmitt Bf.109. The control column is much too tall for a fighter, being almost up to the height of Reincke's chin (the real Priller was only 5ft 4in in height, but not even he would have had to hold such a tall yoke as is shown here). The cockpit windows are noticeably tall and large, suggesting the aircraft it has been taken from had a spacious cabin with good visibility.

Research reveals that the cockpit layout used for Priller's Messerschmitt Bf.109 matches that of the SIPA S.12 training and liaison aircraft, also used by the French Armee de l'Air in the counterinsurgency role against Algerian rebels between 1956 - 1958. Like the Nord 1000 series, the SIPA S.10 - S.12 family were French-built versions of a Luftwaffe type constructed in Nazi Occupied France, the Arado Ar.39. An example is the SIPA S.121 that appears as an Arado Ar.396 in "The Eagle Has Landed" (1977), reviewed in Chapter Five. More than likely this cockpit came from a struck off charge SIPA S.12, again perhaps part of Alexandre Renault's collection of retired French military light aircraft.

As the camera focuses on Reincke in the SIPA S.12 cockpit, a back drop filmed air-air shot of Wodarczyk's 'Messerschmitt Bf.109' can be clearly seen closing up and formating just off what would be Priller's starboard wing. It has been painted in a blotch-style camouflage scheme that is definitely not accurate for a Luftwaffe fighter. The small air filter atop the nose identifies this 'Messerschmitt Bf.109' is being played by Nord 1002M F-BGVU, as of the two Pinguoin IIs it was the one that had this modification. The Nord 1002M manoeuvres really close to the camera-ship, which may have been Nord 1002 F-BFYX - as is seen shortly, a camera was placed in one of these two Pinguoin IIs.

There is a goof in this back drop shot of Wodarczyk's 'Messerschmitt Bf.109' seen through the cockpit windows of Priller's 'Messerschmitt Bf.109': the Swastika on the tail is the wrong way round, meaning this imagery has been reversed. Quite possibly the reason for this is that Reincke as Priller is filmed in the SIPA S.12 cockpit from the port side, which means that Wodarczyk's 'Messerschmitt Bf.109' beyond him has to be seen flying to starboard. However, because the Swastika on Wodarczyk's 'Messerschmitt Bf.109' is reversed means that when it was filmed air-air, it was actually flying in formation on the port side with the camera aircraft, which would have then produced imagery of the Swastika facing in the correct direction. The imagery had to be reversed for the back drop shot when, for whatever reason, Reincke was filmed from the port side in the cockpit of Priller's 'Messerschmitt Bf.109' (the editor could have just reversed the whole scene, which would have had Wodarczyk's 'Messerschmitt Bf.109' flying in the correct direction; one wonders why he did not do this).

"Follow me. Do everything I do!", Priller tells Wodarczyk, before beginning his dive. Wodarczyk waves his acknowledgement.

How he heard Priller, and how Priller got his message through to his wingman is a miracle of the airwaves, seeing as how Priller is not speaking into a radio mike! In their real attack early in the morning of 6th June 1944, Priller and Wodarczyk flew at 50 feet in a classic Luftwaffe 'Rotte', spread apart with Wodarczyk offset slightly behind Priller. The leader would not have instructed his wingman to follow right behind him, because that would have reduced the effectiveness and destructiveness of their cannon fire. Priller actually calls "Rotte" into his non-existent radio before commencing his attack. However, the scriptwriter responsible for this scene makes the mistake of having Priller order Wodarczyk to fly in line astern.

Director Annakin, on the other hand, has actually staged the 'Gold - Juno' Beach set-piece with the 'Messerschmitts' attacking in a 'Rotte', so good for him. Very clearly, though, more than one pass was made by the two Nord 1002s, as a second shot shows the two flying in line astern. This is immediately followed by a shot filmed from the right hand seat in the cockpit of the second Nord 1002, looking straight ahead as the two 'Messerschmitt Bf.109s' strafe the British and Canadian troops, with the lead Nord 1002 very low down on the deck before pulling up. The pilots who flew these two Nord 1002 Pinguoin IIs in "The Longest Day" have not been identified, but it is thought that Marine Nationale pilots who flew the type in Aeronavale service may have carried out the task.

Priller's dive and strafe was most likely filmed from Nord 1002M F-BGVU, with the camera attached beneath one of the wings to obtain a clear and unobstructed view. This set-piece was very obviously not filmed from within the cockpit, as the follow-up shot from this position shows it was not possible to get the clear, unobstructed view that Annakin wanted. It has been suggested that a helicopter was used to obtain the shot of Priller's strafe attack, but this seems unlikely as a sustained dive at a steep angle would be very risky for a rotary wing machine, while the speed flown low over the beaches indicates that it was a propeller-driven aircraft that was being used as the camera-ship. A pity about the Stuka-like wail in the dive, but how often have we seen and heard this device used for dramatic effect, no matter how inaccurate it is.

The final shot is of Priller laughing mockingly in his cockpit, while sarcastically claiming, "The Luftwaffe has had its great moment!". Beyond him, Nord 1002M F-BGVU swings in a second time to close up in the same back drop shot used before. This scene creates the impression that the strafe by Priller and Wodarczyk was the sole attack by the Luftwaffe on D-Day: this is inaccurate, Kampfgeschwader 54, with its Heinkel He.111s and Junkers Ju.88s, attacked later on D-Day but faced overwhelming Allied air superiority over the beachheads and suffered accordingly. Zanuck would have had to have resorted to using studio miniatures of the KG.54 bombers if he wanted to depict this action in the film.

The one other prominent scene in "The Longest Day" that uses actual aircraft is the very realistically created strafe attack by two RAF Spitfires on a German vehicle convoy. Here, Zanuck is absolutely on the money in using exactly the correct Marque of Spitfire that operated over Normandy on 6th June 1944 and which would have carried out just such an attack as seen in the

film. They are Vickers Supermarine Spitfire LF.Mk.IXs, adapted for low-level attacks with their distinctive clipped wings. Rare is it that the correct type or version of a particular aircraft of the World War Two era is used in war films on either side of the Atlantic, so Zanuck deserves all the credit for getting it so right with the use of these two Low Flying Spitfires. How did he achieve it?

Firstly, Zanuck was clearly under the misapprehension in 1961 that there were no flyable Spitfires in Britain, which every British pilot, aviation enthusiast and historian of the time could have told him was palpable nonsense. Nonetheless, he believed this to be the case. Why? Could a gentleman by the name of Pierre Laureys hold the answer? Monsieur Laureys had been brought into the production team as a co-ordinator for Spitfires to be flown in the film. He was well placed to do so, with the scene involving the Spitfires to be shot in his country. But his principal credit was that Monsieur Laureys was a former Spitfire pilot. He had served with No.340 (Free French) Squadron in the RAF, which formed part of the 'Ile de France' Fighter Group. Monsieur Laureys would have experienced flying the Spitfire Mk.IX with No.340 Squadron, although it would have been the High Flying HF.IX Marque that this 'Ile de France' unit operated between October 1942 and March 1945, when it converted onto the Mk.XIV. No.340 Squadron was in action over Normandy on D-Day, providing fighter cover for ground-attack Typhoons and day bombers.

The influence of Pierre Laureys has to explain why the Spitfire LF.IXs in "The Longest Day" are in No.340 Squadron markings, as there is no other obvious explanation for why Free French Spitfires appear in the film. Could a little Gallic creativity have led Monsieur Laureys to convince Darryl F Zanuck that there was nil pointe in looking for Spitfires in Britain? Even if a little subterfuge was employed, nonetheless Monsieur Laureys did manage to get exactly the correct Marque and type of Spitfire of the D-Day period. And he must have known where to find them.

They are former Belgian Air Force armament trainers which had been taken on charge by the COGEA Nouvelle company at Middelkirke Airport near Ostend, where they were being operated as target-tugs on a contract with the Belgian armed forces. All of them were in clipped-wing configuration and bore silver and blue COGEA colour schemes.

COGEA agreed to provide four Spitfire LF.IXs to 20th Century Fox for "The Longest Day". The company also agreed to paint them in RAF camouflage of the period, together with D-Day stripes and No.340 Squadron codes. The camouflage paint schemes aren't exactly accurate, along with the wrong size and style of code lettering, while the Cross of Lorraine symbol is different from that carried by actual No.340 Squadron Spitfire HF.IXb Marques.

The four Spitfire LF.IXs were, with their Belgian civil registrations given first and their original RAF serials following in brackets: OO-ARA (MH434), OO-ARB (MK297), OO-ARD (MH415) and OO-ARF (MK923). Straightaway, we could have a debate as to whether OO-ARA (MH434) does appear in "The Longest Day". There are various sources which quote four Spitfires from COGEA being provided for the film, including the Spitfire Mk.IX we all know today, and many love, as MH434 of the Old

Flying Machine Company. There are other sources that claim three COGEA Spitfires were made available, and that MH434 was not among them. Photographic evidence is available of OO-ARB, OO-ARD and OO-ARF in "The Longest Day" 'wardrobe', as applied by COGEA at Middelkirke. There has also been a photograph published, the caption for which claims that it is of MH434 in its "The Longest Day" markings.

The Old Flying Machine Company list "The Longest Day" in their film credits for Spitfire HF.IXb MH434, and as owner and operator they obviously know their aircraft's history. Nonetheless, there is no shortage of sources on the Web who state that "Operation Crossbow" (1965) saw MH434's first starring role. The contradiction can be explained. Although COGEA provided four Spitfires for "The Longest Day", that does not mean all four were used. MH434 might have been held in reserve as a back-up, if needed, or maybe it went 'tech' and couldn't be used. In the film industry, if you sign up to be an extra in a production you are still part of the production team even if you are not actually called to appear before the cameras: you wait to hear if you are going to be called and don't leave the film set until you are actually told you are not needed. You are still paid for turning up and could be asked to come back the next day. The same principal applies to vehicles, like historic aircraft or cars, hired to be used in films. Perhaps MH434 was hired by 20th Century Fox for "The Longest Day", but, for whatever reason, did not get in front of the cameras. It would still be entitled to a film credit, though.

There is one instance in the film which indicates that four Spitfires were actually used; however, this is audible, not visual, evidence. Throughout the film aircraft are heard but not seen flying overhead. What is noticeable, though, is that the aircraft engines are distinctly Rolls Royce Merlins. In one scene involving American Paratroopers passing by German soldiers at night four fighter aircraft are heard to roar past overhead, one after the other. Careful replay of this scene confirms that there is no break in the soundtrack, meaning that it is of four aircraft recorded flying low past the sound mike in quick succession, not that of two aircraft flying by one after the other more than once, then taped together to make it sound like four fighters flying overhead. Four recorded fighters with Rolls Royce Merlin engines must mean they were the four COGEA Spitfire LF.IXs, including OO-ARA (MH434).

Spitfire HF.IXb MH434's history, filmography and current status is well documented elsewhere in this book, so it is the histories, careers and fate of its three former COGEA colleagues that were used in the film which we now follow:

Vickers Supermarine Spitfire LF.IXb MH415, Belgian registration OO-ARD. Painted to represent Spitfire Mk.IX coded GW-R of No.340 (Free French) Squadron in the film.

Spitfire LF.IXb MH415 was taken on charge by the RAF on 11th August 1943 and delivered to No.129 (Mysore) Squadron at Hornchurch, before joining No.222 (Natal) Squadron in October the same year. This was another short stay because on 2nd January 1944 MH415 was transferred to the Air Fighting Development Unit, then based at RAF Wittering. It served with the AFDU until

it was transferred to No.126 Squadron at Bradwell Bay, Essex, in September 1944. Something caused it to be sent to Vickers Armstrong at Oxford for repairs and re-fitment in January 1945, after which MH415 spent the whole of 1945 in storage, except for an overhaul by de Havillands at Witney, Oxfordshire.

Spitfire LF.IXb MH415 was one among a batch of Spitfire IXs acquired by the post-War Dutch government in August 1946 and shipped to the Dutch East Indies (today, Indonesia) where it was operated in the ground-attack role by No.322 Squadron LSK from Java against Indonesian Nationalist Forces, initially carrying the code H-108 and later H-65. Subsequently, Spitfire LF.IXb MH415 was one of the batch of ex-Royal Netherlands Air Force (LSK) Spitfire IXs to be acquired by the Belgian Air Force in April 1953 as an armaments trainer with l'Ecole de Chasse at Koksijde, coded SM-40. It served in this role until it was struck off charge by the Belgian Air Force and transferred to the COGEA company at Middelkirke, Ostend, for target-towing duties under a contract with the Belgian military and with NATO forces.

In "The Longest Day", Spitfire LF.IXb OO-ARD/MH415/GW-R was the personal mount of Pierre Laureys himself. When filming was complete, Laureys made an unexpected appearance in MH415 at the Battle of Britain RAF 'At Home' Day display held at Biggin Hill during September 1961, still in No.340 Squadron 'wardrobe'. Laureys was by now the proud owner of this Spitfire, which was registered to Rousseau Aviation and based at Dinard. It was stored in the open but kept in flying condition, making a second film appearance when Laureys flew it to portray a Spitfire LF.IX strafing the train of the title of the excellent John Frankenheimer French/US co-production, "The Train" (1964), starring Burt Lancaster. MH415 then went on to appear in two Franco-British co-productions filmed in France, "Triple Cross" (1966) and "The Night of the Generals" (1967), again flown by Pierre Laureys. It remained at Dinard until 'Hamish' Mahaddie came calling for Spitfires to be used in "Battle of Britain" (1969). After being registered G-AVDJ to Mahaddie on 29th December 1966, Spitfire LF.IXb MH415 underwent the prerequisite overhaul and test flights before joining the growing fleet of Spitfires and the few Hurricanes at RAF Henlow (see the review of "Battle of Britain" later in this Chapter for its performances in that film).

Following completion of "Battle of Britain", MH415, now in HF.IXb configuration with elliptical wingtips, was laid up at Bovingdon Airfield but was soon purchased by one of the American pilots contracted to fly in that film, Wilson 'Connie' Edwards, who also swept up many of the ex-Spanish Air Force Buchons used as Messerschmitt Bf.109s in "Battle of Britain". At Edwards's request, Simpsons Aero Services stripped MH415 down and arranged for its shipment, along with all the Buchons, to Houston, Texas, to arrive in January 1969. Once in the States, Spitfire HF.IXb MH415 became N415MH on the US civil register and was based at Edwards' ranch at Big Springs, Texas, where it was painted as a No.222 (Natal) Squadron Spitfire with the codes ZD-E. As happened with many of the aircraft in 'Connie' Edwards's collection, Spitfire N415MH did little flying and spent much of its life in storage at Big Springs. It is still there under wraps, but its Certification of Airworthiness was renewed on 13th July 2011, extended to 31st July 2014, so it is still live and kicking.

Vickers Supermarine Spitfire LF.IXc MK297, Belgian registration OO-ARB. Painted to represent Spitfire Mk.IX coded GW-O of No.340 (Free French) Squadron in the film.

Spitfire LF.IXc MK297 was taken on charge by the RAF and delivered to No.6 MU at RAF Brize Norton on 30th January 1944. Although it was assigned to No.411 (RCAF) Squadron, it was quickly transferred on to No.66 Squadron on 17th February 1944, with which it served until it was transferred again in October 1944, this time to No.132 Squadron at RAF Hawkinge. In February the following year, MK297 was passed to AST, Ltd, at Hamble for a major inspection, after which it was stored with No.33 MU. On 27th September 1946, MK297 became H-116 with the Royal Netherlands Air Force, later becoming H-55 and being operated in the ground-attack role (alongside MH415 and MH434) by No.322 Squadron LSK in the Dutch East Indies against Indonesian Nationalist Forces. In September 1953, the same Spitfire LF.IXc had joined the Belgian Air Force, coded SM-43. After serving as an armaments trainer, SM-43 was one among the number of Spitfire LF.IXs that were acquired in May 1956 by COGEA to serve as target-tugs, registered OO-ARB.

Following its appearance in "The Longest Day", OO-ARB remained with COGEA but retained its No.340 Squadron markings. It was then placed on the British civil register as G-ASSD on 28th April 1964, registered under the ownership of Film Aviation Services. Spitfire LF.IXc G-ASSD was flown to Biggin Hill in May 1964 but was stored at Swanton Morley Airfield in Norfolk, apparently advertised for sale for the then not exactly substantial sum of £4,000.

The Confederate Air Force at Harlingen, Texas, were seeking a Spitfire to buy in England and made a bid for G-ASSD. It was intended that it would be transferred to the USA on 1st September 1965, but this did not go ahead; G-ASSD was then registered to Captain John Crewdson, who then passed it on to one of his partners in the film aviation world, Alan 'Taff' Rich. During this time, G-ASSD was being prepared for shipment to the USA, but, with the passage of time, the massive production of "Battle of Britain" (1969) was underway and the Confederate Air Force agreed to contract to Spitfire Productions, Ltd, for the use of G-ASSD/MK297 in that film and, like Spitfire Mk.IXb MH415, was fitted with elliptical wingtips.

Now a Spitfire HF.IXc, G-ASSD/MK297 was transferred to US ownership on 18th April 1969, registered as N1882 with the Confederate Air Force and based at Harlingen; its registration was later changed to NX9BL. It was flown by the CAF with the personal codes 'D-B' of Group Captain Douglas Bader, an Honorary Colonel with the CAF. On 15th May 1981, Spitfire NX9BL was seriously damaged in a crash at Palacious, Texas, but was fully repaired and continued to be flown at airshows across North America. It suffered a fateful incident when it was performing at the Hamilton International Air Show, Ontario, Canada, in 1990, during which its propeller was struck by an object as the Spitfire was taxying in. Repairs with exactly the

correct kind of propeller blade were difficult to achieve at the time, so an agreement was reached between the CAF and the Canadian Warplane Heritage (CWH) that NX9BL/MK297 would remain at Hamilton, Ontario, during which time it would be stripped down and completely refurbished, to emerge in its original wartime markings. The plan was that MK297 would be operated as a joint CWH/CAF project, along with the CWH's Lancaster and Hurricane as the Canadian Memorial Flight. Tragically, this dream literally went up in smoke when MK297 was destroyed in a hangar fire at Hamilton on 15th February 1993, which not only took MK297 but the CWH's Hurricane as well. There is mention on a Website of the remains being used in a possible restoration project, but no details are to hand at this stage.

Vickers Supermarine Spitfire LF.IXc MK923, Belgian registration OO-ARF. Painted to represent Spitfire Mk.IX coded GW-U of No.340 (Free French) Squadron in the film.

Spitfire LF.IXc MK923 was taken on charge by the RAF on 24th March 1944 when it was delivered to No.9 MU at RAF Cosford, remaining in storage until it was allocated to No.126 Squadron stationed at Sawbridgeworth in Hertfordshire on 10th May 1944, coded 5J-Z. It remained with No.126 throughout most of 1944, undergoing three base relocations with the squadron and at one time was the personal mount of the CO, Squadron Leader W W Swinden. Spitfire LF.IXc MK923 has two 'kills' to its credit, both achieved on the same day and on the same Raid, 'Rodeo 202' on 14th August 1944, when Pilot Officer Risley claimed two Messerschmitt Bf.109Gs south of Paris. No.126 swapped its Spitfire LF.IXs for Mustang IIIs in December 1944, as a result of which MK923 went to No.32 MU at RAF St Athan, South Wales, for a full inspection and overhaul. Back on line by April 1945, the closing stages of the War meant that MK923 went into storage with No.39 MU at RAF Colerne, Wiltshire, where it remained until it was selected for sale to the Dutch government in May 1947.

That same month MK923 was shipped to India before onward transfer to Kalidjati in the Dutch East Indies. Given the code H-104, the Spitfire was operated like its future COGEA brethren with No.322 Squadron LSK and flew a total of 24 bombing missions against nationalist rebels, some as H-61. In March 1952, MK923 was sold to the Belgian Air Force, earlier than its future COGEA colleagues. Given the code SM-37, it, like the others, served as an armaments trainer with the Belgian Air Force until it was passed on to COGEA, being registered on 25th April 1958 as OO-ARF, later than the other COGEA Spitfires flown in "The Longest Day".

It is known that Hollywood film actor Cliff Robertson had sought to purchase a Spitfire when his attempt to acquire a Mosquito, resulting from his starring role in "633 Squadron" (1964), came to nought. Having learnt in 1963 that Spitfires were for sale in Belgium, Robertson negotiated the purchase of one of these, the chosen one being OO-ARF. Robertson asked his friend, test pilot and British National Aerobatic Champion, Neil Williams, to fly the Spitfire from Belgium to Britain, which Williams duly undertook, routeing from Ostend to Southend via Swanton Morley, before finally completing the journey at Biggin Hill. There, Film Aviation Services stripped the Spitfire down in readiness for its flight across 'The Pond' aboard a Flying Tigers Canadair CL-44. Once in the States, MK923 was at first registered as N93081 and painted dark blue overall following a full overhaul, making her first test flight in the USA in 1964. Later, the registration was changed to N512R.

Cliff Robertson joined forces with the only other Spitfire owner in America at the time, the late Bill Ross, who owned Spitfire Mk.XVI SL721. They decided to completely rebuild MK923, which was carried out at Ross's own facility at Dupage County Airport, near Chicago. On Ross's recommendation, Robertson contracted the very experienced Spitfire pilot, Canadian Jerry Billing, to fly his Spitfire on his behalf, which Billing did for more than 22 years throughout the USA and Canada, only finally retiring at the tender age of 75 in 1994. An attempt was made to repaint MK923 in its original No.126 Squadron colours and markings, with the code 5J-Z, but the camouflage was unfortunately not accurate. Nonetheless, Cliff Robertson's Spitfire - which had also been converted into an HF.IX with elliptical wingtips when it was rebuilt - was a very busy performer on the North American airshow scene. Robertson finally sold MK923 in 1996 to Craig McCaw of California, who continued to display it up till 2000, flown by Bud Granley who used it to lead the Canadian Forces Snowbirds Display Team at Abbotsford that year.

When another full overhaul was needed, the cost involved led to the decision to place Spitfire HF.IXc MK923 on display in a museum. It can be seen today exhibited in the Seattle Museum of Flight in Washington, DC.

No more than two Spitfire LF.IXs are seen in "The Longest Day" for the strafing sequence of German reinforcements struggling to reach the Normandy beachhead. It is a very dramatically staged sequence, with SFX charges set off accurately in front of the Spitfires as they tear in out of their dive and rake the German troops with machine gun and cannon fire. Pierre Laureys was one of the pilots of the Spitfires, reprising his real wartime role in a No.340 (Free French) Squadron Spitfire Mk.IX. There can't be many pilots in films who got the job of practically repeating their actual wartime experiences in an aircraft identical to the type they actually flew in the War. And Pierre Laureys's influence didn't end there: he managed to make sure he got himself in front of the camera as well. That's him in the close-up of a Free French Air Force RAF pilot, in a studio mock-up of a Spitfire cockpit wearing his actual wartime uniform and flying helmet, with the Cross of Lorraine patch just below the shoulder. He deserves the accolade for his ingenuity in obtaining the COGEA Spitfire LF.IXs, even if it did mean he allegedly might have 'diverted' Zanuck's attention away from Britain as a source for Spitfires, but for that he shouldn't be begrudged for making sure he and his famous Free French fighter squadron got on film.

With the Spitfires strafing sequence, aviation departs from "The Longest Day". Zanuck strove for authenticity with his enormous epic on such a grand scale. Although inevitably he had to make adjustments, for the most part he succeeded in producing a spectacular recreation of "the longest day in history".

THE WAR LOVER

(Released: October 1962, USA)

Almost a decade earlier, director Philip Leacock and his cameraman Stephen Dade had created some of the most evocative shot angles of Avro Lancaster bombers seen in any film, starting engines, taxiing and flying for "Appointment in London" (1953). Now Leacock was to repeat this process with the Lancaster's American contemporary, the Boeing B-17 Flying Fortress, in this wartime drama and love triangle featuring two US Eighth Air Force aircrewmen and a young Englishwoman.

As with the earlier film, Leacock brings to bear his creative eye to film the B-17s in dramatic close-ups and from inventive angles that fully illustrate the power of the Flying Fortresses' airframes and the energy of their radial engines. Leacock was aided in achieving this dramatic imagery by renowned aerial cameramen Skeets Kelly, who, three years earlier had worked on "Sink the Bismarck!" (1960), and Ron Taylor, who later would work with Richard Attenborough and share an Oscar for his camera work on the epic, "Ghandi" (1982). (Leacock himself would make only two more films after "The War Lover", choosing to spend the remaining 22 years of his directorial career filming a host of TV series in the USA).

The filming of "The War Lover" and the use of the B-17s which star in it has been covered in other publications, most notably by Scott A Thompson in his meticulously researched study of all surviving post-War Flying Fortresses, "Final Cut", and by Martin Caidin in his 1964 book of the daunting ferry flight across the Atlantic by the film's three B-17s, "Everything But the Flak". Reference to "Final Cut" has been made in this review, but not to Caidin's book.

For the record, three Boeing B-17 Flying Fortress bombers were acquired in the United States for the production by the Film Aviation Services company, headed by an adventurous character named Captain John Crewdson who had flown troop-carrying gliders with the British Army Glider Pilot Regiment during the War. Crewdson had set up Film Aviation Services to do what its title said on the tin, provide aviation services to the (largely) British film industry. He was among the first to utilise helicopters as camera platforms for film and television productions in Britain, and had just returned from Jordan, where he had flown one of the two Tiger Moths in "Lawrence of Arabia" (1962) masquerading as Turkish Ottoman Air Force Rumpler C1s, when he was contracted by Columbia Studios to locate the B-17s and to arrange their aerial sequences in "The War Lover".

At first Crewdson believed he could obtain surplus B-17s that had been clandestinely acquired by the fledgeling Israeli Air Force in the Fifties and which were now grounded. However, when he got to Israel, Crewdson found that they had been scrapped apart from the fuselage of a Boeing B-17G Flying Fortress identified only by its original Fiscal Year (FY) serial of 44-83811. Crewdson purchased the fuselage to be used as a studio prop and for a crash scene.

He then went to the USA, finishing up at Ryan Field near Tucson, Arizona, located close to Davis-Monthan AFB where literally thousands of surplus US military aircraft were lined up cocooned in the desert. The USAF was in the process of retiring its last Boeing VB-17 staff transport variants of the Flying Fortress and one of them, Boeing VB-17 44-83563, had been acquired by Ryan Field-based Aero American Corp and placed on the US civil register as N9563Z. Aero American Corp was run by aviation businessman (let's respectfully call him that), Gregory Board, a former Australian Brewster Buffalo pilot in World War Two who reputedly liked to fly close to the edge in the legal sense. Four years after his involvement with "The War Lover", Board would be forced to do a flyer out of the USA when the FBI accused him of trying to illegally export Douglas B-26 light bombers to Portugal without a licence to do so.

However, all that was in the future; in the meantime, Board agreed not only to sell VB-17 N9563Z to Crewdson, but offered to show him where he could acquire the two more B-17s he needed. These were owned by American Compressed Steel Corp of Cincinatti, Ohio, of which Board's Aero American Corp was a subsidiary, and were located at Dallas-Love Field in Texas. They were part of a batch of six ex-US Navy Boeing PB-1W airborne early warning variants that had been retired to the Naval Aircraft Storage Center at Litchfield Park, Arizona, in 1956 and then sold the following year to American Compressed Steel Corp, a scrap dealer, and kept in storage at Love Field.

Crewdson purchased Boeing PB-1Ws N5229V (ex-44-83883) and N5232V (ex-44-83877). Both needed considerable attention after being stored in the open for nearly five years, but Board's Aero American team brought them back into flying condition before Board and Crewdson flew them back to Ryan Field. By mid-September 1961, VB-17 N9563Z and PB-1Ws N5229V and N5232V - the latter both still in their US Navy blue colour schemes - had set out on the arduous trek to England, arriving at London Gatwick Airport on 8th October, two days before the film's schedules were due to begin.

It would be right and proper to refer the reader to Scott A Thompson's "Final Cut" and to Martin Caidin's "Everything But the Flak" for details of the ferry flight across the Atlantic. Veteran American pilot Don Hackett made up the third aircraft commander besides Crewdson and Board. Two former USAF Lieutenant Colonels - William Tesla and Robert F Spence - were brought in by Columbia Studios as Flying Fortress Adviser and General Technical Adviser respectively.

Bovingdon Airfield in Hertfordshire provided the location for the 324th Bomb Squadron of the 91st Bomb Group B-17Gs that appear in the film, the first of five British war film productions to be made at this once busy RAF air station: "633 Squadron" (1964), "Mosquito Squadron" (1969), "Battle of Britain" (1969) and "Hanover Street" (1979) would likewise re-create RAF and USAAF air base scenes there. Manston Airport in Kent was also utilised as a base from where scenes involving air-air shots of B-17s over the English Channel were filmed. Filming with the B-17s took place between October - December 1961.

The key B-17 is named The Body, flown by Steve McQueen's disturbed, risk-taking 'Buzz' Rickson. No single B-17 played The Body exclusively; all three B-17s adopted different identities

throughout the production, to create the impression of extra Flying Fortresses. Crewdson had obtained gun turrets and other B-17 equipment in the States before flying them over on the ferry flight, then had them all fitted at Bovingdon to bring each Flying Fortress up to external B-17G configuration, while also having the three B-17s painted in reasonably accurate Eighth Air Force B-17G colour schemes. One unexplained error by the film's art department was to paint the fuselage 'Star and Bar' symbols smaller and further forward than was actually applied to wartime USAAF B-17Gs.

The VB-17 and two PB-1Ws were the only aircraft, apart from the fuselage of the ex-Israeli Air Force B-17G, that were actually acquired for use in "The War Lover". But the choice was made to make the film in black-and-white so that archive and other footage could be used as well, mixing as naturally as possible with the actual film material. "The War Lover" makes more use of wartime archive footage than any other British World War Two war film. Out-takes from other war films featuring B-17s are also used.

An archive shot used early in the film shows 24 B-17s flying in three separate formations of eight B-17s apiece, while no less than 40 B-17s are seen in an air-air archive shot filmed at considerable height. Another air-air has eight B-17Fs flying in three sections, two of three aircraft each leading the third as a pair which are almost out of shot; although it would be difficult for the audience to discern, these eight Flying Fortresses are in natural metal colour schemes, whereas the three B-17s used in "The War Lover" are all in olive drab.

Nine more B-17s are seen as silhouettes flying in three sections of three; 13 B-17Gs stand out starkly against the white carpet of clouds below them; another archive shot of 11 B-17Gs appears to show part of this same group, as the cloud cover below them is very similar. A good look-down air-air onto six B-17s clearly reveals their camouflage schemes, while a shot from the dorsal turret of one B-17 looking rearwards shows the antenna wire whipping in the airstream ahead of eight B-17s passing behind. Another dorsal turret shot has six B-17Gs flying below in two 'Vics' of three, framed by the camera-ship B-17G's tailplane. For a bomb run on Kiel's U-Boat pens, a rough shot of an unidentifiable B-17 - both as variant and of which Bomb Group - dropping bombs is used.

The quality of all this archive footage is variable; they contrast with the very sharp imagery of the actual three B-17s flown in the film. The source of all this archive footage was possibly the US government's National Archives Establishment.

An air-air study of three B-17s flying in 'Vic' formation is an out-take from the 20th Century Fox movie, "Twelve O'Clock High" (1950). The B-17s are filmed silhouetted against bright sunlit clouds, but this cannot disguise the fact that the two nearest the camera (filmed from a B-25) are both B-17Gs, while the third distant aircraft appears to be a B-17F, confirmed by the lack of chin turret compared with the other two. These three B-17s were part of a dozen Flying Fortresses gathered together at Eglin AFB, Florida, in 1949 to film "Twelve O'Clock High", some coming from the Eglin-based 1st Experimental Guided Missile Group and consisting of DB-17G and QB-17G drone control variants. They were 'dressed up' to appear as either B-17Fs or B-17Gs.

To portray attacking Luftwaffe fighters, archive imagery of two Republic P-47 Thunderbolts is briefly used. Their imagery appears to have been filmed from the waist gun position of a B-17 and may have been filmed during wartime air combat training. Another shot of a single P-47 Thunderbolt flying right at the B-17 filming it clearly shows that it is a USAAF 'Jug', and not a Luftwaffe FW.190 or Bf.109. This same shot is repeated, but in the reverse direction, while more archive footage shows either another pair of P-47s, or the same two as before, 'attacking' from a different direction. The Eighth Air Force maintained a P-47 Thunderbolt training unit at RAF Alconbury, Huntingdonshire, so it is possible that the attacks by the P-47s seen here are being made at B-17s by USAAF fighters to train newly arrived aircrew in defensive tactics against enemy fighters.

An air-air of a B-17, filmed from the bombardier's glazed nose position and showing the Flying Fortress ahead to be slightly below the following camera-ship, has a fighter running in head-on but underneath it which, through freeze-frame analysis, proves itself to be a Spitfire. Again, this almost certainly is archive footage of air combat training or tactics development, this time involving an RAF Spitfire as the attacker.

A B-17 that is hit and blows up is a rather obvious studio miniature. A shot depicting B-17s returning from a raid and breaking formation to land is an out-take of the ten B-17Gs of the 384th Bomb Group put up for "The Way to the Stars" (1945), filmed over RAF Grafton-Underwood 16 years before "The War Lover".

A scene in which Steve McQueen's character, 'Buzz' Rickson, lives up to his name by 'buzzing' the base at low-level, was flown solo by John Crewdson in one of the PB-1Ws. As it streaks low over Bovingdon's ramp, a visiting RAF Vickers Varsity T.1 can be seen parked in the background! Almost unavoidably, more modern-day (for 1961) RAF aircraft, of the type that were based at Bovingdon, appear in shot, filmed from the glazed nose of the PB-1W as it tears over the tarmac at what cannot be more than 50 feet. They comprise six Avro Anson C.19 communications aircraft, operated by the Bovingdon-based Southern Communications Squadron of RAF Transport Command, plus a visiting de Havilland Vampire T.11 jet trainer.

What is noteworthy is that as the PB-1W runs in towards the Ansons and Vampire, a USAF Boeing C-97G can be seen parked on the ramp in the distance. USAF aircraft were no strangers to Bovingdon in 1961, as the 7,531st Air Base Squadron with its C-47 Skytrains were based there at the time - one C-47 is seen in the film undergoing maintenance in a hangar, appearing as a backcloth to the 91st Bomb Squadron CO in his office when Rickson's B-17 roars past his window. Also, the nearby location of USAF Third Air Force Headquarters at RAF South Ruislip, Middlesex, meant that visiting USAF VIP and transport aircraft were a regular sight at Bovingdon.

One can guess that both the RAF and USAF senior staff at Bovingdon were extremely unhappy at Crewdson's low-level flying, as he passes right between buildings and just over hangars,

with no margin for error. It is rumoured he flew this scene as the last to be filmed at Bovingdon, so that Leacock's production crew did not risk being expelled for taking an unacceptable risk. The Ministry of Civil Aviation, which owned Bovingdon Airfield, could have ordered the B-17s to be grounded for such a breach of flight safety rules.

As low as John Crewdson got, famous film stunt pilot Paul Mantz got even lower. He is filmed belly landing a B-17, flying alone. This is a famous out-take from "Twelve O'Clock High" which is used in "The War Lover" to depict a shot-up 91st Bomb Group B-17G crash landing. Mantz flew the B-17 alone, minus its chin and ball turrets so as not to impede the Flying Fortress's progress along the grass and through a row of tents.

The B-17 Mantz flew to destruction was an actual in-service USAF aircraft about to be struck off charge, being DB-17G 44-83592 of the 1st Experimental Guided Missile Group, Eglin AFB. The crash landing was filmed at an auxiliary field to Eglin AFB in Florida, which had been 'dressed up' to appear as a USAAF air base in wartime England.

The finale to "The War Lover" is a one thousand bomber raid on Leipzig. Another out-take of the ten B-17Gs of the 384th BG from "The Way to the Stars" is used to depict B-17s en route to the target. A massive archive shot showing 191 - yes, 191 (!) - B-17s flying en masse, with the contrails of many more flying much higher, illustrates impressively how the Eighth Air Force could congregate so many bombers in one area of sky. Another archive shot of six B-17Gs shows clearly the large Bomb Group code letter 'C' on a black square on their tail fins, denoting the 96th Bomb Group at Shetterton Heath. More air-air archive imagery has 12 B-17Gs in loose formation showing white pyramidal code patches on their tail fins, but their Bomb Group code letter cannot be discerned. In a back drop to a ball turret shot, five B-17Gs of the 96th BG can clearly be seen.

To depict a mass attack by Luftwaffe fighters, a mix of archive footage and studio miniatures is used. One brief shot has very poor imagery of five Messerschmitt Bf.109s breaking formation. Another is of two P-47s, probably the same pair seen earlier, followed by a solo example, again likely to be the same one as before.

A particularly telling aerial archive shot is that of gun-camera footage of a B-17 taking hits from a German fighter. The clarity of this imagery and the concentrated area of fire from a central position in the attacking aircraft suggests it may have been taken from the nose cannon of a Messerschmitt Me.262 jet fighter. More imagery of what is meant to be four Luftwaffe fighters attacking from the rear reveals itself to be that of two Lockheed P-38 Lightnings! No mistaking the next shot of two Messerschmitt Bf.109s, though - they are filmed flying steadily in trail to the camera aircraft, not aggressively at all, so this cannot be air combat footage.

With the attack beaten off, archive footage shows 13 B-17s progressing towards their target. More gun-camera footage shows a Focke Wulf FW.190 taking hits and the pilot bailing out - the countryside below it has the appearance of the wooded plains of central Germany. Another air-air looking down on eight B-17s has the patchwork quilt-like countryside of England below them. A very scratchy piece of archive footage has two Messerschmitt Bf.109s performing a hard turn. Another rough piece of archive is meant to convey two attacking fighters, but in fact is a Bf.109 in pursuit of a Spitfire; it is of too poor quality to be the Crown Film Unit's imagery of a captured Bf.109 and RAE Spitfire, so presumably is actual air combat footage or that of a captured Spitfire being filmed chased by a Luftwaffe Bf.109. Another shot of a single Spitfire running in behind the camera aircraft is of very similar quality, so it may be the same Spitfire in the same film shoot. Suspicion is confirmed when this Spitfire makes a curved pass across the camera aircraft with the Bf.109 coming in behind it; freeze-frame analysis shows it to be a Bf.109G 'Gustav', so whenever this footage was filmed it could not have been before mid-1942.

Actual shoot-down imagery of a B-17 spinning down with its starboard outer engine ablaze appears next. During this sequence, a close-up of one of the three B-17s in "The War Lover" shows that it was flown with its port outer engine shut completely down and with its bomb doors open, the starboard door being made to look badly shot up.

Back to more archive footage, this time of five B-17s filmed from the dorsal turret of a sixth B-17 below them. A sudden attack by a Bf.109 is portrayed by a very grainy archive shot of a Bf.109G variant which can clearly be seen to be armed with a gondola cannon kit attached beneath each wing. It appears again in another shot and seems to have been filmed from the ground while making fast, low passes in front of the camera. More archive imagery of ten B-17s in three separate tight sections, then the first out-take from the William Wyler documentary of B-17F Memphis Belle is used to show a B-17F flying amid flak bursts. Art work is used to 'paint' flak bursts onto an archive shot of six B-17s that we have seen used earlier in the film.

A much closer shot of five B-17Fs also has flak bursts painted onto it, but we can identify one of them once we get past the irritation of having to use a mirror to do so because the editor has cut this shot into the film in reverse. Nearest the camera is a B-17F coded GK-R and revealing '613' as the last three numbers of its FY serial. We can nail this B-17F down to being 42-3613/GK-R. This B-17F and its four companions are all 91st Bomb Group B-17Fs, with the 91st BG code letter 'A' clearly displayed on a white triangle on the tail fins. The 91st BG featured in the wartime documentary, "Memphis Belle" (1944). Much of this same imagery of its B-17Fs was used as backcloth not only in "The War Lover", but also in the earlier "Twelve O'Clock High" (1950) and the later "1,000 Plane Raid" (1969) B-17 movies. This has resulted in the B-17s actually used in each of these three film productions being painted with the white triangle and letter 'A' of the 91st Bomb Group, in order to match with the out-takes of 91st BG B-17Fs from the "Memphis Belle" documentary. Because the B-17F coded GK-R and carrying '613' as the last three of its Fiscal Year serial is so visibly prominent in the air-air shots from "Memphis Belle", it was decided that the DB-17G that Paul Mantz would crash land in "Twelve O'Clock High" would be painted as this same 91st BG B-17F. It clearly can be seen carrying the serial 23613 as well as the GK-R code as it bellies in, which matches with the B-17F in the foreground of the

"Memphis Belle" air-airs, confirming the identity of the real GK-R as being FY 42-3613.

Incidentally, all three B-17s flown in "The War Lover" carried 'DF-' codes, that of the 324th Bomb Squadron, in order to match with "Memphis Belle" out-takes of B-17Fs from the real 324th BS which are used in the documentary film.

An archive air-air of a 305th BG B-17F, carrying the codes 'JJ-' of the 422nd BS, is shown unloading its bombs, with three more B-17Fs below it. Genuine wartime footage of bomb strikes is used to depict the attack on Leipzig's chemical and oil refineries. More archive footage of another but unidentifiable B-17F dropping a stick of bombs appears; camera shake makes this Flying Fortress impossible to detect. Another archive shot of a B-17G, this time with bomb doors open, shows a flak burst very close to it.

The Body is in bad shape, with one engine out and a bomb hung up in the bomb bay. It comes under attack by German fighters again. More footage of P-47s and P-38s is used - why, only the director and editor know. Could not real air combat footage from the "Memphis Belle" documentary of Focke Wulf FW.190s attacking B-17s have been inserted here instead, giving complete reality to these shots? Maybe, for some reason, they were not available to Leacock, while perhaps the National Archive Establishment did not possess actual combat footage of Luftwaffe fighters engaging B-17s, but could offer air combat training and tactics footage as a reasonably realistic alternative.

Gun-camera footage of another FW.190 being shot down does appear, this one taking a hit directly on its underfuselage fuel tank, which erupts into flame. Then another shot is shown of a Spitfire making an attacking run, filmed from the dorsal turret of a B-17, presumably during air combat training or tactics trials for USAAF aircrew. The two Bf.109s seen earlier are shown again, this time with their footage reversed. An aircraft that is difficult to identify by type, due largely to the poor quality of the footage, is shown taking hits before gun-camera footage of what looks like a twin-engined aircraft exploding in a mass of flame appears - the editor has cut the film so that most of the aircraft's shape is obscured by the fireball. A brief shot of a Focke Wulf FW.190 passing beneath an aircraft may have been filmed from a B-17 during actual air combat - if it is, it's the only actual air combat footage used in "The War Lover". That cannon-toting Bf.109G reappears, image reversed.

The final act of the film has the crew of The Body bailing out over the English Channel; parachutists actually bailed out of one of the B-17s for this scene. The image is very realistically created of a badly damaged B-17 struggling to remain airborne. Rogue pilot Rickson stays with The Body, which crashes into the white cliffs of Dover - this is achieved by a studio miniature B-17. The actual flying in this sequence over the Channel with one engine stopped, the starboard undercarriage leg lowered and smoke trailing, is among the most dramatic and challenging of any aerial re-enactment seen in a film, and may explain why two of the three B-17s did not survive the film production.

Apparently the more than 50 hours of gruelling filming was too much for the two PB-1Ws: after the production had been completed, they were broken up at Manston. VB-17 N9563Z was more robust: it was flown back to the USA and used by Columbia Studios on a promotional tour for "The War Lover". It then served as a camera-ship, filming low-level flight scenes that were used to depict the perspective from a B-52D making a nuclear bomb attack run in the satirical Cold War film, "Dr Strangelove" (1962). In February 1963, N9563Z was sold to Aviation Specialties and was converted into an air tanker. Four years later it was one of five B-17s that were hired to appear in "Tora! Tora! Tora!" (1970), then returned to air tanker duties before it was bought in an auction by the National Warplane Museum of Geneseo, New York, in 1986. N9563Z has had an active life on the warbird scene in the USA; she still flies, being now operated as 42-97400/Fuddy Duddy by the Lyon Air Museum at John Wayne/Orange County Airport in California.

"The War Lover" is a fine film, with excellent performances by its cast, and creates a quite believable representation of characters under stress within an Eighth Air Force Bomb Group in 1943. It is certainly worth having in one's collection for the many superb flying sequences involving B-17 Flying Fortresses, as well as a great deal of fascinating archive footage.

MYSTERY SUBMARINE

(Released: 1963)

A sea hunt war film in which the Royal Navy use a captured Kriegsmarine U-Boat to lure a Wolf Pack of U-Boats into a trap prepared for them by a squadron of destroyers. The aviation content is limited and consists entirely of archive material.

The Kriegsmarine headquarters is bombed by the US Eighth Air Force, depicted by archive air-airs of four Boeing B-17G Flying Fortresses and six Consolidated B-24 Liberators. However, using this Eighth Air Force material is a serious goof because the time period in which the action is taking place is in 1941, due to a reference to the Bismarck being a threat. America wasn't even at war then.

Because the captured U-Boat is being crewed by British submariners, they have to avoid RAF Coastal Command maritime patrol aircraft whose aircrew would be unaware of the deception. Sure enough, the U-Boat is targeted by an RAF Catalina. To depict this the film editor has used archive footage of a Coastal Command Consolidated Catalina I, clearly carrying the code letter 'A' next to its fuselage roundel and the large number '10' on the forward fuselage. Part of this footage appears to be the same as that of the Catalina seen in "Sink the Bismarck!" (1960), only shown flying in the opposite direction. No other aircraft footage is shown in "Mystery Submarine".

Curiously, there was a Hollywood made film of the same title released in 1950, but with a very different story about a US Intelligence Officer trying to track down a U-Boat operating off South America. Whether the British "Mystery Submarine" was influenced by the former film is not known.

THE GREAT ESCAPE

(Released: July 1963, USA) Hollywood 'British' war film

Let's get one thing straight - "The Great Escape" IS a British war film. It may have been produced by the Mirisch Corporation (the same film production company that made "The Magnificent Seven", 1960, and the classic Marilyn Munroe/Jack Lemmon/Tony Curtiss comedy, "Some Like It Hot", 1959); its producer/director, John Sturges, may have been more famous for Westerns than war films ("The Magnificent Seven" again); its instantly recognisable and much parodied theme music might have been composed by Elmer Bernstein, another afficionado of Westerns whose compositions for "The Magnificent Seven" and "The Comancheros" (1961) were equally as recognisable; while its all-American lead star, Steve McQueen, was undoubtedly the 'King of Cool' at the time, but his character - Hilts, 'The Cooler King' - was created solely to bring an American into a prime position in what is otherwise an almost entirely British World War Two story.

To 'American-ise' the film even more, the distributor, United Artists, insisted on more American actors taking prime roles, even though no American PoW took part in the mass escape on 24th March 1944 from Stalag Luft III. McQueen's character Hilts is believed to be an amalgam of a USAAF flight commander on the Doolittle Raid over Japan who was later shot down and captured in Europe, an American OSS Colonel captured in North Africa who disguised himself as a USAAF flyer by borrowing a flight jacket from a fellow PoW to avoid being shot as a spy, and a British Squadron Leader who escaped seven times from German PoW camps.

McQueen is joined by James Garner, a very popular film and TV actor in the Sixties and the Seventies (notably, "The Rockford Files" private investigator TV series), who plays an American Flight Lieutenant who joined the Royal Air Force before the United States entered the War and served with RAF 'Eagle' Squadrons, thus bringing an acknowledgment of American volunteers in the RAF, even though the 'Eagle' Squadrons had been transferred to the USAAF by the time the real escape took place; Charles Bronson, who plays a Polish Air Force officer who has escaped to fly with the RAF, thus paying a tribute to Polish airmen as well as making a link with the actual location of Stalag Luft III in Sagan, now Zagan in Poland; and rising star James Coburn, who acts the role of an Australian RAF pilot to acknowledge the number of Commonwealth officers who took part in the escape.

Taking prominent roles alongside the Yanks are a number of strong British character actors, not the least of which is Richard Attenborough who had by now forged an admirable portfolio of film roles ever since his uncredited debut as the rating who deserts his post in Noel Coward's "In Which We Serve" (1942). Attenborough was among a number of British actors in "The Great Escape" who had not only served their country during World War Two, but who also appear in various films reviewed in this book both during and after the War itself, including in his case, "Journey Together" (1945), "A Matter of Life and Death" (1946), "School for Secrets" (1946), "The Gift Horse" (1952) and

"Dunkirk" (1958), among others. Attenborough plays Squadron Leader Roger Bartlett, or 'Big X', the organiser of the break-out, based on the real Squadron Leader Roger Bushell, the actual 'Big X' who escaped from Stalag Luft III on 24th March 1944 and was among the 'Fifty' who were shot by the Gestapo.

Alongside Attenborough are wartime veterans Gordon Jackson ("The Foreman went to France", 1942, "Millions Like Us", 1943, "San Demetrio London", 1943, and "Against the Wind", 1948), James Donald ("In Which We Serve", 1942, "Went The Day Well?", 1942, "San Demetrio London", 1943, "The Way Ahead", 1944, "The Gift Horse", 1952, and "The Bridge on the River Kwai", 1957), and Donald Pleasence, who had actually been shot down and imprisoned during the War. Pleasence was a wireless operator aboard Avro Lancaster Mk.III NE112/AS-M of No.166 Squadron when it was shot down on 9th September 1944, nearly six months after the actual 'Great Escape'. His biography on the IMDb Website says he was sent as a PoW to Stalag Luft I, where he organised amateur dramatic plays to help pass the time for himself and his fellow captives until their liberation in 1945. Notably, Pleasence would play Reichsfuhrer-SS Heinrich Himmler, who ordered in secret the murder of the 'Fifty', in "The Eagle Has Landed" (1977).

As fans of "The Great Escape" know, aviation only features in one section of the film, but it is an important part. Flight Lieutenant Hendley (Garner) plans to steal a Luftwaffe aeroplane and fly it to Switzerland. He takes with him Flight Lieutenant Blythe (Pleasence), the 'Forger', who produced all the essential documents the escapees need and who is suffering from progressive myopia due to the strain his eyes have suffered as a result. We aren't shown how, but the pair manage to break into a German airfield in Bavaria. Among the parked fighters Hendley sees "a trainer I could fly". He kicks an armed guard unconscious, then positions Blythe beside the nose so that Blythe can work the primer handle as he, Hendley, pumps in the fuel. The engine catches, Hendley gets Blythe into the cockpit, and they take off before officers in the air traffic control tower can alert the guards. It looks like they are going to make it to Switzerland, but the trainer's engine starts to fail and Hendley is forced to crash land the little aircraft. It plunges into trees and catches fire, but Hendley and Blythe manage to get out. Blythe staggers into the open, unable to see where he is going. German troops pull up on the road below the hill where he is standing and a soldier armed with a telescopic-sighted sniper's rifle deliberately and needlessly shoots Blythe dead. Hendley is re-captured.

The scene where Hendley and Blythe steal the trainer aeroplane was filmed on an air base in Bavaria. The aircraft used as props to represent Luftwaffe fighters are all CCF Harvard Mk.IV trainers, the first type issued to the newly constituted Bundesluftwaffe (Federal Air Force) after West Germany (the Federal Republic of Germany) joined NATO in 1955. At the time when "The Great Escape" was in production in Bavaria during the summer of 1962, Schule 1 (School 1) of the Flugsdienstaffel Technische (Technical Flying Squadron) was based at Kaufbeuren in the Schwaben region of Southern Bavaria. It was one of two such units in the Bundesluftwaffe that was equipped with the CCF Harvard Mk.IV.

Although not confirmed, it seems most likely that it is the Harvard Mk.IVs located at Kaufbeuren that appear in "The Great Escape", and that Kaufbeuren itself is the air base which provided the location for Hendley's and Blythe's escape scene.

Freeze-frame analysis indicates that a minimum of seven Harvards were used as props. "The Great Escape" was one of the first major feature films that used the North American T-6 Texan/Harvard variants as doubles for Axis Powers fighters, culminating in 1969 with their ultimate expression as Texans and Harvards converted into Japanese Zero look-alikes for "Tora! Tora! Tora!" (1970). In "The Great Escape", the Luftwaffe fighter type that the Harvards are impersonating is the Focke Wulf FW.190, both having radial engines.

All the CCF Harvard IV s were repainted in spurious Luftwaffe camouflage and markings, but with completely unrealistic serials and codes for German World War Two-era aircraft. As Garner and Pleasence sneak into an aircraft shelter - again, untypical of a 1944-period Luftwaffe airfield - they pause beside a Harvard that clearly carries the (fake) serial of '1-37'. The colour scheme that all the Harvards bore in Bundesluftwaffe service was all-over yellow, apart from a matt black top from engine cowling to the cockpit front as anti-dazzle paint for the student pilot, green cowling band and black-and-white checkerboard square. The serials for all the Harvards based at Kaufbeuren began with the letters 'BF-', then had a three-digit number to follow, the first digit always being '0'. It's possible that the Harvard bearing the fake serial '1-37' was actually BF-037, with the last two '37' being retained in the fake serial so that the real identification could be visible while the aircraft was in 'wardrobe'. Another Harvard can be seen to carry the fake serial, '1-56'. If these Harvards are BF-037 and BF-056 respectively, their serials would have been separated by the Bundesluftwaffe Iron Cross symbol, making them appear as BF+037 and BF+056 on their fuselage sides.

When the escape scene was filmed at Kaufbeuren, it appears to have been completed in a single day. The reason for guessing this was the case is that the taxy-tracks and hard parking areas outside individual aircraft shelters are all wet throughout the scene, indicating that it had rained quite heavily before shooting took place.

The aircraft that Hendley and Blythe steal is the only type that is not a Harvard. It is, in fact, a training aircraft of genuine Luftwaffe World War Two vintage, a Bucker Bu.181 Bestmann. It is unlikely that this Bestmann was in service with the Bundesluftwaffe when it was used in the film, as the Bestmann was withdrawn along with all other Deutsches Luftwaffe types following the Wehrmacht surrender in 1945. It could have been a real former Luftwaffe aircraft, however, as the Bestmann served in large numbers as the primary German trainer throughout World War Two. If so, this Bestmann could be the first genuine German World War Two aircraft to appear in a Hollywood movie. How many Bestmann were in flying condition in Germany in 1962 - if any, as the German historic aircraft preservation scene was in its infancy at the time - cannot be guessed at, but the Mirsch Corporation could have obtained an example from other sources, the Swiss Air Force being one possibility, as it was still operating the Bestmann when the film was made; ex-Swedish Air Force Sk.25s were another source.

It has to be stated that there is no doubt that this Bestmann was sacrificed by the Mirisch Corporation's film production team for its role in "The Great Escape". It is not a full-scale facsimile of the Bestmann that is fast-taxyied across grass and through trees into a copse beyond; it is the actual aircraft under power from its own Hirth HM 504A 105hp piston engine. Careful freeze-frame analysis shows no sign of guidance wires pulling the aircraft along the ground, as other crash scenes in films have used.

The crash is filmed from two camera positions. The first is positioned close to the aircraft as it passes by, continuing to film it as it travels at speed towards the trees. The shot is cut the instant the Bestmann mounts a slight rise in the ground, with its port wing striking a slender sapling.

The second camera position is fixed in the copse close to the sapling that the Bestmann strikes. At no time does the camera move. The Bestmann appears from screen right, mounting the rise in the ground to enter the copse as its port wing strikes the sapling tree's trunk. The wing is completely severed as the Bestmann powers through under its own momentum into the copse. For a very brief second the Bestmann is airborne as it leaps over the rise, banking slightly with its starboard wing low which strikes a more substantial tree trunk, causing the wing to break off backwards from the fuselage. The forward fuselage disappears out of shot at screen left, at which point the aircraft clearly impacts an unseen obstacle not in view, bringing a complete halt to the airframe's forward momentum and causing the Bestmann to collapse, partly on its right side, partly on its belly in the copse.

Examination of the wreckage in this crash sequence leaves no doubt it is the Bestmann that was effectively driven through the two trees into the copse. It was almost certainly under the control of a stunt pilot in the cockpit, as ground-running the Bestmann without any control severely risked the aircraft losing direction and ground-looping. The aircraft must have impacted something like an aircraft crash barrier set up out of shot, which would have brought it to an immediate stop and helped to have protected the pilot who, almost certainly, would have had protective padding and strapping in the cockpit. Firecrews with hand-held extinguishers and cutting equipment would have been on hand behind the fixed camera in the copse, to effect a rescue if necessary.

Aviation enthusiasts of today's film audience may berate the destruction of a valuable historic aircraft as nothing short of movie industry vandalism, but they need to take into account the attitudes of the times when "The Great Escape" was made. Much of the cinema audience would have been made up of people on both sides of the Atlantic for whom World War Two would still be of recent memory, while those of the Sixties generation - of which the author is one - were brought up on tales of good Allies versus evil Nazis, as evidenced in many films and documentaries. The sight of a German military aircraft carrying Balkenkreuze and Swastika symbols being trashed in a war film was not a displeasing one in 1963. Future aircraft preservation of historic wartime Luftwaffe types was not even a distant dream in those days, and

the attitude of the Hollywood producers of "The Great Escape" almost certainly would have been , "Hey, so what? It's a Kraut airplane, after all".

TORPEDO BAY (FINCHE DURA LA TEMPESTA)

(Released: September 1963, Italy) International 'British' war film

This international hotch-potch of a production has both Italian and French backing, as well as both British and Italian film directors. The British director is Charles Frend, who has "The Big Blockade" (1942) propaganda drama-doc and "The Cruel Sea" (1953) among his credits.

The storyline has an Italian Navy submarine being hunted in the Mediterranean during 1941 by a Royal Navy destroyer. The submarine puts into the neutral port of Tangiers for repairs, as does the destroyer. The Italian and British Captains forge a diplomatic friendship until they both have to put to sea again.

The only aviation content in the film occurs right at the beginning, when archive footage of Allied aircraft that are meant to be searching for the submarine is shown. First up is a Blackburn Skua, with the sub-Flight code of 'H', taking off from the deck of an aircraft carrier. The shot that immediately follows is taken from an unidentified aircraft, with only part of the tail plane in view, as it departs an aircraft carrier: what is of interest in this shot is that the bow end of the flight deck has an extension for aircraft taking off under their own power but clearly shown are two catapult launch systems, one each side of the forward flight deck, confirming that this method of launching aircraft was operational on British carriers during World War Two (as is seen being operated in the 1944 'drama-doc', "The Volunteer", reviewed in Chapter One).

The next shot to follow shows two USAAF Lockheed P-38 Lightnings departing RAF Gibraltar, with a Boeing B-17 Flying Fortress parked below The Rock. This is an error on the part of the film editor because the United States hadn't entered the War in the 1941 period represented in the film, while USAAF aircraft didn't begin flying from Gibraltar until very late in 1942. Finally, two air-airs of a Martin Maryland flying over the sea appear.

THE VICTORS

(Released: November 1963)

"The Victors" is fully representative of the argument about a film's nationality: is it American or British? Columbia Pictures Corporation financed, presented and distributed it, so that makes it American. The Open Road film company, formed by producer/director Carl Foreman to make "The Guns of Navarone" (1961) and for which "The Victors" was its second production, was based in Britain and used British film studios, technicians and crew.

As stated at the beginning of this book, a film made by a British film company using British film crew members is a British film, even if the backer and distributor is American. By that definition, "The Victors" is a British war film. Perhaps it should be regarded as a British-US co-production.

Having said that, its subject is most definitely American, despite the book on which it is based having been written by a British author. Foreman changed the characters in the book from being British troops to American GIs, to improve the film's chances in America, and follows their fortunes of war across Europe from 1942 to the post-War Occupation of Berlin in 1946. It is fair to say that it is not the kind of film about GIs in World War Two that Hollywood would want to see made today. "Band of Brothers" it is not, although there are some similarities between this film and the celebrated TV series made in the 21st Century based on the same time period in the War.

The film opens with a pre-title credits montage of shots created by graphic designer Saul Bass, showing the sequence of events leading from the end of World War One up to the Battle of Britain in World War Two. Among these images created by Bass are blended images of Hawker Hurricanes, Vickers Supermarine Spitfires, Messerschmitt Bf.109s and Junkers Ju.87 Stukas. What Bass has done is to take one image of one aircraft from archive footage, then multiply it many times over in silhouette so that the impression of hordes of aircraft flying over is shown on screen. One mistake that Bass has made, however, is to use the image of an early model B-17 which he has multi-layered like all the others, but in its case upside down!

Aviation only appears briefly in "The Victors", and exclusively in archive and newsreel form. In depicting the Allied advance across northern Europe amid the deep snows of the winter of 1944 - '45, Foreman selected a variety of archive shots showing army trucks sliding and GIs slithering on icy roads. But really dramatic footage shows a USAAF Republic P-47D Thunderbolt losing complete traction on an ice-bound runway, with its undercarriage collapsing as its slides off onto the snow and hurtles out of control into another parked Republic P-47D Thunderbolt. The impact forces the parked P-47D into the air before it crashes back down again, while a groundcrewman who had been working on it has a miraculous escape as he tries to flee the oncoming Thunderbolt.

The P-47D which loses control on landing is coded C4-N, while the P-47D it collides with is C4-B. This makes both Thunderbolts as being on strength with the 388th Fighter Squadron, part of the 365th Fighter Group in the USAAF's Ninth Air Force. A Web page on Wikipedia for the 365th Fighter Group shows a photograph of a P-47D of the 388th Fighter Squadron coded C4-T, parked on an identical snowy airfield as seen in the archive footage of the collision in "The Victors". The caption to this photograph states it was taken at RAF Beaulieu. The 365th FG, with its three Fighter Squadrons, including the 388th FS, was stationed at RAF Beaulieu in Hampshire from 4th March 1944 until the entire Group moved to Azeville in France on 28th June 1944, post-D-Day. Therefore, this footage of P-47D C4-N colliding with P-47D

C4-B was almost certainly filmed at RAF Beaulieu, most likely during a wintry March 1944.

The only other imagery in "The Victors" involving aviation is newsreel footage, probably from CBS as its microphones are the only ones visible in shot. It shows an amusing scene with the then new First Lady, 'Bess' Truman, wife of new President of the United States, Harry S Truman, at what the newsreel narrator describes as "the National Airport" performing a launch ceremony for "new flying ambulances". The "National Airport" would have to be Washington National Airport (today, Ronald Reagan International), with the launch ceremony being held on 30th May 1945. It was 'Bess' Truman's first public appearance as First Lady, and was not one she would forget.

No matter how hard she tried, the champagne bottle she repeatedly hit against the nose of one of the "flying ambulances" refused to shatter. Apparently the bottle had not been weakened, as would normally be the case with champagne bottles used in ceremonial launches of ships or of aircraft, in order to ensure they shattered easily.

Two aircraft were lined up nose-to-nose for the launch ceremony at the National Airport. Both are versions of the Douglas C-54 Skymaster. The example on the right of the screen which the First Lady continues to batter with the unco-operative champagne bottle is an unidentifiable Douglas C-54D of the USAAF's Air Transport Command. The example on the left can be identified, as its Bureau Number (BuNo) 56509 is clearly visible on the nose. This makes it Douglas R5D-3 BuNo 56509 of the United States Navy, which was originally manufactured for the USAAF as C-54D 42-72580 and was among 202 examples diverted to the US Navy, in whose service they were designated R5D. This particular aircraft would later become Douglas DC-4 N62433 on the US civil register.

"The Victors" is a highly regarded war film for which Carl Foreman received much praise for its realism and the balance it strikes in creating both sympathy and dismay with the behaviour of its central characters in war. Unlike co-producers Steven Spielberg and actor Tom Hanks, with their TV joint venture, "Band of Brothers", Foreman avoids making his equivalent of 'Easy' Company heroic and admirable, just honestly human. He is also respectful in his treatment of British characters in the film, unlike Spielberg who cannot resist making British troops look ineffective compared with their American counterparts. "The Victors" will be high up on any list of best war films ever made, and should be an important component of any war film historian's collection.

633 SQUADRON

(Released: April 1964)

As every aviation enthusiast and British war film fan will attest, the stars of "633 Squadron" are not actors Cliff Robertson, George Chakiris and Maria Herschey, but four out of 11 examples of the de Havilland Aircraft Company's finest ever creations: Mosquito fighter-bombers.

Much has been said and written about "633 Squadron", so to simply rehash well worn tales about the filming and how the aircraft were used in the production could lead to the accusation that material printed here has been 'borrowed' from other published sources. Instead, the focus will be on each aircraft's character, history and fate where known, in keeping with the broad theme of this book. Some extra information not published before is also added.

The film's titles credits are played out over that aerial shot of that swirling cloud caused by the vortex from the camera aircraft, accompanied by the film titles and that perennially played theme music composed by Ron Goodwin. Matched only by the theme music for "The Dam Busters" (1955), "The Great Escape" (1963) and "Where Eagles Dare" (1968, and Ron Goodwin again), "633 Squadron" will always be credited with having the most immediately recognisable musical accompaniment.

And then we have three fabulous Mosquitos roaring low in 'Vic' formation over The Black Swan pub and breaking to land abreast the control tower of the fictional air station of RAF Sutton Craddock. In one memorable zoom shot we see a close-up of the three 'Mossies', filmed from the control tower and looking right down their swirling twin props, taxiing in towards their dispersal. They look and sound every inch the part of wartime Mosquito FB.VIs, for which the art department did an excellent job in dressing them up to appear as.

All aviation film fans and historians know that the majority of the Mosquitos appearing in "633 Squadron" were target-towing Mosquito TT.35 variants. The art department painted over their glazed noses so that each TT.35 had grey-green camouflage nose tops and all-grey undersides, then had dummy cannon and machine guns installed. That made them almost indistinguishable from the FB.VIs they were portraying. However, look closely at the zoom shot, as well as at other close-ups in the film, and you cannot fail to detect the oval, painted-over flat panel of the bomb aimer's glass in the nose - not a quibble but a credit, in fact, on how good a job the art department had done on each Mosquito TT.35.

In total, 11 Mosquitos were acquired for "633 Squadron", nine de Havilland Mosquito TT.35 and two de Havilland Mosquito T.3 versions. Their identities have appeared in a number of publications and Websites, but for whatever reason most sources quote a total of nine Mosquitos, overlooking two that were dismantled for various scenes. The majority were sourced from No.3 Civil Anti-Aircraft Co-Operation Unit (No.3 CAACU) at Exeter Airport, Devon (the same unit which had provided three Spitfire LF.XVIs for "Reach For The Sky", 1956). Officially, some had been struck off charge and were no longer in RAF service by the time of their acquisition in August 1962 by Mirisch Films, Ltd, the British subsidiary company of the US Mirisch Films Corporation that was the production company for "633 Squadron".

Filming was intended to take place during September and October 1962, but a delay in releasing from service those Mosquitos still in flying condition prevented this schedule from being met. No.3 CAACU was the sole source for a suitable number of airworthy Mosquitos to appear in the film. They were dedicated

to aerial towing sleeve targets for Army, Navy and RAF Regiment gunners to practice against, a task from which they could not be spared until replacement aircraft came on line. Mirisch Films, which had bought the film rights to "633 Squadron" from the author of the original novel, Frederick E Smith, had to wait until the remaining flyable Mosquito TT.35s were finally taken out of service, which occurred in May 1963.

Of the nine TT.35s, five were still based in varying states of condition at Exeter Airport, three more had flown into storage with No.27 MU at RAF Shawbury, while the ninth example had been retained by the MoD and had been allocated to the Central Flying School at RAF Little Rissington. The two T.3 trainers were both earmarked for preservation, one held by the Ministry of Defence's Air Historical Branch (AHB) that was keeping it in store at RAF Henlow in readiness for display in the future RAF Museum, while the other was to be preserved by the Imperial War Museum and was being kept at Exeter until its transfer to Lambeth.

Filming took place at Bovingdon Airfield, Hertfordshire, between July - September 1963, the same location that, two years earlier, had hosted the three Boeing B-17 Flying Fortresses for "The War Lover" (1962). Just as in that film, the Avro Anson C.19s of the RAF Transport Command's Southern Communications Squadron were still based at Bovingdon and inevitably get into shot on occasion, as happened in "The War Lover": when three Mosquitos land in succession, seven Anson C.19s can be seen parked on their ramp in the distance. There was equally the constant risk of visiting transport aircraft getting into shot: when two 'Messerschmitt Bf.109s' strafe the airfield, a Handley Page Hastings C.1 transport can be seen parked in the far distance as the Luftwaffe fighters depart. Also, Bovingdon's relatively close location to London Heathrow Airport (it was then, and still is today after the closure of the airfield, one of the 'Stacks' for holding airliners in-bound to Heathrow) meant that intruding airliners were likewise a risk, as evidenced by the contrails in the sky unavoidably getting into shot of the two 'Messerschmitts' departing.

All the Mosquitos used in "633 Squadron" are detailed below, with their film roles, their known histories and their fates explained. All wore 'HT-' squadron codes in the film, which in reality had been carried by No.154 Squadron (Spitfires) between November 1941 - November 1942 and again between June 1943 - October 1944, as well as by No.601 Squadron (Vampire F.3s) between November 1949 - April 1951.

de Havilland Mosquito T.3 TV959, static prop as 'MM398/HT-P'. Built at Leavesden and taken on charge by the RAF in 1945. Accepted by No.13 Operational Training Unit (OTU) at RAF Middleton St George, Durham, then served with the following units between 1946 - 1950: No.266 Squadron, No.54 OTU, No.228 Operational Conversion Unit (OCU) and No.22 MU at Silloth, where it was stored until it was transferred to No.204 Advanced Flying School in July 1951. Whilst there, TV959 was damaged and underwent repair by Brooklands Aviation at Sywell. It returned to RAF service in February 1952 and from then onwards spent varying periods of time either in store with various Maintenance Units or being operated by the Home Command

Examination Unit at White Waltham, Berkshire. On 30th April 1959, TV959 was assigned to No.3 CAACU with whom it was operated alongside Mosquito T.3 TW117 on pilot conversion, aircrew standardisation and general 'hack' tasks. TV959 remained with No.3 CAACU at Exeter until it was loaned to Mirisch Films in July 1963 for "633 Squadron".

In the film, TV959 was already in a stripped down condition, in being prepared at Exeter for its forthcoming display in the Imperial War Museum at Lambeth, South London. It appears as a wingless airframe in a couple of background shots, portraying a Mosquito undergoing repair and maintenance at RAF Sutton Craddock.

Of course, many will remember the incongruous sight of TV959 suspended from wires at Lambeth, with its starboard wing severed. It was rescued from this undignified fate in 1989 when it was removed from Lambeth and put into storage at Duxford. While there, it was acquired in August 1992 by The Fighter Collection (TFC), with a view to long-term restoration to fly again. This was not proceeded with and TV959 was sold by TFC in April 2003 to Paul G Allen's Flying Heritage Collection at Paine Field, Everett, Washington State. It was placed in storage in Norfolk pending a decision as to how to proceed to full restoration, due to the problems caused by the severing of the starboard wing inboard of the engine nacelle; even though the severed wing had been preserved, it was not possible to re-attach it due to the unconventional way it was dismantled from the airframe. A completely new wing and spar will have to be built from the correct type of wood to match with the rest of the airframe, a skill that has been developed in New Zealand. Consequently, Mosquito T.3 TV959 has been shipped to Ardmore, New Zealand, where experienced Mosquito restorer AvSpecs has been contracted to undertake this challenging project during the second decade of the 21st Century.

de Havilland Mosquito T.3 TW117, flyer as 'HR115/HT-M'. Built at Leavesden in 1945 and accepted into RAF service in August that year. On 30th May 1946 TW117 was placed in storage with No.15 MU at Wroughton, Wiltshire, before being assigned to No.2 Armament Practice Station, RAF Acklington, North Yorkshire, on 22nd July 1947. Two years later it found itself assigned to the Station Flight at RAF Linton-on-Ouse, Yorkshire, where it was used to convert pilots onto the Mosquito's short-lived successor, the de Havilland Hornet. In July 1951, TW117 joined No.204 Advanced Flying School alongside its future No.3 CAACU and film-mate, Mosquito T.3 TV959, until it came on charge in February 1953 as a pilot conversion trainer, standardisation flight examination aircraft and general 'hack' with No.58 Squadron based at RAF Benson, the RAF's last dedicated Mosquito photo reconnaissance unit. It was with No.58 Squadron that Mosquito T.3 TW117 received the PR blue and green camouflage scheme that it retained when it spent the years 1954 - 1960 stored with various Maintenance Units, and continued to do so after it joined No.3 CAACU on 31st March 1960. In September 1962, Mosquito T.3 TW117 made a rare public appearance when it was flown at the Farnborough Air Show, in a special programme on the Public Days dedicated to historic British aircraft.

When No.3 CAACU gave up its Mosquitos in May 1963, TW117 was selected for preservation and display with the future RAF Museum and was flown from Exeter to RAF Henlow for storage with the AHB collection. However, Film Aviation Services, on contract to Mirisch Films, came calling and the decision was made to loan TW117 for a role in "633 Squadron". It needed no conversion, as it was manufactured with a solid nose and did not carry target-towing gear as did the TT.35s. It was one of the five flying Mosquitos in the film, but was used as a reserve and as the aircraft on which all the pilots contracted to fly the Mosquitos were checked out on.

After filming, Mosquito T.3 TW117 returned to AHB store at RAF Henlow where it remained until it went on display at the RAF Museum from 1972 - 1991. In November 1991 it was acquired by Tacair Systems of Toronto, Canada, but for what purpose is not known. In any case, it never made the journey to Canada and was instead loaned to the Royal Norwegian Air Force Museum at Gardermoen Air Base, Norway, in February 1992, painted with the codes KK-T to represent a Mosquito FB.VI flown by Norwegian pilots with No.333 Squadron between November 1943 - February 1945. Today, this Mosquito is publicly displayed at the National Museum of Aviation at Bodo, Norway.

de Havilland Mosquito TT.35 RS709, flyer as 'HR113/HT-D/HT-G'. Purchased by Mirisch Films and registered as G-ASKA. This Mosquito began life as a B.35, constructed by Airspeed at Christchurch, Hampshire, in 1946 and serving with No.109 and No.139 (Jamaica) Squadrons until it was sent for conversion into TT.35 target-towing configuration in late 1952. It was then operated by No.3 CAACU for ten years until it was transferred to No.27 MU, RAF Shawbury, at the end of May 1963. It was one of the three Mosquito TT.35s acquired by Mirisch Films for the sole purpose of being used in "633 Squadron" and had a leading role in the film.

When filming was complete, Group Captain 'Hamish' Mahaddie, the film's aviation technical adviser, purchased Mosquito TT.35 RS709 from Mirisch Films in August 1964. But within two months Mahaddie had sold RS709 on to Peter Thomas, who displayed the Mosquito at Staverton Airport, Gloucestershire, in his Skyfame Museum collection, keeping it in its FB.VI disguise. In 1968, Mosquito TT.35 RS709 was in front of the cameras again at Bovingdon for "Mosquito Squadron" (1969), then in August the following year it began the first of its two sojourns to the United States. Ed Jurist of Vintage Aircraft International based RS709 at Nyack, New York State, from August 1969 until 1971, when it joined the Confederate Air Force at Harlingen, Texas, registered as N9797. This Mosquito stayed at Harlingen until 1975, when David Tallichet acquired it for his Yesterday's Air Force collection at Chino, California. Tallichet loaned the Mosquito for display by the Combat Air Museum at Topeka, Kansas, until 1979, during which time it was allowed to fall into non-airworthiness condition.

In November 1979, this Mosquito returned to the UK under the ownership of Doug Arnold, who registered it as G-MOSI with his Warbirds of Great Britain collection at Blackbushe Airport, Surrey, and restored it to flying condition, it taking to the air again in September 1983. However, G-MOSI did not stay long in the UK before it was acquired by David Zeuschel of Van Nuys, California, in 1984. In February 1985, this Mosquito made its last flight to date when it was flown to Dayton, Ohio, for display at the National Museum of the United States Air Force. Today, it is exhibited there as a Mosquito PR.XVI, painted as NS519, a weather reconnaissance version operated by the 653rd Bombardment Squadron based in England between 1944 - 1945.

de Havilland Mosquito TT.35 RS712, flyer as 'RF580/HT-F'. Purchased by Mirisch Films and registered as G-ASKB. Constructed by Airspeed as a B.35 in the same batch as RS709, it had a short service career with No.13 OTU at RAF Middleton St George before it went straight into storage, where it remained until it was delivered to Sywell in November 1951 for conversion by Brooklands into a TT.35. Following conversion it had another spell in storage before it was assigned to No.1 CAACU at Hornchurch right at the end of 1953. In February 1958, Mosquito TT.35 RS712 was transferred to West Germany for operation within the 2nd Tactical Air Force, serving with the Target Towing Flight of the Armament Practice Section at Schleswigland, but within two months it had been transferred on again to No.3 CAACU at Exeter.

Mosquito TT.35 RS712 was placed in storage with No.27 MU after it was taken out of service with No.3 CAACU at the end of May 1963. It became the second of the three Mirisch-owned Mosquitos that did much of the flying in Scotland. RS712 was chartered by 'Hamish' Mahaddie after filming was completed, who based it first at RAF Henlow, then at RAF West Malling in Kent. Like RS709, it too returned to Bovingdon in 1968 for its role in "Mosquito Squadron", followed by a further spell in storage at West Malling until, in September 1972, the entrepreneureal Sir William Roberts acquired it for his Strathallan Collection in Scotland.

One of Britain's most famous airshow and experienced test pilots, Neil Williams, had an 'interesting' flight in this Mosquito when, after completing a check ride with Personal Plane Services at Booker, he attempted a go-around from Wycombe Air Park's Runway Two Five. As Williams opened the throttles, the starboard engine choked, leaving onlookers to watch helplessly as the Mosquito disappeared from sight into the valley at the end of Two Five. Expecting to see a mushroom ball of flame and smoke, they could only watch in wonder as Williams continued with all his experience to maintain the boost and coax RS712 on its single live port engine towards RAF Benson, to make a successful emergency landing. On 8th November 1975, Neil Williams made the successful ferry flight from West Malling to Strathallan.

History records that the Strathallan Collection went into receivership in 1981. Mosquito RS712 was acquired by Kermit Weeks in the auction of the Strathallan Collection on 14th July 1981. It remained in storage in the UK for several years before it was transferred back to Personal Plane Services at Booker on 21st December 1984, to begin the long programme of preparation for the trans-Atlantic flight to Florida. It was painted to represent the No.487 Squadron Mosquito flown by Group Captain P C Pickard in the attack on Amiens Prison in 1944, coded EG-F, and displayed at the 1987 Biggin Hill Air Fair, its last public appearance in the UK. On 29th September 1987, RS712 began its long flight from Britain to Florida where it joined Kermit Weeks's Fantasy of Flight collection, registered as N35MK. Today, it is displayed statically by the EAA Museum at Oshkosh, Wisconsin.

de Havilland Mosquito TT.35 RS715, studio prop and set-dressing. Another Airspeed-built Mosquito B.35 in 1946, RS715 was, like others of its kind that year, placed straight into storage following acceptance by the RAF. There it remained until November 1951 when it was sent to Sywell for conversion into TT.35 status by Brooklands. After completion of the conversion, RS715 went back into storage with No.27 MU until it was summoned for duty with No.3 CAACU at Exeter, then again with No.4 CAACU at Llandow; it was still target-towing with the latter when No.4 CAACU combined with its No.3 sister unit, meaning a return to Exeter. Mosquito TT.35 RS715 served out the remainder of its flying career at Exeter, until it was struck off charge on 18th September 1961. As proof that the Mirisch Corporation planned well in advance of actual filming to make "633 Squadron", the entire airframe of RS715 was purchased by Mirisch Films in August 1962 and stored in sections at MGM British Film Studios, Borehamwood, with the expectation that they could be used in set-dressing for crash scenes or selected close-ups. The airframe remains were acquired by the MGM Studios after filming for future productions, but were sold in 1973. Currently, the rear fuselage is being used in the restoration of Mosquito NF.XI HJ711 with the Yorkshire Air Museum. Because Mosquito TT.35 RS715 was purchased much earlier than when nearly all the other Mosquitos were obtained, and then dismantled, it is often overlooked by those sources which list Mosquitos appearing in "633 Squadron".

de Havilland Mosquito TT.35 RS718, taxyable and static prop as 'HJ662/HT-C' and 'HJ898/HT-G', the latter being the Mosquito assigned to Wing Commander Roy Grant, played by Cliff Robertson (incidentally, HJ662 was actually the serial number of the Mosquito FB.VI prototype in 1942). It was used to film the crash landing scene when Grant, with navigator 'Thistle', is forced into a wheels-up failure at Sutton Craddock after returning from the raid on the Gestapo headquarters in Bergen, where Erik Bergmann was being tortured under interrogation.

Again, another of the Airspeed batch of B.35s built at Christchurch in 1946, RS718's early career took a different path from its compatriots, being delivered to Marshalls on 11th October 1946. In early 1947, it was transferred to the BTU at West Freugh. It suffered a flying accident on 12th July that year and underwent repairs at de Havillands before being placed in storage with No.19 MU in April 1949. There is some suggestion that RS718 spent some time with No.98 Squadron, but it was in storage again when it was sent for conversion into TT.35 status by Brooklands in late 1953. On 17th May 1954, Mosquito TT.35 RS718 began operations with No.1 CAACU, with which it served for three years before being returned to storage with several different MUs. It was assigned to the Target Towing Flight of the Armament Practice Station at Schleswigland in November 1957, but stayed no longer than six months. After returning to the UK, RS718 was sent on its final tasking with No.3 CAACU.

Mosquito TT.35 RS718 suffered a second flying accident on 31st May 1962 that brought an end to its career. It was struck off charge on 19th June and was due to be transferred to No.71 MU for scrapping, but was saved from this fate through being purchased by Mirisch Films in August 1962. It appears an agreement was reached with the MoD that RS718 would be retained at Exeter until all the Mosquitos were transferred to Bovingdon for filming. The author can personally confirm this because he photographed RS718 in the static park of the Exeter Air Day held on 22nd June 1963, still in its target-tug markings. Within a few weeks it had been road-freighted to Bovingdon, where it received its "633 Squadron" 'wardrobe'.

On 8th August 1963, John Crewdson performed the wheels-up crash landing: study of this film stunt shows that Crewdson began a high speed run across grass with the tail high, before lowering the tail as he came abreast the camera position, at which point he deliberately retracted the undercarriage, resulting in RS718 slamming down onto its belly, bouncing the tail into the air and then pounding down again with such force that the fabric covering the rudder shattered, while an elevator broke off completely. The Mosquito slewed round in a complete 90 degrees before coming to a stop. Mosquito RS718 was then set up where it lay to film Grant escaping from the cockpit, with flames pouring from the port engine which actually set fire to the flying suit worn by the stuntman filling in for Cliff Robertson. The scene continues with actual Bovingdon Airfield firecrew hacking their way into the blazing cockpit to rescue the trapped 'Thistle'.

This same crash was also filmed from a camera position ahead of Mosquito RS718, with Crewdson collapsing the undercarriage and RS718 slewing round 90 degrees just before reaching the camera. This shot was used right at the end of the film, when Grant's and Hoppy's Mosquito crashes in Norway after completing the attack on the rocket fuel plant that 633 Squadron have been sent to destroy. The art department matte painted a background scene of mountains and forest trees onto the imagery of this crash, effectively creating the impression the Mosquito really was crashing in Norway. The broken airframe of another Mosquito, understood to be TT.35 TA642, was used to film Grant and Hoppy being rescued by a woodsman. Thus it was that Mosquito TT.35 RS718 was destroyed on the "633 Squadron" film set at Bovingdon, with its remains torched, then buried, along with the other two Mosquitos in the production to suffer the same fate.

de Havilland Mosquito TT.35 TA639, flyer as 'HJ682/HT-B'. Despite the sequence of the serials, TA639 is older than all the above listed TT.35s, having been built by de Havillands at Hatfield as a B.35 and taken straight into storage at No.27 MU on 16th April 1945. There it remained completely inactive until May 1952, when it underwent the TT.35 conversion course at Sywell with Brooklands. On 17th October 1952, Mosquito TT.35 TA639 joined the RAF Ballykelly Station Flight in Northern Ireland, serving there for two months before it transferred to the RAF Aldergrove Station Flight, with which it remained in Northern Ireland until it returned to storage with No.38 MU during December 1954. It remained locked away with both No.38

and No.27 MUs until it was taken out, dusted down and sent to No.3 CAACU at Exeter during September 1959.

Mosquito TT.35 TA639 was struck off charge on 31st May 1963, but was retained by the MoD and assigned to the Central Flying School (CFS) at RAF Little Rissington for display flying and personal use by the CFS Commandant. From there it went to Bovingdon in July 1963 for its role in "633 Squadron", being the other of the two MoD-owned Mosquitos (alongside T.3 TW117) which flew in the film but not in the flying sequences filmed in Scotland.

This Mosquito returned to RAF Little Rissington after completing its role in "633 Squadron". It seems that some controversy became attached to this aircraft, especially as to whether it was maintained in airworthy condition. A book published in 2006 about the CFS at Little Rissington has made the claim that Ground Engineering Wing staff resented being given the task of maintaining not only an extra aircraft in addition to all the Jet Provost T.4 trainers they had to care for, but of a type and method of construction that they had no experience of working on before. The book alleges they intentionally placed the Mosquito in the sole heated hangar at RAF Little Rissington, making sure it was placed with its tail positioned under a canvas hot air duct. This caused the glued joints in the wooden airframe to progressively fail, making the Mosquito unsafe to fly. In March 1966, a glued joint inspection took place, which found that the joints had deteriorated to such an extent that the aircraft was not only unsafe to fly, but unsafe to taxy.

Another mystery attached to Mosquito TT.35 TA639 is an event that the author himself was witness to in 1965, but the significance of which he was unaware at the time. Mosquito TA639 was an extra and undeclared flying display item at the Exeter Air Day on 26th June 1965. TA639 was still carrying its "633 Squadron" camouflage and roundels, but its fake code and serial had been removed. It flew as the final item in the flying display, not listed in the published flying programme. What is mystifying is that this demo is not mentioned in TA639's flight record that is in the possession of the RAF Museum at Cosford and is obtainable Online. Its absence from TA639's flight record suggests that this demo might have been unauthorised and, thus, may have been illegal.

Suffice it to say, Mosquito TT.35 TA639 did not fly again after it was grounded in March 1966. It was transferred to the AHB collection store at RAF Henlow in August 1967, listed for display in the future RAF Museum. In September 1969, it had been placed in storage at RAF Cosford and went on display at the then Cosford Aerospace Museum during the Seventies. In 1988, it was repainted to represent the Pathfinder Mosquito B.XX flown by Wing Commander Guy Gibson, VC, coded AZ-E of No.627 Squadron, in which he lost his life on a sortie during 19th/20th September 1944. TA639 retains these markings to this day with the RAF Museum collection at Cosford.

de Havilland Mosquito TT.35 TA642, intended as a flyer as 'HX835' but written out of the film when it suffered an undercarriage collapse on landing on 1st August 1963. The damaged airframe was used for the crash scene at the end of the film, when the Norwegian woodsman helps 'Hoppy' rescue Grant from the burning wreckage. Its remains were also used as the flaming wreck of the Mosquito in the film which crashes while training for the mission in Scotland, with another Mosquito over-flying it to represent Grant performing his salute to fallen comrades.

This Mosquito was built as a B.35 by de Havillands at Hatfield and was delivered to the RAF in 1945 just as the War in Europe was coming to an end. Little is known about its service record, but it was converted into a TT.35 in 1951 and was operated by both Nos.1 & 3 CAACUs. It was struck off charge on 31st May 1963, but was clearly still airworthy when it joined its compatriots for filming at Bovingdon. After it was dismantled and burnt for the two crash scenes, Mosquito TT.35 TA642 was reportedly buried at Bovingdon along with the remains of RS718 and the third Mosquito that was destroyed during filming, TA724.

de Havilland Mosquito TT.35 TA719, flyer as 'HJ898/HT-G', Wing Commander Grant's Mosquito. Purchased by Mirisch Films and registered as G-ASKC. Built as a B.35 at Hatfield, TA719 was placed into storage after being accepted by the RAF in June 1945. There it was to remain, completely inactive, until it was sent to Sywell on 15th August 1953 for conversion into TT.35 configuration. When completed, it was first stored with No.22 MU before being allocated to No.4 CAACU. On 30th June 1954, it was transferred to No.3 CAACU and served out the rest of its career at Exeter until it was retired in November 1962. It remained at Exeter after being purchased by Mirisch, awaiting "633 Squadron" duty.

After filming was completed, Mosquito TT.35 TA719 was sold to Peter Thomas at Staverton Airport for his Skyfame Museum collection, much to the reported annoyance of actor Cliff Robertson - himself a very experienced pilot in the States - who had been so taken with this Mosquito that he wanted to purchase it when filming was completed. Robertson allegedly blamed 'Hamish' Mahaddie, who handled the disposal of the three Mirish-owned Mosquitos post-filming, for blocking the deal and selling TA719 on to Peter Thomas, especially as Mahaddie sold RS709 to Thomas as well two months later while chartering RS712 himself from Mirisch. Robertson is quoted on his own Website as saying, "I tried to buy one, so I could bring it back to America, but I was subverted by someone who will remain nameless, who screwed things up so nobody got them". One possible explanation for Robertson not getting his hands on one of the Mirisch Mosquitos is that the studio, Columbia Pictures, to whom Robertson was contracted, did not want the actor to own what they perceived as a high risk machine, so perhaps Mirisch Films were instructed not to approve the sale to him.

Thomas intended to keep TA719 in flying condition, and in B.35 configuration, together with RS709. This meant that, along with Hatfield-based Mosquito T.3 RR299, MoD-owned TA639 at RAF Little Rissington, ex- No.3 CAACU Mosquito TT.35 TA634 acquired by the Liverpool Corporation at Speke, and the Mahaddie-chartered RS712 stored at RAF Henlow, there were six airworthy Mosquitos in the UK at the end of 1963. Today there isn't one. However, by 27th July 1964 that total was reduced

to five when TA719 was badly damaged at Staverton during a deadstick landing, especially to the port wing outboard of the engine. The damage was too extensive for Skyfame to repair, but it was used as a static prop with a fake port outer wing when "Mosquito Squadron" was filmed at Bovingdon in 1968. The Imperial War Museum acquired TA719 in 1978 after taking over most of Thomas's collection following the closure of the Skyfame Museum and transferred it to Duxford, where it has remained ever since. Today, Mosquito TT.35 TA719 is suspended from the ceiling in the AirSpace Hall at Duxford, beautifully restored in its silver-yellow-black target-tug colours.

de Havilland Mosquito TT.35 TA724, taxyable and static prop, with no serial but as 'HT-R'. Built in 1946 by Airspeed at Christchurch as a B.35, this Mosquito, like so many others, went straight into storage after delivery to the Royal Air Force. It seems to have remained there until 1951, when it took the TT.35 conversion course and at some stage in time arrived at Exeter with No.3 CAACU. Purchased by Mirisch Films, it was selected to be used in the crash scene when a Mosquito is shot up on the runway by a Messerschmitt Bf.109 and runs out of control into a petrol bowser. To achieve this, a brace was attached to the tail wheel and fitted to the fuselage underside, in order to prevent the tail wheel from turning and thus ensure the pilotless Mosquito - naturally there was no one in the cockpit - taxyied under its own power in a straight line right into the bowser on 10th August 1963. According to Robertson, "…they had this special effects guy running behind it with long wires, so he was able to trigger it off when it hit this truck. It exploded. That broke my heart. Then we watched it burn…That central spar was made of very highly compressed wood. I watched it burn for over three hours, and that spar was still intact. It was amazing how strong it was".

de Havilland Mosquito TT.35 TJ118, cockpit section only for filming in MGM British Film Studios in Borehamwood and set-dressing at Bovingdon. Built in 1945 by de Havillands at Hatfield, TJ118 was originally ordered as a B.XVI but was produced as a B.35. Like so many 1945-delivered B.35s, it was placed straight into storage by the RAF with the War in Europe over. It probably remained locked away until July 1953, when it went to Brooklands at Sywell for conversion into a TT.35. It, too, was acquired by Mirisch Films in August 1962 as a grounded airframe with inhibited engines. All the cockpit scenes in "633 Squadron" were filmed at Borehamwood using the nose section of TJ118; it was used likewise in "Mosquito Squadron". The separated wing section of TJ118 appears in "633 Squadron", set up on a low loader with 'Erks' working on it just before the attack by the two Messerschmitts; the wings had not been repainted, the yellow-black target-tug scheme clearly visible in shot. Today, Mosquito TT.35 TJ118's nose and fuselage sections are in the possession of the de Havilland Aircraft Heritage Centre at London Colney, Hertfordshire.

On 9th May 1963, six Mosquitos of No.3 CAACU made a farewell fly-past over their Exeter Airport base. They comprised T.3 TW117 and TT.35s RS709, RS712, TA634, TA639 and TA719, although TA639 suffered a port engine failure and had to make an emergency landing. This was the last formation of de Havilland Mosquitos in RAF history. The final fly-past had been expected to take place the previous August, but delays in the delivery of the Mosquito TT.35s' replacements with No.3 CAACU, Gloster Meteor TT.20s, meant that the 'Mossies' had to continue sleeve target-towing until May 1963. This is what caused the delay in the filming schedule.

No.3 CAACU was the last RAF unit to operate the Mosquito. Their presence at Exeter Airport made the South Devon regional airfield a uniquely interesting place to visit in the early Sixties. The No.3 CAACU pilots had a neat party trick that they performed at the annual Exeter Air Day held every June. Three Mosquito TT.35s would take off in quick succession. Two would disappear to the South, the third to the North. They would all then return at very low-level, the two spaced well apart while the solo, approaching from the opposite end, would pass right between them. As they converged, all three Mosquitos would release their sleeve targets, which would strike the ground before they sprang open! They would then all dumbbell turn with their targets still in tow and then return to pass again, only this time when they passed through each other they simultaneously released their targets.

A little known airshow appearance by the three Mirisch-owned Mosquito TT.35s - RS709/G-ASKA, RS712/G-ASKB, TA719/G-ASKC - took place on 14th September 1963 at the Biggin Hill Battle of Britain 'At Home' Day. All three made low fly-bys in 'Vic' formation, still in "633 Squadron" camouflage and with their codes, but with their real serials restored. They were accompanied by another "633 Squadron" aircraft, the camera-ship which also had a role in the film, North American B-25J Mitchell N9089Z, named Moviemaker II. This B-25J was in the ownership of a company named Aero Associates based at Ryan Field, Tucson, Arizona, when it was brought over to Bovingdon to film the air-airs of the Mosquitos. Aero Associates was a subsidiary company of Aero American Corp run by Australian Greg Board, who we met in "The War Lover" (1962). Board had teamed up with a colourful and soon-to-become controversial character, John 'Jeff' Hawke, who we shall be meeting a number of times in this book.

Hawke was the pilot of the B-25J, as well as being contracted to fly one of the Mirisch Mosquitos plus a third aircraft in the film that we shall be looking at shortly. Moviemaker II was literally abandoned at Biggin Hill by Hawke after its appearance in the Battle of Britain airshow, largely because his partner in the USA was having an interesting time with his business affairs there and was not interested in the fate of his World War Two bomber. B-25J Mitchell N9089Z was impounded by the CAA due to the non-payment of parking fees at Biggin Hill, and was then passed over free of charge to the Historic Aircraft Preservation Society at the Kent airfield. On 19th July 1967, the B-25J was road-freighted to Southend Airport to go on display with the British Historic Aircraft Museum, painted as an RAF Mitchell, HD368/VO-A of No.98 Squadron. Curiously, it came briefly under the ownership of John Hawke's Visionair International company on 10th May 1983, but the following year it was acquired by Aces High, the

aviation film and services company we shall be dealing with quite a bit in this book.

Aces High had N9089Z displayed statically at Duxford between 1984 - 1987, after which it was transferred by road again to Aces High's North Weald base. It was then re-painted in a USAAF scheme as 430861/Bedsheet Bomber. The Fighter Collection (TFC) acquired it in 1989, in whose ownership it was left out in the open at North Weald while it was used as a spares source to support TFC's operation of its B-25D Mitchell Grumpy. Today, what remains of B-25J N9089Z is believed to be in the ownership of Barry Penrose at Wycombe Air Park, with a view to a restoration, although it is not known if this will involve N9089Z itself or if surviving sections of this B-25 will be used to restore another Mitchell.

The role B-25J N9089Z performs in the film is to portray an RAF Mitchell that parachutes Erik Bergmann into Norway. Its colour scheme was white fuselage top, upper wings and tail fins, with silver lower fuselage and under the wings. RAF roundels were applied, while its US civil serial was shortened to 'N908' to give it an approximate British military identity. The colour scheme was, of course, completely wrong for an RAF Mitchell, and RAF Special Duties squadrons never operated this type of aircraft. However, "633 Squadron" film director Walter E Grauman must have appreciated having the B-25J on set because he flew 56 missions over Europe in B-25s with the USAAF's 12th Air Force, winning the Distinguished Service Cross.

Two more aircraft that appear in "633 Squadron" are, of course, the enemy. They are meant to be Messerschmitt Bf.109s strafing RAF Sutton Craddock and, in the finale, attacking the Mosquitos as they emerge from the fjord after bombing the German rocket fuel plant. They are instantly recognisable to all aviation enthusiasts and historians as Messerschmitt Bf.108B Taifuns, now well established in the international film industry during the Sixties as the closest substitute for the Bf.109.

Both the Bf.108s in "633 Squadron" are the same two Nord 1002 Pinguoin touring aircraft that appeared two years earlier in "The Longest Day" (1962). Readers can refer to "The Longest Day" review in order to link up with their histories. They had taken up residence at RAF Wattisham, Suffolk, in 1963, sitting at the back of the Station Flight hangar. They had both come into the possession, but not the ownership, of John 'Jeff' Hawke. Cornishman Hawke got into the film industry with aircraft at quite a young age and while he was still a serving Royal Air Force pilot. Twenty-nine year old Flight Lieutenant John 'Corny' Hawke was flying the Hawker Hunter T.7, Gloster Meteor T.7, F.8 and TT.20, plus the Chipmunk T.10, with the RAF Wattisham Station Flight in 1963 when he became involved in "633 Squadron", his first film for which he provided aviation services.

Hawke had the foresight to see that the film industry lacked aircraft representative of World War Two Luftwaffe types and, after seeing the Messerschmitt Bf.108s used to act as Messerschmitt Bf.109s in "The Longest Day", he and fellow Wattisham Station Flight pilot, 'Taff' Rich, set about chartering the two French-registered Nord 1002 Pinguoin, plus a Morane MS.500 Criquet, very rare types to be seen in British skies in the early Sixties. All three were hangared at RAF Wattisham and were painted in accurate Deutsches Luftwaffe colour schemes and markings, thus making the two Nord 1002s representative of the Messerschmitt Bf.108B and the Morane MS.500 identical to a Fieseler Storch. They retained their French registration.

Nord 1002 Pinguoin II F-BFYX is the first of the two 'Messerschmitt Bf.109s' in the film. It was flown by Hawke as the second, and noticeably lower, 'Messerschmitt' in the Sutton Craddock strafe attack set-piece. It was painted at Wattisham in realistic-looking mottled camouflage, with the large code number '14' in white just ahead of the fuselage Balkenkreuze and the 'Ace of Spades' badge of III/JG.53 on the nose, giving it some semblance of authenticity; however, all this decoration seems to have met with little favour with the director, as both Pinguoin IIs had had their 'wardrobe' changed to plain duck egg green-grey, with only Luftwaffe Balkenkreuzen applied, when they went in front of the cameras.

Nord 1002M Pinguoin II F-BGVU is the second 'Messerschmitt Bf.109'. The Aeromovies - Films d'Aviation Website quotes American Martin Caidin as being Hawke's companion pilot in "633 Squadron" and who flew F-BGVU. It had a distinctive feature which made it immediately recognisable, as compared with F-BFYX: it had an air filter mounted atop its nose engine cowling, just behind the spinner, a feature that makes it identifiable as a Nord 1002M (Modernise) variant. It too was painted in mottled camouflage at Wattisham, and had a large Chevron applied ahead of the fuselage Balkenkreuze; but it also lost all this paintwork when it appeared in the film.

Caidin flew Pinguoin II F-BGVU for the air battle scenes between it and a Mosquito filmed air-air from B-25J Moviemaker II: the bulk of the aerial dogfights were achieved with the use of very unconvincing studio miniature Mosquitos and Messerschmitt Bf.108s. F-BGVU is immediately recognisable in the air-air close-ups, due to its clearly seen air filter in front of the cockpit (F-BFYX was not used for the air-airs, a bit difficult with Hawke in the B-25J).

When the filming of "633 Squadron" was completed, Caidin purchased both these Nord 1002 Pinguoin IIs. He was very familiar with the type, having written the maintenance manual for the Messerschmitt Bf.108 which was certified by the Federal Aviation Authority in the USA. Caidin did not retain ownership of both these Nord 1002s for long, both being sold in the States. Hawke and another British pilot, Francis Freeman, were contracted by Caidin to fly both aircraft across the Atlantic in January 1964. However, Nord 1002M F-BGVU didn't make it: an engine failure caused Freeman to ditch it in the icy seas close to the unfortunately fatefully named Cut Throat Island, off the Labrador coast. Nord 1002 F-BFYX became N108U on the US register, but was fated to be damaged in a hangar fire. Subsequently, it was transferred to a German owner and fully restored. Today, it is privately owned as D-ELLM, kept at Immendingen.

Incidentally, Cliff Robertson also became enamoured of the Nord 1002/Messerschmitt Bf.108 while making "633 Squadron" and later acquired an example that he had imported into the United States.

Lastly, the opening sequence: George Chakiris as Norwegian Linge Resistance fighter leader Erik Bergman (a mis-casting of a studio contracted actor if ever there was one) and several other Linge fighters ambush a German staff car. Having killed its occupants in a pointless attack, Chakiris is led into a field where a Miles Messenger light aircraft is waiting, engine turning. Chakiris jumps aboard and the Messenger immediately trundles forward to take off at low-level through trees, just as a pursuing German patrol opens fire.

Well, it's a dramatic opening and sets the tone for what is a dramatically entertaining war film, but one that is all too easily content to stay on the side of superficially stereotypical characterisation. The Germans are just bad; the Norwegians are just good. The RAF pilots are, to a man, all heroic and strong.

Chakiris is escaping from Norway to England…in a Miles Messenger? However, credibility had to be sacrificed for availability, there being no Westland Lysander in flying condition to perform the role of an RAF Special Duties squadron aircraft. Also, the Messenger is obviously not a military machine, being painted dark green overall with red cheat line leading from its nose down to the end of its passenger cabin. No registration is visible, though.

The aircraft's owner at the time this scene was filmed has stated in an Online Forum that he believes an out-and-back Scotland-Norway-Scotland trip in a Messenger was "just do-able. Add another ten gallons of gas in an auxiliary fuel tank and it's a breeze". The Norwegian scenes in "633 Squadron" were filmed in Scotland during 1963, presumably including the opening scene involving the Messenger which was based at Perth during this time.

The Miles M.38 Messenger 2A in question is G-AKBO, registered to Dorran Construction Ltd of Perth, Scotland, between 1961 and 1964, and flown in the film by Neville Browning. This is a former Kings Cup Air Race winner, having won this prestigious event in September 1954 when it was flown by Blackburn Aircraft Ltd's test pilot, Flight Lieutenant Harold 'Timber' Wood. Although a Miles aircraft, Messenger 2A G-AKBO was built and first flown at Newtownards, Northern Ireland, in 1947. It spent much of its earlier career on the air race circuit in England. In total, G-AKBO has been registered to no less than 25 owners in its lifetime and is extant today, registered to a private owner in Cornwall.

The question has often been asked as to who flew the Mosquitos in "633 Squadron". It has frequently been assumed that No.3 CAACU pilots flew them, but they were under contract to the MoD for target-towing and were converting to the late-delivered Meteor TT.20s when filming was in progress, meaning they could not be spared from their tasking. However, No.3 CAACU chief pilot Harry Ellis flew Mosquito T.3 TW117 for the few scenes it appeared in, as well as checking out all the other Mosquito pilots, while the Commandant of the Central Flying School made some flights in the Little Rissington-based Mosquito TT.35 TA639.

The three Mirish Mosquitos, RS709, RS712 and TA719, were flown by the following: John Crewdson of Film Aviation Services, fresh from trying to run down Sean Connery as Secret Agent James Bond 007 in the 'SPECTRE Helicopter' in "From Russia With Love" (1963); the aforementioned John 'Jeff' Hawke, who left the RAF once "633 Squadron" was completed, to set up his Visionair International company for aerial filming work; Martin Caidin; and Flight Lieutenant Neil Williams, RAF test pilot at RAE Farnborough with experience of flying a most diverse number of single-engine and multi-engine types, as well as being British national aerobatic champion. Williams and Cliff Robertson forged a strong friendship during the film production, with the former teaching the latter to fly a Tiger Moth at Fairoaks during their days off. When Robertson's attempt to buy one of the Mosquitos came to nought, he opted to buy one of the Spitfire Mk.IXs operated for target-towing in Belgium and had Williams fly it to Britain for him (as described in the review of "The Longest Day", 1962).

The three Mirisch Mosquitos flew the training sequences filmed in the Scottish Highlands, flying through Larig Ghru Pass close to Aviemore, and the fjord opening attack sequences flown through Loch Morar and Loch Nevis. The Mosquitos were based at Inverness/Dalcross Airport for this phase of filming.

Although there is evidence that the five flyers flew altogether on at least one occasion, no imagery of them filmed air-air as a complete unit appears in the film released to theater. Only one brief shot of a four-ship is seen. Most of the formation shots are of the Mirisch three in 'Vic', flying low-level over the sea filmed from the B-25J that was either flying just ahead and above them or behind them. Pinguoin II F-BGVU was flown by Martin Caidin in head-on runs towards B-25J Moviemaker II, with the cameraman filming the 'Bf.109' in zoom shot from the glass flat-panelled nose. Hawke held the B-25J in a straight line, while Caidin timed his pull-up in a pre-planned manoeuvre to pass safely over the oncoming bomber.

The one weak aspect of "633 Squadron" is the use of very unrealistic miniature Mosquitos for the actual attack on the mountain overhang above the rocket fuel plant. Allowing for the level of SFX technology of the time, the miniatures of the Mosquitos and of the Bf.108s were as crudely obvious to a mid-Sixties cinema audience as they are to owners of the film's DVD today.

Despite its 'Boys Own'-ish heroics and stereotypical acting, "633 Squadron" will always remain one of the most enduring and much watched British war films, for one reason only: those magnificent Mosquitos.

THE SECRET OF BLOOD ISLAND

(Released: December 1964)

A Hammer Films follow up to the same production company's "The Camp on Blood Island" (1958) , two British pilots, one male, one female, bail out over Japanese Occupied Malaya and try to avoid capture. However, their aircraft is not shown.

OPERATION CROSSBOW

(Released: March 1965)

"Operation Crossbow" is the second of two British war films that takes as its subject the Vergeltungswaffen - Retaliation Weapons - which Hitler ordered be directed against London after the invasion of Normandy in June 1944. The first film, "Battle of the V1" (1958), was a much lower budget movie that focused solely upon the Fieseler Fi.103 flying bomb campaign, although it included events pertaining to the V2 rocket but without any reference to that weapon. "Operation Crossbow" tackles both Vergeltungswaffen.

It has been claimed that the title of this film is the principal reason why the entire campaign conducted by British Military and Scientific Intelligence, with the full support of the Royal Air Force, is now called Operation Crossbow, when in fact no such military Operation under this name existed. 'Crossbow' was the name given to the campaign itself and to the Committee which oversaw its conduct; there were, however, many military and intelligence operations carried out against the flying bomb and the artillery rocket that the 'Crossbow' Committee approved and authorised.

Curiously, the term 'Operation Crossbow' is never actually used in the film. One wonders if it was coined for the film's title after the production was completed. The script writing team - and it was a sizeable one, including Emeric Pressburger under the non de plume Richard Imrie - may not have been fully commensurate with the facts relating to the 'Crossbow' Committee because much about it was still classified in 1964 when the film was being made. As will be shown in this review, more details came to light in subsequent years that now challenge the roles certain real individuals are portrayed as performing in "Operation Crossbow", and may explain what seems to be the inexcusable exclusion in the film's plot of one person who was central to the success of the 'Crossbow' campaign itself.

The sight in the pre-credits opening sequence, with extras in period dress and Forties-era vehicles moving along Downing Street, W1, must make a 21st Century audience wonder how it could be possible to move about this famous street so easily, when today it is totally blocked off from public access with huge steel barriers. It shows Duncan Sandys, played by actor Richard Johnson, who physically bore a quite reasonable resemblance to the real Sandys, entering 10 Downing Street. He moves with a pronounced limp. The real Duncan Sandys was wounded in action when fighting in Norway and was left with a permanent limp.

Sandys is let into the Cabinet Room in Number 10: it is the real Cabinet Room, the film production team were given permission to film there during Parliament's summer recess in 1964. Churchill sits alone in the centre behind the long table. He greets Sandys by his first name. There is no reference to the relationship in the screenplay, but Churchill was Sandys's father-in-law: Sandys married Churchill's daughter, Diana, in 1935.

Churchill tells Sandys there is a vital job to be done and the outcome of the War may depend on how he handles it. The Prime Minister wants Sandys to find out if the rocket threat is real and, if so, to recommend how to tackle it. His first task is to collect all the evidence he can and then tell the War Cabinet what he thinks about it.

Here is the conundrum: in mid-1943, when this scene is meant to be taking place, the evidence that the rocket threat was real already existed and a recommendation as to what to be done had been presented. The problem was, the Scientific Intelligence team which had gathered this evidence, with the vital assistance of the RAF Photographic Interpretation Unit at Medmenham, Buckinghamshire, was being excluded from the War Cabinet Committee that Churchill appointed Sandys to Chair, the 'Crossbow' Committee itself. This may have been due to the resentment held by military and government experts towards the Scientific Intelligence Officer in charge of the team, Dr R V Jones, who had a poor opinion of Sandys's capacity to understand the nature of the threat and how to deal with it.

Jones is completely excluded from "Operation Crossbow". Certain other real-life members of the 'Crossbow' Committee are portrayed by well known British character actors of the Sixties, some, like John Mills and Trevor Howard, being real veterans of the War and of films made during and after it. Not least among the personalities that made up the 'Crossbow' Committee is Professor Lindemann, Scientific Advisor to Churchill, who had been tutorial professor to Dr Jones before the War and who opposed Jones's theories about the rocket threat. Nonetheless, Lindemann in real life made certain that Jones attended the crucial meeting of the War Cabinet Defence Committee (Operations), chaired by Churchill in the Cabinet's underground headquarters and held on the evening of 29th June 1943, when the decision was finally made to bomb the test and production facilities for the V2 rocket at Peenemunde.

A version of this meeting appears in the film, but it is by no means an accurate portrayal of it. Totally absent from the meeting is the character of R V Jones, as he is from the entire plot. Excluding him is the equivalent of keeping Dr Barnes Wallis's name out of the invention of the bouncing bomb.

In the film, Sandys is portrayed as the man with the insight to realise the extent of the danger presented by the rocket. In his book, "Most Secret War", R V Jones takes the credit for being the first to identify a rocket from photographic intelligence of Peenemunde, which he claims Sandys ignored. He also claims Sandys was behind the serious effort to exclude him from the 'Crossbow' Committee. No doubt there were serious egos at work here, and Jones has his own point to make, as he does so very clearly in his book. But what is now known today means that, as a film, "Operation Crossbow" is a seriously flawed work, which lessens the effect it has as an otherwise well made, well acted production, based on true-life events that could, and very probably did, save the world from a merciless power that had the will, and nearly the whole means, to produce devastating weapons against which there was no answer - until August 1945.

The question has to be asked, were the producer and the original story writers kept in the dark about some very basic facts, so that a more presentable and acceptable picture of the establishment's role could be shown on screen? Was it easier to

achieve this because the producer, Carlo Ponti, and the original story writers, Duilio Coletti and Vittoriano Pettrilli, were all Italian and, therefore, far less commensurate with what actually took place? It's not as if Duncan Sandys was a sympathetic figure publicly in the mid-Sixties, especially where the aviation industry was concerned: after all, his infamous 1957 Defence White Paper when he was Secretary of State for Defence, along with his enforced amalgamation of many British aviation companies, has been claimed to have done more damage to the Royal Air Force and Britain's aircraft manufacturing capacity than Hermann Goering's Luftwaffe ever achieved.

However, in the film, Duncan Sandys is made to be the central figure of the 'Crossbow' Committee who pulls the entire operation against the V1 and the V2 together. There is the distinct feeling that the establishment, in return for providing full facilities in 10 Downing Street and elsewhere, wanted to ensure that Ponti, Coletti and Pettrilli, plus their very capable director, Michael Anderson ("The Dam Busters", 1955), presented a favourable picture that was to their liking.

What is to the credit of the production team behind "Operation Crossbow" is their very accurate creations of full-scale facsimiles of the Vergeltungswaffen themselves, the Fieseler Fi.103 unmanned flying warhead and the Aggregat Vier (Aggregate Four, or simply A4) ballistic artillery rocket. The Fi.103 was known to British Scientific Intelligence as FZG.76, as explained in the review of "Battle of the V1" in Chapter Three, disguised as a pilotless target drone for Luftwaffe Flak regiments to practice against. No mention of this is made in "Operation Crossbow", not surprising as it was R V Jones who first revealed details of this duplicity by the Luftwaffe when he published his book in 1978, clear proof that he had evidence that Sandys was ignoring and that the establishment made sure Coletti and Pettrilli did not learn about.

A scene has General Linz meeting with General Ziemann and Flugkapitan Hannah Reitsch in an underground bunker where a Fieseler Fi.103 hangs from the roof. The script states that the "pilotless plane" has successfully flown but veers to the right. Hannah Reitsch has assembled a group of test pilots who will try to solve the problem. Linz refuses to endorse such an idea as it is suicidal. He soon changes his mind when Ziemann tells him that the Fuehrer has approved the test flights.

Next they inspect a test model of an Aggregat Vier or A4 rocket, although this terminology is not used in the script - they simply refer to it as the "Rakete" (Rocket). The A4 on its Meillerwagen trailer is the real thing, a genuine V2 rocket painted in black-and-white oblong sections, as were the actual A4 test rockets. It was one of eight V2s assembled in September 1945 under British supervision by the Versuchskommando Altenwalde, or AVKO, made up of surviving officers and troops of the V2 Division (officially, the Division zu Vergeltung: Division of Retaliation) who surrendered to American forces on 1st and 2nd May 1945 at Wootz, on the Elbe River. They came under British command when Operation Backfire was put into place at a location in Western Germany called Cuxhaven, close to the North Sea coast, to test fire V2 rockets. V2 field troops, men who had launched V2s in combat, retained the most practical knowledge of field logistics and operations, so were the best equipped to assemble and test fire the rockets.

Three V2 rockets were fired under Operation Backfire during October 1945. All eight V2s were assembled from 18 incomplete rockets found on an abandoned rail shipment outside of Jerxheim in the British Zone of Occupation, while 12 more were found near Lesse, including one almost complete specimen. The author can only commend the excellent v2rocket.com Website and urge readers to study it in detail, where very full information about Operation Backfire can be obtained.

The five remaining V2 rockets were distributed to various research organisations. The example seen in "Operation Crossbow" was in the possession of the Rocket Propulsion Establishment at the former RAF Westcott in Buckinghamshire and was loaned to MGM British Studios for its appearance in the film. It was also used as a pattern for a full-scale facsimile A4 that appears later to portray a V2 being fired at London. This genuine V2 ballistic rocket is today exhibited in the RAF Museum at Cosford, in exactly the form it appears in the film mounted on its mobile firing stand trolley. "Operation Crossbow" is the only feature film made in which a genuine V2 rocket appears.

We then see the 'Crossbow' Committee meeting for the first time, to assess the reports and intelligence into the long-range rocket. "Not very intelligent", dismisses Professor Lindemann, played by Trevor Howard. Here we have another misrepresentation of actual events: Professor Lindemann was, in real life, unpersuaded that German scientists had been able to progress their rocket research as far as they had, but he was not as obdurate and antagonistic as Howard is required to portray him as being in this film. Moreover, Lindemann made sure Jones's contribution got through to the Committee because, despite his opposition to the stance taken by Jones, he, as a scientist, knew that all views had to be considered, so he fed through Jones's information. In the film, though, Lindemann is made to appear to be prejudiced, one-eyed and downright stubborn in his opposition to the possibility that the Germans had overcome weight and propellant problems that British scientific research into rocketry had been unable to do (Lindemann did not understand the principal of liquid oxygen propellants, which the Germans were using; he believed only in solid fuel propellants that added greatly to the weight of any rocket design, thus revealing why British rocket scientists were far further behind their German counterparts).

In answer to Lindemann's challenge as to what to do, Sandys replies by saying first he would examine all the aerial photographic intelligence and order more if needed, next he would interrogate all the available prisoners, and then send in more agents to gain information on the ground. If all of this confirmed the belief that rockets existed, he would recommend bombing their installations before they got off the ground - Peenemunde, in other words.

This is precisely what R V Jones not only proposed, but which he had been doing with the aid of the RAF Photographic Interpretation Unit and RAF PR pilots. He makes the claim that, in a note he sent to Sandys on 19th June, he told him there was a rocket visible in a photograph of Peenemunde by a PR Spitfire, to

which Sandys failed to respond. Jones then sent him a report on the intelligence he had learnt about the rocket, which included his opinion that Peenemunde must be bombed, the first time anyone had made such a recommendation.

So, the script for "Operation Crossbow" has Duncan Sandys stating the courses of action which he would take that, in real life, R V Jones actually advocated, and is portrayed as being the originator of the recommendation for the bombing of Peenemunde when, in June 1943, Jones was the first to advocate such a course of action in his report to Sandys. Did the real Sandys behave in the way he is portrayed in the film, taking the credit which appears to belong to MI6's Scientific Intelligence Officer?

Another member of the 'Crossbow' Committee is a General Boyd, played by the long-lasting John Mills, who is in command of Allied agents operating behind enemy lines. It is most likely that 'Boyd' is a cover for Major General Sir Colin Gubbins, executive head of the Special Operations Executive, who would have been involved with agents in the manner 'Boyd' is portrayed by Mills as being in the film. If Gubbins was part of 'Crossbow', it is likely that the scriptwriters were told to find a non de plume for him.

The film now switches to the launching rail test site of a Fi.103 at Peenemunde. Only this Fi.103 is different from most that appear in the film - it has a cockpit. This is a reasonably accurate representation of the manned version of the Fi.103, a Fieseler Fi.103R Reichenberg, with the code number 'M23'. Here the film mixes fact with fiction. Manned test flights are to be conducted to find out why the Fi.103 (it should be stated that the designation for the flying bomb is never used in the script) will not maintain controlled flight and keeps veering to the right. The test pilot becomes the fourth of his number to die, while the problem remains unsolved.

Meanwhile, the RAF Photographic Interpretation Unit at Medmenham begins to build up evidence of rocket test firing stands at Peenemunde. Again, actual key personnel are portrayed in the film, the CO of the Unit, Wing Commander Douglas Kendall, being played by another veteran British war film actor, Richard Todd, and the resourceful Photographic Interpreter, Flight Officer Constance Babington Smith, acted by Sylvia Syms, who is credited in real life with being the first to identify from a photo taken by a PR Mosquito a V1 flying bomb on its ramp at Peenemunde (The real Constance Babington Smith makes an uncredited appearance in "Target For Tonight", 1941). Before the War she was an aviation journalist with The Aeroplane magazine, her ability to identify aircraft making her invaluable for Photographic Intelligence. After the War, Constance Babington Smith was one of the original driving forces behind the appeal to create what became the Mosquito Aviation Museum, today the de Havilland Aircraft Heritage Centre.

The scene where Sandys is shown visiting the Photographic Interpretation Unit and looking at a photo of a rocket on its transporter at Peenemunde never took place; Sandys never visited Medmenham, while the Unit always either called in R V Jones or sent their photographs to his team first, for them to collate evidence. Sandys tried to block this by ordering photographs must be sent only to him, but the Unit continued to feed Jones's team without Sandys's knowledge, such was the level of mistrust between Sandys and Jones.

Actual PR photos of Peenemunde are used in this Medmenham sequence, which also has the first aircraft to be used in "Operation Crossbow" making its appearance. This is a Photo Reconnaissance Spitfire landing back at its base from a PR mission over Peenemunde and taxying in, presumably meant to be at RAF Benson. The Spitfire is painted in PR Blue. There is nothing else to identify this Spitfire, but it is in fact one of the most widely used historic aircraft in the history of feature films, Vickers Supermarine Spitfire HF.Mk.IXb MH434. Then owned by Timothy Davies, Spitfire HF.IXb MH434 had been sold by its previous operator, the Belgian COGEA company, and registered as G-ASJV on 3rd July 1963. Tim Davies based MH434 at Elstree Aerodrome in Hertfordshire, still in its COGEA company colours of silver and blue.

It was not a difficult task to give it a quick partial coat of blue, to make MH434 look like a PR 'Spit' - the paint scheme certainly looks very temporary. It was filmed landing and taxying at RAF Abingdon, where another scene in the film was conducted as well. Timothy Davies flew the Spitfire over from its Elstree base for a single day's filming in August 1964.

Various sources give "Operation Crossbow" as Spitfire HF.IXb MH434's first film role, but as we know it has been credited with being one of four Spitfires with COGEA that were hired four years earlier to appear in "The Longest Day" (1962). MH434 has had such a long and active life in films that it will be more pertinent to hold its history and film credits over to a production in which it had an even more active role, "A Bridge Too Far" (1977), in Chapter Five.

One of the key scenes in the film, and which is broadly correct, is the 'Crossbow' Committee meeting when Professor Lindemann's objections were finally overruled and the decision to bomb Peenemunde was taken by Sandys. It was, according to Jones, the War Cabinet Defence Committee (Operations) chaired by Churchill on 29th June 1943 which made the decision at which he was present, and not, as in the film, the 'Crossbow' Committee chaired by Sandys. The real Sandys was at the 29th June meeting and fully advocated the bombing of Peenemunde. Lindemann is shown in the film first claiming that the rocket on a trailer is a barrage balloon, then he changes to claiming it is a torpedo. In the script, General Boyd says no ship could launch a torpedo of the size of the object in the photograph; in the real meeting, Jones says he was interrupted by Lindemann when the former was discounting the latter's theory that it could be a torpedo - "…there was no aircraft in Germany that could carry a torpedo 38 feet long and 6 feet in diameter, or could lift 10 or 20 tons". Lindemann's other theory was the rocket was a hoax, to divert the Allies from the real secret weapon which Lindemann espoused was a pilotless aircraft. As the Fieseler Fi.103 had not been properly identified at this stage, and the 'Crossbow' Committee was focused on searching for the rocket to the exclusion of anything else, he was partially correct.

The scene now changes to where Hannah Reitsch has decided she must take responsibility "…to find out why these damn crates won't fly". She straps herself in to Fi.103R Reichenberg coded 'M28' (the same F/S facsimile with the number '3' rounded out

to '8'). Here again, though, "Operation Crossbow" has been criticised for misrepresenting what actually took place and for allowing a popular myth to become accepted as fact (although, again, whether the scriptwriters actually had all the facts in 1964 is wide open to question). Reitsch did test fly the Fi.103R, but not in the way shown in the film. No pilot could have withstood the G-Forces that they would have encountered in being launched off the rail as the film depicts; in reality, the Fi.103R was air-dropped by a Heinkel He.111 'mother ship'.

Reitsch did not carry out the manned flights in the time period - 1943 - as the film's plot requires, nor for the reasons given in the film, ie, the need to find out why the Fi.103's gyroscopic control appears to be causing it to fly off course and crash. In reality, Reitsch test flew the Fi.103R right towards the end of the War, to see if it was feasible to form a suicide squadron of volunteer pilots, the Leonidas Squadron, which she advocated and reportedly was prepared to be a member of until Hitler vetoed her wish to take part. The squadron never went into action: Hitler was apparently persuaded that suicide soldiers were against the Teutonic warrior tradition. No mention is made in the film of the V1 being planned as a suicide aircraft.

What Reitsch did achieve was to solve the problem test pilots were having in safely landing the Fi.103R, which had a high stall speed. Her experience in flying the rocket-powered Messerschmitt Me.163 and in making simulated landings at height in the Fi.103R helped her to discover that the safest way to land it was to do so at a speed above 200 km/h, which her fellow test pilots had no knowledge of how to achieve. Director Anderson and the scriptwriters used Reitsch's test flights in the Fi.103R for different dramatic purposes, which have now become accepted as fact. The reality is that Hannah Reitsch never flew the Fi.103 from Peenemunde and certainly was not present when RAF Bomber Command attacked the facility, as is shown in the film.

In "Operation Crossbow", Hannah Reitsch is played with dramatic flair by German actress Barbara Rutting, who gives every impression of throwing herself into the role with gusto. Reitsch survived the War and became a world renowned glider pilot, establishing a number of world records, some of which still stand today. She would have been alive when "Operation Crossbow" was released. It would have been interesting to know what she thought of Barbara Rutting's performance of herself, if she had seen the film.

Operation Hydra, the all-out RAF Bomber Command offensive against Peenemunde on the night of 17th/18th August 1943, is depicted only briefly in "Operation Crossbow", with flames symbolically blowing through shattered windows behind a portrait of Adolf Hitler. The image then cuts to an Avro Lancaster bomber landing on an RAF air base. This, as is popularly known, is Avro Lancaster B.I PA474 making its first full screen debut: as explained earlier in this Chapter, PA474 was loaned to appear in "The Guns of Navarone" (1961), but was used only as the pattern aircraft for the studio miniature Lancaster in that film.

Just a few shots of Lancaster B.I PA474 appear in "Operation Crossbow", the first showing the bomber landing in what looks like a bit of a crosswind judging by the starboard wing being high on touch down, which forces an immediate correction to counter-balance the

'Lanc' so that it settles on its two main wheels. Noticeable in the approach shot is that the Lancaster has no gun turrets attached, which was the case with PA474 in 1964. Sandys is seen watching it land, then is standing on the grass leaning on his stick as the Lancaster taxyies in towards him on both its inner engines only.

Lancaster B.I PA474 was in the possession of the Air Historical Branch (AHB) at the time of its appearance in "Operation Crossbow" and was based at Wroughton, Wiltshire, awaiting eventual transfer to the proposed RAF Museum at Hendon. It had been painted in an RAF Bomber Command camouflage scheme but did not carry any squadron codes. In the shots in which it is seen filmed, PA474 is either landing or taxying in head-on towards the camera, so no markings are visible in any case. These shots were filmed at its Wroughton base.

After use in "Operation Crossbow", PA474 was flown to RAF Henlow to join other RAF Museum-assigned aircraft. However, in 1965 the CO of No. 44 (Rhodesia) Squadron at RAF Waddington asked the AHB for permission to take PA474 on charge, particularly as No.44 had been the first Lancaster squadron to form. Permission was granted, so Lancaster B.I PA474 made a single flight from Henlow to Waddington, to join the Avro Vulcan B.1As of No.44 Squadron. There PA474 remained, being progressively overhauled and displayed at airshows between 1967 - 1973. As a sign of things to come, Lancaster B.I PA474 led a three-ship formation with a Hurricane and a Spitfire over the Farnborough Air Show on 21st September 1968 to commemorate the 50th Anniversary of the Royal Air Force, a sight since all too commonplace at many events in Britain after PA474 joined the Battle of Britain Memorial Flight in November 1973. PA474 continues today flying the flag for RAF Bomber Command aircrew who flew in Lancasters during World War Two.

The film script makes the claim that "Peenemunde is smashed to bits", hugely exaggerated as British Intelligence soon discovered. Development work on the A4 rocket was put back two months and much of it was diverted to Blizna in Poland, but Peenemunde soon continued to function. The script describes 571 bombers employed against the target, with 40 losses; recent sources give a total of 596 bombers, with the same number of losses, mostly to Luftwaffe night fighters using the Wilde Sau (Wild Boar) system which required good visibility at night; because the RAF bombers were beyond the range of their radio navigational beams, they had to bomb by moonlight and from a lower altitude (8,000 ft) than they normally would (19,000 ft), which made it easier for the German night fighters to detect them visually. A co-ordinated diversion raid on Berlin by 'Pathfinder' Mosquitos - Operation Whitebait - successfully drew off most of the night fighters before Luftwaffe High Command realised Peenemunde was the main target and directed the fighters against the third and final wave of Operation Hydra, meaning that most of the 40 bombers lost were shot down in this last phase of the raid.

No mention is made in the film that the greater majority of fatalities at Peenemunde were among foreign slave labourers in a concentration camp barracks at the facility. This tragic fact was known about because it is depicted in "Battle of the V1", but

producer Ponti and his script writing team made sure there is no reference to it in "Operation Crossbow".

From this point on in the plot "Operation Crossbow" moves into the fictional element of the film, when agents are recruited to pose as scientific engineers so they can penetrate the underground facility that British Intelligence has discovered is where the rockets are now being produced. No name is given for the facility, only that it is "in this area here", as indicated by General Boyd circling his hand over a map showing a part of Germany south of Hamburg. The underground facility is undoubtedly meant to be Mittelwerk (Central Works), near to the town of Nordhausen and located in the southern part of the Harz Mountains. Here, the V2 was produced by forced labour from the Mittelbau-Dora concentration camp, at great cost of life.

Suffice it to say, no slave labourers are shown in "Operation Crossbow", although the foreign scientists and technicians who are forced to work in the underground facility on rocket development are undoubtedly prisoners. Their fate is not shown, but they would have had no escape from the RAF bombing of the facility in the finale.

The plot follows the recruitment and training of three specific agents played by George Peppard, the token American actor needed to make the film appeal to a US audience, Tom Courtenay and Jeremy Kemp. All three actors have to make real jumps from the parachute training tower at RAF Abingdon, acting their roles as they do so: you wouldn't get Brad Pitt or Tom Cruise doing that today, or their studios letting them do so even if they were prepared to. RAF Abingdon was making its fourth appearance in a British war film, after "The Red Beret" (1953), "The Man Who Never Was" (1956) and "Carve Her Name With Pride" (1958). Peppard's and Courtenay's characters are parachuted into Holland at night from an indistinct Dakota miniature.

The film now moves through a protracted section of the plot that covers the agents' efforts to get into the underground facility. Peppard's and Kemp's characters succeed, Courtenay's is identified by an Abwehr agent played by Anthony Quayle who, for some reason, was called upon to play Germans in a number of films, "Ice Cold In Alex" (1958) and "The Eagle Has Landed" (1977) included. Once inside, Peppard learns that the German scientists are developing a rocket of 100 tons designed to reach New York. This is where "Operation Crossbow" crosses the reality threshold into partial fantasy, largely to appeal to an American audience by making them feel involved in a movie whose plot is concerned with the Nazi threat to Britain, not to the United States. This is achieved by having the Nazis' ultimate aim being to launch a very long-range rocket at New York, which the American and British agents must avert at all costs.

This never happened in reality, of course, but the 'Amerika Rakete' project was real. The A9/A10 was a two-stage rocket on which German scientists started design work in 1940, confirming that Adolf Hitler would have attacked the United States at some stage after Germany had succeeded in subduing Britain and defeating Russia, and once he had the means, even if the USA had remained neutral. The A9 was to be the warhead, the A10 the booster stage. It never got beyond the design stage and certainly was not almost ready for launching across the Atlantic, as the 'New York Rocket' is shown to be in "Operation Crossbow".

The plot moves back to RAF Medmenham in England, with Flight Officer Constance Babington Smith making history when she became the first Photographic Interpretation Officer to identify a small pilotless aircraft on a launching ramp at Peenemunde, and which British Scientific Intelligence deduced was evidence of the testing of a flying bomb. The actual photograph, taken by a PR Mosquito on 28th November 1943, is used in the film (It was due to the efforts of the PR Mosquito crews that Babington Smith became a founder director of the original Mosquito Memorial Appeal Fund, which resulted in the preservation of the prototype Mosquito). It and other photos taken on the same sortie not only confirmed the existence of the flying bomb itself, but that the long rails which Intelligence was calling 'Ski Sites' were the launch platforms. Sandys wastes no time in informing the Prime Minister.

The film immediately cuts to the launching of the first wave of what was to become the Vergeltungswaffe Eins (Retaliation Weapon One, V1). The plot makes the time period appear as if this happens in quick succession to the discovery of the V1 by Babington Smith, when in fact more than six months elapsed from the date of that key reconnaissance photo being taken before the opening salvo of V1 flying bombs were fired at London. This is part of the problem with "Operation Crossbow", it tries to cover too wide a subject in too short a space of time. Oddly, it makes no reference to the 'Crossbow' bombing operations, other than Wing Commander Kendall telling the Committee that, "Altogether, we've destroyed a hundred of these ski sites up till now". As the first sightings of the V1 crossing the Channel coast at Dover are reported to the Committee during this scene, the date of it occurring is obviously meant to be 13th June 1944 (in reality, the first V1 to hit London occurred on the night of 12th/13th June 1944).

The Special FX team that created the V1 flying bombs over-flying London have to be congratulated for such realistic and convincing-looking special effects. They are miniatures, but very realistic miniatures. Most challenging of all is how director Anderson's SFX team achieved the images filmed air-air looking down on a V1 being pursued by a Spitfire. They look believably real. One explanation is that they might be a large-scale radio-controlled model V1 and Spitfire, filmed from a helicopter; however, they appear to be flying too high for R/C models controlled from the ground. There is no known record of a R/C model V1 ever having been flown.

The V1 might, however, be a 'Cottingley Fairey', ie, it genuinely is in the picture but is not exactly what it appears to be. The Cottingley Fairies are five photographs taken by two young girls in 1917 and 1920 that supposedly show fairies. Many experts of the time, including Sir Arthur Conan Doyle, creator of Sherlock Holmes and a world famous spiritualist with a deep interest in the psychic world, believed them to be genuine. Examination by photographic technicians could not find any evidence of tampering or faking, the fairies were in the photos the girls had taken. They were, however, cardboard cut-outs of fairies, which the girls had posed with the support of hatpins and then photographed them.

The V1 filmed flying in "Operation Crossbow" appears to be a Cottingley Fairey. It really is in the picture, there is no SFX artwork or faking, but it is not what it looks like. What is shown is a small, silver aircraft of cruciform shape, with a straight mid-wing layout, a tiny tail-plane arrangement and what looks like flame spurting from its rear. Above the rear fuselage is a black tubular device that has the appearance of being the V1's tail pipe containing its pulse jet engine. However, the emitting flame from the rear is not in line with the tail pipe, as it would have to be if this V1 was real. Also, the 'flame' is emitting from the end of the tail-plane, whereas on the real Fieseler Fi.103 design the tail pipe was fixed above and stretched beyond the tail-plane, so that the rocket flame would be emitting much further away from the V1's airframe than is shown in this image.

The R/C V1 is possibly not too wide of the mark, if the aircraft we see here is a remotely-controlled target drone mocked up to appear like a V1. The Australian-designed Jindivik drone approximates in size and shape to what is seen flying in the film. The 'flame' emitting from the tail-plane would be a streamer attached to create the effect, as the Jindivik's Bristol Siddeley Viper engine was non-afterburning. If not a drone, then Anderson's V1 remains a successfully achieved mystery.

A closer air-air image of the Spitfire has all the signs of it being a genuine aircraft. Freeze-frame analysis shows as clearly as it is possible to discern that it is a Rolls Royce Griffon-engined Spitfire. This rules out Merlin-engined Spitfire HF.IXb MH434 being used again. It is camouflaged, which MH434 was not (it is not credible to claim that the production team would go to the expense of painting MH434 in camouflage for one limited shot). The lengthened spinner of the Griffon Spitfire is discernible, as is the slightly more triangular tail fin compared with the rounded fin that was MH434's feature.

There were three Griffon-engined Spitfires flying in Britain in 1964: the RAF Battle of Britain Flight's Spitfire PR.XIXs PM631 and PS853, plus Rolls Royce's Spitfire F.XIVc G-ALGT. The two PR.XIXs were camouflaged, the F.XIVc was not; also, F.XIVc G-ALGT was clipped-wing, which the Spitfire in the film is definitely not. This suggests that Anderson's 2nd Unit filmed either Vickers Supermarine Spitfire PR.Mk.XIX PM631 or PS853 from a helicopter.

However, there is still a problem: PM631 was painted earth-green camou, whereas the Spitfire in the film is clearly green-grey. It has a light grey spinner; PS853 had a black spinner later in the Sixties.

The terrain over which the Spitfire is pursuing the 'V1' is of note. It is flat. The V1 flies in from over the sea with the Spitfire on its tail. The coastline over which they fly is also flat - it is meant to be Kent, but the straight line of sandy beach below them is the exact opposite of the stark white cliffs of Dover and the pebble beaches bordering them. Kent it is not.

The Fi.103R Reichenberg scenes were filmed on the Norfolk coast. The RAF Battle of Britain Flight had been based at RAF Coltishall in Norfolk since 1st April 1963. Spitfire PR.XIX PS853 had rejoined the Flight in April 1964 after being used by the Central Fighter Establishment at Coltishall to conduct interception trials of high performance piston-engined fighters by RAF Lightning jet interceptors. Jindivik drones were used for gunnery practice on army ranges in East Anglia.

Logic has to be that the 'V1' is an unpainted Jindivik minus its wing-tip tanks (the displayed model bears an almost exact resemblance to that which is seen on screen) being chased by Spitfire PR.XIX PS853 which had probably acquired a light grey spinner and green-grey camouflage scheme in 1964 to match the Spitfire in this aerial action scene. The location would be over the Norfolk coastline and countryside

To his credit, Anderson did not fall victim to the temptation to use black-and-white archive imagery of real V1s and V2s. His team's creation of a full-scale facsimile of the Vergeltungswaffe Zwei (V2) ballistic artillery rocket on its mobile firing stand, complete with Meillerwagen and Opel-Blitz T-Stoffwagen, is admirably realistic. V2 rockets climbing vertically into the sky are studio miniatures, though. The impact of V2s is less effectively achieved, as the full size and sound of the detonations was beyond the means of the production team to achieve. The ghostly loud rush of air immediately following the impact is effectively created, but its significance was lost on a mid-Sixties audience who did not understand the dynamics of rocket flight.

The finale of "Operation Crossbow" is too far-fetched. The Germans did plan to launch V2s from underground facilities, but found the mobile system far more effective and far less vulnerable to the kind of bombing raid as depicted in the film wiping out the facility housing the New York Rocket. Compared with all the SFX used in the film, it is somewhat surprising to see rather poor matte imagery of Lancasters being used to depict the raid.; it has the feel of the production team running out of time and budget, and unable to afford to create more effective miniatures in keeping with the rest of the film. Very briefly, an archive shot of a Martin B-26 Marauder releasing its bombs is cut into this scene. It is the last sight of an aircraft in "Operation Crossbow".

Seen today, with so much that has emerged about the real 'Crossbow' campaign, "Operation Crossbow" is inevitably a flawed film from an historical perspective. That is a pity because it is, as previously stated, a well made, well acted production, with mostly high quality SFX for its time. It is probably a subject worth revisiting in a major new film production that, with good quality CGI, could re-create V2 rocket attacks very impressively. It could also, thanks to what we have learnt courtesy of Dr R V Jones's book (published 13 years after the release of "Operation Crossbow"), bring to light the fascinating scientific detective work that went into discovering and identifying Hitler's Vergeltungswaffen and the counter-measures used against them.

THE HILL

(Released: May 1965)

Set entirely in a wartime British Army prison camp in North Africa, no aircraft at all appear in this film.

VON RYAN'S EXPRESS

(Released: June 1965, USA) Hollywood 'British' war film

This very enjoyable PoW escape romp across Nazi Occupied Italy in August 1943 was popularly received on release in both the USA and Britain. It profited from the public's fascination with PoW escape stories, thanks to the hugely successful Steve McQueen epic, "The Great Escape" (1963), and with wartime adventures onboard trains, due to John Frankenheimer's muchly admired and grittily realistic production of "The Train" (1964). "Von Ryan's Express" was described at the time as "The Great Escape" in "The Train".

It has an excellent cast led by Frank Sinatra as the said 'von Ryan', so named by British PoWs because he mistakenly trusts the brutal Italian Prison Camp Commandant not to betray them to the Germans after he (Ryan) spares his life, resulting in the Commandant informing the Germans of their escape and causing the deaths of a number of the British soldiers. Sinatra is backed up by Trevor Howard - 20 years on from his war film debut in "The Way to the Stars" (1945) - as the crusty but tough Major Fincham, surviving Commanding Officer of the British Army Regiment they are leading to freedom by stealing the train that was transporting them to Germany and taking it across war-torn Italy to neutral Switzerland.

Aviation does not feature on a sizeable scale in "Von Ryan's Express", but where it does it is significant, as in the big battle at the end of the film. The opening pre-credits sequence has Italian soldiers in a truck watching a Lockheed P-38 Lightning fighter trailing smoke as it passes overhead. They follow the stricken USAAF fighter, with the intention of capturing its pilot before the Germans can reach him. Two German officers drinking in a harbour-side café also see the P-38, its engine stuttering, and set off in pursuit in a Kubelwagen. They find the crashed P-38 in a carob grove outside the city port, on fire and with the Italian soldiers indicating that the pilot is dead in the wreckage. The Germans seem satisfied and drive off. The Italians show their contempt for them by making offensive gestures at the officers behind their backs, then get into their truck to reveal the pilot, Colonel Ryan, safely in one piece under their protection and drinking from a bottle of wine they have given him.

Film fans down the years have assumed that the P-38 Lightning they see trailing smoke before the crash scene appears is real. It is not. It is a large-scale radio-controlled miniature P-38, filmed against a blue sky. The shot of a church it is passing behind was filmed entirely separately, as were other buildings the smoke-trailing P-38 is flying over. The church was then merged with the blue sky holding the image of the R/C miniature P-38, using the split-screen technique, creating the impression that the USAAF fighter is flying beyond the church while on fire.

Criticism has been made that the smoke trailing from the P-38 is coming from its centre-section, whereas if it is meant to have one of its twin engines on fire, then the smoke should be coming from either one of its two engine cowlings. That's true, although the central gondola containing the cockpit and nose-mounted cannon and machine guns, also held the P-38's ammunition, which if hit would obviously have produced fire and smoke; however, a hit in the ammunition container would probably result in the P-38 blowing up.

To achieve the effect of the crashed P-38 on fire in the carob grove, the film's art department built a full-scale facsimile of a USAAF P-38 Lightning which was set up on its nose. Freeze-frame analysis shows that the art department team did not go to the extent of completing the F/S facsimile with nose, cockpit, engine cowlings and propellers - these are all missing. The central section is a blazing mass of flame, but the absence of the forward sections of the P-38 is clearly discernable. The art department have also made the error of painting the F/S facsimile P-38 with early period red-white stripes and blue bar on each tail fin, which were no longer in use on USAAF aircraft in 1943, having been replaced by either the Fighter Group or Bomb Group code letter and symbol to show to which unit each aircraft belonged. The F/S facsimile P-38 was built on site in Italy, so perhaps not enough reference was available there as a guide to the correct markings of a 1943-period USAAF fighter.

Aviation does not appear again until one-third of the way into the plot. Ryan, Fincham and the other British and American PoWs have learnt that Italy has surrendered. The Italian guards have fled. The PoWs intend on a mass break-out to the coast, to join up with Allied troops that are pushing the Germans back. Before they can leave the PoW camp, a German fighter suddenly appears and dives down onto them, causing the PoWs to scatter in all directions. The fighter does not fire on them but instead makes a low pass over them. It is a warning that the Germans are still in real strength in Italy.

The fighter which dives onto the PoWs bears a strong resemblance to a Messerschmitt Bf.109. In reality, it is not there - it is another split-screen image, this time of a studio model miniature fighter onto which imagery of the PoW camp film set has been superimposed. In fact, the footage of the studio miniature has been lifted from the major set-piece in the finale when 'von Ryan's express' train is attacked by three rocket-firing Luftwaffe fighters, for which both real and studio miniature aircraft were used.

It is in this final set-piece during the last quarter of the film where aviation really makes an impact in "Von Ryan's Express". The escaping PoWs have almost reached the Swiss - Italian border through the Alps when the pursuing German forces call up the Luftwaffe in a final effort to stop them. What are clearly meant to be Messerschmitt Bf.109 fighters attack the train with rockets. The Bf.109 was a most versatile fighter design and its later variants operated in the fighter-bomber and ground-attack roles, usually armed with an under-fuselage bomb or under-wing cannon. It is possible the later Bf.109G models carried rockets, but there is no recorded mention of their use. The Spanish-built Hispano HA.1112 variant could certainly be armed with rockets, and it is believed that Israel adapted the Czechoslovakian Avia S-199 version of the Bf.109 it acquired to fire rockets as well. But the Luftwaffe tended to regard rockets primarily as air-air weapons

against high-flying USAAF bombers, while the Wehrmacht's ground-attack tactics up until 1943 relied extensively on the Ju.87 Stuka dive bomber and the Ju.88 light bomber, backed up by Bf.109 'Jabos' using a single bomb. From the end of 1943 onwards, Germany was on the defensive, so the need for a single-engine fighter-bomber was much less of a priority.

The use of rocket-firing Messerschmitt fighters in "Von Ryan's Express" is, therefore, not strictly accurate but cannot be ruled out as a possibility during World War Two. There is evidence that Panzerfaust (armour fist) anti-tank weapons were attached to slow-flying aircraft like the Bucker Bestmann and Henschel Hs.126, but this is akin to attaching bazookas to Harvard trainers, nowhere near the hitting power of armour-piercing rockets. One wonders how they would have been fired from an aircraft.

Aviation enthusiasts and historians will know immediately that the 'Bf.109s' are three Messerschmitt Bf.108B Taifun four-seat communications aircraft. The use of the Bf.108 to impersonate its Bf.109 fighter descendant in British and Hollywood war films was now a well-established precedent by the middle of the Sixties. In fact, the three Bf.108B Taifuns used in "Von Ryan's Express" are each Nord 1002 Pinguoin II types, as their Renault 6Q-10 engines' layout confirm. Each have had rocket attachments fitted under their wings, while an attempt to reduce the size of their cockpit cabins, and thus give them a more realistic appearance as fighters, has been achieved by having the quadrant-shaped rear window completely masked by a panel and the centre rectangular window panel covered diagonally in half by more panelling. Accurate-size Balkenkreuzen have been applied to their fuselage and wings, with a chevron ahead of the fuselage kreuze (cross) and a Swastika on the tailfin, giving them a more realistically-attired appearance. However, the yellow and mottled green camouflage schemes carried by each Bf.108B is completely out of place for an action taking place in northern Italy, but the schemes were probably chosen to make the Bf.108Bs stand out effectively on screen, especially when they are filmed air-air over the Alpine scenery below them.

The question has to be, from where did P-R Productions, the film company behind "Von Ryan's Express", source these three Bf.108Bs? It is unlikely they came from Italy, which did not use the Bf.108 in either its military or civil guise. The Swiss Air Force operated the Bf.108B, and due to the Alpine location in which the Taifuns are used in "Von Ryan's Express", Switzerland could have been a very likely source; however, Swiss Air Force Bf.108Bs were fitted with a distinctively serrated style of propeller boss, unique to the Swiss Taifuns, which the Bf.108Bs in the film are definitely not using. This would rule Swiss Air Force Taifuns out.

The most likely source is again the collection of former French Armee de l'Air and Aeronavale Nord 1002 Pinguoin II liaison aircraft owned by Alexandre Renault, referred to in the review of "The Longest Day" (1962). At the time when "Von Ryan's Express" was in production, Alexandre Renault still owned a significant number of ex-French military Nord 1002 Pinguoin IIs of which he was the sole distributor for sale onto the civil market. Adding to the likelihood that Renault was the source of the three Nord 1002s in "Von Ryan's Express" is that three identical aircraft from his collection performed as Messerschmitt Bf.109s in the French war epic, "Week-end a Zuydcoot" ("Week-end at Dunkirk", 1964), filmed just before the Frank Sinatra and Trevor Howard PoW train escape drama went into production. Flying them from France to northern Italy would have been no problem.

Cockpit close-ups of the Luftwaffe Messerschmitt pilots have been filmed in a studio-created Bf.109 narrow single-seat style cabin, conflicting with the wider four-seat cabins of the Bf.108Bs. A fine air-air shot of the middle of the three Bf.108Bs breaking to port towards the camera aircraft gives an excellent study of the Taifun's design and the work done by the art department team to turn it and its comrades into Luftwaffe 'Messerschmitt Bf.109s'.

The scene of the aerial attacks has some strange shots of the Bf.108Bs that appear to have been achieved by some unusual methods. As all three dive into the attack, they fly very fast and close past the camera which appears to be filming them from the same height as they pass. The conclusion is that the camera aircraft was actually a helicopter, and that it was hovering at height as the three Bf.108Bs fly by close to it; it seems impossible to have achieved this shot by any other means.

One thing is for certain, P-R Productions certainly succeeded in adapting the Bf.108Bs to actually launch rockets off either wing at low-level. It is believed the nationalist Spanish forces actually adapted the few Bf.108s they operated during the Spanish Civil War to have an armed role, but "Von Ryan's Express" is the only source to prove it was possible. There is no faking the rockets actually coming off the rails of a Bf.108B and exploding beyond the train in one shot, a risky enterprise but very effectively achieved. The American and British PoWs on the roof of the train fire at the strafing Messerschmitts with MP40 machine pistols (popularly called "Schmeissers") they have captured from their German guards; the MP40 was a short-range weapon and no way could the escaping Yanks and Brits have hoped to have brought any one of the Messerschmitts down with the Schmeissers they are using.

A very hairy-looking shot from the roof of the train has a Bf.108B fly low overhead straight towards the mountain face, unleashing rockets as it does so before it pulls up to miss the rocks. Another shot from the train's roof has a Bf.108B firing rockets in a low-level turn to miss the wooded mountainside as it passes over the camera. An aerial shot shows two rockets streaking over the train and impacting the mountainside it is passing by - scary! Whoever devised these aerial stunts really asked the pilots flying them to take serious risks.

However, there is a change to the method by which more rocket-firing shots are achieved. The lead Messerschmitt pilot sees that the escaping train is going to cross a bridge spanning a ravine and enter a tunnel which leads to the Swiss border. He decides to try and stop the train by firing rockets at the rock wall, causing debris to fall onto the tracks. His Messerschmitt fires two rockets which hit the rock wall. This scene is achieved with a studio model miniature Messerschmitt Bf.109, the same that was seen earlier making a pass over the PoWs in their prison camp. Freeze-frame analysis shows that the Special FX model makers have produced a kind of composite of both the Bf.108 and Bf.109 designs: the fuselage is

much more substantial than the slim Bf.108's and the cockpit is the same as that of a single-pilot Bf.109, but the nose section is a copy of the Taifun's design. When this studio miniature 'Bf.108/9' fires its rockets, no rockets actually leave their rails - the effect was achieved by firing what look like smoke-trailing flares. The scenery of the mountain gorge and the bridge is a studio-created model set.

The reason why studio miniature Messserchmitts are used here is because this part of the action was filmed on a specially created film set in the limestone gorge of el Chorro, close to Malaga in Spain. It was matched with the model set in the studio, hence the need for miniature Bf.109s. There were, in fact, three miniature Bf.109s which are seen flying in one shot in formation: however, the effect is very unrealistic because the three fighters are flying in an inverted 'Vic', with the lead aircraft in the centre but behind the two wingmen, a method of formation flying that would not have been attempted in reality. They also all fly in a curve as one, showing that they were actually linked and being pulled round simultaneously on a wire loop, creating an unrealistic effect.

The Messerschmitts achieve their aim and force the train to stop on the bridge. The prisoners try to escape along a cliff-side foot path that leads round the mountain to safety but are attacked by one of the Bf.109s. It is shown diving down in a rather odd, jerky manner, caused by very obvious stop-motion SFX of one of the studio miniatures. The PoWs manage to shoot the Messerschmitt Bf.109 down with their MP40s - totally unrealistic. A large-scale miniature Bf.109, loaded with fuel and explosives, was released down a guidance wire in the film set of el Chorro gorge to smash into the cliff-face and explode - very realistic. The PoWs cheer but a second Bf.109 destroys the cliff-side foot path, meaning they have to retreat to face the German troop train that is pursuing them, leading into a large-scale gun battle for the finale. The two remaining Bf.109s slew round unconvincingly in formation, confirming again they are studio miniatures linked on a loop, but the two Bf.108Bs which over-fly the troop train in salute are definitely the real thing.

"Von Ryan's Express" is always an enjoyable film to watch, no matter how many times. It is based on a very good novel and follows the very strong Anglo-American theme of the book, hence its status in this publication as an Hollywood 'British' war film.

KING RAT

(Released: October 1965, USA)

Ostensibly an American movie due to the financial backing and distributorship from the USA, "King Rat" is to all other extent and purposes a British film production with its English producer, director and crew. Yet another take on the Japanese PoW theme, it has an Americanised angle thanks to the scrounging, conniving central character who is the film's title, a US Army Corporal with the morals of a rat.

The film has one small piece of aviation in it. Towards the end, when the Japanese Camp Commandant is about to inform the British, Australian and American PoWs that Japan has surrendered, an aircraft flies high overhead streaming contrails. It is meant to be a Boeing B-29, but is probably a jet airliner filmed from a long distance.

THE HEROES OF TELEMARK

(Released: November 1965)

A heavily fictionalised re-creation of the SOE operation using Norwegian Commandos to sabotage a hydro-electric plant in Norway that the Nazis were using to produce heavy water in support of their atomic weapons programme. Much of the film was made in the actual locations in the region of Telemark where SOE's Operation Gunnerside took place in February 1943, particularly on the lake where the Norwegian Commandos sank the ferry in 1944 that was transporting tanks of heavy water to Germany.

Aviation is not a big player in "The Heroes of Telemark" but what there is, is worth looking at. After smuggling micro film of the heavy water plant to London, the two leading characters in the film played by Kirk Douglas (an entirely fictional role as a completely unconvincing Norwegian physicist, created solely to sell the film to an American audience) and Richard Harris (based on the real leader of the Norwegian Commandos) are parachuted back into Norway from an RAF Dakota. Two real Norwegian Commandos are filmed departing a Royal Norwegian Air Force (RNAF) Douglas C-47A Dakota I acting the part of the RAF aircraft. The Dakota is filmed from the ground flying at height, so that its Norwegian markings cannot be seen to give it away.

Norway received 10 C-47As in 1950 under the USA's Mutual Aid Program. By the time "The Heroes of Telemark" was filmed their number had been reduced to just four, the other six having been transferred to Denmark. The four RNAF C-47A Dakota I transports served with 335 Skvadron and were able to operate off snow, using skis in place of wheels.

In the real SOE operation in February 1943, 50 British Commandos were flown into Telemark aboard troop-carrying gliders to assist the Norwegian Commandos in their assault upon the hydro-electric plant. Tragedy struck when the two gliders collided, killing most of the Commandos on board. Those that survived were captured, then interrogated and tortured by the Gestapo before being shot. Following the unsuccessful Commando assault on Dieppe the previous year, Hitler had issued an order that all captured British Commandos were exempt from the Geneva Convention's rules governing the treatment of Prisoners of War and were to be summarily executed after interrogation.

This episode is depicted in the film by SFX art work of a glider-towing aircraft and its glider diving into the mountainside, with explosives set off to simulate their impact. This SFX image suggests that only one glider was carrying all 50 Commandos, which would not have been possible – the maximum load was 30 troops. The film does not depict any surviving Commandos being captured, then shot after interrogation, presumably as this might have been too harsh for a film that, when it was released, had a rating that allowed children accompanied by an adult to see it. The audience is led to believe all 50 Commandos perished in the crash.

Before this scene is played out, the Commandos are seen departing England for Norway in their glider. This is depicted with the use of archive footage of a Short Stirling taking off, followed by that of an Airspeed Horsa I troop glider, carrying the number 292 on its fuselage, starting its take-off roll. Here, director Anthony Mann and his editorial team have either got their facts right or they have scored a lucky hit. The towing aircraft is a Short Stirling IV, recognisable by its lack of mid-upper gun turret, which was developed for glider-towing and supply dropping tasks. More to the point, the actual Stirling IV on film is clearly bearing 'ZO-' squadron code letters, although its individual aircraft code letter has been obscured by D-Day invasion stripes. 'ZO-' were the code letters of No.196 Squadron, equipped with the Stirling IV and dedicated to supporting SOE and SAS operations over Occupied Territory. So, Mann and his team have got footage of exactly the right kind of aircraft from the right squadron that would have carried out such a clandestine insertion of Commandos into Nazi Occupied Norway. The only error is the use of archive footage of a Stirling IV bearing D-Day invasion stripes, placing the time when this film was taken as just before 6th June 1944, not February 1943.

No.196 Squadron was based at Keevil from 14th March 1944 onwards, working up within No.38 Group, Allied Expeditionary Air Force, in preparation for massed troop glider landings as part of Operation Overlord. Almost certainly it was during this training period that this footage was filmed, most likely at Keevil, by the RAF Film Production Unit. It was No.196 Squadron which aero-towed the gliders containing the troops of the 6th Airborne Division in their assault on the Orne River Bridge and Caen Canal Bridge ("Pegasus Bridge") during the early hours of 6th June 1944; they later returned with Horsa gliders during D-Day itself to reinforce the 6th Airborne. So, archive footage of a No.196 Squadron Stirling IV is apt and instructive here.

Another archive shot of a Short Stirling IV lifting off with an Airspeed Horsa I in tow follows. This Stirling also carries invasion stripes but its code letters cannot be seen; however, it almost certainly is a No.196 Squadron aircraft filmed at Keevil. Then an aerial shot of a Horsa being aero-towed by a Stirling IV, taken from probably a small window in the upper fuselage of the aircraft with the Stirling's tail clearly in view, depicts the Commandos en route to Norway; however, there are two other Stirlings towing gliders following in the distance, flying over undulating, rolling countryside, which creates a conflict with the intention of having the Commandos being seen flown entirely within a single glider – this is possibly footage of glider-towing training flights prior to D-Day. The final shot is also an aerial view, this time of a Stirling IV filmed from inside the cockpit canopy of the Horsa glider it is towing, with the towing cable clearly visible. Some of this footage was also used in "Theirs Is The Glory" (1946).

The one problem with using this archive footage is that it is all in black-and-white, meaning that it clashes with the spectacularly colourful imagery of the Norwegian scenery that the story is played out against.

After the loss of their British comrades, the Norwegian Commandos decide to break into the hydro-electric plant themselves and blow up the heavy water in storage there, which they successfully do. But the Germans have had contingency plans in place and quickly restore heavy water production. The decision is now taken to bomb the plant, which the Norwegians had wanted to avoid in order to spare civilian life. Again, black-and-white archive footage is mixed in among the colour film, causing more conflict within the imagery. The air raid was carried out by the USAAF and was not successful. The first archive footage is that of 12 Boeing B-17 Flying Fortress bombers flying in groups of three overhead the camera, followed by aerial footage of six Boeing B-17G Flying Fortresses in close formation and filmed in silhouette (the same archival shot of 96th Bomb Group B-17Gs that was used in "The War Lover", 1962). The rest of the bombing scene is that of explosions among the buildings close to the plant, which remains unscathed. The bomb blasts are too small to be realistic.

In between time, the characters played by Douglas and Harris are hiding out from pursuing German troops in a hut up in the mountains, but have to take to their skis when their hut is bombed by a German 'plane. The 'plane is portrayed by a Piper L-18C Super Cub, 16 of which were in service with the RNAF when the film was made. It is seen making a low pass over the hut, with three small objects representing bombs dropping from it. The Super Cub is clearly seen carrying Luftwaffe Balkenkreuzen on its underwing surfaces and is probably portraying an Henschel Hs.126, which could carry a small bomb load (an archive shot of an Hs.126 appears in "The Day Will Dawn", 1942).

The Piper Super Cub was used in the observation and liaison roles by the RNAF. They were painted in two-tone brown camouflage schemes, with yellow wingtips and tail rudder. Their serials ranged from F-AA – F-AP, with their US fiscal manufacturing serial numbers painted on their tail fins. Which one of them portrayed the Luftwaffe Hs.126 in the film is not known - it noticeably is fitted with skis, to operate off snow.

The same Piper Super Cub is seen towards the end of the film, watched by Douglas as it flies low over the lake as he waits to board the ferry on which the heavy water tanks are going to be placed. Although not discernable in the film, a featurette on the DVD of "The Heroes of Telemark" showing a documentary on the making of the film has a close-up shot of the Super Cub with its markings clearly in view. It is carrying the code letters RJ+NP on the fuselage side and has a Swastika on its tail. As memories of the real sinking of the ferry in 1944 would still have been clear in the minds of some of the surviving population of Telemark 21 years later, seeing one of their own aircraft painted as a Luftwaffe machine might not have been a comforting sight.

"The Heroes of Telemark" is an enjoyable film in its own right, but has been criticised in Norway itself for fictionalising too much of the reality.

IT HAPPENED HERE

(Released: May 1966)

This extraordinary and, at the time of its release, highly controversial film posits the reality of what life could have been like in Britain during 1944 - 1945, had Nazi Germany succeeded in invading the country in 1940. It is extraordinary not only for how frighteningly real a vision it creates of what an Occupied England would look and feel like, but even more so as to how the film came to be made. It was the creation of an 18-year-old future film historian (Kevin Brownlow) and a 16-year-old amateur military history buff (Andrew Mollo), and took eight years to complete entirely on 16mm reel, a world record for a feature film production according to the Guinness Book of World Records.

Brownlow himself published a book describing the production, "How It Happened Here" (The UKA Press, 1968, re-issued 2007), which is highly recommended for those wanting to know how such an individual and unique film came to be made. "It Happened Here" is a must-have for any war film fan's collection, as well as being a disturbing social study of how and why 'good' people can turn 'bad' under an extremely oppressive regime. But for the purposes of aviation enthusiasts, aircraft do not appear in it at all, although vehicle enthusiasts will find it fascinating as Brownlow and Mollo were meticulous in using accurate cars, trucks and buses of the Forties period, plus a genuine Hunting Tiger Panzer tank loaned from the Bovington Tank Museum.

TRIPLE CROSS

(Released: December 1966, France)

A Franco-British co-production filmed mostly in France based on the exploits of real-life pre-War safecracker, Eddie Chapman, who became an Abwehr agent codenamed 'Triple X', but who was also an MI5 double agent known as 'Zigzag'. The plot is a mixture of fact and fiction. Director is Terence Young, who had made "The Red Beret" (1953) along with the Warwick Films team of 'Cubby' Broccoli and Richard Maibaum, all of whom successfully collaborated to create the new cinematic phenomenon of the Sixties, the James Bond series. Young directed Bonds One ("Dr No", 1962), Two ("From Russia With Love", 1963) and Four ("Thunderball", 1965), before he took on "Triple Cross", in which he found a role for Bond girl in "Thunderball", Claudine Auger, as a female French Resistance fighter.

"Triple Cross" is an entertaining World War Two espionage film made very much in the Sixties mould for British spy films (it has a very Sixties music soundtrack for its theme music, not in keeping with the Forties at all). Young isn't able to avoid creating a James Bond-like personality for Eddie Chapman, played by Canadian actor Christopher Plummer, which is at odds with the real Chapman who was an out-and-out 'Jack the Lad' career villain (non-violent, but not averse to blackmailing women he seduced -

this side of his character is not shown in the film).

War films about double agents usually find a role for aviation to play, and "Triple Cross" is no exception. A scene towards the end of the film with the German forces in retreat across France in 1944 has Plummer as Chapman dressed as an Oberleutnant being driven in a staff car past armour and trucks when the column is attacked by Low Flying Spitfires. In reality, just one Spitfire was used for this set-piece but it made repeated runs for the camera, to create the effect of five Spitfires making the strafing attacks.

We have seen this Spitfire before, performing identical low-level attacks in "The Longest Day" (1962) and "The Train" (1964) (not included in this book). It is Vickers Supermarine Spitfire LF.Mk.IXb MH415, owned and flown by Pierre Laureys of Rousseau Aviation. The history of Spitfire Mk.IX MH415 is given in the review of "The Longest Day". In "Triple Cross", though, we see it for the first time in colour, although only from head-on angles. It still has D-Day stripes on its wings and, very effectively, the twin cannon and machine gun ports in each wing appear to have been adapted to flash lights to simulate fire bursts, making it look very realistic as it strafes the armoured column.

However, the aircraft which really draw attention in "Triple Cross" are unusual ones to say the least, not seen before or since in any other British war film. Twin-engined, twin-tail fin transports of an unfamiliar design, they appear twice in the film, both times when Chapman is to be parachuted at night from a Luftwaffe aircraft into England. One example in particular has been painted in spurious Luftwaffe camouflage, using a two-tone grey scheme, and bears Balkenkreuze and Swastika markings. A second, which appears as a background prop, also has a Balkenkreuze on its fuselage and Swastika on one of its tail fins, but no camouflage. All the others are in natural metal scheme. The only notable marking carried by them all is an all-black inverted triangle, bordered in white, borne on either side of the nose.

The camouflaged transport in which Plummer as Chapman is seen boarding in both scenes is notably different in appearance compared with all the others. It has a bulbous, all-Perspex glazed nose, while the others have conventional stepped, pointed covered noses with the cockpit canopy in place atop the forward fuselage, as is typical of many mid-20th Century transport aircraft designs, such as the Douglas DC-3.

So what are these unusual-looking twin-engined transport aircraft? They are French-built SNCAC NC.701 and NC.702 Martinet (Swift) general purpose transports that were operated by l'Armee de l'Air and l'Aeronavale after the War up until the early Sixties. They are themselves a derivative of the German Siebel Si.204 twin piston-engined transport developed during World War Two and which the French SNCAC (Societe Nationale de Constructions Aeronautiques du Centre) company was ordered to build for the Luftwaffe during the Occupation. From 1942 up to the Liberation in June 1944, SNCAC produced 168 Siebel Si.204s out of the 455 that the Luftwaffe had ordered. After the War, SNCAC continued to produce Si.204s for the French military as a freight and communications transport, as well as a multi-engined trainer. Production ceased after CNCAC went into liquidation in 1949.

SNCAC produced two versions, both of which are seen in the film: the NC.701 Martinet based on the Si.204D with its glazed nose and the NC.702 Martinet representing the stepped nose Si.204A variant. Both versions were powered by the Renault 12S piston engine, itself the French version of the German wartime Argus As.411; a principal difference from the Luftwaffe Si.204 series was that they had two-bladed propellers, whereas the French military Martinets had three-bladed props for better performance.

In "Triple Cross", it is a single NC.701 Martinet that has been painted in camouflage and with Balkenkreuzen applied which acts the part of the Luftwaffe aircraft from which Eddie Chapman parachutes into England on two occasions. It is seen on the parking ramp at night starting engines and taxying away, before taking off. It is also the sole example that flies in the film. All the others are NC.702 Martinets parked in a line behind the NC.701. In one shot, four NC.702s can be counted. The exact total is difficult to ascertain because they are filmed from different angles, with never less than two in shot. At a guess, there are probably a total of five NC.702 Martinets filmed in a line as background props of Luftwaffe transport aircraft on what is meant to be a Luftwaffe airfield in Occupied France.

Presumably, these are either Armee de l'Air or Aeronavale Martinets being used here, dressed as Luftwaffe Siebel Si.204s. That would be logical, except that all French military NC.701 and NC.702 Martinets had been withdrawn from service by 1964, more than one year before "Triple Cross" went into production. A small number had been exported to Sweden and to Morocco, but as no filming was conducted in either of those countries their participation can be ruled out.

The almost certain source for the single NC.701 and the five NC.702s was the Institut Geographique Nationale (IGN) at Aerodrome de Creil in Northern France. The IGN had a small number of Martinets in service as photo-mapping aircraft, alongside its better known fleet of ex-USAAF Boeing B-17G Flying Fortress survey aircraft, which it disposed of later in the Sixties. Almost certainly it is the IGN Martinets that appear in "Triple Cross", which means that the Luftwaffe air base scenes would have been filmed at Creil Aerodrome.

The use of the NC.701 Martinet, almost exactly representative of the Luftwaffe Siebel Si.204D, is as close as it was possible to get in the Sixties to having an authentic German aircraft of the World War Two period appear in a film, aside from the Bucker Bu.133 Bestmann in "The Great Escape" (1963) and the Swiss Air Force Junkers Ju.52 in "Where Eagles Dare" (1968). The appearance of Spanish Air Force Hispano HA.1112M1Ls and CASA 2.111Ds as Messerschmitt Bf.109 fighters and Heinkel He.111 bombers in "Battle of Britain" (1969) would, of course, eclipse these achievements.

One other aircraft, also representative of a Luftwaffe type, briefly appears in shot at the Luftwaffe airfield scene at Creil. Parked between two NC.702 Martinets can be seen a Nord 1101 Noralpha single-engined touring aircraft. The Nord 1101 was based on the German Messerschmitt Me.208 design, of which two prototypes were built by Nord (then SNCAN) during the

Occupation. Nord put the Me.208 into production post-War as the Nord 1101 Noralpha, powered by a Renault 6Q 10 engine; presumably the example seen in shot at Creil was also operated by the IGN, possibly as a company 'hack'.

THE NIGHT OF THE GENERALS

(Released: January 1967)

This unusual Franco-British co-production follows on the heels of "Triple Cross" and, although there is no connection between the production companies for the two films, they were both filming at the same time in France in the mid-Sixties. One factor they do have in common is actor Christopher Plummer, star of the previous film but here seen briefly in a cameo role as FeldMarschal Erwin Rommel, performed while Plummer was in France making "Triple Cross". What is significant for our purpose is that Plummer's appearance involves the sole use of wartime aviation in "The Night of the Generals".

The sequence concerns the attack on Rommel's staff car in Northern France on 17th July 1944 by RAF Spitfires. As we have seen, this attack had been staged very effectively before in "The Desert Fox" (1951), reviewed in Chapter Three.

In both films the correct Marque of Spitfire is used, the Spitfire Mk.IX. However, in "The Desert Fox" Spitfires from a former Free French Air Force squadron in the Royal Air Force were used, combining a mix of the High Flying HF.IX and Low Flying LF.IX variants. In "The Night of the Generals", only the correct Low Flying Spitfire LF.IX version is used, although it is a single example seen here whereas in the real attack on 17th July two Spitfire LF.IXs were involved.

The attack is well staged in the film, performed by Pierre Laureys in his Vickers Supermarine Spitfire LF.IXb MH415 soon after its appearance in "Triple Cross". A close-up of its first run shows that the cannon and machine guns have been removed from the wings, and that flashing lights installed in the gun ports simulates the Spitfire strafing. Also, MH415 has lost its D-Day stripes and appears to have had the grey waves of camouflage removed, leaving the airframe painted olive green all over. The 1944-style roundels have been replaced by large red-white-blue RAF roundels on the fuselage sides, untypical of wartime Spitfires, plus a bright tail-fin flash has been applied.

As explained in the review of "Triple Cross", the full history of Spitfire LF.IXb MH415 is given in the review of "The Longest Day" (1962) in this Chapter. In fact, "The Night of the Generals" is the fourth feature film in which Spitfire LF.IXb MH415 had the chance to replay its real low flying attack role in World War Two for the movies. Its final performance was yet to come, in two years time for "Battle of Britain" (1969).

TOBRUK

(Released: February 1967, USA) Hollywood 'British' war film

Directed by Arthur Hiller, scripted by Leo V Gordon and starring Rock Hudson and George Peppard, this American war film, filmed in America by an American film production company and starring two American leading actors of the Sixties, has not a single American character in it. All, bar two Irish Nazi collaborators and the Canadian Major played by Hudson, are either British or German.

"Tobruk" is based on an actual British and Commonwealth Commando operation against the Axis-held Libyan port of Tobruk – Operation Agreement – which took place on 13th September 1942 and turned out to be a military disaster. The film is a fictionalised version of Operation Agreement and tries to portray the Commando raid on the Afrika Korps' extensive fuel storage depot at Tobruk as being more successful than it actually was. The part of the plot which has British soldiers of the Long Range Desert Group (LRDG) acting as prisoners guarded by Palestinian Jews of German origin wearing Afrika Korps uniforms, is factual.

Aviation makes a limited but yet significant appearance in "Tobruk". At the start of the film, Hudson's character, Major Donald Craig, has escaped from German forces in North Africa, only to fall into the hands of the Vichy French in Algiers. He was the brains behind planning the raid on Tobruk that is now being put into action and has to be sprung from the prison ship he is being held in by members of the Special Identification Group (SIG), staffed by German-speaking Palestinian Jews led by Peppard's character. To maintain the impression he is being 'rescued' by German Kommandos, he is flown to 'safety' in an amphibious Luftwaffe aircraft – or so it appears.

The amphibian is an Allied aircraft painted in Luftwaffe markings. Aviation enthusiasts and historians may not be too impressed by the lack of realism here, as the fake Luftwaffe amphibian is all-too obviously an American Grumman G-21 Goose. However, the Goose is portraying a German floatplane that was actually operated in 1942 on clandestine missions from Malta against the North African coastline, a Heinkel He.115. Four Heinkel He.115Ns were pressed into service with the Royal Air Force during World War Two. They were all former Royal Norwegian Navy Air Service aircraft that had escaped Norway just before the country fell to the Germans and were flown to Britain. Two of them were stationed at the seaplane base of Kalafrana, Malta, and carried out several covert operations disguised as Luftwaffe aircraft against Axis-held territories on the North African coast before both were lost in action. One was shot up by Regia Aeronautica aircraft at its moorings at Kalafrana, the other was shot down by Luftwaffe Bf.109s.

The 'He.115/Goose' flies Hudson and Peppard to a desert location which, although not named in the film, is meant to be Kufra, an oasis deep in the Libyan south-eastern desert that was a vitally important staging post for the British 8th Army. Captured from the Italians in 1941, it had a desert airstrip like that seen in the film.

In reality, this scene, like all the desert scenes in "Tobruk", is filmed in the Californian desert. The Goose, therefore, is a US-based aircraft. Its identity, however, has so far escaped detection. In the film, it is painted all-over grey with Luftwaffe Balkenkreuzen on the fuselage and wings, plus a Swastika on each side of the tail fin. But no other marks are shown and research has not thrown up a candidate for it. It was provided by the famous Tallmantz Aviation company but was not in their ownership. There are still a goodly number of Grumman G-21 Goose amphibians flying today in the USA. One noticeable factor about this particular Goose in "Tobruk" is that it has the squared-off wingtips of the earliest G-21A models produced; most surviving Grumman Goose in private ownership today are of the later model G-21G, with extended, rounded wingtips.

Interestingly, the Bundesmarineflieger of the post-War West Germany flew eight examples of the Grumman G-21 Goose's successor, the Grumman HU-16D Albatross, as a search and rescue amphibian from the early Sixties until they were replaced by helicopters in 1972.

The other principal piece of aviation action in "Tobruk" is a very dramatic and well-staged sequence when the LRDG 'prisoners' and their SIG 'guards' are driving through the desert in captured German trucks and half-tracks, and are attacked and strafed by an RAF fighter whose pilot obviously does not know of their disguised mission. The scene has the fighter flying extremely low over the convoy, with SFX cannon fire ripping up the desert floor. The LRDG have no choice but to shoot the fighter down, even though it is one of theirs.

The fighter in question is a Curtiss P-40E Kittyhawk IA bearing the distinctive shark-mouth markings that P-40s came to be associated with. Here, director Hiller and his art work team have tried to be accurate, as the RAF's No.112 Squadron in 1941 were the first to adorn their early model P-40 Tomahawks with the shark-mouth image which they later transposed to their newer model P-40E Kittyhawks in 1942.

It is possible to identify this P-40 in "Tobruk". It is an actual ex-RAF P-40E Kittyhawk IA, so it is performing its real-life ground-attack role in the film. At the time of filming in 1966 it bore the US FAA registration of N1207V, which it wore in large figures on its fuselage side. Although it is not easily seen, part of the serial number is visible as the P-40E flies past the camera position: most of the serial is obscured by the large RAF roundel on the fuselage, but the first letter and number 'N1-' have not been covered. In 1966, P-40E N1207V bore the shark-mouth image and red propeller boss typical of No.112 Squadron Kittyhawks but was painted in grey-green camouflage as seen in the film, which is incorrect; to be representative of RAF P-40s in the North African Campaign, it would have had to be painted in sand-brown camouflage. This P-40E was in the ownership of Tallmantz Aviation at the time, although Tallmantz filmography records do not show Frank Tallman as the pilot.

P-40E N1207V began life in 1941 as a Kittyhawk Mk.IA for the RAF, serial number AL152. It was later transferred to the Royal Canadian Air Force, serialled RCAF 1082. Not long after its

appearance in "Tobruk", N1207V was before the cameras again as one of the two P-40 Warhawks in the Pearl Harbor epic, "Tora! Tora! Tora!" (1970). It was damaged during filming and did not fly again until its maiden post-restoration flight on 15th December 1973, under new ownership. N1207V then went through a number of ownership changes while being a regular on the States-side airshow scene throughout the Eighties and Nineties. On 25th June 1986, it was re-registered with the FAA as N95JB, its current identity today. In 1990, it was acquired by John MacGuire, the founder of the War Eagles Museum at Santa Teresa, New Mexico. Today, P-40E N95JB can be seen on static display, resplendent in 23rd Fighter Group markings in the War Eagles Museum.

THE LONG DAY'S DYING

(Cannes Film Festival, May 1968)

This is the kind of British war film that American movie-going audiences cannot stand. A cerebral study of three British Paratroopers trapped behind enemy lines as the Allies fight their way through Nazi Germany in 1945. It is the kind of war film that Hollywood would never make, concentrating on each individual Para's strengths, weaknesses, doubts and failings, as they struggle with their personal conflicts amid the much wider conflict they are trapped in.

Peter Collinson is the director. He was one of the golden boys of British television and cinema in the Sixties, through his gritty portrayal of back street life in "Up The Junction" (1967), the film version of the widely acclaimed BBC TV play. Collinson made "The Long Day's Dying" immediately following "Junction"; he followed that up with the ever-popular (with English Michael Caine fans, anyway), "The Italian Job" (1968), red, white and blue Austin Minis and all.

Aviation does put in an appearance in "The Long Day's Dying", although only briefly. Sixties English film star David Hemmings as the Para with a conscience spots a Luftwaffe observer 'plane circling over their position, as he and his mates hide in a bombed-out building amid a forest. It is a Messerschmitt Bf.108, the fifth time we have seen one of these drafted in to appear as a Luftwaffe aircraft in a British, or Hollywood 'British', World War Two war film. In this case, it is fair to say that the Bf.108 is acting as itself, as in the closing months of the War the Luftwaffe resorted to using any aircraft that it had available in desperate last measures against the overwhelming might of the Allies. The Messerschmitt Bf.108 Taifun was drafted in as an emergency close-air support or spotter aircraft, roles which made it very vulnerable to anti-aircraft fire.

The principal difference between this Messerschmitt Bf.108 and all the others seen in war films up till now is that this example is a British registered machine. The freezing, muddy woods and copses of Chertsey, Surrey, provided the locations for besieged Germany in early 1945, therefore this Bf.108 has to be a British-owned aircraft. There were three such examples on the British civil aviation register when "The Long Day's Dying" was being filmed during the winter of 1967, all of them French-built Nord

1002 variants. Acting as the Messerschmitt Bf.108 is Nord 1002 Pinguoin II G-ASTG, the former F-BGKI on the French register. It was imported into the UK on 21st May 1964 by the Nipper Flying Group at Elstree Aerodrome. Painted in the unimaginative pale white/cream colour scheme that many Nord 1002 Pinguoin tourers seemed to adopt in France, G-ASTG can be seen in the film flying circles low overhead the camera position, with spurious Luftwaffe Balkenkreuzen on its fuselage and under each wing. The aircraft is only filmed from underneath, so, apart from a final distant shot, no topside view is visible. This is deliberate because G-ASTG had a dark cheat line stretching midway along the fuselage which had to be kept out of shot, otherwise the effect would have been spoilt.

Nord 1002 Pinguoin II G-ASTG stayed with the Nipper Flying Group, aside from an 18 month period when it was chartered, until it was sold in June 1974. On 2nd October that year it was registered to Lindsay Walton of Wisbech, Cambridgeshire, who already owned Nord 1002 G-ATBG, then a very familiar performer on the British airshow circuit (as it still is today, under different ownership); Walton acquired G-ASTG as a spares source to support his operation of G-ATBG painted as a Messerschmitt Bf.108B. Walton retained ownership of G-ASTG right up until May 2011, when, on the 25th of that month, it became registered to Robert Fray of Peterborough. It has now been on long-term rebuild to fly at Duxford and actually made its post-restoration flight in December 2013, painted to represent a Messerschmitt Bf108B after something like 35 years of inactivity.

ATTACK ON THE IRON COAST

(Released: June 1968)

The point in making this film is somewhat difficult to understand, as it is a repeat of the St Nazaire Raid that was re-enacted in "Gift Horse" (1952). It had to be made appealing to the US film market, so American actor Lloyd Bridges plays the lead role of the Commando officer who heads the raid: a compromise is reached by making his character Canadian. St Nazaire is changed into the fictional French port of Le Claire (should have been La Claire, to be grammatically correct), while the Lend-Lease destroyer HMS Campbeltown is changed into a run-down old minesweeper without a name.

At the beginning of the film, Lloyd Bridges's character is seen watching film of a seaborne Commando raid that he had led, but which had been a disaster. Although it is not mentioned, the fact that Bridges's character is a Canadian senior officer implies that this is the Dieppe Raid of 19th August 1942. But the St Nazaire Raid took place five months earlier than Dieppe in March 1942, so historical accuracy is obviously not being applied here.

The film that Bridges is watching actually consists of selected out-takes from "The Next of Kin" (1942), reviewed in Chapter One. It has that film's same mix of wartime archive footage and studio miniatures of Junkers Ju.87 Stukas in action, dive bombing British Commandos during their beach landing raid. The archive footage consists of an air-air shot of nine Stukas in three separate

'Kettes' of three Ju.87s each; two Ju.87s dive bombing, with their bombs clearly seen being released; and two more Ju.87s in vertical dives, one leading the other, which was also used in "Dunkirk" (1958). The remaining footage is of miniature Stukas taken from "The Next of Kin".

Later in "Attack on the Iron Coast", the flotilla that is crossing the English Channel at night to attack Le Claire is bombed by a German aircraft. This is a very obvious miniature of a Messerschmitt Bf.109 which appears, by the way it swings round, to be attached to a rotating wire. This miniature Bf.109 has appeared somewhere before: it has actually been lifted from "Nine Men" (1943), and been colour tinted. Adding to the complete sense of unrealism, it repeatedly bombs the ridiculously miniature flotilla which no Bf.109 would be capable of doing. So, "Attack on the Iron Coast" uses out-takes from two wartime period war films, both made more than 25 years earlier.

The only other piece of aviation in the film involves two brief out-takes of the three Avro Lancaster B.VIIs flown in "The Dam Busters" (1955). The scene used is that of the leading section of three Lancasters taking flak as they fly low over Holland. In "Attack on the Iron Coast", these out-takes are meant to depict a diversionary raid by the RAF. Again, accuracy is out the door here, as the Lancaster had yet to enter service in the time period when the so-called "Attack on the Iron Coast" is meant to be taking place.

This is an example of a minimum budget British war film made with little care for military and historical accuracy, while using very sub-standard special effects, for a late Sixties audience that had become sated with stock fare of this kind from both sides of the Atlantic. It was actually the first in a series of mass produced war films made by a company named Oakmont Productions, a subsidiary of The Mirisch Corporation (see "Mosquito Squadron", 1969, in this Chapter, for more details). Lloyd Bridges was probably just happy to pocket his fee.

WHERE EAGLES DARE

(Release: December 1968)

From the second you hear that first soft, staccato drum beat, building up progressively into a loud, continuous hammering, before exploding into that magnificent, over-exaggerated dramatic film score, you know which film you're about to watch without having to open your eyes. Not many film music composers can claim to have authored a movie theme tune which everyone recognises instantly, as well as the film it introduces, but "633 Squadron" (1964) composer Ron Goodwin scores again with his rousing introduction to "Where Eagles Dare", accompanying the stunning imagery of Junkers Ju.52/3mg4e A-702 swaying in the air currents above the Alpine mountains.

When this air-air opening scene was filmed, in early April 1968 from an Alouette II helicopter, Ju.52/3mg4e A-702 was one of three of its kind still on strength with the Transport Kommando (Transport Command) of the Schweizerische Luftwaffe (Swiss Air

Force), carrying civil registration HB-HOT and based at Flugplatz Dubendorf-Salzburg. Its drab grey Swiss Air Force scheme had been replaced with an Alpine-style camouflage pattern that matched superbly the snow-covered jagged mountains below it, much copied by aero-modellers but completely inauthentic compared with actual Luftwaffe Ju.52 schemes. So taken were the Swiss military with their aircraft's 'wardrobe' in the film that they retained the snow-white/dark green jagged camouflage pattern for the rest of its service career, albeit without the Luftwaffe Balkenkreuzen and Swastika, of course.

At the time of its appearance in "Where Eagles Dare", Ju.52/3mg4e A-702 had notched up 48 years of service with the Schweizerische Luftwaffe, along with two sister ships at Dubendorf, A-701 and A-703, and with all three still going strong today. They represented the then entire military transport aircraft fleet in Switzerland. They had joint military and civil transport roles, hence the joint military and civil serial/registrations (A-701 was HB-HOP, A-703 carried HB-HOS). All three were destined to fly on until taken out of service in 1981, but, as many aviation enthusiasts and historians will know, they were saved for posterity by the VFMF (Association of the Friends of the Swiss Air Force). This resulted in the JU-AIR organisation being formed that continues to fly all three Ju.52/3mg4e from Dubendorf today, and recently with a fourth example, a Spanish-built CASA 352L (HB-HOY), which has now been grounded as a spares source.

In the film, Ju.52/3mg4e A-702 is painted with Luftwaffe codes CN+4V, plus a tail number '9' on the top of its rudder. An Online source suggests that this is a reverse representation of an actual Ju.52 unit, and that a photo exists of such an aircraft coded 4V+CN on the Russian Front, also with a tail number '9'. The aero modeller decals website, Wings Palette, has a side-view profile of a wartime Ju.52/3M coded 4V+CA but states this belongs to an unknown unit.

"Where Eagles Dare" was simultaneously scripted as a film and written as a book by thriller writer Alastair MacLean, he of "The Guns of Navarone" (1961) fame, within six weeks. He was under pressure by film producer, Elliott Kastner, to come up with a story that could go into immediate production. MacLean decided to use a mix of plots, sub-plots, counter-plots, false trails and double dealings, to create one of the most unlikely spy-cum-war film adventure stories that would enthral a Sixties generation cinema audience who had a huge appetite for James Bond/Agatha Christie/Guns of Navarone-size epics.

To call "Where Eagles Dare" believable is like saying one believes in "The Da Vinci Code", but like Dan Brown's convoluted spiritual thriller, it has its basis in fact. The plot has a cover story of a group of British, plus one American, operatives being parachuted into Bavaria to rescue a United States Army General and right hand man to General Eisenhower from the hands of the SS, when in reality the mission is intended to expose the extent to which the German Abwehr has penetrated MI6. It has so many twists and turns, so many crosses and double crosses, that it would be easier to believe that the Pope is the Chief Rabbi of Jerusalem in disguise than to accept MacLean's elaborate storyline.

But the final twist of having the head of MI6 being the Abwehr's chief agent in Britain was not so implausible as one might imagine. Great Britain in the Sixties was riven by the revelations of Russian spies Kim Philby, Guy Burgess and (no relation) Donald MacLean defecting from MI6. Moreover, there were continuing rumours and suspicions about the head of MI5, Sir Roger Hollis, being the so-called "Fifth Man" and that British Prime Minister Harold Wilson was a KGB agent, no less. And there was a huge appetite for John Le Carre's Smiley series of spy novels, full of "Moles" in "the Circus". So, Alastair MacLean was playing on the then current fascination with enemy spies in Britain infiltrating into the highest ranks politically and militarily, both in fact and fantasy.

Richard Burton plays Major John Smith (it must have taken MacLean hours to conjure up that name) who leads the team into Bavaria. Clint Eastwood's fame was rising after "The Man With No Name" series of Italian-made Westerns had led to him starring in two Hollywood productions for the first time, "Hang 'Em High" (1968) and "Coogan's Bluff" (1968), prompting him to take the offer to play Lieutenant Schaffer in a British war film that had box office success stamped on it.

The plot has US General Carnaby flying on a secret mission to meet his Russian opposite number in the Middle East, to discuss plans about the forthcoming Second Front. The timeline appears to be early 1944, with the Second Front being described as the invasion of Europe. Mention is made of a "saturation raid on Nuremburg" which should have drawn off all Luftwaffe fighters from Carnaby's route: this could be a reference to the Nuremburg Raid of 30th/31st March 1944, when Bomber Command suffered its largest number of losses in a single night of the War with 106 bombers destroyed. Carnaby was flying in an RAF Mosquito which supposedly was shot down by a "wandering Messerschmitt patrol" 10 miles from the SS headquarters in Bavaria, the Schloss Adler (Castle of Eagles), where he is now held prisoner. But, as Major Smith later divulges, "The Mosquito was riddled with machine gun holes…British machine gun holes", and deliberately crash landed on Oberhafen Airfield with a fake General Carnaby on board who lets himself be caught by the Germans to spread false information to them.

It isn't the Mosquito that is riddled with holes, it's MacLean's plot.

Firstly, the Abwehr had no success at all in mounting a major intelligence operation within Britain against MI5 and MI6. In fact, it had no strategic plan to do so. However, that fact had not been disclosed when MacLean came up with his plot, and with the then media hysteria about Philby and Soviet moles it was logical to assume the Germans had been as good at having double agents in World War Two as the Russians were proving to have in the Cold War.

Secondly, General Carnaby would not have flown to a clandestine meeting in the Middle East in an RAF Mosquito or any other British 'plane. He would have flown in a grand Douglas C-54 of the United States Army Air Force, as all top ranking US military brass of the time did.

Thirdly, what was he doing being flown to the Middle East over Bavaria? He would have flown the Great Britain - Gibraltar -

Malta - Alexandria route, which in 1944 was far less threatened by Axis Powers fighter aircraft.

Fourthly, how did the Mosquito get riddled with British machine gun holes? Does MacLean ask us to believe it flew all the way from England in such a condition? Or that the pilot deliberately crash landed it at Oberhafen Airfield, five miles from the Schloss Adler, and then shot it up with a machine gun himself? And what became of the pilot, anyway?

Finally, MacLean would have us believe that Carnaby was meeting his Russian opposite number in Crete, which is obviously not in the Middle East. Was MacLean's memory so short that he had forgotten Crete was still occupied by German forces in 1944?

No matter, all this is dramatic licence. Smith's team are to parachute into Bavaria from a captured Junkers Ju.52, dressed in the uniforms of Alpine Korps troops. Schaffer's presence is thought to be needed because 'General Carnaby' is an American, so an American participation in a British operation is required. However, the plot is concealing here the true motivation, that Schaffer being an American means he can't be an Abwehr double agent inside MI6.

In reality, Eastwood's role was needed to make "Where Eagles Dare" acceptable to an American movie theater audience. Schaffer is described as a Lieutenant in the US Rangers. Here is another hole in the plot: the US Rangers were never involved in covert operations as portrayed in this film, although they were modelled on the British SAS and did undertake missions behind enemy lines - however, they always wore their own uniforms and never disguised themselves as enemy soldiers, as Schaffer is depicted doing in "Where Eagles Dare". Later in the plot, Smith describes Schaffer as an assassin from the OSS, the Office of Strategic Services, which would be the correct organisation that carried out covert American operations in a similar fashion to the British SOE (how he could simultaneously be a US Ranger and an OSS agent is an interesting conundrum).

Smith's team are described as being all highly experienced men who have each worked behind the lines before and who all speak fluent German (another error for Schaffer's US Ranger). What unit they belong to isn't mentioned, but, as the story unfolds, we are told by Smith they are MI6. Again, another hole: MI6 did not undertake aggressive or coercive action against German Occupation forces, let alone on German soil itself - that was the role of the SOE and, later in the War, the SAS. MI6 concentrated on Intelligence-gathering in Occupied Territories. So, Smith's team ought to be either SOE or SAS; however, if they are, then there would be serious ill feeling within British Military Intelligence about them sorting out German infiltration of MI6. The SOE and MI6 were often at odds with each other, especially concerning operations within Nazi Occupied France.

The scene depicting the insertion of Smith's team into Bavaria was filmed air-air with Ju.52/3mg4e A-702 over a planned drop zone on the Glacier del Forno, south of Majelapass near to San Moritz. The studio cockpit and cabin interiors were shot at MGM British Studios, Borehamwood. The RAF pilot flying the captured Ju.52 is played by Australian actor, Vincent Ball: he had

acquired something of a reputation in the Sixties for playing pilots in British films and TV series, having been the (uncredited) pilot of the Vickers Wellington bomber in "Very Important Person" (1961) and then played more pilot roles in two 1963 television series, "Zero One" and "The Plane Makers". Being Australian, he would naturally go on to play the part of a pilot in the later TV series, "The Flying Doctors".

According to a Website dedicated to the making of "Where Eagles Dare", the parachutists seen making the static line jumps out of Ju.52/3mg4e A-702 were neither Swiss nor Austrian military Fallschirmspringers, as has long been supposed, but were a team of seven French sky-divers. Freeze-frame analysis confirms that they certainly were not military Paras because the manner of their exit from the Ju.52/3mg4e is decidedly un-military in style. If they were military, they would either exit head up, feet together, arms folded across their chest in the US/British style, in order not to impede the operation of the static line, or spring head first down and out of the aircraft, arms spread out in front of them, to allow the umbilical chord system free access to release their 'chutes in the German style (remember the Reich Propaganda Ministry archive footage used in "Dunkirk" (1958), demonstrating this umbilical system?). Instead, they leap in succession as if they were exiting in free-fall, one even turning in mid air as he leaves the Ju.52/3mg4e to face the next sky-diver behind him - decidedly un-military in style! Apparently they used French parachute harnesses attached to static lines, manufactured by the French EFA company which, at the time, supplied parachute harnesses to the French Army.

The air-airs of the parachute exits are splendidly filmed against the Alpine mountain backdrop. However, the one slight criticism, unavoidable in the circumstances, is that Ju.52/3mg4e A-702 cannot conceal, despite her disguise as Luftwaffe CN+4V, that she is a passenger-carrying aircraft because of her distinct passenger windows: a troop-carrying Ju.52 would have had none. But that is a small quibble to make and was a factor the film production team could do nothing about.

A much bigger quibble arises from the appearance of a Bell 47G Sioux helicopter in "Where Eagles Dare". Factually incorrect but historically more accurate than many might realise, the use of a helicopter in a World War Two film, and in particular a German one in an Alpine setting, is not as far fetched as one might suppose. Germany led the world in helicopter technology both before and during World War Two. Famous female test pilot, Hanna Reitsch, had publicly demonstrated the twin rotor Focke Wulf FW.61 inside the Berlin Deutschalle in February 1938. It was what today would be called a concept demonstrator and never went into production. But during the War, the Flettner Fl.282 inter-meshing twin rotor design was used successfully from Kriegsmarine warships in the Mediterranean and Aegean Seas for submarine spotting and for re-supply in the Baltic, although not on a large scale because there was no practical means of storing the helicopter aboard ship in high seas.

When he wrote the helicopter into both the novel and the screenplay of "Where Eagles Dare", MacLean almost certainly had the Focke-Achgelis FA.223 Drache in mind. This was a sizeable machine that employed the FW.61 twin rotor outrigger concept to enable four people to be carried and to lift underslung loads in a net. It was used by the Wehrmacht towards the end of the War to supply Alpine troops, so a German helicopter in an Alpine setting is historically correct. The problem is, no existing German helicopter of the wartime period was available, so a suitable substitute had to be found.

The Bell 47G was the closest in time to the FA.223 Drache, having first flown in 1947. However, its appearance in "Where Eagles Dare" looks incongruous because all aviation enthusiasts and historians know that this American designed and built machine had nothing to do with World War Two. For this reason alone, "Where Eagles Dare" has drawn much flak. The Bell 47G used in the film painted with Luftwaffe Balkenkreuzen and Swastika could have come from any one of several sources in the Alps. It has been presumed that it was played by an example from the Osterreichische Luftstreitkrafte (Austrian Air Force). However, this is almost certainly unlikely because the constitution of the relatively newly formed Austrian armed forces did not permit them to carry the Swastika on any of their equipment, even temporarily for a film. Another possible candidate would be one of the two Bell 47Gs belonging to HeliSwiss, which had got into the film production business through contributing helicopters to the sixth James Bond film to be made, "On Her Majesty's Secret Service" (1967), that was filmed in the Swiss Alps. All the other aircraft appearing in "Where Eagles Dare" came from Switzerland, so a Swiss source for the Bell 47G and other helicopters supporting the production is quite likely, but its actual identity remains unknown.

The plotline has the helicopter flying General Rosemeyer from Berlin to the Schloss Adler - another Alastair MacLean plot hole. If it had done, it would have had to make a series of refuelling stops en route, very impractical for Herr General. The same would have been the case for the real life FA.223 Drache.

"You like my machine?" asks General Rosemeyer of Colonel Kramer (played by everybody's favourite German, Anton Diffring), pointing at the helicopter. "It looks pretty dangerous", replies Kramer. Such was the opinion of the majority, both military and civil on both sides in the War, about the helicopter, hence its development was limited in the Forties.

The convoluted plot takes us through the confusing cross and double cross by Major Smith until he reveals that the mission has always been to get the names of every Abwehr agent in Britain, especially those who have penetrated MI6. The fight on top of the cable car was apparently inspired by the similar scene in "Night Train to Munich", first shown in the cinema as far back as 1940.

Of course, what we want is the final battle at Oberhafen Airfield, in reality Aigen im Ennstal Flugplatz near Liezen, in the region of Styria south-east of Salzburg. This is still an active air base today, being home to the Kommando Luftunterstutzung's Alouette III helicopter Staffel. In March 1968, it was dressed to appear as a Deutsches Luftwaffe fighter base in Bavaria, supposedly equipped with Focke Wulf FW.190 fighters. Because there was no warbird scene in Europe in the Sixties, the only aircraft type that was available to the film production team was the durable North American T-6 Texan, asked yet again to double up as enemy aircraft.

Four are seen at Aigen im Ennstal Flugplatz, three lined up on what would have been the grass if there were no snow, with the fourth slightly separated from them on the cleared hard surface of the operational ramp. All four were painted in reasonably authentic-looking Luftwaffe Alpine camouflage and markings. The origin of these T-6 Texans has been speculated upon in Online Forums, with the favourite theory that they are all full-scale (F/S) mock-ups. If they were such, they would surely be F/S facsimiles of Focke Wulf FW.190s; there would be no need to reproduce F/S T-6 Texans. They are the real thing, and, yes, they do get trashed for real.

They are four Nooduyn AT-16 Harvard 2Bs of the Schweizerische Luftwaffe, struck off charge machines which had been sold to the film production company of "Where Eagles Dare", Winkast Film Productions, Ltd, on 26th February 1968. In 1949, the Swiss Air Force received 40 former RAF Harvard 2Bs, which it operated until the end of 1967. It was in the process of disposing of these Harvards when "Where Eagles Dare" was going into production, and had no problem with selling four of them on to Winkast. They were purchased as 'empty' airframes, ie, without engines and other useful components, and road-freighted to Aigen im Ennstal where they were re-assembled. To give them a bit more of a FW.190-ish appearance, they were fitted with three-bladed props.

Interestingly, the art department painted the Gruppe badge of I/JG.51 onto the forward fuselages of the Harvards, to give the impression that it is to this famous Luftwaffe fighter unit that the 'FW.190s' belong; at the entrance gate to the Flugplatz, there is a signboard with 'I/JG.51' printed on to it. I/JG.51 never operated the FW.190, it was exclusively a Messerschmitt Bf.109 Gruppe, operating nearly all the different versions produced.

The four Swiss Air Force Harvard 2Bs have been identified as U-311, U-315, U-317 and U-327. All of them perished in the production. We all know how: Major Smith and the surviving members of his team commandeer a bus fitted with a snow plough at the front to escape from the town below the Schloss Adler and use it to drive to the Flugplatz. There, the captured Ju.52 has landed to pick them up. Smith deliberately rams and wrecks the parked 'FW.190s' to prevent them from taking off in pursuit.

The first to go is 'Harvard/FW.190' coded BO+ED parked on the ramp, into the tail of which Smith rams the bus, swinging the fake fighter round. The nose of the 'Harvard/FW.190' smashes into a parked truck, causing a fire to break out. First the truck explodes, then the 'Harvard/FW.190' lights up in a mass of flame.

Next, Smith heads straight for the line of three 'Harvard/FW.190s'; interestingly, the snow had melted when this shot was filmed, with dirty green grass and sludge everywhere. First in the line is 'Harvard/FW.190' coded BO+EH, with BO+EY in the middle and BO+ET the last of the three. Smith rams one after the other in succession, slamming into their tails. The ease with which the three light airframes spin round after being hit confirms they had had their engines stripped out. Also, the rear halves of their cockpits have been removed as well. BO+EH explodes, as does BO+ET. A shot of pursuing German troops in a Kubelwagen shows BO+ET well alight in the background, with the fabric of its rudder burnt completely away. Comments have been made

Online that if Richard Burton were still alive, T-6 lovers would be plotting a suitable fate for him; however, he didn't actually drive the bus into the redundant Harvards, he just acted the part in the studio - a stunt driver did the real damage.

When the bus reaches the waiting Ju.52, the airfield is covered with snow again. 'Tante Ju' takes off amid a hail of Spandau machine gun fire, with a fine shot of Ju.52/mg4e A-702 sweeping up surprisingly fast against the backdrop of the Grimming Mountain. It is possible that the film has been speeded up to achieve the effect.

Comment has not surprisingly been made on Website Forums that the use of the Ju.52 is undoubtedly welcome, but is another hole in MacLean's plot. The Ju.52 is meant to be flying to and from England, something which it simply did not have the range to achieve. In his novel of the same story, MacLean has the team use an RAF Lancaster bomber.

Never mind the holes in MacLean's plot, "Where Eagles Dare" retains its 'Boys Own'-style sense of drama, packed with spectacular action and with a lot of vehicles, buildings, a complete cable car and, yes, aircraft all going bang. Apparently a young Steven Spielberg loved it for its unadulterated sense of adventure and excitement. Others, largely due to the never-ending flow of German troops Eastwood mows down or blows up, regard it as the first of the 'Shoot-'em ups'. Whether that was the reputation Alastair MacLean had in mind for it when he penned both the film and the novel, only he knows. Pity about those Harvards.

HANNIBAL BROOKS

(Released: 1969)

An enjoyable story of a British PoW working in the Munich Zoo in 1944 who escapes to the Swiss border with an elephant in tow! Although there is a scene of a bombing raid by the USAAF on Munich, no actual aircraft are shown.

PLAY DIRTY

(Released: January 1969)

For its time this was an against-the-grain look at British Army Commandos operating behind enemy lines in the North African desert. Michael Caine plays a by-the-book Captain who is forced to join a band of British Army no-gooders sent on a suicidal mission by a ruthlessly ambitious Colonel (Harry Andrews), who is quite prepared to sacrifice them in pursuit of his own interests, and led by a murderous Captain (Nigel Davenport) who doesn't care who he kills or gets killed, German or British. The distinctly cynical and brutal Commandos certainly did not fit the stereotyped image of upstanding, heroic British soldiers that the film industry of the Sixties fostered.

With good all-round acting, and a production that realistically appears to have been made in hard, rough conditions, "Play Dirty" is worth having in one's collection (especially if you're a Michael Caine fan), but no aircraft appear in it.

MOSQUITO SQUADRON

(Released: January 1969)

First things first, "Mosquito Squadron" is not a sequel to "633 Squadron" (1964). It does, however, use a considerable amount of out-take material from that earlier film, which was possible due to both productions being made at the same studio, MGM British Film Studios.

"Mosquito Squadron" was the second of a series of six war films, four British and two American, mass produced in the late Sixties by Oakmont Productions, an Anglo-American subsidiary of the Mirisch Company which specialised in low budget war films. American producer and screenplay writer, John C Champion, was behind Oakmont; Champion had the highly popular Western TV series, "Laramie", to his name and had moved to England in 1967 to work for Mirisch Films which, of course, was the production company behind "633 Squadron". Mirisch Films was the British arm of the Mirisch Company, which in its turn was owned by MGM, but was allowed to produce films independently in MGM's studios in both the USA and the UK.

Oakmont's first outing was the cheaply-made "Attack on the Iron Coast" (1968), which we have lambasted in this book. "Mosquito Squadron" is listed as the second, but in fact it was one of three film productions that Oakmont churned out in short notice for release to the cinema in 1969, including "Submarine X-1", whose review follows this one. Talk about trying to make a quick, and cheap, buck.

Oakmont's style is self-evident in "Mosquito Squadron": stereotypical, one dimensional characters; banal, simple script; mass production quickie takes. The actors are all regular names and faces from British and American TV productions of the Sixties, most notably David McCallum as Squadron Leader Quint Munroe: McCallum was well known at the time for portraying Russian secret agent Ilya Kuryakin in the highly popular TV and movie spy series, "The Man From U.N.C.L.E.". In fact, "Mosquito Squadron" was one of only a few feature films that McCallum made; virtually the whole of his career to follow was in TV productions on both sides of the Atlantic, although mostly in the United States - he's still going strong over there today, at the ripe old age of 80.

McCallum plays opposite Suzanne Neve, a very Sixties British TV actress who was cast in the film on the back of her moving performance in the BBC TV dramatisation of the classic novel, "The Portrait of a Lady". Neve plays Beth who Munroe is privately and guiltily in love with, but she is the wife of Munroe's lifelong chum, 'Scotty', who also just happens to be Munroe's squadron commander. Yes, that's the kind of Mills and Boone background that Oakmont Productions liked to attach to its wartime plots.

It was said by critics at the time of the release of "Mosquito

Squadron" that the 'Wooden Wonders' were not the Mosquitos of the film's title, but the actors. However, it is the real 'Wooden Wonders' in the film that are the objects of our interest, and there are plenty of them. Six de Havilland Mosquitos were used directly in the production - four of them flyers - comprising five de Havilland Mosquito TT.35 ex-target-tugs and one de Havilland Mosquito T.3 trainer. But they are not the first flyers we see in the film.

The opening shot is one we have seen before: the long backtrack down the launch rail of a Fieseler Fi.103 flying bomb, serial numbered 'M23', mounted and being prepared for blasting off against London. This shot is an out-take from "Operation Crossbow" (1965), another MGM British Film Studios' production, and being the scene in that film when the Fi.103 was going through its troublesome flight tests from Peenemunde. In fact, almost a minute's worth of out-takes from "Operation Crossbow", showing V1 flying bombs launching and flying through flak, occupies the pre-credits sequence of "Mosquito Squadron". Did the director, Boris Sagal, really believe that cinema audiences wouldn't know he had lifted the V1 scenes straight from "Operation Crossbow", released only a few years earlier? We can't ask him because Sagal had his long career in US TV productions cut short, literally, in 1982 when he walked into a turning helicopter rotor blade. Sagal and McCallum, incidentally, knew each other well, as Sagal had directed McCallum in two episodes of "The Man From U.N.C.L.E." and its spin-off movie, "The Helicopter Spies" (1968), just before they started making "Mosquito Squadron".

But the next shot is what we want to see, that of the four Mosquitos in 'Finger Four' formation flying low over the waves. A neat effect is the way all four are lit up one by one by the sun as they emerge from shadow cast by clouds. Aerial photography was carried out by film cameraman, Stan Sayer, who had RAE Farnborough's Shackleton MR.3 WR972 trials aircraft, no less, as a camera-ship. What was advantageous in using this Shackleton was that it had clear Perspex nose and tail housings that were devoid of the standard cannon installed in operational Shackleton MR.3s, thus allowing for ideal, unobstructed views for aerial filming. A drawback, though, was the fact that Sayer could do nothing about the rain drops which formed on the Perspex nose, leaving them unavoidably in shot during several air-airs with three Mosquitos.

Bovingdon Airfield was again the location, although unlike "633 Squadron" it is not given any identity in the film. Apparently, at one point in time Bovingdon was crowded with many of the Spitfires, Hurricanes and CASA 2.111s/Heinkel He.111s, plus the B-25 Mitchell camera-ship, of "Battle of Britain" (1969) which was in production at the same time as "Mosquito Squadron", sharing ramp space with the four Mosquitos and the RAE Shackleton. Such a sight must have made Bovingdon an extraordinary venue for spotters in 1968. Some of the scenes shot there for "Mosquito Squadron" bear testament to what a wet summer that year produced, as the rain seen covering the Mosquitos in the film proves. In fact, the amount of wet weather the production team had to put up with was written into the plot, explaining the rain-delayed raid that No.641 Squadron, the Mosquito Squadron of the title, was expected to lead.

There was no operational No.641 Squadron in World War Two, although the rafweb.org Website states that the codes 'EU-' were allocated to this squadron number for the period between April - September 1939, in the event of that squadron being formed.

Another location was the Staff College at Minley Manor, near Farnborough in Hampshire, which actually held the Officers' Mess of Gibraltar Barracks. Minley Manor was used to represent l'Chateau de Charlon, where the Germans have set up an underground facility to produce what in the plot is called a "V3 or V4 rocket". There was a Vergeltungswaffe Drei (V3, Retaliation Weapon Three) in World War Two, but little had been published about it when "Mosquito Squadron" was filmed. V3 was based in France and aimed at London, so "Mosquito Squadron" was on the right track here. V3 was, in effect, a 50-barrelled launch system of finned projectiles, firing at a rate of up to ten per minute and with a velocity of 5,000 feet per second, that was located at Mimoyecques, near the Pas de Calais. British Intelligence knew something existed there, and RAF Bomber Command 'visited' it on a number of occasions; but V3's true function was never discovered until it was overrun by the Canadian 3rd Infantry Division in September 1944. It was never fired at London, largely because the projectiles lost momentum above 3,300 feet and 'toppled', falling a long way short. German scientists and armaments experts were never able to correct the problem (R V Jones, "Most Secret War", Chapter 46 'V3', page 462) .

Also, in 1943 British Intelligence located a number of artificial caves near the French coast, including two behind Cherbourg, that turned out to be storage sites for V1 flying bombs and V2 rockets. So, a tunnel-based rocket site in France wasn't far-fetched either. As we know from "Operation Crossbow" (1965), the V2's actual designation was A4 (Aggregat 4), so the script could be playing on A4 in its use of "V4". The Germans were developing an A4b winged version of A4 that, on re-entry from the atmosphere, would be able to glide to targets in England far further inland than London, or could be launched from more distant sites inside Germany itself. Two were test launched, but A4b never got beyond the trials stage.

So "Mosquito Squadron" was on to something with its use of an advanced rocket targeted against England. However, developing such a weapon would not have taken place in Nazi Occupied France, where the Germans would have been inviting just the kind of raid that No.641 Squadron is ordered to carry out.

The raid is planned to use 'Highball', the smaller version of the spinning 'Upkeep' bomb that was used by No.617 Squadron against the Ruhr Dams and which was re-created in the film, "The Dam Busters" (1955). 'Highball' was designed by 'Upkeep' inventor Dr Barnes Wallis to be dropped by Mosquito B.IVs of No.618 Squadron against Kriegsmarine warships operating out of Norwegian fjords against Allied convoys to Russia, particularly the battleship Tirpitz; it was also to be targeted against the Italian Navy in the Mediterranean and, later, the Japanese Navy in the Pacific. Although No.618's Mosquito pilots underwent extensive training with 'Highball', flying over a Scottish loch, the weapon was never used in anger: No.617 Squadron's Lancasters got there before No.618 and capsized Tirpitz with 'Tallboy' bombs (another Barnes Wallis invention); the Kriegsmarine refused to play in the North Sea; Italy surrendered; while bad-ass attitudes on the part of the US Navy towards RAF aircraft operating in its Pacific theater of operations meant that after No.618's Mosquitos had been shipped out to Narromine in Australia, the squadron was disbanded.

What No.641 Squadron have to do, however, is to skip-bomb 'Highball' into the tunnel at Charlon, where "the Germans are hatching their new bird", says crusty Air Commodore Hufford (played with genuine grit and gusto by Charles Gray, the one actor in the film with a bit of steel in him instead of wood), and "addle their eggs", he tells McCallum's morose Munroe (who, incidentally, wears 'Canada' on the shoulder of his RAF uniform, yet at no time in the film is Munroe referred to as being Canadian!). When "Mosquito Squadron" was released, and up till only quite recently, the well held belief was that 'Highball' was designed to skip across water and not across land. "The Dam Busters" has archive footage of Mosquito B.IV DK290, modified by Vickers Armstrong and de Havilland to conduct 'Highball' trials, releasing such an experimental bomb into the sea beside Chesil Beach. Yet, "Mosquito Squadron" has archive footage of another Mosquito launching 'Highball' from very low-level over land.

This imagery is remarkable for its clarity compared with that of the Mosquito B.IV in "The Dam Busters": in that film the 'Highball' trials aircraft is seen completely in silhouette because it was being filmed from a camera on Chesil Beach facing south directly into sun. The "Mosquito Squadron" archive imagery is, however, perfectly clear. It shows a de Havilland Mosquito B.IV loaded with two 'Highball' trials bombs and flying at extremely low-level: the plot for "Mosquito Squadron" has No.641 Squadron's Mosquitos releasing their bombs at Charlon at a height of 60 feet which, judging from this archive imagery, wasn't dramatic licence on the scriptwriter's part but based on fact, as the Mosquito B.IV shown here is easily flying at just such a minimal height.

This Mosquito B.IV has no squadron codes but does have the large letter 'P' applied in white ahead of its fuselage roundel. The letter 'P' usually denoted 'Prototype' on aircraft built in Britain before, during, and just after World War Two, but mostly the letter would be surrounded by a circle; that is not the case on this Mosquito. Also, the letter has the appearance of being possibly hastily applied, as it is positioned slightly lower down on the fuselage side compared with the normal application of squadron code letters abreast the roundel on Mosquitos. The six Mosquito B.IVs of No.618 Squadron modified for 'Highball' trials in 1943 - DZ524, DZ530, DZ531, DZ534, DZ535 and DZ537 - plus the development Mosquito B.IV DK290 with the A&AEE at Boscombe Down, each carried the letter 'G' on their rear fuselages, which indicated that they were to be kept under armed guard at all times when on the ground, so highly secret were their modifications and trials work. However, there is no such letter 'G' on the Mosquito B.IV seen in the archive imagery used in "Mosquito Squadron". Without the suffix 'G', is there any other way to identify this most mysterious Mosquito?

A more likely explanation is that this Mosquito is an actual No.618 Squadron Mosquito B.IV, filmed during work-up trials. If so, then the letter 'P' is its aircraft identifier, as No.618 Squadron's Mosquitos carried no code letters nor any squadron badge, so secret was their tasking. The serial of this Mosquito B.IV is all but invisible, but there is the suggestion of the numbers '534' on the rear fuselage, while the application of a single, brightly visible letter applied alphabetically to each Mosquito would have been the principal means of their identification. No.618 Squadron Mosquito B.IVs carried the following serial ranges: DZ520, DZ524, DZ529 - 531, DZ533 - 535, DZ537, DZ539, DZ541 - 543, DZ546 - 547, DZ552, DZ554 - 556, DZ559, DZ575, DZ578 - 579, DZ581, and DZ583. If the faintly discernible numbers of '534' are correct for the numerical part of its serial, the identity of this secretive de Havilland Mosquito B.IV becomes DZ534/P. And, if correct, this archive imagery then becomes absolutely priceless, as it makes "Mosquito Squadron" the sole public source of where it is possible to see a No.618 Squadron Mosquito launching a 'Highball'.

No.618 Squadron was formed on 1st April 1943, initially with Bristol Beaufighter Mk.II light bombers, but it was always intended the squadron would operate the Mosquito. Very soon they started receiving the Mosquito B.IVs modified by Vickers Armstrong and de Havilland to carry 'Highball'. Initial trials drops of 'Highball' on water were conducted by No.618 at Reculver in North Kent, the same area where 'Upkeep' was tested, but most of the squadron's training against ships took place at Loch Striven, with the impounded French battleship, Courbet, the target vessel. These trials over water are well documented; not so, the 'Highball' trials of No.618 over land.

Based on what is seen in the archive imagery of the assumed No.618 Squadron Mosquito B.IV releasing 'Highball', the terrain over which it is flying is broadly flat, uncultivated, open land that is mostly heath-like in appearance. There are no trees or bushes or rocks, although a clump of gorse is close to one camera position. A tree-line can be seen in the distance, and there is the suggestion of low hills on the far horizon, but the only distinctive feature is a line of white fence poles running parallel to the Mosquito's line of flight. There is a shallow hollow beyond the attack run because the fencing briefly disappears from sight into it, but then emerges quickly again as the camera pans with the passing Mosquito.

The Mosquito releases its first 'Highball' exactly abreast this camera's position beside the attack run. The pilot immediately starts to bank to port and pull up - the film is played in slow motion, so every detail of the Mosquito's movement is fascinatingly visible. The 'Highball' hits the ground just as the Mosquito starts its pull up, hurling a large burst of what looks like peat-type soil up into the air that doesn't quite reach the bomber. Another camera films the 'Highball' itself making between five or six bounces, with each one becoming less and less impactive, until just as it is running out of momentum the spinning bomb strikes a square, box-like target no bigger than a garden hut. It rebounds off the target without exploding.

A camera filming from a third angle, off the port forward quarter of the Mosquito flying toward it, clearly shows the weapon release and first bounce off the ground - the spread of flying dirt shows that it was vital for the Mosquito pilot to pull up as soon as the bomb fell away, to escape the debris bursting up underneath. The accuracy with which the pilot and his bomb-aimer plant their 'Highball' against the relatively small target shows just how experienced in delivering this weapon they had both obviously become.

The terrain beyond the Mosquito in this shot shows that the countryside surrounding this location was very open and mostly flat. It is known that No.618 Squadron was stationed during one period at RAF Beccles on the Suffolk and Norfolk border. A source on a Website Forum states that Beccles was used by No.618 for trial drops of 'Highball' on land. The same Forum gives Ashley Walk in the New Forest as another test site and claims that No.618 attempted to put no less than 12 'Highballs' into a disused railway tunnel in Wales. An adventurous group of aviation archaeologists retrieved an inert 'Highball' from this railway tunnel, which is now exhibited in the Yorkshire Air Museum.

The most likely location in this imagery is Ashley Walk, as photographs of this open heathland posted on the New Forest National Park Website show a strong similarity with the terrain seen on the archive film. Moreover, there is still physical evidence remaining today of the wartime Ashley Bombing Range in the north of the New Forest, including a small brick observation shelter that appears to be of exactly the same proportions and appearance as the target building being hit by the inert 'Highball' bomb in the film. Whether this surviving observation shelter is the same target building used for trial attack runs by 'Highball'-dropping Mosquitos isn't known.

This film indicates that No.618 Squadron did train for the possible use of 'Highball' against targets on land. However, this imagery also gives indications as to why 'Highball' was not, in the end, used operationally in anger against land-based targets.

Firstly, the Mosquito delivering the weapon had to fly extremely low - 60 feet is almost certainly the exact height. This would expose the bomber to any anti-aircraft defences around the target. Secondly, the 'Highball' bomb would bounce and spin with swiftly decreasing velocity over the ground's surface, which meant that the Mosquito delivering it would have to fly significantly close to the target before releasing it. Losses would probably have been high. Thirdly, what kind of target would 'Highball' be used against on land? It would have to be a fixed target because 'Highball', like 'Upkeep', was a fused weapon - it obviously did not detonate on impact - and therefore would be useless against a moving vehicle. A building? Possibly. A bunker? Yes, but almost certainly more than one 'Highball' would be needed to breach a bunker. A tunnel, as in the film? Most likely, and No.618's delivery of inert 'Highballs' into a railway tunnel suggests this was the kind of target they were aiming at. But railway tunnels, or road tunnels for that matter, are almost always dug into hillsides or mountain sides, making a clear, unobstructed run at their openings very difficult, while clearing away by the attacking aircraft after weapon release would be virtually impossible.

Nonetheless, the fact that 'Highball' was tested on land and delivered down a tunnel is the obvious inspiration behind the plot for "Mosquito Squadron", and the use of this amazing archive imagery of what is most likely a No.618 Squadron Mosquito B.IV delivering 'Highball' is an absolute coup for what otherwise is regarded as an average B-movie war film.

What of the actual source of this imagery? Going back in time to 1968, the Imperial War Museum or the RAF Air Historical Branch were the repositories for all archive imagery showing British military aircraft in action during World War Two. But if

either had possession of this imagery, then it would have been in the public domain. It very clearly wasn't because it had never been seen publicly before "Mosquito Squadron" was made; as stated, archive footage of initial 'Highball' trials carried out on water off Chesil Beach was available and had been used before, but not of 'Highball' used on land. So, how did Oakmont Productions get hold of this apparently unique archive imagery?

An Online Forum quotes a visit to the Bovingdon film set by a member of Barnes Wallis's team, who apparently brought with him pictures of 'Highball' and a can of film. Could this film be that of the No.618 Squadron Mosquito B.IV DZ534/P releasing 'Highball' at Ashley Walk? If so, then it must mean that Dr Barnes Wallis and his team withheld a certain amount of 'Highball' trials film from the Air Ministry and the War Office during and after the War, perhaps because they feared that this precious material portraying an ingenious invention and highly secret weapon system would be destroyed on the orders of callous Whitehall mandarins.

Research conducted by the author in the Imperial War Museum's film and video archive annexe reveals that the IWM do have black-and-white film footage of 'Highball' trial drops on land, delivered by a Mosquito. However, it is not the same film material which appears in "Mosquito Squadron". The IWM's film is from the former Ministry of Technology (MTE) collection and is catalogued under its original library number of MTE 2344. Its existence reveals that 'Highball' trials continued after the War, which probably explains why both 'Highball' and 'Upkeep' were not de-classified for many years.

According to the IWM's archival notes, MTE 2344 was filmed post-War on 25th/26th November 1947 and shows an RAE Mosquito making several 'Highball' attack runs over land. The terrain in the film appears to be the same as that seen in the "Mosquito Squadron" archive imagery, and includes similar white fencing bordering the attack run and the same small, block-type building which the inert bomb strikes. What is different, though, is that the Mosquito is filmed from a position abreast the target building, so that the bomber is seen only head-on as it releases its bomb and in silhouette, making identification impossible. However, the pilot and bomb-aimer were clearly not as experienced as the aircrew in the No.618 Squadron Mosquito B.IV DZ534/P, as they not only miss the target at least once but the pilot flies his aircraft with the starboard wing slightly raised, not straight and level, suggesting some discomfort on his part at having to fly so low.

The IWM's film MTE 2344 confirms that footage of 'Highball' being dropped on land did exist when "Mosquito Squadron" was being made, although probably not de-classified in 1968 and, therefore, not publicly available. Whatever the case, the source of the archive film used by Oakmont Productions is still an unsolved mystery to this day.

'Highball' was not the sole inspiration behind "Mosquito Squadron". Equally so was Operation Jericho, the famous Amiens Prison jail break caused by a low-level attack (planned to be at 65 feet but actually flown at 50 feet) against the outer perimeter walls of the prison by nine Mosquitos on 18th February 1944. A large number of French Resistance fighters and political prisoners were being held in Amiens Prison and were due to be executed on 19th February. A great many escaped after the walls were breached by the Mosquito FB.VIs of No.487 (RNZAF) Squadron and No.464 (RAAF) Squadron. In the film, the perimeter walls of Chateau de Charlon are breached by Munroe's low-flying Mosquito using 'Highball', to enable a large number of RAF aircrew held prisoner there as human shields against an attack on Charlon, to escape.

There is evidence that the original intention in making "Mosquito Squadron" was to have the fictional No.641 Squadron Mosquitos carry 'EG-' codes, which were the code letters of the real No.487 (RNZAF) Squadron. The evidence for this is a shot in the film of a four-ship formation of studio miniature Mosquitos all wearing 'EG-' code letters. However, the decision to use out-takes from "633 Squadron" meant that the Mosquitos in "Mosquito Squadron" had to wear the same 'HT-' code letters as those borne by the Mosquitos used in the first film, for the sake of continuity.

And what of the actual Mosquitos used in the film? All sources referring to "Mosquito Squadron", either in print or Online, quote four Mosquitos as being used. Sorry, they are all wrong. As stated, six de Havilland Mosquitos were actually used: four flyers, one static prop, and one cockpit section in the studio. An either full-scale or large-scale facsimile Mosquito was also built by the art department and destroyed in the production. Unlike "633 Squadron", no real Mosquitos were destroyed in the making of "Mosquito Squadron".

However, add in the out-takes from "633 Squadron", of which there are many, plus the archive imagery of the presumed No.618 Squadron Mosquito B.IV, and the number of Mosquitos in the film increases even more. Two of the four flyers in "Mosquito Squadron" are "633 Squadron" veterans, as is the single static prop, but at least two more from the first film can also be identified from the out-takes they appear in.

There is one shot in "Mosquito Squadron" in which the five complete Mosquitos brought to Bovingdon are all seen together. It is the morning of the raid on Charlon. The aircrew are gathering beside their aircraft. The camera rises up over the wing of a Mosquito in a hangar (the camera was probably on a hoist used by RAF maintenance crewmen) to scan over three more Mosquitos parked outside on a very wet airfield, while in the distance another Mosquito is taxying in next to the camouflaged control tower.

The Mosquitos used in "Mosquito Squadron" are as follows:

de Havilland Mosquito T.3 RR299, registered G-ASKH and owned by Hawker Siddeley Aviation, Ltd. Flyer in the film, as 'HT-E' - note, no fake serials were applied on the Mosquitos in this production, so RR299 appeared as itself, as did all the others but with fictitious 633/641 Squadrons' codes. RR299 retained its 'HT-E' code letters and "Mosquito Squadron" camouflage scheme after filming was completed, becoming a very familiar sight in these markings at airshows throughout Britain for many years.

Mosquito T.3 RR299 was the one solid nose Mosquito used in the film; however, this caused a problem as its nose profile was different to the painted-over glazed noses of the other Mosquitos, while it also did not have the bulged bomb-bays of the four former Mosquito B.35s that it stars with in the film. Nor did it have the Perspex bubble atop the navigator's right seat position in the

cockpits of the ex-B.35s. These significant differences meant that RR299, when in shot, had to be seen in the background or in the distance alongside the other four Mosquitos, as its different appearance would make it stand out (the same problem afflicted the two Mosquito T.3s used in "633 Squadron"). Therefore, Mosquito T.3 RR299 is never seen in close-up as 'HT-E', but it does appear clearly in the four-ship formation shots filmed air-air and from the ground: it is the Mosquito that is the furthest outboard on the starboard side of the 'Finger Four' formation in which all four aircraft are seen flying. In the five-ship shot described in the paragraph above, Mosquito T.3 RR299 is the third and most distant of the three Mosquitos parked outside the hangar, identifiable by its slim-line fuselage compared with the bulged bellies of the other two beside it.

Tracking the history of Mosquito T.3 RR299 hasn't proved easy. It is known that it was built in 1945 and there is mention on a Website of a contributor's father making his final flight in the RAF on board RR299 at Aden in 1946. Like all the Mosquitos used in both "633 Squadron" and "Mosquito Squadron", RR299 served with No.3 CAACU at Exeter Airport, coded 'X'. It was used as an aircrew trainer and general 'hack', painted silver overall and with a yellow training band around its rear fuselage. When Flying Training Command changed its markings from yellow bands to red dayglo strips on the noses, wings and tails of its Vampire T.11s, Meteor T.7s, Jet Provost T.3s, Provost T.1s and Chipmunk T.10s in the early Sixties, Mosquito T.3 RR299 also acquired the same markings, making it uniquely the only Mosquito ever to wear dayglo strips.

Mosquito T.3 RR299 was registered as G-ASKH to Hawker Siddeley Aviation, Ltd, on 12th July 1963 and was based, very appropriately, at Hatfield where so many of its relatives were born; when Hawker Siddeley became part of the British Aerospace group, RR299 was based at Hawarden, near Chester. Until its appearance in "Mosquito Squadron", RR299 flew in an all-silver scheme; as stated, it retained its "Mosquito Squadron" 'wardrobe' for the rest of its life. RR299 had another film part to play, albeit briefly, in "Another Time, Another Place" (1983). Tragically, it was lost in a fatal accident at the Barton Air Show on 21st July 1996, with both its pilot and second pilot killed. It was, at the time, the last example of a de Havilland Mosquito flying anywhere in the world.

de Havilland Mosquito B.IV DZ534/P of No.618 Squadron, appears in anonymous archive film footage used in "Mosquito Squadron". DZ534 was built at Hatfield in March 1943. Issued to Vickers Armstrong at Weybridge for development work on 'Highball', with modifications added on 21st May 1943 at Hatfield. Joined No.618 Squadron at RAF Skitten on 18th September 1943 but only served with the squadron until November 1943 when it returned to Hatfield for further modifications (not carried out); so, if the archive film is of DZ534 with No.618 Squadron, it would have had to be filmed between the latter half of September 1943 and the date in November 1943 when it left the squadron.

DZ534's career changed from 'Highball' to that of being a Pathfinder Force Mosquito, initially with No.627 Squadron on 31st January 1944, but, after only four days, it was transferred to

No.692 Squadron of No.8 Group's Light Night Striking Force. It flew 41 Ops with 692 before being sent back to No.627 Squadron and given the squadron codes of AZ-H. Mosquito B.IV DZ534/AZ-H was ditched off Cherbourg on 26th July 1944 after its pilot sent an SOS. Both he and his navigator were picked up by a US Navy destroyer. (Source: De Havilland Mosquito: An Illustrated History, by Ian Thirsk, Page 76).

de Havilland Mosquito TT.35 RS709, registered G-ASKA and owned by the Skyfame Museum at Staverton Airport, Gloucestershire. A "633 Squadron" veteran and used as a flyer in "Mosquito Squadron", RS709's history and current status is described in the "633 Squadron" review.

de Havilland Mosquito TT.35 RS712, registered G-ASKB and owned by Mirisch Films, Ltd, but chartered to Group Captain 'Hamish' Mahaddie, who based it at RAF West Malling in Kent. Mahaddie was heavily engaged in acquiring Spitfires, Hurricanes, Hispano HA.1112 Buchons and CASA 2.111s on behalf of Spitfire Productions for the "Battle of Britain" film in 1968, but found time to loan RS712 to Oakmont Productions as a flyer for "Mosquito Squadron". Another "633 Squadron" veteran, RS712's history and current status is described in the review of that film.

de Havilland Mosquito TT.35 RS718, out-take from "633 Squadron", in which Captain John Crewdson performs the undercarriage collapse at Bovingdon on 9th August 1963. In that film, RS718 was a taxyer that performed the crash landing by Wing Commander Roy Grant's Mosquito at RAF Sutton Craddock, and also the crash of his replacement Mosquito in Norway. In "Mosquito Squadron", both pieces of footage are used again, firstly to portray Squadron Leader Quint Munroe's crash landing on return from a photo reconnaissance mission over Charlon, then later to portray Munroe's Mosquito crashing next to Charlon after the raid on the tunnel housing the new German rocket. Mosquito TT.35 RS718 was destroyed in the making of "633 Squadron".

de Havilland Mosquito TT.35 TA634, registered G-AWJV and owned by the Liverpool Corporation. Appears as the fourth flyer in "Mosquito Squadron". TA634 was built as a B.35 at Hatfield in 1945 and, like so many of its Marque, was placed immediately into storage after it was accepted by the RAF in April 1945. Seven years later it was transferred to Sywell for the TT.35 conversion course with Brooklands Aviation. Emerging as a target-tug, TA634 joined No.4 CAACU at Llandow in Wales on 31st December 1953. Three years later, TA634 was sent to West Germany to provide target facilities for the 2nd Tactical Air Force and the British Army of the Rhine, operating between March 1956 - June 1957 with the three Armament Practice Stations at Ahlhorn, Schleswigland and Sylt. Following its return to Britain, Mosquito TT.35 TA634 was assigned to the combined No.3/4 CAACU at Exeter on 10th September 1959, where it continued to operate until it took part in the final fly-past of six No.3 CAACU Mosquitos on 9th May 1963. Later that same month TA634 was flown to No.23 MU at Aldergrove in Northern Ireland, where it would have been passed over for scrapping had a group of aviation enthusiasts not stepped in. Its being located in Northern Ireland probably explains how this Mosquito was overlooked for "633 Squadron".

The Merseyside Society of Aviation Enthusiasts in Liverpool were eager to preserve a retired No.3 CAACU Mosquito and persuaded the Lord Mayor and Aldermen of the City of Liverpool to make an offer for TA634. A sum of £720 was accepted by the Ministry of Defence for the sale of this Mosquito to the Liverpool Corporation and it was flown from Aldergrove to Liverpool/Speke Airport (today, John Lennon International) on 6th November 1963. There it languished in a hangar, still in its target-tug markings but without its gear, with no apparent success on the part of the Merseyside Society of Aviation Enthusiasts in finding the best way to display the Mosquito. However, it was maintained in flying condition, albeit without a Permit To Fly, until it was found by the aviation consultant to Oakmont Productions, Air Commodore Allen Wheeler. It was registered as G-AWJV to the City of Liverpool on 21st May 1968 and flown to Bovingdon in July. Following its appearance in "Mosquito Squadron", TA634 returned to Speke and was locked away in a hangar once more until the Liverpool Corporation decided in 1970 to donate it to the Mosquito Aircraft Museum (MAM) at Salisbury Hall, London Colney, Hertfordshire, the birthplace of the Mosquito prototype, W4050. Its civil registration was cancelled on 19th October 1970.

After its arrival at Salisbury Hall, the MAM had Mosquito TT.35 TA634 painted in camouflage and with the codes EG-F, as worn by the Mosquito FB.VI HX922/EG-F of No.487 (RNZAF) Squadron flown by Group Captain Percy Charles Pickard, who led the Amiens Prison raid on 18th February 1944 and who was shot down and killed, together with his navigator, by a Focke Wulf FW.190 just after the raid had been completed. Today, TA634 is one of four Mosquitos on display with the de Havilland Aircraft Heritage Centre, the renamed MAM, including the prototype Mosquito and the cockpit and fuselage sections of another "Mosquito Squadron" participant, TT.35 TJ118.

de Havilland Mosquito TT.35 TA639, out-take from "633 Squadron", in which it is one of four Mosquitos seen taxying in at Bovingdon during an early part of that film and later during a start-up sequence of four Mosquitos. These same two sequences were re-used in "Mosquito Squadron". The history and current status of Mosquito TT.35 TA639 is described in the "633 Squadron" review.

de Havilland Mosquito TT.35 TA719, registered as G-ASKC and owned by the Skyfame Museum. Its civil registration was cancelled on 3rd September 1964 following the crash landing by this Mosquito at Staverton Airport earlier that same year. The third "633 Squadron" veteran and a flyer in that film, TA719 was used as a static prop in "Mosquito Squadron". The out-takes of the three flying Mosquitos performing in "633 Squadron" that are used in "Mosquito Squadron" include TA719, the other two being RS709 and RS712.

TA719 makes two appearances in "Mosquito Squadron", firstly in the scene described earlier involving all five complete Mosquito airframes filmed at Bovingdon: it is the Mosquito in the foreground over which the camera films the four flyable Mosquitos at dispersal outside the hangar TA719 is parked in. However, its most prominent role is to portray Squadron Leader Munroe's crashed Mosquito at Charlon: TA719 was set up on a low loader with its wheels retracted, to create the impression that it was lying on its belly, and with foliage placed around it to conceal the low loader. Fire pots were strategically set up on and around the airframe which, after being lit, create the image of the 'crashed' Mosquito on fire, a familiar film art department trick. Mosquito TT.35 TA719 is recognisable in this crash scene due to its visible severed port wing, which it inherited as a consequence of the crash it suffered at Staverton four years earlier that ended its flying career. The "633 Squadron" review contains TA719's history and current status.

de Havilland Mosquito TT.35 TJ118, cockpit section only, used to film cockpit scenes in MGM British Film Studios at Borehamwood, where it had been retained after its use in "633 Squadron" in the event that it might be useful for another film. This cockpit section was donated by MGM to the Mosquito Aircraft Museum some time after "Mosquito Squadron" was completed; it is today exhibited in the de Havilland Aircraft Heritage Centre.

The Mosquitos in "633 Squadron" are not the only aircraft in that film which appear in out-takes used in "Mosquito Squadron": the two Messerschmitt Bf.108Bs acting as Messerschmit Bf.109s are also worked into the latter film. To be accurate, they are Nord 1002 Pinguoin II F-BFYX and Nord 1002M Pinguoin II F-BGVU, being flown by John 'Jeff' Hawke and Martin Caidin respectively. In fact, the complete airfield attack scene by these two 'Messerschmitt Bf.109s' in "633 Squadron" is re-used in "Mosquito Squadron", as is much of the air-air footage of Nord 1002M F-BGVU dog-fighting with a Mosquito.

The use of so many "633 Squadron" out-takes means that aircraft which appear in the background of these shots in that film, also re-appear in "Mosquito Squadron". The seven Avro Anson C.19 passenger-carrying aircraft of the newly-created RAF Air Support Command's Southern Communications Squadron based at Bovingdon, which are seen parked in the distance on their dispersal as Mosquito TT.35s RS709, RS712 and TA719 land in "633 Squadron", are shown again in "Mosquito Squadron" due to this same sequence being repeated in this film. Also repeated from "633 Squadron" is the shot of the two 'Messerschmitts' departing, meaning that the visiting Handley Page Hastings C.1 parked in the distance that got into this shot likewise re-appears in "Mosquito Squadron".

Five of the same Avro Anson C.19s come into shot during the filming of "Mosquito Squadron" itself, when Mosquitos RR299, RS709, RS712 and TA634 are seen at dispersal close to the control tower, with the Ansons clearly visible in the background. Two were later actually painted up to represent camouflaged Avro Anson Is returning surviving Mosquito aircrew to their base at the end of the film. One of them has the fake serial 'K 516' applied. In fact, six Anson C.19s were based at Bovingdon when "Mosquito Squadron" was filmed there, all of which were struck off charge by the RAF on 28th June 1968 during the course of the production! Which actual two were used in the film isn't known, but all of them went onto the civil register, including two that were purchased to be used to fly relief missions for the famine that arose from the Biafran War in 1968, both coming to grief in Africa.

One other aircraft appears in "Mosquito Squadron", although you have to have sharp eyes to see it. It is another visiting aircraft to Bovingdon that accidentally gets into shot. It actually appears as the final film credits roll: while David McCallum as Munroe and Suzanne Neve as Beth walk off beyond the two parked disguised Anson C.19s, an aircraft can be seen taking off in the distance. Freeze-frame analysis shows that it is not a small aircraft and that it has a twin-boom configuration. Only one aircraft type fits its size and description, a Nord Noratlas military transport, almost certainly from the Armee de l'Air, although a German Air Force example is a possibility. This type of aircraft would have been a familiar visitor to Bovingdon during the Sixties.

The studio miniatures of Mosquitos and two Bf.109s used in the film are actually more effective in " Mosquito Squadron" than their counterparts in "633 Squadron". In fact, the SFX in "Mosquito Squadron" is superior in most respects, especially in the post-opening credits sequence of attacks on V1 launch rails and in the big bang finale of Charlon going up in flame and smoke like a Gerry Anderson set being detonated en masse in "Thunderbirds". Most effective of all are the shots of bombs and 'Highballs' being dropped from a large-scale, realistic-looking facsimile Mosquito in the studio, complete with a motor in each engine nacelle that turned the propellers. It is possibly this large-scale facsimile, painted as Munroe's Mosquito 'HT-G' - note the same code letters as that for Wing Commander Grant's Mosquito in "633 Squadron", which had to match so as to achieve continuity - that is blown up, not a real Mosquito. The SFX in "Mosquito Squadron" was created by an outfit calling itself The Bowie Organisation - no connection with the famous rock musician, but named after its founder, Canadian Special FX expert, Les Bowie, who specialised in working for Hammer Films and Roger Corman in the Sixties.

Key to the success of the production was the role of Personal Plane Services at Wycombe Air Park, which provided the aircrews to fly the three Mosquito TT.35s and groundcrews to service them; the pilots were 'Taff' Rich, Neil Williams and 'Dizzy' Addicott. Hawker Siddeley Aviation looked after their own Mosquito T.3 RR299, flown by Hawker Siddeley Aviation's deputy chief test pilot, Pat Fillingham, but were on hand to provide assistance with the other Mosquitos if needed. Personal Plane Services was founded by pilot/engineer/sailor/racing driver/author and bon vivieur, Doug Bianchi, who, after being contracted to build replica Edwardian-era aeroplanes for the film, "Those Magnificent Men In Their Flying Machines" (1965), realised that the film industry needed professionals like himself who could provide aeronautical services. Thus, he created Bianchi Aviation Film Services for precisely that purpose: "Mosquito Squadron" was the third film that Bianchi worked on, behind "Magnificent Men" and "The Blue Max" (1966).

Alongside him, Bianchi had the invaluable services and experience of Air Commodore Allen Wheeler to call upon as Chief Aeronautical Advisor to Oakmont Productions. Wheeler was closely associated with Personal Plane Services - they maintained his Spitfire Mk.Ia AR213, for one thing - and had worked with Bianchi as technical advisor on "Magnificent Men" and as air supervisor on "The Blue Max". Wheeler had served as a test pilot with the RAF in World War Two and had a host of different aircraft types in his logbook.

Also credited with providing services to the film was L J Hillman Engineering, which, in effect, was Les Hillman who serviced and maintained many aircraft appearing in British films and TV productions during the Fifties and Sixties. Les Hillman was teamed up with Captain John Crewdson's Film Aviation Services company, and had worked with Crewdson on both "The War Lover" (1962) and "633 Squadron", so he was no stranger to Bovingdon. Les Hillman was "the special effects guy" Cliff Robertson was referring to who guided Mosquito TT.35 TA724 into the fuel bowser in "633 Squadron".

There is, then, much more to "Mosquito Squadron" than it is usually given credit for having. It has some fine footage of the 'Wooden Wonder' in action - and I mean the aeroplane this time - and it wins a special place in the pantheon of aviation films not just for showing the unique footage of a No.618 Squadron 'Highball' Mosquito, but for presenting us with the images of four of these magnificent war machines flying in formation, the final time this ever happened. For these reasons alone, "Mosquito Squadron" is definitely a film worth keeping in an aviation enthusiast's and war film historian's library.

SUBMARINE X-1

(Released: June 1969)

This third Oakmont Productions release late in the decade that follows on the heels of "Mosquito Squadron" adopts the same formula as used in most of Oakmont's war movies, that of having an American leading actor playing the commander of a British military operation during World War Two. Also, the plot is again based on an actual wartime action which has also been previously filmed, this time that of Royal Navy X-Class midget submarines targeted against German Kriegsmarine warships berthed in a Norwegian fjord.

The real action was Operation Source, in which X-Class submarines attacked and seriously damaged Schlachtschiffe (battleship) Tirpitz in Kafjord on 22nd September 1943. Operation Source was portrayed in "Above Us The Waves" (1955), briefly mentioned in Chapter Three; again, Oakmont was copying a previously successful British war film.

In "Submarine X-1", rising US movie actor James Caan is called upon to perform the role - woodenly stiff-jawed, typical of Oakmont's style - of a Canadian Commander of a Royal Navy submarine who is in conflict with his crew. His submarine, the Gauntlet, has been sunk by the German battleship Lindendorf - how, we do not see, but the crew blame Caan for the loss of 50 men. Was there ever an occasion when a battleship sank a submarine? Unless the sub was clear on the surface and sunk by gunfire, it does not seem possible, as battleships on either side in World War Two were not equipped with weaponry to attack submarines - not that

any sane-minded Captain of a battleship would dream of doing so, anyway. But Oakmont Productions didn't let military historical inaccuracies get in the way of an intended good story.

Despite the loss of his submarine and most of its crew, Caan's Commander is given the chance to redeem himself by leading an attack by three X-Class subs on the Lindendorf moored in its Norwegian fjord lair, using the survivors from the Gauntlet. All good 'Boys Own' stuff again, typical of Oakmont Productions. Acclaim has to be given to the realistic-looking and performing - on the surface of a Scottish loch - of the mock-ups of the X-Class submarines, and of the underwater miniatures of them. Presumably, this again was the work of Canadian Special FX expert, Les Bowie.

The brief role of aviation in "Submarine X-1" is all black-and-white archive imagery, which jars with the 'Color by De Luxe' texture of the film. Two aircraft are seen, both of them German. The first is good quality air-air footage of an early model Messerschmitt Bf.110 Zerstorer. It is filmed in profile gradually overtaking the camera aircraft. Its Balkenkreuze on the fuselage and Swastika on the port tailfin can be clearly seen. However, it has no unit markings or badge. It looks the part, but does not seem likely to be an actual in-service Luftwaffe Bf.110, especially as its camouflage scheme is very much of the RAF wavy two-shade style.

This archive shot is most likely of captured Messerschmitt Bf.110C-4 AX772 of No.1426 (Enemy Aircraft) Flight, RAF, and formerly 5F+CM of 4(F)/14, Deutsches Luftwaffe, repainted in Luftwaffe markings and probably filmed air-air by the RAF Film Production Unit. We know that this Bf.110C-4 was repainted with German Balkenkreuze and Swastika markings after it was operated in RAF camouflage and roundels by the Air Fighting Development Unit in comparison trials with Allied aircraft. It was seen in repainted Luftwaffe markings in "The Adventures of Tartu" (1943), reviewed in Chapter One.

In "Submarine X-1", this archive shot and one other is used to depict a Luftwaffe reconnaissance aircraft trying to detect the X-Class submarines' hideout in the Scottish loch. In so doing, the film production team have unknowingly reprieved Bf.110C-4 5F+CM's actual wartime role, as it was on a reconnaissance sortie when it was forced down on 21st July 1940 and had to make an emergency landing at Goodwood Aerodrome. The review of "Ferry Pilot" (1941) in Chapter One gives this Zerstorer's history.

Two other archive shots show a Junkers Ju.52/3M dropping a stick of Fallschirmjager (Paratroopers), leading in to a sequence involving German Paratroopers attacking the midget submarines's base (security was obviously lax). The Ju.52/3M is only seen in silhouette.

Incidentally, the miniature Lindendorf which Les Bowie and his team blow up spectacularly in the studio-created fjord is a copy of the Panzerschiff (Armoured Ship) Deutschland, later renamed Lutzow, which was a target of Operation Source on 22nd September 1943 by the X-Class midget submarine X-8 that was damaged and scuttled before it could reach the Norwegian fjord where Lutzow was moored. "Submarine X-1" is the type of war film you watch on a wet winter's afternoon when there is not much else to do.

BATTLE OF BRITAIN

(Premier: 15th September 1969)

This epic has become the defining film on the subject of the Battle of Britain in cinema. It has been reviewed and examined countless numbers of times over the decades since its production during a very un-1940-like summer in Britain of 1968. Leonard Mosley 's book, "Battle of Britain: The Story of a Film" (London: Pan Books, 1969) accompanied its general release and details the making of the production. Robert J Rudhall's, "Battle of Britain: The Movie", is highly recommended by those who have read it. Neither of these works have been used for reference in this review, which is entirely the result of the author's own research. Various Websites are dedicated to "Battle of Britain", detailing the aircraft used in it.

"Battle of Britain" has two specific advantages over its predecessor productions that either focused on or included the Battle in their plots: it was filmed in colour and it staged all the aerial sequences as accurately as it was possible to do.

By my count, a total of 128 aircraft were acquired by or loaned to Spitfire Productions, Ltd, for "Battle of Britain", but that does not mean literally every single one of them appears in the film. The usually quoted figure is 109, but that does not take into account the extra Spitfires, Buchons and one Hurricane which were used as spares sources, plus the infamous 'Proctukas', three Percival Proctors obtained to be converted to appear as scaled-down Ju.87 Stukas (thankfully, the idea did not go beyond one Proctuka and was abandoned after three 'interesting' test flights). The total comprises 50 (at least) Hispano HA.1112M1L Buchons and one two-seat Hispano HA.1112M4K Buchon, 32 CASA 2.111s (almost the entire fleet in the Spanish Air Force in 1968), two CASA 352Ls, 34 Spitfires in nine different Marques and six Hawker Hurricanes. In all, Spitfire Productions were able to claim in 1968 that they owned the 35th largest air force in the world.

Of this total, 12 Spitfires flew in the film, with eight more capable of taxying and a further eight used as static props. Three Hurricanes flew: LF363, PZ865 and Canadian registered Mk.XII CF-SMI, flown by its owner, Bob Diemart – these three were, in 1968, the entire total of airworthy Hurricanes in the world. The number of Buchons was whittled down to 17 (16 single-seaters plus the one two-seater) that were purchased by Spitfire Productions and flown to Duxford, where the operations centre for the flying elements of the film was based. Six more were used as taxyers at Tablada in Spain, plus an unspecified number of grounded examples as set-dressing. It has been said that literally all the 32 CASA 2.111s flew at one time or another in Spain, in massed formations as Heinkel He.111Hs. Careful analysis of the film confirms that a total of 18 CASA 2.111s were mounted together as a formation on one occasion, but whether this was superseded is difficult to confirm because so many of the massed Heinkel shots in "Battle of Britain" are achieved by art work montage special effects (doubling, tripling, the actual number of aircraft flown).

To record the aircraft used in the film, their histories and their fates or status are listed under the Commands of the air forces they represented, beginning with:

Royal Air Force Fighter Command

Aviation critics point to the film's almost exclusive focus on the Spitfire as RAF Fighter Command's primary weapon of choice which, in 1940, it numerically was most definitely not. Obviously the lack of available Hurricanes compared with the 34 'Spits' that Spitfire Productions was able to amass, is the explanation for the 'Hurri's relegated role as support player in the film. Adding to the false impression about the Hurricane is its appearance in "Battle of Britain" as being almost exclusively flown by Polish pilots, which may lead a new audience today to mistakenly think that the Poles were the only squadrons operational on Hurricanes in the actual Battle in 1940.

RAF Fighter Command is represented mostly by No. 11 Group, covering the South-East of England which bore the brunt of the Luftwaffe's attacks, especially on AVM Keith Park's airfields. No. 12 Group, covering the country North of London and the Midlands, comes heavily into the Battle after Luftflotten II and III switched their attacks on Southern England to London. Before this happens, No. 12 Group is portrayed in the film as being fixated on AVM Leigh-Mallory's 'Big Wing' tactic, to the cost of Park's airfields and pilots. This is the exact opposite position to that of "Reach For The Sky" (1956), which, not surprisingly, extols the 'Big Wings' as being Douglas Bader's chosen tactic. No. 13 Group in the North of England and Scotland is shown successfully beating off attacks by Luftflotte V from Norway, although it creates the inaccurate impression the Luftwaffe had no fighter escort due to the long range across the North Sea - the reason simply is that Spitfire Productions had no means of portraying the Messerschmitt Bf.110 fighters which provided escort for the bombers of Luftflotte V.

Here, then, are the Hurricane and Spitfire actors and extras that portray RAF Fighter Command in "Battle of Britain":

Hawker Hurricane Mk.1 P2617, taxyer. In store with the RAF Air Historical Branch, reserved for the future RAF Museum and returned to store after use in the film. Hurricane Mk.1 P2617's history has been detailed in "Angels One Five" (1952), Chapter Three. Extant today, in the RAF Museum, Hendon.

Hawker Hurricane Mk.IIc LF363, flyer. Operated by the Battle of Britain Flight at RAF Coltishall, returned to the Flight after use in the film. Hurricane Mk.IIc LF363's history is detailed in "Angels One Five". Extant today, with the Battle of Britain Memorial Flight at RAF Coningsby.

Hawker Hurricane Mk.IIc LF751, static prop and spares. Was gate guardian at RAF Bentley Priory when Group Captain 'Hamish' Mahaddie recruited it for the film. Hurricane Mk.IIc LF751 was built at Hawker's Langley factory and delivered to the RAF on 19th March 1944. It went to No.22 MU at Silloth before being transferred to No.1681 Bomber Defence Training Flight on 8th April 1944, where it was used as what would be called today an 'adversary' fighter for bomber crews to train against. LF751 did not see front-line service in the War and finished its short flying career with No.27 OTU, being designated an instructional airframe in July 1945. It took up its gate guardian duties at Bentley Priory in 1954 and returned there after its use in the film. It was presented to the Medway Aircraft Preservation Society (MAPS) in 1985 for restoration and display in their museum at RAF Manston, Kent. LF751 is still exhibited by MAPS, as a cannon-armed Hurricane in the markings of BN230/FT-A of No.43 Squadron.

Hawker Hurricane Mk.IIc G-AMAU/PZ865, flyer. Owned by Hawker Siddeley Aviation and based at Dunsfold, returned to HSA after use in the film. Hurricane Mk.IIc PZ865's history is described in "Angels One Five". Extant today, with the Battle of Britain Memorial Flight.

Hawker Hurricane Mk.XII G-AWLW, formerly CF-SMI, flyer. Owned by Bob Diemart in Canada and sold to Samuelson Film Services, Ltd, at Elstree, on behalf of Spitfire Productions, Ltd. Manufactured by the Canadian Car Foundry in 1944 and delivered to the Royal Canadian Air Force as RCAF 5377. Struck off charge on 13th July 1946 and purchased by Jim Roy of Portage la Prairie, Manitoba, who owned it till 1964. It seems CF-SMI fell into disuse until Bob Diemart acquired it in 1964 and restored it to flying condition in the markings of RCAF 5585, in time for it to be recruited for "Battle of Britain". It was airfreighted to the UK aboard an RCAF CC-130 Hercules on 1st June 1967 and was placed on the British register as G-AWLW. After the film, this Hurricane was initially sold to Neville 'Tony' Samuelson before it was acquired by Sir William Roberts at Shoreham in December 1969, and subsequently moved to Sir William's Strathallan Collection, Auchterader, in Scotland, flown as P3308/UP-A. After the Strathallan Collection went into administration, this Hurricane was acquired by the Canadian Warplane Heritage at Hamilton, Ontario, in May 1984 and returned to Canada. Registered C-GCWH, it flew again in Canadian skies on 4th June 1984, now as P3069/YO-A. Tragically, this Hurricane was destroyed in the hangar fire at Hamilton on 15th February 1993, which also took Spitfire Mk.IX G-ASSD/MK297 that likewise appears in "Battle of Britain".

Hawker Sea Hurricane Mk.Ib Z7015, taxyer. Owned by the Shuttleworth Collection and kept in a non-flying condition, returned to the Collection after use in the film. Built by the Canadian Car Foundry, Sea Hurricane Mk.Ib Z7015 was operated by 880 and 801 Squadrons of the Fleet Air Arm between 1941 - '42. Later, it became an instructional airframe with the Loughborough Training College, from where it went to the Shuttleworth Collection in 1961. Shuttleworth's policy then was to ensure as many of its oldest aircraft up to 1939 were kept in flying condition, so Sea Hurricane Mk.Ib Z7015 remained on static display or in storage, along with Spitfire Mk.Vc AR501, which was also loaned to Spitfire Productions for use in the film. In 1981, the decision was taken to restore Z7015 back to flying condition, which took place progressively throughout the Eighties and was completed at Duxford under the auspices of the Imperial War Museum. Sea Hurricane Mk.Ib Z7015 flew again on 16th September 1995, carrying the codes 7-L. It continues to fly with the Shuttleworth Collection today from Old Warden Aerodrome.

Vickers Supermarine Spitfire Mk.Ia G-AIST/AR213, flyer. Owned by Air Commodore Allen Wheeler, who based it at Booker but who had taken it off the civil aviation register until 'Hamish' Mahaddie came calling, as a result it returned to the register in April 1968 for use in the film. Wheeler was aviation consultant for "Mosquito Squadron" at the time, to which Mahaddie had loaned the Mosquito he was operating, so both veteran RAF pilots had a quid pro quo deal between them for the use of their respective aircraft in either film production.

Spitfire Mk.Ia AR213 was the correct Marque for the 1940 period, but was built in 1941 by Westlands at Yeovil, Somerset, and delivered to No.12 MU on 24th July that year. It saw no front-line service, being operated by No.57 OTU and No.53 OTU until it was placed in storage with No.8 MU on 17th August 1944. Struck off charge on 30th November 1945, Spitfire Mk.Ia AR213 was sold to its long-term owner, then Group Captain Allen Wheeler, on 10th March 1947, but had to remain in storage until it was volunteered in 1967 for service in "Battle of Britain". Brought back to flying condition at RAF Henlow along with other Spitfires in the film, AR213 returned to its rightful owner who flew it for several years until it was acquired by the Honourable Patrick Lindsay in 1978. Under Lindsay's ownership, AR213 had an active airshow life throughout the Eighties, flown by Tony Bianchi of Personal Plane Services who also maintained it until Lindsay's death in 1986. It then passed to Victor Gauntlet in 1989 who continued to display it, most notably in the 'Sea Wings 2000' event over Southampton on 4th June 2000 to commemorate the 60th anniversay of the Battle of Britain, when AR213 was one among 13 Spitfires to over-fly Southampton Water, piloted by Jonathan Whaley. Ownership passed to Sheringham Aviation following the death of Victor Gauntlett in 2003. Spitfire Mk.Ia AR213 has undergone an extensive refit with Personal Plane Services, bringing it back to true Marque Ia configuration and flying again in 2007. On 20th June 2011, Spitfire Mk.Ia AR213 was registered to Spitfire The One, Ltd.

Vickers Supermarine Spitfire MK.IIa G-AWIJ/P7350, flyer. The one genuine Battle of Britain Spitfire, P7350 owes its renewed lease of life to "Battle of Britain" the film. It was under the care of the Air Historical Branch at RAF Colerne, Wiltshire, when it was assessed as being capable of being returned to flying condition. Registered to Spitfire Productions, Ltd, Spitfire Mk.IIa P7350 was presented to the Battle of Britain Flight after filming was completed, where it has remained ever since, although it continued to be chartered by Spitfire Productions until ownership was transferred to the MoD on 29th February 1984. Built at Vickers' Castle Bromwich 'shadow' factory, P7350 entered RAF service in August 1940, and flew in the Battle with No.266 Squadron and No.603 (City of Edinburgh) Royal Auxiliary Air Force Squadron. On 25th October 1940, Spitfire Mk.IIa P7350 came off worse in a scrap with Messerschmitt Bf.109s and had to crash land at its Hornchurch base. Swift repair work by No.1 Civilian Repair Unit saw it return to service on 15th November 1940, going on to serve with Nos.616 and 64 Squadrons until it was transferred to second-line duties with the Central Gunnery School. P7350 served out its wartime career with No.57 OTU before being stored with No.19 MU. It would have been scrapped had its historical significance not been spotted by the scrap dealer who had purchased it for £25 and offered it back to the RAF. Apparently, bullet hole repairs can still be seen on P7350's port wing.

Vickers Supermarine Spitfire F.Vb G-AISU/AB910, formerly owned by Vickers Armstrong, Weybridge, and flown by famous wartime Spitfire test pilot, Jeffrey Quill, and post-War test pilot Dave Morgan. Built at Castle Bromwich as a Low Flying Spitfire LF.Vb, AB910 was first allocated to No.222 (Natal) Squadron at RAF North Weald in August 1941, where it would return 27 years later for the "Battle of Britain" film. Soon afterwards it joined No.130 Squadron on convoy patrol duty and escorting daylight bombing raids on the Kriegsmarine Schlacht Kreuzeren (battlecruisers) Scharnhorst and Gneisenau moored in Brest harbour in December 1941. In June 1942, AB910 was on the strength of No.133 (Eagle) Squadron at Biggin Hill and flew four sorties on 19th August engaging in fierce aerial battles supporting the Dieppe Raid. Spitfire LF.Vb AB910 continued its career with two Canadian squadrons, Nos.242 and 402 Squadrons, as well as with No.416 Squadron; with 402 it flew many sorties over the Normandy beachhead on and after D-Day. From mid-July 1944, AB910 found itself on second-line duties with No.53 OTU at Hibaldstow before joining a radar calibration unit, No.527 Squadron, at the same location. It was at Hibaldstow that AB910 had its 15 minutes of fame on 14th February 1945 when it took off with Leading Aircraftwoman Margaret Horton, a WAAF groundcrew fitter, clinging to its tail - a safe landing was enjoyed by all, but not at the time!

Group Captain Allen Wheeler purchased AB910 at about the same time as he bought Spitfire Mk.Ia AR213 in 1947; he put AR213 into storage while he went air racing in AB910. It suffered a heavy landing during the 1953 Kings Cup Air Race, following which it went to Vickers Armstrong for restoration, where it remained. Spitfire AB910 was now an elliptical-winged Spitfire and technically a F.Mk.Vb. In 1965, Vickers Armstrong donated AB910 to the RAF Battle of Britain Flight. It has since been operated by the BBMF, although it experienced a difficult decade in the Seventies when it experienced two landing accidents - Coltishall in October 1972 and Duxford in June 1976 - culminating in a head-on taxying collision with an intruding Harvard at Bex, Switzerland, on 21st August 1978. The Spitfire's wreckage was roadfreighted back to the UK and AB910 underwent a full rebuild at RAF Abingdon (see, Spitfire F.Vb BL614 below); it rejoined the BBMF in October 1981. In April 1997, Spitfire F.Vb AB910 was airfreighted inside a C-130K Hercules C.1 to Nellis AFB, Nevada, to take part in the Golden Air Tattoo, which celebrated the 50th anniversary of the United States Air Force. Spitfire F.Vb AB910 continues to fly with the BBMF today.

Vickers Supermarine Spitfire F.Vb BL614, taxyer. Gate guardian at RAF Credenhill. Spitfire F.Vb BL614 first flew from Castle Bromwich in December 1941 and was delivered to No.8 MU at RAF Little Rissington on 4th January 1942. It joined No.611 (West Lancashire) Squadron at RAF Drem, near Edinburgh, on 7th February 1942; this didn't last long, as it suffered Cat. B damage during Ops one month later. It was back in action with No.242 (Canadian) Squadron at Drem by early June 1942, then transferred to No.222 (Natal) Squadron in August, flying south to RAF Biggin Hill that month to cover the landings at Dieppe. This was an operation that covered three days before the squadron returned to Scotland for convoy patrol tasks. BL614 joined No.64 Squadron in March 1943 and had an active service life conducting 'Ramrod' patrols and fighter escort for USAAF medium day bombers. In September 1943, BL614 was transferred to No.118 Squadron with which it had a busy time until it was demoted to No.3501 Support Unit (General Duties Flight) at RAF Cranfield in November 1943. BL614 was then relegated one month later to being an instructional airframe with No.6 School of Technical Training (SoTT) at RAF Hednesford, Staffs; there it remained, training new 'Erks', until April 1948 when it was transferred to No.7 Recruits Centre, RAF Bridgnorth, Salop. On 3rd March 1955, this Spitfire took up gate guardian duties at RAF Credenhill, where it was misidentified as AB871. When it joined Spitfire Productions, it was still carrying this incorrect serial; it returned to RAF custody on 28th October 1968, still as AB871. Displayed in City of London on 15th September 1969, the day of the premier of "Battle of Britain". Then stored at RAF Wattisham until road-freighted to RAF Colerne in September 1972 to replace Spitfire Mk.IIa P7350. Its true serial was discovered when BL614 was stripped down in 1974 for restoration. It received its original No.222 (Natal) Squadron codes of ZD-F, which it wore on the Dieppe Raid Ops. In January 1980, BL614 was used as a spares source and pattern at RAF Abingdon for the restoration of damaged BBMF Spitfire F.Vb AB910; then, in December 1982, it was put on display in the new Manchester Air & Space Museum, where it stayed until March 1995 when it was taken to Rochester Airport for restoration by MAPS. On 11th September 1997, Spitfire F.Vb BL614 was formally handed over to the RAF Museum, Hendon, where it remains today.

Vickers Supermarine Spitfire F.Vb BM597, pattern for fibre glass full-scale facsimile Spitfires built by Pinewood Studios art department. Gate guardian at RAF Church Fenton. Built at Castle Bromwich and delivered to the RAF on 26th February 1942, stored with No.37 MU at Burtenwood. Spitfire F.Vb BM597 was destined to serve as a Polish squadron Spitfire, first with No.315 Squadron in May 1942, then No.317 Squadron in September the same year, both based at Woodvale. It suffered Cat. B damage in February 1943 and was out of action until June, when it was sent to Vickers Armstrong for undisclosed trials work. It then had a rather undistinguished period being transferred between several storage bases between November 1943 - January 1945 before being allocated to No.58 OTU. BM597 was then sent to No.4 SoTT at RAF St Athan in October 1945. From 1950 onwards, BM597 moved to three different RAF Stations to act as gate guardian: Hednesford (1950 - '55), Bridgenorth (1955 - '60) and Church Fenton (1960 - '67); from the latter it was transferred to Pinewood Studios in January 1967, after being inspected at RAF Henlow. It returned to RAF Church Fenton in 1969, to commence its gate guardian duties once more. Tim Routsis, founder of Historic Flying, Ltd, rescued BM597, along with other Spitfires, from the elements in a deal with the RAF in 1989 and sold it four years later to the Historic Aircraft Collection (HAC). Restoration to original specification was undertaken by Historic Flying as part of the sales agreement. Spitfire F.Vb BM597 flew again in its No.317 (Polish) Squadron markings. During the summer of 2000, BM597 was one of four Spitfires used in the "Pearl Harbor" (2001) movie. In September 2005, BM597 made history when it, in company with Hawker Hurricane 'Z5140', became the first Spitfire to fly over Malta since the filming of "Malta Story" in 1952. It continues to fly with HAC from Duxford today.

Vickers Supermarine Spitfire LF.Vb EP120, static prop. Gate guardian at RAF Wattisham. Built at Castle Bromwich and taken on charge with No.45 MU before it was assigned to No.501 Squadron on 4th June 1942. While with 501 it accounted for a Dornier Do.17 at the hands of the Wing Commander, then went on to achieve six more 'kills' when flown by 501's 'Boss', Squadron Leader Geoffrey Northcott. With seven 'kills' to its credit, Spitfire LF.Vb EP120 is one of the highest scoring surviving World War Two warbirds in the world. An accident brought its time with No.501 to an end. After repairs at Castle Bromwich, EP120 was allocated to No.19 Squadron in Cornwall, then later served with No.402 (Canadian) Squadron. It then went on second-line duties with No.3501 Support Unit and No.53 OTU before becoming an instructional airframe at RAF St Athan from June 1945 - 1955. It is thought that during this period EP120 was one of two Spitfire Mk.Vs used as static props in "Angels One Five" (1952). EP120 went on gate guard duties from 1955 onwards at RAF Stations Wilmslow, Bircham Newton, Boulmer and Wattisham, from where it was taken to RAF Henlow to appear in "Battle of Britain", after which it returned to RAF Wattisham. In 1989, EP120 was one among a number of gate guardian Spitfires that were stored by the RAF pending a decision on their future. In 1993, Spitfire LF.Vb EP120 was liberated by The Fighter Collection and overhauled by Historic Flying at Audley End, flying again after 50 grounded years in 1995. In Year 2000, EP120 was used in two film productions, filmed one after the other: the Czech/British co-production "Dark Blue World" (2001), reviewed in Chapter Eight, and "Pearl Harbor" (2001), both of which used out-takes from "Battle of Britain". Spitfire LF.Vb EP120 has been flown at many airshows by The Fighter Collection at Duxford, and continues to do so today.

Vickers Supermarine Spitfire F.Vc G-AWII/AR501, flyer. Owned by the Shuttleworth Collection and chartered by Spitfire Productions, Ltd. Built by Westlands at Yeovil in 1942 and issued that same year to No.310 (Czech) Squadron at RAF Duxford. It undertook many escort patrols for USAAF Eighth Air Force B-17 and B-24 heavy day bombers. Later in the War, AR501 was assigned to the Central Gunnery School. Post-War, it was used by Loughborough Technical College as an instructional airframe, from where it was obtained by the Shuttleworth Collection in 1961. It was placed into storage in a dismantled condition, with an eventual long-term restoration

in mind while the Shuttleworth Trustees decided on the future operation of the Collection at Old Warden. 'Hamish' Mahaddie borrowed Spitfire F.Vc AR501 when he chartered it and had it restored to flying condition by Spitfire Productions at Henlow for "Battle of Britain". It went back into storage after its use in the film, although Mahaddie continued to charter it. AR501 was brought back into flying condition between 1973 - 1975, appropriately at Duxford, and in No.310 (Czech) Squadron colours and markings. It is the only Spitfire in the world to fly with an original de Havilland three-blade propeller. Ownership was transferred back to the Shuttleworth Collection in October 1981. In April 2000, AR501 was overhauled at Duxford, during which time it had its elliptical wing-tips restored, making it fully representative of its time with No.310 (Czech). That summer it was one of four Spitfires used in "Pearl Harbor", alongside the above recorded BM597 and EP120. Spitfire F.Vc AR501 has had a long career since with the Shuttleworth Collection, appearing regularly at airshows held at Old Warden and Duxford.

Vickers Supermarine Spitfire HF.IXb G-AVDJ/MH415, flyer. Purchased by 'Hamish' Mahaddie from Rousseau Aviation at Dinard, France, and registered in the UK on 29th December 1966. Transferred to the ownership of Spitfire Productions, Ltd, and re-registered on 24th January 1968. Converted at Henlow from clipped-wing LF.IXb configuration to elliptical-winged HF.IXb variant. Spitfire HF.IXb G-AVDJ/MH415 was the sole Spitfire flown from Duxford to Tablada Airfield in Spain, for filming air-airs with massed formations of CASA 2.111s posing as Heinkel He.111Hs. We have already met Spitfire HF.IXb MH415 (as a LF.Mk.IXb) before in "The Longest Day" (1962), "Triple Cross" (1966) and "The Night of the Generals" (1967). The history and status of this Spitfire is recorded in the review of "The Longest Day".

Vickers Supermarine Spitfire HF.IXb G-ASJV/MH434, flyer. Acquired by 'Hamish' Mahaddie on 23rd November 1967, then chartered by him after its purchase by Adrian Swire in 1969. Again, we have met MH434 before, in "Operation Crossbow" (1965). As stated in the review of that film, the life history, status and filmography of Spitfire HF.IXb MH434 will be held over for the review of "A Bridge Too Far" (1977) in Chapter Five, due to the more prominent role it had in that film.

Vickers Supermarine Spitfire LF.IXc G-ASSD/MK297, flyer. Owned by Alan 'Taff' Rich, partner of Captain John Crewdson in Film Aviation Services, Ltd, and who also partnered 'Jeff' Hawke in helping to provide the two Messerschmitt Bf.108s for "633 Squadron" (1964). Spitfire LF.IXc MK297 was, in effect, being held in trust on behalf of the Confederate Air Force (CAF) at Harlingen, Texas, and was being prepared for shipment to the USA when 'Hamish' Mahaddie approached with his request to use this Spitfire in "Battle of Britain". The CAF were already in Spain to purchase four Hispano HA.1112M1L 'Buchons', which they had already agreed could be used in the film, so they had no problem in agreeing to the use of MK297 as well. It was shipped to the USA the year after filming was completed. Spitfire LF.IXc MK297 is another of the four Spitfires hired to appear in "The Longest Day", therefore its history and fate is recorded under the review of that film.

Vickers Supermarine Spitfire LF.IXe MK356, static prop. Gate guardian at RAF Locking. Spitfire LF.IXe MK356 was built at Castle Bromwich and delivered to Digby in March 1944. It was allocated to No.443 'Hornet' Squadron of the Royal Canadian Air Force, part of No.144 Canadian Wing under the command of Wing Commander J E 'Johnny' Johnson. It was heavily involved in the build up to D-Day on fighter and fighter-bomber missions, and on D-Day+1 (7th June 1944) its Canadian pilot, Flying Officer Gordon Ockenden, shared in a 'kill' of a Messerschmitt Bf.109. MK356 had its share of rough experiences, including no less than three belly landings. The third, on 14th June 1944, when it lost a wheel on take-off and was flown by its pilot on its mission before the emergency landing, was one too many and resulted in it being placed in storage with a Maintenance Unit. Like many of its co-stars in "Battle of Britain", Spitfire LF.IXe MK356 survived through being used post-War as an instructional airframe and then as a gate guardian, first at RAF Hawkinge and then at RAF Locking when it was transferred to Henlow for film work. After the film, it was placed with the RAF Museum Reserve Collection at RAF St Athan. In January 1992, restoration to flight status was begun which was completed in November 1997. It made its first flight in 53 years on 7th November 1997, then joined the Battle of Britain Memorial Flight on 14th November. It has remained with the BBMF since then.

Vickers Supermarine Spitfire Tr.9 G-AVAV/MJ772, flyer. Owned by Tony Samuelson at Elstree Aerodrome, leased by Spitfire Productions, Ltd. Built as a Spitfire LF.IX at Castle Bromwich and delivered to No.33 MU, RAF Lyneham, Wiltshire, on 20th December 1943. Assigned to Free French Air Force No.341 'Alsace' Squadron on 20th January 1944, operating from Perranporth, Cornwall, and flying 50 sorties before suffering Cat. A damage. After repairs, MJ772 joined No.340 'Ile de France' Free French Squadron on 22nd June 1944 and flew a number of Ops over the Normandy front. The rest of its War career was rather undistinguished, with MJ772 passing between General Support Units and various Maintenance Units before it had a major post-War inspection by Heston Aircraft and was then placed in storage until 1950.

Spitfire LF.IX MJ772 was destined to become one of a batch of Spitfires that were acquired for the Irish Air Corps and converted by Vickers Armstrong into two-seat Spitfire Tr.9 trainers. It was delivered to Baldonnel in 1951 and remained with the Irish Air Corps until withdrawn from use in 1960. Film Aviation Services at Biggin Hill made a bid for this Spitfire in 1963 and then sold it to COGEA in Belgium as part-payment for their purchase of Spitfire LF.IXc OO-ARB, the former MK297 referred to above which was registered as G-ASSD. However, MJ772 was not delivered to Belgium but was stored at Southend instead. In 1965, it was purchased by Samuelson Film Services and transferred to Elstree, where it was rebuilt by Simpson Aero Services and test flown by Tim Davies in July 1967, registered G-AVAV.

Tony Samuelson leased MJ772 to Spitfire Productions; it was used primarily as the conversion trainer for the RAF pilots who were to fly Spitfires in the film, conducted at Debden. It was also used as the 'shepherd' for the 17 Hispano Buchons flying into Manston from Spain on 14th May 1968. On 9th July, MJ772 made a forced landing at Little Staughton Airfield when flown by CAF pilot 'Connie' Edwards and was badly damaged, meaning its short film career was over. After being road-freighted back to Duxford, Spitfire Tr.9 MJ772 was later delivered to Bovingdon where Simpson Aero Services once again rebuilt it. Back with its owner at Elstree, MJ772 was involved in an abortive attempt by Tony Samuelson to enter it in the Daily Mail London - New York Air Race in 1969; it got no further than RNAS Brawdy, due to fuel starvation. In 1970, Sir William Roberts bought MJ772 for his Strathallan Collection; when Strathallan went bust in 1974, Doug Champlin bid for it in the auction of the Collection for his Champlin Fighter Museum. Another emergency landing on its ferry flight to Mesa, California, resulted in it having to be rebuilt for a third time, this time with the rear cockpit covered over. After flying again as a single-seater in October 1985, Spitfire Mk.IX MJ772 was operated by Champlin in its No.341 Squadron NL-R codes. It was then preserved in the EAA AirVenture Museum at Oshkosh, Wisconsin, between 2004 - 2010 before it was acquired by the Air Fighter Academy at Herringsdorf, Germany, on the Baltic island of Usedom. After a 15 month restoration programme by Meier Motors and registered in Germany as D-FMKN, Spitfire IX MJ772 flew again in the hands of Achim Meier at Bremgarten on 17th March 2012. However, less than two months later, on 3rd May 2012, Spitfire IX MJ772 bellied in again for the third time in its career due to an undercarriage malfunction and is now on long-term rebuild once more by Meier Motors.

Vickers Supermarine Spitfire Tr.9 G-AWGB/TE308, flyer. Owned by Samuelson Film Services and leased to Spitfire Productions, Ltd. Built as a Spitfire LF.IXe at Castle Bromwich, TE308 was delivered to No.39 MU at RAF Colerne on 9th June 1944. From then on it never saw the light of day again until 1950, when it was part of a batch of Spitfire Mk.IXs sold to Vickers Armstrong on 19th July. It became one of six converted into Spitfire Tr.9s for the Irish Air Corps, delivered on 30th July 1951. It flew a variety of missions, including some with bomb racks, until retired in 1961, although it was kept airworthy for instructional purposes. On 4th March 1968 Tony Samuelson purchased this Spitfire along with four other Irish Air Corps examples - including MJ772 above - and registered it as G-AWGB, basing all five at Elstree. It joined MJ772 on "Battle of Britain" film duties and was used primarily as the camera-ship, for air-airs filmed from the forward cockpit to give a Spitfire pilot's perspective. TE308 went back into storage at Elstree after filming was finished and was put up for sale in 1970 along with Samuelson's other three Spitfire Tr.9s. They were bought as a job-lot by Sir William Roberts in April 1970 but not for long as they were all, bar MJ772, sold on. Spitfire Tr.9 TE308 was bought by Canadian businessman, Donald J Plumb, and shipped to Toronto, Ontario, in October 1970. Registered CF-RAF, it was in the early Seventies the only flying Spitfire in Canada, and was displayed across North America, flown by Jerry Billings. It was returned to single-cockpit configuration when the rear cockpit was panelled over in 1972, then repainted as TE308/'RA-F', while it was re-registered C-FRAF. Don Plumb was killed in his P-51D Mustang in 1975, which meant that his Spitfire was sold by his widow in October 1976 to a new owner in Maine. Registered firstly N92477, then N308WK, this Spitfire underwent two further ownership changes in the USA, during which time it was converted back as a two-seat trainer. It now flies today from Aspen, Colorado, in the hands of Bill Greenwood who has owned it since 1983 and has had it painted as TE308/RJ-M.

Vickers Supermarine Spitfire F.XIVc G-ALGT/RM689, flyer. Owned by Rolls Royce, Ltd, and based at Hucknall Aerodrome. Loaned to Spitfire Productions, Ltd. Built by Supermarine at Chattis Hall, Salisbury, in March 1944 and delivered to No.39 MU, RAF Colerne, on 3rd July. Spitfire F.XIVc RM689 was allocated to the Air Fighting Development Unit at RAF Wittering on 5th August and was used to trial a new one-piece wrap-around windscreen before it went to No.33 MU at Lyneham for storage. By February 1945, RM689 was on the strength of No.350 (Belgian) Squadron and was flying armed recce and fighter sweep Ops over the Low Countries. No.350 was assigned to No.125 Wing, No.83 Support Group, of the 2nd Tactical Air Force, with which RM689 supported the Allies' advance into Germany, wearing the squadron codes MN-E. In April 1945 it was withdrawn to No.151 Repair Unit after being damaged and was out of action until it returned to No.350 in July. On 14th January 1946, RM689 joined No.443 (Canadian) Squadron of No.144 Canadian Wing, 2nd TAF, but this was a short stay before it went into storage at RAF High Ercall two months later. There it remained before it was sold to Rolls Royce, Ltd, on 19th February 1949 and was delivered to Hucknall for engine development testing. Civilianised as G-ALGT, Spitfire F.XIVc RM689 was painted silver overall with a blue cheat line and it was in this colour scheme it became a familiar sight at British airshows in the Fifties. 'Hamish' Mahaddie approached Rolls Royce in 1967, to request its use in "Battle of Britain", for which it was repainted in 1940-style Fighter Command camouflage and acquired elliptical wing tips. When it returned to Rolls Royce it was repainted in a new camouflage scheme and given the No.130 Squadron codes of AP-D; however, for some reason Rolls Royce believed its serial was RM619, which was applied. It was also returned to clipped-wing status. It continued to be a regular airshow act, flown by John Lewis throughout the Seventies and taken over by David Moore in the Eighties. By 1987, RM689's true identity had been discovered and it was also re-coded with its original No.350 (Belgian) Squadron MN-E codes. It had also been re-engined with a Griffon taken from a Shackleton and was now operating from East Midlands Airport at Castle Donington under the stewardship of Rolls Royce's Executive Flight. Tragedy struck on 27th June 1992 at British Aerospace's Woodford facility when, during a flying display, RM689 failed to pull out of a loop and crashed in front of the crowd, killing David Moore instantly. The wreckage was held in store until, in 2002, the decision was taken to commence the long-term restoration of Spitfire F.XIVc G-ALGT/RM689, using as many of the original surviving components as possible. The restoration work is still in progress, conducted by Airframe Assemblies on the Isle of Wight.

Vickers Supermarine Spitfire LF.XVIe RW382, static prop. Gate guardian at RAF Leconfield. Built at Castle Bromwich in 1945 and delivered to No.6 MU on 20th July. In April 1947, RW382 was on the strength of No.604 Squadron but was returned to storage with No.33 MU three years later. It then spent four months with No.3 CAACU at Exeter from 11th June 1951, before being transferred to the Control and Reporting School, RAF Middle Wallop, on 17th October. By July 1953, RW382 was back in storage and remained so until it was allocated to No.609 Squadron in November 1955, primarily for static display purposes. In 1959, RW382 took up gate guardian duties at RAF Leconfield, where it remained until 1973 apart from its sojourn with Spitfire Productions in 1968. It was used as a background fill-in prop in "Battle of Britain". On 4th April 1973, RW382 had the honour of becoming the gate guardian of RAF Uxbridge, Middlesex, the Operations Control Centre of No.11 Group, RAF Fighter Command, during the Battle of Britain, and remained so until the RAF decided to put all their gate guardian Spitfires up for disposal. Tim Routsis of Historic Flying acquired it on 26th August 1988, then sold it on to David Tallichet of Chino, California, in 1989. Historic Flying undertook RW382's restoration to flying condition at Audley End on behalf of David Tallichet, it taking to the air again on 3rd July 1991. It stayed at Audley End until it was sold to new owner Bernie Jackson of Minden-Tahoe, Nevada, and was registered in the USA as NX382RW. Spitfire LF.XVIe RW382 then took up a new life on the warbird scene in America but this came to grief on 3rd June 1998 when it crashed in the remote Blue River Canyon, Nevada, while flying back to Minden-Tahoe from an airshow at Chico, California. Apparently its former Canadian Armed Forces pilot, 37-year-old Thomas Jackson and nephew of owner Bernie, was flying through the canyon under dense cloud and collided with the canyon wall when he attempted to turn back. Today, the remains of Spitfire LF.XVIe RW382 are stored on the Isle of Wight, in the ownership of Steve Vizard.

Vickers Supermarine Spitfire LF.XVIe SL574, static prop. Preserved at RAF Bentley Priory. Like RW382, Spitfire LF.XVIe SL574 was used as a background fill-in prop in airfield scenes for "Battle of Britain". It was returned to Bentley Priory after filming was completed in 1968. Spitfire LF.XVIe SL574 had a role in "Reach For The Sky" (1956); its history and current status is recorded in the review of that film.

Vickers Supermarine Spitfire LF.XVIe SM411, taxyer and 'Mark Addie' conversion. Preserved at RAF Wattisham. Built at Castle Bromwich and delivered to No.45 MU, RAF Kinloss, Scotland, in November 1944. Then to No.83 GSU at Westhampnett which allocated SM411 to No.421 'Red Indian' Squadron, No.127 Canadian Wing, with which it saw action as part of 2nd TAF in Belgium, Holland and Germany before returning to No.83 GSU, now at Dunsfold, Surrey, in July 1945. It then went into storage with No.29 MU, High Ercall, until April 1951 when SM411 was assigned to No.102 Flying Refresher School. Two months later it was on the staff of No.103 FRS, Full Sutton, but by October it was back into storage again, this time with No.9 MU at RAF Cosford, where it remained locked up for another two years. In October 1953, SM411 joined No.3 CAACU at Exeter, towing targets until May 1954 when it returned to No.9 MU and was struck off charge in December. Spitfire LF.XVIe SM411 then began a life of display exhibitionism, firstly as a preserved exhibit at RAF Wattisham, then, after its appearance in "Battle of Britain", as a travelling exhibit with the RAF Exhibitions Flight. While at Henlow in 1967 it was converted by Simpsons Aero Services into as close a representation of a Spitfire Mk.I as possible, making it a 'Mark Addie' (a play on 'Hamish' Mahaddie's name), and was brought up to taxying condition. It had a couple of "Oops-a-daisies!" while on film work, twice tipping onto its nose, first at North Weald in May 1968, then at Duxford on 11th August when its three-bladed propeller was damaged, resulting in SM411 being withdrawn from its film extra role. Life was reasonably good for SM411 as it travelled the length and breadth of the country in the Seventies, being admired by the public as a recruitment exhibit. It was then selected for donation to Poland, in return for a de Havilland DH.9a which had somehow managed to survive Nazi Occupation in Krakow throughout the War. Spitfire LF.XVIe SM411 is today displayed as TB995/ZF-O of No.308 'Krakow' Squadron at the Museum of Aircraft and Astronautics, Krakow, Poland.

Vickers Supermarine Spitfire LF.XVIe TB382, taxyer and 'Mark Addie' conversion. Gate guardian at the RAF Hospital, Ely, Cambridgeshire. Built at Castle Bromwich and delivered to No.6 MU, RAF Brize Norton, Oxfordshire, on 19th January 1945. Issued to No.602 (City of Glasgow) Squadron, RAuxAF, at Ludham, Norfolk, on 21st February. Used for dive bombing missions against fast dwindling V1 and V2 sites and armed recce Ops until it was damaged on 12th March. Repairs were conducted on site by Vickers Armstrong 'Techies' and TB382 was back on strength of No.602, now at RAF Coltishall. With the end of the War, it, like so many of its brethren, was placed in storage. Spitfire LF.XVIe TB382 was recalled to duty when it joined the Fighter Command Communications Flight at RAF Northolt on 27th January 1949 and served with the FCCF until a flying accident on 31st May 1951 caused it to be returned to storage. Repairs were affected but TB382 remained with No.29 MU until it was delivered to RAF Thornaby for display purposes. Painted silver overall, TB382 went to RAF Middleton St George in 1956, then transferred to the RAF Hospital, Ely, sometime in the mid-Sixties. By February 1967 it was at RAF Henlow for conversion to 'Mark Addie' status, to approximate a Spitfire Mk.I for taxying roles in "Battle of Britain". When its role as a film extra was completed, TB382 was converted back into LF.XVIe configuration and placed in store at Henlow. Spitfire LF.XVIe TB382 spent many a year from 1969 onwards as a touring exhibit with the RAF Exhibition Flight at RAF Abingdon before it was transferred to RAF Coningsby in 1999 to join the BBMF. It has remained with the BBMF as a spares source for the Flight's airworthy Spitfires.

Vickers Supermarine Spitfire LF.XVIe TD248, reserve and possible spares source. Gate guardian at RAF Sealand, returned to Sealand after film production was completed. Spitfire LF.XVIe TD248 was built at Castle Bromwich and was taken on charge on 11th May 1945, just in time to miss the War. It was delivered to No.9 MU at RAF Brize Norton on 16th May but was quickly allocated to No.695 Squadron at Bircham Newton in Norfolk. TD248 continued to operate with No.695 after the squadron transferred to RAF Horsham St Faith in August, but was withdrawn from service on 31st December 1947 when an inspection revealed substantial but unrecorded damage. It returned to service on 13th May 1948. Spitfire LF.XVIe TD248 became a target-tug with No.2 CAACU at Little Snoring, Norfolk, in August 1951, continuing in this role until its military flying career came to an end in May 1954. After storage with No.9 MU at RAF Cosford, TD248 was offered to No.610 Squadron, RAuxAF, for static display at Hooton Park, Cheshire, then subsequently to the Air Training Corps at Sealand. Sold to Historic Flying in 1988, TD248 was restored to flight in November 1992. It became a familiar sight on the UK airshow scene, painted in a striking silver scheme with red fuselage stripe of a No.41 Squadron Spitfire F.21 that took part in the Blackpool Air Races of 1948 - '49. Sold again in 2005, Spitfire LF.XVIe TD248 is today operated by Spitfire, Ltd, and is maintained at Duxford by the Aircraft Restoration Company. It bears the markings of a No.74 'Tigers' Squadron Spitfire, coded CR-S, as worn in May 1945.

Vickers Supermarine Spitfire LF.XVIe TE311, taxyer and 'Mark Addie' conversion. Gate guardian at RAF Tangmere. Built at Castle Bromwich and delivered to No.39 MU, RAF Colerne, on 16th June 1945 after hostilities in Europe had ceased. On 5th October, TE311 was serving with the Empire Central Flying School's Handling Squadron at Hullavington, Wiltshire, remaining there until 17th February 1946 when it went back into storage, this time with No.33 MU, RAF Lyneham. It remained out of sight for five years, until it was allocated to No.1689 FPT Flight on 31st May 1951. Spitfire LF.XVIe TE311 came under Flying Training Command on 31st July 1952 and joined the Ferry Training Unit at RAF Benson on 9th April 1953. This began a short period when TE311 was moved around between Benson, Lyneham and RAF Langham, Norfolk, where it spent four months with No.2 CAACU before it went back to No.33 MU on 23rd February 1954. There it remained until it was allocated as gate guard to RAF Tangmere, arriving on 11th August 1955, a position it held until it was transferred to Henlow in 1967 for conversion into a taxyable 'Mark Addie'. After its work as a film extra was completed in 1968, TE311 was converted back into LF.XVIe configuration and sent to RAF Benson for display purposes. Within a short space of time, though, TE311 was transferred to RAF Abingdon to replace Spitfire LF.XVIe SM411 with the RAF Exhibition Flight, following SM411's donation to Poland. During its time at Abingdon, TE311 spent some time on loan to the Bayeaux Museum in France where it is believed it actually flew in the markings of MK178/LZ-V of No.66 Squadron. Spitfire LF.XVIe TE311 is now with the BBMF at RAF Coningsby, where it has been on long-term restoration to flight. It finally took to the air again after 58 ground-borne years for a short flight from RAF Coningsby on 19th October 2012, coded as 4D-V of No.74 Squadron.

Vickers Supermarine Spitfire LF.XVIe TE356, taxyer and 'Mark Addie' conversion. Preserved at RAF Bicester. Built at Castle Bromwich and delivered to No.29 MU, High Ercall, on 23rd June 1945. Served with No.695 Squadron from 11th July 1945 to 14th February 1949, by which date the unit was renumbered as No.34 Squadron. Spitfire LF.XVIe TE356 served with No.34 until it was transferred to No.2

CAACU at Little Snoring, Norfolk, on 20th August 1951, remaining there until 1st September 1952. On that date it was relegated to being an instructional airframe but was allocated to RAF Bicester for display purposes. There it remained until it was swooped up among other gate guard Spitfires for conversion into 'Mark Addies' at Henlow in 1967. Taxyable, TE356 even got air under its wheels when it performed an unplanned (?) hop at North Weald. Once filming was finished, TE356 was converted back into a LF.XVIe and sent to No.4 Squadron detachment of the CFS at RAF Kemble, sharing hangar space with the Gnat T.1s of the "Red Arrows". The plan was to restore TE356 back into flying condition but the powers-that-be in Flying Training Command were against the idea, possibly because of the abortive experience the CFS had not enjoyed with the ex-"633 Squadron" Mosquito TT.35 TA634. However, Spitfire LF.XVIe TE356 remained with the CFS wherever the School went until, in 1986, the Ministry of Defence agreed the exchange of TE356 for a P-47D Thunderbolt, to be displayed in the RAF Museum, from Doug Arnold's Warbirds of Great Britain collection. Doug Arnold had TE356 registered as G-SXVI in February 1987 while it was rebuilt by Trent Aero at East Midlands. Spitfire LF.XVIe TE356 flew again on 16th December 1987, after which it was stored with the Warbirds of Great Britain at Biggin Hill until January 1990, when it was sold to Evergreen Ventures of Oregon, USA, registered as N356EV. This was changed to N356TE in March 1991 when Evergreen Ventures became 747 Inc. Today, Spitfire LF.XVIe TE356 is exhibited at the Evergreen Aviation Museum of McMinnville, Oregon, still capable of being made airworthy.

Vickers Supermarine Spitfire LF.XVIe TE384, taxyer and 'Mark Addie' conversion. Instructional airframe at RAF Syerston. Built at Castle Bromwich and delivered to No.6 MU at Brize Norton on 3rd August 1945. There it stayed until it was issued to No.603 (City of Edinburgh) Squadron, RAuxAF, at Turnhouse in May 1947. Spitfire LF.XVIe TE384 then spent four years as a Royal Auxiliary Air Force Spitfire, moving around No.501 (County of Gloucester) and No.612 (County of Aberdeen) Squadrons before it went to Airwork General Trading at Gatwick in July 1951 for overhaul. However, it did not fly again but was stored until 26th August 1955, when it was sent to Wymeswold for display purposes. Not long after this it was transferred to RAF Syerston as an instructional airframe, which was its role in life until it too was called for duty as a 'Mark Addie' in "Battle of Britain". During filming at North Weald in May 1968, TE384 tipped up onto its nose while taxying across rough grass during a Luftwaffe bombing scene; it was left in this position as battle damage set-dressing and can be seen in the background when actress Suzannah York shouts at Michael Bates, "Don't you yell at me, Mister Warwick!". An Online source claims that actor Robert Shaw was in the cockpit of TE384, as 'Skipper', when it tipped up: this is questionable, because to allow an inexperienced actor to take the controls of a 'live' Spitfire seems high risk - in fact, the Special Features section of the DVD has an assistant director saying that the actors were filmed in the full-scale facsimile Spitfires and Hurricanes, which had lawnmower engines installed, enabling them to taxy. They were not in the real things.

Spitfire TE384 was converted back into LF.XVIe configuration and placed in store at Henlow. It was selected for the RAF Museum and remained at Henlow until 1972. It then undertook a new lease of life by being flown to Amberley RAAF base in Australia aboard a Belfast C.1, in exchange for a Supermarine Seagull V amphibian which is now exhibited in the RAF Museum at Hendon. Plans were to restore TE384 to flying condition, but this did not transpire so the Spitfire was placed in storage until J F Czerwinski and Barry Hempel acquired it in September 1983. It was moved to Toowoomba and registered VH-XVI, pending its return to flight on 6th October 1988. TE384 was then sold to Ken McBride of San Martin, California, and registered as N384TE, where it remains today. It is still airworthy, although its engine has been seriously damaged by contaminated oil, meaning Spitfire LF.XVIe TE384 will remain grounded until either a new engine is installed or a decision is taken on its future.

Vickers Supermarine Spitfire LF.XVIe TE476, taxyer and 'Mark Addie' conversion. Gate guardian at RAF Neatishead. Built by Vickers Armstrong at Castle Bromwich, TE476 was delivered to No.39 MU at RAF Colerne on 30th June 1945. It remained in store until 4th July 1951 when it finally got to fly with No.1 CAACU at Hornchurch, serving in the target facilities role until its retirement to No.5 MU, RAF Kemble, on 11th September 1956. Spitfire LF.XVIe TE476 was destined for a public display role during the next few years, beginning with being selected for a part in the Royal Tournament at Earls Court in July 1957. After this, TE476 was one of three Spitfire Mk.XVIs selected to join the new RAF Historic Flight, popularly known as the Battle of Britain Flight, and was restored to flying condition. It joined the Flight at Biggin Hill on 1st March 1958, officially with the Station Flight and subsequently with the same at North Weald and Martlesham Heath, when the Flight moved to these RAF Stations. However, TE476 was involved in a flying accident on 10th September 1959, which was quickly repaired. TE476, along with the other now-recognised Battle of Britain Flight Spitfires and Hurricane, came under No.11 Group Communications Flight that same month. This arrangement lasted until 5th January 1960, when TE476 was struck off charge. It then became an exhibition airframe and was issued to RAF Neatishead for display purposes. It was from there it was transferred to RAF Henlow in 1967, to be 'Mark Addied' into a Spitfire Mk.I taxying look-alike. After its film role and re-conversion back to LF.XVIe status, TE476 was issued to RAF Northolt on 2nd July 1970 for display purposes. It became one of the group of Spitfire gate guardians that Tim Routsis of Historic Flying acquired in June 1988 and registered as G-XVIB on 3rd July 1989. Kermit Weeks of Kissimmee, Florida, bought TE476 in February 1990 and had it shipped to his Weeks Air Museum as N476TE in April 1991. However, the hurricane which did so much damage to his collection meant that Weeks was in recovery mode, so TE476 was shipped back to the UK in May 1992 and was restored to flying condition by Personal Plane Services at Booker, flying again on 20th June 1995. Today, Spitfire LF.XVIe TE476 is displayed at Kissimmee with the Weeks FantasyOfFlight Museum and is still in airworthy condition.

Vickers Supermarine Spitfire PR.XIX PM631, flyer. On strength with the Battle of Britain Flight at RAF Coltishall. Built by Vickers Armstrong at Reading in late 1945 and delivered to No.6 MU, RAF Brize Norton, on 6th November. It then remained in storage for six years, although there is a possibility PM631 spent eight months with No.203 Advanced Flying School between May 1949 - January 1950. On 2nd July 1951, Spitfire PR.XIX PM631 became operational with the Meteorological Research Flight at Hooton Park, only a few days before the Flight moved to Woodvale. Known as the THUM Flight, tasks involved temperature and humidity measurement flights conducted until June 1957, when Mosquitos took over the role. The three THUM Flight Spitfire PR.XIXs, PM631 among them, became the founder Spitfires of the RAF Historic Flight at Biggin Hill, which formed on 11th July 1957 - the forerunner of today's Battle of Britain Memorial Flight. Spitfire PR.XIX PM631 has remained with the BBMF ever since, the longest serving member of the Flight. In "Battle of Britian", it was flown only in large formations at the rear to create numbers because its configuration conflicted so much with the earlier Marques portraying 1940-era Spitfires.

Vickers Supermarine Spitfire PR.XIX PM651, static prop and 'Mark Addie' conversion. Gate guardian at RAF Benson. Built by Vickers Armstrong at Reading, PM651 was issued to the Civilian Repair Depot at White Waltham, Berkshire, on 27th November 1945, possibly because storage space was at a premium post-War in Maintenance Units. By 30th September 1947, PM651 was with No.6 MU at Brize Norton and remained under wraps until it was sent for refurbishment by Airworks General Trading at Gatwick on 15th January 1951. It then went back into hiding with No.6 MU for three more years before it was chosen on 15th March 1954 as the replacement Spitfire PR.XIX for the loss of PM652 with the THUM Flight at Woodvale. Unluckily it suffered a landing accident at Woodvale on 14th April, the damage being assessed as uneconomic to repair. Spitfire PR.XIX PM651 was earmarked as a display airframe, first taking up gate guard duties at Hucknall where Rolls Royce's Spitfire F.XIVc G-ALGT was flying from, then moving on to Andover and Benson. After being used for airfield set-dressing in "Battle of Britain", PM651 was painted in PR Blue for its display on the gate to the wartime PRU headquarters at RAF Benson, dedicated to all Spitfire PR pilots who flew high risk low-level missions over enemy territory to gather vital Photographic Intelligence. PM651 was exhibited in the RAF Museum in 1989 before being stored as part of the RAF Museum Reserve Collection at RAF Stafford, where some of its components were used as spares sources for the BBMF's Spitfire PR.XIXs. In October 2010, PM651 was transferred to the RAF Museum at Cosford, where it is displayed today in the Warplanes Hangar.

Vickers Supermarine Spitfire PR.19 PS853, flyer. On strength with the Battle of Britain Flight at RAF Coltishall. Spitfire PR.19 PS853 was originally intended to be a Spiteful out of a batch of 200 ordered, but when this was cancelled it was re-ordered as one of 79 PR.19s (note, Roman numerals were not used for its Marque Number) built at Southampton. It entered service with the Central PRU at RAF Benson on 13th January 1945 but within

six weeks it was on the strength of No.16 Squadron, No.34 Wing, at Melsbroek in Belgium and soon afterwards Eindhoven in The Netherlands. As the War came to an end in Europe, Spitfire PR.19 PS853 was operating with No.268 Squadron which re-numbered as No.16 Squadron at Celle, British Zone of Occupation, in September 1945. When PS853 returned to the UK in March 1946 it went into storage for four years before being allocated to the Meteorological Research ('THUM') Flight at Hooton Park in July 1950. It served with the THUM Flight until it and its fellow Spitfire PR.XIXs were retired in June 1957. PS853 was another of the three PR.XIX/PR.19s which formed the fledgling 'Battle of Britain Flight' at Biggin Hill, being delivered by no less a personality than Wing Commander 'Johnnie' Johnson on 13th June 1957. It did not stay long with the Flight, being selected to be used by the Central Fighter Establishment at West Raynham on 14th April 1958. This was a strange move because hardly had PS853 arrived at West Raynham, it was grounded and made the gate guard. It was restored to flying condition in 1962 and found itself back with the Battle of Britain Flight at Coltishall on 14th April 1964. It has remained with the BBMF, apart from when it joined Spitfire Productions at Henlow in 1967. Like PR.XIX PM631, it was flown at the rear of large formations to make up numbers of Spitfires in "Battle of Britain". In 1973, Spitfire PR.19 PS853 was painted again in PR Blue, the scheme it still flies in today. In 1995, the BBMF decided to off-load one of its PR Spitfires, selling PS853 to Euan English, but when he died in a flying accident in March 1995 the sale was cancelled. Spitfire PR.19 PS853 was bought by Rolls Royce Aero Engines in September 1996, as a replacement for Spitfire F.XIVc RM689, and was operated from Filton until that airfield closed. At time of writing, PS853 was at Duxford undergoing a major strip-down and overhaul, shared between the Aircraft Restoration Company and Historic Flying, Ltd. The magnificent end result was brought out into the limelight again on 4th October 2012.

Vickers Supermarine Spitfire PR.19 PS915, static prop and 'Mark Addie' conversion. Gate guardian at RAF Leuchars. Spitfire PR.19 was another of the cancelled Spitefuls changed into an order for PR.19s. It was delivered to No.6 MU, RAF Brize Norton, on 17th April 1945 but within nine days it was to be found at RAF Benson. This was to be its home for the next few years, serving with a variety of units at Benson: No.541 Squadron, No.1 Pilots Pool, the PR Development Unit and No.151 RU. On an unspecified date, Spitfire PR.19 PS915 was assigned to No.II Squadron at Wunsdorf, Germany, flying strategic reconnaissance sorties monitoring Soviet forces; it returned to the UK in 1951 and was stored at No.9 MU, RAF Cosford. On 4th June 1954, PS915 joined the THUM Flight at Woodvale, with which it served until the Flight's Spitfire PR.19/XIXs were retired in exchange for Mosquitos. Like PM631 and PS853, Spitfire PR.19 PS915 flew to Biggin Hill on 13th June 1957 to form the genesis of the Battle of Britain Flight. However, it was retired from flying on 31st August and sent to RAF West Malling for display purposes. Later, PS915 was transferred to RAF Leuchars to become gate guardian, from where it was taken in 1967 to RAF Henlow to be 'made up' for "Battle of Britain" film work. It was used for background set-dressing on airfields. Spitfire PR.19 PS915 was then chosen to be the gate guard for RAF Brawdy, but did spend some non-flying time with the BBMF for Griffon 57 engine installation trials, taken from a Shackleton. In 1984, the decision was taken to return PS915 to the air powered by a Griffon 58, carried out by BAe apprentices at Samlesbury. By 1986, Spitfire PR.19 PS915 was flying again and the following year was back on the strength of the BBMF, painted, like PS853, in PR Blue. It remains with the BBMF today.

Vickers Supermarine Spitfire F.21 LA198, static prop and 'Mark Addie' conversion. With No.187 Squadron, Air Training Corps, at Worcester. Spitfire F.21 LA198 was built at South Marston and delivered to No.33 MU at RAF Lyneham on 2nd October 1944. It did not see any operational service until it was allocated to No.1 Squadron at Manston on 3rd May 1945. It went back into store with No.9 MU, RAF Cosford, on 4th October 1946, but on 12th May 1947 LA198 had joined No.602 (City of Glasgow) Squadron, RAuxAF, and flew with this unit for four years as RAI-G. On 19th September 1951, Spitfire F.21 LA198 arrived at Exeter with No.3 CAACU, which became its final operational unit. The Spitfire was sent to Vickers on 19th November 1953 for refurbishment and export, but when this was cancelled it was presented to No.187 Squadron, ATC, Worcester, who took great care of it. 'Hamish' Mahaddie was impressed enough to recruit LA198 as a film extra in 1967. There is imagery on the Special Features disc of the 'Definitive Edition' DVD of "Battle of Britain", showing Spitfire F.21 LA198 being 'Mark Addied' to make it as close as possible in appearance to an early Marque of Spitfire. In 1970, LA198 became gate guard at RAF Locking, Weston-super-Mare, restored in its No.1 Squadron colours. On 25th March 1986, LA198 became gate guard at RAF Leuchars. While at Leuchars it was restored to its No.602 (City of Glasgow) Squadron scheme, with codes RAI-G. In 1989, LA198 was selected for possible RAF Museum display and was stored with the Reserve Collections at St Athan and Cardington until 1997, when it was gifted to the City of Glasgow. Today, Spitfire F.21 LA198/RAI-G is exhibited by the Kelvingrove Art Gallery and Museum, Glasgow.

Six more Spitfires were on the strength of Spitfire Productions' version of RAF Fighter Command, all of them in non-flying condition and all acting as spares sources, therefore not getting in front of the cameras. They comprised:

Vickers Supermarine Spitfire F.Ia K9942. In storage with the Air Historical Branch. The oldest Spitfire recruited by 'Hamish' Mahaddie and although a genuine Battle of Britain veteran, it served with No.57 OTU throughout the Battle. Spent much of its post-War years as an exhibit, including being displayed in the Guildhall in London during the 25th anniversary of the Battle of Britain. It was delivered to the RAF Museum, Hendon, on 9th November 1971. Today, Spitfire F.Ia K9942 is exhibited in the RAF Museum, Cosford, painted in its original colours and markings as SD-D of No.72 (Basutoland) Squadron, the first unit it joined on 24th April 1939.

Vickers Supermarine Spitfire FR.XIVc NH904. Bought by 'Hamish' Mahaddie for Spitfire Productions, Ltd, from a private car dealer in Hoylake, Cheshire. Spitfire FR.XIVc NH904 very

briefly served with No.414 Squadron in Germany as the War in Europe was coming to a close, but its operational career came to an end when, on 15th April 1945, it was damaged in a wheels-up landing. Vickers Armstrong sold it to the Belgian Air Force in November 1950. It went through the hands of a Belgian scrap dealer and an English car dealer before Mahaddie acquired it. Sir William Roberts bought it in 1971 and stored it at Strathallan. British aviation enthusiasts will remember this Spitfire performing at airshows during the early Eighties, painted bright red and registered as G-FIRE, owned by Spencer Flack. Today, Spitfire FR.XIVc NH904 is displayed in the USA with the Palm Springs Air Museum, California, registered as N1148P.

Vickers Supermarine Spitfire F.XIVc RM694, fuselage section only. Owned by Manchester Tankers, Ltd, assessed for possible use in the film and stored at Henlow during the production. Currently believed to be stored at Booker with components of another Spitfire Mk.XIV and a Mk.XVIII for a possible restoration project.

Vickers Supermarine Spitfire LF.XVIe TB863. Owned by Pinewood Studios, minus cockpit section which was owned by MGM British Studios. Appeared in "Reach For The Sky" (1956). Today, TB863 is extant with the Alpine Fighter Collection at Wanaka, New Zealand.

Vickers Supermarine Spitfire LF.XVIe TE184. Static display at RAF Bicester. Built in 1945 at Castle Bromwich, spent most of its operational career in storage. Returned to store after completion of the film and allocated in 1971 to the Ulster Folk and Transport Museum at Cultra Manor, Northern Ireland, to which it was delivered in 1977. Sold to Nick Grace in 1986 and registered G-MXVI with Myrick Aviation Services. Flew again on 23rd November 1990. Chartered by Alan de Cadenet in 1996. Has been seen on the British airshow scene since 2009 with The G2 Trust, but during the course of research for this book ownership of Spitfire LF.XVIe TE184 changed again in April 2011 to a private operator.

Vickers Supermarine Spitfire F.24 PK724. Static display at RAF Gaydon. Possibly the lowest-houred Spitfire in existence, with just seven hours on its airframe! Because PK724 was in such excellent condition Simpsons Aero Services assessed it for restoration to flight condition for "Battle of Britain", but the use of a Spitfire F.24 was not practical due to the considerable changes in airframe configuration between it and the early Marques of Spitfire in the film. Consequently, Spitfire F.24 PK724 had no role, not even as a spares source, but remained at Henlow throughout the production. It has been exhibited in the RAF Museum at Hendon since the Museum opened in 1972.

Luftflotten II, III, & V, Deutsches Luftwaffe

The Spanish Air Force's generosity in providing its entire complement of CASA 2.111D and Hispano HA.1112M1L bombers and fighters to re-create the three Air Fleets (Luftflotten) facing Fighter Command across the Channel in 1940 cannot be over emphasized. The relationship between Britain and Spain in 1968 was, at best, diplomatically cool, due to the differences between the two nations over Gibraltar. Spain was then, de facto, a dictatorship in a largely democratised Western Europe, not part of the NATO alliance against the Soviet Union, and at odds with

Britain historically and politically. Despite this, no barriers were put in the way of Spitfire Productions' use of every single usable CASA 2.111D and HA.1112M1L Buchon, apart, that is, of General Franco's personal CASA 2.111D VIP transport.

Let's not pretend the CASA 2.111Ds and HA.1112M1L Buchons were front-line bombers and fighters in 1968. In fact, that same year the Ejercito del Aire was undertaking an expansive modernisation programme with the latest combat jets, consisting of the McDonnell-Douglas F-4C Phantom and the Northrop F-5A Freedom Fighter. The Buchons, in fact, had all been withdrawn from service. The remaining CASA 2.111Ds still operational were used either as multi-engine pilot and navigational trainers, and as target-tugs; in fact, some of the CASA 2.111Ds being flown as Heinkel He.111Hs can be seen among the formations to be still carrying their target-towing units beneath their forward fuselages. They were still providing target-towing facilities to the Spanish armed forces while being filmed at the same time as Luftwaffe bombers!

While all 32 CASA 2.111Ds were made available to Spitfire Productions for filming at Base Aerea Tablada, outside Seville, there is no confirmation that literally every single one of them was used, or indeed even flown together en masse. As stated above, analysis confirms that 18 CASA 2.111Ds can be counted in one air-air formation shot. The highest total visible on film occurs when Generalfeldmarschall Erhard Milch, Inspector General of the Luftwaffe and played by actor Dietrich Frauboes, arrives at an airfield in Northern France to inspect the Kampfgeschwaderen of Luftflotte Zwei (Air Fleet 2). This is played out as the main titles roll. Milch drives in a staff car down between two lines of Heinkel He.111Hs paraded for his inspection. A count reveals this shot contains 22 CASA 2.111Ds lined up, 11 on either side facing each other. Milch, of course, arrives on board a Junkers Ju.52/3M, played by a Spanish AF CASA 352L filmed air-air as the title credits roll. A second CASA 352L, portraying a Lufthansa Ju.52/3M, is seen filmed at Tablada representing Berlin-Staaken Airport.

Out of the overall total, two CASA 2.111Ds were bought by Spitfire Productions and flown to Duxford, arriving on 14th June 1968, from where they were flown for various close-up aerial shots in action against Spitfires and Hurricanes, plus a third was broken up with its frontal half of its fuselage and cabin being used for cockpit and air gunner shots. The 16 HA.1112M1L Buchons and the sole two-seat HA.1112M4K Buchon were also part of the same package. Their identities and what is known either of their fate or their current status is listed below:

CASA 352L T.2B-176. In service with the Ejercito del Aire during the production as a VIP transport, director Guy Hamilton said the only alteration he had to make to the aircraft before having it painted in Luftwaffe markings was to remove the chintz window curtains. Still in EdA service in 1978, with Ala 72 as 721-8. At some stage it was purchased by an unidentified owner in the USA, registered N99059. On 9th September 1991, this CASA 352L came into the ownership of the Commemorative Air Force Airpower Museum at Odessa Regional/Midland International Airport, Midland, Texas, registered as N352JU. It flew with the

Commemorative Air Force at airshows throughout the USA until 2009 when it was taken on board by the Fighter Factory, located at the Military Aviation Museum, Atlantic Airpark, Virginia Beach, Virginia. However, on 30th August 2010 this CASA 352L was registered NX352JU to Training Services Inc of Virginia Beach, VA, in whose ownership it remains today.

CASA 352L unidentified, in service with the Ejercito del Aire. Fate or status unknown.

CASA 2.111D B.2I-77/G-AWHA. Bought by Spitfire Productions and registered in the UK on 14th May 1968. Flown to Duxford for aerial filming until production was completed in October 1968. This was one of the original batch of CASA 2.111Bs that were powered by Jumo 211 engines, serialled B.2H-25. It was converted into a CASA 2.111D with Rolls Royce Merlin 500 engines on 17th February 1958 and re-serialled as B.2I-77 on 30th August. It then served with Ala de Bombardeo Ligero 64, as 64-15, based at Torrejon until it was re-allocated on 7th February 1961 to Ala de BL.27 at El Rompedizo, Malaga, coded 27-32. CASA 2.111D B.2I-77 ended its days with the Ejercito del Aire when it was struck off charge at Tablada on 9th November 1967. It was sold to Spitfire Productions on 23rd March 1968. After filming was completed, 'Hamish' Mahaddie chartered CASA 2.111D G-AWHA, having it registered to him on 27th February 1969. It was subsequently de-registered on 15th August 1970 and re-registered five days later in West Germany as D-CAGI, making its final flight on 21st September 1970. Today it is displayed in the Deutsches Museum, Oberschleissheim, outside Munich.

CASA 2.111D B.2I-37/G-AWHB. Bought by Spitfire Productions and registered in the UK on 14th May 1968. Flown to Duxford for aerial filming until production was completed in October 1968. After filming was completed, 'Hamish' Mahaddie chartered CASA 2.111D G-AWHB, along with G-AWHA, having it registered to him on 27th February 1969. Both aircraft were stored at West Malling. The charter was terminated on 8th March 1972 and the registration was permanently withdrawn from use on 11th September 1974. CASA 2.111D G-AWHB was exhibited throughout the Seventies at Southend Airport, Essex, as part of the Historic Aircraft Collection, still in its "Battle of Britain" wardrobe as '6J+PR'. Aces High acquired CASA 2.111D G-AWHB in 1983 when the Collection was auctioned off and re-opened its registration on 16th October 1989. It remained in storage at North Weald until it was sold to the Flying Heritage Collection of Washington State, USA, its registration being cancelled on 27th April 2001. The most recent information concerning its status is that it is still in England, stored somewhere in Norfolk. Apparently it has serious corrosion problems.

CASA 2.111D B.2I-20. Cockpit and fuselage freighted to Pinewood Studios for interior shots. Now in private ownership in Austria.

Hispano HA.1112M1L Buchon C.4K-126/G-AWHD. Acquired by Wilson 'Connie' Edwards, stored at Big Springs, Texas, registered as N90603.

Hispano HA.1112M1L Buchon C.4K-31/G-AWHE. Acquired by Wilson 'Connie' Edwards, stored at Big Springs,

Texas, registered as N109ME. Flew with the Confederate Air Force in the Seventies and appeared as a Condor Legion Messerschmitt Bf.109B in the film, "Hindenburg" (1975). Today, re-registered as G-AWHE and owned by Spitfire, Ltd, operating from Duxford.

Hispano HA.1112M1L Buchon C.4K-61/G-AWHF. Acquired by the Confederate Air Force, Harlington, US registration not issued. Ground looped at Duxford on 15th June 1968, registration G-AWHF cancelled on 30th June when the aircraft was declared permanently withdrawn from use.

Hispano HA.1112M1L Buchon C.4K-75/G-AWHG. One of three Buchons converted into P-51B Mustangs ('Messerstangs') for the film, "Patton" (1970). Withdrawn after suffering a take off accident at Le Havre in February 1969. Sold in the USA, registered as N3109. Today, converted into Messerschmitt Bf.109G-4 configuration with Daimler-Benz DB.605 engine and registered D-FWME, owned by the Messerschmitt Stiftung in Germany and sponsored by EADS.

Hispano HA.1112M1L Buchon C.4K-105/G-AWHH. Acquired by Wilson 'Connie' Edwards, stored at Big Springs, Texas, registered as N6036. Purchased by Richard Hansen, Batavia, Illinois.

Hispano HA.1112M1L Buchon C.4K-106/G-AWHI. Acquired by Wilson 'Connie' Edwards, stored at Big Springs, Texas, registered as N90607.

Hispano HA.1112M1L Buchon C.4K-100/G-AWHJ. Displayed in Kalamazoo Aviation History Museum, Portage, Michigan, registered as N76GE.

Hispano HA.1112M1L Buchon C.4K-102/G-AWHK. Acquired by Wilson 'Connie' Edwards, originally registered as N9938, then went on static display in Detroit with the Confederate Air Force, re-registered as N109W. Today, owned by Historic Flying, Ltd, as G-BWUE at Duxford, and operated by the Aircraft Restoration Company.

Hispano HA.1112M1L Buchon C.4K-122/G-AWHL. Another 'Messerstang' conversion for "Patton", which was not proceeded with in the film. Originally displayed with the Champlin Fighter Museum, registered as N109J, and fitted with Daimler-Benz DB.601 engine to convert it into Messerschmitt Bf.109E-3 configuration. Today, displayed in Museum of Flight in Seattle, Washington.

Hispano HA.1112M1L Buchon C.4K-99/G-AWHM. Acquired by Wilson 'Connie' Edwards, stored at Big Springs, Texas, registered as N90604.

Hispano HA.1112M1L Buchon C.4K-130/G-AWHN. Acquired by Wilson 'Connie' Edwards and registered as N90602. Today, displayed at the Tillamook Naval Air Station Museum, Oregon.

Hispano HA.1112M1L Buchon C.4K-127/G-AWHO. Acquired by Wilson 'Connie' Edwards who donated the Buchon in 1979 to the EAA AirVenture Museum at Oshkosh, Wisconsin, where it is displayed today, registered as N109BF.

Hispano HA.1112M1L Buchon C.4K-144/G-AWHP. Acquired by the Confederate Air Force, Harlington, registered as N8575. Destroyed in fatal air accident on 19th December 1987.

Hispano HA.1112M1L Buchon C.4K-152/G-AWHR. Acquired by Wilson 'Connie' Edwards, stored at Big Springs, Texas, registered as N4109G.

Hispano HA.1112M1L Buchon C.4K-170/G-AWHS. The third abortive 'Messerstang' for the "Patton" film. Today, exhibited in the Auto und Technik Museum, Sinsheim, Germany, converted into Messerschmitt Bf.109G-6 configuration.

Hispano HA.1112M1L Buchon C.4K-169/G-AWHT. Acquired by the Confederate Air Force, based at Lancaster Airport, Texas, and registered as N9939. Struck the ground during Airsho 76 at Harlingen and grounded. Restored and re-registered as N109W, displayed at Castle Air Force Base, California. Today, active with the Air Fighter Academy of Heringsdorf, Germany, as D-FMVS, and maintained by MeierMotors at Bremgarten. Advertised for sale.

Hispano HA.1112M4K Buchon C.4K-112/G-AWHC. Two-seat Buchon used as camera-ship for the film. Acquired by Wilson 'Connie' Edwards, stored at Big Springs, Texas, and registered as N1109G.

Ten more Buchons were brought into use, six as taxyers at Tablada and four as spares sources at Henlow. They were:

Hispano HA.1112M1L Buchon C.4K-30, spares at Henlow
Hispano HA.1112M1L Buchon C.4K-107, taxyer at Tablada
Hispano HA.1112M1L Buchon C.4K-114, spares at Henlow
Hispano HA.1112M1L Buchon C.4K-121, taxyer at Tablada
Hispano HA.1112M1L Buchon C.4K-131, taxyer at Tablada
Hispano HA.1112M1L Buchon C.4K-134, taxyer at Tablada
Hispano HA.1112M1L Buchon C.4K-135, taxyer at Tablada
Hispano HA.1112M1L Buchon C.4K-154, spares at Henlow
Hispano HA.1112M1L Buchon C.4K-172, taxyer at Tablada
Hispano HA.1112M1L Buchon C.4K-111, spares at Henlow
and cockpit shots at Pinewood Studios.

The six taxyers were subsequently used in the Italian 'take' on the Battle of Britain, "Eagles Over London" (1969), the review of which appears next. They were then shipped to the Victory Air Museum at Mundelein, Chicago, and left outside in all weathers for years to follow. Several were later sold in the Seventies. It was in Buchon C.4K-107, registered as G-BOML with the Old Flying Machine Company, that Mark Hanna suffered his fatal accident at Sabadell, Spain, in September 1999.

In addition, Pinewood Studios set up an aircraft production line at its Iver, Buckinghamshire, base, turning out full-scale facsimiles of Hawker Hurricanes, Vickers Supermarine Spitfires and Messerschmitt Bf.109s produced from fibre-glass moulds for set-dressing on airfields. An unspecified number of the facsimile Hurricanes and Spitfires were blown up in airfield attack scenes. Some were taxyable, powered by lawnmower engines. The Spitfire facsimiles could, if not handled properly, easily tip up onto their noses, which happened several times. According to a documentary on the 'Definitive Edition' DVD's Special Features disc, it was these taxyable faxsimiles which the actors used, not the real aircraft as has been claimed.

Most of the facsimiles that survived the production have been found homes, as detailed below with the serials and/or codes they carried (note - in some cases, more than one facsimile carried the same serial and codes).

Hawker Hurricane F/S facsimiles, believed modelled on Hurricane Mk.IIc   LF751 as pattern aircraft:

H3246, re-serialled as P3975 - Midland Air Museum

L1592/KW-Z - Kent Battle of Britain Museum

L1592/KW-Z - Torbay Aircraft Museum

P3059 - N/K

P3059/SD-N - Kent Battle of Britain Museum

V7467 - Midland Air Museum

V7767, re-serialled as V6799 - Jet Age Museum

Unid. (P3059 ?) - Omaka Aviation Heritage Centre, NZ

Vickers Supermarine Spitfire F/S facsimiles, believed modelled on Spitfire F.Vb BM597 as pattern aircraft:

N3289/DW-K - Kent Battle of Britain Museum

N3289/QV-K   N/K

N3313/BO-D - Kent Battle of Britain Museum

N3313/BO-D - Norfolk & Suffolk Aviation Museum

P8140/ZF-K - Norfolk & Suffolk Aviation Museum

P9340/KL-B - Norfolk & Suffolk Aviation Museum

MH314, re-serialled N3313 - Torbay Aircraft Museum

Messerschmitt Bf.109 F/S facsimiles, believed modelled on Messerschmitt Bf.109G-2 10639 but not used due to their incompatibility with HA.1112M1Ls:

14 - Kent Battle of Britain Museum

14/KM+JI - Midland Air Museum

1480/6 - Kent Battle of Britain Museum

1480/6   N/K

6357 - Torbay Aircraft Museum

6357/6 - Kent Battle of Britain Museum

Finally, Pinewood Studios' art department produced a substantial number of scale radio-controlled model Spitfires, Heinkel He.111Hs in CASA 2.111D configuration, and, unique for "Battle of Britain", Junkers Ju.87 Stuka dive bombers.

Spitfire F.Vb BM597 is believed to have been the pattern aircraft for the R/C Spitfires, while one of the two CASA 2.111Ds purchased by Spitfire Productions is considered to have done likewise for the R/C He.111Hs. However, for the R/C Stukas there could only be one candidate example of the real thing that the art department could have access to as a pattern aircraft: Junkers Ju.87G-2 Werke Nr 494083, coded RI+JK, with the Axis Aircraft Collection that was part of the Air Historical Branch's fleet stored at RAF St Athan. This was, and still is, one of only two complete Ju.87 Stuka dive bombers preserved anywhere in the world: the other example is Ju.87B-2/Trop Werke Nr 5954, A5+HL, in the Chicago Museum of Science & Industry, Illinois.

The original plan was to actually restore Ju.87G-2 Stuka RI+JK to flying condition for the film. It and other captured Axis aircraft were transferred to RAF Henlow by March 1967. Viv Bellamy is described in the RAF Museum's Individual History for this Stuka as starting the engine on the third pull. However, a full inspection of the airframe revealed that, although the aircraft was in immaculate condition, restoration to flight would take too long and would be too costly. The alternative, and sensibly abandoned, plan to convert three Percival Proctors into 'Proctukas' has long since passed into aviation folk lore.

One problem was that Ju.87G-2 Stuka RI+JK was a model too late for the Battle of Britain period. It actually was a converted specimen, having begun life somewhere between 1943 - '44 as a Ju.87D-5 ground-attack variant, Werke Nr 2883, but was at some point later modified into Ju.87G-2 configuration with underwing mounting points for two 37mm Bk37 cannon. This conversion would have been when it acquired its 494083 Werke Nummer. The art department had gone as far as fitting dummy wooden dive brakes, 'Horns of Jericho' sirens, a fibreglass bomb and a modified rear gun position before the decision was taken not to proceed with the restoration to flight condition. The Stuka had even received its film 'wardrobe', having been repainted with the correct camouflage scheme for the 1940 period of the European Theater and given the codes of W8+A, those of an actual Ju.87 unit in Europe during the Battle of Britain. Several different individual identifier letters would have been added after the 'A' at different times, so that Ju.87G-2 W8+A could have portrayed more than one Stuka.

Having Stukas appear in war films has posed serious challenges for movie productions. The simplest way, if the film was in black-and-white, was to use wartime archive footage of Stukas, although this led to difference in contrast in imagery which all too often defeated the object, as seen in "Dunkirk" (1958). We have seen how the production team for "The Guns of Navarone" (1961) got round the problem with a mix of studio miniatures, real stand-in aircraft and art work. Besides "Battle of Britain", the only other colour film production to attempt to create Stukas has been "Captain Corelli's Mandolin" (2001), 32 years into the future, which was able to exploit computer graphics Special FX that did not exist in 1968.

"Battle of Britain" is the only film to have actual flying Stukas. They are, of course, R/C models. The pity of it is that they obviously are R/C models, flying and manoeuvring unrealistically too fast in relation to size and scale for the real thing. When R/C models have been used in other films, their imagery has usually been reproduced in slower motion, which gives a more realistic effect; it is a puzzle as to why the film editors here did not do the same. The R/C Stukas were able to release bombs when they attack the Chain Home RDF sites, but not in vertical dives, so more of the realism is lost here. They do blow up in mid-air effectively: the Pinewood Studios SFX team had learnt the art of making model aircraft blow up realistically on the James Bond films.

One Stuka, however, is not an R/C model. It is a large-scale miniature and exact reproduction of Ju.87G-2 RI+JK itself. It appears in the final act of the attack on the Dover Chain Home RDF site, as a crippled Stuka making its death plunge right into a hut beside the RDF mast. Freeze-frame analysis shows that the art department have fashioned this Stuka as a perfect imitation of a Ju.87G-2, using RI+JK as the pattern aircraft and with the code W8+FR clearly applied. They have copied the slightly lengthened nose section of this variant and particularly its late model rounded cockpit cabin, instead of the rectangular oblong of the early model Stukas used in the actual Battle. As such, this means that Ju.87G-2 Stuka RI+JK can be credited as appearing in "Battle of Britain", as its full likeness is clearly displayed on screen depicting W8+FR in its death dive.

The author is not going to give the game away as to how this crash sequence was achieved, but instead invites the reader to study the film themselves to discover the trick involved. There is, though, a goof in this sequence: the crashing Stuka is first seen as an R/C model trailing smoke in a dive; then a close-up of the pilot and rear gunner in the cockpit, staring in horror before impact; next, the ground filmed rushing up at them from their perspective; then, finally, the complete Stuka smashing into the hut beside the mast and exploding most satisfactorily. But the goof is that the shot from the cockpit as the stricken Stuka hurtles down shows the same aircraft already on the ground and burning! Quite why the art department and film editor made this goof, only they know.

Despite the huge effort by all involved, "Battle of Britain" suffered at the box office after its release in 1969, being criticised by a non-aviation audience for being too repetitive in having so many air battles; was too British for an international audience, and thus was of insufficient interest for US movie-goers (there are no Americans in it); while the Sixties Generation was decidedly anti-war (thanks to what was happening in Vietnam at the time), who mostly shunned it. The film was also spanked by the critics for having too many stereotypical 'RAF types' in it and was considered to be too vast a subject for a satisfactory production to be made.

However, since its re-release on DVD in 2004, the 'Definitive Edition' of "Battle of Britain" has helped the film find a new and genuinely interested audience in the 21st Century. "Battle of Britain" can claim to be the inspiration behind the large-scale war epics of the Seventies featuring World War Two warbird types, such as "Patton" (1970), "A Bridge Too Far" (1977), and most especially "Tora! Tora! Tora!" (1970), the worthy predecessor to the risible "Pearl Harbor" (2001) which uses (without admitting it) out-takes from both "Tora!" and "Battle of Britain". It is to this film's credit that so many out-takes from it have since been used in other film productions and TV programmes. Finally, Spitfire Productions can justifiably claim that their restoration of so many Spitfires and Buchons in the Sixties led to the historic aircraft preservation movement in the UK taking root, to the level at which it exists today with so many superb examples of warbirds in full flying condition.

EAGLES OVER LONDON (LA BATTAGLIA D'INGHILTERRA)

(Released: September 1969, Italy) International 'British' war film.

Extraordinary to say, and unknown outside of Italy at the time, this Italian 'take' on the Battle of Britain was released to the cinema in that country just five days after the premier of "Battle of Britain" at London Leicester Square. Its existence as a film production remained unknown to British cinema audiences because it never got a release in the UK, and only hit American screens in 1973 as "Battle Command". The reason is that "Battle of Britain" director Guy Hamilton allegedly warned Italian film director Enzo G Castellari and producer Edmondo Amati that legal action could follow if it appeared they were trying to capitalise on the (hoped for) success of the British epic by releasing their version at the same time. The film fell completely out of sight

soon afterwards, except in Italy where it was the highest grossing Italian movie in 1969 - 1970, until it appeared on DVD in 2009.

"Eagles Over London" belongs in a genre of film productions of the Sixties and Seventies known, part-mockingly, part-affectionately, as 'Macaroni Combat' war films. They existed alongside the widely popular 'Spaghetti Westerns' and 'Sword and Sandal' films of the same era, all of them Italian productions which often had Spanish and French involvement as well. Many are unashamed exploitations of the themes explored in successful large-scale war movies, such as "The Dirty Dozen" (1967), of which Castellari's "Inglorious Bastards" (1978) is a prime example.

It has to be stated that "Eagles Over London" has its own plot and storyline that differs markedly from Hamilton's production. Historical accuracy is not a requirement for Amati and Castellari. Rather, they follow the established 'Macaroni Combat' genre in having fanciful and overly-dramatic sub-plots set against the backdrop of actual historic events, with two-dimensional characters playing out a variety of shoot and chase action scenarios. In "Eagles Over London", a crack German Kommando unit shoots up a patrol of British troops in France, steals their uniforms and IDs, then mingles with the thousands of soldiers escaping from Dunkirk, with the aim of infiltrating London society and setting about their mission to destroy Britain's defensive chain of radar sites, as a prelude to invasion by the Wehrmacht. All this takes place as the Battle of Britain, or La Battaglia d'Inghilterra (incorrectly, the Battle of England), rages overhead London.

Castellari and his script writing team (ten of them, would you believe?) don't allow any inhibitions to spoil their imagination as to how they want to re-create the Battle of Britain. The Luftwaffe launches a Thousand Bomber Raid on London at night. Square-jawed American actor Van Johnson, in an as unrealistic a portrayal of an RAF Air Marshall as can be dared, personally leads the fight against the Germans in his own Spitfire, calling on all British fighters to meet over London to defeat the raid: "Send everything that can fly. Hurry it up, or there'll be no more England!".

Frederick Stafford, playing handsome British all-action hero, Captain Paul Stevens, is actually an Austrian-born actor who gave himself an English-sounding name. Having an Austrian play a British wartime hero is not the only reversal of logic that Castellari indulges in here. Stafford finds time to become romantically entangled with glamorous Italian actress, Ida Galli, who does wonders for a WAAF uniform. Best of all is Italian actor Renzo Palmer (he also adopted an English last name), dubbed as a Cockney British Army Sergeant with a penchant for punching French naval officers and who just seems to pop up all over London whenever the action demands.

Some of the most spectacular action sequences in the film are Castellari's re-creations of British troops retreating to Dunkirk and being strafed and bombed on the beaches by Luftwaffe fighters. As seen before, the trusty T-6 Texan is called into action to portray the German aircraft, there being no adequate substitute (Messerschmitt Bf.108s not being called upon here). As the Dunkirk scenes were shot in Spain and the Ejercito del Aire (EdA) was lending support to the production, the question could reasonably be asked as to why EdA Hispano HA.1112 Buchons were not used to act as the Luftwaffe fighters, as they had recently done for "Battle of Britain". The answer appears later in the film, and in a way the viewer would literally not expect to see.

Three North American T-6C Texan trainers of the EdA, painted nearly all-over dark grey but with light grey undersides and bearing German Balkenkreuzen and Swastikas, act the role of the attacking fighter-bombers. They make repeated low-level runs in 'Vic' formation over large numbers of extras in British Army uniforms amid various stranded trucks, with plenty of explosions and machine gun fire spraying across the sand. As a depiction of Dunkirk, it is impressively spectacular on an almost "The Longest Day"-size scale. Castellari certainly has an eye for staging major set-pieces.

The reason why no HA.1112 Buchons were called upon to act as Luftwaffe fighters is revealed when the first German air raids approach the southern English coastline. RAF fighter pilots 'Scramble' to board their Spitfires. Spitfires? Correction, Spanish Buchons painted in RAF markings to act as Spitfires! A panoramic shot over a very Spanish-looking airfield shows what appear to be 15 Hispanic HA.1112M1L Buchon fighters in RAF camouflage and roundels awaiting their pilots running towards them. The sight of the Spanish variant of the Messerschmitt Bf.109 portraying Spitfires must be the wackiest goof of all war films. Another shot shows bombs on racks in front of the 'Spitons' or 'Buchfires'!

Of these 15 Buchons, five are actually seen starting engines and taxiing out amid clouds of un-English-like dust. At no time are they seen getting airborne. These five Buchons are among the same grounded taxyers used as extras at Tablada for "Battle of Britain", and Tablada is almost certainly the same airfield used here in "Eagles Over London". A later shot reveals that the remaining ten Buchons, all seen filmed at a distance in the background, are matte art work creations matched with the images on screen.

A particular feature of Castellari's work in this film is his use of split-screen imagery on what some might regard as an excessive scale. Split-screen became very much in vogue in films during the Sixties: it involves the picture on the screen being divided into two, three or even four segments, each showing different elements of the same scene or of two scenes portrayed in unison with each other. Castellari uses split-screen to show the 'Buchfires' taxiing, divided with wartime archive footage of nine Vickers Supermarine Spitfire Mk.Is taking off in formation in three 'Vics'. Squadron codes are not visible on these Spitfires, which are partially obscured by Castellari's decision to superimpose a close-up of the fuselage roundel and fake code letters of one of the 'Buchfires' over them.

The approaching masses of German bombers and the formations of RAF fighters sent up to intercept them are depicted on matte backgrounds. A high ranking German officer, who is presumably meant to be Generalfeldmarschall Wilhelm Keitel, announces the start of Operation Marine Lion (sic). German bombers are seen flying with studio miniature Spitfires painted in Luftwaffe markings as escorts. Pardon!? What was going on in Castellari's mind, or just how confused was his art department team? The Luftwaffe bomb London at night (it seems they didn't bother attacking RAF Fighter Command's airfields). Castellari again resorts to split-screen tactics and includes among them an

out-take of a Short Stirling miniature from "School for Secrets" (1946) portraying a German bomber - what can you say. The attack by the German Kommandos on what Castellari imagines a Chain Home RDF site looked like - inside Portsmouth harbour (!) - further illustrates the fluidity of his imagination.

The air battle over the English Channel has to be one of the most comical depictions of a dog-fight in any war film. Those studio miniature Luftwaffe Spitfires just keep coming and coming. Ridiculously obvious models of burning fighters go splash into a tank of water representing the Channel. Again, split-screen appears, with an unusually cheerful pilot grinning in his cockpit on one side while the familiar archive shot of Junkers Ju.87 Stuka GU+AC breaking off from the camera aircraft appears on the other. This is followed by that of another Junkers Ju.87 Stuka doing likewise, only it has the letters 'K' on the undersides of either wing tip, while a bomb under the fuselage and two smaller ones under each wing are clearly visible. Then a third archive shot appears of three Ju.87 Stukas in a shallow dive, filmed from a distance.

Archive imagery of British fighters follow. Two early Marque Vickers Supermarine Spitfires are seen head-on in silhouette, followed by blue tainted imagery of a Spitfire Mk.II filmed air-air and close-up breaking into a dive while accompanied by a distinctly un-Merlin-like engine sound. At least these Spitfires appear to be British! Split-screen again, of a pilot in his obviously Buchon cockpit firing his obviously Buchon cannon, while the other image is archive gun-camera material of a Messerschmitt Me.410 receiving tracer fire in its port engine. Familiar US Navy archive imagery of an unidentifiable Japanese fighter-bomber spiralling down amid flak bursts and breaking up appears next, in split-screen shown in four segments. Likewise, that is followed by four segments of archive footage of the Westland Lysander seen before in "Eagle Squadron" (1942), wings vertical to the sea, striking the water and cartwheeling in. Then more US Navy wartime footage of what looks like a Japanese Nakajima Ki-84 Hayate fighter rolling violently down, port wing aflame, followed by that of another Ki-84 Hayate plunging vertically into the sea and detonating so massively that its bomb load must have been still under its wings.

This mix-up of archive imagery from various sources shows that Castellari had scant regard for accuracy, only for effect.

The film builds to its climax with the Thousand Bomber Raid on London. For the first time in the film do we see Heinkel He.111 bombers. These, of course, are EdA CASA 2.111D bomber/target-tugs, the same that were used in "Battle of Britain". Three are seen taxiing, painted in completely inaccurate Luftwaffe markings, confirming that their much more accurate colour schemes used in the previous film had been removed by the time Castellari showed up. More are seen parked on the grass beside quite expansive taxyways, presumably at Tablada. The total number of them is difficult to count because they are only seen in the distance, while the imagery has been darkened in the editing suite to create a day-for-night scene.

This scene is not what it appears. Only four out of the total of what look like Heinkel He.111s are real. The three CASA 2.111Ds seen taxiing do so from a dedicated parking ramp. A fourth CASA 2.111D is seen parked on the grass beyond them, probably a redundant airframe as it appears to have canvas covers over it and is not painted in spurious Luftwaffe colours. As the three 'He.111s' move out they pass what appear to be many more of their kind parked on the grass opposite them. These are fakes. The closest to them as they pass is another He.111, but painted with different markings. Behind it, and parked in serried ranks of three each, are row upon row of Ju.87 Stukas. But they, and the He.111 in front of them, are not there in reality - they are all matte art work, moulded on to the imagery of what is meant to be the start of the Luftwaffe bomber armada against London. However, the art department artist has got his perspective wrong in terms of size: the 'Stukas' are gigantic compared with the real thing, almost the same size as the He.111s!

So, in reality three CASA 2.111Ds were used in "Eagles Over London", with a fourth as a backdrop. None of them are seen flying, only starting engines and taxiing. Also, in one shot of the bomber crews running to their aircraft, a line of nine North American T-6C/T-6D Texan trainers can be seen parked in the background on the grass where the 'Stukas' are meant to be, all in their EdA silver/yellow colour scheme.

In total, then, the EdA contributed five Hispano HA.1112M1L Buchon fighters, three CASA 2.111D bomber/target-tugs, and three North American T-6C Texan trainers to "Eagles Over London", to act the roles of RAF Fighter Command Spitfires and of the Luftwaffe bombing London and the Dunkirk beachhead.

This was a profitable period for the EdA. Not only had they done well out of providing and selling so many Buchons and CASA 2.111Ds in 1968 to Spitfire Productions, Ltd, for "Battle of Britain", but they had followed this up in 1969 by supplying the above number of their aircraft for "Eagles Over London". On top of that, they also provided six T-6 Texans acting as USAAF P-47 Thunderbolts and three CASA 2.111Ds as Heinkel He.111s - possibly the same three CASA 2.111Ds - for the 20th Century Fox epic, "Patton" (1970), which was in production in Spain at the same time.

For the climactic air battle over London, Castellari again mixes archive imagery with his singular use of studio miniature Spitfires and Messerschmitts, and again, some of those treacherous Spitfires have swapped sides. Or has Reichmarschall Goering acceded to General Adolf Galland's alleged request for "a squadron of Spitfires"?

Archive footage of a Spitfire wholly silhouetted and with the clouds behind it tainted blue breaks away from the camera aircraft. This is followed by two Spitfire Mk.Is peeling off against blue tainted clouds, the closest to the camera having the code identifier of 'Q' - almost certainly they are Spitfire Mk.Ia R6627/LO-E and Spitfire Mk.Ia and X4829/LO-Q of No.602 (City of Glasgow) Squadron, as seen in "A Yank in the R.A.F." (1941). Then seven Spitfires peeling off one after the other in the classic attack method devised by RAF Fighter Command during the Battle of Britain, again against a very blue tainted background; the reason for this is that Castellari is having the dog-fight take place at night, which, of course, never happened in the real Battle.

Split-screen again, this time with archive footage of a real Heinkel He.111 unloading its bombs. Due to the heavily tainted blue screen, its codes are not readable. This is followed immediately by another He.111 unloading its bombs. Stukas making dive attacks are surprisingly effective studio art work creations.

When Stafford and Palmer foil the German Kommandos' attack on RAF Uxbridge (yes, there is no limit to Castellari's imagination), London is saved, and with it England, although Air Marshall Van Johnson dies a hero's death in his Spitfire.

It would be easy to dismiss "Eagles Over London" as rank foolishness, the product of an over-imaginative film director and his producer who turn the Battle of Britain into a melodramatic escapade. In fact, in their own way, Castellari and Amati are quite reverential in their treatment of the real gigantic struggle during the summer of 1940. Some critics speculate that Italian fantasy war films of this kind are the product of a nation that was trying to find some way to place itself on the right side of history, following its own less than admirable alliance with Fascism. Whether this is true or not, it is better to view "Eagles Over London" as entertainment, not as an attempt to re-enact war as it happened. But, Oh, those Luftwaffe Spitfires!

HELL BOATS

(Released: March 1970)

"Hell Boats" was the fifth in the series of six war films released by the Anglo-American Oakmont Productions company. It follows the same format as the other five films produced between 1967 - 1969, relying on actors whose careers were mostly achieved in television series on both sides of the Atlantic and on plots that have characters at odds with each other while taking on almost impossible missions. "Hell Boats" joins Oakmont's "Attack on the Iron Coast" (1968), "Submarine X-1" (1969) and "The Last Escape" (1970) in having an American lead actor commanding British forces undertaking a desperate mission against the odds (the two exceptions were "Mosquito Squadron, 1968, which had an all-British cast, and "The 1,000 Plane Raid", 1969, which was almost all-American). In this case, the American lead is familiar Sixties/Seventies US TV series performer, James Franciscus, acting the role of Lieutenant Commander Jeffords, RNVR, commander of a Royal Navy motor torpedo boat (MTB) squadron.

"Hell Boats" also follows Oakmont's style in having an American film director, again with a pedigree mostly in television, directing a British cast and crew. Paul Wendkos was the man in charge: he also directed "Attack on the Iron Coast", which may explain the similarity between the two films, as both have as their focal point of action an attack by British gunboats on a seemingly impregnable German seaport. At least the SFX miniature MTBs and E-Boats in "Hell Boats" are a significant advance in quality over those used in the other film.

Again, typical of Oakmont's style, the characters in the story are one-dimensional and stereotypically obvious. Historical fact is disposed of when it becomes inconvenient to the plot: no American ever commanded British MTBs in World War Two and if a US Navy officer ever did serve aboard one, he would have done so in an observer's capacity, learning Royal Navy MTB tactics to compare with those used by the USN's PT Boat fleets. The way the MTB crew are portrayed in the film is inaccurate as well: instead of being upright and correct, MTB officers and men were the most piratical in character and lifestyle of all Royal Navy seamen, due to the high speed, high risk nature of the kind of warfare they were involved in.

The actual "Hell Boats" themselves are the real stars of the film. Fans of all things nautical will enjoy seeing the three fast boats in action. The irony of it is that the 'MTBs' in the film are not MTBs at all; they distinctly don't carry torpedoes! They have much more the characteristics of Harbour Defence Motor Launches. Whether they were still in service with the Royal Navy in 1968 when the film was made, or were loaned from another source, is not known. The MTB had long gone out of service at this time. Adding to the irony is that the German 'E-Boat' in the film does have torpedo launch tubes, which actual E-Boats (Enemy-Boats) did not have in World War Two. This particular craft is a noticeably more substantial beast than its three co-stars, but, again, its progeny is not known.

Probably the most fascinating feature of "Hell Boats" is that it was filmed entirely on Malta. Anyone who is familiar with and fond of this famous Mediterranean island nation will welcome "Hell Boats" as an opportunity to compare Malta of the late Sixties with Malta in the early 21st Century, the imposing bastions of Valletta serving as an impressive backdrop to a good portion of the action.

The naval historian will be fascinated to observe that the MTB base on Malta is actually the former wartime Royal Navy facility, HMS Phoenicia, on Manoel Island in Sliema Creek, from where British submarines operated in World War Two. The dominating feature of Manoel Island is the imposing 18th Century Fort Manoel, in which HMS Phoenicia had its barracks. The fort and the island were handed over to the Maltese Government in February 1965. Judging by the appearance of the fortifications and their huge internal chambers, as seen in "Hell Boats", Fort Manoel was still in good condition in 1968 three years after the Royal Navy had left. It didn't stay that way; over the next three decades, Fort Manoel fell into a serious state of neglect. However, by the start of the second decade of the 21st Century a great deal of the fort has been carefully restored.

What of aviation in "Hell Boats"? Disappointingly, for a film about World War Two on Malta, there isn't much. What is seen occurs in the early part of the film, when Jeffords flies from Britain to Malta aboard an RAF Dakota. Technically, this is inaccurate; the Douglas C-47 Dakota was in service with the RAF in the summer of 1942, the period that the plot of "Hell Boats" covers, but it was not risked in the air supply of Malta - that all-too-often parlous duty fell to the aircrew of Short Sunderland flying boats or converted Vickers Wellington bombers.

Typical of Oakmont's production values were that in all its six films, actors maintained the fashions of the Sixties even though they were too modern for the wartime Forties. This is amusingly illustrated in "Hell Boats" when, as Jeffords and other servicemen aboard the Dakota are nearing Malta, a female WAAF in smart, tightly fitting uniform and neatly cut hairstyle under her cap, suddenly stands up and, in the precise, middle-class tones of a very professional air stewardess, asks, "Can I have your attention, please".

Then, as if she is addressing the passengers of a modern airliner, she says, "We arrive in Malta in 20 minutes. As you know, the Luftwaffe bases on Sicily are only a few minutes flying time from Malta. They'll be waiting to strafe the airfield when we touch down". Franciscus as Jeffords and the other servicemen watch and listen attentively to her as if she was informing them that the seat belt lights were on and that the toilets may no longer be used until the aircraft has landed - this scene deserves to have come straight from the spoof movie, "Airline" (1980)!

"We have a special procedure for coping with this", the WAAF stewardess goes on in her clipped accent. "As soon as the 'plane stops rolling, all exit doors will be turned open. You'll de-plane as fast as you can and make for the blast shelters alongside the runway. Remain there until the All Clear. One final matter, the motors will not be stopped while we are on the ground. Try to avoid running into the propellers, we will need them after you are gone".

Surely the director Wendkos and the scriptwriting team had their tongues fully in their collective cheeks when they came up with this scene!

As the WAAF speaks, the shots of her are intercut with the Dakota landing at what is meant to be Malta and the passengers on board de-planing amid attacks by Stukas. This scenario is achieved first with footage of a USAF Douglas C-47 Skytrain landing. The action is meant to be taking place at night on Malta, so the imagery of the C-47 is darkened, but not sufficiently for the USAF 'Star-and-Bar' to be invisible on the rear fuselage - obviously it was a goof by the film editor to use film of a USAF C-47 Skytrain to represent an RAF Dakota.

The footage shows the C-47 Skytrain filmed abreast the runway threshold as it lands on. Despite the 'day-for-night' darkening, leafless trees can be seen in the background, showing that the C-47 was filmed somewhere in winter. What is seen of the airfield, which is not much, does not have the appearance of a US-style air base, although it could have been a USAF base in Europe. It would have to be footage shot in the Fifties, as the C-47 has what appears to be the Military Air Transport Service (MATS) band of that period around the top of its tail fin. It also has the code letters 'SN' in white on its forward fuselage, which was difficult to detect at first because the editor has made another goof in showing the footage in reverse, meaning that a mirror had to be used to read the codes.

However, when the Dakota is seen rolling out on what is meant to be the runway of RAF Luqa, RAF Safi or RAF Ta'Qali, a different C-47 is used. The 'SN' code letters are clearly not in place. The scene is again meant to be taking place at night on Malta, so this particular C-47 is very darkened in the shot; but it appears to be painted in a very dark scheme anyway, meaning that no markings of any kind are visible upon it, thus rendering identifying it impossible to achieve.

The background is visible and has a very English countryside look about it. From the lie of the land, it bears quite a strong similarity with the terrain in Wiltshire. The C-47 is rolling out on a perimeter track, not a runway, with sand bags making up blast pens close by. Smoke billows around from simulated bomb blasts. It could be that this scene was filmed at Wroughton Airfield, or even at the A&AEE Boscombe Down, both in Wiltshire. Even so, this does not aid us in identifying this C-47 which has a distinctive feature of what appears to be a small glazed tip to its nose, housing a strobe light, perhaps. As this scene is undoubtedly filmed in England, the C-47 is unquestionably a Douglas C-47 Dakota, but that is as much as we know.

The editor uses archive footage of three Junkers Ju.87 Stukas heading straight for the camera to depict the Luftwaffe's attack as the Dakota's passengers run for the blast pens. He has darkened the imagery and tainted it blue to create the effect of the Stukas attacking at night. In fact, the Stukageschwader rarely made night attacks because having clear sight of their targets was essential for their success. The three Stukas shown are noteworthy in being completely 'clean', ie, no weaponry or stores of any kind carried. Possibly this is footage of Stukas filmed for promotional or propaganda purposes.

It is followed by archive footage of three more - or the same three - Junkers Ju.87 Stukas hurtling past the camera. They, too, are 'clean'. This same footage was used in "Dunkirk" (1958) and has also been tainted blue for "Hell Boats". It is used twice by the editor, the second time reversed so that the Stukas hurtle by in the opposite direction. They are the last aircraft to be seen in "Hell Boats".

THE LAST ESCAPE

(Released: May 1970, USA)

Released in the USA as "The O S S" (quite why, as the OSS gets no mention in the plot), this is the last of the six Oakmont Productions war films and arguably the worst of them. The acting, even by experienced American leading man, Stuart Whitman, is shockingly amateur and one dimensional, the direction is stilted and uninspired, and there is a shameless use of out-takes of aircraft from other Mirisch Films and MGM productions.

The plot has a team of British Commandos in Wehrmacht uniforms, led, of course, by an American parachuted into Bavaria close to the end of the War, to kidnap a German rocket scientist before the Russians can get to him. A poor piece of archive film of a Consolidated B-24 Liberator is used first to portray the aircraft from which they are to jump. Then a colour-tinted out-take of the Lockheed Hudson miniature from the Ronald Reagan early Forties Hollywood vehicle, "International Squadron" (1941), is used for some strange reason. The Liberator archive shot re-appears next, with two parachutes drifting away from it before out-takes of Paratroopers descending from "Against The Wind" (1948) and "The Red Beret" (1953) supplant it.

Most egregious of all are the out-takes of the three Mirisch-owned de Havilland Mosquito TT.35s (G-ASKA/RS709, G-ASKB/RS712 and G-ASKC/TA719) from "633 Squadron" (1964), shown in reverse and dubbed with totally unrepresentative engine sounds, for a bombing attack on the German rocket research site. Mixed in with this are reversed out-takes of the five Lockheed Hudsons used as RAF bombers in "A Yank in the R.A.F." (1941), an extraordinary inclusion by the film editor. More outrage is caused by the reversed out-takes of Mosquito TT.35s RS718 and TA724 being destroyed in "633 Squadron", to simulate Mosquitos being shot down during the attack on the rocket site. Even "Mosquito Squadron" (1969) is raided for out-takes of studio miniature Mosquitos dropping bombs.

The robbing of out-takes from other films doesn't end there. The Commandos have arranged to be picked up by an RAF Lancaster. Simulating this is unused footage of Avro Lancaster B.I PA474, then of the Air Historical Branch collection at Wroughton, filmed approaching to land for the scene in "Operation Crossbow" (1965) of a Lancaster returning to base after the raid on Peenemunde. However, the Lancaster is attacked and shot down by Luftwaffe fighters just before it lands to pick up the Commandos. Once again out-takes of the two Nord 1002 Pinguoin F-BFYX and F-BGVU from "633 Squadron", acting as Messerschmitt Bf.109s, are called upon to depict the Luftwaffe fighters. The Lancaster being shot down is one of the studio miniature Mosquitos being blown up in the air battle at the end of "633 Squadron".

Probably, Oakmont thought it was getting good value for money through the use of all these out-takes, never mind whether the audience were convinced by them or not. "The Last Escape" is the last we shall see of Oakmont Productions, and, as this film unashamedly shows, this decidedly limited film production company saved the worst till last.

TOO LATE THE HERO

(Released: May 1970, USA)

An unusual anti-war film directed by tough US filmmaker, Robert Aldrich. It is said that the film's message was aimed as a protest against the Vietnam War taking place at the time, and apparently came from an unpublished story written by one of Aldrich's co-writers. Despite the alleged anti-Vietnam War message, the theme is very much about a disparate group of British troops occupying one half of an island in the New Hebrides Islands (today, Vanuatu in the South Pacific) while the Japanese occupy the other half. Aldrich wrote much of the screenplay himself, and came up with a very credible English and Scottish script; the inference has been made that he created a British theme to a tropical jungle war story to disguise his anti-Vietnam War message, otherwise the studio, ABC Pictures Corp, would have withdrawn its backing if he had tried to use an American anti-war theme.

Aldrich also drew on British war films set in South-East Asia that he admired, such as "The Bridge on the River Kwai" (1957) and "The Long, and the Short, and the Tall" (1961). He reprised the sub-plot of "Kwai" in having a skiving, amoral US Navy officer (Cliff Robertson) sent against his will on a mission with British troops by his Commanding Officer, who despises him (Henry Fonda, in a guest role), as well as the sub-plot from "LST" of the force being led by a tactically inept officer (Denholm Elliott) who is more of a danger to his own men than the Japanese are. Aldrich apparently preferred the British anti-heroic style of war film involving the Japanese, as opposed to the all-American, all-conquering hero against the Japanese style of war movie that he felt was far from the truth. He also liked making films about flawed characters placed in tough, challenging situations, of which his "The Dirty Dozen" (1967) had to be the epitome.

Two other leading characters complete the picture: a cynical yet professional Cockney soldier played by - who else? - Michael Caine, and, totally against type and stereotype of any British or American war film, a Japanese Major (Ken Takakura) who is the one soldier on either side possessed of any dignity or morality.

The mission is to destroy a Japanese radio station on the far side of the island before it can broadcast a warning to Japanese forces that an American convoy is passing close by. Robertson's character speaks fluent Japanese: it is his task to send a false message in Japanese on the radio before it is destroyed, that will buy the Americans time.

The film was made in the Philippines, and the Philippines Air Force is credited in the opening titles for providing assistance to the production. All the aircraft seen in the film were operated by the Philippines Air Force of the time.

There are only two sequences in which aircraft appear. The first shows Robertson being driven in a jeep to a Douglas C-47 Skytrain numbered 13643, parked on a dusty airstrip with cattle herded beside it! This is very obviously a passenger-carrying C-47, due to its row of cabin windows and clearly visible passenger seats. It is painted silver overall and has a large blue circle containing a white star applied over its Philippines Air Force insignia on the fuselage, to give the impression of it being a USAAF C-47 on a South-East Asian strip - the large 'wings' of the insignia would have had to have silver strips covering them. Later it is seen taxiing in to another and larger air base, probably a different part of the same airfield location in the Philippines, most likely Manila, where two more identical Douglas C-47 Skytrain passenger transports are parked up. Their serial numbers are too distant to read. The silver-overall scheme was how they appeared in Philippines Air Force service, probably as VIP transports, in 1970. Some had been donated as foreign aid from Royal Australian Air Force stocks.

If the serial number 13643 on the tail is both its Philippines Air Force serial and manufacturer's number, then this C-47 is actually a Douglas DC-3C which later came onto the US register as N100DW. Operated by Tol Air Services from Luis Munoz Marin International Airport at Carowina, Puerto Rico, this DC-3C was written off after being damaged beyond economic repair by Hurricane Hugo on 17th September 1989.

The other sequence featuring aviation in "Too Late The Hero" concerns the discovery by the British raiding force of a secret Japanese Air Force jungle air base on the island which the US military has failed to detect. "Three rousing great cheers for American air reconnaissance, eh!", sneers the cynical Caine.

The Philippines Air Force loaned four North American AT-28D Trojan light attack aircraft, including one serialled 77-613, and a single Beech T-34 Mentor to act the role of Japanese Air Force dive bombers and fighters hidden in mud and wood shelters. Presumably the serial that is visible on the T-28 Trojan closest to the camera is its actual Philippines Air Force identity number. The AT-28D served with the 15th Strike Wing of the Philippines Air Force at Sangley Air Base in Cavite, armed with miniguns, general purpose bombs, 81mm cluster grenades and up to 1,200lbs of munitions carried on six underwing pylons. Called 'Tora-Toras', the AT-28Ds saw a lot of action supporting government troops against Communist and Muslim rebels. They did actually operate

as dive bombers, and some reconstructed examples were still on strength until they were retired in late 1992, replaced by SF.260 Warriors. The T-34 served as an armed trainer with the 105th Combat Crew Training Squadron at Basa Air Base; many were Fiji-built examples donated to the Philippines as Japanese war reparations. They were phased out in the late Sixties.

THE MCKENZIE BREAK

(Premier, New York, USA: October 1970)

An unusual and particularly gritty PoW escape story in that the escapees are German Kriegsmarine U-Boat crewmen, not British PoWs. Set in Scotland but filmed in Ireland, this film's plot is based on actual events in Canada that took place in September 1943 when a number of high-ranking U-Boat submariners did actually try to break out of a PoW camp named Bowmanville in Ontario. Their plan was to rendezvous with a U-Boat that would take them back to Germany, but this was foiled by the Canadian authorities.

Camp McKenzie in Scotland substitutes for Camp Bowmanville in Ontario. The U-Boat men, led by a fanatical Nazi Leutnant who was raised in the Hitler Jugend, manage to break out and drive in a truck to the coast where they will be picked up by submarine. As they drive alongside a loch they are spotted by a British patrol aircraft. In this case, it is an Auster VI observation aircraft played by a camouflaged civilianised variant of the same type, an Auster 6A. It is filmed air-air from another aircraft in a very loose, hand-held style which means that there is a lot of camera movement that prevents clear identification of the Auster. Presumably it is an Irish registered Auster 6A.

The other aircraft used in "The McKenzie Break" is a Percival Proctor, which is painted up in unrealistic brown-grey camouflage, plus fuselage roundel and fin flash, to depict a Royal Navy search aircraft. This Proctor carries the serial 'W3480' on its rear fuselage below 'Royal Navy' titling, a serial number which was not allocated to any real aircraft but, if it had been, would have been issued to a Spitfire Mk.V. Presumably, this Proctor, like the Auster, is an Irish registered aircraft but there are no means of identifying it. Of those Proctors that are known to have been registered in the Irish Republic, none were in flying condition by the time "The McKenzie Break" was in production and most had been de-registered, so the mystery remains. Interestingly, this Proctor carries a small, black radome under its fuselage just aft of the wings, most untypical of any member of the Proctor family. From its appearance, it appears to be a Percival Proctor III.

CHAPTER 5

1971-1980

It only needs a quick count of the number of British World War Two war films produced in the Seventies - just 15, including one Hollywood 'British' war film, compared with the massed output of the previous two decades - to realise that the war film genre was now well and truly on the wane.

It is not difficult to understand why. World War Two was far less relevant to the Seventies generation. In the first half of the decade, they were decidedly anti-war, due to what was happening in Vietnam. Moreover, the very real threat of a new war - nuclear - made the subject of war as cinema entertainment far less appealing. Spies like Roger Moore's James Bond, cops like Clint Eastwood's 'Dirty' Harry Callahan, all American romantic rogues, as played by Paul Newman and Robert Redford in "The Sting" (1973), even rogue sharks in the "Jaws" series - definitely; air, sea and land battles - less so.

There were exceptions, of course, especially in the latter half of the decade when "A Bridge Too Far" (1977) showed that there was still an audience for large-scale World War Two epics. For the British war film, the need to appease American distributors' prejudices that the American war hero was even more tough, brave, resolute and attractive to women than his British counterpart, in order for the British product to sell in the USA, gained even greater expression in the Seventies, and never more so on such a debasing scale as in director Richard Attenborough's re-creation of Operation Market Garden.

For aviation in British war films, the Seventies was a far less profitable decade. The world was growing increasingly modern in its use of technology and this was reflected in the use of aviation in the films that were being made. This was the decade of Concorde, the Boeing 747 and wide-body airliners, the Harrier 'Jump Jet' and the Apollo Moon Missions. Extra terrestrial epics in the style of "Close Encounters of the Third Kind" (1977) and the first "Star Wars" (1977) movie, showed that cinema was looking beyond Earth's horizons for new ways to entertain the masses.

Even so, there were opportunities for some familiar aeronautical performers, such as Avro Lancaster PA474 and Spitfire Mk.IX MH434, to find roles in British war films during this period, while the film industry itself continued to contribute to the growing numbers of privately-owned historic aircraft in the UK by making use of them in various film productions. The following reviews reflect this trend.

MURPHY'S WAR

(Released: January 1971)

Filmed entirely on location in Venezuela and Malta, "Murphy's War" – starring Peter O'Toole in the title role – is the story of one man's revenge against an entire German Navy U-Boat crew who not only sank the British merchant ship on which he served, but also massacred all his ship-mates as they struggled helplessly in the water.

Murphy is an Irishman who is the aircraft mechanic that services the ship's amphibious flying-boat. This amphibian tries to attack the U-Boat but is shot down. Murphy believes he is the sole survivor of the massacre, after being nursed back to health by a missionary doctor (played by O'Toole's then real-life wife, Sian Phillips) who provides medical services for the Amazonian natives who save his life. However, the pilot of the flying-boat has survived as well, but he is murdered by the U-Boat Captain who thinks the pilot is the only witness of the massacre. He has reckoned without Murphy.

The Irishman finds the amphibian beached up-river of the natives' camp. He salvages it with the aid of a French oil administrator, Louis, who lives on a large river dredger – actually a genuine World War Two tank landing craft. Murphy intends making the amphibian fly again, and with it to bomb the U-Boat in its hideout up-stream.

The amphibian is a Grumman J2F-6 Duck, a two-seater radial-engined bi-plane which served in World War Two with the United States Navy and the United States Marine Corps, mostly in the Pacific. The Grumman Duck didn't have an offensive role, it was used mainly for supply work, reconnaissance, target-towing, or for air-sea rescue of downed airmen.

The Duck was not operated by the British military services. In the film, it is representing a Fleet Air Arm Fairey Swordfish, floatplane versions of which were carried by armed merchant ships to try and spot U-Boats. They were lowered into the water and recovered by large on-board cranes. The one flying Fairey Swordfish in the world in 1970 when the film was released - LS326 of the RNAS Yeovilton Station Flight, which had appeared in "Sink The Bismarck!" (1960) - could neither be spared nor risked for the type of flying carried out by the Duck in "Murphy's War"; nor would the Fleet Air Arm allow it to be converted into a floatplane. The Grumman Duck became the best available substitute

Two Grumman Ducks were actually used in "Murphy's War", both painted to represent the same aircraft; two were needed in case one pranged and caused a costly delay in the film's production. Both Ducks belonged to legendary airshow and movie stunt pilot, Frank Tallman, a man who physically and characteristically lived up to his name.

Tallman was born to fly, making his first flight in 1924 at the age of five sitting on his father's lap - his father was piloting the 'plane! He served mostly as a flight instructor for the USAAF during World War Two, and after the War built up a collection of pre-1920 vintage aircraft. Throughout the Fifties and the Sixties Tallman developed a growing reputation for airshow performances and television work with his historic aircraft, but the turning point in his career came in 1961 when he merged his collection and business with that of Paul Mantz, the leading Hollywood film pilot of the time: they created Tallmantz Aviation Inc. Mantz was older than Tallman and was looking to do less flying, so Tallman succeeded him as the eminent Hollywood movies stunt pilot. However, 1965 was to become a tragic year for Tallmantz Aviation: Paul Mantz was killed while flying the unique hybrid aircraft built from a crashed Flying Boxcar for the movie, "The Flight Of The Phoenix" (1965), while Tallman had to have a leg amputated after crashing in a go-kart. He had to learn to fly again with a prosthetic leg, but by 1967 he was fully back in business, contracted to provide Paramount Studios with 18 B-25 Mitchell bombers for "Catch 22" (1970).

Frank Tallman's aerial exploits are now the stuff of legend in the film world. Among the most memorable are the Boeing Stearman crop-duster scene he flew over Grand Canyon in "Capricorn One" (1977) and the sequences with his own World War One aeroplanes for "The Great Waldo Pepper" (1975). His flying in "Murphy's War" remains Tallman's other most talked-about movie aerial action scene.

For the film, Tallman's two Grumman Ducks were painted in as near as it could be achieved all-over Royal Navy blue; however, the scheme is still not of the correct shade or hue. As the Duck never flew with the Fleet Air Arm, this error doesn't really matter, as authenticity can't be achieved here anyway. No serial is carried, nor any squadron code letters, but each Duck bears the titling, 'RN/MS Mount Kyle', the name of the ship the flying-boat operated from and denoting the services it belonged to: Royal Navy/Merchant Ship Mount Kyle.

The flying scenes, and nearly all of the film itself, were filmed on and over the Orinco River in Venezuela. Tallman had to fly the Ducks as if it is Murphy in the cockpit: he may have been the aircraft's mechanic, but he has no flying experience at all! This called for some very risky low-level flying over jungle and water. There were times when Tallman had to take off, then stall and impact the water again, flying as Murphy struggling to get the big, snarling Wright 1820G radial-powered amphibian into the air. Tallman is quoted as saying of the terrain over which he had to fly: "This jungle is terrible. If you start to go down in it, you're dead! Don't even bother to reach for your beads".

As it happened, both Peter O'Toole and Frank Tallman were physically very much alike, both being lean and tall, so it was not difficult to have Tallman made up to look like O'Toole as Murphy while flying the Duck. But O'Toole himself actually flew in one of the Ducks, acting as Murphy at the controls; he offered to do so, to add to the realism, especially as none of the film was made in a studio. He flew in the front seat, with a sheet of paper bearing director Peter Yates's typed instructions of what moves he had to make and filmed from a camera strapped to the forward canopy shield, while Tallman controlled the Duck from the rear seat out of shot. When Murphy yells, "Fly, you bastard!", as the Duck refuses to get airborne from the water, O'Toole wasn't just acting! He was also instructed how to water-taxy one of the Ducks, as is clearly seen in one shot.

Murphy believes he has successfully bombed the U-Boat in its hideout up-river by using improvised petrol bombs dropped from the Duck. However, he is badly mistaken and the U-Boat suddenly surfaces to shoot up and destroy the Duck as it is moored beside the natives' camp. This was an accurately created full-scale facsimile of the Duck that was bullet riddled and blown up, so technically there were three Grumman Ducks in the film.

Of the two real Grumman Ducks used in "Murphy's War", both still survive today and both are on view in museum collections in the United States. One is a former US Navy veteran, USN Bureau Number (Bu.N) 36976, which served with US Naval Utility Squadrons 4 and 16 during World War Two, and at some stage operated from the carrier USS Franklin. After being demobbed, this J2F-6 Duck appeared on the US civil register in 1963 and had several owners until it became part of the Tallmantz Aviation fleet. Following its appearance in "Murphy's War", Frank Tallman sold this J2F-6 to Carl Meis in 1972 who, in turn, donated it to the EAA Aviation Foundation with the US civil registration N1196N. Since 1983, this Duck has been exhibited in the EAA's AirVenture Museum at Oshkosh, Wisconsin.

The second Grumman Duck was J2F-6 Bu.N 33587, which became N67790 on the US civil register. Built in 1945, this Duck did not see wartime service. It came onto the US civil register in 1961 when it was used by Aircraft Specialties Inc of Mesa, Arizona, as a fire bomber fitted with a 300 gallon tank. It was then operated between 1966 - '69 by Hart Marine Inc on oil rig support tasks in the Gulf of Louisiana before Frank Tallman acquired it. He flew it from Orange County Airport, California, at many airshows in the United States in US Navy markings as 7790. The prolific aircraft collector, Kermit Weeks, then acquired this Duck in 1985 for display in his Weeks Air Museum at Tamiami, Florida, before he donated it to the National Museum of the United States Air Force at Wright-Patterson Air Force Base, Dayton, Ohio, where it is still displayed today. The USAF operated eight Grumman Ducks under the designation OA-12 in Alaska as rescue aircraft; J2F-6 Duck N67790 has been painted to represent OA-12 48-563.

The Grumman Duck is a popular aircraft with collectors in the United States, there being at least 11 surviving examples in private ownership, some in flying condition. Frank Tallman's exploits in his two Grumman Ducks in "Murphy's War" have been much discussed among fans of this beast of a floatplane.

RAID ON ROMMEL

(Released: February 1971, USA) Hollywood 'British' war film.

How to get two films for the price of one? Simple, lift virtually all the action sequences from "Tobruk" (1967) and fit them around scenes involving actor Richard Burton. He returns for the third time to the North Africa Campaign by the British 8th Army against Rommel's Afrika Korps, after his previous appearances in "The Desert Rats" in 1953 and "Bitter Victory" four years later. Returning too was director Henry Hathaway, 20 years after his first brush with Rommel in "The Desert Fox" (1951). One wonders why Hathaway chose to get involved with this war film on the cheap, which got caned by the critics.

Also lifted from "Tobruk" are the two aircraft in that film, the unidentified Grumman G-21A Goose and Curtiss P-40E Kittyhawk IA N1207V from Tallmantz Aviation. Exactly the same sequences involving these two aircraft in "Tobruk" are re-shown in "Raid on Rommel".

DAD'S ARMY

(Released: March 1971)

The film version of Britain's best ever loved TV comedy series has a limited aviation content, but does benefit from being able to use out-takes from "Battle of Britain" (1969) which was still in recent memory during the early months of 1971. The film itself provided some light relief from the strained industrial relations of the time in the country, but the irony was not lost that while "Dad's Army" poked fun at Hitler's Germany, Britain had actively engaged in changing its coinage from pounds, shillings and pence to decimalisation this year, a move which older generation Brits felt was a dangerous creep towards becoming more European and, therefore, closer to the former enemy.

"Dad's Army" begins with its familiar adopted theme song by Bud Flanagan before changing to sounds and images of Nazi dominance, using archive material. There are several archive shots of Luftwaffe aircraft in parade formations, the first of which is unusual and appears not to have been used in a British war film before. It shows two Dornier Do.215B bombers flying in a tight paired formation over arrays of Nazi flags and banners.

The Do.215B was a modified version of the Do.17Z 'Flying Pencil' medium bomber that appeared in such large numbers over southern England in the summer of 1940. The outwardly visible difference between the Do.17Z and Do.215B - they both utilised the same airframe and bomb-carrying capacity - were the engines: the Do.215B was powered by two Daimler-Benz DB.601 inline engines instead of the Do.17Z's Bramo 323 radial engines. The two Dornier bombers shown in this imagery clearly have inline engines, not radials, therefore confirming they are Do.215Bs, archive footage of which is significantly rare.

What is noteworthy about this footage is that the lead Do.215B is streaming coloured smoke from an outlet under its fuselage, possibly from a flare fixed in its bomb bay. It also bears the red tail band and black Swastika scheme of the pre-War Luftwaffe. Taking into account that the Do.215B was first put into service by the Deutsches Luftwaffe in August 1939, and that all German military aircraft had been painted in tactical camouflage schemes by the time of the invasion of Poland on 1st September that same year, the Do.215Bs seen in this footage must have been filmed over-flying a Nazi rally just before the outbreak of World War Two. As they fly out of shot, two more appear behind them in a similar tight formation and also streaming coloured smoke. Quite likely they were being displayed as the first examples of the then newest bomber design to enter service with the Deutsches Luftwaffe.

Next comes footage of two formations in other different aerial parades, this time with nine Dornier Do.17 medium bombers leading a second wave of nine Heinkel He.111 medium bombers flying at a greater altitude above and behind the 'Flying Pencils'. Finally, the last piece of archive footage used in "Dad's Army" is a goof. It shows a total of 20 high parasol-winged single-engine aircraft, filmed from a distance, flying in a lead formation of 15 in a very wide 'Vee' followed by five more in the slot. The editor might have thought he had got hold of archive film of German observation aircraft over-flying a Nazi rally; however, the style of formation does not correspond with the type of parade formations that the Luftwaffe flew over such rallies in Nuremberg or Berlin during the Thirties. Although it cannot be a definite claim because of the poor quality of the imagery and the small size of the aircraft filmed in silhouette in their formations, they bear a strong resemblance to being 20 ANF Les Mureaux 113 reconnaissance machines, which would make them all French Armee de l'Air aircraft presumably flying in a parade formation during an event before World War Two broke out. The ANF Les Mureaux 113 was militarily not a successful design, many of them being lost to Luftwaffe fighters during the Battle of France in 1940.

Aviation does not feature again in "Dad's Army" until well into the body of the film. Our heroes are about to take part in a military exercise and are cycling as a unit to the camp, together with Corporal Jones's gas-powered butcher's van converted into an armoured car (!), when Captain Mainwaring (pronounced 'Mannering', of course) gives the alert that a Stuka is approaching. Cue panic all round and a mass pile up of bicycles.

The 'Stuka' is nothing of the sort. It happens to be a low-flying Spitfire. It appears in three shots which, unfortunately, are all distant and rather badly filmed, suggesting that this is amateur footage and definitely are not out-takes from "Battle of Britain". This Spitfire is a Merlin-engined variant, but, being so distant and unclear in shot, cannot be identified.

Another scene has the residents of Walmington-on-Sea looking upwards at German fighters flying overhead. Several shots show five fighters flying in a mixed gaggle, rather than in formation. Freeze-framing shows that one of the fighters is larger than the other four and can be identified as a Hawker Hurricane. The other four are all Hispano HA.1112M1L, or Messerschmitt Bf.109J, fighters. Undoubtedly, these are aircraft that were used in the "Battle of Britain" film, made two years earlier than "Dad's Army". However, the footage shown is definitely not out-take material from "Battle of Britain". The Hurricane and four Bf.109Js are filmed from the ground looking directly upwards at the aircraft: no such shot was used in the 1969 film. It is also of much lesser quality than was used in the feature film on release. The fighters are flying at a height somewhere between 2,000 and 3,000 feet, and are probably over-flying one of the airfield locations used in "Battle of Britain". The most likely explanation is that this is part of footage filmed from the ground for the guidance of the aerial co-ordinators of the massed dog-fight sequences, not for release into the main production, but was loaned for use in "Dad's Army".

The finale has a Heinkel He.111 bomber on a photo-reconnaissance mission over the South of England coastline being hit by flak and the three-man crew bailing out. In desperation, they take hostage the residents of Walmington-on-Sea in the village church hall. Captain Mainwaring and his platoon of Home Guards gallantly come to their rescue while the regular Army, Marines and police dither outside.

To depict the He.111 being shot down a number of out-takes from "Battle of Britain" of either of the two CASA 2.111D bombers that were flown to the UK in 1968 for filming with Spitfires and Hurricanes are used. In particular, the imagery of the bail outs from one of these CASA 2.111s, acting as a Luftwaffe He.111 on fire while its crew jump for their lives, that appears in "Battle of Britain", is re-used here in "Dad's Army".

HITLER: THE LAST TEN DAYS

(Released: April 1973)

This British - Italian co-production utilises entirely archive material to illustrate the remorseless destruction of Berlin by the Soviet Red Army as Adolf Hitler repeatedly refuses to accept the reality of Germany's defeat during his final ten days in the Fuhrer Bunker.

The first archive shot to show aircraft appears as the title credits are displayed over imagery of a fly-past by 21 Heinkel He.111 bombers, in seven separate 'Kettes' of three aircraft each. Following the credits and to illustrate the advance of Soviet forces, rough archive footage of four Soviet Red Army Polikarpov I-16 'Ishak' ('Donkey') fighters taking off appears,

followed immediately by two Ilyushin Il-2 Shturmovik (ground-attack aircraft), both filmed air-air firing their cannon.

The only other part of this film in which archive imagery of aviation is used is mid-way through the plot when Hitler denounces the German people for being too feeble, deserving to "go down in a sea of flames, a Viking funeral of the Reich". Immediately the editor cuts to a shot of aircraft diving down into the attack. These are actually 16 US Navy Grumman F-6F Hellcat fighters filmed air-air breaking off one by one and commencing their attacks. Next, a Luftwaffe Messerschmitt Bf.109G is dramatically filmed diving past two Boeing B-17 Flying Fortress bombers of the USAAF's Eighth Air Force. Then two Republic P-47 Thunderbolts roll past the camera position, probably aboard a B-17 during air combat training for Flying Fortress gunners. They are followed by gun-camera footage of a Focke Wulf FW.190 taking hits at low-level. Next, another P-47 'Jug' dives towards the camera, filmed from a B-17 whose tailplane gets into shot as the 'Jug' closes in from behind; an unidentified fighter explodes in a mass of flame; another gun-camera shot, which has been used in many documentaries about the War, shows a Focke Wulf FW.190 at very low-level exploding and instantly rolling left (if the editor had followed through, the FW.190 would have been seen to roll right onto its back and plunge nose first into the ground, but for some reason he cuts this shot before the impact happens); an unidentifiable fighter that is filmed from a ship bursts into flame amid flak and plunges down, streaming fire and smoke.

From this point on no further archive material of aircraft is used, but the film is noteworthy from the aviation historian's perspective for Australian actress Diane Cilento's convincing performance as Hannah Reitsch.

OVERLORD

(Premier: July 1975, Berlin International Film Festival)

This extraordinary film is an exquisite gem, combining its use of contemporarily staged scenes with genuine archive material filmed by military cameramen in World War Two. It is a recently discovered minor masterpiece that was produced in 1975 but did not get a public film release until 2008.

"Overlord" was made by director Stuart Cooper with the full support and assistance of the Imperial War Museum and the Ministry of Defence. Cooper spent an unprecedented amount of time in the IWM's archive; the Museum granted him access to its original nitrate negatives, which, as Cooper states, were of pristine quality. He and his cinematographer, John Alcott, chose to film their staged scenes in black-and-white using period lenses made in Germany in 1936 and 1938, in order to achieve parity between their contemporary footage and the IWM's archive material.

Cooper says of "Overlord", "…the only rival we had in the Museum's archive was 'The World at War', the now-legendary

26-episode TV documentary series. 'Overlord' is the antithesis of 'The World at War', as it was to all other war films of the period".

He could not have expressed it more accurately. "Overlord" stands no comparison with any other war film, made either in Britain or the USA, or anywhere else for that matter.

For the purpose of our review, it is the examination of the amazing amount of archive footage containing wartime aviation which holds our interest. Some of it has been seen before in other feature films, but more of it is entirely unique for this production alone and is of astonishing quality. Cooper was probably able to extract previously unseen material because he was not subject to any time constraints: "Overlord" was his personal project and he could take all the time he wanted to research the kind of footage he was looking for. As he amusingly describes, he originally suggested to the IWM's keeper of film, Anne Fleming, that he examine the entire collection; Ms Fleming was agreeable to this, but pointed out to Cooper that if he came in on Monday - Friday each week between 9-00am - 4-00pm, it would take him approximately nine years to view every part of the 93 million feet of film of World War Two in the Museum's collection.

"Overlord" opens to a black screen, only the growing sound of marching troops and of trains of horses clattering over hardened roads confirming any sign of life. The sounds then merge with imagery of retreating British troops followed by victorious Wehrmacht forces, mixed among refugees streaming out of a shattered city, believed to be Warsaw. A cameraman filming from an aircraft circling over the Arc de Triomphe in Paris shows German troops looking down from the top of the huge monument at the completely deserted rotunda below. Hitler is pictured looking expressionessly out of the window of his personal Focke Wulf FW.200V1 Condor at the Paris scene below him. The aircraft filming over Warsaw drapes its shadow over the shattered city below, its long-legged, insect-like shape making it distinctly identifiable as a Fieseler Storch. Almost certainly this footage is from the same film stock of a bombed-out city that was used as far back as 1941 in "Dangerous Moonlight", depicting the destruction of Warsaw after the Wehrmacht invasion of Poland in September 1939.

What Cooper does in "Overlord" is mix some astonishing archive footage, filmed from a variety of different types of aircraft, both Allied and Axis, as they power low over towns and countryside, with contemporary footage of the principal actors in the story. Matched with these in-flight shots is the recorded sound of powerful aero engines. The effect is dramatic and tells in a simply stark yet awe-inspiring way the progress of the War. They include a close-up of a pilot's foot in the crude metal shoe that controls the rudder of a Heinkel He.111; spent cartridges from the same He.111's forward machine gun lie collected in one of the glass panel frames of the bomber's glazed nose; Cooper uses a close-up of the forward machine gun, showing a merchant ship below it seen through the glazed nose as the He.111 flies low over the sea, matched with audio of a machine gun firing to create the effect of the bomber strafing the ship.

There follows an in-cockpit shot taken presumably from a Junkers Ju.87 Stuka diving almost vertically down on a cargo ship it is targeting, accompanied by the classic scream of the Stuka's

'Horns of Jericho'; footage taken from an unidentified aircraft flying very low past a cargo ship, with more audio of machine gun fire; a semi-sunken merchant ship is seen through an He.111's ventral gondola as the bomber over-flies the stricken vessel; bombs descend from an He.111, again filmed from the ventral gondola, leading into archive footage of the London Blitz which Cooper matches with voice-overs by actors shouting to represent the firemen fighting the blazes.

Further into the body of the film new army recruits are being put under punishing field training amid simulated battle conditions. Cooper uses footage that we saw in "Ferry Pilot" of Vickers Armstrong chief test pilot, Alex Henshaw, aerobating a Vickers Supermarine Spitfire Mk.I, to represent a Spitfire making low-level runs at the recruits. Later, Cooper uses archive footage of two Spitfire Mk.Is making low passes over open countryside. Soon afterwards a dramatic study of an Avro Lancaster filmed head-on appears, taking off directly towards the camera, with a second Lancaster moving out at the far end of the grass runway in preparation for its turn. This is interspersed with shots, both from the air and from the ground, of the ruins of Corfe Castle in Dorsetshire, the insertion of which by Cooper isn't apparently clear unless this footage is meant to convey bombed-out buildings.

What is clear are the beautiful air-airs of Avro Lancaster B.I PA474 of the Battle of Britain Memorial Flight which follow, glistening in the sun over the Avonmouth coastline near to Bristol. Cooper confirms that this imagery was filmed specifically for "Overlord"; the fact that it is shown in black-and-white does not in any fashion detract from the stunning visual quality of these shots. Lancaster PA474 can be clearly seen to be carrying the No.44 Squadron codes of KM-B that it wore during the airshow seasons of the Seventies.

These shots of PA474 are inter-cut with archive footage of night-time bombing raids over German cities. PA474 is now filmed in silhouette against the brilliant sunlight, creating the effect of the Lancaster flying at night and illuminated by the massed fires below it. Cooper cleverly blends PA474's airframe into this imagery of bomb bursts and blazing cities.

A familiar piece of footage of 'Candle' cascading down, with a Handley Page Halifax seen silhouetted against the raging fires below it, comes next. Then, graphic images of charred corpses. A derelict Avro Lancaster on its belly, with the nose completely separated from the fuselage just in front of the cockpit gives the impression of a crashed aircraft, but its engines have been removed, so it almost certainly is a scrapped aircraft; but Cooper achieves the effect he wants. Aerial shots of blasted cities, with not a sign of life except for what looks like washing hanging out on a balcony of a top floor apartment in one building that has miraculously survived intact. A close-up, looking right down, of a Handley Page Halifax posed right above a sea of fire.

Cooper uses a lot of fascinating IWM archive material showing the build-up of the massive Allied forces towards the real Operation Overlord: D-Day. The many extraordinary vehicles and devices which fit into no known category of military warfare illustrate the ingenious inventions that were actually used on the Normandy beaches. In this segment of the film a lot of aerial activity is shown, representing the preparation for the Paratroop landings and glider assaults, plus attacks on vital German communications hubs.

Firstly, two Douglas Boston Mk.III day bombers skimming low over the sea, with the white cliffs of Dover beyond them, is seen - this is the same imagery as used in "For Those in Peril" (1944), only in reverse. Several archive shots of countryside and towns flashing past a twin-engined light bomber flying at very low-level appear next, followed immediately by the same gun-camera footage of a Focke Wulf FW.190 exploding at less than 100 feet above the ground and rolling instantly onto its back, as was used in "Hitler: The Last Ten Days" (1973). Another FW.190 disintegrates, with its left wing flying off and pieces of debris hurtling towards the gun-camera of the fighter which has shot it down. Amazing gun-camera imagery shows a third FW.190 clearly losing part of its starboard wing, two thirds of it having severed completely in one piece, with the fighter entering an uncontrolled roll to port. Yet another FW.190 loses its starboard wing at exactly the same part of the join, the aircraft rolling violently with more pieces flying off it; the pilot would surely not have stood a chance. Gun-camera footage follows an FW.190 which is fully intact and with no sign of fire or smoke, but as it rolls left its pilot can be clearly seen leaving the aircraft and falling away from it as his parachute begins to deploy: this same footage has been used in a number of documentaries.

Mixed between these images from the gun-cameras are several shots of the ground filmed from an aircraft that is weaving from side to side, and with rain splashes on the glass nose canopy through which the camera is filming. In the last of these shots, as the aircraft in which the camera is placed banks to the left, a Douglas Boston suddenly appears in front of it, doing likewise from left to right.

To end this series of shoot-down images, Cooper uses the same gun-camera shot of a pilot hanging below his parachute, filmed from the aircraft that is flying right past him, which appears in "Reach For The Sky" (1956).

Really powerful imagery of a menacing-looking Douglas Boston Mk.II, filmed air-air from above roaring over land and sea, is possibly among the most dramatic pieces of wartime aerial footage to be found anywhere. Cooper's search for the most outstanding imagery in the IWM's archive has turned up a unique piece of film of this most aggressive warplane which has not been used anywhere else before.

The airborne armada of troop-carrying gliders and their tow aircraft is spectacularly illustrated by a shot filmed from an aircraft flying over one of the many airfields in preparation for the huge assault to come. No less than 53 Douglas C-47 Skytrain tow aircraft and 48 Airspeed Horsa gliders are seen packed into dense ranks side by side with each other, while 15 Waco GC-4A Hadrian gliders can be seen beyond them. Interesting to see that all the Horsas are in USAAF markings - as are the C-47s and Hadrians, of course - which is not often seen, confirming that the American forces did make use of large numbers of this British-built glider design, it probably being the most widely used type of any troop glider by the Allies.

More Airspeed Horsas appear, this time RAF gliders filmed from the ground with troops boarding them: seven appear in one shot, six in another. Three North American B-25 Mitchells with D-Day invasion stripes are seen starting engines; the RAF used the Mitchell as a glider-tug aircraft and Cooper has found some fine imagery of one Horsa, with the fleet number of '146' chalked on its side, being towed off by a B-25. Another Horsa lumbers into the air. A third example manages to get airborne a bit more quickly, perhaps being not so heavily loaded. A B-25 is filmed air-air against an evening sky.

The film then cuts to a series of shots of bombs dropping onto what looks like open ground targets, followed by low-level gun-camera footage of attacks on trains, barges and vehicles. This footage is very graphic and shows railway engines towing freight trucks being hit with considerable force and accuracy. Shell splashes in canals demonstrate how ground-attack pilots used the technique of 'walking the bullets' from one target onto the next. One gun-camera shot has a P-47 Thunderbolt pulling up into the smoke generated from an attack, another has a Mosquito strafing a small warship, possibly a minesweeper, ahead of the aircraft filming its own cannon fire streaming onto the same target. A D-Day striped RAF Douglas Boston Mk.II is filmed in flight over shipping below it; this dramatic footage is, in fact, the last aerial image in "Overlord".

This little known film is at last finding an audience which it thoroughly deserves. For aviation historians, it is an absolute must-see, with so much highly-prized archive material used in its 90-minute production. As one of cinema's most renowned film directors, Stanley Kubrick, is quoted as saying of "Overlord",

"There is only one thing wrong with 'Overlord'; it is 90 minutes too short".

OPERATION: DAYBREAK

(Released: February 1976)

This complicated multi-national production is dominated by a strong British cast playing Czechs and Germans and is directed by Briton Lewis Gilbert, a three-time James Bond film director who is credited with directing well-admired British productions like "Alfie" (1966), "Educating Rita" (1983) and "Shirley Valentine" (1989), all of which resulted in Oscar nominations for their leading actors. Gilbert directed no less than four British war films reviewed in this book: "The Sea Shall Not Have Them" (1954), "Reach For The Sky" (1956), "Carve Her Name With Pride" (1958) and "Sink the Bismarck!"(1960) - a record in itself. So, any doubts about this film's British credentials are well and truly erased.

Recounting the real life Operation Anthropoid, the MI6-planned assassination of the ReichsProtector of Bohemia and Moravia in Prague, Czechoslovakia, in June 1942, followed by the terrible reprisals against the civilian population by the SS, this very realistically performed film makes only the briefest use of aviation. This involves a twice-used out-take of the No.138 (Special Duties)

Squadron Handley Page Halifax V filmed air-air in "Now It Can Be Told" (1946), to illustrate the two sequences of Czech agents being parachuted into their occupied home country. The original black-and-white out-take has been tinted in the editing suite, so that the sky is a bright blue, while the Halifax itself remains in total silhouette. In its original imagery, the Halifax was filmed during daylight in silhouette, then the footage was darkened in the editing suite to make it appear as if the aircraft was flying at night. Portraying the Halifax flying in bright blue skies, as it is shown in "Operation: Daybreak", is unrealistic, as the agents' parachute insertion would definitely have taken place at night.

CROSS OF IRON

(Released: January 1977)

This Anglo - German co-production directed by American film director, Sam Peckinpah (noted mostly for Westerns, this is the only war film he directed), was filmed in the former Yugoslavia and tells the story of Wehrmacht soldiers in retreat on the Russian Front. Aviation only makes a very brief, and very inaccurate, appearance during the retreat. Out-takes from the 1976 American TV series, "Blacksheep Squadron", show seven United States Marine Corps Chance Vought F-4U Corsair fighter-bombers being used totally unconvincingly to portray Russian Red Army Shturmoviks (ground-attack aircraft). Obviously no footage of real Il-2 Shturmoviks was available to the production, although as the film was made in Yugoslavia it ought to have been possible to obtain imagery of Yugoslav Air Force Yaks, which would have been more convincing. The US Star-and-Bars on the Corsairs are clearly visible, while the bombs they are dropping are napalm containers. Towards the end of the film, during the final assault, a Red Army fighter strafes the German soldiers. An out-take from an unknown American war film of a North American T-6 or SN-4J is used. "Cross Of Iron" is, like most Sam Peckinpah productions, extremely violent.

THE EAGLE HAS LANDED

(Released: March 1977)

"The Eagle Has Landed" is an enduringly successful war film as far as aviation enthusiasts are concerned, less so with historians because of the teasing tactics by Jack Higgins, author of the novel of the same name, in claiming that fifty per cent of the story is true, the film's audience being invited to decide which fifty per cent they believe in.

The plot is simple, at least as far as SS Reichsfuhrer Heinrich Himmler is concerned: kidnap Winston Churchill and the Allies will sue for a negotiated peace, during which time Germany will rebuild her strength and go on to achieve the victory that has been pre-destined for the Third Reich. An Abwehr agent in Norfolk has discovered that Churchill is due to stay at a country house close to the Norfolk coast after inspecting a bomber base. Insert a team of Wehrmacht Kommandos in a captured RAF Dakota to capture the British Prime Minister, then spirit him to Occupied Holland aboard a captured Royal Navy motor torpedo boat.

The Kommandos will be led by Colonel Steiner, played by Michael Caine, who makes no attempt at all to affect a German accent - very wise of him, but it got him into trouble with some film critics at the time of general release of "The Eagle Has Landed". In fact, Caine's role as Steiner is one of his most admired among his huge legion of fans, so who cares what the critics say.

"The Eagle Has Landed" is a well made, well acted, well directed film which maintains good pace and manages to create a believable scenario out of an event which has some loose basis in fact. Director John Sturges (who died not long after making this film) had proven with "The Great Escape" (1963) that he knew how to bring an American flair for action to a war film with a strong British theme. The film scores highly with its close attention to detail, especially with the aircraft, vehicles and the genuine MTB of World War Two period vintage that were used.

Where the aircraft were concerned, the production company brought in one of the most knowledgeable and influential personalities within the British aircraft preservation community of the Seventies, Doug Bianchi of the highly reputable Personal Plane Services company based at Wycombe Air Park, the home of many fascinating historic and original aeroplanes (as it still is today). Doug Bianchi, an irrepressible character who was well known for his entertaining but entirely detailed articles on aircraft preservation, made certain his wife, Edna, was included as an aviation consultant on the film as well, especially if it meant scouring for aircraft in Europe fortified by some choice wines. Bianchi had, of course, provided aviation services to a number of film productions in the Sixties, of which "Mosquito Squadron" (1969) is referenced in Chapter Four.

The plot called for the use of four aircraft in the film, all of which had to be accurately representative of the actual types that would have been used in a real military operation like Fall Adler (Case Eagle) that was intended to take place in late 1943. Bianchi would probably have had nothing to do with the project had it meant that a Harvard would be painted in Luftwaffe markings, or a twin Beech would be called upon to play the role of a German transport aircraft.

The four aircraft each had a specific role to play:

A light transport aircraft, in which the planner of Case Eagle, Colonel Radl (played by American actor, Robert Duvall, who does affect a creditable and unstereotypical German accent), and Liam Devlin, the IRA operative working for the Abwehr (played totally believably by Canadian actor, Donald Sutherland), fly from Occupied France to Alderney in the Channel Islands;

A fast two-seater aeroplane, from which Devlin will parachute into Northern Ireland and then make his way via Belfast and Liverpool across to the Norfolk village, where the Abwehr agent lives (a South African widow with a hatred of the British for causing the death of her Boer husband in the Boer Wars, played by Jean Marsh, who doesn't look old enough to be a widow from that late 19th Century period) close to where Churchill is due to stay;

A large troop transport aircraft, in which Steiner and his Kommandos will be flown from the Channel Islands to the captured Dutch air base in Holland, from where they will all be flown to Norfolk;

And a captured RAF Dakota, from which Steiner and his men, wearing the uniforms of Polish soldiers, will parachute into England.

A fifth airframe was also available to the production team, as a prop for set-dressing on what is intended to be the captured Dutch air base of Lansvoort.

The first aircraft to be seen in "The Eagle Has Landed" is a Fieseler Fi.156 Storch high-wing, short take-off and landing communications and observation aircraft. It is seen bringing Radl and Devlin to Alderney Airport. If they were doing this for real in 1943, they would have had to make their flight either very early in the morning or during late evening, flying at low-level over the sea, to avoid RAF fighter patrols.

The Storch is seen landing at what is meant to be Alderney Airport, but is actually RAF St Mawgan in Cornwall, being used to represent not only Alderney Airport, but also Lansvoort air base in Holland. St Mawgan was, of course, a fully operational RAF air base when filming took place there in the Autumn of 1976, the production team having to time the scenes they were filming in between the thunderous take-offs by the mighty Nimrod MR.1 maritime patrol jets of No.42 Squadron and No.236 Operational Conversion Unit. There were also scheduled visits throughout the day by Brymon Aviation's Twin Otter commuter taxi which they had to avoid conflicting with.

It is commendable that Sturges and his team were able to create their film sets at St Mawgan in such a way that none of the base's modern infrastructure appears in shot, and certainly not any of the Nimrods. From the angles by which the aircraft appearing in "The Eagle Has Landed" are shot, it is quite believable that they are operating from Alderney Airport, or are parked on Lansvoort air base.

The Storch is first seen floating in over the threshold landing lights of 'Alderney Airport's' runway and touching down on its elastic-like, spindly legs. It pulls up after a very short landing run and immediately spins round in a neat one-eighty right in front of the camera. It is then seen taxiing towards a wooden watch tower set up on the airfield, pulls round and comes to a halt before Radl and Devlin dismount from the rear of the cabin.

The parts of RAF St Mawgan that were used in the film include one of the original short cross runways that were built between 1940 - 1941 and were still active in 1976, although not used by Nimrods! As the Storch settles down onto the runway and runs past the camera, the original control tower can be seen in the background of what was RAF Trebelzue, until the airfield was expanded and renamed RAF St Mawgan on 24th February 1943. Two wartime Nissen Huts can also be seen, long since converted for agricultural use. However, when the Storch is seen in the next shot, taxiing up to the watch tower, it is doing so at a completely different location on base, near to the end of the opposing cross runway with its threshold close to the cliffs overlooking the seaside town of Newquay below (out of sight). This part of St Mawgan was modernised in the Eighties to take nine hardened aircraft shelters (HAS), from which strike jets

could be operated. From the very wet state of the runway's hard surface in the film, it seems the production team caught the first rains following the drought of 1976.

Doug Bianchi had an easy job locating the Fieseler Storch, as it was based at Wycombe Air Park and was restored and maintained by his Personal Plane Services company. It was owned by the Honourable Patrick Lindsay, who had acquired the aircraft in 1972.

Registered G-AZMH, this Storch is actually a French licence-built Morane-Saulnier MS.500 Criquet, complete with the original Argus engine identical to Fieseler-built examples in Germany. It is, therefore, fully representative of the Fieseler Fi.156 Storch, hundreds of which performed extraordinary feats of endurance with the Wehrmacht forces during World War Two, the most famous of which was the mountain-top landing of a Storch to rescue Mussolini after he had been taken prisoner by Italian troops who had joined forces with the Allies. The Hon. Patrick Lindsay had his MS.500's registration adapted so that the code letters on the fuselage side, front and rear of the Balkenkreuze, read 'AZ+MH', which were painted over for its appearance in the film.

This MS.500 was a very familiar and busy performer on the British airshow scene throughout the Seventies and Eighties, not just with the Hon. Patrick Lindsay, but with Brian Woodford's Wessex Aviation & Transport Collection at Chalmington Manor, Dorset, after he acquired it in June 1983. The Luftwaffe-liveried MS.500 flew as a Fieseler Storch in a complementary display act along with Woodford's Westland Lysander, thus showing both the RAF's and the Luftwaffe's most widely used front-line, short field observation and communications aircraft of World War Two.

In June 1997, MS.500 Criquet G-AZMH had its registration cancelled when ownership was transferred to Germany. Today, it is displayed as 7A+WN in the Luftwaffenmuseum at the former RAF Gatow air station outside Berlin.

The aircraft from which Devlin is to parachute into Northern Ireland (one would have thought the Abwehr would have favoured the Republic of Ireland as being far more favourable and safe) posed more of a challenge for Bianchi. For one thing, the Luftwaffe did not convert any of their bombers into paratrooping platforms in the way the RAF did with the Whitley and the Halifax, which were used to insert SOE and MI6 agents. Part of the reason was that the Abwehr did not conduct a strategic espionage and intelligence warfare campaign against Britain in the way that Churchill ordered the SOE, MI6 and, later, the SAS to do against Germany in the occupied countries in Europe. Those Abwehr agents that were parachuted into Britain did so mostly in the way that Devlin is forced to do in the film:

Devlin: "How do I jump out of this thing?"

Pilot: "Release your safety belt. I turn the aircraft upside down, you drop out".

The aircraft type most suited for this ungracious form of exit was the Messerschmitt Bf.110 Zerstorer. Its long 'glasshouse' style cockpit allowed for an easy, unobstructed drop-out by the agent in the rear seat. However, no Messerschmitt Bf.110 was available to be used in the film, although, as we have seen in previous Chapters, a number of captured Zerstorers did initially survive the

War in flying condition. The challenge Bianchi faced was to find a believable alternative. This is where his inexhaustive knowledge and his invaluable contacts within the aviation community throughout Europe came into play.

Bianchi's friendship with French historic aircraft collector and restorer, Jean-Baptiste Salis, resulted in the latter offering him a genuine German World War Two machine as a suitable substitute for a Bf.110. This was an Arado Ar.396, a single-engined advanced pilot trainer that was widely used by the Luftwaffe in a number of variants throughout the War, beginning with the basic Ar.96A and culminating in the Ar.396. As with the Fieseler Storch, variants of the original Ar.96 were built under licence in Occupied France, in this case by the SIPA (Societe Industrielle Pour l'Aeronautique) collective founded in 1938 by famous French aircraft designer, Emile Dewoitine, whose own company had been nationalised by the French government before the War. SIPA manufactured parts for various types of German aircraft during the Occupation, but went on to design and build its own machines following the Liberation. Among these was a version of the Arado Ar.396 designated the SIPA S.10, followed by modified versions as the S.11 and S.12. The ultimate version was the SIPA S.121, 58 of which were built as advanced trainers for the new post-War Armee de l'Air. It is one of these which appears in "The Eagle Has Landed", painted to represent a Luftwaffe Arado Ar.396.

In 1976, SIPA S.121 F-BLKH was part of the Amicale Jean-Baptiste Salis (AJBS) collection at Aerodrome de Cerny-La Ferte Alais, 40km south of Paris. It bore a natural metal scheme with bright orange top surfaces to the nose and fuselage, as well as bordering the leading edges of the wings and tailplanes. The entire tail fin and rudder was painted in orange and white horizontal stripes. The authentic-looking Luftwaffe camouflage scheme and markings were applied specifically for the film, although no codes were used.

In the film, the 'Arado Ar.396' was flown by Jerrard Oosterliuck, whose main job was as an air traffic controller at Aeroport de Orly. As he swings the Ar.396 round, the redundant RAF Trebelzue control tower can again be seen in the background. When he takes off, it is from the then Zero-Five secondary runway which was closed in the Eighties and made into the HAS operational area. The brief shot of it getting airborne shows that the Ar.396 was a racy aeroplane, a good deal faster than its opposite number used by the Allies, the T-6 Texan/Harvard. The Ar.396 was probably more closely related to the Miles Master in performance, as both had light fighter-like qualities and were armed on occasion.

While he was in the country, Oosterliuck flew SIPA S.121 F-BLKH at a Shuttleworth Collection Open Day at Old Warden, still in its Ar.396 'wardrobe'. Tragically, this aircraft was lost in a fatal accident in France two years later. Jean-Baptiste Salis donated the remains to the Deutsches Technikmuseum in Berlin, where they remain in store to this day, with a possible future rebuild in mind using parts of other surviving Ar.96 series aircraft.

Another part of RAF St Mawgan was used to represent Lansvoort air base, the fictional captured airfield in Holland. The area that was used was on the northern side of RAF St Mawgan, located near to the Carloggas entrance gate to the air base just

to the east of where the Newquay International Airport terminal building stands today. At the threshold end of Runway Two-Three, the opposite to Runway Zero-Five that the Ar.396 took off from, a hangar was situated used by the Air Training Corps for Scottish Aviation Bulldog T.1 trainers and Slingsby Sedbergh T.21 gliders during Summer Camps. It was converted by the film production company into a Luftwaffe hangar and is seen in shot as Steiner and his Kommando team arrive with Radl at Lansvoort air base, walking across the airfield apron - actually the end of Runway Two-Three - towards the hangar with the transport aircraft they have flown in from the Channel Islands beyond them.

This was Doug Bianchi's third challenge, to find Steiner's and Radl's transport aircraft. Obviously, a Junkers Ju.52/3M tri-motor was needed. And, by good fortune, there was one in-country in 1976. Doug Arnold had imported a Spanish Air Force CASA 352L, serialled T.2B-176, and had based it with his Warbirds of Great Britain collection at Blackbushe Airfield. It was shown, but not flown, at the Blackbushe Air Festival in August 1976. It still bore its Spanish Air Force markings and colours. If it was to be used in "The Eagle Has Landed", it would have to be repainted in Luftwaffe camouflage with Nazi Swastika and Balkenkreuzen. That would cost a lot of money, plus the hire of the aircraft and of re-locating it for the sequence in which it would appear at RAF St Mawgan. Would the film's budget be able to absorb that cost for a scene in which the Ju.52 would appear only briefly?

In any case, the plan, like a lot of good ones, failed to survive contact with the enemy, in this case the UK Civil Aviation Authority. Since its arrival in Britain during the sweltering summer of '76, the CAA was taking its time in issuing a Certificate of Airworthiness (CofA) to allow the CASA 352L, and the CASA 2.111E which had accompanied it to Blackbushe, to fly in British airspace. The vintage tri-motor was an unknown quantity to the CAA in 1976 and much had to be learnt about its performance and operation before a CofA could be issued. In reality, this meant the CASA 352L would still be grounded during the time period when it would be needed for filming.

There was still the option of painting it as a Luftwaffe Ju.52/3M and filming it as a static prop at Blackbushe, but this would mean re-locating the entire film crew and the actors in the scene, another costly exercise. No, another option needed to be found.

The only other source of Junkers Ju.52/3M tri-motors in Europe during the Seventies, besides the Spanish Air Force, was the Swiss Air Force which had provided one of its three examples for "Where Eagles Dare" (1968). The cost of hiring one of its Ju.52s and flying it to Cornwall for one short scene was obviously prohibitive. So, what to do?

This is where a film production company's art department really prove their worth and earn their money. The answer, like all the best ones, was simple. The scene called for Radl, Steiner and the Kommandos to walk from the Ju.52 following their arrival towards the hangar at Lansvoort air base. They are seen doing so on what was obviously a blustery wet day, judging by the low, grey sky and waterlogged runway. Guards with large dogs watch them pass. In the foreground, wooden barriers covered in barbed wire are placed with a hardboard sign nailed to the top of one barrier carrying the words, "Unbefugten Eintritt Verboten!" (Unauthorised Entry Forbidden). This sign holds the key to solving the problem of having the Junkers Ju.52 in shot.

What the art department have done is to carve an hardboard, two-dimensional cut-out miniature of a 'Junkers Ju.52/3M' in a pose seen from its starboard forward quarter and paint it as such to create a three-dimensional effect. One end of a wooden shaft is then nailed to the reverse side of the miniature cut-out, the other end in its turn is nailed to the hardboard sign atop the barrier. This means that the miniature cut-out 'Ju.52' is being held aloft at the top of the wooden shaft it is nailed on to, projecting up from the barrier. Junkers on a stick, in other words.

The art department team have made sure the 'Ju.52' is aligned with the horizon in the background, so that the miniature transport aircraft appears to be parked on its wheels on the runway. The camera is positioned so that it is lined up with the angle of the hardboard miniature against the horizon, so that when filmed it will appear that the 'Ju.52' is parked in the distance behind the walking Kommandos, when in fact it is a small cut-out pinned to the barrier well ahead of them! Freeze-frame analysis confirms the shaft or pole on which the cut-out 'Ju.52' is attached; however, no one watching the film as this scene is played out would have had the time to spot it, or realise how the effect was achieved.

The trick worked brilliantly, as shown by the amount of debate among film fans and aviation enthusiasts on Online Forums, many of whom believe it is an actual Junkers Ju.52/3M seen in "The Eagle Has Landed". The author admits he too believed it was a real Ju.52 until a lot of careful examination of the footage in which the 'Ju.52' appears revealed how the effect was achieved.

The key question was, why would the film production company pay so much money to hire a real Junkers Ju.52/3M, then place it in the far background for one very short shot? The answer is, they didn't. They called upon the art department to solve the problem, which they did, as described. Using scale models and miniatures matched with background or foreground full-size objects is an old trick in the movie business. It saves a lot of money and gives free reign to the imagination and the creativity of the art department teams in many film productions. Among some of the best examples are the very clever use of the miniature AcroJet appearing to fly into and out of a hangar in the James Bond film, "Octopussy" (1983), and the C-130 Hercules in another 007 adventure appearing to bomb Russian tanks in Afghanistan in "The Living Daylights" (1987).

There is another clever trick used in this scene at Lansvoort air base. To the left of the 'Ju.52', the nose and propeller of another aircraft is protruding into shot, but this is all that is shown of it. However, in another scene where Caine as Steiner debates with his second-in-command, Captain von Neustadt (played by Swedish actor, Sven-Bertil Taube), about the wisdom of conducting the kidnap operation, an aircraft is clearly visible behind them parked close to the hangar. This is not another cleverly positioned and juxtaposed miniature like the cut-out 'Ju.52'; it is a full-size aircraft, but it too has provoked debate among enthusiasts and historians.

It is very obviously an Hispano HA.1112M1L Buchon painted to represent a Messerschmitt Bf.109G, and it is equally obvious by its colour scheme that it was one of the Buchons used in the "Battle of Britain" (1969) film - it bears the same scheme and the identical Luftwaffe markings that all the Buchons in that film bore, including the Chevron on the fuselage side ahead of the German military Balkenkreuze. But the key questions are, which Buchon is it and where did it come from? Especially, as far as it was known, no HA.1112M1L had remained in the country after the filming of "Battle of Britain" was completed. There was certainly no example on the UK flying display scene during the Seventies, nor in Europe.

Speculation Online has suggested the Warbirds of Great Britain as the source, but despite the ever-growing size of Doug Arnold's collection at Blackbushe in the Seventies, there is no evidence that he owned a Buchon in 1976 and he was not in the historic aircraft purchase business when all the HA.1112M1Ls were put up for disposal at the end of 1968. It was known that most of the Buchons were acquired by US collectors, as described in the review of "Battle of Britain"; but that review does give one possible clue to the identity of the Buchon in "The Eagle Has Landed".

The fate of the HA.1112M1L Buchon used at Pinewood Studios for cockpit shots has not been recorded. Film studios are not wasteful of the props they either acquire or create, and often store them for possible future re-use in other productions. They will also hire them out to different film production companies if needed. There is a strong likelihood that Pinewood Studios retained the Buchon they acquired when the filming of "Battle of Britain" was completed, and that this is the same Buchon in "The Eagle Has Landed".

There are several factors to support this, most particularly in the way the Buchon is filmed. Firstly, just the propeller and a short part of its nose is shown in one shot. Why is that, why not show much more of the airframe? Secondly, in the scene between Caine and Taube, the Buchon is positioned some distance away behind them but is clearly in shot. But it is positioned exactly in profile, not at an angle either from the front or the rear. Why is that? Lastly, there are extra markings on this Buchon, suggesting it has been used since in another production. It has what looks like a large letter 'F' on its engine cowling on the port side, and has what appears to be a two-digit number, or two letters, applied between the Chevron and the Balkenkreuze on the fuselage, plus another number or letter on the opposite side of the Balkenkreuze: these numbers or code letters are too small to read, but they do not equate to the style of Geschwader coding system used by the Luftwaffe and were certainly not applied for the "Battle of Britain" film.

Speculation on the Web suggests the Buchon may be one of the full-size replicas built for that film; except, as described in the review of "Battle of Britain" in Chapter Four, Pinewood's art department made the mistake of creating Messerschmitt Bf.109Es, out of wood, using a genuine example as a pattern. They, as described in "Battle of Britain", did not match the Buchons in that film. However, the Buchon in "The Eagle Has Landed" makes another, different appearance: it appears in a publicity still photo and was actually used on one of the film's advertising posters, with Michael Caine standing beside it in his Wehrmacht Colonel's uniform.

This close-up of the Buchon clearly shows the engine exhaust stacks and other details, absolutely confirming it is the real thing and not a replica made out of wood.

There is also something not quite right about this publicity still photo of Michael Caine and the Buchon: it has to do with the position Caine is standing in relation to it, close to the fuselage just behind the cockpit. His positioning finally gives the clue as to what is rather odd about this Buchon and why it is filmed in full only in profile.

It has no wings.

If the wings were attached, Caine could not be standing where he is positioned in relation to the aircraft for the publicity still and poster shot. In the film, it has been placed at an exact broadside angle because any other position would reveal that it is wingless. The art department appear to have either painted wings onto the fuselage sides, or fixed short mock-ups to the wing join, because the Buchon would still look strange if they were not there - the latter is more likely, because there is a trace of a shadow on the ground beneath where the wings would be, were they attached. This would also explain why only the nose and propeller of the Buchon appears in the previous shot, alongside the fake 'Ju.52'.

So, "The Eagle Has Landed" has a Hispano HA.1112M1L Buchon in two scenes, used as a prop to depict a parked Messerschmit Bf.109 on a captured airfield in Holland. If it is the example obtained by Pinewood Studios, and kept by them since for use in other film productions, then it will be HA.1112M1L C.4K-111. One thing is clear, judging by its appearance in "The Eagle Has Landed", it had suffered during its time in film work, as the propeller blade above the nose cone has been bent forward slightly!

Incidentally, these two scenes with the Buchon, plus that of the cut-out 'Ju.52', were cut from the film originally released to the cinema in 1977; not until the full cut was released on DVD did we film fans and aviation enthusiasts ever discover the existence of these two 'aircraft'!

The last aircraft needed for "The Eagle Has Landed" posed Doug Bianchi far less of a challenge, a captured RAF Dakota. Whether he chose the particular aircraft that appears in the film deliberately because he knew of its history cannot be known, but if he did then Bianchi could not have made a more historically appropriate choice. He approached Intra Airways and asked if they would loan him their Douglas C-47D Dakota IV G-AKNB, which happened to be the oldest former RAF Dakota still flying. Intra Airways had no hesitation in agreeing to the loan. They themselves carried out the paint work of applying a reasonably accurate wartime RAF camouflage scheme, at the location of their engineering company at Exeter Airport in Devon, where Dakota IV G-AKNB was regularly serviced.

Intra Airways were a Channel Islands-based airline, set up in 1969 to operate passenger and cargo charters from Jersey's States Airport to England and to the Continent. Dakota IV G-AKNB was their first and, for several years, their sole aircraft. By the time it was loaned for use in "The Eagle Has Landed", it had been joined by four more Dakotas, while Intra had also begun to acquire the first of three Vickers Viscounts. Intra Airways was, in effect, the founding company of today's FlyBe airline, having

merged in 1979 with Bournemouth Airport-based Express Air Freight, Ltd, to create the very successful and long-running Jersey European Airways which, in its turn, evolved into the highly successful FlyBe.

Dakota IV G-AKNB is the former FD789, having been completed at Long Beach, California, as USAAF 42-32817 and delivered to the Royal Air Force under Lend-Lease on 7th March 1943. It served with Nos.24 and 512 Squadrons at RAF Hendon between April 1943 - March 1944, before serving out the remainder of its wartime career with two Transport Operational Training Units. Put into storage with No.22 Maintenance Unit at RAF Silloth, Northumberland, this Dakota was first registered as G-AKNB in November 1947 with Scottish Aviation at Prestwick. This was the start of a lengthy and varied civil career for G-AKNB between 1947 - 1986, during which time it went through ten changes of ownership and was twice operated overseas, in Burma and Ireland, returning afterwards to the British civil register, each time with the same registration as before.

Intra Airways was the eighth company to operate G-AKNB. It was an easy acquisition for the airline to make because G-AKNB was, in 1968, being operated by British United Island Airways (BUIA) out of Jersey, and it was BUIA employees who set up Intra Airways the following year - they simply acquired the same aircraft they had been operating with their former employer.

A significant occurrence in this aircraft's history was its acquisition by Aces High in January 1982, who loaned it to Harvest Air for anti-pollution spraying, operating from Blackpool/Squires Gate Airport. While based there it was damaged by means unknown and was grounded for a short period of time, until Aces High had it repaired. However, during this inactive period G-AKNB took on its former RAF identity when it was painted as Dakota FD789 for an appearance in the film, "The Dirty Dozen: Next Mission" (1985). Aces High retained this paint scheme and based G-AKNB/FD789 at Duxford where, in 1986, it took part in the TV mini-series, "War and Remembrance" (1988).

Following its appearance in that production, Dakota G-AKNB was sold to Northern Airways of Burlington, Vermont, USA, and placed on the US civil register as N459NA. It has remained in the USA ever since, undergoing three more changes of ownership. Today it is operated by the Rare Air Inc collection as N59NA, painted as C-47-DL Skytrain 42-32814/3J/B, named Bones.

Dakota IV G-AKNB appears as RAF Dakota 'CR496' in "The Eagle Has Landed", a fictitious RAF serial. It is first seen in the hangar at Lansvoort air base, where Steiner's Kommandos prepare for their mission. It is later seen filmed air-air before Paratroopers jump from it. This is meant to be taking place over the Norfolk coastline, but actually is filmed over the north Cornish coast. The German Kommandos jumping from the Dakota are actually the eight-man REME (Royal Electrical and Mechanical Engineers) Parachute Display Team of 1976. The air-airs of them jumping from the Dakota were filmed over RAF St Mawgan during a week-end, when the big Nimrods were inactive and when the film company could virtually have the airfield to themselves, apart from scheduled arrivals and departures by

Brymon's Twin Otter. Several jump runs were made, so that both distant and close-up shots of the REME Paras exiting the Dakota by static line could be obtained.

The script, however, called for the Kommandos to be seen landing in what was meant to be Norfolk. Cornwall looks nothing like Norfolk. So, what to do? The answer was, have the Kommandos land on the beach. This inevitably meant some of the Paras risked landing in the sea, which is exactly what happened, so proper rescue facilities had to be laid on, provided by the Padstow RNLI with their RIBs (rubber inflated boats). The jump onto the beach and into the sea was completed safely on a very clear, sunny day, confirming it was filmed on a day different to when the REME Para team made their jumps from the Dakota. Study of the footage confirms that the REME Paras made free fall descents. The 'Kommandos' seen in the film hauling in their parachute canopies from the sea are the REME Paras themselves.

From this point onwards in "The Eagle Has Landed", aircraft no longer feature in the plot.

So, what fifty per cent of the truth in the story do you believe? Well, on 20th May 1994 classified papers dating from late 1943 were released by the British authorities that confirm there was a Nazi plot to assassinate Churchill on his route back to Britain from the Cairo conference. British Intelligence had learnt from Enigma intercepts by Bletchley Park that Churchill's flight plan via Algiers and Gibraltar had been obtained by the Nazis, and four agents had been despatched to Algiers to carry out the assassination. Acting on the advice of 'C', the head of the Secret Intelligence Service, Churchill changed his flight plan to stop off only at Marrakesh. At this same time, the KLM DC-3 carrying the film actor and director Leslie Howard back to Whitchurch, Bristol, from Lisbon was shot down over the Bay of Biscay by Ju.88C-6s of V/JG.40. Accompanying Howard was his accountant and travelling companion, Alfred Tregear Chenhalls, who apparently bore a physical resemblance to Churchill. It has been speculated that German spies in Lisbon mistook Chenhalls for Churchill, alerted Berlin and the attack on the defenceless DC-3 was thus ordered.

Jack Higgins got his inspiration for part of "The Eagle Has Landed" from the 1942 British war film, "Went The Day Well?", mentioned in Chapter One, which opens with a memorial stone in a church graveyard stating that the bodies of German Paratroopers were buried there: Higgins's novel of "The Eagle Has Landed" begins in similar fashion. Made during the War, "Went The Day Well?" is the story of a complete village taken over by German Paratroopers, until the villagers fight back with the aid of British troops coming to their rescue. It is set at the time Britain was preparing for the then expected German invasion.

It is very unlikely a memorial stone for German Paratroopers killed in the attempted assassination of Churchill in Norfolk would be allowed to exist. If the authorities wanted such an event covered up, no such memorial stone would be permitted. Even if it had been placed there clandestinely sometime afterwards beneath another memorial stone for someone else, as Higgins claims in his novel, it certainly won't be there now, thanks to his revelation. And how can such an event be kept secret? The villagers may keep silent during the War years, but somebody is going to speak out sooner or later, especially later generations who wouldn't be made subject to the Official Secrets Act, as the villagers of the time would have been.

The British authorities would not have had the bodies of the dead German Paratroopers buried in the village, anyway; they would have been taken away and, if nothing was to come out in the future, completely disposed of.

Personally, I think Jack Higgins is the Dan Brown of his generation and, like the author of "The Da Vinci Code", had an inventive mind and knew how to tell a good story.

A BRIDGE TOO FAR

(Released: June 1977)

If any British war film took to heart the mantra that Americans must be shown to be strong, courageous, intelligent and determined in action, while the British have to be portrayed as vascillating, vain, snobbish and defeatist in comparison, in order to ensure box office success in America, then "A Bridge Too Far" is streets ahead in this regard of any other production made in Britain before or since. Director Richard Attenborough (Academy Award winner as best director for "Ghandi", 1982) and scriptwriter William Goldman (Academy Award winner for his screenplay for "Butch Cassidy and the Sundance Kid", 1969) leave no stone unturned in their pursuit of stereotyping the main American and British characters in this huge World War Two epic as positively and as negatively in respect of either nationality as it was possible for them to do.

Aviation, of course, plays a major role in this giant re-telling of Operation Market Garden. Not since "Battle of Britain" (1969) and "Tora! Tora! Tora!" (1970) have so many aviation assets been assembled for a war film production. "A Bridge Too Far", based on author Cornelius Ryan's reconstruction of what was, until the Airborne Forces mass drop on the Rhine just over six months later, the largest military airborne assault in history, does gain credit for staging the mass Paratroop landings so realistically (although the film could not show the many different aircraft types involved, obviously, due to most of them no longer existing). In so doing, it is clear that Attenborough, Goldman and father and son producers, Joseph E Levine and Richard P Levine, must have been influenced by the 1945 re-enactment of the assault on Arnhem Bridge in "Theirs Is The Glory" (1946), reviewed in Chapter Two, as there are distinct similarities between various shots and scenes in both films. We will look at these as they occur.

"A Bridge Too Far" opens with archive footage, shown as if it were on a Forties era cinema screen, beginning with a series of flak bursts (actually art work imagery from an unknown wartime film) that are followed by a shot of three Martin B-26 Marauders simultaneously unloading their sticks of bombs as they fly in 'Vic' formation. The camera follows the bombs down, then suddenly film editor Anthony Gibbs freeze-frames the shot. A European-accented woman's voice then speaks, saying, "It is hard to remember now, but Europe was like this in 1944". The film then moves on to show the bombs hitting and detonating - there is no obvious target in sight, so this footage was probably of a fire power demonstration, not that of live combat.

Further on into this opening archive footage an air-air of another Martin B-26 Marauder appears over-flying the D-Day invasion fleet. General Eisenhower is seen exiting a Douglas C-47 Skytrain, the serial of which is in shot but camera blur is such that the number is unreadable. The tail of a C-47, possibly the same one, is seen in another shot as 'Ike' pours over a map with his Generals. The C-47 was possibly Eisenhower's personal transport, but research has not revealed its identity.

The voice of the woman giving the opening monologue, which is played as more archive film is rolled showing Hitler, Churchill and Montgomery among others, is that of Norwegian actress Liv Ullmann. This pale, Nordic beauty was very much in vogue in both European and American cinema of the Seventies, due to her compelling and sensuous roles in films made by famous Swedish director, Ingmar Bergman. Ullmann is actually speaking in her voice-over as Dutch housewife Kate ter Horst, who she portrays later in the film: the real Kate ter Horst nursed more than 250 wounded and dying British Paratroopers in her home during the battle for Arnhem, and can be seen as herself in "Theirs Is The Glory". However, when "A Bridge Too Far" was released, neither British nor American cinema audiences understood the significance of Liv Ullmann's monologue, or even why a European-accented woman was speaking.

The monologue, written by Goldman, is factually inaccurate. Ullmann has to say that the War was in its fifth year and still going Hitler's way. In the first half of 1944, that was decidedly not so: the Wehrmacht had suffered crushing defeats in North Africa and Russia; Italy and Sicily had left the Axis Powers and joined with the Allies; the Mediterranean and the Middle East were controlled by the British; Occupied Bulgaria, Yugoslavia and Greece were isolated and breaking up into factional local wars which Germany could not control; and the U-Boat threat to Britain was considerably diminished. Following the D-Day landings in June 1944, the Wehrmacht forces were being sytematically pushed back through France and Belgium towards the Rhine.

Goldman uses Ullmann's monologue to perpetuate the American myth that Eisenhower's "two most famous generals, Patton in the South and Montgomery in the North (after D-Day), disliked each other intensely. Their longstanding rivalry had never been more fierce".

In reality, Patton and Montgomery had little to do with each other while serving under Supreme Allied Commander, General Dwight D Eisenhower. Both had real personality problems, not only with their opposite numbers among the Allies, but with their own Generals and fellow officers in their own respective armies.

The myth that Patton and Montgomery were rivals to each other was fostered by director Franklin J Schaffner and screen writers Francis Ford Coppola and Edmund H North in their otherwise excellent Academy Award-winning production of "Patton" (1970). It is exaggerated even more by Goldman and Attenborough in "A Bridge Too Far". The film fails to acknowledge

that Montgomery was superior in rank and command to Patton at the time of Market Garden, who wasn't even involved in the assault on the Rhine bridges.

Goldman also propagates the additional myth that Montgomery and Patton were in a race with their respective armies to get to Berlin before the other; palpable nonsense because 'Monty' was in command of an entire Army Group, made up of the British and Canadian Armies, while Patton had only been brought into action one month earlier than Market Garden as Commander of the US Third Army, and was subordinate to US General Bradley (who disliked Patton intensely). If Montgomery was superior in command to Patton and had under him a complete Army Group, while Patton was Commander of only one Army, how could Patton be Montgomery's rival?

Following the title credits, the film opens with German forces retreating through Holland ahead of the Allies' advance. A curious shot shows a close-up of a young woman's face amid the German troops. As with the Liv Ullmann monologue, there is no explanation for the audience to understand the reason for her presence. She is actually a Dutch collaborator played by a Dutch actress. This scene was filmed not just for "A Bridge Too Far", but also for a Dutch film, "Soldier of Orange", which was produced jointly with the Levines' production and shared various facilities, scenes and assets. These included a number of the aircraft in "A Bridge Too Far", as will be described.

Goldman's and Attenborough's treatment of the character of the Deputy Commander of the First Allied Airborne Army, and Operational Commander of Operation Market Garden, Lieutenant General Frederick Browning (played by Dirk Bogarde), has become one of the most controversial elements of the film and certainly sets the tone for the director's and screenwriter's combined denigration of most of the British personalities in the plot in favour of the upstanding, worthy American ones. Bogarde plays Browning as being supercilious, mocking and effete, everything that the real General Browning was not. Bogarde apparently protested to Attenborough about having to play Browning in this fashion, with good reason because Bogarde knew Browning at the time of Market Garden, he having been a British Army Intelligence Officer on Browning's staff. To no avail; one wonders why Bogarde didn't walk off set.

Bogarde is one among a number of well known British actors who played challenging, memorable roles in British war films after World War Two itself, but who are forced to debase themselves in "A Bridge Too Far": Jeremy Kemp ("The Blue Max", "Operation Crossbow") as a quite stupid and unbelievably embarrassing RAF briefing officer, Denholm Elliott ("They Who Dare", alongside Bogarde) as a weakly apologetic RAF Met. Officer, and Edward Fox ("Battle of Britain") as a plummy Lieutenant General Brian Horrocks, Commander of XXX (30) Corps, the Garden ground forces element of the Operation (although Fox is on record as claiming his portrayal of Horrocks to be his favourite film role and one that he believes to be accurate). Attenborough himself made some outstanding performances as an actor in British war films ("Journey Together", "Gift Horse", "Sea of Sand", "Dunkirk"), ever since his uncredited debut in "In Which We Serve" (1942) as a petrified sailor who deserts his post. It is a real shame he allowed himself to direct this travesty of British servicemen in war, in order to appeal to American prejudices about British military personnel.

The aviation elements provide some of the best scenarios in the film. A total of 28 aircraft, powered and glider, were assembled together for the production. Although the scenes showing the aerial armada taking off on the opening day of Operation Market Garden are meant to be taking place at airfields in England, they are all shot at the Royal Netherlands Air Force base of Deelen in Holland. Much of the aerial filming took place between 31st August - 21st September 1976.

Eleven Douglas C-47 Dakotas from four separate sources were either purchased by or loaned to Visionair, which operated them on behalf of Joseph E Levine Presents Incorporated. One of them was a genuine Operation Market Garden veteran. The Portuguese Air Force sold two C-47s to the company, with serials FAP 6153 and FAP 6171, which were registered N9984Q and N9983Q respectively. Two more C-47s owned by Air Djibouti that were operating from Djibouti, the capital of French Somaliland, with the registrations F-OCKU and F-OCKX, were also acquired and re-registered as N9986Q and N9985Q with Visionair (apparently, the British Paratroopers jumping from the C-47s in the film nicknamed the two Air Djibouti aircraft, 'Jam Butty Airlines'). The Royal Danish Air Force and the Finnish Air Force agreed to loan C-47 Dakotas that they still had in service: three came from the Danes, serialled K-685, K-687 and K-688, while the Finns provided the final four marked as DO-4, DO-7, DO-10 and DO-12.

All eleven Dakotas were painted to represent USAAF Douglas C-47 Skytrain or C-53 Skytrooper transports for the air drop scenes. Some briefly wore RAF roundels to represent RAF C-47 Dakotas. While they look very convincing in their scenes, in fact a major goof was made in painting the C-47s in sand brown colour schemes. USAAF C-47s did wear this style of colour scheme for operations in North Africa, Sicily and Italy, but by the time the invasion of Europe was due to take place in Normandy they had all adopted olive drab paint schemes. How and why this mistake was made by the art department is not known. Considering the number of military advisers the film makers had available to them to consult, this was an error that should have been avoided. The RAF never adopted the sand brown scheme for their Dakotas, so the sight of them in the film with roundels is incongruous to the collective eye of the enthusiast and the historian.

The most interesting aircraft in the film are the four North American (or, more correctly, Noorduyn) AT-16 Harvard IIs which are pressed into service as Allied fighter-bombers. They all underwent ingenious conversions into USAAF P-47 Thunderbolts and RAF Hawker Typhoons. It was these four Harvards which were shared with the "Soldier of Orange" production, when they adopted the guise of Luftwaffe Focke Wulf FW.190s and made very convincing-looking Luchtvaartafdeling (Dutch Army Aviation Group) Fokker D.XXIs, the principal Dutch fighter at the time of the Nazi invasion of the Netherlands in May 1940.

Two of the Harvards, serialled B-64 and B-118, were still on the strength of the Royal Netherlands Air Force (RNLAF) and were loaned for the production. Two more, on the Dutch civil register as PH-BKT and PH-KLU, were ex-RNLAF machines then being operated by the Gilze-Rijen Aero Club, located at the Gilze-Rijen air base. The conversions into American, British, Dutch and German fighters were all conducted by the Gilze-Rijen Aero Club, who also provided the pilots, all either serving or former officers of the RNLAF.

The Harvards were capable of releasing dummy bombs, as they are seen doing when, as Hawker Typhoons, they attack entrenched Wehrmacht defences to clear the way for XXX Corps. In this large-scale set-piece, the 'Typhoons' are seen carrying 'HF-' code letters. These almost certainly relate to No.183 Squadron, a Hawker Typhoon Ib unit which bore these codes when it was operating in the Netherlands during 1944 - '45, covering the Allies' push towards the Rhine. Curiously, one of the Harvards painted in RAF green-brown camouflage has a red tail rudder with white flash towards the top. This almost certainly has been left in place after the same Harvard had doubled as a Fokker D.XXI for its appearance in "Soldier of Orange".

The Gilze-Rijen Aero Club also provided the Auster III PH-NGK, which acts the role of an Auster VI delegated to General Browning as his personal liaison aircraft. The Auster is accurately painted in the correct camouflage and markings of the 1944 period. It was given the serial RT607, which actually had belonged to an Auster AOP.V.

A timid and wretched British Army Intelligence Officer timorously suggests to Browning that another low-level photo reconnaissance of the drop zones be ordered because he feels uncertain the intelligence about the German defences being manned by old men and Hitler Youth is correct. Attenborough lays it on thick with this stammering officer, sweaty, tie askew in most un-British Army fashion, confessing that "I know that everyone thinks I'm over anxious". It is true that Browning ignored photo intelligence of German armour and allegedly later had the Intelligence Officer removed on health grounds, but this weak, sad individual is just not credible. He does get his PR sortie, though.

For British aviation enthusiasts, the scene with the PR Spitfire appearing like a winged ghost above the road on which a boy is cycling in Holland is one of the most magical in the film. It is played by Vickers Supermarine Spitfire HF.Mk.IXb MH434, making its fourth film appearance. It is flown in the film by one of Britain's most celebrated pilots of the time, Neil Williams, British National Aerobatic Champion, who was denied being made World Aerobatic Champion in Kiev the same year that filming took place by conniving Soviet judges. The way Williams just appears above the road in MH434 as if out of nothing is the hallmark of his skill as a pilot.

Spitfire MH434 was not painted in 'wardrobe' for its appearance in "A Bridge Too Far"; it bears the markings it wore for much of the airshow seasons in Britain throughout the Seventies, particularly the 'AC-S' codes which were not squadron code letters, but the initials of its then owner, Adrian Swire, Chairman of Cathay Pacific Airways.

Tragically, Neil Williams was killed, along with his wife and two aircrewmen, just six months after the release of "A Bridge Too Far" when they were ferrying back to Britain an ex-Spanish Air Force CASA 2.111 (one of the many that had been used in "Battle of Britain") that crashed into a Spanish mountain.

Built especially for the film were ten Airspeed Horsa troop-carrying assault gliders. These were full-scale static props, not new-build aircraft. Some were 'shells', partially completed airframes easily dismantled for set-dressing. However, not only were they accurately created, but equally they were accurately painted in the correct camouflage and matt black schemes as borne by Horsas used for Operation Market Garden in September 1944. Adding to their realism are the chalked numbers and names on their fuselage sides. Shown is Horsa numbered '683' with the name 'London Pride', presumably associated with the brand of real ale of that name produced by the brewery Fuller's Ales in Chiswick, West London. Three other Horsas are numbered '611', '463' and '261' respectively. Presumably, these numbers and markings were researched from archive material, almost certainly including "Theirs Is The Glory".

Without any Short Stirling or Handley Page Halifax converted bombers that were used in 1944 available, the film production team had to resort to using the C-47 Dakotas as glider-tugs, painted with RAF roundels. Or so it appears; in reality, carefully managed and inter-cut shots of Dakotas beginning to roll and of Horsas starting to move with tow ropes attached create the impression that the big gliders are actually being aero-towed off the ground by the Dakota transports.

One shot appears to have been filmed from a glider's cockpit as it lifts off the runway of Deelen air base, with the Dakota towing it clearly in view ahead. The tow rope extends from beneath the Dakota's tail and appears to have been attached to its tail wheel. This system would never have been used in reality: the tail wheel would have been wrenched off. Instead, dedicated towing apparatus was built in to the rear fuselage of the RAF C-47 Dakota and USAAF C-47 Skytrain glider-tugs.

This aero-tow shot was achieved by having the Dakota tow a LET L-13 Blanik sports glider off the runway. This must have been a challenge because the wake wash from the Dakota would surely have caused the small glider behind it to wobble quite a lot, while the take off itself would have been at a much higher speed than if the Blanik was being aero-towed by the usual type of small, single-engined light aircraft normally employed by gliding clubs. The Blanik was probably airborne before the Dakota had rolled more than 50 feet. Judging by the angle of the shot from the cockpit, the Blanik pilot climbed quickly to get above the towing Dakota and just held his glider there, well out of the Dakota's wake wash. Eight other C-47s and two Horsas had been set up on either side of the runway as set-dressing for this shot.

The take offs by the C-47s were filmed over and over again from a whole variety of angles, some from within a C-47, to create the impression of the departure by the massive aerial armada. Shots are then seen of the huge numbers of C-47s over-flying a church and a street scene in England, with people watching from the ground. This is a direct copy of similar shots seen in "Theirs Is The

Glory", confirming that the 1946 production definitely influenced parts of "A Bridge Too Far". The effect is achieved by the split screen technique to create imagery of greater numbers of C-47s than were actually filmed, which is then used as a matte overlay onto the shots of the church and the street buildings. When the extras in the street were filmed looking up at the streams of C-47s passing overhead, the aircraft weren't there.

Similarly, when aerial shots are shown of so many C-47s in formation, the split screen technique is used to create the effect of large numbers of troop transports in the air. The air-air shots of Dakotas towing Horsas has been achieved with the Dakota towing the Blanik superimposed onto a matte painting of Dakotas towing the big gliders - the giveaway is that none of the matte Dakotas and Horsas are moving, only the real flying Dakota!

The air drop shots are the best part of "A Bridge Too Far". Very impressively staged, up to 1,000 Paratroopers were used from 1st Battalion, 16th Parachute Brigade, the Parachute Regiment, all jumping for real from ten out of the eleven C-47s: the 11th C-47 was used as an airborne camera platform amid the formation. Other aerial shots were achieved from a Piper Aztec camera-ship, painted the same sand brown colour as the C-47s, and from an Alouette helicopter.

Again, the influence of "Theirs Is The Glory" is apparent here, especially with the camera shot from one of the actual para-jumpers amid the mass of Paratroops in the air. The drops were very carefully pre-planned and went ahead without a hitch. All the Paras rehearsed jumping out of the C-47s on the ground, to make certain they exited the venerable troop transports correctly. Practice jumps were also made from Dakota C.3 ZA947, then with the Royal Aerospace Establishment, at a week-end over its base at RAE Farnborough, right next door to the Parachute Regiment's barracks at Aldershot.

The 1st Battalion, 16th Parachute Brigade, treated the jump scenes as a full military exercise. They considered it a special honour because the drop zones used were the same as in September 1944, so the Paras really felt they were re-creating history while honouring their former comrades who fell in the battle at Arnhem.

Some of the Horsa gliders were set up as set-dressing on the drop zones. This, however, is inaccurate: glider landing zones and Paratroop landing zones were mostly kept separate, unless the Paratroops landed first to clear the area for the gliders which landed later. Having the Paratroops landing with the gliders already in place is a goof. The Horsas also had to double for USAAF gliders, which the US Airborne did use, but the troop glider that would have been more accurate for them was the Waco GC-4A Hadrian.

The mass drop attracted significant media attention at the time. Hollywood star, Robert Redford, who appears in the film, came to watch the drop and was willing to be interviewed by BBC TV as it took place. Redford called over a Para who landed near him with a large bruise on his face. Redford was impressed, thinking the bruise had been inflicted as the Paratrooper hit the ground, and asked the Para just how dangerous it was making the jump. The Para replied with a grin that he had got the bruise in a bar fight the night before.

Following the mass landings and the attacks by the Hawker Typhoons on Wehrmacht artillery positions concealed in a forest, aviation does not feature again in "A Bridge Too Far" until towards the end when the C-47s make supply drops in desperate attempts to relieve the besieged 1st Airborne Division in Arnhem.

What happened to all the aircraft that appeared in "A Bridge Too Far"? Three out of four of the Harvards are alive and kicking, while seven out of the 11 C-47s are extant, although the condition of two of them is not thought to be healthy. The Auster III is still active. And, of course, the 'PR' Spitfire is a long-standing airshow favourite. All bar one of the Horsa facsimiles failed to survive the film production: they weren't made with preservation in mind and, with no future use earmarked for them as props, were chopped up and burnt. The one that did survive - at least, temporarily - is believed to have been bought by a collector, but, when it was left outside during a damp winter, it deteriorated so quickly that it too was disposed of.

Here is a resume of the fate of all the aircraft that appear in "A Bridge Too Far":

Auster III PH-NGK. Owned by the Stichting Vliegsport Gilze-Rijen, which translates into English as the Gilze-Rijen Aero-Sport Foundation (the correct title for the Gilze-Rijen Aero Club). Former Koninklijke Luchtmacht (Royal Netherlands Air Force) Auster AOP.3, coded R-18. Served with the RNLAF between the Fifties and Sixties. Today, forms part of the Stichting Koninklijke Luchtmacht Historische Vlucht (RNLAF Historical Flight Foundation), based at Gilze-Rijen, still in flying condition painted in its original RNLAF colours and code.

Douglas C-47A K-685 (USAAF 42-100828), Royal Danish Air Force, returned to Denmark after completing filming. One of three RDAF C-47As purchased by the Valiant Air Command of Tico, Titusville, in August 1983. Was used as a jump-ship by the United States Army Parachute Team, The Golden Knights, that same year in the USA. Sold to Seco Aviation Company, registered as N3240A, with whom it still operates in Augusta, Georgia, today.

Douglas C-47A K-687 (USAAF 42-100737), Royal Danish Air Force, returned to Denmark after completing filming. After retirement from RDAF service, K-687 was selected for preservation, firstly in the Danmarks Flyvemuseum (Danish Aviation Museum) at Bilund, now today with the Dansk Veteranflysambling (Danish Collection of Flying Vintage Aircraft) at Stauning.

Douglas C-47A K-688 (USAAF 43-15652), Royal Danish Air Force, returned to Denmark after completing filming. After retirement from RDAF service, K-688 was presented to the Militaire Luchtvaart Museum (Dutch Military Aviation Museum) and displayed as a Dutch-East Indies Air Force C-47 with the code 'T-443'. Although still with the Museum, this C-47A was stored at Soesterberg air base by the end of 2011, along with other aircraft from the same collection, pending a decision as to where the Museum will be sited.

Douglas C-47A DO-4 (USAAF 43-48254), Finnish Air Force, returned to Finland after completing filming. Today, displayed in its original markings at the Keski-Suomen Ilmailumuseo (Aviation Museum of Central Finland), Tikkakoski.

Douglas C-47A DO-7 (USAAF 42-100646), Finnish Air Force, returned to Finland after completing filming. Was purchased by the Dutch Dakota Association (DDA), registered PH-DDA, and flown throughout Western Europe in the Eighties and the Nineties at airshows and on pleasure flights. Tragically, was lost in a fatal accident on 25th September 1996 when PH-DDA crashed on a mud flat, killing all 32 people on board.

Douglas C-47A DO-10 (USAAF 42-92268), Finnish Air Force, returned to Finland after completing filming. On 3rd October 1978, DO-10 crashed into Lake Juuruvesi when trying to return to Kuopio Airport, from where it had departed on a military flight to Helsinki Airport but had suffered engine failure on take-off.

Douglas C-47A DO-12 (USAAF 42-93096), Finnish Air Force, returned to Finland after filming. This C-47A was the one genuine Market Garden veteran to take part in the film, having dropped the 506th 'Pathfinders' in the opening phase of the Operation. It was sold to the USA in the late Eighties, as N58NA with Saber Aviation of Charlotte, North Carolina, with whom it operates today. This C-47A is displayed on the US airshow circuit in its original Ninth Air Force markings, coded 8Y and named Haawka.

Douglas C-47B F-OCKU (USAAF 43-48549) of Air Djibouti. Registered N9986Q with Visionair for the film. Sold afterwards to Ethiopian Airlines as ET-AHR. Written off in December 1981 after it was struck by a crashing helicopter on 7th October that same year.

Douglas C-47B F-OCKX (USAAF 43-49954) of Air Djibouti. Registered N9985Q with Visionair for the film. Sold afterwards to African Air Carriers, then later operated by Interocean Airways. Reportedly donated to the Dakota Association of South Africa, but also reported to have been scrapped at Lanseria, near Johannesburg.

Douglas C-47B FAP 6171 (USAAF 44-77200), Portuguese Air Force. Registered N9983Q with Visionair for the film. On 16th July 1976, six weeks before filming began, Visionair ferried N9983Q to Sweden for its new owners, Stiftelse for Flyghjal. Registered SE-GUL, it was allowed to continue to participate in the film. Afterwards, it was sent to RRC Air Service (RRC: Ethiopian Relief and Rehabilitation Commission) in Ethiopia. Subsequently, it was 'parted out' as ET-AHS with Ethiopian Airlines. Last seen in derelict condition at Bole Airport in Addis Ababa.

Douglas C-53D FAP 6153 (USAAF 42-68741), Portuguese Air Force. Registered N9984Q with Visionair for the film. Former TAP aircraft, as CS-TDE, this C-53D is recorded as being written off in February 1959. It was probably one of five TAP/FAP C-47s/C-53s sold to DETA in Mozambique. All five were taken back on charge with the FAP again in 1971. In 1976, C-53D FAP 6153 and C-47B FAP 6171 were both being operated in the aerial photography role by AB.1 (Portelo) when they were sold to Visionair. Noted in 1977 as being 9Q-CYC with Air Kasai in Zaire. Later with Regie des Vois Aeriennes. Believed to be currently stored at Ndjili, Kinshasa, condition unknown.

Noorduyn AT-16 Harvard IIb B-64, Royal Netherlands Air Force, airworthy, but in use as an instructional airframe. Appears as Hawker Typhoon coded 'HF-J' in the film. Extant today as PH-LSK with the RNLAF Historical Flight Foundation.

Noorduyn AT-16 Harvard IIb B-118, Royal Netherlands Air Force, also in use as an instructional airframe but capable of flying. Appears as Hawker Typhoon 'HF-N' in the film. Extant today as PH-IIB with the RNLAF Historical Flight Foundation.

Noorduyn AT-16 Harvard IIb PH-BKT of the Gilze-Rijen Aero-Sport Foundation. Originally B-135 with the RNLAF. Appears as Hawker Typhoon 'HF-L' in the film; was to have appeared as Focke Wulf FW.190 '-+5' as well, and to have been shot down, but this sequence not used (appeared in the same FW.190 markings in "Soldier of Orange", along with at least one other Harvard in the same FW.190 guise). Later, lost in a fatal accident that cost the lives of its pilot and passenger.

Noorduyn AT-16 Harvard IIb PH-KLU of the Gilze-Rijen Aero-Sport Foundation. Originally B-59 with the RNLAF. Registration PH-KLU is a salute to the Koninklijke Luchtmacht (KLu). Appears as Hawker Typhoon 'HF-S' and P-47 Thunderbolt 'MX-W'. Also converted into Focke Wulf FW.190 '-+7' for the film, but again not used (although is used as such in "Soldier of Orange"). Extant today with the RNLAF Historical Flight Foundation.

Vickers Supermarine Spitfire HF.Mk.IXb MH434/AC-S (G-ASJV), owned by Adrian Swire and based at Wycombe Air Park, Booker. Arguably the most filmed Spitfire in history, MH434 already had three film credits to its name ("The Longest Day", 1962, "Operation Crossbow", 1965, and "Battle of Britain", 1969) when it appeared in "A Bridge Too Far". However, its appearance in this film marks its most prominent role to date, as a photo-reconnaisance Spitfire making a low-level PR sortie over the Arnhem drop zone area.

Spitfire HF.IXb MH434 appears as itself in the film, wearing the D-Day invasion stripes and the 'AC-S' initials of its owner as its code letters, in which markings it appeared at many airshows in the Seventies. It was synonymous then, as it always has been, with the pilot who flew it for four decades, giving so many spectacular aerobatic displays: former Red Arrows team leader, Squadron Leader Ray Hanna. But, in "A Bridge Too Far", it is British Aerobatic Champion and former RAF test pilot, Flight Lieutenant Neil Williams, who makes the swooping low-level passes over the son of a Dutch Resistance leader in the film. In fact, during the mid-Seventies, Neil Williams flew MH434 more often than Ray Hanna, who was mostly occupied at the time flying Convair 880s and Boeing 707s for Cathay Pacific out of Hong Kong. MH434 was maintained by Personal Plane Services at Booker, for whom Neil Williams was CAA examiner for all the historic aircraft PPS operated, restored and serviced. When Hanna was not available, the agreement was that Williams would display it.

Spitfire Mk.IXb MH434 was air tested on its first flight from Castle Bromwich in August 1943 by another Spitfire 'great', Vickers' test pilot Alex Henshaw. That same month, MH434 was issued to No.222 (Natal) Squadron, coded ZD-B. It was flown by South African Flight Lieutenant Henry Lardner-Burke, DFC, who claimed 7½ 'kills', plus 3 damaged: four of these victories he attained in MH434, consisting of two FW.190s, a half-share in the 'kill' of a Bf.109G, and damaging a third FW.190, all over the Normandy and Northern France areas between 27th August - 8th September 1943.

MH434 was transferred to No.350 Squadron in March 1944 before returning for a second spell with No.222, during which time it flew missions over Normandy on D-Day 6th June 1944, when No.222 was part of No.135 Wing, 18 Sector, 2nd TAF; it completed 79 operational sorties overall during World War Two.

Post-War, MH434 was put up for disposal in 1946. It was acquired by the Royal Netherlands Air Force in 1947 and allocated to the Dutch-East Indies Air Force, joining No.322 Squadron in Java where it operated in the classic ground-attack role in clipped-wing configuration, coded H-105 and H-68. A belly landing at Semarang, Java, on 7th May 1949 forced it into storage and a return to Holland, where it remained before flying again on 10th March 1953. Later that same year, MH434 was sold to the Belgian Air Force with which it operated for three years as SM-41, flown by the Advanced Pilot School at Koksijde and with No.13 Wing at Brustem. On 26th March 1956, MH434 began a new career as a target-tug operated by the Belgian COGEA company at Ostende with the civil registration OO-ARA, on a contract to the Belgian and NATO forces. It was during this time that it became one of the four Spitfires loaned by COGEA to 20th Century Fox for use in the Darryl F Zanuck epic, "The Longest Day" (1962), although it is believed that it may have had a technical fault, or its pilot became indisposed, which prevented it from acting the role of an RAF Free French Squadron Spitfire LF.IXb. However, being listed as an extra for the film entitles it to a credit.

In 1963, Spitfire Mk.IXb MH434 was acquired by Tim Davies who based it at Elstree Aerodrome in Hertforshire, still painted in its COGEA blue-silver colour scheme and retaining its clipped-wing configuration. Registered as G-ASJV, the Spitfire was universally known as 'Juliet Victor' and was equipped to fly Airways by Davies, fitted with IFR radio, transponder and long-range fuel tanks. He soon refitted 'Juliet Victor' with elliptical wing-tips, in which guise it appeared in PR Blue as a photo-reconnaissance Spitfire in "Operation Crossbow" (1965). By November 1967, MH434 had joined 'Hamish' Mahaddie's collection of Spitfires and Hurricanes at RAF Henlow in preparation for "Battle of Britain" (1969). Mahaddie chartered MH434 after filming was completed until February 1972, during which time it is believed it appeared in a US made-for-TV movie as an 'Eagle' Squadron Spitfire, as it was seen bearing No.121 (Eagle) Squadron AV-H codes between 1971 -'72. Ray Hanna made his first check flight in Spitfire Mk.IXb MH434 on 21st February 1970 from Leavesden, lasting 15 minutes. He gave his first public aerobatic display in MH434 at an event at Southend Airport in May 1970 and followed this up with displays at the Biggin Hill International Air Fair later the same month. The rest, as they say, is history. Spitfire HF.Mk.IXb MH434 is, of course, very active today at Duxford with the Old Flying Machine Company, painted in its original No.222 Squadron markings as ZD-B.

Spitfire HF.Mk.IXb MH434 has 13 film and television appearances to its credit, possibly more than any other World War Two warbird in the world, of which seven meet the criteria for this book and are described here. To come are "Hope and Glory" (1987) in Chapter Six, "Land Girls" (1998) in Chapter Seven and "Dark Blue World" (2001), Chapter Eight.

As a film, it is a serious disappointment that such a well crafted production on an epic scale - which "A Bridge Too Far" undoubtedly is, with a great deal of attention paid to accurately-staged realism - should be so marred by Goldman's British-baiting screenplay and by Attenborough's directorial collusion with him, all to make a predominately British-populated war film acceptable to American audiences, while propagating strongly-held prejudices in the USA about the characters of senior British Army officers in relation to their US Army counterparts in World War Two. The aviation scenes in "A Bridge Too Far" are unquestionably its best part.

FORCE 10 FROM NAVARONE

(Released: December 1978)

"History", pronounced Henry T Ford, founder of the Ford Motor Company, "is bunk". It certainly is where this sequel to both the novel and the immensely popular film of "The Guns of Navarone" (1961) is concerned. It is also another blatant example of a British war film twisting historical fact in order to appease American popular opinion and thus achieve box office success in the United States - in fact, it achieved neither.

The plot of the film "Force 10 from Navarone" has very little in common with that of the Alastair MacLean novel from which it shamelessly takes its title, apart from two of the leading characters in both it and "Guns", Captain (now Major) Keith Mallory and Corporal (now Sergeant) 'Dusty' Miller, plus its location, Nazi Occupied Yugoslavia. The screenplay by Robin Chapman and screen story by "Guns" producer and scriptwriter, Carl Foreman (also executive producer of "Force 10"), adds three more characters who don't appear in the novel, all of them American. By doing so, Chapman and Foreman prove Ford's theory about history to be correct: US forces had nothing to do with the Yugoslav theater of war, apart from shot down USAAF airmen being sheltered and liberated by Yugoslav Partizans, hence the bunk.

The American characters have all been created to make the film appeal to US movie audiences. MacLean's original story involves an all-British military action which Foreman obviously thought would not sell in the USA, even though the novel had been popular there. Two of the three Americans are part of a US Rangers Commando Unit named 'Force 10', sent to Yugoslavia to blow up a vital road bridge spanning a gorge across which the Wehrmacht is planning to launch three Panzer divisions against Partizan Resistance fighters. The third character is representative of what had become a common feature of Hollywood movies in the Seventies, the 'token black actor' amid an all-white cast to appeal to the African-American community in post-Civil Rights America, in this case a 'busted' (for what, the plot never explains) US Army Sergeant who somehow gets in on the act.

In historical reality, all Allied operations in Occupied Yugoslavia were conducted by the SOE. No US Army Ranger ever set foot there in World War Two. Foreman's screen story is implausible because the SOE never operated alongside the Rangers

in any theater of war, and certainly never had need to make use of any form of American sabotage unit, being the masters of sabotage themselves. The US Rangers were a Commando-style unit within the US Army itself, and did not operate behind enemy lines in disguise as depicted in "Force 10 from Navarone" (US Army Rangers did operate with the post-War British SAS, although this was never officially admitted to by either unit and certainly not by either the US or British governments).

"Force 10" only went into production 17 years after its hugely successful forebear because of the never-ending popularity of repeats of "Guns" on TV. Foreman, however, made a serious mistake in having "Force 10" lead directly from "Guns" because he makes a major change to a particular event in the first film that has a direct bearing on one of the sub-plots in the sequel. He has Mallory and Miller (played, as we know, by Gregory Peck and David Niven respectively in "Guns", but by Robert Shaw and Edward Fox in "Force 10") sent along with the 'Force 10' unit for the express purpose of unmasking and eliminating the German spy who had betrayed their sabotage team on Navarone, and who British Intelligence has discovered has penetrated the Yugoslav Partizans. Three previous Allied missions into Yugoslavia have failed because of this spy. Only Mallory and Miller can identify him.

The problem is, there was no German spy in the film version of "The Guns of Navarone". Mallory, Miller and their comrades were betrayed by a female Greek Resistance fighter who had been caught and tortured by the Germans, before being released with the promise to spare her life if she worked as a double agent for them. This very obvious conflict between the separate plots of the two films is a major flaw in "Force 10 from Navarone", and possibly explains one reason why the film did so badly at the box office. Not even the presence of, then, new star Harrison Ford, fresh from his debut as Han Solo in "Star Wars: Episode Four" (1977), as the leader of 'Force 10', could save it.

Aviation only features in the plot when 'Force 10' is inserted into Yugoslavia, and, in so doing, Foreman and Chapman ramp up the implausibility factor even further. They have the US Rangers highjack an RAF Avro Lancaster from an air base in Italy. More bunk is added to the plot, not only because Lancasters never operated from Italy, but in having 'Termoli Air Base' being "HQ 17th CORP USAF" on its entrance sign: "CORP" should have been spelt "CORPS", but is incorrect anyway because there was no Corps structure within the United States Air Force, while "USAF" should obviously have been "USAAF". British director Guy Hamilton, of "Battle of Britain" (1969) fame, and his art department team have seriously goofed here.

Harrison Ford (no relation to Henry), Mallory, Miller and 'Force 10' break into Termoli Air Base through the perimeter wire to steal a Lancaster parked just beyond. This 'Lancaster' is portrayed by a very obvious and unconvincing-looking two-dimensional hardboard prop. They get caught in the act by a bunch of US military policemen who are escorting the black US Army Sergeant prisoner to the brig. A fine old fist fight ensues, during which the Sergeant escapes from the MPs and jumps on board the Lancaster that 'Force 10' are highjacking.

For the actual highjack and in-flight shots of the stolen Lancaster, plus its subsequent attack and shoot-down by Luftwaffe fighters, Hamilton has resorted to a number of sources. Firstly, he uses two take off shots. They are of two different Avro Lancasters. Look carefully at the first shot: the Lancaster is 'up on the step', as its take off roll with the tail raised was called, in silhouette against a dark sky at night. In fact, this shot was taken in daylight and has been darkened in the editing suite to make it 'day for night'. It is also a black-and-white shot that the editor has very effectively 'coloured' with a dark blue sky, allowing him to darken the Lancaster as well.

This piece of footage is actually an out-take of an Avro Lancaster B.VII taking off from RAF Kirton-in-Lindsay, filmed for "The Dam Busters" (1955) but not actually used in the production of that film released to the cinemas. How can we be sure of that? For a number of reasons: (a) the Lancaster is taking off from a grass runway, which Kirton-in-Lindsay had; (b) the grass itself is covered with dandelions, as Kirton-in-Lindsay was when it appeared in "The Dam Busters" representing RAF Scampton; (c) the Lancaster itself is devoid of a mid-upper turrent, as all the Lancaster B.VIIs used in that film were; and (d) freeze-frame analysis confirms the presence of the same Avro Anson T.21 visible in the background that appears in "The Dam Busters" when Wing Commander Guy Gibson's Lancaster lands back after the Dams' Raid.

After a brief shot of Harrison Ford at the controls (Ford went on to become a very accomplished pilot in real life in the USA, but where did he as a US Rangers Colonel learn how to fly a 'Lanc'?), another take off shot appears but this is of a different Avro Lancaster. The difference is immediately apparent in freeze-frame analysis because it shows this Lancaster has a mid-upper turret. It is also glinting around the nose area, revealing that this shot was taken in bright sunlight which has also been turned 'day for night' in the editing suite; the sky beyond, however, has no cloud feature as the previous footage has, indicating that the sky is a cloudless blue. The imagery here looks very clean, suggesting that this was a modern-day shot and almost certainly was of the RAF Battle of Britain Memorial Flight's Avro Lancaster B.I PA474.

There is no question that all the air-airs which follow are of Lancaster B.I PA474 itself. The only question is, where did Hamilton obtain this footage? The BBMF could have made PA474 available for air-air filming for "Force 10 from Navarone", but if they did why would Hamilton have bothered to use an out-take from "The Dam Busters" for one of the take off shots? There was the possibility these air-airs were unused out-takes of aerial footage of PA474 filmed for "Overlord" (1975), also coloured in the editing suite, but a quick comparison between both in-flight imagery shows that this cannot be the case: in "Force 10", PA474 has a mid-upper turret, in "Overlord" it hasn't (PA474 was fitted with a mid-upper turret during 1975 that had been located in Argentina, but not before it was filmed for "Overlord").

It is likely, then, that PA474 was either filmed air-air specifically for "Force 10", or that Hamilton acquired imagery of the Lancaster from another source, possibly RAF Strike Command's public relations section at High Wycombe. "Force 10 from Navarone" was Avro Lancaster PA474's fourth film role,

behind "The Guns of Navarone" (1961, as a pattern for the studio miniature Lancaster in that film), "Operation Crossbow" (1965) and "Overlord" (1975).

For the shoot-down of the Lancaster by Luftwaffe Messerschmitt Bf.109s, Hamilton has made use of an out-take of two Hispano HA.1112M1L Buchons from his own creation, "Battle of Britain" (1969). He also uses the same wartime archive imagery of a Messerschmitt Bf.109E-4, filmed from the dorsal turret of a bomber and with SFX-created cannon fire bursting from its wings, that appears in "Reach For The Sky" (1956). A goof is the close-up of four Browning machine guns firing from the wings, most un-Messerschmitt Bf.109-like. The Lancaster that explodes in mid-air is a very impressively created SFX studio miniature.

From here on, all the action in "Force 10 from Navarone" takes place against the spectacular back drop of the mountains of Montenegro, with no further aviation elements (the bombing of Partizans is achieved without showing the aircraft doing it).

ESCAPE TO ATHENA

(Released: January 1979)

This entirely fictional and implausible Prisoner of War – cum – treasure heist action adventure was one of a series of spectaculars made by Sir Lew Grade's ITC company in the Seventies, and trades on particularly popular star film and TV names of the era, among them: Roger Moore (James Bond), equally implausible as the Austrian PoW camp commander; Telly Savalas ("Kojak"), as a Greek Resistance leader; Stephanie Powers ("Hart to Hart"), an American troop entertainer; and Richard Rountree ("Shaft"), as a US Army Sergeant. The scene of the action is the Greek island of Rhodes and utilises some of the locations that were used 18 years earlier in "The Guns of Navarone".

No aviation elements appear in "Escape to Athena", although the finale involves a Byzantine monastery that is a secret base for V2 rockets – historically completely incorrect, as the Vergelstungwaffe Zwei was never launched from Greece.

THE PASSAGE

(Released: April 1979, USA)

What induced the well respected film director J Lee Thompson ("The Guns of Navarone", 1961) to get involved with this self indulgently nasty war film, will probably remain a mystery. Mercifully, aviation is spared from having any role in this somewhat typically sadistic film of the Seventies period.

HANOVER STREET

(Released: May 1979)

Is this a British war film? Technically, yes, because although director/scriptwriter Peter Hyams and producer Paul N Lazarus III are both American, almost the entire film crew are British and all the locations used in the film are based in England, most notably Hertfordshire and Oxfordshire. Technically, it is a US-UK co-production.

This is a British war film very typical of its time. As stated in the preamble to this Chapter, the Seventies was a decade when it was felt that British films in general had to pander to the American market, often in terms of having an American lead star in ascendancy over a British counterpart. "Hanover Street" does not debase the British character anything like the extent that "A Bridge Too Far" (1977) does, but it has the same essence of American masculinity and courage overshadowing the weaker English personality in war.

Its lead star, Harrison Ford, was making his third film in Britain in as many years. Having been seen at the end of 1978 breaking historical military fact by acting as an American assisting Yugoslav Partizans in "Force 10 From Navarone", Ford is asked to repeat the dose in "Hanover Street" by playing the part of a USAAF bomber pilot operating in Occupied France with a British SOE agent in a way that no USAAF bomber pilot ever did.

"Hanover Street" is very much Peter Hyams's baby. He says he was influenced by the Hollywood romance movie, "Waterloo Bridge" (1940), which has a similar chance meeting between two lovers that both films are concerned with. However, Hyams also thought it necessary to inject quips into the script when Ford and his aircrew are in action, particularly the bombardier played by Richard Masur who first debates with himself that the bombers shouldn't be able to fly because they are made of metal, then complains that the Germans should be told they are only meant to be shooting light-to-moderate flak on a particular mission, because that's what the briefing officer had told the American bomber aircrews to expect. Such wise guy dialogue was obviously intended to appeal to an American Seventies cinema audience that was fully engaged with the ironic humour of such movies of the day as Woody Allen's classic, "Annie Hall" (1977), which accepted that life could be difficult yet could still have a joke made about it. The effect in "Hanover Street", however, is to encourage the audience to take the bomb attack sequences less seriously than they actually should, and results in Ford and his bomber crew sounding irritating to the point of failing to be credible as they wise crack while flak explodes around them.

The film did not do well at the box office, either in Britain or the USA, largely because it falls between being a wartime romance film and an action movie, failing to deliver satisfactorily on either front. We have to put up with Ford's affair with Lesley-Anne Down, who is the wife of British Intelligence chief, Christopher Plummer. We have to follow Ford's and Plummer's scarcely credible mission in Occupied France, during which they discover they are rivals for the same woman. In between there is some aerial action.

There is no doubt that for aviation enthusiasts the B-25 Mitchells flown in "Hanover Street" are what the film is all about. All the rest of the film's plot is incidental. Their epic flights across the Atlantic and what happened to them after their appearance in the film is what matters most, and is what is of importance to this book. The documentary film that was made about their trans-Atlantic crossing, "Mitchells do fly in IMC" (1983), is one of the most sought after of its kind. The clash of personalities between the two main protagonists of the project behind flying five North American B-25J Mitchell bombers from the USA to the UK is of far greater fascination than the rivalry between Ford and Plummer for Lesley-Anne Down's affections.

The two said protagonists are American David Tallichet and Englishman John 'Jeff' Hawke, both larger-than-life characters (in Hawke's case, physically as well as personally) who, in their individual ways, made an enormous impression on both the aircraft preservation and movie industry scenes on either side of the Atlantic. Hawke we have already met, due to his operating a Mosquito, his B-25 Mitchell and the two Messerschmitt Bf.108s in "633 Squadron" (1964) and his role in flying the 'Psychedelic Monster' B-25 camera-ship for "Battle of Britain" (1969). Tallichet we will come across again, as he was involved with other aviation film projects described in this book; in particular, some information about Tallichet has been held over until the review of "Memphis Belle" (1990) because of his unique personal connection with that film.

Tallichet was an important man behind the project to fly five B-25 Mitchells to the UK for "Hanover Street". A former wartime USAAF B-17 Flying Fortress co-pilot, with the 350th Bombardment Squadron of the 100th Bombardment Group at RAF Thorpe Abbotts, Tallichet had made a lucrative post-War living in the States by pioneering what are known today as Themed Restaurants, but which in the Fifties and Sixties were called Destination Restaurants. So successful was this business that Tallichet used his wealth to set up the Military Aircraft Restoration Corp (MARC) as a subsidiary, specialising in the acquisition, restoration and operation of World War Two and Korean War era aircraft. At one time it was estimated Tallichet owned more than 120 such aircraft, many of which he subsequently sold, but he was considered to still own approximately 50 at the time of his death from complications with prostate cancer on 31st October 2007. He had flown a B-17 at an airshow in the USA only three months before, then being the sole surviving Eighth Air Force B-17 pilot who was able to fly the Flying Fortress in the 21st Century.

Tallichet became heavily involved with the Hollywood film and US television industries by supplying World War Two aircraft for a host of productions. Probably his most well known venture was flying his own B-17G Flying Fortress across the Atlantic in 1989 to take part in the film "Memphis Belle", as described in the review of that film in Chapter Six. Tallichet's company also specialised in building full-size replica aircraft for film productions, such as "Pearl Harbor" (2001) and "Collateral Damage" (2002).

Tallichet was responsible for locating three out of the five B-25J Mitchells used in "Hanover Street", which included his own aircraft based with what he then called Yesterday's Air Force; Hawke obtained the other two Mitchells. As the documentary reveals, both men had a falling-out over the best way to fly the B-25s across the Atlantic. As a FAA-qualified examiner, Tallichet would not support Hawke's plan to take the shorter, more direct route 'over the Pond' via The Azores because the B-25 Mitchell was not an aircraft that had been designed or certificated to fly in Instrumentation Metereological Conditions (IMC), which Hawke's plan would make inevitable due to the weather forecast for the mid-Atlantic in May 1978. Tallichet intended to fly the more traditional, but much longer route from North America via staging posts in Greenland, Iceland and Scotland, while escorted by an executive aircraft with full instrumentation and weather radar.

John 'Jeff' Hawke has inspired much controversy and mystery about his career in aviation. There are no shortages of threads about him on various Online Forums. It would not be inaccurate to describe 'Jeff' Hawke, as he styled himself in association with the British comic book spaceman hero of the same name, as an adventurer in aviation, one who was prepared to not just take risks but who wasn't inhibited in flying wide of the law if it was in his financial interest to do so. He became involved in the same undercover deal to clandestinely deliver Douglas A-26 Invader bombers to Portugal in 1965 that Australian Gregory Board, who helped to provide B-17s for "The War Lover" (1962), was involved in. The A-26s were flown via The Azores, a Portuguese protectorate, and it is believed that Hawke's relationship with the Portuguese authorities through this deal meant he was always welcome on the mid-Atlantic island group, hence his favouring this location for trans-Atlantic flights. It is not surprising he felt confident of taking the B-25s for "Hanover Street" on this route, despite Tallichet's objections.

With the FBI closing in on him, and with his backers refusing to help clear his name, Hawke hit upon an idea of getting free that only a high risk-taker like himself could dream of doing. The A-26 deal also included a B-25 Mitchell. Hawke deliberately flew this B-25 over the forbidden airspace above the White House in Washington, was forced to land by the USAF, and was arrested by the FBI. Under examination, he claimed he was a CIA agent and that the B-25 and A-26s were CIA-acquired aircraft that he was delivering to Portugal for use by the Angolan government against Communist-supported rebels in Angola. The CIA denied all knowledge of this and of Hawke, so the FBI dropped their charges against him. Because of the CIA's denial, they could not claim ownership of the B-25 - Hawke thus acquired a B-25 Mitchell free of charge! He put it to good use in the film industry, as we saw in "Battle of Britain" (1969).

Hawke went on to become aerial co-ordinator for a number of film productions; however, after "Hanover Street" his career appeared to go in other directions away from the film industry. He was certainly active on the airshow circuit in the UK during the Eighties, flying an ex-Spanish Air Force CASA 352L which he had painted as a Luftwaffe Junkers Ju.52/3M, complete with roof-mounted gas-operated machine gun. He also flew a B-25 on the British airshow circuit at the same time.

The rumours about Hawke's exploits are many and his death in (very) mysterious circumstances aboard a Piper Aztec that crashed into the Adriatic Sea in November 1991 has prompted a great deal of speculation as to what he was actually involved in. It was reported at the time his body was discovered in late December 1991, inside the Aztec which had been hauled to the surface of the Adriatic by a fishing trawler, that he had got himself into serious financial difficulties and had allegedly told his wife shortly before his final, and unauthorised, flight that the deal he had secured would solve all their problems. Hawke no longer had any problems after taking off on this flight, but not in the way he intended.

However, in May 1978 five B-25 Mitchells had to be flown across the Atlantic to meet the filming schedule for "Hanover Street". Hawke took four of them on The Azores route, he leading the four-ship through cloud in line astern formation with his B-25 being the sole example fitted with VOR (VHF Omnidirectional Range Radio) for navigation, while Tallichet took the longer, but less risky, Northern route. The "Mitchells do fly in IMC" documentary has Hawke discoursing on his flight plan to his fellow aircrew while indulging his other great passion in life, gourmet, by making light work of a large plate of oysters in The Azores as he speaks contemptuously of "Tallichet and his bullshit". Maybe so, but two members of the four B-25 Mitchells' aircrew refused to fly any further, and demanded to be paid off there and then.

After the B-25s had cleared Customs at Luton Airport, they were all flown to Bovingdon Airfield in Hertfordshire, the main filming location used to portray once more a USAAF Eighth Air Force bomber base in wartime England. Bovingdon was making its fifth, and final, appearance in a war film, after "The War Lover" (1962), "633 Squadron" (1964) "Mosquito Squadron" (1969) and "Battle of Britain" (1969). It had already closed as an active airfield in 1972 but its runways, hard standings, air traffic control tower and fire tender building were still in usable condition.

Hyams was faced with a tricky problem once the five B-25s were assembled and 'dressed' in their film 'wardrobe': how to film them? The budget did not extend to the use of a camera-ship, hence the B-25s are only filmed from the ground. They flew under FAA rules, so they were not transferred to the British civil register; the CAA was reportedly not happy about their condition anyway. Had they been flying under a UK Permit To Fly, the insurance costs would have made their operation prohibitive.

Bovingdon could not be used for filming the B-25s in flight because it was too close to local housing. Noise and the use of explosive maroons to simulate flak bursts made Bovingdon unsafe. An airfield in a rural location was needed, and the former Central Flying School base of RAF Little Rissington in Gloucestershire provided the answer. All the shots of the B-25s flying in formation through flak, with the lead B-25 feathering its starboard propeller, were filmed over Little Rissington. The maroons were fired seriously close to the bombers; they are not CGI Special FX. The bombs shown being released, however, are obviously too lightweight compared with real ordnance because they scatter and tumble too freely, instead of descending horizontally in long vertical streams as genuine bombs would have done.

Of the five B-25s, only one would return to the USA after filming was completed. Four still survive today, in four different countries. Following filming, the four that remained in the UK were left in open storage at Blackbushe Airport near Camberley in Surrey, among stored ex-Spanish Air Force CASA 352Ls and Douglas C-47s, former Moroccan Air Force T-28 Fennecs, retired Belgian Air Force Percival Pembrokes and a myriad of other privately owned military types belonging to the extraordinary Warbirds of Great Britain collection. Many of these aircraft, including two of the four stored B-25s, would appear in "Eye of the Needle" (1981), reviewed in Chapter Six.

All the Mitchells that appear in "Hanover Street" are B-25Js, although some had been converted into TB-25Ns at some stage which meant they were twin-stick trainers. Three out of the five had appeared in "Catch 22" (1970). The identities of each B-25J, their roles in the film and their ultimate fate is described as follows:

North American B-25J Mitchell N7681C (44-86701), appears as '151790 Amazing Andrea', crewed by E Lorentzen, B Maddigan and T Howarth. Taken on charge by the USAAF on an unknown date, remained in service with the USAF, during which it was converted into both a TB-25J and TB-25N, until placed in storage at Davis-Monthan AFB, Arizona, in December 1957. The following year it was soled to Bud Marquis of Marysville, California, for conversion into a crop duster, although this was never carried out, registered as N7681C. It was acquired by Tallmantz Aviation in 1968, then transferred to Filmways Inc, of Hollywood, California, for its appearence in "Catch 22". It was then purchased by David Tallichet in 1972 and flown to Luton Airport, Bedfordshire, in May 1978 for its role in "Hanover Street". Subsequently it was flown to France for an intended appearance in a film production there which did not materialise and was left abandoned. It was stored at Paris-Dugny for static display with the Musee de l'Air at le Bourget, Paris, but was destroyed in a hangar fire in 1990.

North American B-25J Mitchell N9115Z (44-29366), appears as '151645 Marvellous Miriam', crewed by M Wright, B Muszala and D Smith. Taken on charge by the USAAF on an unknown date, remained in USAF service during which time it was converted into a TB-25N trainer before being placed in storage at Davis-Monthan AFB in August 1958. In January 1960, it was purchased by Sonora Flying Service of Columbia, California, registered as N9115Z and converted into a fire tanker with a 1,000 gallon tank in its bomb-bay. It underwent two further changes of ownership between 1964 - 1968 before being acquired by Filmways Inc for its use in "Catch 22". It was acquired by David Tallichet in 1972, who displayed it in his Yesterday's Air Force collection at St Petersburg, Florida, until he flew it across the Atlantic in May 1978 for its appearance in "Hanover Street". After its appearance in the film, N9115Z was stored at Blackbushe Airport and came under the ownership of Warbirds of Great Britain in June 1979. Before that happened, 'Jeff' Hawke flew a most dangerous display in Marvellous Miriam at the 1979 Biggin Hill Air Fair, which included diving into the valley at the southern end of the airfield. N9115Z was one of the two B-25s used as static props in "Eye of the Needle" (1981),

filmed at Blackbushe Airport. In October 1982, it was acquired by the Royal Air Force Museum and has since been on display at Hendon, North London.

North American B-25J Mitchell N9455Z (44-30210), appears as '151863 Big Bad Bonnie', crewed by B Baldwin, V Patman and L Gilbert. Delivered to the USAAF on an unknown date, remained in service with the USAF until 1959 during which time it was converted into both a TB-25J and TB-25N. Declared surplus on 31st December 1959 when it was in open storage at MASDC, Davis-Monthan AFB, it was sold to National Metals of Phoenix, Arizona, on 15th January 1960 and registered as N9455Z. Four months later it was acquired by Les Bowman & Paul Mantz Air Service at Santa Ana, California, and converted into a fire tanker in August 1960. It was deployed to Caracas, Venezuela, in 1961 before returning to Les Bowman's Long Beach facility in California and continued to operate as a tanker until December 1964, when it was sold to Cat-Nat Airways of Grass Valley, California. Quite what the purpose of this acquisition was is not clear because this B-25 was simply put out to grass in open storage at Grass Valley until 1970, when it went into private ownership for five years. David Tallichet acquired N9455Z in 1975; it was flown to Luton on 11th May 1978 for "Hanover Street", then stored first at Blackbushe, later Dublin, for the next three years. 'Jeff' Hawke operated this B-25 on the UK airshow circuit between 1981 - 1983 under The Mitchell Flight banner, flying it a lot more responsibly than he did the B-25s he flew at airshows in 1978 and 1979. However, in common with Hawke's style, he abandoned it in France during July 1982 after it blew an engine over Aix-en-Provence and had to make a forced landing. It remained in situ until it was repaired and flown back to England by the Warplane Flying Group at Wellesbourne Mountford. It was then re-acquired by David Tallichet and ferried to Chino, California, on 1st August 1986. Tallichet loaned this B-25 to the USAF Museum at March AFB, California, as a gift in the USAF's 40th anniversary year for static display between 1987 - 1990, still marked as Big Bad Bonnie; it was then moved back to Chino in 1991 and underwent a major restoration between 1997 - 2000. Still registered to David Tallichet's Military Aircraft Restoration Corp, B-25J N9455Z was lasted listed as being exhibited by the Grissom Air Museum in Indiana.

North American B-25J Mitchell N9494Z (44-30925), appears as '151632 Georgeous George-Ann' - named after Peter Hyams's wife, who was called George-Ann - and crewed by D Halloran, M Myer and J Cimino. Taken on charge on an unknown date by the USAAF and remained in USAF service until it was placed into storage at Davis-Monthan AFB in August 1958. It was bought by National Metals Co of Tucson, Arizona, in 1960 and registered as N9494Z. In July that same year it entered private ownership and then went through three more changes of operator until it was acquired in December 1968 by Filmways Inc, of Hollywood, for use in "Catch 22", in which film it appeared as Laden Maiden. It retained this same identity for the following nine years, during which time it flew with the Confederate Air Force in Texas until its acquisition by Hawke's Visionair International Inc for "Hanover Street". Arriving at Luton Airport on 11th May 1978 flown by Hawke and Eric

Lorentzen, this B-25 at some stage acquired the identity of Thar She Blows but then returned to being Georgeous George-Ann. While in storage at Blackbushe Airport it was the second B-25 used as a static prop in "Eye of the Needle". This B-25 remained grounded for seven years, spending time being road-trucked first to Wellesbourne Mountford in October 1982, then to Coventry/Baginton in 1985. The aviation film company, Aces High at North Weald Aerodrome, acquired this B-25 in August 1995 and had it placed on the UK civil register as G-BWGR. The Imperial Aviation Group at North Coutes acquired G-BWGR in 1998 and stored it at Sandtoft, pending restoration to flight; however, this was never achieved and it was left in a deteriorating condition in the open until it was rescued by the Brussels Air Museum Foundation in 2005 and can be seen on static display in the Brussels Air Museum today.

North American B-25J Mitchell N86427 (44-29121), appears as two different B-25s in the film: '151724 Brenda's Boys' and '151451 Miami Clipper', crewed by Hawke and E Lorentzen. Delivered to the USAAF on an unrecorded date and served with the USAF until it was placed in storage at Davis-Monthan AFB in December 1958. It was sold to National Metals Co of Tucson, Arizona, and registered as N86427. It remained with National Metals until 1962, when it was sold to Compass Aviation Inc, of Richmond, California, in whose ownership it flew in the Doolittle Raid 25th Anniversary fly-past at NAS Alameda, California, in October 1967. In 1969, this B-25 came under the ownership of the American Air Museum at Oakland, California, remaining until 1976 when it was sold into private ownership and appeared on the US airshow circuit as Doolittle Raider. 'Jeff' Hawke acquired it in 1978 and registered it to his Visionair International Inc before having it flown to Luton as Doolittle Raider for "Hanover Street". Hawke retained ownership of N86427 after filming was complete and flew it as '151451 Miami Clipper' on 26th and 27th August 1978 at the USAF Air Fete 78, RAF Mildenhall, Suffolk, in what a photographer on board described as the most dangerous flight he had ever experienced. Hawke abandoned this B-25 at Malaga, Spain, in January 1979 after it was damaged during the filming of "Cuba" (1979). It was impounded by the Spanish authorities and eventually transported by road to Cuatro Vientos at Madrid, where it was restored for static display in the Museuo del Aire and where it can be seen today.

When "Hanover Street" is written about in publications or discussed on Internet Forums, it is invariably the B-25 Mitchells that are the subject of interest, not the film itself. The film has a serious credibility problem with aviation enthusiasts and war movie fans, particularly during the in-cockpit scenes when Ford appears to be just nonchalantly taking his B-25 for an aerial stroll, so relaxed are he and his co-pilot - the wise-cracking during the bomb run may work in Hyams's mind, but not in the mind of any serious student of war films. The idea of having Plummer's Intelligence chief clandestinely undertaking a mission in Occupied France, just to prove to himself he is not a coward, is so far-fetched that it reveals just how far in the unreality stakes that Hyams was prepared to go in his film. Similarly, the task of parachuting Plummer into France being assigned to Ford and his B-25 crew

totally ignores the historical fact of the Special Duties squadrons that would have conducted this operation, and only increases the annoyance felt by the aviation and war film fans towards Hyams's production for playing fast and loose with fact and reality.

Of course, Hyams wanted to play off Ford's tough, romantic, unafraid American pilot lover against Plummer's effete, unconfidant, doubting English husband (and he's a top spy chief!) of the woman Ford is having an affair with, while they are both in Occupied France and need to depend on each other. So, for the sake of dramatic expediency and to ensure a better reception in America, this unbelievable scenario is played out to its inevitable romantic ending. That's the problem with "Hanover Street", it's a romance that doesn't work and a war film that isn't believable, and which spoils what could have been better used aerial scenes.

YANKS

(Released: September 1979)

This sensitive tale about the loves and fortunes of American GIs and the English women they meet, set in the North of England during 1943 and '44, has little room for aviation, but one aircraft makes a short appearance: North American B-25J Mitchell N86427, marked up in "Hanover Street" wardrobe as '151451 Miami Clipper'. N86427 is shown both air-air above clouds and making a landing on a very wet runway, in a scene when American Captain William Devane spirits English aristocrat Vanessa Redgrave away aboard the B-25 on a clandestine flight to Ireland for a little hanky-panky. Devane and Redgrave are seen leaving the Mitchell on a rain-soaked airfield, with its Miami Clipper nose paintwork in the background behind them. They are also shown smooching in the bombardier's nose position.

This scene with B-25J N86427 must have been filmed early in the production of "Yanks", as owner 'Jeff' Hawke had abandoned the Mitchell at Malaga, Spain, in January 1979, eight months before the release of the film. The fate of N86427 is described above in the review of "Hanover Street".

THE SEA WOLVES

(Released: August 1980)

A multi-national British war film, Anglo-American-Swiss, with much of it filmed on location in India and Portuguese Goa, "The Sea Wolves" is a fictionalised re-creation of an actual SOE operation in March 1943 that remained classified by the British government until 1978. Sub-titled, "The Last Charge by the Calcutta Light Horse", it re-enacts the (deniable) assault by retired members of an old territorial regiment on three German merchant ships moored in the neutral waters of Portuguese Goa, from which information about Allied ships was being transmitted to U-Boats operating in the Indian Ocean. It is a story that does not need aviation in it.

CHAPTER 6

1981-1990

The fact that we are now down to just seven film productions in this decade shows that World War Two was no longer a bankable subject in British cinema. Of the seven war films produced, only two have any substantial aviation content, although the final production reviewed in this Chapter contains such a substantial amount of aircraft that, it alone, illustrates just how far advanced the warbird preservation scene had become in Britain and in other European countries by the end of the Eighties.

The Eighties saw a shift in tone and style with some war films, concentrating much more on the civilian population at home and on how the War affected them personally and emotionally. "Another Time, Another Place" (1983) and "Hope and Glory" (1987) fully reflect this. The fascination with British PoWs enduring the privations of Japanese Prisoner of War camps returned, for some reason, during this decade. Of the seven films listed in this Chapter, just one qualifies as a Hollywood 'British' war film.

ESCAPE TO VICTORY

(Released: July 1981, USA) Hollywood 'British' war film

An original PoW story of a football match played in Nazi Occupied Paris as a propaganda coup by the German High Command between German footballers and Allied PoW football players. The Allied PoWs plan an escape during the match. Apart from starring Sylvester Stallone and Michael Caine, the cast was made up of many actual professional international footballers, most notably Pele (Brazil), Bobby Moore (England), Osvaldo Ardiles (Argentina), and particularly seven from the then very successful Ipswich Town Football Club. However, aviation does not feature at all in this John Huston-directed war movie.

EYE OF THE NEEDLE

(Released: July 1981, USA)

Having acted as a Nazi spy only four years previously in "The Eagle Has Landed" (1977), Donald Sutherland invades England again, this time as a psychopathic killer for the Fatherland who is known as 'Der Nadel' (The Needle) due to his preference for using a stiletto knife when despatching his victims. "Eye of the Needle" is a well made and very well acted film, utilising a blend of actors of the period who had fine reputations, especially Kate Nelligan, who plays the young wife of a disabled RAF fighter pilot who has a fatal affair with the Needle.

However, despite the fine performances, good script and the realistic re-creation of wartime Britain four decades after World War Two, Sutherland and Co are let down by the actual plot of the film itself, which is rather far-fetched and not really believable. It is, in effect, a vehicle for a study of love, lust and betrayal involving three people on a remote island off the West Coast of Scotland. How they end up there is part of the unreality of the film's plot, particularly in the light of the hard economic and severely rationed times when the events they are involved in are occurring.

The Needle is assigned a mission by the Fuhrer himself in early 1944 to get photographic evidence that the Allies will invade Occupied France in the Pas de Calais area, using a massive army led by the American General George Patton. He is to photograph the build up of the army in East Anglia (where Sutherland had spied before in "The Eagle Has Landed"), then make his way to the West Coast of Scotland from where he will be picked up by a German U-Boat and taken back to Germany. He is to deliver his photographs in person to Hitler, who needs the evidence to confirm his conviction the invasion will take place at the Pas de Calais in order to discount his astrologer, who has warned him that the Allies will invade Normandy.

The Needle carries out his mission but discovers that Patton's army assembled in East Anglia is entirely fake. He realises this means that the real army must be assembled in the south of England and that Normandy has to be the real target. It is vital he gets to Berlin to warn the Fuhrer. The Security Service, MI5, are hot on his tail but he manages to keep one jump ahead of them. He gets to Storm Island off Scotland, from where he tries to make contact with the U-Boat.

It is at this point that the film, in the second half, gets bogged down with Sutherland's affair with Nelligan, who plays the wife of a Spitfire pilot who was crippled on the day of their wedding four years earlier after driving recklessly and crashing their car. He has lost the use of his legs and has become embittered as a result. Somehow, he and his wife have ended up on Storm Island to farm sheep. This is scarcely credible and it is at this point that the film falls into a quagmire of sexual betrayal and murder. It ends when Nelligan finally shoots the Needle as he tries to escape the island to reach the waiting U-Boat.

So, where does aviation fit into this convoluted plot? It actually does so quite effectively in the first half by using a large collection of aircraft which are accurately representative of the types flown during the latter part of the War years; however, aviation goes into an overdrive of unreality during the film's second half, particularly in the finale.

For aviation enthusiasts, "Eye of the Needle" provides a nostalgic sight of a once impressive but mysterious collection of historic aircraft which were always known about but which were often frustratingly kept well away from public view, guarded by an owner who had a reputation for being very threatening. This is the Warbirds of Great Britain collection, then based at Blackbushe Airport outside Camberley in Surrey, owned and operated by the now late Doug Arnold.

At the time of "Eye of the Needle" being filmed, Doug Arnold also owned and operated Blackbushe Airport itself. It was a well known location to aviation enthusiasts in the Seventies and Eighties for having an extraordinary collection of World War Two-vintage aircraft stored out in the open on-field, but, according to many reports and comments, Mr Arnold did not encourage visitors - or, his Doberman Pincher dogs certainly did not. However, some of his warbirds were performers at airshows in the Eighties, particularly the Biggin Hill Air Fair; his Warbirds of Great Britain collection was subsequently re-located at Biggin Hill after leaving Blackbushe.

Two principal scenes involving aviation take place during the first half of "Eye of the Needle". Both were filmed at Blackbushe Airport.

The first involves a British Army soldier who had previously known the Needle, and who can identify him, being flown to meet the MI5 officer who is on the trail of the German agent. A C-47 Dakota is seen taxiying to a stop, bearing the title Windsor Castle on its nose. The MI5 staff car drives past parked aircraft to greet the Dakota and its passenger.

All the aircraft used in this scene were residents at Blackbushe Airport at the time they were filmed. The C-47 is Douglas C-47A Dakota III G-BGCE of Fairoaks Aviation Services, which officially owned many of the aircraft in Doug Arnold's Warbirds of Great Britain collection. Dakota G-BGCE came onto the British civil register on 20th November 1978, being part of a batch of C-47s that had been retired by the Spanish Air Force and acquired by Arnold. It carried the Spanish military serial T.3-2. For its role in "Eye of the Needle", Dakota G-BGCE was painted (on the port side, at least) in all-over olive drab, which is not accurate for RAF Dakotas during World War Two. However, the film's art department has tried to be accurate in portraying a real-life Dakota that carried the name Windsor Castle: this was FD772/ZK-Y of No.24 Squadron, based at RAF Hendon. As we discovered in "I Was Monty's Double" (1958), No.24 Squadron was the Royal Air Force's principal VIP transport unit during and after World War Two. The serial 'FD772' has been painted on the rear fuselage of Dakota G-BGCE, incorrectly above the code letter identifier; the fuselage roundel has been incorrectly applied as well. After its use in "Eye of the Needle", Dakota G-BGCE was sold to a private owner in Texas and registered N37529 in the USA.

The MI5 staff car passes two other aircraft of World War Two vintage parked on the apron at Blackbushe. Both of these aircraft were to become very well known to British aviation enthusiasts attending airshows in the Eighties, and help to convey in the film a realistic impression of a British military air base in 1944.

The first is Westland Lysander Mk.IIIA G-BCWL, which was known in 1980 to carry (incorrectly) the military serial V9281. When used in "Eye of the Needle", Lysander G-BCWL was on strength with the Warbirds of Great Britain collection and was undergoing refurbishment following its restoration to flight for its previous owner in the Seventies. In the film, it can be seen to have an upper fuselage and top wings coating of dark grey, while its under surfaces are in light grey. However, the 'waves' of green camouflage have yet to be added, while no national markings or squadron code letters have been applied.

Lysander G-BCWL was restored by Personal Plane Services at Wycombe Air Park as a composite airframe from the components of three different Canadian-built Lysanders. The restoration was carried out on behalf of its original owner, the prolific historic aircraft collector Philip Mann, who, under the banner of his Shipping and Airlines import-export business, owned a large number of vintage aircraft types spread between Wycombe Air Park and Biggin Hill Airport during the Seventies and early Eighties. Lysander G-BCWL made its post-restoration maiden flight on 1st March 1974, the first time a Lysander had flown in Britain since 1958 when the RAF Museum's Lysander R9125 flew in the Woolwich Tattoo during that year's Battle of Britain Week (see, "Now It Can Be Told", 1946, in Chapter Two).

Mann had established for himself a respected reputation as a collector, having been the first to import rare (at the time) Russian Yak 11 and Finnish Valtian Viima II World War Two trainers, among others, onto the British civil register. However, the Lysander presented more challenges than were anticipated and, as Philip Mann wanted to focus on vintage light aircraft, it was put up for sale in 1979.

Lysander G-BCWL was acquired by the Arnold group in June 1979 and remained as part of the Warbirds of Great Britain collection until February 1985. It was painted in a Special Duties colour scheme and flown on a few occasions. But the challenges posed by such a demanding and intricate aircraft - culminating in it suffering a forced landing at Bobbington Airfield on 21st August 1983, with it turning over onto its back - meant that it would need an operator able to devote time and resources in ensuring its successful airshow programme. That operator turned out to be Wessex Aviation and Transport, based at Chalmington Manor in Dorsetshire, which acquired G-BCWL in March 1985 and set about making sure this Lysander enjoyed a busy series of airshow seasons in the Eighties and the Nineties, flying with the serial V9545 and the codes BA-C of No.277 Squadron, an air-sea rescue unit based at Stapleford Tawney, Essex, during World War Two.

In June 1999, Lysander G-BCWL left the British shores for a new life in the United States, where it has remained ever since as a static exhibit in Kermit Weeks's Florida Air Museum at Lakeland, Florida.

The other aircraft appearing in this first scene parked beside the Lysander in the background is Noorduyn AT-16 Harvard IIb G-AZSC, clearly identifiable by its RAF serial of FT323. This Harvard was already a well known performer on the British airshow circuit when it was used as a background prop in "Eye of the Needle", flown by its owner, experienced aerobatics pilot Mike Stowe, who based it at Blackbushe.

Harvard G-AZSC began life as a licence-built AT-6A (designated AT-16 in Canada) by the Canadian Noorduyn company and taken on charge by the USAAF as 43-13064 in November 1943. It was immediately allocated to the Royal Air Force, with the serial FT323, and shipped from Newark, New Jersey, to Liverpool Docks in December that same year. It spent most of its wartime career in storage at No.46 MU, RAF Speke, Liverpool, before it was donated to the new post-War Royal Netherlands Air Force, coded B-19. It appears to have had an inconspicuous service career until it emerged as PH-SKK on the Dutch civil register, performing as a skywriting aircraft advertising a brand of Dutch beer.

In April 1972, Doug Arnold acquired this Harvard and registered it as G-AZSC with his Fairoaks Aviation Services company. Arnold had the Harvard repainted in RAF colours, with the serial FT830; however, this was an error and subsequently the correct serial of FT323 was applied. Mike Stowe acquired G-AZSC in November 1977 and aerobat'd it at various airshows in the UK until he re-sold it to the Arnold group in January 1981.

Now enter a familiar name on both the British airshow and rock music scenes - Gary Numan. He purchased G-AZSC in February 1984, registered it to his Machine Music company and had it painted it to represent a Japanese 'Zero' fighter. Together with the late Norman Lees, Newman formed 'The Radial Pair' aerobatic duo of two Harvards, which expanded into the five-ship 'Harvard Formation Aerobatic Team' of the Eighties. Newman retained ownership of G-AZSC until October 2005, when he sold the Harvard to its current owners, Goodwood Aero Club, based at the famous Goodwood Aerodrome and vintage road racing circuit. Today, it is operated as a tail-wheel veteran aircraft trainer for pilots learning to fly warbirds and is painted in a spurious US Navy-

style all-over gloss black colour scheme. It is still a familiar sight at various aviation events in Britain. On 22nd July 2011 it was forced to make a wheels-up landing in a field next to Goodwood Aerodrome due to a fuel feed failure; damage was minor.

The second main scene in which aviation features in "Eye of the Needle" involves the Needle himself reconnoitring what he believes is a large military airfield in East Anglia where invasion forces have been stored prior to invading mainland Europe at the Pas de Calais. He breaks into the airfield with remarkable ease and discovers that all the parked aircraft are full-scale plywood facsimiles. He realises that the fake invasion forces in East Anglia means that Pas de Calais is a deception and that Normandy is the real location for the landings.

Blackbushe Airport was very cleverly disguised as the fake invasion airfield. It is initially seen in a panoramic shot, filmed from the Needle's perspective as he surveys the air base from trees he is hiding among. The shot shows rows of military aircraft and vehicles occupying just about every space available on the airfield. However, this is a clever art department creation. In the foreground, the Nissan huts, rows of parked vehicles and the immediate row of aircraft lined up on the nearest runway, are all genuine. But the dozens of aircraft and vehicles covering acres of grass space stretching into the distance beyond are matte artwork on imagery of the real Blackbushe Airport, completely changing its normal shape and lay-out.

A significant number of aircraft from the Warbirds of Great Britain collection were used for this invasion force scene. But not all of them were real. Two, in fact, were quite realistic-looking (from a distance) full-scale facsimiles of Boeing B-17 Flying Fortress bombers; the Needle only realises they are fake when he accidentally knocks the wooden propeller off one of them. In this case, the art department has created these facsimile B-17s as clear fakes because that is what they are intended to be in the film's plot. To add depth to the scene, two-dimensional art department hardboard cut-outs of another B-17 and two P-51D Mustangs have been placed in the background.

However, all the other aircraft parked around the two dummy B-17s are certainly real, and all of them are from Warbirds of Great Britain. Five of them are Douglas C-47 Dakota troop transports, all painted to represent USAAF C-47 Skytrains; or at least on their port sides, the angle from which they are intended to be filmed - they retained their normal paint schemes on their (meant to be) unseen starboard sides (betrayed in one shot when two of the five C-47s are clearly seen to have their standard white-and-bare-metal schemes on their starboard sides clashing with their temporarily applied USAAF-style olive drab 'wardrobe' on their port sides). Four are ex-Spanish Air Force C-47A and C-47B Dakotas; the fifth was a US-registered C-47A. They, and four former Spanish Air Force CASA 352Ls (licence-built Junkers Ju.52 tri-motors), were a regular feature at Blackbushe in the early Eighties until buyers were found for them.

Of the five C-47s used in the film as USAAF Skytrains, one was the previously used G-BGCE (42-108953/T.3-2) as the RAF Dakota Windsor Castle. The other four were G-BFPW (44-77272/T.3-40), G-BGCF (43-16130/T.3-33), G-BGCG (43-15536/T.3-27) and N54607 (42-24211). Their fates were as follows:

C-47A N54607, formerly owned by Visionair International, Inc, was transferred to Liverpool/Speke Airfield (today, John Lennon International Airport) in August 1982 and remained there with Keenair until February 1989, when it came onto the British register as G-BPMP, owned by Cherkley Aviation, Ltd, at Coventry/Baginton Airport. Lord Beaverbrook planned to restore this C-47A to its original configuration as Skytrain 42-24211 with the 313th Troop Carrier Group, which operated it during the invasions of Sicily, Italy and Normandy. However, Kuwait Oil were sponsoring the restoration project but had had its assets frozen as a result of Saddam Hussein's invasion of Kuwait in August 1990, therefore no more money. The C-47A was then acquired by Coventry-based Air Atlantique as a spares source for its large DC-3 Dakota fleet, and was eventually broken up on 7th April 1995.

C-47B G-BFPW came onto the British register with Warbirds of Great Britain in April 1978 and had already been sold to an American owner by the time of its brief use in "Eye of the Needle"; it departed the UK soon afterwards.

C-47A G-BGCF was registered in November 1978 to Fairoaks Aviation Services and had also been sold to an American owner when it was used in the film; it became N3753C on the US register and is preserved today with the Eighth Air Force Museum at Barksdale Air Force Base, Louisiana.

C-47A Dakota III G-BGCG was registered at the same time as 'CF to Fairoaks Aviation Services and likewise had been taken on charge as N5595T by the same American owner as the previous two C-47s; however, it never left the UK shores, being stored and used as a spares source by Skysports at Thruxton Airfield. It was re-registered as G-BGCG in October 1984 to Datran Holdings, Ltd, of London, remaining so until cancelled by the CAA in April 1989. Reportedly its remains are today stored at a farm in Bedfordshire.

In another part of the same scene, two more aircraft are shown among the parked C-47s that would be recognisable to aviation enthusiasts from their previous appearance in a British war film released just two years earlier than "Eye of the Needle". These are two of the five North American B-25J Mitchell bombers that were flown across the Atlantic for "Hanover Street" (1979). This particular pair had since been stored at Blackbushe. The two B-25J Mitchells were N9115Z (44-29366), which played '151645/Marvellous Miriam' in "Hanover Street", and N9494Z (44-30925), previously owned by John Hawke's Visionair International, Inc, and still wearing its costume as '151632/Georgeous George-Ann'. The histories of both these B-25s are described in the "Hanover Street" review.

Two more historic American warbirds need to be accounted for in "Eye of the Needle". One of them is only briefly seen in two passing shots and can, therefore, be easily missed; however, freeze-frame analysis confirms its appearance. This is what was a very rare warbird on the British aviation scene in the early Eighties: a Republic P-47D Thunderbolt, the first of its kind to be seen in Britain since the Forties ('seen' is perhaps a very loose-meaning description here, as Doug Arnold kept this 'Jug' well away from enthusiasts' eyes for virtually the whole of the time he owned it).

The P-47D Thunderbolt in question is N47DE, an ex-Peruvian Air Force 'Jug', with which it flew as FAP 122. It was actually a two-seat 'Razor Back' P-47 that had been taken on charge by the USAAF as 45-49205. It arrived in Britain in 1979 to join the Warbirds of Great Britain collection at Blackbushe and briefly came onto the UK civil register as G-BLZW in July 1985, when Stephen Grey at Duxford acquired it from Doug Arnold; but this was cancelled the following November when this P-47D was sold back to the USA, joining Robert Pond's Planes of Fame East collection. It flew again in June 1986. It is now registered as N47RP and flies on the US warbird circuit as 228473/2Z-P Big Chief, with Ray Stutsman of Elkhart, Indiana.

The other warbird which clearly comes into view as the Needle runs through the midst of packed C-47s and B-25s is North American P-51D Mustang N166G, wearing fake code letters of 'LH-O' and carrying D-Day invasion stripes. This P-51D arrived in the UK with Warbirds of Great Britain the same time as did P-47D N47DE. It began life as 44-63788 and served mainly as a US Air National Guard fighter until struck off charge in 1957. This P-51D then went through a series of private ownerships and registration changes in the USA before Doug Arnold acquired it in 1979. "Eye of the Needle" was the first of this Mustang's two movie appearances: it had a static role in this film, but would go into action as a USAAF P-51D in Steven Spielberg's "Empire of the Sun" (1987), by which time it had been bought by Stephen Grey who registered it in the UK as G-PSID. Grey later sold G-PSID to a French owner, who in his turn had it registered in France as F-AZFI; tragically it was lost in a fatal airshow accident in June 1988, resulting in the death of its pilot and his passenger.

Mention now has to be made of the most erroneous aircraft type to appear in this invasion airfield scene, and also in the finale to "Eye of the Needle". For whatever reason known to them, director Richard Marquand and scriptwriter Stanley Mann have chosen to include a helicopter. Neither can surely claim ignorance of the historical fact that helicopters were not used by the Allies in World War Two, except in very limited rescue operations by the United States Army in Burma and China towards the end of the War.

It seems that Marquand and Mann are trying to portray a Sikorsky R-4 Hoverfly as a helicopter type that was supposedly in service with both the US Army and the British Army in the run-up to D-Day, as the invasion airfield scene has a helicopter bearing unconvincing US Army markings parked among all the other aircraft, while towards the end of the film a British Army helicopter tries to intercept the Needle.

Very simply, neither the US Army nor the British Army had anything to do with helicopters in Europe during 1944. The British had been loaned two R-4 Hoverfly prototypes for evaluation by the RAE, but neither saw operational service. A small number of R-4 Hoverfly helicopters would briefly enter service with the Royal Air Force in January 1945, before they were assessed as having little operational value and were then passed on to the Fleet Air Arm for evaluation in the air-sea rescue role.

The helicopter in "Eye of the Needle" is, at first sight, something of a mystery. It is, to all appearances, a Westland Dragonfly, a licence-built version of the Sikorsky S-51. But there were no Westland Dragonfly helicopters flying anywhere in the world when "Eye of the Needle" was in production in 1980. So, how do we account for this one?

The answer appears to be that it is a converted version of the civil variant of the Westland Dragonfly, a Westland Widgeon Srs 2, a modernised conversion of a Dragonfly offering a slightly larger cabin and using the gearbox, rotor head and blades of the more powerful Westland Whirlwind. Or, so it appears. Careful freeze-frame analysis reveals the art department trick that has been used to make the Widgeon appear like a Westland Dragonfly.

Instead of being a reverse-engineered version of the Widgeon that has been turned back into a Westland Dragonfly, with the latter's all-glass glazed nose in place of the former's solid metal proboscis, what the art department have done is build a temporary wooden and Perspex cockpit frame and fitted it neatly over the Widgeon's nose and windscreen. This meant the pilot had to fly the helicopter while looking through two sets of cockpit windows ahead of him, which must have made for challenging flying, especially among rocky Scottish scenery. The effect, though, is very convincing and gives the Widgeon a very realistic Westland Dragonfly-style appearance. The codes 'NE-X' have been applied to the tail boom which were actually used by Nos.143 and 63 Squadrons during World War Two, neither of which had anything to do with helicopters.

The actual Widgeon concerned is G-ANLW, owned at the time by Helicopter Hire at Southend Airport, a company which contributed a number of helicopters to British films and TV productions during the Sixties, Seventies and Eighties. Subsequently, this Widgeon came into the ownership of Sloane Helicopters at Shoreham Airport and was donated by Sloanes on permanent loan to the Norfolk and Suffolk Aviation Museum at Flixton, Suffolk, where it remains on display to this day.

ANOTHER TIME, ANOTHER PLACE

(Released: July 1983)

World War Two provides no more than the background to what is a romantic story involving the love affair between the young wife of a farmer in Scotland and an Italian Prisoner of War. No action is involved, although British Aerospace-owned de Havilland Mosquito T.3 RR299/HT-E puts in a brief appearance to remind us that the War was still on.

MERRY CHRISTMAS, MR LAWRENCE

(Released: August 1983)

A Japanese PoW story based partly on the real-life experiences of journalist/author/philosopher/explorer, Laurens van der Post, when he was held prisoner by the Japanese, and starring David Bowie as the British Army officer who challenges the Samurai code of the Camp Commandant. A very well received film internationally; however, aviation does not feature in it.

HOPE AND GLORY

(Released: September 1987)

It's hard to imagine that this film was nominated for the Best Picture 'Oscar' at the 1988 Academy Awards ceremony, along with other 'Oscar' nominations, none of which it won. It may be genteel, humorous, and beautifully filmed and acted, but the characters portrayed are just not interesting enough to sustain the sympathy and the attention of the audience. The latter half of the film is uneventful in terms of drama and tension.

Based on the wartime experiences of film director John Boorman, when he was an eight-year-old boy growing up in London during The Blitz of 1940 - 1941, it is at its best when it shows how children turn bomb sites into playgrounds and create fantasy roles for themselves to ameliorate the terrors of the bombing. The final scene when Billy, the nine-year-old boy who is the central character, joins in the celebrations of his schoolmates when they find their school has been hit by a stray bomb the night before the start of a new term, meaning all lessons are cancelled, is genuinely funny in illustrating how destruction could be made welcome.

As with films made about The Blitz during the War itself - "Fires Were Started" (1943) and "The Bells Go Down" (1943) - the Luftwaffe bombers devastating London are never seen. Nor are they heard, as they are in the two wartime productions, which is a strange elimination of detail by Boorman as he must have listened to the demoralising drone of the Dorniers and Heinkels if he was in the midst of the actual Blitz in the way Billy and his family are portrayed in the film.

However, what is seen is the shoot-down of a Messerschmitt Bf.109 by a Spitfire which Billy, his family and friends all witness. The Messerschmitt passes across the street where Billy lives, trailing smoke, and is immediately followed by the victorious Spitfire making a fast, low pass over the houses as the children cheer, before pulling up into a classic 'Victory Roll'.

We know this Spitfire well: Vickers Supermarine Spitfire HF.Mk.IXb MH434 (G-ASJV), almost certainly being flown by Ray Hanna. Freeze-framing reveals MH434's instantly recognisable ZD-B codes of No.222 (Natal) Squadron. This, of course, is technically incorrect for the 1940 period being depicted, as the Spitfire Mk.IX would not appear on the scene for another two years, while no Battle of Britain Spitfires were armed with the cannon that MH434 is seen toting here. No.222 (Natal) Squadron was, however, an actual Battle of Britain No.11 Group squadron, as we have discovered in reviews of war films in Chapter One.

The street scene itself is filmed at the former Vickers airfield of Wisley in Surrey, where the Vickers Viscount airliner and Valiant V-Bomber made their first flights. A complete 650-acre film set of a suburban London street, with very realistic semi-detached houses, was created at Wisley airfield, over which Hanna is filmed making his characteristic curved top-side pass that was his trademark entry manoeuvre at the start of his aerobatic displays in Spitfire HF.IXb MH434.

But what of the Messerschmitt Bf.109 seen trailing smoke? It, too, is seen in shot just before the Spitfire sweeps in. It is not, as might be supposed, an Hispano HA.1112M1L Buchon, as used in "Battle of Britain" (1969). It is, in fact, another aircraft owned by Ray Hanna and his Old Flying Machine Company at Duxford in the Eighties, Pilatus P-2-05 G-BJAX. This ex-Swiss Air Force trainer was actually based on the Messerschmitt Bf.109 design. Pilatus P-2 G-BJAX was painted in the mid-Eighties in the colours of a Bf.109 flown by JG.71 Richtofen, marked as 'Red 14' and with high visibility yellow nose, and would have carried this scheme when it was flown in "Hope and Glory". It makes another appearance later in the film, as a Bf.109 'Jabo' when it bombs the River Thames close to where Billy and his younger sister are fishing - the explosion stuns dozens of fish, which Billy and his sister scoop up. This Pilatus P-2 was probably being flown by the late Flight Lieutenant John Watts in both these scenes, as he regularly displayed G-BJAX at this time.

Just before the shoot-down of the Bf.109, Billy is sitting in a cinema with his mother and sisters watching a newsreel of a dog-fight between RAF and Luftwaffe fighters. These newsreel shots are actually out-takes from "Battle of Britain" (1969), both used and unused in that original film, shown in black-and-white on the cinema screen to create the newsreel effect. The first out-take is of a Spitfire shooting down a Hispano HA.1112M1L Buchon, which blows up in the rather ineffective SFX used in "Battle of Britain". A second out-take has another Spitfire chasing a smoke-trailing Buchon. A third has a studio miniature of a Heinkel He.111 exploding in a mass of flame, which for whatever reason was not used in the original film but was made use of 32 years later in the Czech production of "Dark Blue World" (2001).

The cinema audience are shown a message on the screen as the 'newsreel' is in progress, informing them that an air raid is taking place and they are advised to leave for the shelters. As they get up from their seats, the cinema screen has an unused out-take of four Hispano HA.1112M1L Buchons breaking from echelon starboard formation to attack. This is immediately followed by the aerial shot that was used in "Battle of Britain" to show Squadron Leader Harvey's Spitfire being hit. It is the last of the out-takes used.

The problem in Boorman choosing to use these out-takes is that they are not realistic of actual newsreels of the period: air-air shots of aerial dog-fights were hardly ever available for these screened news reports in 1940.

The only other form of aviation in "Hope and Glory" appears in the shape of a barrage balloon that is set up close to Billy's home; there is an entertaining scene when it breaks loose from its mooring ropes and floats like a large, out-of-control bloated whale over the rooftops of the houses in Billy's street.

RETURN FROM THE RIVER KWAI

(Released: April 1989)

When this film was released, it was burdened from the outset by its title. The production company, Roadshow Productions, probably hoped to capitalise on the "River Kwai" element for obvious reasons, but its distributor in the UK, J Arthur Rank Film Distributors, was forced to show a disclaimer before the opening credits, stating that the film was neither related, nor was a sequel, to the famous Academy Award-winning movie, "The Bridge on the River Kwai" (1957). In the United States, Universal Studios were prevented by legal action from releasing the film to theater at all.

A claim is made on the DVD release that "Return from the River Kwai" is based on fact. If so, the fact has been considerably fictionalised by the director, Andrew V McLagen, and the scriptwriters, Sargon Tamimi and Paul Mayersberg. Using the book of the same title by Joan and Clay Blair, Jnr, as its inspiration, the film "…tells the true story of what happened to 2,218 British and Australian POWs - and a lone American - who survived the brutal hardships of building the jungle railway in Japanese-occupied Thailand" (actually, Siam in 1945).

In actuality, the notorious bridge built over the supposed River Kwai (probably the Siamese Khwae Yai River) by Commonwealth, Dutch and American Prisoners of War, to link Siam with Burma, only appears right at the beginning of the film when it is bombed by USAAF fighter-bombers, killing both Allied PoWs and Japanese guards in the process. Aside from this scene, anything to do with the River Kwai is absent from the plot. In reality, the book on which the film claims to be based deals mostly with the fate of British and Australian PoWs aboard two Japanese prison ships that were conveying them to Japan in 1945, when they were torpedoed by US Navy submarines. Elements of this event are portrayed towards the end of the film, but do not reflect the ordeal of the surviving PoWs left to drift for days in the Sea of Japan, which is the principal theme of the book.

Aviation features in two segments of the film: the bombing of the supposed River Kwai bridge at the beginning and the escape in a Japanese fighter-bomber by a captured USAAF fighter pilot two-thirds of the way through the story. To enact both these sequences, four North American AT-28D Trojans of the Philippines Air Force are called upon to act as both American and Japanese warplanes, just as a similar number of AT-28Ds from the 15th Strike Wing, Philippines Air Force, were required to perform the same role as Japanese dive bombers in "Too Late The Hero" (1970): the AT-28Ds in "Return from the River Kwai" were from the same Strike Wing.

An unusual opening shot has a statement reflected onto a close-up of one panel of a pair of eye shades, saying, "In February 1945, planes from the 493rd Squadron of the US Army Air Corps bombed and destroyed the bridges on the River Kwai in Japanese-occupied Thailand". As stated, Thailand was Siam in 1945, while the United States Army Air Corps had been subsumed within the overall United States Army Air Force structure by 9th March 1942. Quite why "the 493rd Squadron" is quoted is not obvious: there was a 493rd Fighter Squadron (Single Engine) active within the US Army Air Force in February 1945, but it was operational at that time with P-47 Thunderbolts from Liberated France over Germany, not over Siam. Scriptwriters Tamimi and Mayersberg were obviously not too preoccupied with the facts.

There is one theoretical explanation for this curious opening shot. The eye shade in the close-up is very similar in style to that favoured by USAF combat jet pilots; it is certainly too modern for the 1945 period. Also, no one wears eye shades in the film itself (not exactly standard issue to Commonwealth PoWs or Japanese guards). The thinking is that McLagen and his scriptwriters may have been making a nod towards the involvement of the modern-day 493rd Tactical Fighter Squadron (TFS), the Grim Reapers, in the most widely talked-about air combat mission by the USAF of the time since the Vietnam War: Operation Elderado Canyon, the attack on Tripoli in April 1986 by the 48th Tactical Fighter Wing, of which the 493rd TFS was a part. This punishment attack on Colonel Gaddafi's regime, which had organised the terrorist bombing of US servicemen in a nightclub in West Berlin 10 days earlier, was still widely celebrated in the USA during 1988 when "Return from the River Kwai" was in production.

If there is another explanation for the out-of-synch opening eye shade shot, along with the reference to the 493rd Squadron, then it is most certainly not obvious in the film.

Two AT-28Ds make repeated runs over the 'River Kwai Bridge' acting as fictional 493rd Squadron P-47s, and can actually be seen dropping (albeit small) ordnance from their outer underwing hardpoints. One of the AT-28Ds has to stream white smoke from an underwing flare, to depict being hit by Japanese ground fire, from which a US Army Air Force pilot parachutes to safety and eventually joins up with the PoWs, played by American actor Christopher Penn. The Trojans are clearly painted overall dark olive green, obviously untypical of actual Air Corps P-47s, but quite likely this was the natural colour scheme of the Philippines Air Force AT-28D 'Tora Toras' in 1988, as most of their operational sorties against Communist and Islamist rebels took place over jungle terrain. This colour scheme naturally adapted the AT-28Ds into Imperial Japanese Air Force fighter-bombers later in the film, when Lieutenant Crawford, played by Penn, steals one of them to make his escape.

These four AT-28Ds are first seen in their Japanese markings parked on the ramp of what is meant to be an air base in Siam, viewed by Crawford from the prison train in which he and his fellow PoWs are being conveyed to Saigon in Japanese Occupied French Indo-China. Crawford resolves to escape in one of them.

This scene is almost certainly filmed at Sangley Air Base, Cavite, home to the AT-28D-equipped 15th Strike Wing until 1992. The four AT-28D 'Tora Toras' are clearly marked with code numbers in white on their tail fins. These are different to the code numbers that AT-28Ds bore in "Too Late The Hero", which seemed in that film to have been based on their actual original US serials that Philippines Air Force aircraft carried. In "Return from the River Kwai", the code numbers appear to be invented Imperial Japanese Air Force codes.

The four 'Japanese' AT-28Ds can be identified as being: '01-06', '01-07', '01-08' and '03-09', the latter being the aircraft which Crawford steals with ridiculous ease. In so doing, he shoots up an armed jeep on the runway, using an Eighties-era underwing minigun that the attack version of the T-28 Trojan was equipped with. The jeep rams into fuel drums, which explode into flame - a stuntman acting as a Japanese soldier rolling on the ground looks uncomfortably close to the exploding drums, which could have sent flames in any direction! There is a nice study of AT-28D '03-09' retracting its

undercarriage, with minigun pods clearly attached beneath both wings. The North American AT-28D counterinsurgency version of the long-serving T-28 Trojan trainer served the Philippines Air Force well for several decades, until they were phased out in favour of the SIAI-Marchetti SF.260W Warrior in 1992.

"Return from the River Kwai" is a quite fast-paced war movie, filmed in obviously steamy locations in Malaysia, the Philippines and Thailand. Its claim to be based on fact is selective, but McLagen knows how to keep the action moving, however unlikely some of it may be in comparison to the (very) grim reality. Perhaps the real truth (pardon the double negative) of what happened to the Commonwealth PoWs in 1945 in Japanese Occupied Siam and French Indo-China (today, Vietnam) needs to be put on screen, but if so, it will make very hard watching.

MEMPHIS BELLE

(Released: October 1990)

What was meant to be a stellar box office hit of a war movie, celebrating the memory of both an historic wartime documentary and of its illustrious Hollywood director, William Wyler, turned out instead to be one big flop of a turkey with film fans. Why? One of its two producers was David Puttnam, whose own star had ridden high throughout the Eighties due to his Oscar-winning and nominated film productions, such as "Chariots of Fire" (1982), "The Killing Fields" (1985) and "The Mission" (1987); it had what was considered to be the ideal crop of young American actors representative of the recently retired President Ronald Reagan's USA; and it had 17 genuine World War Two warbirds filmed in aerial action on a superbly colourful tapestry. How could it go wrong?

The answer is simple: the film is boring. It just does not have an adequate enough story to tell. Ten young men flying their bomber's 25th and final bombing mission before it was sent back home just doesn't offer sufficient interest to a movie-going audience 47 years after the actual events took place. In 1943, when the real Memphis Belle was in action over the Ruhr - yes; when it involved young American men fighting and dying in the skies above Nazi Germany - yes; when the documentary by William Wyler created valuable propaganda for the American people to admire about their Army Air Force - yes. But in 1990, and in years to follow, when America and the western world were adjusting to the fall of the Soviet Union, wondering what consequences would result from the invasion of Kuwait by Saddam Hussein's Iraq, and preparing for "the new world order to come", as the newly incumbent President George H W Bush was calling it - no.

Yet it wasn't simply about bad or unfortunate timing, or being overwhelmed by new and unexpected events, which might have made this film's subject irrelevant: it would have flopped anyway. The ten characters in the film are just not interesting enough to make the audience care whether they get through their 25th bombing mission aboard Memphis Belle or not. There isn't sufficient time for the audience to get to know the crew of the Memphis Belle and to find any empathy with them.

They are all composites of supposed young American manhood of the Forties, including the innocent kid from a large family, who worked in the family diner before signing up; the ex-reform school yahoo from Chicago; the sensitive, religious 19-year-old from Cleveland; the self-promoting 18-year-old supposed ladies man; the farmer's son who had to play piano in a New Orleans cat house when his father lost the farm in a poker game; the 'Irishman'; the lifeguard; the apparently genuine medical student; and the Captain who pilots the Belle, a serious-faced businessman. Not one of them is interesting.

Not only that, they are so obviously Eighties generation young American actors portraying what Eighties generation young Americans thought Forties generation young Americans behaved like. Or, what the director, Scotsman Michael Caton-Jones, and scriptwriter, American Monte Merrick, thought they had to get from the Memphis Belle aircrew in order to appeal to young Americans of 1990. This was the era of "Top Gun", right? Cool dude aircrew shout in action, right? So what do Caton-Jones and Merrick have the men of Memphis Belle do? They have them shout in action, like tough, gung ho, "Top Gun" dudes. They have them 'horsin' around on the airplane' while en route to the target. No wonder this got up the noses of genuine ex-Eighth Air Force vets, who felt that the way the Memphis Belle aircrew are portrayed was not only unrealistic, but laughable.

How Merrick got chosen to write the script for "Memphis Belle" is a mystery, he only wrote one screenplay for a feature film before this one, according to his screen biography. And Caton-Jones seemed an odd choice as director as well, with no major feature film to his credit prior to "Memphis Belle" apart from the well-received in Britain film re-creation of the John Profumo/Christine Keeler scandal of the Sixties, the appropriately titled "Scandal" (1989).

Furthermore, the sense of drama is dampened by George Fenton's all-too glorious music score, played using the 'wash-around' soundtrack style so favoured in big budget films of the Eighties: it is meant to sound impressive on the ear, but the score has no depth, no tension, no sense of emotion. It sounds glorious, but no more.

It is a curiosity as to why David Puttnam had wanted to get involved with a film like "Memphis Belle" in the first place. After all, it didn't seem to be a subject that would normally be associated with him. Moreover, he had just emerged bruised and battered from the unhappy, year-long experience of being head of Columbia Pictures, from which he had been fired in a boardroom revolt against him. Puttnam had wanted to take Columbia away from the Rambo-style and Terminator-type 'shoot-'em-ups' that had become the gore-fest fare of Eighties American (and plenty of British) movie fans. However, he had reckoned without the junk food-addicted/reversed baseball cap-wearing/Rambo-wannabe/ PlayStation-hooked young Americans that the Columbia Pictures board members wanted to cultivate and service, so the cultured Puttnam was thrown to the Reaganite wolves.

It has been suggested that Puttnam had long wanted to make a film about RAF Bomber Command, not as a "Dam Busters"- style piece with heroic stiff-upper-lipped Brits to the fore, but as a study of the emotional and psychological effects of being the crew members of a Lancaster bomber on a night-time raid over Nazi Germany. It is thought that Puttnam had a film version of Len Deighton's novel, "Bomber", in mind, especially as the plot would have had the fire storm of Dresden included as a counterbalance to the experiences of the Lancaster aircrew, thus making it an anti-war film. Apparently Puttnam couldn't get any backers for it, while the film distributor he was dealing with advised him that war films in which the action takes place at night were a loser with the audience.

How the connection came about is not entirely known, but the daughter of William Wyler, Catherine Wyler, who wanted to make "Memphis Belle" as a tribute to her father, may have learnt of Puttnam's interest in making a film about World War Two bomber pilots by two possible means: firstly, through her own work as a film producer (she mostly made documentaries, particularly several about her father), and secondly, through her uncle, David Tallichet, whose sister, Margaret, was Catherine Wyler's mother. David Tallichet we know about, through his involvement with providing B-25 Mitchell bombers for "Hanover Street" (1979) a decade earlier.

The combination of having William Wyler's daughter join with her aviation expert uncle and with the British film industry's most talented producer, is what became the driving force behind the making of "Memphis Belle".

But there were historical precedents that could have alerted Puttnam and Catherine Wyler to the risks involved: previous blockbusters about factual aerial battles, such as "Battle of Britain" (1969) and "Tora! Tora! Tora!" (1970), had gone down like loss-making lead balloons following their release.

But proceed they did, and spared no expense in hiring some of the best and most knowledgeable warbird experts from both sides of the Atlantic to acquire aircraft, pilots and support equipment for the all-important aerial scenes. David Tallichet was obviously in at the start, and has to be credited with ensuring that the B-17 Flying Fortresses used in the film were all converted to appear as the B-17F model. The time period was the summer of 1943 and the B-17F was then the most modern version of the Flying Fortress being operated by the Eighth Air Force in Britain. Ray and Mark Hanna had impressed producer/director Steven Spielberg with their flying sequences with P-51D Mustangs for his "Empire of the Sun" (1987) epic, and had just come off the back of flying and co-ordinating Spitfires and Messerschmitt Bf.109Js in the British TV production, "A Piece of Cake" - they were obvious candidates to do a similar job for "Memphis Belle". Ray was appointed chief pilot, while Mark undertook the role of aerial co-ordinator, as well as flying both of the Old Flying Machine Company (OFMC) warbirds which appear in the film. Mike Woodley's Aces High company had acquired for itself a strong reputation as a provider of aviation assets to the film industry in the UK, and was the natural choice to organise all the aircraft appearing in Puttnam's and Wyler's co-production as well as providing the camera aircraft. Retired RAF Air Vice-Marshall Ron Dick had the job of co-ordinating the air-air filming.

By July 1989, 17 warbirds had been assembled at Duxford Aerodrome, which was to be the operational base for "Memphis

Belle". The former RAF Lightning base of Binbrook in Lincolnshire was used for most of the scenes filmed at Memphis Belle's airfield in England (the real Memphis Belle flew from Bassingbourn in Cambridgeshire, which could not be used as most of its runways had been turned over to agriculture, while the air base's infrastructure was now used as an Army barracks).

Detailed below are all 17 of the aircraft that appear in "Memphis Belle", with their actual roles and individual histories described:

Boeing B-17F Flying Fortress: N17W (42-29782), owned by Robert Richardson of Seattle, Washington, and flown by him and his second pilot, Donald Clark. Carried the serial 124299 and the code DF-X in the film, acting the roles of B-17s C-Cup and Kathleen. N17W was the one genuine B-17F Flying Fortress in "Memphis Belle" and, since its appearance at Binbrook and Duxford in 1989, has the distinction of being the last such 'F' Model B-17 to fly in British skies. It came into USAAF service in February 1943 and appears to have spent its wartime career entirely States-side with various training units until it was demobbed in November 1945. It then became a war memorial at the city of Stuttgart, Arkansas, but was still the property of the federal government. This became an issue of dispute when the city authorities allowed a local resident of Stuttgart to remove the B-17F without charge and to sell it to three businessmen in 1953. The federal government then moved in and, through the Civil Aeronautics Authority - forerunner of the Federal Aviation Administration - requested that no civil registration be allocated until the ownership dispute was settled. The businessmen eventually agreed to pay the government $20,000 and the registration N17W was issued. This B-17F then spent the period between 1954 - 1961 as an aerial sprayer before it was sold to Abe Sellards of Safford, Arizona. Sellards helped form the Aviation Specialties company in 1963, which, as mentioned in "The War Lover" (1962) review, operated a large fleet of B-17s as fire fighting aerial tankers. This was N17W's occupation until 1985. However, it also developed a role as a film actor, appearing as a B-17F in "The 1,000 Plane Raid" (1968) and standing in for a B-17D in "Tora! Tora! Tora!" (1970). After completing its work on "Memphis Belle" in August 1989, B-17F N17W was flown back to the USA and displayed on the American airshow circuit for several years. N17W is today with the Museum of Flight at Boeing Field, Seattle, on permanent exhibition representing all the B-17s that originated from this world famous aircraft manufacturing plant.

Boeing B-17G Flying Fortress: N3703G (44-83546), owned by David C Tallichet's Military Aircraft Restoration Corp of Long Beach, California. Flown in the film by David Tallichet himself, B-17G N3703G was skilfully converted into a very realistic representation of an earlier model B-17F and, as it was the only one of the five B-17s used in the film to have a working under-fuselage ball turret, was chosen to take the starring role of the Memphis Belle herself. It also acted as Mary Lou and carried the serials and codes of 121485/DF-H, 124485/DF-H, 124485/DF-A (that of Memphis Belle) and 124495/DP-A, without any name: quite why a 'DP-' code was used is not known - B-17G G-BEDF did likewise - unless this was an art department error. B-17G N3703G began life when it was accepted as 44-83546 by the USAAF in April 1945

and spent most of its service career as firstly a CB-17G personnel transport, then a VB-17G staff transport, conducting much of its tasking with the Far East Air Force at Haneda, Japan, during the Korean War. It was put up for disposal in April 1959 and was auctioned off in a job-lot including other B-17s, finishing up with Fast-Air, Inc, of Long Beach, California, and being converted in 1960 into a tanker for fire fighting. N3703G plied her trade, first with Fast-Air, then with TBM, Inc, of Tulare, California, as an air tanker until the late Seventies when it was sold to David Tallichet. Tallichet was operating a B-17 on loan from the USAF Museum with his Yesterday's Air Force; now that he owned a B-17 outright, he could return the loaned example and bring N3703G back into full military configuration. Tallichet chose to create a very realistic B-17F model-like Flying Fortress with most parts, like the bomb doors and Norden bombsight, actually working. Since its starring performance in "Memphis Belle", this B-17 has been a big hit on the US airshow circuit and still flies every year at many events, now in B-17G configuration and bearing the identity 124485/DF-A/ Memphis Belle. In 2010, it made the return journey across 'The Pond' to its film location at Duxford Aerodrome, where it took centre stage at that year's Flying Legends Air Show. For Tallichet, flying his B-17 in "Memphis Belle" must have been a very déjà vu-like experience, as he had been an Eighth Air Force co-pilot with the 100th Bomb Group in England during World War Two. As previously mentioned in the "Hanover Street" (1979) review, Tallichet recently succumbed to prostate cancer.

Boeing B-17G Flying Fortress: G-BEDF (44-85784), owned by B-17 Preservation based at Duxford Aerodrome and flown in the film by chief pilot, Captain Keith Sissons, with second pilot Alan Walker. It acted the roles of a number of B-17s in "Memphis Belle", including My Zita, Lady Jane, Gee Whiz and Windy City, carrying the identities of 22360/DF-O, 22960/DF-M and 124888/ DP-O. This Flying Fortress needs no introduction to British aviation enthusiasts: it has been displaying in Britain since 1975 and is known to one and all as Sally B (not the name of any actual B-17, but the affectionate nickname of its owner, Elly Sallingboe, given to her by her former partner - both in the professional and personal sense of the word - the late Ted White, who acquired this B-17G in 1975). Sally B actually appears as herself, configured as a B-17F, in the shot of the B-17 aircrews driving out to their bombers. B-17G 44-85784 came on strength with the USAAF just after World War Two had ended (in Europe) and spent its military career as a test and trials aircraft. Under the designation EB-17G, it was "Exempted" from all but urgent technical orders for the type, so as to permit it to conduct whatever role was assigned to it while not having to comply with any new such technical orders applied to all remaining B-17s. At one point in time, it had manned wing-tip gun turrets installed, which must have been interesting. From 1954 onwards, this B-17 became one among 13 Flying Fortresses operated by the Institut Geographique Nationale (IGN) at Creil in France, under the French civil registration F-BGSR, and operated on aerial survey missions throughout the world. The IGN retired F-BGSR in 1970, after which it languished until acquired by Ted White and Duane Igli, two Americans who operated an all-purpose aviation company named Euroworld from

Biggin Hill Airport. Registered N17TE, this B-17G arrived during a very wet Biggin Hill Air Fair on 18th May 1975, beginning a long career on the British airshow circuit. It was subsequently re-registered as G-BEDF in 1976 under the ownership of Mark Campbell, then was registered to B-17 Preservation, Ltd, at Duxford on 30th April 1985. Since then, Sally B has operated from Duxford.

Boeing B-17G Flying Fortress: F-AZDX (44-8846), owned by the Association Forteresse Tourjours Volante at Melun-Villaroche, France, and flown by chief pilot, Andre Domine, with co-pilot Michel Bezy. This B-17 appeared as Mother and Country and Pink Lady in "Memphis Belle", carrying the identity of 25703/DF-S. B-17G 44-8846 was taken on charge by the USAAF in January 1945 and was in time to see action with the 511th Bomb Squadron of the 351st Bomb Group, named Half Pint. It flew six missions before the War ended, resulting in being transferred to the 365th BS of the 305th BG which re-located to Lechfeld in Germany. It then became part of the 95th Reconnaissance Squadron, converted to RB-17G status, and remained in Germany at Wiesbaden until its return States-side in early 1953. After being struck off charge in November 1954, 44-8846 was quickly on her way to France to join the IGN at Creil, registered as F-BGSP. Together with the future Sally B and other IGN B-17s, it was operated worldwide on aerial survey and research work, including a survey project in South Africa during 1965. B-17G F-BGSP was placed in storage in 1979, but was brought back to life again to take part in the 40th anniversary of the Liberation of France in 1984. The following year it was re-registered as F-AZDX and operated as Lucky Lady under a joint partnership between the Association Forteresse Tourjours Volante and the Amicale Jean-Baptiste Salis. After its appearance in "Memphis Belle", F-AZDX retained its olive drab colour scheme and flew as Pink Lady at many airshows throughout Europe, bearing its original serial code from its days with the 511th BS. Although still in flying condition, B-17G Pink Lady has been placed in open storage at La Ferte Alais due to the high cost of maintaining and operating this classic World War Two bomber. Recently this B-17 was put back into the air again for its appearance in the new war film, "Red Tails".

Boeing B-17G Flying Fortress: F-BEEA (44-85643) of the Institut Geographique National at Creil, flown by Captain Jean-Pierre Gattegno. Appears in the film as Baby Ruth, with the serial and code 124292/DF-U. This B-17's military service role is believed to have been very short as it is reported as being the first of 13 examples to operate with the IGN, being bought in December 1947 and flown under the identity of Chateau de Verneuil. It was used on aerial survey work in various parts of the world. One of its most unusual tasks was to film high and low-level over Iceland and Greenland the scenic views of mountains and icebergs that were used in the satirical Cold War film, "Dr Strangelove" (1962). During one of these photo shoots, B-17G F-BEEA was forced down into making an emergency landing on a glacier in Greenland by F-102A Delta Darts of the 57th Fighter Interceptor Squadron out of Keflavik, Iceland, when the B-17 over-flew classified US military listening posts in Greenland monitoring Soviet Navy nuclear submarines. B-17G F-BEEA crashed on take off during filming at the former RAF Binbrook on 25th July 1989 and was destroyed in the ensuing fire, fortunately without any casualties among the 12 people on board.

Commonwealth CA-18 Mustang 22: G-HAEC, owned by the Old Flying Machine Company based at Duxford Aerodrome. Appears as 44-72917/AJ-A, named as Ding Hao!. Mustang G-HAEC differs from the other six P-51Ds in "Memphis Belle" in being a licence-built CA-18 Mustang Mk.22 manufactured by the Commonwealth Aircraft Company (CAC) in Australia and first flew on 8th March 1951. The customer was the Royal Australian Air Force (RAAF), with which it entered service as A68-192. In 1958, it was struck off charge and was placed on the Australian civil aircraft register as VH-FCB. In 1969 it was acquired by Prontino Inc of the Philippines as PI-C651, but crashed on landing four years later. Rebuilt using components from a retired Philippines Air Force Mustang (44-72917, the serial it carries in "Memphis Belle") by the Hong Kong Aero Engineering Company (HAEC), it flew again in 1981 as VR-HIU for Patina, Ltd, Ray Hanna's holding company based in Jersey. Hanna brought this CA-18 Mustang to the UK in 1983, to join the collection that he and his son Mark were building up at Duxford as the Old Flying Machine Company (OFMC). It was re-registered in the UK as G-HAEC, in recognition of the Hong Kong company that restored it, and carried its RAAF serial and markings as A68-192/CV-H. In 1987, Ray Hanna flew G-HAEC in Stephen Spielberg's "Empire of the Sun" as USAAF Fifth Air Force P-51D 44-72917, named Missy Wong from Hong Kong. Subsequently, the Hannas repainted G-HAEC in all-over silver RAAF markings carrying its original serial of A68-192 and flew it for several years on the Australasian airshow circuit in the Nineties. G-HAEC was acquired by Rob Davies in 1997, based at Woodchurch, Kent, who had it painted as 44-72218/WZ-I/Big Beautiful Doll of the 78th Fighter Group that operated from RAF Duxford during 1944. In February 2011, it was re-registered to the Air Fighter Academy GmbH in Rangsdorf, Germany, but retained its identity as G-HAEC. This Mustang was involved in a very public accident when it collided with Douglas Skyraider F-AZDP on 10th July 2011 at the Flying Legends Airshow held at Duxford - Rob Davies successfully bailed out at approximately 300 feet. At time of writing, it is not known if a restoration is possible.

North American P-51D Mustang: G-BIXL, owned by and flown in the film by Robs Lamplough and based at North Weald Aerodrome. Appears as 44-72216/AJ-L, named as Miss L. Mustang G-BIXL began its career as a post-War Eighth Air Force P-51D 44-72216 with the 487th FS, 352nd FG, coded HO-M at Bodney and flown as Miss Helen by Captain Raymond Littge and later as Miss Nita by Lieutenant Russell Ross. In 1948, it was acquired by the Swedish Air Force, serving as Fv26116/gF with first Flygflotti 4 (F4), then F16. In 1953, this P-51D was part of a batch acquired by the Israeli Air Force and went into action against the Egyptian Armed Forces in the Sinai during the '100 Days War'. In 1976, it was one of four ex-Israeli AF P-51Ds acquired by aircraft collector Robs Lamplough and registered as G-BIXL in 1981. It was restored to flying condition in 1987, using components from P-51D 44-72770 and flying as 44-72216/HO-L. After its appearance in "Memphis Belle", G-BIXL initially retained its markings as Miss L but was repainted in its original 487th FS colours as 44-72216/HO-M/Miss Helen. Today, G-BIXL is still owned by Robs Lamplough; it experienced an emergency landing in 2004, requiring repairs which saw it fly again in 2007, but was believed to be up for sale in 2011 since its owner had ceased flying.

North American P-51D Mustang: G-SUSY, owned by Charles Church Displays at Roundwood, Micheldever, Hampshire. Appears as 44-72773/AJ-C, named as Susy, which was its identity with Charles Church. Mustang G-SUSY began as P-51D 44-72773 that was accepted by the USAAF on 13th February 1945. It spent much of its early military career in storage before being assigned in 1951 to the USAF Tactical Air Command's 131st FS at George AFB in California. Later, in 1954, it was on the strength of the Texas ANG's 182nd FS at Brooks AFB, San Antonio. In 1958, this P-51D was declared surplus and sold to the Nicaraguan Air Force, where it operated until it was registered in 1963 in the USA as N12066, passing through two owners until Charles Church acquired it in 1987, naming it Susy after his wife. The late Charles Church was killed in 1990 when the Spitfire he was flying crashed in a field and burst into flames after its engine failed, resulting in his aircraft collection being put up for auction. P-51D G-SUSY was acquired by Paul Morgan, who retained its identity as Susy but had it re-registered as G-CDHI. Morgan himself was to lose his life in a Hawker Sea Fury, resulting in his P-51D being purchased in 2002 by The Real Aeroplane Company in Yorkshire, under which it operated until 2007 when it was sold to Meier Motors in Germany. Now registered as D-FPSI, this Mustang is today owned by Christoph Nothinger of Switzerland and flies as Lucky Lady VII.

North American P-51D Mustang: N51JJ, owned by The Fighter Collection at Duxford Aerodrome. Appears as 44-63221/AJ-S, named as Candyman/Moose; the FY serial and identity are the same as this P-51D adopted at the time in TFC ownership, although neither are correct for this actual Mustang. This P-51D was originally 44-73149 and is believed by some historians to have been operated by the 357th FG of the Eighth Air Force in 1945. Two years later it was part of the first batch of Mustangs delivered to the Royal Canadian Air Force, taken on charge as RCAF 9568. It was sold in 1957 and came onto the US register as N6340T. This Mustang became recognisable as an Unlimited Air Racer at Reno, painted all-red with the race number '7'. In 1980, it was overhauled in Oakland, California, then ferried by John Crocker to Geneva, Switzerland, for its new owner, English businessman Stephen Grey. This P-51D now carried the serial 44-63221 and the code G4-S of the 357th FG, named Candyman/Moose, under which identity it made its British airshow debut at the 1981 Biggin Hill Air Fair. Two years later it became a founder member of Stephen Grey's The Fighter Collection, which he set up at Duxford in 1983 and which still operates from there today. In 1986, this P-51D was re-registered as N51JJ. Two years after "Memphis Belle" finished filming, P-51D N51JJ changed hands at Duxford from TFC to the OFMC and was re-registered again in 1991, this time as G-BTCD on the British civil register. Today, it flies with the OFMC as 44-13704/B7-H, named as Ferocious Frankie of the 361st FG. P-51D G-BTCD has

the distinction of being the longest serving, longest flying Mustang on the British and European airshow circuit.

North American P-51D Mustang: N167F, owned by the Scandinavian Historic Flight (SHF) and flown in the film by SHF founder and owner, Anders Saether. Appears as 44-73877/AJ-N, named as Cisco, although it also carried another FY serial of 44-14450 in the film as well. This P-51D began life in 1951 with the Royal Canadian Air Force as RCAF 9279, with which it operated until struck off charge in April 1958. It was then registered in the US as N6320T to Intercontinental Airways in New York State before coming under the ownership of Aero Enterprises, Indiana, in 1960. However, that same year it was acquired by Neil McClain of Strathmore, Alberta, and returned to Canada as CF-PCZ. Eight years later this P-51D returned to the USA under the ownership of Paul D Finefrock in Oklahoma and received its current registration of N167F. On 1st September 1969, N167F collided with P-51D N2870D while taxying for an air race in Texas. After rebuild, this Mustang went through two more owners during the next 14 years before it was purchased by Anders Saether in 1984 and ferried to Norway two years later. Since this time P-51D N167F has been operated by the Scandinavian Historic Flight, firstly as 44-73877/E2-D/Detroit Miss before adopting its current identity as 44-14450/B6-S/Old Crow. These are the markings of Bud Anderson's P-51D when he flew the original Old Crow with the 363rd FS of the 357th FG. Bud Anderson has flown N167F in the UK; it has been seen at many airshows throughout Europe. This P-51D was also flown in the George Lucas "Red Tails" movie, filmed in the Czech Republic.

North American P-51D Mustang: N314BG, owned by the late Doug Arnold's Warbirds of Great Britain collection, then based at Biggin Hill Airport. Reportedly Doug Arnold would not agree to N314BG being repainted in olive drab for its film role, so it was flown in distance shots only to add numbers to both P-51D and Bf.109J formations. P-51D N314BG is another former RCAF Mustang, being taken on charge as RCAF 9567 in June 1947 and remaining in service until September 1960. Like P-51D N167F it was acquired by Intercontinental Airways of New York State, registered as N6337T, and was then sold to Aero Enterprises in Indiana but remained stored in Canada until April 1964. It came onto the US register as N169MD and was flown as an air racer with race number '71' until 1978. It then underwent a registration and ownership change as N51N, being held by Aerodyne Sales of El Reno, Oklahoma, before being acquired by the Canadian Warplane Heritage, Ontario. It was placed on the Canadian civil register as C-FBAU and painted in its original colours as RCAF 9567/BA-U. However, on 7th July 1984 it crashed while making a forced landing at Massey, Ontario, and suffered serious fire damage. Its remains and identity were then transferred to a restoration project for another P-51D Mustang and went through several owners before finally being re-registered in the USA as N314BG. It was rebuilt by Pioneer Aero Service at Chino, California, flying again on 25th July 1988. By this time it had been acquired by Doug Arnold and delivered to Biggin Hill in 1988, flying as 44-14151/HO-M/Petie 2nd. It remained with the Warbirds of Great Britain when the collection transferred to Bournemouth/Hurn Airport, then, after Doug Arnold's death, passed to his son David Arnold's Flying A Services at North Weald in 1995, where it was stored until it was acquired by Ice Strike Corp of Rockford, Illinois, that same year. P-51D N314BG returned to the USA in 2001, was brought back into flying condition by Pioneer Aviation at Chino, and today is owned and flown by Les Heikkila from Creve Couer, Missouri.

North American P-51D Mustang: N1051S, owned and flown in the film by Spencer Flack. As with Doug Arnold's N314BG, Spencer Flack would not agree to his P-51D N1051S being repainted in olive drab 'wardrobe', so it too was flown only in distance formation shots. This Mustang was delivered as 45-11371 to the California Air National Guard (ANG) in 1945 and went on to serve with the Air Defense Command at Yuma, Arizona, the New Hampshire ANG and the Illinois ANG before being sold to the Nicaraguan Air Force, along with the former G-SUSY, in May 1958 and was operated as GN121. It was purchased by MACO Sales Financial Corp of Chicago in July 1963 and registered as N12067. It then underwent a number of changes of ownership and registration between 1963 - 1987, during which time it was twice registered as N1051S and was finally in the possession of the Breckenridge Air Museum in Texas when Spencer Flack's Myrick Aviation acquired it. P-51D N1051S was delivered to the UK on 22nd June 1987 and was based at Southend Airport, Essex, flown as 45-11371/VF-S/Sunny VIII. This Mustang did not stay long in the UK, returning to the USA in 1992 with Spencer Flack's American company, Flakair Inc, where it was re-registered as N51KF. It spent several years with the US Army Air Corps Museum at Dover, Delaware. Mustang N51KF was destroyed in an airshow accident at Malone Airport, New York, on 2nd July 1995, with its pilot, George Krieger, fatally injured. The NTSB Accident Report found that Krieger had not acquired sufficient time and experience on the P-51D Mustang to competently display it at an airshow.

Hispano HA.1112M1L Buchon: G-BOML, owned by the Old Flying Machine Company. This Ha.1112 Buchon was operated by the Spanish Air Force as C.4K-107 and was one of the seven non-flying Buchons used in 1968 at Tablada as Messerschmitt Bf.109 props by Spitfire Productions, Ltd, for the "Battle of Britain" (1969) film. The CAA Airworthiness Approval Notice for a Permit To Fly issued on 12th August 1988 states that it was sold to a number of buyers in the USA, with the US civil registration of N170BG, before it was purchased by the late Nick Grace and registered by him with the CAA as G-BOML on 15th April 1988. It was acquired without any airframe records and with the number of airframe hours unknown, but Nick Grace carried out a successful restoration to the CAA's satisfaction before selling this Buchon to the OFMC on 21st February 1989. It was operated by the OFMC on the British and European airshow circuit up to 5th September 1993, when it was damaged in a wheels-up landing at Duxford on returning from an airshow in Belgium. After being repaired it continued to be displayed by the OFMC. As aviation enthusiasts will be aware, it was in HA.1112 Buchon G-BOML that Mark Hanna was fatally injured in a landing accident during an airshow at Sabadell Airport in Spain on 25th September 1999. Its registration was cancelled by the CAA on 29th March 2000.

Hispano HA.1112M1L Buchon: G-HUNN, owned by Charles Church Displays at Micheldever. This aircraft was assembled in 1944 as a Messerschmitt Bf.109G-2 using German manufactured components and converted into an HA.1112 Buchon in 1958, after which it served with the Spanish Air Force as C.4K-172. Interestingly, the CAA Airworthiness Approval Notice for a Permit To Fly issued on 24th March 1988 states that the wing tips are those of the rounded type as fitted to the Bf.109E, rather than the pointed type normally fitted to Spanish Buchons, probably carried out by Spitfire Productions, Ltd. One of the batch of Buchons flown in the "Battle of Britain" film in Spain, England and France during 1968, this HA.1112 was subsequently sold in the USA. Restored by Sim Ron Aviation of Tulsa, Oklahoma, in 1977, it suffered a ground loop accident later that same year. Robs Lamplough acquired this Buchon in 1982 and registered it as G-BJZZ on 30th March, making it the first HA.1112 to fly in British airspace since the filming of "Battle of Britain" 14 years earlier. Not for long, though, as it suffered a second ground loop and propeller damage, occurring during its airshow debut at the Biggin Hill Air Fair on 15th May 1982. After a brief sojourn on the airshow circuit in 1983, Buchon G-BJZZ had its registration cancelled on 21st December 1983 after it had gone on display at Revue Bar impresario Paul Raymond's Whitehall Theater of War in London's West End. Charles Church acquired it in 1987 and had it re-registered as G-HUNN, bringing it back onto the airshow scene. Following Charles Church's death, G-HUNN returned to the USA in 1991 and has since been registered as N109GU with the Cavanaugh Flight Museum of Addison in Texas. It has been converted into Messerschmitt Bf.109E configuration, fitted with a Daimler Benz DB.601 engine, but there have been problems in getting it flying again because of the shorter length of the HA.1112's undercarriage oleos (as compared with those of the Bf.109E) restricting the propeller's ground clearance.

Hispano HA.1112M1L Buchon: D-FEHD, owned by Hans Ditte and operated by Daimler Benz Aerospace (DASA). Flown in the film as 'Black 15' by well known German warbird pilot, Walter Eichhorn, who displayed it at various airshows throughout the Eighties, most notably the 50th Anniversary Battle of Britain Airshow at A&AEE Boscombe Down in 1990. It is believed to have operated as C.4K-40 with the Spanish Air Force, but is more likely to be a composite airframe. There is no record of it being used in the "Battle of Britain" film. It has since been converted into Messerschmitt Bf.109G-10 configuration, with a Daimler Benz DB.605 engine, as well as using some parts from real Bf.109G-10 Werke Nr 151591. Today, it is operated by the EADS Messerschmitt Stiftung (Foundation), registered D-FDME and painted as 'Black 2' of I/NJG.11.

Douglas C-47A Skytrain: G-DAKS (42-100884) of Aces High, Ltd, at North Weald Aerodrome. This C-47A appears as a ground-based prop for scenes filmed at RAF Binbrook and does not fly in "Memphis Belle". It served with the Royal Air Force as Dakota III TS423 before being purchased by Mike Woodley in September 1979 and registered to his Aces High company in May 1980. Initially, G-DAKS was based at Fairoaks Airport in Surrey, Aces High's first operating base, during which time it made its acting debut in the popular TV series, "Airline", about a risk-taking private airline boss. Dakota G-DAKS has been a very hard-working C-47 and has proved itself a very useful earner, especially in TV commercials, for Mike Woodley. In 1995, it was placed on the US civil register as N147DC and is today displayed by Aces High in its original guise as C-47A Skytrain 42-100884. Its most recent screen appearance was as a USAAF Skytrain in the acclaimed Steven Spielberg/Tom Hanks co-produced TV series, "Band of Brothers".

North American VB-25N Mitchell: N1042B (44-30823/69), owned by Aces High and used as the principal camera aircraft for filming the air-air scenes, flown by veteran pilot, 'Dizzy' Addicott. Previously owned by David Tallichet, who had it converted into a camera-ship, it went 'tech' during filming and was relegated to being a prop at RAF Binbrook for scenes shown at the beginning of "Memphis Belle". Aces High operated this B-25 painted as 430823/69, named Dolly. It was sold in 1995 to World Jet Inc, at Kissimee, Florida, who converted it back into B-25N configuration by replacing its camera nose with a standard 'glasshouse' nose. Today, this B-25 is a regular performer on the US airshow circuit with Jim Terry, painted as Pacific Prowler.

The fighter pilots listed in the film credits who flew the Mustangs and Buchons are Ray Hanna as chief pilot, with Chris Bevan, Paul Chaplin, Rod Dean (wrongly credited in the film as Rob Dean), Walter Eichhorn, Stephen Grey, Reg Hallam, Mark Hanna, Pete Jarvis, Pete John, Rolf Meum, Hoof Proudfoot, Anders Saether, Carl Schofield and Brian Smith.

One effective scene in the film utilises archive and gun-camera footage of B-17s taking hits played out not to cannon fire or dramatic music, but to voice-over readings from letters written by parents of aircrew in response to being informed that their son has been lost in action. It is one of the most genuinely moving moments in the film. Some of these archive shots have been used in other war films and documentaries, others may not have been seen before. They are as follows:

A B-17 taking hits in its starboard outer wing;

A B-17 spinning down out of control (believed to be from the original documentary, "Memphis Belle");

Gun-camera footage taken from a German fighter making a pass at a B-17 from its starboard rear quarter, with pieces flying from the Flying Fortress;

More gun-camera footage, taken from a fighter which is closing fast from the rear on four B-17s, the nearest of which bursts into flame when both its port engines explode - possibly the attacking fighter was a Messerschmitt Me.262, judging by the speed at which it was flying;

Another gun-camera shot, which first shows two B-17s higher up streaming contrails, but the view point changes as the fighter from which the film is taken swings to starboard to line up behind five more B-17s at the same height and attacks the rearmost of the group, scoring hits on the starboard inner engine and the fuselage - again, the speed with which the attacker closes on the target suggests it may have been a Me.262 jet fighter;

A shot, probably filmed from a B-17 directly below, of a single B-17 in silhouette above streaming fire and smoke from its damaged port inner engine;

The next shot is quite telling, as it is clearly a 324th Bomb Squadron B-17F that is in trouble, its 'DF-' code and 91st Bomb Group white triangle bearing the Group code letter 'A' clearly visible; however, its individual code letter is obscured by the starboard wing. This B-17F banks to port away from the camera, with what looks like fuel venting from underneath its forward fuselage;

Briefly, a couple of fighters are filmed hurtling past the B-17 that is filming them - they appear to be Focke Wulf FW.190s, but the speed at which they are passing, camera shake and poor image quality makes that difficult to confirm;

The next is a very dramatic gun-camera shot from a fighter attacking a quartet of B-17Fs from head on through black puffs of flak, clearly scoring hits on one of them;

The editor then cuts back to the 324th BS B-17F, now sliding away and starting to dive down;

An archive shot that was used in "The War Lover", of a B-17 spiralling down, with roads clearly seen below, is followed immediately by the gun-camera footage used in that same film of a B-17 receiving hits, which may have been filmed from a Me.262 because the cannon fire is very concentrated in the centre of the shot, suggesting the weapons were located in the nose of the fighter, as was the case with the Me.262 jet;

This cuts to the first B-17 that is shown in this sequence, likewise taking hits;

Then a B-17 seen from directly in its Six-o'-Clock, taking a real pounding from a fighter that has closed right up behind the bomber and just continues to pour fire into its port engines and rear fuselage. This is the final archive shot of this moving sequence.

The aerial battles involving the three Hispano HA.1112M1L Buchons, often referred to as Messerschmitt Bf.109Js, against the B-17s and the P-51D Mustangs is very well choreographed and realistically filmed from inside at least one Flying Fortress. The late Mark Hanna was on record as saying that these flying sequences were among the most arduous he had ever flown. The team put together by Ray Hanna to fly them were already well experienced in aerial filming, not least the three Bf.109J pilots - Walter Eichhorn, Charles Church and Mark Hanna - who had flown the same three Buchons the previous year for the British TV series about the Battle of Britain, "A Piece of Cake". To help swell the numbers of Luftwaffe "One Nineties", as the Memphis Belle's waist gunners call them, up to four of the Mustangs filled in the back row behind the three Bf.109Js in the foreground - all filmed from a distance - as they run in towards the B-17s. From certain shot angles, it is obvious that the Buchons were choreographed to fly past and close to the bombers. They and the Mustangs had electrically-operated firing mechanisms attached to gas guns in the wings, which very realistically spit fire.

It is a moot point to now realise, but four of the pilots in "Memphis Belle" - Ray and Mark Hanna, Hoof Proudfoot and B-25 pilot, 'Dizzy' Addicott - are no longer with us.

The actual bomb run over Bremen - the target is a Focke Wulf FW.190 works - has attracted criticism from veterans who dispute the way the crew of the Memphis Belle are portrayed as behaving - shouting, yelling, one of them trying to press the bombardier's bomb release button to drop the bombs and thus override the Captain's order to make a second run through heavy flak. In particular, Matthew Modine's line as the Belle's Captain, that "There are innocent people down there" - the works is next to a hospital and a school - would have drawn considerable derision from real Eighth Air Force aircrew, and is obviously been put in the script to make a 1990 audience believe that B-17 aircrew tried to avoid civilian casualties in World War Two. And the prospect of the tail gunner allowing the co-pilot to take over his guns, just so he can tell the folks back home he shot at enemy fighters, is just pure baloney. Despite this, the bomb run sequence is effectively created through its use of SFX.

Mention must be made of the extremely realistic 1:6 scale model B-17s that are used in the film, created by the specialist Model Effects group from Watford. This company created the impressively realistic B-29 Superfortress model for Spielberg's "Empire of the Sun" (not many people realised it was a model, they thought it was the Confederate Air Force's B-29, Fifi) and would go on to contribute many equally effective aviation and marine model miniatures for the Pierce Brosnan series of James Bond films.

Five model B-17s were used in "Memphis Belle", two of which were radio-controlled (R/C) flyers. One is seen performing the one-wheel crash landing at the beginning of the film, running directly into the camera! The effect is dramatically real, though. The other R/C B-17 was used for the single-engine landing by Memphis Belle in the film's finale, when fake feathered props on three engines were attached behind the actual turning ones - because the flight sequence of the models was reproduced in slow motion, the blade motion of the 'live' engines do not show.

Also, the art department created a number of full-size facsimiles of B-17s, known as studio B-17s, as well as some two-dimensional hardboard frames of B-17s which were set up to fill the background. It is one of the studio B-17s which was blown up after the crash landing at the beginning of the film: fire pots of petroleum were placed in the wreckage and lit.

Rumour has it that it was the remains of B-17G F-BEEA which were set alight for this scene. However, from a legal standpoint, this seems unlikely. The wreckage of F-BEEA would have had to be left where it was until the Air Accidents Investigation Branch completed its examination. The remains were still the property of the IGN, and insurance requirements would almost certainly have forbidden any further interference with F-BEEA's remains.

Speculation has also suggested a static B-17 was used for the interior shots of the Memphis Belle. However, all of these shots were filmed at Pinewood Studios, using a very realistically-created B-17 shell based on the actual interior of B-17G N3703G and which included actual equipment and components borrowed from the Imperial War Museum's Mary Alice. The Imperial War Museum confirms that its B-17G Flying Fortress, the former F-BDRS of the IGN - normally displayed in the American Air Museum at Duxford as 42-31983 Mary Alice of the 615th BS, 401st BG, but now undergoing a completely

new restoration - was the pattern aircraft for the F/S facsimile studio B-17s and the R/C model miniatures, so technically it can be claimed that six B-17s appear in "Memphis Belle".

The film has attracted a lot of criticism in terms of detail and accuracy, which must be a frustration for David Puttnam, as he reputedly went to great lengths to make "Memphis Belle" be as accurate as possible. But the following are all too obvious:

Note in the scene when the aircrew are being driven out to their bombers, then are forced to wait while weather over the target clears, the contrast between the wet, muddy peri-track and grass compared with the hot, dry August cornfields in background shots soon afterwards - an unavoidable continuity clash, perhaps, due to the vagaries of the English summer;

The take-off shots of Memphis Belle filmed airborne along Binbrook's secondary runway crosses Binbrook's main runway, which is very modern tarmac'd;

Memphis Belle is coded DF-A, but in other shots she is DF-H and even DF-O, a problem perhaps caused by having three separate B-17s represent her;

Matthew Modine wears his Captain's cap throughout the mission, and so do the other officer aircrew - surely they would have worn flight helmets like the rest of the crew! Cosmetic reasons?

The bombardier lights a cigarette right underneath a B-17's wing close to the engines, with oil almost certainly leaking and lying in patches on the ground!

There is a silly scene when the tail gunner rides a farmer's plough, while arguing with the co-pilot about whether the latter should be allowed to fire the tail guns when under attack by fighters;

At 30 degrees below zero, Modine and his co-pilot are still only wearing their normal uniform, when they should have been in their fleece-lined flight jackets;

And, as previously mentioned, shouting and 'horsin' around by the waist gunners before and after attacks by enemy fighters is unrealistic of how aircrew would have really behaved, and which would have earned them a disciplinary hearing back at base;

And, of course, using P-51D Mustangs may have been exciting and effective, but they were a year too early for 1943.

Interestingly, in the real "Memphis Belle" documentary, the B-17Fs of the 324th BS were unescorted. Would excluding escorts and their consequent dog-fights have reduced the visual impact of the film? Possibly. This is a film, after all, and accuracy can so easily get in the way of dramatic effect.

So, "Memphis Belle" is a flawed production despite the considerable amount of time, money and dedication that went into making it. Nonetheless, it definitely has its adherents among the aviation community, especially those who appreciate seeing B-17s and P-51Ds collectively in colour.

Now we are down to just three British World War Two war films in the Nineties, but three very original productions, it has to be noted. War films were being made in Hollywood, but they almost exclusively focussed on American heroism in Iraq against Saddam Hussein's forces, thanks to Operation Desert Storm in early 1991. War films were no longer the exclusive preserve of World War Two.

CHAPTER 7

1991-2000

In the final decade of the 20th Century, the world was looking ahead and preparing for the New Millenium. The past was definitely the past.

THE ENGLISH PATIENT

(Released: November 1996)

For our purpose, the only reason for watching "The English Patient" is to see two bi-planes flying against the Tunisian desert and ravines, echoing - and probably inspired by - the converted Tiger Moths flown over the Jordanian desert in "Lawrence of Arabia". One is a de Havilland DH.82A Tiger Moth, carrying the serial 'G-AFFC' (in reality, a de Havilland Rapide) but actually G-AJHU. This aircraft was owned in Italy when it was used in the film, but was retained on the British civil register. It was flown by Clive Watson.

The other is a Boeing A75 Stearman, the former N88ZK that was owned and flown in the film by Italian pilot and collector Franco Actis. It carries the registration 'G-AFEA' that had actually belonged to a Percival Vega Gull. The Stearman that crashes is a SFX miniature.

THE BRYLCREEM BOYS

(Released: April 1998)

A very original take on the PoW theme, but one that is based quite accurately on fact. The neutral Republic of Ireland interned any belligerent military personnel from both the Allies and Axis nations who were captured on Irish soil for the duration of the War - in the same prison camp.

An RAF bomber crew - the 'Brylcreem Boys', as RAF aircrew were nicknamed throughout World War Two, for their fashion of using Brylcreem hair oil to maintain their hairstyle - are shot down over Ireland and are interned. So, too, is the Luftwaffe night fighter pilot who they shot down as he was in the act of shooting them down. This is the opening scene of the film, all of which is acted within the bomber's cabin. Only a brief and not very effective SFX image of a Vickers Wellington going down behind the pilot and another crew member, hanging - again, not very convincingly - from their parachute harnesses, is shown.

Perhaps the one main flaw in the film's plot is that the bomber crew and the night fighter pilot all believe they are over France when they engage each other. Is it really plausible that not only could they each be so wildly off course, but likewise so seriously in error in their judgement of their respective positions? Aircrew on both sides made serious navigational errors on numerous occasions, but the plot is asking the audience too much to believe that the British bomber crew and the German fighter pilot had somehow flown across the Channel and right over England into the airspace of Ireland without knowing it. It would have been more plausible if the scriptwriter had made the bomber a Coastal Command aircraft lost after a patrol over the Atlantic and the pursuing night fighter a Junkers Ju.88 operating out of an airfield in Brittany.

The only actual image of an aircraft in the film comes right at the very end, using an out-take of Vickers Wellington Mk.Ic P2517/OJ-F, 'F for Freddie', of No.149 Squadron, from "Target for Tonight" (1941) peeling off in an air-air above clouds.

"The Brylcreem Boys" is a well-acted, well-directed, British war film unique in concept that convincingly creates the feel and atmosphere of Ireland during the latter months of 1941, the period in which the story is set. It was actually made on the Isle of Man, but you wouldn't have known it. Well worth having in your film library, whether you are an aviation enthusiast, war film historian, or not.

THE LAND GIRLS

(Released: September 1998)

This British - French co-production is the feature film version of the BBC TV series of the same title. Quite why French TV and film production company, CanalPlus, wanted to put money into it is a puzzle, as there is no French angle or content in the story at all.

"The Land Girls" are three young members of the Women's Land Army who took the place of young men from farms across the country called up for duty in World War Two. It is a beautifully crafted and well acted film, and looks convincingly like it was filmed in Dorset where the story takes place but in fact no location in that richly rural county was used at all - most of it was filmed in Somerset and Devon, utilising the West Somerset Steam Railway for period locomotive shots.

Aviation might not seem a likely participant in a story like this, but in fact two elements in the plot require the appearance of aircraft. Firstly, the small town close to the farm where the three 'Land Girls' are working has raised funds to buy a Spitfire. A special celebration involving the whole town is put on, which includes having 'their' Spitfire over-fly the rooftops. No prizes for guessing which Spitfire acts the role of 'their' Spitfire: who else but Vickers Supermarine Spitfire HF.Mk.IXb MH434 of the Old Flying Machine Company, making its sixth feature film appearance in an acting career now spanning 36 years.

This time it is Mark Hanna flying MH434, with the familiar ZD-B codes clearly visible. The time period for the story is meant to be late 1941, so the Spitfire Mk.IX was the wrong Marque for the sequence in which it is seen in the film; but it would be churlish to criticise MH434's appearance in "The Land Girls" as it certainly looks the part. If the production company had wanted to be exactly correct in their choice of a genuine 1941-era Spitfire in 1997, they would have had to request either the Spitfire Mk.IIa or the Spitfire Mk.Vb of the Battle of Britain Memorial Flight to act the role.

It is not clear at which countryside location Mark Hanna is flying MH434, but he is seen diving down into a valley and then pulling up over a hill head on towards where the camera is filming, very Alex Henshaw. Mark Hanna is also seen performing two climbing rolls in the Spitfire Mk.IXb, again a la Henshaw. This short sequence replicates almost exactly the identical sequence of Henshaw flying a Spitfire Mk.Ia in "Ferry Pilot" (1941), reviewed in Chapter One, in which he dives the Spitfire into a valley, pulls up in front of the camera, then is seen performing two climbing rolls in succession - Mark Hanna's performance can only have been an intentional copy of this sequence.

However, the second aircraft which appears in "The Land Girls" is one that aviation enthusiasts and historians would relish seeing flying again. The scene in which it appears requires Joe, the young farmhand, to run to the rescue of Stella, the 'Land Girl' he is in love with, who is in danger of being struck by a crashing German fighter. The enemy aircraft is a Messerschmitt Bf.109. The example seen being shot down in the film is a completely genuine World War Two version, in fact the only genuine Bf.109 flying anywhere in the world when it was used for this role.

This is Messerschmitt Bf.109G-2/Trop G-USTV, or 'Black 6' as it was known when it was active on the British airshow scene in the Nineties. It is filmed here making a low, weaving run to simulate the pilot making a desperate attempt to keep it flying. Smoke streams from a small 'tray' attached to the under fuselage between the wing join. Flying it in the film is Paul Bonhomme (wrongly given as Paul Bonhom in the end film credits), today a pilot synonymous with his exploits as a Champion Red Bull Air Race winner. In 1997, Bf.109G-2 G-USTV was being operated by The Fighter Collection at Duxford, on loan from the Ministry of Defence. It had undergone an extensive and lengthy restoration to flying condition and was flown at airshows in the Nineties by Defence Evaluation and Research Agency (DERA, today Qinetiq) test pilot, Squadron Leader Dave Southwood, and Air Chief Marshall Sir John Allison. When it appears in "The Land Girls", it was probably flown by Bonhomme at some period during the winter of 1996 - 1997, judging by the leafless trees it is seen passing. By the end of 1997 it was in a somewhat sorry state, having suffered a crash landing at Duxford after completing its last planned flight.

Messerschmitt Bf.109G-2/Trop G-USTV joins the exclusive list of genuine World War Two Luftwaffe combat aircraft that have appeared in British war films. It began life as Werke Nr 10639 at Leipzig in September 1942, built initially as a Bf.109F-3 by Erla Maschinenwerk GmbH but converted into Bf.109G-2/Trop configuration during construction. Trop meant that it would be operated in hot climatic conditions. Given the factory code of PQ+QJ, this Bf.109G-2 was allocated to III/JG.77 and collected by that Staffel at Munchen-Reim airfield on 21st October 1942. It was flown that same day to Vicenza, North Italy, and then on to Jesi. The following day it was flown to Foggia and then to Bari, where the Staffel code number 'Black 6' replaced the factory code. By 28th October, 'Black 6' had arrived at Tobruk.

On 4th November 1942, 'Black 6' was operating from Bir el Abd landing ground. On this day it flew its only known operational sortie, having re-located to Quotifaiya from where it was flown against a group of South African Air Force Bostons being escorted by USAAF P-40s. The pilot of 'Black 6' was slightly injured in this combat but he managed to get the Bf.109G-2 back to Quotifaiya, from where it was immediately ferried to landing ground (LG 139) Gambut Main. This airfield was overrun by Allied troops on 11th November. 'Black 6' was discovered two days later by personnel of No.3 Squadron, Royal Australian Air Force, abandoned with some damage to its cockpit canopy, propeller, tail fin and tail wheel, probably from its engagement with the USAAF P-40s. Using parts of other wrecked aircraft, including that of Bf.109F Werke Nr 9678, a replacement tail fin, tail wheel and canopy were fitted. 'Black 6' then temporarily became CV-V, the personal code of Squadron Leader R H Gibbes, who flew it all the way to Heliopolis (Cairo) via various desert airfields, arriving on 2nd December 1942.

No.209 (Fighter) Group, RAF, had ordered that the Bf.109G-2 be flight tested, as it was one of the first 'Gustav' models to be captured by the Allies. No.451 Squadron, RAAF, prepared the aircraft before completing three flight tests in late December 1942. It was then handed over to the Lydda Communications Flight before more tests were flown, including one by a Rolls Royce pilot to investigate the Bf.109G-2's inverted flying capabilities. While in Egypt, 'Black 6' was flown against a Spitfire Mk.Vc. In 1943, 'Black 6' was packed and crated for shipping to the UK, where it was allocated the serial RN228 and further flight tested by No.1426 (Enemy Aircraft) Flight at RAF Collyweston. From February 1944 onwards it underwent comparison trials against a variety of British and American combat types, including the Tempest V, Mustang III, Spitfire XIV, Seafire III, Corsair, Hellcat and even three Mosquitoes. It then went on various demonstration tours to RAF and USAAF air bases throughout Britain until No.1426 (EA) Flight was disbanded on 21st January 1945. The Bf.109G-2 was then transferred to the Enemy Aircraft Flight of the Central Fighter Establishment at RAF Tangmere in March 1945, where it stayed until it was inspected by the Air Historical Branch in March 1946 for possible museum display.

From this time onwards, the Messerschmitt Bf.109G-2 was stored at various locations along with other captured Luftwaffe aircraft preserved from scrapping and was exhibited at certain displays. By September 1960, it had found a corner of a hangar at RAF Wattisham where Flight Lieutenant John Hawke - the same John 'Jeff' Hawke who has put in a number of appearances in this book - and a volunteer team made a serious attempt to restore the 'Gustav' back to flying condition by August 1962. However, the cost in terms of resources and man-hours meant that this ambitious project was later abandoned, while Hawke, of course, had left the RAF to concentrate on flying aircraft for film productions.

'Black 6' was sent to RAF Henlow in May 1967 for possible use in the "Battle of Britain" film, along with other former Axis aircraft, which wasn't proceeded with. In September 1972, it was air freighted in sections aboard two C-130 Hercules transports to RAF Lyneham where Flight Lieutenant Russ Snadden, who was to have more to do with this Messerschmitt Bf.109G-2's restoration than anyone, began what was to become a 19-year-long project before it flew again as 'Black 6' on 17th March 1991. It was painted in its correct Flieger Afrika tan brown and sky blue colour scheme, identical to that which it wore when found abandoned on the North African desert landing ground 49 years earlier. Now registered G-USTV, 'Black 6' made its first airshow appearance at Duxford, appropriately on 15th September 1991 - Battle of Britain Day - flown by Dave Southwood.

'Black 6' went on to enjoy a six-year period of airshow flying, although this was interrupted for little more than a year between August 1993 and September 1994 due to fuel leak problems. On its final flight on 12th October 1997 at Duxford's Autumn Airshow, 'Black 6' overshot the runway and landed in a ploughed field, where it turned over onto its back, fortunately not causing any injury to its pilot, ACM Sir John.

Today, 'Black 6' sits in the Milestones of Flight building, part of the RAF Museum at Hendon. Curiously, the RAFM's individual history for 'Black 6' makes no mention of its flight appearance in "The Land Girls". Freeze-frame analysis shows that temporary dark green camouflage has been applied to its fuselage and wings over its tan brown and sky blue scheme, while a 'Red 3' has been taped over its 'Black 6' number. However, the Balkenkreuzen on the fuselage and wings, the Swastika on the tail fin, the white band around the rear fuselage and the III/JG.77 badge on the nose all remain in place. It is a quite effective disguise. The art department also created a very accurate looking full-scale facsimile of the Bf.109G-2, painted exactly as 'Black 6' appears in the film, lying crashed in a field and which is blown up.

CHAPTER 8

2001-CURRENT

Into the 21st Century and British World War Two war films appear to have had a mini revival in the first decade. However, where aviation is concerned this is not entirely a good thing. The new century has, not surprisingly, brought with it new technology, especially in the film industry. This is the age of CGI: computer graphic imagery. As we shall discover, CGI does not necessarily make a good substitute for the real thing. For some Special FX dudes, the temptation to make aircraft perform in exaggerated fashion through the use of CGI is something they have proven unable to resist, to the detriment of the films in which CGI-created aviation appears. In others, 21st Century ideas of what attitudes and lifestyles were like during the War years jar uncomfortably.

Nonetheless, in this final Chapter there are still some interesting and impressive aircraft to discover, including one that can only be described as oddball.

TO END ALL WARS

(Released: 2001, USA) Hollywood 'British' war film

It was somewhat surprising that, when this film was released, the production companies involved believed that there was still a public appetite in the cinema for yet more sufferings by Allied (mostly British, and, in this case, troops from the Argyll and Sutherland Highlanders) Prisoners of War of the Japanese. Added to that, how many more treatments of the Burma-Siam 'Death Railway' can the film industry offer, over and above those that have already been shown on the screen in the past decades? Note, the opening preamble to the film makes the same mistake as other productions by referring to Japanese Occupied Siam as Thailand.

Aviation features in a minor capacity in "to END all WARS" (this is how the title is reproduced in the film's opening credits) but, as stated in the above introduction, we have now entered the CGI age, so it is no surprise that all bar one aircraft in the

film are digitally reproduced SFX images. Right at the beginning, as the Japanese take the Scottish troops prisoner, a CGI-created Mitsubishi A6M Zero over-flies the scene. It is reasonably realistic in its flight characteristics and in shape, and is seen only very briefly.

Nothing is seen again of aviation until close to the end of the film when USAAF bombers over-fly the Prisoner of War Camp in Siam and later attack it, mistaking it for a Japanese military base in the jungle. The bombers are a mix of between six and seven Consolidated B-24 Liberators. Their appearance confirm to the emaciated and brutalised prisoners that the Japanese are losing more and more territory, and that their ordeal is closer to being over.

What is puzzling is that the final credits list America by Air Stock Footage and the Producer's Library Service, both US organisations, as providing "bomber formation footage", presumably of the B-24s. However, the B-24s seen in the film are unquestionably CGI creations, not stock footage of real wartime Liberators. Again, they are, like the Zero, quite realistic in their imagery as they bomb the PoW camp, although as they fly overhead and away into the distance after dropping their bombs the SFX team have reproduced them as moving far too fast.

The one real aircraft which appears in the film is a Douglas C-47 acting the role of a British Far East Air Force Dakota. It is only seen from beneath - acting the role of dropping canisters by parachute containing leaflets informing the PoWs that Japan has surrendered - but RAF roundels under the wings are visible. However, the art department which applied the roundels has made the mistake of applying red-white-blue roundels, when South-East Asia Command blue-white circles should have been painted on instead. The only thing known about this actual C-47 is that it may have been Hawaii-based, as most of the filming took place on Hawaii in Year 2000; if not, it would have come from the mainland USA.

CHARLOTTE GRAY

(Released: February 2001)

The problem with this beautifully filmed wartime drama is just that, it is too beautiful to be a war film. It is also too slow and too long, although its portrayal of the treatment of the Jewish population in Vichy France is both very convincing and moving.

Apparently the character Charlotte Gray is meant to be a composite of female SOE agents Pearl Witherington, Nancy Wake, Odette Sansom and Violet Szabo. Compared with the earlier cinematic treatment of female agents reviewed in this book, Charlotte Gray is all too obviously fictitious and not very believable as a real person. The portrayal of SOE staff officers as either cynical or somewhat callous does not ring true either: the SOE 'Baker Street Firm' had an almost familial feel to it and was very loyal to its operatives, according to the various histories written about the Special Operations Executive.

Aviation only features in "Charlotte Gray" when the time comes for the character of the title (played by Cate Blanchett) to be parachuted into Vichy France (there is a supply drop scene later in the film, but the Dakota making the drop is a CGI SFX image). For this scene, Charlotte is presented with her documentation inside a Nissen-style hangar. Completely in shadow in the background - almost unnoticeable, in fact - is a Beech 18.

Charlotte Gray is then driven in a car to her waiting aircraft. The Australian director of the film, Gillian Anderson, says this was filmed at "a real Army base, outside of London. Apart from wheeling out a few 'planes, a lot of it is still as it was in the Forties". Hmm, that does not help us much, Ms Anderson. She does not give the name of the base and no reference work on the film "Charlotte Gray" lists any such as a location. It very clearly is an airfield, as the World War Two era hangar in the background and aerial shot of the runway attest. The likelihood is that it is North Weald, although the infrastructure that appears in shot is not recognisable.

The scene is obviously meant to be RAF Tempsford. Charlotte Gray is given her mission briefing in the car in which she is being driven to the aircraft from which she is to make her drop into France, totally against all commonsense reality! The car drives past a parked Douglas C-47 Dakota. Standing looking up at it are two men in modern clothing, one wearing jeans! How Ms Anderson allowed that goof to get into shot is hard to believe.

The car pulls up beside a C-47 Dakota, presumably the same C-47 seen in the previous shot filmed from a different angle. It has an RAF roundel on the port rear fuselage and carries the codes NF-A painted in red. Somebody has done their homework here, as the 'NF-' codes were borne by No.138 Squadron aircraft during World War Two. This, as we know from "Now It Can Be Told" (1946) in Chapter Two, was one of the two Special Duties squadrons that operated from RAF Tempsford; however, it never operated the Dakota. The serial of the Dakota is not visible on screen. Its paint scheme is olive drab, not correct for an RAF machine but correct for a USAAF C-47 Skytrain. It has passenger windows, so is a civilianised DC-3 painted to represent an RAF Dakota.

Gillian Anderson says, "This 'plane is one of the last Dakotas that can still fly", which, again, does not help very much. In 2000, when the film was in production, there were a number of Dakotas flying in the UK, the majority, of course, in the hands of Air Atlantique at Coventry.

The most likely candidate is Douglas DC-3 Dakota 3 N147DC, the former G-DAKS of Aces High, then based at North Weald but today operating from Dunsfold. N147DC carried a USAAF olive drab paint scheme and markings in 2000, but it would be an easy task for an experienced outfit in the film aviation business like Aces High to change it from an Eighth Air Force Skytrain into an RAF Dakota. Confirmation of this appears in a photograph of N147DC wearing the 'NF-A' codes on static display at the Royal International Air Tattoo 2002, identical to the Dakota in "Charlotte Gray".

Aces High also owned Beech C-45H Expeditor G-BKRG at the time, which must be a strong candidate for the shadowy Beech 18 seen in the hangar. Today, this C-45H is on display at the Aviodrome at Lelystad Airport in the Netherlands. It was originally imported into the UK in the Eighties by Aces High's Mike Woodley for use in the James Bond film, "Octopussy" (1983).

CAPTAIN CORELLI'S MANDOLIN

(Released: May 2001)

This over-long, overly drawn out wartime romance has no real aviation in it apart from two newsreel shots of Junkers Ju.87 Stukas, shown in the town square of Argostoli when the townspeople on the Greek island of Cephallonia watch on the public cinema screen the news of the German occupation of parts of Greece. One shot shows a five-ship echelon of Ju.87 Stukas, the other a close-up of four Ju.87B Stukas whose individual code letters of the two closest to the camera can be read, but not their Stukageschwader codes.

Those other aircraft seen in "Captain Corelli's Mandolin" are either created by CGI or are Special FX miniatures. The CGI-created Regia Aeronautica transport aircraft supposedly dropping Italian Paratroopers on Cephallonia bear no resemblance to any known type, they just seem to be what the film's SFX team thought Italian military transports might appear like.

It is the attack by Ju.87 Stukas which really catch the eye. The film's production team have done their research work and have realistically created a CGI formation of seven Ju.87D Stukas in correct Mediterranean Luftwaffe schemes of the September 1943 period. Their attacks on the Italian Aquina Division now defending Argostoli are achieved by a mix of CGI images and studio miniature Stukas. The latter are propelled by wires that have then been 'digitalised out' by the editing team after their images have been cut into the action depicted on screen. The SFX team faced the same problem as did their counterparts 33 years earlier in "Battle of Britain" (1969) in not being able to solve the problem of how to depict

Ju.87s making vertical dive attacks; like their predecessors they had to make their Stukas perform low-level attacks at relatively benign dive angles, which is not representative of how the dreaded Stuka achieved its 'kills'.

DARK BLUE WORLD (TMAVOMODRY SVET)

(Released: May 2001, Czech Republic) International 'British' war film

If there was an Academy Award for a war film that could be described as beautiful, then "Dark Blue World" would be a strong contender for such an Oscar. It is a beautifully staged, beautifully filmed motion picture, aided by the most accurate and effective use of CGI as compared with any other film reviewed in this book.

"Dark Blue World" is not simply about the experiences of Czechoslovakian fighter pilots who flew with the RAF in World War Two. It has a separate theme of how the friendship of two men can be challenged and invaded when they both fall in love with the same woman, while from a Czech perspective alone there is a sub-plot concerning the post-War persecution of Czechoslovakian pilots who flew for the West in the War by the Communist regime which took over Czechoslovakia in 1948.

The film is a joint Czech - German production and was, in 2001, the most expensive film ever made in the history of Czech cinema. It was filmed almost exclusively in the Czech Republic, although the author attests that for most of the time he was successfully convinced by its Academy Award-winning director, Jan Sverak (for "Kolya", 1997 Academy Award for Best Foreign Language film), that much of it was actually staged in England. The convincing factor was the English-style house - actually in the Czech Republic - and the correct period-style British cars of the Forties era in a very English-like rural setting.

For us, the stars of the film are the aircraft that appear in it, and there is no shortage of them. Judging by what the author found in Online Forums, there is equally no shortage of question and debate about the actual aircraft concerned. The number claimed for the Spitfires used in the production vary between two and four in total, with different serials and Marques being quoted, while the most scratch-your-head question concerns the unfamiliar-looking Czechoslovakian Air Force bi-plane trainers seen right at the beginning of the film.

The time period is 1939, just prior to the Nazi Occupation of Czechoslovakia. A small bi-plane buzzes at low-level a train station, watched by a young woman hanging out her washing - the pilot is her lover. The 'plane is then filmed landing at what is meant to be Olomouc Airfield, a Czechoslovakian Air Force training base. The small bi-plane in olive green colour scheme and Czechoslovakian AF military markings has proved to be one of the most difficult aircraft for the author to identify. It was not a type he could recognise. Website research confirmed that he was not alone: Forum contributors veered from suggesting it was

an R/C model to a full-scale mock-up. However, one contributor accurately pinned it down, so to him many thanks.

It is a genuine aircraft and is a modern-day version of a type that would have been correct for the period, although not flown by the Czechoslovakian Air Force: a Platzer Kiebitz UL designed by Michael Platzer of Germany based upon the Focke Wulf S.24 Kiebitz (Peewit), a light aeroplane design which first flew in 1927. The 18th April 1929 issue of Flight devotes a full page to the Focke Wulf Kiebitz and unreservedly congratulates British influence upon the German 'light 'plane' industry: "One of the latest German firms to produce a light 'plane after the British pattern is the Focke-Wulf Flugzeugbau, of Bremen. The new machine, known as the type S.24 "Kiebitz", bears unmistakable evidence of British influence in its whole general conception, although the detail work remains, naturally enough, typically German". The "British influence" was that the S.24 Kiebitz was the first German light 'plane to have sufficient flexibility and imagination in its design to allow it to have folding wings and the ability to be towed behind a car. The "typically German" element is that the Kiebitz was the heaviest of the then light 'plane class of aircraft.

The S.24 Kiebitz had no military application in its day, so its appearance in "Dark Blue World" as a Czechoslovakian Air Force trainer is inaccurate; it is, though, a design that would still have been in contemporary use as a sport 'plane within Central European nations in 1939. Michael Platzer flew his modernised version for the first time in 1984 and has since sold more than 300 Kiebitz UL home-built sports 'planes throughout Europe. The example flown in the film has not been identified but is believed to have come from Germany. It carries the fake Czechoslovakian AF serial of '12K' and is used to introduce the audience to the two central characters of the film, Franta Slama, the senior pilot played by Ondrej Vetchy, and the young Karel Vojtisek, portrayed by Krystof Hadek: Karel hero worships the older man but is destined to feel betrayed by him when Franta takes away the Englishwoman whom Karel has fallen in love with.

Also included in this introductory scene are four more bi-planes which have a more recognisable look. They appear to be Bucker Bu.131 Jungmann trainers, again painted olive green and bearing Czechoslovakian Air Force markings. Three out of the four can be seen to carry the codes '3K', '6K' and '8K'; the fourth is not visible. Technically, yes, they are Bucker Jungmann trainers, but actually they are all Aero C-104 derivatives. The Czech Aero company mass produced the Bucker Jungmann during the War under Nazi Occupation; following Liberation, the company decided there was still a market for the type in Central Europe and built approximately 250 more between 1947 - '49, marketed as the Aero C-104, without bothering with the need for a licence from the now defunct Bucker Flugzeugbau, of course.

Some Online sources claim these bi-planes are Tatra T.131 aircraft. This is very unlikely: the Czech car manufacturer, Tatra, acquired a licence from Bucker in 1938 to build the Bu.131, which it marketed as the Tatra T.131. Twelve in total were built and were offered to the Czechoslovakian Air Force, but the offer was turned down. A few of these original Tatra T.131 bi-planes exist in museums, but today it is the far more numerous examples of the Aero C-104 which can be seen flying throughout Central Europe and which appear in "Dark Blue World". As a design, they are correct for the 1939 period, but not as Czechoslovakian Air Force training aircraft of that time. The Aero C-104 did serve with the post-War Czechoslovakian AF. Again, unfortunately, the identities of the four Aero C-104s in the filmare obscure.

The main story in the film follows the experiences of Franta and Karel when they fly with RAF Fighter Command during the Battle of Britain and beyond. This is where the British war film element occurs, with a great deal of action taking place in the skies above England and France. All of it, however, was filmed in the Czech Republic, with the former Soviet Air Army base of Hradcany, north of Prague, doubling as an RAF Fighter Command air station where the Czechoslovakian pilots are flying from. The Russians operated a MiG-21 air regiment from Hradcany, plus having surface-to-surface missiles located there pointing the wrong way towards Western Europe. Marek Petru, technical and historic advisor to "Dark Blue World", was a former Czechoslovakian Air Force pilot based at Hradcany before the Russian invasion in 1968. In the official published record of the film, he describes what happened at Hradcany after the Russians departed.

"The Russians left in 1990, leaving behind them a big environmental disaster. The surrounding areas were land mined and the ground was very polluted by chemicals. Their left-over kerosene was dumped into the ground and the contaminated top soil has been taken away and stored in warehouses. As a result, no one is really permitted to live near the base, as there could be mines anywhere and the experts are still working every day, dismantling and exploding them. There are certain areas in the forests where the public are not allowed to walk. It will be some time before there is any commercial activity around the air base". The documentary on the making of the film included in the DVD shows the entire production team walking in a line across the deserted Hradcany airfield, picking up every stone they could find before any aircraft could fly from there.

And the aircraft, of course, were Spitfires. Online Forums claim between two and four Spitfires appearing in "Dark Blue World", the latter number largely quoted because four Spitfires were used during the same summer - 2000 - for "Pearl Harbor" (2001) that was being filmed at the same time, with the assumption made by some sources that the same Spitfires were used in both film productions. In fact, two out of these four Spitfires were to appear in both films.

For "Dark Blue World", three Spitfires were hired. They were Vickers Supermarine Spitfire LF.Vb EP120 (G-LFVB) from The Fighter Collection (TFC), Vickers Supermarine Spitfire HF.VIIIc MV154 (G-BKMI) belonging to Robs Lamplough, and Vickers Supermarine Spitfire HF.IXb MH434 (G-ASJV) of the Old Flying Machine Company (OFMC), all based at Duxford. All three had to be dressed in wardrobe, which meant they were made to appear grimy all over, with oil, exhaust and gunport stains. Flying them were Nigel Lamb, Robs Lamplough and Ray Hanna respectively.

In actuality, Spitfire Vb EP120 and Spitfire VIIIc MV154 were the flyers; Spitfire IXb MH434 remained ground-borne among a number of very accurate full-scale facsimile Spitfires created by

GB Replicas in the UK and freighted to Hradcany. Why MH434 did not fly in the film is not known; if it had done so it would have appeared more representative of early Marques than Spitfire VIIIc MV154, whose 'shark-finned' style of tail makes it stand out incongruously when filmed air-air alongside the correct rounded configuration of EP120's tail fin.

Ray Hanna's name is listed among the 'Period Plane Pilots' given in the film's final credits; however, Spitfire IXb MH434 is only seen as part of a line up of Spitfires on the grass at Hradcany waiting to 'Scramble', both it and Spitfire VIIIc MV154 spoiling the realism of the 1940-period scene with their 1942-era four-bladed propellers among the three-blades of Spitfire Vb EP120 and of the GB Replicas' Spitfires. The possibility is that either MH434 had a problem that kept it grounded, or that Ray Hanna himself became indisposed. OFMC had been contracted to supply the Spitfires and the pilots: OFMC were by now, in 2000, very experienced in the art of flying aircraft in film productions, with "Empire of the Sun" (1987) and "Tomorrow Never Dies" (1997) among their extensive credits. Logically, it would have been expected that Hanna and Lamb would have flown the sequences in "Dark Blue World" because of their collective experience of flying together within OFMC, especially in the "Breitling Fighters" display team of warbirds that was very active on the European airshow scene in 2000; but instead Robs Lamplough joined Lamb in the air in his own Spitfire. Lamplough comments in the official record of the film:

"I've not flown with Nigel Lamb before. We have to fly very close together and the overall effect is that it should look easy… Squeezing two planes in formation amongst trees and hills is a risky business. Wearing the costumes with the flying jacket, the May (sic) West life-jacket, helmet and goggles makes it authentic, but not so easy for us - the chaps flying in the War were in their early 20s and perhaps not the same physical proportions as us!".

Apparently, Spitfire HF.VIIIc MV154 was fitted with an underwing camera in order to achieve some aerial shots. Lamplough says, "You have to carry various aero-dynamic loads to compensate for the weight and disturbance caused by the camera on the wing. It's tricky to keep the other plane in shot so the preparation on the ground first is essential. It's a technical exercise flying the plane in a particular position at relative angles. Both Nigel Lamb and I have had experience of this before. The camera angles are very tight to give the best dramatic effect and there's no space either side of the plane so you have to hit your target".

Spitfires Vb EP120 and IXb MH434 have had their histories and careers assessed elsewhere in this book. Spitfire VIIIc MV154 is new to the war film world. Built at Southampton in 1944, MV154 was part of a batch that was delivered by sea to Sydney, Australia, arriving on 24th November. Allocated RAAF serial A58-671, this Spitfire was placed in storage at No.2 Aircraft Depot, Richmond, on 28th November and there it remained until it was struck off charge on 24th May 1948. It was then delivered in its original crate to the School of Aircraft Construction at Sydney on 1st December 1948, but nothing more happened with it until October 1961 when the test pilot for De Havilland Aircraft Pty acquired it for restoration as a memorial to Australian Battle of Britain pilots. It was moved to Bankstown Airport for reassembly but this fell through as well. The Spitfire was bought by Sid Marshall of Marshall Airways for his museum. At some stage it was reassembled but when Robs Lamplough found it, it was back in its crate again.

"It's one that was forgotten by the War", says Lamplough, on the "Dark Blue World" website, "it never caught up and never saw any action. I brought it back to England where we started to work on it and the whole renovation took 10 years. The major structures are all original, but the rivets needed replacing, all 133,000 of them. The engine was stripped down and a few minor adjustments were made, but its basically as it was when it came out of the factory".

Registered G-BKMI, Spitfire HF.VIIIc MV154 literally made its first flight on 28th May 1994, from Filton, 50 years after it was built. Like Spitfire Vc EP120, it took part in the "Pearl Harbor" movie, filmed after its appearance in "Dark Blue World". It has been seen regularly at airshows staged at Duxford, carrying the serial MT928 and coded 'ZX-M' of No.145 Squadron. In February 2010 Robs Lamplough sold MV154 to Max Alpha Aviation in Bremgarten, Germany, where it is operated today still in the same markings.

One possible reason why some enthusiasts believe the same four Spitfires that flew in "Pearl Harbor" did likewise in "Dark Blue World", may be due to a scene depicting a 'Scramble' with four Spitfires getting airborne. Unfortunately, anyone thinking that four Spitfires are actually 'Scrambling' is being spoofed by some very clever split-screen SFX. There are four Spitfires in shot, but they are EP120 and MV154 filmed twice taking off, then their images are spliced together in the editing suite, a method known as layers in progress in film terminology. "Dark Blue World" has some of the best split-screen SFX to be seen in any film, literally making it appear that there are twice as many Spitfires on screen as were actually present at Hradcany.

Mention must be made of the full-scale facsimile Spitfires created by GB Replicas. This Great Yarmouth-based company produced a number of Spitfire Mk.II and Mk.IX facsimiles for the film, of which two were capable of taxying, powered by small engines. It was in these replica Spitfires that the actors were filmed, not in the real Spitfires. In one shot, Ondrej Vetchy as Franta Slama is seen in the cockpit of his Spitfire, leading his section of four 'Spits' as they taxy across the airfield: in fact, the 'Spitfire' Vetchy was in was one of the facsimiles with its wheels in a jig that was attached to a trailer, which, in its turn, was pulling the Spitfire along the peri track while its propeller turned, creating the impression of Vetchy actually taxying the aircraft himself. Some of the facsimiles have survived and can be found in an outdoor aircraft display in the Czech Republic, while one other has made its way to an artist's garden in Cornwall. At least one was destroyed in the filming process, during an airfield bombing scene.

Spitfire LF.Vb EP120 wore 'AI-A' and 'AI-H' codes in the film, as did Spitfire HF.VIIIc MV154. These were essential, as they had to bear the same codes as used by Spitfires in "Battle of Britain" (1969), to match with the many out-takes used from that film in "Dark Blue World". Spitfire AI-H was Franta's

aircraft, while AI-A was assigned to Karel - he gets shot down twice in it, which is quite a feat.

One other aircraft was used in the film. This was North American B-25J Mitchell N6123C of the Austrian Flying Bulls collection. It was used primarily as the camera-ship, but does make a short appearance as a shot-up USAAF bomber making an emergency landing on one engine. The B-25 pilot was actually John Romain of the Aircraft Restoration Company, also based at Duxford. His long-term experience of flying with both Nigel Lamb and Robs Lamplough was crucial, which explains why Romain took the controls of B-25J N6123C: "The low-level flying between the hills is very risky, but the display flying gives us all the training we need and I've flown with Nigel Lamb and Robert Lamplough a lot before, so the trust is already there. The more important thing is to know the other pilots you're flying with". The original plan had been to use the B-25 Mitchell owned by The Dukes of Brabant, but that World War Two bomber went 'tech' just before filming was due to take place between 17th - 27th April 2000, so Flying Bulls stepped in with their B-25 instead. It was rewarded with an appearance in the film, although its all-silver colour scheme is completely unrealistic.

There are, of course, an extraordinary number of out-takes from "Battle of Britain" used in "Dark Blue World", all to excellent effect. It is a complete compliment to "Battle of Britain" that, 32 years after its release to theater, it was able to provide a 21st Century film production with such everlastingly clear imagery. In fact, "Battle of Britain" did it twice in 2001, as more of its imagery was used that same year in "Pearl Harbor". Out-takes from the "Battle of Britain" epic have appeared in a series of documentaries on the Battle itself shown on the History Channel, while selected sequences have appeared in the London Weekend Television mini-series, "A Piece of Cake" (1988), and were also used in the "Into The Storm" (2009) TV film, among others. We have found out-takes from "Battle of Britain" in other film productions, such as "Dad's Army" (1971) and "Hope and Glory" (1987).

Likewise, two out-takes from "Memphis Belle" (1990) also appear. What is significant about the out-takes from "Battle of Britain" in "Dark Blue World" is that all bar six of the total of 57 sequences inserted into the latter film to depict dog-fights over England were not used in the original production - director Jan Sverak and editor Alois Fisarek have very carefully selected the pieces they wanted to use, and have done so in a most imaginative way. What is more, the DVD released in 2004 contains a fascinating insight into how Sverak and Fisarek manipulated the images from "Battle of Britain", using CGI technology to both enhance them and to match them with the imagery of the Spitfires they had filmed in the Czech Republic. What this all means is, of course, that there are a great many more aircraft in "Dark Blue World" than the three Spitfires, four Aero C-104s, the solo Kiebitz and the single B-25 Mitchell filmed at Hradcany. Detailed below are how the out-takes from "Battle of Britain", plus "Memphis Belle", are used in "Dark Blue World", along with the aircraft shown in them (those which were used in the original films as well are referred to in brackets).

Out-take 1 - Spitfire four-ship, representing Spearhead Blue Section led by Franta Slama. This is an in-transit formation filmed by 'Skeets' Kelly from the 'Psychedelic Monster'; 'Skeets' Kelly reportedly filmed everything he could from the B-25, whether the subject aircraft were flying according to their pre-briefed sequence or not. Sverak and Fisarek must have studied reams of used and unused footage filmed for "Battle of Britain", and selected this formation shot to show Franta Slama leading his Spearhead Blue Section on their first sortie after being declared operational. Of this quartet, the leader carries the codes AI-H, the left wingman bears AI-A while his opposite number on the right is AI-J. The fourth Spitfire in the slot is too far behind and too distant for its codes to be read. The lead Spitfire and the slot are clearly Mk.IXs as their double radiators show, while the two wingmen are flying earlier Marques of Spitfire.

They are believed to be Spitfire Mk.IXc MK297 (G-ASSD) leading as AI-H, Spitfire Mk.IIa P7350 (G-AWIJ) on the left wing as AI-A and Spitfire LF.Vb AB910 (G-AISU) on the opposite side as AI-J, as these three were known to carry these codes in "Battle of Britain" at certain times. The fourth Spitfire in the slot is either HF.IXb MH415 (G-AVDJ) or MH434 (G-ASJV).

Out-take 2 - four Spitfires diving in loose 'Trail'; it is not obvious if they are the same four seen in the previous shot.

Out-take 3 - CASA 2.111D two-ship and one Spitfire. An unused out-take of a Spitfire attacking two Heinkel He.111H bombers. The two 'Heinkels' are undoubtedly CASA 2.111D B.2I-77 (G-AWHA) and CASA 2.111D B.2I-37 (G-AWHB), which were purchased by Spitfire Productions, Ltd, and flown to England in May 1968 for filming along with the assembled fleet of Hurricanes, Spitfires and Buchons at Duxford. The Spitfire in this shot could be any one of the nine Merlin-engined examples flown in "Battle of Britain" (it is not a Griffon-engined Spitfire), but is not identifiable.

Out-take 4 - Seven Hispano Ha.1112M1L Buchons, acting as Messerschmitt Bf.109Es, breaking from echelon starboard to attack.

Out-take 5 (used in "Battle of Britain") - A massed dog-fight, with a large number of fighters wheeling about the sky in the distance. Freeze-frame analysis reveals that they are all Hispano HA.1112M1L Buchons, amounting to 17 in all. As the airborne camera films them, a Spitfire trailing smoke flies across the screen from right to left in front of the simulated dogfight, with another, and 18th, HA.1112M1L Buchon pursuing it from directly behind. Almost certainly this sequence was filmed in Spain, with the many Buchons in the background portraying both Spitfires and Bf.109s - the audience would not have had time to detect the deception. This means that the Spitfire on fire flying past the camera is Spitfire HF.IXb MH415 (G-AVDJ), the one Spitfire that was flown out to Tablada in Spain for filming there. In "Dark Blue World", it is being used to portray the Spitfire flown by Czech pilot Tom-Tom being shot down.

Out-take 6 - Solo Spitfire trailing smoke, again portraying Tom-Tom's stricken aircraft. The actual Spitfire used is not identifiable.

Out-take 7 - Solo Spitfire trailing smoke from its exhaust,

filmed from the two-seat Hispano HA.1112M4K Buchon C.4K-112 (G-AWHC) that was used as a camera-ship in "Battle of Britain" to film aerial scenes from a Luftwaffe fighter pilot's perspective. The port wing of the Buchon is clearly in shot in the forefround, with the smoke-trailing Spitfire beyond it. It appears to be carrying the codes AI-E, which were borne by Spitfire Mk.IIa P7350 in "Battle of Britain".

Out-take 8 (used in "Battle of Britain") - solo Spitfire breaking left on fire. In "Battle of Britain", this shot was used to depict the Spitfire flown by Squadron Leader Harvey (played by Christopher Plummer) taking a hit. Which Spitfire it is cannot be identified, but it is one of the early Marque 'Spits'.

Out-take 9 - solo Spitfire rolling over onto its back and diving down towards the sea, with the White Cliffs beyond. A very similar shot is used in "Battle of Britain", when Sergeant Pilot 'Andy' (acted by Ian McShane) is shot down into the Channel. It appears that this out-take was not used for that scene, possibly because the preferred piece of footage was more clear and had the Bf.109 that got 'Andy' in shot as well.

Out-take 10 - Radio-controlled model Spitfire diving vertically into the sea.

Out-take 11 - Formation shot, with two Hawker Hurricanes leading and breaking away from a following element of six Spitfires, which in turn are being followed by no less than eight 'Hurrischmitts' - HA.1112M1L Buchons that were painted to represent Hurricanes flown in the distance. It is likely that "Battle of Britain" film director, Guy Hamilton, rejected this formation shot because it is too unrealistic - Hurricanes and Spitfires did not fly in formation together, while the aircraft in the background are visibly not representative of either type.

Out-takes 12, 13 & 14 - HA.1112M1L Buchon chasing Spitfire (Karel's aircraft), which is shot down. Sverak and Fisarek have added CGI tracer fire for effect.

Out-take 15 - Red propeller-bossed HA.1112M1L Buchon firing cannon, with CGI cannon shots added to the imagery.

Out-takes 16 & 17 - More shots of the Spitfire being pursued by the Buchon.

Out-take 18 - View of the stricken Spitfire seen from the Buchon's cockpit and viewed through the German pilot's gun-sight.

Out-take 19 - The victorious red-bossed Buchon breaking away.

Out-take 20 - Lovely shot of two Spitfires, coded AI-A and AI-H (Franta and Karel), flying together with the White Cliffs behind them. In fact, there were three Spitfires in the original footage; one has been CGI'd out by Sverak and Fisarek in the editing suite (the original shot with the three Spitfires is shown on the 'Special Features' section of the DVD). In "Battle of Britain", this shot was filmed for the sequence in which Spitfires on patrol break up to attack Stukas that are dive bombing Dover's radio direction finding antenna site. It was probably not used by Guy Hamilton for precisely the reason it is used by Sverak - it is a lovely shot, beautifully serene against stunning scenery, and really celebrates the beauty of the Spitfire; it would have been too beautiful to use as a lead-in to an aerial battle sequence, which is almost certainly why Hamilton rejected it. This shot was undoubtedly filmed from the Sud Aviation Alouette Astazou helicopter, G-AWAP, that was used for aerial shots from a static position in "Battle of Britain".

Out-take 21 - Beautiful air-air of what is meant to be the same two Spitfires in echelon starboard. The example nearest to the airborne camera (possibly filmed from two-seat Spitfire Tr.9 TE308) is an early Marque, carrying the codes AI-A' and is believed to be Spitfire Mk.IIA P7350; while the leading Spitfire beyond it is clearly a Mk.IX variant, coded AI-H, and is thought most likely to be Spitfire HF.IXb MH434 (G-ASJV). The codes of both Spitfires are CGI fakes: the 'Special Features' section of the Disk shows the same shot, but the Spitfires are coded CD-M and CD-F respectively, for "Battle of Britain". Sverak and Fisarek have deleted them in the editing suite and CGI'd in the 'AI-' codes in their place! The codes CD-M are reported to have been borne by Spitfire IIa P7350 in "Battle of Britain", while Spitfire IXb MH434 is likewise quoted as having carried CD-F.

Out-take 22 - Another air-air immediately follows, filmed from a static position, so the camera was almost certainly on board the Alouette Astazou helicopter hovering above clouds, with 'Johnny' Jordan filming. However, the Spitfire two-ship are now in echelon port. They carry the same codes, with AI-A leading AI-H. What is distinct is that they are not the same two Spitfires in the previous out-take: they are both Spitfire Mk.IXs, as their matched double radiators under their wings attest. They are probably carrying the codes they carried in "Battle of Britain", so this is probably not CGI-altered footage. All three Mk.IXs which flew in "Battle of Britain" carried the AI-A codes at some stage, but only Spitfire LF.IXc MK297 (G-ASSD) reportedly flew as AI-H. This being the case, it means that out-takes of Spitfire HF.IXb MH415, Spitfire HF.IXb MH434 and Spitfire LF.IXc MK297 from "Battle of Britain" all appear in "Dark Blue World".

Out-take 23 - Another air-air of Spitfire IIa P7350 and the probable Spitfire HF.IXb MH434 in formation, breaking to attack a lone Heinkel He.111H that Karel has spotted.

Out-takes 24, 25 & 26 - Lone CASA 2.111D as a Heinkel He.111H over very English urban and rural scenery, filmed from behind taking hits and trailing white smoke from the port engine. Tracer fire has been CGI'd in.

Out-take 27 - Single CASA 2.111D filmed from a distance, breaking left with smoking port engine. A fighter is climbing away above it, which is meant to be a Spitfire but freeze-frame analysis confirms that it is a Hawker Hurricane.

Out-take 28 - Another shot of the CASA 2.111D filmed from the rear, taking hits.

Out-take 29 - Reversed imagery of Harvey's Spitfire breaking off after being hit, used to represent Karel's Spitfire being shot down.

Out-take 30 - Filmed from inside one of the Duxford-based CASA 2.111Ds, showing the nose gunner firing at a Spitfire which is rolling and trailing smoke, again to portray Karel's Spitfire being hit.

Out-take 31 - Of CASA 2.111D trailing black smoke over the English countryside, as seen from Franta's perspective in his Spitfire as he closes in for the kill.

Out-take 32 (used in "Battle of Britain") - Air-air of the CASA 2.111D trailing white smoke from the port engine, with

Franta's Spitfire curving in behind. This same air-air footage was used in "Battle of Britain" when Pilot Officer 'Archie' (played by Edward Fox) shoots down the Heinkel He.111H which crashes into Victoria Station.

Out-take 33 - CASA 2.111D as the Heinkel He.111H being shot up from behind by Franta - all the smoke, tracer fire and flying debris have been CGI'd in very realistically by Sverak and Fisarek.

Out-take 34 - Spitfire breaking away from smoke-trailing CASA 2.111D.

Out-take 35 - Long distance air-air of crew bailing out by parachute from the stricken Heinkel He.111H. A close-up air-air was used in "Battle of Britain" of parachutists jumping out of one of the two CASA 2.111Ds owned by Spitfire Productions, but not the shot which Sverak and Fisarek have used here. The imagery of the Heinkel He.111H exploding in mid-air is a studio miniature filmed for "Battle of Britain", but was not used; however, it did appear in black-and-white as a newsreel shot in "Hope and Glory" - Sverak and Fisarek have added CGI-created debris flying off, including a propeller, for "Dark Blue World".

Out-take 36 - Very fine air-air of Spitfire Mk.IX flying over sun-dappled English countryside, bearing the codes AI-H, so presumably this is MK297. The fake serial 'N3317' can be clearly read on the rear fuselage, which was also borne by MK297, so this seems to confirm this Spitfire's identity.

Out-take 37 - A section of the same mixed bag formation used earlier, led by the two Hawker Hurricanes, this time filmed above strato-cumulus clouds but showing just a portion of the formation following behind, consisting of five Spitfires and four 'Hurrischmitt' Buchons in shot.

Out-take 38 - Fine air-air of eight Spitfires in formation, believed to be the largest number of 'Spits' filmed together for "Battle of Britain". One Spitfire breaks formation, to depict a Czech pilot who keeps losing his nerve in the air and fakes reasons for avoiding action. The Spitfire breaking away is a CGI SFX image created for "Dark Blue World".

Out-take 39 (used in "Battle of Britain") - One Spitfire IX curving in to line up on another Spitfire IX. This imagery was used in "Battle of Britain" to portray 'Skipper' (played by Robert Shaw) making a fake attack on the luckless rookie pilot, Simon (Nicholas Pendleton), shouting "Dacka, Dacka, Dacka!" into the radio. This imagery reveals that they are the same two Spitfire IXs used in the previous shots of Franta and Karel flying together in AI-A and AI-H.

Out-take 40 - Four-ship of HA.1112M1L Buchons depicting two 'Rottes' diving into attack.

Out-take 41 - Air-air of a single HA.1112M1L Buchon portraying a Messerschmitt Bf.109E coded 'White 13'.

Out-takes 42, 43 & 44 - Spitfire pursuing an HA.1112M1L Buchon trailing smoke.

Out-take 45 - Clever CGI insert of smoke-trailing B-25 Mitchell (also a CGI image) onto footage of an HA.1112M1L Buchon flying above clouds.

Out-takes 46 & 47 - More air-air footage of a Spitfire pursuing a Buchon.

Out-take 48 - Static air-air filmed from the helicopter of a smoke-trailing Buchon flying past below with what is meant to be - in "Dark Blue World" - a Spitfire in hot pursuit, but which is actually a Hawker Hurricane (pity this footage was not used in "Battle of Britain", to show that Hurricanes did have success against Messerschmitts). Part of an airfield can be seen below showing a modern peri-track, but beyond it can be seen the original peri-track and aircraft revetments. This looks very much like the south side of what was RAF Duxford.

Out-take 49 (used in "Battle of Britain") - Radio-controlled model of a Buchon blowing up.

Out-take 50 - Long distance air-air of a Spitfire flying back over the White Cliffs.

Out-take 51 - Dog-fight filmed above clouds, showing a Hawker Hurricane, seven Buchons and both Spitfire Productions'-owned CASA 2.111Ds.

Out-take 52 (used in "Battle of Britain") - Radio-controlled model Spitfire on fire.

Out-take 53 - Radio-controlled model Spitfire trailing smoke and curving into the sea.

Out-take 54 - Spitfire being pursued by a Buchon, which in its turn is being chased by another Spitfire.

Out-take 55 - Buchon going down, trailing white smoke, and followed by Spitfire.

Out-take 56 - Beautiful air-air of the eight-ship formation of Spitfires, filmed over a coastline with the sun shimmering on the sea behind and below them. However, this shot was not used in "Battle of Britain", probably because the coastline is decidedly un-English in appearance, being very flat and curved. It is almost certainly the French coastline near to Montpelier in the South of France, with the sea being that of the Mediterranean, not the English Channel close to Dover with its very distinctive cliffs. Some air-air filming was completed in the South of France because of the atrocious weather in England during the summer of '68.

Out-take 57 - Five-ship formation of Spitfires above clouds. Leading is a Spitfire Mk.IX, the two following behind it are both early Marque Spitfires, while the fourth beyond is Spitfire F.XIVc RM689. The fifth and final Spitfire in the distance is another early Marque version. Almost certainly these are the five Spitfires that were flown in the sequence in "Battle of Britain" following the airfield attack by the Luftwaffe; they were probably filmed from the 'Psychedelic Monster' in transit by 'Skeets' Kelly, either prior to or following on from acting out that scene.

As mentioned, "Battle of Britain" is not the only film from which out-takes are used in "Dark Blue World". To illustrate the Czech Spitfire squadron's role in escorting USAAF B-17 Flying Fortress bombers - the plot does not mention it, but clearly the time frame has moved forward to 1943 - two out-takes from "Memphis Belle" are shown. The first has two Boeing B-17F Flying Fortress aircraft flying in close formation, one above the other. This actual shot appears in "Memphis Belle": in that film, it depicts the B-17F Memphis Belle nearly colliding with another B-17 in cloud soon after take off. This sequence was flown with David Tallichet's Boeing B-17G Flying Fortress N3703G acting as Memphis Belle and Boeing B-17G Flying Fortress G-BEDF, known to all her fans

as Sally B of B-17 Preservation, but acting the role of another 324th Bombardment Squadron B-17F in the film "Memphis Belle".

The second out-take was not used in the original film. As it appears in "Dark Blue World", it has seven B-17s flying over the English coastline seen from directly above with Spitfires flying top cover as escort. In the "Special Features" section of the DVD, the actual out-take itself is shown, with all five B-17s that were flown in "Memphis Belle" filmed from directly above as they pass in formation over the coast on their outward passage towards the European mainland. What Sverak and Fisarek have done in the editing suite is to first 'lift' the planform imagery of one of the five B-17s and 'place' it twice in two different positions adjacent to the formation of five, thus increasing the size of the formation to seven B-17s; they have then added atmospheric effects to the imagery by having CGI-created contrails stream from behind each bomber (not created in the original shot); finally, Sverak and Fisarek used CGI imagery of Spitfires which they have 'overlaid' above the B-17s below, to create the effect of the American bombers being escorted by British fighters.

There are one or two goofs in "Dark Blue World" which could have been avoided. The Heinkel He.111H that Franta shoots down is called "one Junkers" by him, while aeroplane models suspended from the ceiling in the crewroom for the Czech pilots in England include a P-38 Lightning, a C-47 Dakota and a TBM-3 Avenger, none of which were in service during 1940 and, even if they were, would have been inappropriate American aircraft models - only British and German aeroplane models would have been hung from the ceiling, to aid recognition. Film set designers can make the mistake in assuming the audience would not know the difference, but this is always a high risk attitude to take with today's knowledgeable film fans.

The final shot of the Spitfire F.VIIIc and the Spitfire LF.Vb filmed air-air against a burning orange setting sun must be one of the most beautiful ways of ending what is a very fine war film, Czech made, German financed and with a very strong British content. "Dark Blue World" is, without question, one of the best aviation movies made anywhere in the world.

ENIGMA

(Released: September 2001)

Much criticised version of the novel "Enigma" by Robert Harris, centred upon the Bletchley Park codebreakers of the German Enigma intelligence system. The only aviation element in the film involves Special FX CGI-created RAF Coastal Command Consolidated PBY-5 Catalina flying boats attacking a U-Boat during the finale.

TWO MEN WENT TO WAR

(Released: November 2002)

A comedy drama about two real life Royal Army Dental Corps soldiers, one a drill Sergeant, the other a private, who literally carried out their own two-man invasion of Nazi Occupied France in 1942 - without any official sanction, although they did send a letter to Prime Minister Winston Churchill, informing him of their intentions.

It seems hardly credible that two 'passed-over' soldiers could successfully achieve what the Dieppe Raid of the same year catastrophically failed to do, but apparently both men, each now deceased, did land in France using a small fishing boat they stole in South-West England and spent several days trying to attack the Nazi war machine with Webley revolvers and a back pack containing some grenades. They eventually had to 'hop it smartish' when German troops started taking them seriously and spent eight days adrift in the Channel aboard a small French boat they had stolen. Their lives were saved when they were spotted by a RAF Coastal Command aircraft, but had to face a Courts Martial, resulting in the Sergeant being demoted to private and his comrade spending six months in Colchester Military Prison.

Apparently the most damage they inflicted upon the German occupying forces was the cutting of some telegraph wires and slightly bending one side of a railway line with a grenade. Both events are shown in the film, but the plot significantly embellishes their achievements by having them become involved, entirely by chance, in the Bruneval Raid by the 1st Airborne Division (the script incorrectly attributes the Raid to the Parachute Regiment, which had yet to be formed). The plot also coalesces into a matter of days other military events in 1942, such as Operation Chariot against the port of St Nazaire and the Channel Dash by the Schlacht Kreusers Scharnhorst and Gneisenau (the battlecruisers were the original targets of the intrepid duo, which they planned to attack in Brest Harbour by planting a grenade in the boiler of each warship!).

The film is entertaining, amusing and well acted, but does aviation feature in it at all? Yes, in fact it does, albeit very briefly. The Sergeant and the private originally think they have lost their way in sea mist and landed back in Cornwall because they can hear women speaking in English about various food recipes (it is actually a German radio operator listening in to the BBC and piping the women's voices through a loud speaker). The Sergeant's belief they have failed and are back in England is reinforced when a Low Flying Spitfire suddenly appears and passes over his head. The version shown is a Spitfire LF.IX, which was not yet operational in the early 1942 period that the plot is set in. It is seen only making one low, fast pass; whether it was filmed by a 2nd Unit, or whether it is footage obtained from a separate source, is not known.

The Spitfire in question is Vickers Supermarine Spitfire LF.IXc MK912, carrying the SH-L codes of the 1st (Belgian) Squadron and registered G-BRRA to Historic Flying Limited (HFL) at Duxford. "Two Men Went To War" was in production between September - November 2001, so it may be that MK912 was filmed during this period, probably over-flying Duxford.

Spitfire LF.IXc MK912 was built at Vickers' shadow factory in Birmingham and delivered to the RAF in late March 1944, going immediately into store with No.8 MU at Little Rissington, Gloucestershire. In May, it was issued to No.84 Group Support Unit at RAF Aston Down. It was in action in the days following

D-Day with No.312 (Czech) Squadron and had to make a forced landing on Liberated French soil when loose radio equipment threatened a loss of control. MK912's sojourn with the Czechs was brief, as it returned to No.84 GSU later in June 1944 before being sent to Exeter for an overhaul by Service Training, Ltd. It seems that any record of further operational use by this Spitfire has not been traced, but by April 1945 it was in store with No.33 MU at Lyneham, Wiltshire.

MK912 followed a familiar post-War path taken by other Spitfire Mk.IXs described in this book in being taken on charge by the Royal Netherlands Air Force and operated in the Dutch East Indies between 1947 - 1950. Similarly, it joined the Belgian Air Force along with other Mk.IXs in 1953, serving as an armaments trainer at Koksijde. In June 1953, MK912 had a Cat. 3 accident and was withdrawn from use, going into storage at Brustem and being struck off charge in August 1955. It avoided the COGEA target-tug fate of its colleagues by being assigned as a display aircraft at the Belgian Air Force Technical School, Saffraenberg, mounted on a plinth for more than 30 years. In 1997, MK912 was rescued by an aircraft collector from Jersey who sold it to HFL two years later. HFL undertook the full restoration of MK912 for Karel Bos, making its first flight in 47 years on 8th September 2000 from Audley End, Essex, registered as G-BRRA. It was painted in the 'MN-' markings of No.350 (Belgian) Squadron. For whatever reason, Karel Bos did not take up ownership of this Spitfire. Instead, it was offered for sale by HFL in October 2000; it did not find a buyer.

By now, MK912 was carrying the SH-L codes of a 1st (Belgian) Squadron Spitfire LF.IX, as it is seen in the film. In May 2003, Ed Russell of Niagra South, Ontario, Canada, purchased MK912 for a reported £1 million and had it shipped to Canada in September. It then spent the next eight years making selected airshow appearances in Canada, being flown variously alongside Ed Russell's Hurricane XII and Messerschmitt Bf.109E, as well as the Canadian Warplane Heritage's Avro Lancaster. However, by June 2011 MK912 had been re-registered as G-BRRA for its return to the UK. It was imported by Peter Monk, but within less than three months had passed to the ownership of Paul Andrews, with whom it remains today.

THE LAST DROP

(Released: May 2005, Cannes Film Festival)

This entertaining "Kelly's Heroes"-style mission to rescue, but in reality, steal, valuable art treasures in Holland which are being plundered by the SS is well made when the action is ground-borne, but not when it is airborne.

"The Last Drop" is a classic example of the over-indulgence in the film industry during the past two decades in the use of CGI to depict aircraft in flight. Director Colin Teague makes every mistake in the book in using CGI art work to make aircraft appear like cartoon creations and to perform manoeuvres that are either exaggerated or are shown from angles that could not be achieved in reality. Thus, the mass formations of C-47 Dakotas aero-towing troop-carrying gliders in the opening phase of Operation Market Garden are so obviously CGI cartoons that any sense of dramatic reality is totally lost. Similarly, the crashing Airspeed Horsa glider is made to fly at such crazy angles and speeds that only a PlayStation geek could be taken in by it. And as for the comical Focke Wulf FW.190, which performs like it is in a Walt Disney cartoon…the least said the better.

Director Teague does make use of genuine aircraft in "The Last Drop", the film's title referring to a fictional 1st Airborne Division battalion making the last drop of the airborne armada parachuted or glider-flown into Holland on 17th September 1944. He uses archive footage showing gliders and their tow aircraft departing England which appears to be the same wartime film material that was used in "The Heroes of Telemark" (1965), as described in Chapter Four.

We see the same footage of an Airspeed Horsa I glider numbered '292' starting its take off run behind its tow aircraft that appears in the 1965 film. Then a fine study of a Short Stirling IV coded 'X9-' powering down a runway. This footage is not used in the "Telemark" film, but it almost certainly comes from the same source and was shot on the same day and at the same airfield location. This Stirling IV is a No.299 Squadron aircraft: No.299 was a Special Duties squadron that was formed in November 1943 to operate in support of the French Resistance. It was equipped with the Stirling IV, the Special Duties version of the original bomber design, from January 1944 onwards, becoming operational on the type in April that year and continued to operate the same aircraft until the end of the War.

No.299 Squadron took part in the night-time Paratroop dropping over Normandy that was the opening phase of the D-Day invasion, using all 24 of its Stirling IVs before returning during the daylight phase on 6th June 1944 with 16 Stirlings aero-towing gliders; it lost two aircraft during this action. No.299 also took part in Operation Market Garden, making 54 glider-towing sorties during the first three days of the assault upon Arnhem and then carrying out a further 72 re-supply drops, losing five Stirlings in the process. As with the squadron shown in the "Telemark" film, No.196 Squadron, RAF Keevil was the base from which No.299 Squadron operated and almost certainly is the airfield shown in this archive footage: the runway from which the Stirling IV marked 'X9-' is filmed taking off from is exactly the same runway that the Stirling IVs are seen using in "The Heroes of Telemark".

The Stirling IV carrying the 'X9-' code is unidentifiable because it has invasion stripes painted right over its individual aircraft code letter, which are also obscuring all the digits apart from the letter 'P' of its serial; however, it does have the number '510' on its nose. Curiously, No.299 Squadron had two different code systems on its aircraft at the same time: some of its Stirlings also carried the code '5G-'. This may have been because No.299 Squadron was an unusually large squadron in the RAF's No.38 Group, with a complement of 24 Stirlings in total, possibly divided into two separate Flights of 12 each, carrying out different specialised roles, hence the simultaneously carried two code system. As soon as the 'X9-' coded Stirling IV passes the camera, a second Short Stirling IV with a '5G-' code is shown taking off as well, with an

Airspeed Horsa I in tow behind it. Finally, the same footage of an unidentifiable Short Stirling IV lifting off with another Airspeed Horsa I climbing away in its wake, that was used in "The Heroes of Telemark", gets another showing in "The Last Drop", and, in so doing, confirms that all this archive material seen in both films was taken at the same airfield location in 1944, almost certainly RAF Keevil, either just prior to the D-Day invasion on 5th/6th June or the glider and Paratroop assault on Arnhem three months later.

So, if Teague was aware of the fact he was using archive footage of aircraft that were from a squadron that was involved in the real Arnhem operation, then he needs to be credited with the accuracy of his choice. However, he ruins this achievement immediately with his use of CGI C-47 Dakotas towing gliders in the footage which follows, a continuity clash of such obviously large proportions that even a non-aviation-minded cinema audience could not fail to spot it. What Teague was thinking of in making such an immediately obvious goof only he knows, and it has already been remarked upon in an Online Website devoted to movies (although that comment mistakenly identifies the Short Stirlings as "Brit Lancasters"). As he was using CGI, what was stopping Teague from using CGI-created Short Stirlings? And in between this imagery Teague inserts another piece of wartime archive footage of a massed formation of 27 Douglas C-47 Skytrain transports.

The use of black-and-white wartime film footage to link with the action in an all-colour modern production always clashes, unless it is used creatively, which Teague does not. He tries to cover for this by having his own footage appear for a few seconds in black-and-white following the appearance of archive film, after which it changes into colour, but this does not ameliorate the conflict between the two sources of imagery in "The Last Drop".

Another unrealistic element to the film is in having American actor Billy Zane play a British Glider Regiment glider pilot. OK, he is meant to be Canadian, but if he was he would be carrying a Canadian flag patch and the word 'Canada' on his uniform's shoulder - Zane isn't, he's wearing an obviously American military jacket, and note the modern earphones and mike headset he has donned as well. The goof of taking a heading "south and east on two-seven-nine" has also been remarked upon Online - a heading of 279 degrees is in exactly the opposite north and west direction! We then have a poor quality air-air image of an Handley Page Halifax aero-towing an Airspeed Horsa I over a coastline, the use of which conflicts completely with the action in colour taking place inside the studio glider set.

Only one actual aircraft appears in "The Last Drop", and in a ridiculously comic guise. It is an Antonov An-2 which, believe it or not, has been dressed up to play the part of a Luftwaffe seaplane. To achieve this, the set designer and his team have lopped off completely the upper wing of the world's largest single-engined bi-plane and have replaced its undercarriage with what are meant to be floats, but which look simply like two large railway sleepers. The whackiest part of the whole creation is that the set team have tried to give the An-2 a Junkers-tri-motor-like appearance, by fixing a fake engine to each wing in addition to its big single rotary up front! The whole effect just looks hilarious, especially when it taxyies across water on a lake with its fake engines turning. Imagery of it flying is of pure, and poor, CGI.

Although the action is taking place in Nazi Occupied Holland, the film was made in Romania, so this is obviously a Romanian Antonov An-2. As most examples in that country were military, it is most likely an ex-Romanian Air Force An-2 and probably one of the many that had been discarded on various airfields in Romania. Presumably it was scrapped after filming was completed.

As one of the British Paras says of the Billy Zane pilot character, "I don't believe it, Canada. I've only flown with you twice, and both times you've crashed". Very much like this film, which tries to bring too much of a "Kelly's Heroes" get "Lock, Stock and Two Smoking Barrels" type of action to a British World War Two war film plot.

ATONEMENT

(Released: September 2007)

Whatever the merits of any particular production, and "Atonement" was a huge critical and box office success, historical error is what it is - historical error. The bomber that one of the leading characters sees flying over his home in 1936 could not possibly be the Avro Lancaster that is shown: the Lancaster had another five years in the design and the making before such an event could take place. Surely the director must have known that a Lancaster was the wrong typHeinkel He.111 Luftwaffe bombers flying above three British soldiers making their way towards Dunkirk. No other aircraft scenes appear in "Atonement".

FEMALE AGENTS (LES FEMMES DE L'OMBRE)

(Released: March 2008, France) International 'British' war film

The actual title of this French production translates into English as "The Women of the Shadows", yet it was released onto the English language cinema circuit as simply "Female Agents", an accurate but far less imaginative and creative heading. Its central characters are French female agents recruited into the SOE, with its leading personality played by French actress Sophie Marceau as Louise Desfontaines. Reputedly, she is based on real-life French SOE agent, Lise de Baissac; if so, it is a very loose connection, as the operations and mission Louise Desfontaines undertakes with four other female French SOE operatives bear little comparison to the actual operations Lise de Baissac undertook in Nazi Occupied France during 1944 in the run-up to D-Day.

The main action does take place in France, and in Paris in particular, but the build-up occurs in England where Louise and her colleagues are recruited in London by Major Maurice Buckmaster, head of SOE's F Section (French). Part of their mission is to rescue a British Army geologist caught by the Germans reconnoitring

the Normandy beaches two weeks before D-Day. He had been collecting samples of sand that he was due to take back to London by RAF Special Duties aircraft (a Lysander, most likely, but the type is not mentioned): this is artistic licence on the part of director/writer Jean-Paul Salome, as no such military geologist was used by the Allies prior to D-Day to collect sand samples for geological study to ensure the beaches could safely support the forces that were to be landed (samples were collected by Royal Navy divers who swam ashore from X-Craft mini-submarines). However, there is a loose link that Salome may have been trying to make with Lise de Baissac here, as her cover in France was that she was an amateur archaeologist collecting rock samples while she reconnoitred landing and drop zones for Special Duties aircraft.

Salome was correct to identify RAF Tempsford as the airfield from which the Special Duties aircraft would carry the female agents of the story into Normandy. In fact, he can be credited as being the only film director to actually use the name of Tempsford in a feature film about the SOE, as all previous British productions like "Now It Can Be Told" (1946), "Against The Wind" (1948) and "Carve Her Name With Pride" (1958) were made when the identity and location of RAF Tempsford was still classified.

In "Les Femmes de l'Ombre", however, it is described as 'Aerodrome de Tempsford', with no RAF title. Even more so, the selection of the types of aircraft shown parked on Tempsford create a completely inaccurate representation of the real RAF Tempsford, as shown in detail in "Now It Can Be Told" (1946). This is because all the aircraft shown are American types in various US military markings, apart from one type in a spurious RAF scheme. The result is that Salome's representation of Tempsford creates the impression of it being an American military air base in England.

To be fair to Salome, he had to go with what was available to him, especially as the film was made in France. All the aircraft assembled for the Tempsford scenes and for the night-time landings in Occupied Territory belonged to French collections, none of which owned types that could be representative of RAF Special Duties squadrons. However, the errors in types and colour schemes are glaring to aviation historians.

Tempsford appears right at the beginning of the film, with a tracking shot along parked aircraft in front of very un-RAF like hangars. The first to be seen is a Beech C-45 Expeditor with RAF camouflaged top surfaces and fuselage, plus all yellow undersides - fairly realistic of an RAF communications Beech C-45 of the World War Two era, but totally unlike a Special Duties squadron machine. It is possible that the colour scheme may have been chosen because the few C-45 Expeditors flown by the RAF in the European theater (the majority of RAF C-45s were operated in the Far East by SEAC) bore a very similar scheme to the example in "Les Femmes de l'Ombre", and may have been copied from photographs of a similarly-painted RAF Beech C-45 flown with the Commemorative Air Force in Texas. The fake serial of 'ZZ429' seen under the starboard wing, however, is very far ahead of its time!

The more likely explanation is that it is Beech E18S F-AZEJ, which, at the time the film was made, bore green-brown camouflage top surfaces and fuselage sides, plus all-yellow undersides, but carried completely erroneous US Army markings and the large code letter 'V' on its twin tail fins. It would have been an easy job to apply large RAF roundels over the US blue circle with white star on each side of the fuselage. Beech 18S F-AZEJ was operated by the Amicale Jean-Baptiste Salis (AJBS) at Aerodrome de Cerny-La Ferte Alais. This Beech is also seen at night in two scenes involving the insertion and extraction of agents, in which it could be said to be impersonating an RAF Special Duties Lockheed Hudson, both types being broadly similar in appearance, although the Beech was smaller in size.

The camera pans on from the Beech and passes right in front of a Douglas C-47 Skytrain in USAAF colour scheme. Beyond it, and just outside one of the hangars, can be seen a North American P-51D Mustang. As the camera passes across the scene, the wing of a second Douglas C-47 appears, but the shot is cut before the whole aircraft appears in view.

In the scene where the female SOE agents all arrive at Tempsford, a North American T-6 Texan can be seen in the background painted in pre-1941 USAAC markings, another serious error not only in time but in aircraft type, as no USAAC Texans ever appeared at Tempsford. This is almost certainly North American T-6G Texan F-AZMP operated by the AJBS in the markings of 493056/X-56, as its scheme appears identical to the T-6 seen in the film.

The P-51D is seen twice in the background from a distance, and both times surrounded by props of vehicles and various equipment which obscure its code letters. However, the aircraft identification code of 'C' is discernable in one shot, while in another it can be seen that this P-51D has a red-yellow checkerboard band around its nose immediately aft of the propeller, plus it is in natural metal scheme. This corresponds to the same paint scheme borne by the AJBS North American P-51D Mustang F-AZSB, which carries the markings of 44-11622/G4-C and is named Nooky Booker IV. P-51D F-AZSB was imported into France by Christophe Jacquard in 1998, who operated this Mustang in the same markings (those of Major Leonard 'Kit' Carson of the 363rd Fighter Squadron, 357th Fighter Group, USAAF Eighth Air Force) until he sold it to the AJBS in 2006.

With three AJBS aircraft used as props for 'Aerodrome de Tempsford', the film location for the Special Duties squadron base can only be Aerodrome de Cerny-La Ferte Alais.

The aircraft which features most prominently in "Les Femmes de l'Ombre" is the USAAF C-47 Skytrain that flies the SOE agents into France. An historical error is the appearance of this C-47, as the SOE never used the famous USAAF transport aircraft for agent insertion missions. RAF C-47 Dakotas were used on Special Duties missions over the Balkans, operating from Italy, as well as in Burma, and only occasionally in the Occupied Territories in Europe. It is painted with the USAAF serial and codes of 313142/17-N and has D-Day stripes, another error because the agents are parachuting into France from it in late May, at least a week before D-Day, a time period too early for the application of these stripes. Another incongruity are the scenes filmed inside the C-47 which show that it has passenger windows, something which a military Skytrain would not have, confirming that it is in reality a civil Douglas DC-3.

The film credits give the name of the pilot as Gabriel Leveque of France DC-3. This being the case, the C-47 is Douglas DC-3 Dakota III F-AZTE operated by l'Amicale France DC-3, an association dedicated to keeping airworthy a DC-3 in Air France colours carrying the registration F-BBBE. It is a former USAAF C-47 Skytrain, flying from Long Beach, California, on 5th March 1943 and taken on charge as 42-23310. Post-War, it was purchased by Scottish Aviation at Prestwick and registered as G-AGZF, but was requisitioned by the British government for use in the Berlin Airlift. It subsequently was taken on charge by the l'Armee de l'Air in 1952 as a VIP transport before undergoing a series of civil registration changes in France. It was operated as F-GDPP by Publi-Air, formed by Air Inter at Aeroport de Orly to preserve a working DC-3, before this association evolved into l'Amicale France DC-3.

In the film, DC-3 F-AZTE is seen releasing five parachutists to represent the female SOE agents parachuting into France, a task it was familiar with as it had been used as a jump platform a number of times during its service history, both military and civil, including dropping Paras during the 40th Anniversary D-Day celebrations on 6th June 1984. Other in-flight scenes consist of a CGI-created depiction of the C-47 avoiding flak.

"Les Femmes de l'Ombre" doesn't lose out in the action and drama stakes, but with its 21st Century approach to a war film it does stretch the credibility factor in a number of ways, not just where historical accuracy with the aircraft that appear in it is concerned, but in having a disparate group of female French agents with tangled private lives that are more soap opera than World War Two. One of them is the escaped lover of the SS Colonel in Paris who is hunting them down, while another is a former stripper in Soho who has murdered her (presumably English) pimp and is due to be hanged in Holloway Prison unless she agrees to take part in the mission to rescue the captured English geologist. Neither would have stood the ghost of a chance of being recruited into the real-life Special Operations Executive.

BROTHERS WAR

(Released: 2009) Hollywood 'British' war film

This low budget, "Band of Brothers"-influenced, American war film has the unusual plotline of a German Hauptmann (Captain) and a British Army Major joining forces as Freemasons to warn the Allies that the Russians plan to take over Europe after the defeat of Nazi Germany. It plays around with history by moving the Katyn Forest Massacre of Polish politicians and intellectuals by the Soviet NKVD from April and May 1940 to April 1945. It is riddled with more holes and continuity goofs than a Schmeisser MP40 could inflict. As far as aviation is concerned, all the aircraft shown are CGI-created and very poorly at that.

GLORIOUS 39

(Released: November 2009)

An extraordinarily beautiful film that is by no means a normal or familiar British war film. Its focus is on secret manipulations by members of the British establishment to exploit the appeasement movement at the outbreak of World War Two, during the glorious summer of 1939 in Britain, to try and create a pact with Hitler that will see their interests and way of life preserved in exchange for undermining those like Winston Churchill who advocate resisting Germany's National Socialism. The events are seen through the eyes of the naïve young actress daughter of an upper class family, who gradually comes to realise her whole family are involved in the appeasement conspiracy. It is a first class film that deserves to be in anyone's collection of productions about World War Two but, despite the image of an indistinct twin-engined aircraft on the poster, no aircraft has any role in "Glorious 39".

AGE OF HEROES

(Released: May 2011)

Inspired by James Bond creator Ian Fleming's clandestine 30 Commando Assault Unit, and probably in the title by the current Help for Heroes campaign for assistance to British service personnel injured in action in Afghanistan and Iraq, this is a questionably accurate portrayal of an insertion of a Commando team into Nazi Occupied Norway to capture intelligence on the German Freya radar system. I say questionable because military scientist R V Jones, in Most Secret War, explains that "…they (the Germans) would almost certainly bring some of their radar equipment forward to the Channel coast. Indeed we already knew that they had done so, and that the name of their basic equipment was Freya" (Chapter 23, 'Freya', page 189).

Channel coast meant Nazi Occupied France, not Norway. And as Freya was a detection system targeting both aircraft and ships, France was the obvious country in which to locate it as part of the defence against RAF bomber raids and Royal Navy attacks on captured Channel ports. Thus, the reason for basing the story in Norway probably has more to do with this film being a British - Norwegian co-production, rather than any basis in historical fact.

For our purpose with aviation in mind, it is a very disappointing production. The two poster covers for the film both show aircraft prominently to the fore, suggesting that aerial action plays a significant part in it. In reality, only extremely limited CGI of three Stuka-like machines and of a Handley Page Halifax appear. That is in keeping with the whole production, which has a very low budget feel to it. And, as some reviewers on Website Forums have asked, what happened to Sean Bean at the end? Like him, the story just disappears.

FINAL CUT

It's been an epic production. Seventy-four years long and covering more than 180 British World War Two war films, including a variety of Hollywood 'British' and international 'British' films among them. And we have made some remarkable and unexpected discoveries which, in aviation history, have either never been revealed before or were not, until now, fully recognised for what they are.

The six actual war years of World War Two are rich with aircraft action in British films. The War Office, the Air Ministry and the Ministry of Information actively encouraged and supported the appearance of front-line fighters and bombers in an extraordinary variety of film productions created as Great Britain fought for her life and for the free world. We have discovered that film directors and film editors working in Ealing Studios, British MGM Film Studios and other production houses actually fought their own war against the Deutsches Luftwaffe raining bombs on cities in England. Their weapons were the deliberate reversing of, and even inverting, images of Heinkels, Dorniers and Messerschmitts, to portray the enemy aircraft as twisted and deformed, a calculated insult in the editing suite that the suffering British people could take courage from, but which, up till now, has always been misunderstood to be thought simply bad, error-ridden film editing.

Even more notable is the discovery and identity of actual captured Luftwaffe aircraft appearing in British World War Two war films, which is unique to the British film industry. Six captured German bombers and fighters were used in seven film productions:

Messerschmitt Bf.110C-4 5F+CM of 4(F)/14 in "Ferry Pilot" (1941) and "The Adventures of Tartu" (1943); Heinkel He.111H-3 1H+EN of II/KG.26 in "The First of the Few" (1942); Junkers Ju.88A-6 M2+MK of II/KGr.106 in "In Which We Serve" (1942) and "The Adventures of Tartu" (1943); Messerschmitt Bf.110G-4 3C+BA of NJG.4 as a wrecked fighter in "Angels One Five" (1952); Junkers Ju.87G-2 RI+JK, today painted as being from II/SG.3, as pattern for a large-scale facsimile Stuka in "Battle of Britain" (1969); and Messerschmitt Bf.109G-2 'Black 6', owned by the Ministry of Defence and operated by The Fighter Collection, in "The Land Girls" (1998). Out-takes of Junkers Ju.88A-6 M2+MK served five other British war films made in the Fifties.

Films made during the War years have thrown up the following discoveries:

The first British World War Two film, "The Lion Has Wings" (1939), is the sole public source of film of Adolf Hitler's personal VIP Focke Wulf FW.200 airliner filmed before the War;

"Dangerous Moonlight" (1941) is the first film to feature the Battle of Britain;

"The Next of Kin" (1942) was the first film to make extensive use of archive imagery of the Junkers Ju.87 Stuka in action;

"Ships With Wings" (1942) has footage of the actual Fairey Swordfish torpedo bombers from HMS Ark Royal which attacked the battleship Bismarck;

In "Flying Fortress" (1942), the early model Boeing B-17 is made out to be a success as a high altitude bomber in RAF service, when in fact it was a failure;

"The Volunteer" (1944) has some of the most valuable film footage of wartime Fleet Air Arm aircraft in action off Royal Navy aircraft carriers, especially of the earliest steam catapults launching Martlets and Seafires;

"The Way to the Stars" (1945) has archive footage of the first USAAF Eighth Air Force B-17 to complete 25 missions, and it is not Memphis Belle. The Bristol Blenheim Mk.Is seen in the same film were hired from the Finnish Air Force.

Another wartime discovery is that No.222 (Natal) Squadron's Spitfires appear in more British war films than any other RAF Fighter Command Squadron, while No.149 Squadron does likewise for RAF Bomber Command.

More historic discoveries occur in film productions released to the cinema just after the War's end, then into the Fifties and beyond:

"Now It Can Be Told" (1946) is the sole public source available that portrays in detail the activities of the secretive RAF Tempsford and its Special Duties squadrons, only recently released on DVD by the Imperial War Museum;

"Odette" (1950) has very rare footage of the Boeing B-17G Flying Fortress in a parachute supply dropping role;

It can be confirmed that a total of 10 Hawker Hurricanes were used in "Angels One Five" (1952) - including both LF363 and PZ865 - not six, as is popularly supposed;

The four Lancaster bombers used in "Appointment in London" (1953) are not, as it has been claimed, all the same Lancasters as used in "The Dam Busters" (1955);

The four Spitfires used in "Malta Story" (1953) have been tracked down and identified, they having remained a mystery for so long;

"The Red Beret" (1953) has film - in colour - of the last flying Vickers Wellingtons in RAF service;

"They Who Dare" (1954) has unique footage of the last flying Savoia-Marchetti SM.79 Sparveiro bomber/transports, typical of those flown by the wartime Italian Regia Aeronautica, and again in colour;

"Reach For The Sky" (1956) makes an extraordinary use of out-takes from other British war films, with much of it inserted in reverse direction by the editor;

The first war film made anywhere to use the Messerschmit Bf.108 as a stand-in for Luftwaffe Messerschmitt Bf.109s was "Operation Amsterdam", filmed in 1958 in The Netherlands;

"Foxhole in Cairo" (1960) has footage of the most amazing escape by parachute at low-level of the dorsal turret gunner from a crashing bomber;

The much-criticised "Mosquito Squadron" (1969) has archive footage unseen anywhere else in the public domain of a No.618 Squadron Mosquito releasing 'Highball' over land. The same film also has the last ever footage taken of de Havilland Mosquitos flying in formation;

The scene in "Battle of Britain" (1969) showing the attack on the Ventnor RDF Chain Home Station is an almost direct copy of the same scene shown 23 years earlier in "School For Secrets" (1946);

Similarly, the massed parachute drops sequences in the re-creation film about Arnhem, "Theirs Is The Glory" (1946), was copied in part in "A Bridge Too Far" (1977).

More discoveries reveal that a number of World War Two warbirds used in British or Hollywood 'British' war films made in the Sixties and Seventies reprised their actual wartime roles in these productions. They include:

The four Spitfire LF.Mk.IXs used in "The Longest Day" (1962);

The P-40E Kittyhawk Mk.IA in "Tobruk" (1967);

Spitfire Mk.IIa P7350 in "Battle of Britain" (1969), the one genuine veteran used in that film of the real Battle in 1940;

Spitfire Mk.Vb AB910, which was a No.222 Squadron aircraft based at RAF North Weald in August 1941 when part of "Eagle Squadron" (1942) was being filmed there;

Spitfire LF.IXb MH415 is accurately representative of Low Flying Spitfires strafing with cannon, as seen in "Triple Cross" (1966) and "The Night of the Generals" (1967) - so too are the Low Flying Spitfires seen shooting up Rommel's staff car in "The Desert Fox" (1951);

One of the 11 Douglas C-47/C-53 Skytrain/Skytrooper transports appearing in "A Bridge Too Far" (1977) was a genuine Operation Market Garden veteran;

A genuine V2 rocket appears in "Operation Crossbow" (1965), a captured example discovered by British forces following the collapse of Nazi Germany - the same V2 can be seen preserved today in the RAF Museum at Cosford.

And no prizes for identifying which warbird has acted more roles in British World War Two war films than any of its contemporaries - Spitfire HF.Mk.IXb MH434.

We have found that film production companies had to be creative in the Fifties and the Sixties by having various aircraft types represent certain actual World War Two machines which either no longer existed or were not in flying condition. The famous T-6 Texan/Harvard has played the roles of being Luftwaffe Focke Wulf FW.190s, USAAF P-47 Thunderbolts and RAF Hawker Typhoons, both in British and Hollywood war film productions. In no less than five similar such productions, the slim Messerschmitt Bf.108B Taifun tourer has play-acted the part of its Messerschmitt Bf.109 fighter offspring. Austers, the Fairchild Argus and the de Havilland Canada Beaver have all been called upon act as Westland Lysanders in films featuring agents of the Special Operations Executive being landed secretly at night in Nazi Occupied France.

Especially in the Fifties, certain 'goofs' proved unavoidable when modern day aircraft accidentally crept into shot or were deliberately used as props for similar-looking World War Two types. Witness the Canberra jet which suddenly appears in the background amid No.617 Squadron's Lancaster bombers in "The Dam Busters" (1955), plus on-base Avro Lincolns doubling up for their famous forebears in the same production, as well as in "Appointment in London" (1953). The Lancaster's maritime patrol descendent, the Avro Shackleton, is used to represent its ancestor twice in British World War Two war films made during the Fifties at RAF Gibraltar. Late model Avro Ansons can't avoid getting into shot at Bovingdon, where they were based, as B-17s and Mosquitos roar down the runway in "The War Lover" (1962), "633 Squadron" (1964) and "Mosquito Squadron" (1969).

The surging warbird movement of the Seventies onwards increasingly allowed for the 'real thing' to be used in World War Two movies. Various historic aircraft collections, such as the Old Flying Machine Company at Duxford and Personal Plane Services at Wycombe Air Park, have proved invaluably expert at providing aircraft, pilots and support services to film productions featuring World War Two themes.

21st Century digital electronic technology has proven itself to be both a blessing and a curse in the way certain film directors and editors use it to depict World War Two aircraft in action. CGI can be used very effectively, as in "Dark Blue World" (2001), or to the point of exaggerated ridiculousness, such as in "The Last Drop" (2005). The amount of flak directed by both critics and the public at the recently released Hollywood World War Two movie, "Red Tails", about which producer/director George Lucas has openly admitted to using greatly exaggerated CGI SFX of 'Tuskegee Airmen' P-51D Mustangs in air combat, in order to appeal to American teenagers hooked on computer simulator play stations, suggests that audiences are no longer willing to be convinced that such over indulgent Special Effects should replace reality. CGI has its place, but to enhance the representation of reality in war films, not to make air battles look like digitally enhanced outer space warfare.

As the 21st Century progresses, it is difficult to predict how World War Two will be portrayed in future film productions or even if there will be a demand for the subject. But one thing is for certain, the opportunity to use genuine military aircraft of the 1939 - 1945 time period in films remains as strong as ever. The potential for Spitfire Mk.IX MH434 and its co-stars to be in demand for war films appears to be limitless.

DIRECTORY
OF
AIRCRAFT APPEARING IN BRITISH WAR FILMS

FILM TERMINOLOGY

ACTOR - Individual playing identified role.

EXTRA - Further individual playing non-speaking role.

PROP - Any item used as physical part of a scene.

SET DRESSING (S/D) - Item or items used to physically add to a scene.

FOREGROUND (F/G) - Any item which happens to be in the foreground of a scene.

BACKGROUND (B/G) - Any item which happens to be in the background of a scene.

BACK DROP (B/D) - Filmed item seen on screen filling background to the main subject filmed in the foreground of a scene.

OUT-TAKE (O/T) - A scene or image taken from one film and used again in another film.

ARCHIVE - Film taken from newsreels or other sources held in store and edited in to fit with sequences filmed for the main production;

STOCK - Film footage made for organisations or companies, and held in store by them to be used in films, newsreels or promotional material.

DOC. - Documentary.

MINIATURE (M/T) - Model of real item being filmed.

F/SF - Full scale facsimile or accurate copy of real item, substituting for same real item in the film production.

SFX - Special Effects;

U/U - Unused material.

DEFINITIONS

1.ANS - No.1 Air Navigation School; 2TAF - 2nd Tactical Air Force; a/c - aircraft; A&AEE - Aircraft & Armaments Experimental Establishment; AB - Air Base; AF - Air Force' AFDU - Air Fighting Development Unit; AHC - Aircraft Heritage Centre; AJBS - Amicale Jean-Baptiste Salis; ASR - Air-Sea Rescue; ATA - Air Transport Auxiliary; ATAF - Allied Tactical Air Force; ATC - Air Training Corps; BCATP - British Commonwealth Air Training Plan; BDTF - Bomber (Defence) Training Flight; BFTS - British Flying Training School; BG - Bombardment Group; BS - Bombardment Squadron; CAACU - Civil Anti-Aircraft Co-Operation Unit; CFS - Central Flying School; CFU - Crown Film Unit; Co. - Company; COI - Central Office of Information; Comms - Communications; Corp. - Corporation; docu. - documentary; E-Stelle - Erprobungsstelle; FG - Fighter Group; Flt - Flight; FS - Fighter Squadron; FTC - Flying Training Command; HAC - Historic Aircraft Collection; HMS - His Majesty's Ship; I/D - Identification; IWM - Imperial War Museum; Ltd. - Limited; MAEE - Marine Aircraft Experimental Establishment; MAPS - Medway Aircraft Preservation Society; MARC - Military Aircraft Restoration Corporation; MATS - Military Air Transport Service; Met. - Metereological; Min. - Ministry; Mk. - Mark, or Marque; MoI - Ministry of Information; MU - Maintenance Unit; NAA - North American Aviation; NCO - Non-Commissioned Officer; N/K - Not Known; NZ - New Zealand; OFMC - Old Flying Machine Company; OTU - Operational Training Unit; PR - Photo Reconnaissance; RAE - Royal Aircraft Establishment; RAF - Royal Air Force; RAF AHB - RAF Air Historical Branch; RAF BBMF - RAF Battle of Britain Memorial Flight; RAF FPU - RAF Film Production Unit; RAAF - Royal Australian Air Force; RCAF - Royal Canadian Air Force; R/C - radio-controlled; recon. - reconnaissance; RNAF - Royal Norwegian Air Force; RNAS - Royal Naval Air Station; RNHF - Royal Navy Historic Flight; SA - South Africa; SAAF - South African Air Force; SKHV - Stichting Koninklijke Luchtmacht Historische Vlucht; SOC - Struck Off Charge; SOE - Special Operations Executive; Sqn - Squadron; TFC - The Fighter Collection; TOC - Taken On Charge; UL - Ultralight; Unid. - Unidentified; USAAC - United States Army Air Corps; USAAF - United States Army Air Force; USNAE - United States National Archive Establishment; V/S - Vickers Supermarine; WAAF - Women's Auxiliary Air Force; WFU - Withdrawn From Use; W/O - Written Off; YAM - Yorkshire Air Museum

THE LION HAS WINGS (RELEASED: NOVEMBER 1939)

AIRCRAFT	I/D OR TOTAL	SOURCE/OPERATOR	ROLE/MATERIAL	STATUS/FATE
Airspeed Queen Wasp	K8887	Airspeed, Ltd	Archive: 1937 RAF Display	RAF, later WFU
Avro 652A Anson Mk.I	x 30	224 Sqn, RAF	Archive: 1937 RAF Display	All: SOC 1946
Bristol Blenheim Mk.I	x 5	Royal Air Force	Stock: MoI	All: SOC 1944
De Havilland DH.91 Albatross	E.2	de Havilland Aircraft Co.	Archive: 1937 RAF Display	Crashed 11/4/41 Reykjavik
Dornier Do.23G	x 18	Deutsches Luftwaffe	Archive: Reich Propaganda Min.	All: WFU 1939
Fairey P.4/34	K7555	Fairey Aviation Co.	Archive: 1937 RAF Display	Flight test with Fairey, WFU
Fairey Battle	x 6	Royal Air Force	Stock: MoI	All: SOC 1941
Fairey Battle	x 5	Royal Air Force	Stock: MoI	All: SOC 1941
Fairey Battle	Unid.	Royal Air Force	Stock: MoI	SOC by 1941
Focke Wulf FW.200V3	D-2600 (?)	Regierungsstaffel (?)	Stock: Newsreel	Bombed 18/7/44 Tempelhof
Gloster F.5/34	K5604	Gloster Aircraft Co.	Archive: 1937 RAF Display	WFU 05/41
Gloster Gauntlet	x 5	66 Sqn, RAF	Archive: 1937 RAF Display	All: SOC 1943
Gloster Gauntlet	x 100	Royal Air Force	Archive: 1937 RAF Display	All: SOC 1943
Hawker Fury I	x 4: K2043 K2879 K2881 K5673	All: 1 Sqn, RAF	Archive: 1937 RAF Display	All: SOC 1943
Hawker Fury I	x 9, inc: K2051 K2053 K2055	25 Sqn, RAF	Archive: 1937 RAF Display	All: SOC 1943
Hawker Henley	K5115	Hawker Siddeley Aircraft	Archive: 1937 RAF Display	SOC 25/03/41
Hawker Hind	x 100	Royal Air Force	Archive: 1937 RAF Display	All: SOC 1943
Heinkel He.51C	x 13	Deutsches Luftwaffe	Archive: Reich Propaganda Min.	All: WFU 1942
Heinkel He.51C	x 9	Deutsches Luftwaffe	Archive: Reich Propaganda Min.	All: WFU 1942
Heinkel He.111	x 3	Deutsches Luftwaffe	Archive: Reich Propaganda Min.	All: WFU 1945
Junkers Ju.52/3M	x 27	Deutsches Luftwaffe	Archive: Reich Propaganda Min.	All: WFU 1945
Junkers Ju.52/3M	Unid.	Lufthansa	Archive: N/K	N/K
Vickers Wellesley	x 3	Royal Air Force	Stock: MoI	All: SOC 1940
Vickers Wellington I	L4229/OJ-K	149 Sqn, RAF	Itself	N/K
Vickers Wellington I	L4259/OJ-L	149 Sqn, RAF	Itself	Shot Down 04/09/39
Vickers Wellington I	L4214/OJ-G (?)	149 Sqn, RAF	Itself	N/K
Vickers Wellington Ia	N2867/OJ- (?)	149 Sqn, RAF	Itself	N/K

Vickers Wellington Ia	Masked/OJ-T	149 Sqn, RAF	Itself	N/K
Vickers Wellington I	-----/OJ-J	149 Sqn, RAF	Itself	N/K
Vickers Wellington I	-----/OJ-O	149 Sqn, RAF	Itself	N/K
Vickers Wellington I	-----/OJ-Q	149 Sqn, RAF	Itself	N/K
Vickers Wellington I	L4346/UX-	214 Sqn, RAF	Itself	N/K
Vickers Wellington I	-----/VF-G	99 Sqn, RAF	Itself	N/K
V/S Spitfire Ia	x 6	74 Sqn, RAF	Actors: 299 & 301 Squadrons	All: SOC 1945
V/S Spitfire Ia	x 3	Royal Air Force	Stock: MoI	All: SOC 1945

NIGHT TRAIN TO MUNICH (RELEASED: AUGUST 1940)

AIRCRAFT	I/D OR TOTAL	SOURCE/OPERATOR	ROLE/MATERIAL	STATUS/FATE
Hawker Hart Trainer ?	Unid.	Royal Air Force	B/G: aircraft at 'Prague Airport'	N/K
Lockheed Super Electra	G-AFGN	British Airways	Newsreel	WFU 11/08/39
Messerschmitt Bf.110	x 12	Deutsches Luftwaffe	Stock: MoI, from clandestine source	All: SOC 1945

CONVOY (RELEASED: SEPTEMBER 1940)

AIRCRAFT	I/D OR TOTAL	SOURCE/OPERATOR	ROLE/MATERIAL	STATUS/FATE
Fairey Swordfish Mk.I	Unid.	Fleet Air Arm	Stock: MoI	All: SOC 1945
Fairey Swordfish Mk.I	x 2	Fleet Air Arm	Stock: MoI	All: SOC 1945
Hawker Osprey	K----/034	Fleet Air Arm	Stock: MoI	All: SOC 1939
Saro London	N/K	Royal Air Force	Stock: MoI	All: SOC 1941

DANGEROUS MOONLIGHT (RELEASED: JUNE 1941)

AIRCRAFT	I/D OR TOTAL	SOURCE/OPERATOR	ROLE/MATERIAL	STATUS/FATE
Bristol Blenheim Mk.I	N/K	Royal Air Force	Stock: MoI	All: SOC 1944
Bristol Blenheim Mk.I	x 3	Royal Air Force	Stock: MoI	All: SOC 1944
Dornier Do.17	N/K	Deutsches Luftwaffe	Archive: Reich Propaganda Min.	All: SOC 1945
Dornier Do.17	x 30	Deutsches Luftwaffe	Archive: Reich Propaganda Min.	All: SOC 1945
Heinkel He.111	N/K	Deutsches Luftwaffe	Gun camera: MoI	Shot down, date N/K
Heinkel He.111	N/K	Deutsches Luftwaffe	Gun camera: MoI	Shot down, date N/K
Heinkel He.111	x 5	Deutsches Luftwaffe	Archive: Reich Propaganda Min.	All: SOC 1945
Heinkel He.111H	9K+FP	KG.51, Deutsches Luftwaffe	Archive: Reich Propaganda Min.	N/K
Messerschmitt Bf.109	x 18	Deutsches Luftwaffe	Archive: Reich Propaganda Min.	All: SOC 1945
Messerschmitt Bf.110	x 9	Deutsches Luftwaffe	Archive: Reich Propaganda Min.	All: SOC 1945
V/S Spitfire Mk.I	x 6	19 Sqn, RAF	Stock: MoI	All: SOC 1945

V/S Spitfire Mk.Ia	R6774	RAE Farnborough	Actor: Radetsky's Spitfire & Polish AF fighter	Grounded 02/03/43
V/S Spitfire Mk.IIa	Unid.	Royal Air Force	Actor: Radetzky's Spitfire	N/K
V/S Spitfire Mk.IIa -	----/ZD-A	222 Sqn, RAF	Itself	N/K
V/S Spitfire Mk.IIa	-----/ZD-B	222 Sqn, RAF	Itself	N/K
V/S Spitfire Mk.IIa	-----/ZD-D	222 Sqn, RAF	Itself	N/K
V/S Spitfire Mk.IIa	-----/ZD-G	222 Sqn, RAF	Itself	N/K
V/S Spitfire Mk.IIa	-----/ZD-J	222 Sqn, RAF	Itself	N/K
V/S Spitfire Mk.IIa	-----/ZD-R	222 Sqn, RAF	Itself	N/K
V/S Spitfire Mk.IIa	-----/ZD-V	222 Sqn, RAF	Itself	N/K
V/S Spitfire Mk.IIa	x 12	222 Sqn, RAF	Extras: Polish RAF Spitfires	All: SOC 1945

TARGET FOR TONIGHT (RELEASED: JULY 1941)

AIRCRAFT	I/D OR TOTAL	SOURCE/OPERATOR	ROLE/MATERIAL	STATUS/FATE
Avro 652A Anson Mk.I	N/K	Royal Air Force	Itself: RAF recon. aircraft	All: SOC 1945
Gloster Gladiator	Unid.	Royal Air Force	B/G: to RAF Met. Unit	All: SOC 1943
Vickers Wellington Ic	P2517/OJ-F	149 Sqn, RAF	Itself: 'F for Freddie'	To No.3 GTF, 09/41
Vickers Wellington Ic	-----/OJ-A	149 Sqn, RAF	Itself: 'A for Apple'	N/K
Vickers Wellington Ic	-----/OJ-B	149 Sqn, RAF	Itself: 'B for Bertie'	N/K
Vickers Wellington Ic	-----/OJ-C	149 Sqn, RAF	Itself: 'C for Charlie'	N/K
Vickers Wellington Ic	-----/OJ-R	149 Sqn, RAF	Itself: 'R for Robert'	N/K

FERRY PILOT (RELEASED: 1941)

AIRCRAFT	I/D OR TOTAL	SOURCE/OPERATOR	ROLE/MATERIAL	STATUS/FATE
Airspeed Oxford	Unid.	Royal Air Force	Stock: MoI/CFU	All: SOC 1956
Airspeed Oxford	Unid.	Royal Air Force	Stock: MoI/CFU	All: SOC 1956
Armstrong Whitworth Whitley V	Z6635	Royal Air Force	Actor: Bomber on delivery	N/K
Armstrong Whitworth Whitley V	Z6669/ZA-B	10 Sqn, RAF	Stock: MoI/CFU	Crashed 28/12/42 Lewannick
Armstrong Whitworth Whitley V	-----/ZA-O	10 Sqn, RAF	Stock: MoI/CFU	All: SOC 1944
Armstrong Whitworth Whitley	Unid.	Royal Air Force	Stock: MoI	All: SOC 1944
Avro 652A Anson Mk.I	L7909/5	Air Transport Auxiliary	Itself: ATA taxi	Sold March 1948
Avro 652A Anson Mk.I	N5089	Air Transport Auxiliary	Itself: ATA taxi	All: SOC 1946
Avro 652A Anson Mk.I	N5100	Air Transport Auxiliary	Itself: ATA taxi	All: SOC 1946
Avro 652A Anson Mk.I	N5289	Air Transport Auxiliary	Itself: ATA taxi	All: SOC 1946
Avro 652A Anson Mk.I	N9719	Air Transport Auxiliary	Itself: ATA taxi	All: SOC 1946
Avro 652A Anson Mk.I	N9972	Air Transport Auxiliary	Itself: ATA taxi	All: SOC 1946

Avro 652A Anson Mk.I	Unid.	Air Transport Auxiliary	Itself: ATA taxi	All: SOC 1946
Avro 652A Anson Mk.I	Unid.	Air Transport Auxiliary	Itself: ATA taxi	All: SOC 1946
Avro 652A Anson Mk.I	Unid.	Air Transport Auxiliary	Itself: ATA taxi	All: SOC 1946
Avro 652A Anson Mk.I	Unid.	Air Transport Auxiliary	Itself: ATA taxi	All: SOC 1946
de Havilland DH.87B Leopard Moth	Unid.	Air Transport Auxiliary	Itself: ATA taxi	All: SOC 1945
de Havilland DH.89A Dominie	Unid.	Air Transport Auxiliary	Itself: ATA taxi	All: SOC 1946
Hawker Hart Trainer	Unid.	Royal Air Force	Stock: MoI/CFU	All: SOC 1943
Hawker Hurricane	Unid.	Royal Air Force	B/G: RAF fighter	All: SOC 1947
Heinkel He.111B-2	72+OIG	KG.157, Deutsches Luftwaffe	Archive: Reich Propaganda Min.	N/K
Heinkel He.111H	9K+FR	KG.51, Deutsches Luftwaffe	Archive: Reich Propaganda Min.	N/K
Heinkel He.111H	V4+AU	KG.1, Deutsches Luftwaffe	Archive: Reich Propaganda Min.	N/K
Heinkel He.111H	x 3, inc: --+BL	Deutsches Luftwaffe	Archive: Reich Propaganda Min.	All: SOC 1945
Heinkel He.111	Unid.	Deutsches Luftwaffe	Archive: Reich Propaganda Min.	All: SOC 1945
Heinkel He.111	Unid.	Deutsches Luftwaffe	Stock: Gun-camera footage	Shot down, date N/K
Junkers Ju.88	Unid.	Deutsches Luftwaffe	Stock: MoI	Shot down, date N/K
Messerschmitt Bf.110C-4	5F+CM AX772	4(F)/14, Luftwaffe AFDU	Actor: Bf.110 Zerstorer	Captured 21/7/40 Scrapped 1947
Messerschmitt Bf.110C	Unid.	Deutsches Luftwaffe	Archive: Reich Propaganda Min.	All: SOC 1945
Messerschmitt Bf.110C	x 2	Deutsches Luftwaffe	Archive: Reich Propaganda Min.	All: SOC 1945
Messerschmitt Bf.110	x 8	Deutsches Luftwaffe	Archive: Reich Propaganda Min.	All: SOC 1945
Messerschmitt Bf.110	x 4	Deutsches Luftwaffe	Archive: Reich Propaganda Min.	All: SOC 1945
Miles M.14 Magister	x 5	Royal Air Force	B/G: RAF primary trainers	All: SOC 1948
Miles M.19 Master Mk.II	T8902	Royal Air Force	Itself: RAF advanced trainer	All: SOC 1945
Miles M.19 Master Mk.II	Unid.	Royal Air Force	Itself: RAF advanced trainer	All: SOC 1945
NAA BC-1 Harvard I	N7126/49	Royal Air Force	F/G: RAF advanced trainer	All: SOC 1942
NAA BC-1 Harvard I	N7128/51	Royal Air Force	F/G: RAF advanced trainer	All: SOC 1942
NAA BC-1 Harvard I	P5856	Royal Air Force	F/G: RAF advanced trainer	All: SOC 1942
Vickers Wellington Ia	OJ-	149 Sqn, RAF	O/T: "The Lion Has Wings"	All: SOC 1952
Vickers Wellington Ia	OJ-	149 Sqn, RAF	O/T: "The Lion Has Wings"	All: SOC 1952
Vickers Wellington I	Unid.	RAF Bomber Command	Stock: CFU	All: SOC 1952
Vickers Wellington I	x 3	RAF Bomber Command	Stock: CFU	All: SOC 1952

V/S Spitfire Mk.Ia	R7157	Royal Air Force	Itself: RAF fighter	Crashed 26/09/42 Quedgeley
V/S Spitfire Mk.Ia	No serial	Vickers Armstrong	Itself: RAF fighter	All: SOC 1945
V/S Spitfire Mk.Ia	Unid.	Royal Air Force	Itself: RAF fighter	All: SOC 1945
V/S Spitfire Mk.I	Unid.	Royal Air Force	Itself: RAF fighter	All: SOC 1945
V/S Spitfire Mk.I	Unid.	Royal Air Force	Itself: RAF fighter	All: SOC 1945
V/S Spitfire Mk.I	Unid.	Royal Air Force	Itself: RAF fighter	All: SOC 1945
V/S Spitfire Mk.I	Unid.	RAF Fighter Command	Stock: MoI	All: SOC 1945
V/S Spitfire Mk.I	x 6	19 Sqn, RAF	Stock: MoI	All: SOC 1945
V/S Spitfire Mk.IIa	P8441	RAE Farnborough	Actor: RAF Spitfire	SOC 30/12/44
V/S Spitfire Mk.IIa	P799-	Royal Air Force	Itself: RAF fighter	All: SOC 1945
V/S Spitfire Mk.IIa	P80--	Royal Air Force	Itself: RAF fighter	All: SOC 1945
V/S Spitfire Mk.II	-----/UO-O	266 Sqn, RAF	Stock: MoI	All: SOC 1945
V/S Spitfire Mk.II	-----/UO-	266 Sqn, RAF	Stock: MoI	All: SOC 1945
V/S Spitfire Mk.II	x 2	Royal Air Force	Stock: CFU	All: SOC 1945
V/S Spitfire Mk.I/II	x 3	RAF Fighter Command	Stock: MoI	All: SOC 1945
V/S Spitfire Mk.I/II	x 2	RAF Fighter Command	Stock: MoI	All: SOC 1945
V/S Spitfire PR.V	N3111	RAE Farnborough	PR.V prototype as Spitfire on delivery flight	Crashed 27/03/43 Worlington
Westland Lysander	Unid.	Royal Air Force	Stock: CFU	All: SOC 1948

A YANK IN THE R.A.F.
(HOLLYWOOD 'BRITISH' WAR FILM. RELEASED: SEPTEMBER 1941, USA)

AIRCRAFT	I/D OR TOTAL	SOURCE/OPERATOR	ROLE/MATERIAL	STATUS/FATE
Bristol Blenheim I	Unid.	RAF Fighter Command	RAF night fighter	All: SOC 1944
Lockheed Hudson V	AM870	Lockheed Corp. / RAF	B/G: Lend-Lease Hudson	All: SOC 1945
Lockheed Hudson V	2970	Lockheed Corp. / RAF	Prop: RAF bomber	All: SOC 1945
Lockheed Hudson V	Unid.	Lockheed Corp. / RAF	Extra: Baker's ferry aircraft	All: SOC 1945
Lockheed Hudson V	x 5	Lockheed Corp. / RAF	Extras: RAF bombers	All: SOC 1945
Lockheed Hudson V	x 5	Lockheed Corp. / RAF	B/G: Lend-Lease Hudsons	All: SOC 1945
Lockheed Hudson V	x 3	Lockheed Corp. / RAF	Extras: RAF bombers	All: SOC 1945
'Messerschmitt Bf.109'	No serial	20th Century Fox Studios	F/SF: shot down Bf.109	Retained by Studio
NAA AT-6 Harvard II	RCAF 3016	NAA / RCAF	BCATP trainer	All: SOC 1945
NAA AT-6 Harvard II	RCAF 3781	NAA / RCAF	BCATP trainer	All: SOC 1945
NAA AT-6 Harvard II	RCAF 3817	NAA / RCAF	BCATP trainer	All: SOC 1945

NAA AT-6 Harvard II	x 8, inc: RCAF 3027	NAA / RCAF	BCATP trainers	All: SOC 1945
NAA AT-6 Harvard II	x 8, inc: RCAF 3763	NAA / RCAF	BCATP trainers	All: SOC 1945
NAA AT-6 Harvard II	x 6	NAA / RCAF	BCATP trainers	All: SOC 1945
NAA AT-6 Harvard II	x 4	NAA / RCAF	BCATP trainers	All: SOC 1945
V/S Spitfire Ia	x 12, inc: R6627/LO-E X4829/LO-Q -----/LO-B -----/LO-C -----/LO-D -----/LO-R	602 Sqn, Royal Air Force	Extras: RAF fighters	All: SOC 1945 W/O 18/8/44 Lost at sea 07/12/44
V/S Spitfire Ia	x 3, inc: -----/SH-D -----/SH-E -----/SH-J	64 Sqn, Royal Air Force	Stock: MoI	All: SOC 1945
V/S Spitfire Ia	x 10	RAF Fighter Command	Stock: MoI	All: SOC 1945

INTERNATIONAL SQUADRON
(HOLLYWOOD 'BRITISH' WAR FILM. RELEASED: AUGUST 1941, USA)

AIRCRAFT	I/D OR TOTAL	SOURCE/OPERATOR	ROLE/MATERIAL	STATUS/FATE
Airspeed Oxford I	Unid.	RAF Flying Training Command	Stock: MoI	All: SOC 1956
Avro 652A Anson Mk.I	Unid.	Royal Air Force	Stock: MoI	All: SOC 1946
Brown B-3	NX266Y	Brown Aircraft Co, Montebello, California	Actor: new fighter & Spitfire	Destroyed hangar fire, 1943
de Havilland DH.82A Tiger Moth II	N9621/4	RAF Flying Training Command	Stock: MoI	All: SOC 1951
Heinkel He.111B	Unid.	Deutsches Luftwaffe	Archive: Reich Propaganda Min.	All: SOC 1945
Heinkel He.111H	x 2	Deutsches Luftwaffe	Archive: Reich Propaganda Min.	All: SOC 1945
Heinkel He.111P	Unid.	Deutsches Luftwaffe	Archive: Reich Propaganda Min.	All: SOC 1945
Heinkel He.111P	Unid.	Deutsches Luftwaffe	Archive: Reich Propaganda Min.	All: SOC 1945
Heinkel He.111	Unid.	Deutsches Luftwaffe	Archive: Reich Propaganda Min.	All: 1945
Junkers Ju.52/3M	Unid.	Deutsches Luftwaffe	Archive: Reich Propaganda Min.	All: SOC 1945
Junkers Ju.87B-1 Stuka	x 3	Deutsches Luftwaffe	Archive: Reich Propaganda Min.	All: SOC 1945
Junkers Ju.87D-5 Stuka	x 3	Deutsches Luftwaffe	Archive: Reich Propaganda Min.	All: SOC 1945
Junkers Ju.87R Stuka	x 3	Deutsches Luftwaffe	Archive: Reich Propaganda Min.	All: SOC 1945
Junkers Ju.87 Stuka	x 3	Deutsches Luftwaffe	Archive: Reich Propaganda Min.	All: SOC 1945
Junkers Ju.88 ?	Unid.	Deutsches Luftwaffe	Stock: MoI	Shot down 1940

Messerschmitt Bf.109E	'2'	JG.51, Deutsches Luftwaffe	Archive: Reich Propaganda Min.	All: SOC 1945
Messerschmitt Bf.109E-3	'Yellow 5'	VI/JG.51, Deutsches Luftwaffe	Archive: Reich Propaganda Min.	All: SOC 1945
Messerschmitt Bf.109E-3	'Yellow 12'	VI/JG.51, Deutsches Luftwaffe	Archive: Reich Propaganda Min.	All: SOC 1945
Messerschmitt Bf.109E-3	Unid.	VI/JG.51, Deutsches Luftwaffe	Archive: Reich Propaganda Min.	All: SOC 1945
Lockheed Hudson V	Unid.	Lockheed Corp. / RAF	Prop: RAF bomber	All: SOC 1945
Ryan ST-A Special	Unid.	N/K	Prop: Spitfire	N/K
Ryan ST-A Special	Unid.	N/K	Prop: Spitfire	N/K
Travel Air D-4000	NC406N	N/K	O/T: "Murder In The Sky"	Extant: private owner, USA
Travel Air 'Mystery Ship'	NR613K	Paul Mantz	Prop: Spitfire	Extant: Skyfire Corp, Delaware
Vickers Wellington	Unid.	Royal Air Force	Stock: MoI	All: SOC 1952
V/S Spitfire Mk.I	x 3	19 Sqn, RAF	Stock: MoI	All: SOC 1945
V/S Spitfire Mk.Ia	x 3	74 Sqn, RAF	O/T: "The Lion Has Wings"	All: SOC 1945
V/S Spitfire Mk.IIa	Unid.	AFDU, Royal Air Force	Stock: CFU/MoI	All: SOC 1945
Westland Lysander	Unid.	Royal Air Force	Stock: MoI	Shot down 1940

49TH PARALLEL (RELEASED: NOVEMBER 1941)

AIRCRAFT	I/D OR TOTAL	SOURCE/OPERATOR	ROLE/MATERIAL	STATUS/FATE
Douglas Digby I	RCAF 744/PB-D	10(BR) Sqn, Royal Canadian Air Force	Actor: RCAF patrol aircraft	Crashed at sea 29/12/41
Douglas Digby I	x 2	Eastern Air Command, Royal Canadian Air Force	Extras: RCAF patrol aircraft	All: SOC 1946
Fairchild 71C	CF-BJE	Canadian Airways Ltd.	Actor: hijacked supply aircraft	Crashed 04/1/43 Franquelin, PQ,
Lockheed Hudson III	RCAF 778/OY-P	11(BR) Sqn, Royal Canadian Air Force	Actor: RCAF patrol aircraft	Crashed 26/5/41 Dartmouth, NS,
Lockheed Hudson III	x 4	Eastern Air Command, Royal Canadian Air Force	Extras: RCAF patrol aircraft	All: SOC 1945
Lockheed Lodestar	CF-TCH	Trans-Canada Air Lines	Stock: TCAL ?	N/K
Westland Lysander II	Unid.	Royal Canadian Air Force	Extra: RCAF patrol aircraft	All: SOC 1946

SHIPS WITH WINGS (RELEASED: NOVEMBER 1941)

AIRCRAFT	I/D OR TOTAL	SOURCE/OPERATOR	ROLE/MATERIAL	STATUS/FATE
Blackburn Skua Mk.II	L2967/6M	800 Sqn, HMS Ark Royal	Doc.: "Find, Fix and Strike"	All: SOC 1945
Blackburn Skua Mk.II	-----/6A	800 Sqn, HMS Ark Royal	Doc.: "Find, Fix and Strike"	All: SOC 1945
Blackburn Skua Mk.II	-----/6B	800 Sqn, HMS Ark Royal	Doc.: "Find, Fix and Strike"	All: SOC 1945

Blackburn Skua Mk.II	-----/6K	800 Sqn, HMS Ark Royal	Doc.: "Find, Fix and Strike"	All: SOC 1945
Blackburn Skua Mk.II	Unid.	800 Sqn, HMS Ark Royal	Doc.: "Find, Fix and Strike"	All: SOC 1945
Blackburn Skua Mk.II	Unid.	800 Sqn, HMS Ark Royal	Doc.: "Find, Fix and Strike"	All: SOC 1945
Blackburn Skua Mk.II	-----/7K	803 Sqn, HMS Ark Royal	Doc.: "Find, Fix and Strike"	All: SOC 1945
Blackburn Skua Mk.II	Unid.	Fleet Fighter School, RNAS Yeovilton	Doc.: "Find, Fix and Strike"	All: SOC 1945
Blackburn Skua Mk.II	Unid.	Fleet Fighter School, RNAS Yeovilton	Doc.: "Find, Fix and Strike"	All: SOC 1945
Fairey Fulmar Mk.I	Unid.	Fleet Fighter School, RNAS Yeovilton	Doc.: "Find, Fix and Strike"	All: SOC 1945
Fairey Fulmar Mk.I	Unid.	Fleet Fighter School, RNAS Yeovilton	Doc.: "Find, Fix and Strike"	All: SOC 1945
Fairey Fulmar Mk.I	Unid.	Fleet Fighter School, RNAS Yeovilton	Doc.: "Find, Fix and Strike"	All: SOC 1945
Fairey Swordfish Mk.I	-----/2A	810 Sqn, HMS Ark Royal	Doc.: "Find, Fix and Strike"	All: SOC 1945
Fairey Swordfish Mk.I	-----/2C	810 Sqn, HMS Ark Royal	Doc. "Find, Fix and Strike"	All: SOC 1945
Fairey Swordfish Mk.I	-----/2F	810 Sqn, HMS Ark Royal	Doc.: "Find, Fix and Strike"	All: SOC 1945
Fairey Swordfish Mk.I	-----/2L	810 Sqn, HMS Ark Royal	Doc. "Find, Fix and Strike"	All: SOC 1945
Fairey Swordfish Mk.I	-----/2Q	810 Sqn, HMS Ark Royal	Doc. "Find, Fix and Strike"	All: SOC 1945
Fairey Swordfish Mk.I	P4219/5A	818 Sqn, HMS Ark Royal	Doc.: "Find, Fix and Strike"	All: SOC 1945
Fairey Swordfish Mk.I	L9726/5C	818 Sqn, HMS Ark Royal	Doc.: "Find, Fix and Strike"	All: SOC 1945
Fairey Swordfish Mk.I	-----/5F	818 Sqn, HMS Ark Royal	Doc.: "Find, Fix and Strike"	All: SOC 1945
Fairey Swordfish Mk.I	-----/5G	818 Sqn, HMS Ark Royal	Doc.: "Find, Fix and Strike"	All: SOC 1945
Fairey Swordfish Mk.I	-----/5H	818 Sqn, HMS Ark Royal	Doc.: "Find, Fix and Strike"	All: SOC 1945
Fairey Swordfish Mk.I	K8357/4H	820 Sqn, HMS Ark Royal	Doc.: "Find, Fix and Strike"	All: SOC 1945
Fairey Swordfish Mk.I	-----/4G	820 Sqn, HMS Ark Royal	Doc.: "Find, Fix and Strike"	All: SOC 1945
Fairey Swordfish Mk.I	L2865/V	Fleet Air Arm	Stock: MoI	All: SOC 1945
Fairey Swordfish Mk.I	-----/B	Fleet Air Arm	Stock: MoI	All: SOC 1945
Fairey Swordfish Mk.I	-----/F	Fleet Air Arm	Stock: MoI	All: SOC 1945
Gloster Sea Gladiator	-----/E	Fleet Fighter School, RNAS Yeovilton	Doc.: "Find, Fix, Strike"	All: SOC 1943
Gloster Sea Gladiator	Unid.	Fleet Fighter School, RNAS Yeovilton	Doc.: "Find, Fix, Strike"	All: SOC 1943
Gloster Sea Gladiator	Unid.	Fleet Fighter School, RNAS Yeovilton	Doc.: "Find, Fix, Strike"	All: SOC 1943

305

THE BIG BLOCKADE (RELEASED: MARCH 1942)

AIRCRAFT	I/D OR TOTAL	SOURCE/OPERATOR	ROLE/MATERIAL	STATUS/FATE
Handley Page Hampden I	-----/XG-A	16 OTU, RAF Lindholme	Actor: 'T for Tommy'	All: WFU 09/43
Handley Page Hampden I	-----/VN-A	50 Sqn, RAF Lindholme	Itself: filmed at RAF Lindholme	All: WFU 09/43
Handley Page Hampden I	-----/VN-D	50 Sqn, RAF Lindholme	Itself: filmed at RAF Lindholme	All: WFU 09/43
Handley Page Hampden I	Unid.	16 OTU, RAF Lindholme	Actor: 'T for Tommy'	All: WFU 09/43
Handley Page Hampden I	Unid.	RAF Lindholme Wing	Itself: filmed at RAF Lindholme	all: WFU 09/43
Handley Page Hampden I	Unid.	RAF Lindholme Wing	Itself: filmed at RAF Lindholme	All: WFU 09/43
Handley Page Hampden I	Unid.	RAF Lindholme Wing	Itself: filmed at RAF Lindholme	All: WFU 09/43
Handley Page Hampden I	Unid.	RAF Lindholme Wing	Itself; filmed at RAF Lindholme	All: WFU 09/43
Handley Page Hampden I	Unid.	RAF Lindholme Wing	Itself: filmed at RAF Lindholme	All: WFU 09/43
Handley Page Hampden I	Unid.	RAF Lindholme Wing	B/G: Lindholme	All: WFU 09/43
Handley Page Hampden I	Unid.	RAF Lindholme Wing	B/G: Lindholme	All: WFU 09/43
Handley Page Hampden I	Unid.	RAF Lindholme Wing	B/G: Lindholme	All: WFU 09/43
Heinkel He.111	x 9	Deutsches Luftwaffe	Archive: Reich Propaganda Min.	All: SOC 1945
Heinkel He.111H-3	6853/1H+EN	See: "First of the Few"	Stock: MoI	Crashed: 11/43
Junkers Ju.52/3M	Unid.	Deutsches Luftwaffe	Archive: Reich Propaganda Min.	All: SOC 1945
Junkers Ju.87 Stuka	x 3	Deutsches Luftwaffe	Archive: Reich Propaganda Min.	All: SOC 1945
Vickers Wellington I	Unid.	RAF Bomber Command	B/G: Lindholme	All: SOC 1952
V/S Spitfire Mk.I	Unid.	RAF Fighter Command	Stock: MoI	All: SOC 1945
V/S Spitfire Mk.I	Unid.	RAF Fighter Command	Stock: MoI	All: SOC 1945
V/S Spitfire Mk.IIa	Unid.	AFDU, Royal Air Force	Stock: MoI	All: SOC 1945

ONE OF OUR AIRCRAFT IS MISSING (RELEASED: APRIL 1942)

AIRCRAFT	I/D OR TOTAL	SOURCE/OPERATOR	ROLE/MATERIAL	STATUS/FATE
Short Stirling Mk.I	Unid.	RAF Bomber Command	Actor: 'B for Bertie' crew's new bomber	All: WFU 09/44
Short Stirling Mk.I	-----/MG-B	7 Sqn, RAF	Stock: MoI	All: WFU 09/44
Short Stirling Mk.I	-----/MG-E	7 Sqn, RAF	Stock: MoI	All: WFU 09/44
Short Stirling Mk.I	-----/MG-K	7 Sqn, RAF	Stock: MoI	All: WFU 09/44
Short Stirling Mk.I	-----/MG-P	7 Sqn, RAF	Stock: MoI	All: WFU 09/44
Short Stirling Mk.I	-----/MG-W	7 Sqn, RAF	Stock: MoI	All: WFU 09/44
Short Stirling Mk.I	-----/MG-Z	7 Sqn, RAF	Stock: MoI	All: WFU 09/44
Short Stirling Mk.I	Unid.	7 Sqn, RAF	Stock: MoI	All: WFU 09/44
Short Stirling Mk.I	Unid.	7 Sqn, RAF	Stock: MoI	All: WFU 09/44

Short Stirling Mk.I	Unid.	7 Sqn, RAF	Stock: MoI	All: WFU 09/44
Short Stirling Mk.I	Unid.	7 Sqn, RAF	Stock: MoI	All: WFU 09/44
Vickers Wellington Ic	-----/KO-B ?	115 Sqn, RAF	Actor: 'B for Bertie'	All: SOC 1952
Vickers Wellington Ic	Unid.	115 Sqn, RAF	Itself: 115 Sqn aircraft	All: SOC 1952
Vickers Wellington Ic	Unid.	115 Sqn, RAF	Itself: 115 Sqn aircraft	All: SOC 1952
Vickers Wellington Ic	Unid.	115 Sqn, RAF	Itself: 115 Sqn aircraft	All: SOC 1952
Vickers Wellington Ic	Unid.	115 Sqn, RAF	Itself: 115 Sqn aircraft	All: SOC 1952
Vickers Wellington Ic	Unid.	115 Sqn, RAF	Itself: 115 Sqn aircraft	All: SOC 1952
Vickers Wellington Ic	Unid.	115 Sqn, RAF	Itself: 115 Sqn aircraft	All: SOC 1952

THE DAY WILL DAWN (RELEASED: JUNE 1942)

AIRCRAFT	I/D OR TOTAL	SOURCE/OPERATOR	ROLE/MATERIAL	STATUS/FATE
Armstrong Whitworth Whitley	Unid.	Royal Air Force	Stock: Crown Film Unit	All: SOC 1944
Bristol Blenheim IV	x 4	Royal Air Force	Stock: Crown Film Unit	All: SOC 1944
Dornier Do.17	x 30	Deutsches Luftwaffe	Archive: Reich Propaganda Min.	All: SOC 1945
Heinkel He.111H	x 3	Deutsches Luftwaffe	Archive: Reich Propaganda Min.	All: SOC 1945
Henschel Hs.126	N/K	Deutsches Luftwaffe	Archive: Reich Propaganda Min.	All: SOC 1945
Messerschmitt Bf.109	x 18	Deutsches Luftwaffe	Archive: Reich Propaganda Min.	All: SOC 1945
Messerschmitt Bf.110	x 9	Deutsches Luftwaffe	Archive: Reich Propaganda Min.	All: SOC 1945
Vickers Wellington Ic	P2517/OJ-F	149 Sqn, RAF	O/T: "Target for Tonight"	All: SOC 1952

THE NEXT OF KIN (RELEASED: JUNE 1942)

AIRCRAFT	I/D OR TOTAL	SOURCE/OPERATOR	ROLE/MATERIAL	STATUS/FATE
Armstrong Whitworth Whitley	Unid.	Royal Air Force	Stock: MoI	All: SOC 1944
Bristol Beaufort	x 2	RAF Coastal Command	Extras: RAF bombers	All: SOC 1945
Bristol Blenheim IV	x 2	RAF Coastal Command	Extras: RAF bombers	All: SOC 1944
Curtiss Tomahawk IIb	x 3	Royal Air Force	Extras: RAF fighter-bombers	All: SOC 1943
Heinkel He.111B-2	72+OIG	KG.157, Deutsches Luftwaffe	Archive: Reich Propaganda Min.	N/K

Heinkel He.111H	x 4	Deutsches Luftwaffe	Archive: Reich Propaganda Min.	All: SOC 1945
Heinkel He.111H	x 2	Deutsches Luftwaffe	Archive: Reich Propaganda Min.	All: SOC 1945
Junkers Ju.52/3mge	ZS-AFD	South African Airways	Archive: South African Airways	Crashed 29/3/40 Salamandar
Junkers Ju.87 Stuka	GU+AC	E-Stelle, Rechlin ?	Archive: Reich Propaganda Min.	All: SOC 1945
Junkers Ju.87 Stuka	TK+HG	E-Stelle, Rechlin ?	Archive: Reich Propaganda Min.	All: SOC 1945
Junkers Ju.87 Stuka	x 7	Deutsches Luftwaffe	Archive: Reich Propaganda Min.	All: SOC 1945
Junkers Ju.87 Stuka	x 4	Deutsches Luftwaffe	Archive: Reich Propaganda Min.	All: SOC 1945
Junkers Ju.88	Unid.	Deutsches Luftwaffe	Archive: Reich Propaganda Min.	All: SOC 1945
V/S Spitfire Mk.IIa	x 4, inc: -----/LZ-A -----/LZ-F	66 Sqn, RAF	Extras: RAF fighters	All: SOC 1945

THEY FLEW ALONE (RELEASED: JUNE 1942)

AIRCRAFT	I/D OR TOTAL	SOURCE/OPERATOR	ROLE/MATERIAL	STATUS/FATE
Airspeed Oxford Mk.I	T1041	Air Transport Auxilliary	Prop: Airspeed Oxford V3457	All: SOC 1956
Bristol Blenheim Mk.I	x 5	Royal Air Force	Stock: MoI	All: SOC 1944
De Havilland DH-60G Gipsy Moth	'G-AAAH' 'VH-UFT'	N/K	Actor: Amy Johnson's and Jim Mollinson's aircraft	N/K
De Havilland DH.80A Puss Moth	G-ABXY	Harold Brooks, Sherburn	Archive: Movie-tone News	WFU 02/12/34
De Havilland DH.80A Puss Moth	'G-ABXY' 'G-ACAB'	N/K	Actor: Amy Mollinson's and Jim Mollinson's aircraft	N/K
De Havilland DH.84 Dragon	G-ACCV	Amy Mollinson, CBE	Archive: Movie-tone News	WFU ?/11/33
De Havilland DH.87B Leopard Moth	Unid.	Air Transport Auxiliary	O/T: "Ferry Pilot"	N/K
Vickers Wellington	Unid.	Royal Air Force	B/G: Wellington for delivery	All: SOC 1952
V/S Spitfire Mk.Ia	Unid.	Royal Air Force	Stock: MoI	All: SOC 1945
V/S Spitfire Mk.IIa	Unid.	Royal Air Force	B/G: Spitfire on delivery	All: SOC 1945
V/S Spitfire Mk.IIa	Unid.	Royal Air Force	Stock: MoI	All: SOC 1945
V/S Spitfire Mk.IIa	x 7	222 Sqn, RAF	O/T: "Dangerous Moonlight"	All: SOC 1945

FLYING FORTRESS
(HOLLYWOOD 'BRITISH' WAR FILM. RELEASED: JUNE 1942, UK)

AIRCRAFT	I/D OR TOTAL	SOURCE/OPERATOR	ROLE/MATERIAL	STATUS/FATE
Beech AT-7 Kansan	Unid.	United States Army Air Corps	Stock: USNAE	Survivors rebuilt to C-45G, 1950s
Beech D.17S Staggerwing	NC180JA ?	N/K	O/T: unknown Warner Bros film	N/K
Boeing Model 299	NX13372	Boeing Aircraft Company Seattle, Wa	Stock: Boeing ?	Crashed 30/10/35
Boeing B-17C Flying Fortress	x 6	Boeing / Royal Air Force	Stock: MoI	All: WFU 1944
Boeing B-17C Flying Fortress	x 3	United States Army Air Corps	Stock: Boeing ?	All: up-graded to B-17D
Boeing Fortress I	AN530/WP-P	90 Sqn, RAF	Actor: Richard Greene's Fortress	All: WFU 1944
Boeing Fortress I	AN536/WP-M	90 Sqn, RAF	Actor: Fortress bombing Berlin	All: WFU 1944
Boeing Fortress I	Unid.	90 Sqn, RAF	Extra: Fortress bombing Berlin	All: WFU 1944
Buhl CA-6 Air Sedan	NC8446	S J Coughran, Fullerton, Ca	O/T: unknown Warner Bros film	w/o a/c destroyed in film, 1940
Consolidated Liberator I	x 4	Atlantic Return Ferry Service	Stock: MoI	All: SOC 1945
Junkers Ju.52/3M	Unid.	Deutsches Luftwaffe	Archive: Reich Propaganda Min.	All: SOC 1945
Junkers Ju.87D Stuka	x 4	Deutsches Luftwaffe	Archive: Reich Propaganda Min.	All: SOC 1945
Junkers Ju.87D Stuka	x 4	Deutsches Luftwaffe	Archive: Reich Propaganda Min.	All: SOC 1945
Junkers Ju.87R Stuka	x 3	Deutsches Luftwaffe	Archive: Reich Propaganda Min.	All: SOC 1945
Junkers Ju.88	Unid.	Deutsches Luftwaffe	Stock: MoI	Shot down 1940
Messerschmitt Bf.109E-3	'2'	JG.51, Deutsches Luftwaffe	Archive: Reich Propaganda Min.	All: SOC 1945
Messerschmitt Bf.109E-3	'Yellow 5'	VI/JG.51, Deutsches Luftwaffe	Archive: Reich Propaganda Min.	All: SOC 1945
Messerschmitt Bf.109E-3	'Yellow 12'	VI/JG.51, Deutsches Luftwaffe	Archive: Reich Propaganda Min.	All: SOC 1945
Messerschmitt Bf.109E-3	Unid.	VI/JG.51, Deutsches Luftwaffe	Archive: Reich Propaganda Min.	All: SOC 1945
NAA AT-6 Texan	2 x ranks	United States Army	Stock: USNAE	All: SOC 1959
V/S Spitfire Mk.IIa	Unid.	AFDU, Royal Air Force	Stock: CFU/MoI	All: SOC 1945

EAGLE SQUADRON (HOLLYWOOD 'BRITISH' WAR FILM. RELEASED: JUNE 1942, USA)

AIRCRAFT	I/D OR TOTAL	SOURCE/OPERATOR	ROLE/MATERIAL	STATUS/FATE
Messerschmitt Bf.109	Unid.	Deutsches Luftwaffe	Stock: MoI	All: SOC 1945
Vickers Wellington	Unid.	Royal Air Force	Stock: MoI	All: SOC 1952
V/S Spitfire Mk.Ia	X4829/LO-Q	602 Sqn, Royal Air Force	Stock: MoI	Lost at sea 07/12/44
V/S Spitfire Mk.Ia	-----/LO-B	602 Sqn, Royal Air Force	Stock: MoI	All: SOC 1945
V/S Spitfire Mk.Ia	x 8, inc: -----/LO-R	602 Sqn, Royal Air Force	Stock: MoI	All: SOC 1945
V/S Spitfire Mk.Ia	-----/MV-?	53 OTU, Royal Air Force	Extra: 'Eagle' Sqn Spitfire	All: SOC 1945
V/S Spitfire Mk.Ia	x 3	53 OTU ?	Extras: 'Eagle' Sqn Spitfires	All: SOC 1945
V/S Spitfire Mk.Vb	x 5, inc: -----/XR-A -----/XR-C -----/XR-L -----/XR-P ?	71 (Eagle) Sqn, RAF Fighter Command	Extras: 'Eagle' Sqn Spitfires	All: SOC 1955
V/S Spitfire Mk.Vb	-----/ZD-Y	222 Sqn, Royal Air Force	Itself: 222 Sqn Spitfire	All: SOC 1955
V/S Spitfire Mk.Vb	x 12, inc: -----/PK-A -----/PK-E -----/PK-R -----/PK-V	315 Polish Fighter Sqn, RAF Fighter Command	Extras: 'Eagle' Sqn Spitfires	All: SOC 1955
V/S Spitfire Mk.I or II	Unid.	RAF Fighter Command	Stock: MoI	Shot down 1940
Westland Lysander	-----/TV-?	4 Sqn, Royal Air Force	Itself: ASR a/c	All: SOC 1948
Westland Lysander	Unid.	Royal Air Force	Itself: ASR a/c	All: SOC 1948

THE GOOSE STEPS OUT (RELEASED: AUGUST 1942)

AIRCRAFT	I/D OR TOTAL	SOURCE/OPERATOR	ROLE/MATERIAL	STATUS/FATE
Heinkel He.111B	Unid.	Deutsches Luftwaffe	Archive: N/K	All: SOC 1945

UNPUBLISHED STORY (RELEASED: AUGUST 1942)

AIRCRAFT	I/D OR TOTAL	SOURCE/OPERATOR	ROLE/MATERIAL	STATUS/FATE
Messerschmitt Bf.109	x 18	Deutsches Luftwaffe	Archive: Reich Propaganda Min.	All: SOC 1945
Messerschmitt Bf.110	x 9	Deutsches Luftwaffe	Archive: Reich Propaganda Min.	All: SOC 1945

THE FIRST OF THE FEW (RELEASED: SEPTEMBER 1942)

AIRCRAFT	I/D OR TOTAL	SOURCE/OPERATOR	ROLE/MATERIAL	STATUS/FATE
Bristol Blenheim Mk.IV	Unid.	RAF FPU	Camera aircraft	All: SOC 1944
Dornier Do.17Z-2	2361/F1+FH	I/KG.76, Deutsches Luftwaffe	Archive: British Pathe	Shot down 15/09/40
Heinkel He.111	x 11	Deutsches Luftwaffe	Archive: Reich Propaganda Min.	All: SOC 1945
Heinkel He.111H-3	6853/1H+EN AW177	II/KG.26, Luftwaffe 1426 (Enemy Aircraft) Flt	Actor: Luftwaffe bomber	Captured 09/2/40 Crashed 11/43
Lohning Lo-100 Zwergrieher	Unid.	N/K	Archive: German Glider	N/K
Messerschmitt Bf.109E	x 4	Deutsches Luftwaffe	Archive: Reich Propaganda Min.	All: SOC 1945
Supermarine Sea Lion III	G-EBAH	Supermarine Aviation	Archive: MoI	Crashed Felixstowe 1923
Supermarine S.4	G-EBLP	Supermarine Aviation	Archive: MoI	Crashed USA 23/10/25
Supermarine S.5	'N220'	British Aviation Pictures	F/SF: S-5 Racer	Dismantled post-production
Supermarine S.6A	N247/2	RAF High Speed Flight	Archive: MoI	Crashed Calshot 1931
Supermarine S.6B	S1596	RAF High Speed Flight	Archive: MoI	Sank Calshot 1931
V/S Spitfire Mk.I	'K5054'	Vickers Supermarine Co.	Actor: Spitfire Prototype	Prototype Crashed 04/09/39
V/S Spitfire Mk.Ia	x 9, inc: R6627/LO-E X4829/LO-Q -----/LO-B -----/LO-C -----/LO-D -----/LO-R	602 Sqn, Royal Air Force	Stock: Air Min. & O/T "A Yank in the R.A.F."	All: SOC 1945 W/O 18/8/44 Lost at sea 07/12/44
V/S Spitfire Mk.IIa	P8664/SD-C	501 Sqn, RAF	Extra: 'Hunter' Sqn Spitfire	Crashed Spey Bay 14/06/43
V/S Spitfire Mk.IIa	P8256/SD-D	501 Sqn, RAF	Extra: 'Hunter' Sqn Spitfire	SOC 30/10/44
V/S Spitfire Mk.IIa	P8074/SD-L	501 Sqn, RAF	Actor: 'Hunter' Sqn Spitfire	Force landing in Ireland attacking He.111 30/11/41
V/S Spitfire Mk.Vb	-----/NK-B	118 Sqn, RAF	Actor: Niven's Spitfire	N/K
V/S Spitfire Mk.Vb	P8789/'SD-E'	118 Sqn, RAF	Actor: Sqn Ldr Howell's Spitfire	Engine failure, abandoned English Channel 01/06/42
V/S Spitfire Mk.Vb	W3840/SD-G	501 Sqn, RAF	Extra: 'Hunter' Sqn Spitfire	Shot down nr Cherbourg 25/04/42
V/S Spitfire Mk.Vb	W3626/SD-K	501 Sqn, RAF	Extra: 'Hunter' Sqn Spitfire	Missing over Belgium 01/6/42

V/S Spitfire Mk.Vb	-----/'SD-W'	118 Sqn, RAF	Extra: 'Hunter' Sqn Spitfire	N/K
V/S Spitfire Mk.Vb	-----/'SD-X'	118 Sqn, RAF	Extra: 'Hunter' Sqn Spitfire	N/K
Wright NW-2	A.6554	United States Navy Schneider Trophy Team	Archive: MoI	Sank Cowes 24/09/23

IN WHICH WE SERVE (RELEASED: SEPTEMBER 1942)

AIRCRAFT	I/D OR TOTAL	SOURCE/OPERATOR	ROLE/MATERIAL	STATUS/FATE
Curtiss P-40 Tomahawk	Unid.	Royal Air Force	Archive: MoI	All: SOC 1943
Heinkel He.115 ?	Unid.	Deutsches Luftwaffe	Archive: MoI	Shot down, date N/K
Junkers Ju.88A-5	6073/M2+MK HM509	II/KGr.106, Luftwaffe 1426 Enemy Aircraft Flt	Actor: German bomber	Captured 26/11/41 W/O 19/05/44
V/S Spitfire (Mk.V ?)	x 4	Royal Air Force	Archive: MoI	All: SOC 1955

DESPERATE JOURNEY (HOLLYWOOD 'BRITISH' WAR FILM. RELEASED: SEPTEMBER 1942, USA)

AIRCRAFT	I/D OR TOTAL	SOURCE/OPERATOR	ROLE/MATERIAL	STATUS/FATE
Boeing B-17B Flying Fortress	Unid.	7th Bomb Group, USAAC	Actor: RAF bomber	All: SOC 1944
Lockheed Hudson III	T9386	Lockheed / RAF	Actor: captured RAF bomber	All: SOC 1945
Stinson Model A	Unid.	N/K	Actor: Luftwaffe Junkers Ju.52	N/K
V/S Spitfire Mk.I or II	x 3	RAF Fighter Command	Stock: MoI ?	All: SOC 1945

SECRET MISSION (RELEASED: OCTOBER 1942)

AIRCRAFT	I/D OR TOTAL	SOURCE/OPERATOR	ROLE/MATERIAL	STATUS/FATE
Armstrong Whitworth Whitley V	-----/OA-D	Parachute Exercise Sqn, RAF ?	Stock: MoI	All: SOC 1944
Armstrong Whitworth Whitley V	-----/OA-S	Parachute Exercise Sqn, RAF ?	Stock: MoI	All: SOC 1944
Armstrong Whitworth Whitley V	x 5	Parachute Exercise Sqn, RAF ?	Stock: MoI	All: SOC 1944

COMMANDOS STRIKE AT DAWN
(HOLLYWOOD 'BRITISH' WAR FILM. RELEASED: DECEMBER 1942, USA)

AIRCRAFT	I/D OR TOTAL	SOURCE/OPERATOR	ROLE/MATERIAL	STATUS/FATE
Bristol Bolingbroke IV	Unid.	Royal Canadian Air Force	Prop: Luftwaffe Junkers Ju.88	All: SOC 1945
Bristol Bolingbroke IV	Unid.	Royal Canadian Air Force	Prop: Luftwaffe Junkers Ju.88	All: SOC 1945
Douglas DC-3	Unid.	N/K	Stock: N/K	N/K
Handley Page Hampden	x 7	32 OTU, Royal Air Force, Patricia Bay, BC, Canada	Themselves	All: WFU 09/43
Heinkel He.111	Unid.	Deutsches Luftwaffe	Archive: N/K	All: SOC 1945
Heinkel He.111	Unid.	Deutsches Luftwaffe	Archive: N/K	All: SOC 1945
Westland Lysander	Unid.	Royal Canadian Air Force	Prop: Luftwaffe Henschel Hs.126	All: SOC 1946
Westland Lysander	Unid.	Royal Canadian Air Force	Prop: Luftwaffe Henschel Hs.126	All: SOC 1946

TONIGHT WE RAID CALAIS
(HOLLYWOOD 'BRITISH' WAR FILM. RELEASED: APRIL 1943, USA)

AIRCRAFT	I/D OR TOTAL	SOURCE/OPERATOR	ROLE/MATERIAL	STATUS/FATE
Lockheed Hudson V	x 5	Lockheed Corp. / RAF	O/T: "A Yank in the R.A.F."	All: SOC 1945

UNDERCOVER (RELEASED: JULY 1943)

AIRCRAFT	I/D OR TOTAL	SOURCE/OPERATOR	ROLE/MATERIAL	STATUS/FATE
CANT Z.1007	x 2, inc: '21'	Regia Aeronautica	Stock: MoI	All: WFU 1945

THE FLEMISH FARM (RELEASED: SEPTEMBER 1943)

AIRCRAFT	I/D OR TOTAL	SOURCE/OPERATOR	ROLE/MATERIAL	STATUS/FATE
Hawker Hurricane Mk.II	Unid.	RAF Fighter Command	Actor: Belgian AF Hurricane	All: SOC 1947
Hawker Hurricane Mk.II	Unid.	RAF Fighter Command	Actor: Belgian AF Hurricane	All: SOC 1947
Hawker Hurricane Mk.II	Unid.	RAF Fighter Command	Extra: Belgian AF Hurricane	All: SOC 1947
Hawker Hurricane Mk.II	Unid.	RAF Fighter Command	Extra: Belgian AF Hurricane	All: SOC 1947
V/S Spitfire Mk.I	x 9	19 Sqn, RAF	Stock: MoI	All: SOC 1944
V/S Spitfire Mk.Vb	-----/NK-X	118 Sqn, RAF	O/T: "The First of the Few"	N/K
V/S Spitfire Mk.Vb	-----/SD-A	501 Sqn, RAF	O/T: "The First of the Few"	N/K

| V/S Spitfire Mk.Vb | -----/SD-Y | 501 Sqn, RAF | O/T: "The First of the Few" | N/K |
| V/S Spitfire Mk.Vb | x 2 | 118 Sqn, RAF | O/T: "The First of the Few" | All: SOC 1955 |

THE VOLUNTEER (PRE-RELEASE PUBLIC SHOWING: OCTOBER 1943)

AIRCRAFT	I/D OR TOTAL	SOURCE/OPERATOR	ROLE/MATERIAL	STATUS/FATE
Consolidated Catalina	x 3	RAF Coastal Command	Ship's film: moored at Gib.	All: SOC 1945
Fairey Albacore I	Unid.	831 Sqn, FAA, HMS Indomitable	Stock: Landing on Indomitable	All: SOC 1946
Fairey Albacore I	Unid.	Fleet Air Arm	Stock: Albacore crashed on deck	All: SOC 1946
Fairey Albacore I	x 2	831 Sqn, FAA, HMS Indomitable	Stock: Albacores on deck at Gib.	All: SOC 1946
Fairey Fulmar I	-----/LSR	739 Sqn, FAA, RNAS Lee-on-Solent	B/G: Delivery Unit aircraft	All: SOC 1945
Fairey Fulmar II	Unid.	Fleet Air Arm	Stock: Fulmar on carrier deck	All: SOC 1945
Fairey Swordfish I	-----/5Z	HMS Formidable Air Group	Ship's film: itself taking off carrier	All: SOC 1945
Fairey Swordfish I	Unid.	HMS Formidable Air Group	Ship's film: itself taking off carrier	All: SOC 1945
Fairey Swordfish	Unid.	Fleet Air Arm	Prop: Swordfish in Argus's hangar	All: SOC 1945
Grumman F-4F-4A Martlet II	-----/07-B	888 Sqn, FAA, HMS Formidable	Stock: catapult launch training	All: SOC 1946
Grumman F-4F-4A Martlet II	-----/07-D	888 Sqn, FAA, HMS Formidable	Stock: Martlet engine running	All: SOC 1946
Grumman F-4F-4A Martlet II	-----/07-W	888 Sqn, FAA, HMS Formidable	Stock: catapult launch training	All: SOC 1946
Grumman F-4F-4A Martlet II	Unid.	888 Sqn, FAA, HMS Formidable	Stock: catapult launch training	All: SOC 1946
Grumman F-4F-4A Martlet II	Unid.	Fleet Air Arm	Stock: Martlet on carrier hangar lift	All: SOC 1946
Grumman F-4F-4A Martlet II	Unid.	Fleet Air Arm	Stock: Martlet landing on carrier	All: SOC 1946
Grumman F-4F-4A Martlet II	x 3	Fleet Air Arm	B/G: Martlets in Argus's hangar	All: SOC 1946
Grumman F-4F-4A Martlet II	x 2	Fleet Air Arm	B/G: Martlets at Lee-on-Solent	All: SOC 1946
Grumman F-4F-4B Wildcat IV	FN123/07-J	888 Sqn, FAA, HMS Formidable	Stock: Wildcat tipping onto nose	All: SOC 1946
Grumman F-4F-4B Wildcat IV	x 4, inc. FN121/09-Z	893 Sqn, FAA, HMS Formidable	Stock: Wildcats on carrier deck	All: SOC 1946
Heinkel He.111	Unid.	Deutsches Luftwaffe	Stock: MoI	All: SOC 1945
Junkers Ju.87 Stuka	Unid.	Deutsches Luftwaffe	Stock: MoI	All: SOC 1945
Junkers Ju.88	Unid.	Deutsches Luftwaffe	Stock: MoI	All: SOC 1945
Savoia-Marchetti SM.79II Sparviero	Unid.	Regia Aeronautica	Stock: MoI	All: SOC 1944

Supermarine Walrus I	Unid.	Fleet Air Arm	Itself: Amphibian transport aircraft	All: SOC 1947
Vought OS2U-3 Kingfisher I	Unid.	765 Sqn, FAA, Sandbanks, Dorset	Actor: Ralph Richardson's a/c	All: Returned USA 1944
V/S Seafire Ib	MK345/K	885 Sqn, FAA, HMS Formidable	Stock: taking off Formidable	Damaged 21/11/45. w/o ?
V/S Seafire Ib	-----/G	885 Sqn, FAA, HMS Formidable	Stock: Seafire parked on deck	All: SOC 1946
V/S Seafire Ib	Unid.	885 Sqn, FAA, HMS Formidable	Stock: Seafire being waved off	All: SOC 1946
V/S Seafire Ib	Unid.	885 Sqn, FAA, HMS Formidable	Stock: Seafire landing on	All: SOC 1946
V/S Seafire Ib	Unid.	885 Sqn, FAA, HMS Formidable	Stock: Seafire parked on deck	All: SOC 1946
V/S Seafire Ib	Unid.	Fleet Air Arm	Itself: Seafire on carrier hangar lift	All: SOC 1946
V/S Seafire Ib	x 3	Fleet Air Arm	Stock: Seafires on carrier deck	All: SOC 1946
V/S Seafire IIc	MB182/06-F	885 Sqn, FAA, HMS Formidable	Stock: Seafire beside 4.5in guns	N/K
V/S Seafire IIc	MB307/8D	807 Sqn, FAA, HMS Indomitable	Itself: taking off HMS Indomitable	SOC 1945
V/S Seafire IIc	MB309/L	884 Sqn, FAA, Edinburgh/Turnhouse	Prop: 'Fred's' Seafire	Missing 19/06/43
V/S Seafire IIc	-----/06-A	885 Sqn, FAA, HMS Formidable	Stock: Seafire catapult launched	All: SOC 1948
V/S Seafire IIc	-----/8F	807 Sqn, FAA, HMS Indomitable	Stock: Seafire parked on deck	All: SOC 1948
V/S Seafire IIc	-----/8Y	807 Sqn, FAA, HMS Indomitable	Itself: taking off HMS Indomitable	N/K
V/S Seafire IIc	Unid.	807 Sqn, FAA, HMS Indomitable	Itself: taking off HMS Indomitable	All: SOC 1948
V/S Seafire IIc	Unid.	807 Sqn, FAA, HMS Indomitable	Itself: taking off HMS Indomitable	All: SOC 1948
V/S Seafire IIc	Unid.	807 Sqn, FAA, HMS Indomitable	Stock: Seafire on HMS Indomitable	All: SOC 1948
V/S Seafire IIc	Unid.	Fleet Air Arm	Prop: 'Fred's' Seafire	All: SOC 1948
V/S Seafire Ib or IIc	Unid.	HMS Formidable Air Group	Ship's film: on deck in Algiers	All: SOC 1946 or 1948
V/S Seafire Ib or IIc	Unid.	HMS Formidable Air Group	Ship's film: on deck in Gibraltar	All: SOC 1946 or 1948
V/S Seafire Ib or IIc	x 5	HMS Formidable Air Group	Ship's film: on deck in Algiers	All: SOC 1946 or 1948
V/S Seafire Ib or IIc	x 5	HMS Formidable Air Group	Ship's film: on deck in Gibraltar	All: SOC 1946 or 1948

MILLIONS LIKE US (RELEASED: NOVEMBER 1943)

AIRCRAFT	I/D OR TOTAL	SOURCE/OPERATOR	ROLE/MATERIAL	STATUS/FATE
Avro Lancaster	x 12	RAF Bomber Command	Stock: MoI	All: SOC 1954
Avro Lancaster	Unid.	RAF Bomber Command	Stock: MoI	All: SOC 1954
Avro Manchester	Unid.	RAF Bomber Command	Stock: MoI	All: WFU 06/42
Short Stirling Mk.I	Unid.	Air Ministry / Austin Aero	Stock: MoI	All: SOC 1944
Short Stirling Mk.I	Unid.	Air Ministry / Austin Aero	Stock: MoI	All: SOC 1944
Short Stirling Mk.I	Unid.	Air Ministry / Austin Aero	Stock: MoI	All: SOC 1944
Short Stirling Mk.IV (Mk.I conversion)	W74--/---O	Air Ministry / Austin Aero	Prop: Fred Blake's Stirling	All: SOC 1945
V/S Spitfire Mk.V	x 6	302 Polish Fighter Sqn, RAF Fighter Command	B/D: Spitfires	All: SOC 1955

THE ADVENTURES OF TARTU (RELEASED: NOVEMBER 1943)

AIRCRAFT	I/D OR TOTAL	SOURCE/OPERATOR	ROLE/MATERIAL	STATUS/FATE
Bristol Blenheim Mk.IV	Unid.	RAF Ferry Command	Newsreel: "Fly Away Peter"	All: SOC 1944
Junkers Ju.88A-6	6073/M2+MK HM509	II/KGr.106, Luftwaffe 1426 (Enemy Aircraft) Flt	Actor: German bomber	Captured 26/11/41 W/O 19/11/44
Lockheed Hudson	Unid.	Royal Air Force	B/G: Parked at RAF Collyweston	All: SOC 1945
Messerschmitt Bf.110C-4	2177/5F+CM AX772	4(F)/14, Luftwaffe 1426 (Enemy Aircraft) Flt	Actor: German fighter	Captured 21/7/40 Scrapped 1947
Short Stirling	x 3	Royal Air Force	B/G: Parked at RAF Collyweston	All: SOC 1944

BIG PACK (RELEASED: 1944)

AIRCRAFT	I/D OR TOTAL	SOURCE/OPERATOR	ROLE/MATERIAL	STATUS/FATE
Armstrong Whitworth Whitley	Unid.	Royal Air Force	B/G: itself	All: SOC 1944
Armstrong Whitworth Whitley	Unid.	Royal Air Force	B/G: itself	All: SOC 1944
Avro 652A Anson I	Unid.	Royal Air Force	B/G: itself	All: SOC 1946
Bristol Blenheim IV	Unid.	Royal Air Force	B/G: itself	All: SOC 1946
Handley Page Halifax II	Unid.	Royal Air Force	Itself: Halifax being maintained	All: SOC 1952
Hawker Hurricane Mk.IIb	x 7	Royal Air Force	Extras: formation fly-by, RAF FPU	All: SOC 1947
Hawker Hurricane Mk.IIc	HV340	Royal Air Force	Itself: under-going mod. fit	N/K
Hawker Hurricane Mk.IIc	HV551	Royal Air Force	Itself: ground attack Hurricane	Sold Turkish AF 31/01/43
Hawker Hurricane Mk.IIc	HV745	Royal Air Force	Itself: ground attack Hurricane	N/K

Hawker Hurricane Mk.IIc	HV863	Royal Air Force	Itself: ground attack Hurricane	N/K
Hawker Hurricane Mk.IIc	HW267	Royal Air Force	Extra: parked Hurricane	N/K
Hawker Hurricane Mk.IIc	Unid.	Royal Air Force	Actor: Hurricane delivered by ATA	All: SOC 1947
Hawker Hurricane Mk.IIc	Unid.	Royal Air Force	B/G: undergoing mod. fit	All: SOC 1947
Hawker Hurricane Mk.IIc	Unid.	Royal Air Force	Itself: ground attack Hurricane	All: SOC 1947
Hawker Hurricane Mk.IIc	Unid.	Royal Air Force	Itself: being dismantled	All: SOC 1947
Hawker Hurricane Mk.IIc	Unid.	Royal Air Force	Archive: MoI	All: SOC 1947
Hawker Hurricane Mk.IIc	Unid.	Royal Air Force	Archive: MoI	All: SOC 1947
Hawker Hurricane Mk.IIc	Unid.	Royal Air Force	Archive: MoI	All: SOC 1947
Hawker Hurricane Mk.IIc	Unid.	Royal Air Force	Archive: MoI	All: SOC 1947
Hawker Hurricane Mk.IIc	x 4	Royal Air Force	Themselves: being rolled out	All: SOC 1947
Hawker Hurricane Mk.IIc	x 4	Royal Air Force	Extras: parked Hurricanes	All: SOC 1947
Hawker Hurricane Mk.IIc	x 3	Royal Air Force	RAF FPU footage	All: SOC 1947
Hawker Hurricane Mk.IIc	x 2	Royal Air Force	Extras: parked Hurricanes	All: SOC 1947
Hawker Hurricane Mk.IIc	x 2	Royal Air Force	Archive: MoI	All: SOC 1947
Heinkel He.111 (Captured He.111 ?)	Unid.	Deutsches Luftwaffe	Archive: MoI	All: SOC 1945
Junkers Ju.87 Stuka	GU+AC	E-Stelle, Rechlin ?	Archive: Reich Propaganda Min.	All: SOC 1945
Junkers Ju.87 Stuka	TK+HG	E-Stelle, Rechlin ?	Archive: Reich Propaganda Min.	All: SOC 1945
Junkers Ju.87 Stuka	Unid.	Deutsches Luftwaffe	Archive: Reich Propaganda Min.	All: SOC 1945
Junkers Ju.87 Stuka	Unid.	Deutsches Luftwaffe	Archive: MoI	Shot down, date N/K
Junkers Ju.88A-6	6073/M2+MK HM509	II/KGr.106, Luftwaffe 1426 (Enemy Aircraft) Flt	O/T: "In Which We Serve"	Captured 26/11/41 W/O 19/11/44
Lockheed Hudson I	NZ7211	RAF FPU	Actor: RAF transport aircraft	N/K
Messerschmitt Bf.110C-4	2177/5F+CM AX772	4(F)/14, Luftwaffe AFDU	O/T: "Ferry Pilot" Archive: CFU	Captured 21/7/40 Scrapped 1947
Messerschmitt Bf.110C	Unid.	Deutsches Luftwaffe	Archive: Reich Propaganda Min.	All: SOC 1945
Messerschmitt Bf.110	Unid.	Deutsches Luftwaffe	Gun camera: MoI	Shot down, date N/K
NAA P-51A Mustang II	x 2	RAF Army Co-Operation Command	Archive: MoI	All: SOC 1947
NAA P-51A Mustang II	Unid.	RAF Army Co-Operation Command	Archive: MoI	All: SOC 1947
Vickers Wellington III	BJ959	Royal Air Force	Itself: RAF transport aircraft	N/K
Vickers Wellington	x 2	Royal Air Force	B/G: themselves	All: SOC 1952

Aircraft	I/D or Total	Source/Operator	Role/Material	Status/Fate
Vickers Wellington	Unid.	Royal Air Force	Itself: Wellington being loaded	All: SOC 1952
V/S Spitfire Mk.I or II	x 12	RAF Fighter Command	Stock: MoI	All: SOC 1945
V/S Spitfire Mk.I or II	x 9	RAF Fighter Command	Stock: MoI	All: SOC 1945
V/S Spitfire Mk.I or II	Unid.	RAF Fighter Command	Stock: MoI	All: SOC 1945
V/S Spitfire Mk.II or V	x 8	Royal Air Force	B/G: themselves	All: SOC 1945
V/S Spitfire Mk.II or V	Unid.	Royal Air Force	Itself: fighter landing	All: SOC 1945
V/S Spitfire Mk.IIa	P8441	RAE Farnborough	O/T: "Ferry Pilot" Archive: CFU	SOC 30/12/44
V/S Spitfire PR.V	N3111	RAE Farnborough	O/T: "Ferry Pilot" Archive: RAF FPU	Crashed27/03/43 Worlington
V/S Spitfire Mk.Vc	x 8, inc: BR4--/AN-V -----/AN-T -----/AN-W -----/AN-Y	417 Sqn (RCAF), RAF	Stock: RAF FPU	All: WFU 1944
V/S Spitfire Mk.Vc	Unid.	Royal Air Force	Stock: RAF FPU	All: WFU 1944
V/S Spitfire Mk.Vc	Unid.	Royal Air Force	Stock: RAF FPU	All: WFU 1944
V/S Spitfire LF.IX	MJ223/B	RAF Fighter Command	Stock: RAF FPU	Shot down 29/09/44
V/S Spitfire LF.IX	-----/WR-C	40 Sqn (SAAF), RAF	Stock: RAF FPU	All: SOC 1955
V/S Spitfire LF.IX	-----/WR-D	40 Sqn (SAAF), RAF	Stock: RAF FPU	All: SOC 1955
V/S Spitfire LF.IX	x 3	RAF Fighter Command	Stock: RAF FPU	All: SOC 1955

WESTERN APPROACHES (RELEASED: 1944)

AIRCRAFT	I/D OR TOTAL	SOURCE/OPERATOR	ROLE/MATERIAL	STATUS/FATE
Consolidated Catalina II	Unid.	RAF Coastal Command	ASR amphibian	All: SOC 1945
Grumman F-6F Hellcat	Unid.	Fleet Air Arm	Lend-Lease fighter	All: SOC 1946
Grumman F-6F Hellcat	x 4	Fleet Air Arm	Lend-Lease fighters	All: SOC 1946

CANDLELIGHT IN ALGERIA (RELEASED: MARCH 1944)

AIRCRAFT	I/D OR TOTAL	SOURCE/OPERATOR	ROLE/MATERIAL	STATUS/FATE
Douglas DB-7 Havoc	x 6	ex-Vichy French ?	Archive: N/K	TOC by Free French AF 1943

THE WAY AHEAD (RELEASED: JUNE 1944)

AIRCRAFT	I/D OR TOTAL	SOURCE/OPERATOR	ROLE/MATERIAL	STATUS/FATE
Heinkel He.111	x 6	Deutsches Luftwaffe	Archive: MoI	All: SOC 1945
Heinkel He.111H-1	Unid.	Deutsches Luftwaffe	Archive: MoI	All: SOC 1945
NAA P-51A Mustang II	Unid.	RAF Army Co-Operation Command	Archive: MoI	All: SOC 1947

FOR THOSE IN PERIL (RELEASED: JUNE 1944)

AIRCRAFT	I/D OR TOTAL	SOURCE/OPERATOR	ROLE/MATERIAL	STATUS/FATE
Bristol Blenheim Mk.IV	Unid.	Royal Air Force	Stock: CFU camera aircraft	All: SOC 1944
Douglas Boston Mk.II	-----/OA-	342 (Free French) Sqn	Stock: MoI	Transferred to French AF 1945
Douglas Boston Mk.II	x 3	342 (Free French) Sqn	Stock: MoI	Transferred to French AF 1945
Douglas Boston Mk.III	x 2	Royal Air Force	Stock: MoI	All: SOC 1945
Douglas Boston	Unid.	Royal Air Force	Stock: MoI	All: SOC 1945
Douglas DB-7 Havoc	x 6	ex-Vichy French ?	Archive: N/K	TOC by Free French AF 1943
Douglas Marauder	Unid.	USAAF	Stock: MoI	All: SOC 1946
Heinkel He.111	x 3, inc: --+BL	Deutsches Luftwaffe	Archive: MoI	All: SOC 1945
Messerschmitt Bf.110C-4	5F+CM AX772	4(F)/14, Luftwaffe AFDU	Stock: MoI RAF FPU	Captured 21/7/40 Scrapped 1947
NAA P-51A Mustang II	x 3	RAF Army Co-Operation Command	Extras: German fighters	All: SOC 1947
Supermarine Walrus Ia	W2797	277 Sqn, RAF Shoreham	Actor: Air Sea Rescue Walrus	SOC 11/1945
V/S Spitfire	x 8	RAF Fighter Command	Stock: MoI	All: SOC 1945
V/S Spitfire Mk.I	Unid.	RAF Fighter Command	Stock: MoI	All: SOC 1944
V/S Spitfire Mk.I	x 3	RAF Fighter Command	Stock: MoI	All: SOC 1944
V/S Spitfire PR.V	N3111	Royal Air Force	O/T: "Ferry Pilot"	Crashed 27/03/43
V/S Spitfire Mk.Ia	Unid.	Royal Air Force	O/T: "Ferry Pilot"	All: SOC 1945
V/S Spitfire Mk.IIa	P8441	RAE Farnborough	Stock: MoI RAF FPU	SOC 30/12/44
V/S Spitfire Mk.IIa	Unid.	277 Sqn, RAF Shoreham	Extra: Air Sea Rescue Spitfire	All: SOC 1945
V/S Spitfire Mk.IIa	Unid.	Royal Air Force	Stock: MoI	All: SOC 1945

THE WAY TO THE STARS (RELEASED: JUNE 1945)

AIRCRAFT	I/D OR TOTAL	SOURCE/OPERATOR	ROLE/MATERIAL	STATUS/FATE
Avro 652A Anson Mk.1	R9647	Royal Air Force	Actor: RAF transport aircraft	All: SOC 1946
Boeing B-17F Flying Fortress	41-24577/VK-G Hell's Angels	358th BS, 303rd BG, USAAF 8th Air Force	O/T: W. Wyler 8th AF Doc. (u/u)	N/K
Boeing B-17G Flying Fortress	43-38016/SU-R	544th BS, 384th BG, USAAF 8th Air Force	Actor: 'B-Baker' Hollis's B-17G	N/K
Boeing B-17G Flying Fortress	44-6923/DJ-J (Should be:JD-J)	545th BS, 384th BG, USAAF 8th Air Force	Extra: USAAF B-17G	Crashed 4/6/45
Boeing B-17G Flying Fortress	44-6909/---H (Should be:BK-H)	546th BS, 384th BG, USAAF 8th Air Force	Extra: USAAF B-17G	N/K
Boeing B-17G Flying Fortress	42-30757/SO-L	547th BS, 384th BG, USAAF 8th Air Force	Extra: USAAF B-17G	Crashed 05/45

Boeing B-17G Flying Fortress	x 9	384th Bomb' Group, USAAF 8th Air Force	Extras: B-17s fly-over on Raid	All: SOC 1949
Boeing B-17G Flying Fortress	x 10	384th Bomb' Group, USAAF 8th Air Force	Extras: B-17s return from Raid	All: SOC 1949
Boeing B-17G Flying Fortress	x 3	384th Bomb' Group, USAAF 8th Air Force	F/G: To B-17s in return from Raid	All: SOC 1949
Boeing B-17G Flying Fortress	x 4	384th Bomb' Group, USAAF 8th Air Force	Extras: USAAF B-17s taxying	All: SOC 1949
Boeing B-17G Flying Fortress	x 2	384th Bomb' Group, USAAF 8th Air Force	Extras: USAAF B-17s taxying	All: SOC 1949
Bristol Blenheim Mk.II	'-----/PJ-A'	Finnish Air Force	Actor: RAF Blenheim I	All: SOC 1957
Bristol Blenheim Mk.II	'-----/PJ-B'	Finnish Air Force	Extra: RAF Blenheim I	All: SOC 1957
Bristol Blenheim Mk.II	'-----/PJ-H'	Finnish Air Force	Actor: John Mills' Blenheim	All: SOC 1957
Bristol Blenheim Mk.II	Unid.	Finnish Air Force	Extra: RAF Blenheim I	All: SOC 1957
Bristol Blenheim Mk.II	Unid.	Finnish Air Force	Extra: RAF Blenheim I	All: SOC 1957
Douglas Boston Mk.IIIA	-----/OA-B	342 Sqn, Free French Air Force	Actor: RAF Boston	All: SOC 1945
Douglas Boston Mk.IIIA	-----/OA-P	342 Sqn, Free French Air Force	Actor: RAF Boston	All: SOC 1945
Douglas Boston Mk.IIIA	-----/OA-T	342 Sqn, Free French Air Force	Actor: RAF Boston	All: SOC 1945
Hawker Hurricane Mk.IIc	-----/HQ-H	56 OTU, RAF	Extra: RAF Hurricane	All: SOC 1947
Hawker Hurricane Mk.IIc	-----/HQ-V	56 OTU, RAF	Prop: RAF Hurricane	All: SOC 1947
Hawker Hurricane Mk.IIc	-----/3K-C	1695 BDTF, RCAF	Extra: RAF Hurricane	All: SOC 1947
Hawker Hurricane LF.IV	-----/3K-H	1985 BDTF, RCAF	Extra: RAF Hurricane	All: SOC 1947

JOURNEY TOGETHER (RELEASED: OCTOBER 1945)

AIRCRAFT	I/D OR TOTAL	SOURCE/MATERIAL	ROLE/MATERIAL	STATUS/FATE
Avro 652A Anson Mk.I	MG108/33	RAF Flying Training Command	Itself: Multi-engine trainer	All: SOC 1946
Avro 652A Anson Mk.V	RCAF 6331	3 Air Observers School, RCAF	Itself: RCAF navigator trainer	All: SOC 1962
Avro Lancaster B.I	NF972/OJ-H	149 Sqn, RAF	B/G: '522 Sqn' bomber	All: SOC 1954
Avro Lancaster B.I	NG355/OJ-L, or NG387/OJ-L	149 Sqn, RAF	Actor: '522 Sqn' bomber	All: SOC 1954
Avro Lancaster B.I	Unid.	149 Sqn, RAF	Itself: RAF heavy bomber	All: SOC 1954
Avro Lancaster B.I/B.III	x 77	RAF Bomber Command	Stock: MoI/RAF FPU	All: SOC 1954
Avro Lancaster B.I	x 5	RAF Bomber Command	Stock: MoI/RAF FPU	All: SOC 1954

Avro Lancaster B.I	x 4	149 Sqn, RAF	B/G: '522 Sqn' bombers	All: SOC 1954
Avro Lancaster B.I	x 2	149 Sqn, RAF	B/G: '522 Sqn' bombers	All: SOC 1954
Boeing PT-17 Stearman	1	4 BFTS, Falcon Field, Mesa, Arizona	Itself: USAAC pilot trainer	All: SOC 1946
Boeing PT-17 Stearman	2	4 BFTS, Falcon Field, Mesa, Arizona	Itself: USAAC pilot trainer	All: SOC 1946
Boeing PT-17 Stearman	4	4 BFTS, Falcon Field, Mesa, Arizona	Itself: USAAC pilot trainer	All: SOC 1946
Boeing PT-17 Stearman	8	4 BFTS, Falcon Field, Mesa, Arizona	Itself: USAAC pilot trainer	All: SOC 1946
Boeing PT-17 Stearman	13	4 BFTS, Falcon Field, Mesa, Arizona	Itself: USAAC pilot trainer	All: SOC 1946
Boeing PT-17 Stearman	14	4 BFTS, Falcon Field, Mesa, Arizona	Itself: USAAC pilot trainer	All: SOC 1946
Boeing PT-17 Stearman	23	4 BFTS, Falcon Field, Mesa, Arizona	Itself: USAAC pilot trainer	All: SOC 1946
Boeing PT-17 Stearman	25	4 BFTS, Falcon Field, Mesa, Arizona	Itself: USAAC pilot trainer	All: SOC 1946
Boeing PT-17 Stearman	28	4 BFTS, Falcon Field, Mesa, Arizona	Itself: USAAC pilot trainer	All: SOC 1946
'Boeing PT-17 Stearman'	'13'	RAF Film Production Unit	F/SF: Attenborough's PT-17	Disposed of post-production
de Havilland DH.82A Tiger Moth II	R5035/11	RAF Flying Training Command	Itself: RAF basic trainer	Sold 29/03/1951
de Havilland DH.82A Tiger Moth II	DF188/50	2 Flying Grading School, RAF	Itself: RAF basic trainer	Scrapped 28/03/1950
de Havilland DH.82A Tiger Moth II	-----/3	2 Flying Grading School, RAF	Itself: RAF basic trainer	All: SOC 1951
de Havilland DH.82A Tiger Moth II	-----/14	2 Flying Grading School, RAF	Itself: RAF basic trainer	All: SOC 1951
de Havilland DH.82A Tiger Moth II	-----/53	2 Flying Grading School, RAF	Itself: RAF basic trainer	All: SOC 1951
de Havilland DH.82A Tiger Moth II	-----/101	2 Flying Grading School, RAF	Itself: RAF basic trainer	All: SOC 1951
de Havilland DH.82A Tiger Moth II	-----/107	2 Flying Grading School, RAF	Itself: RAF basic trainer	All: SOC 1951
Douglas Boston Mk.III	Unid.	RAF Bomber Command	Actor: RAF Spotter aircraft	All: SOC 1945
NAA AT-6 Texan	EP-227	4 BFTS, Falcon Field, Mesa, Arizona	Itself: USAAC advanced trainer	All: SOC 1959
NAA AT-6 Texan	x 17	4 BFTS, Falcon Field, Mesa, Arizona	USAAC advanced trainers	All: SOC 1959

NOW IT CAN BE TOLD (RELEASED: 1946)

AIRCRAFT	I/D OR TOTAL	SOURCE/OPERATOR	ROLE/MATERIAL	STATUS/FATE
Armstrong Whitworth Whitley V	x 5	297 Sqn, RAF ?	Stock: COI	All: SOC 1945
Handley Page Halifax A.III	-----/9W-T	296 Sqn, RAF	Actor: Special Duties Halifax	All: SOC 1952

Handley Page Halifax A.III	x 4	296 Sqn, RAF	Scene: RAF Earls Colne ?	All: SOC 1952
Handley Page Halifax A.V.Srs.1a	Unid. Haggis/Big Chief	138 Sqn, RAF	Itself: Special Duties Halifax	All: SOC 1952
Handley Page Halifax B. ?	Unid.	RAF Bomber Command	Stock: COI	All: SOC 1952
Lockheed Hudson V	FK803/MA-N	161 Sqn, RAF	Itself: Special Duties Hudson	N/K
Short Stirling IV	-----/NF-J	138 Sqn, RAF	B/G: RAF Tempsford	All: SOC 1946
Short Stirling IV	Unid.	138 Sqn, RAF	B/G: RAF Tempsford	All: SOC 1946
Short Stirling IV	Unid.	138 Sqn, RAF	B/G: RAF Tempsford	All: SOC 1946
Westland Lysander III	R9125/JR-M	161 Sqn, RAF	Itself: Special Duties Lysander	Extant: RAF Museum, Hendon

THE CAPTIVE HEART (RELEASED: APRIL 1946)

AIRCRAFT	I/D OR TOTAL	SOURCE/OPERATOR	ROLE/MATERIAL	STATUS/FATE
Boeing B-17 Flying Fortress	x 48	USAAF	Stock: MoI/COI	All: SOC 1949

THEIRS IS THE GLORY (RELEASED: OCTOBER 1946)

AIRCRAFT	I/D OR TOTAL	SOURCE/OPERATOR	ROLE/MATERIAL	STATUS/FATE
Airspeed Horsa	Indeterminate number	Royal Air Force	Archive: COI	All: SOC 1945
Airspeed Horsa	111	Royal Air Force	Archive: COI	All: SOC 1945
Airspeed Horsa	297	Royal Air Force	Archive: COI	All: SOC 1945
Airspeed Horsa	304	Royal Air Force	Archive: COI	All: SOC 1945
Airspeed Horsa	402	Royal Air Force	Archive: COI	All: SOC 1945
Airspeed Horsa	D5/Cynthia	Royal Air Force	Archive: COI	All: SOC 1945
Airspeed Horsa	The Obstinate Virgin	Royal Air Force	Archive: COI	All: SOC 1945
Airspeed Horsa	Scrounger's Roost	Royal Air Force	Archive: COI	All: SOC 1945
Airspeed Horsa I	HG790	Royal Air Force	Prop: RAF assault glider	SOC 1945
Airspeed Horsa I	x 3	Royal Air Force	Props: RAF assault gliders	All: SOC 1945
Consolidated B-24 Liberator	x 3	USAAF	Archive: COI	All: SOC 1952
Consolidated B-24 Liberator	Unid.	USAAF	Archive: COI	Shot down 09/44
Curtiss C-46 Commando	Unid.	USAAF	Archive: COI	Shot down 09/44
Douglas C-47 Skytrain	YAW	USAAF	Prop: C-47 Skytrain	All: Retired by 1960s
Douglas C-47 Skytrain	YCW	USAAF	Extra: C-47 Skytrain	All: Retired by 1960s

Douglas C-47 Skytrain	Unid.	USAAF	Archive: COI	Shot down 09/44
Douglas C-47 Skytrain	Unid.	USAAF	Archive: COI	Shot down 09/44
Douglas C-47 Skytrain	Indeterminate number	USAAF	Archive: COI	All: Retired by 1960s
General Aircraft Hamilcar	Unid.	Royal Air Force	Archive: COI	All: SOC 1945
Handley Page Halifax	Unid.	38 Group, RAF	Archive: COI	All: SOC 1952
Hawker Typhoon	x 4	2TAF, RAF	Archive: COI	All: WFU 1945
NAA B-25 Mitchell	Unid.	38 Group, RAF	Archive: COI	All: WFU 1945
Short Stirling IV	-----/ZO-	196 Sqn, RAF	Archive: COI	All: SOC 1946
Short Stirling IV	-----/8Z-G	295 Sqn, RAF	Archive: COI	All: SOC 1946
Short Stirling IV	-----/5G-	299 Sqn, RAF	Archive: COI	All: SOC 1946
Short Stirling	Indeterminate number	38 Group, RAF	Archive: COI	All: SOC 1946
Waco GC-4A Hadrian	x 2	USAAF	Archive: COI	All: SOC 1945

A MATTER OF LIFE AND DEATH (RELEASED: NOVEMBER 1946)

AIRCRAFT	I/D OR TOTAL	SOURCE/OPERATOR	ROLE/MATERIAL	STATUS/FATE
de Havilland Mosquito	Unid.	RAF Coastal Command ?	Itself: Mosquito	All: WFU 1963

SCHOOL FOR SECRETS (RELEASED: DECEMBER 1946)

AIRCRAFT	I/D OR TOTAL	SOURCE/OPERATOR	ROLE/MATERIAL	STATUS/FATE
Bristol Blenheim Mk.II	x 5	Finnish Air Force	O/T: "The Way to the Stars"(u/u)	All: SOC 1957
Handley Page Halifax A.6	RG876/AD-?	113 Sqn, RAF	Prop: RAE trials aircraft	All: SOC 1952
Handley Page Halifax VI	-----/DY-C	102 Sqn, RAF	Archive: CoI	All: SOC 1952
Handley Page Halifax	Unid.	RAF Bomber Command	Archive: CoI	All: SOC 1952
Handley Page Halifax (Tail section)	Unid.	Air Ministry	Prop: crashed Halifax	Scrapped 1946
Heinkel He.111	x 13	Deutsches Luftwaffe	Archive: CoI	All: SOC 1945
Messerschmitt Bf.110C-4	AX772	AFDU	Archive: CoI	Scrapped 1947
Messerschmitt Me.410	Unid.	Deutsches Luftwaffe	Gun camera: CoI	Shot down, date N/K
Short Solent Mk.3	G-AHIU	Ministry of Supply	Prop: Short Sunderland	WFU 14/05/56
Short Sunderland Mk.V	Unid.	N/K	Archive: CoI	All: SOC 1959
Short Sunderland	Unid.	RAF Coastal Command	B/D: Sunderland at mooring	All: SOC 1959
V/S Spitfire Mk.II	Unid.	RAF Fighter Command	Archive: CoI	All: SOC 1945
V/S Spitfire Mk.IIa	P8441	RAE Farnborough	Archive: CoI	SOC 30/12/44
V/S Spitfire Mk.IIa	-----/ZD-	222 Sqn, RAF	Archive: CoI	All: SOC 1945
V/S Spitfire Mk.IIa	-----/ZD-	222 Sqn, RAF	Archive: CoI	All: SOC 1945
V/S Spitfire HF.IX	x 3	Royal Air Force	Archive: CoI	All: SOC 1950
V/S Spitfire LF.IX	x 3	Royal Air Force	Archive: CoI	All: SOC 1950

AGAINST THE WIND (RELEASED: 1948)

AIRCRAFT	I/D OR TOTAL	SOURCE/OPERATOR	ROLE/MATERIAL	STATUS/FATE
Avro Anson C.19	Unid.	Royal Air Force	Prop: Special Duties aircraft	All: SOC 1968
Handley Page Halifax V	-----/NF-T	138 Sqn, RAF	O/T: "Now It Can Be Told"	All: SOC 1952
Handley Page Halifax A.9	RT901/G	Royal Air Force	Actor: No.138 Sqn aircraft	All: SOC 1952
Westland Lysander III	R9125/JR-M	161 Sqn, RAF	O/T: "Now It Can Be Told"	Extant: RAF Museum, Hendon
'Westland Lysander' (Partial F/S facsimile)	'KY-L'	Ealing Film studios	F/SF: Lysander	Disposed of post-production?

LANDFALL (RELEASED: OCTOBER 1949)

AIRCRAFT	I/D OR TOTAL	SOURCE/OPERATOR	ROLE/MATERIAL	STATUS/FATE
Avro 652A Anson Mk.X	NK583/'MK-L'	Royal Air Force or Air Ministry	Actor: Coastal Command Anson	All: SOC 1949
Avro 652A Anson Mk.X	Unid.	Royal Air Force or Air Ministry	Extra: Coastal Command Anson	All: SOC 1949
Avro 652A Anson Mk.X	Unid.	Royal Air Force or Air Ministry	Extra: Coastal Command Anson	All: SOC 1949
Avro 652A Anson Mk.X	Unid.	Royal Air Force or Air Ministry	Extra: Coastal Command Anson	All: SOC 1949
Vickers Wellington XVI ?	Unid.	Royal Air Force	Actor: missile test aircraft	All: SOC 1953
V/S Spitfire	x 5	Royal Air Force	B/G: at North Weald?	All: SOC 1956

THEY WERE NOT DIVIDED (RELEASED: MARCH 1950)

AIRCRAFT	I/D OR TOTAL	SOURCE/OPERATOR	ROLE/MATERIAL	STATUS/FATE
Armstrong Whitworth Whitley	Unid.	Royal Air Force	Archive: COI	All: SOC 1945
Douglas B-26 Marauder	x 35	USAAF	Archive: COI	All: SOC 1947
Douglas C-47A Skytrain	Unid.	MATS, United States Air Force	Prop: USAAF C-47 Skytrain	All: Retired by 1960s
Douglas C-47A Skytrain	Unid.	N/K	Prop: USAAF C-47 Skytrain	All: Retired by 1960s
Douglas C-47A Skytrain	Unid.	USAAF	Archive: COI	All: Retired by 1960s
Douglas C-47A Skytrain	x 34	USAAF	Archive: COI	All: Retired by 1960s
Hawker Typhoon	Unid.	2TAF, Royal Air Force	Archive: COI	All: SOC 1945
Hawker Typhoon	x 4	2TAF, Royal Air Force	Archive: COI	All: SOC 1945

ODETTE (RELEASED: OCTOBER 1950)

AIRCRAFT	I/D OR TOTAL	SOURCE/OPERATOR	ROLE/MATERIAL	STATUS/FATE
Auster 6A	Unid.	N/K	Actor: Special Duties Lysander	N/K
Boeing B-17G Flying Fortress	x 14	USAAF 8th Air Force	Archive: IWM	All: SOC 1949
Boeing B-17G Flying Fortress	x 8	USAAF	Archive: IWM ?	All: SOC 1949
Douglas Boston IIIA	-----/OA-L	342 (Free French) Sqn, Royal Air Force	Archive: IWM	All: SOC 1945
Fairchild F-24W Argus II	Unid.	N/K	Actor: Special Duties Lysander	N/K
Handley Page Halifax II/I	Unid.	Royal Air Force	Archive: IWM	All: WFU 1945
Handley Page Halifax II/I	Unid.	Royal Air Force	Archive: IWM	All: WFU 1945
Handley Page Halifax II/I	Unid.	Royal Air Force	Archive: IWM	All: WFU 1945
Handley Page Halifax II/I	Unid.	Royal Air Force	Archive: IWM	All: WFU 1945
Handley Page Halifax II/I	Unid.	Royal Air Force	Archive: IWM	All: WFU 1945
Handley Page Halifax II/I	Unid.	Royal Air Force	Archive: IWM	All: WFU 1945
Handley Page Halifax A.9	RT901/G	Royal Air Force	O/T: "Against The Wind"	All: SOC 1952
Martin B-26 Marauder	x 7	N/K	Archive: IWM	All: USAAF SOC 1946
NAA B-25 Mitchell	x 4	Royal Air Force	Archive: IWM	All: SOC 1945
V/S Spitfire Mk.V	Unid.	Royal Air Force	Archive: IWM	All: WFU 1944
V/S Spitfire Mk.IX	x 12	RAF Fighter Command	Archive: IWM	All: SOC 1950

THE DESERT FOX (HOLLYWOOD 'BRITISH' WAR FILM. RELEASED: OCTOBER 1951, USA)

AIRCRAFT	I/D OR TOTAL	SOURCE/OPERATOR	ROLE/MATERIAL	STATUS/FATE
Curtiss P-40 Warhawk	x 17	United States Army Air Force	Archive: US source	All: SOC 1945
Douglas C-47 Skytrain	x 45	United States Army Air Force	Archive: US source	All: Retired by 1960s
Grumman TBM-3 Avenger	Unid.	United States Navy	Archive: US source	All: Retired by 1960s
V/S Spitfire HF.IX	Unid.	Armee de l'Air	Actor: RAF Spitfire Mk.IX	All: SOC 1950
V/S Spitfire LF.IXe	Unid.	Armee de l'Air	Actor: RAF Spitfire Mk.IX	All: SOC 1950

ANGELS ONE FIVE (RELEASED: MARCH 1952)

AIRCRAFT	I/D OR TOTAL	SOURCE/OPERATOR	ROLE/MATERIAL	STATUS/FATE
Avro Anson C.12	PH606	RAF Training Command	Prop and camera aircraft	All: SOC 1968
Hawker Hurricane Mk.I	L1591	RAF Air Historical Branch, sold to Templar Film Studios	Studio Prop: cockpit shots	Broken up and disposed of after filming

Hawker Hurricane Mk.I	L1592	RAF Air Historical Branch	Prop: at RAF Kenley	Extant: London Science Museum
Hawker Hurricane Mk.I	P2617	RAF Air Historical Branch	Actor: Septic's Hurricane	Extant: RAF Museum, Hendon
Hawker Hurricane Mk.IIb	544	Portuguese Air Force	Extra: RAF Hurricane	All: SOC 1954
Hawker Hurricane Mk.IIb	554	Portuguese Air Force	Extra: RAF Hurricane	All: SOC 1954
Hawker Hurricane Mk.IIc	600	Portuguese Air Force	Extra: RAF Hurricane	All: SOC 1954
Hawker Hurricane Mk.IIc	601	Portuguese Air Force	Extra: RAF Hurricane	All: SOC 1954
Hawker Hurricane Mk.IIc	624	Portuguese Air Force	Extra: RAF Hurricane	All: SOC 1954
Hawker Hurricane Mk.IIc	LF363	Station Flt, RAF Hendon	Extra: RAF Hurricane	Extant: RAF BBMF
Hawker Hurricane Mk.IIc	PZ865	Hawker Aircraft Co., Langley	Actor: Septic's Hurricane	Extant: RAF BBMF
Messerschmitt Bf.110G-4 1	80580/3C+BA	NJG.4, Luftwaffe Air Ministry Collection	Prop: shot down Bf.110	Buried 1951
Noorduyn AT-16 Harvard T.2B	FX311	RAF Training Command	Extra: at RAF Kenley	All: WFU 1952
Noorduyn AT-16 Harvard T.2B	Unid.	RAF Training Command	Extra: at RAF Kenley	All: WFU 1952
V/S Spitfire Mk.I	x 6	RAF Fighter Command	Archive: COI	All: SOC 1945
V/S Spitfire Mk.Vb ?	BL614 ?	RAF Instructional Airframe ?	Prop: at RAF Kenley	Extant: RAF Museum, Hendon
V/S Spitfire Mk.Vb ?	EP120 ?	RAF Instructional Airframe ?	Prop: at RAF Kenley	Extant: TFC, Duxford

GIFT HORSE (RELEASED: JULY 1952)

AIRCRAFT	I/D OR TOTAL	SOURCE/OPERATOR	ROLE/MATERIAL	STATUS/FATE
Bristol Blenheim Mk.II	x 5	Finnish Air Force	O/T: "The Way to the Stars"	All: SOC 1957
Bristol Blenheim Mk.IV	x 2	RAF Coastal Command	Archive: COI RAF FPU	All: SOC 1944
Junkers Ju.87 Stuka	Unid.	Deutsches Luftwaffe	Archive: COI	All: SOC 1945
Junkers Ju.87 Stuka	Unid.	Deutsches Luftwaffe	Archive: COI	All: SOC 1945
V/S Spitfire Mk.I	Unid.	RAF Fighter Command	Archive: COI	Shot down 1940

APPOINTMENT IN LONDON (RELEASED: FEBRUARY 1953)

AIRCRAFT	I/D OR TOTAL	SOURCE/OPERATOR	ROLE/MATERIAL	STATUS/FATE
Avro Lancaster B.I	-----/OL-F	83 Sqn, Royal Air Force	Stock: COI	N/K
Avro Lancaster B.I	TW862/'IH-S'	RAF Upwood Wing	Actor: Lancaster 'S - Sugar'	SOC by 1955
Avro Lancaster B.VII	NX673/'IH-B'	RAF Upwood Wing	Actor: Lancaster 'B - Baker'	SOC by 1955

Avro Lancaster B.VII	NX782/'IH-V'	RAF UpwoodWing	Actor: Lancaster 'V - Victor'	SOC by 1955
Avro Lancaster B.VII ?	NX679/'IH-C' ?	RAF Upwood Wing ?	Extra: Lancaster coded 'IH-C'	N/K
Avro Lincoln B.I	Unid.	RAF Bomber Command	Extra: Lancaster	SOC by 1955
Avro Lincoln B.II	RF289	RAF Upwood Wing	Prop: Lancaster	SOC by 1955
Avro Lincoln B.II	RF344	RAF Upwood Wing	Prop: Lancaster	SOC by 1955
Avro Lincoln B.II	Unid.	RAF Upwood Wing	Extra: Lancaster	SOC by 1955
Avro Lincoln B.II	Unid.	RAF Upwood Wing	Extra: Lancaster	SOC by 1955
Avro Lincoln B.II	Unid.	RAF Upwood Wing	Extra: Lancaster	SOC by 1955
de Havilland DH.82A Tiger Moth II	T7187	RAF Training Command	Actor: Station 'hack'	Extant: G-AOBX privately owned
Focke Wulf FW.190	Unid.	Deutsches Luftwaffe	Stock: COI	All: SOC 1945
Focke Wulf FW.190	x 3	Deutsches Luftwaffe	Stock: COI	All: SOC 1945
Messerschmitt Bf.109D	x 2	Deutsches Luftwaffe	Stock: COI	All: SOC 1945

THE DESERT RATS (HOLLYWOOD 'BRITISH' WAR FILM. RELEASED: MAY 1953, USA)

AIRCRAFT	I/D OR TOTAL	SOURCE/OPERATOR	ROLE/MATERIAL	STATUS/FATE
Grumman TBM-3 Avenger	Unid.	United States Navy	O/T: "The Desert Fox"	All: Retired by 1960s
V/S Spitfire HF.IX	Unid.	Armee de l'Air	O/T: "The Desert Fox"	All: SOC 1950
V/S Spitfire LF.IXe	Unid.	Armee de l'Air	O/T: "The Desert Fox"	All: SOC 1950

MALTA STORY (RELEASED: JUNE 1953)

AIRCRAFT	I/D OR TOTAL	SOURCE/OPERATOR	ROLE/MATERIAL	STATUS/FATE
Avro Tudor I	G-AGRI	Ministry of Civil Aviation	B/G: War Office Contract	WFU: 11/12/58
Avro Tudor I	G-AGRJ	Ministry of Civil Aviation	B/G: War Office Contract	WFU: 11/12/58
Bristol Beaufighter	-----/2-O	Royal Air Force	Archive: IWM	All: SOC 1959
Bristol Beaufighter	Unid.	Royal Air Force	Archive: IWM	All: SOC 1959
Bristol Beaufort Mk.I	-----/TU-Z	1 Torpedo Unit, RAF	Archive: IWM	All: SOC 1945
Bristol Beaufort Mk.I	-----/Z	Royal Air Force	Archive: IWM	All: SOC 1945
Bristol Beaufort Mk.I	-----/-D-T	Royal Air Force	Archive: IWM	All: SOC 1945
Bristol Beaufort Mk.I	Unid.	Royal Air Force	Archive: IWM	All: SOC 1945
Bristol Beaufort Mk.I	Unid.	Royal Air Force	Archive: IWM/ RAF FPU	All: SOC 1945
Bristol Beaufort Mk.I	x 2	1 Torpedo Unit, RAF	Archive: IWM	All: SOC 1945
Bristol Blenheim Mk.V	Unid.	Royal Air Force	Archive: IWM/ RAF FPU	All: SOC 1944
Consolidated B-24 Liberator	Unid.	United States Army Air Force	Archive: IWM	All: SOC 1953
Douglas C-47 Dakota III	Unid.	Royal Air Force	Archive: IWM	All: SOC by 04/04/1970

Fairey Albacore Mk.I	Unid.	Air Ministry Storage ?	Prop: Torpedo bomber	All: SOC 1945
Fairey Firefly AS.5 (Wings, centre section)	Unid.	Fleet Air Arm	Prop: wreckage	All: SOC 1958
Junkers Ju.87 Stuka	Unid.	Deutsches Luftwaffe	Archive: IWM	All: SOC 1945
Junkers Ju.87 Stuka	x 3	Deutsches Luftwaffe	Archive: IWM	All SOC 1945
Junkers Ju.87 Stuka	x 2	Deutsches Luftwaffe	Archive: IWM	All SOC 1945
Junkers Ju.87 Stuka (Wing section)	Unid.	Deutsches Luftwaffe	Archive: IWM	Shot down Malta 1942
Junkers Ju.88	Unid.	Deutsches Luftwaffe	Archive: IWM	All: SOC 1945
Junkers Ju.88	Unid.	Deutsches Luftwaffe	Archive: IWM	Shot down ?
Junkers Ju.88	Unid.	Deutsches Luftwaffe	Archive: IWM	Shot down ?
Junkers Ju.88A-6	6073/M2+MK HM509	II/KGr.106, Luftwaffe 1426 Enemy Aircraft Flt	O/T: "In Which We Serve"	Captured 26/11/41 W/O 19/11/44
Macchi MC.202	'20'	Regia Aeronautica	Archive: IWM	All: SOC 1944
Messerschmitt Bf.109E (Burning airframe)	Unid.	Deutsches Luftwaffe	Archive: IWM	All: SOC 1945
Messerschmitt Me.410 ? (Burning airframe)	Unid.	Deutsches Luftwaffe	Archive: IWM	All: SOC 1945
Savoia-Marchetti SM.79II Sparveiro	Unid.	Regia Aeronautica	Archive: IWM	All: SOC 1944
Savoia-Marchetti SM.79II Sparveiro	Unid.	Regia Aeronautica	Archive: IWM	All: SOC 1944
Vickers Wellington T.10	HF626 or NB113	No.3 Overseas Ferry, Unit, RAF Abingdon	Prop: Wellington bomber	SOC 1953
V/S Seafire F.XVII (Wing, fuselage, tail)	SX---/133	Fleet Air Arm	Prop: wreckage	All: WFU 1951
V/S Spitfire Mk.I or II	x 3	RAF Fighter Command	Archive: IWM	All: SOC 1945
V/S Spitfire Mk.II	x 11	RAF Fighter Command	Archive: IWM	All: SOC 1945
V/S Spitfire Mk.II	x 8	RAF Fighter Command	Archive: IWM	All: SOC 1945
V/S Spitfire Mk.V	--536/J	RAF Fighter Command	Archive: IWM	All: WFU 1944
V/S Spitfire Mk.V	Unid.	RAF Fighter Command	Archive: IWM	All: WFU 1944
V/S Spitfire Mk.Vb	x 9	Overflying HMS Furious	Archive: IWM	All: WFU 1944
V/S Spitfire Mk.Vb	x 3	Launched off HMS Furious	Archive: IWM	All: WFU 1944
V/S Spitfire Mk.Vb	-----/C	1425 Sqn, RAF Ta'Qali	Archive: IWM	All: WFU 1944
V/S Spitfire Mk.Vb	-----/Z	1425 Sqn, RAF Ta'Qali	Archive: IWM	All: WFU 1944
V/S Spitfire Mk.Vb	Unid.	1425 Sqn, RAF Ta'Qali	Archive: IWM	All: WFU 1944
V/S Spitfire Mk.Vb	Unid.	1435 Sqn, RAF Luqa	Archive: IWM	All: WFU 1944
V/S Spitfire Mk.Vb	Unid.	1435 Sqn, RAF Luqa	Archive: IWM	All: WFU 1944
V/S Spitfire Mk.Vb	Unid.	Royal Air Force	Archive: IWM	All: WFU 1944
V/S Spitfire LF.XVI	TE178	Air Ministry Storage	Extra: Malta Spitfire	Sold for scrap 15/05/56
V/S Spitfire LF.XVI	TE241	Air Ministry Storage	Extra: Malta Spitfire	Sold for scrap 28/11/53
V/S Spitfire LF.XVIe	RW352	Air Ministry Storage	Extra: Malta Spitfire	Sold for scrap 05/04/57
V/S Spitfire LF.XVIe	TB245	Air Ministry Storage	Actor: PR Spitfire	Sold for scrap 15/05/56
'V/S Spitfire'	Facsimile	Theta Film	Prop: wreckage	Disposed of after filming

THE RED BERET (RELEASED: AUGUST 1953)

AIRCRAFT	I/D OR TOTAL	SOURCE/OPERATOR	ROLE/MATERIAL	STATUS/FATE
Bristol Beaufighter TT.10	Unid.	No.5 CAACU, RAF Llanbedr	Prop: Luftwaffe Junkers Ju.88	All: SOC 1959
de Havilland DH.82A Tiger Moth II	Unid.	ATC or RAF Abingdon Station Flight	Prop: RAF trainer	N/K
Douglas C-47A Dakota III	'HJ252/E'	l'Armee de l'Air	Prop: USAAF C-47 Skytrain	N/K
Douglas C-47A Dakota III	'NU-'	N/K	Prop: USAAF C-47 Skytrain	N/K
Douglas C-47B Dakota IV	Unid.	Royal Canadian Air Force	Actor: USAAF C-47 Skytrain	All: SOC 1989
Douglas C-47A Skytrain	43-16048	United States Air Forces in Europe	Actor: USAAF C-47 Skytrain	All: Retired by 1960s
Douglas C-47A Skytrain	Unid.	United States Air Forces in Europe	Prop: USAAF C-47 Skytrain	All: Retired by 1960s
Douglas C-47	Unid.	N/K	Prop: USAAF C-47 Skytrain	N/K
Douglas C-47 Skytrain	x 12	United States Army Air Force	Archive: possibly Dept. of Air Force	All: Retired by by 1960s
Douglas C-47 Skytrain	x 7	United States Army Air Force	Archive: possibly Dept. of Air Force	All: Retired by by 1960s
Fairchild C-119 Flying Boxcar	x 3	United States Air Forces in Europe	Stock: COI or early MoD	All: SOC 1962
Handley Page Hastings C.1	TG602	RAF Transport Command	Actor: USAAF C-47 Skytrain	Crashed Fayid, Egypt, 12/1/53
Handley Page Hastings C.1	Unid.	RAF Transport Command	Actor: RAF Wellington	All: SOC 1968
Handley Page Hastings C.1	Unid.	RAF Transport Command	Actor: USAAF C-47 Skytrain	All: SOC 1968
Vickers Wellington T.10	HF626	No.3 Overseas Ferry Unit, RAF Abingdon	Actor: RAF Wellington	SOC 1953
Vickers Wellington T.10	NB113	No.3 Overseas Ferry Unit, RAF Abingdon	Actor: RAF Wellington	SOC 1953
Vickers Wellington T.10	Unid.	No.3 Overseas Ferry Unit, RAF Abingdon	Actor: RAF Wellington	SOC 1953
Vickers Wellington T.10	-----/FF-KP	1 ANS, RAF Flying Training Command	Extra: RAF Wellington	SOC 1953
Vickers Wellington T.10	Unid.	1.ANS, RAF Flying Training Command	Extra: RAF Wellington	SOC 1953
Vickers Wellington T.10	Unid.	1.ANS, RAF Flying Training Command	Extra: RAF Wellington	SOC 1953
Vickers Wellington T.10	Unid.	1.ANS, RAF Flying Training Command	Extra: RAF Wellington	SOC 1953

THEY WHO DARE (RELEASED: 1954)

AIRCRAFT	I/D OR TOTAL	SOURCE/OPERATOR	ROLE/MATERIAL	STATUS/FATE
Savoia-Marchetti SM.79L Sparviero	L-111	Lebanese Air Force	Actor: German/ Italian bomber	Extant: in Italy

329

Savoia-Marchetti SM.79L Sparviero	L-112	Lebanese Air Force	Actor: German/ Italian bomber	Extant:Italian Air Force Museum
Savoia-Marchetti SM.79L Sparviero	L-113	Lebanese Air Force	Prop: German/ Italian bomber	Extant: Museo dell'Aero- nautical Gianni Caproni
Savoia-Marchetti SM.79L Sparviero	L-114	Lebanese Air Force	Prop: German/ Italian bomber	Extant: in Israel

THE PURPLE PLAIN (RELEASED: SEPTEMBER 1954)

AIRCRAFT	I/D OR TOTAL	SOURCE/OPERATOR	ROLE/MATERIAL	STATUS/FATE
Avro Anson C.19	TX181	RAF Negombo, Ceylon ?	Itself	N/K
de Havilland DH.98 Mosquito T.3	-----/Z	RAF Negumbo scrapyard	Prop: Mosquito on airstrip	WFU 1954
de Havilland DH.98 Mosquito PR.34	Unid. 'FP136/TF510'	81 Sqn, RAF Seletar, Singapore	Actor: Forrester's Mosquito	N/K
de Havilland DH.98 Mosquito PR.34	Unid.	RAF Negombo scrapyard	Prop: crashed Mosquito	WFU: remains destroyed in film
NAA AT-6C Harvard 2B	Unid.	RAF Negombo, Ceylon ?	Prop: Harvard on airstrip	N/K

THE SEA SHALL NOT HAVE THEM (RELEASED: NOVEMBER 1954)

AIRCRAFT	I/D OR TOTAL	SOURCE/OPERATOR	ROLE/MATERIAL	STATUS/FATE
Avro Lancaster B.VII	NX782	RAF Upwood Wing	O/T: "Appoint- ment in London"	Scrapped 1955 ?
Lockheed Hudson	Unid.	Lockheed Corporation ? For Royal Air Force ?	O/T: Unknown Hollywood film	All: SOC 1945
Lockheed Hudson V	Unid.	Air Ministry storage	Prop: ditched Hudson	Sunk in production ?
Short S.45 Seaford	NJ201	MAEE, Felixstowe	Prop: RAF Sunderland	Sold 1953 to Aquila Airways, wrecked 1956
Short S.45a Solent III	WM759	MAEE, Felixstowe	Prop: RAF Sunderland	Broken up, date N/K
Supermarine Sea Otter I	JM909	MAEE, Felixstowe	Actor: Royal Navy Sea Otter	N/K

THE DAM BUSTERS (RELEASED: MAY 1955)

AIRCRAFT	I/D OR TOTAL	SOURCE/OPERATOR	ROLE/MATERIAL	STATUS/FATE
Avro Anson T.21	Unid.	RAF Flying Training Command	B/G: at RAF Kirton-in-Lindsay	All: SOC 1968
Avro Lancaster B.VII	NX673/'AJ-P'	Air Ministry storage, RAF Aston Down	Actor: 617 Sqn Lancaster 'P - Popsy'	Scrapped 1955 ?

Avro Lancaster B.VII	NX679 'ED932/AJ-G	Air Ministry storage, RAF Aston Down	Actor: 617 Sqn Lancaster 'G - George'	Scrapped 1956 ?
Avro Lancaster B.VII	NX739	A&AEE, Boscombe Down	2nd Camera aircraft	Scrapped 02/57
Avro Lancaster B.VII	NX782/'ZN-G'	Air Ministry storage, RAF Aston Down	Actor: 106 & 617 Sqns Lancaster	Scrapped 1955 ?
Avro Lancaster B.VII	RT686/'AJ-M'	Air Ministry storage, RAF Aston Down	Actor: 617 Sqn Lancaster 'M - Mother'	Scrapped 1955 ?
Avro Lincoln B.II	RF446	Air Ministry storage, RAF Hemswell	B/G: demobbed Lincoln B.II	Scrapped 1955 ?
Avro Lincoln B.II	Unid.	Air Ministry storage, RAF Hemswell	Prop: 617 Sqn Lancaster	All: SOC 1955
Avro Lincoln B.II	Unid.	Air Ministry storage, RAF Hemswell	Prop: 617 Sqn Lancaster	All: SOC 1955
Avro Lincoln B.II	x 3	Air Ministry storage, RAF Hemswell	B/G: demobbed Lincoln B.II	All: SOC 1955
de Havilland DH.98 Mosquito B.IV	DK290/G	Air Ministry A&AEE Boscombe Down	Archive: COI	Grounded 03/12/43
de Havilland DH.98 Mosquito PR.34 ?	Unid.	58 Sqn, RAF Wyton ?	Prop: 'Highball' trials aircraft	All: SOC 1956
English Electric Canberra B.2	Unid.	199 Sqn, RAF Hemswell	Goof: B/G shot	All: SOC 1961
Vickers Wellington III	BJ895/G	Vickers, Ltd	Archive: COI or Vickers, Ltd	All: SOC 1953
Vickers Wellington T.10	MF628	19 MU/RAF Hemswell Station Flight	Camera aircraft & 'Upkeep' trials aircraft	Extant: RAF Museum, Hendon

COCKLESHELL HEROES (RELEASED: NOVEMBER 1955)

AIRCRAFT	I/D OR TOTAL	SOURCE/OPERATOR	ROLE/MATERIAL	STATUS/FATE
Vickers Valetta C.1	Unid.	RAF Transport Command	Stock: RAF Public Relations	All: SOC 1969

A TOWN LIKE ALICE (RELEASED: MARCH 1956)

AIRCRAFT	I/D OR TOTAL	SOURCE/OPERATOR	ROLE/MATERIAL	STATUS/FATE
de Havilland DH.89A Dragon Rapide	VH-AHI or VH-BKR	Connellan Airways, Alice Springs	Itself: 'Bush' airliner	Wfu 1958
de Havilland DH.90 Dragonfly	VH-UTJ	Connellan Airways, Alice Springs	Itself: 'Bush' airliner	Destroyed 9/8/55
Douglas DC-3 Dakota	VH-TAN	Trans-Australian Airlines	Itself: TAA airliner	Scrapped 1978

THE MAN WHO NEVER WAS (RELEASED: MARCH 1956)

AIRCRAFT	I/D OR TOTAL	SOURCE/OPERATOR	ROLE/MATERIAL	STATUS/FATE
de Havilland DH.98 Mosquito FB.VI	'SB-F'	de Havilland Aircraft Co, Hatfield ?	Actor: RAF Mosquito	Export aircraft
de Havilland DH.98 Mosquito FB.VI	'SG-'	de Havilland Aircraft Co, Hatfield ?	Extra: RAF Mosquito	Export aircraft
de Havilland DH.98 Mosquito FB.VI	Unid.	de Havilland Aircraft Co, Hatfield ?	Extra: RAF Mosquito	Export aircraft

REACH FOR THE SKY (RELEASED: JULY 1956)

AIRCRAFT	I/D OR TOTAL	SOURCE/OPERATOR	ROLE/MATERIAL	STATUS/FATE
Avro 504K	D7560	British Science Museum, London	Prop: as CFS Trainer	Extant: London Science Museum
Avro 504K	G-ACNB 'E3404'	Avro, Woodford	Actor: as RAF Cranwell trainer	Extant: Shuttleworth Collection
Bristol F.2B	G-AEPH/D8096	Shuttleworth Collection, Old Warden	Camera Aircraft & Prop	Extant: Shuttleworth Collection
Bristol Blenheim Mk.II	x 5	Finnish Air Force	O/T: "The Way To The Stars"	All: SOC 1957
Bristol Bulldog Mk.IIa	G-ABBB 'K2496'	British Science Museum, London	Prop: static, as itself	Extant: RAF Museum, Hendon
'Bristol Bulldog Mk.IIa'	'K2494'	Angel Productions	F/SF: 23 Sqn Bulldog IIa	Disposed of post-production ?
Dornier Do.17Z-2	2361/F1+FH	1./KG.76, Luftwaffe	Archive: IWM	Shot down 15/09/40
Focke Wulf FW.190	Unid.	Deutsches Luftwaffe	Archive: gun camera footage	Shot down, date N/K
Focke Wulf FW.190	Unid.	Deutsches Luftwaffe	Archive: gun camera footage	Shot down, date N/K
"Hawker Hurricane" ' (F/S Facsimile)	R7141'	Angel Productions	F/SF: static, as R7141/SD-T, SD-W, SD-X	N/K
Hawker Hurricane Mk.I	L1592	RAF Air Historical Branch	Extra: taxyer, as V5276/SD-W, SD-Y	Extant: London Science Museum
Hawker Hurricane Mk.I	P2617	RAF Air Historical Branch	Extra: taxyer, as T4107/SD-P, SD-W, SD-X	Extant: RAF Museum, Hendon
Hawker Hurricane Mk.IIc LF363		Station Flight, RAF Biggin Hill	Actor: flyer, as T4125/SD-K, SD-N, SD-R, SD-W, SD-X	Extant: RAF BBMF
Hawker Hurricane I & II	x 5	Portuguese Air Force	O/T: "Angels One Five"	All: SOC 1954
Heinkel He.111	x 7	Deutsches Luftwaffe	Archive: IWM	All: SOC 1945
Heinkel He.111	x 2	Deutsches Luftwaffe	Archive: IWM	All: SOC 1945

Heinkel He.111	Unid.	Deutsches Luftwaffe	Archive: gun camera footage	Shot down, date N/K
Heinkel He.111	Unid.	Deutsches Luftwaffe	Archive: gun camera footage	Shot down, date N/K
Heinkel He.111H	1G+GT or GY	KG.27, Deutsches Luftwaffe	Archive: IWM	All: SOC 1945
Heinkel He.111H-3	6853/1H+EN AW177	II/KG.26, Luftwaffe 1426 Enemy Aircraft Flt	O/T: "The First Of The Few"	Captured 09/02/40 Crashed 11/43
Junkers Ju.87	Unid.	Deutsches Luftwaffe	Archive: IWM	All: SOC 1945
Junkers Ju.87B	6U+AC	ZG.1, Luftwaffe ?	Archive: IWM	All: SOC 1945
Junkers Ju.88 ?	Unid.	Deutsches Luftwaffe ?	Archive: IWM	Shot down, date N/K
Messerschmitt Bf.109	x 21	Deutsches Luftwaffe	Archive: IWM	All: SOC 1945
Messerschmitt Bf.109	Unid.	Deutsches Luftwaffe	Archive: gun camera footage	Shot down, date N/K
Messerschmitt Bf.109	Unid.	Deutsches Luftwaffe	Archive: gun camera footage	Shot down, date N/K
Messerschmitt Bf.109E-4	Unid.	Deutsches Luftwaffe	Archive: IWM	All: SOC 1945
Messerschmitt Bf.109G	'G' / 'E'	Deutsches Luftwaffe	Archive: IWM	All: SOC 1945
Messerschmitt Bf.110	x 9	Deutsches Luftwaffe	Archive: IWM	All: SOC 1945
Messerschmitt Bf.110C-4	2177/5F+CM AX772	4(F)/14, Luftwaffe AFDU, Royal Air Force	Archive: IWM CFU	Scrapped 11/47
Spartan Arrow	G-ABWP	Shuttleworth Collection, Old Warden	Prop: static, at Woodley Airfield	Extant: private ownership
V/S Spitfire Mk.IIa	P8774	RAE Farnborough	Archive: IWM CFU	SOC 30/12/1944
V/S Spitfire Mk.IIa	P8074/SD-L	501 Sqn, RAF	O/T: "The First Of The Few"	Force landing in Ireland 30/11/41
V/S Spitfire LF.XVIe	RW345	Air Ministry storage	Prop: static, as TA614	Scrapped 1956
V/S Spitfire LF.XVIe	RW352	3 CAACU, RAF	Extra: flyer, as RA617/QV-S	Scrapped 1957
V/S Spitfire LF.XVIe	SL574	3 CAACU, RAF	Extra: flyer, as RV214/QV-R	Extant: Air & Space Museum, San Diego, Ca
V/S Spitfire LF.XVIe	SL745	Air Ministry storage	Prop: static, as TR627/QV-T	Scrapped 1956
V/S Spitfire LF.XVIe	TB293	Air Ministry storage	Prop: static, as RV415/QV-U	Scrapped 1956
V/S Spitfire LF.XVIe	TB863	MGM British Studios (ex-3 CAACU)	Studio prop	Extant: Temora Aviation Museum Australia
V/S Spitfire LF.XVIe	TB885	Air Ministry storage	Prop: static, as R1247/QV-V	Buried RAF Kenley 1958, excavated 1982, storage until 2008, under restoration to fly
V/S Spitfire LF.XVIe	TE288	RAF Instructional Airframe	Extra: taxyer, as AR251/QV-X	Extant: RNZAF Museum, Wigram, NZ

V/S Spitfire LF.XVIe	TE341	Air Ministry storage Sold to Pinewood Studios	Prop: cockpit interior shots	Broken up at Pinewood Studios 1956
V/S Spitfire LF.XVIe	TE358	103 Flying Refresher School, RAF	Extra: flyer, as AR251/QV-X	Scrapped 1957
V/S Spitfire LF.XVIe	TE456	3 CAACU, RAF	Extra: flyer, as TE425/PD-9 (?)	Extant: Auckland War Memorial Museum, NZ

THE BATTLE OF THE RIVER PLATE (RELEASED: NOVEMBER 1956)

AIRCRAFT	I/D OR TOTAL	SOURCE/OPERATOR	ROLE/MATERIAL	STATUS/FATE
de Havilland DH.82A Tiger Moth II	Unid.	Fleet Air Arm (?)	Actor: ship's spotter	N/K
'Fairey Seafox' (Studio miniature)	No I/D	Arcturus Productions	M/T: ship's spotter	Disposed of post-production

ILL MET BY MOONLIGHT (RELEASED: JANUARY 1957)

AIRCRAFT	I/D OR TOTAL	SOURCE/OPERATOR	ROLE/MATERIAL	STATUS/FATE
Morane-Saulnier MS.505 Criquet	Unid.	Armee de l'Air ?	Actor: Luftwaffe Fieseler Storch	N/K

THE BRIDGE ON THE RIVER KWAI (RELEASED: OCTOBER 1957)

AIRCRAFT	I/D OR TOTAL	SOURCE/OPERATOR	ROLE/MATERIAL	STATUS/FATE
Vickers Valetta C.1	Unid.	RAF Far East Air Force	Prop: RAF Dakota	All: SOC 1969

THE ONE THAT GOT AWAY (RELEASED: DECEMBER 1957)

AIRCRAFT	I/D OR TOTAL	SOURCE/OPERATOR	ROLE/MATERIAL	STATUS/FATE
DHC Chipmunk T.10	Unid.	RAF Training Command	B/D: goof	All: SOC 1996
Hawker Hurricane Mk.IIc	LF363	RAF Historic Flight, RAF Biggin Hill	Actor: aircraft von Werra steals	Extant: RAF BBMF
'Messerschmitt Bf.109E-4' (Full-scale facsimile)		The Rank Organisation	F/SF: Bf.109E-4 of JG-3	Destroyed in another film

CARVE HER NAME WITH PRIDE (RELEASED: FEBRUARY 1958)

AIRCRAFT	I/D OR TOTAL	SOURCE/OPERATOR	ROLE/MATERIAL	STATUS/FATE
Blackburn Beverley C.1	Unid.	47 Sqn, RAF Abingdon	Camera ship & SOE jump ship	All: SOC 1969
Blackburn Beverley C.1	Unid.	RAF Transport Command	B/G: goof	All: SOC 1969

DHC Beaver 1	G-AMVU	de Havilland Aircraft Co.	Actor: 161 (SD) Sqn Lysander	Sold to Sierra Leone 1956
Handley Page Halifax V	-----/NF-T	138 (Special Duties) Sqn, Royal Air Force	O/T: "Now It Can Be Told"	All: SOC 1952
Handley Page Halifax A.9	RT901/G	Royal Air Force	O/T: "Against The Wind"	All: SOC 1952

DUNKIRK (RELEASED: MARCH 1958)

AIRCRAFT	I/D OR TOTAL	SOURCE/OPERATOR	ROLE/MATERIAL	STATUS/FATE
Bristol Blenheim Mk.I	Unid.	Royal Air Force	Archive: IWM	All: SOC 1944
Junkers Ju.52/3M	x 3	Deutsches Luftwaffe	Archive: IWM	All: SOC 1945
Junkers Ju.87B	x 6	Deutsches Luftwaffe	Archive: IWM	All: SOC 1945
Junkers Ju.87R	x 3 (inc. +LH/12)	1/StG.1, Luftwaffe	Archive: IWM	All: SOC 1945
Junkers Ju.88A-6	6073/M2+MK	II/KGr.106, Luftwaffe	O/T: "In Which We Serve"2	Captured
	HM509	1426 Enemy Aircraft Flt		6/11/41
				W/0 19/05/44

THE SILENT ENEMY (RELEASED: MARCH 1958)

AIRCRAFT	I/D OR TOTAL	SOURCE/OPERATOR	ROLE/MATERIAL	STATUS/FATE
Avro Shackleton MR.2	WL741	244 Sqn, RAF Gibraltar	Prop: RAF Lancaster	Burnt & scrapped Manston 1987
Avro Shackleton MR.2	WL792/K	244 Sqn, RAF Gibraltar	Prop: RAF Lancaster	Crashed, W/O 14/09/57
Avro Shackleton MR.2	-----/O	244 Sqn, RAF Gibraltar	B/G: RAF Gibraltar	All: WFU 1966
Avro Shackleton MR.2	x 2	244 Sqn, RAF Gibraltar	B/G: RAF Gibraltar	All: WFU 1966
Handley Page Halifax A.9	RT901/G	Royal Air Force	O/T: "Against The Wind"	All: SOC 1952

THE CAMP ON BLOOD ISLAND (RELEASED: APRIL 1958)

AIRCRAFT	I/D OR TOTAL	SOURCE/OPERATOR	ROLE/MATERIAL	STATUS/FATE
Handley Page Hastings C.1	x 2	RAF Transport Command	Stock: COI	All: SOC 1968
'Messerschmitt Bf.109E-4' (Full-Scale facsimile)		The Rank Organisation	Prop: Crashed US Navy fighter	Destroyed post-filming ?

ICE COLD IN ALEX (RELEASED: JUNE 1958)

AIRCRAFT	I/D OR TOTAL	SOURCE/OPERATOR	ROLE/MATERIAL	STATUS/FATE
Bristol Beaufighter TT.10	RD788	Malta Communications and Target Towing Sqn, RAF Ta'Qali	Actor: RAF fighter-bomber	All: SOC 1959

BATTLE OF THE V1 (RELEASED: AUGUST 1958)

AIRCRAFT	I/D OR TOTAL	SOURCE/OPERATOR	ROLE/MATERIAL	STATUS/FATE
Avro Lancaster	Mass raid	RAF Bomber Command	Archive: IWM	All: SOC 1954
Douglas C-47B Dakota	A65-73/OM-P	37 Squadron, RAAF	Archive: IWM	Extant: Beck Collection, Mareeba, Qld, Australia
Douglas C-47B Dakota	G-AMSU or 'SS	Dan-Air London, Blackbushe	Actor: RAF Dakota	Either, WFU 26/2/1973 or sold to Persia 1968
Fieseler Fi.103 V1	Unid.	FZG.76, Deutsches Luftwaffe	Archive: IWM	All: Captured or destroyed 1945
Fieseler Fi.103 V1	Unid.	FZG.76, Deutsches Luftwaffe	Archive: IWM	Shot down by fighter, 1944 – 1945
Fieseler Fi.103 V1	Unid.	FZG.76, Deutsches Luftwaffe	Archive: IWM	All: Captured or destroyed 1945
Fieseler Fi.103 V1	Unid.	FZG.76, Deutsches Luftwaffe	Archive: IWM	All: Captured or destroyed 1945
Fieseler Fi.103 V1	Unid.	FZG.76, Deutsches Luftwaffe	Archive: IWM	Destroyed, dives into field
Fieseler Fi.103 V1	Unid.	FZG.76, Deutsches Luftwaffe	Archive: IWM	Destroyed, dives into ground
Fieseler Fi.103 V1	Unid.	FZG.76, Deutsches Luftwaffe	Archive: IWM	Shot down by Ack-Ack, Dover
Fieseler Fi.103 V1	Unid.	FZG.76, Deutsches Luftwaffe	Archive: IWM	Destroyed, dives into sea
'Fieseler Fi.103 V1' (Full-Scale facsimile)	No serial	Criterion Films	F/SF: Fieseler Fi.103 V1	Disposed of by Criterion Films
Handley Page Halifax	Unid.	RAF Bomber Command	Archive: IWM	All: SOC 1952
Handley Page Halifax	Unid.	RAF Bomber Command	Archive: IWM	All: SOC 1952

THE KEY (RELEASED: SEPTEMBER 1958)

AIRCRAFT	I/D OR TOTAL	SOURCE/OPERATOR	ROLE/MATERIAL	STATUS/FATE
Junkers Ju.88A-6	6073/M2+MK HM509	II/KGr.106, Luftwaffe 1426 Enemy Aircraft Flt.	O/T: "In Which We Serve"	Captured 26/11/41 W/O 19/05/44

I WAS MONTY'S DOUBLE (RELEASED: OCTOBER 1958)

AIRCRAFT	I/D OR TOTAL	SOURCE/OPERATOR	ROLE/MATERIAL	STATUS/FATE
Avro Shackleton MR.2	Unid.	244 Sqn, RAF Gibraltar	B/G: RAF Gibraltar	All: WFU 1966
Avro York I	G-AHF? 'MW101'	Skyways of London	Actor: Monty's York C.1 MW101	All: WFU 1964
Focke Wulf FW.190A-2	Unid.	Deutsches Luftwaffe	Archive: IWM	All: SOC 1945

Messerschmitt Bf.109E-3	'White 5'	I/JG.26, Deutsches Luftwaffe	Archive: IWM	All: SOC 1945
Messerschmitt Bf.109G-2	Unid.	Messerschmitt GmbH ?	Archive: IWM	All: SOC 1945
V/S Spitfire Ia	-----/WZ-H	19 Sqn, RAF	Archive: IWM	N/K
V/S Spitfire Ia	-----/WZ-S	19 Sqn, RAF	Archive: IWM	N/K
V/S Spitfire Ia	x 3	19 Sqn, RAF	Archive: IWM	All: SOC 1944
V/S Spitfire Ia	x 10	602 Sqn, RAF	O/T: "A Yank in the R.A.F."	All: SOC 1944
V/S Spitfire IIa	x 9	RAF Fighter Command	Archive: IWM	All: SOC 1945

THE TWO-HEADED SPY (RELEASED: NOVEMBER 1958)

AIRCRAFT	I/D OR TOTAL	SOURCE/OPERATOR	ROLE/MATERIAL	STATUS/FATE
Heinkel He.111	x 21	Deutsches Luftwaffe	Archive: IWM	All: SOC 1945
Junkers Ju.87B	x 3	Deutsches Luftwaffe	Archive: IWM	All: SOC 1944
Junkers Ju.87D	Unid.	Deutsches Luftwaffe	Archive: IWM	All: SOC 1945
Junkers Ju.87D-2	Unid.	Deutsches Luftwaffe	Archive: IWM	All: SOC 1945
Junkers Ju.87D-5	x 2	Deutsches Luftwaffe	Archive: IWM	All: SOC 1945
Junkers Ju.88A-4	Unid.	Deutsches Luftwaffe	Archive: IWM	All: SOC 1945
Martin B-26 Marauder	x 6	USAAF	Archive: IWM	All: SOC 1946
Martin B-26 Marauder	x 5	USAAF	Archive: IWM	All: SOC 1946
Martin B-26 Marauder	x 3	USAAF	Archive: IWM	All: SOC 1946
Messerschmitt Bf.110	x 9	Deutsches Luftwaffe	Archive: IWM	All: SOC 1945

OPERATION AMSTERDAM (RELEASED: JANUARY 1959)

AIRCRAFT	I/D OR TOTAL	SOURCE/OPERATOR	ROLE/MATERIAL	STATUS/FATE
Bristol Blenheim II	x 5	Finnish Air Force	O/T: "The Way To The Stars"	All: SOC 1957
Junkers Ju.52/3M	x 3	Deutsches Luftwaffe	Archive: IWM	All: SOC 1945
Junkers Ju.88A-6	6073/M2+MK HM509	II/KGr.106, Luftwaffe 1426 Enemy Aircraft Flt	O/T: "In Which We Serve"	Captured 26/11/41 W/O 19/05/44
Messerschmitt Bf.108D-1	PH-PBC	Schreiner & Co NV, Den Haag	Actor: German Bf.109 fighter	Extant: as D-EHAF

THE ANGRY HILLS (RELEASED: JULY 1959, USA)

AIRCRAFT	I/D OR TOTAL	SOURCE/OPERATOR	ROLE/MATERIAL	STATUS/FATE
Junkers Ju.87 Stuka	x 6	Deutsches Luftwaffe	Archive: IWM	All: SOC 1945

SINK THE BISMARCK! (RELEASED: FEBRUARY 1960)

AIRCRAFT	I/D OR TOTAL	SOURCE/OPERATOR	ROLE/MATERIAL	STATUS/FATE
Consolidated Catalina I	Unid.	RAF Coastal Command	Archive: IWM	All: SOC 1945
Fairey Swordfish Mk.II	G-AJVH LS326/'5A'	Fairey Aviation Co., White Waltham	Actor: 825 and 818 Sqn aircraft	Extant: RNHF, RNAS Yeovilton
Fairey Swordfish Mk.III	NF389 'LS423/5B'	781 Sqn, Fleet Air Arm, RNAS Lee-on-Solent	Actor: 825 and 818 Sqn aircraft	Extant: RNHF, RNAS Yeovilton
V/S Spitfire Mk.IIa	P8074/SD-L	501 Sqn, RAF	O/T: "The First of the Few"	Force landing in Ireland 30/11/41
V/S Spitfire Mk.IIa	P8441	RAE Farnborough	Archive: IWM (RAF FPU)	SOC 30/12/1944
V/S Spitfire LF.XVIe	TE341	Pinewood Studios	Prop: Spitfire Cockpit section	Stored, Pinewood Studios
V/S Spitfire	Unid.	RAF Fighter Command	Archive: IWM	N/K

FOXHOLE IN CAIRO (RELEASED: OCTOBER 1960)

AIRCRAFT	I/D OR TOTAL	SOURCE/OPERATOR	ROLE/MATERIAL	STATUS/FATE
Hawker Hurricane Mk.II	Unid.	Royal Air Force	Archive: IWM	Shot down, date N/K
Heinkel He.111F	RD+NZ	Deutsches Luftwaffe	Archive: IWM	All: SOC 1945
Martin Maryland II	Unid.	Royal Air Force	Archive: IWM	Shot down, date N/K
Messerschmitt Bf.109F	2+-	Fliegerfuhrer Afrika, Deutsches Luftwaffe	Archive: IWM	All: SOC 1945
Messerschmitt Bf.109F	Unid.	Fliegerfuhrer Afrika, Deutsches Luftwaffe	Archive: IWM	All: SOC 1945
Messerschmitt Bf.110E	3U+GT	IX/ZG.26, Deutsches Luftwaffe	Archive: IWM	All: SOC 1945

THE GUNS OF NAVARONE (RELEASED: ROYAL PREMIER, APRIL 1961)

AIRCRAFT	I/D OR TOTAL	SOURCE/OPERATOR	ROLE/MATERIAL	STATUS/FATE
Armstrong Whitworth Whitley	x 2	Royal Air Force	Archive: IWM	All: SOC 1945
Avro Lancaster B.I	PA474	College of Aeronautics, Cranfield	Pattern: studio M/T Lancaster	Extant: BBMF, RAF Coningsby
Bristol Beaufort	x 7	Royal Air Force	Archive: IWM	All: SOC 1945
Consolidated PBY-5 Catalina	'5583/Z' ?	N/K	Actor: RAF Catalina	N/K
Douglas Boston Mk.III	x 13	RAF Bomber Command	Archive: IWM	All: SOC 1945
NAA T-6G Texan	x 2	Royal Hellenic Air Force	Extras: 'Stukas'	N/K
Piper L-21B Cub	Unid.	Royal Hellenic Army	Actor: Luftwaffe Henschel Hs.126	N/K
Short Stirling	Unid.	RAF Bomber Command	Archive: IWM	All: SOC 1946
Short Stirling	Unid.	RAF Bomber Command	Archive: IWM	All: SOC 1946
Sikorsky UH-19D Chickasaw	Unid.	Royal Hellenic Army	B/G: 'Henschel HS.126'	N/K

| Vickers Wellington | Unid. | RAF Bomber Command | Archive: IWM | All: SOC 1952 |
| Vickers Wellington | Unid. | RAF Bomber Command | Archive: IWM | All: SOC 1952 |

VERY IMPORTANT PERSON (RELEASED: APRIL 1961)

AIRCRAFT	I/D OR TOTAL	SOURCE/OPERATOR	ROLE/MATERIAL	STATUS/FATE
Vickers Wellington Ic	-----/'B'	XV Sqn, RAF Bomber Command	O/T: "One of our aircraft is missing"	All: SOC 1952

THE VALIANT (INTERNATIONAL 'BRITISH' WAR FILM. RELEASED: JANUARY 1962)

AIRCRAFT	I/D OR TOTAL	SOURCE/OPERATOR	ROLE/MATERIAL	STATUS/FATE
Junkers Ju.88	Unid.	Deutsches Luftwaffe	Archive: IWM ?	All: SOC 1945

THE LONGEST DAY (HOLLYWOOD 'BRITISH' WAR FILM. RELEASED: SEPTEMBER 1962, FRANCE)

AIRCRAFT	I/D OR TOTAL	SOURCE/OPERATOR	ROLE/MATERIAL	STATUS/FATE
Airspeed Horsa (F/S non-flying airframe)	Unid.	20th Century Fox Film Corporation	F/SF: RAF assault glider	N/K
Airspeed Horsa (F/S non-flying airframe)	Unid.	20th Century Fox Film Corporation	F/SF: RAF assault glider	N/K
Douglas AD-4 Skyraider	x 4	United States Navy	Extras: USAF attack aircraft	All: to Vietnam by 1968 or WFU
Nord 1002 Pinguoin II (Messerschmitt Bf.108B)	F-BFYX	Alexandre Renault, Mureaux	Actor: Luftwaffe Bf.109	Extant: private owner, Germany
Nord 1002M Pinguoin II (Messerschmitt Bf.108B)	F-BGVU	Alexandre Renault, Mureaux	Actor: Luftwaffe Bf.109	Lost at sea, off Labrador coast, Canada, 01/1964
SIPA S.12 (Cockpit section)	Unid.	Alexandre Mureaux ?	Studio prop: Bf.109 cockpit	N/K
V/S Spitfire LF.IXb	OO-ARA MH434	COGEA, Middelkirke, Ostend	Reserve or withdrawn ?	Extant: OFMC, Duxford
V/S Spitfire LF.IXb	OO-ARD MH415	COGEA, Middelkirke, Ostend	Actor: Free French Spitfire	Extant: 'Connie' Edwards, Texas
V/S Spitfire LF.IXc	OO-ARB MK297	COGEA, Middelkirke, Ostend	Actor: Free French Spitfire	W/O: hangar fire, Ontario, 15/02/93
V/S Spitfire LF.IXc	OO-ARF MK923	COGEA, Middelkirke, Ostend	Actor: Free French Spitfire	Extant: Museum of Flight, Seattle

THE WAR LOVER (RELEASED: OCTOBER 1962, USA)

AIRCRAFT	I/D OR TOTAL	SOURCE/OPERATOR	ROLE/MATERIAL	STATUS/FATE
Avro Anson C.19	x 6	Southern Comms Sqn, RAF Bovingdon	Based aircraft at Bovingdon	All: SOC 1968
Boeing B-17 Flying Fortress	x 191	USAAF 8th Air Force	Archive: USNAE	All: SOC 1949
Boeing B-17 Flying Fortress	x 40	USAAF 8th Air Force	Archive: USNAE	All: SOC 1949
Boeing B-17 Flying Fortress	x 24	USAAF 8th Air Force	Archive: USNAE	All: SOC 1949
Boeing B-17 Flying Fortress	x 13	USAAF 8th Air Force	Archive: USNAE	All: SOC 1949
Boeing B-17 Flying Fortress	x 10	USAAF 8th Air Force	Archive: USNAE	All: SOC 1949
Boeing B-17 Flying Fortress	x 9	USAAF 8th Air Force	Archive: USNAE	All: SOC 1949
Boeing B-17 Flying Fortress	x 8	USAAF 8th Air Force	Archive: USNAE	All: SOC 1949
Boeing B-17 Flying Fortress	x 8	USAAF 8th Air Force	Archive: USNAE	All: SOC 1949
Boeing B-17 Flying Fortress	x 6	USAAF 8th Air Force	Archive: USNAE	All: SOC 1949
Boeing B-17 Flying Fortress	x 5	USAAF 8th Air Force	Archive: USNAE	All: SOC 1949
Boeing B-17 Flying Fortress	Unid.	USAAF 8th Air Force	Archive: USNAE	All: SOC 1949
Boeing B-17 Flying Fortress	Unid.	USAAF 8th Air Force	Archive: USNAE	All: SOC 1949
Boeing B-17 Flying Fortress	Unid.	USAAF 8th Air Force	Archive: IWM	Shot down, date N/K
Boeing B-17 Flying Fortress	Unid.	USAAF 8th Air Force	Archive: IWM	Shot down, date N/K
Boeing B-17F Flying Fortress	x 8	USAAF 8th Air Force	Archive: USNAE	All: SOC 1949
Boeing B-17F Flying Fortress	x 5, inc: 42-3613/GK-R	91st Bomb' Group, USAAF 8th Air Force	O/T: "Memphis Belle" docu.	All: SOC 1949 N/K
Boeing B-17F Flying Fortress	Unid.	91st Bomb' Group, USAAF 8th Air Force	O/T: "Memphis Belle" docu.	All: SOC 1949
Boeing B-17F Flying Fortress	JJ-	305th Bomb' Group, USAAF 8th Air Force	Archive: USNAE	All: SOC 1949
Boeing B-17F Flying Fortress	Unid.	USAAF 8th Air Force	Archive: USNAE	All: SOC 1949
Boeing B-17G Flying Fortress (Fuselage only)	44-83811	Ex-Israeli Air Force	Prop: studio interior shots	Disposed of post-filming
Boeing B-17G Flying Fortress	x 13	USAAF 8th Air Force	Archive: USNAE	All: SOC 1949
Boeing B-17G Flying Fortress	x 12	USAAF 8th Air Force	Archive: USNAE	All: SOC 1949
Boeing B-17G Flying Fortress	x 10	384th Bomb' Group, USAAF 8th Air Force	O/T: "The Way to the Stars"	All: SOC 1949
Boeing B-17G Flying Fortress	x 6	96th Bomb' Group, USAAF 8th Air Force	Archive: USNAE	All: SOC 1949
Boeing B-17G	x 6	USAAF 8th Air Force	Archive: USNAE	All: SOC 1949

Flying Fortress				
Boeing B-17G	x 5	96th Bomb' Group,	B/D: "Memphis	All: SOC 1949
Flying Fortress		USAAF 8th Air Group	Belle" docu.	
Boeing B-17G	Unid.	USAAF 8th Air Group	Archive: USNAE	All: SOC 1949
Flying Fortress				
Boeing DB-17G	44-83592	1st Experimental Guided	O/T: "Twelve	Controlled crash
Flying Fortress	'42-3613/GK-R'	Missile Group, USAF	O'Clock High"	09/1949
Boeing DB-17G/QB-17G	x 3	1st Experimental Guided	O/T: "Twelve	All: SOC 1959
Flying Fortress		Missile Group, USAF	O'Clock High"	
Boeing VB-17	N9563Z	Aero American Corp	Actor: 324th BS	Extant: Lyon Air
Flying Fortress	(44-83563)		B-17Gs	Museum, Ca.
Boeing PB-1W	N5229V	American Compressed	Actor: 324th BS	Broken up,
	(44-83883)	Steel Corp	B-17Gs	Manston 01/1962
Boeing PB-1W	N5232V	American Compressed	Actor: 324th BS	Broken up,
	(44-83877)	Steel Corp	B-17Gs	Manston 01/1962
Boeing C-97G	Unid.	USAF Strategic Air	Visiting aircraft	All: SOC 1978
Stratofreighter		Command	to Bovingdon	
de Havilland	Unid.	RAF Training Command	Visiting aircraft	All: SOC 1966
Vampire T.11			to Bovingdon	
Focke Wulf FW.190	Unid.	Deutsches Luftwaffe	Archive: IWM	Shot down,
				date N/K
Focke Wulf FW.190	Unid.	Deutsches Luftwaffe	Archive: IWM	Shot down,
				date N/K
Focke Wulf FW.190	Unid.	Deutsches Luftwaffe	Archive: IMW	All: SOC 1945
Lockheed P-38 Lightning	x 2	USAAF 8th Air Force	Archive: USNAE	All: SOC 1949
Messerschmitt Bf.109	x 5	Deutsches Luftwaffe	Archive: IWM	All: SOC 1945
Messerschmitt Bf.109	x 2	Deutsches Luftwaffe	Archive: IWM	All: SOC 1945
Messerschmitt Bf.109	x 2	Deutsches Luftwaffe	Archive: IWM	All: SOC 1945
Messerschmitt Bf.109G	Unid.	Deutsches Luftwaffe	Archive: IWM	All: SOC 1945
Messerschmitt Bf.109G	Unid.	Deutsches Luftwaffe	Archive: source	All: SOC 1945
			N/K	
Republic P-47	x 2	USAAF 8th Air Force	Archive: USNAE	All: SOC 1949
Thunderbolt				
Republic P-47	Unid.	USAAF 8th Air Force	Archive: USNAE	All: SOC 1949
Thunderbolt				
Vickers Varsity T.1	Unid.	RAF Training Command	B/G: visiting	All: SOC 1976
			Bovingdon	
V/S Spitfire	Unid.	RAF AFDU (?)	Archive: USNAE	All: SOC 1945
V/S Spitfire	Unid.	Captured Spitfire (?)	Archive: source	N/K
			N/K	

MYSTERY SUBMARINE (RELEASED: 1963)

AIRCRAFT	I/D OR TOTAL	SOURCE/OPERATOR	ROLE/MATERIAL	STATUS/FATE
Boeing B-17G	x 4	USAAF 8th Air Force	Archive: IWM	All: SOC 1949
Flying Fortress				
Consolidated B-24	x 6	USAAF 8th Air Force	Archive: IWM	All: SOC 1953
Liberator				
Consolidated Catalina I	-----/A:10	RAF Coastal Command	Archive: IWM	All: SOC 1945

THE GREAT ESCAPE (HOLLYWOOD 'BRITISH' WAR FILM. RELEASED: JULY 1963)

AIRCRAFT	I/D OR TOTAL	SOURCE/OPERATOR	ROLE/MATERIAL	STATUS/FATE
Bucker Bu.181 Bestmann	N/K	The Mirisch Corp	Actor: stolen German trainer	Destroyed in film production
CCF Harvard Mk.IV	BF+037 ?/'1-37'	Schule 1, Flugsdienstaffel Technische, Kaufbeuren	Prop: Focke Wulf FW.190	All: sold 1966
CCF Harvard Mk.IV	BF+056 ?/'1-56'	Schule 1, Flugsdienstaffel Technische, Kaufbeuren	Prop: Focke Wulf FW.190	All: sold 1966
CCF Harvard Mk.IV	x 5	Schule 1, Flugsdienstaffel Techniische, Kaufbeuren	Props: Focke Wulf FW.190s	All: sold 1966

TORPEDO BAY (INTERNATIONAL 'BRITISH' WAR FILM. RELEASED: SEPTEMBER 1963, ITALY)

AIRCRAFT	I/D OR TOTAL	SOURCE/OPERATOR	ROLE/MATERIAL	STATUS/FATE
Blackburn Skua	-----/H	Fleet Air Arm	Archive: IWM	All: SOC 1945
Boeing B-17 Flying Fortress	Unid.	United States Army Air Force	Archive: IWM	All: SOC 1949
Lockheed P-38 Lightning	x 2	United States Army Air Force	Archive: IWM	All: SOC 1949
Martin Maryland II	Unid.	Royal Air force	Archive: IWM	All: SOC 1945

THE VICTORS (RELEASED: NOVEMBER 1963)

AIRCRAFT	I/D OR TOTAL	SOURCE/OPERATOR	ROLE/MATERIAL	STATUS/FATE
Douglas C-54D Skymaster	Unid.	Air Transport Command, USAAF	Newsreel: CBS	All: WFU 1972
Douglas R5D-3	BuNo 56509	United States Navy	Newsreel: CBS	Converted to DC-4 N62433
Republic P-47D Thunderbolt	-----/C4-B	388th FS, 365th FG, USAAF	Archive: USNAE	Damaged by C4-N, 03/1944 ?
Republic P-47D Thunderbolt	-----/C4-N	388th FS, 365th FG, USAAF	Archive: USNAE	Collided with C4-B, 03/1944 ?

633 SQUADRON (RELEASED: APRIL 1964)

AIRCRAFT	I/D OR TOTAL	SOURCE/OPERATOR	ROLE/MATERIAL	STATUS/FATE
Avro Anson C.19	x 7	Southern Comms Sqn, RAF Bovingdon	Based aircraft at Bovingdon	All: SOC 1968
de Havilland DH.98 Mosquito T.3	TV959	MoD, donated to IWM Ex-3 CAACU, Exeter	Prop: Mosquito MM398/HT-P	Extant: Under restoration by AvSpecs, NZ
de Havilland DH.98 Mosquito T.3	TW117	MoD/AHB, RAF Henlow Ex-3 CAACU, Exeter	Actor: Mosquito HR115/HT-M	Extant: National Museum of Aviation, Norway

de Havilland DH.98 Mosquito TT.35	G-ASKA RS709	Mirisch Films, Ltd Ex-3 CAACU, Exeter	Actor: Mosquito HR113/HT-D/G	Extant: National Museum of the USAF, Dayton
de Havilland DH.98 Mosquito TT.35	G-ASKB RS712	Mirisch Films, Ltd Ex-3 CAACU, Exeter	Actor: Mosquito RF580/HT-F	Extant: EAA Museum, Oshkosh
de Havilland DH.98 Mosquito TT.35	RS715	Mirisch Films, Ltd Ex-3 CAACU, Exeter	Studio prop and set dressing	Extant: rear fuselage with YAM
de Havilland DH.98 Mosquito TT.35	RS718	Mirisch Films, Ltd Ex-3 CAACU, Exeter	Extra: Mosquito HJ662/HT-C HJ898/HT-G	Destroyed in production 08/08/1963
de Havilland DH.98 Mosquito TT.35	TA639	CFS, RAF Little Rissington	Actor: Mosquito HJ682/HT-B	Extant: RAF Museum, Cosford
de Havilland DH.98 Mosquito TT.35	TA642	MoD Ex-3 CAACU, Exeter	Extra: Mosquito HX835	Destroyed in production 08/1963
de Havilland DH.98 Mosquito TT.35	G-ASKC TA719	Mirisch Films, Ltd Ex-3 CAACU, Exeter	Actor: Mosquito HJ898/HT-G	Extant: IWM, AirSpace Hall, Duxford
de Havilland DH.98 Mosquito TT.35	TA724	Mirisch Films, Ltd Ex-3 CAACU, Exeter	Extra: Mosquito -----/HT-R	Destroyed in production 10/08/1963
de Havilland DH.98 Mosquito TT.35	TJ118	MGM British Film Studio Ex-3 CAACU, Exeter	Studio prop and set dressing	Extant: parts donated to de Havilland AHC
HP Hastings C.1	Unid.	RAF Transport Command	Visiting aircraft to Bovingdon	All: SOC 1968
Miles Messenger 2A	G-AKBO	Dorran Construction, Ltd, Perth	Actor: escape aircraft	Extant: private owner, Cornwall
NAA B-25J Mitchell	N9089Z Moviemaker II	Aero Associates, Ryan Field, Tucson, Az	Camera ship and actor: RAF B-25	Extant: private owner, Booker
Nord 1002 Pinguoin II (Messerschmitt Bf.108B)	F-BFYX	Chartered: John Hawke, RAF Wattisham	Actor: Luftwaffe Bf.109	Extant: private owner, Germany
Nord 1002M Pinguoin II (Messerschmitt Bf.108B)	F-BGVU	Chartered: John Hawke, RAF Wattisham	Actor: Luftwaffe Bf.109	Lost at sea, off Labrador coast, Canada, 01/1964

OPERATION CROSSBOW (RELEASED: MARCH 1965)

AIRCRAFT	I/D OR TOTAL	SOURCE/OPERATOR	ROLE/MATERIAL	STATUS/FATE
Aggregat 4	Unid.	Heeresversuchsanstalt Peenemunde	Archive: RAF PR photograph	Wooden test round, w/o 1945
Aggregat 4/V2		Rocket Propulsion Establishment, Westcott	Itself: Operation Backfire V2	Extant: RAF Museum, Cosford
'Aggragat 4/V2' (Facsimile)	Unid.	MGM British Studios	F/SF: V2 rocket of V2 Division	N/K
Avro Lancaster B.I	PA474	Air Historical Branch, RAF Wroughton	Actor: Operation Hydra Lancaster	Extant: BBMF, RAF Coningsby
Fieseler Fi.103	Unid.	FZG.76, Deutsches Luftwaffe	Archive: RAF PR photograph	Presumed test launch into Baltic

'Fieseler Fi.103' (Facsimile)	Unid.	MGM British Studios	F/SF: Fi.103 prototype	Extant: donated to IWM Duxford
'Fieseler Fi.103R Reichenberg' (Facsimile)	'M23' 'M28'	MGM British Studios	F/SF: Fi.103R Reichenberg	N/K
GAF Jindivik	Unid.	Flight Refuelling	Extra: portraying V1	Presumably expended ?
Martin B-26 Marauder	Unid.	USAAF 8th Air Force	Archive: IWM	All SOC: 1947
V/S Spitfire HF.IXb	G-ASJV MH434	Timothy Davies, Elstree	Actor: PR Spitfire	Extant: OFMC, Duxford
V/S Spitfire PR.XIX	PS853	Battle of Britain Flight, RAF Coltishall	Extra: Spitfire attacking V1	Extant: Rolls-Royce Aero Engines

VON RYAN'S EXPRESS (HOLLYWOOD 'BRITISH' WAR FILM. RELEASED: JUNE 1965, USA)

AIRCRAFT	I/D OR TOTAL	SOURCE/OPERATOR	ROLE/MATERIAL	STATUS/FATE
'Lockheed P-38 Lightning' (facsimile)	No serial	P-R Productions	F/SF: shot down P-38 Lightning	Destroyed on set
Nord 1002 Pinguoin II (Messerschmitt Bf.108B)	Unid.	Alexandre Renault Collection ?	Actor: Luftwaffe Bf.109	N/K
Nord 1002 Pinguoin II (Messerschmitt Bf.108B)	Unid.	Alexandre Renault Collection ?	Actor: Luftwaffe Bf.109	N/K
Nord 1002 Pinguoin II (Messerschmitt Bf.108B)	Unid.	Alexandre Renault Collection ?	Actor: Luftwaffe Bf.109	N/K

THE HEROES OF TELEMARK (RELEASED: NOVEMBER 1965)

AIRCRAFT	I/D OR TOTAL	SOURCE/OPERATOR	ROLE/MATERIAL	STATUS/FATE
Airspeed Horsa I	292	Royal Air Force	Archive: IWM	All: SOC 1945
Airspeed Horsa I	Unid.	Royal Air Force	Archive: IWM	All: SOC 1945
Airspeed Horsa I	Unid.	Royal Air Force	Archive: IWM	All: SOC 1945
Airspeed Horsa I	Unid.	Royal Air Force	Archive: IWM	All: SOC 1945
Boeing B-17 Flying Fortress	x 12	USAAF 8th Air Force	Archive: IWM	All: SOC 1949
Boeing B-17G Flying Fortress	x 6	USAAF 8th Air Force	Archive: IWM	All: SOC 1949
Douglas C-47A Dakota I	Unid.	335 Skv, RNAF	Actor: RAF Dakota	All: WFU 1974
Piper L-18C Super Cub	F-A?	Observer Service, RNAF	Actor: Luftwaffe Henschel Hs.126	All: WFU during 1970s
Short Stirling IV	-----/ZO-	196 Sqn, RAF	Archive: IWM	All: SOC 1946
Short Stirling IV	N/K	196 Sqn, RAF	Archive: IWM	All: SOC 1946
Short Stirling IV	N/K	No.38 Group, RAF	Archive: IWM	All: SOC 1946
Short Stirling IV	N/K	No.38 Group, RAF	Archive: IWM	All: SOC 1946

TRIPLE CROSS (RELEASED: DECEMBER 1966, FRANCE)

AIRCRAFT	I/D OR TOTAL	SOURCE/OPERATOR	ROLE/MATERIAL	STATUS/FATE
Nord 1101 Noralpha	Unid.	Institut Geographique Nationale, Creil	B/G: Luftwaffe Me.208	N/K
SNCAC NC.701 Martinet	Unid.	Institut Geographique Nationale, Creil	Actor: Luftwaffe Siebel Si.204D	WFU: 1960s
SNCAC NC.702 Martinet	Unid.	Institut Geographique Nationale, Creil	B/G: Luftwaffe Siebel Si.204A	WFU: 1960s
SNCAC NC.702 Martinet	Unid.	Institut Geographique Nationale, Creil	B/G: Luftwaffe Siebel Si.204A	WFU: 1960s
SNCAC NC.702 Martinet	Unid.	Institut Geographique Nationale, Creil	B/G: Luftwaffe Siebel Si.204A	WFU: 1960s
SNCAC NC.702 Martinet	Unid.	Institut Geographique Nationale, Creil	B/G: Luftwaffe Siebel Si.204A	WFU: 1960s
SNCAC NC.702 Martinet	Unid.	Institut Geographique Nationale, Creil	B/G: Luftwaffe Siebel Si.204A	WFU: 1960s
V/S Spitfire LF.IXb	MH415	Rousseau Aviation, Dinard	Actor: Spitfire strafing troops	Extant: 'Connie' Edwards, Texas

THE NIGHT OF THE GENERALS (RELEASED: JANUARY 1967)

AIRCRAFT	I/D OR TOTAL	SOURCE/OPERATOR	ROLE/MATERIAL	STATUS/FATE
V/S Spitfire LF.IXb	MH415	Rousseau Aviation, Dinard	Actor: Spitfire strafing Rommel	Extant: 'Connie' Edwards, Texas

TOBRUK (HOLLYWOOD 'BRITISH' WAR FILM. RELEASED: FEBRUARY 1967, USA)

AIRCRAFT	I/D OR TOTAL	SOURCE/OPERATOR	ROLE/MATERIAL	STATUS/FATE
Curtiss P-40E Kittyhawk IA	N1207V	Tallmantz Aviation Inc	Actor: No.112 Sqn P-40E Kittyhawk	Extant: War Eagles Museum, Santa Teresa, New Mexico
Grumman G-21A Goose	Unid.	via Tallmantz Aviation	Actor: 'German' He.115 floatplane	N/K

THE LONG DAY'S DYING (CANNES FILM FESTIVAL, MAY 1968)

AIRCRAFT	I/D OR TOTAL	SOURCE/OPERATOR	ROLE/MATERIAL	STATUS/FATE
Nord 1002 Pinguoin II (Messerschmitt Bf.108)	G-ASTG	Nipper Flying Group, Elstree	Actor: German spotter 'plane	Extant: post-restoration flight 12/2013

ATTACK ON THE IRON COAST (RELEASED: JUNE 1968)

AIRCRAFT	I/D OR TOTAL	SOURCE/OPERATOR	ROLE/MATERIAL	STATUS/FATE
Avro Lancaster B.VII	x 3	Air Ministry	O/T: "The Dam Busters"	Scrapped 1955 ?
Junkers Ju.87 Stuka	x 9	Deutsches Luftwaffe	O/T: "The Next of Kin"	All: SOC 1945
Junkers Ju.87 Stuka	x 2	Deutsches Luftwaffe	O/T: "The Next of Kin"	All: SOC 1945
Junkers Ju.87 Stuka	x 2	Deutsches Luftwaffe	O/T: "The Next of Kin"	All: SOC 1944

WHERE EAGLES DARE (RELEASED: DECEMBER 1968)

AIRCRAFT	I/D OR TOTAL	SOURCE/OPERATOR	ROLE/MATERIAL	STATUS/FATE
Bell 47G Sioux	Unid.	N/K	Actor: Luftwaffe helicopter	N/K
Junkers Ju.52/3mg4e	A-702 HB-HOT	Schweizerische Luftwaffe	Actor: Captured Luftwaffe Ju.52	Extant: JU-AIR, Dubendorf
Noorduyn AT-16 Harvard 2B	U-311	Schweizerische Luftwaffe	Prop: Luftwaffe FW.190	Destroyed in production 03/68
Noorduyn AT-16 Harvard 2B	U-315	Schweizerische Luftwaffe	Prop: Luftwaffe FW.190	Destroyed in production 03/68
Noorduyn AT-16 Harvard 2B	U-317	Schweizerische Luftwaffe	Prop: Luftwaffe FW.190	Destroyed in production 03/68
Noorduyn AT-16 Harvard 2B	U-327	Schweizerische Luftwaffe	Prop: Luftwaffe FW.190	Destroyed in production 03/68

MOSQUITO SQUADRON (RELEASED: JANUARY 1969)

AIRCRAFT	I/D OR TOTAL	SOURCE/OPERATOR	ROLE/MATERIAL	STATUS/FATE
Avro Anson C.19	Unid. 'K 516'	Southern Comms Sqn, RAF Bovingdon	Actor: RAF Anson I	SOC 28/06/68
Avro Anson C.19	Unid.	Southern Comms Sqn, RAF Bovingdon	Actor: RAF Anson I	SOC 28/06/68
Avro Anson C.19	x 3	Southern Comms Sqn, RAF Bovingdon	Based aircraft at Bovingdon	All: SOC 28/06/68
Avro Anson C.19	x 7	Southern Comms Sqn, RAF Bovingdon	O/T: "633 Squadron"	All: SOC by 28/06/68
de Havilland DH.98 Mosquito T.3	G-ASKH RR299/HT-E	Hawker Siddeley Aviation, Hatfield	Actor: 641 Sqn Mosquito	Fatal crash Barton 21/7/96
de Havilland DH.98 Mosquito B.IV	DZ534/P	618 Sqn, Royal Air Force	Archive: source N/K	Ditched Cherbourg 26/7/44
de Havilland DH.98 Mosquito TT.35	G-ASKA RS709	Skyfame Museum, Staverton	Actor: 641 Sqn Mosquito	Extant: National Museum of the USAF, Dayton
de Havilland DH.98 Mosquito TT.35	G-ASKB RS712	Charterer: Thomas Gilbert Mahaddie	Actor: 641 Sqn Mosquito	Extant: EAA Museum, Oshkosh

de Havilland DH.98 Mosquito TT.35	RS718	Mirisch Films, Ltd Ex-3 CAACU	O/T: "633 Squadron"	Destroyed in production 08/08/1963
de Havilland DH.98 Mosquito TT.35	G-AWJV TA634	Liverpool Corporation, Speke	Actor: 641 Sqn Mosquito	Extant: DH Aircraft Heritage Centre
de Havilland DH.98 Mosquito TT.35	TA639	CFS, RAF Little Rissington	O/T: "633 Squadron"	Extant: RAF Museum, Cosford
de Havilland DH.98 Mosquito TT.35	G-ASKC TA719	Skyfame Museum, Staverton	Prop: 641 Sqn Mosquito	Extant: IWM AirSpace Hall, Duxford
de Havilland DH.98 Mosquito TT.35 (Cockpit section only)	TJ118	MGM British Film Studios, Borehamwood	Studio prop: cockpit shots	Extant: DH AirSpace Hall, Duxford
'Fieseler Fi.103' (F/SF V1 Flying Bomb')	'M23'	MGM British Film Studios, Borehamwood	O/T: Operation Crossbow	Donated to IWM, Duxford
HP Hastings C.1	Unid.	RAF Transport Command	O/T: "633 Squadron"	All: SOC 1968
Nord 1002 Pinguoin II (Messerschmitt Bf.108B)	F-BFYX	Charterer: John Hawke, RAF Wattisham	O/T: "633 Squadron"	Extant: private owner, Germany
Nord 1002M Pinguoin II (Messerschmitt Bf.108B)	F-BGVU	Charterer: John Hawke, RAF Wattisham	O/T: "633 Squadron"	Lost at sea, off Labrador coast, 01/1964
Nord 2501 Noratlas	Unid.	Armee de l'Air ?	B/G: visiting aircraft	WFU: 1989

SUBMARINE X-1 (RELEASED: JUNE 1969)

AIRCRAFT	I/D OR TOTAL	SOURCE/OPERATOR	ROLE/MATERIAL	STATUS/FATE
Junkers Ju.52/3M	Unid.	Deutsches Luftwaffe	Archive: IWM	All: SOC 1945
Messerschmitt Bf.110C-4	2177/5F+CM	4(F)/14, Luftwaffe	Archive: IWM	Captured 21/7/40
	AX772	1426 (Enemy Aircraft) Flt	RAF FPU	Scrapped 1947

BATTLE OF BRITAIN (PREMIER: 15TH SEPTEMBER 1969)

AIRCRAFT	I/D OR TOTAL	SOURCE/OPERATOR	ROLE/MATERIAL	STATUS/FATE
CASA 352L	T.2B-176	Ejercito del Aire	Actor: Milch's Junkers Ju.52	Extant: Training Services, Inc. Virginia Beach
CASA 352L	T.2B- ?	Ejercito del Aire	Prop: Lufthansa Junkers Ju.52	N/K
CASA 2.111D	B.2I-77 G-AWHA	Ejercito del Aire Spitfire Productions, Ltd	Actor: Luftwaffe Heinkel He.111H	Extant: Deutsches Museum, Oberschleissheim
CASA 2.111D	B.2I-37 G-AWHB	Ejercito del Aire Spitfire Productions, Ltd	Actor: Luftwaffe Heinkel He.111H	Extant: stored Norfolk, England
CASA 2.111D (Forward fuselage)	B.2I-20	Ejercito del Aire Spitfire Productions, Ltd	Studio prop: interior shots	Extant: private owner, Austria
CASA 2.111D	x 30	Ejercito del Aire	Extras: Heinkel He.111s	Some scrapped, some preserved

Hawker Hurricane Mk.I	P2617	Air Historical Branch, RAF Museum Store	Extra: RAF Hurricane	Extant: RAF Museum, Hendon
Hawker Hurricane Mk.IIc	LF363	Battle of Britain Flight, RAF Coltishall	Actor: RAF Hurricane	Extant: BBMF, RAF Coningsby
Hawker Hurricane Mk.IIc	LF751	Gate Guardian, RAF Bentley Priory	Prop & Spares	Extant: MAPS, Manston
Hawker Hurricane Mk.IIc	PZ865 G-AMAU	Hawker Siddeley Aviation, Dunsfold	Actor: RAF Hurricane	Extant: BBMF, RAF Coningsby
Hawker Hurricane Mk.XII	G-AWLW ex-CF-SMI	Spitfire Productions Formerly Bob Diemart	Actor: RAF Hurricane	Destroyed in fire, Hamilton 15/2/93
Hawker Sea Hurricane Ib	Z7015	Shuttleworth Collection, Old Warden	Extra: RAF Hurricane	Extant: Shuttle-worth Collection
'Hawker Hurricane'	'H3246' 'P3975'	Pinewood Studios	F/SF: RAF Hurricane	Extant: Delabole, Cornwall
'Hawker Hurricane'	'L1592/KW-Z'	Pinewood Studios	F/SF: RAF Hurricane	Extant: Kent Battle of Britain Museum
'Hawker Hurricane'	'L1592/KW-Z'	Pinewood Studios	F/SF: RAF Hurricane	Extant:Torbay Aircraft Museum
'Hawker Hurricane'	'P2640'	Pinewood Studios	F/SF: RAF Hurricane	Extant: New Zealand
'Hawker Hurricane'	'P3059'	Pinewood Studios	F/SF: RAF Hurricane	N/K
'Hawker Hurricane'	'P3059/SD-N'	Pinewood Studios	F/SF: RAF Hurricane	Extant: Kent Battle of Britain Museum
'Hawker Hurricane'	'V7467'	Pinewood Studios	F/SF: RAF Hurricane	Extant: Midland Air Museum
'Hawker Hurricane'	'V7767'	Pinewood Studios	F/SF: RAF Hurricane	Extant: Gloucest-ershire Aviation Collection
Hispano HA.1112M1L	C.4K-126 G-AWHD	Ejercito del Aire Spitfire Productions, Ltd	Actor: Luftwaffe Bf.109E	Extant: stored Big Springs, Tx
Hispano HA.1112M1L	C.4K-31 G-AWHE	Ejercito del Aire Spitfire Productions, Ltd	Actor: Luftwaffe Bf.109E	Extant: Spitfire, Ltd, Duxford
Hispano HA.1112M1L	C.4K-61 G-AWHF	Ejercito del Aire Spitfire Productions, Ltd	Actor: Luftwaffe Bf.109E	Damaged 15/6/68 PWFU 30/6/68
Hispano HA.1112M1L	C.4K-75 G-AWHG	Ejercito del Aire Spitfire Productions, Ltd	Actor: Luftwaffe Bf.109E	Extant: Messer-schmitt Stiftung
Hispano HA.1112M1L	C.4K-105 G-AWHH	Ejercito del Aire Spitfire Productions, Ltd	Actor: Luftwaffe Bf.109E	Extant: Private, Batavia, Illinois
Hispano HA.1112M1L	C.4K-106 G-AWHI	Ejercito del Aire Spitfire Productions, Ltd	Actor: Luftwaffe Bf.109e	Extant: stored Big Springs, Tx
Hispano HA.1112M1L	C.4K-100 G-AWHJ	Ejercito del Aire Spitfire Productions, Ltd	Actor: Luftwaffe Bf.109E	Extant: Kala-mazoo Aviation History Museum
Hispano HA.1112M1L	C.4K-102 G-AWHK	Ejercito del Aire Spitfire Productions, Ltd	Actor: Luftwaffe Bf.109E	Extant: Historic Flying, Duxford
Hispano HA.1112M1L	C.4K-122 G-AWHL	Ejercito del Aire Spitfire Productions, Ltd	Actor: Luftwaffe Bf.109E	Extant: Museum of Flight, Seattle
Hispano HA.1112M1L	C.4K-99 G-AWHM	Ejercito del Aire Spitfire Productions, Ltd	Actor: Luftwaffe Bf.109E	Extant: stored Big Springs, Tx
Hispano HA.1112M1L	C.4K-130 G-AWHN	Ejercito del Aire Spitfire Productions, Ltd	Actor: Luftwaffe Bf.109E	Extant:Tillamook NAS Museum,Or

Hispano HA.1112M1L	C.4K-127 G-AWHO	Ejercito del Aire Spitfire Productions, Ltd	Actor: Luftwaffe Bf.109E	Extant: EAA Air-Venture Museum
Hispano HA.1112M1L	C.4K-144 G-AWHP	Ejercito del Aire Spitfire Productions, Ltd	Actor: Luftwaffe Bf.109E	Destroyed fatal accident 19/12/87
Hispano HA.1112M1L	C.4K-152 G-AWHR	Ejercito del Aire Spitfire Productions, Ltd	Actor: Luftwaffe Bf.109E	Extant: stored Big Springs, Tx
Hispano HA.1112M1L	C.4K-170 G-AWHS	Ejercito del Aire Spitfire Productions, Ltd	Actor: Luftwaffe Bf.109E	Extant: Auto und Technik Museum
Hispano HA.1112M1L	C.4K-169 G-AWHT	Ejercito del Aire Spitfire Productions, Ltd	Actor: Luftwaffe Bf.109E	Extant: Air Fighter Academy
Hispano HA.1112M4K	C.4K-112 G-AWHC	Ejercito del Aire Spitfire Productions, Ltd	Camera ship	Extant: stored Big Springs, Tx
Hispano HA.1112M1L	C.4K-30	Ejercito del Aire	Spares source, RAF Henlow	N/K
Hispano HA.1112M1L	C.4K-107	Ejercito del Aire	Extra: Bf.109E at Tablada	Crashed Sabadell, Spain 25/09/99
Hispano HA.1112M1L	C.4K-111	Pinewood Studios	Cockpit studio shots	Retained by Pinewood Studios
Hispano HA.1112M1L	C.4K-114	Ejercito del Aire	Spares source, RAF Henlow	N/K
Hispano HA.1112M1L	C.4K-121	Ejercito del Aire	Extra: Bf.109E at Tablada	N/K
Hispano HA.1112M1L	C.4K-131	Ejercito del Aire	Extra: Bf.109E at Tablada	N/K
Hispano HA.1112M1L	C.4K-134	Ejercito del Aire	Extra: Bf.109E at Tablada	N/K
Hispano HA.1112M1L	C.4K-135	Ejercito del Aire	Extra: Bf.109E at Tablada	N/K
Hispano HA.1112M1L	C.4K-154	Ejercito del Aire	Spares source, RAF Henlow	N/K
Hispano HA.1112M1L	C.4K-172	Ejercito del Aire	Extra: Bf.109E at Tablada	N/K
Junkers Ju.87G-2	Werk Nr.494083 RI+JK	Air Historical Branch, RAF St Athan	Pattern: Large scale facsimile	Extant: RAF Museum, Hendon
'Junkers Ju.87G-2'	'W8+FR'	Pinewood Studios	Large scale facsimile Stuka	Destroyed in production
'Messerschmitt Bf.109'	'14'	Pinewood Studios	F/SF: Luftwaffe Bf.109, not used	Extant: Kent Battle of Britain Museum
'Messerschmitt Bf.109'	'14/KM+JI'	Pinewood Studios	F/SF: Luftwaffe Bf.109, not used	Extant: Midland Air Museum
'Messerschmitt Bf.109'	'1480/6'	Pinewood Studios	F/SF: Luftwaffe Bf.109, not used	Extant: Kent Battle of Britain Museum
'Messerschmitt Bf.109'	'1480/6'	Pinewood Studios	F/SF: Luftwaffe Bf.109, not used	N/K
'Messerschmitt Bf.109'	'6357'	Pinewood Studios	F/SF: Luftwaffe Bf.109, not used	Extant: Torbay Aircraft Museum
'Messerschmitt Bf.109'	'6357/6'	Pinewood Studios	F/SF: Luftwaffe Bf.109, not used	Extant: Kent Battle of Britain Museum
V/S Spitfire F.Ia	K9942	Air Historical Branch, RAF Museum Store	Spares source	Extant: RAF Museum, Cosford

V/S Spitfire Mk.Ia	AR213 G-AIST	Air Cdre Allan Wheeler, Wycombe Air Park	Actor: RAF Spitfire	Extant: Spitfire The One, Ltd
V/S Spitfire Mk.IIa	P7350 G-AWIJ	Gate Guardian, RAF Colerne	Actor: RAF Spitfire	Extant: BBMF, RAF Coningsby
V/S Spitfire F.Vb	BL614	Gate Guardian, RAF Credenhill	Extra: RAF Spitfire	Extant: RAF Museum, Hendon
V/S Spitfire F.Vb	BM597	Gate Guardian, RAF Church Fenton	Pattern: for F/SF Spitfires	Extant: HAC, Duxford
V/S Spitfire LF.Vb	AB910 G-AISU	Battle of Britain Flight, RAF Coltishall	Actor: RAF Spitfire	Extant: BBMF, RAF Coningsby
V/S Spitfire LF.Vb	EP120	Gate Guardian, RAF Wattisham	Prop: RAF Spitfire	Extant: TFC, Duxford
V/S Spitfire LF.Vc	AR501 G-AWII	Shuttleworth Collection, Spitfire Prod'ns charter	Actor: RAF Spitfire	Extant: Shuttle-worth Collection
V/S Spitfire HF.IXb	MH415 G-AVDJ	'Hamish' Mahaddie ex-Rousseau Aviation	Actor: RAF Spitfire	Extant: stored, Big Springs, Tx
V/S Spitfire HF.IXb	MH434 G-ASJV	'Hamish' Mahaddie ex-Tim Davies, Elstree	Actor: RAF Spitfire	Extant: OFMC, Duxford
V/S Spitfire LF.IXc	MK297 G-ASSD	Alan Rich, on behalf of Confederate Air Force	Actor: RAF Spitfire	Destroyed in fire, Hamilton 15/2/93
V/S Spitfire LF.IXc	MK356	Gate Guardian, RAF Locking	Prop: RAF Spitfire	Extant: spares source, BBMF
V/S Spitfire Tr.9	MJ772 G-AVAV	Samuelson Film Services Spitfire Prod'ns lease	Conversion a/c for Spitfire pilots	Extant: Air Fighter Academy, Herringsdorf
V/S Spitfire Tr.9	TE308 G-AWGB	Samuelson Film Services Spitfire Prod'ns lease	Camera ship & RAF Spitfire	Extant: private, Aspen, Colorado
V/S Spitfire F.XIVc	RM689 G-ALGT	Rolls Royce, Ltd	Extra: RAF Spitfire	Fatal airshow crash 27/6/92, under restoration
V/S Spitfire F.XIVc	RM694	Manchester Tankers, Ltd	Spares source Booker	Parts stored (Fuselage section)
V/S Spitfire FR.XIVc	NH904	Spitfire Productions, Ltd	Spares source	Extant: Palm Springs Air Museum, Ca
V/S Spitfire LF.XVIe	RW382	Gate Guardian, RAF Leconfield	B/G prop: RAF Spitfire	Fatal crash, Nevada, 3/6/98
V/S Spitfire LF.XVIe	SL574	RAF Bentley Priory	B/G prop: RAF Spitfire	Extant:San Diego Air & Space Museum, Ca
V/S Spitfire LF.XVIe	SM411	RAF Wattisham	Extra: 'Mark Addie'	Extant: Museum of Aircraft & Astronautics, Krakow, Poland
V/S Spitfire LF.XVIe	TB382	Gate Guardian, RAF Hospital, Ely	Extra: 'Mark Addie'	Extant: spares source, BBMF
V/S Spitfire LF.XVIe (Minus cockpit)	TB863	Pinewood Studios	Spares source	Extant: Alpine Fighter Collec-tion, Wanaka, NZ
V/S Spitfire LF.XVIe	TD248	Gate Guardian, RAF Sealand	Reserve & spares source	Extant: Spitfire, Ltd, Duxford
V/S Spitfire LF.XVIe	TE311	Gate Guardian, RAF Tangmere	Extra: 'Mark Addie'	Extant: BBMF, for restoration

V/S Spitfire LF.XVIe	TE356	RAF Bicester	Extra: 'Mark Addie'	Extant:Evergreen AviationMuseum, Oregon
V/S Spitfire LF.XVIe	TE384	Instructional Airframe, RAF Syerston	Extra: 'Mark Addie'	Extant: Private, San Martin, Ca
V/S Spitfire LF.XVIe	TE476	Gate Guardian, RAF Neatishead	Extra: 'Mark Addie'	Extant: Weeks FantasyOfFlight Museum, Florida
V/S Spitfire PR.XIX	PM631	Battle of Britain Flight, RAF Coltishall	Extra: RAF Spitfire	Extant: BBMF, RAF Coningsby
V/S Spitfire PR.XIX	PM651	Gate Guardian, RAF Benson	B/G prop: 'Mark Addie'	Extant: RAF Museum, Cosford
V/S Spitfire PR.19	PS853	Battle of Britain Flight, RAF Coltishall	Extra: RAF Spitfire	Extant: Rolls-Royce Aero Engines,
V/S Spitfire PR.19	PS915	Gate Guardian, RAF Leuchars	B/G prop: 'Mark Addie'	Extant: BBMF, RAF Coningsby
V/S Spitfire F.21	LA198	187 Sqn, ATC, Worcester	B/G prop: 'Mark Addie'	Extant: Kelvingrove Museum, Glasgow
V/S Spitfire F.24	PK724	RAF Gaydon	Stored, RAF Henlow	Extant: RAF Museum, Hendon
'V/S Spitfire'	'N3289/DW-K'	Pinewood Studios	F/SF: RAF Spitfire	Extant: Kent Battle of Britain Museum
'V/S Spitfire'	'N3289/QV-K'	Pinewood Studios	F/SF: RAF Spitfire	N/K
'V/S Spitfire'	'N3313/KL-B'	Pinewood Studios	F/SF: RAF Spitfire	Extant: Kent Battle of Britain Museum
'V/S Spitfire'	'N3313/BO-D'	Pinewood Studios	F/SF: RAF Spitfire	Extant: Norfolk & Suffolk Aviation Museum
'V/S Spitfire'	'P8140/ZF-K'	Pinewood Studios	F/SF: RAF Spitfire	Extant: Norfolk & Suffolk Aviation Museum
'V/S Spitfire'	'P9340/KL-B'	Pinewood Studios	F/SF: RAF Spitfire	Extant: Norfolk & Suffolk Aviation Museum
'V/S Spitfire'	'MH314' 'N3313'	Pinewood Studios	F/SF: RAF Spitfire	Extant: Torbay Aircraft Museum

EAGLES OVER LONDON (LA BATTAGLIA D'INGHILTERRA) (INTERNATIONAL 'BRITISH' WAR FILM. RELEASED: SEPTEMBER 1969, ITALY)

AIRCRAFT	I/D OR TOTAL	SOURCE/OPERATOR	ROLE/MATERIAL	STATUS/FATE
CASA 2.111D	Unid.	Ejercito del Aire	Actor: Luftwaffe Heinkel He.111	N/K
CASA 2.111D	Unid.	Ejercito del Aire	Actor: Luftwaffe Heinkel He.111	N/K
CASA 2.111D	Unid.	Ejercito del Aire	Actor: Luftwaffe Heinkel He.111	N/K

CASA 2.111D	Unid.	Ejercito del Aire	B/G: at Tablada ?	N/K
Heinkel He.111	Unid.	Deutsches Luftwaffe	Archive: IWM ?	All: SOC 1945
Heinkel He.111	Unid.	Deutsches Luftwaffe	Archive: IWM ?	All: SOC 1945
Hispano HA.1112M1L	C.4K-121	Ejercito del Aire	Actor: RAF Spitfire	N/K
Hispano HA.1112M1L	C.4K-131	Ejercito del Aire	Actor: RAF Spitfire	N/K
Hispano HA.1112M1L	C.4K-134	Ejercito del Aire	Actor: RAF Spitfire	N/K
Hispano HA.1112M1L	C.4K-135	Ejercito del Aire	Actor: RAF Spitfire	N/K
Hispano HA.1112M1L	C.4K-172	Ejercito del Aire	Actor: RAF Spitfire	N/K
Junkers Ju.87 Stuka	GU+AC	E-Stelle, Rechlin ?	Archive: IWM ?	All: SOC 1945
Junkers Ju.87 Stuka	Unid.	Deutsches Luftwaffe	Archive: IWM ?	All: SOC 1945
Junkers Ju.87 Stuka	x 3	Deutsches Luftwaffe	Archive: IWM ?	All: SOC 1945
Messerschmitt Me.410	Unid.	Deutsches Luftwaffe	Archive: IWM ?	All: SOC 1945
NAA T-6C Texan	Unid.	Ejercito del Aire	Actor: Luftwaffe fighter bomber	All: WFU 1986
NAA T-6C Texan	Unid.	Ejercito del Aire	Actor: Luftwaffe fighter bomber	All: WFU 1986
NAA T-6C Texan	Unid.	Ejercito del Aire	Actor: Luftwaffe fighter bomber	All: WFU 1986
NAA T-6C/T-6D Texan	x 9	Ejercito del Aire	B/G: at Tablada ?	All: WFU 1986
Nakajima Ki-84 Hayate ?	Unid.	Japanese Imperial Navy	Archive: IWM ?	Shot down, date N/K
Nakajima Ki-84 Hayate ?	Unid.	Japanese Imperial Navy	Archive: IWM ?	Shot down, date N/K
V/S Spitfire Mk.Ia	R6627/LO-E	602 Sqn, Royal Air Force	O/T: "A Yank in the R.A.F."	W/O 18/08/44
V/S Spitfire Mk.Ia	X4829/LO-Q	602 Sqn, Royal Air Force	O/T: "A Yank in the R.A.F."	Lost at sea, 07/12//44
V/S Spitfire	Unid.	RAF Fighter Command	Archive: IWM ?	N/K
V/S Spitfire Mk.I	x 9	RAF Fighter Command	Archive: IWM ?	All: SOC 1945
V/S Spitfire Mk.I	x 7	RAF Fighter Command	Archive: IWM ?	All: SOC 1945
V/S Spitfire Mk.I	x 2	RAF Fighter Command	Archive: IWM ?	All: SOC 1945
V/S Spitfire Mk.II	Unid.	RAF Fighter Command	Archive: IWM ?	All: SOC 1944
Westland Lysander	Unid.	Royal Air Force	Archive: IWM ?	Crashed at sea, date N/K

HELL BOATS (RELEASED: MARCH 1970)

AIRCRAFT	I/D OR TOTAL	SOURCE/OPERATOR	ROLE/MATERIAL	STATUS/FATE
Douglas C-47 Dakota	Unid.	N/K	Actor: RAF C-47	N/K
Douglas C-47 Skytrain	-------/SN	MATS, USAF	Stock: N/K	N/K
Junkers Ju.87 Stuka	x 3	Deutsches Luftwaffe	Archive: IWM	All: SOC 1945

THE LAST ESCAPE
(HOLLYWOOD 'BRITISH' WAR FILM. RELEASED: MAY 1970, USA)

AIRCRAFT	I/D OR TOTAL	SOURCE/OPERATOR	ROLE/MATERIAL	STATUS/FATE
Avro Lancaster B.1	PA474	Air Historical Branch, Wroughton	O/T: "Operation Crossbow"	Extant: BBMF
Consolidated B-24 Liberator	Unid.	United States Army Air Force	Archive: IWM ?	All: SOC 1953
de Havilland DH.98 Mosquito TT.35	G-ASKA RS709	Mirisch Films, Ltd Ex-3 CAACU, Exeter	O/T: "633 Squadron"	Extant: National Museum of the USAF, Dayton
de Havilland DH.98 Mosquito TT.35	G-ASKB RS712	Mirisch Films, Ltd Ex-3 CAACU, Exeter	O/T: "633 Squadron"	Extant: EAA Museum, Oshkosh
de Havilland DH.98 Mosquito TT.35	G-ASKC TA719	Mirisch Films, Ltd Ex-3 CAACU, Exeter	O/T: "633 Squadron"	Extant: IWM AirSpace Hall, Duxford
de Havilland DH.98 Mosquito TT.35	RS718	Mirisch Films, Ltd Ex-3 CAACU	O/T: "633 Squadron"	Destroyed in "633 Squadron"
de Havilland DH.98 Mosquito TT.35	TA724	Mirisch Films, Ltd Ex-3 CAACU, Exeter	O/T: "633 Squadron"	Destroyed in "633 Squadron"
Lockheed Hudson V	x 5	Lockheed / Air Ministry	O/T: "A Yank in the R.A.F."	All: SOC 1945
Nord 1002 Pinguoin II (Messerschmitt Bf.108B)	F-BFYX	Charterer: John Hawke, RAF Wattisham	O/T: "633 Squadron"	Extant: private owner, Germany
Nord 1002M Pinguoin II (Messerschmitt Bf.108B)	F-BGVU	Charterer: John Hawke, RAF Wattisham	O/T: "633 Squadron"	Lost at sea, off Labrador coast, 01/1964

TOO LATE THE HERO
(HOLLYWOOD 'BRITISH' WAR FILM. RELEASED: MAY 1970, USA)

AIRCRAFT	I/D OR TOTAL	SOURCE/OPERATOR	ROLE/MATERIAL	STATUS/FATE
Beech T-34 Mentor	Unid.	105 CCTS, Philippines AF	Extra: Japanese AF fighter	WFU: 1969
Douglas DC-3C	13643	Philippines Air Force	Actor: USAAF C-47 Skytrain	W/O: Hurricane Hugo 17/09/89
Douglas DC-3	x 2	Philippines Air Force	Extras: USAAF C-47 Skytrains	Sold 70's or converted AC-47
NAA AT-28D Trojan	x 4, inc: 77-613	15th Strike Wing, Philippines AF	Extras: Japanese AF dive bombers	WFU: 1992

THE MCKENZIE BREAK (US PREMIER: OCTOBER 1970)

AIRCRAFT	I/D OR TOTAL	SOURCE/OPERATOR	ROLE/MATERIAL	STATUS/FATE
Auster 6A	Unid.	N/K	Actor: Auster AOP.6	N/K
Percival Proctor III	Unid. 'W3480'	N/K	Actor: RN search aircraft	N/K

MURPHY'S WAR (RELEASED: JANUARY 1971)

AIRCRAFT	I/D OR TOTAL	SOURCE/OPERATOR	ROLE/MATERIAL	STATUS/FATE
Grumman J2F-6 Duck	N1196N	Tallmantz Aviation Inc	Actor: Murphy's floatplane	Extant: AirVenture Museum Oshkosh, Wis
Grumman J2F-6 Duck	N67790	Tallmantz Aviation Inc	Actor: Murphy's floatplane	Extant: USAF National Museum, Dayton, Ohio
'Grumman J2F-6 Duck'	No serial	Hemdale	F/SF: facsimile of floatplane	Destroyed in film production

RAID ON ROMMEL (HOLLYWOOD 'BRITISH' WAR FILM. RELEASED: FEBRUARY 1971, USA)

AIRCRAFT	I/D OR TOTAL	SOURCE/OPERATOR	ROLE/MATERIAL	STATUS/FATE
Curtiss P-40E Kittyhawk IA	N1207V	Tallmantz Aviation Inc	O/T: "Tobruk"	Extant: War Eagles Museum, Santa Teresa, New Mexico
Grumman G-21A Goose	Unid.	via Tallmantz Aviation	O/T: "Tobruk"	N/K

DAD'S ARMY (RELEASED: MARCH 1971)

AIRCRAFT	I/D OR TOTAL	SOURCE/OPERATOR	ROLE/MATERIAL	STATUS/FATE
ANF Les Mureaux 113 ?	x 20	Armee de l'Air ?	Archive: IWM	All: W/O 1940
CASA 2.111D	B.2I-77 G-AWHA	Spitfire Productions, Ltd	O/T: "Battle of Britain"	Extant: Deutsches Museum
CASA 2.111	B.2I-37 G-AWHB	Spitfire Productions, Ltd	O/T: "Battle of Britain"	Extant: Stored in Norfolk, England
Dornier Do.17	x 9	Deutsches Luftwaffe	Archive: IWM	All: SOC 1945
Dornier Do.215B	x 4	Deutsches Luftwaffe	Archive: IWM	All: SOC 1945
Hawker Hurricane Mk.IIc or Mk.12	Unid.	Spitfire Productions, Ltd.	O/T: "Battle of Britain"	Possibly extant: RAF BBMF
Hispano HA.1112M1L	x 4	Spitfire Productions, Ltd.	O/T: "Battle of Britain"	All: sold privately, USA
Heinkel He.111	x 9	Deutsches Luftwaffe	Archive: IWM	All: SOC 1945
V/S Spitfire	Unid.	Either RAF or private	Amateur film ?	N/K

HITLER: THE LAST TEN DAYS (RELEASED: APRIL 1973)

AIRCRAFT	I/D OR TOTAL	SOURCE/OPERATOR	ROLE/MATERIAL	STATUS/FATE
Boeing B-17 Flying Fortress	x 2	USAAF 8th Air Force	Archive: IWM	All: SOC 1949

Boeing B-17 Flying Fortress	Unid.	USAAF 8th Air Force	Archive: IWM	All: SOC 1949
Focke Wulf FW.190	Unid.	Deutsches Luftwaffe	Archive: IWM	Shot down, date N/K
Focke Wulf FW.190	Unid.	Deutsches Luftwaffe	Archive: IWM	Shot down, date N/K
Grumman F-6F Hellcat	x 16	United States Navy	Archive: IWM	All: SOC 1952
Heinkel He.111	x 21	Deutsches Luftwaffe	Archive: IWM	All: SOC 1945
Ilyushin Il-2 Shturmovik	x 2	Soviet Red Air Force	Archive: IWM	All: SOC 1945
Messerschmitt Bf.109G	Unid.	Deutsches Luftwaffe	Archive: IWM	All: SOC 1945
Polikarpov I-16 'Ishak'	x 4	Soviet Red Air Force	Archive: IWM	All: SOC 1943
Republic P-47 Thunderbolt	Unid.	USAAF 8th Air Force	Archive: IWM	All: SOC 1949
Republic P-47 Thunderbolt	x 2	USAAF 8th Air Force	Archive: IWM	All: SOC 1949

OVERLORD (PREMIER: JULY 1975, BERLIN INTERNATIONAL FILM FESTIVAL)

AIRCRAFT	I/D OR TOTAL	SOURCE/OPERATOR	ROLE/MATERIAL	STATUS/FATE
Airspeed Horsa I	Unid.	Royal Air Force	Archive: IWM	All: SOC 1945
Airspeed Horsa I	Unid.	Royal Air Force	Archive: IWM	All: SOC 1945
Airspeed Horsa I	Unid.	Royal Air Force	Archive: IWM	All: SOC 1945
Airspeed Horsa I	x 48	USAAF	Archive: IWM	All: SOC 1945
Airspeed Horsa I	x 7	Royal Air Force	Archive: IWM	All: SOC 1945
Airspeed Horsa I	x 6	Royal Air Force	Archive: IWM	All: SOC 1945
Avro Lancaster B.I	PA474/KM-B	BBMF, Royal Air Force	Itself	Extant: BBMF, RAF Coningsby
Avro Lancaster	x 2	RAF Bomber Command	Archive: IWM	All: SOC 1957
Avro Lancaster (Derelict remains)	Unid.	RAF Bomber Command	Archive: IWM	W/O ?
de Havilland Mosquito	Unid.	Royal Air Force	Archive: IWM	All: SOC 1962
Douglas Boston	Unid.	Royal Air Force	Archive: IWM	All: SOC 1945
Douglas Boston Mk.II	Unid.	Royal Air Force	Archive: IWM	All: SOC 1945
Douglas Boston Mk.II	Unid.	Royal Air Force	Archive: IWM	All: SOC 1945
Douglas Boston Mk.III	x 2	Royal Air Force	Archive: IWM	All: SOC 1945
Douglas C-47 Skytrain	x 53	USAAF	Archive: IWM	All: SOC 1960s
Fieseler Storch (Shadow on film)	Unid.	Deutsches Luftwaffe	Archive: IWM	All: SOC 1945
Focke Wulf FW.190	Unid.	Deutsches Luftwaffe	Archive: IWM	Shot down, N/K
Focke Wulf FW.190	Unid.	Deutsches Luftwaffe	Archive: IWM	Shot down, N/K
Focke Wulf FW.190	Unid.	Deutsches Luftwaffe	Archive: IWM	Shot down, N/K
Focke Wulf FW.190	Unid.	Deutsches Luftwaffe	Archive: IWM	Shot down, N/K
Focke Wulf FW.190	Unid.	Deutsches Luftwaffe	Archive: IWM	Shot down, N/K
Focke Wulf FW.200V1 (Cabin interior)	D-2600	Regierungsstaffel	Archive: IWM	Bombed 18/7/44 Tempelhoff
Handley Page Halifax	Unid.	RAF Bomber Command	Archive: IWM	All: SOC 1952
Handley Page Halifax	Unid.	RAF Bomber Command	Archive: IWM	All: SOC 1952
Heinkel He.111 (Cockpit interior)	Unid.	Deutsches Luftwaffe	Archive: IWM	All: SOC 1945

Heinkel He.111 (From within gondola)	Unid.	Deutsches Luftwaffe	Archive: IWM	All: SOC 1945
Heinkel He.111 (From within gondola)	Unid.	Deutsches Luftwaffe	Archive: IWM	All: SOC 1945
Junkers Ju.87 Stuka (From within cockpit)	Unid.	Deutsches Luftwaffe	Archive: IWM	All: SOC 1945
NAA B-25 Mitchell Unid.		Royal Air Force	Archive: IWM	All: SOC 1945
NAA B-25 Mitchell	Unid.	Royal Air Force	Archive: IWM	All: SOC 1945
NAA B-25 Mitchell	x 3	Royal Air Force	Archive: IWM	All: SOC 1945
Republic P-47 Thunderbolt	Unid.	USAAF 8th Air Force	Archive: IWM	All: SOC 1949
V/S Spitfire Mk.I	Unid.	Vickers Supermarine Air Ministry	O/T: "Ferry Pilot"	All: SOC 1944
V/S Spitfire Mk.I	x 2	RAF Fighter Command	Archive: IWM	All: SOC 1944
Waco GC-4A Hadrian	x 15	USAAF	Archive: IWM	All: SOC 1945

OPERATION: DAYBREAK (RELEASED: FEBRUARY 1976)

AIRCRAFT	I/D OR TOTAL	SOURCE/OPERATOR	ROLE/MATERIAL	STATUS/FATE
Handley Page Halifax V	Unid.	138 (Special Duties) Sqn., RAF Tempsford	O/T: "Now It Can Be Told"	All: SOC 1952

CROSS OF IRON (RELEASED: JANUARY 1977)

AIRCRAFT	I/D OR TOTAL	SOURCE/OPERATOR	ROLE/MATERIAL	STATUS/FATE
Chance Vought F-4U Corsair	x 7	Private operators, USA	O/T: "Black sheep Squadron"	N/K
NAA T-6 / SN-4J	Unid.	Private operator, USA	O/T: N/K	N/K

THE EAGLE HAS LANDED (RELEASED: MARCH 1977)

AIRCRAFT	I/D OR TOTAL	SOURCE/OPERATOR	ROLE/MATERIAL	STATUS/FATE
Douglas C-47D Dakota IV	G-AKNB	Intra Airways, States Airport, Jersey	Actor: Captured RAF Dakota	Extant: Rare Air Inc., USA
Hispano HA.1112M1L Buchon (partial airframe)	C.4K-111	Pinewood Studios	Prop: Messerschmitt Bf.109G	N/K
Morane-Saulnier MS.500 Criquet (Fieseler Storch)	G-AZMH	Hon. Patrick Lindsay, Wycombe Air Park	Actor: Fieseler Storch	Extant: Luftwaffenmuseum
SIPA S.121 (Arado Ar.396)	F-BLKH	Amicale Jean-Baptiste Salis, La Ferte Alais	Actor: Arado Ar.396	W/O: Crashed France 1978

A BRIDGE TOO FAR (RELEASED: JUNE 1977)

AIRCRAFT	I/D OR TOTAL	SOURCE/OPERATOR	ROLE/MATERIAL	STATUS/FATE
Auster III	PH-NGK	Stichting Vliegsport Gilze-Rijen	Actor: RAF liaison Auster	Extant: SKHV, Gilze-Rijen
Douglas C-47 Skytrain	Unid.	Gen. Eisenhower's personal aircraft ?	Archive: IWM or USNAE	N/K
Douglas C-47A	K-685	Royal Danish Air Force	Extra: C-47 in Market Garden	Extant: Seco Aviation, USA
Douglas C-47A	K-687	Royal Danish Air Force	Extra: C-47 in Market Garden	Extant: Dansk Veteranfly-sambling
Douglas C-47A	K-688	Royal Danish Air Force	Extra: C-47 in Market Garden	Extant: stored, Soesterberg AB
Douglas C-47A	DO-4	Finnish Air Force	Extra: C-47 in Market Garden	Extant: Keski-Suomen Ilmailomuseo
Douglas C-47A	DO-7	Finnish Air Force	Extra: C-47 in Market Garden	Crashed 29/9/96, as PH-DDA
Douglas C-47A	DO-10	Finnish Air Force	Extra: C-47 in Market Garden	Crashed Lake Juuruvesi 7/10/78
Douglas C-47A	DO-12	Finnish Air Force	Extra: C-47 in Market Garden	Extant: Saber Aviation, USA
Douglas C-47B	N9983Q FAP 6171	VisionAir Ex-Portuguese Air Force	Camera aircraft & Extra: C-47 in Market Garden	Derelict: Bole Airport, Addis Ababa
Douglas C-47B	N9985Q F-OCKX	VisionAir Ex-Air Djibouti	Extra: C-47 in Market Garden	Scrapped: Lanseria, SA
Douglas C-47B	N9986Q F-OCKU	VisionAir Ex- Air Djibouti	Extra: C-47 in Market Garden	W/O: 7/10/81, Ethiopia
Douglas C-53D	N9984Q FAP 6153	VisionAir Ex- Portuguese Air Force	Extra: C-47 in Market Garden	Stored: Ndjili, Kinshasa ?
Martin B-26 Marauder	Unid.	USAAF 8th Air Force	Archive: IWM	All: SOC 1947
Martin B-26 Marauder	x 3	USAAF	Archive: IWM or USNAE	All: SOC 1947
Noorduyn AT-16 Harvard IIb	B-64	Koninklijke Luchtmacht	Extra: RAF Typhoon 'HF-J'	Extant: SKHV, as PH-LSK
Noorduyn AT-16 Harvard IIb	B-118	Koninklijke Luchtmacht	Extra: RAF Typhoon 'HF-N'	Extant: SKHV, as PH-IIB
Noorduyn AT-16 Harvard IIb	PH-BKT B-135	Stichting Vliegsport Gilze-Rijen	Extra: RAF Typhoon 'HF-L'	Crashed, date N/K
Noorduyn AT-16 Harvard IIb	PH-KLU B-59	Stichting Vliegsport Gilze-Rijen	Extra: RAF Typhoon 'HF-S' P-47 'MX-W'	Extant: SKHV, Gilze-Rijen
V/S Spitfire HF.IXb	MH434/AC-S G-ASJV	Adrian Swire, Wycombe Air Park	Actor: PR Spitfire	Extant: OFMC, Duxford

FORCE 10 FROM NAVARONE (RELEASED: DECEMBER 1978)

AIRCRAFT	I/D OR TOTAL	SOURCE/OPERATOR	ROLE/MATERIAL	STATUS/FATE
Avro Anson T.21	Unid.	RAF Flying Training Command	O/T: "The Dam Busters"	All: SOC 1968
Avro Lancaster B.1	PA474	BBMF, RAF Coningsby	Actor: RAF Lancaster	Extant: BBMF, RAF Coningsby
Avro Lancaster B.VII	Unid.	Air Ministry storage, RAF Aston Down	O/T: "The Dam Busters"	All: SOC 1957
Hispano HA.1112M1L	x 2	Spitfire Productions	O/T: "Battle of Britain"	All: sold USA post-filming
Messerschmitt Bf.109E-4	Unid.	Deutsches Luftwaffe	O/T: "Reach For The Sky"	All: SOC 1945

HANOVER STREET (RELEASED: MAY 1979)

AIRCRAFT	I/D OR TOTAL	SOURCE/OPERATOR	ROLE/MATERIAL	STATUS/FATE
NAA B-25J Mitchell	N7681C/151790 Amazing Andrea	Military Aircraft Restoration Corp.	Actor: B-25 Amazing Andrea	Destroyed 1990, Dugny, France
NAA B-25J Mitchell	N9115Z/151645 Marvellous Miriam	Military Aircraft Restoration Corp.	Actor: B-25 Marvellous Miriam	Extant: RAF Museum, Hendon
NAA B-25J Mitchell	N9455Z/151863 Big Bad Bonnie	Military Aircraft Restoration Corp.	Actor: B-25 Big Bad Bonnie	Extant: Grissom Air Museum, In.
NAA B-25J Mitchell	N9494Z/151632 Georgeous George-Ann	Visionair International Inc	Actor: B-25 Georgeous George-Ann	Extant: Brussels Air Museum, Belgium
NAA B-25J Mitchell	N86427/151724 Brenda's Boys 151451 Miami Clipper	Visionair International Inc	Actor: B-25s Brenda's Boys & Miami Clipper	Extant: Museuo del Aire, Madrid

YANKS (RELEASED: SEPTEMBER 1979)

AIRCRAFT	I/D OR TOTAL	SOURCE/OPERATOR	ROLE/MATERIAL	STATUS/FATE
NAA B-25J Mitchell	N86427/151451 Miami Clipper	Visionair International Inc	Actor: B-25 Miami Clipper	Extant: Museuo del Aire, Madrid

EYE OF THE NEEDLE (RELEASED: JULY 1981, USA)

AIRCRAFT	I/D OR TOTAL	SOURCE/OPERATOR	ROLE/MATERIAL	STATUS/FATE
'Boeing B-17 Flying Fortress'	No I/D	Kings Road Entertainment	F/SF: facsimile of USAAF B-17	Disposed of post-production
'Boeing B-17 Flying Fortress'	No I/D	Kings Road Entertainment	F/SF: facsimile of USAAF B-17	Disposed of post-production
Douglas C-47A	N54607	Warbirds of Great Britain, Blackbushe	Prop: USAAF C-47 Skytrain	Scrapped 7/5/95

Douglas C-47A Dakota	G-BGCE/T.3-2 'FD772/ZK-Y'	Fairoaks Aviation Services, Blackbushe	Actor: Dakota Windsor Castle	Sold USA 1980
Douglas C-47A	G-BGCF/T.3-33	Fairoaks Aviation Services, Blackbushe	Prop: USAAF C-47 Skytrain	Extant: 8th Air Force Museum, Barksdale AFB
Douglas C-47A	G-BGCG/T.3-27	Fairoaks Aviation Services, Blackbushe	Prop: USAAF C-47 Skytrain	Broken up 04/89, remains stored
Douglas C-47B	G-BFPW/T.3-40	Warbirds of Great Britain, Blackbushe	Prop: USAAF C-47 Skytrain	Sold USA 1980
NAA B-25J Mitchell	N9115Z/151645 Marvellous Mirium'	Warbirds of Great Britain, Blackbushe	Prop: USAAF B-25 Mitchell	Extant: RAF Museum, Hendon
NAA B-25J Mitchell	N9494Z/151632 Georgeous George-Ann'	Warbirds of Great Britain, Blackbushe	Prop: USAAF B-25 Mitchell	Extant: Brussels Air Museum
NAA P-51D Mustang	N166G	Warbirds of Great Britain, Blackbushe	Prop: USAAF P-51 Mustang	Crashed France 06/88
Noorduyne AT-16 Harvard IIb	G-AZSC/FT323	Mike Stowe, Blackbushe	Prop: RAF Harvard	Extant: Goodwood Aero Club, Goodwood
Republic P-47D Thunderbolt	N47DE	Warbirds of Great Britain, Blackbushe	Prop: USAAF P-47 Thunderbolt	Extant: Private owner, USA
Westland Lysander IIIA	G-BCWL	Warbirds of Great Britain, Blackbushe	Prop: RAF Lysander	Extant: Florida Air Museum, Lakeland, USA
Westland Widgeon Srs.2 'Westland Dragonfly'	G-ANLW 'NE-X'	Helicopter Hire, Southend	Actor: British Army helicopter	Extant: Norfolk & Suffolk Aviation Museum

ANOTHER TIME, ANOTHER PLACE (RELEASED: JULY 1983)

AIRCRAFT	I/D OR TOTAL	SOURCE/OPERATOR	ROLE/MATERIAL	STATUS/FATE
de Havilland DH.98 Mosquito T.3	G-ASKH RR299/HT-E	British Aerospace, Hawarden	Actor: RAF Mosquito	Fatal crash Barton 21/7/96

HOPE AND GLORY (RELEASED: SEPTEMBER 1987)

AIRCRAFT	I/D OR TOTAL	SOURCE/OPERATOR	ROLE/MATERIAL	STATUS/FATE
Hispano HA.1112M1L Buchon	x 4	Spitfire Productions, Ltd	O/T: "Battle of Britain"	All: Sold USA, 1968
Hispano HA.1112M1L Buchon	Unid.	Spitfire Productions, Ltd	O/T: "Battle of Britain"	Sold USA, 1968
Hispano HA.1112M1L Buchon	Unid.	Spitfire Productions, Ltd	O/T: "Battle of Britain"	Sold USA, 1968
Pilatus P-2-05	'Red 14' G-BJAX	Old Flying Machine Company, Duxford	Actor: Luftwaffe Bf.109s	PWFU 15/04/94
V/S Spitfire HF.IXb	MH434/ZD-B G-ASJV	Old Flying Machine Company, Duxford	Actor: RAF Spitfire	Extant: OFMC, Duxford
V/S Spitfire	Unid.	Spitfire Productions, Ltd	O/T: "Battle of Britain"	N/K

V/S Spitfire	Unid.	Spitfire Productions, Ltd	O/T: "Battle of Britain"	N/K
V/S Spitfire	Unid.	Spitfire Productions, Ltd	O/T: "Battle of Britain"	N/K

RETURN FROM THE RIVER KWAI (RELEASED: APRIL 1989)

AIRCRAFT	I/D OR TOTAL	SOURCE/OPERATOR	ROLE/MATERIAL	STATUS/FATE
NAA AT-28D Trojan	'01-06'	15th Strike Wing, Philippines Air Force	Prop: Japanese fighter bomber	All: WFU 1992
NAA AT-28D Trojan	'01-07'	15th Strike Wing, Philippines Air Force	Prop: Japanese fighter bomber	All: WFU 1992
NAA AT-28D Trojan	'01-08'	15th Strike Wing, Philippines Air Force	Prop: Japanese fighter bomber	All: WFU 1992
NAA AT-28D Trojan	'03-09'	15th Strike Wing, Philippines Air Force	Actor: Japanese fighter bomber	All: WFU 1992

MEMPHIS BELLE (RELEASED: OCTOBER 1990)

AIRCRAFT	I/D OR TOTAL	SOURCE/OPERATOR	ROLE/MATERIAL	STATUS/FATE
Boeing B-17 Flying Fortress	x 7	USAAF 8th Air Force	Archive: IWM	All: SOC 1949, one damaged
Boeing B-17 Flying Fortress	x 4	USAAF 8th Air Force	Archive: IWM	One shot down, date N/K
Boeing B-17 Flying Fortress	Unid.	USAAF 8th Air Force	Archive: IWM	Damaged in air combat, date N/K
Boeing B-17 Flying Fortress	Unid.	USAAF 8th Air Force	Archive: IWM	Shot down, date N/K
Boeing B-17 Flying Fortress	Unid.	USAAF 8th Air Force	Archive: IWM	Damaged in air combat, date N/K
Boeing B-17 Flying Fortress	Unid.	USAAF 8th Air Force	Archive: IWM	Damaged in air combat, date N/K
Boeing B-17 Flying Fortress	Unid.	USAAF 8th Air Force	Archive: IWM	Shot down, date N/K
Boeing B-17 Flying Fortress	Unid.	USAAF 8th Air Force	Archive: IWM	Shot down, date N/K
Boeing B-17 Flying Fortress	Unid.	USAAF 8th Air Force	Archive: IWM	Shot down, date N/K
Boeing B-17F Flying Fortress	x 4	USAAF 8th Air Force	Archive: IWM	All: SOC 1945, one damaged
Boeing B-17F Flying Fortress	DF/-?	324th Bomb' Sqn, 91st Bomb' Group, 8th AF	Archive: IWM	Shot down, date N/K
Boeing B-17F Flying Fortress	N17W	Robert Richardson, Seattle	Actor: C-Cup & Kathleen	Extant: Museum of Flight, Seattle
Boeing B-17G Flying Fortress	N3703G	David Tallichet, March AFB, California	Actor: Memphis Belle, Mary Lou	Extant: MARC
Boeing B-17G Flying Fortress	G-BEDF Sally B	B-17 Preservation, Duxford	Actor: My Zita, Lady Jane	Extant: with same owner
Boeing B-17G Flying Fortress	F-AZDX Pink Lady	Association Forteresse Tourjours Volante	Actor: Mother and Country	Extant: Stored, La Ferte Alais

Boeing B-17G Flying Fortress	F-BDRS Mary Alice	Imperial War Museum, Duxford	Pattern: for F/SF & R/C B-17s	Extant: IWM, Duxford
Boeing B-17G Flying Fortress	F-BEEA	Institut Geographique National	Actor: Baby Ruth	Crashed 25/7/89 RAF Binbrook
CAC Mustang Mk.22	G-HAEC	Old Flying Machine Co, Duxford	Actor: Ding Hao!	Airshow crash Duxford, 10/07/2011
Douglas C-47A Skytrain	G-DAKS	Aces High, North Weald	Prop: USAAF C-47	Extant: with same owner
Focke Wulf FW.190	x 2	Deutsches Luftwaffe	Archive: IWM	All: SOC 1945
Hispano HA.1112M1L Buchon	G-BOML	Old Flying Machine Co, Duxford	Extra: Bf.109J	Crashed 25/9/99 Sabadell, Spain
Hispano HA.1112M1L Buchon	G-HUNN	Charles Church Displays, Micheldever	Extra: Bf.109J	Extant:Cavanan - augh Flt Museum
Hispano HA.1112M1L Buchon	D-FEHD	Hans Ditte / DASA	Extra: Bf.109J	Extant: Messer - schmitt Stiftung
NAA VB-25N Mitchell	N1042B	Aces High, North Weald	Prop: B-25 & camera ship	Extant: Jim Terry USA
NAA P-51D Mustang	G-BIXL	Robs Lamplough, North Weald	Actor: Miss L	Extant: with same owner
NAA P-51D Mustang	G-SUSY	Charles Church Displays, Micheldever	Actor: Susy	Extant: Christoph Nothinger
NAA P-51D Mustang	N51JJ	The Fighter Collection, Duxford	Actor: Moose / Candyman	Extant: OFMC, Duxford
NAA P-51D Mustang	N167F	Scandinavian Historic Flight, Norway	Actor: Cisco	Extant: with same owner
NAA P-51D Mustang	N314BG	Warbirds of Great Britain, Biggin Hill	Extra: P-51D / Bf.109J	Extant: Les Keikkila, USA
NAA P-51D Mustang	N1051S	Spencer Flack, Southend	Extra: P-51D / Bf.109J	Crashed 2/7/95 Malone, NY

THE ENGLISH PATIENT (RELEASED: NOVEMBER 1996)

AIRCRAFT	I/D OR TOTAL	SOURCE/OPERATOR	ROLE/MATERIAL	STATUS/FATE
Boeing A75 Stearman	N88ZK	Franco Actis, Italy	Actor: Clifton's Stearman	Extant: Italy
de Havilland DH.82A Tiger Moth	G-AJHU	Guijeppe Valenti, Italy	Actor: Madox's Tiger Moth	Extant: Italy

THE BRYLCREEM BOYS (RELEASED: APRIL 1998, SWEDEN)

AIRCRAFT	I/D OR TOTAL	SOURCE/OPERATOR	ROLE/MATERIAL	STATUS/FATE
Vickers Wellington Ic	P2517/OJ-F	149 Sqn, RAF	O/T: "Target for Tonight"	To No.3 GTF, 09/41

THE LAND GIRLS (RELEASED: SEPTEMBER 1998)

AIRCRAFT	I/D OR TOTAL	SOURCE/OPERATOR	ROLE/MATERIAL	STATUS/FATE
Messerschmitt Bf.109G-2	'Black 6' G-USTV	MoD, on loan to the Fighter Collection	Actor: crashing Bf.109	Extant: RAF Museum, Hendon
'Messerschmitt Bf.109G'	'Red 3'	Intermedia Films	F/SF: crashed Bf.109G	Destroyed in production
V/S Spitfire HF.IXb	MH434/ZD-B G-ASJV	Old Flying Machine Company, Duxford	Actor: publicly funded Spitfire	Extant: OFMC, Duxford

TO END ALL WARS (HOLLYWOOD 'BRITISH' WAR FILM. RELEASED: 2001, USA)

AIRCRAFT	I/D OR TOTAL	SOURCE/OPERATOR	ROLE/MATERIAL	STATUS/FATE
Douglas C-47	Unid:	N/K	Actor: RAF C-47	N/K

CHARLOTTE GRAY (RELEASED: FEBRUARY 2001)

AIRCRAFT	I/D OR TOTAL	SOURCE/OPERATOR	ROLE/MATERIAL	STATUS/FATE
Beech C-45H Expeditor	G-BKRG	Aces High, North Weald	B/G: Prop	Extant: Aviodrome, Holland
Douglas C-47A Dakota 3	N147DC	Aces High, North Weald	Actor: 138 Sqn aircraft	Extant: Aces High, Dunsfold

CAPTAIN CORELLI'S MANDOLIN (RELEASED: MAY 2001)

AIRCRAFT	I/D OR TOTAL	SOURCE/OPERATOR	ROLE/MATERIAL	STATUS/FATE
Junkers Ju.87B Stuka	x 4	Deutsches Luftwaffe	Deutsches Bundesarchiv	All: SOC 1945
Junkers Ju.87 Stuka	x 5	Deutsches Luftwaffe	Deutsches Bundesarchiv	All: SOC 1945

DARK BLUE WORLD (TMAVOMODRY SVET) (INTERNATIONAL 'BRITISH' WAR FILM. RELEASED: MAY 2001, CZECH REPUBLIC)

AIRCRAFT	I/D OR TOTAL	SOURCES/OPERATOR	ROLE/MATERIAL	STATUS/FATE
Aero C-104A	Unid. / '6K'	N/K	Extra: Czechoslovakian trainer	N/K
Aero C-104A	Unid. / '8K'	N/K	Extra: Czechoslovakian trainer	N/K
Aero C-104A	Unid. / '?K'	N/K	Extra: Czechoslovakian trainer	N/K
Aero C-104S	Unid. / '3K'	N/K	Extra: Czechoslovakian trainer	N/K
Boeing B-17F Flying Fortress	N17W	Robert Richardson, Seattle	O/T: "Memphis Belle"	Extant: Museum of Flight, Seattle

Boeing B-17G Flying Fortress	N3703G	David Tallichet, California	O/T: "Memphis Belle"	Extant: with same owner
Boeing B-17G Flying Fortress	G-BEDF	B-17 Preservation, Duxford	O/T: "Memphis Belle"	Extant: B-17 Preservation
Boeing B-17G Flying Fortress	F-AZDX	Association Forteresse Tourjours Volante	O/T: "Memphis Belle"	Extant: Stored, La Ferte Alais
Boeing B-17G Flying Fortress	F-BEEA	Institut Geographique Nationale	O/T: "Memphis Belle"	Crashed 25/7/89 RAF Binbrook
CASA 2.111D	B.2I-77 G-AWHA	Spitfire Productions, Ltd	O/T: "Battle of Britain"	Extant: Deutsches Museum
CASA 2.111D	B.2I-37 G-AWHB	Spitfire Productions, Ltd	O/T: "Battle of Britain"	Extant: Stored in Norfolk, England
Hawker Hurricane Mk.IIc	LF363 ?	Battle of Britain Flight, RAF Coltishall	O/T: "Battle of Britain"	Extant: BBMF, RAF Coningsby
Hawker Hurricane Mk.IIc	PZ865 ? G-AMSU	Hawker Siddeley Aviation, Dunsfold	O/T: "Battle of Britain"	Extant: BBMF, RAF Coningsby
Hispano HA.1112M1L	x 18	Ejercito del Aire	O/T: "Battle of Britain"	All: see "Battle of Britain"
Hispano HA.1112M1L	x 7	Spitfire Productions, Ltd	O/T: "Battle of Britain"	All: see "Battle of Britain"
Hispano HA.1112M1L	x 4	Spitfire Productions, Ltd	O/T: "Battle of Britain"	All: see "Battle of Britain"
Hispano HA.1112M4K	C.4K-112 G-AWHC	Spitfire Productions, Ltd	O/T: "Battle of Britain"	Extant: Stored Big Springs, Tx
NAA B-25J Mitchell	N6123C	Flying Bulls, Austria	Camera ship & USAAF B-25	Extant: Flying Bulls
Platzer Kiebitz UL	Unid. / '12K'	N/K	Actor: Czecho-slovakian trainer	N/K
V/S Spitfire Mk.IIa	P7350 G-AWIJ	Spitfire Productions, Ltd	O/T: "Battle of Britain"	Extant: BBMF, RAF Coningsby
V/S Spitfire LF.Vb	AB910 G-AISU	Battle of Britain Flight, RAF Coltishall	O/T: "Battle of Britain"	Extant: BBMF, RAF Coningsby
V/S Spitfire LF.Vb	EP120 G-LFVB	The Fighter Collection, Duxford	Actor: Czech RAF Spitfire	Extant: TFC, Duxford
V/S Spitfire F.Vc	AR501 G-AWII	Shuttleworth Collection	O/T: "Battle of Britain"	Extant: Shuttle-worth Collection
V/S Spitfire HF.VIIIc	MV154 G-BKMI	Robs Lamplough, Duxford	Actor: Czech RAF Spitfire	Extant: Maxi Gainza, Germany
V/S Spitfire HF.IXb	MH415 G-AVDJ	'Hamish' Mahaddie	O/T: "Battle of Britain"	Extant: Stored Big Springs, Tx
V/S Spitfire HF.IXb	MH434 G-ASJV	Old Flying Machine Co., Duxford	Prop: Czech RAF Spitfire	Extant: OFMC, Duxford
V/S Spitfire LF.IXc	MK297 G-ASSD	Confederate Air Force	O/T: "Battle of Britain"	Destroyed in fire, Hamilton 15/2/93
V/S Spitfire F.XIVc	RM689 G-ALGT	Rolls Royce, Ltd	O/T: "Battle of Britain"	Fatal airshow crash 27/6/92
V/S Spitfire	x 8	All: leased by Spitfire Productions, Ltd	O/T: "Battle of Britain"	All: see "Battle of Britain"
'V/S Spitfire Mk.II' (Full-scale facsimile)	'P5411' 'DU-W'	GB Replicas, Ltd	F/SF: RAF Spitfire II	Extant: Czech Rep. air park
'V/S Spitfire Mk.II' (Full-scale facsimile)	'R6811' 'AI-D' / 'CD-N'	GB Replicas, Ltd	F/SF: RAF Spitfire II	Extant: Czech Rep. air park
'V/S Spitfire Mk.II' (Full-scale facsimile)	'R6813' 'AI-N' / 'CD-N'	GB Replicas, Ltd	F/SF: RAF Spitfire II	Extant: Czech Rep. air park

| 'V/S Spitfire Mk.IX'' (Full-scale facsimile) | N3317' 'AI-A' | GB Replicas, Ltd | F/SF: RAF Spitfire II | Extant: Cornwall |
| 'V/S Spitfire Mk.IX' (Full-scale facsimile) | Unid. | GB Replicas, Ltd | F/SF: RAF Spitfire II | Destroyed in production |

TWO MEN WENT TO WAR (RELEASED: NOVEMBER 2002)

AIRCRAFT	I/D OR TOTAL	SOURCES/OPERATOR	ROLE/MATERIAL	STATUS/FATE
V/S Spitfire LF.IXc	MK912/SH-L G-BRRA	Historic Flying, Ltd, Duxford	Actor: Low Flying Spitfire	Extant: Paul Andrews

THE LAST DROP (PREMIER: MAY 2005, CANNES FILM FESTIVAL)

AIRCRAFT	I/D OR TOTAL	SOURCES/OPERATOR	ROLE/MATERIAL	STATUS/FATE
Airspeed Horsa I	292	Royal Air Force	Archive: IWM	All: SOC 1945
Airspeed Horsa I	Unid.	Royal Air Force	Archive: IWM	All: SOC 1945
Airspeed Horsa I	Unid.	Royal Air Force	Archive: IWM	All: SOC 1945
Airspeed Horsa I	Unid.	Royal Air Force	Archive: IWM	All: SOC 1945
Antonov An-2 (Converted airframe)	Unid.	Romanian Air Force ?	Actor: Luftwaffe seaplane	N/K, probably scrapped
Douglas C-47 Skytrain	x 27	USAAF	Archive: IWM	All: Retired by 1960s
Handley Page Halifax	Unid.	No.38 Group, RAF	Archive; IWM	All: SOC 1952
Short Stirling IV	--510/X9-?	299 Sqn, RAF	Archive: IWM	All: SOC 1946
Short Stirling IV	-----/5G-?	299 Sqn, RAF	Archive: IWM	All: SOC 1946
Short Stirling IV	Unid.	No.38 Group, RAF	Archive: IWM	All: SOC 1946

FEMALE AGENTS (LES FEMMES DE L'OMBRE) (INTERNATIONAL 'BRITISH' WAR FILM. RELEASED: MARCH 2008, FRANCE)

AIRCRAFT	I/D OR TOTAL	SOURCES/OPERATOR	ROLE/MATERIAL	STATUS/FATE
Beech 18S	F-AZEJ	Amicale Jean-Baptiste Salis, La Ferte Alais	Actor: RAF Hudson	Extant: AJBS, La Ferte Alais
Douglas DC-3 Dakota III	F-AZTE '313142/17-N'	Amicale France DC-3	Actor: USAAF C-47 Skytrain	Extant: Amicale France DC-3
NAA P-51D Mustang	F-AZSB 44-11622/G4-C	Amicale Jean-Baptiste Salis, La Ferte Alais	Prop: aircraft at RAF Tempsford	Extant: AJBS, La Ferte Alais
NAA T-6G Texan	F-AZMP 493056/X-56	Amicale Jean-Baptiste Salis, La Ferte Alais	Prop: aircraft at RAF Tempsford	Extant: AJBS, La Ferte Alais

LEADING AVIATION FILM STARS

Spitfire HF.IXb	MH434	The Longest Day	D-Day Spitfire
		Operation Crossbow	PR Spitfire
		Battle of Britain	Battle of Britain Spitfire
		A Bridge Too Far	PR Spitfire
		Hope and Glory	Battle of Britain Spitfire
		The Land Girls	Village funded Spitfire
		Dark Blue World	Battle of Britain Spitfire
Spitfire LF.IXb	MH415	The Longest Day	D-Day Spitfire
		The Train	Spitfire strafing the train
		Triple Cross	Spitfires strafing armoured column
		The Night of the Generals	Spitfire strafing Rommel
		Battle of Britain	Battle of Britain Spitfire
Hurricane IIc	LF363	Angels One Five	Battle of Britain Hurricane
		Reach For The Sky	Douglas Bader's Hurricane
		The One That Got Away	Hurricane von Werra nearly steals
		Battle of Britain	Battle of Britain Hurricane
Lancaster B.1	PA474	The Guns of Navarone	Pattern for studio miniature
		Operation Crossbow	Operation Hydra Lancaster
		Overlord	RAF Bomber Command Lancaster
		Force 10 from Navarone	Lancaster stolen by US Rangers

WARTIME SQUADRONS, UNITS AND ESTABLISHMENTS WHICH CONTRIBUTED AIRCRAFT TO BRITISH WORLD WAR TWO WAR FILMS AND HOLLYWOOD 'BRITISH' WAR FILMS

IV Squadron	Lysander	Eagle Squadron (1942)
7 Squadron	Stirling I	One of our Aircraft is Missing (1941)
50 Squadron	Hampden I	The Big Blockade (1942)
66 Squadron	Spitfire IIa	The Next of Kin (1942)
71 (Eagle) Squadron	Spitfire Vb	Eagle Squadron (1942)
74 Squadron	Spitfire Ia	The Lion Has Wings (1939)
90 Squadron	Fortress I	Flying Fortress (1942)
115 Squadron	Wellington Ic	One of our Aircraft is Missing (1941)
118 Squadron	Spitfire Vb	The First of the Few (1942)
149 Squadron	Wellington Ia	The Lion Has Wings (1939)
	Wellington Ic	Target for Tonight (1941)
	Lancaster B.I	Journey Together (1945)
222 Squadron	Spitfire IIa	Dangerous Moonlight (1941)
	Spitfire Vb	Eagle Squadron (1942)
277 Squadron	Spitfire IIa	For Those In Peril (1944)
	Walrus Ia	For Those In Peril (1944)
315 (Polish) Squadron	Spitfire Vb	Eagle Squadron (1942)
342 (Free French) Sqn	Boston IIIA	The Way to the Stars (1945)
501 Squadron	Spitfire Vb	The First of the Few (1942)

602 Squadron	Spitfire Ia	A Yank in the R.A.F. (1941)
16 OTU	Hampden I	The Big Blockade (1942)
32 OTU	Hampden I	Commandos Strike at Dawn (1942)
53 OTU	Spitfire IIa	Eagle Squadron (1942)
56 OTU	Hurricane IIc	The Way to the Stars (1945)
2 Flying Grading School	Tiger Moth II	Journey Together (1945)
3 Air Observers School	Anson V	Journey Together (1945)
4 BFTS	PT-17 Stearman	Journey Together (1945)
1695 BDTF	Hurricane IV	The Way to the Stars (1945)
1426 (EA) Flight	He.111H-3	The First of the Few (1942)
	Ju.88A-6	In Which We Serve (1942)
	Ju.88A-6	The Adventures of Tartu (1943)
	Bf.110C-4	The Adventures of Tartu (1943)
AFDU	Bf.110C-4	Ferry Pilot (1941)
739 Squadron, FAA	Fulmar I	The Volunteer (1943)
765 Squadron, FAA	Kingfisher I	The Volunteer (1943)
807 Squadron, FAA	Seafire IIc	The Volunteer (1943)
884 Squadron, FAA	Seafire IIc	The Volunteer (1943)
384th BG, USAAF	B-17G	The Way to the Stars (1945)
ATA	Oxford I	They Flew Alone (1942)
RAF FPU	Blenheim IV	The First of the Few (1942)
	Hudson I	Big Pack (1944)
RAE Farnborough	Spitfire Ia	Dangerous Moonlight (1941)
	Spitfire IIa	Ferry Pilot (1941)

REFERENCE

WEBSITES

104thlocking.org.uk
384thbombgroup.com
602 (City of Glasgow) Squadron Museum website: 2175atc.co.uk
a2zeemodels.co.uk
aeroarchaeology.com
aeromovies.fr
aerovintage.com
af.mil.com
airfixtributeforum.org
AirlineFan.com
airliners.net
airpages.ru
airpixbycaz.co.uk
airplane-pictures.net
airport-data.com
AirTeamImages.com
airwaysmuseum.com
angelfire.com
asisbiz.com/Wildcat
aussieairliners.org
austinmemories.com
Avia Déjà Vu - crimso.msk.ru
aviation-ancienne.fr

aviationphotocompany.com
avrolancaster.co.uk
axisaircraft.org
axishistory.com
bbc.co.uk/shropshire
belgian-wings.be
BFI: screenonline.org.uk
bredow-web.de
briandesmondhurst.org
canadianwings.com
CanMilAir website
chinaburmaindiawwii.devhub.com
collectair.com/woodason.html
"Dark Blue World" official website
Davis-Monthan Aviation Field website
de Havilland Mosquito, An Illustrated History, by Ian Thirsk
derelictplaces.co.uk
dhc-2.com
douglasdc3.com
dv-photo.co.uk
ebay.co.uk
edcoatescollection.com
eduard.com
encyclopedia.jrank.org/The-Emerging-War-Film

DIRECTORY OF AIRCRAFT APPEARING IN BRITISH WAR FILMS

fanpix.com

fighterfactory.com

filmcenter.cz

fleetairarmarchive.net

flickr.com

flightaware.com

flightglobal.com

flyingheritage.com

flyingmule.com

forum.keypublishing.com

fotocommunity.de

fotolibra.com

Fourthfightergroup.com

Friends of the DC-3 website

GINFO: caa.co.uk/application

historicaircraft.org

historyofwar.org

hmsformidable.com

hmvf.co.uk

HyperScale.com: The Grumman Wildcat in FAA Service, by Bruce Archer

imdb.com: Internet Movie Database

impdb.org: Internet Movie Plane Database

jetphotos.net

jr-creative-images.co.uk

k5054.com

KBismarck.com

lancaster-archive.com

largescaleplanes.com

lookerun.com

luftkrigsskolen.no

madasafish.com

Matterhorn Circle website

MeierMotors website

mh434.com

Military Aviation Movie List

militaryaircraft.de

militaryimages.net

militaryplanes.co.uk

monash.edu.au

MovieGoods.com

moviepostershop.com

museumofflight.com

MyAviation.net

myweb.tiscali.co.uk/olliesweb…is%20Belle.htm

na3t.org

napoleon130.tripod.com

nationalmuseum.af.mil

navalhistory.flixco.info

new-forest-national-park.com

nigelblake.co.uk

northbaddesleyvillage.co.uk/4history-1939-1945

oldprops.ukhome.net

pipex.com

pixstel.com

pjhughes.co.uk

PlanePictures.net

planetalk.net

polishairforce.pl

powell-pressburger.org

PPRuNe Forums

preservedaxisaircraft.com

pyperpote.tonsite.biz

raf.mod.uk/bbmf

rafcodes.html

rafweb.org

RalphLuntPhotography.com

rcgroups.com

richard-seaman.com

richkurz.com

ruudleeuw.com

scribd.com

sepsy.de

simouthouse.com

skhv.nl

skytamer.com

sonsofdamien.co.uk

South Wales Aviation Group website

spitfireforums.com

spitfiresite.com

spitfire-society.org.uk

spitfires.ukf.net

spyflight.co.uk

TCM Movie Database

team-merlin.com

The Longest Headache, by Richard Oulahan, Jr.

thenorthernecho.co.uk

Touchdown Aviation website

ubi.com

UK Airshows Review website

UK Serials Resource Centre website

v2rocket.com

vmiengineering.com

warbirdinformationexhange.org

warbirdregistry.org

warbirdsresourcegroup.org

warbirdz.net

wikimedia.org

wikipedia.org

wilmslow.org.uk

Wings Over New Zealand Forum

Wings Palette / wp.scn.ru

ww2Aircraft.net

ww2images.com

wwiivehicles.com

xuite.net

zap16.com

PUBLICATIONS

De Havilland Mosquito: An Illustrated History, Ian Thirsk
First Light, Geoffrey Wellum, 2003, Penguin Books
Most Secret War, R V Jones, 1978, Penguin Books
The Defence of the Realm: The Authorised History of MI5, Christopher Andrew, 2009, Penguin Books
The Women Who Lived For Danger, Marcus Binney, 2002, Coronet Books, Hodder & Stoughton
When Hollywood Loved Britain: The Hollywood 'British' Film 1939 - 1945,
H. Mark Glancy, 1999, Manchester University Press

BIBLIOGRAPHY

After The Battle, Battle of Britain Intl. Ltd
Aircraft magazine, July 2011, Ian Allan Publishing
Final Cut by Scott A. Thompson, Pictorial Histories Publishing Company
Flight International, Reed Business Information Ltd
Mosquito: A Celebration of de Havilland's 'Wooden Wonder', Key Publishing
Short S.45 Seaford by Bill Mortimer, Wingspan

DOCUMENTATION

Deutsches Bundesarchive
FlightGlobal/Archive
Imperial War Museum Film and Video Archive
RAF Museum Individual Aircraft Histories

DVD SOURCES

allwar.com
Amazon.com
Amazon.co.uk
Imperial War Museum Collection

ONLINE FILM SOURCES

FantaTunes
YouTube